PORTSMOUTH

THE MODERN ERA

– A Complete Record –

DESERT ISLAND FOOTBALL HISTORIES

CLUB HISTORIES	ISBN
ABERDEEN: A CENTENARY HISTORY 1903-2003	1-874287-57-0
ABERDEEN: CHAMPIONS OF SCOTLAND 1954-55	1-874287-65-1
ABERDEEN: THE EUROPEAN ERA – A COMPLETE RECORD	1-874287-11-2
BRISTOL CITY: THE MODERN ERA – A COMPLETE RECORD	1-874287-28-7
BRISTOL CITY: THE EARLY YEARS 1894-1915	1-874287-74-0
CAMBRIDGE UNITED: THE LEAGUE ERA – A COMPLETE RECORD	1-905328-06-0
CAMBRIDGE UNITED: 101 GOLDEN GREATS	1-874287-58-9
THE STORY OF THE CELTIC 1888-1938	1-874287-15-5
CHELSEA: CHAMPIONS OF ENGLAND 1954-55	1-874287-94-5
COLCHESTER UTD: GRAHAM TO WHITTON – A COMPLETE RECORD	1-874287-27-9
COVENTRY CITY: THE ELITE ERA – A COMPLETE RECORD	1-874287-83-X
COVENTRY CITY: AN ILLUSTRATED HISTORY	1-874287-59-7
DUNDEE: CHAMPIONS OF SCOTLAND 1961-62	1-874287-86-4
DUNDEE UNITED: CHAMPIONS OF SCOTLAND 1982-83	1-874287-99-6
HISTORY OF THE EVERTON FOOTBALL CLUB 1878-1928	1-874287-14-7
HALIFAX TOWN: FROM BALL TO LILLIS – A COMPLETE RECORD	1-874287-26-0
HEREFORD UNITED: THE LEAGUE ERA – A COMPLETE RECORD	1-874287-18-X
HUDDERSFIELD TOWN: CHAMPIONS OF ENGLAND 1923-1926	1-874287-88-0
IPSWICH TOWN: THE MODERN ERA – A COMPLETE RECORD	1-874287-43-0
IPSWICH TOWN: CHAMPIONS OF ENGLAND 1961-62	1-874287-63-5
BINMEN AND BUDGIES: IPSWICH V NORWICH	1-905328-12-5
KILMARNOCK: CHAMPIONS OF SCOTLAND 1964-65	1-874287-87-2
LEYTON ORIENT: A SEASON IN THE SUN 1962-63	1-905328-05-2
LUTON TOWN AT KENILWORTH ROAD: A CENTURY OF MEMORIES	1-905328-10-9
LUTON TOWN: THE MODERN ERA – A COMPLETE RECORD	1-874287-90-2
LUTON TOWN: AN ILLUSTRATED HISTORY	1-874287-79-1
MANCHESTER UNITED'S GOLDEN AGE 1903-1914: DICK DUCKWORTH	1-874287-92-9
THE MATT BUSBY CHRONICLES: MANCHESTER UNITED 1946-69	1-874287-96-1
MOTHERWELL: CHAMPIONS OF SCOTLAND 1931-32	1-874287-73-2
NORTHAMPTON TOWN: A SEASON IN THE SUN 1965-66	1-905328-01-X
NORWICH CITY: THE MODERN ERA – A COMPLETE RECORD	1-874287-67-8
PETERBOROUGH UTD: THE MODERN ERA – A COMPLETE RECORD	1-874287-33-3
PETERBOROUGH UNITED: WHO'S WHO?	1-874287-48-1
PLYMOUTH ARGYLE: THE MODERN ERA – A COMPLETE RECORD	1-874287-54-6
PLYMOUTH ARGYLE: 101 GOLDEN GREATS	1-874287-64-3
PLYMOUTH ARGYLE: SNAKES & LADDERS	1-874287-82-1
PORTSMOUTH: THE MODERN ERA	1-905328-08-7
PORTSMOUTH: FROM TINDALL TO BALL – A COMPLETE RECORD	1-874287-25-2
PORTSMOUTH: CHAMPIONS OF ENGLAND – 1948-49 & 1949-50	1-874287-50-3
THE STORY OF THE RANGERS 1873-1923	1-874287-95-3
THE ROMANCE OF THE WEDNESDAY 1867-1926	1-874287-17-1
SEVENTEEN MILES FROM PARADISE: SAINTS V POMPEY	1-874287-89-9
STOKE CITY: THE MODERN ERA – A COMPLETE RECORD	1-874287-76-7
STOKE CITY: 101 GOLDEN GREATS	1-874287-55-4
POTTERS AT WAR: STOKE CITY 1939-47	1-874287-78-3
SWANSEA CITY: SEASONS IN THE SUN	1-905328-02-8
THIRD LANARK: CHAMPIONS OF SCOTLAND 1903-04	1-905328-03-6
TOTTENHAM HOTSPUR: CHAMPIONS OF ENGLAND 1950-51, 1960-61	1-874287-93-7
WEST HAM: FROM GREENWOOD TO REDKNAPP	1-874287-19-8
WEST HAM: THE ELITE ERA – A COMPLETE RECORD	1-905328-07-9
WIMBLEDON: FROM SOUTHERN LEAGUE TO PREMIERSHIP	1-874287-09-0
WIMBLEDON: FROM WEMBLEY TO SELHURST	1-874287-20-1
WIMBLEDON: THE PREMIERSHIP YEARS	1-874287-40-6
WREXHAM: THE EUROPEAN ERA – A COMPLETE RECORD	1-874287-52-X

WORLD CUP HISTORIES	
ENGLAND'S QUEST FOR THE WORLD CUP – A COMPLETE RECORD	1-874287-61-9
SCOTLAND: THE QUEST FOR THE WORLD CUP – A COMPLETE RECORD	1-897850-50-6
IRELAND: THE QUEST FOR THE WORLD CUP – A COMPLETE RECORD	1-897850-80-8

MISCELLANEOUS	
RED DRAGONS IN EUROPE – A COMPLETE RECORD	1-874287-01-5
THE BOOK OF FOOTBALL: A HISTORY TO 1905-06	1-905328-00-1
FOOTBALL'S WAR & PEACE: THE TUMULTUOUS SEASON OF 1946-47	1-874287-70-8

PORTSMOUTH

THE MODERN ERA
— A Complete Record —

Series Editor: Clive Leatherdale
Series Consultant: Leigh Edwards

Colin Farmery

DESERT ISLAND BOOKS LIMITED

First Published in 2005
(an earlier edition, *Portsmouth: From Tindall to Ball,* was published in 1999)

DESERT ISLAND BOOKS LIMITED
7 Clarence Road, Southend-on-Sea, Essex SS1 1AN
United Kingdom
www.desertislandbooks.com

The right of Colin Farmery to be identified as author of this work has been
asserted under The Copyright Designs and Patents Act 1988

British Library Cataloguing-in-Publication Data
A catalogue record for this book is available from the British Library

ISBN   1-905328-08-7

Printed in Great Britain
by
Biddles Ltd, King's Lynn

Photographs in this book are reproduced courtesy of:
The News, Portsmouth, Portsmouth FC, Steve Reid, Mike Jones,
Author's collection, Chris Gibbs' collection

CONTENTS

AUTHOR'S NOTE

When I wrote the original version of this book back in 1999 I mused that Pompey were a club whose story had 'more character than most'. Six years on, that statement holds true more than ever, as this new volume weaves the highs and lows of the Milan Mandaric era into the rich tapestry that is the history of Portsmouth FC.

Mandaric had just taken over Portsmouth FC in the summer of 1999, and I then looked forward to the reign of this Serbo-American silicon-chip magnate. Like his predecessors John Deacon and Jim Gregory – self-made men themselves who devoted countless hours of time and energy into trying to take Pompey forward – Milan was a 'football man' by dint of his spell as a professional in his native Yugoslavia and his subsequent ownership of clubs in the United States and France.

His aim was to stir a so-called 'sleeping giant' who had become virtually comatose as the new millennium dawned. His initial three-year plan to establish the club in the Premiership and build a state-of-the-art stadium quickly unravelled as the club's historical fault-lines undermined his lofty ambitions. By 2004, however, no one could argue that Milan hadn't delivered, on the field at least. His appointment of Harry Redknapp as manager in 2002 was a masterstroke, and the club's record-breaking surge to the first division championship in 2003 finally gave that generation of fans brought up on the sepia-tinted nostalgia of the championship sides of 1949 and 1950 a team of heroes to call their own. In my book *Portsmouth: Champions of England* (2000) I wrote that I hoped one day that book would have a sequel. It is the sad structure of the modern game that means the momentous 2002-2003 season will be probably as close as we will get to a repeat of those immediate post-war glory years.

There are many people I need to thank for their help in making this book as comprehensive and accurate as I trust it is. My long-standing friend Chris Gibbs – we first met in 1977 – was a tremendous help, tracking down elusive attendances and match reports, as well as delving into his picture collection. Steve Reid, the talented *News* photographer, gave invaluable assistance, supplying many of the pictures in the later years, some of which are published for the first time. Mike Jones, another photographer, also supplied some previously unseen images.

Peter Jeffs offered constructive criticism of the new chapters, as well as having helped on the original version. Other people who contributed to the first edition included Alan Loader, who I 'employed' as a research assistant. No doubt the experience stood him in good stead for his history degree at Sussex, which he passed with flying colours.

Former club director Jim Sloan and honorary club historian Richard Owen read the final draft of the first version and their knowledge and constructive criticism was appreciated. Mick Cooper also assisted with tracking down statistics.

I must also thank *The News*, especially Steve Bone and Sports Editor Colin Channon, for their support. The first 27 years of this book drew heavily on the work of *News* Chief Sports Writer Mike Neasom, sadly no longer with us, but his successor Mark Storey has taken on the mantle and continues, with his colleagues, to provide first-class, comprehensive coverage of the Pompey scene.

I have now worked on four books with my editor and publisher Clive Leatherdale. The experience has never been anything less than invigorating. Our occasionally feisty, yet ever-friendly, relationship as we debate the nuances of my writing remains a quality control measure *par excellence*. Via Clive I also 'know' Donal Cullen as stats-checking wizard who, not for the first time, laid bare the inadequacies of my first draft of the statistical summaries. My eternal appreciation is extended for your phenomenal attention to detail, Donal.

Last, but by no means least, my wife Di Lloyd, remains my strongest supporter. Not only does she get on with the day-to-day necessities of life while I pore through dusty volumes and then turn my research into prose, but she is also my most-trusted proof-reader, although I fear the skills she has developed have taken the edge off her novel-reading pleasure for good. No book by me next summer. Promise.

COLIN FARMERY
September 2005

INTRODUCTION

When Milan Mandaric arrived at Portsmouth Football Club many fans believed finally a 'sleeping giant' was about to stir. However, six years on, with Pompey established in the Premiership, the very term 'sleeping giant' has been rendered meaningless as the ruthless capitalism of the modern game has left former 'giants' – such as Tottenham, Everton and Aston Villa – relative pygmies by comparison with Roman Abramovic's multi-million pound revolution at Chelsea. Barring the improbable arrival of a mega-rich sugar-daddy, Pompey cannot compete in those spheres. But at this juncture in the club's history significant challenges lie ahead for Milan Mandaric, or perhaps those who will inevitably, one day, succeed him. They must ensure that the last three seasons will be judged as a staging post on a journey to real success – perhaps a Cup or at least European football – rather than as a 'golden age' for a generation or two of Pompey fans.

Besides, in the summer of 1999 even the term 'sleeping giant' attached to the club was an embarrassment. 'Comatose' would have been a better description, as the club had slithered perilously close to becoming one of the 'also-rans' of the first division – having more in common with the likes of Port Vale and Tranmere than West Brom, Ipswich or even Barnsley, who had just enjoyed a brief sojourn in the Premiership. Pompey had struggled to adjust to the inflationary football world and almost paid the price of extinction, until Mandaric and his dollars rolled into town. What marked Pompey's pretensions to greatness as unusual was that, unlike their other dozing companions – such as Birmingham, Sunderland and Manchester City – prior to Mandaric's arrival, in the previous 40 years they had spent just one season in the top flight they left in 1959. That sad record is compounded by Pompey's lack of success in the cups. Since winning the FA Cup in 1939, two semi-finals (in 1949 and 1992) are the closest they have come. And yet fans and officials alike cling on to the perception that, with the right backing, the glory years of the 1930s, 1940s and 1950s can be recaptured.

The evidence suggested they had a case, although the reality of Premiership football in 2005 has tempered that optimism. As travel became both easier and cheaper in the late 20th century, it might be suggested that the 'size' of a club is perhaps better reflected by the travelling support it can muster. In the 1960s and 1970s Pompey fans always had a reputation for following their club in great numbers to cup-ties – 15,000 went to Tottenham in 1967, 10,000 to Arsenal in 1971 and 10,000 to Charlton in 1976. Increasingly, that passion was been reflected in the day-to-day grind of league existence, despite Portsmouth's geographical isolation, which makes most 'local' derbies a minimum 150-mile round trip. But whenever a hint of glory surfaced, Pompey fans were renowned for travelling in droves – proportionally dwarfing their nominal average home attendance. QPR were not the first hosts to be caught out by unanticipated demand, when 4,000 Pompey fans descended on Loftus Road in March 1997 to cheer on their play-off chasing team. Although Pompey's home gates, when considered over the last 30 years, make less compelling inspection, when the good times do roll, their potential backing was seen as a force to be reckoned with and it was that potential into which Mandaric invested.

When Pompey squeezed out of the fourth division in 1979-80, four home attendances that season exceeded 20,000. Indeed, in October 1979, Pompey beat Bradford City 4-1 in front of 23,871 – an attendance bigger than five in the old first division that afternoon. Twelve months later, an estimated 15,000 made the 500-mile round trip to Liverpool to see their side lose 1-4 in the League Cup, by which time Pompey's phenomenal support brooked no argument. When the Premiership beckoned fleetingly in the spring of 1993, each of the last four home games was watched by an average of 22,000. The remarkable backing, following Alan Ball's return in January 1998, was a decisive factor in rescuing the team from apparently inevitable relegation.

To put this into a wider context, home gates have rarely been the 'be all and end all' in terms of measuring potential. In the 1970s and 1980s, Newcastle, Sunderland and Middlesbrough all saw their gates drop below five figures from time to time – fewer than 5,000 saw Middlesbrough play Pompey in January 1985 – and over the past 30 years or so each of these clubs boasted a track record far better than Pompey's. Inclusion of Portsmouth's name among clubs which have become icons for football passion is intended, and chairman Milan Mandaric's plan for a state-of-the-art 35,000-seater stadium seemed far from pie in the sky in the late 1990s. The words 'Pompey', 'potential' and 'unfulfilled' used to provide a neat answer to a word-association problem. They had also seduced successful businessmen in the past, intent on restoring the club to its former glory.

The efforts of Southampton-based property developer John Deacon in the 1970s and 80s, and London garage owner Jim Gregory (former QPR chairman) in the 1990s, to turn Pompey round form the backbone of this book. Both men were committed and ruthless in their ambition, but still found the burden of expectation weighed heavily on their shoulders. For all their undoubted loyalty, Pompey's fans are never slow to vent their feelings if they feel they are being short-changed, as both Deacon and Gregory found when their promised success was slow to materialise. Mandaric too, would find the challenge of revitalising Pompey equally as taxing, only to find that when 'nirvana' was reached, the shifting sands of the football world had rendered traditional measures of 'potential' obsolete. Football 21st-century style is measured in different terms. The 'working class' core of Pompey's traditional support has been squeezed by rising ticket prices. Even that famed away following has shrunk to the hard core.

A consistent sub-plot attending Pompey's usually abortive bids to return to the big time had been the emergence of Southampton. Worse, Saints claimed the FA Cup in 1976 for the only time in their history – ironically the season Pompey tumbled into the third division. In 1984, under Lawrie McMenemy, Southampton even finished second in the old first division. While Pompey's fortunes have waxed and waned, the Saints since 1966 had spent all but four seasons in the top division. Their second promotion in 1978 coincided with Pompey falling through the trapdoor into the fourth division for the first time. Over the years a bitter rivalry has built up, with Pompey fans resting on their fading laurels, while Saints relied on their Houdini-like ability to cheat relegation and maintain a Premiership presence south of London.

The roots of this rivalry are far from clear-cut. There are few precedents in the football world for two clubs quite so far apart – 17 miles of motorway separate them – to have a passion that clearly runs deep. One theory is based on the relative civic status of the cities. Southampton was only granted city status in 1964, while Portsmouth was designated a city by virtue of its Cathedral and Royal Charter dating from 1194, although the civic designation would have to wait until the 1920s. Similarly the traditional rivalry between the Merchant and Royal Navies has been cited as a contributory factor. In the last 30 years, ironically, Portsmouth has replaced much of its dependency on the Senior Service by using its communications links to poach some of Southampton's traditional sea-going trade in the shape of the cross-channel ferries.

However, it seems tenuous to suggest that these factors unduly affect the passions of fans. The answer is probably simpler. Pompey fans regard their club as being – potentially at least – a 'big' club. Not on the Chelsea, Manchester United or Arsenal scale, but certainly on the coat-tails of Middlesbrough, West Ham or Newcastle, all of whom have been second-flight companions in the not too distant past. The fact that Southampton failed to do much more with their elevated status than retain it was regarded by Pompey fans with disdain. Victims of an illustrious past, the best part of 50 years' under-achievement by their own club is glossed over. Southampton, on the other hand, are also hampered by their roots. An undoubted football power-house at the turn of the 19th century, until the mid-1960s Saints were plodders who shuffled between the old second and the third division (south), rarely threatening Pompey's ascendancy. Despite more than 115 years of history, Saints' sole mark on football's honours board is still the 1976 FA Cup, acting as a constraining influence on their perceived status. Pompey's supposed superiority complex – however misplaced by accomplishments on the field – remained to Saints fans an irritant, as Southampton's undoubted achievements – not least the construction (and filling) of the impressive 32,000 capacity St Mary's – have never enabled them to clearly establish themselves as the South's leading club.

Couple this with the fact that in the 30 years until 2003 the clubs faced each other just eight times, creating a recipe where old grudges festered and new ones developed as, in this case, a lack of familiarity bred contempt. Those rare derby days became a focus for tension and score-settling. Saints' win at Fratton in 1976 relegated Pompey; twelve years is a long time to have to wait for revenge. Ten seasons together in the same division – any division – could be therapeutic for both sets of fans. The irony was that once the two clubs finally met in the top flight, even six meetings in two seasons couldn't put the bitterness to rest. Redknapp's perceived treacherous defection to St Mary's poisoned relations and Saints' relegation from the Premiership, albeit leaving Pompey top dogs, means that the rivalry has some way to go to achieving maturity.

With the Southampton rivalry often put into cold storage, other clubs have stepped in to spice up life. In the 1970s clashes with Millwall were frequently tight affairs, but it was the hooligan fringe that largely explained the tenseness. In the 1980s, matches with Huddersfield were eagerly anticipated as both clubs' fall from grace and subsequent revival ran in tandem. Huddersfield found themselves in division four after dropping two divisions in the mid-1970s, and by 1978 Pompey had followed suit. In 1980 and 1983 both clubs shared promotions and a total of almost 39,000 fans watched two epic Fratton battles. In 1993 Swindon earned the scorn of Pompey fans, who held their players guilty of 'not trying' against promotion rivals West Ham. Swindon went on to win the play-off final against Leicester, who had beaten Pompey in the semi-finals, partly thanks to a goal which appeared to be yards offside. Between them, those two villains were regarded as having denied Pompey their supposedly rightful place in the top flight.

However muted the 'Pompey Chimes' have been in the last 40 years – until recently – the song itself remains one of football's enduring classics. Its origins are more clear-cut than the nickname 'Pompey', which is a term widely used to refer not just to the football club, but to the whole city. The name 'Pompey' is almost certainly of naval extraction and Mike Neasom's book *Pompey: The History of Portsmouth Football Club* sets out three main theories. Legend has it that a snoozing, drunken sailor interrupted a lecture on the Roman Empire given by a naval temperance worker. Upon hearing that an emperor of that name had died, the sailor shouted out 'Poor old Pompey'.

More substantive evidence records a group of Portsmouth-based sailors, who scaled Pompey's Pillar near Alexandria, Egypt, in 1781 and became known as the 'Pompey Boys', while others claim the name originates from a French battleship *La Pompée*, captured in 1793 and which eventually became the guardship to Portsmouth Harbour. The Chimes – the slow intonation of 'Play up Pompey, Pompey play up' – is derived from the hour chime of the city's Guildhall clock, and the song is first recorded as being heard at the ground in the early 1900s. Although of undeniably Portsmouth origins, it has been plagiarised by others as both a term of endearment – 'Ay-o Barnsley, Barnsley ay-o,' for instance – or derision – 'Bye-bye Pompey, Pompey bye-bye!' – to suit the occasion. Devotees of Italian football, too, will have come across the chant given a more staccato, Latin-esque feel. Another noteworthy song 'By far the greatest city' refers to 'Portsmouth *City* FC' – a name by which the club has never been known – reflecting the identification by fans not only with the club, but also the city it represents.

But the recurring question for serious students of Pompey's history is how did it all go so wrong. In 1951 the club had the world at its feet, literally. Portsmouth FC were invited to represent the FA on a tour of South America, having won the League Championship in the previous two years. Gates of 40,000 at Fratton Park were the norm and the likes of Jimmy Dickinson, Jimmy Scoular and Peter Harris were household names. Within 20 years the club were at a dead end in division two and going nowhere fast.

The seeds of the championship-winning team had been sown during the war years, when Jack Tinn introduced several promising players. Harris was a flying young winger; wing-half Dickinson had been recommended by his Alton schoolteacher Eddie Lever; and Scottish wing-half Scoular was a sailor stationed locally. Tinn announced his retirement at the end of the 1946-47 season, but the appointment of the charismatic Bob Jackson as his successor proved popular. Dickinson's performances were attracting rave reviews, and Duggie Reid, Jack Froggatt and Harris between them claimed forty of the 68 goals scored by a Pompey team widely tipped for success as the club approached its Golden Jubilee year.

Chairman Vernon Stokes called for the anniversary to be marked by the winning of the League Championship. The team made a superb start to 1948-49, with six wins in the first seven matches. That jubilee season included a 'birthday' match in the league against Arsenal in November and the celebrations, led by club president Lord Montgomery, were climaxed by a 4-1 win over the mighty Gunners. Underrated and overlooked by the national press, the team played swift attacking football, with the flying wingers, Harris and Froggatt, acting as the springboards. It was the FA Cup run which brought a record attendance which still stands: 51,385 saw Pompey beat Derby 2-1 in the quarter-finals to earn a semi-final place against lowly Leicester from division two.

Pompey faced the prospect of becoming the first side in the 20th century to achieve the elusive League and Cup double. It was therefore a shattering disappointment for the 25,000 fans from the south coast who travelled to Highbury, when the red-hot favourites sank 1-3 to a Don Revie-inspired Leicester. Back in the league, Pompey more than atoned for their cup disappointment and stormed to their first championship. By now, Dickinson and Harris had achieved England recognition, soon to be followed by Froggatt. Pompey won the title the following season, too, mainly due to a storming finish that saw seventeen points picked up from the last eleven games. The outcome went down to the final moments of the final match, at home to Aston Villa. Goal-average was likely to prove decisive, and in the event a 5-1 victory put Pompey two-fifths of a goal better off than challenging Wolves.

In the early 1950s Pompey consolidated their place in the top flight but then slowly slid into decline as the championship-winning players began to age. It was during this period that Fratton Park staged one of its most memorable post-war contests. The FA Cup quarter-final tie against Newcastle in March 1952 was rated by the eminent journalist Geoffrey Green of *The Times* as one of the best three club matches he had seen in 30 years of reporting football. A rousing contest had seen the Jackie Milburn-inspired Geordies sweep to a 4-2 victory.

In the summer of 1952 Bob Jackson left to manage Hull City, and reserve-team manager Eddie Lever replaced him. The championship team was breaking up, but had not been adequately replaced. The 1954-55 season brought a flattering fourth place, but from then on Lever struggled, and endured several relegation-haunted campaigns before being replaced by the former Bournemouth manager Freddie Cox. His era was to be one of controversy and acrimony, and positively disastrous. His first season, 1958-59, was calamitous, with relegation the inevitable outcome following a miserable twenty defeats in the last 24 matches, and only 21 points secured for the whole season. The fall into division two brought no respite, and midway through his second season in the lower league Cox was dismissed.

The appointment of George Smith in April 1961 came too late to save Pompey from a slide into division three after 37 years. The outspoken, often controversial, Smith was one of the best coaches in the country and was known for his strict discipline and 'commando-style' form of training. Smith stabilised the club, and helped by some inspired signings – wingers Tony Barton and Dave Dodson in particular – guided his team to promotion at the first attempt under the captaincy of the seemingly ageless Jimmy Dickinson. The 37-year-old played his 600th league appearance that season and compensated for his age and lack of speed with his unique positional sense and anticipation. Smith's arrival had revived a previously depressed and dispirited club, and his coming had proved the spur that encouraged Dickinson to play on and on and aim for the record books.

Pompey fans had to settle regularly for a mid-table place in the second division through the 1960s, without the resources or ambition to go further. Centre-forward Ron Saunders proved to be an outstanding goalscorer amidst the mediocrity around him, and by the time he was surprisingly sold to Watford, in September 1964, he had notched 145 league goals from 236 appearances. Approaching his fortieth birthday, Dickinson announced that he would retire at the end of the 1964-65 season, and it was a dramatic finale. Pompey had struggled all season and needed at least a point in the final match at Northampton to survive. Curiously, the league allowed the match to kick-off at 7.30pm, by which time results elsewhere meant Pompey knew exactly what was required.

The team were a goal down – an own-goal from forward Johnny Gordon – with just six minutes remaining. Pompey's last-ditch life-saver came from full-back Alex Wilson, who had only scored one other goal in a long career. That precious goal enabled Dickinson to be chaired from the pitch in triumph, retiring after a playing career spanning twenty years and 764 league appearances. Pompey will never see the likes of such as Dickinson again. A unique, loyal one-club man, Dickinson was universally known as 'Gentleman Jim' and was never once cautioned or spoken to by a referee. Unobtrusiveness, soundness and consistency were the hallmarks of his play, and his record of service to the club was to extend, in various capacities, right up to his death in 1982.

George Smith, meanwhile, was intent on revolutionising the way the club was organised. He disbanded the reserve and youth teams, leaving a first-team squad of just sixteen players. Savings of £20,000 annually were projected as Smith explained, mischievously, that 'there was nothing but fish in the sea around Portsmouth'.

Season 1966-67 was notable for Pompey's FA Cup run. A marathon three-game tie against Hull included an astonishing 33,107 Fratton Park crowd, which served to highlight the club's potential. In the next round, over 15,000 fans travelled to White Hart Lane to see Spurs dash Pompey's hopes. In the following season, 1967-68, home gates were regularly topping 20,000, encouraged by a nine-match unbeaten run up to September which saw Pompey perched on top of the division. At Christmas, more than 35,000 fans packed Fratton to see Pompey beat their then main rivals Blackpool 3-1 in what was probably the most memorable match of the 1960s.

However, despite the arrival for a club record £40,000 of striker Mike Trebilcock, Pompey's challenge faltered. The new striker failed to score the number of goals expected from him, and just three wins from the last thirteen league games meant the team had to settle for a disappointing fifth place. The following season local boy Ray Hiron finished top scorer with seventeen goals, but his contribution could not lift Pompey above mid-table. By now the pressure on Smith was intensifying, as fans stayed away and attendances plummeted to 10,000 levels. The first-team squad system – a consequence of the abolition of the reserve and youth teams – had failed to achieve the desired results. At the close of the 1969-70 season Smith was moved upstairs to become general manager, and Ron Tindall, a former player, assumed control of team affairs.

As Pompey approached the 1970s, the challenge of 'waking the sleeping giant' had barely been taken up. Pompey fans were having to come to terms with the fact that theirs was a 'second division' club, and that a return to their rightful place in division one seemed as far away as ever.

## 1

FREEFALL
1970-1978

LEAGUE DIVISION 2   **1970-71**
Division 2   16th
League Cup   3rd Round
FA Cup   4th Round

Portsmouth Football Club in the summer of 1970 was in transition. The glory days of the late 1940s were becoming a distant memory and even the promised land of the first division, vacated in April 1959, was an unknown quantity for a whole generation of supporters. The club had become an archetypal 'sleeping giant'. The board acted in April 1970 by moving manager George Smith 'upstairs' to become general manager and giving 34-year-old former player Ron Tindall control of team affairs.

The change was radical. Smith was from the old school of management – discipline and hard work at the core of his values – but although he had brought the club back to respectability, his approach had not produced a return to the first division. Many supporters felt that his decision to axe the reserve and youth teams in 1965 had set the club back considerably, whatever the apparent financial merits of that arrangement.

Tindall, on the other hand, was to be one of the new breed of tracksuit managers; a players' man who would coax the best from a squad which contained its fair share of individuals who had yet to fulfil their potential. Goalkeeper Milkins was widely regarded as being one of the best outside the top flight, defender Eoin Hand had recently been capped by the Republic of Ireland, and Nicky Jennings was a goalscoring winger with a fine reputation. More intriguingly, Mike Trebilcock – scorer of two FA Cup winning goals for Everton in 1966 – had yet to justify the club-record £40,000 spent on him in 1968.

Although the club were still in dire financial straits, the board gave Tindall £50,000 to spend during the summer. Most of it went on signing up England Under-23 international Norman Piper from third division Plymouth Argyle, in a deal that equalled the club-record outlay. At the time, the transfer was considered rather a coup, as Piper's services had been coveted by a number of first division clubs. Tindall also signed two Burnley defenders, full-back Fred Smith and centre-half Colin Blant, as well as covering the goalkeeping department by recruiting veteran Jim Standen from Millwall.

The board used their evident ambition as justification for another hike in admission prices – the best seats now cost 14 shillings (70p) – and as the season got underway it seemed Tindall had done the trick. Five wins and a draw in the first six league and cup matches at Fratton saw the team handily placed in the top half of the table and through to the third round of the League Cup and the prospect of an attractive tie at Manchester United.

By the end of October that early optimism had largely evaporated. The rot set in on 30 September, when Sheffield United recorded their second 5-1 league win at Fratton in thirteen months. Four consecutive league defeats in October – plus a single goal defeat against United – meant the club were back in familiar territory near the foot of the table.

Not even two October hat-tricks by the enigmatic Trebilcock, the first securing a 5-0 win over Watford in his first appearance of the season, the second seeing off Blackburn Rovers 4-1, could lift the gloom. The attendance against Rovers dipped to 9,936 – the first sub-10,000 league gate at Fratton since December 1965. Supporters and officials were casting increasingly envious glances along the coast to Southampton, who were steadily establishing themselves as a first division force and assuming the mantle of the south's top club.

Tindall's problem was that he was no more successful than Smith at realising a consistent performance from his players. Solid home form kept Pompey out of the two relegation places, but on the road the team were performing pitifully. The nadir was reached in December when promotion-chasing Carlisle United put six goals past Milkins. Injury meant the team would be deprived the service of stalwart midfielder Albert McCann for the rest of the season.

As the New Year dawned – after unseasonable snow in Portsmouth had meant the postponement of a potentially lucrative Boxing Day match with Bristol City – it was the FA Cup which once again was to provide a little spice for the jaded palettes of supporters. On the face of it, Sheffield United were the last team Pompey would have wanted to face – even though the tie was at home – when the third round draw was made. A crowd of more than 20,000, however, was persuaded that all bad runs have to end sometime and they were rewarded with a coupon-busting 2-0 win, thanks to goals from Gosport-born centre-forward Ray Hiron and Trebilcock, whose Cup pedigree was long established.

The fourth round draw pitted Pompey against championship chasing Arsenal and the scene was set for the club's biggest match since the mid-1950s. Eventually the Gunners were to shoot down Pompey 3-2 in a controversial replay at Highbury, but only after two titanic struggles which saw Fratton Park attract a near 40,000 gate and Trebilcock etch another entry on his FA Cup roll of honour with a dramatic injury-time equaliser.

The fact that Pompey could live with the best did little to inspire league form, however. An unlikely first, and only, away win of the season was achieved at promotion-chasing Hull City at the end of January thanks to a last minute goal from Hiron. From then on, however, Pompey were to win just twice more, including an ominous run of ten winless matches to the end of the season.

A groin injury suffered by Milkins, which contributed to Sheffield Wednesday's 3-1 home win in March, allowed Standen the chance to extend his football career. The curtain finally came down on a season that only flattered to deceive when Leicester City gained a 2-1 win at Fratton which ensured the Midlands club were promoted as champions. That match also saw the last appearance of Harry Harris, who signed for the club in 1958 from Newport County, and in recognition of his long service he was asked to captain the team for the last time.

The board must have been less than impressed with a final position of sixteenth – although it meant saving money on position bonuses promised – but the reality of Pompey's increasingly precarious financial position was underlined when the club's accounts to June 1971 showed an overall loss of almost £58,000. With the transfer market poised to become increasingly inflationary, the club were far from able to compete to buy the calibre of player needed to turn first division aspirations into reality.

Match of the Season 1970-71

Portsmouth 1 Arsenal 1

FA Cup, 4th Round, 23 January 1971

As dramatic climaxes go, there are few in Pompey's history which match the intensity of excitement of this one. The die had been cast a little under three weeks previously, when the draw for the fourth round was made. Pompey, fresh from a surprise victory over Sheffield United, were drawn at home to Yeovil Town or Arsenal.

Provided the championship-chasing Gunners could shoot down their Southern League opponents at their sloping Huish home, the scene would be set for the biggest game Fratton had known since the mid-1950s.

Arsenal duly obliged 3-0 and the city of Portsmouth went Cup Crazy. The match was immediately made all-ticket and the board cannily announced that the next home match against Cardiff would enable fans to collect a voucher entitling them to a ticket for the big game. Almost 25,000 turned up – nearly double the average gate for the season – only for City to win 3-1 against an insipid Pompey, who offered little suggestion they could cause an upset.

The national press, too, chose to focus on what was undoubtedly the most intriguing tie of the round. Celebrated *Daily Mirror* photographer Monte Fresco turned up to shoot a pre-match feature and Mike Trebilcock was in demand for pictures of him and that Cup medal which his two goals for Everton had helped earn in the 1966 final.

BBC TV Match of the Day cameras were there to capture the action as Pompey, attacking the Milton End in the first half, set about an Arsenal side packed with household names including Bob Wilson, Ray Kennedy, John Radford, George Armstrong and Frank McLintock. It was the London side, however, who went ahead in the 35th minute when Peter Storey converted a penalty after George Ley had punched a goal-bound shot off the line.

The second half was virtually one-way traffic as Pompey pinned Arsenal back in an increasingly vain search of an equaliser. Wilson kept Arsenal in the game with a string of fine saves, but as the game slipped into injury-time he was finally undone as Fred Smith's cross eluded everyone except Trebilcock, who sent more than 39,000 fans wild as he slotted home from two yards out.

Seconds later the final whistle went and Pompey left the field to a deserved standing ovation. The replay – originally scheduled for 26 January – was postponed due to a waterlogged pitch until Monday 1 February. Thousands of fans travelled from the south coast, only to see Arsenal finally break Pompey's resistance in the dying minutes to secure a 3-2 win and a fifth round trip to Manchester City. The Gunners went on to win the league and cup double. For Pompey it was back to the humdrum world of the second division.

LEAGUE DIVISION 2   **1971-72**
Division 2   16th
League Cup   1st Round
FA Cup   5th Round

During the summer of 1971, Pompey finally rid themselves of the last vestiges of the Smith era. The former manager had been relieved of his general manager role on amicable terms in March, and as the club approached the start of the season the final details of a revolutionary link up with Waterlooville FC, newly promoted to the Division One South of the Southern League, were finalised.

When Pompey axed their reserve and youth set up in 1965 on the advice of Smith – who felt the Portsmouth area had little to offer in terms of young footballers – many felt it was a step backwards. The reasoning was partly financial. By simply having a first-team squad of seventeen players or so, the argument went that running costs could be kept to a minimum. But as the club's ever-widening balance sheet showed, the experiment was a failure. Now Pompey were to start running a 'reserve' set-up of sorts, with assistant coach Bobby Campbell taking over as 'Ville manager, enabling squad players to play competitive football rather than be forced to kick their heels on a Saturday. The relationship between the two clubs was further cemented by the announcement that 'Ville chairman Peter Faulkner was to join the board. Pompey also decided to re-establish its youth policy and start playing fixtures in the South West Counties League.

Against this backdrop, Tindall was given little room to sign new players. In the close season £20,000 was found to recruit Tottenham left-back John Collins, but the only other move was to recruit Plymouth forward Richard Reynolds on a free transfer. Initially, Pompey started brightly – although a first round exit from the League Cup at third division Bournemouth proved embarrassing – and when Hull City were convincingly beaten 3-1 at Boothferry Park in September, hopes rose that a top half of the table position was within reach. Alas, inconsistency was again to dog the team's progress. A run of poor results in October and November put the team in the bottom third of the table and when promotion-chasing Birmingham mauled Pompey 6-3 in early January relegation was a real possibility.

That month Tindall shuffled his squad, allowing midfielder Brian Bromley to move along the coast to Brighton – where he had been on loan since November – in a £15,000 deal and at the same time £25,000 was splashed out to sign Blackburn Rovers' experienced defender Billy Wilson.

DID YOU KNOW?

Portsmouth FC were one of the pioneers of ground-sharing. In the early 1970s they hosted several matches of Waterlooville, Pompey's nursery side.

The FA Cup once again provided a welcome distraction from league worries and temporarily lifted form to ensure a tension-free run-in to the season. After Northern Premier League side Boston United had been somewhat fortuitously seen off in the third round and third division Swansea City dispatched in round four, Pompey were drawn away to Birmingham City. Interest in Portsmouth was great and two special trains, 'Royal Blue Rockets' – as they were dubbed – were chartered to take more than 4,000 fans to St Andrews. There was to be no fairytale ending though, and despite seeing their side take an early lead thanks to a Reynolds goal, City were good value for their 3-1 win.

As in the previous season, league form dipped alarmingly after the cup exit, although the team did produce a fine display in March to beat champions-elect Norwich 2-1 at Fratton. Attendances meanwhile were slipping towards an all-time low. Four figure gates were the norm during March and April, and when Burnley arrived for the last game of the season, which coincided with dreadful weather, the final count saw just 5,885 fans in the ground – the lowest-ever attendance for a league game at Fratton.

Pompey finished the season in sixteenth place – the same as the previous season – and a return to the first division was looking more remote than ever. The link with Waterlooville was also beginning to unravel. The Southern League was unhappy with the arrangement and objected to both the Football Association and Football League, forcing a premature end to the experiment.

When the club's retained list was announced in May, goalkeeper Standen, journeyman striker Jim Storrie, defender Mike Travers and former England international centre-forward Ray Pointer were not on it. Neither was defender Tommy Youlden, defender Blant and, more controversially, Trebilcock, who was allowed to return to his native West Country at Torquay on a free transfer. Pointer was retained to help develop the new youth set-up. Fortunately for them, those players weren't around for the final humiliation of the season when local rivals Southampton came to Fratton to play a well-earned testimonial for goalkeeper John Milkins. Ninety torrid minutes later the Saints – who had narrowly escaped relegation to the second division – had run out 7-0 winners and Milkins was left to count the cost to his pride and disappointing receipts from another sub-6,000 gate.

DID YOU KNOW?

In 1965, Pompey's then manager George Smith scrapped the club's youth team on the grounds that there is 'nothing around Portsmouth except fish'.

The financial position was worsening, with the accounts due to show a loss of more than £90,000. As with many clubs, the increasing cost of running a professional football club against the backdrop of falling attendances made the traditional board of directors (comprising local businessmen and dignitaries) look increasingly anachronistic. Pompey needed substantial capital investment. Previous loan schemes and promised American investment had proved to be blind alleys, but unknown at the time, over the horizon, hope was springing eternal. Not, however, before the existing board decided to have one last throw of the dice.

Match of the Season 1971-72
Portsmouth 6 Fulham 3

Division 2, 23 October 1971

Pompey went into this match with newly promoted Fulham having failed to win in five matches. The apparent promise of September was giving way to a feeling of *déjà vu*, as the team drifted towards the relegation zone. Pompey were also missing striker and joint-leading scorer Ray Hiron, left out after the 1-1 midweek draw with Bristol City, all of which made the events that unfolded that afternoon all the more remarkable.

Pompey's hero was 5ft 5in winger Nicky Jennings who was drafted in to replace Hiron for his first full start of the season, having been out for six months with a fractured collarbone. After a fumbling opening fifteen minutes, Jennings seized on a half-clearance, then shortly afterwards he was involved with Trebilcock to set up Reynolds for his second goal.

After the break the game went goal-crazy, with a calculator needed to keep track of the score. Piper, who had been given the freedom of Fulham's back-four, flicked a cross into Trebilcock's path and the shot exploded past Webster. Hand then nodded in Treb's corner.

Munks then floored Johnston and Jim Conway converted a twice-taken penalty, only for the action to bounce to the other end. Fulham's offside trap came apart at the seams and right-back Fred Smith lobbed his one and only Pompey goal. Conway and Barrett stabbed home from corners to send a frisson of anxiety through the home crowd, but Jennings skipped past two defenders to finish the rout.

Fulham chairman and comedian Tommy Trinder saw the funny side afterwards, ruefully pointing to the 'Match Off' notice stored under the stand. 'Perhaps they should have put that out before we started!' he commented. Fulham were struggling to adjust to second division football after their promotion, and this result took their tally of goals conceded on their travels to 21 in seven matches. They would escape the drop, but only just.

For Pompey, it was their biggest win since Orient were beaten by an identical score at Brisbane Road in October 1963 and the largest victory at Fratton since Middlesbrough were also beaten 6-3 in December 1959. To no avail, however, as Pompey too, flirted with the relegation zone right until the penultimate match.

LEAGUE DIVISION 2   **1972-73**
Division 2   17th
League Cup   2nd Round
FA Cup   3rd Round

The start of the 1972-73 season proved to be another false dawn. Despite the tight financial circumstances, the board had sanctioned the purchase of West Ham centre-half Alan Stephenson for £32,000 and highly rated Peterborough and Wales Under-23 striker Peter Price for £27,000. Promising 17-year-old Arsenal reserve goalkeeper Graham Horn was signed on loan as cover for Milkins and was pitched into action for the opening-day clash at Nottingham Forest, who had just been relegated. Horn emerged with his goal intact and Pompey with an encouraging point. Wins in the next two matches, at home to Cardiff and away at Millwall, hinted at promising things to come. Midfielder Brian Lewis, who had been re-signed at the end of the previous season from Colchester for £8,500, was in particularly fine form, scoring three times in the two victories.

Within a week three home defeats had put things into clearer perspective. More than 16,000 were persuaded into Fratton for a top-of-the-table midweek meeting with Huddersfield. Not for the first time, the team fluffed their lines as Town went away with a 2-1 win. By the time Burnley collected two easy points on the following Saturday, 5,000 fans had abandoned a clearly leaky vessel. On the following Tuesday third division Chesterfield secured a 1-0 League Cup victory with rather more comfort than the scoreline suggested and the gate had plummeted to below 7,000.

More significantly, Price had been laid low by a back injury sustained on the opening day, which was to plague his Pompey career and, as autumn set in, it was evident that the signing of Stephenson had done little to shore up the porous defence. In September Tindall was forced to sell full-back George Ley for £28,000 to newly promoted Brighton in order to stem the increasing losses as gates averaged no more than 8,000. The board's gamble had failed and Pompey were doomed to yet another season of struggle.

When Pompey played host to fellow strugglers Sunderland on 9 December, the team had won just once in ten matches. Not surprisingly the attendance set a new all-time low of just 5,783, and the team contrived to throw away a 2-1 lead in the dying minutes by conceding two goals. The result dumped the club into 20th position – one above the two relegation places.

Action was urgently needed and the following Saturday rumours gained substance concerning a local property investor who was looking to invest a substantial amount of capital into the club in return for a place on the board. Bramwell John Deacon was invited by the directors to attend the home match against Middlesbrough as their guest and immediately afterwards entered into negotiations. On 27 December it was announced that Deacon would join the board.

Two days later the team celebrated by gaining a useful 2-0 win at Cardiff to lift the team out of the danger zone and Deacon's money was immediately put to work with the re-signing of former favourite Bobby Kellard from Crystal Palace. Within the week winger Ken Foggo arrived in a £25,000 deal from Norwich City and despite a disappointing FA Cup exit at the hands of Bristol City, league form improved dramatically.

Three consecutive wins in late January and early February, including a spectacular 5-0 demolition of Preston at Deepdale (which ironically cost Alan Ball's father the manager's job at North End), seemed to remove the threat of relegation. The last match of an unbeaten seven-game run saw Pompey beat Nottingham Forest 2-0 at Fratton, with the second goal coming from Ray Hiron, his 100th in the league. Not a bad record for the gangly forward who had been discovered playing for Hampshire League side Fareham Town in 1964.

But then things began to go wrong. Goalkeeper Horn, who had emerged as a young man with great potential, was recalled from his loan by Arsenal and promptly sold to Luton Town. Ron Tilsed, another Highbury reserve, arrived as his replacement. The run of good form ended with a three goal defeat at Middlesbrough, and just two further wins from the next ten matches left the relegation equation in the balance.

Pompey faced a tricky trip along the coast on Easter Monday for their penultimate game of the season to face Brighton. Albion had rallied from a virtually impossible position at Christmas to be within striking distance of safety as the season entered the final strait. On the last day of the season Pompey were also away at Huddersfield, another team fighting for their lives, but the situation was clear. Provided Pompey took a point from the two games they would be safe. Ironically Pompey's saviour at the Goldstone was to be veteran centre-forward Ray Pointer, now 36 years old, who had been coaxed out of retirement to cover a paper-thin squad. His goal ensured a share of the spoils in a 1-1 draw and the Deacon revolution could begin in earnest.

Although relegation had been a real possibility, the main talking point among fans as the season drew to a close had been the promise that Deacon was to back his dream to take Pompey back to

Division One by buying and buying big. They did not have to wait long to see words turned into action. Tindall, closely monitored by Deacon, had already spent £45,000 on Southampton's Welsh international forward, Ron Davies, in April, before splashing out £55,000 on Bristol Rovers' Welsh international full-back Phil Roberts, and, most sensationally of all, £100,000 to bring in Arsenal's talented, but misfit, winger Peter Marinello. Each transfer deal in turn shattered the club's record transfer outlay, and the publicity generated was enormous.

The chief beneficiary in the short term was long-serving midfielder Albert McCann, who had signed for the club from Coventry City back in 1962. McCann had a testimonial scheduled for May against West Ham, and as Pompey paraded their new signings in their line-up more than 22,000 fans turned up to see the new dawn. And very impressed they were, too. With Marinello at his tricky, teasing best and Davies rolling back the years to grab a hat-trick, Hammers were trounced 4-2. Even McCann got in on the act with a goal.

In retrospect, the expectations that that result produced were probably unrealistic. A week previously Hull City had put five past West Ham, and the London team used the Pompey game to blood one or two younger players. But the result certainly whetted Pompey fans' appetite for the coming season, in which the club would celebrate its 75th anniversary. Twenty five years before, the team had served up a first division championship for the club's Golden Jubilee and hopes were high that 1973-74 could be just as memorable.

Match of the Season 1972-73

Portsmouth 0 Middlesbrough 0

Division 2, 16 December 1972

It was on this chilly December afternoon that Portsmouth Football Club – a proud institution not far short of its 75th birthday – touched the first of what were to prove a steady stream of low points during the 1970s, which eventually culminated with the club's relegation to Division Four.

The attendance against Sunderland the previous week had set a Football League low for the club, but with pre-Christmas shopping likely to create an unwelcome diversion, the indications were that even that unwanted record was under threat. Once the turnstiles had stopped revolving, just 4,688 paying customers had made it to the match – a still unchallenged nadir.

DID YOU KNOW?

As a Fourth Division club in 1979-80, Pompey had four League attendances in excess of 20,000.

However, things were shortly to take a turn for the better. Among the guests in the directors' box was Bramwell John Deacon, a Southampton-based property magnate. He had been invited by vice-president Sir Alfred Blake, aware of the club's increasingly desperate search for an individual with the necessary wherewithal to secure the financial future of the club.

Deacon, too, was keen to become involved in football. A brief courtship with Southampton had been politely, but firmly, rebuffed, but seventeen miles down the road he found an apparently tailor-made suitor. Pompey had all the pedigree one could ask for – two championships and an FA Cup triumph attained within living memory, plus a latent rather than a loyal fan base, which if tapped could still compete with the biggest, should glory be glimpsed.

All that was needed was someone willing and able to stump up the cash required to build a promotion-winning team and the crowds, money and, perhaps most important of all, adulation, would start to roll in.

That was the dream that seduced John Deacon. His apparent fortune, based on the booming property market of the late 1960s and early 1970s, was the factor which turned the head of a board keen to see Pompey back where they and the club's supporters felt they belonged.

Happily, the dream survived a nondescript encounter with Middlesborough. After a featureless 0-0 draw, Pompey slipped to 21st place in the second division. Only Brighton, who were sinking without trace, kept the team off the foot of the table.

Shortly after the end of the match, negotiations were underway which were to culminate with Deacon taking full control of Portsmouth FC by May 1973. It was announced on 27 December that he would be joining the board, promising to get Pompey out of the second division in three years. He was to prove as good as his word.

LEAGUE DIVISION 2   **1973-74**
Division 2   15th
League Cup   2nd Round
FA Cup   5th Round

Having before the end of May invested the best part of £200,000 in players for the coming season, it was no surprise to find little more transfer activity during the summer of 1973. The only other signings were England amateur international winger Mick Mellows from non-league Winchester City, and Paul Smith, a midfielder who had been freed by Manchester City.

However, behind the scenes the managerial structure of the club was being revamped. Firstly, came the inevitable move in May, when Dennis Collett stood down as chairman, allowing Deacon to take over. Shortly afterwards it was announced that John Mortimore, who at the time was coaching in Greece, would be returning to England to take charge of team affairs at Fratton. Tindall would become the club's general manager.

Deacon also decided Pompey needed a new-look on the field. As the club approached its 75th-anniversary season, supporters were invited to submit designs for a new strip in a competition run by *The News*. The winning entry dispensed with the traditional blue shirts and instead featured a predominantly white shirt, with blue trim and two vertical blue bands down the left side. At the time, it was felt the design was in keeping with a modern, continental image, but overall it was an unpopular move, as well as ultimately becoming synonymous with a period of dramatic decline for the club.

The club also revealed that it would be entering a reserve team in the Midweek Football League – an application to join the Football Combination having been rejected – and that the youth team, which was progressing steadily, would re-join the South East Counties League.

In pre-season, Pompey attempted to organise a south-coast cup tournament, but unfortunately Southampton were unenthusastic. This left what were effectively warm-up matches with third division neighbours Brighton and Bournemouth, played on a home and away basis. Three draws and a win, 4-1 at home to Brighton, were hardly the stuff of champions, but nevertheless almost 20,000 fans were attracted to the opening league fixture of the season, a home match with Middlesbrough, now managed by former World Cup winner Jack Charlton.

Characteristically, Pompey failed to make the most of their big opportunity to impress and Boro's 1-0 win was the first of many *en*

route to their second division championship. It took Pompey until
October to secure their first home win, with only some good away
form keeping the team out of trouble. By the time home form did
pick up during the autumn, the team were beginning to unravel on
their journeys. Notably third division Plymouth thrashed them 4-0
in the League Cup and Blackpool did likewise 5-0 in the league.
This was clearly not what Deacon had in mind, especially after all
the money he had spent.

December's AGM revealed a loss of more than £167,000, up to
the end of June 1973, by which time the club's overall debt was not
far short of £300,000. At that meeting Deacon announced a new
150,000 share issue, which he and his Superior Properties company
took up entirely, giving him a 69 per cent controlling interest in the
club. At the same time, Mortimore was given money to spend and
the club's record transfer fee was broken again to sign Fulham
centre-half Paul Went for £155,000. Another £55,000 was found to
buy Leicester City defender Malcolm Manley.

The Went-Manley partnership at the heart of the defence
brought a much-needed element of stability to the team and a New
Year's Day victory at Fratton over Cardiff City, in front of more
than 20,000 spectators, saw the team edge into the top ten of the
division.

These were the days of petrol crises, three-day weeks, striking
miners and power cuts, and Pompey were not immune to their
effects. The Cardiff game kicked off at 2pm, to ensure that it was
completed in daylight, thereby saving scarce fuel, and the match
programme was reduced to a four-page black and white affair
costing 2p. To circumvent the floodlight ban, Pompey introduced
their own generator for the next home league fixture, against promotion-chasing Luton Town, and attracted a larger than average
gate in excess of 18,000. Unfortunately, the experiment ended
embarrassingly when the makeshift generator conked out midway
through the second half. The club attracted some unwanted adverse
publicity as the mains had to be switched on to ensure public
safety.

A handy FA Cup run was also taking shape, despite a scare
when lowly Swindon took a 3-1 half-time lead in the third round at
Fratton. A replay victory on the following Tuesday afternoon – that
floodlight ban again – set up a fourth round home tie with Orient,
who had been the surprise package of the second division and were
looking good for promotion.

Despite Deacon's misgivings – he was a devout Christian – the
club took advantage of a special dispensation by the Football Association in these chaotic times which allowed clubs to stage games on

Sundays. The response of the public was overwhelming and the club's biggest gate in three years, 32,838, turned up to see a goalless draw. Another afternoon replay, this time at Brisbane Road, failed to separate the teams and it took a third match, at neutral Selhurst Park – this time under lights – to put Pompey in the fifth round for the second time in three years. Their opponents would be Nottingham Forest at the City Ground.

By the time the tie came around in February, Manley's Pompey career was in tatters, his knee shattered the previous week at Notts County. He was to play just once more for the club before being forced to retire, and what many regarded as the most promising defensive partnership the club had enjoyed in years was broken. Once again thousands followed the team in search of cup glory, with hopes of a quarter-final appearance for the first time since 1952, but those dreams were dashed as Forest won by a single goal in front of more than 38,000.

At the turn of the year Pompey had placed eleven players on the transfer list, as the club sought to generate income and cut a huge wagebill. In the event, only one player actually departed – defender David Munks joining Swindon. However, having seen Tilsed concede three goals at Oxford in his comeback after breaking an arm at Luton in September, Mortimore decided in March he needed a third goalkeeper, and spent £22,500 on Ipswich's David Best. The writing was also on the wall for long-serving keeper Milkins, who played his last game for the club in February against Sheffield Wednesday, before being allowed to join Oxford in the close season.

Yet again, Pompey's season fizzled out after the cup disappointment. Any hopes of a late push for promotion, in what was a distinctly average division – Carlisle were promoted in third place with just 49 points – faded away. The season ended with just two wins in the last nine matches. However, two products of the reinstated youth policy made encouraging debuts. Striker Andy Stewart, just seventeen years old, made a sensational impact with two goals in the last four matches of the season and in the final match, which saw Nottingham Forest stroll to a 2-0 win, he was joined by 18-year-old defender and former Southern Grammar schoolboy Peter Ellis.

The reserve team completed a league and cup double, but these were mere consolations to Deacon, who had seen all that money and effort rewarded with fifteenth position – just two places better than the previous season. The time was ripe for a clear out as it became obvious that Deacon's pockets were not bottomless. In fact, they were far from it. There were to be testing times ahead for Pompey and their fans.

Match of the Season 1973-74

Orient 0 Portsmouth 2

FA Cup, 4th Round, second replay, 5 February 1973

When Deacon took over, it was nights such as these that he envisaged as the rewards of owning a football club. His expensively assembled team had pushed an Orient team who were on-course for promotion to the first division all the way during the first two drawn instalments of this FA Cup fourth round tie.

In those times, second replays were generally staged at a neutral venue, and Selhurst Park, home of Crystal Palace, was deemed to be a suitable stage for what was to prove to be the decider.

Pompey, despite having failed to reach the quarter-final stage of the FA Cup for more than twenty years, had established a reputation of being a cup team and frequently took a large following with them, out of proportion to the club's league attendances. This match proved to be no different.

The A3 Portsmouth to London road was a sea of blue and white as Pompey fans made up the bulk of the 20,000 gate. Mortimore announced an unchanged team from the one which had been held to a draw at home by West Brom on the previous Sunday.

It was Mortimore's first-choice team and they did not disappoint on a wet evening. Kellard drew first blood in the 27th minute with a thunderous 30-yarder. The Chimes boomed out in the second half as Orient tried to force their way back, but it was Davies who made the game safe three minutes from time, elegantly wrong-footing two defenders before rifling home. George Petchey's Orient were left to concentrate on the league, but even that turned sour, their promotion push pipped at the last by Carlisle United.

As for Pompey, the win proved to be the high water-mark of the Mortimore regime. The fifth round came to anticlimactic end at Forest and the hopes of a late run for promotion never materialised.

With hindsight, it could be argued that Mortimore's team was ageing almost before it took shape. Without a legacy of young players to call upon – the youth squad having been abandoned in 1965 – he was almost working with one arm tied behind his back. It would not be long before he became the first, and by no means the last, manager to pay the price for failing to deliver Deacon's dream.

LEAGUE DIVISION 2   **1974-75**
Division 2   17th
League Cup   2nd Round
FA Cup   3rd Round

Pompey's players reported for pre-season training in July 1974 with no new signings on parade. However, several familiar faces had departed in a financially-driven end-of-season purge. McCann had moved to South Africa in the spring, while Jennings had joined Exeter City on a free transfer, and full-back Fred Smith joined Halifax on a similar basis. By the time the season began, Tilsed too had been given a free transfer, only to drift into non-league, Milkins had joined Oxford for a nominal fee, and Collins had been allowed to join Smith at the Shay for £8,000.

After an unconvincing series of friendly matches Pompey began with a tough trip to Bolton, shorn of the services of Went, Marinello and Kellard due to suspension, and the unfortunate Manley, who was facing a series of knee operations to try to save his career. Wanderers' comprehensive 3-0 win set the tone for a difficult autumn, which started sensationally on the morning of the home match with West Brom on 7 September. Deacon announced, to the surprise of all concerned, that Mortimore had been suspended for failing to deliver success. Tindall was to be put in charge of the team on a caretaker basis, pending the search for a successor.

Three defeats later, which included a derby loss at Southampton and Derby County's humiliating 5-1 win at Fratton in the second round of the League Cup, Deacon was able to announce on the eve of the midweek trip to Nottingham Forest that he had got his man. The former Liverpool and Scotland striker, and manager of Motherwell, Ian St John, was to take charge. The players responded well, following an initial meeting with their new boss at a Midlands hotel, by beating Forest 2-1, momentarily lifting the gloom which had enveloped Fratton.

It proved to be yet another false dawn, however, and a run of six matches without a goal in October-November saw Pompey sink to the bottom of the league and face an uphill struggle to avoid relegation. St John had been assured a transfer budget, but it was slow to materialise – indeed, money would have to be raised through sales – and he was forced to juggle his slender resources in late November by swapping striker Davies for Manchester United midfielder George Graham.

Graham's class galvanised the side and, coupled with the return of Hiron to the attack, results improved during January and February. A 3-0 home win against Orient actually lifted the side to the heady heights of seventeenth place. The only disappointment was the ignominy of becoming the first team to be knocked out of the FA Cup third round. This was on Friday night at Notts County, a game brought forward to avoid clashing with Forest's home tie with Tottenham.

The relegation battle was still touch and go, and it took consecutive Easter victories over fellow strugglers Bristol Rovers and Millwall to finally kill off fears of the drop. A 2-2 draw at Fulham on the penultimate Saturday, following a brace of goals by Richie Reynolds, saved a point against the FA Cup finalists and removed even the mathematical possibility of going down.

In the boardroom, changes were afoot. Certain long-established directors found it difficult to come to terms with the football club having effectively become a subsidiary – and not a very successful one at that – of a property company. In April 1975 David Sparshatt left the board after six years service. He was the first of what was to prove a steady stream of departures as personalities clashed with Deacon's autocratic regime.

Of direct concern was the mounting financial crisis surrounding the club. The buoyant property market of the late 1960s had been replaced by a period of deep recession, along with the rest of the economy, and Deacon's company found it increasingly difficult to find the £1,500 or so each week needed to offset Pompey's day-to-day losses. In the financial year ending June 1974, Pompey lost more than £400,000, and it was clear that further economy measures, not to mention a hike in admission prices to 60p for terrace admission and £1.50 for the best seats, were called for.

During the season, the injury-plagued Peter Price was allowed to leave to try to rebuild his career at fourth division Barnsley, but the real carnage was to come as the season came to a close. In April, Kellard followed McCann's route to South African pastures, but when the club's retained list was announced in May some significant names did not appear. Stephenson, Foggo, Best and Lewis – all in their thirties and past their peak – were given free transfers, but most controversially striker Hiron, with more than 350 matches under his belt and 117 goals, was also deemed by St John to be surplus to requirements.

Hiron had just had his testimonial match, against Southampton, and it was a bitter-sweet affair for the Gosport lad who had served his local professional team so loyally. A glowing tribute by St John in the programme sat uneasily with his decision to allow the striker to leave. Hiron's goalscoring record of six goals in seventeen appearances that season compared favourably with most, and his return to the team coincided with the club's best run of the season.

The gate of less than 6,000 for his testimonial must have been somewhat of a disappointing reward for eleven years' service, but he bowed off the Fratton stage with two goals. A 2-1 win went some way to avenge a league double inflicted during the course of the season by the men from the Dell.

Hiron signed for Reading and was to play a significant role in their fourth division championship the following season, scoring vital goals. These were all the more galling for Pompey fans as the catastrophic events of the 1975-76 season were to unfold.

Match of the Season 1974-75
Portsmouth 4 Sunderland 2

Division 2, 11 January 1975

One of the joys of football is that every so often a result comes along that turns the form-book on its head. So it proved at Fratton Park on this unseasonably mild January afternoon.

At kick-off, few of the 14,000 spectators at the game would have given lowly Pompey much hope against a promotion-chasing Sunderland team who were neck-and-neck with Manchester United at the top of the table. Bob Stokoe's side still contained the bulk of the team which had sensationally won the FA Cup as a second division side in 1973 against Leeds, including Jim Montgomery in goal and centre-half Dave Watson dominating a defence which had conceded just seventeen goals in 24 games.

Pompey, by contrast, were rooted in the bottom three. The previous week they had bowed out of the FA Cup at Notts County and manager St John reacted to that defeat by leaving out young striker Andy Stewart and pushing recent signing George Graham up front to partner Hiron. Brian Lewis came into midfield for his first game since coming on as a substitute against Bolton on the opening day.

At half-time, all seemed to be going according to the script as 'Pop' Robson's goal for Sunderland separated the teams. Shortly after the interval, however, Hiron got ahead of Moncur to slot home the equaliser and within twenty minutes Fratton was in raptures as Pompey led 3-1. Prompted by man-of-the-match Lewis, centre-half Went waltzed forward to score his first goal for the club, then Hiron and Graham combined to put Mellows clear. His cross was volleyed home by Piper for a memorable goal. Graham put the icing on the cake with his 100th league goal five minutes from the end, and not even Vic Halom's late consolation could take the gloss off what *The News* described as a 'magic show' by Pompey.

DID YOU KNOW?

In 1974-75 Mick Mellows was Pompey's leading scorer with eight goals. In 1969 he had scored at Wembley, for Sutton United in the Amateur Cup final.

It was without doubt St John's finest moment as Pompey manager, and it proved to be the springboard to an eight-match unbeaten home run which was to effectively banish relegation fears. For Sunderland it was the beginning of the end of their promotion campaign. They eventually slipped to fourth place, pipped by Norwich, who ironically clinched promotion on the last day of the season by ending Pompey's run of home form, winning 3-0.

Twelve months later, in April 1976, Pompey and Sunderland were to meet again, this time at Roker Park. By then the two clubs' fortunes had diverged dramatically.

LEAGUE DIVISION 2   **1975-76**
Division 2   22nd (relegated)
League Cup   2nd Round
FA Cup   4th Round

If St John thought his purge of the club's deadwood would per-suade his employer to allow him to spend in order to strengthen a squad that was now short on experience, he was to be disap-pointed. The only players to arrive at Fratton in the summer of 1975 came on free transfers. First was centre-back Paul Cahill, who had been on loan from Coventry at the end of the previous season. He was joined by midfielder Allan Kane, who had been released by Hibernian, Motherwell forward Bobby McGuinness, and goalkeeper Graeme Lloyd, surplus to requirements at Liverpool.

Very quickly it became apparent that the squad was out of its depth and that goals were going to be at a premium. The first seven matches produced just six and a solitary victory at Orient – and that only thanks to a Bobby Fisher own-goal. Some encouraging draws, against newly relegated Chelsea and at home to first division Leices-ter in the League Cup, merely papered over the deficiencies.

The rot set in with a vengeance at the end of September when Southampton demolished Pompey 4-0 in front of the ITV cameras at the Dell. Stung pride helped to force draws in the next three matches, including one at home to Sunderland, but the 1-1 draw with Hull City on 20 October was to prove the last point Pompey were to gain until the mid-December. And points were only half the problem. When Peter Marinello tucked away a late consolation as Bristol Rovers gained a 2-1 victory at Fratton three days later, it was to be last home goal fans were to celebrate until January.

St John tried everything, to no avail. He pitched in promising young midfielder Chris Kamara and Portsmouth-born centre for-ward Steve Foster – both products of an increasingly successful youth policy – long before they were sufficiently mature. He signed midfielder Ian Collard on loan from Ipswich, only to see him in-jured in his one and only league appearance, at Carlisle. Midfielder Tony Macken arrived from Derby, temporarily for an unproductive ten-game spell, as did St John's former Liverpool team-mate John McLaughlin for an equally forgettable five matches, until a knee injury ended the loan.

At the end of October St John again returned to his former Anfield stamping ground, this time to sign former England interna-tional full-back Chris Lawler on a free transfer. Shoring up an increasingly leaky defence was the easy part. Finding the man who could score the goals that would give Pompey a fighting chance of

staying up, however, looked a task beyond an increasingly belea-
guered St John.

As the defeats mounted, even 21st place looked to be fast disap-
pearing over the horizon. The nightmare run finally ended after a
club-record ninth consecutive loss at West Brom in December.
Pompey's consolation goal, as Albion won 3-1, was scored by
Marinello, that six-figure icon of hope back in May 1973, who had
failed ever since to deliver the goods on a consistent basis. It was to
prove to be his last act in a Pompey shirt. Within days he had been
sold to Motherwell for a cut-price £35,000; revenue that was desperately needed to pay off the most pressing creditors, now circling the
club like vultures.

Briefly Pompey rallied. McGuinness's second goal that season
gave the team an unlikely 1-0 win at Nottingham Forest. On Boxing
Day the team scored more than once in a league game for the first
time to beat Charlton 3-1. Sandwiched between those results, however, was 21st placed York City's 1-0 win at Fratton. Two steps
forward, one step back.

The FA Cup proved a distraction. In the third round, first division Birmingham City attracted a 19,000 gate to Fratton. The Midlanders were stunned when another product of Pompey's youth
policy, striker Billy Eames, levelled Trevor Francis's early goal. It
was Portsmouth's first home goal in more than 450 minutes of
football. On the Tuesday, the teams met again at St Andrews for
the right to meet Charlton away. McGuinness scored probably his
most famous Pompey goal to secure an improbable upset. The
fourth round proved to be a typical let down, however, with Charlton winning comfortably in a Fratton replay, watched by more than
31,000.

In the league Pompey just about managed to keep in touch with
the 19th place that would mean salvation (three clubs now being
relegated), but too often good results – such as a 3-0 win at Blackburn in February – were followed by poor displays – consecutive
defeats by Chelsea and Notts County. The shocking form of the
autumn was to ultimately prove crucial in sending Pompey down.

Ironically, the last straw was snatched away by Southampton in
early April. The Saints arrived at Fratton fresh from a 2-0 FA Cup
semi-final success over Crystal Palace – thus securing their first
Wembley appearance. Their Tuesday night visit to Fratton – rearranged from the Saturday – attracted a crowd of more than 24,000.
To be fair, Pompey outplayed their neighbours for long periods
with just that all-important cutting edge missing. In the last minute
Pompey succumbed to a sucker punch from Mick Channon, which
meant any hopes of a miraculous redemption were all but buried.

Oldham's 5-2 win at Boundary Park four days later confirmed relegation to the third division for the first time since 1962.

Pompey ended the season with two consecutive defeats. The first, by one goal at Bristol City, ensured the West Country club's return to the first division for the first time in more than 60 years. The second, at Roker Park in front of more than 40,000, crowned Sunderland as champions. The contrasts could not be starker.

Financial storm clouds also continued to gather as Pompey's bankers took fright at the prospect of reduced income from third division football. A public meeting was called at the Guildhall in April where, before more than 1,000 fans, Deacon spelled out the drastic financial plight facing the club. In pursuing his dream of turning Pompey into a promotion chasing team, he had spent the best part of £500,000 and, in addition, guaranteed bank loans to the tune of £350,000. A whip-round on the night raised over £1,000 towards a fighting fund target of £100,000, and even though supporters formed the Pompey Action Group, pledged to raise funds for the club, the outlook was clearly bleak. The club even approached the city council for a loan but were, not surprisingly, turned down.

St John used his Scottish contacts to organise a fund-raising friendly in May against Celtic. Despite their traditional large away following, less than 10,000 turned up for the game, which was barely enough to cover expenses. In the circumstances the Celts' 6-1 win on the night was the least of Pompey's worries and St John was ordered to pare the wage-bill still further. Coach Pat Wright was the principal victim, though Reynolds and Hand found that their Pompey contracts, and therefore their Fratton careers, were at an end. They sought alternative employment in Holland and South Africa respectively.

Match of the Season 1975-76

Portsmouth 0 Charlton Athletic 3

FA Cup, 4th Round replay, 27 January 1976

The capacity for Portsmouth Football Club to shoot itself in the foot, while simultaneously slitting its own throat, was probably never better (or should that be worse?) illustrated than by the events of this evening fixture.

After a catastrophic autumn, the team were showing signs of a long-overdue renaissance. A run of three wins in six matches (the previous nine had been lost) had built fragile hopes that relegation might just prove not to be inevitable. At the same time the team had

---

DID YOU KNOW?

Several players and managers joined Pompey twice – Kellard, Lewis, Hand, Kamara,
Walsh, Wood, Claridge, Whittingham, Burrows, Alan Ball and Jim Smith.

---

confounded the critics by knocking first division Birmingham out of
the FA Cup in a third round replay at St Andrews.

In the fourth round a typically-large following from the south
coast had swelled the Valley attendance to more than 26,000, with a
late Norman Piper goal earning Pompey a deserved draw with
Charlton and a much-needed, money-spinning replay. The fifth
round draw also offered the opportunity of an equally lucrative visit
to Wolverhampton Wanderers.

St John named an unchanged team for the replay, with 18-year-
old Emsworth-born Billy Eames continuing to shoulder the attacking
responsibility with Bobby McGuinness. Between them the two had
scored three goals so far in January. The Scotsman had secured the
vital win at Birmingham and Eames scored the goal against City at
Fratton and, more importantly, the goal which earned Pompey their
first home league win of the season against Carlisle.

Typically, Pompey fans turned out in droves, but the queues
meant many didn't get in until half-time. That might not have
mattered had the team not self-destructed. Charlton dominated the
first half, but couldn't capitalise, Hunt going closest when Lloyd
turned his shot onto the bar. St John's interval tongue-lashing failed
to deliver the desired effect. In the 54th minute, Hope danced
round Cahill as he slipped and crossed for Powell. The deficit was
doubled when Flanagan slid in to convert Hales' centre three minutes later, the ball slipping from Lloyd's grasp. The tie was effectively dead.

By the time Hope netted Charlton's third goal near the end,
rounding Lloyd and clipping past Cahill's despairing hack, most
fans were on their way home. They were totally frustrated by their
team's inability to see off a side that Pompey, even in their parlous
state, had comprehensively beaten just one month previously.

In effect, Pompey's season ended that night. Even though the
arithmetic decreed Pompey could conceivably still get out of trouble, the collective morale of players, officials and supporters was
shattered.

LEAGUE DIVISION 3   **1976-77**
Division 3   20th
League Cup   1st Round
FA Cup   3rd Round

As temperatures soared during the summer of 1976, the simmering financial crisis at Fratton was set to boil over and threaten the very existence of the club itself. St John by now had resigned himself to trawling the free transfers in a bid to reinforce his squad. The only player to arrive was Luton striker Matt Pollock.

Pre-season saw Pompey take part in the Kent Cup, upsetting the Hampshire FA by not asking for permission to play in it. This cup was a slightly more competitive variation on the traditional friendly, and the team performed creditably, drawing with Oxford, beating Watford 4-2 and losing only to second division Luton. Optimism was high that Pompey might be able to at last find relative success on the field, but for their final friendly St John took his first team to Sussex League club Horsham, who won 1-0, and confidence was once again shattered.

As the league season got underway – Crystal Palace having already dumped Portsmouth out of the League Cup before the official start – Pompey were struggling. By early September they had won just once and were in the bottom third of the table. Gates were now averaging less than 8,000 and questions were increasingly raised over whether Pompey could survive the season. In mid-September Deacon was forced to admit that Pompey were in severe danger of folding and called on supporters to raise £35,000 in six weeks. Otherwise it might be too late.

Backed by an SOS – save our soccer – campaign organised by *The News* and chaired by local businessman Harry Garcia, money began to roll in. The club's troubles were attracting nationwide publicity. Deacon even called a truce with his long-time adversary in the boardroom, previous chairman Dennis Collett, as the 'save Pompey' spirit took hold. The one boardroom casualty was director and Southern TV presenter Peter Clark, who resigned as the crisis deepened. Few mourned his leaving, having wondered why he had been invited to join in the spring, so apparently tenuous were his Portsmouth connections.

On the field, things were almost as desperate. Following Shrewsbury's comprehensive 4-1 win in early October, St John sold Paul Went to Cardiff for £25,000. Although the sale was primarily aimed at shifting one of the highest paid players out of the club and earning some revenue to pay the most pressing creditors, there was little doubt that Went and St John failed to see eye to eye. In desperation, the manager had pushed the strapping defender into attack from the start of the season, but just one goal in six matches told its own story.

The team finally hit rock bottom on a Friday night at Northampton, where an experienced team, including the likes of Billy Wilson, Phil Roberts and Norman Piper, gifted the Cobblers a 3-1 win. St John reacted to the defeat by dropping a number of senior players and the team he named to play Port Vale the following Saturday was probably the least experienced in the club's history. Seven of the twelve players were aged 20 or under and had come through the youth ranks. A 1-1 scoreline was followed by an impressive 2-2 draw at high-flying Rotherham. The 'Pompey Babes' were born.

By November more than £20,000 had been raised by the SOS fund – nuggets of Fratton turf had been sponsored by the square foot – and the immediate threat of bankruptcy passed. New blood was recruited to the boardroom in the shape of Gordon Gauntlett and Jim Sloan, both local men with impeccable Pompey credentials, and manager St John was even able to shuffle his squad.

George Graham and St John had fallen out ever since the former Arsenal midfielder was dropped, following Chesterfield's 1-0 win at Fratton in August. The chance to swap him, not to mention his wage packet, for the 23-year-old Crystal Palace striker Dave Kemp, who had impressed with a brace of goals in the League Cup against Pompey back in August, was too good to resist.

Kemp's impact was almost immediate. He made his debut in mid-November and his first goal arrived three games later to secure a less than convincing FA Cup win over Southern League Minehead at Fratton Park.

December was also the month when any goodwill behind the scenes was blown apart. At the AGM, Deacon calculatingly removed Collett from the board after 21 years service. Three directors were up for re-election, including Collett. At the start of the meeting it was announced that the election would be on a one share, one vote basis, on which basis Deacon's keenest critic in the boardroom didn't have a hope.

On the field, however, things were improving. At last Pompey had a striker capable of scoring on a more or less regular basis and as results picked up over Christmas, the team pulled themselves out of the bottom four. A 1-0 victory over promotion-chasing Sussex rivals Brighton on Boxing Day was watched by more than 32,000 spectators.

The FA Cup almost brought more cheer for the club too, but despite a brave performance, Birmingham showed too much class for Pompey, who had been reduced to ten men after Paul Cahill was

---

DID YOU KNOW?

Between Boxing Day 1970 (v Bristol C) and February 1978 (v Exeter) Fratton Park did not have any first-team game postponed because of the weather.

---

sent off. The first division team sneaked through 1-0. A third share of another 30,000 plus gate helped to soften the blow, as did the fact that Pompey continued to pick up points to keep relegation fears at bay.

In March the money St John was promised back in September 1974 finally materialised. £5,000 was spent to sign Southampton striker Paul Gilchrist. No doubt St John afforded himself a wry smile as the ink dried on the cheque. The SOS fund was finally closed, having raised more than £30,000 in six months and earned itself a deserved niche in Pompey folklore.

When promotion-hopefuls Rotherham were walloped 5-1 on a sunny April afternoon, with Kemp scoring a hat-trick, thoughts of relegation seemed to have been banished for good, but a four-match losing run dramatically altered the picture and St John was doomed.

Mansfield's 2-0 victory on 2 May clinched the Stags' promotion to the second division for the first time. Pompey's fourth defeat in a row also sealed St John's fate as manager – he had come in for increasing criticism from the terraces – and the following day Deacon announced St John's suspension.

With three games left to play, and Pompey's hopes of staying out of the fourth division on a knife-edge, Deacon used all his persuasive powers to convince Jimmy Dickinson, 764 league appearances, two championship medals and now club secretary, that he was the man who could save Pompey from the ultimate ignominy.

And so he did, with a game to spare. Old heads Wilson and Roberts were back in the team as a priceless point was ground out at Preston. Companions in distress York City arrived at Fratton the following Saturday knowing that defeat would send them down and keep Pompey up. Once again the fans responded, with more than 14,000 inside Fratton to see two goals from another youth team product Clive Green, added to Kemp's fifteenth goal in 30 appearances, ensure a 3-1 win. The pitch invasion on the final whistle would have done justice to winning the FA Cup.

Pompey were seemingly back in business in more ways than one, and as fans drifted happily home they contented themselves with the thought that surely no season could be more traumatic than the one just experienced. Little did they realise this nightmare had a few more twists to come before it would be over.

Match of the Season 1976-77

Portsmouth 5　Rotherham United 1

Division 3, 16 April 1977

Anyone who was a Pompey fan in the 1970s will agree on one thing. Big victories were something that happened to other clubs. When Rotherham brought their promotion credentials to Fratton, a thrashing was probably as far from their minds as it was from the 10,482 fans who turned up to see one of the more remarkable performances from a Pompey side during this grim era.

The last time a Pompey side had scored more than four goals in any match was more than four years previously – a 5-0 win at Preston in February 1973. To unearth a similar feat at Fratton it was necessary to go back another eighteen months for the famous 6-3 mauling of Fulham. As for hat-tricks from Pompey players, step forward Mike Trebilcock, the last player to do so, against Blackburn in October 1970.

A glance at the league table prior to the game also indicated why a goal avalanche seemed unlikely. Rotherham were in fourth position, tucked in behind the leaders Brighton, Wrexham and Palace. Pompey, on the other hand, could still be sucked into the relegation mire, and recent form was cause for concern, with just one win in the previous seven games. Despite the signing of David Kemp – twelve strikes in 23 matches – goals were still hard to come by, and just one had been forthcoming in the previous four matches.

St John gambled by pitching muscular midfielder Denyer into the forward line and it paid off spectacularly. He nodded in Clive Green's cross after just seven minutes, then ten minutes later Foster flicked on Pullar's corner and Kemp's lunging head did the rest at the far post.

Phillips' 25-yarder pulled one back against the run of play, but after the break Pompey were irresistible, scoring twice in the first nine minutes. Kemp received Kamara's throw and turned to fire a deflected goal past McAllister; then he angled in from the left and from fifteen yards completed the first hat-trick of his career. In the 57th minute Denyer finished things off with a shot into the roof of the net after Kemp's shot was blocked.

The result should have been the springboard for Pompey to pull clear of the relegation zone. Instead, in typical fashion, the following Tuesday, with almost 13,000 fans attracted to Fratton, they were comprehensively outplayed by fellow strugglers Tranmere Rovers, who easily won 3-0. It took a victory in the penultimate game to kill off the threat of the dreaded drop.

LEAGUE DIVISION 3   **1977-78**
Division 3   24th (relegated)
League Cup   3rd Round
FA Cup   2nd Round

During the summer of 1977 hopes were high that a realistic promotion bid could be mounted during the coming season. The promise shown by the young players to emerge under St John had helped the reserves to the Midweek league championship. This was coupled with the 'feel-good factor', engendered by the escape from relegation and the appointment of Dickinson, which laid the grounds for that optimism. However, there was still precious little money around Fratton, despite the club having one of the best average attendances in the division, and Dickinson was forced to scour the bargain basement for additions to the squad.

Behind the scenes, youth coach Ray Crawford had been promoted to become the new manager's right-hand man and goalkeeper Steve Middleton arrived from Southampton on a free transfer. He was joined by his former team-mate at the Dell, Portsmouth-born striker Bobby Stokes, who sixteen months previously had scored the winning goal for the Saints at Wembley in the FA Cup final. His arrival on a free was only completed at the end of August, after Stokes had spent the summer playing in the United States for the Washington Diplomats.

Just before the start of the season Dickinson surprised everyone by selling promising midfielder Chris Kamara – one of St John's 'babes' – to Swindon for £17,500. The shock soon subsided as the team made a promising start, climaxing with a 2-0 win over first division Leicester in the second round of the League Cup, thanks to late goals from David Kemp and Clive Green. Four days later Chesterfield were defeated 3-0 at Fratton, due to a brace from Kemp and a debut goal from Stokes in front of more than 13,000 spectators, close to the break-even figure.

Within weeks, however, the club's bright start had clouded over. Even a six-match unbeaten run in September-October was marred by including a club-record five successive draws. The wheels came off Pompey's wagon when they travelled to Shrewsbury in late October only for the hosts to thrash them 6-1. In mitigation it could be pointed out that one of the Shrews' goals actually went wide of the post, bouncing back into play from the wall behind the goal, while another two were suspect penalties, but the effect on collective morale was corrosive.

Four consecutive league defeats dumped Pompey into the drop zone, with Tranmere's 5-2 win at Fratton the most disheartening

result, as Pompey had led 2-0. The team were also knocked out of
the League Cup in a replay at Swindon by the odd goal in seven in
a thriller that went to extra-time. The run was broken by a draw
with Port Vale, followed by back-to-back wins over Hereford in the
league – the first since September – and in the FA Cup against
Western League Bideford. To try to improve his squad, Dickinson
signed Brighton midfielder John Ruggiero on loan, and sought to
shore up his leaky defence by recruiting a familiar face: Eoin Hand
returned to Fratton after an 18-month spell in South Africa.

Leading Pompey's fight against the drop was Kemp, who scored
ten goals in ten matches during November and December and was
attracting the attention of clubs in higher divisions. Pompey resisted
the temptation to cash in on their prized asset, but as the New Year
dawned a calamitous relegation to Division Four looked increasingly
inevitable, especially after hopes of a lucrative FA Cup run were cut
short by a replay defeat at fourth division Swansea City. Gates were
still holding up, however, and more than 12,000 saw Pompey defeat
relegation rivals Bradford City on 2 January. Kemp opened the
scoring with his 21st league and cup goal of the season. Typically,
that promising performance was followed by an inept display at
fellow strugglers Port Vale, 2-0 winners, after which Ruggiero was
allowed to return to the Goldstone.

The Bradford City result proved to be Pompey's last win for nine
long weeks. By the time Shrewsbury became Pompey's next victims
in mid-March, the landscape at Fratton had changed fundamentally.
Off the field, Dickinson's assistant Crawford had left the club in
acrimonious circumstances in mid-January, to be replaced by Swindon's coach Frank Burrows, who was seen as the track-suited
'hands-on' type of coach who would complement Dickinson's more
traditional approach. It was under Burrows' eye that Pompey at last
moved into the transfer market to shore up an inadequate squad.
Full-back Tony Taylor arrived from Bristol Rovers for a nominal fee,
£15,000 was invested in Huddersfield winger Jim McCaffery, and
£25,000 went along the coast to Brighton to sign midfielder Steve
Piper.

Results remained poor, the latest nadir being Colchester's 4-0
eclipse of an awful team in early March. Another shuffle of playing
staff saw Norman Piper and Stokes have their contacts terminated,
while Pompey finally accepted the inevitable and allowed Kemp to
leave in a £75,000 deal for Carlisle United. Ironically, the striker had
failed to score in nine matches, but it was still somewhat of a surprise that he was allowed to join a club from the same division. As
part of the deal, midfielder John Lathan arrived at Fratton and
£25,000 was reinvested to replace Kemp with Colchester's journey-

man striker Colin Garwood. These arrivals were never going to stave off inevitable relegation, which was mathematically confirmed by Oxford's 2-0 victory at Fratton in early April.

For most fans, however, relegation was finally accepted four days after a 2-0 win over Shrewsbury, when Malcolm Allison, newly installed as manager of Plymouth, saw his team rip Pompey apart 5-1 in front of an 11,000 Fratton crowd. Mike Neasom opened his report in *The News* the following day: 'Where is Southport?'

With the pressure off, once relegation was confirmed, Pompey rounded off the season with consecutive away victories at Hereford and Rotherham, sandwiching a home defeat which saw Preston clinch promotion with two late goals. The contrast between two famous old clubs could not be more marked. In the last game of the season, at Millmoor, Dickinson gave a first start to youth team goalkeeper Alan Knight, who became the club's youngest-ever first team goalkeeper.

Knight's day was still to come for Pompey, but the club needed short-term solutions to ensure any stay in the Football League's basement was short and sweet. Paul Cahill and Mick Mellows were given free transfers, and they were joined on the 'not retained' list by young goalkeeper Phil Figgins and striker Clive Green, whose goals twelve months previously had helped to keep the team up. It set the scene for a busy summer of comings and goings.

Match of the Season 1977-78

Portsmouth 2 Tranmere Rovers 5

Division 3, 5 November 1977

As results go, it would take something spectacular by a Pompey team to produce a more wretched one than this. At half-time, 21st-placed Pompey were 2-0 up and cruising against their promotion-chasing rivals. By the final whistle they had been comprehensively beaten in ninety – or more accurately forty-five – wretched minutes in which the team showed itself for what it was; on the fast track to Division Four.

Ironically the team went into the match heartened by their performance, if not the result, at Swindon in midweek which saw them lose in a thrilling League Cup third round replay. Town eventually won 4-3 after extra-time. Goalkeeper Steve Middleton and his defence, however, were having a tough time, conceding fourteen goals in the previous four games. Ex-Saint Middleton was particularly feeling the pressure, as it had been his late slip against Swindon which had necessitated the replay in the first place.

DID YOU KNOW?

Q. When did Pompey drop a player but leave the team-sheet unchanged?
A. In February 1978 v Lincoln. Dickinson replaced Norman Piper with Steve Piper.

Tranmere had proved to be one of the surprise packages, mounting a promotion bid on the back of a stable team which had remained unchanged since the start of the season. Quickly, though, Pompey had their measure and Kemp stabbed in at the far post as the rain teemed down. Rovers earned a penalty, but Allen's effort thumped the bar, then Kemp showed him the way after Mellows was up-ended in the box.

Ronnie Moore pulled one back shortly after the break and Pompey were rocking. Then Flood stepped up to thrash a free-kick past Middleton in the 63rd minute and the knock-out punch was delivered two minutes later when Foster handled on the line and Allen made no mistake a second time.

By the time James sauntered round a static defence for the fifth, large sections of the crowd had already left the ground. Those that remained were too stunned even to manage a derisory chorus of 'What a load of rubbish'. For that is what it had been.

Middleton carried the can and wasn't seen in the first team again until March, along with Cahill, who was frozen out of the frame until February. But it made little difference. Pompey finally succumbed to the inevitable drop in early April.

Not that Tranmere prospered on the back of Pompey's generosity. When the teams met again in December a 2-0 win kept Rovers in the promotion picture, but their challenge faded in the New Year and they ended up in mid-table. Almost two years later the clubs' paths crossed again. By this time they were both in Division Four.

## 2

RESPECTABILITY
1978-1983

LEAGUE DIVISION 4	**1978-79**
Division 4	7th
League Cup	1st Round
FA Cup	2nd Round

During the summer of 1978 Jimmy Dickinson and Frank Burrows looked to bring in experienced professionals to form the backbone of a squad charged with the task of providing instant promotion. The fourth division was an unfamiliar place for a club who had two Football League championships and an FA Cup to its name. Only Huddersfield Town, relegated three seasons previously and whose own 'glory days' were further back in history than Pompey's, provided a link with a glorious past and a shared uncertain future.

The management duo had to cut their cloth according to their surroundings. £15,000 was found to sign Bury midfielder Jimmy McIlwraith, but the other signings were all on free transfers. Experienced Hereford goalkeeper Peter Mellor, who had kept goal in an FA Cup final for Fulham in 1975, was joined by his striking team-mate Steve Davey, who had spent most of his career with Plymouth. The final piece in the jigsaw was Port Vale striker Jeff Hemmerman, whose main claim to fame was to have scored on Match of the Day in March 1977 while playing for his hometown club Hull City. One other addition to the backroom staff was Burrows' former Swindon team-mate Stan Harland, who was appointed youth team coach.

Hopes were lifted by an encouraging pre-season, which included a 1-1 draw with first division Chelsea, but when the real action got underway fears that the club might fail to prosper even in their present modest surroundings seemed justified. Bradford City pinched the points on the opening day at Fratton, and on the following Tuesday York City took advantage of some generous defending to win 5-3 and send Pompey to 91st place in the Football League. Three days later Pompey were in action at Hartlepool and when Ian Crumplin gave the north east team the lead the foot of the table beckoned. That fate was averted when Davey scored his first goal of the season with ten minutes remaining, to the delight of the band of hardy fans who had made the journey north.

That goal and that point galvanised the side and a post-war league record of six consecutive clean sheets (by goalkeeper Mellor), brought five wins and put the club into the promotion picture. Not even the loss in early November of Steve Piper with the knee injury that was to finish his career – Piper had slotted comfortably into the centre-back role – succeeded in interrupting the momentum. Davey showed his versatility by filling the gap so admirably that the new clean-sheet record was equalled before the turn of the year. The final victory in that run, 4-0 at home to promotion rivals Reading in front of more than 12,000 fans, put the team in second place behind pace-setters Wimbledon.

As well as a tight defence, instrumental in Pompey's renaissance were the goals of Hemmerman, who by Christmas had scored fourteen in all competitions. He netted his fifteenth in a memorable 4-2 win at Plough Lane on Boxing Day as Pompey came from behind to close the gap on the leaders to one point. After that prolific start, however, his goals dried up as the New Year dawned and hopes of immediate promotion began to fade. Pompey's cause was not helped by a severe winter, even in the south of England, which meant a fixture pile-up. A break in the weather allowed Pompey to go top of the table in mid-January, although it took a last-minute equaliser by Leigh Barnard against struggling Rochdale to achieve the feat. The rhythm of the team was broken and even a series of friendlies, including a notable 2-0 win over the first division leaders West Brom, could not compensate. In February the club were also honoured when highly regarded young defender Foster was called up for the England Under-21 squad, although the game with Holland fell victim to the icy weather.

In a bid to freshen up the team, Dickinson used the fast improving financial position – gates were averaging around 11,000, unprecedented for Division Four – to sign striker Derek Showers for £15,000 from Bournemouth. His arrival made little difference as the team slithered out of contention. In late February – in front of the Match of the Day cameras, which were making a rare excursion into the lower leagues – promotion rivals Grimsby won 3-1 at Fratton Park, with experienced defender Billy Wilson gifting the Mariners two goals. A week later Pompey lost at a snowy Shay to give Halifax their first league win (2-0) at home since August, and as a result the team dropped out of the top four for the first time since October.

DID YOU KNOW?

When Pompey lost to Bradford City in August 1978 in their first Division 4 match, it was the first time they had ever lost their first match in a new competition.

Again Dickinson delved into the transfer market. £15,000 was needed to buy Northampton midfielder Steve Bryant, while Blackpool full-back Larry Milligan was signed on loan as deadline-day approached. It was late March when the team finally recaptured their form in a thrilling 1-1 draw at Oakwell against promotion rivals Barnsley. After the game a massive heart-attack put Dickinson on the critical list in a South Yorkshire hospital. The man who was Pompey through and through, with a record 764 league appearances behind him, not to mention spells as public relations officer, secretary and now manager, had found the responsibility of restoring the club to even a shadow of its former self increasingly burdensome. The fact that he paid the price with his health shocked everyone connected with the club to the core.

In the short term, Burrows assumed the role of caretaker manager. Though Dickinson slowly rebuilt his health, the team were unable to provide the best possible tonic as the effects of twelve matches in six weeks took its toll. Promotion hopes were finally extinguished when Barnsley arrived at Fratton in early May for the return, and clinched their own elevation, thanks to a Derek Bell goal. By this time, Dickinson was off the danger list, although it went without saying that his days as manager were over.

As the season petered out, it offered an odd postscript. In the penultimate match, on FA Cup final eve, Darlington won 2-0 at Feethams. The attendance of 1,140 was the lowest league gate ever for a match involving the club. That month, Dickinson resigned as manager and, unsurprisingly, Burrows was installed as his successor with Harland stepping up to be his assistant. Chairman John Deacon prepared to spend big for the second time in five years, but this time the rebuilding of the squad was on firmer foundations: in June, Steve Foster was sold to Brighton, newly promoted to Division One, for £150,000.

Match of the Season 1978-79

Portsmouth 4 Reading 0

Division 4, 23 December 1978

A league table with Pompey sitting in the top four was a novel experience for many younger fans. The first real test of the club's promotion potential came in this top-of-the-table clash with Maurice Evans' Reading, who were currently one point ahead of Pompey in second place.

The edge had been slightly taken off the match, as the previous Saturday the two clubs had met at the same venue in the second round of the FA Cup. Reading had won more convincingly than the 1-0 scoreline suggested, in front of a crowd of more than 17,000.

Dickinson made just one change to the side, with Davey moving up front to replace Garwood, and Billy Wilson stepping up from substitute to take his place as Foster's partner at the heart of the defence. Jimmy McIlwraith – in and out of the side since his summer arrival – was named as substitute.

It was the Saturday before Christmas, but the gate of 12,500 fans was from Pompey's point of view a slightly disappointing attendance, even in the context of fourth division football. However, those paying customers were soon to realise there was to be no repeat of the disappointment seven days earlier.

Despite playing into a stiff wind and driving rain, Pompey had the game sewn up by half-time after Peter Denyer and Leigh Barnard, both products of the club's youth policy, had left Reading reeling with a close-range strike and a thumping volley in the eleventh and nineteenth minute respectively.

Attacking the Fratton End after the break, Pompey turned on the style. Jeff Hemmerman scored his fourteenth goal of the season in the 48th minute, after being unleashed by a huge, wind-assisted drop-kick from goalkeeper Peter Mellor. It was Davey who completed the rout, when he stole in at the far post to convert a tricky chance from a narrow angle.

Three days later the club narrowed the odds on an instant return to the third division still further with a 4-2 Boxing Day victory at Wimbledon. It included a rare strike by Wilson, who curiously had swapped his number six shirt for Davey's number nine in a tactical ploy to confuse the Dons.

The quality of both performances made Pompey's subsequent dip in form all the more difficult to fathom. Eventually they finished in seventh place, nine points adrift of fourth-placed Barnsley, while champions Reading and Wimbledon both went on to clinch promotion with matches to spare.

LEAGUE DIVISION 4   **1979-80**
Division 4   4th (Promoted)
League Cup   1st Round
FA Cup   3rd Round

New manager Frank Burrows knew his squad needed reinforcing if promotion was to be ensured. Armed with Deacon's chequebook he embarked on one of the busiest summers in the transfer market the club had ever known. Rules regarding the transfer of players out of contract had changed, with clubs being forced to go to Football League arbitration if a fee could not be agreed. Burrows used all his persuasive powers to encourage Swindon's out-of-contract centre-half Steve Aizlewood and his right-back team-mate John McLaughlin to drop down a division and sign for Pompey. Ultimately, the Wiltshire club were upset to receive just £90,000 for the pair, but Burrows had acted decisively to cut short any criticism by supporters over the sale of Foster. Alan Rogers, the Plymouth winger, was also out of contract and he signed for Pompey in a £25,000 deal. Also arriving were Doncaster midfielder Joe Laidlaw for £15,000, Charlton midfielder Terry Brisley on a free transfer and Archie Styles, the former Everton and Birmingham left-back, who had been released by Peterborough.

Joining Foster through the Fratton Park exit door were his former youth team colleagues Denyer and Pullar, who joined Northampton and Exeter respectively. McIlwraith also cut short an unproductive stay in the south, rejoining Bury. By the time the players assembled for pre-season training in early July, Burrows had given the squad a distinctly 'third division' feel to it and was still in credit with his transfer dealings. A mixed pre-season saw Pompey beat first division Coventry 1-0, but that was offset when Southern League Dorchester turned them over 3-2. In addition, there was yet another League Cup exit at the hands of Swindon. By the end of September, however, Pompey were threatening to rewrite the record books.

The league season began with a flattering 3-0 win at Hartlepool, which might have turned out somewhat differently had Bryant not given Pompey the lead while half the opposing team were still celebrating a 'goal' of their own, unaware it had been ruled out for offside. Four more wins in a row, twelve goals scored and just two conceded, meant Pompey topped the table in early September and gates climbed towards the 15,000 mark. Even Tranmere's 4-1 win on a Friday night, in which McLaughlin was sent off, merely prompted another five straight wins with sixteen more goals in the process.

The team were playing thrilling football and the fans responded in numbers unheard of in the fourth division in recent times.

Around 15,000 saw Bournemouth and York beaten, approaching 17,000 watched a seven-goal thriller against Darlington. That match also heralded the fairytale two-goal debut of Phil Ashworth, signed by Burrows on a free transfer from Rochdale as cover for Derek Showers, who had been ruled out for the rest of the season by a knee injury.

Matching Pompey virtually point for point and goal for goal were old rivals Huddersfield Town and their Yorkshire neighbours Bradford City. By a quirk of the fixture list, Pompey faced both teams on successive Saturdays in October 1979. Two handsome wins – 3-1 at Leeds Road and 4-1 at home to Bradford City – virtually persuaded the bookmakers to stop taking bets on promotion. Then the first niggling doubts set in. The flow of goals had deflected attention from a porous defence, and twice within a fortnight Newport County exposed those frailties, winning 2-0 at Fratton in front of more than 20,000 and then 4-3 at Somerton Park. Those defeats were sandwiched between another at Doncaster Rovers, and a less than convincing last-gasp win in the return with Hartlepool.

As Christmas approached, the team recovered their poise to record their 50th league goal of the season in a 4-0 thrashing of Lincoln, while Newport were made to pay for their earlier impudence, losing to Brisley's early goal at Fratton in the first round of the FA Cup. However, Burrows moved again in the transfer market to eradicate any signs of complacency. Port Vale midfielder Kenny Todd had already arrived in October for £20,000 and he was joined in Pompey's reserve team by Wigan winger Ian Purdie in November for a similar fee. Just before Christmas, Burrows shocked everyone by shelling out £60,000 on Bury striker David Gregory and another £15,000 on Plymouth forward Steve Perrin. Goals were hardly a problem, with Colin Garwood particularly prolific, netting his seventeenth of the season in a 3-1 win over Halifax in early December before injury ruled him out for six weeks.

The benefits of having such a large squad were underlined on Boxing Day when a patched up team ground out a 0-0 draw at Hereford. Nearly all the regulars were back in the side for the last match of the 1970s at Fratton, when Pompey closed the account on a painful decade in style, thrashing Northampton 6-1. One of the bonuses for Burrows had been the emergence of 18-year-old goalkeeper Alan Knight to challenge Mellor. Since November he had been keeping the popular veteran out of the team, but on New Year's Day he had a nightmare as Aldershot underlined their own promotion potential winning 3-1 in front of a stunned Fratton crowd of more than 23,000.

```
DID YOU KNOW?

Pompey were drawn against Swindon Town in the League Cup in three successive
seasons (1977-78, 1978-79, and 1979-80) and lost all three.
```

Mellor was back between the posts for a delayed FA Cup second round, second replay, at third division Wimbledon, with the prize a crack at first division Middlesbrough at home the following Wednesday. A Hemmerman goal set up the biggest cup game at Fratton since Arsenal in January 1971. The match generated tremendous interest in the city and reinforced the prevailing view that Pompey were truly a 'sleeping giant'. More than 31,000 witnessed a titanic struggle, which would have gone Pompey's way had a linesman's flag not ruled out a late Hemmerman 'winner' after Brisley had levelled Terry Cochrane's opener. Boro won the replay 3-0 and the defeat took much of the fizz out of the team's season.

Between January and March the team won just three out of fourteen matches and what once looked like the formality of promotion became increasingly uncertain as Walsall, Huddersfield, Bradford City and Newport continued to set a ferocious pace. Garwood had also been sold, controversially to Aldershot for £60,000 in February, and the money invested in Watford centre-back Alan Garner, only for injury to restrict his appearances to just three. Midfielder Jimmy Brown also arrived from a spell in Greece on a short-term contract. The team finally found form in April, winning three matches away from home, but promotion still remained in the balance as first struggling Hereford and then their companions-in-distress Crewe eked out unlikely draws at Fratton.

Though Peterborough were beaten 4-0 in the last home match of the season – thanks in part to two own-goals – promotion was out of the team's own hands. Assuming Pompey won at Northampton, either Newport or Bradford City would have to slip up in the last week of the season, if the club were to go up by virtue of superior goal-difference. Newport opened the gates by losing in midweek to Rochdale, when a draw would have guaranteed them promotion. Buoyed by that result, more than 8,000 Pompey fans turned the County Ground into a sea of blue and white. Despite having a squad ravaged by flu the week before, Pompey duly fulfilled their side of the bargain, winning 2-0 thanks to goals from Steve Davey and Ian Purdie, who was making a rare appearance for the unwell Rogers. Attention now turned to the Newport and Bradford City results. Word filtered through that the Welsh team had won 4-2 at Walsall, but that Bradford City had lost at Peterborough by a single goal. Pompey were up! Scenes of unprecedented celebration followed as players, supporters and officials shared in the relief of emerging from a seemingly endless journey through a dark tunnel, which at times had threatened the very existence of the club.

The party continued on Monday as Brighton were beaten 1-0 in a friendly, organised as part of the Foster deal, and later that week the club was honoured by the city council with a civic reception. Thousands of fans lined the streets to acclaim the team on the open-top bus ride to the Guildhall. Burrows was not fooled by the euphoria, however. He knew further strengthening was needed if Pompey were to compete at the higher level.

Match of the Season 1979-80

Portsmouth 4 Bradford City 1

Division 4, 23 October 1979

Pompey's start to the season had been virtually perfect. Of ten matches played, nine had been won and 36 goals scored. The Saturday prior to Bradford City's arrival had produced a top class performance to see off Huddersfield, who boasted a similarly impressive record, despite having two-goal striker Jeff Hemmerman sent off. That was to prove to be just the appetiser.

For the main course, the team served up a sumptuous perform-ance against a Bradford City team who had promotion pretensions themselves. At kick-off they lay a point behind Pompey in third place; by the end of it they seemed light years behind.

Manager Frank Burrows made just one change, with Phil Ashworth, signed on a free from Rochdale four weeks previously and already with two goals from his only appearance against Darlington, coming in for the suspended Hemmerman. Interest in Pompey's powerful start had generated tremendous interest with gates averaging around 15,000, but it now reached surreal propor-tions. The attendance of 23,871 provided a gate better than five first division games that day.

Within two minutes Ashworth must have thought Roy of the Rovers was his scriptwriter as his deft flick from close range put Pompey one up. On 42 minutes he knew that was the case, when his turn and instant shot fizzed into the bottom corner to send the crowd wild. Little did he know, but Ashworth was to play just twice more in the first team. In between, winger Alan Rogers had produced an audacious piece of skill in the 34th minute to chip the City keeper Steve Smith, before nodding home.

After the interval City rallied and sent one or two shivers of anxiety through the crowd as Terry Dolan pulled a goal back with a

20-yard shot. The crowd's nerves were finally quelled with three minutes to go, when Colin Garwood poached his ninth goal of the season.

It had been captivating stuff and few of those present doubted that the rest of the division would be competing for the remaining promotion places behind Pompey come May. As it turned out, three days later the team lost their perfect home record, as Newport won 2-0. By the last day of the season it was in fact Bradford City who were in the promotion driving seat and Pompey who needed a slice of luck if they were not to miss out. City duly obliged, losing in their last match.

LEAGUE DIVISION 3   1980-81
Division 3   6th
League Cup   4th Round
FA Cup   1st Round

After the frenetic wheeling and dealing of the previous summer, Burrows restricted himself to just one signing as the club prepared for third division football for the first time in three years. The forward line was bolstered by the arrival of Mick Tait from Hull City for £100,000, a player who had been the scourge of Pompey's defence at his previous clubs. Leaving the club was striker Ashworth, who joined Scunthorpe on a free transfer. Midfielder Jimmy Brown also departed, despite the best efforts of fans in the Guildhall celebrations chanting: 'Give him a contract!' Injury forced full-back Archie Styles to retire and he became youth coach.

Optimism was high that a second successive promotion could be achieved, the bookies installing the team as one of the favourites. The positive approach was reflected in a new shirt, which featured white epaulettes on the traditional blue and a new, 'copyrightable' crest featuring a football on a crossed sword and anchor. The only hitch in the pre-season preparations was the knee injury suffered by striker Jeff Hemmerman, which ruled him out until December.

Pompey began in fine fettle, despatching divisional rivals Plymouth on aggregate in the League Cup, before winning their first four league games. The backbone of the team was the one that had won promotion, with a fit-again Alan Garner forming a formidable partnership with Aizlewood. The fact that Tait struggled initially to find his way was offset by the return of a resurgent Derek Showers after almost a year out injured. The League Cup was offering additional interest, as second division Oldham were beaten by virtue of the away-goals rule, to provide a welcome distraction as the early league momentum subsided. The third round saw Pompey drawn away to another second division team, Bristol Rovers. After a creditable 0-0 draw at Ashton Gate (Rovers' Eastville ground was out of action due to a fire), more than 18,000 turned up for the replay to decide who would meet the reigning League Champions Liverpool at Anfield. Once Gregory had scored early on there was only one outcome and Perrin's late second was merely icing on a very big cake. The seeds of one of the greatest nights in Pompey folklore had been sown.

Portsmouth succumbed to the mighty Reds, but Liverpool's 4-1 victory flattered them. The experience helped to galvanise Pompey's performances in the league and five successive wins in late October and early November carried the team up into second place. The final victory in that run, 2-0 at Swindon, proved to be the swan-song for scorers Showers and Laidlaw, who were both allowed to move to Hereford shortly afterwards.

At the end of November, the club balloted fans on plans to introduce a Rugby League club to the city, using Fratton Park on alternate weeks, rather like Fulham were doing at Craven Cottage. A resounding 'no' vote condemned the scheme to the dustbin. On the pitch, Pompey suddenly found goals at a premium. This cost the club a potential FA Cup run, as the team tamely surrendered at Colchester, losing by three goals. Burrows took decisive action as Christmas approached, persuading chairman Deacon to spend £200,000 to sign midfielder Bobby Doyle from Blackpool and ever-green striker Billy Rafferty from Newcastle. Around this time, winger Ian Purdie, who had failed to make any impression, had his contract paid up and moved to Australia.

League form remained inconsistent, however, and although the team kept in touch with the leading pack, the prospect of a second successive promotion was all but extinguished by Easter. Too often a good result, such as a 3-1 win at fellow promotion outsiders Burnley in late January, was followed up by a poor one, in this case league leaders Rotherham strolled to a 3-0 home win. February also saw Tait begin to carve himself into the affections of the fans with a five-minute hat-trick during a 5-0 demolition of Exeter City, who seemingly had more than one eye on their forthcoming FA Cup fifth round tie at Newcastle.

The team also had to contend with injury problems in defence, as both the unfortunate Garner and his deputy Davey fell victim to long-term absences. Burrows swooped to sign Hull defender Stuart Croft until the end of the season to fill the gap.

Against the wishes of Deacon, the club repeated the experiment of Sunday football for the first time since 1974, when Oxford were the visitors in late March. The disappointing crowd of 12,000 meant the trial would not be repeated, although the foul weather that afternoon might have explained the below expected turnout. That match also saw the full debut of winger Neil Ayrton, signed earlier in the season from Alliance Premier League Maidstone. Highly rated when he arrived, he struggled to make an impact and returned to the Kent club in the summer.

The season finished on a high note, as Gregory's 13th goal of the campaign earned a 1-0 win at Chester and ensured a respectable final placing of sixth, but for some of Burrows' squad it was time to move on. Experienced professionals Steve Davey and Terry Brisley, who had played a key role in promotion the previous season, found themselves released.

DID YOU KNOW?

Pompey's third division match with Huddersfield Town in December 1980 meant the two clubs had played each other in all four divisions.

Match of the Season 1980-81
Liverpool 4 Portsmouth 1

League Cup, 4th Round, 28 October 1980

On the face of it, a heavy defeat at a far from critical stage of a lesser cup competition ought not be among the seminal results for supporters of Portsmouth FC. However, it surely is. The credit for that rests with the fans themselves, who in an astonishing show of fervour travelled in their thousands 250 miles on an October evening to see if their team could do the impossible and topple the reigning League Champions at their Anfield home.

When the draw had been made, Pompey still had to beat second division Bristol Rovers in the third round. The mere prospect of Pompey, fresh from promotion from Division Four, being able to lock horns with the best, persuaded more than 18,000 along to the replay, which was won 2-0.

To suggest that Liverpool under-estimated the size of Pompey's potential following was an understatement. Despite warnings from Fratton Park that it would far from satisfy demand, the Anfield club sent down an allocation of just 6,500 tickets, with the promise of more if they sold out. They did within hours. Three times Pompey went back to Liverpool playing 'Oliver' and asking for more, and eventually the whole of the Anfield Road end was given over to those in blue and white, with several thousand more seated in the Kemlyn Road stand.

And when Alan Kennedy inadvertently turned in Alan Rogers' cross in the 36th minute to equalise Dalglish's opener, pockets of Pompey fans revealed themselves all over the ground, even on the legendary 'Kop'. At the final count it was estimated up to 15,000 fans had made the journey. When the teams trotted out, the end housing the Pompey fans became a blizzard of tickertape, which remains the club's supporters' trademark to this day, along with the Pompey 'Chimes' which boomed out throughout the game.

On the field, a minute after Pompey's equaliser David Johnson slid the ball past Mellor. Despite huffing and puffing, a second equaliser rarely threatened. Liverpool got the benefit of an offside decision, which allowed Johnson to run clear and make the game safe. Souness's volley late on merely rubbed salt in the wound.

LEAGUE DIVISION 3   **1981-82**
Division 3   13th
League Cup   2nd Round
FA Cup   1st Round

Despite the frustration at missing out on promotion in 1980-81, there was no doubting that the club had made significant progress in the three years Frank Burrows had been involved at the club. During the summer there was an expectation that the team would go one better next time around. The manager felt he had the nucleus of a squad which could challenge for promotion and he limited his transfer dealings to a double raid on Swindon to sign central defender Andy Rollings on a free and £45,000 midfielder Chris Kamara, who had made the opposite journey four years previously.

In pre-season it also became clear that Burrows intended to allow 21-year-old goalkeeper Alan Knight the chance to stake his claim for a first-team spot in place of the popular Mellor. Indeed, it was Knight who started the campaign in the home match against newly promoted Lincoln, in front of almost 11,000, but it took a late strike from Billy Rafferty to rescue a point. The disappointing start continued and it took Pompey until 23 September to claim their first-ever three points for a win, following the Football League's summer decision to change the system. Two home wins in quick succession against Bristol City and Exeter put a rosier tint on things, with the former match featuring a spectacular goal by 18-year-old Gosport-born midfielder Steve Berry, who had forced his way into Burrows' thinking.

It was a false dawn, ruthlessly exposed by second division Queens Park Rangers in the second round of the League Cup, when they thrashed Pompey 5-0 on their newly-installed plastic pitch at Loftus Road. Even the arrival of former Scotland international midfielder Alex Cropley in September, following a protracted transfer from Canadian club Toronto Blizzard, failed to disguise the ordinariness of the team. Between October and the beginning of February the team won just three times in eighteen matches and were dumped out of the FA Cup. In October, Burrows had astounded everyone by transferring Chris Kamara to Brentford, just eleven matches into his return, in exchange for winger David Crown, who had impressed during the Bees' 2-2 draw at Fratton in September.

Crown never displayed his Brentford form in a Pompey shirt, and the crowd were becoming increasingly restless as the team slid into the relegation zone and gates slipped below 8,000. John Deacon was becoming more and more alarmed at the loss of revenue and it was clear that Burrows was coming under mounting pressure to come up with some results. The loan signing of Brian Bason from Crystal Palace in early January did little to help and the team touched the depths in a midweek rearranged fixture at Chester in the middle of that month. The Sealand Road club were bottom of the table and without a home win all season, but some shocking defending in the last fifteen minutes allowed a 2-1 lead to become a 3-2 Chester victory and relegation suddenly was a real possibility.

Initially it was Burrows' assistant Stan Harland who paid the price, sacked by Deacon and replaced by former Pompey wing-half Bobby Campbell as coach in early February. A flurry of form with just two defeats in thirteen matches killed off the spectre of relegation, but even that was not enough ultimately to save Burrows. That run included a 5-1 demolition of promotion-chasing Chesterfield, but the match was marred by a serious knee injury to the classy but injury-prone Cropley, which cut short his Pompey career and forced him to retire. To shore up a suspect defence, Hereford left-back Colin Sullivan, who had top-flight experience at Norwich under his belt, arrived on a free transfer in late February.

Shortly before his own departure, Burrows had pitched 21-year-old centre-forward Trevor Senior into action, making his debut at home to promotion-chasing Fulham. Spotted while playing in the Southern League, where he had scored a hat-full of goals, Pompey gambled £35,000 in November on his raw potential after Bournemouth had knocked his club Dorchester out of the FA Cup. By the time Senior scored his first Pompey goals, on Easter Monday against Reading, Burrows was, temporarily at least, part of Pompey's history. On 31 March Deacon announced that the club had parted company with the man who had guided the club to its first promotion in eighteen years. He was to be replaced, initially on a caretaker basis, by Campbell.

Also making his senior debut as a substitute against Reading was 17-year-old Havant-born midfielder Paul Wimbleton. As Campbell shaped the team in his own image, the youngster was on the point of staking a claim for a permanent first-team place when he twisted awkwardly on the turf during a match at Huddersfield in April and wrecked his knee ligaments. It was to take nearly two years and two operations before he featured in the first team again.

The curtain came down on the season with a home match against Millwall on FA Cup final eve, which had the unwelcome distinction of becoming the second-lowest ever attendance – just 4,902 – at Fratton Park for a Football League match. The decision to make the match all-ticket on police advice, after rival fans had clashed earlier in the season at the FA Cup match between the teams, contributed significantly to the low turnout.

For two players, that match spelled their last in Pompey colours as Campbell set about building a squad to seriously challenge for promotion. Left-back Keith Viney, who had been one of St John's original Pompey 'babes' in 1976, was given a free transfer, just twelve months after he had been voted player of the season by supporters, and, more controversially, striker Jeff Hemmerman was also released. They were joined on the 'surplus to requirements' list by midfielder Leigh Barnard, as Campbell cleared the decks for a hectic summer of wheeling and dealing.

With Portsmouth Football Club now a wholly owned subsidiary of Deacon's Superior Properties company, the chairman was determined to continue bankrolling his dream of putting Pompey back in the big time, and he saw Campbell as the ideal man for the job. The club's change of status meant any losses could now be offset against the profits of the parent company. This had been achieved after Deacon had acquired additional shares – from, of all people, former boardroom rival Dennis Collett – to take him over the 75% threshold needed to effect the deal.

Match of the Season 1981-82

Portsmouth 5   Chesterfield 1

Division 3, 13 February 1982

Promotion-chasing Chesterfield had conceded just nineteen goals in 25 matches prior to this game, while Pompey were labouring at the foot of the table, with just seven goals in eight win-less games. In midweek, a livid Burrows had laid into his team after a tame home 1-1 draw with Oxford United, but the verbal mauling seemed to trigger the right response from a team whose lowly league position seemed out of proportion to the size of salaries the players were drawing.

Burrows decided to gamble on the fitness of striker Tait – who had been doubtful beforehand with a stomach muscle strain – and it immediately paid off as his flick found centre-half Aizlewood, improbably trundling through the middle to score after just four minutes. Within three more minutes it was 2-0, as loan-signing Bason put Crown away to score his first Pompey goal.

The stunned Spireites reeled, but regained their composure to score with their first attack, Bonnyman calmly beating Knight after Crawford's pull-back. Would Pompey crack, as they had done at Chester four weeks previously?

DID YOU KNOW?

Pompey did not take kindly to QPR's new plastic pitch. In 1981-82 the first team lost 0-5 in the League Cup, while the juniors lost 0-10 in the Youth Cup.

The answer was an emphatic no, as Garner and Aizlewood went on to reduce Bonnyman and Kowalski to anonymity. The only blot came when Kowlaski's yellow card challenge on Cropley forced the former Scotland international midfielder to limp off before half-time with a recurrence of a knee injury that would force his summer retirement.

After the interval, Pompey capitalised on some increasingly uncertain defending, as Rafferty hardly had to jump to beat Green to Crown's cross. Chesterfield briefly rallied, with Knight making a flying save to deny Wilson, but in the last ten minutes Rafferty turned the game into a personal triumph.

First he latched onto Doyle's floated pass and angled home as the linesman's flag stayed down, then substitute Gregory's shot was fumbled by Turner and Rafferty was on hand to complete the first hat-trick of his Pompey career.

The result eased the mounting pressure on Pompey at the foot of the table and within six weeks they would be safe after a run of just two defeats in thirteen games. Not enough to save Burrows job, though, for he was sacked at the end of March and replaced by newly appointed coach Bobby Campbell.

Chesterfield boss Frank Barlow fumed: 'We were a disgrace to ourselves and our fans who travelled. It could have been eight.' After this result their season fell away and they finished in mid-table – just three points ahead of Pompey.

LEAGUE DIVISION 3   **1982-83**
Division 3   1st (Champions)
Milk Cup   1st Round
FA Cup   2nd Round

Once appointed permanently, Bobby Campbell set about utilising his extensive contacts to shake up the squad. After finishing his playing days at Fratton Park in the 1960s, he had gone on to coach at Pompey, before becoming manager at Fulham in 1976, where he pulled off the unlikely coup of persuading both Rodney Marsh and George Best to sign for the riverside club.

Before returning to Pompey he had been coaching in the Persian Gulf, but soon showed he had lost none of his persuasive qualities when, in the space of ten hectic days in early June he added three players to the squad. Central defender Ernie Howe, out of contract at QPR, and former England winger Dave Thomas from Middlesbrough fell under Campbell's spell and agreed to drop down a division. The jewel in the crown, however, was the capture from under the noses of several first division teams of 18-year-old England Under-21 international Neil Webb from Reading. The starlet was out of contract at Elm Park and the arbitrated fee of £87,500 was ultimately to prove one of the bargains of this or any other season.

During the pre-season fixtures, Campbell's charges drew praise from several visiting first division managers, notably from former Pompey stalwart Tony Barton, now manager of European Cup winners Aston Villa. The Midlands club paraded the trophy around Fratton Park before a testimonial match for the unfortunate Alex Cropley.

On the eve of the season, however, Campbell played one more ace when he stunned the football world – well, managers of third division clubs at least – when he signed striker Alan Biley from first division Everton for £100,000. It was the final piece in the jigsaw and Pompey set about the third division with a vengeance. Biley, Webb and Howe all scored on their debuts as more than 13,000 saw their team thrash newly promoted Sheffield United 4-1 at Fratton. By the end of September the team was second in the table, with only a shock home defeat by Newport County and a spirited exit from the League Cup against second division Crystal Palace to cloud the skies.

October proved more problematic as it became clear that Pompey had become 'the' team to beat in the division. The month started badly as Southend won 4-0 in a match which saw striker Billy Rafferty, who was proving the perfect foil for Biley, sent off for violent conduct. His suspension gave Trevor Senior a chance, but he looked out of his depth and missed enough chances to have won the game against Bournemouth single-handed. Doubts about the team's ability to fulfil their potential surfaced as the month ended with a defeat at promotion rivals Cardiff. Ironically City's goal was scored by their leading marksman, Jeff Hemmerman.

The team bounced back to take runaway leaders Lincoln City apart, 4-1 at a foggy Fratton Park, but ten days later Bristol Rovers exposed fundamental defensive weaknesses at Eastville. A shell-shocked Campbell was left to explain away Rovers' 5-1 win, that left Pompey off the pace. After the match, full-back Trevor Ross, signed on loan from Everton, was allowed to return to Merseyside, with only five appearances and a missed penalty against Gillingham to show for his stay at Fratton. The manager challenged his players to prove their quality and they responded with a devastating burst of form which by the end of February seemed to put the promotion question beyond doubt.

A run of twelve wins and a draw in fifteen matches was sparked by the sad news that another heart attack had claimed the life of Jimmy Dickinson. He had never fully regained his health following a coronary after a match at Barnsley in 1979, but his death was still a huge shock and left a large gap at the club. A minute's silence was observed before the first round FA Cup-tie with fourth division Hereford United at Fratton, ultimately won 4-1, but ironically it was the Cup that proved the only blot on the landscape. In December Hampshire rivals Aldershot, from Division Four, strolled to a 3-1 win at Fratton in round two. That month also saw the publication of the annual accounts, which showed Deacon had ploughed more than £250,000 of his fortune into the club, though he still failed to convince all fans that his intentions were entirely as they would have wished.

January and February saw the club finally take an apparently unshakeable grip on the championship with a club-record seven successive league victories, including crucial wins over promotion challengers Lincoln and Huddersfield. It might have been eight in a row but for a curious penalty jinx which was affecting the team. When Colin Sullivan's spot-kick was saved by the Wigan keeper with five minutes to go on 1 March, ensuring a 0-0 draw in front of just over 16,000 fans at Fratton, he became the sixth Pompey player to have missed from the spot that season.

During March it seemed as though some of those misses might prove crucial, as a four-match winless – and goalless – run put paid to thoughts of a straightforward procession to the championship. To calm everyone's nerves, however, Campbell employed his renowned expertise in the transfer market to buy Birmingham midfielder Kevin Dillon, a regular in their first division team at the time, who arrived in a £140,000 deal shortly before transfer deadline day. Deacon found another £50,000 to sign West Ham reserve striker Nicky Morgan, so that everything seemed set for the final push.

At first, form remained patchy. A victory against Bristol Rovers merely heralded another three matches without a win, then defeat against Bradford City on 9 April left Cardiff, Huddersfield and Newport in pole positions. At least, the penalty problems appeared solved, Dillon's double from the spot salvaging a 2-2 draw at home to Reading.

Pompey travelled to South Wales for effectively a do-or-die clash with Newport. More than 3,000 travelling fans swelled the gate to over 10,000 and they saw a commanding second-half performance produce a 3-0 win, courtesy of Rafferty and Biley. The result was therapeutic and the team accepted their destiny, winning five and drawing the other of their final six matches. They secured promotion with two matches to spare when Southend were beaten 2-0 in front of more than 18,000 fans, initiating a pitch invasion at the final whistle. Up in the directors box, the players acknowledged the support of the fans, who had turned up in numbers both home and away, but Campbell, ever the professional, refused to celebrate until the championship was secure.

Three days later a 1-0 home win over Walsall, this time before more than 22,000, all but clinched the club's second third division title, making them the first club to achieve the feat. A 1-0 win at Plymouth, marred only by the loutish behaviour of a small minority of fans travelling to the West Country, gave the club a divisional points record of 91.

The key to Campbell's success had been the signing of Biley, who had become an instant hit with supporters with his Rod Stewart lookalike haircut and infectious enthusiasm for the game. An ever-present with 26 league and cup goals, he was the obvious choice for player of the season, but even he would acknowledge the part the wily Rafferty – nineteen goals in all competitions – had played in his success.

The season ended with a second open-top bus parade and civic reception in three years. The style with which Pompey had won the championship immediately installed the club among the favourites for yet another promotion the following season. And Campbell, voted Bells' Division Three Manager of the Season, was already plotting another transfer coup to try to ensure that it would happen.

Match of the Season 1982-83

Lincoln City 0 Portsmouth 3

Division 3, 16 February 1983

In November, Pompey had ruthlessly exposed Lincoln's promotion credentials 4-1 in the Fratton fog, but by the time the return fixture came around the Imps were still short-priced favourites for the title and hell-bent on avenging that defeat.

However, Pompey had won their previous four matches and Cardiff's defeat at Bradford City in the afternoon had opened the way for Pompey to go top of the table on goal-difference if they won. Lincoln had slipped a little of late, having led the table by six points in the autumn, but had games in hand to overhaul the teams ahead of them.

Lincoln swarmed forward from the start, but Shipley and Burke were both narrowly off-target. Aizlewood was booked for a clumsy tackle on Lincoln's 23-goal leading scorer Bell, but soon atoned, rising to head home Sullivan's cross at the near post, after a short corner routine involving Rogers.

Webb and Biley quickly combined to set up Rafferty, who was denied by the diving Felgate. After that it was backs-to-the-wall, but with every player covering and tackling, Knight only knew one difficult moment, but Hobson headed straight at him.

After the interval, Pompey soon took a grip on the game, despite losing Howe early on with a bruised knee, to be replaced ably by the long-serving Ellis. Felgate made one superb save to keep out Rafferty's shot, but the ex-Wolves striker wasn't to be denied, looping home a header from Biley's cross in the 55th minute. Six minutes later it was all over, as Felgate again excelled to save from Biley, but Rafferty fed off the rebound.

Afterwards an elated Campbell paid tribute to his side: 'We were magnificent. They tried to intimidate us and found they couldn't – I'm proud of them all.' Only four bookings by fussy referee John Key and the news that following the game three Pompey fans were hospitalised after being set upon with copper piping, slightly marred an almost perfect evening.

Lincoln's season would never recover from the blow and they eventually slumped to sixth place, six points away from promotion.

## 3

DEACON'S DREAM FULFILLED
1983-1988

LEAGUE DIVISION 2   **1983-84**
Canon Division 2   16th
Milk Cup   2nd Round
FA Cup   4th Round

The championship celebrations had barely subsided when Bobby Campbell – having signed a new three-year contract – out-foxed his managerial colleagues once again. By signing the out-of-contract Coventry and England Under-21 centre-forward Mark Hateley, one of the hottest properties around at the time, he announced to the world that the club's ambition was undimmed. And it demonstrated once again the canny Liverpool-born manager's powers of persuasion, as Hateley took an apparent step backward to move forward. When the Football League arbitrated the fee at around £220,000, a host of rivals were left astonished by Campbell's audacity. Coventry were merely left fuming as their prized asset was allowed to leave for what they regarded as a pittance.

Pompey had also appointed its first woman director the previous December, Deacon's wife Joan. She was a member of the board that took the unpopular decision in July to install perimeter fences around the Fratton pitch, sparking a predictably unhappy response from supporters.

Other changes included the appointment of Alan Ball as youth coach, while Trevor Senior, who had been loaned to Aldershot and who now saw his position compromised by the arrival of Hateley, agreed to join Reading for £35,000. Rafferty refused Pompey's offer of a new contract and never featured in the first team again before moving to Bournemouth in February. Shortly before the start of the season, as Pompey enjoyed a productive pre-season with wins over Arsenal and West Ham, Campbell signed former Fulham and Liverpool defender Richard Money for £50,000 from Luton.

Two goals against the Gunners established Hateley as a crowd favourite, but first-day visitors Middlesbrough failed to read the script, pinching a 1-0 win at Fratton. Gloom descended three days later when fourth division Hereford came from behind to take a 3-2 first-leg lead at Edgar Street in the League Cup, despite Hateley's first competitive goal. However, he was on the mark, so to speak, again when Fulham presented the team with their first win of the season at Craven Cottage, Alan Biley also scoring in a 2-0 win. A prolific partnership was born.

Unfortunately, the team were also liable to leak goals alarmingly and it soon became clear Pompey had much work to do if they were to match divisional pace-setters Newcastle United, inspired by Kevin Keegan, Chelsea and Sheffield Wednesday. The League Cup – once Hereford had been put in their place – provided a minor distraction. Aston Villa scored two late goals to rescue a second round, first leg draw at Fratton, then struck late in the return to take the tie into extra time and a 3-2 win for the Midlanders. During that match Money sustained knee-ligament damage, which was to keep him out of contention until March.

In the league, Pompey's inconsistency was well illustrated in early November, when Hateley's two hat-tricks in four days secured 5-0 and 4-0 wins over Cambridge and Grimsby respectively, only for the team to take just one point from their next four matches and approach Christmas languishing in mid-table. To shore things up, Sunderland defender Rob Hindmarch was signed on loan, but he made only two appearances before returning north. The festive period started brightly as Pompey strolled to a 4-0 Boxing Day win over Charlton. The next day the team produced one of their best performances of the season to hold second-placed Chelsea at Stamford Bridge. The New Year hangover arrived a day early, however, as Fulham comprehensively avenged their defeat earlier in the season by winning 4-1 on 31 December.

The FA Cup soon lifted the atmosphere as 'super sub' striker Nicky Morgan came off the bench to earn a 2-1 win over Grimsby at Fratton and set the scene for the fourth round draw which paired Pompey with arch-rivals Southampton. Within days the match was a 36,000 all-ticket sell out, but it would end in tears as Steve Moran slid home an injury-time winner.

That disappointment was the unpalatable filling in a sandwich which saw just three points earned out of 24 in the league. By the end of February Pompey were feeling the chill wind of a relegation struggle at their backs. Some impressive away form eased the threat, but it took a sensational five-goal second-half burst to see off Brighton 5-1 at the end of March and give Pompey their first home league win since Boxing Day. Campbell also had another stab at trying to build defensive stability, signing former Southampton defender Malcolm Waldron from Burnley for £50,000 earlier in the month.

It was back to more mediocre fare in April, four defeats and a draw out of five matches. The public's patience finally snapped and gates slumped to below 8,000, well short of Deacon's break-even figure of around 13,000. The vultures were gathering around Campbell, who appeared increasingly isolated as the season wore on. The final straw was a two-goal defeat in the penultimate match of the season at already-relegated Derby, which left the team in 21st position; safe, but by just one place. Two days later Campbell was confronted by his chairman to account for a season which had seen 21 league defeats. The inevitable outcome was the sack.

Ball was put in temporary charge of the team and they bowed out in style, thrashing doomed Swansea 5-0 in front of just 7,359 Fratton fans, with Biley finally emerging from the 22-goal Hateley's shadow to notch his second Pompey hat-trick. Ultimately Campbell had paid the price for too cavalier an approach to the club's first second division campaign in eight years. The team conceded 64 goals, half of them at home, and not even the thrilling Hateley-Biley tandem could compensate.

Hateley also showed that moving down a division to Fratton had done his international prospects little harm. He was called up for the England tour of South America, and became the first Pompey player to earn full England honours since the days of Jimmy Dickinson in 1956 when Hateley played and scored in the Maracana against Brazil. The new manager would have to take tough decisions when the fans' favourite returned from South America.

Match of the Season 1983-84
Portsmouth 0 Southampton 1

FA Cup, 4th Round, 28 January 1984

If ever an FA Cup-tie captured the imagination of the Hampshire public, this was it. The rivalry between Pompey and Southampton goes deeper than many might imagine, fuelled partly by the fact that the two teams have met on comparatively few occasions, despite being similar cities in terms of size and profile.

Pompey fans claim the high ground of three FA Cup finals – one won in 1939 – and two league championships, all achieved between 1929 and 1950, while the Saints' fans delight in pointing out an unbroken run – bar four seasons – in the top flight since 1966. Not forgetting of course the FA Cup of 1976. The winning goal was scored, ironically, by Portsmouth-born Bobby Stokes.

DID YOU KNOW?

In May 1984 Mark Hateley became the first Pompey player to play for England since Jimmy Dickinson in 1956. He scored in a 2-0 win v Brazil.

So, tickets were in heavy demand for the first competitive meeting of the sides since 1976 and the first in the FA Cup since 1906. With Southampton entitled to 9,000 – out of the 36,000 available – it was inevitable that many people would be upset at missing out. Once season-ticket holders had had their share, the remainder sold out in a matter of hours, prompting a flood of sob stories in the local press.

The game was featured on BBC TV's Match of the Day – for most of those in the crowd it was the match of the century – and the atmosphere inside Fratton was feverish as the teams came out. A scrappy first-half saw chances at a premium, but Pompey were more than matching their neighbours, who boasted a number of class acts brought together by the astute Lawrie McMenemy, including Peter Shilton, Mick Mills (rejected by George Smith as a junior), Frank Worthington and David Armstrong.

The second half opened up a little, but still chances were few and far between. Possibly the turning point came when volatile full-back Mark Dennis shaped to take a throw and was felled by a coin thrown from the Pompey fans behind. Those extra seconds would prove crucial.

The game looked set to prompt a yet more frantic ticket rush for the replay, scheduled for Tuesday in the half-pint pot Dell, which could have easily sold a quart's-worth of tickets, when Biley blazed a glorious chance over the bar with three minutes remaining.

With the clock ticking towards 4.50 pm and referee Shapter still disinclined to blow his whistle, as he added on stoppages, Worthington sent Armstrong scuttling away down the right. His cross was true and Steve Moran nipped in ahead of Aizlewood to stab the ball home. The Milton End erupted; the three other sides of the ground were stunned.

Southampton had stolen victory – the poetic justice of its injury 'timing' lost to this day on all Pompey fans – but fate had a possibly crueller end up its sleeve for Saints. They crashed out in the semi-finals to Everton's extra-time winner.

LEAGUE DIVISION 2   **1984-85**
Canon Division 2   4th
Milk Cup   2nd Round
FA Cup   3rd Round

In the wake of Campbell's dismissal, the identity of his successor was one of the worst kept secrets in Portsmouth. The fact that Alan Ball had been asked to take charge for the last game of the season was a pretty big hint. Deacon maintained a sort of suspense however, by advertising for the post and drawing up a short-list while allowing Ball to release Steve Aizlewood, John McLaughlin, the injury-jinxed Ernie Howe and former youth-team product Peter Ellis.

As the pretence of a vacancy persisted, the new manager in all but name proceeded to revamp the heart of the defence by signing Crystal Palace hard man Billy Gilbert for £100,000 and Middlesbrough's Mick Baxter on a free transfer. Ball returned to Ayresome Park to invest another £100,000 of his employer's money in midfielder Mick Kennedy. When the press conference to announce Campbell's successor finally took pace in early June, the odds of anyone other than a red-haired, former England World Cup winner from Lancashire were zero.

And then came the Hateley conundrum. His goals could have undoubtedly been instrumental in finally fulfilling Deacon's dream of returning Pompey to the big-time, but it was one goal – that one in the Maracana – that had suddenly put Hateley in a bigger league altogether. Ten days after he had scored it, Italian giants AC Milan had tabled a £915,000 offer, with a two-legged friendly thrown in. Its acceptance was a formality and Hateley was off to sample *la dolce vita* in the San Siro.

To appease fans, within two days Ball had swooped to sign Manchester United striker Scott McGarvey, whose first-team chances had been limited, for £85,000. As pre-season training got underway confidence was growing. The team seemed altogether better prepared for a promotion challenge, but the club was rocked ten days before the start of the season when it was announced that new centre-half Mick Baxter had been diagnosed with Hodgkinson's Disease and his career was over. The loss was immediately covered with the signing of Birmingham centre-half Noel Blake for £150,000, who made his debut in the final friendly, at home to Queens Park Rangers.

The league campaign started with a gritty 1-0 win over Middlesbrough, thanks to a goal from the ever-reliable Biley five minutes from time, and it sparked a ten-match unbeaten run in the league, the best start to a season since 1961. The highlights of that run were back-to-back 1-0 victories at likely promotion rivals Leeds and Birmingham, countering sceptical views about the team's ability to go the distance after a 0-0 draw at home to Barnsley.

The League Cup also provided evidence of the quality of Ball's squad, as first division Nottingham Forest were beaten 1-0 in front of more than 20,000 at Fratton in the first leg of a second round match. The second leg at the City Ground was a classic, with Forest finally prevailing with two extra-time goals. The first league defeat of the season followed shortly afterwards, with Wimbledon claiming a 3-2 win at Plough Lane, thanks in part to a bizarre own-goal by Blake. Alan Cork had just given the Dons the lead, and Alan Knight had hurt his knee in attempting to save. From the re-start the ball was played back to Blake, who knocked it on to Knight, having failed to notice his team-mate was more preoccupied with his injury. The frantic shouts of Pompey fans behind the goal alerted Knight to the danger too late. Despite a spirited second-half performance, the damage had been done.

Confidence faltered as, a week later, lowly Wolves inflicted a first home defeat, and both Blake and McGarvey were on the receiving end of the crowd's frustration. Blake soon proclaimed his unhappiness at Fratton, citing racist elements in the crowd who were making his life a misery, and Deacon, to his credit, acted immediately, threatening to ban any fans who were caught making remarks of that kind.

In late November Ball went into the transfer market again to widen his tactical options. Since Alan Rogers had been allowed to move to Southend the previous spring, the team had no natural wide-man, but £85,000 rescued former Crystal Palace winger Vince Hilaire from an unhappy spell at Luton. His impact was immediate as he scored on his debut to earn a 2-2 draw with promotion rivals Blackburn. That match also saw Gilbert pick up an injury which was to keep him out for six matches and which saw a previously frugal defence concede fifteen goals, which in retrospect cost the team promotion.

However, that run also saw one of the most dramatic climaxes to a match at Fratton ever. Going into injury-time against league leaders Oxford three days before Christmas, Pompey were a goal down. In 120 glorious seconds, added on for a pitch invasion by Santa Claus, Biley buried two headers and secured an improbable victory amid scenes of delirium. It was to prove the last win for two months – even a 4-0 half-time lead against Fulham on New Year's Day wasn't enough to secure maximum points – and by the end of February the third promotion spot was drifting away. The FA Cup had also passed the club by, with Blackburn finally winning a twice-postponed third round replay at Ewood Park on fourth round day.

By then, Ball had strengthened his squad still further. Just before Christmas he had signed strikers Paul Sugrue and Dave Bamber from Northampton and Walsall respectively for nominal fees. Those decisions seemed curious as neither player was to feature prominently in his plans. In January he also signed veteran midfielder Gerry Francis from Swansea until the end of the season; then in February Yugoslav right-back Ivan Golac came on loan from Southampton, and Ipswich winger Kevin O'Callaghan on a similar basis with a view to a £100,000 transfer. The arrival of the latter pair galvanised a flagging team, and a 5-1 thrashing of Oldham thanks to a pair of Kevin Dillon penalties and a brace from recalled striker Biley heralded a ten-match unbeaten run which was to take the club to the brink of promotion.

The key to the team's success was the imposing Blake and Gilbert partnership, which ensured that teams rarely scored more than once against Pompey whenever they were playing in tandem. Since his unhappiness in the autumn, Blake was more settled, a couple of crucial goals had helped endear him to the crowd, and the club profited. O'Callaghan, who had impressed, was signed permanently, but Golac was released.

Even the shock sale of crowd favourite Biley to promotion rivals and neighbours Brighton for £65,000 on transfer deadline day was forgotten as Neil Webb took on the striking mantle with aplomb. His two goals at Fulham on Easter Monday, taking him to five in three matches, earned Pompey a 3-1 win and took them into the third promotion spot. Webb had become a sought after player, with scouts from several top clubs tracking his progress, and significantly he was out of contract in the summer. If Pompey were to keep him they had to go up.

Almost 24,000 turned up for the promotion showdown with Birmingham, only to be bitterly disappointed as City strolled to a 3-1 win and Blake was forced to suffer the taunts from Blues fans over his decision to leave St Andrews the previous August. Promotion was still there to be taken, but a defeat at Crystal Palace meant the game with Manchester City on 27 April was effectively a promotion decider. More than 22,000 turned up for the contest and once Nicky Morgan grabbed a second-half equaliser there seemed only one winner, until Paul Simpson's audacious lob with six minutes to go put City five points clear in third place with just three games to go.

Pompey needed a miracle, but it nearly happened. City drew and lost their next two games, while Pompey won 1-0 at Blackburn then 3-1 at home to Carlisle to set up a thrilling climax. If City beat Charlton they were up by virtue of their superior goal-difference, but any other result meant a Pompey victory at Huddersfield would ensure promotion. 10,000 Pompey fans made the journey north to see goals from O'Callaghan and Hilaire ensure a 2-0 win. On a day which was ultimately overshadowed by the fire at Bradford City's Valley Parade ground, however, there was no happy ending as City used teenage Charlton goalkeeper Lee Harmsworth for target practice as they cruised to a 5-1 win.

As Pompey came to terms with their disappointment, Francis and Waldron were released, but the question on everyone's lips was could Ball persuade Neil Webb that his dream of first division football could be realised at Fratton Park.

Match of the Season 1984-85
Portsmouth 4 Fulham 4

Division 2, 1 January 1985

Pompey would end the 1984-85 season missing promotion on goal-difference to Manchester City. It wouldn't take Sherlock Holmes – whose creator, Sir Arthur Conan Doyle, played for one of Portsmouth FC's forerunners in the 1890s – to discover when the crucial point went astray.

The loss of Billy Gilbert to injury in early December had unhinged a previously rock-solid back line, and goals had been shipped at an alarming rate. The previous Saturday, four had been conceded in the second half at Sheffield United.

Blake and Waldron were given the benefit of the doubt and kept their places, but Webb and Biley were paired up front, with the aim of providing more punch. Before the first half was over, Fulham were apparently out for the count as, backed by a fierce wind, Pompey roared into a 4-0 lead.

One goal had already been disallowed before keeper Jim Stannard failed to hold Kennedy's free-kick and Waldron tapped in his first goal for the club. Webb then hit the bar and Biley scrambled home the rebound. The pantomime – or should that be farce – continued as referee Brian Stevens limped off to be replaced by senior linesman John Carter.

Stannard then turned clown once more, appearing to lose the flight of a wind-assisted clearance by Knight, allowing Webb to nip in. Then Stannard was forced to watch in horror as Hopkins smashed a clearance into Biley's face and it drifted over the stranded keeper.

DID YOU KNOW?

Q. In October 1984, how did Wimbledon score without touching the ball?
A. From the kick-off the ball was played back to Noel Blake, who own-goaled.

With the wind now at their backs, Fulham were rewarded when Blake missed Lewington's cross and Coney forced home in the 48th minute. Within seconds Pompey had a good penalty shout waved aside as Hopkins clattered into Webb, but two goals in three minutes – Rosenior clipping over Knight in the 74th minute, then Gary Barnett's free header – had Fulham sensing a 'Great Escape'.

With all around them losing their heads – especially Blake, who chopped down Cliff Carr as he burst into the box in injury-time – Kevin Lock kept his and stepped up to send Knight the wrong way. The Case of the Missing Points? Elementary, my dear Watson. Pompey just threw them away.

LEAGUE DIVISION 2   **1985-86**
Canon Division 2   4th
Milk Cup   Quarter-finals
FA Cup   3rd Round

Within days of the 1984-85 season concluding, Webb had decided to exercise his freedom of contract, signing for first division Nottingham Forest. Rather than take the risk of a tribunal, Pompey negotiated a fee of £250,000, but as pre-season started there was little evidence that Ball was going to invest that money. The only new arrival, veteran full-back Kenny Swain, made the reverse journey from the City Ground on a free.

Rumours of a swoop for Aston Villa striker Peter Withe were sunk when he elected to join Sheffield United, but when Pompey lined up for their first home friendly – against Forest – among the squad was former Southampton striker Mick Channon, whom Ball had recruited on a month-to-month contract. The match was played with the South Stand closed. In the wake of the Bradford City fire, clubs had been forced to upgrade their facilities and the tight pre-season schedule meant work was only just completed on time. The work meant the disappearance of the distinctive metal facade – also to be found at Ibrox and Roker Park – incorporated by architect Archibald Leitch when he designed the stand back in 1925.

On the eve of the season, which kicked off away at newly promoted Hull, Pompey were quoted at 6-1 for the title, but they soon set about making those odds look generous. Four wins and a draw in the opening five fixtures took the team to the top of the table. The start was a personal triumph for striker Nicky Morgan who, partnered with Channon, emerged from the shadows to set a club record by scoring in the each of those games. By the end of August Channon's contribution was recognised with a season-long contract, but leaving Fratton was 31-year-old midfielder Bobby Doyle, who joined Hull in a £30,000 deal.

The club maintained pole position – despite their first league defeat at Oldham – throughout September, as chairman John Deacon revealed he had been approached about the possibility of involving the club in the setting up a 'Super League'. Dreams of Pompey playing among the elite were quickly shattered by first division Chelsea's 3-0 win in the newly created Full Members' Cup, but that proved to be Portsmouth's only defeat in October, a month which culminated with an emphatic 4-0 victory at old rivals Millwall.

The month ended with Pompey eight points clear at the top and, thanks to a brace of Kevin Dillon penalties against Stoke, through to the fourth round of the Milk Cup, where they were drawn away to Tottenham Hotspur. The bookmakers had virtually stopped taking bets on the team going up, but by the end of November the season was taking on a slightly different complexion. Defeat at Leeds on 2 November was followed by a similar outcome at Grimsby. When a Withe-inspired Sheffield United destroyed Pompey's perfect home record the alarm bells rang loud and clear. Three consecutive defeats cut Pompey's lead to just two points, but a 0-0 draw at White Hart Lane set up a lucrative replay at Fratton, which was to end in another goal-less stalemate and frustration for thousands of fans locked out of the match while holding valid tickets.

At the end of extra-time the toss of a coin decreed Fratton would host the second replay – all-ticket from the start – and provide the club with much needed revenue and a realistic chance of making the fifth round for the first time since 1961. The financial imperative had been underlined by the accounts for the previous season, which had revealed a loss of £431,000 and a significant increase in both the wage-bill and the money Deacon had loaned to the club.

Pompey began December with another disappointing defeat at Bradford City's temporary Odsal Stadium, hastily rearranged after the previous Saturday's fixture had been postponed. Supporters were becoming increasingly frustrated and a hike in admission prices did little for their mood, but the team responded magnificently to silence the doubters.

Starting with an emphatic 3-1 win at Sunderland and ending on New Year's Day with an identical result at promotion rivals Wimbledon, the team took thirteen points out of a possible eighteen and dumped Tottenham out of the Milk Cup. The match at Plough Lane marked a personal triumph for Channon, who had initially struggled to overcome his Southampton connections, but two slickly-taken goals changed all that.

However, in January and February the team flattered only to deceive as injury and suspensions forced Ball into a number of reshuffles. The FA Cup ended in disappointment, with Aston Villa sneaking a replay with a late equaliser at Fratton, then winning the rearranged second match 3-2 in extra-time. Of greater significance than the Cup exit was the broken cheekbone sustained by goal-keeper Alan Knight, which would keep him out for the best part of two months.

Reserve goalkeeper Andy Gosney made his league debut in a top of the table clash with Norwich, only for two late goals to spoil his day. Four days later he would be disappointed once more as first division Oxford ended dreams of a trip to Wembley, winning the much-anticipated Milk Cup quarter-final at the Manor Ground 3-1.

To use the old cliché, Pompey could now concentrate on the
league, but their progress remained erratic. A handling error by
Gosney gifted lowly Oldham three points at the end of February,
leaving the team six points adrift of leaders Norwich. Within a
fortnight Oldham's 23-year-old forward Mick Quinn arrived at
Fratton in a £150,000 deal as Ball's quest for the cutting edge to
ensure promotion finally materialised.

His debut was a winning one – a crucial 2-1 win at Charlton –
which prompted their manager, Lennie Lawrence, to claim that
Pompey and Norwich were as good as up and they and Wimbledon
were playing for third place. Ten days later he scored his first goal
for the club – his 100th – in a brutal 2-1 win over Millwall, which
meant Pompey looked as good as up. Deadline day came and went
with just Paul Wimbleton being allowed to leave for Gola League
Barnet on loan.

Easter Saturday saw the return with Wimbledon – reinforced by
the signing of muscular Millwall striker John Fashanu – and another
physical contest saw Pompey's promotion chances fatally undermined. The 1-1 draw, played in front of more than 18,000, was a
sound enough result, but injuries to Mick Tait and Kevin Dillon,
coupled with Gary Stanley's long-term absence with a serious back
problem, left the midfield looking under-resourced. An Easter
Monday win over south-coast rivals Brighton put the team nine
points clear of fourth place, but ominously the chasing pack had
games in hand.

April started disastrously and got rapidly worse. Lowly Leeds
came from behind to win 3-2 at Fratton, the result compounded by
a booking for captain and midfielder Mick Kennedy which meant a
suspension. Within four days Pompey's Crystal Palace jinx struck
again as Andy Gray scored an extraordinary winner, then a missed
Quinn penalty at Middlesbrough allowed the relegation-threatened
Tees-siders to steal a 1-0 win against a depleted Pompey side
reduced to ten men by Kevin Ball's sending off. Even international
call-ups for Kennedy and Kevin O'Callaghan by the new Republic
of Ireland manager Jack Charlton couldn't lift the gloom.

Lightning had struck for the second time as a three-match losing
run had taken promotion out of the team's own hands. The next
match against Grimsby was crucial, but in the build-up the club
received another blow as safety inspectors declared the upper tier of

the Fratton End unsafe; the sea-dredged aggregate of thirty years earlier was rusting the steel-reinforced concrete. The return of Dillon was a boost and Scott McGarvey's first goal in eighteen months helped secure a 3-1 win, but Charlton and Wimbledon were keeping the pressure on. When Pompey cracked again at Stoke City in a rearranged midweek match, limply surrendering to two first-half goals, promotion was looking an increasingly forlorn hope. A 0-0 draw at Sheffield United in the penultimate match kept Pompey clinging to third place, but by the time Bradford City brought the curtain down on a season that had promised so much, the team had slipped out of the top three for the first time. A 4-0 win was mere consolation as away wins for the south London duo secured their respective places in the top flight.

In the post-mortem that followed, speculation was rife that Ball's contract would not be renewed. Chief scout Derek Healy was the first casualty of Deacon's promise to cut costs. Six players – Dave Thomas, Channon, Stanley, the unfortunate Wimbleton, Brendan O'Connell and Jake Findlay, signed in January as cover for Gosney – were all released. However, Ball was given a year's extension to his contract.

Match of the Season 1985-86

Portsmouth 1 Tottenham 0
> Milk Cup, 4th Round, second replay, 10 December 1985

Star-spangled Spurs had already had two chances to see off second division pretenders Pompey for the right to meet Oxford in the fifth round. They drew 0-0 at White Hart Lane, before extra-time failed to produce a goal in the Fratton replay, which was marred by thousands of ticket-bearing fans denied access to the ground as police shut the gates.

The key to Pompey's success was their willingness to graft for one another, which Peter Shreeve's team were never able to match. So it proved on this occasion, as an all-ticket crowd urged Pompey to their best Cup result since the mighty Gunners were delayed on their way to the 'double' in 1971.

Shreeve brought back Hoddle – injured for the first replay – and recalled million pound man Clive Allen to partner Mark Falco up front. Kennedy's spiky competitiveness nullified the former, while Blake and Gilbert's assurance reduced the strikeforce to half-chances. With young Sandford chipping in to reduce the effectiveness of newly capped England winger Chris Waddle, the platform for victory was built.

DID YOU KNOW?

Pompey were undefeated under the Fratton Park floodlights in league and cup between October 1980 and August 1987 – a run of 37 matches.

The glory went to Blake, who out-jumped Mabbutt and Danny Thomas to head past Clemence in the 44th minute, but even then Knight was called upon in first-half injury-time to keep out efforts from Falco and Hoddle. The second half saw Pompey soak up tremendous pressure, but only once was their lead threatened. With three minutes left, Waddle, for once, got away from Sandford and drifted a cross-shot over the stranded Knight, only to see it come back off the angle of post and bar.

Pompey's first appearance in the quarter-finals of the League Cup since 1961 ended in a tame defeat at the Manor Ground, Oxford winning 3-1.

LEAGUE DIVISION 2 **1986-87**
Today Division 2   2nd (Promoted)
Littlewoods Cup   3rd Round
FA Cup   4th Round

In response to missing out on promotion, manager Ball transfer-listed strikers Morgan and McGarvey, midfielder Dillon, defender Kevin Ball and goalkeeper Gosney. Knight had also refused a new contract, but in the end only one of these players moved – McGarvey ending an unhappy spell at Fratton by joining Carlisle United.

Arriving on a free transfer were Southampton midfielder Eamonn Collins – a player Ball had introduced to the first team aged fourteen during Ball's unsuccessful spell at Blackpool – and Finnish forward Marcus Winter, who ultimately had to return home as EEC work-permit regulations didn't extend to non-members Finland. As the players reported back for pre-season training a new disciplinary code was introduced by chairman Deacon. The club had appeared in front of the FA at Lancaster Gate for the second summer in a row. They were fined £250, with the previous year's suspended fine of £1,000 activated. Mick Kennedy was also stripped of the captaincy and responded by asking for a transfer.

The club also announced another round of price increases, but increasing supporter dissatisfaction was partially assuaged when, on the eve of the club's pre-season tournament in the Isle of Man, Arsenal and former England international striker Paul Mariner joined the club. The first game of the season was at Brighton, and new skipper Kenny Swain could be pleased with a solid 0-0 draw.

A shock transfer request by Noel Blake on the eve of the first home match of the season was soon forgotten, along with Kennedy's, as the team put together a twelve-match unbeaten start in the league and cups. Just three goals were conceded and Pompey headed the table in mid-October. Even news that Mick Tait's knee ligament injury, sustained in training, would keep him out until Christmas failed to interrupt momentum.

A first defeat, at Leeds, was quickly out of the system when three nights later Mick Quinn scored a second-half hat-trick to secure a 3-1 win over Derby under the Fratton floodlights. The League Cup, now sponsored by Littlewoods, proved only to be a passing distraction, ended by Bradford City.

Cup interest was confined to the much-maligned Full Members' Cup, which Ball used as an extension of training, experimenting with tactics and allowing fringe players competitive action. Wins over Crystal Palace, Millwall and Sheffield Wednesday put the team into the quarter-finals and within sight of a trip to Wembley, but compared to the objective of promotion, it was considered low key in the extreme.

In the transfer market, Ball speculated £40,000 by signing the 23-year-old Dulwich Hamlet striker Andy Perry. At the start of November he recouped the fee by allowing Nick Morgan to join Stoke, initially on a month's loan. The annual accounts revealed a profit of more than £400,000, as the cash for Hateley and Webb filtered through, but the operating loss remained more than £250,000.

On the pitch, some occasionally suspect away form was offset by a perfect home record since August. The week before Christmas Barnsley came within a minute of drawing, only for a late penalty to put Pompey back on the top of the table, seven days after they had lost that advantage in strange circumstances at Bramall Lane. In a well-contested first half, referee Kelvin Morton, in those pre-FIFA directive days, stuck to the letter of the law and sent off four players – including Pompey's Tait, Dillon and Billy Gilbert. The eight men held out until the 69th minute, when a Mariner own-goal gave Sheffield United the points. For their part in the proceedings Tait and Gilbert were fined by the FA for bringing the game into disrepute.

A 3-2 win at Plymouth on Boxing Day was marred by an injury to full-back Paul Hardyman, which was immediately covered by the loan signing of young Arsenal defender Michael Thomas. The post-Sheffield United suspensions also put the squad under pressure, but consecutive home wins over Shrewsbury and Reading made light of the disruption. Momentum was briefly halted by a 1-0 defeat at Blackburn. Ironically, Ball had virtually a full strength squad to call upon, but more worrying was the impending court case featuring leading scorer Quinn, who was due to appear at Havant magistrates on motoring offence charges. Shortly before the case Pompey learned that his natural understudy, Paul Wood, would be out for the rest of the season with a pelvic injury.

Quinn faced imprisonment, leaving Pompey short of forwards for the league game with Brighton and the fourth round FA Cup-tie at Wimbledon. Ball reverted to his 'lone striker' system, perfected in the Full Members' Cup, to cover his absence and the Seagulls paid the price, as Pompey won 1-0. At Wimbledon, however, it was men against boys and the Dons underlined how far Pompey still had to go to be first division quality, winning easily 4-0.

A bitter Ball accused his players of 'surrender', but, lifted by the return of Quinn, the team responded in style to defeat promotion outsiders Ipswich 1-0 at Portman Road. The following week Hull were beaten by the same score, thanks to Quinn's 22nd of the season, despite the fact that half Ball's team were suffering from chest infections. By the Tuesday the bug meant Pompey had just five fit players and the Football League agreed to their request to postpone the Full Members' Cup quarter-final at Norwich.

That match took place seven days later and the first division side prevailed 3-1, thanks to two late goals, but the disappointment was soon forgotten as the team put together a five-match unbeaten run. The only downside came when Leeds ended a run of fourteen consecutive home victories by stealing a point on 10 March. Transfer deadline day came with little activity, but a 3-1 win over Sunderland two days later left the team four points clear of third placed Oldham, with nine matches to play.

As April arrived, Noel Blake and Mick Quinn were named in the Professional Footballers Association second division team of the season, but a single-goal defeat at lowly Bradford City had fans wondering whether the team was going to choke yet again with promotion tantalisingly close. The answer seemed to be no, as Oldham were seen off 3-0 at Fratton Park in front of more than 19,000 spectators. A point at Reading on Easter Saturday put Pompey top with a match in hand.

However, two days later Plymouth ended Fratton's fortress reputation and although a win against relegation-haunted Grimsby seemed to have wrapped things up, another odd-goal defeat at West Brom meant the champagne would have to remain on ice. With three matches left Pompey needed four points to be certain of a return to Division One. Three of them were gained with a 2-0 home win over Millwall, before attention turned to Selhurst Park on May Bank Holiday. 10,000 fans made the journey but with three minutes to go Ian Wright popped up to poop the party. Celebrations were only delayed a little over 24 hours as Shrewsbury beat Oldham Athletic 2-0, but it was something of an anti-climatic way to clinch promotion. The season ended with Fratton Park packed to the rafters for the visit of Sheffield United. The kick-off was delayed as spectators spilled into the closed upper tier of the Fratton End, but an outside chance of clinching the title was ended as United won 2-1.

The following day, chairman Deacon joined manager Alan Ball in front of thousands of fans in the Guildhall square after an open-top bus ride through the city. Having arrived at the club fifteen years previously, promising Division One in three years, he had spent countless thousands of pounds pursuing his dream, only to see the club plumb the depths of the Football League. This was his moment.

```
DID YOU KNOW?

Q. What was odd about Kevin Dillon's hat-trick against Millwall in November 1986?
A. It was a Full Members' Cup match and all three goals were penalties.
```

Match of the Season 1986-87
Crystal Palace 1 Portsmouth 0

Division 2, 4 May 1987

This May bank holiday afternoon should have been the match which clinched Pompey's return to the big-time, 28 years after they left it with a lowest points total in the club's history and most goals conceded in a season.

As the game drifted into the last five minutes, the necessary point looked to be in the bag and 10,000 fans on the Holmesdale Road end prepared to party. But hang on a minute. Being Pompey fans they should have known better. The previous two seasons had seen promotion cruelly torn from their grasp as the team collapsed in April, within sight of the finish line. Surely lightning wasn't going to strike for a third time?

Well, no, not exactly. Third-placed Oldham were six points adrift with only two to play (and with an inferior goal-difference), but when Alan Irvine got away down the right and pumped a hopeful cross into the box with three minutes remaining, somehow you knew what was going to happen next.

Palace's 17-year-old substitute, John Salako, knocked the ball back across the six-yard line and there was Ian Wright on hand to sweep it home. The collective feeling was 'typical'. To add insult to injury, Hilaire allowed his frustration to get the better of him and his push on Andy Gray meant he became the fifth Pompey player to be dismissed during the season.

To add to the 'if onlys' that would haunt all concerned for the next thirty hours or so, Mariner had had a seemingly good goal disallowed, but the linesman ruled Quinn to be offside. Pompey's promotion was still in their own hands, with Sheffield United due to visit Fratton on Saturday, but relegation-threatened Shrewsbury could spare any chewing of fingernails, by avoiding defeat the following night at home to Oldham.

Deacon and his wife Joan spend the night at the theatre – watching *Les Miserables!* They were among the last people connected with the club to learn that the Shrews' 2-0 win over Oldham meant Pompey were finally up, although any hopes of pinching the title from Derby ended with Sheffield United winning 2-1 at Fratton.

LEAGUE DIVISION 1   **1987-88**
Barclays Division 1   19th (relegated)
Littlewoods Cup   2nd Round
FA Cup   Quarter-finals

As the euphoria of promotion subsided, Ball – presented with a new three-year contract by Deacon – set about planning his strategy for keeping the club up. First to arrive was young American striker John Kerr from non-league Wycombe, who had impressed on trial in the spring. He was quickly joined by QPR and Northern Ireland international winger Ian Stewart on a free, forwards Terry Connor from Brighton for £200,000 and Ian Baird from Leeds for £285,000, plus midfielder Mick Fillery, who came on a free transfer as a result of an administrative error at QPR. Also arriving were West Brom utility player Clive Whitehead on a free and promising Welsh Under-21 international midfielder Barry Horne for £60,000. Young striker Kevin Russell made the opposite move to Wrexham. More controversially, winger Kevin O'Callaghan returned to his first club Millwall for £100,000, but that was nothing compared to the shock at Ball's sale of Mick Tait on the eve of the season to Reading for £35,000.

That decision soon came to haunt the manager as centre-half Noel Blake badly injured his knee in training and Ball was forced to press Paul Mariner into emergency defensive cover for the first three matches of the season. These saw just one point gained and nine goals conceded. The gap was plugged when £70,000 was spent on Oxford defender Malcolm Shotton, but the newcomer could not disguise deficiencies in the squad, which were brutally exposed at the end of August by Arsenal 6-0.

A league run of three wins, three draws and just one defeat propelled the team as high as eleventh in mid-October, but that was offset by third division Swindon's embarrassing 6-2 aggregate thrashing in the Littlewoods Cup. Three straight defeats put the team back in the relegation mire by the end of October and two more points were tossed away when Kevin Dillon's usual penalty accuracy deserted him and Spurs escaped from Fratton with a draw.

Of equal concern was the growing financial crisis enveloping Fratton. The anticipated boom in attendances that top-flight football was meant to bring failed to materialise, with average gates little better than the previous season. Matters came to a head when a puzzled Deacon asked where the fans had gone after the Tottenham match attracted fewer than 16,000 spectators. The Hampshire Constabulary's insistence that nearly every game should be all-ticket probably went a long way towards answering his question.

DID YOU KNOW?

The first Football League substitute to be substituted was Pompey's American-born striker John Kerr, against Watford in September 1987.

By this time, a knee injury had claimed Shotton's Fratton career and he signed for Huddersfield on his recovery. The team's patched up defence was struggling to cope, while Baird's one goal in thirteen appearances made it impossible for him to live down his Southampton connections with the fans. The nadir was reached when second division Stoke won a Simod Cup-tie at Fratton against virtually Ball's first-choice eleven with contemptuous ease. Nottingham Forest followed up on the Saturday with a 5-0 pasting that put Pompey in the relegation zone. Players were up for sale and Dillon nearly went to Watford for £150,000, until uncertainty over a takeover by Robert Maxwell scuppered the deal.

By Christmas, things were becoming desperate, compounded by just one point gleaned over the festive period from games against companions-in-distress Charlton and Watford. However, with the return of Blake, and with striker Connor – whose Pompey debut was put on hold until October, following an injury in pre-season – finally getting off the mark, things began to look up.

Another 'TC' goal on New Year's Day looked set to exact revenge for that August thrashing at Highbury until Alan Smith's late equaliser. Even that wouldn't have mattered had Dillon not collected an unwanted north London 'double', missing another spot-kick in the dying minutes. Two days later Connor's third goal in as many matches clinched a joyful 2-0 win over arch-rivals Southampton and suddenly Pompey were pulling away from trouble. It was now that Deacon dropped the bombshell.

Ball had made his spiky midfielder Mick Kennedy captain for the game at the Dell for good reason. It would be his last Pompey appearance because the club had agreed to sell him to second division Bradford City for £250,000. The sale was intended to ease the cash-flow crisis that had come to a head. A High Court winding-up petition brought by the Inland Revenue was due to be heard in February. The money from Kennedy's sale helped settle the debt, but collective belief in the club's ambition was shattered.

Ironically, the team found its best form of the season, spurred by a developing run in the FA Cup which accounted for second division Blackburn and Sheffield United in rounds three and four. The fifth round draw paired the club with, of all teams, Bradford City, but Kennedy's return was far from happy as more than 19,000 saw Pompey cruise into the quarter-finals for the first time since 1952.

With the winding-up order rescinded and an unbeaten league run stretching back to Boxing Day, Pompey allowed themselves to dream of Wembley. The awakening was rude.

At the end of February, Pompey finally displayed first division pulling power as more than 28,000 turned up to see runaway leaders Liverpool – 28 games unbeaten – gain a 2-0 win. A fortnight later Pompey's Cup dreams ended in tears as Quinn was sent off for elbowing former Pompey centre-half Steve Foster during Luton's 3-1 win at Kenilworth Road.

The question now was could the team stay up, but with the only activity in transfer deadline week being the sale of Baird back to Leeds for a cut-price £185,000, the signs were not good. After the Cup exit a run of five defeats in six matches effectively sealed the club's fate. The break in that sequence was a 1-0 win at Tottenham, courtesy of a Horne goal. The Welshman had been one of the few players to enhance his reputation during the campaign and the result briefly raised hopes that the team might just claim eighteenth position and a relegation play-off place. Play-offs nowadays involve only those clubs who narrowly failed to make automatic promotion, but in the first years of its operation they included the team just above the automatic relegation zone. This was the position Pompey hoped to occupy.

Their hopes were finally doused by a controversial penalty goal at Coventry, hard on the heels of successive 2-2 draws against Wimbledon and Norwich. The match at Plough Lane also saw Alan Knight hospitalised with a fractured cheekbone, following a fearsome first-half clash with Eric Young and John Fashanu.

Pompey bowed out of the first division after just one season at Old Trafford, when Manchester United won 4-1. Ball handed a full debut to 18-year-old Sutton-born winger Mark Kelly, who had been the subject of a tug-of-war between the Football Associations of England and Ireland. Having represented both countries in friendly matches – he even gained a full cap for the Republic before his first league appearance – Kelly eventually plumped for his Irish roots. For Ball, he represented one of the club's brightest prospects for many years.

As the season ended, most attention was focused on rumours of an imminent buy-out of John Deacon's stake in the club. The financial strain of trying to keep Pompey in Division One had taken its toll on the ageing property magnate. Although he had denied stories in the national press indicating that London garage owner Jim Gregory was keen to acquire the club – Gregory having recovered from the heart attack that forced him to sell QPR in 1986 – the rumours refused to go away.

DID YOU KNOW?

Sunderland-born midfielder Kevin Dillon has been sent off at all three major north-
east clubs: Middlesbro (Jan 85), Newcastle (Dec 87), Sunderland (Dec 88).

In this fevered atmosphere, Ball's decision to release out-of-
contract defender Noel Blake almost passed unnoticed. Shortly
before the Cup final it was announced that Gregory and Deacon
had agreed a deal, which included Deacon's son David and Jim
Sloan remaining on the board. The scene was set for the busiest
summer Fratton had ever known.

Match of the Season 1987-88
Portsmouth 3 Luton 1

Division 1, 10 October 1987

For most Pompey fans there is only one match of this particular
season. And this isn't it. The date 3 January 1988 is etched into club
folklore when Southampton finally got their come-uppance, and at
the Dell to boot.

However, the match with Luton has a case to be heard, in a
season largely dominated by doom, gloom and assorted visits to the
High Court to stave off winding-up orders. This was the day that
Pompey reached the dizzy heights of eleventh place – with Southampton six points adrift in the bottom three – and the team fleetingly promising to establish themselves in the first division.

A catastrophic start had been mended – just one defeat in the
last six games, that at all-conquering Liverpool the previous weekend – and in the 55th minute Pompey had the benefit of an
outstanding strike by Dillon, which suddenly turned a match of
base metal into gold.

Dillon's 30-yard half-volley out of nothing, as Baird flicked on
Knight's drop-clearance, fizzed past Les Sealey and in off the post.
Seventeen minutes later he played Hilaire clear and his dramatic
tumble over Sealey's plunge at his feet was 'bought' by referee
Buksh. The spot-kick was unerringly drilled home. Dillon capped a
virtuoso display by chasing substitute Mariner's pass to the bye-
line, before pulling the ball back for the ex-Arsenal and England
striker's head to seal the points.

Buksh again showed his penalty generosity in the last minute,
deeming Kevin Ball's interception of Ricky Hill's point-blank shot to
be deliberate handball, and Mick Harford pulled one back for his
namesake Ray's team. Luton could point to a double-dose of bad

luck midway through the first half, when Micky Weir headed against the bar and Danny Wilson thrashed the rebound against a post, but in the end the points were deservedly Pompey's.

The following Saturday, Pompey had a blank weekend, as the Football League's bid to restructure the competition meant there were just 21 teams in the first division this season. Among others, Southampton took advantage of one of their games in hand to tighten things up at the foot of the table.

Just one point from the next eighteen was gleaned and Pompey didn't win at home again until February. The relegation-battle die was quickly re-cast, but for one weekend in October at least, the uplands of the first division – third-placed Arsenal were only seven points away – were briefly glimpsed.

## 4

THE JIM GREGORY YEARS
1988-1994

LEAGUE DIVISION 2   **1988-89**
Barclays Division 2   20th
Littlewoods Cup   2nd Round
FA Cup   3rd Round

From the moment Jim Gregory arrived it was clear he did not want to waste time taking stock. His immediate priority was to bring Fratton Park up to date after years of neglect. In early June contractors moved in to strip the North and South Stands of their cladding, with an end of August deadline to have refurbished their interior and exterior completely. New terracing was to be installed under the South Stand, and the Fratton End top tier – unused since 1986 – was demolished with the promise of a new covered terrace by the end of the season.

The pace of change was breathtaking, and was matched by the revamping of the squad. Ominously for Ball, his job title changed from 'manager' to 'chief coach', although it was stressed that his role had not changed, and his assistant Graham Paddon was demoted to youth coach. Gregory brought in his namesake John, the former QPR, Derby and England international midfielder, as Ball's assistant. Ball was given money to spend: £200,000 brought in Sheffield Wednesday winger Mark Chamberlain, £110,000 signed QPR full-back Warren Neill, and £150,000 was spent on Manchester United centre-half Graeme Hogg. To help balance the books, Vince Hilaire was allowed to join Noel Blake at Leeds for £185,000, but on the eve of the season Ball was allowed to break the club record transfer fee. He paid Aston Villa £315,000 for Warren Aspinall, a striker with a bad-boy image who he had long admired.

Ironically, suspension kept Aspinall out for the first three matches, but the team started like an express train with ten points from the first twelve, including a 4-0 home thrashing of Leeds in front of more than 15,000 crammed into a partially open ground. September and early October were less fruitful and the team slipped into mid-table and were unceremoniously dumped out of the Littlewoods Cup by league newcomers Scarborough. It took the arrival of midfielder Martin Kuhl for £125,000 from Watford to put some much-needed bite into the team.

Pompey were back on top of the table after a 3-0 win over Barnsley on 19 November, the final result in a run of seventeen points taken out of 21. Aspinall and Mick Quinn were proving to be a potent force and when the team beat Brighton 2-0 on the Saturday before Christmas, the play-offs seemed the minimum expectation of the season.

Within four weeks the situation had altered dramatically. Form slumped with three successive league defeats and an FA Cup third round exit at the hands of Swindon in a replay. Injuries and loss of form forced Ball at Leicester to hand a debut to 17-year-old defender Kit Symons, who partnered Gavin Maguire, making his league debut after a £225,000 move from QPR. Tottenham loan signing Paul Moran was also in the starting line-up for the first time and Mick Fillery made his first appearance of the season. City's 2-1 win spelt the end for Ball after almost five years in charge. He was replaced by John Gregory.

The fans were clearly disillusioned and the gate for his first match, at home to Shrewsbury, dipped below 9,000 for the first time that season. A 2-0 win lifted spirits, as did Jim Gregory's announcement of ambitious plans to build a new 'Super Stadium' for the club on the railway goods-yard site behind Fratton Park.

In footballing terms, however, John Gregory had a baptism of fire. Four out of the next five were lost by a single goal and the sole point gained was at home to bottom placed Walsall in front of just over 7,000 fans. Promotion was by now a forlorn hope, although consecutive 1-0 wins over Plymouth and Birmingham in early March briefly brought the play-offs back into focus.

One win in the final thirteen matches, including a six-match consecutive losing run to end the season, meant that Pompey finished just two places and nine points above the relegation places. To stop the rot, the 'manager' – for that was his title – was given money to spend before the transfer deadline, but full-back John Beresford, a £300,000 signing from Barnsley, broke his ankle on his first full appearance, at home to Watford on Easter Monday. Gregory's other signing was Nottingham Forest winger Steve Wigley, bought for a similar fee. To pay for the signings Gregory had to generate income. When first division Southampton offered £700,000 for Barry Horne, it was too good an offer to refuse, and the Welsh international became one of only a handful of players who have ever made the move from Fratton to the Dell.

DID YOU KNOW?

Carlton Palmer was the first opponent to be sent off at Fratton Park for two different teams – WBA in 1988 and Sheffield Wednesday in 1991.

The final game of the season saw Mick Quinn grab a consolation goal from the penalty spot as Chelsea, now managed by Bobby Campbell, clinched the championship with a 3-2 win. The fact that Quinn threw his boots and shirt to his adoring fans on the still truncated Fratton End suggested he was not going to renew his contract, which was about to expire.

His replacement, although no one knew it at the time, finally put pen to paper in the May. The princely sum of £450 bought 24-year-old striker Guy Whittingham out of the Army, where his non-league career had blossomed at Yeovil Town. Whittingham's arrival stemmed from a deal ironically set up by his predecessor, Ball. At the same time, John Gregory started clearing out what he regarded as the club's 'dead wood'. Kevin Dillon, Billy Gilbert and Clive Whitehead were released, but negotiations opened to keep defender Paul Hardyman at the club. Quinn was also offered a contract, but with little hope of it being accepted.

Match of the Season 1988-89
Portsmouth 4 Leeds United 0
Division 2, 3 September 1988

This win represented the high-watermark of optimism which the new Jim Gregory regime, installed at the end of May, insisted was about to propel the club into a new era of prosperity. Alas, it arrived just three games into the season.

A whirlwind summer had seen Fratton Park turned into a building site – 15,000 was the capacity while work was finished off – and more than £1 million had been invested in new players, including Warren Neill, Graeme Hogg and Mark Chamberlain, all of whom started this match. A club-record fee had also been shelled out for a long-time Ball target, striker Aspinall, but he missed the game through suspension carried over from his previous club.

During the summer, Ball had also off-loaded two of his stalwarts – Noel Blake, controversially, on a free transfer, and tribunal-arbitrated £185,000 Vince Hilaire – both of whom ended up at Elland Road. Also in the Leeds line-up was Fratton flop Ian Baird, who had rejoined the club in March after an unhappy eight months at Fratton. Although their halcyon days of the late 60s and 70s had long gone, Leeds were always short-priced favourites for a return to the first division. A good test of Pompey's mettle was in prospect.

Blake received a warm welcome, but it soon cooled after he clattered Horne early on. Pompey went ahead when Dillon's corner was nodded goalwards by Hogg, and Taylor could only divert the ball in. The second was a strike of stunning class, as Chamberlain found Neill overlapping and his far-post cross was buried by Quinn's head.

Leeds were on the rack and Pompey were not going to let them off it. Connor wrapped the points up with a shot from an acute angle after Quinn had turned Blake, then Chamberlain brought the house down with a languid run, ending with a devastating shot in off the far post. Blake handled, but Quinn skied the penalty. However, Leeds' misery was complete when the mercilessly-taunted Baird was sent off for tangling with Hogg.

Quickly, Pompey's fortunes nose-dived. The next win was more than a month, and six games, away and despite briefly regaining top spot in November, a four-match losing run at the turn of the year did for Ball. His replacement, John Gregory, failed to stop the rot and Pompey would end up 20th. Leeds' promotion bid stalled too, but by the time the teams met again on Easter Saturday, mid-fielder Gordon Strachan's experience had been recruited and they wouldn't fall short the following season.

LEAGUE DIVISION 2   **1989-90**
Barclays Division 2   12th
Littlewoods Cup   2nd Round
FA Cup   3rd Round

After the hectic summer twelve months previously, this time around Pompey's novice manager restricted himself to just one new signing, with Hearts midfielder Kenny Black arriving in a £250,000 deal. That fee was more or less recouped when Paul Hardyman exercised his freedom of contract and joined Sunderland for an arbitrated fee. Quinn, too, left for the north east, Newcastle his destination, and Pompey had to settle for another arbitrated fee of £650,000. John Gregory made a popular move when he appointed former Fratton boss Frank Burrows as his assistant.

A series of pre-season 'friendly' defeats, including one by South American touring side Botofogo, hinted that the manager was still struggling to blend his squad satisfactorily. Hopes of a bright start were shattered on the opening day, when Watford sneaked a 1-0 win and Warren Aspinall was ruled out for several months with a broken leg. Things quickly went from bad to worse and it took until the seventh match of the season to record a league win. A narrow aggregate defeat by Manchester United promised better things, but newly promoted Wolves' 5-0 thrashing was more typical of the state the team was in.

The only redeeming feature was the way Whittingham had taken his chance to step up from non-league football. A goal helped salvage a point against Hull on his second appearance as substitute. He also scored on his full home debut in that first win against Middlesbrough and by the end of October he had seven goals, including a bizarre brace scored in stoppage time against Leeds which earned an unlikely point. With Terry Connor clearly out of sorts, £215,000 was found to bring striker Jimmy Gilligan from Burrows' former club Cardiff. This was intended to give Whittingham experienced support to nurture his developing talent.

Results improved during November and December, with just one defeat in the league, at home to Watford, but the team was far from out of the relegation woods. The year ended on a high with Whittingham scoring his first league hat-trick to secure a 3-3 draw at promotion-chasing Oldham. That promise was quickly undermined on New Year's Day, however, as Leicester came from two goals down to win, and within 48 hours John Gregory was part of Pompey's history.

Burrows was appointed caretaker for the FA Cup third round tie at first division Crystal Palace, which saw a spirited performance end with a last-minute defeat to a controversial penalty. The players clearly responded to Burrows and he was given the job until the end of the season, immediately signing £100,000 Chelsea midfielder Micky Hazard and Tottenham defender Gary Stevens on loan to reinforce the squad. Hazard scored on his debut to secure a vital win at relegation rivals Stoke, now managed by Alan Ball, and the following week Stevens was on the mark to see off another struggling side, Bradford City, at Fratton.

With hindsight, the Pompey job had clearly come far too early in John Gregory's managerial career – having to deal with the club's volatile combination of highly-talented under-achievers – but Burrows' no-nonsense approach brought an element of much-needed stability. His determination not to allow individuals to harm the collective spirit was clearly illustrated by his handling of Hazard. After eight enigmatic appearances, which had seen the midfielder substituted four times, Burrows' patience snapped after his contribution to a home defeat by Wolves. The former Chelsea man found himself frozen out and his attitude questioned by his boss. He never kicked a ball for Pompey again and eventually moved to Swindon.

A run of four defeats out of five matches in March threatened to drag the team back into the relegation scuffle, but a run of six wins and three draws in the run-in eventually averted fears of a catastrophic demotion and raised real hopes for the following season. Among Pompey's scalps were eventually-promoted Sheffield United and an Oldham side whose FA Cup and Littlewoods Cup exploits meant they just missed out.

The real bonus was the emergence of Whittingham as a forward of real potential. His 23 goals in 42 league appearances earned him a deserved player of the year award. The club could also face the future with confidence after the exploits of the youth team, which reached the semi-finals of the FA Youth Cup, beating Liverpool on the way to an aggregate defeat by Middlesbrough. Defenders Kit Symons and Andy Awford, along with striker Darryl Powell, had already appeared in the first team, while Darren Anderton had been marked as a winger of immense promise.

It was no surprise when Jim Gregory summoned Burrows to his Blue Star Garages' headquarters at Roehampton shortly after the end of the season to offer him the manager's job on a permanent basis. New contracts were offered to Kevin Ball and Terry Connor, but the new manager's main preoccupation would be to find a striking partner for Whittingham to ensure the goals that could turn the team into true promotion candidates. He would have to break the club's transfer record to do so.

DID YOU KNOW?

Before the England Youth international v Czechoslovakia at Fratton Park in
November 1989, the referee noticed the crossbars were too low.

Match of the Season 1989-90
Stoke City 1 Portsmouth 2

Division 2, 13 January 1990

Alan Ball probably relished this match. Installed as Stoke manager,
he was undoubtedly looking forward to putting one over on his
former employers, who were just three points ahead of his team in
this relegation clash. However, some of the spice was lost since
John Gregory – Ball's 'assistant' who ended up getting his job – had
fallen victim to Jim Gregory's impatience ten days earlier.

Ball was diplomatic, claiming he was looking forward to seeing
old friends, but added: 'It promises to be some match. Motivation
shouldn't be too difficult for me!' Gregory's assistant, Frank
Burrows, had been put in temporary charge and reinforced the
squad by signing Stevens and Hazard. Rock-bottom Stoke, needing
a win, included three former Pompey players: Chris Kamara, Dave
Bamber and Lee Sandford, who had joined Stoke in December.

A large Pompey following gave Ball a generous reception. Their
mood brightened further when Wigley raced away and crossed for
Whittingham to bury a header. Stoke were further rocked when
Biggins was carried off after an aerial clash with Kevin Ball. Pompey
should have gone further ahead when Fox felled Chamberlain for a
penalty. Black's kick hit the post and he instinctively knocked in the
rebound, before realising his mistake. Five minutes later, though,
Whittingham set up Hazard for a debut goal.

Ball re-jigged his team at half-time, but still they struggled until
Kamara flighted a corner to the far post and Sandford's gentle
header crept in. Bamber thrashed a shot wide. Then Kamara's free-
kick was fisted clear by Knight. According to the *Sports Mail* the
Pompey penalty area resembled the 'Alamo'. Hogg could be
counted among the wounded as he was stretchered off with two
minutes to go with a head injury and replaced by Beresford.

The win lifted Pompey out of the bottom three, six clear of
bottom-placed Stoke. Under Burrows' guidance they would end up
twelfth. Poor old Potters were doomed, however, securing just
fifteen more points and never moving off the foot of the table. Ball
would remain in charge, but once Stoke's bid to bounce back
immediately fell apart he was sacked and replaced by Lou Macari.

LEAGUE DIVISION 2   **1990-91**
Barclays Division 2   17th
Rumbelows Cup   3rd Round
FA Cup   5th Round

Burrows' planning for the new season was disrupted early on when it became clear that Kevin Ball was disinclined to accept the club's contract offer. Eventually he moved to Division One new-boys Sunderland, while Pompey had to make do with the arbitrated transfer fee. Terry Connor also decided it was time to move on, to third division Swansea, and Jimmy Gilligan shortly joined him, recouping most of the money John Gregory had paid for him.

However, the money received gave Burrows the opportunity to spend a club record fee of £450,000 to sign QPR's Northern Ireland international forward Colin Clarke, who he saw as the ideal foil for Whittingham's pace. He also added Tottenham midfielder Shaun Murray to the squad for £100,000 and appointed Tony Barton – who had won the European Cup as Aston Villa manager – as his assistant. A sound set of pre-season performances, including a 2-1 win over first division QPR, persuaded more than 12,000 to turn up for the opening match at home to West Brom. It took a late goal from Whittingham to save a point and 'Corporal Punishment', as he was now known, also scored in a 1-1 draw at West Ham three days later.

His third goal in as many games wasn't enough to avoid defeat at Oldham, however, and an injury ruled him out for the next five weeks, during which time the team won just twice, losing five games. During this period Burrows dropped Alan Knight, giving Andy Gosney his chance in goal, and Gregory found £325,000 to sign Tottenham centre-half Guy Butters in September, but results didn't improve at all as Clarke and Whittingham failed to hit it off. By the time Pompey slumped to an unlucky defeat at Sheffield Wednesday on 29 December – their sixth in a ten-match winless run – the team was just one off the bottom and looking short-priced for the drop. In November, the League Cup, by now sponsored by Rumbelows, should have provided a lift as Pompey led first division Chelsea 2-0, until three late goals in a third round replay gave the Londoners a place in the next round.

The FA Cup had provided a tricky third round draw away to Vauxhall Conference side Barnet and, sensing a shock, BBC TV's Match of the Day was there to record the highlights. Bolstered by a 5-1 win over bottom club Hull on New Year's Day, Pompey cruised home 5-0. Whittingham grabbed a hat-trick to enhance his reputation on a national stage. Confidence was high, and in the next round an openly impudent Bournemouth team from Division Three were sent packing 5-1 in front of more than 15,000. The reward was a home tie with Tottenham, who included the hero of England's Italia '90 bid, Paul Gascoigne, in their ranks. Within hours the match was an all-ticket sell-out, but the home fans were disappointed as the formbook prevailed and Gascoigne scored twice in the second half to seal a 2-1 win.

Three wins and a draw in February, including a first win at Middlesbrough since 1949, seemed to have banished thoughts of relegation, only for March to reveal all the old frailties. It was too much for Burrows, who resigned in the wake of a 0-0 home draw with Millwall, allowing Barton – a former player and scout for the club in the 60s and 70s – to be given the manager's job he coveted until the end of the season. Initially he made little impact, as a return of just one point out of nine left Pompey fourth from bottom by Easter.

But then the pieces all fell into place, as Butters and Maguire returned to the defence and £80,000 full-back Ray Daniel – whom Burrows' signed from Cardiff the day before his resignation – stiffened the left-hand side. Even Clarke finally gained grudging acceptance from the fans as his hat-trick helped thrash promotion chasing Bristol City 4-1 at Fratton. Three more wins and a draw virtually ensured safety, although it took a 3-1 victory over Bristol Rovers in the final home match of the season to mathematically kill the possibility of relegation.

The end of the season also brought the unfortunate news that Republic of Ireland international Mark Kelly's long battle against a knee injury had been lost. The slender winger's desire to live up to his billing as the 'new George Best' had frequently been sabotaged by protracted periods on the treatment table and he finally bowed to the inevitable retirement at just 22 years of age.

Despite a disappointing end as Wolves won 3-1 on the last day, Barton certainly felt he had done enough to gain the manager's job on a permanent basis, having steered the club to safety. But he was left a bitter man as the expected summons to Roehampton never materialised. Instead, Gregory decided he had burned his fingers once already with Burrows by appointing a 'Pompey man' to the job, so he turned to one of his trusted former managers in Jim Smith, who had taken QPR to Wembley in the Milk Cup in 1986.

Smith's appointment was welcomed by players and supporters alike. He had a reputation of getting clubs promoted, while still sticking to his principles of playing attractive football. He soon realised what an abundant crop of talent he had to harvest at Fratton.

DID YOU KNOW?

Three Pompey players have scored two hat-tricks in the same month: Mike
Trebilcock (Oct 1970), Mark Hateley (Nov 1983), Guy Whittingham (Jan 1991).

Match of the Season 1990-91

Portsmouth 1   Tottenham 2

FA Cup, 5th Round, 16 February 1991

Paul Gascoigne's contribution to the 1991 FA Cup is well docu-
mented – a curling free-kick that destroyed Arsenal in a Wembley
semi-final and that notorious challenge on Gary Charles in the final
which crocked his own knee, nearly putting paid to his multi-
million pound transfer to Lazio. However, none of that would have
been possible without a virtuoso second-half performance at Fratton
Park in the fifth round, in which he single-handedly rescued his
team from impending ignominy.

Before the game Gazza had been doubtful after injuring himself
in England's friendly game with Cameroon, but nevertheless tickets
for the tie had been snapped up quickly. Terry Venables' Spurs still
boasted quality performers such as Gary Lineker, Paul Walsh and
Gary Mabbutt. Hopes of a shock were high, as Spurs had just one
league win in six under their belts since Christmas, while Pompey's
Cup run had seen them score ten goals in two games, with
Whittingham grabbing seven of them.

In the pre-match warm-up those hopes received a further boost
when Terry Fenwick pulled up and had to be replaced by Justin
Edinburgh. In a fiercely competitive first half, Gazza curled one
free-kick just wide from 25 yards and Lineker saw a shot fizz just
over, but it was no surprise when Aspinall's deflected shot fell into
Chamberlain's path and he drilled a shot past Thorstvedt four
minutes from the break. Kuhl almost doubled the lead with a free-
kick and at half-time the BBC Match of the Day team seemed to
have a shock result developing.

Whittingham was close to a goal with a header shortly after the
break, but Gosney excelled to block Paul Allen's shot as the action
ebbed and flowed. Then Gazza took over. He initiated the move
which ended with him powering a header past Gosney from Allen's
cross. He then picked up Van den Hauwe's pass, shimmied past a
despairing challenge and bent a shot in from the edge of the area.

Spurs would go on and lift the Cup in May, but Pompey could
hold their heads high. Only a few hot-heads who held up the match
near the end by invading the pitch slightly marred the day.

LEAGUE DIVISION 2   **1991-92**
Barclays Division 2   9th
Rumbelows Cup   3rd Round
FA Cup   Semi-final

Despite Jim Smith's high-profile appointment, the club's involvement in the close season transfer market was limited to £25,000
spent on Cheltenham Town's 23-year-old midfielder Chris Burns,
who readily swapped his day job as a bricklayer for the challenge of
becoming a professional footballer. Out-of-contract centre-half
Graeme Hogg was the only significant departure, failing to agree
terms with the new manager and joining Scottish Premier Division
club Hearts.

During pre-season, Smith used the opportunity to give all his
squad the chance to show what they could do, but his first team-
sheet for the away match at Blackburn – who had just started to flex
the financial muscle afforded them by benefactor Jack Walker – still
raised a few eyebrows. Senior professionals such as Aspinall,
Wigley and Neill found themselves excluded, while Chamberlain
had to make do with a place on the bench. The thirteen-man squad
included the backbone of the team which had done so well in the
FA Youth Cup two seasons previously, not to mention a rags-to-
riches tale for 'brickie' Burns. This new crop of Pompey 'babes'
came within a minute of a sensational win at Ewood Park, but
Kevin Moran's injury-time equaliser cancelled out an outrageous
opening goal from Darren Anderton shortly after the interval.

Smith took the view that if they were good enough they were
old enough and Awford, Symons, Anderton and Powell became
regular fixtures in the side as Pompey's promising start developed.
The main problem holding the team back was scoring goals,
although three in the first six matches were enough to secure two
wins and two draws. By the end of October the team were comfortably placed and the Rumbelows Cup had given the team the
chance to perform creditably against the best, as Manchester United
won a compelling third round tie at Old Trafford 3-1.

It was only when Guy Whittingham – the start of his season
disrupted by loss of form and injury – got back into the groove with
the winner against Leicester at Fratton on 5 November that people
began to sit up and take notice of Smith's south-coast revolution.
Four more wins in seven matches took Pompey into the play-off
places after a 2-0 home win over Bristol Rovers on Boxing Day. Two
days later leaders Middlesbrough brought their championship
credentials to Fratton and left on the receiving end of a 4-0 thrashing. Automatic promotion was now a distinct possibility.

DID YOU KNOW?

Pompey have only had one serious penalty shoot-out. It cost them the 1992 FA Cup semi-final against Liverpool, when three Pompey players missed.

Consistency in the league deserted the team in January and February as attention switched to the FA Cup. A hard-fought win over Exeter – their manager Alan Ball receiving a standing ovation from Pompey fans before the start – was followed by a fourth round home tie with fourth division Leyton Orient. Weather had played havoc with the fixture list and consequently the relatively mild south coast was seen as a safe bet by the producer of Match of the Day. It was the game that launched willowy winger Anderton into the national consciousness as his two goals – one of them a stunning volley – put Pompey into the fifth round for the second consecutive season.

Most assumed Pompey's chances of progression had ended when Middlesbrough exacted partial revenge for their December pummelling by sneaking a late equaliser at Fratton Park. By the time the replay came round eleven days later Smith had moved in the transfer market to bolster his squad with the signing of Southampton's unsettled Republic of Ireland international midfielder Alan McLoughlin for £440,000. It proved to be a masterstroke, although 'Macca' watched the Ayresome Park tie from the stands. That night saw Smith's young team come of age as Anderton and Clarke shared the goals in a memorable 4-2 win in extra time to seal a sell out Fratton quarter-final with Brian Clough's first division Nottingham Forest.

McLoughlin scored on his home debut against Tranmere, but seven days later he repaid a huge slice of his transfer fee when his toe-poked goal put Pompey in the semi-finals of the FA Cup for the first time since 1949. The draw could have pitted Pompey with divisional rivals Sunderland, or even Norwich or Southampton who had to replay. Instead it was Liverpool who came out of the hat and supporters began a mad scramble for the 19,000 tickets allocated for the Clock End at neutral Highbury.

In the meantime, promotion was still possible, at least via the play-offs, and the Cup success inspired two consecutive wins against Millwall (6-1) and Southend (3-2). Pompey went into the semi-final in poor form, however, as one point in nine, albeit with games in hand, left the team in mid-table.

If the fifth round tie at Middlesbrough was when Smith's team came of age, Highbury was where they showed maturity beyond their years. After an even ninety minutes with chances at both ends, the reigning league champions had been taken to extra-time. Then, just when everyone thought their resolve would crack, Neill's long pass set Anderton clear. His shot was straight and true, Bruce Grobbelaar's hand could only help it into the corner of the net and Pompey were six minutes from Wembley. Only then did they betray themselves momentarily. With the clock ticking down, Awford's rash challenge halted Steve Nicol's surge on the edge of the area. John Barnes floated the free-kick against a post and Ronnie Whelan was on hand to break 19,000 hearts. The same Whelan whose crude foul on Chamberlain meant he limped out of the match and the rest of the season.

Eight days later another army of fans made the trip to Villa Park for the replay, only for fate to conspire once more. Six minutes from the end of normal time McLoughlin rattled the bar. An extra thirty minutes failed to produce a goal and the mighty Reds proficiency from the penalty-spot cruelly exposed Pompey's profligacy, as only Symons scored, while Kuhl, Neill and Beresford all missed. So near, yet so far.

A backlog of fixtures also put paid to any lingering play-off hopes, five games in twelve days producing just five points, but everyone at Fratton was convinced the club was on the verge of great things, provided the team could be kept together. Smith's first real test would be how to handle the out-of-contract Beresford and the inevitable attention Anderton was attracting from clubs with money to burn in the newly formed Premier League. It promised to be a more interesting summer than usual.

Match of the Season 1991-92

Portsmouth 1 Nottingham Forest 0
                                    FA Cup, quarter-final, 7 March 1992

The last time Pompey made it to the semi-finals in 1949, most fans in the 25,402 all-ticket crowd weren't even born. Most of the home support in the ground will remember this occasion for the rest of their lives. Confidence was high in Portsmouth, after the 4-2 win at Middlesbrough in the fifth round replay and, certainly, Brian Clough's Forest were far from a vintage crop. They came to Fratton on the back of seven league matches without a win and only a series of kind home draws – pitting them against lower league opposition – had smoothed their path to the quarter-finals.

Although a division beneath their visitors, Pompey were a different proposition and they were given the perfect start when Stuart Pearce fouled Anderton. From Beresford's free-kick, Forest keeper Crossley fumbled the cross and McLoughlin poked home from three yards. Soon afterwards Knight had to be at his best to keep out Pearce's flicked header, and Roy Keane appealed in vain for a penalty after Beresford was forced into a last-ditch tackle.

After the break, both teams continued to threaten, although Clough substituted his out-of-sorts striker Teddy Sheringham, who had been bottled up by Symons. In the 65th minute Forest were reduced to ten men when Laws' crude late challenge from behind on Beresford saw red, but Pompey were fortunate when Awford similarly clattered Nigel Clough, but was only booked.

Pompey made their advantage tell and Beresford's drive might have added to the score. At the end, thousands invaded the pitch and grown men were seen openly weeping at the joy of seeing their team one step from Wembley. The dream was to be cruelly shattered by a penalty shoot-out defeat at Villa Park against Liverpool.

LEAGUE DIVISION 1 (NEW)   **1992-93**
Barclays Division 1   3rd
Coca-Cola Cup   3rd Round
FA Cup   3rd Round

Out-of-contract Beresford soon decided his chances of playing in the newly-formed Premier League were better served away from Fratton Park. After his impressive performances against Liverpool in the semi-final it was little surprise when the Anfield club agreed a £700,000 deal with Pompey for his services. However, a failed medical ended his dream move, allowing Kevin Keegan, recently installed as Newcastle manager, the opportunity to sign him as he sought to turn the Geordies from relegation fodder to championship contenders.

Pompey's other jewel was Darren Anderton, particularly coveted by Terry Venables at Tottenham. In early June an offer of £1.7 million was accepted, but it still took several days agonising by the 20-year-old before he agreed to sign. Jim Smith immediately used £400,000 to return to White Hart Lane and snap up Paul Walsh, the perennially promising 30-year-old, whose career had taken one or two false turns, despite having played at the highest level with Liverpool.

The move was to prove inspirational – not only for Walsh, who suddenly found his talents completely to the taste of Smith and the Fratton faithful – but also for Whittingham, who had laboured for much of the previous season, scoring just eleven goals in the league in 35 appearances. Whit's opening day hat-trick earned a point at newly promoted Bristol City, which he followed up by scoring the winner at home to Barnsley. Walsh was slower off the mark, enduring public criticism by Smith after a poor performance in a defeat at Leicester, but once the effects of a virus had cleared the partnership was to become one of the most prolific in the club's history. August also saw director Jim Sloan retire at the AGM.

Shortly before a televised single goal home defeat by West Ham on 27 September, which left the team in mid-table, Smith courted controversy by selling popular midfielder Kuhl to divisional rivals Derby for £650,000, prompting accusations from fans of a lack of ambition. However, a run of just two defeats in thirteen games bounced the team into play-off contention just before Christmas, although the automatic promotion places were seemingly being sewn up by West Ham and an inspired Newcastle. Ironically the most disappointing result of that sequence was a draw, as two ultimately crucial points were dropped when Oxford scored twice in injury-time to secure an improbable 5-5 draw.

DID YOU KNOW?

The lowest ever attendance for a first-team fixture involving Pompey is 502, for an Anglo-Italian Cup match at Ascoli in December 1992.

Leading the way was Whittingham, thriving on the time and space the astute Walsh created for him, with 21 goals in league and cup. Three of those goals had come in the club's first excursion into 'Europe' in the guise of the Anglo-Italian Cup, organised between teams from the English second tier and the Italian *Serie B*. Having qualified by eliminating Charlton and Millwall, almost 5,000 turned up at Fratton to see a 2-0 win over Cesena. That gate was halved for the next home game against Lucchese, but was still huge when compared with the two sub-1,000 gates for the games in Italy at Bari – where Pompey fans made up almost half the official attendance of 837 – and Ascoli. No one was unduly bothered when the team failed to qualify for the semi-finals.

Of increasing excitement, though, was the gathering promotion push, especially after Pompey found the FA Cup 'giant-killing' boot on the other foot as second division local rivals Brighton pinched a 1-0 third round win at the Goldstone. After Whittingham had battered Bristol Rovers, scoring all four in a 4-1 win on Boxing Day and another two against Derby in a 4-2 win, the team secured thirteen points out of the next 21. The only downside was a nasty knee injury sustained in a reserve match by Colin Clarke, which ruled him out for the rest of the season. The climax of the run was a 2-0 home win over runaway leaders Newcastle in February in front of more than 21,000, thanks to first-half goals by Symons and the inevitable Whittingham strike – his 31st of the season.

Smith also moved to strengthen his squad, as Neill was ruled out for a couple of months with a back injury. The £50,000 signing of Chris Price, a veteran full-back also surplus to requirements at Ewood Park, proved astute. The former Aston Villa defender slotted into Neill's position comfortably and he was a regular as the club embarked on the most remarkable run of results in its history.

After losing to a late goal at fellow play-off contenders Swindon on 27 February, the team were in fifth place, nine points behind second-placed West Ham. Six straight wins in March eliminated that gap and put even leaders Newcastle in Pompey's sights. In the run-up to transfer deadline day Smith shuffled his pack, allowing Maguire to end a turbulent spell at Fratton with a move to Millwall, while he reinforced the midfield by signing Danish international Bjorn 'Benny' Kristensen from Newcastle. Another £100,000 was invested in the raw potential of Torquay winger Paul Hall. Smith's

other signing, the plucking 30-year-old former Southampton and
Oxford striker George Lawrence from the obscurity of Beazer
Homes League Weymouth, smacked of tightening purse-strings at
Fratton. Smith had desperately needed cover up front since Clarke's
injury, but the club had baulked at paying the going rate for Bristol
Rovers' striker John Taylor or the £250,000 demanded by Southamp-
ton for the services of veteran Scotland international David Speedie,
who signed instead for West Ham.

It all seemed academic as the team clearly had the bit between its
teeth. Even when Price dropped a toolbox on his toe, breaking a
bone, his loss was offset by Neill's return to fitness. A draw at
Millwall preceded another five straight wins, the fourth of which –
1-0 at Notts County – put Pompey in second place. During the
following week the club revealed plans to build a new 25,000 capacity stadium and retail development called 'Parkway', at Farlington,
near to the A27 and main railway line to London. By the time it was
due to be completed in 1995 it was clearly expected Pompey would
have established themselves in the Premier League. A 2-0 win over
Wolves in the 44th match of the season put the team briefly on top
of the table. A win and a draw from the final two games would put
Pompey up.

The penultimate game of the season was at relegation-haunted
Sunderland. Pompey had sold its 6,000 allocation of tickets in no
time, but as a catastrophic ninety minutes unfolded, with the hosts
winning 4-1, the club's destiny was suddenly out of its own hands.
Almost as important as the defeat was the sending off of Walsh –
the three-match ban would encompass the play-offs, should they
prove necessary. What price Speedie or Taylor now?

West Ham sensed their chance and 24 hours later cruised past an
unmotivated Swindon – their play-off berth secure. The London
club were level on points with Pompey, but crucially had scored
two goals more. They had the marginally harder task on the final
Saturday; at home to a Cambridge side desperate for a win to avoid
relegation, while Pompey were at home to mid-table Grimsby.

On a gripping afternoon, in front of an all-ticket crowd of almost
25,000, the outcome remained hanging in the balance until the
dying minutes. Despite trailing at half-time, news that West Ham
were only drawing spurred Pompey on. But for the heroics of the
Mariners' goalkeeper Wilmot, Pompey might have had half a dozen
goals rather than the two they finally had to settle for. West Ham
eventually won 2-0, but a disallowed Cambridge 'equaliser' at
Upton Park twelve minutes before the Hammers' last-minute
clincher, added to the sense that the fates had conspired against the
club.

The fates had one more trick to play, however, as Smith rallied his dispirited troops for the play-off semi-final with Leicester. The first leg was at Nottingham Forest's City Ground (Filbert Street was under renovation), and Julian Joachim's late winner was poor reward for a solid, but relatively toothless display, which saw Whittingham struggle in the absence of his foil, Walsh. The second leg was another Fratton sell-out, and when Alan McLoughlin squared things early in the second half, Wembley beckoned for the second time in thirteen months. Within minutes, however, neither the referee nor linesman saw 6ft 4in Ian Ormondroyd apparently standing yards offside as he sidefooted an equaliser. The game ended 2-2 and it was ultimately Swindon – two places and twelve points behind Pompey's total of 88 – who booked their place among the elite.

For the second time in eight seasons Pompey had been pipped to promotion by the narrowest of margins. For Jim Smith, the challenge was to persuade Whittingham – at the end of his contract and in high demand – that his Premiership ambitions could be fulfilled at Fratton. For the club, the challenge was to persuade a sceptical city council that its ambitions should be fulfilled at Parkway.

Match of the Season 1992-93

Portsmouth 2 Wolves 0

Division 1, 24 April 1993

Back in January, Pompey were nineteen points adrift of league leaders Newcastle. Victory against Wolves, though, would put Pompey on top of the table – for 24 hours at least, until the Magpies played at home to Sunderland – on the back of a run of ten wins and a draw in eleven matches, stretching back to March.

Jim Smith's team had come from play-off contenders to favourites for automatic promotion thanks to the prolific partnership of Whittingham and Walsh and the surge towards top-flight football had attracted the public back to Fratton in their droves. Nearly 24,000 had seen the Easter Monday win over Derby and a similar sized crowd turned up expecting to see Graham Turner's Wolves muzzled.

Symons kept his place in defence after Pompey's successful appeal to FIFA over Wales' insistence that he be released for international duty, but Wolves had a point to prove: the previous Saturday's home defeat by Tranmere had seen nine first-teamers pressed into reserve action during the week.

DID YOU KNOW?

In November 1981, furious manager Frank Burrows pitched his feeble first-team
against Exeter reserves as a punishment. They only drew 0-0.

Pompey generally had the better of the opening exchanges and
Wolves' Portsmouth-born keeper Mike Stowell had to be alert to
keep out a Whittingham shot. Gradually Wolves began to wear
down Pompey's threat and their own counter-attacking style began
to pose increasing problems. Frustrations showed after the break
when Butters was booked for an angry clash with Andy Mutch.

Daniel was denied by Stowell's reflexes, but in the 61st minute
the breakthrough came when Walsh held the ball up before laying it
off to Daniel, who drilled his shot just inside the near post. With
the minutes ticking away, Smith brought on his talisman substitute
Lawrence, who immediately made an impact, firing just over, then
crossing for Walsh to make the points safe with a header off the
underside of the bar.

For 24 hours the soon-to-be christened Premiership was tantalisingly within Pompey's grasp, until Newcastle restored their top
position with a 1-0 win. During the week, Sky TV covered
England's Under-21 international with Holland, using the occasion
to measure up their pitch angles for live TV coverage next season.
Their efforts were in vain. A crushing defeat at Sunderland took the
promotion equation out of Pompey's hands and West Ham took full
advantage. The play-offs were destined to provide still more heart-
ache.

LEAGUE DIVISION 1   **1993-94**
Endsleigh Division 1   17th
Coca-Cola Cup   Quarter-finals
FA Cup   3rd Round

Smith was limited in his scope for manoeuvre, as he was only able to release young striker Micky Ross, who had failed to make an impact, and George Lawrence. The news that Clarke's injury was so serious he would have to retire made the search for a new striker imperative, especially as Whittingham was refusing to sign a new contract. However, despite his record-breaking feats the previous season, Premiership clubs were hardly queuing up to sign him.

Smith gambled £200,000 on the volatile Oxford striker John Durnin, who had gained a troublesome reputation on and off the pitch, and who came complete with a four-match suspension with which to start the season. By the time pre-season training got underway Smith had also added Newcastle full-back Mark Stimson – who had had a spell on loan the previous season – to the squad. Middlesbrough defender Jon Gittens also trained with the club, as Smith held out the prospect of a permanent contract, which was accepted after a successful trial.

During a warm-up tournament in Finland it became clear Whittingham wanted to leave the club, and his presence was becoming increasingly unsettling. Eventually Pompey struck a £1.2 million deal with Aston Villa, with their England Under-21 international Mark Blake arriving at Fratton as part of the deal. The club's striking resources were clearly depleted, however, and on the eve of the season Smith announced he had signed 33-year-old Leeds striker Lee Chapman for £250,000.

A two-goal debut for Chapman was marred by a controversial odd goal defeat at Oxford. His home debut ended in disaster as a naughty elbow produced a red card and a three-match ban. By the time it was served he had gone – the first division was apparently beneath him – and Pompey recouped their money from West Ham. The team struggled for form, not helped by an injury to Knight which saw his understudy, Brian Horne, signed from Millwall the previous December as cover, concede nine goals in three games. The eventual arrival of Durnin galvanised things, however, and by mid-November – although the team were still short of goals – they were well on course for another promotion tilt. A move for Norwich's Lee Power was aborted two games into a loan spell, and the only arrivals in the autumn were Blackburn defender Tony Dobson, initially on loan, and young Weymouth defender Robbie Pethick for £35,000.

DID YOU KNOW?

Goalkeeper Alan Knight has played for Pompey in every possible domestic competition bar one – the Premiership.

There was also a developing run in the League Cup – now in its Coca-Cola guise – which saw Rotherham, Swindon and then Peterborough, after an extra-time replay, accounted for *en route* to a much-anticipated clash with Manchester United in the quarter finals.

Off the field, attention was focused on the increasingly problematic bid to secure planning permission for the Parkway stadium and retail development. Residents at Farlington were appalled at the prospect of a football ground on their doorsteps, and local retailers were unhappy at another out-of-town shopping development which contravened the published council structure plan, not to mention government guidelines. The conservationist lobby also chipped in with their concern for the nesting and breeding grounds of Brent Geese, even though they were apparently unperturbed by a nearby six-lane carriageway. Despite these objections, the planning committee voted in favour of the scheme at the end of October. The margin was a single vote, after one councillor changed his mind shortly before the crucial count. By December, however, the Department of the Environment had become involved and a Public Inquiry called. It would be twelve more months before this argument was settled.

Results deteriorated as the team's lack of firepower was exposed over Christmas and New Year, which accumulated just one goal and three points out of twelve. It was with some trepidation that Pompey faced cup visits to Premiership leaders Manchester United and second placed Blackburn in the space of five days. However, McLoughlin – who in November had booked the Republic of Ireland's trip to USA '94 with a goal against Northern Ireland – went a long way to ensuring his place in the squad with a stunning hat-trick at Ewood Park to earn a third round FA Cup replay. At Old Trafford, Walsh rolled back the years to score twice and Fratton looked forward to hosting another couple of huge occasions.

The lack of league goals, however, was cruelly underlined by a shock home defeat against lowly Peterborough in front of 19,000 fans, many seeking vouchers for the United game. The board acted and a new club record fee of £650,000 was found to sign Celtic striker Gerry Creaney, in whom Everton had shown a brief interest. Smith's initial target had been former apprentice Brett Angell, now leading scorer at Southend, but a failed medical halted the transfer.

Creaney made his debut as Manchester United won their replay more easily than the 1-0 scoreline suggests. Seven days earlier Rovers had made their class tell 3-1 and Pompey were left with the challenge of getting their promotion bandwagon back on course.

However, a miserable February brought just one win – including Creaney's first three goals – at home to Grimsby. After another home defeat, by promotion-chasing Crystal Palace on 5 March, the team were becoming increasingly preoccupied by events at the foot of the table. The board, over which the ailing Jim Gregory was exerting less and less influence, were concerned by a gaping hole in the balance sheet as gates slipped below 8,000. To balance the books, Smith stunned everyone by selling crowd favourite Walsh to Premiership strugglers Manchester City for £750,000. His justification – not without substance – that this was a good price for a 32-year-old, cut little ice with supporters furious at the way in which the promise of the previous season was being unravelled.

Walsh's 'replacement' had, in fact, arrived a couple of weeks earlier, as £35,000 was found to enable Smith to re-sign Alan Ball's former protégé, Paul Wood, from Bournemouth. The permanent signing of Dobson, after his loan period expired, had also been confirmed.

A 3-0 win over Wolves – who ironically included loaned Villa misfit Whittingham in their line-up – lifted spirits. As transfer deadline day approached, Smith also off-loaded his own misfit, Blake, who had failed to settle in the south, to promotion-chasing Leicester for £400,000. Coming in was Dutch striker Jerome Boere, on loan from West Ham, but an unproductive five matches proved he was not the answer to the team's needs. The spectre of relegation was lifted only with a run of four wins and two draws around Easter, including a satisfying 3-0 win at Filbert Street against Leicester.

The season ended disappointingly with four consecutive defeats – three at Fratton – all against teams with more to play for at their respective ends of the table than Pompey. The last game ended with scenes of pandemonium as West Brom avoided relegation with a 1-0 win, while 10,000 Albion fans swelled the gate to more than 17,000, the second highest of the season.

Smith's retained list had no room for Chamberlain, while Aspinall and Burns, who had struggled to progress after appearing in an FA Cup semi-final in his first season, had already been allowed to move on. While hardly clearing the decks, it gave some room for manoeuvre for a manager who was well aware that his squad was going to need considerable work to turn it into promotion material.

Match of the Season 1993-94

Blackburn 3 Portsmouth 3

FA Cup, 3rd Round, 8 January 1994

To state that cup draws had not been kind to Pompey in December 1993 was an understatement. No sooner had the League Cup quarter-final paired them with Premiership leaders Manchester United at Old Trafford, along came the FA Cup third round draw and a trip to second-in-the-table Blackburn. And all in the space of five days!

The portents did not look too promising either. The team had lost its scoring touch over Christmas and New Year, three 0-0 draws and a two-goal defeat at Barnsley knocking Pompey out of the play-off zone. And Kenny Dalglish's £20 million Rovers had yielded just eight goals at home in the Premiership all season.

However, Pompey had just the man for the big occasion in the shape of Republic of Ireland international midfielder Alan McLoughlin. On the coach to the team hotel, a video was shown of the FA Cup semi-final replay with Liverpool two seasons previously, and Macca took some stick from his team-mates as he was forced to relive a late miss which rapped the bar when it seemed easier to score. His answer now was sweet!

Moneybags Rovers, who had left their old second division sparring partners Pompey well behind on the substantial depths of Jack Walker's pockets, went ahead when ex-Saint Alan Shearer rammed the taunts of the visiting fans down their throats with his 21st goal of the season in the 21st minute.

Pompey battled back, though, and Blackburn went in at the break lucky still to be ahead. McLoughlin finally levelled in the 49th minute, as he exchanged passes with Walsh before rounding Flowers. Rovers reclaimed the lead with a sharp finish from Gallacher, only for McLoughlin to be given the freedom of the Rovers area for a second time.

When Tim Sherwood's shot skipped over Knight's dive, it looked as if former Rovers' boss Jim Smith was going to leave Ewood with only pride to show for his team's efforts. With thirty seconds on the watch remaining, Ray Daniel swung over a free-kick, Walsh and Symons got touches, and there was McLoughlin with the ball at his feet to complete his first hat-trick for the club.

On the Wednesday, Pompey held Manchester United to a 2-2 draw. Walsh scored both goals. But class finally told with a pair of replay defeats, whereupon Pompey's season fell apart. Four losses to end the season meant the club was grateful for its good autumn form which spared relegation embarrassment.

## 5

THE MARTIN GREGORY YEARS 1994-1999

LEAGUE DIVISION 1	**1994-95**
Endsleigh Division 1	18th
Coca-Cola Cup	3rd Round
FA Cup	4th Round

Jim Gregory's failing health meant that his son Martin, for whom football was very much a secondary interest, was increasingly taking the day-to-day decisions. A significant slice of income had been directed towards the costs of the Parkway project, which still hung in the balance as a government-appointed inspector weighed the options after the Public Inquiry had closed. However, Smith was allowed to spend £100,000 on Everton and Yugoslavian international winger Predrag Radosaviljevic – 'Preki' to the uninitiated – and a further £200,000 on Estonian goalkeeper Mart Poom, signed from Swiss club FC Wil. Luton midfielder and Wales international Jason Rees arrived on a free transfer. The tone was set for the season as Preki broke his arm in pre-season training and was ruled out until September.

Designed to put pressure on the 33-year-old Knight, the arrival of the 6ft 2in Poom clearly had the desired effect as Pompey's veteran goalkeeper was inspired as the team took eight points from the first four matches. The Estonian had to make do with a couple of appearances in the Coca-Cola Cup against Cambridge. During September form dipped, although a 2-0 win at West Brom lifted the team to within striking distance of the play-off places, only for the result to be marred by Awford's broken leg, which ruled him out for the season. The Coca-Cola fizzed briefly as Creaney made Everton boss Mike Walker pay for not signing him in January. His brace helped earn a 3-2 win at Goodison Park; then Hall's late leveller at Fratton ensured a third round home tie with Derby, who won 1-0 thanks to Simpson's goal.

With Creaney and Powell struggling to hit it off up front, the team failed to find consistency and a five-match losing run in

November and December produced a solitary goal. Attendances slumped to just over 5,000 for the home defeat by Stoke. As the pressure mounted on Smith, former Coventry midfielder Lloyd McGrath arrived in October and in a desperate search for goals Aiden Newhouse was signed on loan from Wimbledon. The only one he bagged helped the team to a 3-0 win over Barnsley on 27 December, in a run of three wins in five matches which lifted the team clear of the relegation zone.

The worst result of December happened off the pitch – the verdict of the government inspector, who comprehensively rejected the Parkway dream. The proposed retail development was the prime stumbling block, but the habitat of the nearby Brent Geese was a significant contributory factor in his decision. Effectively it meant eighteen months' effort and the best part of £500,000 down the drain, while Fratton Park was no nearer meeting the already deferred criteria for conversion to an all-seater stadium.

A 3-1 FA Cup third round win over high-flying Bolton, inspired by two-goal Preki, hinted that perhaps the depths had finally been plumbed, only for two dropped points against Bristol City and a three-goal televised drubbing at Derby to turn the screw again. Smith, his tactics and team selection coming increasingly under scrutiny, desperately needed to avoid defeat in the forthcoming FA Cup fourth round tie with first division Leicester. On a quagmire of a Fratton pitch, however, circumstances conspired to leave Pompey a goal down and with just nine men on the field by the finish.

It was the final straw for Gregory junior, who offered Smith the chance of a sabbatical until the end of the season. His pride stung, Smith predictably declined and was sacked. Earlier that day he had agreed a deal to borrow Coventry's Mick Quinn for a month, but that deal was shelved by his replacement Terry Fenwick, an ambitious coach who had recently found himself out in the cold at Swindon. Sceptical supporters pointed to his QPR connections – he had played at Wembley with Rangers while Gregory senior was in control there – but his initial impact was impressive. One of his first acts was to sign Crystal Palace goalkeeper Jimmy Glass on loan, while Knight served a suspension and Poom recovered from a long-standing knee injury.

Three wins and a draw in Fenwick's first four matches seemed to have banished the relegation blues and had the *Sports Mail* claiming he had the 'Midas touch'. At the same time, Pompey's post-Parkway plans were revealed. The club teamed up with supermarket chain Safeway for a joint plan to re-build the Fratton End, linking it to construction of a store on the now derelict goods yard site. For director David Deacon, who had presided over the

Parkway project, it was a last chance to regain credibility. Immediately the Co-op, with their own rival store nearby, raised objections. When the scheme foundered, Deacon quit the board.

Fenwick's touch also deserted him, as just one win in the next eight games suggested the team were more incorrigible than he might have thought. That win – 3-2 against Millwall – had its downside, as the impressive McGrath suffered a knee ligament injury that was ultimately to finish his career. Hopes of avoiding the drop were largely riding on 19-goal top scorer Creaney, who was at last living up to his record fee. His 20th stopped the rot by condemning Sheffield United at Fratton on 8 April, but six days later his season was over. An evening out at a Southsea night-spot ended on the Common with the Scot attacked and his face rearranged by a gang of thugs.

A single goal defeat at Barnsley on Easter Saturday left the team with four games in which to save themselves, including crucial trips to relegation rivals Burnley and Swindon. Fenwick's options were reduced further by the news that Powell, too, was ruled out by injury for the season, forcing him to pitch in 18-year-old Deon Burton alongside Durnin, who had only recently returned to full fitness himself. The pair responded with the goals that beat Watford 2-1 on Easter Monday, and another one apiece against Swindon and Burnley respectively. The three successive wins secured first division status again, but many wondered whether Fenwick would be any more able than Smith to turn around the club's fortunes on an increasingly fraying shoestring budget.

Match of the Season 1994-95

Portsmouth 3 Bolton 1

FA Cup, 3rd Round, 7 January 1995

Jim Smith's position was becoming increasingly tenuous during the autumn of 1994. Heady days of FA Cup semi-finals, promotion pushes and glory nights against the Premiership big-boys were receding fast as a run of five consecutive defeats in November and December dumped Pompey in the relegation zone. The team had managed to revive somewhat over Christmas and New Year, but this clash with Bruce Rioch's unlikely Premiership promotion contenders looked at the time to be make or break.

The old maestro showed he hadn't lost his touch completely and Wanderers were swept aside. The key was the scintillating form of Serbian winger Preki, who was at last beginning to justify the £100,000 paid for his services. He had been on target in the 2-0 win over Burnley five days previously, on the same day that Bolton had beaten Tranmere 1-0 to go second in the table.

Within seconds of the start, Preki sent a shot searing just over Branagan's bar. A 25-yard free-kick arrowed just wide as Pompey took the game by the scruff of the neck. They went ahead in the 31st minute when Pethick sent Powell away to burst into the area and tee up Creaney. McAteer set up Bolton's equaliser, wrestling the ball from McGrath allowing Sneekes to fire home from twenty yards.

A frantic start to the second half saw Preki appealing for a penalty; then on the hour he fired home Butters' lay-off to restore Pompey's advantage. Knight quickly had to block Coleman's shot. Rioch brought on wide-men Lee and Thompson to try to unlock an increasingly assured defence. With time running out, Pompey countered when Knight's goal-kick was helped on to Preki, who cut in from the right before leaving the keeper helpless from the edge of the box.

Before the match Smith had reckoned this game would reveal to what extent his side had got their autumn nightmare out of their systems. The response was apparently emphatic, but within four weeks Smith was out of the job. Bolton, on the other hand, picked up the pieces and ended the season as play-off winners and Coca-Cola Cup runners-up to Liverpool.

LEAGUE DIVISION 1   **1995-96**
Endsleigh Division 1   21st
Coca-Cola Cup   1st Round
FA Cup   3rd Round

Had Terry Fenwick expected that transfer funds would be made available to him, the summer of 1995 quickly disabused him. Speculation centred more on who was most likely to leave, under the threat of an ever-widening balance sheet. In pole position was striker Creaney, his reputation enhanced by 33 goals in 64 league and cup appearances, and his sentimental attachment to the south coast somewhat loosened by his night-club beating. Second in line was young defender Symons, a reluctant departure, yet cashing in on his promise looked more and more irresistible.

During pre-season, Fenwick insisted no one was going anywhere – until Darryl Powell was sold to Derby for £750,000. However, a useful tour of Scotland, including a 3-0 win over Premier Division Falkirk, boded well. Fenwick had even been allowed to invest a hefty signing-on fee to recruit former Liverpool and Arsenal winger Jimmy Carter. A star of the Scottish tour had been 20-year-old Cowes-born forward Lee Bradbury, bought out of the Army, following in Whittingham's illustrious footsteps. The opening day saw Creaney back in the groove with a brace against Southend, but the 4-2 win fooled no one. Symons was omitted from the side which slumped at home to third division Cardiff in the Coca-Cola Cup. The next day he was off to Manchester City in a £1.5 million deal, which included ex-Swindon winger Fitzroy Simpson and ex-Shrewsbury striker Carl Griffiths making the opposite journey.

With cash purchases still out of the question, it was no surprise when Fenwick wheeled and dealed again in early September to send Creaney on his way. He returned to Maine Road, setting up a cash plus player deal for the sulky Scot which saw Pompey's prodigal son Paul Walsh return to Fratton Park. The move put 6,000 on the gate for his second coming, ironically against a Derby side now managed by former boss Jim Smith, but it took an injury-time header from McLoughlin to rescue a point. Less happy with Walsh's return was Griffiths, who had left City to get away from his main obstacle to a first team place – Walsh! Also making his home debut was Martin Allen, signed on loan from West Ham, as the precursor to what was to prove a protracted permanent transfer.

Having shuffled his pack, Fenwick still found it difficult to play his hand on the pitch. A 4-2 win over companions-in-distress Watford was the only victory in a run of thirteen matches which saw the team dumped at bottom of the division by late November.

Off the field, however, rumours that Martin Gregory was finally ready to relinquish his family's controlling stake in the club gained credence. London-based businessman Warren Smith had attended several matches during the autumn cultivating fan support for a take-over bid which he was fronting on behalf of a consortium based in the north of England.

Negotiations opened in earnest in early December and the team were lifted by the increasing optimism – not to mention the calming influence of defender Adrian Whitbread, signed on loan from West Ham in mid-November – and reeled off back-to-back victories at home to struggling Oldham and away at Tranmere. Smith and Gregory had toasted a deal in principle and shortly after the Rovers' match the draw for the third round of the FA Cup pitched Pompey against their bitter rivals Southampton at the Dell to lift spirits still further. Within days the bubble burst as Gregory announced the deal was off, each side blaming the other. It was to be the first spat in what was to prove an acrimonious on-off take-over during the next three months.

The fuss did not affect the team unduly. Walsh continued to weave his magic and victories over Luton and Norwich at Fratton Park pulled Pompey clear of danger. Christmas and New Year yielded just a solitary point out of nine to remind everyone that the club was far from safe, but optimism was high as Fenwick prepared his men for the Sunday 'high noon' shoot-out with Southampton.

His plans had been thrown into disarray as uncertainty over the take-over had deprived him of Allen and Whitbread; both of whom were ineligible as their transfers had not been made permanent. Spirits were buoyed on the eve of the game, however, as Smith resurfaced, keen as ever, announcing he had an Asian 'billionaire' to back his vision of Pompey's future. Unfortunately the match proved to be no contest as the Premiership side showed more than enough class to win the day.

As a hard winter bit into the fixtures, the south coast remained largely untouched, and the team continued to collect points happily into March. The blow of losing Walsh, permanently as it transpired, to a knee injury sustained in a 2-1 win over Leicester in February, was apparently ridden by the emergence of 19-year-old Burton.

By this time the take-over saga was declared dead. Martin Gregory insisted, to the fury of many supporters, that Smith's plans were too flimsy to risk his family's considerable investment in the club. Director Terry Brady – who was still waiting to have his position ratified by the league on the grounds of his daughter Karren's involvement with Birmingham City – found £500,000 to finally sign Allen, but Whitbread had returned to his club.

DID YOU KNOW?

Up to 2004-05, Pompey have a 100% record against non-league opponents in the FA Cup. Their scalps are Boston, Minehead, Bideford and Barnet.

After a 1-1 draw at Norwich, Pompey sat comfortably in mid-table with 45 points from 35 matches and relegation seemed a remote threat. Within four weeks that notion had been exploded as the threadbare nature of Fenwick's squad was exposed. A run of just one point out of fifteen at home put the team on the brink of the second division. The penultimate match of the season saw Ipswich pinch their customary win at Fratton, leaving the team two points adrift of safety.

Happily the record books show that catastrophe was averted, thanks to Millwall's astonishing collapse of form and a breathless final day victory at Huddersfield, but it was merely the precursor to the start of surely the oddest period in Pompey's topsy-turvy existence.

Match of the Season 1995-96

Huddersfield 0 Portsmouth 1

Division 1, 5 May 1996

Over the years Pompey have found themselves in numerous relegation scrapes. A last-ditch leveller at Northampton in 1965; a 3-1 win over York in the penultimate game of 1976-77; a burst of form in April 1991 to pull clear of danger, to name but three.

However, the club had never known the agony of a last-day demotion. On the five previous occasions when the club had gone down, everything was done and dusted by the time of the last match. That looked set to change at Huddersfield's still-glistening McAlpine Stadium.

Only Millwall's apparently terminal decline from being top-of-the-table in December was keeping Pompey's survival hopes alive. But, if the Lions won at Ipswich it was all over. And if Pompey did not win, it was all over anyway. Results in midweek had removed fellow-strugglers Reading and Oldham from the equation, but at least Huddersfield's defeat at Ipswich had ended their play-off hopes, while keeping the East Anglian side's alive.

More than 2,500 fans travelled north, more in hope than anticipation. A run of just one win in twelve matches (with one point out of eighteen gleaned at Fratton) since early March had inevitably sapped the confidence of players and supporters alike. Manager

Fenwick remained bullish, but one sensed he was whistling in the dark.

The pendulum of the afternoon's events swung Pompey's way quicker than expected. Town's leading-scorer, Andy Booth, was carried off after just five minutes, when he collided with Knight. Three minutes later Carter's free-kick was flicked on by Thomson and Burton etched his name in Pompey folklore, thrashing home from eight yards. By the interval, Pompey could have made the game safe, but Terriers' keeper Steve Francis produced a point-blank save from McLoughlin.

With Butters and Thomson strong at the back, and stand-in full-back Jason Rees outstanding, Knight hardly had a save to make, and suddenly the pressure was on Millwall to come up with a goal themselves as the minutes ticked away. As the game drifted into injury-time a huge roar from the Pompey fans indicated Millwall and Ipswich had deadlocked each other's hopes. Time was comfortably played out and initial relief could then turn to wild celebration.

LEAGUE DIVISION 1   **1996-97**
Nationwide Division 1   7th
Coca-Cola Cup   2nd Round
FA Cup   Quarter-finals

During the summer of 1996 football 'came home' as the nation focused on England's – not to mention Scotland's – attempts to win the European Championship. However, Pompey fans had more than a passing interest in the outcome as, not for the first time, speculation was rife that England boss Terry Venables was poised to take over at Fratton. This time the rumours had more substance than the usual connections with the Gregory family. Since the collapse of the Warren Smith buy-out, Gregory had announced he was actively seeking the finance which would allow Pompey to compete in the post-'Bosman ruling' world of spiralling transfer fees.

And Venables was clearly going to be short of a job at the end of 'Euro 96' as his high-profile court cases had precipitated his resignation from the England job.

Shortly following England's penalty demise against the Germans, Venables confessed he had been in negotiations with Gregory. For some fans, however, frustrated by an inactive summer in the transfer market, it appeared to be another smokescreen. Their frustrations boiled over in a pre-season friendly at Honfleur against French first division side Le Havre. Unfortunately, their intended 'peaceful' pitch invasion protest was hijacked by more malevolent followers, the game abandoned and the club left highly embarrassed.

A week later, however, Gregory had sealed his coup. Venables appeared in the directors' box for the friendly with Bristol City. By the following Tuesday the 'i's' had been dotted and the 't's' crossed on a 'consultancy' role at Fratton Park. Venables also had a three-year option to buy the club for a nominal sum. As summer turned to autumn, results on the pitch were none too impressive. Goals were at a premium and the team hovered around the relegation zone. Also it became clear that not everyone was happy with the arrival of Venables, nor that of his personal assistant Eddie Ashby, who was running things on a day-to-day basis. An acrimonious board meeting following a 1-1 draw with Birmingham saw director Brady resign, citing his unease with the way things were being run. Before long Brady sued for the return of his £500,000 loan, which had covered Allen's transfer fee.

On the pitch the turning point came against a West Brom team which boasted the proud record of only having lost once at Fratton since 1954. By half-time Pompey were 4-0 up, with Lee Bradbury finally emerging as a striker of tremendous promise, netting his sixth goal in seven matches. Also on the mark, for the first time, was winger Andy Turner, who had become the first signing in the Venables era, from Spurs for £250,000 in September. His arrival had been offset by the sale of Guy Butters to Gillingham in October.

The Venables influence had also extended to the stadium. During the summer Pompey had finally been forced to conform to the all-seater requirements of the Taylor Report, but Gregory was still counting the pennies. When Fratton opened for business in August a mere 5,000 seats had been installed under the South Stand and on the old Milton End and North terraces, leaving the ground with an unviable capacity of fewer than 12,000. Within weeks Venables had ordered extra seats to be installed on the Fratton End as well as filling the remaining two terraces, bringing the capacity to nearer 17,000.

The sense of purpose was refreshing after so many years of neglect. The new seating arrangements were 'christened' with a 2-1 win over Manchester City in front of a gate of nearly 13,000. Venables also ventured to reassure fans still sceptical of his commitment to the club. Their worst fears seemed to be confirmed when Pompey's 'consultant' was named as the new part-time manager of the Australian national team, with the brief of seeing them qualify for the forthcoming World Cup in France. The plot thickened when Venables also announced that he was to become Pompey chairman, filling a post that had been vacant since Jim Gregory had been forced him to step down in 1994 through ill-health.

On the transfer front, Fenwick was able to move again, signing Arsenal midfielder David Hillier, who marked his debut by being sent off at Oldham. In early December the club signed Mathias Svensson, car salesman and part-time striker for Swedish second division club Elfsborg. The official fee was £75,000, although publicly the amount ranged between £150,000 and £250,000. The transfer was a protracted affair, having been agreed in principle in early November. The Swede had been spotted by chief scout Ted Buxton, an old friend of Venables, who had joined the staff earlier in the season. Svensson's impact was immediate. Two goals on his full debut helped see off Huddersfield, but in his next match he found himself sent off at Reading.

As the New Year dawned, form remained inconsistent. Two defeats in early January meant the chill wind of the relegation zone whistled around Fratton once more. A 2-1 win at promotion-chasing Crystal Palace – Pompey's first victory at Selhurst Park since 1966 –

was the springboard for an unbeaten run of six wins and two draws which put the team on the fringes of play-off contention. Of greater significance was a blossoming FA Cup run, started by a 2-1 win at Wolves – the first there since 1951 – and carried on by a 3-0 home demolition of Reading. The fifth round saw possibly one of the best Pompey performances of the decade as Premiership Leeds were beaten more comprehensively than the 3-2 scoreline suggested. Stars of the performance were Bradbury and Svensson, who were developing into one of the most potent strikeforces in the first division. Prior to the tie, Venables had announced that he was going to exercise his right to buy a controlling interest in the club – the nominal sum usually mentioned was £1; it made for good copy anyway! The Cup-run was ended in the quarter-finals by Ruud Gullit's cosmopolitan Chelsea outfit, as Premiership class finally told in a 4-1 Sunday lunch-treat served up for the benefit of Sky TV viewers.

The play-offs were not out of the question and three home wins on the trot, offset by a disappointing defeat at doomed Southend, apparently opened the door for Fenwick's team. Three defeats in the last five matches proved decisive, however, and Pompey ended the season one place and three points short of their target. Optimism was high however that this young team could develop still further, provided they could be kept together. Bradbury had been called up for the England Under-21 squad and Svensson for the full Sweden team, while planning permission and finance had at long last been raised for the construction of a £2.5 million stand on the Fratton End. This had been a source of bitter resentment among fans ever since its closure in 1986. It seemed Venables, and the oft-maligned Fenwick, could do no wrong ...

Match of the Season 1996-97

Leeds United 2 Portsmouth 3

FA Cup, 5th Round, 15 February 1997

Despite having a reputation as FA Cup fighters over the years, Pompey's recent record in the competition is relatively poor. The semi-finals in 1992 and the sixth round in 1988 are the only time a trip down Wembley Way has been as much as sniffed. So when the fifth round draw pitted Pompey away to the winners of the rear-ranged Arsenal – Leeds tie, hopes of further progress were deemed somewhat optimistic. Most seemed to prefer the Arsenal option, but George Graham's side created a minor upset of their own by winning at Highbury.

DID YOU KNOW?

In 1998, Jamaica's Fitzroy Simpson and Paul Hall became the first Pompey players
to play in the World Cup since Northern Ireland's Uprichard in 1958.

Pompey's ticket allocation of 4,500 was quickly sold on the back
of a five-match winning run, that had banished relegation fears.
Leeds though, were back to their defensively mean best, having not
conceded a goal in five league or cup games. Extra spice was added
by the prospect of Pompey chairman Venables coming up against
his old Chelsea mate (and former Pompey midfielder) Graham.

By then end of 90 frantic minutes, Leeds' reputation was in
tatters. As early as the seventh minute, their defence was opened
up and McLoughlin nodded in Bradbury's cross, although he
injured his leg in the process and had to limp off. That proved
expensive when Kelly handled Bradbury's header, so Fitzroy
Simpson stepped up to the spot, only to see Martyn save his weak
shot.

No doubt Graham had his say at half-time and Leeds were soon
back in it. Bowyer eased home Wallace's pass, but Pompey continued to make the running and it was no surprise when Svensson
scored the goal of the game, turning Molenaar inside out before
firing across the keeper. Bradbury's close-range effort wrapped it
up, despite Bowyer's header deep into injury time.

At the end Pompey's players conga-ed their way across the pitch
to celebrate probably the greatest act of giant-killing in the club's
history. Although dreams of a final appearance were ruthlessly
exposed by Chelsea in the next round, Fenwick had seemingly won
over a sceptical crowd and his team went on to get within an ace of
the play-offs. Venables preferred to talk up the huge potential of his
nominal investment, but within a year they would both be part of
Pompey's history.

LEAGUE DIVISION 1   **1997-98**
Nationwide Division 1   20th
Coca-Cola Cup   1st Round
FA Cup   3rd Round

The impending World Cup focused the minds of several players. McLoughlin, a veteran of USA '94, was a regular in the Republic of Ireland squad, while, more curiously, Wiltshire-born Fitzroy Simpson, Ashford-born Burton and Manchester-born Hall's Jamaican roots had seen them seconded to a romantic qualification adventure in the Conacaf (Central and North American) zone. Club chairman Terry Venables, too, was preoccupied on the other side of the globe with Australia's apparently untroubled progress to the finals.

Not that there was any lack of activity closer to home. A new sponsorship deal with mobile phone company KJC had been signed and a new shirt design by manufacturers Admiral unveiled, while Venables found time to pose for the cameras on a mechanical digger in his hard hat to begin work on the new Fratton End. The ground improvements also included a roof over the old North Terrace and hospitality facilities under the new stand.

During the summer, Fenwick spent much of his time with Venables tracking Australia's progress, but it was only when the players reported back for pre-season training that the reason for the trip became apparent. Subject to work permits and international clearance, Aussie international midfielders Craig Foster and Robbie Enes, goalkeeper Zeljco Kalac and promising young strikers Paul Harries and Hamilton Thorp were to join the club. They were soon to be joined by Australia's striker John Aloisi, who slotted straight into the squad by virtue of his Italian passport, but by then the bombshell had dropped. To make way for the arrivals, Burton and Bradbury were on their respective ways to Premiership Derby for £1.5 million and divisional rivals Manchester City for a club record £3.5 million.

In the cold light of day, the deals can be seen as good business for a club that from the 1960s had increasingly become a 'selling' club, developing talent for fish in bigger ponds to swallow. But for Fenwick and Venables, they sowed the seeds of their own destruction as the pledges of the previous spring quickly evaporated.

On the pitch Aloisi proved an instant hit. He upstaged the debut-making Bradbury at Maine Road on the opening day by scoring after just five minutes, although it was left to Hall to save a point with ten minutes to go. The former Cremonese striker scored twice more as two home wins lifted the team into sixth place, but the cracks were already showing as third division Peterborough dumped the club out of the Coca-Cola Cup.

Another brace of Aloisi goals, this time against newly promoted Crewe, failed to prevent defeat. This was the first of six consecutive losses which left the team rooted one off the bottom. Two draws followed. One of these was against Bradford City, and it nearly had to be postponed as the shadow cast by the almost-complete Fratton End (or KJC Stand as it was known) plunged one goalmouth into darkness. The new stand finally opened at another evening game, with Swindon, but the team's Sky TV jinx was reinforced by a single-goal reverse.

Fenwick was becoming increasingly hampered by international call-ups by the Jamaican, Australian and Irish federations, which at best caused a fixture pile-up and at worst deprived him of key men for league matches. The Australian contingent – Aloisi apart – were also struggling to live up to expectations, with Foster, who cost £300,000, often a peripheral figure. The first win since August, 2-0 at Bury on 8 November, briefly raised spirits, but a week later Sunderland's comprehensive 4-1 win at Fratton planted the team at the foot of the table.

Just when it seemed things couldn't get any worse they did. Since September, when he was convicted of business irregularities, Venables' right-hand man, Ashby, had been relieved of his duties at Fratton. With TV otherwise engaged with the World Cup and international call-ups causing the scheduled home match with Wolves to be postponed, the club was engulfed by a cash-flow crisis. As a result, November's salaries went unpaid and it took a loan from the Professional Footballers' Association, plus a cash injection from Martin Gregory, to ensure belated payment. Collective morale was further dented as Australia's World Cup bid was shattered by two late Iranian goals, although Hall and Simpson booked their place in France when Jamaica got the point they needed against Mexico.

Gregory's timely reappearance coincided with a mounting rumour that Venables' option to buy a controlling stake in the club was not as secure as it had seemed. Back in August, American-based entrepreneur Vince Wolanin and his rock-star friend and lifelong Pompey fan Brian Howe had expressed interest in investing in the club, but had seemingly been rebuffed by Venables. Gregory announced he was going to meet with the duo in Paris early in the New Year.

Amid the rumours and counter-rumours, three home wins in December briefly lifted the team out of the relegation zone. With Venables and, by association, Fenwick's tenure looking increasingly tenuous, the team came within three minutes of knocking Premiership Aston Villa out of the FA Cup. However, the following week the crowd's frustrations were directed at the two Terries as relegation-rivals Manchester City strolled to a 3-0 win at Fratton.

By the Monday, Venables had gone – not before he had negotiated a handsome pay-off to relinquish the disputed option to buy – and the next day Fenwick followed him. It was left to assistant manager Keith Waldon to prepare the team for the Cup replay at Villa and another six-pointer at Port Vale. Gregory installed himself as chairman and Terry Brady returned to the fold as his adviser. The pair flew to Paris to meet with Wolanin for apparently fruitful talks, against the backdrop of an increasingly desperate league position.

Waldon made his only signing on the eve of a rearranged match at Oxford on FA Cup fourth round day, recruiting Leicester striker, and former Pompey apprentice, Steve Claridge on loan. It was no happy return, as Oxford stole an injury-time winner to condemn the team to their fourth defeat in a row. The plot took a bizarre twist that night, as Howe announced on BBC Radio Solent that Alan Ball would be returning to the club as manager, following an approach to the former World Cup winner who had guided Pompey to the first division in 1987.

Many assumed that this meant the Americans, and their promise of multi-million pound investments, were all but in control. The reality, however, was that the proposed move infuriated Gregory and the prospects of a take-over receded as the season progressed. Ball evoked the club's battling spirit and, reinforced by the arrival of Greek defender Michalis Vlachos and Southampton full-back Matt Robinson, began to turn the team around. But not before the nadir was reached with a defeat at Crewe, which left the team seven points adrift of safety. The response of both team and fans was to roll up their sleeves and battle. A 1-0 win over Stockport, courtesy of Claridge's first goal for his hometown club, in front of less than 9,000 looks, on the face of it an unremarkable result. The incessant chanting of the fans as visiting attacks were desperately repulsed in the second half was not, and a new legend was born.

Four weeks later, with seventeen points gained out of 21, an improbable escape beckoned. Claridge's return to Filbert Street – Pompey could not afford him – pitched the team back into trouble as the goals dried up. A run of just two points out of the next 21 put the team back in penultimate place and Division Two beckoned. To their credit, the fans did not lose faith. More than 14,000 turned out for the last home game of the season against Huddersfield, two days after Ball had been handed a four-year contract by Gregory.

Inspired by Durnin and the reinstated Svensson, the team cruised to a 3-0 win and results elsewhere put destiny back in the team's own hands. The 3,500 visitors' allocation for the last day at Bradford City were sold in no time, and Durnin maintained his habit of scoring vital goals for the club with a double that sealed a 3-1 win. It confirmed survival in a switchback season of epic proportions. Stability at the club was desperately needed, and Ball's contract promised that, but as events were to prove it would be the last thing that happened.

Match of the Season 1997-98

Portsmouth 1 Stockport 0

Division 1, 17 February 1998

To say that Portsmouth was a club in crisis in February 1998 would be an understatement. Despite the universally-popular re-appoint-ment of Ball as manager in January, his influence had yet to translate into deeds on the pitch. On Saturday, his team had surrendered, as Crewe's 3-1 win left Pompey adrift at the foot of the division. Take-over talks between Gregory and Wolanin had gone sour and an uncertain future lay ahead on and off the pitch.

The one consolation emerging from the Crewe debacle had been the response of the fans, who, at three goals down had started an incessant chant of 'Alan Ball's Blue and White Army' to try to raise spirits. Ball reacted to the result by axing veteran keeper Knight, who had been at fault for one of the goals and Australian interna-tional midfielder Foster, who had looked uninterested.

By the fourteenth minute of a dour game, Pompey had the lead presented to them by ex-apprentice Claridge's header. Gary Megson's Stockport had made a competent debut in Division One and were unlikely play-off contenders, thanks to some impressive form at Edgeley Park, including a 3-1 defeat of out of sorts Pompey back in October.

The question was, could Pompey protect their lead, as County, spearheaded by former Fratton apprentice Brett Angell, stepped up the pressure in the second half. Although that pressure was largely punchless, the tension was unbearable as Pompey sought their first win of 1998. With the game bogged down in midfield, suddenly the

Fratton End started up that chant of 'Alan Ball's Blue and White Army' again. Within minutes the South and North Stands had picked up the incessant rhythm and for fifteen minutes or more the crowd and team joined forces to repel the threat, helped by stand-in keeper Flahaven's assured handling.

The win was crucial to collective morale. Four wins and a draw in the next five games built the foundations of the eventual miraculous escape from the drop. A bond between players, manager and supporters had been made. It would prove invaluable in the trying sixteen months to come.

LEAGUE DIVISION 1   **1998-99**
Nationwide Division 1   19th
Worthington Cup   2nd Round
FA Cup   4th Round

During the summer of 1998, Ball set about restructuring his side. One of his first jobs was to cut the wage-bill, and pay-offs were negotiated for the Australian contingent, bar Aloisi. Foster would re-surface at Crystal Palace, to join up with Fenwick and Venables again. Striker Svensson and winger Turner would tread the same path to Selhurst Park. The arrivals at Fratton saw Ball using his continental contacts. Greek striker Nikos Kyzeridis signed for £200,000 – but would be back home by October – and on the eve of the season Danish utility player Thomas Thogersen arrived in a six-figure deal from Brondby. French midfielder Jean-Francois Peron – known as Jeff – arrived from Walsall for £150,000. Ball also signed Leek Town midfielder Steve Soley for £35,000, after the player had impressed in a trial. These transfers were offset by the shock departure of Jamaican World Cup star Hall, who joined Premiership Coventry for a cut-price £300,000. Ball evidently decided to cash in while he could on a player who would be a free agent in twelve months' time.

Pre-season matches included a tour of the Republic of Ireland, followed by the club's Centenary tournament at Fratton Park, which proved to be a financial disaster as less than 3,000 fans turned up. The competition was won by French side Sochaux, who beat Genoa in the final. Pompey finished fourth, Wimbledon winning a play-off 3-1.

However, optimism was high and the opening league game at home to new-boys Watford was watched by more than 16,000. Two late goals turned the game on its head, although Ball took comfort from his side's first-half showing. The next three games were drawn, while third division Plymouth were seen off in the Worthington Cup. By the time QPR were beaten 3-0 at Fratton on August bank holiday, Ball had added £200,000 striker Claridge from Wolves and Manchester City winger Martin Phillips to his squad.

Inconsistent form in September was overshadowed by goalkeeper Aaron Flahaven's mysterious black-out in the penalty area against Swindon, and the sowing of the seeds of the financial crisis that would threaten the club's existence later in the season. Finance director and company secretary Brian Henson became embroiled in a war of words with *The News* over the reporting of the club's AGM in August, in which a trading loss of £1.5 million was revealed, offset by £1.9 million in transfer revenues. The accounts also showed the Gregory family had loaned the club around £3.5 million. A sub-text to the proceedings was a further bid from American businessman Vince Wolanin and his partner Brian Howe, which was rejected by chairman Martin Gregory in a terse faxed reply which found its way into *The News*. Gregory later apologised for his rudeness.

Negotiations were also on-going to purchase the goods yard site behind Fratton Park, to widen options for redevelopment of the stadium. In a statement in the Sunderland programme at the end of September, Gregory asserted that the club were 'under no pressure financially' and also denied he was in the process of trying to sell Aloisi, at the time the leading scorer in the country. He reshuffled the boardroom, appointing Jeremy Keith and soon afterwards Les Parris. In the same month former chairman Jim Gregory died following a long illness.

A run of just two wins in ten matches in October and November plunged the team into the relegation zone. The only bright spot was the emergence of 17-year-old striker Luke Nightingale, who scored twice on his debut as a substitute at home to West Brom, turning the game. By the start of December it was clear the club was far from financially secure, as for the second year running only a PFA loan prevented November's wages from going unpaid.

Matters came to a head in the run-up to the Sky TV clash with Grimsby. Wolanin and Howe were still watching developments, along with Warren Smith's consortium, which had reappeared. Gregory stunned everyone by announcing that he was taking away Ball's power to buy and sell players, handing them over to London-based agent Athole Still. It became clear that Gregory's intent was to raise cash quickly, but the players pledged not to be sold on the cheap, showing their loyalty to Ball and the fans. Before the game the team warmed up in T-shirts indicating their 'price' – 50p here, £2.50 there – and the fans staged a peaceful half-time pitch invasion to make their point. Soon, director and TV presenter Fred Dinenage resigned in protest, too.

The only player to leave was Aloisi – a full international and the second top-scorer in the country – for just £690,000 to Premiership Coventry, although other deals were mooted. With the fans and most of the team and management by now in open rebellion, Gregory finally resigned as chairman just before Christmas after he claimed one of his daughters had received a death threat. However, he retained his family's controlling stake. Parris took over, pledging to sort out the mess. On 23 December the situation seemed to have been resolved when it was announced that Warren Smith's consortium were taking over and a press conference called for the following week. To the surprise of no one, the take-over never materialised.

Instead, the club were threatened with impending bankruptcy as Try Build, the company which had constructed the KJC Stand, issued a winding up petition for £400,000 owed, to be heard in the High Court in January. At once the Inland Revenue joined in to protect their £750,000 debt and the future of the club hung in the balance.

On the field, consecutive defeats at Bolton and Ipswich plunged the team into the relegation zone, but things picked up in the New Year. Premiership Nottingham Forest were beaten in the FA Cup and the team embarked on an eight-match unbeaten league run, which ultimately saved them from the drop. A home draw in the fourth round of the Cup against Premiership Leeds United ensured some vital income. Director Brady allowed Ball to recruit former favourite Guy Whittingham on loan from Sheffield Wednesday – Brady agreed to pay the player's wages – to give him some striking cover.

After a couple of adjournments, the High Court case was finally heard in early February. An Administrator appointed by the court gave the club until the end of May to resolve its financial problems. Tom Burton and John Ariel of accountants Kidson Impey were the men charged with the task of turning Pompey around. They appealed to the fans to turn out in force in the club's time of need. To cut costs, several long-standing employees were made redundant and Parris was sacked as chairman. Pethick, Thomson and Hillier also left the club, all joining Bristol Rovers, leaving Ball's squad paper-thin for the relegation run-in.

Burton and Ariel advertised the club as a going concern in the Financial Times and a number of enquiries were followed up, including one from Portsmouth United, a fan-led organisation, whose aim was to turn Pompey into a 'community club' along the lines of south coast neighbours Bournemouth. A public subscription raised more than £400,000, but it soon became apparent that the preferred outcome was an outright sale to a group with the financial clout to give the club the investment it needed.

As spring arrived it was clear Ball's side was running out of steam. Whittingham had returned to Sheffield Wednesday, while loaned keeper Petterson, signed back in November, returned to Charlton. A deadline-day move for ex-Norwich and Manchester United striker Mark Robins foundered, but young American-based Brazilian midfielder Stefani Miglioranzi – of Italian extraction – brought his cosmopolitan talents to the club until the end of the season.

> **DID YOU KNOW?**
>
> Between August 1996 and December 1998 Pompey had seven of their matches covered live on Sky TV. They lost all of them.

Four defeats around Easter put the relegation threat back on the agenda, but a 3-1 win over Stockport County in the penultimate home game all but ensured safety. Results during the following week made the drop only a faint possibility, due to the team's impressive 'goals for' tally, which had replaced goal-difference in the Football League.

At the end of April, Burton and Ariel received the final bids of the prospective buyers – including Wolanin and Howe and a mysterious Arab businessman. It soon became clear, however, that the preferred bidder was American-based Serbian businessman Milan Mandaric, who was assisted by Ball's former Arsenal team-mate Bob McNab and former director David Deacon. Their consortium was formally unveiled at a press conference after the final game of the season and their take-over confirmed by a meeting of the creditors in late June. Their first match in control saw Premiership West Ham beaten 1-0 in a testimonial for ex-player, trainer and kit man Gordon Neave, who was retiring after more than forty years' service to the club.

Mandaric pledged to get the club into the Premiership within three years, confirmed Ball as manager and said he was looking to build a new 35,000 stadium to support his bid to put Pompey back in the top flight. Dinenage also returned as a director, while Deacon took responsibility for the day-to-day running of affairs at Fratton. A new era was dawning.

Match of the Season 1998-99
Swindon 3   Portsmouth 3

Division 1, 21 February 1999

In a season dominated by matters off the field, it seems fitting to feature a match which will long be remembered for its thrills and spills on the pitch, not to mention one of the greatest fight-backs against the odds in the club's history.

On the face of it, a visit to Jimmy Quinn's team, with both teams safely in lower mid-table, looked a routine fixture. Earlier in the season Pompey had produced one of their best performances to beat the Robins 5-2, although Flahaven's mysterious collapse had added a bizarre twist to the plot.

By the time the return came around, Flavs was back between the posts for the first time since October – a raft of tests had found nothing wrong – as on-loan keeper Petterson had been recalled by Charlton. Events were to prove Flav's luck had yet to change.

In the 30th minute he failed to collect Ndah's straightforward shot and Chris Hay gobbled up the rebound, then soon afterwards he went for a high ball on the edge of the area and was clattered by Iffy Onoura. No free-kick was given, but quickly a doctor was called for as the keeper had sustained severe facial injuries and had to be stretchered off.

After more than five minutes' delay, the game resumed, with substitute Perrett pulling on the gloves and within thirty seconds Hay curled in a second. Claridge seized on a Howe's poor back-pass to beat Talia, but on the stroke of half-time Howe atoned by crossing for Onoura's header.

Backed by 4,000 travelling fans, who had claimed both ends of the ground, Pompey dug deep, showing the spirit that had carried them through the financial troubles of December and January. Pinning Swindon back, Claridge grabbed a lifeline in the 72nd minute, reacting first when Talia pushed Whittingham's shot against the bar. Six minutes later Peron's 20-yard shot arrowed into the corner and a precious point was saved.

Perrett hardly had a save to make, but he was grateful to Robinson and McLoughlin, who both cleared off the line in stoppage time. 'I went in goal in similar circumstances at Lymington and the boys are telling me I must report for goalkeeper training next week,' said the defender, who borrowed Knight's gloves when he came on.

By the end of the season, both sides were sucked back into the relegation dog-fight, but Pompey were more grateful than most for this unlikely point earned. They missed the drop on goals-scored.

## 6

THE MILAN MANDARIC ERA
From 1999

LEAGUE DIVISION 1   **1999-2000**
Nationwide Division 1   18th
Coca-Cola Cup   2nd Round
FA Cup   3rd Round

Once formal approval of Milan Mandaric's takeover came in late June, manager Alan Ball was quickly given the wherewithal to re-shape his squad into one which could challenge for promotion, signing a mixture of promising youngsters, such as Arsenal trainee Jason Crowe, along with solid experience in the shape of Ipswich defender Jason Cundy. By the time Mandaric jetted in from the USA to see how his investment was shaping up, bolstered by £1 million spent on Spurs striker Rory Allen, Pompey had already seen off Southern League sides Tiverton and Weymouth. Dorchester were expected to be similarly sacrificial lambs for the new chairman. Ninety humiliating minutes later Pompey had been beaten 0-3 by a side who just narrowly escaped relegation. Worse, Pompey would be without utility man John Durnin for a while. He dislocated his elbow when the golf buggy he was driving at the team's training base in Devon flipped over.

With hindsight, that setback was the beginning of the end for Ball but, initially at least, he seemed to have finally got the formula right. Sheffield United came to town on 7 August for the opening match, duly won 2-0, thanks to goals from Stefani Miglioranzi and Guy Whittingham. Team-building continued, with the accent on the future, as young striker Steve Lovell signed from Bournemouth for £250,000 and French defender Noe Pamarot arrived on loan from Nice. As Pompey headed north on the final Saturday of the opening month, they were unbeaten and through to the next round of the Worthington Cup – a second-string side having seen off Torquay. Barnsley, beaten play-off finalists, would prove a good test of the team's mettle. By the 34th minute Pompey, sporting their new 'Brazil-style' second strip, were down to nine men. Once the Tykes took the lead, five second-half goals followed, leaving the travelling support to earn the man-of-the-match award!

In a move he would be quick to regret, Mandaric offered Ball a new four-year deal. Ball was soon shelling out £500,000 to buy the Australian Aris Salonika winger Mike Panopoulos. September proved to be inconsistent. No better was that illustrated than by the fortunes of two of the club's goalkeepers. Aaron Flahavan had endured a nightmare year after his first fainting fit, then sustaining a serious facial injury at Swindon in February. Now understudy to the permanently signed Andy Petterson, he got another chance in the Worthington Cup-tie with Blackburn, only to collapse on the pitch. Rovers striker Nathan Blake earned the admiration of the home fans for tending the stricken player rather than poking the ball into an unguarded net. Shell-shocked Pompey also collapsed, conceding three late goals. With the tie all but lost, Flahavan's plight ironically made easier Ball's gesture of putting long-serving Alan Knight on the bench for the return leg. With seven minutes to go, and Pompey 1-5 down overall, 38-year-old Knight replaced Petterson to a standing ovation from all sides, as he made his 800th competitive appearance for the club.

A 4-2 win at Tranmere in mid-September had left Pompey tucked in the leading pack. By then Allen had succumbed to an ankle ligament injury that would keep him out until December. For a team with Premiership aspirations, the arrival of Grimsby a week later should have been the opportunity to stamp their credentials. Instead, another insipid performance saw the ten-man visitors go away with a well-deserved three points. A week later an equally supine performance saw Crystal Palace win 4-0. Ball's mood wasn't helped as former favourite Matt Svensson – whom Ball had allowed to leave eighteen months beforehand – was among the goals. With the tea-cups flying across the dressing room at the final whistle, he privately, then publicly, declared many of that team would never play for him again. He later back-tracked, claiming the 'heat of the moment', but any chance of Ball recapturing the backing of the dressing room ended that afternoon.

A surprise signing in October was Crystal Palace striker Lee Bradbury, for a cut-price £350,000 as the cash-strapped Londoners felt the pinch of administration as Pompey had done nine months beforehand. Sold for £3 million to Manchester City in 1997, having been found for nothing in the Army, pound for pound Bradbury is surely one of the best-value players the club has ever had. And he scored his first goal in his 'second coming' at the end of October to help beat his old team-mates 3-1 and avenge that drubbing earlier in the month; a drubbing he'd helped inflict!

DID YOU KNOW?

**In 1999-2000, Pompey used a record 41 players during the season.
They were drawn from nine different nationalities.**

On the field it remained one step forward and two back, and in November the wheels came off spectacularly. The problem was a frail defence and, by the time the on-off signing of Bradford City centre half Darren Moore finally materialised in mid-month for £750,000, Pompey had lost two consecutive away games – both to injury-time goals – at Fulham and West Brom. A third defeat at home to bottom-of-the-table Crewe was unthinkable on Moore's debut, but it came to pass. For all his investment, Mandaric's side was barely better off than it had been twelve months previously under the chaotic final days of the Martin Gregory regime.

Dressing room discontent was underlined by midfielder Alan McLoughlin's reluctance to move to Wigan unless he got a pay-off from Pompey. Ball was trying to purge those he saw as his dressing room enemies, and Jeff Peron was similarly packed off to the ambitious Lancashire side, while Fitzroy Simpson left for Hearts. By early December McLoughlin, too, had finally agreed to leave, and Ball felt he was getting things back on an even keel.

For the trip to Sheffield United on 4 December he called once more upon Cundy – whose recent return helped grind out a gutsy draw with high-flying Bolton – and Allen made his long-awaited reappearance. In the eighteenth minute Allen broke his other ankle. Two minutes later Paul Devlin's goal condemned Pompey to another defeat, and the following Thursday the axe fell: for the second time Ball was fired by an ambitious new chairman, unhappy at not seeing immediate results. That all had been far from well under the former World Cup winner was underlined by the anonymous player who commented to *The News*: 'There are not too many players disappointed at the manager going. There are a lot of players unhappy with the way they were being treated. Morale was at an all-time low.' Ironically, on the same day McLoughlin's move to Wigan was finally sealed after a protracted medical.

In Ball's place came Bob McNab, the American-based former Huddersfield and Arsenal double-winning full-back as caretaker. McNab had been involved in introducing Mandaric and he felt obliged to help his friend out. His tenure would be brief – until a new manager could be found – but he was abrasive in his criticism of Ball's regime. Coaches Kevin Bond and Ted MacDougall stepped down soon afterwards and Dave Kemp, a favourite at Fratton in the mid-1970s, was drafted in as first-team coach.

Wins were still few and far between as Pompey slipped into the relegation zone for Christmas. Former Stoke boss Gary Megson was hot favourite, with Jim Jefferies, the Hearts boss, also interviewed. With Pompey out of the FA Cup – the third round taking place in December – the season had become a damage-limitation exercise and the man who finally emerged to stop the rot was somewhat surprising. Tony Pulis had done well at Gillingham, hauling them to the brink of the First Division before falling out with his chairman Paul Scally. His latest job at Bristol City was not going well behind the scenes and Pompey's decision to recruit him suited all parties. His first game ended in defeat, 2-3 at home to Wolves after Pompey had led 2-0, but he soon set about instilling some long-overdue discipline into the squad.

Midfielder Ceri Hughes arrived from Wimbledon and goalkeeper Russell Hoult from Derby. Steve Claridge's hat-trick on 29 January secured the team's first win in fifteen matches, and that was trumped by an even more impressive 1-0 win at play-off contenders Huddersfield, again courtesy of 'Super Steve'. Things took a turn for the worse that month, though, with a couple more defeats and the news that Allen and Flahavan were facing court action over a fracas at a Fareham restaurant. March began no better – with a 1-2 home defeat to Tranmere – and Pompey were in the bottom three again. A 1-0 win at promotion-chasing Ipswich may have owed as much to a defiant rearguard as to Claridge's sharp header, but was offset by a 0-1 defeat at Birmingham. Pulis signed Spurs defender Justin Edinburgh and Derby winger Kevin Harper. Things still looked grim and when relegation rivals Forest took the lead ten minutes from the end of a crunch game at Fratton, things looked bleaker still. Tommy Thogersen headed an equaliser, then in the last minute Claridge angled an unexpected winner.

Another £650,000 was found to sign Sheffield United midfield hard-man Shaun Derry ahead of transfer deadline day and he took his place as Pompey cruised past Crewe 3-1, then scored as strugglers West Brom were beaten 2-0 at home. The month ended with a 4-1 win over doomed Swindon, a seven-minute Bradbury hat-trick meaning that relegation had all but been avoided. Security was finally assured with a 2-2 home draw with Manchester City, who were headed for consecutive promotions, on Easter Monday. Losing the last two games was offset by the return of Allen for QPR, against whom he scored.

In late May, Mandaric and Pulis met in Miami to discuss future requirements. After a good run-in, hopes were high that 2000-01 would be the season Pompey finally realised the long-smouldering potential Mandaric had invested in twelve months beforehand.

Match of the Season 1999-2000

Portsmouth 2 Sheffield United 0

Division 1, 7 August 1999

Not since John Deacon's arrival as chairman in 1973 had an opening fixture generated such optimism. Alan Ball had seemingly bought well. Former Chelsea and Spurs centre-back Jason Cundy came on a free transfer from Ipswich and a product of Arsenal's youth academy, right-back Jason Crowe, cost £500,000. Goalkeeper Andy Petterson, midfielder Stefani Miglioranzi and former favourite Guy Whittingham – who had spent time at the club the previous season – had signed permanent contracts, and another promising youngster, Adam Newton, arrived on loan from Premiership West Ham. Mandaric had also shattered Pompey's transfer record to land Spurs striker Rory Allen for £1 million.

Before the kick-off Mandaric, basking in the adulation of a near-capacity crowd, took the microphone: 'Thank you for your support for our football team. I am delighted to be here and will do everything humanly possible to take this club back where it belongs.' On the pitch, the team didn't disappoint. They had wasted several chances before they went ahead. Jeff Peron spotted Miglioranzi's run into the box and his inch-perfect pass was stroked first time under Simon Tracey. Newton fired wide when through and Tracey had to be alert to block Whittingham's effort.

Pompey could have done with the half continuing, but instead they had to take a break and almost at once they looked set to pay for their profligacy. Miglioranzi's tackle on the edge of the box looked fair, but referee Tony Bates thought otherwise and Paul Devlin stepped up to take the spot-kick. His effort finished high on the Milton End, massed with Sheffield United supporters, and Pompey could resume their arrogant control. Peron fired just over, then Tracey somehow kept out Allen's close-range header.

With the clock running down, Blades' midfielder Axel Smeets was sent off for a second yellow when he clattered McLoughlin. Then Andy Awford played the ball forward and Allen nodded it back into the path of Whittingham who fired beyond Tracey from fifteen yards.

At the end of that broiling afternoon the Premiership must have seemed but a short step away for Mandaric. Touched by his reception, afterwards he revealed: 'I turned to my wife Gordana and said that was probably the nicest moment I had enjoyed in football,' adding 'I could see people appreciated me, but I have only scratched the surface with what I want to do at this football club.'

LEAGUE DIVISION 1	2000-01
Nationwide Division 1	20th
Coca-Cola Cup	2nd Round
FA Cup	3rd Round

Pulis started pre-season training with just two new signings – out-of-contract defender Linvoy Primus from Reading, and midfielder Tom Curtis from Chesterfield. His conservatism was understandable perhaps, given his spree the previous spring. The first friendly, a 2-0 win at Dorchester, at least laid one ghost to rest, but Pulis was also being hampered in his team-building by the perception that Pompey were not a 'big club'. An abortive bid to sign Bristol Rovers hot-shot Jason Roberts, who opted for West Brom instead, underlined the point.

Mandaric's appointment of former Leicester Chief Executive Barrie Pierpoint, who was given the brief of bringing the club's commercial facilities into the 21st century, looked a step in the right direction. £1 million eventually found its way into Bradford City's coffers for striker Lee Mills. Another big-money move for Manchester City striker Robert Taylor, which fell through, lifted spirits a notch. An additional arrival was unsettled Nottingham Forest midfielder Nigel Quashie for £500,000. He had cost £2 million two years before when he left QPR for the Midlands.

Once again Sheffield United were the first-day opponents, this time at bogey ground Bramall Lane, where no Pompey side had won since 1956. True to form, the day started badly and got worse. Justin Edinburgh tripped Paul Devlin, who didn't waste his chance from the spot, then defender Andy Awford was stretchered off in a neck brace after an awkward fall. Mills fired blanks, then a cock-up late on saw Primus slice the ball into his own net. A home draw with Grimsby the following Saturday confirmed the deepening pessimism, and the fact Mariners' boss Alan Buckley was fired after the match – a point at Fratton Park used to be a good result – was an ironic reminder of how low Pompey's standing was these days. Pompey's and Pulis's season was stuttering. A Steve Claridge hat-trick against Wolves, amid rumours of player dissent at the manager's methods, seemed to kick-start things, only for a miserable September to unpick the good work. Four defeats, including a 0-4 hiding at Blackburn in the Worthington Cup, meant the writing was on the wall. The second leg attracted fewer than 3,000 fans – the lowest first-class competitive gate at Fratton – and now Pompey faced tricky trips to Burnley and Stockport. Two draws looked good but given the fact Pompey led until late on in both games meant they tasted of defeat.

DID YOU KNOW?

Since the inauguration of the Premier League in 1992, Guy Whittingham is the record goalscorer for a season in the Football League, with 42 in 1992-93.

The following week saw rumours sweeping the Fratton Park corridors. By Thursday Pulis had been given 'leave of absence' to fight a lawsuit he had brought against his former employer at Gillingham, Paul Scally, and Pompey had a new boss. Step forward home-town boy Claridge, who assembled a coaching 'dream team' of Pompey legend Guy Whittingham and Awford, who had decided to retire from playing. Three straight wins, including an improbable 3-2 success at Crystal Palace after Pompey had trailed 0-2, nurtured hopes that promotion was not out of reach.

At the same time, plans to build a new stadium on the goods yard site, now overseen by Pierpoint, were almost ready to go. Although the size and financing of the project had yet to be agreed, the CEO expected the ground to be in place by the start of 2003-04. Mandaric dampened enthusiasm somewhat by saying he preferred an initial 26,500 development which could be expanded at a later date: 'I expected to lose £500,000 last year, but lots of things came out of the closet and I lost £3 million. It's not a lot of fun, so I don't want hidden costs to emerge over the stadium. I want to get the plans right before making promises.'

On the field, Claridge's honeymoon was short. A string of draws maintained his unbeaten record, but when Pompey lost 1-3 at Fulham on 18 November, with Primus and Hughes sent off, the rot set in and his side didn't win again for two months, sliding down the league and dumped out of the FA Cup at home by Tranmere. Mandaric was also increasingly frustrated by the club's financial position. With losses heading towards £6 million for the year, he charged new director Paul Mitchell with finding out why. In December Chief Executive Pierpoint was scapegoated – despite only having been in the job for seven months. He was replaced by Martin Murphy, owner of Portsmouth printing company and club sponsor Bishops Printers.

The team's relatively healthy league position was being whittled away and Claridge's dream of managing his home-town club was fast turning into a nightmare. A run of one point from four matches saw him axed on the eve of the trip to West Brom on 24 February, to be replaced by Graham Rix. Bizarrely, Claridge had just been handed £700,000 to make his only permanent signing, Jamie Vincent. Stranger still, he was asked to take the team for the game, which was lost 0-2. The soon-to-be former player-manager made his

Fratton swansong as a second-half substitute. Although Mandaric wanted him to stay as a player, Claridge went on loan to Millwall. Rix, despite the baggage of imprisonment, was seen as a promising young manager, who had played a key role as a coach in the success Chelsea had enjoyed under Ruud Gullit.

Home wins over Burnley and Stockport propelled the team nine points clear of the drop zone with just ten games to play. A point at Tranmere kept momentum going, but a 0-1 defeat at Crewe suddenly had the club looking over their shoulder. A break for an international week proved costly and when Pompey conceded four second-half goals at lowly Huddersfield another relegation scrap loomed. Three draws, two of them against high-flying Fulham and Birmingham, kept their heads above water, but defeat at Blackburn meant the relegation issue went to the final week. Pompey had a game in hand at home to fellow strugglers Crystal Palace, but it all went wrong and a 2-4 defeat left Rix sweating on his team beating Barnsley at Fratton on the final Sunday and hoping results elsewhere went his way.

What relegation would have spelled for the Mandaric era can only be surmised, but before the Barnsley game he pledged to stay regardless. He revealed his accountant had drawn up two sets of figures detailing the consequences of staying up and going down. In the end, Pompey collected three points against unmotivated opposition, while Huddersfield's home defeat to Birmingham sent the Terriers down. 'This will never happen again,' roared Rix defiantly on the microphone after incoming results confirmed his team were safe.

Mandaric pledged to back his new boss, as he had Ball and Pulis before, with cash. He told *The News*: 'I never want to go through that again. We would have lost a tremendous amount of money if we had gone down and our dream would have taken a lot longer. We will bring quality players to the club and right now Graham is looking at two or three players. I will give him the green light to move for them, there is no problem there.' Milan had his eye on a player too, who he felt could give something not just to the team but also to the fans, whose loyalty to him had yet to waver.

Match of the Season 2000-01

Portsmouth 2 Crystal Palace 4

Division 1, 2 May, 2001

The mathematics were straightforward. Despite a run which had seen Pompey pick up just three points from 21 since mid-March,

victory over a Crystal Palace side whose slump was deeper still –
two wins in 16 matches since January – would condemn Palace to
the drop. In the process, Pompey would save not only themselves,
but also Grimsby and Huddersfield, who were similarly hovering
over the edge. With 3,000 fans from South London, Fratton was a
sell out for only the second time since Mandaric had arrived. The
match had also taken a new dynamic as Palace had fired manager
Alan Smith after the previous weekend's capitulation at home to
Wolves. In his place came Palace legend Steve Kember. It was an
old trick, but would it work?

From the outset it became clear it probably would. Pompey froze
and Palace were first to every ball and won every 50:50 tackle. Aki
Riihilahti and Dougie Freedman wasted chances before a quick free-
kick allowed Freedman to scoot away, draw Aaron Flahavan and
cross for Mikel Forssell to head into an empty net. Seven minutes
later a carbon-copy move saw Riihilahti provide the finish. Pompey
were reeling. Goal-difference meant the Blues were now in the
bottom three for the first time all season, but on half-time Palace
keeper Alex Kolinko fumbled Lee Sharpe's deep cross and Lee Mills
bundled the ball over the line – 1-2. Things could only get better.
But wait. From the kick-off Carl Tiler – a £500,000 Rix signing in
March – gave the ball away 30 yards out and Freedman raced clear
to angle home and restore the two-goal advantage.

At that point the crowd turned. Pompey's fans have a reputation
for loyalty – invariably in adversity – but the down-side of their
backing is that when their patience finally gives way, it does so with
a vengeance. In that 60 crazy seconds of hope then despair they
snapped. A chant of 'You're not fit to wear the shirt!' rained down
from stands and as skipper Scott Hiley acknowledged afterwards,
the fans were right. 'They [Palace] wanted it more than us, which I
know is a shocking thing to say,' he confessed. With Pompey
trailing 1-4 deep into the second half, after another defensive calam-
ity let Clinton Morrison score from close range, one fan couldn't
contain his frustration and ran on to remonstrate with striker Lee
Bradbury. Ironically, Bradbury was one player on the night who
could hold his head up.

With three minutes to go, villain Tiler's powerful header reduced
the deficit, but it seemed too little, too late. Certainly Tiler's Fratton
career never recovered and he left the club a year later. But with
that goal hope sprang eternal. Pompey could stay up even if they
lost at home to Barnsley, provided Palace lost by three goals at
Stockport. In the end it was more comfortable than that.

LEAGUE DIVISION 1   **2001-02**
Nationwide Division 1   17th
Worthington Cup   1st round
FA Cup   3rd round

Rix used his Chelsea connections to build a team in his own image, persuading midfielder Neil Barrett and winger Courtney Pitt to join Pompey from his old club. He also persuaded Mandaric to find £1.25 million to buy 20-year-old Peter Crouch from relegated QPR, beating off competition from Burnley. However, ultimately the most significant arrival was Harry Redknapp – recently eased out of West Ham – as Director of Football. Redknapp and Mandaric went back a long way – to the 1970s and the chairman's involvement with the Major Soccer League in the United States – and despite the press conference smiles there is little doubt the move was hardly welcome for Rix. Even Pompey's squad-building had Harry's stamp, as young AS Roma defender Alessandro Zamperini – a former trialist at Upton Park – was offered a contract.

The underlying anxiety was not helped by the pre-season friendlies. A 1-0 win over Southern League Newport (IW) was overshadowed by unconfirmed reports that goalkeeper Aaron Flahavan's 'stomach upset' which forced him out of the warm up, was, in fact another fainting fit. Premiership Spurs then outclassed Pompey 5-2 at Fratton in front of 15,000, although two impressive Crouch headers had even Spurs' boss Glenn Hoddle singing his praises.

The squad numbers also left a huge question unanswered, as the No 8 shirt was left vacant, fuelling speculation Mandaric's Croatian connections were about to persuade chain-smoking midfield playmaker Robert Prosinecki to add 'Portsmouth' to a CV which included Real Madrid, Barcelona and Red Star Belgrade. By the time he eventually signed on 1 August, Rix's regime was in chaos after a 1-2 defeat at Conference side Yeovil and a 0-0 draw with Southern League Tiverton Town. Rix and his assistant Jim Duffy sensed they were being undermined, reinforced by Mandaric's apparent reluctance to sanction talks with Celtic about signing striker Mark Burchill, the second part of a 'little and large' double act up front envisaged by Rix.

Pompey's final friendly at home to Premiership Leicester saw a last-minute Rowan Vine goal secure a morale-boosting 2-1 win. In the stands was goalkeeper Flahavan, who had discharged himself from hospital after minor surgery in a bid to alleviate his condition. Eight hours after the final whistle he was dead. While driving on the A338 towards Bournemouth, his BMW crashed. The 25-year-old was flung from the car and he was pronounced dead at the scene.

Football was put into true perspective and fans from all clubs, including Flahavan's native Southampton, came together to pay their respects. It was decided to go ahead with the opening game, at Wolves, with Pompey – appropriately enough – drafting in ex-Saint veteran Dave Beasant to fill the breach. Within 20 minutes Pompey led 2-0, Crouch and Crowe stunning the bookies' favourites for promotion, although the home side fought back to earn a draw.

In the week of Flahavan's funeral, the gloom was marginally lifted by news that Prosinecki had won his appeal against the rejection of his work permit application. His cameo as a sub against Bradford City couldn't prevent a 0-1 defeat, but his full debut, three days later, couldn't have been worse. Second Division Colchester ran Pompey ragged in the Worthington Cup first round. Pompey were in turmoil. Signing Burchill in a £650,000 deal was offset by selling skipper Darren Moore to West Brom for £1 million.

Part of the problem was who was pulling the strings at Fratton. Rix had finally got Burchill, but Prosinecki seemed Mandaric-wrapped – his 'gift to the fans' – while Redknapp inadvertently revealed in a local newspaper that part of his remit was to track down players: 'I was two days late to sign Pearcey [Stuart Pearce] for Pompey'. Even though ten points from four matches hoisted Pompey to second by mid-September, a barely-concealed whispering campaign against Rix was under way. Mandaric was forced to publicly back his manager after the high spot of Rix's reign – a 4-2 demolition of Crystal Palace in which Prosinecki scored a sublime free-kick. Even Redknapp seemed uncomfortable in his Director of Football role, reportedly mulling over a chance to take charge at Leicester, and briefing his numerous media buddies that he was missing the 'day-to-day stuff' of management.

Despite Mandaric's overt backing, Rix's luck ran out. On the eve of a top-of-the-table clash at relegated Coventry, Prosinecki clipped Burchill's heels in a training ground accident. Burchill tore his cruciate knee ligament and was out for the season. Pompey lost the game 0-2, with several hundred 'fans' going on the rampage at half-time, and the season never regained its momentum. Not that there weren't a few more bizarre twists to come, none more so than the signing of Japan goalkeeper Yoshikatsu Kawaguchi for a club-record £1.8 million in October. Lured by the bonanza of replica shirt-sales to the Far East, Pompey instead got their fingers burned. The diminutive goalie proved an adequate shot-stopper, but lacked the physical presence to deal with brutish centre-forwards. Poor Rix was saddled with the responsibility of playing a keeper he clearly didn't want – he would have preferred to sign Sasa Ilic, who had deputised for Beasant after he broke a hand at Stockport in August. Kawaguchi conceded his first goal just 26 seconds into his debut against Sheffield Wednesday. Although Pompey came back to win 3-2, Kawaguchi's career peaked early – he made crucial saves to help beat Manchester City – then nosedived.

Grimsby proved to be his nemesis. On 29 December two misjudgements from corners just before the interval cost two goals and set up the Mariners for their first win since August. A week later Pompey crashed out of the FA Cup, beaten 1-4 at home by Third Division Leyton Orient. Although only one goal could be laid at his door, Yoshi's career in England was effectively over, along with the mirage of untold merchandising riches. Kawaguchi let in 25 goals in 12 games, and hopes of promotion had turned to fears of relegation. That Orient result almost did for Rix. Subsequently Redknapp revealed it was only his reluctance to take over in the post-match boardroom inquest which saved Rix's skin – but it was only prolonging the inevitable. Rix's assistant, Duffy, was relieved of his duties and Redknapp was asked to 'help' the manager.

Also eased out was Managing Director Murphy – Rix's strongest backer in the boardroom, who had urged his appointment in the first place. Murphy was replaced in December by former Notts County Chief Executive Peter Storrie, also a former colleague of Redknapp's at West Ham, thereby weakening Rix's position still further. Initially Murphy was asked to renegotiate the deal to build the new stadium, which was becoming increasingly mired in disputes, not to mention a falling out with the company which was redeveloping the goods yard site. By February Murphy was off the board for good.

Beasant returned in the wake of the Orient debacle at Bradford City and duly let in three (and another three in his next match for good measure) to underline Pompey's problems went deeper than the man between the sticks. Now the battle was for Pompey to grind out the 50 points needed to ensure staying up. The sublime Prosinecki, coupled with the emergence of Crouch as a true striking talent, meant goals were not in short supply, but seven in two matches against Barnsley and Sheffield United could earn no more than a point. Almost a year to the day he arrived, on 23 February, Rix took a Pompey team to West Brom. With old boys Russell Hoult and Darren Moore in commanding form, Albion led 4-0 at the break and declared at five. The relegation places were just nine points away with 12 games left.

Before he was finally fired – on the eve of the visit of Sheffield Wednesday four weeks later – Pompey had their 50 points. In the end Rix will not go down as one of Pompey's greatest managers.

DID YOU KNOW?

In February 2002 Robert Prosinecki became the first Pompey player since 1928 to bag a hat-trick in a home League game and not end up on the winning side.

Rix's concept of building a team around young players was never going to wash with Mandaric, who three years into his spell as chairman, perhaps understandably now wanted results yesterday. His epitaph would be a pre-season claim he would be 'happy-with mid-table mediocrity'. His chairman was anything but. However, Rix will certainly be remembered for his stoic and dignified manner as his time in the Fratton hot-seat began to unravel almost from the moment it began.

To the surprise of no one, Rix's replacement was Redknapp and at last Mandaric struck gold. Harry's wheeler-dealer, East End wide-boy persona, coupled with a knack for creating attractive, attacking football teams, had found perhaps its perfect niche, despite his initial reluctance to take the Fratton manager's job – given the parlous state of the squad. However, Redknapp's style fitted Pompey and its fans' expectations like a hand in a glove. A revolution was underway. Even Rix's declared 'last signing' – £750,000 Bulgarian striker Svetoslav Todorov from West Ham – was anything but. Rix did not even appear at the press conference to unveil him. With six days to play with, Harry sold Crouch to Aston Villa for £5 million and bought Eddie Howe from Bournemouth, loaned Scott Wilson from Rangers, and signed Mark Summerbell from Middlesbrough on a short-term contract.

Just two points from his first six games hardly bode well, but the man who declared in February that more than half the squad 'were not good enough' knew how to sort that out. The stage was set for possibly the busiest summer Portsmouth FC had ever known.

Match of the Season 2001-02

Portsmouth 4 Barnsley 4

Division 1, 2 February 2002

If one match captured the essence of a season which hurtled from the sublime to the 'cor blimey', it had to be this one. After flirting with the play-offs until early December, Pompey had plummeted like a stone, despite the presence of Prosinecki, whose talents had been offset by the impossibility of incorporating him into a team structure. When Pompey went forward they could be as devastating as anyone in the division. When they had to defend they were a man light, as the Croat's reported 40-a-day habit wrecked what was left of his fitness. Three days before Barnsley's visit Pompey had pulled out of their nosedive – which had seen them win just once in eight games and been dumped from the FA Cup – with a 1-0 win at Nottingham Forest thanks to Prosi's late free-kick.

The arrival of struggling Barnsley seemed the ideal opportunity to cement the renaissance and rekindle hopes of a blind-side run at the play-off places. Within four minutes Prosinecki nonchalantly dispatched a penalty after Pitt had been up-ended. But the Tykes were showing all their battling qualities and Chris Lumsdon found the top corner from 25 yards. Then Gary Jones hit a post. Primus restored Pompey's lead with a near-post header from Pitt's cross, but just after the interval Chris Barker ran unchallenged into the penalty area to prod Mike Sheron's pass beyond Beasant – 2-2.

Cue Prosinecki. With Pompey struggling, the Croat suddenly reminded everyone why he was earning a reported £10,000 per week. Primus made a timely interception in his own box and Harper and Crouch combined to find Prosi 30 yards out. A jinking run had yellow-shirted defenders retreating and he even slipped on the greasy surface in curling the ball into the net from the edge of the area. That was the *hors d'oeuvre*. When Pompey won a free-kick on the left-hand corner of the penalty area it might as well have been a spot-kick as Prosinecki fired an unstoppable swirling shot into the top corner of the net. Game over, surely, as Prosi now laid on his full repertoire of flicks and tricks to leave lesser mortals looking ridiculous.

Not quite. This was a season when Pompey were never more than a goal from panic stations. With seven minutes left referee Phil Prosser spotted a punch by Primus in the box. Even the Barnsley players were amazed when they got a penalty, with the Pompey man seeing red. Chris Barker converted the kick and now Pompey were clinging on at 4-3. Crowe kicked one off the line, before one cross too many was slung into the Pompey box and Sheron glanced home an unlikely equaliser. A withering Prosinecki commented afterwards: 'I cannot believe it. You saw what happened out there. What can you say about that? It was a hat-trick for nothing.' A suitable epitaph for Prosinecki's brief career at Fratton Park.

LEAGUE DIVISION 1   **2002-03**
Nationwide Division 1   Champions
Worthington Cup   2nd round
FA Cup   3rd round

For a club accustomed to false dawns, the summer of 2002 hinted at something better than the usual August optimism, which would give way to October recrimination. For a start, with Redknapp identifying the targets and Storrie doing the deals, Pompey were capable of stealing a march on their rivals in the transfer market. They were helped by the fact that the previous spring the ITV Digital contract with the Football League had fallen apart as the would-be alternative to Sky TV collapsed. As a result, the majority of clubs – committed to salary deals in anticipation of the TV lucre – were facing financial meltdown.

But Mandaric, buoyed by the £5 million banked for Crouch, seemed prepared to spend. As a result, by early June midfielder Richard Hughes had been signed for a song from Bournemouth, promising Juventus striker Vincent Pericard arrived on loan, Luton's 20-year-old left-back Matt Taylor was 'stolen', according to his manager Joe Kinnear, for a tribunal fee rising to £750,000, and Wigan's captain Arjan De Zeeuw and West Ham defender Hayden Foxe had been recruited on free transfers. Harry had also brought in former Fratton favourite Jim Smith as his assistant.

By the time pre-season training started, West Ham's out-of-contract goalkeeper Shaka Hislop agreed to drop down a division, while Wolves' midfielder Carl Robinson was given a three-month contract to prove his fitness. Mandaric summed up the prevailing mood: 'I believe that this time we are finally getting it right. I have good feelings about this season, probably more than ever before.' A 2-3 defeat by Celtic, a 1-3 reverse against Premiership Chelsea, and a 1-1 draw with Spanish top-flight side Alaves did not dampen the expectant mood.

Five days before the opening game, Redknapp signed 34-year-old Paul Merson. His name had first surfaced in May – as had Paul Gascoigne, David Ginola and even Romario – but it was only when Merson's relationship with Villa boss Graham Taylor broke down that a deal was brokered. On his arrival, he was clear about his role: 'It's my job to get us into the Premiership.'

The season started with a visit from Nottingham Forest and Fratton was virtually a sell out. Not that Redknapp hadn't already encountered problems. With Rory Allen primed to return from injury to lead the attack alongside Pericard – in the absence of the suspended Todorov – the news that Allen had broken down again

in training was the last thing the boss needed. After a flurry of
mobile phone calls, ex-Pompey striker Deon Burton – out of favour
at Derby – was signed on loan to cover. Burton scored after just
seven minutes of his 'second' debut and the blue touch paper had
been lit. Even the early loss of defender Howe with a serious knee
injury was offset by the assurance of his replacement, Primus.

Buoyed by a 2-0 win, Pompey proceeded to sweep all before
them, picking up a point at Sheffield United and coming from 0-2
down to beat Crystal Palace – who had earlier signed Shaun Derry –
at Selhurst Park, with three goals in five minutes. On Bank Holiday
Monday, Mark Burchill's late goal secured a 1-0 win at Grimsby
which put Pompey top of the table, having won four and drawn
one of their opening five games.

Redknapp continued to wheel and deal. Middlesbrough's
Gianluca Festa joined for a year in a deal which saw the Riverside
club pay most of his wages, while talk of signing Derby striker
Fabrizio Ravanelli persisted for months. Similar talk about Spurs'
midfielder Tim Sherwood would finally come to fruition in February. With the August Manager of the Month award in the bag,
Redknapp was pleased to see it wasn't the usual kiss of death. Four
more League wins saw Pompey two points clear of Leicester. They
were four clear of third-placed Norwich, despite the Canaries inflict-
ing their first defeat earlier in September.

October started with a 1-3 defeat to Wimbledon in the Worthington Cup, as Redknapp rested one or two players, but the signing of
Ivory Coast international Lassina Diabaté freshened things up. The
points continued to accrue at a healthy rate, as did the arrivals.
Redknapp's ability to lure experienced pros with a point to prove
was underlined again as he persuaded Villa's right midfielder Steve
Stone to sign. Stone's debut was at in-form Burnley, but Pompey
won 3-0 to leave even the most pessimistic fans thinking the Premiership dream could become reality.

A week later their hopes were dented by a 0-2 home defeat by
Leicester which saw Festa stretchered off with a knee injury. The
Foxes were the only team keeping pace with Pompey, but the
'match of the season' to date was rendered farcical by a pre-match
thunderstorm which flooded the pitch. Any hopes the rest of the
division might have had that Pompey's stride would be checked
were quickly dashed. Four more wins and a draw at Wolves in the
rest of November took Pompey beyond the 50-point 'safety' mark
unseasonably early. They found themselves seven points clear at
the top and 12 clear of third-placed Forest.

The comings and goings continued unabated too, with Manchester City defender Paul Ritchie having a short loan spell, while the

luckless Rory Allen sensationally walked out on the club to join the 'Barmy Army' watching the England cricket team in Australia. In early December Burton signed a permanent deal, having returned to Derby in September when he broke a bone in his foot. 'Old guard' recruits, including Neil Barrett and Tom Curtis, moved to lower division clubs, while Burchill was, surprisingly for some, packed off on loan to Dundee.

When at last Pompey had their 'blip', it was no worse than five draws in six matches, the other being a vital 2-1 win at Forest. But suddenly the fans were fretting at the sight of the chasing pack, although with 19 games left the gap over third-placed Sheffield United was still a healthy eight points. A knee injury for De Zeeuw, whose towering performances at the back were fast acquiring cult status, was quickly masked by the loan signing of Arsenal's young Greek Stathis Tavlaridis, who debuted in the FA Cup at Old Trafford of all places, as Pompey and their 9,000 travelling fans had a presumed foretaste of the Premiership. Two late United goals in their 4-1 win distorted the balance of play.

Of more pressing concern was the impending visit of Sheffield United. Victory meant it would be hard to see anyone denying Pompey an automatic promotion place. Instead, the Blades sneaked a late win and suddenly they were only five points behind. Throw in another injury to the recently returned Festa, and Pompey were wobbling.

As ever, Harry had an ace up his sleeve – Maacabi Haifa's Nigerian striker Ayegbeni Yakubu. With a goal in the Champions League against Manchester United to his name, and Alex Ferguson's endorsement, the 20-year-old looked an exciting prospect. The Yak's debut would have to await the granting of a work permit, but his introduction with Pompey 0-1 down at bottom-of-the-table Brighton sparked an equaliser and Pompey never looked back. On his home debut against Grimsby he scored inside four minutes, and a brace in a 6-2 win over Derby a week later had Pompey up and running again. Sherwood had also finally arrived to give the squad a 'Premiership' feel to it.

A draw at a sell-out Walkers Stadium against nearest challengers Leicester kept the Foxes at bay. Successive wins over Gillingham (home) and Millwall (5-0, away) consolidated their lead. The game at the New Den was watched by 2,000 fans on the big screen at Fratton. Pompey had been denied tickets as a consequence of trouble between the sides in September. A 1-2 defeat at Wimbledon, where Pompey had 9,000 fans in the 10,000 gate, barely broke their stride. Home wins over play-off contenders Norwich and Wolves inside three days in March meant promotion was tantalisingly close.

DID YOU KNOW?

Pompey are one of only 8 clubs to have played in all 4 divisions and the Premiership.
The others are Bradford C, Bolton, Coventry, Palace, Oldham, Sheffield U, and Wolves.

The points (and goals) kept coming. A 4-0 romp at Coventry included a rare left-footer from Merson. Then Yakubu scored again to earn a point at Preston, 12 months to the weekend since Redknapp had taken charge. The transformation was stunning, as Redknapp reflected later: 'I didn't fancy the job to be honest with you. Even after I took it I was asking myself why, but the lads have been fantastic. They have worked their socks off. We have lost four games all season, so it's been an incredible turnaround.'

Redknapp tried to use the transfer deadline to bolster his squad for the Premiership, but Charlton got wind of his hush-hush move for Ipswich defender Herman Hreidarsson from cash-strapped Ipswich and the lure of 'jam today' won out. A 2-1 win at Walsall – Redknapp dedicated the victory to Pompey fans serving on *HMS Ark Royal* in the Gulf – looked set to open the door to the promised land. Bottom-of-the-table Sheffield Wednesday rolled into town to become the ritual slaughter that confirmed promotion, but Redknapp left nothing to chance. Injuries to Péricard and Yakubu persuaded him to recall striker Lee Bradbury from his loan, ironically at Hillsborough. Making his first start of the season, Bradbury scored the goal which would have guaranteed promotion, but for two late Owls strikes which pooped the party and knocked Pompey off the top for the first time in six months.

That shock defeat merely delayed the inevitable by three days, until Burnley came to Fratton for a re-arranged game. Todorov, who had matured into a striker of quality, saw his close-range shot trickle over the line to propel Pompey into the Premiership. On the final whistle the crowd invaded the pitch and chaired off their hero Merson – who had secretly restarted therapy for his gambling addiction – giving him one of the best 'natural highs' of his career. 'To go up this season is the feat of all feats. It's an honour to be part of this team,' he said.

The next question was whether Pompey could clinch the title. Leicester had stuck doggedly to their heels and when Redknapp's 'hung-over' team crashed 0-3 at Ipswich on Good Friday, the initiative switched back to the Foxes, who booked their own place in the elite by beating Brighton 2-0 at home. But then it was Leicester's turn to slip up, losing at Sheffield United, allowing Pompey to regain top spot with a 3-0 home thumping of Reading. When Leicester failed to beat Norwich the following Sunday lunchtime, the scene was set for Pompey to clinch the championship later that day in front of the Sky cameras and over 19,000 fans by beating Rotherham 3-2. The curtain came down on Pompey's best season in more than half a century with another five-goal bonanza at Bradford City – watched by 7,000 travelling fans who had snapped up tickets weeks before – with Todorov scoring a ten-minute hat-trick which enabled him to land the division's golden boot award for his 26 goals.

It was the stuff of dreams for Pompey fans reared on the dross regularly served up in the 1960s, 1970s and 1990s, but the challenge was now to establish the club in the Premiership. Promotion also meant the revival of the Hampshire derby, but with Southampton in the FA Cup final and well established in their state-of-the-art St Mary's home, Mandaric's banner 'Step Aside Saints' still looked a tall order in the short term.

Match of the Season 2002-03

Portsmouth 6 Derby County 2

Division 1, 1 February 2003

In a campaign when there were so many contenders, this clash with Derby had pretty much everything. Pre-match, the encounter was spiced up by the fact that the Rams' boss was former Pompey manager John Gregory, who had endured a miserable 18 months at Fratton Park in the late 1980s. Throw in the fact that Pompey's latest signing, Yakubu, might have been playing for the opposition, had his work permit application not been refused in the summer. Subsequently the Yak found a Portuguese wife which smoothed the path of his move from Maccabi Haifa somewhat. The connections were reinforced by the fact that ex-Ram Deon Burton was on the Pompey bench, while long-time Pompey target Fabrizio Ravanelli was on Derby's. Oh, and how could I forget, Pompey's assistant manager Jim Smith had enjoyed a productive spell as Derby's boss, taking them into the Premiership in 1996.

Pompey had hauled themselves out of a mid-season slump, beating Grimsby 3-0 at Fratton to cement their status as odds-on favourites for promotion. Mid-table Derby had enjoyed a similarly emphatic victory over Rotherham, but their hopes of an immediate return to the Premiership had stalled as the financial reality of lower division football bit deep into their resources. They were facing an uphill battle to keep out of administration.

From the off Pompey tore into their opponents, and in the third minute Merson raced 50 yards to get on the end of Yakubu's cross, poking the ball home after his first effort came off the bar. Yakubu then swivelled to thump home Taylor's cross. Taylor himself could hardly miss as he strolled onto Todorov's defence-splitting pass to make it 3-0.

Poor Gregory had to endure his own supporters calling for his head and Pompey's ironically joining in. After the interval Derby got their act together and Georgi Kinkladze finally started to make inroads. On the hour Quashie lost possession in his own half and the Georgian dribbled 60 yards. His shot was parried by Hislop to Lee Morris, who reduced the arrears. When Kinkladze converted a spot-kick, after Warren Barton's tumble under Todorov's challenge, Fratton Park held its breath. Memories of losing leads – 12 months before, Pompey were leading Barnsley 4-2 with seven minutes to go – were fresh. The class of '03 were made of sterner stuff and once Todorov clipped home after being played through by Yakubu's flick, their arrogant control was restored. Gregory's misery was compounded as he was sent to the stand for rowing with the officials. Todorov repaid Yak's compliment to make it 5-2. The Nigerian cracked home a fierce cross-shot, then with five minutes left the Bulgarian grabbed his fourteenth goal of the season, scoring from a narrow angle after his first shot had been saved.

If there was a moment at which Pompey's promotion became a formality, this was probably it. Standing fourteen points clear of third-placed Sheffield United, with just 15 games to play, Harry Redknapp's men had seen off their mid-season hiccup in style and proved themselves a cut above the First Division. For the fans it was time to sit back and enjoy the best Pompey side in memory.

PREMIERSHIP   **2003-04**
Barclaycard Premiership   13th
Carling Cup   4th round
FA Cup   Quarter-finals

Even before the open-top bus ride round the city and a rain-soaked parade on Southsea Common, Redknapp was preoccupied with signing the players needed to ensure Pompey might stay up and not go straight back down. The likes of Yakubu and Sherwood had been signed in January with that in mind, as was his abortive move for Hreidarsson in March. Old stager Teddy Sheringham was being touted, and by Easter Pompey had been linked with Liverpool's soon-to-be free agent Patrik Berger.

There was also the knotty question of Captain Catalyst Paul Merson. Pompey were getting cold feet about retaining him, but Merse's decision to forsake the promotion celebrations to watch his son play rugby – a gesture which hurt Mandaric – provided the pretext. Walsall made enquiries and Pompey were prepared to help to pay his wages if he joined them, a reasonably honourable, if not entirely satisfactory resolution. Merson deserved a better send off.

Other promotion heroes departed: Festa returned, as planned, to his native Cagliari, while Diabaté wasn't retained. Crowe was given a free transfer, as was Carl Tiler.

Pompey's potential recruits were constantly in the limelight, especially now that the club's elevation accorded them wall-to-wall coverage on Sky Sports News. By the end of May almost 30 players had cropped up on the rumour mill. Berger, also courted by Leeds, made a whistle-stop tour of Portsmouth and agreed to sign almost on the spot. For many it was proof-pudding that Pompey were now in the big time. A record £1.85 million was paid to Vitesse Arnhem for ex-Sheffield Wednesday defender Dejan Stefanovic, in the face of competition from Rangers, and £400,000 to Juventus brought Péricard on board. Croatian defender Boris Zivkovic from Bayer Leverkusen took Prosinecki's recommendation and signed, as did Harald Wapenaar from Holland as goalkeeping cover.

Not all deals went as smoothly. Matt Holland preferred Charlton, as did Paolo Di Canio. Stephen Reid of Millwall preferred Blackburn, while a double deal for Reo-Coker and McAnuff with the administrators of Wimbledon mysteriously collapsed. A fax requesting to sign Cameroon star Marc Vivien Foé – known to Redknapp at West Ham – was sent shortly before the player's death on the field during the Confederations Cup.

Sheringham, 38, also agreed to hitch his star to Harry's bandwagon, persuaded to take a drop in wages, and it has to be said

Pompey were looking a half-decent squad. A tour of Scotland was inconclusive; a 5-0 win at Kilmarnock promising rather more than a 0-1 reverse at Dunfermline. At Rugby Park, Redknapp fielded a trialist called 'Andy Henry' – alias Auxerre midfielder Amdy Faye – and another of Harry's capers was unfolding. His pleading to the inquisitive FA that he had misunderstood the player's accent would never have been accepted from anyone else.

The rest of the tale, however, was the stuff of *Carry On* movies. First came reports of torn up faxes to Pompey's Scottish hotel (vehemently denied), informing Faye of Middlesbrough's interest. Then Redknapp dashed to the airport to stop Faye – supposedly guarded by Smith and coach Kevin Bond – flying back to France. Finally, Harry stationed his bulldogs outside Faye's room in his house, where he had holed him up to ensure he didn't leave until he had signed for Pompey for £1.5 million. Faye was in the team, officially this time, as Pompey beat Feyenoord 2-0. Redknapp's striking options were, however, wrecked when Todorov snapped a cruciate ligament. He would be out until March.

Fratton Park saw a minor re-vamp. Extra seats had been installed, so that 20,000 were able to cram in for the opening fixture of the Premiership campaign, a Sky-televised clash with Aston Villa. This was the moment of truth. Did Pompey have what it takes? The answer was an emphatic 'yes'. Villa were poor, but Pompey's 2-1 win took them top of the league for a couple of hours. And when Bolton were swatted 4-0 a week later Pompey stayed top for a good 24 hours. For the fans it was time to pinch themselves.

With the newly imposed transfer window snapping shut, Harry was still dealing. Ajax's Andre Bergdolmo didn't fancy Pompey, long-running sagas over Eyal Berkovic and Darren Anderton came to naught, as did a short trial by Georgi Kinkladze. Russia captain Alexei Smertin did arrive. He had been signed by Chelsea from Bordeaux for £3.5 million and was promptly loaned to Pompey for the season. West Ham's right-wing-back, Sebastian Schemmel, shunned by manager Glenn Roeder, also signed, along with ex-Newcastle keeper Pavel Srnicek and West Brom striker Jason Roberts on loan. Pompey's adrenaline-fuelled entry into the big time survived a 0-0 draw at Wolves and a trip to Highbury. In the end a 1-1 draw felt like robbery, after Robert Pires' dive earned the penalty which stole a draw. However, Pompey had announced themselves on the big stage. Well not quite.

Within a month three straight defeats had removed the gloss, and although a 1-0 win over a diminished Liverpool restored spirits, back-to-back spankings at Newcastle and Manchester United had Pompey in the bottom third of the table by early November.

DID YOU KNOW?

When Arsenal won The Premiership in 2003-04 without losing a game, the only teams they failed to beat were Manchester United and Portsmouth.

At least the ground redevelopment was taking shape. Ambitious plans for a 28,000 stadium, financed by controversial plans to build 500 apartments, called the Pompey Village, were unveiled, but a dispute over a sliver of land crucial to the development left a sour taste, not least the evidence presented by former director David Deacon, who had left the board soon after Mandaric's arrival.

Back on the field, hapless Leeds were crushed 6-1, but injuries and suspensions were also beginning to bite. Quashie had risen to the challenge of top-flight football, but also harvested five bookings and an inevitable ban. Péricard's thigh strain wouldn't clear up, and Hislop succumbed to a hernia, underwent surgery, and missed the 0-2 loss at Fulham. Berger was sent off for verbally abusing the referee – the first Pompey player red-carded in 20 months. Hislop's replacement, Wapenaar, was hardly to blame, but he was more culpable as Leicester won 2-0 at Fratton.

This was hardly ideal preparation for the first Hampshire derby in eight years, when Pompey travelled up the M27 for a fourth round Carling Cup-tie. On the way, the team bus only narrowly avoided a multiple pile-up. Srnicek replaced Wapenaar, but was no more convincing. Saints' 2-0 win owed little to De Zeeuw's late red card for fouling James Beattie in the box.

Three weeks later, on 23 December, the pair were at it again. Pompey had picked up a point at Middlesbrough but then lost at home to Everton. Wapenaar was back in goal, flapped at a corner, and sparked a 0-3 defeat that left Pompey just outside the bottom three (while Saints were in a Champions League spot). Redknapp responded by 'cancelling' Christmas, which had the desired effect as a Berger brace defeated Spurs on Boxing Day.

Redknapp was plotting his transfer strategy for the January transfer window and Mandaric was clearly expected to bankroll Harry's choice. Newcastle's unhappy striker Lomano LuaLua arrived on loan. Ajax's Finnish defender Petri Pasanen signed for the rest of the season, while the moody Zivkovic fell out with Redknapp and joined Dortmund. Harry also prised Berkovic, not to mention his wage packet, from Manchester City. The Israeli's debut on 10 January was against his former team and he pulled the strings in a 4-2 win.

The key to Pompey's survival was getting Yakubu back in the goalscoring groove. He had returned to England in the summer with malaria and, although recovered, he had looked a shadow of himself. But a goal in the 1-2 defeat at Villa, the winner against Blackpool in the FA Cup, and then two goals against City saw him firing on all cylinders – at which point he departed for the African Nations Cup. Faye was supposed to go too, with Senegal, but pulled out with injury. On the eve of the Wolves game Yakubu was sent home by Nigeria in disgrace after breaking a curfew (claims he took women back to his room were denied). A police escort from the airport saw him come on as a sub in a 0-0 draw. Making his debut that day was £400,000 Anderlecht striker Ivica Mornar and, true to form, as the final minutes ticked away to the transfer deadline, Leicester full-back John Curtis arrived on a free transfer.

Had Redknapp's transfers done enough? Initially the jury was out. Having scored just three away goals all season, Pompey doubled that in one game at Spurs but still lost 3-4. Defeat at home to title-chasing Chelsea was no disgrace and the fifth round FA Cup replay win over Liverpool hinted at better things. On 29 February Newcastle led 1-0 at Fratton going into the last minute, but Sir Bobby Robson was rendered speechless as LuaLua volleyed the equaliser and backflipped his way into the affections of Pompey fans forever. 'It means one of our players has taken points off us,' spluttered Robson. 'We thought there might be a ban on LuaLua, but there wasn't so I got my pen out and quickly signed the agreement,' beamed Storrie.

Still Pompey stuttered. Arsenal humiliated them on national TV, winning 5-1 in the FA Cup quarter-final at Fratton Park. The fans won acclaim by backing their side in adversity and their sporting appreciation of their vastly superior opponents. Consecutive defeats at Everton and Liverpool in mid-March dumped Pompey in the bottom three ahead of the return derby with Saints, put back until Sunday, 21 March. Yakubu's 68th-minute goal gave Pompey their first League win in two months and their first at home against Saints since 1963. It was if a curse had been lifted. Suddenly points were gobbled up like it was summer again. Three vital ones came at fellow strugglers Blackburn and one more at Charlton.

One benefit of losing to Arsenal in the Cup was that the League appointment on semi-final day now had to be postponed, otherwise Pompey feared another walloping. On Easter Monday they dispatched Birmingham 3-1 at Fratton, and when a dogged rearguard action protected Stone's first-half goal against Manchester United, safety was within touching distance. A 2-1 win at sinking Leeds was more convincing than the score-line suggested, and results elsewhere the following week ensured Pompey's survival earlier than had been anticipated.

Colin Blant on
the attack
against Bolton
(August 1970)

Skipper Jim Storrie (right) introduces Round the World Yachtsman
Chay Blyth to Ray Hiron (August 1971)

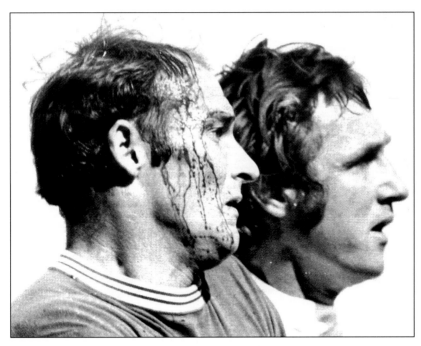

A bloodied Richie Reynolds against Luton (April 1972)

Eoin Hand cannot prevent Bristol City scoring (October 1972)

Ray Hiron receives the match ball from assistant manager Pat Wright
after his 100th goal (February 1973)

Pompey on the defensive at FA Cup finalists Sunderland (April 1973)

Peter Price gets in a header against Middlesbrough (August 1973)

Ron Tilsed (left) breaks his arm against Luton, watched by
Alan Stephenson and referee Bill Hall (September 1973)

Alan Stephenson on the attack against West Brom (September 1974)

George Graham
wins a header
against Orient
(February 1975)

Bobby McGuinness in action against Brighton in a pre-season friendly
(August 1975)

Mike Flanagan
ends Pompey's FA
Cup hopes, despite
Phil Roberts'
challenge
(January 1976)

Norman Piper in action against Reading (September 1976)

Pompey fans in confident mood before the game with York (May 1977)

Striker David Kemp gets in a header against Millwall (August 1977)

Bobby Stokes had an unhappy time at his home-town club (January 1978)

Colin Garwood's goals couldn't keep Pompey in Division Three (March 1978)

David Pullar gets in a shot against Hereford (October 1978)

Joe Laidlaw scores against Darlington (October 1979)

Jeff Hemmerman
gets in a cross
against Huddersfield
(October 1979)

The Pompey team celebrate promotion at Northampton (May 1980)

The News covers Pompey's visit to Anfield (October 1980)

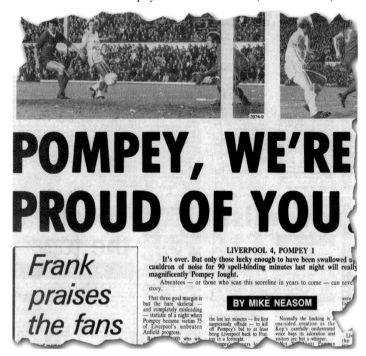

Bobby Doyle gets in a header against Oxford (March 1981)

John Deacon introduces the summer signings:
(from left) Thomas, Biley, Howe, and Webb (August 1982)

Peter Ellis gets in a tackle against Sheffield United (August 1982)

Mick Tait gets in a header against Newport (September 1982)

Mark Hateley scores in the 5-1 thrashing of Brighton (March 1984)

Alan Biley scores a swan-song goal against Oldham (February 1985)

Kevin
O'Callaghan
in action
against
Birmingham
(April 1985)

Nicky Morgan scores against Norwich (August 1985)

Noel Blake makes his point against Barnsley (March 1986)

Mick Quinn scores on his home debut against Millwall (March 1986)

Noel Blake gets in
a header against
Sunderland
(October 1986)

£285,000 flop
Ian Baird
fails to score
against
Everton
(December
1987)

Vince Hilaire is brought down by Warren Neill of QPR (March 1988)

Jim Gregory gives Fratton Park a revamp (July 1988)

Record signing
Warren Aspinall
gets in a header
against Oldham
(October 1988)

Steve Wigley on the
ball against Ipswich
(October 1989)

Guy Whittingham on the prowl against Oxford (March 1990)

Martin Kuhl scores from the spot against Notts County (February 1991)

Lee Russell tangles with Gary Lineker of Spurs in the FA Cup (February 1991)

Darren Anderton puts Pompey ahead against Liverpool (April 1992)

Kit Symons makes a splash against Southend (January 1993)

Alan
McLoughlin
scores a hat-
trick against
Blackburn
(January 1994)

Andy Turner in
action against
Wimbledon
(September 1996)

Matt Svensson scores on
his debut against
Huddersfield
(December 1996)

Paul Hall takes on Aston Villa in the FA Cup (January 1998)

Steve Claridge loses out to Jonathan Woodgate of Leeds in the FA Cup (January 1999)

Pompey defend against Crystal Palace:
(from left) Whitbread, Thogersen, Petterson, Robinson (October 1999)

The wall does its job against Bolton: (from left) Brown, Igoe,
McLoughlin, Bradbury, Awford, Simpson (November 1999)

Manager Graham Rix jumps for joy as Pompey avoid relegation against Barnsley (May 2001)

Lewis Buxton wins a header against Rotherham (February 2002)

Robert Prosinecki in action against Manchester City (April 2002)

Paul Merson signs for Pompey (August 2002)

Svet Todorov challenges
Brighton's Guy Butters
(August 2002)

Nigel Quashie makes a splash against Leicester (November 2002)

We are the Champions! (April 2003)

Pompey parade the First Division trophy around the city on an open-top bus (May 2003)

Patrik Berger celebrates
Pompey's second goal
against Aston Villa
(August 2003)

Pompey celebrate their first Premiership goal, scored by
Teddy Sheringham against Aston Villa (August 2003)

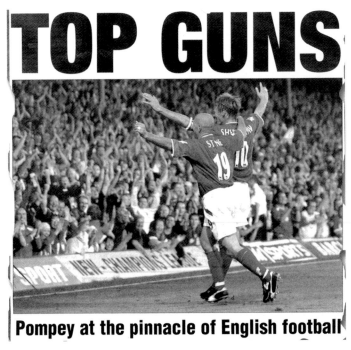

Pompey go top of the Premiership. *The News* tells the tale (August 2003)

Yakubu has just given Pompey the lead against Saints (March 2004)

Milan threatens to 'strangle'
Harry at their joint press
conference ... if he moves to
Saints (November 2004)

Lomano LuaLua
somersaults to
celebrate his fist
goal against
Southampton
(April 2005)

The re-arranged clash with unbeaten champions Arsenal on 4 May ended 1-1, as both sets of fans and players celebrated their respective and relative success. Thierry Henry walked off at the end wearing a Pompey shirt, to the applause of all four sides of the ground. Everything was sweetness and light.

If only. After losing against already relegated Leicester on 8 May murmurings circulated that Redknapp and Mandaric had fallen out. According to Redknapp, Milan wanted Jim Smith sacked. Mandaric replied that Pompey's coaching needed modernising and getting rid of Smith was actually Harry's idea. Fuelled by the voracious appetite for 'news' demanded by a 24-hour sports service like SSN, the pair washed each others' dirty linen in public for the next six days, their egos ruling out a curt 'no comment'. No longer could the matter be settled behind closed doors. With Harry accusing Milan of 'lying', things looked irretrievable, but a last-ditch, uneasy truce was brokered ahead of the last game with Middlesbrough. Pompey incredibly won 5-1, Yakubu cracking four goals. 'We want Milan, with Harry and Jim!' bellowed a bemused crowd. What do they say? Be careful what you wish for. Sometimes wishes come true.

Match of the Season 2003-04

Portsmouth 1   Southampton 0

Premiership, 21 March 2004

For more than 40 years the balance of power in south-coast football terms had lain to the west. Saints had spent most of that time in the top flight, winning the FA Cup in 1976, while Pompey had roller-coastered through the divisions before climbing out of the second tier rut they had been in for almost 20 years. When Pompey won the First Division title, Saints trumped them by reaching the FA Cup final. Even now as 'equals', Saints had the upper hand. Comfortably above Pompey in the league, they also had a shiny new 32,000-capacity stadium and a youth academy boasting some of the brightest talents in the country. And yet . . .

Two months earlier Saints' talismanic boss Gordon Strachan had suddenly upped sticks and resigned, claiming he wanted a break from the game. After an uneasy hiatus, in which Saints didn't win a game, Paul Sturrock – who had taken Plymouth from nowhere to the brink of the First Division – had been appointed their new boss, even though he had had no experience at Premiership level. Some of the Saints persuasion hinted he was the cheap option, but his start had been solid enough as Saints beat Liverpool 2-0 at St Mary's a week before their visit to Fratton.

Pompey simply needed a win. Their Premiership lifeblood was draining away, as just one win in 2004 had dumped them into the bottom three. Even the return of Todorov, at Liverpool in midweek, had gone sour as he lasted just 45 minutes. What the Fratton Faithful needed was a sign. Twenty minutes before the kick-off it duly arrived. With most of the 2,000 Saints fans assembled in the open Milton End, Pompey's antiquated facilities provided a portent. A violent hailstorm whipped up off the Solent and deposited itself on those wretched Southampton supporters. The more the icy pellets bounced and ricocheted off the roofs over the remaining three sides of the ground, the brighter the mood became. Unbeknown, another drama was taking place. During the warm up, Michael Svensson, Saints' classy Swedish central defender, crocked his knee and had to be replaced at short notice.

The game itself was dreary. The first half was bad enough and if anything the second half was worse. This was two poor, shambling sides, a shadow of their relatively recent selves. Beattie's pathetic attempt to shoot from 40 yards earned him derision. Then in the 68th minute Smertin played the ball wide to Stone, whose cross was arrowed in to Yakubu, who buried his shot from three yards. Cue pandemonium in the Pompey ranks.

At the prospect of victory, nerves set in. Saints threw caution to the wind. Subs Fabrice Fernandes and Marian Pahars caused problems and in the final minute a loose ball fell to the normally deadly Kevin Phillips ten yards out. His deliberately placed shot gently kissed the upright and bounced out. Defender Primus, a revelation since being called up for his first Premiership appearance in December, hoofed the ball to safety. Hislop smothered Claus Lundekvam's header in the final action and Pompey's demons had been exorcised. Sad then, that 400 of them rioted in their own backyard after the match, attacking the police when their attempts to get at the Saints fans were thwarted.

The pendulum had started to swing back. Few could imagine how quickly it would be swinging a year later.

PREMIERSHIP   **2004-05**
Barclaycard Premiership   16th
Carling Cup   Quarter-finals
FA Cup   4th round

Even as Euro 2004 in Portugal shifted attention elsewhere, the Fratton arrival turnstile kept ticking over. Newcastle's Andy Griffin and Reading's 23-year-old goalkeeper Jamie Ashdown were signed, but with Svet Todorov needing further surgery to rebuild his knee a new striker was paramount. The prime target was LuaLua, whose maverick skills had helped lift Pompey clear of danger. Only when promoted West Brom had their £1.75 million offer accepted by Newcastle did Pompey swoop to tie up a deal.

Pompey breezed through pre-season unbeaten, the defence bolstered by the signing of Everton stalwart David Unsworth. The arrival of Aliou Cissé from Birmingham for £300,000 was scant consolation for Redknapp, who wanted West Ham's Michael Carrick, and the Senegal midfielder barely featured.

The season got underway with a home draw with Birmingham. A 1-2 defeat at Charlton meant that, because Pompey's midweek clash with Liverpool had been called off, they were bottom of the table when they faced Fulham. Harry's squad had been bolstered by a 'pay-as-you-play' deal with Preston for Ricardo Fuller. More excitingly, a £2.3 million 'record' deal had been done with Italian side Modena for Senegalese striker Diomansy Kamara.

A couple of defeats in September were offset by an unbeaten October, which brought draws at Norwich and Middlesbrough and home wins over Spurs and Manchester United. With hindsight, Pompey had probably reached the high-water mark of Harry's reign, although the loss of Kamara for eight weeks with a knee injury took off a little of the gloss. Ninth in the table, with a game in hand on most of those above them, the juxtaposition of 'Portsmouth' and 'Europe' no longer seemed a pipe-dream.

The speed at which the tide receded was breathtaking. Villa's 3-0 win showed Pompey to be as travel sick as ever. In the Carling Cup, having knocked out Tranmere and Leeds, Pompey reached the quarter-finals for only the fourth time, beating Cardiff 2-0 at Ninian Park. That same evening it was reported that Panathinaikos Sporting Director Velimir Zajec was set to join Pompey in a similar role. With Harry expressing surprise, the tabloids had a field day – *Harry Down the Pan* was surely the best. The thin ice supporting manager and chairman finally gave way – hardly the best preparation for the visit to Southampton. With Saints, under former Pompey winger Steve Wigley, without a win since August, there

was no better time to lay the St Mary's jinx. Instead, Pompey lost
the game 1-2 and lost Yakubu for six weeks to a nasty tackle.

A week later Pompey lost miserably at home to Manchester City,
with Zajec and Redknapp sitting awkwardly next to one another in
the directors box, but the end was nigh. In the run up to the trip to
Bolton on 27 November, Jim Smith resigned in protest at the way
Redknapp had been treated. The next day Harry followed suit,
claiming he needed a break from the game. It was a tearful departure as Harry was mobbed by fans wishing him well. When fans
urged him not to take the Southampton job if it arose, Harry replied: 'I will not go down the road. No chance.'

Zajec picked the team for the trip to Bolton, in conjunction with
the two remaining coaches – Kevin Bond and Joe Jordan – the latter
having only joined in the summer. The players responded with a
rare away win, thanks to De Zeeuw's goal, although all the headlines focused on El Hadji Diouf spitting in his face. Still the Harry
saga wouldn't die. When tabloids reported Mandaric bemoaning the
£3.4 million agents' fees the club had paid under Redknapp, Harry
demanded a joint press conference with Milan at which both insisted Redknapp had had no part in the financial aspects of transfers. It was a pity the press conference was on the day of the Carling Cup quarter-final at Watford. Pompey capitulated 0-3.

It took a couple of late goals against West Brom to turn defeat
into victory against the League's bottom side, but it was the latest
twist in the Redknapp saga which was about to turn south coast
football on its head. After Saints' latest defeat, Wigley lost his job.
His replacement was Redknapp. 'Judas' and 'Traitor' were two of
the more printable terms applied to the 'fallen' hero. It was rumoured, falsely, that Redknapp had agreed to move to Saints before
the derby day defeat. Within days Saints' new back-up team was
also in place: Jim Smith and Kevin Bond.

Pompey's crowing neighbours chanted 'Harry and Jim, in Red
and White' – a spoof version of Pompey's Championship season
chant 'Top of the League, with Harry and Jim'. For the moment,
the joke was on Saints, as Pompey continued to gather points while
their neighbours failed to reap the 'new manager' effect. In an
ironic twist, former Saints boss Gordon Strachan, who had resigned
in January, emerged as the favourite for the Pompey job, although
the Scot eventually ruled himself out.

By the New Year Pompey were lower mid-table with 27 points,
twelve clear of their neighbours, who were second from bottom. But
this sub-plot had plenty more chicanes to negotiate. First of all, fate
couldn't resist plucking Saints' and Pompey's balls out of the bag in
succession to set up an FA Cup fourth round showdown at St

Mary's. Then came the unsettling of Pompey's players during the January transfer window. Hislop, De Zeeuw and Berger were considered 'close' to Redknapp and likely targets. Midfielder Quashie went for £2 million, after he tried to negotiate a pay rise to match the money Saints were offering. Fuller, too, was the subject of an enquiry. Pompey's form was worrying – one point out of twelve in January – and morale was further sapped as the Cup-tie was lost in controversial circumstances. In stoppage time David Prutton's cross struck Taylor high on the arm and the assistant referee flagged for a penalty. Former Pompey striker Peter Crouch netted, and another Saints chip was carved on Pompey's shoulder.

Quashie's loss was filled when Zajec went back to Greece to sign Giannis Skopelitis. Pompey also added Slovenian striker Aleksander Rodic to the squad, as well as goalkeeper Kostas Chalkias from Panathinaikos. Chalkias seemed an odd signing, but Hislop seemed to have been marginalised. The newcomer had a nervy debut against Saints, let in a soft goal in a 2-1 win over Middlesbrough and looked unconvincing in the 1-3 defeat at Spurs. First impressions are invariably the lasting ones, and fans had already written his obituary. But it took another soft goal conceded in the 0-3 defeat at Arsenal for Chalkias to be axed.

Ashdown was restored, but by now Pompey were in real trouble. Since Boxing Day they had won just once in ten matches. With Saints and Crystal Palace reviving, the gap between Pompey and the bottom three was down to six points. Pompey had also courted controversy by announcing plans for the rebuilding of Fratton Park. The Pompey Village development had received planning permission in July, but construction, initially set to start early in 2005, hadn't, prompting speculation that the necessary funding wasn't in place. When the prices for new season tickets were announced, North Stand patrons would be getting a discount.

Plans to rotate the pitch 90 degrees over the summer were shelved. Instead it would be done in three weeks, in November 2005, with the North Stand being demolished at the same time, leaving ticket holders 40 yards from the action. Under the supposed weight of protests the idea was scrapped, but at the cost of putting the redevelopment a year behind schedule.

Crucial to any redevelopment was staying in the Premiership. A woeful second-half display at Fulham, which turned a 1-0 lead into a 1-3 defeat, left Pompey teetering four points above the trap door with seven games to go. Drastic action was needed, and on 7 April Pompey announced their new manager, several weeks ahead of schedule. Alain Perrin had made his reputation guiding Troyes from the lower reaches of the French leagues to qualification for the

UEFA Cup. He then took Olympique de Marseille into the Champions League in his first season, before results began to wane and he found himself out of work in January 2004. After a spell in Qatar he was in the job market again and a move to Fratton in the summer had been quietly negotiated. The dire position of the club saw him parachuted in early, to be helped by former Spurs manager David Pleat in the short term. The shock tactic worked.

The svelte Perrin paced the technical area for the visit of Charlton and made a double substitution at 2-2, pitching two extra strikers into the fray. He was rewarded with a pressure-easing 4-2 win. A point at Birmingham in his next game meant that a win over either Liverpool or Southampton would all but ensure safety. The Liverpool game was narrowly lost, but the 4-1 win against Saints will go down in history as one of the finest, and most crucial, results in the club's history. More to the point, Perrin had earned the kudos to start the task of reshaping Pompey.

Mission accomplished. Pompey had three games left and the last one, at West Brom, was to provide a deliciously ironic postscript. Relegation-threatened Baggies were vying with Saints, Palace and Norwich for the three drop positions. Saints lost at home to Manchester United, ensuring their relegation, but with Albion winning 2-0 it was a happy Hawthorns on all sides as the curtain came down on one of the more bizarre seasons in Pompey's history.

Match of the Season 2004-05

Portsmouth 4 Southampton 1

Premiership, 24 April 2005

It was always going to come to this. Ever since Harry had decided his ego was big enough and his skin thick enough to decamp for St Mary's, Sunday, 24 April had been ringed as D-Day. The FA Cup-tie back in January, far from lancing Pompey's boil, had only heightened the pain. What's more, Southampton's New Year revival had been matched by Pompey's slump. The arrival of Alain Perrin had lifted spirits, but this was still a relegation six-pointer. Should Saints win, Pompey too would be fighting for their lives. If Portsmouth won, not only would Redknapp and his lackeys – Quashie, Smith, and Bond – be vanquished, Pompey would confirm their status as top dogs in Hampshire for the first time since 1960.

Death threats to Redknapp were taken seriously enough to have bodyguards protect him. Kick-off had been set for noon – to cut out pre-match drinking – and, indeed, the pre-match atmosphere outside the ground didn't have the ugly edge of the previous season.

DID YOU KNOW?

**Pompey played Saints six times in 20 months between 2003 and 2005.
It had taken 20 years for the previous six matches between the clubs.**

Inside, a rash of anti-Harry banners were unfurled, but the overwhelming feeling was one of fear of the result. The teams, and Harry, emerged, to a cacophony of 'Judas!' Former Fratton favourite Crouch, finally showing his Premiership class, was out with a pulled hamstring. In his place came Henri Camara, the Senegalese striker who had arrived at St Mary's on loan in January and was looking to keep a third successive relegation off his CV.

The Pompey team went into one of those huddles. But this was no pretentious team-building affair. It lasted less than ten seconds, as skipper De Zeeuw and his colleagues realised that the Saints had bottled it. 'We looked at each other and then we looked at them in the tunnel and we knew we were going to make the better start. You could see it in their faces,' said De Zeeuw afterwards. And how. Taylor's crunching tackle inside 15 seconds set the mood. After three minutes O'Neil's chip over the top wrong-footed Saints' lumbering centre-backs. Keeper Antti Niemi brought down LuaLua and Yakubu chipped the spot-kick high into the net. Southampton were like a balloon that had burst.

When Quashie fouled Stone, Berger – allegedly one of Red-knapp's targets – whipped in a free-kick for De Zeeuw to head into the net. But two minutes later Camara sped away to fire across Jamie Ashdown from the edge of the penalty box.

Which way would the game turn? Almost at once two Saints defenders got in a tizzy, Niemi raced out and was stranded as LuaLua hooked the ball from 25 yards into an empty net. As the scorer backflipped his celebrations he tweaked a muscle in his thigh. Pompey were preparing to substitute him when the ball broke to LuaLua on the edge of the box. His instant half-volley ricocheted into the net off the post. Portsmouth 4 Southampton 1, and just 26 minutes on the clock. Perhaps the most remarkable 26 minutes Fratton Park has ever witnessed.

Saints had been bullied and battered into submission. For the rest of the game Pompey toyed with them in the manner of a cat and a mouse. Had the shooting of LuaLua's replacement – Kamara – been less wayward, there might have been more goals. The important thing was that a ghost had been exorcised. As Harry magnanimously conceded afterwards, his side had been outclassed. You could almost feel sympathy for the man who had seen his undeniable achievements at Fratton Park forever tarnished. Almost . . .

PORTSMOUTH'S FRIENDLY, TESTIMONIAL, AND MINOR CUP FIXTURES

Season	Date	Venue	Opponents	Res	F-A	Scorers	Att	Competition
1970-71	1/8	H	WEST HAM	L	0-2		13,986	Friendly
	5/8	H	BRIGHTON	L	0-1		5,836	Friendly
	8/8	A	PLYMOUTH	L	3-4	Jennings, Hiron 2	5,139	Friendly
	11/8	H	FULHAM	L	1-3	Youlden	5,382	Friendly
	16/9	A	MSV DUISBURG	L	0-4			City Twinning
	14/10	H	MSV DUISBURG	L	0-2		4,414	City Twinning
1971-72	31/7	H	IPSWICH	D	0-0		5,775	Friendly
	4/8	A	ALDERSHOT	D	2-2	Hand, Storrie	3,611	Friendly
	7/8	A	READING	W	3-0	Reynolds, Piper, Trebilcock	1,949	Friendly
	9/8	A	MANSFIELD	D	1-1	Storrie	3,498	Friendly
	5/10	A	BASINGSTOKE	W	2-1	Storrie, Jennings		Opening of lights
	21/12	A	BOGNOR R	W	3-0	Jennings 2, Hiron	1,000	Friendly
	11/1	A	WATERLOOVILLE	W	5-2	Reynolds 2, Hiron 2, McCann		Friendly
	5/3	A	GUERNSEY	W	5-0	Not recorded		Friendly
	5/5	H	SOUTHAMPTON	L	0-7		8,793	J Milkins Testimonial
	10/5	A	YEOVIL	W	2-1	Plumb (guest), Reynolds		Benefit
1972-73	29/7	A	BRENTFORD	W	1-0	Price	5,750	Friendly
	2/8	H	MORTON	W	1-0	Wilson	4,028	Friendly
	7/8	H	PARTICK T	D	0-0		4,727	Friendly
	15/11	A	BROCKENHURST	W	5-0	Reynolds 4, Lewis		Friendly
	2/2	H	BIRMINGHAM	L	0-2		3,608	Friendly
	25/3	A	SOUTHEND	W	3-2	Lewis, Jennings, Reynolds		Friendly (Guernsey)
	2/5	A	GUILDFORD	W	2-0	Piper, Lewis		T Burge Testimonial
	9/5	H	WEST HAM	W	4-2	Davies 3, McCann	22,070	A McCann Test.
1973-74	11/8	A	BOURNEMOUTH	D	0-0		6,653	Friendly
	15/8	H	BRIGHTON	W	4-1	Marinello, Price, Davies 2	5,920	Friendly
	17/8	H	BOURNEMOUTH	D	1-1	Davies	4,359	Friendly
	18/8	A	BRIGHTON	D	2-2	Lewis, Davies	4,222	Friendly
	5/11	H	ARSENAL	W	2-1	Piper, Davies	8,859	75th Anniversary
	4/12	H	MANCHESTER U	D	1-1	Piper	17,226	75th Anniversary
	3/5	H	SOUTHAMPTON	D	0-0		8,322	G Neave Testimonial
	9/5	H	GOALDIGGERS XI	W	4-3	Reynolds 2, Marinello, Stewart	1,737	Charity
1974-75	3/8	A	BRENTFORD	W	4-0	Davies 2, Piper, Mellows		Friendly
	5/8	A	READING	L	0-1		2,746	Friendly
	7/8	H	TOTTENHAM	L	0-2		6,259	Friendly
	10/8	H	IPSWICH	L	0-2		4,845	Friendly
	28/10	A	BOGNOR	D	0-0		1,500	Friendly
	19/11	A	HUELVA (Spain)	D	1-1	Foggo		Friendly
	24/1	H	STOKE	W	2-0	Lewis (pen), Piper	11,230	Friendly
	14/2	H	MANCHESTER C	D	3-3	Mellows, Graham, Piper	8,603	Friendly
	16/3	A	GOS'/ FAREHAM XI	D	3-3	Mellows, Hiron, Crawford	1,500	Hiron Test. (Gosport)
	6/5	H	SOUTHAMPTON	W	2-1	Hiron 2	5,374	R Hiron Test.
	9/5	A	KETTERING	D	1-1	Foster	4,000	Friendly
1975-76	2/8	H	BRIGHTON	W	2-1	Marinello, Went (pen)	2,447	Friendly
	4/8	H	SWINDON	L	0-1		1,800	Friendly
	6/8	A	BRENTFORD	W	1-0	Marinello	955	Friendly
	9/8	A	BOURNEMOUTH	W	1-0	Graham	1,952	Friendly
	12/8	H	WIMBLEDON	D	2-2	Marinello, McGuinness	1,669	Friendly
	2/4	A	NUNEATON	L	1-2	Kamara (pen)	683	Friendly
	27/4	H	LEICESTER	W	3-1	Wilson, Foster, Graham	3,216	M Manley Testimonial
	19/5	H	CELTIC	L	1-6	Mellows	9,279	Friendly
1976-77	31/7	A	OXFORD	D	2-2	McGuinness, Piper	1,500	Kent Cup
	3/8	H	WATFORD	W	4-2	Kamara (pen), Piper 2, Foster	2,690	Kent Cup
	7/8	H	LUTON	L	0-2		3,330	Kent Cup
	10/8	A	HORSHAM	L	0-1			Friendly
	15/11	A	NEWPORT (IOW)	W	4-0	McGuinness, Pollock, Kemp, Foster	2,700	SOS Fund
	8/3	A	GOSPORT B	W	1-0	Barnard	2,500	SOS Fund

Season	Date	H/A	Opponent	Result	Score	Scorers	Attendance	Competition
1977-78	30/7	H	FULHAM	L	0-1		4,183	Friendly
	3/8	H	ALDERSHOT	L	0-1		2,256	Friendly
	6/8	H	MILLWALL	D	1-1	Gilchrist	3,424	Friendly
	8/8	A	POOLE	W	3-1	Kemp 3	558	Friendly
	22/8	A	GOSPORT B	W	2-0	Kemp, Stokes	1,500	Friendly
	8/11	A	CRAWLEY	D	3-3	Mellows 2, Stokes	1,078	Maggs Testimonial
	7/12	A	ROYAL NAVY	L	0-1		100	Friendly (Abandoned)
	13/2	H	FORT LAUDERDALE	D	2-2	Piper N, Piper S	6,027	Friendly
1978-79	29/7	A	YEOVIL	W	2-0	Hemmerman, Denyer	782	Friendly
	5/8	H	CHELSEA	D	1-1	Viney	8,477	Friendly
	9/10	H	TULSA ROUGHNECKS	L	0-2		2,791	Friendly
	23/10	A	NEWPORT (IOW)	W	4-1	Foster, Davey, Denyer, McIlwraith	3,000	Friendly
	24/1	A	BIRMINGHAM	L	0-1		4,347	Friendly
	31/1	H	CAMBRIDGE	W	2-0	Pullar 2	2,110	Friendly
	6/2	H	WEST BROM A	W	2-0	Hemmerman 2	8,522	Friendly
	12/2	H	MIDDLESBROUGH	L	1-2	o.g.	1,344	Friendly
	18/4	H	REP OF IRELAND XI	D	2-2	Garwood, Kemp (guest)	6,878	E Hand Testimonial
	21/5	A	LEATHERHEAD	D	1-1	Denyer	500	Dave Reid Test.
	23/5	A	CHICHESTER	W	2-0	Hemmerman, Tindal	950	Friendly
1979-80	28/7	H	COVENTRY	W	1-0	Garwood (pen)	4,257	Friendly
	30/7	H	WEST HAM U	L	1-2	Garwood	6,099	Friendly
	4/8	H	STOKE	L	0-3		3,583	Friendly
	7/8	A	DORCHESTER	L	2-3	Garwood, McLaughlin		Friendly
	10/9	A	WATERLOOVILLE	W	3-2	Laidlaw, Rogers, Hemmerman	1,242	A Stones Testimonial
	26/11	A	NEWPORT (IOW)	W	2-1	Todd, Hemmerman	700	Curling Memorial
	5/5	H	BRIGHTON	W	1-0	Brown	14,346	Friendly
	16/5	H	SOUTHAMPTON	L	2-4	Perrin 2	11,233	Duggie Reid Test.
1980-81	20/7	A	ATHLONE	L	0-1			Ireland Tour
	22/7	A	LIMERICK	W	3-0	Barnard 2, Davey	1,113	Ireland Tour
	28/7	A	WIMBLEDON	D	1-1	Laidlaw		Friendly
	30/7	H	TOTTENHAM	L	1-2	Laidlaw	9,934	Friendly
	4/8	H	CHELSEA	D	0-0		5,771	Friendly
	14/10	H	CRYSTAL PALACE	L	2-3	Kemp (guest), Tait	3,143	S Piper Testimonial
	13/12	H	ALDERSHOT	L	2-3	Davey, Tait	3,120	Friendly
	16/12	H	ROYAL NAVY	W	3-0	Ellis, Doyle, Gregory		Friendly
	3/5	A	CHICHESTER	W	3-1	Doyle (pen), Rafferty, Hemmerman	650	Friendly
1981-82	8/8	A	WEYMOUTH	W	2-1	Hemmerman, Doyle (pen)	885	Friendly
	11/8	A	BOURNEMOUTH	L	0-1		2,398	Friendly
	14/8	H	WEST HAM	L	0-2		6,512	Friendly
	17/8	A	IOW SELECT XI	L	0-2		650	Friendly (at Ryde)
	22/8	H	ARSENAL	L	0-1		6,706	Friendly
	22/12	H	SOUTHAMPTON	W	2-1	Crown, Hemmerman	6,649	Hants Prof Cup SF
	30/12	H	MANCHESTER U	L	0-3		13,917	Friendly
	27/4	H	ALDERSHOT	W	1-0	Aizlewood	3,821	HPC Final
1982-83	8/8	H	LIVERPOOL	L	0-3		15,355	Friendly
	17/8	H	COVENTRY	D	1-1	Wimbleton	3,066	S. Atlantic Fund
	20/8	H	IPSWICH	L	0-2		3,919	Friendly
	23/8	H	ASTON VILLA	L	3-4	Rafferty, Senior, Crown	4,519	A Cropley Testimon
	26/10	A	DORCHESTER	W	4-0	Biley 3, Webb	555	Friendly
	8/1	A	JERSEY FA XI	W	1-0	Howe	359	Friendly
	1/2	A	ALDERSHOT	W	4-2	Howe, Aizlewood, Rafferty, Biley	1,132	HPC SF
	19/4	H	BOURNEMOUTH	L	1-3	Morgan	2,621	HPC Final
1983-84	6/8	A	FARNBOROUGH	W	3-0	Morgan 2, Biley	300	Friendly
	9/8	H	TOTTENHAM H	L	1-3	Biley	10,911	Friendly
	17/8	H	WEST HAM U	W	3-1	Biley 2, Hateley	6,024	Friendly
	20/8	H	ARSENAL	W	2-1	Hateley 2	9,128	Friendly
	20/11	A	ST MARTIN'S (Guern)	W	5-0	Ball A, Rogers, Morgan, Dillon, Webb	400	Lights Opening
	13/3	A	ALDERSHOT	L	2-3	Webb, Souter o.g.	1,433	HPC SF
	16/5	H	ASTON VILLA	W	1-0	Biley	2,652	Friendly

Season	Date	H/A	Opponent	Res	Score	Scorers	Att	Competition
1984-85	8/8	A	HILLINGDON	W	5-0	McGarvey (pen), Webb 2, Biley, Wood		Friendly
	11/8	A	SALISBURY	W	2-0	McGarvey 2 (1 pen)		Friendly
	15/8	A	HASTINGS	W	3-0	Dillon, McGarvey 2	302	Friendly
	20/8	H	QP RANGERS	L	0-2		6,099	Friendly
	7/11	H	NEW ZEALAND	W	3-2	McGarvey 2, Walsh	1,889	Friendly
	30/1	H	ALDERSHOT	W	3-0	Sugrue 2, McGarvey (pen)	771	Hants Senior Cup SF
1985-86	31/7	A	ALDERSHOT	D	1-1	Kennedy		Friendly
	6/8	A	BOURNEMOUTH	W	1-0	Hilaire	1,725	1984/85 HSC Final
	7/8	H	NOTTINGHAM F	L	1-3	Morgan	3,781	Friendly
	10/8	H	ARSENAL	L	0-1		5,625	Friendly
	17/9	H	CHARLTON	W	4-0	Blake, Morgan, Wood 2	3,074	Full Members Cup
	2/10	A	CHELSEA	L	0-3		6,833	FMC
1986-87	27/7	IOM	ISLE OF MAN XI	W	3-1	Hilaire, Kennedy, Dillon (pen)		Manx Cup
	29/7	IOM	NEWCASTLE	D	2-2	O'Callaghan, Dillon (pen)		Manx Cup
	30/7	IOM	BLACKBURN	W	1-0	Morgan		Manx Cup
	2/8	IOM	WIGAN	L	0-1	(after extra-time)	1,100	Manx Cup Final
	9/8	H	WATFORD	W	3-0	Mariner 2, Blake	2,269	Friendly
	13/8	A	EXETER	L	0-1		499	Friendly
	16/8	H	QP RANGERS	D	0-0		1,732	Friendly
	19/8	H	REAL SOCIEDAD	W	1-0	Dillon	3,217	Friendly
	16/9	H	CRYSTAL PAL	W	4-0	Dillon, Hilaire, O'Callaghan, Wood	2,515	FMC Rd 1
	4/11	H	MILLWALL	W	3-2	Dillon 3 (all pens)	3,900	FMC Rd 2
	25/11	A	SHEFFIELD W	W	1-0	Hilaire	7,846	FMC Rd 3
	25/2	A	NORWICH	L	1-3	O'Callaghan	9,204	FMC QF
	31/3	A	FARNBOROUGH	W	2-1	Collins, Birch	488	HSC SF
	12/5	H	ROAD SEA	W	2-0	Birch, Russell		HSC Final
1987-88	23/7	A	SALA	W	4-0	Horne, Baird, Quinn, Stewart	1,803	Swedish Tour
	25/7	A	SODERHAMNS	W	4-1	Mariner 2, Hilaire, Kennedy	700	Swedish Tour
	27/7	A	LEKSANDS	W	7-0	Connor 2, Mariner 2, Quinn 3	1,000	Swedish Tour
	28/7	A	FILMS SK	W	3-1	Quinn, Baird, Gilbert	900	Swedish Tour
	30/7	A	SANVIKENS	W	3-1	Quinn, Baird, Hilaire	659	Swedish Tour
	3/8	A	HELENELUNDS	D	2-2	Hilare, Dillon (pen)		Swedish Tour
	6/8	H	SEATTLE STORM	W	3-1	Kerr, Baird, Birch	2,684	Friendly
	9/8	A	BOGNOR R	W	1-0	Dillon	750	Friendly
	10/11	H	STOKE	L	0-3		3,228	Simod Cup Rd 1
1988-89	10/8	A	BOGNOR R	W	2-0	Connor (pen), Horne		Friendly
	17/8	A	POOLE	W	1-0	Quinn		Friendly
	8/11	H	HULL	W	2-1	Quinn, Hardyman	2,717	Simod Cup Rd 1
	21/12	A	MIDDLESBROUGH	L (aet)	1-2	Powell	6,853	Simod Cup Rd 2
	15/5	A	WATERLOOVILLE	D	1-1	Turner		B Cole Testimonial
1989-90	1/8	A	BOGNOR R	W	1-0	Black		Friendly
	4/8	A	GOSPORT	W	2-0	Aspinall 2	1,000	G Juryeff Testimonial
	8/8	H	BOTOFOGO	L	0-2		4,500	Friendly
	11/8	A	SOUTHEND	L	1-2	Aspinall		Friendly
	15/8	H	TOTTENHAM	L	0-1		7,670	Friendly
	5/12	H	WIMBLEDON	L	0-1		2,499	ZDS Cup Rd 1
	22/1	H	CAEN	W	5-1	Connor 4, Chamberlain	1,730	NSPCC Centenary
	7/5	A	E COWES VICS	W	5-4	Chamberlain, Gilligan, Ball 3	750	Reed Memorial
1990-91	4/8	A	GOSPORT	W	2-0	Aspinall (pen), Chamberlain	1,158	K Findlay Testimonial
	8/8	A	CHELTENHAM	W	2-0	Whittingham, Beresford	599	Friendly
	11/8	A	CARDIFF	L	0-1		1,389	Friendly
	14/8	A	SWANSEA	W	2-1	Clarke, Chamberlain	1,215	Friendly
	18/8	H	QP RANGERS	W	2-1	Whittingham, Kuhl	3,541	Friendly
	12/12	A	OXFORD	L	0-1		1,055	ZDS Cup Rd 2
1991-92	24/7	A	GLASTONBURY	W	2-0	Doling Symons		L Heal Testimonial
	27/7	A	DORCHESTER	W	2-1	Whittingham, Clarke	964	Friendly
	30/7	A	BRENTFORD	W	2-0	Clarke, Ross	1,231	Friendly
	3/8	A	BOURNEMOUTH	W	1-0	Daniel	3,500	Friendly
	5/8	A	GOSPORT	W	3-0	Chamberlain, Ross (pen), Wigley	1,404	Friendly
	7/8	A	FULHAM	W	2-1	Burns, Kuhl (pen)	1,029	Friendly

Season	Date	Venue	Opponents	Res	F-A	Scorers	Att	Competition
1991-92	9/8	H	SHEFFIELD W	D	1-1	Kuhl	2,672	Friendly
(cont)	1/10	A	PLYMOUTH	L	0-1		2,303	ZDS Cup Rd 1
	6/5	A	HASTINGS	L	2-4	Burt (og), Kuhl	1,240	P Petkovic Testimon
1992-93	24/7	A	WEYMOUTH	W	3-0	Doling, Whittingham, Clarke	1,149	Friendly
	28/7	A	READING	W	1-0	Whittingham		Friendly
	1/8	A	FOREST GREEN	W	6-0	Ross 3, Wigley, Whit', Chamberlain		Friendly
	3/8	A	BOURNEMOUTH	D	0-0			Friendly
	7/8	H	ASTON VILLA	W	1-0	Walsh	4,658	Friendly
	10/8	H	TOTTENHAM H	W	4-2	Walsh (pen), Powell, Murray, Asp (p)	10,929	Friendly
	15/9	A	CHARLTON	W	3-1	Aspinall, Clarke, Whittingham	1,853	Anglo-Italian Cup (Grp)
	29/9	H	MILLWALL	D	1-1	Whittingham	2,535	AIC (G)
	11/11	H	CESENA	W	2-0	Symons, Walsh	4,752	AIC (International)
	24/11	A	BARI	L	0-3		837	AIC (I)
	8/12	H	LUCCHESE	W	2-1	Powell 2	2,363	AIC (I)
	16/12	A	ASCOLI	W	2-1	Aspinall, Whittingham	502	AIC (I)
1993-94	20/7	A	RYDE SPORTS	W	5-0	Walsh, Whit' 2, Durnin, Symons	2,000	Friendly
	27/7	A	AJAX	L	0-2		2,500	Mypa Tournament
	29/7	A	MYPA (Finland)	W	2-0	Kristensen, Durnin	4,000	Mypa Tournament
	4/8	A	READING	W	1-0	Walsh		Friendly
	7/8	A	WYCOMBE	W	3-0	Walsh 2, McLoughlin	2,712	M West Testimonial
	9/8	H	REAL SOCIEDAD	W	3-0	Chapman 2, Blake	8,485	Friendly
	31/8	H	BRISTOL C	W	3-1	Burns, Daniel, Powell	2,318	AIC (G)
	14/9	A	OXFORD	W	2-0	Hall, Durnin	2,987	AIC (G)
	12/10	A	PADOVA	D	0-0		1,117	AIC (I)
	9/11	A	PESCARA	L	1-2	Doling	2,000	AIC (I)
	16/11	H	COSENZA	W	3-0	Kristensen, Walsh 2	2,961	AIC (I)
	22/12	H	FIORENTINA	L	2-3	Hall, Dobson	4,338	AIC (I)
	1/2	A	BICESTER	W	3-0	Creaney 2, Powell	955	Lights Opening
	10/5	A	SOUTHAMPTON	L	1-5	Knight (pen)	16,900	A Knight Testimonial
	13/5	A	AEK ATHENS	D	4-4	Creaney 3 (1 pen), Powell (won pens)	1,800	Thrace Cup (Greece)
	15/5	A	COVENTRY	W	1-0	Hall	1,000	Thrace Cup
1994-95	21/7	A	WEYMOUTH	W	3-0	Creaney 3	642	Friendly
	26/7	A	HAVANT	W	2-1	Creaney, McLoughlin		Friendly
	29/7	A	BRENTFORD	W	2-1	Creaney (pen), Powell		Friendly
	2/8	A	METROPOLITAN POL	W	5-0	Creaney 2, Powell, McLoughlin, Hall		Friendly
	6/8	H	WEST HAM U	D	1-1	Creaney	4,622	Friendly
	8/8	H	MANCHESTER C	L	1-2	Powell	6,468	Friendly
1995-96	19/7	A	YEOVIL	W	3-1	Hall 2, Burton	1,498	Friendly
	22/7	A	TORQUAY	W	2-1	Powell, Durnin		Friendly
	24/7	A	TIVERTON	W	7-1	Hall 3, Burton 2, Rees, Symons		Friendly
	29/7	A	CLYDE	W	2-0	Butters, Creaney	645	Scotland Tour
	31/7	A	MONTROSE	W	3-0	Burton 2, Creaney		Scotland Tour
	3/8	A	AYR	W	3-0	Bradbury 2, Hall		Scotland Tour
	5/8	A	FALKIRK	W	3-0	Butters, Burton, Bradbury		Scotland Tour
	8/8	H	ASTON VILLA	L	0-2		8,924	Friendly
1996-97	23/7	A	BATH	W	2-0	Bradbury, Simpson		Friendly
	25/7	A	YEOVIL	D	1-1	Rees		Friendly
	27/7	A	EXETER	W	3-0	Burton 2, Rees		Friendly
	29/7	A	TORQUAY	D	2-2	McLoughlin, Simpson (pen)	724	Friendly
	31/7	A	BRIGHTON	D	1-1	Burton		Friendly
	3/8	A	LE HAVRE	D	1-1	Butters		Friendly (Abandoned)
	10/8	H	BRISTOL C	W	1-0	McLoughlin (pen)	2,701	Friendly
	13/8	A	BOGNOR R	W	3-0	Burton, Bradbury, More		Friendly
	3/12	A	LYMINGTON	L	0-1			Friendly
	18/2	H	WIDZEW LODZ	L	2-5	Simpson, Whitbread	1,100	Friendly
1997-98	15/7	A	BOURNEMOUTH	L	0-1			Friendly
	20/7	A	VIDAR STAVANGER	W	4-3	McLoughlin, Burton 2, Durnin		Norway Tour
	22/7	A	KVINNHERAD	W	6-1	Hall, Bur', Thorp, Bradb' Turner, Igoe	695	Norway Tour
	24/7	A	SKEID OSLO	D	0-0			Norway Tour
	26/7	A	DUNDEE	D	1-1	Burton		Friendly

Season	Date	Venue	Opponents	Res	F-A	Scorers	Att	Competition
1997-98	28/7	A	BRECHIN	W	3-1	Bradbury, Thorp	325	Friendly
(cont)	30/7	H	CHELSEA	L	1-4	Burton	7,851	Friendly
1998-99	13/7	A	BOURNEMOUTH	L	0-1		4,850	Friendly
	15/7	A	TORQUAY	L	1-2	Aloisi	671	Friendly
	17/7	A	EXETER	W	2-0	Soley, Alosi		Friendly
	20/7	A	BOHEMIANS	D	1-1	McLoughlin		Ireland Tour
	22/7	A	FINN HARPS	W	2-0	Aloisi 2		Ireland Tour
	24/7	A	MONAHAN	W	7-0	Aloisi 3, McNevin 2, McL' (pen), Hall		Ireland Tour
	25/7	A	DERRY CITY	W	1-0	Aloisi		Ireland Tour
	27/7	A	SLIGO ROVERS	W	5-0	Aloisi 2, Kyzeridis, Durnin, Whitbread		Ireland Tour
	29/7	A	MILLWALL	L	0-2			Friendly
	1/8	H	GENOA	D	2-2	Durnin, Aloisi (lost 5-6 on pens)	3,100	Centenary Tourn
	2/8	H	WIMBLEDON	L	1-3	Durnin	1,950	Centenary Tourn
	18/5	H	WEST HAM	W	1-0	Whittingham (guest)	4,285	G Neave Testimonial
1999-00	14/7	A	TIVERTON	W	2-0	Phillips, Nightingale	664	Friendly
	17/7	A	WEYMOUTH	W	2-1	Awford, Whittingham		Friendly
	19/7	A	DORCHESTER	L	0-3		879	Friendly
	21/7	A	EXETER	W	2-1	Thogersen, Whittingham		Friendly
	24/7	H	LEICESTER	W	2-1	Whittingham, Nightingale	4,985	Friendly
	28/7	A	BOURNEMOUTH	W	2-0	McLoughlin (pen), Whittingham		Friendly
	31/7	A	BRENTFORD	W	1-0	Whittingham		Friendly
	9/5	H	TOTTENHAM	W	4-2	Bradbury, Allen, Edinburgh 2	6,757	J Edinburgh Test
2000-01	14/7	A	DORCHESTER	W	2-0	Harper, Lustu (tr)	675	Friendly
	17/7	A	EXETER	W	2-1	Bradbury, Harper	1,256	Friendly
	19/7	A	TORQUAY	D	1-1	Harper (pen)	894	Friendly
	21/7	H	COVENTRY	D	1-1	Nightingale	6,810	Friendly
	4/8	A	WOKING	W	1-0	Curtis		Friendly
2001-02	21/7	A	NEWPORT(IW)	W	1-0	Crouch	2,900	Friendly
	25/7	H	TOTTENHAM	L	2-5	Crouch 2	15,144	Friendly
	28/7	A	YEOVIL	L	1-2	Pitt	1,668	Friendly
	30/7	A	TIVERTON	D	0-0		743	Friendly
	1/8	A	BRENTFORD	D	2-2	Crouch, Pitt	1,361	Friendly
	4/8	H	LEICESTER	W	2-1	Bradbury (pen), Vine	6,804	Friendly
2002-03	10/7	H	CELTIC	L	2-3	Hughes, Primus	11,553	Friendly
	17/7	A	NEWQUAY	W	5-0	Todorov, Tiler, Péricard, Harper 2	200	Friendly
	20/7	A	TORQUAY	W	4-1	Foxe, Todorov, Konovalov (tr), Pitt	1,420	Friendly
	27/7	H	CHELSEA	L	1-3	Péricard	10837	Friendly
	3/8	H	ALAVES	D	1-1	Allen	3,301	Friendly
2003-04	19/7	A	BOURNEMOUTH	L	4-5	Fletcher (og), Todorov, Quashie, Sher'	6,646	S Fletcher Test
	16/7	A	EXETER	W	4-0	Todorov, Sher', Robinson, Harper	3,163	Friendly
	25/7	A	SWINDON	D	2-2	Zivkovic, Todorov	5,108	Friendly
	29/7	A	KILMARNOCK	W	5-0	Yakubu 2, Sheringham, Stone, o-g	3,837	Friendly
	2/8	A	DUNFERMLINE	L	0-1			Friendly
	5/8	A	BRENTFORD	W	1-0	Péricard	3,080	Friendly
	9/8	H	FEYENOORD	W	2-0	Berger, Yakubu	6,020	Friendly
2004-05	21/7	A	WYCOMBE	W	2-0	Yakubu, Harper	2,270	Friendly
	24/7	A	TORQUAY	W	4-1	De Zeeuw, Taylor 2, Yakubu	2,875	Friendly
	28/7	A	PLYMOUTH	W	5-1	LuaLua, Yakubu 3, O'Neil	6,964	Friendly
	30/7	A	BRISTOL C	D	0-0		8,338	B Tinnion Test
	3/8	A	RUSHDEN & DIA	W	2-1	Mornar, O'Neil	2,097	Friendly
	7/8	H	PANATHINAIKOS	D	0-0		6,523	Friendly

GUIDE TO SEASONAL SUMMARIES

Col 1:   Match number (for league fixtures); Round (for cup-ties).
      e.g. 2:1 means 'Second round; first leg.'
      e.g. 4R means 'Fourth round replay.'

Col 2:   Date of the fixture and whether Home (H), Away (A), or Neutral (N).

Col 3:   Opposition.

Col 4:   Attendances. Home gates appear in roman; Away gates in *italics*.
      Figures in **bold** indicate the largest and smallest gates, at home and away.
      Average home and away attendances appear after the final league match.

Col 5:   Respective league positions of Portsmouth and their opponents after the match.
      Portsmouth's position appears on the top line in roman.
      Their opponents' position appears on the second line in *italics*.
      For cup-ties, the division and position of opponents is provided.
      e.g. *2:12* means the opposition are twelfth in Division 2.

Col 6:   The top line shows the result: W(in), D(raw), or L(ose).
      The second line shows Portsmouth's cumulative points total.

Col 7:   The match score, Portsmouth's given first.
      Scores in **bold** indicate Portsmouth's biggest league win and heaviest defeat.

Col 8:   The half-time score, Portsmouth's given first.

Col 9:   The top lines shows Portsmouth's scorers and times of goals in roman.
      The second line shows opponents' scorers and times of goals in *italics*.
      A 'p' after the time of a goal denotes a penalty; 'og' an own-goal.
      The third line gives the name of the match referee.

Team line-ups: Portsmouth line-ups appear on the top line, irrespective of whether
      they are home or away. Opposition teams appear on the second line in *italics*.
      Players of either side who are sent off are marked !
      Portsmouth players making their league debuts are displayed in **bold**.

Substitutes: Names of substitutes appear only if they actually took the field.
      A player substituted is marked *
      A second player substituted is marked ˆ
      A third player substituted is marked "
      These marks do not indicate the sequence of substitutions.

N.B.   For clarity, all information appearing in *italics* relates to opposing teams.

LEAGUE DIVISION 2 — Manager: Ron Tindall — SEASON 1970-71

No	Date	Opponents (V)	Res	F-A	H-T	Pos	Pt	Att	1	2	3	4	5	6	7	8	9	10	11	12 (sub)
1	15/8	NORWICH (A)	D	1-1	0-0	–	1	15,100	Milkins	Smith	Ley	Piper	Blant	Munks	McCann	Storrie	Hiron	Bromley	Jennings	
									Keelan	*Butler*	*Black*	*Mallander*	*Forbes*	*Howard*	*Briggs*	*Bennett*	*Silvester*	*Paddon*	*Foggo*	
2	22/8	BOLTON (H)	W	4-0	1-0	4	3	15,703	Milkins	Smith	Ley	Piper	Blant	Munks	McCann	Storrie	Hiron	Bromley	Jennings	
									Clarke	*Ritson**	*Farrimond*	*Williams*	*Hulme*	*Rimmer*	*Wharton*	*Byron*	*Hunt*	*Greaves*	*Taylor*	*Hurley*
3	29/8	MILLWALL (A)	D	0-0	0-0	7	4	8,909	Milkins	Smith	Ley	Piper	Blant	Munks	McCann	Storrie	Hiron	Bromley	Jennings	
									King	*Brown B*	*Cripps*	*Dorney*	*Kitchener*	*Burnett*	*Possee*	*Jacks*	*Bolland**	*Dunphy*	*Alder*	*Brown S*
4	2/9	ORIENT (H)	D	1-1	0-1	4	5	15,218	Milkins	Smith	Ley	Piper	Blant	Munks	McCann	Storrie	Hiron	Bromley	Jennings	
									Goddard	*Jones*	*Rofe*	*Taylor*	*Mancini*	*Allen*	*Lazarus*	*Bullock*	*Fairbrother*	*Dyson*	*Brabrook*	*Youdlen*
5	5/9	SHEFFIELD WED (H)	W	2-0	2-0	2	7	18,712	Milkins	Smith	Ley	Piper	Blant	Munks	McCann	Storrie	Hiron	Bromley	Jennings	
									Grummitt	*Prophett**	*Wilcockson*	*Todd*	*Ellis*	*Craig*	*Sinclair*	*Young*	*Downes*	*Prendergast*	*Sissons*	*Pugh*
6	12/9	SWINDON (A)	L	1-2	0-2	5	7	14,662	Milkins	Smith	Ley	Piper	Blant	Munks	McCann	Storrie	Hiron	Pointer	Jennings	
									Downsboro'	*Thomas*	*Trollope*	*Butler*	*Burrows*	*Harland*	*Smith*	*Gough*	*Horsfield*	*Noble*	*Rogers*	
7	19/9	BIRMINGHAM (H)	W	1-0	1-0	4	9	18,037	Milkins	Smith	Ley	Piper	Blant	Munks	McCann	Storrie	Hiron	Bromley	Jennings	
									Kelley	*Martin*	*Green*	*Hockey*	*Sleeuwenh'k*	*Robinson*	*Francis*	*Vowden*	*Hynd*	*Pendrey*	*Summerill*	
8	26/9	LEICESTER (A)	L	0-2	0-1	6	9	25,613	Milkins	Smith	Ley	Piper	Blant	Munks*	McCann	Storrie	Hiron	Bromley	Jennings	
									Shilton	*Whitworth*	*Nish*	*Manley*	*Sjoberg*	*Cross*	*Farrington*	*Partridge*	*Brown*	*Kellard*	*Glover*	*Travers*
9	30/9	SHEFFIELD UTD (H)	L	1-5	0-0	11	9	16,587	Milkins	Smith	Ley	Piper	Blant	Munks	McCann	Storrie	Hiron	Bromley	Jennings	
									Crawford	*Badger*	*Hemsley*	*Powell*	*Tudor*	*Barlow*	*Woodward*	*Reece*	*Dearden*	*Currie*	*Salmons*	
10	3/10	WATFORD (H)	W	5-0	0-0	7	11	15,712	Milkins	Smith	Ley	McCann	Blant	Munks	Storrie	Treblicock	Hiron	Piper	Jennings	
									Walker	*Welbourne*	*Williams*	*Lugg*	*Lees**	*Eddy*	*Scullion*	*Wigg*	*Garbett*	*Walley*	*Woods*	*Packer*

Scorers, Times, and Referees

1. Piper 86 / Silvester 46. Ref: K Burns (Stourbridge)

2. McCann 1, Hiron 48, 78, Jennings 90. Ref: R Johnson (Lowestoft)

3. Ref: K Styles (Barnsley)

4. Hiron 85 / Bullock 44. Ref: T Reynolds (Swansea)

5. Hiron 9, Jennings 22. Ref: T Dawes (Norwich)

6. Storrie 80 / Noble 19, Horsfield 32. Ref: G Kew (Leeds)

7. Hiron 39. Ref: W Gow (Swansea)

8. Glover 45, Farrington 90. Ref: W Johnson (Kendal)

9. Munks 82 / Woodward 78, 85, 89, Dearden 55, [Reece 86]. Ref: B Daniels (Rainham)

10. Treblicock 50, 60, 82, Piper 73, [Jennings 64]. Ref: G Hartley (Wakefield)

Match reports

1. Pompey put a disappointing pre-season behind them to claim a deserved point. Silvester puts Ron Saunders' City ahead by bundling home Foggo's cross but new-boy Piper caps a fine debut by volleying home after Jennings' cross-shot comes back of the bar. Milkins was on form.

2. Bolton never recover from falling behind after just 24 seconds: Bromley sent Jennings away and his cross was swept in by McCann. Hiron seizes on a loose ball as Storrie challenges Clarke, then Williams hits the post twice, before Hiron's thunderbolt and Jennings' magic seal it.

3. Benny Fenton's Millwall put Pompey under intense pressure, but fail to make it pay on a tropical afternoon. Bobby Brown nearly broke the deadlock shortly after the break with a cross-shot, but Ley almost stole the points with a long-range effort which King saved at full stretch.

4. An impressive performance is rewarded as Hiron's drive enters the net 'like a steam train' after Piper and Ley combined to make space. Orient lead from the break, as Bullock pounces on Allen's saved shot, while Munks is off the pitch with a cut head. Rofe hits the underside of the bar.

5. Hiron sets up Pompey with a far-post header after Bromley linked with Jennings to create the chance. Jennings then takes advantage of four static defenders to head home from Piper's free-kick. Prophett is booked for a foul then subbed. 'Once again we looked solid,' said Tindall.

6. Poor defending costs Pompey their unbeaten start in torrential rain. Noble dives in front of Milkins to nod home Trollope's cross and Horsfield scores after the ball squirms through a crowded box. Storrie nets after Jennings' shot was cleared off the line. Bookings for Smith and Blant.

7. Birmingham's dour tactics, often nine men back, are rumbled by Hiron's volley as Smith's cross flicks Sleeuwenhoek's head. Storrie hits the bar in a second-half break, but Tindall refuses to criticise Brum who have Hockey booked. 'I'd have done the same in their position,' he said.

8. Controversy at Filbert Street as Storrie's 17th-minute headed 'goal' is missed by the officials as the ball hits the stanchion and comes out. City make the most of their let-off and Kellard's run sets up Glover for the opener. Farrington wraps up the points with a fine shot in injury-time.

9. Lightning strikes twice as the Blades win 5-1 at Fratton for the second time in 13 months. Woodward's rocket seals it after Currie puts Dearden away. Munks' shot goes in off the bar, but Reece nets and Woodward completes his hat-trick in a frantic finale. United get a standing ovation.

10. Watford's four-man midfield frustrates Pompey until Treblicock, in his first game for six months, volleys in Smith's centre. He then flicks in Ley's free-kick and darts between two defenders for his hat-trick. Jennings heads in from Ley's cross and Piper scores from Storrie's pass.

11 · A MIDDLESBROUGH · 10/10 — 2-3 (L)
Figures: 10 · 7 · 11 · Att 18,775
Scorers: McCann 8, 27p, McIlmoyle 45 87, Hickton 56.
Ref: V Batty (Helsby)

Pompey	Middlesbrough
Milkins	*Whigham*
Hand	*Madden*
Ley	*Jones*
McCann	*Smith G*
Blant	*Gates*
Munks	*Spraggon*
Storrie	*Mills*
Trebilcock	*McMordie*
Hiron	*McIlmoyle*
Piper	*Hickton*
Jennings	*Laidlaw*

McCann nets from an acute angle, then slots in a penalty after Jones fouled Storrie. On half-time Boro's pressure pays as McIlmoyle nets from close in. He then sets up Hickton with a nod down and scores the winner. Hiron hits the post at the end. Boro have scored 15 goals in four.

12 · H NORWICH · 17/10 — 0-2 (L)
Figures: 11 · 7 · 11 · Att 15,064
Scorers: Self 10, Howard 22.
Ref: J Yates (Redditch)

Pompey	Norwich
Milkins	*Keelan*
Hand	*Payne*
Ley*	*Black*
Piper	*Mallender*
Blant	*Forbes*
Munks	*Howshall*
McCann	*Howard*
Storrie	*Bennett*
Hiron	*Self*
Bromley	*Paddon*
Jennings	*Anderson*
(sub) Travers	

A poor show by Pompey gifts City their first win in seven as their 4-4-2 formation baffles the Blues. Young striker Self is helped to the opener by Anderson's cross, then Howard nets from Bennett's pass. Ley's substitution infuriates the crowd and Piper's goal is ruled out for handball.

13 · A QP RANGERS · 24/10 — 0-2 (L)
Figures: 18 · 9 · 11 · Att 14,709
Scorers: Clement 79, Morgan 82.
Ref: D Howell (North Shields)

Pompey	QP Rangers
Milkins	*Parkes*
Hand	*Clement*
Ley	*Gillard**
Piper	*Hunt*
Blant	*Mobley*
Munks	*Hazell*
McCann	*Morgan*
Trebilcock	*Venables*
Hiron	*Francis*
Storrie	*Marsh*
Jennings	*Ferguson*
	(sub) *McCulloch*

More woe on the road as Tindall plays five at the back to try to stop Marsh. Hand marks him out of the game, apart from one brilliant effort saved by Milkins. Pompey are on for a point until Clement loops in a header from a corner, then Morgan finds himself unmarked six yards out.

14 · A CARDIFF · 28/10 — 0-1 (L)
Figures: 18 · 6 · 11 · Att 18,529
Scorers: Toshack 62.
Ref: J Taylor (Wolverhampton)

Pompey	Cardiff
Milkins	*Eadie*
Hand	*Carver*
Ley	*Bell*
Piper	*Sutton*
Blant	*Murray*
Munks	*Harris*
McCann	*Gibson*
Storrie	*Woodruff*
Hiron	*Phillips*
Bromley	*Toshack*
Jennings	*King*

City's 21-year-old keeper Eadie is the hero as he denies Storrie, Piper and Hiron in the first half. Pompey are aggrieved when Milkins appears to be fouled from Gibson's corner, but Toshack heads home. In injury-time Hiron's header slips through Eadie's fingers, but a defender clears.

15 · H BLACKBURN · 31/10 — 4-1 (W)
Figures: 16 · 21 · 13 · Att 9,936
Scorers: Trebilcock 8, 15, 16, Pointer 81; Knighton 85.
Ref: R Tinkler (Boston)

Pompey	Blackburn
Milkins	*Jones*
Hand	*Wilson*
Ley	*Wood*
Piper	*Hunter*
Blant	*Mulvaney*
Munks	*Eccles*
Pointer	*Goodwin**
Storrie	*Knighton*
Trebilcock	*Conlon*
Bromley	*Kerr*
Jennings	*Hill*
	(sub) *Metcalfe*

Trebilcock's second hat-trick of the month destroys feeble Rovers. Jennings crosses for the first, then Piper picks him out, before Hunter's back-pass is gleefully seized upon. Pointer's goal is set up by Jennings as chairman Collett's £85,000 debt revelation is temporarily forgotten.

16 · A CHARLTON · 7/11 — 2-2 (D)
Figures: 13 · 22 · 14 · Att 8,420
Scorers: Bromley 20, Jennings 23; Plumb 55, Kenning 90.
Ref: P Baldwin (Middlesbrough)

Pompey	Charlton
Milkins	*Wright*
Hand	*Curtis*
Ley	*Bruck*
Piper	*Moore**
Blant	*Went*
Munks	*Shipperley*
Trebilcock	*Davies*
Storrie	*Treacy*
Hiron	*Plumb*
Bromley	*Bond*
Jennings	*Peacock*
	(sub) *Kenning*

Sub Kenning hits the top corner from 20 yards to save it. Earlier Bromley volleyed home from a corner, then Piper crossed for Jennings to score via the post. Plumb's volley brought the Valiants back, but Hiron was denied by Wright's boot and a clearance when the ball looked in.

17 · H SUNDERLAND · 14/11 — 2-1 (W)
Figures: 12 · 10 · 16 · Att 10,474
Scorers: Trebilcock 46, Hiron 63; Kerr 18.
Ref: K Sweet (Aberdare)

Pompey	Sunderland
Milkins	*Montgomery*
Hand	*Malone*
Ley	*Irwin*
Piper	*Todd*
Blant	*Pitt*
Munks	*Porterfield*
McCann	*Harvey*
Trebilcock	*Kerr*
Hiron	*Baker*
Bromley	*Chambers*
Jennings	*Hughes*

Sunderland's Billy Hughes brightens up a bleak day with his white boots, but his late shot against a post means gloom for Alan Brown's team. McCann beat the boo-boys to star. Trebs stroked home Piper's pass before Hiron thumped his first goal for two months after Porterfield's slice.

18 · A LUTON · 21/11 — 1-2 (L)
Figures: 13 · 2 · 16 · Att 16,876
Scorers: McCann 9; Ryan John 8, Givens 50.
Ref: J Thacker (Scarborough)

Pompey	Luton
Milkins	*Read*
Hand	*Ryan John*
Ley*	*Slough*
Piper	*Hoy*
Blant	*Nicholls*
Munks	*Moore**
McCann	*Ryan Jim*
Trebilcock	*Keen*
Hiron	*MacDonald*
Bromley	*Givens*
Jennings	*Busby*
(sub) Travers	(sub) *Bannister*

Tindall describes Pompey's defending as 'comic' after MacDonald's head deflects Givens' shot past Milkins for the winner. John Ryan's free-kick had given Luton the lead, only for McCann to elude two defenders from Hiron's nod down and score left-footed directly from the re-start.

19 · H HULL · 28/11 — 2-2 (D)
Figures: 14 · 5 · 17 · Att 13,360
Scorers: Jennings 77, 83; Butler 63, Chilton 68.
Ref: D Turner (Rugeley)

Pompey	Hull
Milkins	*McKechnie*
Hand	*Banks*
Ley	*Beardsley*
Piper	*Wilkinson*
Blant	*Neill*
Munks	*Simpkin*
McCann	*Lord*
Trebilcock	*Houghton*
Hiron	*Chilton*
Bromley	*Greenwood*
Jennings	*Butler*

The Tigers lead as Chilton heads in from a disputed Lord free-kick, then the same scenario sees Butler's shot creep in. Player-manager Terry Neill's earlier composure disappears when a cross-shot dips into the top corner, then Hiron dummies Treb's cross for Jennings to square it.

20 · A CARLISLE · 5/12 — 0-6 (L)
Figures: 14 · 6 · 17 · Att 7,540
Scorers: Owen 2, 23, Hatton 6, 12, 77, 82.
Ref: C Fallon (Blackpool)

Pompey	Carlisle
Milkins	*Ross*
Hand	*Balderstone*
Ley	*Gorman*
Piper*	*Ternent*
Blant	*Winstanley*
Munks	*Kinsella*
McCann	*Murray*
Pointer	*Barton*
Hiron	*Hatton*
Bromley	*Owen*
Jennings	*Davis*
(sub) Trebilcock	

Milkins has an off-day as Owen nets from Kinsella's pass, then he drops a corner for the lurking Hatton. A rebound off the ref helps set up his second, before Hiron's shot is turned onto the post by Ross. Owen and Hatton complete the rout to silence the jeers of an over-critical crowd.

21 · H OXFORD · 12/12 — 1-0 (W)
Figures: 14 · 8 · 19 · Att 11,456
Scorers: Hiron 28.
Ref: W Castle (Dudley)

Pompey	Oxford
Milkins	*Kearns*
Hand	*Lucas*
Ley	*Shuter*
Piper	*Smithson*
Blant	*Clarke C*
Munks	*Thompson*
Storrie	*Sloan*
Trebilcock	*Atkinson G*
Hiron	*Skeen*
Bromley	*Cassidy*
Jennings	*Atkinson R*

Tindall is off checking the form of a transfer target, despite funds being apparently short. He misses Hiron's floating header past Kearns after Ley's clever throw let Jennings cross. Pompey miss McCann, ruled out by a strained knee on Friday. Gerry Summers' side are on the slide.

LEAGUE DIVISION 2   Manager: Ron Tindall   SEASON 1970-71

Player cells are given as **Portsmouth / Opponent**. The Pos column is given as **Portsmouth position / opponent position**.

No	Date	Att	Pos	Pt	F-A	H-T	Scorers, Times, and Referees	1	2	3	4	5	6	7	8	9	10	11	12 sub used
22	A BOLTON 19/12	5,528	14 / 17	D 20	1-1	1-1	Pointer 37 / Manning 45; Ref: R Kirkpatrick (Leicester)	Milkins / Boswell	Smith / Ritson*	Travers / McAllister	Piper / Williams	Blant / Hulme	Munks / Rimmer	Pointer / Jones G	Trebilcock / Byrom	Hiron / Manning	Bromley / Greaves	Jennings / Phillips	Wharton
23	A SHEFFIELD UTD 9/1	18,665	15 / 4	L 20	0-2	0-1	Tudor 4, Currie 87; Ref: K Walker (Bearsted, Kent)	Milkins / Hodgkinson	Smith / Badger	Youlden / Hemsley	Hand / Powell	Blant / Colquhoun	Munks / Barnwell	Pointer / Woodward	Trebilcock / Tudor	Hiron / Dearden	Bromley / Currie	Jennings / Salmons	
24	H CARDIFF 16/1	24,747	16 / 3	L 20	1-3	0-2	Youlden 58 / Murray 22, Warboys 27, 59; Ref: R Capey (Crewe)	Milkins / Eadie	Smith / Carver	Ley / Bell	Piper / Sutton	Blant / Murray	Munks / Harris	Storrie / King	Trebilcock / Gibson*	Hiron / Warboys	Bromley / Phillips	Jennings* / Rees	Youlden / Clark
25	A HULL 30/1	19,958	15 / 1	W 22	1-0	0-0	Hiron 88; Ref: R Lee (Cheadle)	Milkins / McKechnie	Smith / Banks	Ley / De Vries*	Hand / Wilkinson	Blant / Neill	Munks / Simpkin	Piper / Lord	Youlden / Greenwood	Hiron / Chilton	Bromley / Wagstaffe	Pointer / Butler	Houghton
26	H CARLISLE 6/2	13,219	16 / 7	L 22	1-4	1-1	Hiron 39 / Winstanley 38, Owen 54, Hatton 62, [Murray 90]; Ref: R Challis (Tonbridge)	Milkins / Ross	Smith* / Balderstone	Ley / Gorman	Hand / Ternent	Blant / Winstanley	Munks / Sutton	Piper / Murray	Trebilcock / Martin	Hiron / Owen	Bromley / Hatton	Jennings / Davis	Youlden
27	H LUTON 20/2	13,661	17 / 3	L 22	0-1	0-1	Givens 45; Ref: A Oliver (Leigh-on-Sea)	Milkins / Read	Smith / Ryan John	Ley / Slough	Piper / Hoy	Blant / Nicholls	Munks / Moore	Storrie / Ryan Jim	Pointer* / Givens	Hiron / MacDonald	Travers / Keen	/ Anderson	Youlden
28	A BLACKBURN 27/2	7,269	18 / 19	D 23	1-1	0-1	Pointer 83 / Eccles 5; Ref: C Howell (North Shields)	Milkins / Jones	Smith / Goodwin	Ley / Wood	Hand / Hunter	Youlden / Fazackerley	Munks / Knighton	Piper / Metcalfe*	Pointer / Atherton	Hiron / Eccles	Storrie / Rogers	Jennings / Russell	Charter
29	H QP RANGERS 6/3	10,402	18 / 16	W 25	2-0	0-0	Blant 60, Hiron 64; Ref: I Jones (Treharris)	Milkins / Parkes	Youlden / Watson	Ley* / Clement	Hand / McGovern	Blant / Hunt	Munks / Sibley	Piper / Francis	Pointer / Wilkes	Hiron / Leach	Bromley / Marsh	Jennings / Ferguson	Trebilcock
30	H BRISTOL CITY 10/3	8,676	17 / 19	D 26	1-1	0-1	Hand 75 / Garland 19; Ref: C Thomas (Treorchy)	Milkins / Gibson	Smith / Jacobs	Youlden* / Drysdale	Hand / Winshurst	Blant / Parr	Munks / Hill	Piper / Wilson	Pointer / Garland	Hiron / Galley	Bromley / Gow	Jennings / Tainton	Trebilcock
31	A SUNDERLAND 13/3	10,827	17 / 11	D 27	0-0	0-0	Ref: H Williams (Sheffield)	Milkins / Montgomery	Youlden / Malone	Travers* / Irwin	Hand / Harvey	Blant / Pitt	Munks / Harris	Piper / Park*	Pointer / Kerr*	Storrie / Watson	Bromley / Hughes	Hiron / Tueart	Jennings / Porterfield

Match reports

22 – Bolton: Pompey sacrifice entertainment for points with four in midfield. A first away win looks on when Jennings' cross is rifled home by Pointer, but Bolton level as Manning's 30-yard shot leaves Milkins unsighted. Byrom then hits a post and Gary Jones knocks the rebound over the bar.

23 – Sheffield Utd: The Blades exact revenge for their FA Cup exit after Tudor gives them the perfect start converting Woodward's cross. Milkins makes several good saves and with time running out Trebilcock lifts the siege but his shot hits a defender in the face. From a retaken corner Currie clinches it.

24 – Cardiff: City stun a large crowd after vouchers for the Arsenal cup-tie. Jennings misses a one-on-one with Eadie even before Murray's 25-yard opener. Warboys then heads in Rees' cross. Sub Youlden heads his first Pompey goal, but the rally ends when Warboys follows up his own shot.

25 – Hull: Sandwiched between the Arsenal cup games Pompey stun highflying Hull as Pointer spearheads a late counter attack, draws Terry Neill and plays a perfect pass for Hiron to score and silence the crowd. The Tigers force 17 corners, but prove toothless as Milkins is in inspired form.

26 – Carlisle: After heroics against the Gunners, Pompey capitulate against a United side on the fringes of the promotion race. Winstanley takes advantage of some untidy defending, only for Hiron to cut in and level. After Owen's lob it's all over. Hatton scores before Murray slides in on the whistle.

27 – Luton: Pompey, short of the injured Bromley, struggle to break down a Luton side which has conceded just 19 goals in 27 matches. Don Givens heads the vital goal after Milkins misjudges the cross. Piper can celebrate being called up for an FA squad to tour Australia in the summer.

28 – Blackburn: With Blant and Hiron ruled out by illness just before the kick off, re-shuffled Pompey go behind when Eccles heads in a corner. Second-half pressure sees Storrie head against the bar before Pointer squeezes home a shot after his first one was blocked. Jones denies Storrie at the death.

29 – QP Rangers: QPR miss the hurt Venables, but Pompey have to reshuffle early on when Ley injures knee ligaments after colliding with Milkins. Hand does a terrific job to shackle Marsh, and Blant heads his first Pompey goal. The corner routine works again as Hiron's effort goes in off a defender.

30 – Bristol City: In a match rearranged from Boxing Day, City almost pull off their first away win of the season after Garland's instant control and shot from Tainton's pass beats Milkins. The Robins shut up shop and Milkins hits the post before Hand's free-kick clips off the defensive wall to creep in.

31 – Sunderland: Tindall plays five at the back to stifle Sunderland, but Travers is forced to scuff £100,000-rated Dave Watson's effort off the line. Bromley also blocks shots from Pitt and Hughes. Hiron goes closest, forcing Montgomery to save a cross-shot. Rokermen have no goals or wins in six now.

32 H 20/3 CHARLTON — 10,294 — 16 — W 2-0 — 22 — 29
Hand 60, Jennings 84
Ref: E Wallace (Swindon)
Portsmouth: Milkins, Travers, Youlden, Hand, Blant, Munks, Piper, Pointer, Hiron*, Bromley*, Jennings, Trebilcock
Charlton: *Wright, Curtis, Bruck, Reeves, Went, Shipperley, Treacy, Bond, Endean, Hunt*, Peacock, Plumb*
Charlton boss Theo Foley fumes 'We were utter rubbish and got what we deserved.' Pompey shrug off their injury crisis to take the lead when Jennings keeps the ball in, Treb's flick is saved and Hand scores from a yard. Travers' 50-yard pass sets up Jennings for a memorable goal.

33 A 24/3 OXFORD — 7,517 — 16 — D 1-1 — 14 — 30
Pointer 40; Atkinson G 1
Ref: L Callaghan (Merthyr Tydfil)
Portsmouth: Milkins, Travers, Youlden, Hand, Blant, Munks, Piper, Pointer, Hiron, Bromley, Jennings, Trebilcock
Oxford: *Kearns, Lucas, Shuker, Roberts, Clarke C, Evanson, Sloan, Atkinson G, Skeen, Clarke D, Atkinson R*
A vintage 25-yarder from veteran Pointer levels after Travers' cross fall to him. Oxford score after 45 seconds when Evanson's free-kick sees Ron Atkinson set up his brother Graham with a simple chance. A U's fan runs on and berates the referee after he turned down a late penalty.

34 A 30/3 SHEFFIELD WED — 14,134 — 16 — L 1-3 — 12 — 30
Piper 80; Sinclair 77, Prendergast 81, Sunley 90
Ref: G Jones (Lancaster)
Portsmouth: Milkins*, Youlden, Travers, Hand, Blant, Munks, Piper, Pointer, Hiron, Bromley, Jennings, Trebilcock
Sheffield Wed: *Grummitt, Rodrigues, Burton, Thompson, Prophett, Pugh, Sinclair, Craig, Sunley, Prendergast, Sissons*
Milkins limps off on the hour with a groin strain and Pointer goes in goal, but he can't stop Prendergast's knock-back to Sinclair. Piper levels from Youlden's pass, but Prendergast's looping header, then Sunley's follow-up header after he had hit the bar, seals a flattering result.

35 H 3/4 MILLWALL — 9,668 — 17 — L 0-2 — 10 — 30
Bridges 70, Bolland 87
Ref: J Yates (Redditch)
Portsmouth: Standen, Hand, Youlden, Piper, Blant, Munks, Pointer, Trebilcock, Hiron, Bromley, Jennings
Millwall: *King, Brown B, Cripps, Dorney, Kitchener, Burnett, Possee, Bolland, Bridges, Dunphy, Coxhill*
Standen plays his first league game in 16 months, after former-Chelsea forward Barry Bridges and then Gordon Bolland he is powerless to stop the rebounds. Tindall refuses to criticise the Lions' negative approach 'We would have done the same.'

36 A 9/4 WATFORD — 12,826 — 17 — D 0-0 — 18 — 31
Ref: B Daniels (Rainham)
Portsmouth: Standen, Smith, Youlden, Hand, Blant, Munks, Piper, Pointer, Hiron, Bromley, Jennings
Watford: *Walker, Butler, Packer, Garbett, Lees, Eddy, Scullion, Sinclair, Wigg*, Walley, Woods, Franks*
Tindall is as good as his word, often getting ten men behind the ball to draw the Hornets' sting. Watford boss Ken Furphy phoned the Football League beforehand to ask if Pompey could play on-loan keeper Dave Hollins (from Aldershot) if Standen failed to get over a training injury.

37 A 10/4 BRISTOL CITY — 14,663 — 17 — L 0-2 — 18 — 31
Garland 30, Tainton 86
Ref: A Hart (London)
Portsmouth: Standen, Youlden, Travers, Hand, Blant, Munks, Piper, Storrie, Hiron, Bromley, Jennings, Fear
Bristol City: *Cashley, Jacobs, Drysdale, Tainton, Rooks, Merrick, Wilson, Garland, Galley*, Winshurst, Gow*
With the threat of the drop all but gone, Pompey create just two chances. Storrie misses early on, then Youlden has a shot tipped over near the end. Only Standen's brilliance prevents a rout, but Garland's volley from Rooks' knock-down and Tainton's finish from sub Fear's pass seal it.

38 H 12/4 SWINDON — 10,987 — 17 — L 0-2 — 12 — 31
Peplow 12, 79
Ref: T Reynolds (Swansea)
Portsmouth: Standen, Downsbro'*, Travers, Hand, Blant, Munks, Piper, Pointer, Hiron, Bromley, Jennings
Swindon: *Thomas, Trollope, Butler, Burrows, Harland, Peplow, Smart, Jones C, Noble, Porter*
Fred Ford's Swindon claim only their second away win. Tindall, away scouting, misses Peplow's angled shot after being set up by future Fratton coach Stan Harland. His second sees him nod in after his shot hit the bar. Youlden is unlucky when his shot hits the bar near half-time.

39 H 17/4 MIDDLESBROUGH — 8,916 — 17 — D 1-1 — 6 — 32
Trebilcock 30; McIlmoyle 86
Ref: R Crabb (Exeter)
Portsmouth: Standen, Whigham, Youlden, Pointer, Blant, Munks, Jennings, Trebilcock, Hiron, Piper, Travers
Middlesbrough: *Smith A, Jones, Laidlaw, Gates, Madden, McMordie, McIlmoyle, Hickton, Murray, Downing*, Mills*
Injury-hit Pompey, with five men out, rue Hiron's shot which hit both posts after 65 minutes and another off the bar soon after. Earlier, Piper and Jennings had set up the opener, but Stan Anderson's Boro levelled when McIlmoyle's header off the bar rolled in off Standen's heel.

40 A 24/4 BIRMINGHAM — 19,440 — 16 — D 1-1 — 9 — 33
Hiron 70; Latchford 8
Ref: A Bone (Sunderland)
Portsmouth: Standen, Kelley, Youlden, Pointer, Hand*, Munks, Jennings, Trebilcock, Hiron, Bromley, Travers
Birmingham: *Martin, Page, Pendrey, Hynd, Robinson, Campbell, Francis, Latchford R, Summerill, Taylor, Harris*
Veterans Standen and Pointer star as patched up Pompey pinch a point when Hiron glances home Jennings' centre to cancel out Latchford's early shot. Flu victim Hand is taken off at half-time to allow Harris a rare outing. 'Our full side couldn't have done as well!' beamed Tindall.

41 A 26/4 ORIENT — 3,941 — 16 — D 1-1 — 17 — 34
Hiron 8; Lazarus 61
Ref: M Kerkhof (Bicester)
Portsmouth: Standen, Goddard, Ley, Pointer, Youlden, Munks, Jennings, Trebilcock, Hiron, Bromley, Travers
Orient: *Jones, Rofe, Bennett, Mancini, Allen, Lazarus, Riddick*, Bullock, Dyson, Fairbrother, Brabrook*
Before the game Pompey reveal they turned down Orient's 'derisory' £2,000 offer for Trebilcock. Pompey are cruising against The O's, who haven't won at home in two months, after Hiron's majestic header from Jennings's 'away swinger', but Lazarus's header silences the jeers.

42 H 1/5 LEICESTER — 18,795 — 16 — L 1-2 — 1 — 34
Hiron 90; Farrington 8, Brown 25
Ref: K Burns (Dudley)
Portsmouth: Standen, Smith, Youlden, Pointer, Hand*, Munks, Piper, Trebilcock, Hiron, Harris, Jennings, Travers
Leicester: *Shilton, Whitworth, Nish, Kellard, Manley, Cross, Farrington, Brown, Fern, Carling*, Stringfellow, Partridge*
Frank O'Farrell's side clinch the championship, backed by a large contingent. Farrington curls home the opener, then Ally Brown reacts first to float in Kellard's slice. Harris is skipper for his last Pompey game after 13 years, but Hiron's fierce shot on time can't provide a happy ending.

Home 13,792
Away 13,519
Average 13,792

LEAGUE DIVISION 2 (CUP-TIES)   Manager: Ron Tindall   SEASON 1970-71

League Cup

1 — H PLYMOUTH, 19/8 — W, F-A 2-0, H-T 0-0 — 12,846 (3)
Scorers, Times, and Referees: McCann 51p, Storrie 67. Ref: M Kerkhof (Bicester)

	1	2	3	4	5	6	7	8	9	10	11	12 sub used
Pompey	Milkins	Smith	Ley	Piper	Blant	Munks	McCann	Storrie	Hiron	Bromley	Jennings	
Plymouth	*Dunne*	*Woolbridge*	*Sullivan*	*Hore*	*Molyneux*	*Saxton*	*Maher**	*Allen*	*Bickle*	*Burnside*	*Hutchins*	*Rickard*

Frittered chances in the first half are forgotten when Woolbridge's backpass forces Dunne to bring down Storrie and McCann converts. Storrie then scores from close range after Hiron diverts the ball past the keeper. Man of the Match is Jennings, returning to his orthodox left-wing role.

2 — H WALSALL, 9/9 — W, F-A 1-0, H-T 1-0 — 15,967 (3:16)
Scorers, Times, and Referees: Piper 8. Ref: C Nicholls (Plymouth)

	1	2	3	4	5	6	7	8	9	10	11	12 sub used
Pompey	Milkins	Smith	Ley	Piper	Blant	Munks	McCann	Storrie	Hiron	Bromley	Jennings	
Walsall	*Wesson*	*Harrison*	*Evans*	*Bennett*	*Jones*	*Atthey*	*Morris*	*Baker*	*Woodward*	*Penman*	*Taylor*	

A fifth clean sheet in seven games fails to disguise a laboured win over the plucky third division side. Piper scores with a deft shot after Ley's corner is half-cleared. Blant courageously plays on with a neck injury, but almost concedes a penalty with a clumsy challenge on Woodward.

3 — A MANCHESTER U, 7/10 — L, F-A 0-1, H-T 0-0 — 32,080 (1:14)
Scorers, Times, and Referees: Charlton 61. Ref: D Lyden (Birmingham)

	1	2	3	4	5	6	7	8	9	10	11	12 sub used
Pompey	Milkins	Smith	Ley	McCann	Blant	Munks	Storrie	Trebilcock	Hiron	Piper	Jennings	
Manchester U	*Rimmer*	*Donald*	*Burns*	*Fitzpatrick*	*Ure*	*Sadler**	*Morgan*	*Gowling*	*Charlton*	*Kidd*	*Best*	*Aston*

The agility of Jimmy Rimmer denies Storrie then McCann in the dying minutes, as Pompey lose their record of never losing in a Cup at Old Trafford. A Charlton 25-yard 'special' meant an uphill struggle from then on, especially when Smith was carried off with a serious knee injury.

FA Cup

3 — H SHEFFIELD UTD, 2/1 — W (17), F-A 2-0, H-T 0-0 — 20,556 (2:4)
Scorers, Times, and Referees: Hiron 57, Trebilcock 85. Ref: D Lyden (Birmingham)

	1	2	3	4	5	6	7	8	9	10	11	12 sub used
Pompey	Milkins	Smith	Youlden	Hand	Blant	Munks	Trebilcock	Piper	Hiron	Bromley	Jennings	
Sheffield Utd	*Hodgkinson*	*Badger*	*Hemsley*	*Powell*	*Colquhoun*	*Barnwell*	*Woodward*	*Tudor*	*Dearden*	*Currie*	*Salmons*	

Pompey blunt a Blades team who had scored 15 goals in the three previous meetings between the clubs. Youlden's pass sets up Hiron to ease the tension, then Bilco caps one of his best performances with a 25-yard shot from Hiron's pass. 'Give the team credit,' said chairman Collett.

4 — H ARSENAL, 23/1 — D (16), F-A 1-1, H-T 0-1 — 39,659 (1:2)
Scorers, Times, and Referees: Trebilcock 90 / *Storey 35p*. Ref: R Johnson (Lowestoft)

	1	2	3	4	5	6	7	8	9	10	11	12 sub used
Pompey	Milkins	Smith	Ley	Hand	Blant	Munks	Piper	Trebilcock	Hiron	Bromley	Jennings	Pointer*
Arsenal	*Wilson*	*Rice*	*McNab*	*Storey*	*McLintock*	*Simpson*	*Armstrong*	*Sammels*	*Radford*	*Kennedy*	*George*	*Youlden*

Cup specialist Trebilcock pops up at the far post to convert Smith's cross, after Radford had lost possession, to seal a famous result. In driving rain Pompey push the championship chasers all the way after Storey had opened the scoring from the a spot after Ley's punch off the line.

4R — A ARSENAL, 1/2 — L (15), F-A 2-3, H-T 1-2 — 47,865 (1:2)
Scorers, Times, and Referees: Piper 5, Ley 58 / *George 13, Simpson 32, Storey 84p*. Ref: R Johnson (Lowestoft)

	1	2	3	4	5	6	7	8	9	10	11	12 sub used
Pompey	Milkins	Smith	Ley	Hand	Blant	Munks	Piper	Trebilcock	Hiron	Bromley !	Jennings	
Arsenal	*Wilson*	*Rice*	*McNab*	*Storey*	*McLintock*	*Simpson*	*Armstrong*	*Sammels*	*Radford*	*Kennedy*	*George*	

Storey slots in a late penalty to settle a niggling affair. Piper nets from Jennings' corner, but George's fizzing shot and Simpson's close-range effort put the Gunners on top. Ley's half-hit shot levels it before the finale which also sees Bromley sent off later on for alleged retaliation.

League Table

	P	Home					Away					Pts
		W	D	L	F	A	W	D	L	F	A	
1 Leicester	42	12	7	2	30	14	11	6	4	27	16	59
2 Sheffield Utd	42	14	6	1	49	18	8	6	7	24	21	56
3 Cardiff	42	12	7	2	39	16	8	6	7	25	25	53
4 Carlisle	42	16	3	2	39	13	4	10	7	26	30	53
5 Hull	42	11	5	5	31	16	8	8	5	23	25	51
6 Luton	42	12	7	2	40	18	6	6	9	22	25	49
7 Middlesbro	42	13	6	2	37	16	4	8	9	23	27	48
8 Millwall	42	13	5	3	36	12	6	4	11	23	30	47
9 Birmingham	42	12	7	2	30	12	5	5	11	28	36	46
10 Norwich	42	11	8	2	34	20	4	6	11	20	32	44
11 QP Rangers	42	11	5	5	39	22	6	5	10	19	31	43
12 Swindon	42	12	7	2	38	14	3	5	13	23	37	42
13 Sunderland	42	11	6	4	34	21	4	6	11	18	33	42
14 Oxford	42	8	8	5	23	23	6	6	9	18	25	42
15 Sheffield Wed	42	10	7	4	32	27	2	5	14	19	42	36
16 PORTSMOUTH	42	9	4	8	32	28	1	10	10	14	33	34
17 Orient	42	5	11	5	16	15	4	5	12	13	36	34
18 Watford	42	6	7	8	18	22	4	6	11	20	38	33
19 Bristol City	42	9	6	6	30	28	1	5	15	16	36	31
20 Charlton	42	7	6	8	28	30	1	8	12	13	35	30
21 Blackburn	42	5	8	8	20	28	1	7	13	17	41	27
22 Bolton	42	6	5	10	22	31	1	5	15	13	43	24
	924	225	141	96	697	444	96	141	225	444	697	924

Appearances and Goals

	Appearances						Goals			
	Lge	Sub	LC	Sub	FAC	Sub	Lge	LC	FAC	Tot
Blant, Colin	37		3		3		1			1
Bromley, Brian	33		2		3		1			1
Hand, Eoin	29				3		2			2
Harris, Harry	1	1								
Hiron, Ray	39		3		3		13	1		14
Jennings, Nicky	40	1	2		2		8			8
Ley, George	28		3		2				1	1
McCann, Albert	18						3		1	4
Milkins, John	34		3		3					
Munks, David	42		3		3		1			1
Piper, Norman	42		3		3		3	1	1	5
Pointer, Ray	20				1		4			4
Smith, Fred	23		3		3					
Standen, Jim	8									
Storrie, Jim	21		3				1	1		2
Travers, Mick	11	4								
Trebilcock, Mike	19	5	1		3		8		2	10
Youlden, Tommy	17	5			1	1	1			1
18 players used	462	10	33		33	1	46	3	5	54

Odds & ends

Double Wins: (0).

Double Losses: (6) Cardiff, Carlisle, Leicester, Luton, Sheffield Utd, Swindon.

Won from behind: (1) Sunderland (h).

Lost from in front: (1) Middlesbrough (a).

High spots: Mike Trebilcock's two hat-tricks in October.

The two FA Cup matches with Arsenal.

Winning 1-0 at promotion chasing Hull in January.

Seven match unbeaten start to the season in league and cup.

Low spots: Losing 1-5 at home to Sheffield Utd for the second season in a row.

Failing to win any of the last ten league matches.

Losing 0-6 at Carlisle for the heaviest defeat since 1965.

Just a solitary away win all season at Hull.

Player of the Year: David Munks.

Hat-tricks: Mike Trebilcock (2).

Ever-presents: (2) Norman Piper and David Munks.

Leading Scorer: Ray Hiron (14).

LEAGUE DIVISION 2 — Manager: Ron Tindall — SEASON 1971-72

No	Date	Venue	Opponent	Att	Pos (Pompey/opp)	Pt	Res	F-A	H-T	Scorers, Times, and Referees
1	14/8	H	MIDDLESBROUGH	15,649		2	W	2-1	1-1	Storrie 19, McCann 90 / Vincent 43 / Ref: A Hart (London)
2	21/8	A	NORWICH	13,787	15 / 5	2	L	1-3	1-3	Reynolds 20 / Darling 3, Silvester 22, Foggo 44 / Ref: D Corbett (Wolverhampton)
3	28/8	H	BIRMINGHAM	14,729	10 / 14	4	W	1-0	1-0	Trebilcock 13 / Ref: K Sweet (Aberdare)
4	1/9	H	BLACKPOOL	16,058	15 / 1	4	L	1-3	1-2	Hand 18 / Burns 1, James 15, 86 / Ref: F Bassett (Swindon)
5	4/9	A	SHEFFIELD WED	13,170	13 / 22	5	D	1-1	1-1	Hiron 8 / Joicey 4 / Ref: V Batty (Helsby)
6	11/9	H	ORIENT	10,966	9 / 14	7	W	3-2	1-1	Trebilcock 14, Hand 64, Hiron 70 / Brisley 25, Bowyer 78 / Ref: G Hill (Leicester)
7	18/9	A	HULL	14,363	6 / 14	9	W	3-1	0-0	Piper 70, Hand 72, McCann 74 / Pearson 85 / Ref: R Matthewson (Manchester)
8	25/9	H	MILLWALL	15,485	10 / 4	10	D	1-1	1-1	Hiron 43 / Bridges 20 / Ref: G Pugh (Chester)
9	2/10	A	WATFORD	11,633	12 / 19	10	L	0-1	0-0	Williams 76 / Ref: F Nicholson (Manchester)
10	9/10	H	PRESTON	12,749	12 / 16	11	D	1-1	1-1	Trebilcock 7 / McIlmoyle 23 / Ref: R Toseland (Kettering)

Line-ups (columns 1–12 sub used)

No	Team	1	2	3	4	5	6	7	8	9	10	11	12
1	Pompey	Milkins	Smith	Ley	McCann	Blant	Youden	Piper	Reynolds	Hiron	Collins	Storrie	Hand
1	Middlesbrough	Whigham	Maddren	Jones	Stiles	Boam	Spraggon	Downing	Mills	Hickton	Vincent	Laidlaw*	Allen
2	Pompey	Milkins	Smith	Ley	McCann	Hand	Youden	Piper	Reynolds	Hiron	Collins*	Storrie	Travers
2	Norwich	Keelan	Payne	Butler	Stringer	Forbes	Anderson	Darling	Silvester	Livermore	Paddon*	Foggo	Howard
3	Pompey	Standen	Smith	Ley	Hand	Blant	Youden	Piper	Reynolds	Hiron	McCann	Trebilcock	
3	Birmingham	Latchford D	Martin	Page	Smith	Hynd	Pendrey	Campbell	Bowker*	Latchford R	Summerill	Taylor	Robinson
4	Pompey	Standen	Smith	Ley	Hand	Blant	Youden	Piper	Reynolds	Hiron	McCann	Trebilcock	
4	Blackpool	Burridge	Hatton	Bentley	Booth	Alcock	Suddaby	Burns	Green	James	Suddick	Hutchinson	
5	Pompey	Standen	Smith	Ley	Hand*	Blant	Youden	Piper	Reynolds	Hiron	McCann	Trebilcock	Munks
5	Sheffield Wed	Grummitt	Rodrigues	Thompson	Prophett	Holsgrove	Clements	Sinclair	Craig	Joicey	Prendergast	Sissons	
6	Pompey	Standen	Smith	Ley	Hand*	Blant	Youden	McCann	Reynolds	Hiron	Piper	Trebilcock	Munks
6	Orient	Goddard	Jones	Rofe	Allen	Mancini	Harris	Lazarus	Brisley	Bullock*	Dyson	Bowyer	Sewell
7	Pompey	Milkins	Smith	Ley	Hand	Blant	Youden	McCann	Reynolds	Hiron	Piper	Trebilcock	
7	Hull	McKechnie	Banks*	De Vries	Wilkinson	Neill	Knighton	Greenwood P	Simkin	Pearson	Wagstaffe	Butler	Lord
8	Pompey	Milkins	Smith	Ley	Hand	Blant	Youden	Piper	Reynolds	Hiron	McCann	Trebilcock	
8	Millwall	King	Brown B	Cripps	Dorney	Kitchener	Burnett	Possee	Bolland	Bridges	Smethurst	Allder	
9	Pompey	Milkins	Smith	Ley	Hand	Blant	Youden	Piper	Reynolds	Hiron	McCann	Trebilcock	
9	Watford	Walker M	Butler	Williams	Welbourne	Woodfield*	Walley	McGettigan	Eddy	Wigg	Lindsay	Franks	Lugg
10	Pompey	Milkins	Smith	Ley	Hand	Blant	Youden*	Piper	Reynolds	Hiron	McCann	Trebilcock	
10	Preston	Kelly	McMahon	McNab*	Bird	Hawkins	Spavin	Heppolette	Ham	McIlmoyle	Lyall	Ingram	Spark

Match reports

1 — Middlesbrough: Lone yachtsman Chay Blyth is guest of honour as McCann's 18-yard shot from Piper's pass seals the points at the death. Earlier, new-boy Collins and Hiron had combined to set up Storrie to flick home, then Vincent surprised Milkins on his near post after cutting in from the left.

2 — Norwich: Tindall concedes the score flattered Pompey. Darling opens by latching on to Silvester's flick, but Reynolds levels despite a strong challenge as he shoots. Immediately, Milkins flapped at a corner and Silvester prodded in. City clinch it as Pompey lose the ball and Foggo runs clear.

3 — Birmingham: Referee Sweet turns sour for Pompey as he rules out goals for Reynolds and Hand, and then turns down a clear penalty when Pendrey flattens Reynolds. However, the 13th minute proves lucky for Trebilcock, as Ley's shot hits his back and sends Dave Latchford the wrong way.

4 — Blackpool: Newly-relegated Pool show their class, racing ahead after 40 seconds when Burns glances home Suddaby's centre. Defender-turned-striker James then follows suit, but Hand drags Pompey back with a brave diving header. Suddaby hits a post, before James' glancing header seals it.

5 — Sheffield Wed: Brian Joicey makes a stunning debut after his £100,000 joint move from Coventry, with Clements, intercepting Blant's back pass and slotting home. Trebilcock and Ley then work a short corner and Hiron turns in the cross. Hand has seven stitches after a clash of heads with Holsgrove.

6 — Orient: Trebilcock's stunning volley from Reynolds' quick break opens the scoring. Brisley levels, but Pompey take control when Hand, with seven stitches in a cut head, sees his shot deflect in. Hiron heads a third, but Standen's dropped cross lets in Bowyer and sets up a tense finish.

7 — Hull: Hull player-manager Terry Neill is forced to leave the field with a nose injury and it turns the match. Piper nets at once from Trebilcock's pass, then good work from Hiron allows Hand to score from close in. McCann wraps it up despite a defender's efforts, with Neill about to return.

8 — Millwall: Tindall praises Millwall keeper Bryan King after he defies Pompey: 'His save from Hiron turned the game.' Old-stager Barry Bridges latches on to McCann's bad backpass for a flick finish. Hiron earns a deserved point when his fine control and shot from Reynold's pass squeezes in.

9 — Watford: Tindall is bitterly disappointed with his team, as lowly Watford show more grit. Milkins turns Franks' shot against the post in the first minute, but Williams run and 25-yard shot doesn't settle it until late on. Pompey's best efforts see Trebs hit Mike Walker's legs, then he heads wide.

10 — Preston: An imperious finish by Trebilcock after Reynolds had headed into his path proves the high-spot, as promoted Preston take control. Before McIlmoyle heads the equaliser, the striker missed a twice-taken penalty following Smith's handball. 'We looked very ordinary', said Tindall.

Portsmouth 1971–72 — match log (games 11–21)

#	Venue	Opponent	Date	Pos	Res	Score	Att		
11	A	MIDDLESBROUGH	16/10	14	L	1-2	16,376	5	11
12	H	BRISTOL CITY	20/10	13	D	1-1	12,575	3	12
13	H	FULHAM	23/10	10	W	6-3	14,172	20	14
14	A	QP RANGERS	30/10	9	D	1-1	15,934	6	15
15	H	SUNDERLAND	6/11	10	D	2-2	14,387	8	16
16	A	CARLISLE	13/11	10	L	0-1	7,955	11	16
17	H	OXFORD	20/11	11	W	2-0	10,423	17	18
18	A	LUTON	27/11	11	L	2-3	9,910	16	18
19	A	CARDIFF	1/12	11	L	2-3	10,268	21	18
20	H	CHARLTON	4/12	12	D	0-0	10,007	13	19
21	A	BURNLEY	11/12	11	W	3-1	11,338	8	21

---

11 — A MIDDLESBROUGH, L 1-2
Scorers: Reynolds 27 / Hickton 1, Vincent 10
Ref: C Fallon (Blackpool)
Pompey: Milkins, Smith, Ley, Hand, Blant, Munks, Piper, Reynolds, Hiron, McCann, Trebilcock*, (sub) Jennings
Middlesbrough: Platt, Craggs, Jones, Moody, Boam, Gates, Laidlaw, McMordie, Maddren, Hickton, Vincent

Pompey slump to their ninth successive defeat at Ayresome Park as some inept defensive work allows Hickton and then Vincent the freedom of the penalty area to head home. Reynolds heads home Trebilcock's corner, and nearly levels before half-time, but shoots just over.

12 — H BRISTOL CITY, D 1-1
Scorers: Ley 57 / Spring 82
Ref: B Daniels (Rainham)
Pompey: Milkins, Smith, Ley, Hand, Youlden, Munks, Piper, Reynolds, Hiron, McCann, Trebilcock, (sub) Jennings
Bristol City: Cashley, Wimshurst, Drysdale, Emanuel, Rooks, Merrick, Tainton, Spring, Galley, Sweeney, Gow

City keep their good start going when Gow surges past three defenders to set Spring up for a spectacular shot, then a rash tackle on the same player by Munks almost earns a penalty. Earlier, Ley's bending free kick had put Pompey on top after Milkins denied Galley in the first half.

13 — H FULHAM, W 6-3
Scorers: Jen 25, 87, Rey 31, Treb 54, Smith 71 / Conway 67p, 79, Barrett 81 [Hand 57.]
Ref: R Crabb (Exeter)
Pompey: Milkins, Smith, Ley, Hand, Youlden, Munks, Piper, Reynolds, Trebilcock, McCann, Jennings
Fulham: Webster, Pentecost, Callaghan, Richardson, Matthewson, Dunne, Conway, Jim Johnston, Earle, Lloyd, Barrett

Fulham director, comedian Tommy Trinder, was still smiling despite this mauling, recorded by ITV. Recalled Jennings is inspired, steering in a poor clearance, then finishing the rout after skipping past two defenders. Smith lobs his only Pompey goal in the best home win since 1959.

14 — A QP RANGERS, D 1-1
Scorers: Piper 68 / Morgan 75
Ref: D Laing (Preston)
Pompey: Milkins, Smith, Ley, Hand, Youlden, Munks, Piper, Reynolds, Trebilcock, McCann, Jennings
QP Rangers: Parkes, Hazell, Clement, Venables, Hunt, Mancini, Busby*, Francis, O'Rourke, Marsh, Saul

The team's Loftus Road bogey – three 0-2 defeats in a row – is laid, but Tindall claims 'We should have won comfortably.' Trebilcock hit a post early on, but Piper volleyed in from Reynolds' flick. QPR levelled out of the blue when sub Morgan netted from the edge of the box.

15 — H SUNDERLAND, D 2-2
Scorers: Piper 9, Trebilcock 38p / Watson 44, Tueart 89
Ref: R Challis (Tonbridge)
Pompey: Milkins, Smith, Ley, Hand, Youlden, Munks, Piper, Reynolds, Trebilcock, McCann, Jennings
Sunderland: Montgomery, Malone, Coleman, Harvey, Pitt, McGiven, Chambers, Kerr, Watson, Hughes, Tueart

Sunderland earn a draw at the death when Tueart hits the bar, then nets Hughes' cross from the rebound. Pompey led when Ley and Jennings combined for Piper's calm header. Trebs scored from the spot after Chambers fouled Piper, but Watson's 20-yarder set up the comeback.

16 — A CARLISLE, L 0-1
Scorers: Martin 63
Ref: D Turner (Rugeley)
Pompey: Milkins, Smith, Ley, Hand, Youlden, Munks, Piper, Reynolds, Trebilcock, McCann, Jennings*
Carlisle: Ross, Hemstead, Gorman, Ternent, Winstanley, Barton, Balderstone, Martin, Owen*, Webb, Bowles, (sub) Sutton

Alan Ashman's Carlisle pin Pompey back for long spells, but Tindall reacts angrily to suggestions that his team were defensive. 'We played 4-2-4 against their 4-3-3,' he said. The crucial goal comes after a third successive corner, when Martin's header deflects in via Smith's shoulder.

17 — H OXFORD, W 2-0
Scorers: Jennings 70, Trebilcock 88
Ref: J Yates (Redditch)
Pompey: Milkins, Smith, Ley, Hand, Youlden, Munks, Piper, Reynolds, Trebilcock, McCann, Jennings
Oxford: Burton, Lucas, Shuker, Roberts, Clarke C, Evanson, Sloan, Atkinson G, Cassidy, Clarke D, Aylott

This match was heading for a stalemate when the floodlights failed early in the second half. After a short delay, because the timer had been set an hour too early, Jennings's topped shot deflected in off Shuker, then Trebilcock's near post shot finished it. Cassidy had two disallowed.

18 — A LUTON, L 2-3
Scorers: Reynolds 5, 40 / Keen 50, Hindson 57, Anderson 85
Ref: C Nicholls (Plymouth)
Pompey: Standen, Smith, Ley, Hand, Youlden, Munks, Piper, Reynolds, Trebilcock, McCann, Jennings
Luton: Reed, Ryan John, Slough, Court, Nicholl, Moore, Anderson, Busby*, Givens, Keen, Halom

According to Tindall 'We scaled the heights and plumbed the depths', as Luton hit back. Reynolds sharp reaction from a misplaced header, and a fierce shot after McCann's skill, seems enough. Luton level through Keen, then Hindson's 30-yarder. Givens seals it via Munks' legs.

19 — A CARDIFF, L 2-3
Scorers: Hiron 54, Trebilcock 75 / Gibson 37p, Clark 40, Woodruff 78
Ref: G Kew (Leeds)
Pompey: Milkins, Smith, Ley, Hand, Youlden, Munks, Piper, Reynolds, Hiron, McCann, Jennings
Cardiff: Irwin, Carver, Bell, Phillips, Morgan, Derrett, Villars*, Clark, Couch, Woodruff, Rees

Pompey claw back from two-down when the returning Hiron converts Piper's square pass. Then Trebilcock nets after Derrett slips, but Munks misses Gibson's pass to allow Woodruff to clinch it. Earlier Smith's handball allowed Gibson to score from the spot and Clark headed home.

20 — H CHARLTON, D 0-0
Ref: D Biddle (Bristol)
Pompey: Milkins, Smith, Collins, Pointer, Blant, Munks, Piper, Reynolds, Trebilcock, McCann, Hiron*
Charlton: Dunn, Reeves, Warman, Bond, Went, Shipperley, Davies, Treacy, Hunt, Rogers, Peacock

Charlton keeper John Dunn quipped 'Tell me when they're coming!' to photographers as the fog swirled around. Collins, in his first game for three months, was impressive, and McCann nearly pinched a goal at the end. 'I thought it was a good game,' was Tindall's minority view.

21 — A BURNLEY, W 3-1
Scorers: Nutty 35 (og), McCann 62, Reynolds 82 / Waldron 21
Ref: J Hunting (Leicester)
Pompey: Milkins, Smith, Collins, Pointer, Blant, Munks, Piper, Reynolds, Trebilcock, McCann, Jennings
Burnley: Mellor, Docherty, Nutty, Bellamy, Waldron, Dobson, Thomas, West, Fletcher, Casper, James

Burnley take advantage of the strong breeze as Waldron's left-foot volley finds the top corner, but then Nutty's back-pass sails over his keeper before half-time. Pointer stars against his former club. McCann scores from just inside the box. Reynolds' volley seals a famous Pompey win.

LEAGUE DIVISION 2 Manager: Ron Tindall SEASON 1971-72

No	Date	Att	Pos	Pt	F-A	H-T	Scorers, Times, and Referees	1	2	3	4	5	6	7	8	9	10	11	12 sub used
22	H SHEFFIELD WED 18/12	10,280	12 *10*	L 21	1-2	0-0	Trebilcock 87 / Pugh 49, Craig 66p / Ref: K Walker (Ashford)	Milkins	Smith	Collins	Pointer	Hand	Blant	Piper	Reynolds	Trebilcock	McCann	Hiron	
							(opp)	*Grummitt*	*Rodrigues*	*Clements*	*Prophett*	*Holsgrove*	*Pugh*	*Sinclair*	*Craig*	*Joicey*	*Prendergast*	*Sissons*	

Owls¹ – one loss in ten - midfield overwhelms Pompey. Sissons and Clements work a free-kick to Prendergast to set up Pugh, then Collins brings down Sinclair in the box for Craig to make the game safe for Derek Dooley's men. Trebs' heel deflects Smith's shot, but it's too late.

No	Date	Att	Pos	Pt	F-A	H-T	Scorers, Times, and Referees	1	2	3	4	5	6	7	8	9	10	11	12 sub used
23	A SWINDON 27/12	20,494	13 *14*	L 21	1-3	0-1	Piper 83 / Bunkell 7, Rogers 46, 65 / Ref: P Walters (Bridgwater)	Milkins	Smith	Ley	Piper	Hand	Blant	Jennings	Reynolds	Trebilcock	McCann	Hiron	
							(opp)	*Allan*	*Thomas*	*Trollope*	*Butler*	*Burrows*	*Mackay*	*Dangerfield*	*Bunkell*	*Horsfield*	*Noble*	*Rogers*	

Missed chances cost Pompey dear in this Boxing Day clash. Before Rogers raced away from Trollope's pass, Trebilcock should have levelled Bunkell's early shot which deflected in off Hand. Rogers' superb left-footer sealed it, but Piper replied, turning in Hiron's knock-down.

No	Date	Att	Pos	Pt	F-A	H-T	Scorers, Times, and Referees	1	2	3	4	5	6	7	8	9	10	11	12 sub used
24	H HULL 1/1	8,665	14 *21*	D 22	0-0	0-0	Ref: D Corbett (Wolverhampton)	Milkins	Smith	Collins	Piper	Hand	Blant	Jennings	Reynolds	Hiron	Ley	McCann	
							(opp)	*McKechnie*	*Banks**	*De Vries*	*Wilkinson*	*Green*	*Knighton*	*McGill*	*Lord*	*Pearson*	*Wagstaffe*	*Butler*	

Chairman John Collett toasts the New Year with champagne in the club's traditional Loving Cup ceremony, but there is little to cheer. Knighton's lobbed back-pass forces his anxious keeper to crash into a post. Tindall, scouting in Scotland, is set to bid for Dumbarton striker McCormack.

No	Date	Att	Pos	Pt	F-A	H-T	Scorers, Times, and Referees	1	2	3	4	5	6	7	8	9	10	11	12 sub used
25	A BIRMINGHAM 8/1	22,410	17 *5*	L 22	3-6	2-3	McC'n 7, Ley 21, Hiron 72 [Francis 88] / Hat' 26, 42, Latch' 83, 90, Camp' 30p / Ref: G Jones (Lancaster)	Milkins	Smith	Collins	Piper	Hand	Blant	Jennings	Trebilcock	Hiron	Ley	McCann	
							(opp)	*Cooper*	*Carroll*	*Pendrey**	*Page*	*Hynd*	*Harrison*	*Campbell*	*Francis*	*Latchford R*	*Hatton*	*Taylor*	*Smith*

Teenager Francis is on song, but Pompey race away through McCann's and Ley's free-kick. Hiron's error lets in Hatton, and Hand's foul gives away a penalty. Hiron levels Hatton's second, but Francis volleys the best goal and Latchford seals a happy debut for keeper Cooper (18).

No	Date	Att	Pos	Pt	F-A	H-T	Scorers, Times, and Referees	1	2	3	4	5	6	7	8	9	10	11	12 sub used
26	H CARDIFF 22/1	11,039	16 *20*	W 24	2-0	2-0	Trebilcock 7, Ley 23 / Ref: D Smith (Stonehouse)	Milkins	Smith	Collins	Wilson	Hand	Blant	Piper	Reynolds	Trebilcock	Ley	Jennings	
							(opp)	*Irwin*	*Carver*	*Bell*	*Phillips*	*Murray*	*Sutton*	*Gibson*	*Clark*	*Warboys*	*Woodruff*	*Foggon**	*King*

Wilson starts after a £15,000 move from Blackburn, but Irwin's howlers make the headlines. First he doesn't see Reynolds nip in as he rolls the ball out to set up Trebilcock, then he takes his eyes off Ley's low cross. 'He had a bad one,' says City boss and Fratton old-boy Jimmy Scoular.

No	Date	Att	Pos	Pt	F-A	H-T	Scorers, Times, and Referees	1	2	3	4	5	6	7	8	9	10	11	12 sub used
27	A BRISTOL CITY 29/1	10,949	15 *14*	D 25	1-1	1-1	Jennings 25 / Galley 21 / Ref: B Homewood (Sunbury)	Milkins	Smith	Collins	Wilson	Hand	Blant	Piper	Reynolds	Trebilcock	Ley	Jennings	
							(opp)	*Bond*	*Jacobs*	*Drysdale*	*Gow*	*Bruton*	*Merrick*	*Tainton*	*Wilson*	*Galley*	*Sweeney*	*Bartley*	

In injury-time Piper slots home after collecting a ricochet from a defender, only for a linesman's flag to rule out the goal to the bemusement of everyone. City ease ahead when Galley's mis-hit shot deflects in, but Collins hits back at once and his shot is parried for Jennings to pounce.

No	Date	Att	Pos	Pt	F-A	H-T	Scorers, Times, and Referees	1	2	3	4	5	6	7	8	9	10	11	12 sub used
28	A FULHAM 12/2	8,390	14 *20*	D 26	1-1	0-1	Reynolds 78 / Cross 27 / Ref: I Jones (Treharris)	Milkins	Smith	Collins	Wilson	Hand	Blant	Piper	Reynolds	Trebilcock*	Ley	Jennings	McCann
							(opp)	*Webster*	*Moreline*	*Callaghan*	*Brown*	*Richardson*	*Matthewson*	*Conway*	*Jim Cross*	*Earle*	*Lloyd*	*Barrett*	

Tindall says it was the 'worst performance of the season', but Pompey nearly pinch it when Reynolds goes close. Earlier, Cross seized on confusion between Blant and Hand, but Reynolds levelled from Ley's corner. Their new £250,000 Riverside Stand opens soon against Benfica.

No	Date	Att	Pos	Pt	F-A	H-T	Scorers, Times, and Referees	1	2	3	4	5	6	7	8	9	10	11	12 sub used
29	H QP RANGERS 19/2	15,563	12 *13*	W 28	1-0	0-0	Reynolds 71 / Ref: P Walters (Bridgwater)	Milkins	Smith	Collins	Wilson	Hand	Blant	Piper	Reynolds	Hiron	Ley	Jennings	
							(opp)	*Parkes*	*Clement*	*Hazell*	*Busby*	*Hunt*	*Mancini*	*O'Rourke*	*Francis*	*Leach*	*Marsh*	*Ferguson*	

Young QPR keeper Phil Parkes stood between his team and a thrashing with a string of fine saves. Reynolds finally scored with an unstoppable shot into the roof of the net from 18 yards. Earlier, O'Rourke had clipped the outside of the post and Leach had spooned over from six yards.

No	Date	Att	Pos	Pt	F-A	H-T	Scorers, Times, and Referees	1	2	3	4	5	6	7	8	9	10	11	12 sub used
30	A SUNDERLAND 1/3	8,273	13 *3*	L 28	2-3	0-1	Piper 71p, Wilson 87 / Lathan 20, 48, 59 / Ref: V Batty (Helsby)	Milkins	Smith	Collins	Wilson	Hand	Blant	Piper	Reynolds	Hiron	Ley	Storrie	
							(opp)	*Forster*	*Malone*	*Coleman*	*Harvey*	*Pitt*	*Porterfield*	*McGiven*	*Kerr*	*Watson*	*Lathan*	*Tueart*	

The miners' strike means a midweek daytime kick-off to avoid the risk of power cuts. Lathan (19), later to play for Pompey, is set up twice by Watson, before claiming a treble with a close-range header. Forster fouls Reynolds for the penalty, then Wilson's 25-yarder means a tense end.

No	Date	Att	Pos	Pt	F-A	H-T	Scorers, Times, and Referees	1	2	3	4	5	6	7	8	9	10	11	12 sub used
31	H CARLISLE 4/3	9,098	13 *7*	W 30	1-0	0-0	Ley 49 / Ref: R Crabb (Exeter)	Milkins	Smith	Collins	Wilson	Hand	Blant	Piper	Reynolds	Hiron	Ley	Storrie	
							(opp)	*Ross*	*Hemstead*	*Gorman*	*Tennent*	*Delgado*	*Bowles**	*Barton*	*Martin*	*Owen*	*Train*	*Balderstone*	*Webb*

According to The News, defensive Carlisle put up a 'Hadrian's Wall' as Reynolds and Piper have efforts hacked clear in the first half. Ley's decisive 25-yard scorcher is rubbed in as the U's make for their long coach ride home; Pompey's team are off to fly to Guernsey for four days.

Portsmouth (Pompey) — match record, games 32–42

#	V	Opponent	Date	Att	Opp pos	Res	Score		Pts
32	A	PRESTON	11/3	10,575	15	L	0–4	10	30
33	H	NORWICH	18/3	13,902	12	W	2–1	1	32
34	A	ORIENT	24/3	9,492	13	L	1–2	19	32
35	A	MILLWALL	31/3	21,919	2	L	0–1	13	32
36	H	SWINDON	1/4	12,157	14	L	1–2	12	32
37	H	WATFORD	3/4	7,909	16	D	2–2	22	33
38	A	OXFORD	8/4	6,933	14	D	2–2	13	34
39	H	LUTON	15/4	8,552	17	L	0–3	13	34
40	A	CHARLTON	22/4	7,351	18	D	1–1	20	35
41	A	BLACKPOOL	24/4	10,507	15	W	2–1	6	37
42	H	BURNLEY	29/4	5,885	16	L	1–2	7	37

Average: Home 11,917 — Away 12,477

Line-ups (Pompey in roman / opponent in italic), scorers, referee and report

32 · A PRESTON — Milkins, Smith (*McNab*), Collins* (*Connor*), Wilson (*Bird*), Hand (*Hawkins*), Youlden (*Spavin*), Piper (*Heppolette*), Reynolds (*Young*), Trebilcock (*McIlmoyle*), Ley (*Lyall*), Hiron (*Tarbuck*), Pointer. Opp also *Kelly*.
Scorers: *McIlmoyle 8, Young 44, Tarbuck 75, [Lyall 85p]*. Ref: R Raby (Leeds)
A bumpy pitch and strong wind are no excuse for dispirited Pompey. Collins goes off with a cut face and Preston take charge as McIlmoyle's shot loops in off Youlden. Young strides through on half-time, before Tarbuck heads in and is then fouled for Lyall to score from the spot.

33 · H NORWICH — Milkins (*Keelan*), Smith (*Payne*), Collins (*Black*), Wilson (*Stringer*), Hand (*Forbes*), Munks (*Anderson*), Piper (*Livermore*), Reynolds (*Bone*), Trebilcock (*Cross**), Ley (*Paddon*), Hiron (*Foggo*), Pointer (*Howard*).
Scorers: Hiron 20, 32 / *Howard 86*. Ref: W Gow (Swansea)
Bone rattles the bar, but then Pompey take over. Reynolds hits the woodwork, but Hiron secures the win, then he cleverly hooks in a cross. Howard can't console fuming Norwich boss Ron Saunders: 'The worst we've played in two years.' Some of City's 1,000 fans came by air.

34 · A ORIENT — Milkins (*Goddard*), Smith (*Hoadley*), Collins (*Rofe*), Wilson (*Bennett*), Hand (*Harris*), Munks (*Allen*), Piper (*Fairbrother*), Reynolds* (*Dyson*), Trebilcock (*Bullock*), Ley (*Walley*), Hiron (*Bowyer*), Pointer.
Scorers: Hand 61 (og), *Allen 65*. Ref: M Washer (Bristol)
Tindall adopts a defensive 5-3-2 formation, but despite taking the lead when Reynolds forces his way past three defenders to shoot home, Pompey capitulate. Hand nods an innocuous cross past Milkins after a misunderstanding, then Peter Allen trickles a shot through a sea of legs.

35 · A MILLWALL — Milkins (*King*), Smith (*Brown B*), Collins (*Cripps*), Wilson (*Dorney*), Hand (*Kitchener*), Munks (*Burnett*), Piper (*Bridges*), Reynolds (*Bolland*), Pointer* (*Saul*), Ley (*Smethurst*), Hiron (*Allder*), Youlden.
Scorers: *Bridges 54*. Ref: E Wallace (Swindon)
Youlden almost scores a point against promotion-chasing Millwall, but his header in the dying seconds is saved by King. Bridges' shot from Collins' poor clearance that settles the points, at which point the Lions stopped playing. Tindall declares, 'This was a travesty of a result.'

36 · H SWINDON — Milkins (*Downsboro'*), Smith (*Thomas*), Collins (*Trollope*), Wilson (*Bunkell**), Hand (*Burrows*), Munks (*Butler*), Piper (*Hubbard*), Reynolds (*Smart*), Trebilcock (*Horsfield*), Ley (*Noble*), Hiron (*Rogers*), Youlden (*Mackay*).
Scorers: Ley 54 / *Noble 82, 88*. Ref: B Daniels (Rainham)
Cultured winger Don Rogers was the architect of Swindon's win. With time running out, his inch-perfect pass found Noble in space to score, then his corner found the same player's head. Ley's perfectly placed 20-yarder had earlier looked set to ease Pompey's relegation fears.

37 · H WATFORD — Milkins (*Walker M*), Smith (*Butler*), Collins (*Williams*), Wilson (*Lugg*), Hand (*Franks*), Munks (*Eddy*), Piper (*Kenning*), Reynolds (*Wigg**), Trebilcock* (*Jennings*), Ley (*Lindsay*), Hiron (*Welbourne*), Youlden (*Lees*).
Scorers: Hiron 44, Wilson 68 / *Eddy 60p, 61*. Ref: C Nicholls (Plymouth)
Wilson's shot earns a lucky point. Eddy converted a penalty after Bill Jennings was tripped, then he finished Kenning's flicked-on corner to turn the game after Hiron's header. Referee Nicholls will report PFC after a blonde woman ran on and thumped him after he disallowed a goal.

38 · A OXFORD — Milkins, Smith (*Burton*), Collins (*Lucas*), Blant (*Stuker*), Youlden (*Smithson*), Munks (*Skeen*), Piper (*Sloan*), Reynolds (*Atkinson G*), Trebilcock* (*Clarke D*), Wilson (*Cassidy*), Hiron (*Fleming*).
Scorers: Piper 16p, 42 / *Sloan 14, Clarke D 64p*. Ref: R Crabb (Exeter)
Pompey bounce back from a poor Easter with a spirited display. Sloan's volley opens things, but Smith is tripped in the box by Shuker and Piper scores. Piper's header finishes the move-of-the-game he began. Blant's clumsy foul on Cassidy lets Derek Clarke level from the spot.

39 · H LUTON — Milkins (*Barber*), Smith (*Slough*), Collins (*Shanks*), Blant (*Keen*), Youlden (*Garner*), Munks (*Moore*), Piper (*Wainwright*), Reynolds (*Halom*), Hiron (*Givens*), Wilson (*Ryan John*), Hiron (*Hindson*).
Scorers: *Givens 15p, Ryan John 32 67*. Ref: N Paget (Coventry)
Tindall refused to talk after Town's stroll. Blant handles Shanks' cross, as Hiron prods home when Munks' shot is only half-saved. Piper and Hiron go close to clinching it, before Peacock lashes in the equaliser after a goal-mouth scramble. One point will make Pompey safe.

40 · A CHARLTON — Milkins (*Dunn*), Smith (*Bruck*), Collins (*Warman*), Munks* (*Went*), Blant (*Shipperley*), Youlden (*Davies*), Piper (*Bond*), Reynolds (*Hunt*), Hiron (*Givens*), Wilson (*Treacy*), Ley (*Peacock*), Youlden (*Flanaghan*).
Scorers: Hiron 67 / *Peacock 80*. Ref: K Styles (Barnsley)
Relegation-haunted Charlton are denied the win to take them above Pompey, as Hiron lashes down Pompey take over. Hiron's dummy allows Hand to score from close in.

41 · A BLACKPOOL — Milkins (*Wood*), Smith (*Hatton*), Collins (*Bentley*), Hand (*Suddaby*), Youlden (*James*), Blant (*Simpkin**), Piper (*Hutchinson*), Reynolds (*Suddick*), Hiron (*Dyson*), Wilson (*Hardcastle*), Ley (*Burns*), Youlden (*Ainscow*).
Scorers: Piper 44, Hand 71 / *Hutchinson 30*. Ref: K Wynn (Wolverhampton)
The relegation threat ends against a Pool team looking for goals in pursuit of a Watney Cup place. Hutchinson's first of the season is no more than they deserve, but after Piper's volley from Reynolds' knock down Pompey take over. Hiron's dummy allows Hand to score from close in.

42 · H BURNLEY — Stevenson (*Docherty*), Smith (*Nuity*), Collins (*Dobson*), Wilson, Hand (*Rodaway*), Blant (*Thomson*), Piper (*Ingham*), Reynolds (*Casper*), Hiron* (*Fletcher*), Ley (*Probert*), Lewis (*James*), Pointer.
Scorers: Reynolds 60 / *Dobson 35, Thomson 78*. Ref: R Perkin (Stafford)
Youthful Burnley win in front of the lowest recorded attendance at Fratton. Lewis makes his second Pompey debut, but Fletcher had already hit the bar before Dobson headed in Casper's cross. Reynolds beats three men before slotting home, but Thomson's first of the season sealed it.

LEAGUE DIVISION 2 (CUP-TIES)

Manager: Ron Tindall — **SEASON 1971-72**

League Cup

1   A   BOURNEMOUTH   17/8   —   15,382   3   —   L   1-2   H-T 0-0
Scorers: McCann 53; MacDougall 64, 71
Ref: R Crabb (Exeter)

	1	2	3	4	5	6	7	8	9	10	11	12 sub used
Pompey	Milkins	Smith	Ley	McCann	Hand	Youlden	Piper	Reynolds	Hiron	Collins	Storrie	
Bournemouth	*Davies*	*Benson*	*Stocks*	*Davidson*	*Kitchener*	*Powell*	*Cave*	*MacDougall*	*Boyer*	*Miller*	*Scott*	

Pompey look on-course after McCann scores with a shot from outside the box and Davies makes two sharp saves from Reynolds. MacDougall equalises after his header rebounds to him, then he scores again despite being surrounded. Reynolds misses from an acute angle at the end.

FA Cup

3   A   BOSTON   15/1   17   —   11,000 NPL   —   W   1-0   H-T 0-0
Scorer: Jennings 53
Ref: R Kirkpatrick (Leicester)

	1	2	3	4	5	6	7	8	9	10	11	12 sub used
Pompey	Milkins	Smith	Collins	Piper	Hand	Blant	McCann	Hiron	Reynolds	Ley	Jennings	
Boston	*White*	*Lakin*	*Pilgrim*	*Smith*	*Bate*	*Howells*	*Hughes*	*Svarc*	*Froggatt*	*Coates*	*Wilkinson*	

Boston, player-managed by Jim Smith, put Pompey under pressure and see two penalty appeals refused after Blant's handball and Jennings' elbow. After the break, Jennings hooks home from Piper's free-kick, but Milkins is the hero at the death, pushing Svarc's shot onto the post.

4   H   SWANSEA   5/2   15   —   19,782   3:5   —   W   2-0   H-T 0-0
Scorers: Williams 62 (og), Trebilcock 82
Ref: A Oliver (Leigh-on-Sea)

	1	2	3	4	5	6	7	8	9	10	11	12 sub used
Pompey	Milkins	Smith	Collins	McCann	Hand	Blant	Piper	Reynolds	Trebilcock	Ley	Jennings	
Swansea	*Millington*	*C Jones*	*Screen A*	*Williams*	*Evans K*	*Slattery*	*Screen W*	*Thomas**	*Davies*	*Gwyther*	*Rees*	*Evans W*

A determined rearguard action by the Swans is undone when Alan Williams, pressured by Piper, flicks the ball over his shoulder into his own net. Jennings' header off the underside of the bar is finished off by Trebs, ensuring Pompey are in the fifth round for the first time since 1968.

5   A   BIRMINGHAM   26/2   14   —   43,886   4   —   L   1-3   H-T 1-2
Scorers: Reynolds 5; Hatton 10, Latchford R 26, 51
Ref: R Matthewson (Manchester)

	1	2	3	4	5	6	7	8	9	10	11	12 sub used
Pompey	Milkins	Smith	Collins	McCann	Hand	Blant	Piper	Reynolds	Trebilcock*	Munks	Ley	Storrie
Birmingham	*Cooper*	*Carroll*	*Pendrey**	*Page*	*Hynd*	*Harrison*	*Campbell*	*Francis*	*Latchford R*	*Hatton*	*Taylor*	*Smith*

Hopes of reaching the quarter-finals are dashed for 2,000 fans who travel to St Andrews. With Jennings and Hiron ruled out, Pompey defy the odds by going ahead when Piper finds the unmarked Reynolds. After Hatton equalises it is all over. Latchford is then twice set up by Hatton.

League Table

Pos	Team	P	Home W	D	L	F	A	Away W	D	L	F	A	Pts
1	Norwich	42	13	8	0	40	16	8	7	6	20	20	57
2	Birmingham	42	15	6	0	46	14	4	12	5	14	17	56
3	Millwall	42	14	7	0	38	17	5	10	6	26	29	55
4	QP Rangers	42	16	4	1	39	9	4	10	7	18	19	54
5	Sunderland	42	11	7	3	42	24	6	9	6	25	33	50
6	Blackpool	42	12	6	3	43	16	8	1	12	27	34	47
7	Burnley	42	13	6	4	43	22	2	12	7	27	33	46
8	Bristol City	42	14	3	4	43	22	7	10	4	18	27	46
9	Middlesbro	42	16	4	1	31	11	3	14	4	19	37	46
10	Carlisle	42	12	6	3	38	22	5	13	3	23	35	43
11	Swindon	42	12	6	5	29	16	6	10	5	18	31	42
12	Hull	42	10	6	5	33	21	4	13	4	16	32	38
13	Luton	42	7	8	6	25	24	3	10	8	18	24	38
14	Sheffield Wed	42	11	7	3	33	22	2	5	14	18	36	38
15	Oxford	42	10	8	3	28	17	2	6	13	15	38	38
16	PORTSMOUTH	42	9	7	5	31	26	3	6	12	28	42	37
17	Orient	42	12	4	5	32	19	2	5	14	18	42	37
18	Preston	42	11	6	4	32	21	1	8	12	20	37	36
19	Cardiff	42	9	7	5	37	25	1	7	13	19	44	34
20	Fulham	42	10	7	4	29	20	2	3	16	16	48	34
21	Charlton	42	9	7	5	33	25	3	2	16	22	52	33
22	Watford	42	5	5	11	15	25	0	4	17	9	50	19
		924	249	131	82	760	434	82	131	249	434	760	924

Appearances and Goals

Player	App Lge	Sub	LC	Sub	FAC	Sub	Goals Lge	LC	FAC	Tot
Blant, Colin	27									
Bromley, Brian		1				3				
Collins, John										
Hand, Eoin	24		1		3		5			5
Hiron, Ray	40		1	2			9			9
Jennings, Nicky	33	2			1	2	4		2	6
Lewis, Brian	1									
Ley, George	39		1		3		5			5
McCann, Albert	25	1	1		3	1	4		1	5
Milkins, John	37		1		3					
Munks, David	17	3			1					
Piper, Norman	42		1		3		8			8
Pointer, Ray	4	3								
Reynolds, Richard	41		1		3		10	1		11
Smith, Fred	42		1		3		1			1
Standen, Jim	5									
Storrie, Jim	4				1	1	1			1
Travers, Mick		1								
Trebilcock, Mick	29		1	2			9			9
Wilson, Billy	17						2			2
Youlden, Tommy	22	3	1				1		1	2
(own-goals)										
21 players used	462	14	11	2	33	1	59	1	4	64

Odds & ends

Double wins: (0).

Double Losses: (2) Swindon, Luton.

Wins from behind: (2) Burnley (a), Blackpool (a).

Lost from in front: (4) Luton (a), Birmingham (a), Orient (a), Swindon (h).

High spots: 6-3 thrashing of Fulham in October.

2-1 victory over league leaders Norwich in March.

Six-match unbeaten league and cup run in January and February.

3-1 win at Burnley in December.

Low spots: Southampton thrash Pompey 7-0 in May 1972 in John Milkins' testimonial.

One win in last nine league matches.

Lowest-ever home league gate against Burnley on the last day of the season.

Player of the Year: Richard Reynolds.

Ever presents: (2) Fred Smith, Norman Piper.

Hat tricks: (0).

Leading scorer: Richard Reynolds (11).

LEAGUE DIVISION 2 — Manager: Ron Tindall — SEASON 1972-73

No	Date	V	Opponent	Att	Pos	Pt	F-A	H-T	Result
1	12/8	A	NOTT'M FOREST	13,175	–	1	0-0	0-0	D
2	19/8	H	CARDIFF	14,067 *14*	4	3	3-1	0-1	W
3	26/8	A	MILLWALL	12,421 *11*	2	5	2-0	1-0	W
4	30/8	H	HUDDERSFIELD	16,419 *7*	6	5	1-2	0-1	L
5	2/9	H	BURNLEY	11,701 *1*	10	5	0-2	0-1	L
6	9/9	A	SHEFFIELD WED	17,830 *1*	12	5	1-2	1-1	L
7	16/9	H	PRESTON	6,965 *12*	16	5	0-1	0-1	L
8	23/9	A	SWINDON	9,431 *15*	17	6	1-1	1-0	D
9	27/9	H	OXFORD	7,385 *7*	15	8	1-0	1-0	W
10	30/9	H	BRIGHTON	15,726 *21*	13	10	2-0	1-0	W

---

1. A NOTT'M FOREST — 12/8

	1	2	3	4	5	6	7	8	9	10	11	12 sub used
Pompey	Horn	Smith	Collins	Wilson	Stephenson	Hand	Piper	Reynolds	Price*	Ley	Hiron	Munks
Forest	*Barron*	*Fraser*	*Gemmill*	*Serella*	*Chapman*	*Robertson*	*McIntosh*	*Lyall*	*McKenzie*	*Richardson*	*O'Neill*	

Ref: P Baldwin (Middlesbrough)

Piper strokes a penalty wide after Hiron is fouled in the first half, but on-loan Horn (17) from Arsenal keeps a clean sheet against relegated Forest, who need to spend Cormack and Storey-Moore's fees quickly. Stephenson looks solid, but striker Price injures his back on his debut.

2. H CARDIFF — 19/8

	1	2	3	4	5	6	7	8	9	10	11	12 sub used
Pompey	Horn	Smith	Collins	Wilson	Stephenson	Hand	Piper	Reynolds	Hiron	Ley	Lewis	
Cardiff	*Irwin*	*Carver*	*Bell*	*Foggon**	*Murray*	*Larmour*	*Gibson*	*Clark*	*Phillips*	*Warboys*	*Showers*	*Woodruff*

Scorers: Lewis 61, Piper 81, Reynolds 90 / Showers 35
Ref: H Davey (Mansfield)

It takes a fine save from Horn, after Lewis slides home Reynolds cross, to set up the win. Showers, who will join Pompey in 1979, volleys in superbly for mauve and yellow-shirted City, but Reynolds beats Larmour to set up Piper, then nets a solo goal. Fans brawl on the Milton End.

3. A MILLWALL — 26/8

	1	2	3	4	5	6	7	8	9	10	11	12 sub used
Pompey	Horn	Smith	Collins	Wilson	Stephenson	Hand	Piper	Reynolds	Hiron	Ley	Lewis	
Millwall	*King*	*Brown B*	*Burnett*	*Dorney*	*Kitchener*	*Bolland*	*Brown S*	*Smethurst*	*Wood*	*Possee*	*Allder*	

Scorers: Lewis 14, 88
Ref: E Jolly (Manchester)

Horn is the hero as he defies a heavy blow to the head from Alf Wood to help ensure Millwall's run of 29 unbeaten matches at the Den comes to an end. Lewis ghosts in at the far post to nod in Hiron's cross, then Piper slips a free-kick to Lewis, whose shot deflects in off the wall.

4. H HUDDERSFIELD — 30/8

	1	2	3	4	5	6	7	8	9	10	11	12 sub used
Pompey	Horn	Smith	Collins	Wilson	Stephenson	Hand	Piper	Reynolds	Hiron	Ley*	Lewis	Jennings
Huddersfield	*Wood*	*Jones*	*Smith D*	*Pugh*	*Dolan*	*Nicholson*	*Fairclough*	*Lawson*	*Gowling*	*Smith S*	*Chapman*	

Scorers: Reynolds 49 / Gowling 33, 53
Ref: D Biddle (Bristol)

Pompey would have gone top of the table with a draw, but slick Town spoil the party. Graduate Alan Gowling, a £70,000 signing from Man U, nods home Pugh's quick free-kick, then converts from a Chapman's corner. In between, Hiron forces Wood into an error to set up Reynolds.

5. H BURNLEY — 2/9

	1	2	3	4	5	6	7	8	9	10	11	12 sub used
Pompey	Horn	Smith	Collins	Munks	Stephenson	Hand	Piper	Reynolds	Hiron	Wilson	Lewis	Jennings
Burnley	*Stevenson*	*Docherty*	*Newton*	*Dobson*	*Waldron*	*Thomson*	*Thomas*	*Casper*	*Fletcher*	*Collins*	*James*	

Scorers: Fletcher 7, Thomas 63
Ref: M Paget (Coventry)

Tindall concedes that in-form Burnley were an unlikely source of points. Stephenson is at fault, missing the flight of Waldron's clearance, allowing Fletcher to roll home despite slipping as he shoots. His foul then allowed Dave Thomas, later to play for Pompey, to drive home.

6. A SHEFFIELD WED — 9/9

	1	2	3	4	5	6	7	8	9	10	11	12 sub used
Pompey	Horn	Smith	Collins	Wilson	Stephenson	Hand	Piper	Reynolds	Hiron	Ley	Lewis	Jennings
Sheff Wed	*Grummitt*	*Rodrigues*	*Clements*	*Holsgrove*	*Swan*	*Craig T*	*Henderson**	*Eustace*	*Joicey*	*Prendergast*	*Sissons*	*Sunley*

Scorers: Hiron 11 / Prendergast 38, Sunley 85
Ref: D Laing (Preston)

Owls go top as sub David Sunley reacts quickest to a half-clearance of Sissons' cross to nod home. Tindall played deeper and Ley, wanted by Brighton, is moved out wide. Hiron steered home, but then Hand loses a contact lens, misjudges a cross and Horn is left rooted for the leveller.

7. H PRESTON — 16/9

	1	2	3	4	5	6	7	8	9	10	11	12 sub used
Pompey	Milkins	Smith	Collins	Munks	Stephenson	Hand	Piper	Reynolds	Hiron	Wilson*	Lewis	Jennings
Preston	*Kelly*	*McMahon*	*McNab*	*Bird*	*Hawkin*	*Spavin*	*Heppolette*	*Spark*	*Tarbuck*	*Young*	*Wilson*	

Scorers: Tarbuck 38
Ref: R Kirkpatrick (Leicester)

Pompey slump to a fifth consecutive loss. Wilson's cross sets up a simple goal. Late on skipper Hand almost levelled then Hiron's drive was closer still. The ref's ebullience livens things up and Tindall's search for a midfielder continues as Fulham's Barry Lloyd turns down a move.

8. A SWINDON — 23/9

	1	2	3	4	5	6	7	8	9	10	11	12 sub used
Pompey	Milkins	Smith	Wilson	Hand	Stephenson	Munks	Piper	Reynolds	Price*	McCann	Lewis	
Swindon	*Allan*	*Thomas*	*Trollope*	*Howell*	*Potter*	*Butler*	*Peplow*	*Hubbard**	*Treacy*	*Noble*	*Rogers*	*Moss*

Scorers: Piper 20 / Rogers 76
Ref: J Williams (Wrexham)

A reshuffled side stops the rot and manager Tindall celebrates his birthday with a deserved point. Allan missed McCann's cross for Piper to stroke home, and he should have made it 2-0 after good work by Price. Rogers looks offside, but races on to Noble's pass to equalise.

9. H OXFORD — 27/9

	1	2	3	4	5	6	7	8	9	10	11	12 sub used
Pompey	Milkins	Smith	Collins	Hand	Stephenson	Munks	Piper	Reynolds	Price	McCann	Lewis	
Oxford	*Burton*	*Lucas*	*Shuker*	*Roberts*	*Clarke C*	*Evanson*	*Sloan*	*Skeen*	*Clarke D*	*Cassidy*	*Aylott*	

Scorers: Clarke C 44 (og)
Ref: R Crabb (Exeter)

Colin Clarke, under pressure from Reynolds, inadvertently slices the decisive goal from Lewis's low cross, then his brother Derek Clarke, adjusting to a higher level. Milkins saves from Derek Clarke, then his brother Colin almost atones, but his header grazes the bar late on.

10. H BRIGHTON — 30/9

	1	2	3	4	5	6	7	8	9	10	11	12 sub used
Pompey	Milkins	Smith	Collins	Hand	Stephenson	Munks	Piper	Reynolds	Hiron	McCann	Lewis	
Brighton	*Powney*	*Murray*	*Ley*	*Lutton*	*Gall*	*Templeman*	*Bridges*	*Spearitt*	*Irvine**	*Bromley*	*O'Sullivan*	*Beamish*

Scorers: Reynolds 16, Piper 83
Ref: G Hill (Leicester)

Piper's midfield guile is crucial as Pompey carve out chance after chance and Albion look out of their depth, despite a large following. The crowd only breathes easy when McCann, Reynolds and Hiron set up Piper. The returning Bromley is hampered by Hand's early foul.

No		Opponent	Date	Pos			Att	Res	FT	HT
11	H	BRISTOL CITY	7/10	16	10	10	9,375	L	0-3	0-1
12	A	HULL	14/10	17	10	10	9,513	L	1-5	0-4
13	A	LUTON	18/10	17	5	11	9,813	D	2-2	2-2
14	H	ASTON VILLA	21/10	17	3	11	13,524	L	0-1	0-1
15	A	CARLISLE	28/10	20	19	11	6,361	L	0-1	0-0
16	A	OXFORD	4/11	17	12	13	8,714	W	3-1	2-0
17	H	LUTON	11/11	18	4	14	7,571	D	2-2	2-0
18	A	FULHAM	18/11	18	9	15	9,624	D	0-0	0-0
19	H	QP RANGERS	25/11	20	2	15	8,460	L	0-1	0-0
20	A	BLACKPOOL	2/12	20	3	15	8,409	L	1-3	0-2
21	H	SUNDERLAND	9/12	21	19	15	5,783	L	2-3	1-1

11 — H BRISTOL CITY 7/10
Pompey: Milkins, Smith, Wilson, Hand, Stephenson, Munks, Piper, Reynolds, Hiron, McCann, Lewis*, Price
Bristol City: Cashley, Wilson, Drysdale, Emanuel, Rodgers, Merrick, Tainton, Spiring*, Galley, Gow, Sweeney, Ritchie
Sweeney 4, 59, Emanuel 54
Ref: J Thacker (Scarborough)
Pompey lurch from one extreme to another as Peter Spiring (20) is the tormentor-in-chief. Defensive chaos allows Sweeney to stab home, then his sidefoot past an exposed Milkins seals it after Emanuel's fierce volley. Price's appearance pepped up the attack, but McCann went closest.

12 — A HULL 14/10
Pompey: Milkins, Smith, Wilson, Hand, Stephenson, Munks, Piper, Reynolds, Price, McCann*, Lewis, Hiron
Hull: Wealands, Banks, De Vries, Kaye, Neill*, Knighton, McGill, Houghton, Pearson, Holme, Butler, Wilkinson
Price 63 / Holme 3, Pearson 9, 11, 27, 79
Ref: R Perkin (Stafford)
Chairman Collett moans 'Finding the right player is the problem, rather than the money,' after this first-half debacle assures Hull's first win over Pompey since 1966. Tindall's interval chat has the desired effect, however. Reynolds hits a post, then he releases Price for his first goal.

13 — A LUTON 18/10
Pompey: Horn, Smith, Collins, Wilson, Stephenson, Munks, Piper, Reynolds, Price, McCann, Lewis*, Hiron
Luton: Barber, Ryan John, Thomson, Anderson, Faulkner, Slough, Ryan Jim, Fern, Busby, Halom, Aston
Lewis 3, Price 20 / Halom 30, Busby 45
Ref: R Tinkler (Boston)
Collins returns at left-back after training with the Welsh squad, while Wilson covers for Hand on duty for Eire. Reynolds is involved in both goals, cleverly setting up Price. Halom thrashes home John Ryan's knock-down, then Busby slots in from an acute angle, but Pompey hold out.

14 — H ASTON VILLA 21/10
Pompey: Horn, Smith, Collins, Wilson, Stephenson, Hand, Piper, Reynolds, Price, McCann, Lewis*, Hiron
Aston Villa: Cumbes, Gidman, Aitken, Rioch B, Rioch N, Turnbull, Graydon*, Evans, Ross, Vowden, Anderson, Little
Vowden 31
Ref: P Walters (Bridgwater)
Villa manager Vic Crowe shuts up shop after Horn and Smith's misunderstanding presents Vowden with a simple chance. The link with Waterlooville is underlined as their manager Pat Wright is in charge while Tindall scouts. Police separate fighting fans on the Fratton End.

15 — A CARLISLE 28/10
Pompey: Horn, Wilson, Collins, Hand, Stephenson, Munks, Piper, Reynolds, Price, McCann, Lewis*, Hiron
Carlisle: Clarke, Balderstone, Gorman, Tiler, Winstanley, Tennant, Train, Martin, Owen, Wilson, Laidlaw
Balderstone 79
Ref: W Castle (Dudley)
Boss Tindall moans 'We should have had a penalty when Price was impeded in the first half.' A deserved point is snatched away when Joe Laidlaw's shot rebounds to makeshift full-back Chris Balderstone, who shows his striking instincts by firing into the roof of the net.

16 — A OXFORD 4/11
Pompey: Horn, Wilson, Collins, Hand, Stephenson, Munks, Piper, Reynolds, Hiron, McCann, Lewis, Jennings
Oxford: Burton, Lucas, Shuker, Roberts, Clarke C, Evanson, Sloan, Skeen*, Curran, Cassidy, Aylott, Bray
Piper 14, 53, Jennings 43 / Curran 83
Ref: R Capey (Crewe)
Piper makes his 100th consecutive league appearance and celebrates with a breakaway goal after Curran's tumble in the box is waved aside. Tindall defends his team's robust approach which sees the returning Jennings score from Hiron's centre before Piper seals it from Price's pass.

17 — H LUTON 11/11
Pompey: Horn, Wilson, Thomson?, Hand, Stephenson, Munks, Piper, Reynolds, Hiron, McCann, Jennings
Luton: Barber, Ryan John, Thomson, Slough, Garner, Ryan Jim*, Fern, Hindson, Halom, Aston, Goodeve
Piper 10, Jennings 12 / Stephenson 62 (og), Fern 67
Ref: T Reynolds (Swansea)
A concussed Wilson is forced into action despite suffering from double-vision at half-time because Pompey's sub is a striker. Goodeve's introduction changes the game as John Ryan pushes forward and his centre is sliced in by Stephenson. Fern then slams in a rebounding shot.

18 — A FULHAM 18/11
Pompey: Horn, Wilson, Collins, Hand, Stephenson, Munks, Price, Reynolds, Hiron, McCann, Jennings
Fulham: Mellor, Cutbush, Callaghan, Mullery, Dunne, Went, Conway J'n, Earle, Mitchell, Lloyd, Strong*, Moreline
Ref: M Sinclair (Guildford)
A hamstring strain means Piper misses his first game for the club. Price replaces him, but is clearly troubled by his back injury. In the dying seconds former England star Alan Mullery's indirect free-kick from four yards out is blocked and Mitchell hits the post from the rebound.

19 — H QP RANGERS 25/11
Pompey: Horn, Wilson, Collins, Hand, Stephenson, Munks, Price, Reynolds, Hiron, McCann, Jennings
QP Rangers: Parkes, Clement, Gillard, Venables, Mancini, Hazell, Francis, Morgan, Bowles, Givens, Leach
Givens 48
Ref: N Burtenshaw (Gt Yarmouth)
Venables lays off Bowles' pass into the path of Givens, who fires past Horn to seal the points, but Pompey come back strongly and Piper nets from close range at the death, only for a free-kick to be given. Off the field, Smith's transfer request is rejected, but Jennings remains listed.

20 — A BLACKPOOL 2/12
Pompey: Horn, Hatton?, Collins, Hand, Stephenson, Munks, Lewis, Reynolds, Hiron, McCann, Jennings
Blackpool: Burridge, Hatton, Bentley, Alcock, Suddaby, Hardcastle, Burns, Rafferty, Dyson*, Ainscow, Suddick, James
Hiron 88 / Dyson 30, Ainscow 43, Suddick 65
Ref: D Turner (Rugeley)
The referee's leg strain means he can't carry on and a volunteer from the crowd runs the line as the senior linesman takes over. Managerless Pool's sharpness makes the difference. Ainscow and Dyson combine twice to set each other up before half-time; then Suddick chipped in.

21 — H SUNDERLAND 9/12
Pompey: Horn, Wilson, Collins, Hand, Stephenson, Munks, Piper, Reynolds, Hiron, McCann, Lewis
Sunderland: Montgomery, Malone, Coleman, Horswill, Watson, Porterfield, Chambers*, Kerr, Hughes W, McGiven, Tueart, Tones
Lewis 42p, Jennings 54 / Watson 35, Hughes 87, Kerr 89
Ref: I Jones (Treharris)
Bob Stokoe's Roker revival starts here and ends in Wembley glory. Hughes nods in Porterfield's effort, then Kerr stoops to shatter the lowest crowd in Pompey's history. Horswill's foul on Reynolds for a penalty had looked like setting up a win. Wright deputises as Tindall has flu.

LEAGUE DIVISION 2

Manager: Ron Tindall   SEASON 1972-73

No	Date	Team	Att	Pos	Res	Pt	F-A	H-T	Scorers, Times, and Referees	1	2	3	4	5	6	7	8	9	10	11	12 sub used
22	H 16/12	MIDDLESBROUGH	4,688	21 (*8*)	D	16	0-0	0-0	Ref: C Thomas (Treorchy)	Horn	Smith	Collins	Hand	Stephenson	Munks*	Piper	Reynolds	Hiron	Wilson	Jennings	Lewis
		(opp)								*Platt*	*Craggs*	*Jones*	*Gates*	*Madren*	*Taylor*	*McMordie*	*Hickton*	*Smith*	*Mills*	*Armstrong*	
23	A 23/12	ORIENT	4,466	20 (*21*)	W	18	1-0	0-0	Hiron 52. Ref: J Hunting (Leicester)	Horn	Smith	Collins	Hand*	Stephenson	Munks	Piper	Reynolds	Hiron	Wilson	Jennings	Lewis
		(opp)								*Goddard*	*Arber*	*Wall*	*Allen*	*Linton*	*Hoadley*	*Downing*	*Brisley*	*Queen*	*Bullock*	*Bowyer*	
24	H 26/12	SWINDON	7,941	17 (*15*)	D	19	1-1	0-0	Lewis 57, Noble 55. Ref: P Walters (Bridgwater)	Horn	Wilson	Collins	Hand	Stephenson	Munks	Piper	Reynolds	Hiron	Lewis	Jennings	
		(opp)								*Allan*	*Thomas*	*Trollope*	*Bunkell*	*Burrows*	*Potter*	*Jenkins*	*Howell*	*Treacy*	*Noble*	*Butler*	
25	A 29/12	CARDIFF	12,382	17 (*20*)	W	21	2-0	0-0	Hand 69, Hiron 75. Ref: A Hart (London)	Horn	Wilson	Collins	Hand	Stephenson	Munks	Lewis	Reynolds	Hiron	Piper	Jennings	
		(opp)								*Irwin*	*Dwyer*	*Bell*	*Phillips*	*Morgan R*	*Impey*	*Kellock*	*McCulloch*	*Woodruff*	*Vincent*	*Reece**	*Couch*
26	H 6/1	MILLWALL	10,031	17 (*14*)	D	22	1-1	0-0	Reynolds 56, Wood 81. Ref: F Bassett (Swindon)	Horn	Wilson	Collins	Hand	Stephenson	Munks	Piper	Reynolds	Hiron	Kellard	Jennings	
		(opp)								*King*	*Brown B*	*Cripps*	*Dorney*	*Kitchener*	*Burnett*	*Brown S**	*Bolland*	*Wood*	*Dunphy*	*Allder*	*Smethurst*
27	H 27/1	SHEFFIELD WED	9,705	16 (*9*)	W	24	1-0	1-0	Jennings 44. Ref: B Daniels (Rainham)	Horn	Smith	Wilson	Piper	Stephenson	Munks	Foggo	Reynolds	Hiron	Kellard	Jennings	
		(opp)								*Springett*	*Craig J*	*Clemets*	*Thompson*	*Holsgrove*	*Craig T*	*Henderson*	*Coyle*	*Sunley**	*Prudham*	*Sissons*	*Eustace*
28	A 10/2	PRESTON	6,230	15 (*14*)	W	26	5-0	2-0	Piper 32, 57 Kellard 39, Jennings 87, [Hiron 90]. Ref: L Hayes (Doncaster)	Milkins	Wilson	Collins	Hand	Stephenson	Munks	Foggo	Piper	Hiron	Kellard	Jennings	
		(opp)								*Kelly*	*McMahon*	*McNab*	*Bird*	*Hawkins*	*Spavin*	*Tarbuck**	*Young*	*McIlmoyle*	*Spark*	*Bruce*	*Clark*
29	H 17/2	NOTT'M FOREST	11,151	13 (*15*)	W	28	2-0	2-0	Jennings 29, Hiron 43. Ref: G Kew (Leeds)	Milkins	Wilson	Collins	Piper	Stephenson	Munks	Foggo	Reynolds	Hiron	Kellard	Jennings	
		(opp)								*Barron*	*Hindley*	*Winfield*	*Chapman*	*Serella*	*Fraser*	*McIntosh*	*Robertson*	*Martin*	*Galley*	*Lyall*	
30	A 24/2	MIDDLESBROUGH	7,038	14 (*6*)	L	28	0-3	0-0	Foggon 61, Stiles 72, Hickton 78. Ref: I Smith (Accrington)	Milkins	Wilson	Collins	Piper	Stephenson	Munks	Foggo	Reynolds	Hiron	Kellard	Jennings	
		(opp)								*Platt*	*Craggs*	*Spraggon*	*Stiles*	*Boam*	*Maddren*	*Gates*	*Smith*	*Hickton*	*Mills**	*Souness*	*Foggon*
31	A 3/3	BRISTOL CITY	10,977	14 (*11*)	L	28	1-3	0-2	Hiron 81. Gow 10, 64, Fear 32. Ref: A Jones (Ormskirk)	Milkins	Wilson	Collins	Hand	Stephenson	Munks	Foggo	Reynolds	Hiron	Kellard	Jennings*	Lewis
		(opp)								*Bond*	*Sweeney*	*Drysdale*	*Emanuel*	*Rodgers*	*Merrick*	*Tainton*	*Ritchie*	*Woods*	*Gow*	*Fear*	

22. Potential investor John Deacon's arrival in the Directors' Box is the highlight in front of Pompey's lowest-ever league gate: Boro's World Cup winner Nobby Stiles is suspended and Hiron hit the bar with time running out. Over-zealous ref Clive Thomas awards a total of 40 free-kicks.

23. Pompey ride their luck to earn a vital win over fellow strugglers in the East End. With only 13 fit players available, Stephenson is outstanding as the team clings to Hiron's clinical finish from 15 yards. Bowyer twice clips the bar, then Horn's superb stop denies Bullock on the whistle.

24. With only ten fit outfield players, Pointer is drafted in from 'Ville as sub. A meagre Boxing Day crowd sees a rousing second half. Noble rolls home Treacy's cross against the run of play, only for Lewis to convert Hiron's deflected cross. Wilson heads against the bar near the end.

25. Cardiff's run of five consecutive home wins is ruthlessly ended. Hand thunders in his first of the season from Collins' curling free-kick, then Hiron thrashes home Jennings' centre. Hiron's turn and shot late on draws a murmur of approval from John Charles in the press box.

26. The return of midfielder Kellard from Crystal Palace swells the gate by 2,000 and prospective signing Ken Foggo from Norwich is in the stand. A slick move lets Reynolds open the scoring, but familiar defensive failings allowed the Lions to break away and leave Wood unmarked.

27. Four months without a home win comes to an end when Wilson bursts through to angle his shot past the keeper and leave Jennings with the formality of turning the ball in. Ex-England international Ron Springett keeps the Owls in it, but Prudham almost snatches an equaliser.

28. Pompey keep their league run going when Hand's blocked shot sets up Piper, and is followed by Kellard's scorching drive. Collins crosses for Piper's diving header, then Jennings seizes on a mistake and Hiron sweeps home. Young hits the bar, but Preston boss Alan Ball Snr is sacked.

29. Hiron nets his 100th league goal with a terrific diving header – a carbon copy of his first – when Foggo's persistence works space for a cross. Jennings is Pompey's main threat, earning Hindley a booking for scything him after he netted the first with a header from Foggo's corner.

30. A second-half collapse sees Pompey's eight-match unbeaten run come to an end and re-awakens relegation fears. Foggon angles the first after Stiles shot deflects to him, then the former England man nets from five yards. Hickton quashes any comeback hopes by sweeping in the third.

31. City strikers Spiring and Gould are out but, even so, Fear had hit the bar before Gow pounced on Milkins' error. He then skips past a creaking defence to set up Fear and, in the second half, hits the post from the spot after a foul, then Piper set up Hiron.

32 H HULL 10/3 — 1-1 / 2-2 / 1-1 — 14 D 29 — 8,139 13
Kellard 42, Reynolds 60
Holme 12, Kaye 50
Ref: K Baker (Rugby)

Milkins · Hand · Wilson · Piper · Stephenson · Munks! · Foggo · Reynolds · Hiron · Kellard · Jennings
McKechnie · Banks · Beardsley · Kaye · Neill · Knighton · McGill · Houghton · Pearson* · Holme · Greenwood · Blampey

An all-action game sees Munks sent off for scuffling with Greenwood in the 36th minute, by which time City were already leading thanks to Holme's curler. Kellard has his penalty saved but nets the rebound, only for Kaye to thump the Tigers' second. Reynolds' header nicks a point.

---

33 A ASTON VILLA 17/3 — 0-2 / 0-2 — 14 L 29 — 18,432 6
Vowden 10, McMahon 21
Ref: P Baldwin (Middlesbrough)

Milkins · Hand · Wilson · Piper · Stephenson · Munks · Foggo* · Reynolds · Hiron · Kellard · Jennings
Cumbes · Robson · McDonald · McMahon · Nicholl · Turnbull · Garydon · Brown · Evans · Vowden · Lochead · Collins

Ex-Liverpool striker Alun Evans inspires Villa, but some slack defending helps, as Vowden and McMahon are left unmarked. Pompey look tighter after the break, but Reynolds' glancing header and Jennings' shot at Cumbes' legs hardly disconcert Villa's lowest gate of the season.

---

34 A BURNLEY 20/3 — 0-4 / 0-4 — 14 L 29 — 13,569 1
Nulty 10, Casper 18, 35, Fletcher 29
Ref: J Taylor (Wolverhampton)

Milkins · Lewis · Collins · Pointer · Stephenson · Hand · Foggo · Reynolds · Hiron · Kellard · Piper
Stevenson · Docherty · Newton* · Dobson · Waldron · Thomson · Nulty · Casper · Fletcher · Collins · James · Probert

Tindall maintains Pompey were better than of late, but Burnley are irresistible. Nulty's gentle overhead starts the rush, but Casper's penalty has already been blocked. He makes up with two classy finishes, sandwiched by Fletcher's follow-up after Nulty's lob was hacked clear by Hand.

---

35 H CARLISLE 24/3 — 0-0 / 0-0 — 15 D 30 — 5,346 17
Ref: R Perkin (Stafford)

Tilsed · Lewis · Collins · Wilson · Stephenson · Hand · Foggo · Reynolds · Hiron · Kellard* · Piper · Jennings
Ross · Carr · Gorman · O'Neill · Winstanley · Tiler · Martin · Train · Owen · Balderstone · Laidlaw

The back-pass count makes 43 in this dreary draw. Kellard's hamstring strain disrupts Pompey early on, then Hiron sees his angled shot saved while Reynolds shoots straight at Ross. Carlisle gain their first away point of the year and Ron Tilsed makes his debut on loan from Arsenal.

---

36 A QP RANGERS 31/3 — 0-5 / 0-5 — 17 L 30 — 14,086 2
Thomas 4, Lewis 49 (og), Venables 78, [Leach 82, Mancini 87]
Ref: D Biddle (Bristol)

Tilsed · Lewis · Collins · Wilson · Stephenson · Hazel · Foggo · Reynolds · Hiron* · Kellard · Collins
Parkes · Clement · Watson · Venables · Mancini · Hazell · Thomas · Francis · Leach · Bowles · Givens

Pompey slump nearer the drop zone after Tilsed's punch falls to Thomas who scores. Lewis places a back-pass wide of the keeper shortly after the interval and rampant Rangers stretch Pompey's winless run to seven matches. Keeper Parkes denies Kellard and Piper before a late rush.

---

37 H BLACKPOOL 7/4 — 1-0 / 1-0 — 16 W 32 — 6,768 4
Hiron 46
Ref: K Wynn (Wolverhampton)

Tilsed · Lewis · Wilson · Hand · Stephenson · Munks · Foggo · Reynolds · Hiron* · Piper · Jennings
Wood · Hatton · Bentley · Alcock · James · Suddaby · Burns* · Suddick · Rafferty · Dyson · Ainscow · Lennard

Pool's promotion hopes are ended by a great strike by Hiron 30 seconds into the second half. He pulls down Wilson's cross, skips past James, then slots the ball past Wood as he narrows the angle. However, his season is over when he limps off with knee-ligament trouble near the end.

---

38 A SUNDERLAND 14/4 — 0-2 / 0-1 — 16 L 32 — 31,430 11
Kerr 42, Tueart 84p
Ref: R Porthouse (Carnforth)

Tilsed · Lewis · Wilson · Hand · Stephenson · Munks · Foggo · Reynolds · Pointer · Piper · Jennings
Montgomery · Malone · Guthrie · Horswill · Watson · Pitt · Kerr · Hughes* · Halom · Porterfield · Tueart · Young

FA Cup finalists Sunderland are clapped onto the pitch by Pompey, who soak up early pressure only to see Porterfield's curling cross elude the defence for Kerr to nod a simple goal. Hopes of a point disappear as Stephenson fouls Tueart in the box and the striker strokes the clincher.

---

39 H ORIENT 20/4 — 1-0 / 1-0 — 17 W 34 — 8,954
Foggo 28
Ref: W Gow (Swansea)

Tilsed · Lewis · Wilson · Hand · Stephenson · Munks · Foggo · Reynolds · Piper · Kellard · Jennings
Goddard · Hoadley · Downing · Linton · Harris · Allen · Bowyer · Brisley · Fairbrother · Queen · Heppolette* · Bullock

Wales striker Ron Davies, just signed from Saints (£40,000) but unable to play while vital points are at stake, sees good chances go begging at either end. The O's, with just one away win, look marginally better, but Pompey are almost safe after Foggo unleashed a fierce drive.

---

40 H FULHAM 21/4 — 1-2 / 1-2 — 16 L 34 — 9,192 4
Cutbush 69 (og)
Conway John 27, 32
Ref: R Toseland (Kettering)

Tilsed · Lewis · Wilson · Hand · Stephenson · Munks · Foggo · Reynolds · Hiron* · Kellard · Jennings
Mellor · Cutbush · Moreline · Mullery · Went · Horne · Conway J'n · Earle · Mitchell · Lloyd · Barrett

Fulham gain their first-ever win at Fratton, despite falling behind when Cutbush was left helpless by Foggo's firm cross. Prompted by former England and Spurs star Mullery, John Conway guides in his free-kick, then Conway's shot deceives Tilsed to leave five defenders crestfallen.

---

41 A BRIGHTON 23/4 — 1-1 / 0-0 — 16 D 35 — 15,535 22
Pointer 69
Bridges 84
Ref: C Nicholls (Plymouth)

Tilsed · Lewis · Wilson · Hand · Stephenson · Munks · Foggo · Reynolds · Pointer · Kellard · Piper
Powney · Templeman · Ley · Howell* · Gall · Spearritt · Robertson · Murray · Beamish · O'Sullivan · Towner · Bridges

Pointer (36), in his last season, shows more class than most, converting Piper's cross at the second attempt for his 179th and last goal. He then set up Piper, but Powney smothered. Doomed Albion rally, but Murray's penalty is turned onto the bar, although Bridges salvages local pride.

---

42 A HUDDERSFIELD 28/4 — 0-2 / 0-1 — 17 L 35 — 8,993 21
Fairclough 35, Summerill 88
Ref: A Hart (London)

Tilsed · Lewis · Wilson · Hand · Stephenson · Munks · Foggo · Reynolds · Piper · Kellard · Pointer*
Poole · Clarke · Garner · Pugh · Saunders · Marshall · Hoy · Fairclough · Gowling · Dungworth* · Lawson · McCann · Summerill

Virtually-relegated Terriers finish in style, but to no avail as Preston draw. Fairclough nips in for the opener after Tilsed fails to hold Lawson's shot, then sub Summerill muscles his way past Wilson to bury number two. However, it is little consolation for a second successive drop.

Home 9,471 · Away 11,830
Average

LEAGUE DIVISION 2 (CUP-TIES) Manager: Ron Tindall SEASON 1972-73

League Cup

	F-A	H-T	Scorers, Times, and Referees	1	2	3	4	5	6	7	8	9	10	11	12 sub used
1 A TORQUAY 16/8 W 2-1 5,202 4	2-1	0-0	Hiron 56, Reynolds 66 *Trebilcock 85p* Ref: T Spencer (Wootton Bassett)	Horn *Mahoney*	Smith *Sandercock K Stocks*	Collins	Wilson *Harrison*	Stephenson ! *Edwards*	Hand *Boulton !*	Piper *Stuckey*	Reynolds *Gough*	Hiron *Trebilcock*	Ley *Twitchin*	Jennings *Jackson**	*Sandercock P*
2 H CHESTERFIELD 6/9 L 0-1 10 6,972 3:4	0-1	0-0	*Moss 51* Ref: G Kew (Leeds)	Horn *Tingay*	Smith *Holmes*	Collins *Tiler*	Wilson *Barlow*	Stephenson *Bell*	Hand *Phelan*	Piper *McHale*	Reynolds *Moss*	Hiron *Downes*	Ley *Bellamy*	Lewis *Wilson*	

1. Both teams consider a joint appeal to the FA after the referee dismisses Boulton and Stephenson for fighting and books five more. Hiron's drive, then Reynolds' diving header, underline Pompey's superiority, but old-boy Trebilcock scores from the spot after Collins fouls Stuckey.

2. The crowd gives Pompey the slow hand-clap after a shock third home defeat in ten days. It might have been different had Hiron's third-minute effort not been disallowed for offside. The impressive Tingay tips away Hand's shot, then Moss dives in to head home from Wilson's cross.

FA Cup

	F-A	H-T	Scorers, Times, and Referees	1	2	3	4	5	6	7	8	9	10	11	12 sub used
3 H BRISTOL CITY 13/1 D 1-1 17 15,177 10	1-1	0-0	Piper 64 *Gould 90* Ref: R Crabb (Exeter)	Horn *Bond*	Wilson *Sweeney*	Collins *Drysdale*	Hand *Emanuel*	Stephenson *Rodgers*	Munks *Merrick*	Piper *Tainton*	Reynolds *Spring*	Hiron *Gould*	Kellard *Gow*	Jennings *Fear**	*Hall*
3R A BRISTOL CITY 16/1 L 1-4 17 16,699 10	1-4	0-1	Hiron 86 [Gow 88pj] *Gould 27, Tainton 74, Sweeney 84,* Ref: R Crabb (Exeter)	Horn *Bond*	Wilson *Sweeney*	Collins* *Drysdale*	Hand *Emanuel*	Smith *Rodgers*	Munks *Merrick*	Piper *Tainton*	Reynolds *Spring*	Hiron *Gould*	Kellard *Gow*	Price *Bartley*	Lewis

3. Gould pays back a slice of his £70,000 fee from WBA when he nets from close in from a corner. Eleven Pompey players were protecting Piper's curling free-kick from 20 yards. Horn claims he kept the ball out, but Pompey were on top when City broke to force the fateful kick.

3R. City will meet Wolves away, as reshuffled Pompey surrender. Stephenson is banned and Jennings injured, then Gould's header leaves Horn fuming as he felt he was fouled. City's late flourish gives the score a fairer hue, with Gow's penalty sealing it off after Munks fouled Tainton.

Home / Away League Table

		P	W	D	L	F	A	W	D	L	F	A	Pts
1	Burnley	42	13	6	2	44	18	11	8	2	28	17	62
2	QP Rangers	42	16	4	1	54	13	8	9	4	27	24	61
3	Aston Villa	42	12	5	4	27	17	6	9	6	24	30	50
4	Middlesbro	42	12	6	3	29	15	5	7	9	17	28	47
5	Bristol City	42	10	7	4	34	18	7	5	9	29	33	46
6	Sunderland	42	12	6	3	35	17	5	6	10	24	32	46
7	Blackpool	42	12	4	5	37	17	6	4	11	19	34	46
8	Oxford	42	14	2	5	36	18	5	5	11	16	25	45
9	Fulham	42	11	6	4	32	16	5	6	10	26	33	44
10	Sheffield Wed	42	14	4	3	40	20	3	6	12	19	35	44
11	Millwall	42	12	5	4	33	18	4	5	12	22	29	42
12	Luton	42	6	9	6	24	23	9	2	10	20	30	41
13	Hull	42	12	5	5	39	22	5	5	11	25	37	40
14	Nott'm Forest	42	12	5	4	32	18	2	7	12	15	34	40
15	Orient	42	11	6	4	33	18	1	6	14	16	35	36
16	Swindon	42	8	9	4	28	23	2	7	12	18	37	36
17	PORTSMOUTH	42	8	8	5	21	22	1	7	13	21	37	35
18	Carlisle	42	10	5	6	40	24	1	7	13	10	28	34
19	Preston	42	6	8	7	19	25	5	4	12	18	39	34
20	Cardiff	42	11	4	6	32	21	0	7	14	11	37	33
21	Huddersfield	42	7	9	5	21	20	1	8	12	15	36	33
22	Brighton	42	7	8	6	32	31	1	5	15	14	52	29
		924	232	133	97	722	434	97	133	232	434	722	924

Odds & ends

Double Wins: (3) Oxford, Orient, Cardiff

Double Losses: (6) H'field, Burnley, Bristol C, Aston Villa, QPR, Sun'land.

Won from behind: (1) Cardiff (h).

Lost from in front: (3) Sheffield Wed (a), Sunderland (h), Fulham (h).

High spots: 5-0 away win at Preston in February.
Eight game unbeaten run from December to February, which eased relegation fears.
Ray Hiron's 100th league goal, against Nottingham Forest.

Low spots: Losing 2-3 at home to Sunderland after leading with three minutes to go.
Four defeats in a row in August and September, which quickly evaporated any early season optimism.
A 1-5 thrashing at Hull in October in which Stuart Pearson grabbed four of the goals.
Bobby Gould's injury-time equaliser for Bristol C in the FA Cup Round 3.

Player of the Year: Not awarded.

Ever Present: (0).
Hat-tricks: (0).
Leading Scorer: Ray Hiron (10).

Appearances and Goals

	Appearances						Goals			
	Lge	Sub	LC	Sub	FAC	Sub	Lge	LC	FAC	Tot
Collins, John	26	2	2		2		1			1
Foggo, Ken	16						1			1
Hand, Eoin	39		2		2		1			1
Hiron, Ray	31	2	2		2		8	1	1	10
Horn, Graham	22		2		2					
Jennings, Nick	24	3	1		1		6			6
Kellard, Bobby	15						2			2
Lewis, Brian	24	5	1		2	1	6			6
Ley, George	5		2							
McCann, Albert	14	1					2			2
Milkins, John	12									
Munks, David	33	1								
Piper, Norman	40		2		2		8		1	9
Pointer, Ray	4	1					1			1
Price, Peter	10	1			1					
Reynolds, Richard	40		2		2		5	1		6
Smith, Fred	18		2		1					
Stephenson, Alan	41		2		1					
Tilsed, Ron	8									
Wilson, Billy	40		2		2		2			2
(own-goals)										
20 players used	462	16	22		22	1	42	2	2	46

LEAGUE DIVISION 2

Manager: John Mortimore

SEASON 1973-74

No	Date		Att	Pos	Pt	F-A	H-T	Scorers, Times, and Referees	1	2	3	4	5	6	7	8	9	10	11	12 sub used
1	25/8	H MIDDLESBROUGH	19,799		L 0	0-1	0-1	Foggon 21 Ref: C Thomas (Treorchy)	Tilsed *Platt*	Roberts *Craggs*	Wilson *Spraggon*	Piper *Boam*	Stephenson *Taylor*	Munks *Madren*	Marinello *McMordie*	Kellard *Mills*	Davies *Hickton**	Foggo *Foggon*	Price *Armstrong*	Smith *Smith*
								New Boro boss Jack Charlton accepts: "To the uncommitted, 1-1 would have been fair.' Big-spending Pompey's chins drop once McMordie's floated pass allows Foggon a nudged finish. Former Gunner Marinello sparkles after half-time and Davies almost salvages it, but raps the bar.												
2	1/9	A CARDIFF	10,110	16 *12*	D 1	1-1	1-0	Piper 44 McCulloch 49 Ref: R Toseland (Kettering)	Tilsed *Irwin*	Roberts *Dwyer*	Wilson ! *Bell*	Piper *Smith*	Stephenson *Murray*	Munks *Phillips*	Marinello *Villars*	Kellard *McCulloch*	Davies *Woodruff*	Foggo *Vincent**	Reynolds* *Anderson*	Lewis *King*
								Ten-man Pompey re-group well after Wilson is controversially dismissed for two bookings after he fouls Anderson, then kicks the ball away. From the kick McCulloch sweeps home King's knock-down. Earlier Piper clipped home Davies' header and had a goal ruled out for offside.												
3	8/9	H BOLTON	13,367	20 *3*	L 1	0-2	0-1	Byron 33, 66 Ref: G Kew (Amersham)	Tilsed *Siddall*	Roberts *Ritson*	Wilson *McAllister*	Piper *Rimmer*	Stephenson *Jones*	Munks* *Waldron*	Marinello *Byrom*	Kellard *Nicholson*	Davies *Greaves*	Foggo *Lee*	Reynolds *Phillips*	Lewis
								The gate has already slipped below break-even level. Pompey fail to get to grips with Jimmy Armfield's newly-promoted Bolton, who field seven players under 21. However, it is old-hand Byrom who makes the most of defensive errors to convert Waldron's cross, then volley home.												
4	11/9	H SUNDERLAND	18,989	20 *7*	D 2	1-1	1-1	Hiron 27 Halom 1 Ref: M Kerkhof (Bicester)	Tilsed *Montgomery*	Roberts *Malone*	Wilson *Guthrie*	Piper *McGivern*	Stephenson *Watson*	Hand *Pitt*	Marinello *Kerr*	Kellard *Halom*	Davies *Porterfield*	Lewis *Tueart*	Hiron	
								Cup holders Sunderland stun Pompey after just nine seconds when Halom's soft shot hits a divot and spins over Tilsed's shoulder. Dave Watson, later to play for England, is lucky when his 'tackle' on Davies in the box is unpunished, but Marinello's flick sets up Hiron to nod in.												
5	15/9	A LUTON	11,552	19 *10*	D 3	3-3	1-2	Kellard 17, Lewis 64p, Davies 71 Thomson 33, Garner 35, Finney 75 Ref: W Hall (Preston)	Tilsed *Horn*	Roberts *Shanks*	Wilson *Thomson*	Piper *Anderson*	Stephenson *Faulkner*	Hand *Garner*	Marinello *Ryan Jim*	Kellard *Ryan John*	Davies *Butlin*	Lewis *Finney*	Hiron *Aston*	
								Keeper Tilsed plays the last 20 minutes with a broken arm and is out for six weeks. Luton take charge with Thomson's volley and Garner's back-header after a short-corner routine sets up Kellard. Garner handles for the penalty then Davies opens his account, only for Finney to level.												
6	18/9	A CARLISLE	6,416	14 *20*	W 5	2-0	0-0	Hiron 53, Davies 80 Ref: P Willis (Meadowfield)	Milkins *Ross*	Roberts *Carr*	Wilson *Gorman*	Piper *Ternant*	Stephenson *Green*	Hand *Tiler*	Marinello *O'Neill*	Kellard *Barry*	Davies *Laidlaw*	Lewis *Martin*	Hiron *Balderstone*	
								Alan Ashman's Carlisle, who will go up at the end of the season, are never in it, but the first half is a dour stalemate. Lewis floats the ball over Ross for Hiron to head home. Davies' near-post diving header from Wilson's cross makes sure for Deacon's expensively assembled squad.												
7	22/9	H NOTTS CO	14,443	16 *14*	L 5	1-2	1-1	Hiron 40 Mann 5, Bradd 47 Ref: A Oliver (Leigh-on-Sea)	Milkins *McManus*	Roberts *Brindley*	Wilson *Worthington Masson*	Piper *Needham*	Stephenson *Stubbs*	Hand *Nixon*	Marinello *Randall*	Kellard* *Bradd*	Davies *Probert*	Lewis *Mann*	Hiron	Reynolds
								Milkins defies Stubbs three times from the spot as the ref orders two retakes following a foul on Bradd, but the keeper was at fault for letting in Mann's corner. Hiron's glorious volley levels, but Stephenson slips to let in Bradd. 'Their goals were like a park game,' moaned Mortimore.												
8	29/9	A PRESTON	10,640	21 *9*	L 5	1-2	1-0	Davies 44 Baxter 47, Bruce 55 Ref: K Burns (Dudley)	Milkins *Brown*	Roberts *McMahon*	Wilson *McNab*	Piper *Baxter*	Stephenson *Hawkins*	Hand *Stiles*	Marinello *Lamb*	Kellard *Bruce*	Davies *Holden**	Lewis* *Burns*	Hiron *Young*	Foggo *Williams*
								Points go begging as first Baxter, who went on to suffer a serious illness after signing for Pompey, fires home, then Bruce is left free at the far post to volley in. Earlier, Preston were run ragged and Davies nudged in Piper's flick. Mortimore claims: 'I haven't seen a better side than us.'												
9	2/10	H CARLISLE	10,796	17 *18*	W 7	2-1	1-0	Hand 12, 88 Owen 74 Ref: M Sinclair (Guildford)	Milkins *Ross*	Roberts *Carr*	Wilson *Gorman*	Piper *O'Neill*	Stephenson *Green*	Hand *Tiler*	Marinello *Martin*	Kellard *Barry*	Davies *Clarke F**	Lewis *Delgado*	Hiron *Laidlaw*	Owen
								New £10,000 floodlight lamps – donated by the Supporters' Club – are switched on, but it is Hand who lights things up when he blasts home Davies' knock-down. The same routine had set up the opener, but U's levelled when Laidlaw and O'Neill set up Owen for an astute finish.												
10	6/10	H OXFORD	11,669	14 *21*	W 9	2-1	1-0	Piper 39, Davies 49 Cassidy 61 Ref: P Walters (Bridgwater)	Milkins *Burton*	Roberts *Lucas*	Wilson *Shuker*	Piper *Roberts*	Stephenson *Lowe*	Hand *Clarke C*	Marinello *Clarke D*	Kellard *Skeen*	Davies *Cassidy*	Lewis *Curran*	Hiron *Jeffrey*	
								Any home jinx is buried against uninspired Oxford. Roberts' burst through the middle sets up Lewis to weight a perfect pass to Piper to angle in, then Davies scooped home Marinello's cross. Cassidy's clever header from Jeffrey's cross gave Gerry Summers' side a glimmer of hope.												

Match Record

11 — A SHEFFIELD WED · 13/10
10 W · 2-1 · Att 12,690 · 16 · 11
Davies 52, Piper 55 / Joicey 25
Ref: J Goggins (Manchester)

Milkins	Roberts	Collins	Piper	Stephenson	Hand	Marinello	Kellard	Davies	Lewis*	Foggo	Mellows
Springett	Rodrigues	Shaw	Craig T	Thompson	Mullen	Kent*	Knighton	Joicey	Prendergast	Henderson	Sunley

The game is turned on its head as Davies rises majestically to head home Piper's corner, then debut-making sub Mellows, a former England Amateur, centres for Piper to finish off a post. The Owls only had Joicey's lofted shot over Milkins to show for their first-half dominance.

12 — A HULL · 20/10
14 L · 1-4 · Att 6,874 · 11 · 11
Hand 39 [Hawley 76] / Greenwood 23, Wagstaff 34, 66,
Ref: J Wrennall (Eccleston)

Milkins	Wealands	De Vries	Galvin*	Deere	Blampey	Hawley	Lord	Pearson	Wagstaff	Greenwood	O'Riley

Terry Neill's side are inspired by Ken Wagstaff. First he makes space for Greenwood to score, then finishes accurately from Lord's deflected shot. Hand heads in Collins' cross, but a counter-attack sees Wagstaff beat the offside trap, then Jon Hawley (18) scores his first league goal.

13 — H SWINDON · 27/10
13 W · 3-1 · Att 11,819 · 21 · 13
Piper 4, 31, Kellard 8p / Treacy 69
Ref: R Perkin (Stafford)

Milkins	Roberts	Collins	Piper	Stephenson	Hand	Marinello	Kellard	Davies	Lewis	Foggo	Mellows
Allan	Thomas	Butler	Gabriel	Burrows	Potter	Moss	McGovern	Treacy	Syrett	Jenkins	

Man-of-the-Match Piper opens the scoring by stealing past two defenders to finish a good move, then he taps in after Allan's error. In between Foggo's dramatic tumble earned a penalty. Boss Les Allen fired up Town at half-time and Treacy hit the bar, before diverting Syrett's shot in.

14 — A BLACKPOOL · 3/11
15 L · 0-5 · Att 6,535 · 7 · 13
[Alcock 90] Suddick 18, Walsh 24, Burns 68, 87
Ref: V James (York)

Milkins	Burridge	Collins	Piper	Stephenson	Hand	Marinello*	Kellard	Davies	Lewis	Foggo	Mellows
Burridge	Curtis	Hatton	Alcock	James	Suddaby	Burns	Suddick	Dyson	Bentley	Walsh	

Philanthropic Pompey enjoy plenty of possession, but Pool have all the fireworks. Stephenson's foul allows Suddick to bend in a free-kick, then Roberts' error is compounded by Hand and Walsh is free to score. Burns angles in, then poaches another before Adcock rubs in salt.

15 — H ASTON VILLA · 10/11
14 W · 2-0 · Att 12,678 · 2 · 15
Piper 40, Davies 89
Ref: B Homewood (Sunbury)

Milkins	Roberts	Collins	Piper	Stephenson	Munks	Marinello	Kellard	Davies	Lewis	Foggo	Mellows
Cumbes	Gidman	Aitken	Hockey	Nicholl	Ross	McMahon	Brown	Evans	Hamilton	Little	

Piper's knee gets the credit for the first goal, but he tries to hand it to Marinello afterwards as the winger's shot was inadvertently deflected in. Kellard claims the 'Battle of the Beards' in midfield with Trevor Hockey. 'The best performance under my command,' purrs Mortimore.

16 — A FULHAM · 17/11
16 L · 0-2 · Att 8,403 · 14 · 15
Mitchell 4, Barrett 46
Ref: J Taylor (Wolverhampton)

Milkins	Roberts	Collins	Piper	Stephenson	Munks	Marinello	Kellard	Davies	Lewis	Foggo*	Mellows
Webster	Cutbush	Slough	Mullery	Went	Dunne	Conway	Earle	Mitchell	Lloyd	Barrett	

Fulham claim their first home win over Pompey after 50 years trying. Mitchell's shot deflects off Stephenson for an untidy goal that sums up the first half. Kellard then loses possession and Barrett's effort creeps in. Went is in imperious form and will join Pompey within a fortnight.

17 — H CRYSTAL PALACE · 24/11
15 D · 2-2 · Att 14,212 · 22 · 16
Reynolds 6, 55 / Rogers 15p, 33
Ref: D Turner (Cannock)

Milkins	Roberts	Collins	Piper	Stephenson	Munks	Marinello*	Kellard	Davies	Reynolds	Foggo	Mellows
Hammond	Mulligan	Taylor T	Jeffries	Anderson	Cannon	Possee	Whalley	Rogers	Taylor P		

Malcolm Allison's under-achievers (11 defeats so far) draw as Mortimore laments: 'We must beat sides at the bottom'. Reynolds' flick finish is single-handedly cancelled out by Rogers, who nets after Possee is fouled, then he cracks in a rising drive. Reynolds is left unmarked to level.

18 — H BRISTOL CITY · 8/12
15 W · 1-0 · Att 13,178 · 11 · 18
Davies 57
Ref: A Hart (London)

Milkins	Roberts	Collins	Piper	Stephenson	Manley	Marinello	Kellard	Davies	Reynolds	Foggo	Mellows
Bond	Tainton	Merrick	Sweeney	Rodgers	Collier	Whitehead*	Ritchie	Gillies	Gow	Fear	Emanuel

Pompey unveil Went (£155,000) and Manley (£55,000 from Leicester) to stabilise the defence. However, the team make heavy weather of beating City, who cost less than the £40,000 paid for ex-Saint Davies, who settles it by thrashing in a volley in from the edge of the box.

19 — A WEST BROM · 15/12
15 W · 2-1 · Att 11,213 · 6 · 20
Piper 7, Davies 51 / Cantello 27
Ref: I Smith (Accrington)

Milkins	Roberts	Collins	Piper	Stephenson	Manley	Marinello	Kellard	Davies	Reynolds	Foggo	Mellows
Latchford	Nisbet	Wilson	Cantello	Wile	Robertson	Johnston	Brown T	Shaw	Hartford	Glover	

Furious Albion protest Piper was offside as he taps in Roberts' mis-hit shot, but the referee says Wilson was playing him on. Cantello replies with a swift shot after Milkins had saved from Robertson, but Latchford then fumbled Marinello's centre and Davies poached the winner.

20 — H PRESTON · 22/12
14 W · 3-0 · Att 13,957 · 15 · 22
Reynolds 1, Piper 62, Davies 78
Ref: J Bent (Hemel Hempstead)

Milkins	Roberts	Collins	Piper	Stephenson	Manley	Marinello	Kellard	Davies	Reynolds	Foggo	Mellows
Healey	McMahon	Snookes	Stiles	Hawkins	Bird	Sadler	Burns	Bruce	Holden	Young	

Man-of-the-Match Mellows plays a part in all three goals, hitting the post early on for Reynolds to hook in the rebound. His through-ball then allows Piper to judge a lob perfectly, then his cross-field pass is nodded into Davies' path by Kellard. Went faces suspension after a booking.

21 — A MILLWALL · 26/12
12 D · 1-1 · Att 9,797 · 16 · 23
Davies 37 / Wood 14
Ref: T Reynolds (Swansea)

Milkins	Roberts	Collins	Piper	Stephenson	Manley	Marinello	Kellard	Davies	Reynolds	Foggo	Mellows
King	Donaldson	Jones	Dorney	Kitchener	Alder	Bolland	Clark	Wood	Saul	Hill	

Milkins is inspired as Millwall have 12 shots on target to four. He pushes Hill's volley onto the post and Lions' boss Benny Fenton says: 'He had no right to stop that one'. Wood nets his 12th of the season, but Mellows' chase of an apparent lost cause allows him to cross for Davies.

LEAGUE DIVISION 2

Manager: John Mortimore

SEASON 1973-74

No	Date	Att	Pos	Pt	F-A	H-T	Scorers, Times, and Referees	1	2	3	4	5	6	7	8	9	10	11	12 sub used
22	A BOLTON 29/12	13,684	13 / 18	L 23	0-4	0-2	[Whatmore 64, 84] Jones G 13p, Byrom 18. Ref: R Lee (Cheadle). *Mortimore complains about the fairness of the loan system as Thompson, borrowed from Liverpool, rips Pompey apart. He is fouled for the penalty, then his delicate chip gives Byrom an easy header. Teenager Neil Whatmore taps in Paul Jones nod-down, then hits a searing shot.*	Milkins / Siddall	Roberts / Ritson	Collins / McAllister*	Piper / Rimmer	Went / Jones P	Manley / Waldron	Marinello / Byrom	Kellard / Jones G	Davies / Greaves	Reynolds / Whatmore	Mellows / Thompson	Nicholson
23	H CARDIFF 1/1	20,062	10 / 17	W 25	1-0	0-0	Kellard 62. Ref: H Powell (Stourport). *Struggling City are unlucky in front of the largest crowd of the season. The goal comes from nothing as Davies touches a throw-in-field to see skipper Kellard's well-struck shot catch the keeper unsighted. The three-day-week means a four-page, black and white programme costing 2p!*	Milkins / Irwin	Roberts / Dwyer	Collins / Bell	Piper / Powell*	Went / Murray	Manley / Villars	Marinello / Farrington	Kellard / McCulloch	Davies / Phillips	Reynolds / Carlin	Mellows / Anderson	Impey
24	H LUTON 12/1	18,476	10 / 3	D 26	0-0	0-0	Ref: R Kirkpatrick (Leicester). *Pompey achieve national notoriety during the energy crisis when their hired generator fails and they are forced to switch on the mains after a 24-minute stoppage. Harry Haslam's Division One-bound side almost snatch it after the restart when Manley slices against his own bar.*	Milkins / Horn	Roberts / Ryan John	Collins / Thomson	Piper / Shanks	Went / Faulkner	Manley / Garner	Marinello / Ryan Jim	Kellard / Finney	Davies / Anderson	Reynolds / West	Mellows / Aston	
25	A MIDDLESBROUGH 19/1	21,774	10 / 1	L 26	0-3	0-0	Foggon 49, Smith 74, Souness 76. Ref: D Civil (Birmingham). *A second-half onslaught sees Pompey wilt and turns Ayresome into a 'cauldron of delight.' Davies should have punished frustrated Boro, but missed from six yards before the break. Foggon then efficiently despatched Boam's knock-down, then sub Smith sealed it with his first touch.*	Milkins / Platt	Roberts / Craggs	Hand / Spraggon	Piper / Souness	Went / Boam	Manley / Maddren	Marinello / Murdoch	Kellard / Foggon	Davies / Mills	Reynolds / Hickton*	Mellows / Armstrong	Smith
26	H WEST BROM 3/2	19,789	10 / 6	D 27	1-1	0-0	Piper 72. Went 67 [og]. Ref: R Challis (Tonbridge). *Pompey's first Sunday league game sees skipper Kellard vowing to contest a first-half dismissal. High-flying WBA led when Glover's long-range drive deflected in off Went, but Piper levelled after Hiron's shot was saved. Davies hit a post and Shaw was sent off in a frantic finale.*	Milkins / Latchford	Roberts / Nisbet	Collins / Wilson	Piper / Cantello	Went / Wile	Manley / Robertson	Marinello / Johnston	Kellard ! / Brown T	Davies / Shaw !	Hiron / Hartford	Mellows / Glover	
27	A NOTTS CO 9/2	8,664	10 / 8	L 27	0-4	0-1	[Roberts 87og] Randall 8, 78, Masson 67p. Ref: A Jones (Ormskirk). *A 'League Liner' special train takes 400 fans to Meadow Lane, but their morale is sapped by Manley's career-finishing cartilage injury and a thrashing rounded off by Roberts' flick past Milkins, which replicated his similar o.g. against County the previous season with Bristol Rovers.*	Milkins / McManus	Roberts / Brindley	Collins / Stubbs	Piper / McVay	Went / Needham	Manley* / Mann	Marinello / Randall	Kellard / Masson	Davies / Bradd	Hiron / Probert	Mellows / Carter	Lewis
28	H SHEFFIELD WED 20/2	8,699	12 / 19	D 28	1-1	1-0	Davies 43. Potts 90. Ref: B Homewood (Sunbury). *A midweek afternoon fixture – due to the on-going strikes – has a pre-season atmosphere, as the Owls nick a point 15 seconds from time. Potts takes advantage of hesitant defending to level. Davies converted Piper's cross with a smart shot and Price played after six months out.*	Milkins / Ferguson	Roberts / Rodrigues	Wilson / Knighton	Piper / Thompson	Went / Eustace	Hand / Shaw	Price / Coyle	Kellard* / Sunley	Davies / Joicey*	Mellows / Craig T	Jennings / Potts	Lewis / Prendergast
29	A OXFORD 23/2	7,765	14 / 19	L 28	0-3	0-0	Aylott 51, Gough 78, Curran 85. Ref: R Capey (Crewe). *Without a win since 1 January, Pompey slip nearer the relegation battle after a side shorn of Milkins, Kellard and Piper is no match for Oxford. Went's blunder lets in Aylott, then Hand dallies and Gough takes advantage. Curran's fantastic shot secured the U's first win bonus of 1974.*	Tilsed / Burton	Roberts / Light	Wilson / Shuker	Lewis / Roberts	Went / Clarke C	Hand / Briggs	Jennings / Gough	McCann / Atkinson	Davies / Clarke D	Price / Curran	Mellows* / Aylott	Reynolds
30	H MILLWALL 2/3	11,004	15 / 13	D 29	0-0	0-0	Ref: D Smith (Stonehouse). *Keeper Dave Best, signed from Ipswich for £35,000, produces a tremendous save from Hill's lob in injury-time to save a point. McCann, in his first game since his testimonial ten months ago, stars, but Pompey fail to trouble a side which had leaked nine in their last two away games.*	Best / King	Lewis / Brown N	Collins / Cripps	Piper / Dorney	Went / Kitchener	Hand / Alder	Marinello / Bolland	McCann / Clark	Davies / Wood	Wilson / Smethurst	Hiron* / Hill	Jennings
31	A SUNDERLAND 5/3	8,142	15 / 9	L 29	0-3	0-0	Tueart 74p, 80, Kerr 83. Ref: M Lowe (Sheffield). *Roberts' foul on Tueart on the edge of the box is judged a penalty and Pompey never recover. Heads drop after that and Tueart thrashes home Porterfield's cross, before Kerr's topped shot loops in off Kellard. Piper's early effort is mysteriously disallowed in another afternoon kick-off.*	Best / Montgomery	Wilson / Malone	Collins / Bolton	Piper / Longhorn	Went / Watson	Hand / Belfitt	Marinello / Kerr	Kellard / Hughes	Davies / Halom	Wilson / Porterfield	Hiron* / Tueart	Jennings

Results

#	Date	Venue	Opponent	Pos	Result	Score	Att.	Opp pos	Pts
32	9/3	A	SWINDON	13	W	2:1	5,364	22	31
33	16/3	H	HULL	11	W	3:1	9,838	9	33
34	23/3	A	ASTON VILLA	15	L	1:4	15,517	11	33
35	26/3	A	NOTT'M FOREST	15	L	0:2	14,040	4	33
36	30/3	H	BLACKPOOL	15	D	0:0	9,693	3	34
37	6/4	A	CRYSTAL PALACE	15	D	0:0	23,662	19	35
38	12/4	H	ORIENT	15	D	0:0	10,944	4	36
39	13/4	H	FULHAM	15	W	3:0	12,054	14	38
40	15/4	A	ORIENT	16	L	1:2	11,540	4	38
41	20/4	A	BRISTOL CITY	14	W	2:0	11,143	16	40
42	27/4	H	NOTT'M FOREST	15	L	0:2	11,765	6	40

Home Average 13,677 · Away 11,215

---

32 — A SWINDON, 9/3 — W 2:1
McCann 18, Marinello 24 / McLaughlin 83
Ref: K Baker (Rugby)
Portsmouth: Best, Roberts, Collins, Piper, Hand, Lewis, Marinello, McCann, Davies, Wilson, Mellows* — sub Smith
Swindon: Spratley, McLaughlin, Trollope, Butler, Potter, Munks, Moss, Dixon, Compton*, Syrett, Jenkins — sub Legg

With chairman Deacon's lecture still fresh, Piper is pushed forward and he creates space for Marinello's confidence-boosting goal. Earlier, McCann's lob bounced over the keeper and in. Town rallied, but Jenkins' pen was saved before McLaughlin (19) netted from an acute angle.

33 — H HULL, 16/3 — W 3:1
Marinello 3, 60, Davies 44 / Pearson 65
Ref: A Hart (London)
Portsmouth: Best, Roberts, Collins, Piper, Went*, Hand, Marinello, McCann, Davies, Wilson, Lewis — sub Mellows
Hull: Wealands, McGill, De Vries, Burnett, Deere, Blampey, Lord, Grimes, Pearson, Hemmerman, Greenwood

Marinello demonstrates his new-found belief with a solo goal, then his mis-hit slips under Wealands. Davies nodded in Collins' free-kick. Transfer-listed Wilson is outstanding at left-back, but even he can't stop Pearson pulling one back. Hand covers for Went after his ankle injury.

34 — A ASTON VILLA, 23/3 — L 1:4
Piper 20 / McMahon 54, 80, Morgan 67, 86
Ref: P Willis (Meadowfield)
Portsmouth: Best, Roberts, Collins, Piper, Stephenson, Hand, Marinello, McCann, Davies, Wilson, Lewis* — sub Foggo
Aston Villa: Cumbes, Gidman, Aitken, Ross, Nicholl, Turnbull, McMahon, Little, Morgan, Hamilton, Leonard

Dismal away form remains after a second-half collapse. Marinello's pace sets up Piper to glance in off the far post, but after the interval Villa turn up the heat and McMahon's 30-yarder levels. Morgan stabs home from close in and it's over. Pompey have let in more away than anyone.

35 — A NOTT'M FOREST, 26/3 — L 0:2
Lyall 19, Hand 90 (og)
Ref: J Rice (Leyland)
Portsmouth: Best, Roberts, Collins*, Piper, Stephenson, Hand, Marinello, McCann, Davies, Lewis, Mellows — sub Foggo
Nott'm Forest: Barron, O'Kane, Winfield, Chapman, Cottam, Richardson, McKenzie, Lyall, Martin, Robertson, Bowyer

Increased work-rate after the Villa debacle is no consolation as Best's poor clearance is nodded back by Lyall, forcing Hand to back-head into his own net in injury-time. By then Fratton favourite Allan Brown is in front, thanks to Lyall's opener from Bowyer's flick.

36 — H BLACKPOOL, 30/3 — D 0:0
Ref: G Kew (Amersham)
Portsmouth: Best, Roberts, Wilson, Hand, Went, Stephenson, Marinello, Kellard, Davies, Piper, Foggo
Blackpool: Burridge, Harrison, Hatton, Alcock, James, Suddick, Burns, Suddaby, Davies, Evanson, Ainscow

An unbeaten home run stretching to 17 matches couldn't disguise the lack of quality on offer. Fans were streaming out of the sun-drenched ground long before the end. Pool would have snatched it, but Micky Burns, wanted by Pompey and Saints earlier in the season, booed twice.

37 — A CRYSTAL PALACE, 6/4 — D 0:0
Ref: R Crabb (Exeter)
Portsmouth: Best, Roberts, Wilson, Hand, Went, Stephenson, Marinello, Kellard, Davies, Piper, Foggo
Crystal Palace: Hammond, Mulligan, Jump, Blyth, Barry, Johnson, Possee, Jeffries, Whittle, Rogers, Taylor P

Went puts longer studs in his boot at half-time after a slip put him on his back and allows Rogers a free shot, which inches wide. Stephenson and Kellard impress against their old club. Piper misses an easy header, but relegation-bound Palace rally late on and Jump rattles the bar.

38 — H ORIENT, 12/4 — D 0:0
Ref: M Sinclair (Guildford)
Portsmouth: Best, Roberts, Wilson, Hand, Went, Stephenson, Marinello, Kellard, Davies, Piper, Foggo
Orient: Goddard, Payne, Downing, Allen, Hoadley, Walley, Fairbrother, Brisley, Bullock, Queen, Heppolette

Davies' aerial mastery of Walley creates enough chances to have won the game, but increased security has been offset by a lack of firepower. The O's rarely threaten and boss George Petchey wails: 'If we beat Pompey on Monday we will go up, as we will have done the impossible.'

39 — H FULHAM, 13/4 — W 3:0
Went 23, Piper 59, 67
Ref: J Taylor (Wolverhampton)
Portsmouth: Best, Roberts, Wilson, Hand, Went, Stephenson, Marinello, Kellard, Davies, Piper, Stewart
Fulham: Mellor, Strong, Dunne*, Mullery, Fraser, Howe, Conway, Cutbush, Busby, Moore, Barrett — sub Lloyd

Debut-making apprentice Stewart (17), in for Foggo, impresses as Went ends the goal-famine by pulling down Roberts' cross and firing home against his old club. Mellor, later to join Pompey, is hurt as Piper snaps up Hand's blocked shot, then Piper arrows home a half-cleared corner.

40 — A ORIENT, 15/4 — L 1:2
Stewart 73 / Queen 13, 44
Ref: P Reeves (Leicester)
Portsmouth: Best, Roberts, Wilson, Hand, Went, Stephenson, Marinello, Kellard*, Davies, Piper, Stewart — sub Mellows
Orient: Goddard, Payne, Downing, Allen, Hoadley, Walley, Fairbrother, Brisley, Bullock, Queen, Heppolette

Petchey must have been pleased with the result, but the O's fail to clinch promotion in the end. Stewart's brave finish as he was clattered by Hoadley produces a grandstand climax, but earlier Queen had seen a soft shot creep in, then apparently sewn things up with a diving header.

41 — A BRISTOL CITY, 20/4 — W 2:0
Davies 13, Stewart 77
Ref: T Bosi (Codsall)
Portsmouth: Best, Roberts, Wilson, Hand, Went, Stephenson, Marinello, Kellard, Davies, Piper, Stewart
Bristol City: Cashley, Sweeney, Drysdale, Gow, Collier, Merrick, Tainton, Ritchie, Fear, Gillies*, Emanuel — sub Hunt

Stewart is instrumental in setting up this first win at Ashton Gate in a decade. City had nabbed seven points out of the last eight, but Stewart's distracting run allows Davies to stroke home. The youngster then smashed a perfect shot past Cashley, but he claimed: 'I just hit and hoped.'

42 — H NOTT'M FOREST, 27/4 — L 0:2
McKenzie 76, 88
Ref: I Jones (Treharris)
Portsmouth: Best, Roberts, Wilson, Hand, Stephenson, Ellis, Foggo, Kellard, Davies, Piper, Stewart
Nott'm Forest: Peacock, Serella, O'Kane, Chapman, Cottam, Richardson, McKenzie, Lyall, Martin, Jackson, Woodcock

Having spent £400,000 on talent, Pompey wind up nearer the drop than promotion. £250,000 of that is ruled out as Went and Marinello start two-match bans and it shows. Former Southern Grammar boy Ellis (18) does well, but McKenzie nets twice late on to end up with 28 goals.

LEAGUE DIVISION 2 (CUP-TIES)

Manager: John Mortimore

SEASON 1973-74

League Cup

				W/D/L	F-A	H-T	Att	Scorers, Times, and Referees
1	H	SOUTHEND	28/8	W	2-1	1-0	9,652 / 3	Davies 16, Reynolds 79 / Taylor 48 / Ref: A Lees (Street)
2	A	PLYMOUTH	9/10	L	0-4	0-2	13,202 / 3:14	Machin 8, Davey 42, 87, Mariner 64 Furnell / Ref: D Smith (Stonehouse)

Match	1	2	3	4	5	6	7	8	9	10	11	12 sub used
1 Pompey	Tilsed	Roberts	Wilson	Piper	Stephenson	Munks*	Marinello	Kellard	Davies	Foggo	Reynolds	Lewis
1 Southend	*Mackay*	*Smith*	*Ford*	*Elliott*	*Albeson*	*Moody*	*Booth*	*Johnson*	*Moore*	*Guthrie*	*Taylor*	
2 Pompey	Milkins	Roberts	Wilson	Piper	Stephenson	Hand	Marinello	Kellard	Davies	Lewis	Hiron	
2 Plymouth	*Furnell*	*Webb*	*Sullivan*	*Hore*	*Saxton*	*Hague*	*Welsh*	*Davey*	*Mariner*	*Machin*	*Rogers*	

Match 1: The third division side cause a few flutters, but Reynolds converts Foggo's cross to win it after Mackay's poor goal-kick had been cut out by Marinello. Taylor, later to play for England while at Div Three Palace, catches the eye and levels Davies' header thanks to a defensive disaster.

Match 2: Pompey are sunk deeper than Plymouth Sound as Argyle get a standing ovation. Sullivan, called up by England U-23s and later to join PFC, crosses for Mariner (19), fresh from the Lancs League, to nod the clincher. Davey, also to end up at Fratton, is set up by Rogers (ditto) late on.

FA Cup

				W/D/L	F-A	H-T	Att	Scorers, Times, and Referees
3	H	SWINDON	5/1	D	3-3	1-3	16,682 / 21	Davies 20, Went 78, Kellard 90p / Jenkins 4, Moss 23, Trollope 45 / Ref: B Daniels (Rainham)
3R	A	SWINDON	9/1	W	1-0	0-0	10,021 / 21	Kellard 58 / Ref: B Daniels (Rainham)
4	H	ORIENT	27/1	D	0-0	0-0	32,838 / 2	Ref: D Smith (Stonehouse)
4R	A	ORIENT	29/1	D	1-1	1-1	14,879 / 2	Mellows 2 / Fairbrother 29 / Ref: D Smith (Stonehouse)
4 RR	N	ORIENT	5/2	W	2-0	1-0	19,595 / 2	Kellard 27, Davies 87 / Ref: M Sinclair (Guildford)
5	A	NOTT'M FOREST	17/2	L	0-1	0-0	38,569 / 7	McKenzie 65p / Ref: K Burns (Dudley)

Match	1	2	3	4	5	6	7	8	9	10	11	12 sub used
3 Pompey	Milkins	Roberts	Collins	Piper*	Went	Manley	Marinello	Kellard	Davies	Reynolds	Mellows	Lewis
3 Swindon	*Allan*	*Dixon*	*Trollope*	*Munks*	*Burrows*	*Stroud*	*Moss*	*Hubbard*	*Eastoe*	*Butler*	*Jenkins*	
3R Pompey	Milkins	Roberts	Collins*	Lewis	Went	Manley	Marinello	Kellard	Davies	Reynolds	Mellows	Hand
3R Swindon	*Allan*	*Dixon*	*Trollope*	*Munks*	*Burrows*	*Stroud*	*Moss*	*Hubbard*	*Eastoe*	*Butler*	*Jenkins*	
4 Pompey	Milkins	Roberts	Collins	Piper	Went	Manley	Marinello	Kellard	Davies	Hiron	Mellows	
4 Orient	*Goddard*	*Hoadley*	*Payne*	*Boyle*	*Linton*	*Walley*	*Fairbrother*	*Brisley*	*Bullock*	*Queen*	*Heppolette*	
4R Pompey	Milkins	Roberts	Collins	Piper	Went	Manley	Marinello	Kellard	Davies	Hiron	Mellows	
4R Orient	*Goddard*	*Hoadley*	*Payne*	*Boyle*	*Linton*	*Walley*	*Fairbrother*	*Brisley**	*Bullock*	*Queen*	*Heppolette*	*Downing*
4RR Pompey	Milkins	Roberts	Collins	Piper	Went	Manley	Marinello	Kellard	Davies	Hiron	Mellows	
4RR Orient	*Jackson*	*Hoadley*	*Payne*	*Boyle*	*Harris*	*Walley*	*Fairbrother*	*Brisley*	*Bullock**	*Queen*	*Heppolette*	*Downing*
5 Pompey	Milkins	Roberts	Wilson		Went	Hand	Marinello*	Kellard	Davies	Hiron	Mellows	Lewis
5 Forest	*Barron*	*O'Kane*	*Winfield*	*Chapman*	*Cottam**	*Richardson*	*McKenzie*	*O'Neill*	*Martin*	*Jackson*	*Bowyer*	*Serella*

Match 3: Kellard's glance at the programme pic of him scoring a penalty against Town in October proves vital, as Lewis tumbles under Butler's tackle deep into injury-time. 'I thought the keeper would go the same way, so I put in the opposite corner,' he smiled. Pompey are lucky to survive.

Match 3R: The three-day week strikes again with an afternoon kick-off and only a teamsheet for a programme. Kellard is the hero again in a mudbath as he rifles home after Mellows' shot is hacked off the line. A large Pompey following 'Chime' on their team, who set up a home tie with Orient.

Match 4: Fans flock to the first Sunday game at Fratton, ensuring the biggest gate since Arsenal in 1971, including several thousand visitors. Orient, with just one away defeat so far, live dangerously, but Pompey rely on Milkins to make two fine stops from Brisley early on, then at the death.

Match 4R: Davies' extra-time goal is ruled out by a dubious offside flag and means the teams will have to slug it out again at neutral Selhurst Park for the right to meet Forest. Mellows gave Pompey a dream start after Marinello set him up for a header, but Manley's error allowed the equaliser.

Match 4RR: Pompey survive Orient's opening onslaught, before poaching the lead when Davies' knock-down was met 30 yards out by Kellard and his left-footer exploded into the roof of the net. Davies' perfectly-placed shot made things safe to send 10,000 fans happily back home down the A3.

Match 5: Hand's return for Manley turns sour when his ill-timed tackle on Bowyer lets McKenzie calmly beat Milkins. Forest force ten corners in just half an hour, with McKenzie hitting the bar, but as the game wore on a replay looked on until Hand dashed the hopes of a visiting army of fans.

League table

	Team	P		Home						Away					Pts
			W	D	L	F	A	W	D	L	F	A			
1	Middlesbro	42	16	4	1	40	8	11	7	3	37	22			65
2	Luton	42	12	5	4	42	25	7	7	7	22	26			50
3	Carlisle	42	13	5	3	40	17	7	4	10	21	31			49
4	Orient	42	9	8	4	28	17	6	10	5	27	25			48
5	Blackpool	42	11	5	5	35	17	6	8	7	22	23			47
6	Sunderland	42	11	6	4	32	15	8	3	10	26	29			47
7	Nott'm Forest	42	12	6	3	40	19	3	9	9	17	24			45
8	West Brom	42	8	9	4	28	24	6	7	8	20	21			44
9	Hull	42	9	9	3	25	15	4	8	9	21	32			43
10	Notts Co	42	8	6	7	30	35	7	7	7	25	25			43
11	Bolton	42	12	5	4	30	17	3	7	11	14	23			42
12	Millwall	42	10	6	5	28	16	4	8	9	23	35			42
13	Fulham	42	11	4	6	26	20	5	6	10	13	23			42
14	Aston Villa	42	9	8	4	33	21	5	6	10	19	24			41
15	PORTSMOUTH	42	9	8	4	26	16	5	4	12	19	46			40
16	Bristol City	42	9	5	7	25	20	5	5	11	22	34			38
17	Cardiff	42	8	7	6	27	20	2	9	10	22	42			36
18	Oxford	42	8	8	5	27	21	2	8	11	8	25			36
19	Sheffield Wed	42	9	6	6	33	24	3	5	13	18	39			35
20	Crys Palace	42	6	7	8	24	24	5	5	11	19	32			34
21	Preston *	42	7	8	6	24	23	2	6	13	16	39			31
22	Swindon	42	6	7	8	22	27	1	4	16	14	45			25
		924	212	143	107	665	441	107	143	212	441	665			923

* deducted 1 pt

Odds & ends

Double wins: (3) Carlisle, Swindon, Bristol C.
Double losses: (4) Middlesbrough, Bolton, Notts Co, Nott'm F.

Won from behind: (1) Sheff Wed (a).
Lost from in front: (2) Preston (a), Aston Villa (a).

High spots: Completing double over promoted Carlisle.
Beating Orient 2-0 in a FA Cup second replay at Selhurst Park.
18-match unbeaten home run in league and cup from October to April.

Low spots: Losing 0-5 at Blackpool in November.
Being knocked out of the FA Cup at Nott'm F.
Losing 0-4 at third division Plymouth in the League Cup.
Conceding more goals away than anyone else in the division.
A run of three successive 0-0 draws in March and April.
Taking only one point from eight in the first four home matches.

Pompey played enough FA Cup matches (6) to have played in the final,
but only reached the fifth round!

Player of the Year: Paul Went.
Ever Presents: (1) Ron Davies.
Hat-tricks: (0).
Leading Scorer: Ron Davies (13).

Appearances and Goals

Player	Appearances Lge	Sub	LC	Sub	FAC	Sub	Goals Lge	LC	FAC	Tot
Best, David	13									
Collins, John	21				5					
Davies, Ron	42		2		6		13	1	2	16
Ellis, Peter	1									
Foggo, Ken	13	3	1				3			3
Hand, Eoin	27		1		1	1	3			3
Hiron, Ray	10		1		4					
Jennings, Nick	3	1								
Kellard, Bobby	36		2		6		3		3	6
Lewis, Brian	14		1		1	2	1			1
Manley, Malcolm	10				5					
Marinello, Peter	39		2		6		3			3
McCann, Albert	7									
Mellows, Mick	20	3			6				1	1
Milkins, John	23		1		6					
Munks, David	6		1							
Piper, Norman	41		2		5		12			12
Price, Peter	3									
Reynolds, Richard	11	2	1		2		3	1		4
Roberts, Phil	41		2		6					
Smith, Paul			1							
Stephenson, Alan	26		2		2					
Stewart, Andy	4				1		2			2
Tilsed, Ron	6		1							
Went, Paul	21				6		1		1	2
Wilson, Billy	24		2		1					
26 players used	462	17	22		66	3	44	2	7	53

LEAGUE DIVISION 2 — Manager: Mortimore ⇨ Ian St John — SEASON 1974-75

Match summary

No	Date	Opponent	Att	Pos	Pt	F-A	H-T	Scorers, Times, and Referees
1	A 17/8	BOLTON	12,776		L 0	0-3	0-2	Jones P 28, 53 Byrom 42 — Ref: K Styles (Barnsley)
2	H 24/8	NOTT'M FOREST	11,340	14 / 21	W 2	2-0	1-0	Mellows 29, Reynolds 75 — Ref: M Sinclair (Guildford)
3	A 28/8	MANCHESTER U	42,547	1 / 17	L 2	1-2	0-1	Davies 88p; Daly 15p, McIlroy 80 — Ref: P Willis (Meadowfield)
4	A 31/8	ORIENT	6,861	16 / 15	D 3	1-1	1-0	Reynolds 24; Bullock 80 — Ref: R Kirkpatrick (Leicester)
5	H 7/9	WEST BROM	9,158	20 / 13	L 3	1-3	0-3	Stephenson 54; Johnston 23, Shaw 38, Merrick 45 — Ref: B Daniels (Rainham)
6	A 14/9	SOUTHAMPTON	19,361	21 / 15	L 3	1-2	0-1	Davies 59p; Osgood 44, 78 — Ref: C Thomas (Treorchy)
7	A 17/9	NOTT'M FOREST	9,534	17 / 14	W 5	2-1	2-1	Davies 7, 24; Jones 25 — Ref: J Williams (Wrexham)
8	H 21/9	CARDIFF	9,519	17 / 22	D 6	2-2	0-2	Mellows 51, Piper 66; Showers 31, Vincent 44 — Ref: A Hart (London)
9	H 24/9	OLDHAM	9,671	18 / 11	D 7	1-1	1-0	Kellard 44; Young 55 — Ref: C White (Harrow)
10	A 28/9	YORK	6,177	19 / 7	L 7	0-3	0-2	Seal 22, Holmes 32p, Wann 48 — Ref: I Smith (Accrington)

Line-ups (Pompey roman; opponent *italic*)

No	1	2	3	4	5	6	7	8	9	10	11	12 sub used
1	Best	Roberts	Wilson	Hand	Stephenson	Ellis	Piper	Reynolds	Davies	Mellows	Stewart*	Lewis
1	*Siddall*	*Ritson*	*Dunne*	*Nicholson*	*Jones P*	*McAllister*	*Byrom*	*Waldron*	*Lee*	*Whatmore*	*Thompson*	
2	Best	Peacock	Wilson	Piper	Went	Stephenson	Marinello*	Hand	Davies	Reynolds	Mellows	Stewart
2		*O'Kane*	*Jones*	*Chapman*	*Cottam*	*Richardson*	*Dennehy*	*Lyall*	*Galley*	*Woodcock*	*Jackson*	*Serella*
3	Best	Roberts	Wilson*	Piper	Went	Stephenson	Marinello	Hand	Davies	Reynolds	Mellows	Ellis
3	*Stepney*	*Forsyth*	*Houston*	*Greenhoff*	*Holton*	*Buchan*	*Morgan*	*McIlroy*	*Pearson*	*Martin*	*Daly*	
4	Best	Ellis	Roberts	Piper	Went	Stephenson	Marinello	Hand	Davies	Reynolds	Mellows	Kellard
4	*Jackson*	*Fisher*	*Roffey*	*Hoadley*	*Harris*	*Walley*	*Fairbrother*	*Brisley*	*Bullock*	*Queen*	*Possee*	
5	Best	Ellis	Roberts	Hand	Went*	Stephenson	Marinello	Reynolds	Davies	Piper	Mellows	Kellard
5	*Latchford*	*Nisbet*	*Wilson*	*Cantello*	*Wile*	*Robertson*	*Merrick*	*Brown T*	*Shaw*	*Glover*	*Johnston*	
6	Best	Peacock	Wilson	Piper	Went	Stephenson	Marinello	Kellard	Davies	Reynolds	Mellows	Ellis
6	*Turner*	*Mills*	*Peach*	*Fisher*	*Bennett*	*Steele !*	*Gilchrist*	*Channon*	*Osgood*	*O'Neil*	*O'Brien*	*Stokes*
7	Best	Peacock	Wilson	Piper	Ellis	Stephenson	Marinello	Kellard	Davies	Hiron	Mellows	Hand*
7		*O'Kane*	*Jones*	*Chapman*	*Cottam*	*Robertson*	*Dennehy*	*Lyall*	*Martin*	*Bowyer*	*O'Neill*	*Jackson*
8	Best	Peacock	Wilson	Roberts	Ellis	Hand	Marinello	Kellard	Davies	Piper	Mellows	
8	*Healey*	*Impey*	*Pethard*	*Villars*	*Murray*	*Powell*	*Farrington*	*Charles*	*Showers*	*Vincent*	*McInch*	*Sayer*
9	Best	Ellis	Wilson	Piper	Hand	Went	Foggo	Kellard	Jones	Reynolds	Mellows	
9	*Ogden*	*Wood*	*Whittle*	*Blair*	*Hicks*	*Edwards*	*Lochhead*	*Bell*	*Jones*	*Robins*	*Groves*	*Young*
10	Best	Ellis	Wilson	Piper	Went	Hand	Foggo	Kellard	Davies	Reynolds	Mellows	
10	*Crawford*	*Hunter*	*Oliver*	*Holmes*	*Swallow*	*Topping*	*Lyons*	*Cave*	*Seal*	*Hinch*	*Wann*	

Match reports

1. Pompey leave Burnden Park well beaten, but wonder what might have been, had the ref given a penalty early on, rather than an indirect free-kick, when Davies seemed to be shoved. Jones claims two gifts, first from Stewart's misplaced back-pass, then when Best drops a simple cross.

2. Anyone watching the brawling fans on the Milton End, rather than the game, would have missed Reynolds' spectacular shot to seal two points. Mellows opened the scoring after swapping passes with Marinello, but Forest, shorn of McKenzie's goals (to Leeds), couldn't take advantage.

3. It takes 86 minutes for Stepney to be troubled, but United are unconvincing. Sub Ellis acquits himself well and Buchan trips the youngster for the penalty, which is the first goal the Reds have let in so far. Stephenson's handball led to the opener, then McIlroy's cross-shot settled it.

4. Mortimore is off scouting, so misses what turns out to be his last match in charge. Coach Wright claims a win was thrown away, but O's boss Petchey begs to differ. Reynolds' 25-yarder trumps Jackson, but it is Pompey's only worthwhile shot. Bullock's downward header rescues it.

5. Tindall is in temporary charge after Mortimore's shock sacking. Went's injury allows WBA to take over but Stephenson nudges home a corner and Deacon praises the team for their second half. Pompey are said to be talking to Alf Ramsey and eyeing a move for QPR's Stan Bowles.

6. Davies gets a standing ovation before the start. Osgood's brilliance settles a bad-tempered derby, as he volleys in Channon's cross from an acute angle, then converts O'Neil's pass. In between, Davies nets after Turner's foul and late on Steele is sent off for body-checking Marinello.

7. New boss St John arrives in Deacon's limo after a hotel meeting with the team. With Hiron recalled, Davies is back to form, finishing a five-man move, before heading in Piper's free-kick. Gosport-born Jones replies, but Pompey hold on and Forest fans howl for Allan Brown's head.

8. Pompey fans are warned by St John that they will have to get used to 'possession' football. They had showed their frustration as an equaliser took time to come. Slack defending lets City in twice, but then it's one-way traffic. Mellows scores from 20 yards, then Piper hooks home.

9. Latics' 17-year-old sub, Alan Young, crowns an impressive debut with a fierce drive after Roberts' error. It mars a better second-half showing by Pompey. Earlier, Kellard's ferocious 20-yard shot earned a lucky half-time lead. 'A stupid goal cost us a point,' bemoaned Ian St John.

10. Deacon maintains St John has yet to mention the subject of the transfer market, but on this showing it can't be long in coming. New-boys York go ahead when Seal's knee unwittingly diverted the ball in, then Wann's dramatic fall lets Holmes' spot-kick put the game beyond Pompey.

Match 11 — A NOTTS CO, 5/10
Att: 8,573 · Pos: 19 · 11 · D 1-1 (HT 0-1) · 8
Davies 47 / Stubbs 7
Ref: J Goggins (Manchester)

Pompey: Best, Ellis, Wilson, Piper, Went, Stephenson, Foggo, Kellard, Davies, Hand, Marinello
Notts Co: Brown, Brinley, O'Brien, Masson, Needham, Stubbs, Randall*, Probert, Bradd, Mann, Scanlon, Carter

St John's drive for fitness on the training field earns dividends, but he blames 'stiff-leggedness' for a poor first-half, in which Stubbs' header from Masson's free-kick was the least County deserved. Recalled winger Foggo crossed for Davies' head to level, then Pompey dominated.

Match 12 — H FULHAM, 12/10
Att: 12,520 · Pos: 18 · 8 · D 0-0 (HT 0-0) · 9
Ref: R Crabb (Exeter)

Pompey: Best, Ellis, Wilson, Piper, Went, Stephenson, Foggo, Kellard, Davies, Hand, Marinello
Fulham: Mellor, Cutbush, Strong, Mullery*, Lacy, Moore, Conway, Slough, Busby, Lloyd, Barrett, Mitchell

Afterwards St John growls: 'We're having the ball frequently,' following former-England star Moore's apparent handball shortly after the break. Almost at once, the roving Marinello is up-ended by Cutbush, but again the referee waves away penalty appeals and Fulham hang on.

Match 13 — H MANCHESTER U, 15/10
Att: 25,608 · Pos: 17 · 7 · D 0-0 (HT 0-0) · 10
Ref: P Walters (Bridgwater)

Pompey: Best, Ellis, Wilson, Piper, Went, Stephenson, Foggo, Kellard, Davies, Hand, Marinello
Manchester U: Stepney, Forsyth, Albiston, Greenhoff, Holton, Buchan, Morgan*, McIlroy, Macari, McCalling, Daly, McCreery

An absorbing, rather than exciting, game has United thanking full-back Forsyth for a goal-line clearance which denies Kellard 12 minutes from the end. Playing with composure and style, Pompey must have impressed a crowd more than twice the average, as they match the leaders.

Match 14 — A NORWICH, 19/10
Att: 20,899 · Pos: 20 · 3 · L 0-2 (HT 0-1) · 10
Stringer 15, Boyer 59
Ref: H Hackney (Barnsley)

Pompey: Best, Ellis*, Wilson, Piper, Went, Stephenson, Foggo, Kellard, Davies, Hand, Marinello
Norwich: Keelan, Butler, Sullivan, Morris, Forbes, Stringer, Machin, MacDougall, Boyer, Suggett, Powell, Roberts

Ex-Bournemouth star Boyer's £145,000 fee scared off Pompey in February, but on this evidence he seems a bargain. First he harried Went into conceding the corner from which Stringer scored, then his persistence let him regain possession three times before scooping the ball over Best.

Match 15 — H BLACKPOOL, 26/10
Att: 10,143 · Pos: 19 · 11 · D 0-0 (HT 0-0) · 11
Ref: D Civil (Birmingham)

Pompey: Best, Roberts, Wilson, Piper, Went, Stephenson, Foggo, Kellard, Davies*, Hand, Marinello, Stewart
Blackpool: Burridge, Hatton, Harrison, Curtis, Hart, Suddaby, Walsh, Tong, Evanson, Bentley, Ainscow

After this dreadful show which saw the crowd slow-handclapping, St John hints for the first time that Deacon's promised transfer funds may not be forthcoming. 'Any changes will have to come from within the club,' he warned. Substitute Stewart, the only bright spot, went closest.

Match 16 — H BRISTOL CITY, 2/11
Att: 9,590 · Pos: 20 · 5 · L 0-1 (HT 0-0) · 11
Gow 60
Ref: M Taylor (Deal)

Pompey: Best, Roberts, Wilson, Piper, Went, Stephenson, Marinello, Reynolds, Stewart, Hand*, Mellows, Foggo
Bristol City: Cashley, Sweeney, Drysdale, Mann, Collier, Merrick, Tainton, Ritchie, Fear, Gow, Emanuel

The goal-less run stretches to five, but a better performance pleases St John, who gives rookie striker Stewart, in for Davies, a rough ride. Gerry Gow earns the win with a dipping 25-yarder, while Went came closest for Pompey with a booming long-range shot.

Match 17 — A OXFORD, 9/11
Att: 6,402 · Pos: 22 · 11 · L 0-1 (HT 0-0) · 11
McCulloch 62
Ref: G Trevett (Eccles)

Pompey: Best, Roberts, Wilson, Piper, Went, Stephenson, Marinello, Reynolds, Clarke D, Hiron*, Mellows, Foggo
Oxford: Milkins, Light, Shuker, Roberts, Clarke C, Briggs, Aylott, Duncan, McCulloch*, Sims, Gough

Pompey's shot-shy attack (just 12 goals in 17 games) is defied by old-boy Milkins, sold in August. However, the bar saves him (48), first from own defender Colin Clarke then Wilson's shot. McCulloch's speculative effort settles it, but St John laments: 'We had five shots for their one.'

Match 18 — H HULL, 16/11
Att: 9,045 · Pos: 22 · 8 · D 1-1 (HT 1-1) · 12
Piper 4 / Wood 37
Ref: D Biddle (Bristol)

Pompey: Best, Roberts, Hand, Piper*, Went, Stephenson, Marinello, Reynolds, Davies, Wilson, Mellows, Foggo
Hull: Wealands, Banks, De Vries, Galvin, Croft, Blampey, McGill, Lord, Wood, Wagstaff, Hawley

A 9-0 midweek bonanza, albeit against Guernsey behind closed Fratton doors, heralds the end of a 581-minute goal drought. Piper defies a slight strain to calmly shoot over Wealands, but once he limps off, Hull take over. Wood deflects home after Best's error leads to a corner.

Match 19 — A ASTON VILLA, 23/11
Att: 16,821 · Pos: 22 · 4 · L 0-2 (HT 0-2) · 12
Hamilton 3, Little B 22
Ref: E Garner (Maghull)

Pompey: Best, Roberts, Hand, Foggo, Went, Stephenson, Marinello, Reynolds*, Davies, Wilson, Mellows, Stewart
Aston Villa: Cumbes, Robson, Aitken, Phillips, Nicholl, Ross, Graydon, Brown, Little B, Hamilton, Carrodus

New recruit George Graham watches from the stands as Pompey huff and puff but rarely threaten Villa's early grip on the game. First Brown floats a cross and Hamilton heads home, then Wilson's clearance takes a deflection and puts Graydon away to set up the second for Little.

Match 20 — H SHEFFIELD WED, 30/11
Att: 9,786 · Pos: 21 · 19 · W 1-0 (HT 0-0) · 14
Stewart 47
Ref: A Lees (Street)

Pompey: Best, Roberts, Hand, Piper*, Went, Stephenson, Marinello, Graham*, Davies, Wilson, Mellows, Foggo
Sheffield Wed: Springett, Shaw, Rodrigues, Dowd, Thompson, McMordie, Potts, Harvey, Ferguson, Craig, Sunley

Graham's debut, finalised by Davies' move to Man U in exchange, lasts just 33 minutes as he suffers a hamstring pull. However, his signing spurs the team to their second win in 13 games, thanks to Stewart's neat finish. Potts hits the post for Owls, then Went heads a penalty late on.

Match 21 — A SUNDERLAND, 7/12
Att: 25,926 · Pos: 22 · 2 · L 1-4 (HT 0-1) · 14
Mellows 54 / Halom 31, Hughes 57p, Malone 61, [Robson 72]
Ref: G Flint (Kirkby)

Pompey: Best, Roberts, Hand, Piper, Went, Stephenson, Marinello, Foggo, Stewart, Wilson, Mellows, Foggo
Sunderland: Montgomery, Malone, Guthrie, Moncur, Watson, Porterfield, Kerr, Hughes, Halom, Robson, Towers

Halom's sprawl under pressure from Stephenson convinces the referee and Hughes deflates Pompey's confidence from the spot. Mellows had just levelled after Marinello's magic, but Malone then angles only his second in 200 games and Robson, looking offside, flatters Sunderland.

LEAGUE DIVISION 2 — Manager: Mortimore ⇒ Ian St John — SEASON 1974-75

Column headings (for the stats trio): **Att | Pos | Pt**, followed by **F-A | H-T** and **Scorers, Times, and Referees**; player columns **1–11** plus **12 sub used**.

---

22 — 14/12 · H BOLTON (21) W

Att	Pos	Pt	F-A	H-T
7,612	14	16	2-0	1-0

Scorers: **Mellows 14, Bartlett 85.** Ref: R Challis (Tonbridge)

	1	2	3	4	5	6	7	8	9	10	11	12 sub used
Pompey	Best	Roberts	Hand	Piper	Went	Stephenson	Marinello	Foggo	Stewart*	Wilson	Mellows	**Bartlett**
Bolton	*Siddall*	*Ritson*	*Dunne*	*Nicholson*	*Jones P**	*Rimmer*	*Smith*	*Curran*	*Lee*	*Greaves*	*Thompson*	*Jones G*

Storybook stuff as substitute Bartlett (19) earns his 15 minutes of fame, by clinching the points after Piper's header was saved. Former teacher Mellows gave a lesson in finishing, slamming home Marinello's pass, but Bolton never recover from losing defender Paul Jones early on.

---

23 — 21/12 · A BRISTOL ROV (18) W

Att	Pos	Pt	F-A	H-T
9,262	12	18	1-0	1-0

Scorers: **Piper 40.** Ref: M Sinclair (Guildford)

	1	2	3	4	5	6	7	8	9	10	11	12 sub used
Pompey	Best	Roberts	Hand	Piper	Went	Stephenson	Marinello	Graham*	Stewart	Wilson	Mellows	Foggo
Bristol Rov	*Eadie*	*Jacobs*	*Parsons*	*Aitken*	*Taylor*	*Prince*	*Britten*	*Stanton**	*Warboys*	*Bannister*	*Fearnley*	*Staniforth*

Piper's finish, after Eadie pushed out Mellows' shot, deservedly lifts Pompey out of the drop zone. However ragged Rovers almost save it, but Wilson hacks Fearnley's shot clear. The ref angers St John by refusing a prone Went treatment for several minutes and Graham limps off again.

---

24 — 26/12 · H SOUTHAMPTON (18) L

Att	Pos	Pt	F-A	H-T
19,534	15	18	1-2	0-2

Scorers: **Piper 87.** *Osgood 13, Peach 16.* Ref: J Taylor (Wolverhampton)

	1	2	3	4	5	6	7	8	9	10	11	12 sub used
Pompey	Best	Roberts	Hand	Piper	Went	Stephenson	Marinello	Foggo	Stewart*	Wilson	Mellows	**Bartlett**
Southampton	*Turner*	*Mills*	*Steele*	*Fisher*	*Bennett*	*Blyth*	*Stokes*	*Chatterley*	*Osgood**	*Peach*	*O'Brien*	*Holmes*

It's a derby disaster for Pompey at blustery Fratton. Went thumps a post from 25 yards, but within six minutes Saints' two-goal salvo seals it. Osgood loops a header over Best, then Portsmouth-born Stokes puts Peach clear. Piper seizes on O'Brien's error, but it is too little, too late.

---

25 — 28/12 · A MILLWALL (20) D

Att	Pos	Pt	F-A	H-T
8,116	22	19	0-0	0-0

Scorers: — Ref: P Reeves (Leicester)

	1	2	3	4	5	6	7	8	9	10	11	12 sub used
Pompey	Best	Roberts	Hand*	Piper	Went	Stephenson	Marinello	Hiron	Stewart	Wilson	Mellows	Foggo
Millwall	*King*	*Hazell*	*Moore*	*Donaldson*	*Kitchener*	*Dorney*	*Saul*	*Summerill**	*Baldwin*	*Clark*	*Hill*	*Allder*

Euphoria over a gritty point earned evaporates as all Pompey's rivals win and they are back in trouble. The back-four is re-jigged after Hand is kicked, but Hiron, out for six weeks with a broken toe, returns. Wilson saves the point with a late goal-line clearance from Tommy Baldwin.

---

26 — 11/1 · H SUNDERLAND (19) W

Att	Pos	Pt	F-A	H-T
14,133	2	21	4-2	0-1

Scorers: **Hiron 50, Went 66, Piper 73.** *Robson 21, Halom 87* [Graham 85]. Ref: T Reynolds (Swansea)

	1	2	3	4	5	6	7	8	9	10	11	12 sub used
Pompey	Best	Roberts	Wilson	Piper	Went	Stephenson	Marinello	Lewis	Graham*	Hiron	Mellows	Foggo
Sunderland	*Montgomery*	*Malone*	*Bolton*	*Moncur*	*Watson*	*Longhorn**	*Kerr*	*Hughes*	*Halom*	*Robson*	*Towers*	*Ashurst*

Pompey demolish a Sunderland team who had not let in a league goal for five weeks. St John's half-time 'Riot Act' sees Hiron and Went net their firsts of the season, then Piper volleys 'a goal in a thousand'. Graham's sidefoot is his 100th goal, but Halom's miss at 1-1 is expensive.

---

27 — 18/1 · A SHEFFIELD WED (18) W

Att	Pos	Pt	F-A	H-T
11,032	22	23	2-0	0-0

Scorers: **Lewis 60, Marinello 87.** Ref: D Wallace (Crewe)

	1	2	3	4	5	6	7	8	9	10	11	12 sub used
Pompey	Best	Roberts	Wilson	Piper	Hand	Stephenson	Marinello	Lewis	Graham	Hiron	Mellows	Foggo
Sheff Wed	*Fox*	*Rodrigues*	*Knighton*	*Thompson**	*Mullen*	*Shaw*	*Potts*	*Harvey*	*Sunley*	*McIver*	*Brown*	*Ferguson*

Angry Owls fans hurl cushions from the stand as Marinello's curler pushes Wednesday nearer the drop. Earlier Lewis – St John's Man of the Match last week – had broken the deadlock with a glorious 18-yard drive. Pompey are the form team of the division with nine points from 12.

---

28 — 1/2 · H OXFORD (17) W

Att	Pos	Pt	F-A	H-T
13,123	8	25	2-1	1-0

Scorers: **Graham 20, Foggo 60.** *McCulloch 70.* Ref: A Hamil (Wolverhampton)

	1	2	3	4	5	6	7	8	9	10	11	12 sub used
Pompey	Best	Roberts*	Ellis	Piper	Hand	Stephenson	Marinello	Lewis	Graham	Hiron	Mellows	Foggo
Oxford	*Burton*	*Light*	*Shuker*	*Roberts**	*Clarke C*	*Jeffrey*	*Aylott*	*Duncan*	*Clarke D*	*McCulloch*	*Heron*	*Briggs*

St John quips that injury worries beforehand meant he even considered playing. Hiron's shot hits the underside of the bar, leaving Graham with the formality of a header. Foggo's deft volley seemed enough, but McCulloch's head kept things boiling, as Hiron hit a post and Foggo the bar.

---

29 — 8/2 · A BRISTOL CITY (18) L

Att	Pos	Pt	F-A	H-T
13,802	5	25	1-3	1-0

Scorers: **Hiron 38.** *Stephenson 48 (og), Sweeney 50, Gillies 62* [Gillies 62]. Ref: J Bent (Hemel Hempstead)

	1	2	3	4	5	6	7	8	9	10	11	12 sub used
Pompey	Best	Roberts	Hand	Piper	Went	Stephenson	Marinello	Lewis*	Graham	Hiron	Mellows	Foggo
Bristol City	*Cashley*	*Sweeney*	*Drysdale*	*Emanuel*	*Collier*	*Merrick*	*Tainton*	*Mann*		*Fear*	*Brolly*	*Gillies*

Alan Dicks' City team turn the game on its head, seconds after Hiron was inches from making it 2-0. A quick counter-attack earns Fear a free-kick and Stephenson's head leaves his own keeper stranded. Sweeney then nets at the second attempt, and more defensive chaos lets in Gillies.

---

30 — 18/2 · H ASTON VILLA (19) L

Att	Pos	Pt	F-A	H-T
13,355	4	25	2-3	2-3

Scorers: **Mellows 34p, Graham 37.** *Carrodus 1, Graydon 21, Little 38.* Ref: I Jones (Treharris)

	1	2	3	4	5	6	7	8	9	10	11	12 sub used
Pompey	Best	Roberts*	Ellis	Piper	Went	Manley	Marinello	Foggo	Graham	Hiron	Mellows	**Stewart**
Aston Villa	*Cumbes*	*Robson*	*Aitken*	*Ross*	*Rioch*	*McDonald*	*Graydon*	*Little B*	*Leonard*	*Phillips*	*Carrodus*	

Injuries force Manley, due to recuperate in South Africa for four months, to play. Graydon is the tormentor throughout, making the first, then tapping in, before having a goal ruled out. Mellows' twice-taken pen creeps in and Graham levels, only for Little to slide home from the restart.

---

31 — 22/2 · A HULL (18) D

Att	Pos	Pt	F-A	H-T
6,919	10	26	0-0	0-0

Scorers: — Ref: R Perkin (Stafford)

	1	2	3	4	5	6	7	8	9	10	11	12 sub used
Pompey	Best	Ellis	Piper	Hand	Went	Cahill	Marinello	Foggo	Graham	Hiron	Mellows	
Hull	*Wealands*	*Banks**	*Daniel*	*Galvin*	*Deere*	*Roberts*	*McGill*	*Lord*	*Hemmerman*	*Blampey*	*Greenwood*	*Fletcher*

Teenager Cahill, loaned from Coventry to cover Manley, is pressed into an early debut and he lives up to his 'competitor' tag by earning a booking for a late tackle. Hull's threat is snuffed out by Hand's towering performance, but Marinello scorns two second-half chances to win it.

Match log (matches 32–42)

No	Venue	Opponent	Date	Att	Pos	—	Pts	Res	Score	HT	Scorers	Referee
32	H	ORIENT	28/2	11,619	17	15	28	W	3-0	3-0	Hiron 7, 9, Foggo 26	T Spencer (Wootton Bassett)
33	A	OLDHAM	8/3	10,303	18	17	28	L	0-2	0-0	Robins 48, Groves 87	D Civil (Birmingham)
34	H	YORK	15/3	9,906	17	14	30	W	1-0	1-0	Hiron 37	A Jones (Ormskirk)
35	A	WEST BROM	22/3	10,017	18	7	30	L	1-2	0-1	Reynolds 55; Brown T 6, Wilson 88	P Willis (Meadowfield)
36	H	BRISTOL ROV	29/3	12,261	17	19	32	W	3-0	2-0	Mellows 21, 65, Hiron 29	T Bosi (Codsall)
37	H	MILLWALL	31/3	14,329	15	19	34	W	1-0	0-0	Kitchener 65 (og)	D Turner (Cannock)
38	A	CARDIFF	2/4	9,892	15	19	34	L	0-1	0-1	Sayer 31	K Baker (Rugby)
39	A	BLACKPOOL	5/4	6,543	16	6	35	D	2-2	2-2	Mellows 80, Marinello 86; Walsh 10, 68p	G Hill (Leicester)
40	H	NOTTS CO	12/4	10,960	15	14	36	D	1-1	0-0	Went 90; Scanlon 87	A Hart (London)
41	A	FULHAM	19/4	17,580	16	9	37	D	2-2	2-2	Reynolds 76, 89; Mitchell 20, 86	J Hunting (Leicester)
42	H	NORWICH	26/4	18,977	17	3	37	L	0-3	0-1	McGuire 26, Peters 79, Boyer 87	C Newsome (Broseley)

Home Average 12,485 — Away 13,302 — Average 13,302

32. ORIENT
Pompey: Best, Ellis, Piper, Reynolds, Hand, Cahill, Marinello, Foggo, Graham, Hiron, Mellows; sub Lewis
Orient: Jackson, Fisher, Payne, Allen, Hoadley, Walley, Cunningham, Grealish, Queen, Heppolette, Possee*; sub Mooney

Orient are locked in their dressing room for 30 minutes after one of the best defensive records is destroyed. Patched-up Pompey storm ahead as Hiron first poaches off Mellows' miscue, then snaps up Graham's knock-down. Foggo sweeps home Hiron's set up and the O's give up.

33. OLDHAM
Pompey: Best, Ellis, Piper, Reynolds, Hand, Stephenson, Marinello, Foggo*, Graham, Hiron, Mellows; sub Lewis
Oldham: Ogden, Wood, Whittle, Bell, Hicks, Holt, McVitie, Robins, Young, Chapman, Groves

Graham accepts the blame for the goal that put the skids under Pompey. He fails to block Young's cross and Robins stoops to head in. Foggo's 'goal' before half-time is disallowed for a foul. Oldham make it two, but punchless, pressure, and Groves' cool finish seals it.

34. YORK
Pompey: Best, Roberts, Went, Piper, Hand, Stephenson, Marinello, Reynolds, Graham, Hiron, Mellows
York: Crawford, Calvert, Oliver, Holmes, Swallow, Topping, Pollard, Cave, Seal, Jones, Lyons

York's first-ever visit to Fratton is so sterile, but Hiron is put clear by Reynolds to earn the points. City boss Wilf McGuinness orders his side to show more enterprise at half-time, but they barely trouble Best. Graham stands out from the rest, making St John's swap deal look shrewd.

35. WEST BROM
Pompey: Best, Roberts, Went, Reynolds, Hand, Stephenson, Marinello, Piper, Graham, Hiron*, Mellows; sub Foggo
West Brom: Ward, Nisbet, Wilson, Cantello, Wile, Rushbury, Glover, Brown T, Edwards, Trewick*, Johnston; sub Shaw

Albion left-back Wilson, just two goals in 200 games, lashed in with his 'standing' foot from 25 yards near the end. Tony Brown's unmarked finish was just reward after the visitors endured a torrid spell, but once Reynolds thrashed in Graham's pull-back, Pompey looked like winners.

36. BRISTOL ROV
Pompey: Best, Roberts, Went, Piper, Hand, Stephenson, Marinello, Reynolds, Graham, Hiron, Mellows
Bristol Rov: Eadie, Jacobs, Bater, Aitken, Day, Prince, Stanton, Smith, Warboys, Bannister*, Fearnley; sub Staniforth

Mellows, branded 'too nice' by St John in the autumn, proves his boss wrong with an aggressive display and two goals which make him leading scorer with seven. First he follows up his blocked shot, then he thunders home a 30-yarder. Hiron slots in Marinello's deflected shot.

37. MILLWALL
Pompey: Best, Roberts, Went, Piper, Hand, Stephenson, Marinello, Reynolds, Graham, Hiron, Mellows
Millwall: King, Evans, Moore, Dorney, Kitchener, Saul, Hazell, Burnett, Kelly C, Summerill, Hill

Chris Kelly, the 'Leatherhead Lip' signed by the Lions after the non-league striker's Cup exploits, sees his one chance saved by Best. Pompey are four points clear of the drop zone after Kitchener diverts Reynolds' pass past his own keeper. 'We need three more points,' says St John.

38. CARDIFF
Pompey: Best, Roberts, Went, Reynolds, Hand, Cahill, Marinello, Piper, Graham, Hiron*, Mellows; sub Foggo
Cardiff: Irwin, Attley, Pethard, Buchanan, Morgan, Larmour, Anderson, Charles, Showers, Dwyer, Sayer

Cardiff, without a home win since January, look ripe for the taking early on, as Hiron flashes a shot blocked by Irwin, then Piper flashes a shot just too high. City sneak ahead when Sayer deceives Best, who anticipated a cross. From then on Pompey's five-point Easter target is doomed.

39. BLACKPOOL
Pompey: Best, Roberts, Went, Reynolds, Hand, Cahill, Foggo, Piper, Graham, Lewis*, Mellows; sub Marinello
Blackpool: Burridge, Curtis, Harrison, Hart, Alcock, Walsh, Hatton, Ainscow, Davies, Suddaby, Evanson

Mellows' close-range effort stands after the officials consult and Pompey sense an escape. Marinello rescues the point with a 15-yard shot that Burridge sees too late. Earlier Walsh had finished a quick Pool break, then blasted home after Cahill felled Ainscow. Hatton missed a penalty.

40. NOTTS CO
Pompey: Best, Roberts, Went, Reynolds, Hand, Cahill, Marinello, Piper, Graham, Hiron*, Mellows; sub Foggo
Notts Co: McManus, Brindley, O'Brien, Bolton, Needham, Stubbs, Carter, McVay, Randall, Probert, Scanlon

County's tactics strangle the game, but St John refuses to criticise his old friend Jimmy Sirrell's approach. Pompey's increasingly desperate forays are punished when Scanlon is put clear to score by Randall, who had earlier hit a post. Went's low left-footer ensured justice was done.

41. FULHAM
Pompey: Figgins, Piper, Went, Reynolds, Hand, Cahill, Marinello, Foggo, Graham, Stewart*, Mellows; sub Kane
Fulham: Mellor, Fraser, Strong*, Mullery, Lacy, Moore, Dowie, Mitchell, Busby, Slough, Barrett; sub Cutbush

St John is already in the tunnel and assumes the roar is for FA Cup finalists Fulham's third. Instead Went's run and tackle sets up Reynolds to sign off, before his summer at Dallas Tornado, in style. Mitchell's goal from a neat corner routine had looked like ruining Figgins (19) debut.

42. NORWICH
Pompey: Figgins, Piper, Went, Kane, Hand, Cahill, Marinello, Foggo, Graham, Stewart, Mellows
Norwich: Keelan, Butler, Sullivan, Morris, Forbes, Powell, McGuire, MacDougall, Boyer, Suggett, Peters

Norwich cruise to promotion as St John accuses his senior players of forgetting the basics in the second half. It might have been different had Piper's free-kick not hit the post at 0-1. Instead, Peters' header makes it safe. Then Suggett and Ted MacDougall combine to set up Phil Boyer.

LEAGUE DIVISION 2 (CUP-TIES)

Manager: Mortimore ⇨ Ian St John

League Cup

			F-A	H-T	Scorers, Times, and Referees	1	2	3	4	5	6	7	8	9	10	11	12 sub used
1	A SWINDON 20/8	W	1-0	0-0	Piper 68	Best	Roberts	Wilson	Piper	Went	Stephenson	Marinello	Hand	Davies	Reynolds	Mellows	
	4,779 *3*				Ref: J Taylor (Wolverhampton)	*Barron*	*McLaughlin*Trollope*		*Hubbard*	*Potter*	*Munks*	*Moss*	*Dixon*	*Eastoe*	*MacLean*	*Jenkins*	*Burrows*

Pompey get their opening-day thrashing at Bolton out of their system as Piper takes advantage of an overstretched Town defence to hook in the winner after Barron stopped his first effort. Referee Jack Taylor, fresh from controlling the World Cup final, draws praise from all sides.

			F-A	H-T	Scorers, Times, and Referees	1	2	3	4	5	6	7	8	9	10	11	12 sub used
2	H DERBY 11/9	20 L	1-5	0-2	Marinello 79 *[Roberts 81 (og)]*	Best	Roberts	Wilson	Piper	Went	Stephenson	Marinello	Kellard	Davies*	Reynolds	Hand	Ellis
	13,582 *1:10*				*Hector 10, 48, Lee 29, Rioch 46,*	*Boulton*	*Webster**	*Nish*	*Rioch*	*Daniel*	*Todd*	*Powell*	*Gemmill*	*Davies*	*Hector*	*Lee*	*Newton*
					Ref: R Toseland (Kettering)												

First division pretentions are exposed by Dave Mackay's team, who will go on to win the league. Only caretaker boss Tindall thinks the score flattered Derby. At half-time Went goes up front, but two quick goals send him back. Roberts' deflection sends fans scurrying for the exits.

FA Cup

			F-A	H-T	Scorers, Times, and Referees	1	2	3	4	5	6	7	8	9	10	11	12 sub used
3	A NOTTS CO 3/1	20 L	1-3	0-2	Marinello 73	Best	Roberts	Wilson	Piper	Went	Stephenson	Marinello	Graham	Stewart*	Hiron	Mellows	Foggo
	14,723 *9 9*				*Needham 10, Randall 29, 66*	*McManus*	*Brinley*	*Richards*	*Bolton*	*Needham*	*Stubbs*	*Carter*	*Probert*	*Randall*	*Bradd*	*Mann*	
					Ref: T Spencer (Wootton Bassett)												

Pompey are the first team to be knocked out of the 3rd round in this Friday-night tie, due to Forest's pairing with Spurs. Pompey had worked all week on stopping County's far-post knock-down tactic, only to be undone by it twice in the first half. 'It makes you sick,' moaned St John.

League Table

#	Team	P	Home W	D	L	F	A	Away W	D	L	F	A	Pts
1	Manchester U	42	17	3	1	45	12	9	6	6	21	18	61
2	Aston Villa	42	16	4	1	47	6	9	4	8	32	26	58
3	Norwich	42	14	3	4	34	17	6	10	5	24	20	53
4	Sunderland	42	14	6	1	41	8	5	7	9	24	27	51
5	Bristol City	42	14	5	2	31	10	7	3	11	16	23	50
6	West Brom	42	13	4	4	33	15	5	5	11	21	27	45
7	Blackpool	42	12	6	3	31	17	2	11	8	7	16	45
8	Hull	42	12	8	1	25	10	3	6	12	15	43	44
9	Fulham	42	9	8	5	29	17	4	8	9	15	22	42
10	Bolton	42	9	7	5	27	16	6	5	10	18	25	42
11	Oxford	42	14	3	4	30	19	1	9	11	11	32	42
12	Orient	42	8	9	4	17	16	3	11	7	11	23	42
13	Southampton	42	10	6	5	29	20	5	5	11	24	34	41
14	Notts Co	42	7	11	3	34	26	5	5	11	15	33	40
15	York	42	9	7	5	28	18	5	3	13	23	37	38
16	Nott'm Forest	42	7	7	7	24	23	5	7	9	19	32	38
17	PORTSMOUTH	42	9	7	5	28	20	3	6	12	16	34	37
18	Oldham	42	10	4	7	28	16	0	8	13	12	32	37
19	Bristol Rov	42	7	7	7	25	23	2	7	12	12	41	35
20	Millwall	42	8	9	4	31	19	2	3	16	13	37	32
21	Cardiff	42	7	8	6	24	21	2	6	13	12	41	32
22	Sheffield Wed	42	3	7	11	17	29	2	4	15	12	35	21
		924	232	139	91	658	378	91	139	232	378	658	924

Appearances and Goals

Player	Lge	Sub	LC	Sub	FAC	Sub	Goals Lge	LC	FAC	Tot
Bartlett, Gordon							1			1
Best, David	40	2								
Cahill, Paul	7									
Davies, Ron	17		2				5			5
Ellis, Peter	16	2	2		1					
Figgins, Phil	2					1				
Foggo, Ken	18	10					2			2
Graham, George	19				1		3			3
Hand, Eoin	40		2							
Hiron, Ray	17			1			6			6
Kane, Alan	1	1								
Kellard, Bobby	11	1	1	1			1			1
Lewis, Brian	5	2					1			1
Manley, Malcolm	1									
Marinello, Peter	38	1	2		1		2	1	1	4
Mellows, Mick	36		1		1		8			8
Piper, Norman	41		2		1		5	1		6
Reynolds, Richard	23	1	2		1		5			5
Roberts, Phil	31	1	2		1					
Stephenson, Alan	31		2		1		1			1
Stewart, Andy	10	4			1		1			1
Went, Paul	34		2		1		2			2
Wilson, Billy	24		2		1					
(own-goals)							1			1
23 players used	462	25	22	1	11	1	44	2	1	47

Odds & ends

Double wins: (3) Nott'm Forest, Bristol Rov, SheffWed.

Double losses: (5) West Brom, Bristol City, Southampton, Aston Villa, Norwich.

Won from behind: (1) Sunderland (h).

Lost from in front: (1) Bristol City (a).

High spots: Beating second placed Sunderland 4-2 in January.

Collecting 11 points out of 14 between December and February.

Six home wins in seven from January to March.

Gordon Bartlett (19) scoring within ten minutes of making his debut as a substitute against Bolton in December.

Low spots: Southampton completing a double on Boxing Day.

Six match goal-less run from October to November.

First team knocked out of the FA Cup 3rd Round, 1-3 at Notts Co on the Friday night.

Losing 1-5 to Derby in the League Cup 2nd Round.

Six match goal-less run between October and November.

Player of the Year: Mick Mellows.

Ever presents: (0).

Hat-tricks: (0).

Leading scorer: Mick Mellows (8).

LEAGUE DIVISION 2   Manager: Ian St John   SEASON 1975-76

Results

No	Date	Att	Pos	Pt	Cum	F-A	H-T	Scorers, Times, and Referees
1	A YORK 16/8	4,602	21	L	0	1-2	1-1	Piper 30 / Lyons 36, McMordie 82 / Ref: G Nolan (Hazel Grove)
2	H NOTT'M FOREST 23/8	10,655	21 (8)	D	1	1-1	0-1	Went 86 / Bowyer 15 / Ref: B Daniels (Rainham)
3	A ORIENT 29/8	5,056	20 (13)	W	3	1-0	1-0	Fisher 27 (og) / Ref: L Shapter (Paignton)
4	H LUTON 6/9	9,835	20 (6)	L	3	0-2	0-1	King 39, Alston 55 / Ref: C White (Harrow)
5	A CARLISLE 13/9	7,316	22	L	3	1-2	1-1	McGuinness 31 / Prudham 7, Clarke 74 / Ref: G Flint (Kirkby-in-Ashfield)
6	H OLDHAM 20/9	8,079	21 (8)	D	4	1-1	1-1	Piper 44 / Groves 6 / Ref: J Yates (Redditch)
7	H CHELSEA 23/9	16,144	21 (9)	D	5	1-1	1-1	Reynolds 24 / Garner 37 / Ref: T Spencer (Wootton Bassett)
8	A SOUTHAMPTON 27/9	17,310	21 (5)	L	5	0-4	0-1	Channon 40, 63, 80, Peach 54 / Ref: P Reeves (Leicester)
9	H SUNDERLAND 4/10	13,098	22 (1)	D	6	0-0	0-0	Ref: A Hamil (Wolverhampton)
10	A BLACKPOOL 11/10	8,351	22 (8)	D	7	0-0	0-0	Ref: R Tinkler (Boston)

Line-ups (top row = Pompey; italic row = opponents)

No	1	2	3	4	5	6	7	8	9	10	11	12 sub used
1	Lloyd	Roberts	Ellis	Piper	Went	Hand	Marinello	Kane*	Graham	McGuinness	Mellows	Reynolds
	Crawford	*Oliver*	*Downing*	*Holmes*	*Swallow*	*Topping*	*Lyons*	*Cave*	*Seal*	*Jones*	*McMordie*	
2	Lloyd	Roberts	Ellis	Piper	Went	Hand	Marinello	Kane	Graham	McGuinness*	Mellows	Reynolds
	Middleton	*Anderson*	*Clark*	*O'Kane**	*Chapman*	*Richardson*	*Robertson*	*McGovern*	*O'Hare*	*Bowyer*	*Lyall*	*O'Neill*
3	Lloyd	Roberts	Ellis	Reynolds	Went	Hand	Marinello	Kane	Graham	Foster	Mellows*	Ellis
	Jackson	*Fisher*	*Grealish*	*Queen*	*Hoadley*	*Walley*	*Cunningham*	*Bennett*	*Bullock*	*Heppolette*	*Allder*	
4	Lloyd	Roberts	Ellis	Piper	Went	Hand	Marinello	Kane	Graham	Foster	Kamara	
	Barber	*Ryan John*	*Buckley*	*Anderson*	*Faulkner*	*Futcher P*	*King*	*Chambers*	*Futcher R*	*Spiring*	*Alston*	
5	Lloyd	Roberts	Piper	Kane	Went	Hand	Marinello	Reynolds	Graham	Collard	Kamara	Eames
	Burleigh	*Spearritt*	*Gorman*	*Barry*	*Green*	*Carr*	*Martin*	*Hindson**	*Prudham*	*Laidlaw*	*Clarke*	*O'Neill*
6	Lloyd	Roberts	Cahill	Piper	Went	Hand	McGuinness*	Reynolds	Graham	Wilson	Mellows	
	Ogden	*Branagan*	*Whittle*	*Bell*	*Hicks*	*Holt*	*Blair*	*Jones*	*Wood !*	*Chapman*	*Groves**	*Robins*
7	Lloyd	Roberts	Cahill	Piper	Went	Hand	McGuinness*	Reynolds	Graham	Wilson	Mellows	Marinello
	Sherwood	*Harris*	*Hay*	*Stanley*	*Droy*	*Dempsey*	*Britton*	*Wilkins R*	*Bason*	*Langley*	*Garner*	
8	Lloyd	Roberts	Cahill	Piper	Went	Hand	McGuinness*	Reynolds	Graham*	Wilson	Mellows	
	Middleton	*Rodrigues*	*Peach*	*Holmes*	*Bennett*	*Blyth*	*Channon*	*Fisher*	*Osgood*	*McCalliog*	*Stokes*	
9	Lloyd	Roberts	Cahill	Piper	Went	Hand	Marinello	Reynolds	Graham*	McLaughlin	Mellows	Foster
	Montgomery	*Malone*	*Bolton*	*Towers*	*Clarke*	*Moncur*	*Kerr*	*Hughes*	*Halom*	*Robson*	*Porterfield*	
10	Lloyd	Roberts	Cahill	Piper	Went	Hand	Marinello*	Reynolds	Graham	McLaughlin	Mellows	Kamara
	Wood	*Curtis*	*Bentley*	*Hart*	*Suddaby*	*Hatton*	*Tong**	*Saddick*	*Walsh*	*Moore*	*Ainscow*	*Harrison*

Match notes

1. A dismal performance in unseasonably blustery conditions underline the weaknesses in St John's squad. At the back, too many free-kicks are conceded, making life difficult for new keeper Grahame Lloyd. Up front Reynolds looks far from sharp after his summer sojourn in the States.

2. Went is the hero with his bullet-header, but the late drama was thanks to Lyall, who rolled a penalty wide after Ellis fouled Anderson, later to be the first black England player. Alarm bells are ringing, as Pompey hardly threaten after Bowyer's close-range header from a corner flick-on.

3. Fisher's panic-stricken lob, under pressure from Marinello, leaves Jackson stranded and gifts the points. Cunningham impresses, but the O's scorn his creativity. Young striker Foster – later to become an England centre-half – is denied a debut goal by the keeper's smart interception.

4. St John gambles with youth, but Luton have too much know-how. Kamara is pitched into midfield and impresses for half-an-hour until the pace tells and the ends his game with a booking. Town lead through King, then Aussie World Cup star Alston turns and shoots home in the six-yard box.

5. United's opener hinges on the interpretation of offside. Laidlaw's free-kick is turned in by Prudham, but the flag is over-ruled as a deflection 'played him on'. Eames (17), hat-trick hero for the youth team last week, comes on, while Collard (on loan from Ipswich) makes his only start.

6. Went's volley smashes against the post in the dying seconds to frustrate Pompey, up against ten-man Oldham. Wood was sent off by a fussy referee for an injudicious remark. Groves' 25-yard shot put the Latics in charge, but Piper snapped up McGuinness' blocked shot on the break.

7. Chelsea are a pale imitation of their early-70s side, but still attract double Saturday's crowd. Pompey look on course when Reynolds flings himself at Piper's corner to head home, but slack marking allows Garner the chance to nod in future Fratton full-back Stanley's hopeful cross.

8. TV highlights do Pompey no favours, editing out Reynolds' shots against post and bar. Channon is the difference between the sides, making it 0-3 from an impossible angle, but the telly shows Cahill was fouled in the build-up. Wilson's block on Fisher lets Peach to bend in a free-kick.

9. A point is not enough to haul Pompey off the bottom, as goal-average separates four teams on six points. St John's old Liverpool team-mate McLaughlin looks short of fitness at the start of his loan, while another old pal, Lawler, is in the stand. Neither side create a clear-cut chance.

10. Pompey force their solitary corner after 85 minutes, but that apart it's backs-to-the-wall. St John claims Blackpool never caused his side any trouble; perhaps he was looking the other way when Hart and Walsh both extended Lloyd, then Ainscow misses after rounding the keeper.

Portsmouth Match Records

#	Venue	Opponent	Date	Attendance	Pld	Result	Score	HT	Pos
11	H	HULL	18/10	8,155	20	D	1-1	0-0	11 / 8
12	H	BRISTOL ROV	21/10	9,078	20	L	1-2	0-0	5 / 8
13	A	NOTTS CO	25/10	9,594	21	L	0-2	0-0	5 / 8
14	H	FULHAM	1/11	11,441	21	L	0-1	0-0	4 / 8
15	A	BOLTON	4/11	18,538	21	L	1-4	1-1	2 / 8
16	A	PLYMOUTH	8/11	13,885	21	L	1-3	0-0	16 / 8
17	H	BLACKBURN	15/11	7,323	22	L	0-1	0-0	13 / 8
18	A	HULL	22/11	4,549	22	L	0-1	0-0	16 / 8
19	H	OXFORD	29/11	8,648	22	L	0-2	0-2	20 / 8
20	A	WEST BROM	6/12	15,325	22	L	1-3	0-1	5 / 8
21	A	NOTT'M FOREST	13/12	11,343	22	W	1-0	0-0	11 / 10

11 — HULL (H), 18/10
Scorers: Piper 56 / Grimes 85. Ref: J Bent (Hemel Hempstead)

Pompey: Lloyd, Roberts, Cahill, Piper, Went, Hand, Marinello, McLaughlin, Graham, McGuinness, Mellows
Hull: Wealands, Banks, De Vries, Galvin, Croft, Roberts, Lord, McGill, Grimes, Wagstaff, Greenwood

Grimes levels late for John Kaye's men, then 300-goal Wagstaff misses from six yards out, avoiding a worse fate. Earlier Piper's 12-yard shot looked to have earned a first home win and if McGuinness' first-half header had gone in, rather than hit a post, the game would have been safe.

12 — BRISTOL ROV (H), 21/10
Scorers: Marinello 82 / Staniforth 65, Bannister 68. Ref: K Salmon (Barnet)

Pompey: Lloyd, Roberts, Cahill, Piper, Went, Hand, Marinello, Reynolds, Graham, McLaughlin, Mellows
Bristol Rov: Eadie, Williams, Parsons, Day, Taylor, Smith, Fearnley, Prince, Staniforth, Bannister, Dobson

Frugal Rovers, with just three goals conceded in five away games, hang on. Pompey create 30 chances (compared to Rovers' four) and take just one. Worst culprit is Went, whose first-half penalty after Taylor handles, hits Eadie. Bannister sets up the first, then nets from close range.

13 — NOTTS CO (A), 25/10
Scorers: Scanlon 89p, Probert 90. Ref: R Matthewson (Bolton)

Pompey: Lloyd, Roberts, Cahill, Lawler, Went, Hand, Kamara, Foster, Graham, McLaughlin*, Mellows (Wilson)
Notts Co: McManus, Richards P, O'Brien, Bolton, Needham, Stubbs, Randall*, McVay, Bradd, Probert, Scanlon (Vinter)

'A disgraceful decision,' fumes St John after Went's innocent-looking jump with Bradd ends with Scanlon burying the penalty for only Notts Co's fourth goal at home. Insult is added, when Graham helps Probert's shot in. Free transfer Lawler (ex-Liverpool), finds the pace 'rushed'.

14 — FULHAM (H), 1/11
Scorers: Slough 68. Ref: P Walters (Bridgwater)

Pompey: Lloyd, Roberts, Wilson, Piper, Lawler, Hand, Marinello, Reynolds, Graham, McGuinness*, Mellows (Kamara)
Fulham: Mellor, James, Strong, Mullery, Lacy, Moore, Conway, Dowie, Busby, Slough, Barrett (Stewart)

It's the same old script as Pompey dominate, but squander what chances come their way. The composed Lawler somehow heads wide from Graham's flick and Kamara (17) catches the eye as he ruffles World Cup-winner Moore's renowned unflappability. Slough's header nicks it.

15 — BOLTON (A), 4/11
Scorers: Kamara 23 [Whatmore 80] / Jones P 4, Jones G 62, 70. Ref: P Partridge (Bishop Auckland)

Pompey: Lloyd, Roberts, Wilson, Lawler, Went, Hand, Marinello, Reynolds, Graham, Kamara, Mellows
Bolton: Siddall, Ritson, Dunne, Greaves, Jones P, Allardyce, Byrom, Whatmore, Jones G, Reid, Thompson

Pompey match Ian Greaves' high-riding side, except in taking chances. St John's high-tempo tactics pay off when Kamara cuts out Dunne's back-pass to level with his first senior goal, but once Garry Jones blasts home unmarked, then chips in despite a vain offside appeal, it's over.

16 — PLYMOUTH (A), 8/11
Scorers: Piper 82 / Johnson 52, Rafferty 84, 90. Ref: W Gow (Swansea)

Pompey: Lloyd, Roberts, Wilson, Piper, Went, Lawler, Marinello, Hand, Graham, Kamara*, Mellows (Cahill)
Plymouth: Aleksic, Darke, Burrows, Delve, Rioch, Green, Foster, Johnson, Mariner, Rafferty, Pearson

Pompey's winless run stretches to 13. Piper angles a late equaliser at his old club, only for Rafferty, who will later join Pompey, to power past three tackles and rifle into the roof of the net. Earlier Johnson's attempted cross deceived Lloyd. Rafferty is then put clear to stroke home.

17 — BLACKBURN (H), 15/11
Scorers: Beamish 84. Ref: M Taylor (Deal)

Pompey: Lloyd, Lawler, Wilson, Roberts, Went, Hand, Marinello, Reynolds, Graham, McGuinness*, Mellows (Kamara, Hawkins)
Blackburn: Jones, Wilkinson*, Wood, Metcalfe, Wood, Fazackerley, Beamish, Svarc, Hindson, Oates, Parkes

Pompey's season is becoming a well-worn cliché as chances go begging again. Dour Rovers had settled for a draw when Svarc's quick break allows Hindson to set up Beamish. Early on Marinello went close when his chip hits first the underside of the bar, then the inside of the post.

18 — HULL (A), 22/11
Scorers: Galvin 77. Ref: K Ridden (Colchester)

Pompey: Lloyd, Lawler, Mellows, Roberts, Went, Cahill, Marinello, Reynolds, Graham, McGuinness*, Macken (Kamara)
Hull: Wealands, Daniel, Devries, Galvin, Wood, Haigh, Gibson, Grimes, Hawley, Wagstaff, Greenwood

St John's latest loanee, Tony Macken (from Derby), makes little impact, as a solid defence is finally unlocked by Gibson (17), who opens the way for Galvin. Four gilt-edged chances are missed, the worst when Reynolds dragged wide late on. Hull took 40 minutes to muster a shot.

19 — OXFORD (H), 29/11
Scorers: Tait 34, 44. Ref: R Challis (Tonbridge)

Pompey: Lloyd, Lawler, Mellows, Roberts, Went, Cahill, Marinello, Piper, Foster, Kamara*, Reynolds (Tait, Foley)
Oxford: Burton, Taylor, Shuter, Lowe, Clarke C, Jeffrey, Houseman*, Tait, Clarke D, McCulloch, Aylott

'On a clear day you can see division three' says The News, after this latest disaster against fellow strugglers. 18-year-old Mick Tait, who will sign for Pompey, cracks home from 20 yards, then shows maturity to coolly slot past Lloyd. By contrast, Foster, also 18, fluffs a one-on-one.

20 — WEST BROM (A), 6/12
Scorers: Marinello 90 / Brown A 10, 70, Brown T 52p. Ref: R Lee (Cheadle)

Pompey: Lloyd, Lawler, Mellows, Roberts, Went, Cahill, Marinello, Piper, Graham, Kamara, Macken
West Brom: Osborne, Mulligan, Wilson, Martin, Robertson, Robson, Brown T, Mayo, Brown A, Giles, Johnston

Macken successfully shackles Albion player-boss Johnny Giles and it takes a contested penalty to settle it. Cahill blocks Mulligan's shot, but the referee decides he handled. Marinello's 'dipper' is a parting shot, as in the week he moves to Motherwell for £35,000 to cut the wage bill.

21 — NOTT'M FOREST (A), 13/12
Scorers: McGuinness 55. Ref: K Baker (Rugby)

Pompey: Lloyd, Lawler, Mellows, Roberts, Went, Cahill, McGuinness, Piper, Graham, Kamara*, Macken
Nott'm Forest: Wells, Anderson, Clark, McGovern, Chapman, Robertson, Curran, O'Neill, Butlin, Bowyer, Eames

A tiny knot of Pompey fans savour the win which avoids the ignominy of ten defeats in a row. McGuinness is put clear by Piper for the goal and he went close twice more. Lloyd hasn't a save to make, but only Went's injury-time goal-line clearance ensures the first win since August.

LEAGUE DIVISION 2   Manager: Ian St John   SEASON 1975-76

No	Date	Att	Pos	Pt	F-A	H-T	1	2	3	4	5	6	7	8	9	10	11	12 sub used	Scorers, Times, and Referees
22	H YORK 20/12	7,903	22 21	10	0-1	0-1	Lloyd	Lawler	Mellows	Roberts	Went	Cahill	McGuinness	Piper	Graham	Eames	Macken		Hinch 14
							Crawford	*Hunter*	*Woodward*	*McMordie*	*Swallow*	*Topping*	*Hosker*	*Holmes*	*Seal*	*Hinch*	*Cave*		Ref: H Robinson (Norwich)

Lloyd is the villain in a tale of two keepers, as he flaps at a corner and Hinch taps in. Meanwhile, Crawford's string of stops frustrate Pompey, but the bar saves him when Topping deflects Eames' shot. 'There are still 40 points at stake,' raps St John, his side now nine away from safety.

No	Date	Att	Pos	Pt	F-A	H-T	1	2	3	4	5	6	7	8	9	10	11	12 sub used	Scorers, Times, and Referees
23	A CHARLTON 26/12	10,736	22 19	12	3-1	2-0	Lloyd	Tutt	Mellows	Roberts	Went	Cahill	Eames	Piper	Graham	Reynolds	McGuinness		Piper 22, Graham 40, Roberts 64
							Curtis	*Warman*	*Bowman*	*Giles*	*Goldthorpe*	*Powell*	*Hales*	*Flanaghan*	*Hunt*	*Peacock*			Flanaghan 72
																			Ref: M Sinclair (Guildford)

A Christmas 'miracle' sees Pompey net more than once for the first time. Piper hits the post, then Lloyd keeps out Warman's header. Piper's nod from close in and Graham's back-header are capped by Roberts' power-drive. Birmingham's watching Cup spies must have left bemused.

No	Date	Att	Pos	Pt	F-A	H-T	1	2	3	4	5	6	7	8	9	10	11	12 sub used	Scorers, Times, and Referees
24	H BRISTOL CITY 27/12	14,315	22 3	12	0-1	0-1	Lloyd	Lawler	Mellows	Roberts	Went	Cahill	Eames	Piper	Foster	Reynolds	McGuinness* Hand		Ritchie 8
							Cashley	*Sweeney*	*Drysdale*	*Gow*	*Collier*	*Merrick*	*Tainton*	*Ritchie*	*Mann*	*Brolly*	*Fear*		Ref: B Daniels (Rainham)

It is now 458 minutes since Pompey scored at home. This gloomy statistic disguises another passionate, but punch-less performance. Div One-bound City are put on the rack, but Ritchie nicks it when his soft shot eludes Lloyd. 'I feel so sorry for the players and fans,' laments St John.

No	Date	Att	Pos	Pt	F-A	H-T	1	2	3	4	5	6	7	8	9	10	11	12 sub used	Scorers, Times, and Referees
25	H CARLISLE 10/1	11,430	22 16	14	1-0	0-0	Lloyd	Lawler	Mellows	Roberts	Went	Cahill	McGuinness	Piper	Graham	Reynolds	Eames		Eames 48
							Ross	*Carr*	*Gorman*	*O'Neill*	*Green*	*Parker*	*McVitie*	*Train*	*Clarke*	*McCartney* Martin*	*Laidlaw*		Ref: D Lloyd (Fernhill Heath)

Eames leaves with a £100 leather coat, donated by a fan to the scorer of the first goal in a home win. His near-post shot is muffed by Ross and ends a barren run back to 31 March. United boss Dick Young heaps on praise: 'Pompey are as good as any we've met lately.'

No	Date	Att	Pos	Pt	F-A	H-T	1	2	3	4	5	6	7	8	9	10	11	12 sub used	Scorers, Times, and Referees
26	A LUTON 17/1	10,464	22 8	14	1-3	0-2	Lloyd	Lawler*	Mellows	Roberts	Went	Cahill	McGuinness	Piper	Graham	Reynolds	Eames	Wilson	Piper 70
							Barber	*Ryan John*	*Buckley*	*Chambers*	*Faulkner*	*Futcher P*	*Husband*	*King*	*Futcher R*	*West*	*Aston*		Faulkner 8, King 28, Futcher R 57
																			Ref: D Richardson (Clayton-le-Dale)

Ron Futcher's apparent handball is missed by the referee and in the ensuing action he nets the killer third while looking offside. The goal ends Pompey's encouraging fight-back, after Town had threatened to run riot following Faulkner's six-yard header and King's spectacular volley.

No	Date	Att	Pos	Pt	F-A	H-T	1	2	3	4	5	6	7	8	9	10	11	12 sub used	Scorers, Times, and Referees
27	A BRISTOL ROV 31/1	6,133	22 9	14	0-2	0-2	Lloyd	Lawler	Mellows	Roberts	Went	Cahill	McGuinness	Piper	Graham	Reynolds	Kamara		Britten 18, Bannister 44
							Eadie	*Bater*	*Williams*	*Aitken*	*Taylor*	*Prince*	*Stephens*	*Smith*	*Warboys*	*Bannister*	*Britten*		Ref: K Burns (Dudley)

Grim-faced St John and Deacon stalk away from Eastville without comment, but assistant Willie Hunter sighs: 'We've seen that a few times.' Slack marking allows Warboys two free headers in the box to set up Britten and Bannister. Pompey now need 22 points from 30 to be safe.

No	Date	Att	Pos	Pt	F-A	H-T	1	2	3	4	5	6	7	8	9	10	11	12 sub used	Scorers, Times, and Referees
28	H BOLTON 7/2	8,958	22 1	14	0-1	0-1	Lloyd	Lawler	Mellows	Roberts	Went	Cahill	McGuinness	Piper	Graham	Busby	Macken		Went 42 (og)
							Siddall	*Ritson*	*Dunne*	*Greaves*	*Jones P*	*Allardyce*	*Byrom*	*Whatmore*	*Jones G*	*Reid*	*Thompson*		Ref: D Turner (Cannock)

Bolton go top thanks a solitary on-target effort. Went's knee diverts Ritson's terrace-bound shot and relieved boss Ian Greaves accepts: 'They murdered us.' Piper screws a shot horribly from six yards and angles wide after a one-two with Wilson. QPR loanee Busby is still settling in.

No	Date	Att	Pos	Pt	F-A	H-T	1	2	3	4	5	6	7	8	9	10	11	12 sub used	Scorers, Times, and Referees
29	H PLYMOUTH 14/2	9,509	21 17	16	2-0	1-0	Lloyd	Lawler	Wilson	Roberts	Mellows	Cahill	McGuinness	Piper	Busby	Macken	Kamara		Busby 12, Macken 67
							Furnell	*Horswill*	*Burrows*	*Sutton*	*Green*	*Delve*	*Randell*	*Foster*	*Mariner*	*Rafferty*	*McAuley*		Ref: C Newsome (Broseley)

Kamara retaliates after Horswill's OTT foul, but earns little sympathy from his boss. His rashness left Pompey 48 minutes to hold out for the win that lifts them above York. Macken, back for a second loan, clinches it with an instant, return volley from Green's drop-ball clearance.

No	Date	Att	Pos	Pt	F-A	H-T	1	2	3	4	5	6	7	8	9	10	11	12 sub used	Scorers, Times, and Referees
30	A BLACKBURN 21/2	8,067	21 19	18	3-0	1-0	Lloyd	Lawler	Wilson	Reynolds	Macken	Cahill	McGuinness	Piper	Graham	Busby	Hird		Graham 37, Piper 47, 74
							Jones	*Wilkinson*	*Wood*	*Metcalfe*	*Hawkins*	*Fazackerley Beamish**	*Oates*	*Svarc*	*Parkes*	*Kanyon*			Ref: R Toseland (Kettering)

A 'Great Escape' seems possible after Rovers are outclassed. McGuinness' crossing ability and deft control makes goals for Graham and Piper respectively. Hawkins' suicidal back-pass gifts Piper the second. 'We were brilliant,' said St John, whose side at last earn back-to-back wins.

No	Date	Att	Pos	Pt	F-A	H-T	1	2	3	4	5	6	7	8	9	10	11	12 sub used	Scorers, Times, and Referees
31	A CHELSEA 25/2	12,709	21 12	18	0-2	0-2	Lloyd	Lawler	Wilson	Macken	Went	Cahill	McGuinness	Piper	Graham	Busby	Mellows		Cooke 26, Locke 35
							Bonetti	*Locke*	*Harris*	*Stanley*	*Wicks*	*Hay*	*Britton*	*Wilkins R*	*Finnieston*	*Swain*	*Cooke*		Ref: A Porter (Bolton)

Chelsea gain their first home win since December. Veteran Scots international Cooke fires in from future Fratton defender Swain's pull-back, then Locke angles home. Pompey dominate the second half, but scorn their chances. With eleven games left, the team are eight points adrift.

32 H NOTTS CO 28/2 — 9,135 — 21 L 4 18 — **1-3** (0-1)

Kamara 51
Bradd 28, 84, Scanlon 71
Ref: T Reynolds (Swansea)

Lloyd · Lawler · Wilson · Macken · Cahill · Busby · McGuinness* · Piper* · Graham · Kamara · Mellows · Foster
McManus · Brinley · O'Brien · Probert · Needham · Stubbs · Bolton · Sims* · Bradd · Mann · Scanlon · Vinter

Chaotic defending all but ends hope of avoiding relegation. After St John's blunt half-time talk, things improve and Kamara thumps home Piper's nod down, but then Cahill blunders and lets Bradd set up Scanlon. 'I saw Foster warming up and hoped I was coming off,' he said.

---

33 A FULHAM 6/3 — 6,928 — 21 W 13 20 — **1-0** (0-0)

Piper 70
Ref: D Biddle (Bristol)

Figgins · Lawler · Wilson · Macken · Cahill · Busby · Viney · Piper · Graham · Kamara · Mellows
Mellor · Curtbush · Slough · Mullery · Lacy · Moore · Mitchell · Strong · Busby · Lloyd · Barrett* · Dowie

Veteran Fulham boss Alex Stock suffers virulent abuse from the crowd at the end, less than 12 months after he guided his team to Wembley. Pompey have more appetite for the battle and St John singles out tough-tackling debutant Keith Viney (18), who plays a part in Piper's goal.

---

34 H BLACKPOOL 13/3 — 8,394 — 21 W 16 22 — **2-0** (0-0)

Kamara 50p, Piper 87
Ref: T Bosi (Codsall)

Figgins · Lawler · Wilson · King · Cahill · Viney · Foster · Piper · Graham · Kamara · Mellows* · Denyer
Wood · Hatton · Harrison · Alcock · Suddaby · McEwan · Weston* · Ainscow · Walsh · Smith · Bentley · Evanson

St John quips: 'We could do with the season being extended to 52 matches,' as this fourth win in six trims the safety gap to five points. Jeff King, on loan from Derby, makes an assured debut and Kamara shrugs off a missed penalty in training, to thump home after Hatton's handball.

---

35 A OXFORD 20/3 — 6,928 — 21 L 20 22 — **0-1** (0-0)

Foley 48
Ref: E Read (Bristol)

Figgins · Lawler · Wilson* · King · Cahill · Viney · Foster · Piper · Graham · Kamara · Denyer · McGuinness
Burton · Taylor · Shuker · Lowe · Clarke C · Briggs · Houseman · Foley · Clarke D · Gibbins · Tait

Gibbins 'assault' on Figgins forces him to spill the ball and Foley jabs home, but there is no whistle, to St John's fury. Even Oxford boss Mick Brown accepts Pompey were unlucky, especially when King hits the post in the first-half. Pompey must win their remaining games to stay up.

---

36 H WEST BROM 27/3 — 10,617 — 21 L 4 22 — **0-1** (0-0)

Cantello 48
Ref: A Grey (Great Yarmouth)

Figgins · Lawler · Wilson · King · Cahill · Viney · Foster* · Piper · Graham · Kamara · Mellows · McGuinness
Osborne · Mulligan · Robson · Brown T · Wile · Robertson · Martin · Cantello · Mayo · Giles · Johnston

Mathematically Pompey can stay up, but the gap is now nine after Blackburn beat two table-topping teams in a week. Cantello wins a race with Mayo to convert Wile's cross. It would have been worse but for Figgins' brilliance, although he is relieved to catch Johnston's shot of a post.

---

37 H SOUTHAMPTON 6/4 — 24,115 — 21 L 5 22 — **0-1** (0-0)

Channon 90
Ref: R Capey (Crewe)

Figgins · Lawler · Ellis · Roberts · Cahill · Viney · Piper · King · Graham · Kamara · Mellows
Turner · Rodrigues · Peach · Holmes · Blyth · Bennett · Gilchrist · Channon · Earles · Williams · Stokes

Cruelty knows no limit as rivals Saints, clapped on after making the FA Cup Final, hammer the final nail in the coffin. Channon's strike from Earles' lay-back silences the 'Chimes', but it could have gone either way. Earles hit the bar, but Turner excelled to keep out Ellis and Mellows.

---

38 A OLDHAM 10/4 — 6,672 — 22 L 12 22 — **2-5** (0-3) [Shaw 84]

Piper 55, Kamara 78p
Hicks 22, Rob' 24, Grov' 44, Whit' 76, Shaw 84
Ref: H Davey (Mansfield)

Figgins · Ellis · Lawler · Cahill · Viney ! · Roberts* · McGuinness · Piper · Graham · Kamara · Mellows · Denyer
Platt · Wood · Whittle · Hicks · Edwards · Holt · Bell · Shaw · Robins · Chapman · Groves

Viney troops off close to tears after chopping down Groves, and with it goes any comeback hopes. Six minutes earlier Piper had stabbed in, but the first half was a shambles. Groves' free-kick, taken as the referee got the wall back, rankled, but Kamara was barely touched for the penalty.

---

39 H ORIENT 13/4 — 5,069 — 22 W 17 24 — **2-1** (2-0)

Wilson 14, McGuinness 42
Queen 47
Ref: M Taylor (Deal)

Figgins · Ellis · Wilson · Eames · Cahill · Denyer · McGuinness · Piper · Graham* · Kamara · Mellows · Pullar
Jackson · Fisher · Payne · Bennett · Hoadley · Walley · Possee · Grealish · Mooney* · Heppolette · Queen · Allder

Veteran full-back Wilson hadn't scored for four years, but he makes up by blitzing home a 30-yarder. Youthful Pompey, down to three 'senior' players when Graham limps off, then see McGuinness gratefully accept Walley's 'gift'. The lowest gate since late-1972 spells bankruptcy.

---

40 H CHARLTON 17/4 — 7,992 — 22 D 9 25 — **2-2** (0-0)

Mellows 59, 70
Hales 76, 82
Ref: J Taylor (Wolverhampton)

Figgins · Ellis · Wilson* · Cahill · Denyer · Roberts · McGuinness · Piper · Eames · Kamara · Mellows · Viney
Wood · Campbell · Berry · Young T · Curtis* · Powell · Hales · Flanaghan · Hunt · Harrison · Bowman

The curtain comes down typically as Pompey throw it away. Mellows ends his season-long famine with a glancing header and thunderous shot, only for the predatory Hales to draw within two goals of a £10,000 prize for 30-in-a-season. Just 14 home points from 42 sums up a sad season.

---

41 A BRISTOL CITY 20/4 — 27,300 — 22 L 2 25 — **0-1** (0-1)

Whitehead 3
Ref: J Homewood (Sunbury)

Figgins · Ellis · Roberts · Cahill · Eames · McGuinness · Piper · Graham · Kamara · Mellows
Cashley · Sweeney · Drysdale · Collier · Merrick · Tainton · Ritchie · Gillies · Cheesley · Whitehead

City are back in Division One after a 65-year gap, but this showing suggests it will be hard for them. The crowd is still arriving as Whitehead, looking yards offside, nets his first since October. Despite the start, City are on edge throughout, and Merrick is almost harried in an own-goal.

---

42 A SUNDERLAND 24/4 — 40,515 — 22 L 1 25 — **0-2** (0-2)

Bolton 27, Hughes 30
Ref: R Chadwick (Darwen)

Figgins · Ellis · Went · Denyer · Eames* · Piper · Graham · Kamara · Mellows · Wilson
Swinburne · Malone · Bolton · Train · Ashurst · Moncur · Kerr · Towers · Holden · Robson · Hughes

Pompey at least have the consolation of their share of the gate money, as Sunderland clinch the title. Joe Bolton's hopeful shot trumps the otherwise impressive Figgins, but the keeper is helpless for Hughes' close-range header. Swinburne blocks the only chance Pompey create.

Home 10,471 — Away 12,015 — Average 10,471

LEAGUE DIVISION 2 (CUP-TIES) — Manager: Ian St John — SEASON 1975-76

League Cup — Match details

No	Venue	Date	Opponent	Res	F-A	H-T	Attendance	Pos	Scorers, Times, and Referees
1	A	20/8	ALDERSHOT	D	1-1	1-1	6,274	3	Graham 3 / Warnock 16 — Ref: R Challis (Tonbridge)
1R	H	26/8	ALDERSHOT	W	2-1	2-0	7,049	3:23	Marinello 21, Reynolds 28 / Warnock 55 — Ref: R Challis (Tonbridge) (Pompey won 3-2 on aggregate)
2	H	9/9	LEICESTER	D	1-1	0-0	10,629	1:16	Eames 78 / Garland 82 — Ref: R Crabb (Exeter)
2R	A	17/9	LEICESTER	L	0-1 aet	0-0	11,055	1:17	Sammels 118 — Ref: M Lowe (Sheffield)

League Cup — Line-ups (opponents in italics)

Match	Team	1	2	3	4	5	6	7	8	9	10	11	12 sub used
1	Portsmouth	Lloyd	Roberts	Ellis	Piper	Went	Hand	Marinello	Kane	Graham	McGuinness	Mellows	
1	Aldershot	*Johnson*	*Walden*	*Wallis J*	*Sainty*	*Jopling*	*Walker*	*Walton**	*Morrissey*	*Howarth*	*Brodie*	*Warnock*	*Bell*
1R	Portsmouth	Lloyd	Roberts	Ellis	Piper	Went	Hand	Marinello	Kane	Graham	Foster	Mellows	
1R	Aldershot	*Johnson*	*Walden*	*Wallis J*	*Crosby*	*Richardson*	*Jopling*	*Walton*	*Morrissey*	*Howarth*	*Bell*	*Warnock*	
2	Portsmouth	Lloyd	Roberts	Ellis	Piper	Went	Hand	Marinello*	Reynolds	Graham	Collard	Mellows	Eames
2	Leicester	*Wallington*	*Whitworth*	*Rofe*	*Kember*	*Sims*	*Woollett*	*Weller*	*Lee*	*Worthington*	*Sammels*	*Garland*	
2R	Portsmouth	Lloyd	Roberts	Cahill	Piper	Went	Hand	McGuinness*	Reynolds	Graham	Wilson	Mellows	Marinello
2R	Leicester	*Wallington*	*Whitworth*	*Yates*	*Kember*	*Sims*	*Birchenall*	*Weller*	*Lee*	*Tomlin**	*Sammels*	*Garland*	*Alderson*

Match 1: Keeper Lloyd, a 'free' from Motherwell, endears himself by saving Walker's pen after Mellows handles in the 46th minute. Graham's classy finish is cancelled out by Warnock, when Walden's shot is blocked. 'Playing at Fratton will be a treat,' says Shots' boss Tommy McAnearney.

Match 1R: Pompey should have made sure in the first half and are left hanging on. After a panicking Ellis' heads against his own post early on, Marinello fires in and Reynolds' 25-yarder leaves Johnson groping. Warnock lifts Shots' hopes, only to have Walton's joy cut short by an offside flag.

Match 2: Striker Billy Eames (17) makes a sensational debut, scoring from 12 yards, just eight minutes after substituting the less-than happy Marinello. Giant-killing hopes are soon dashed, as Jimmy Bloomfield's men finally stir. Garland coolly chips in after Lloyd blocked Kember's effort.

Match 2R: City drop a pre-match bombshell by leaving out England international striker Worthington. He is missed as Leicester fail to unravel Pompey's blanket defence. Weller blasts wide from five yards in normal time, but as the game peters out, Sammels' low-drive avoids a second replay.

FA Cup — Match details

No	Venue	Date	Opponent	Res	F-A	H-T	Attendance	Pos	Scorers, Times, and Referees
3	H	3/1	BIRMINGHAM	D	1-1	1-1	19,414	1:19	Eames 14 / Francis 3 — Ref: J Bent (Hemel Hempstead)
3R	A	6/1	BIRMINGHAM	W	1-0	1-0	26,106	1:19	McGuinness 45 — Ref: J Bent (Hemel Hempstead)
4	A	24/1	CHARLTON	D	1-1	0-1	26,333	16	Piper 86 / Curtis 25p — Ref: A Grey (Great Yarmouth)
4R	H	27/1	CHARLTON	L	0-3	0-0	31,722	16	Powell 55, Flanagan 58, Hope 86 — Ref: A Grey (Great Yarmouth)

FA Cup — Line-ups (opponents in italics)

Match	Team	1	2	3	4	5	6	7	8	9	10	11	12 sub used
3	Portsmouth	Lloyd	Lawler	Mellows	Roberts	Went	Cahill	McGuinness	Piper	Graham	Reynolds	Eames	
3	Birmingham	*Latchford*	*Osborne*	*Want*	*Kendall**	*Gallagher*	*Burns*	*Page*	*Francis*	*Withe*	*Hatton*	*Hibbitt*	*Pendrey*
3R	Portsmouth	Lloyd	Lawler	Mellows	Roberts	Went	Hand	McGuinness	Piper	Graham	Reynolds	Eames	
3R	Birmingham	*Latchford*	*Martin*	*Want*	*Pendrey*	*Gallagher**	*Burns*	*Page*	*Francis*	*Withe*	*Hatton*	*Bryant*	*Calderwood*
4	Portsmouth	Lloyd	Lawler	Mellows	Roberts	Went	Cahill	McGuinness	Piper	Graham	Reynolds	Eames	
4	Charlton	*Tutt*	*Penfold*	*Warman*	*Hunt*	*Giles*	*Curtis*	*Powell*	*Hales*	*Hope*	*Peacock*	*Flanagan*	
4R	Portsmouth	Lloyd	Lawler	Mellows	Roberts	Went	Cahill	McGuinness	Piper	Graham	Reynolds	Eames*	Wilson
4R	Charlton	*Tutt*	*Penfold*	*Warman*	*Hunt*	*Giles*	*Curtis*	*Powell*	*Hales*	*Hope*	*Peacock*	*Flanagan*	

Match 3: Relieved Blues boss Willie Bell acknowledges: 'We knew they would make it hard, but not that hard.' Francis sprinted away for the opener, but Piper responded by rattling the bar. Just afterwards, Eames deflected Reynolds' shot in, then Piper, McGuinness and Roberts all go close.

Match 3R: Blues miss Kendall's inspiration and end up a well-beaten team in front of their disbelieving fans. Lloyd had only one save to make as Hand (in for the injured Cahill), Lawler and Roberts bottle up Withe, Francis and Hatton. McGuinness slots home from 12 yards after robbing Burns.

Match 4: Piper keeps Pompey's season alive with a deft finish from Graham's nod down. Earlier, as the TV highlights proved, Cahill tripped Hope just inside the area and Curtis converted. Had Flanagan not spooned over from five yards right on half-time, there would have been no way back.

Match 4R: FA Cup 'magic' lures thousands back to Fratton, many not getting in until half-time. Pompey spurn the chance to make friends, not to mention money from a 5th round tie at Wolves, by producing a pathetic display. The terraces are bare by the time Hope skips round Lloyd to seal it.

		P	Home					Away					Pts
			W	D	L	F	A	W	D	L	F	A	
1	Sunderland	42	19	2	0	48	10	6	6	10	19	26	56
2	Bristol City	42	11	7	3	34	14	8	8	5	26	21	53
3	West Brom	42	10	9	2	29	12	10	4	7	21	21	53
4	Bolton	42	12	5	4	36	14	8	7	6	28	24	52
5	Notts Co	42	11	6	4	33	13	8	5	8	27	28	49
6	Southampton	42	18	2	1	49	16	3	5	13	17	34	49
7	Luton	42	13	6	2	38	15	8	5	11	23	36	48
8	Nott'm Forest	42	13	1	7	34	18	8	6	11	21	22	46
9	Charlton	42	11	5	5	40	34	4	7	10	21	38	42
10	Blackpool	42	9	9	3	26	22	5	5	11	14	27	42
11	Chelsea	42	7	9	5	25	20	9	5	9	28	34	42
12	Fulham	42	9	8	4	27	14	6	6	11	18	33	40
13	Orient	42	10	6	5	21	12	3	8	10	16	27	40
14	Hull	42	8	5	7	29	23	5	6	10	16	26	39
15	Blackburn	42	8	6	7	27	22	4	8	9	18	28	38
16	Plymouth	42	13	4	4	36	20	0	8	13	12	34	38
17	Oldham	42	11	8	2	37	24	2	4	15	20	44	38
18	Bristol Rov	42	9	9	5	20	15	4	7	10	18	35	38
19	Carlisle	42	9	8	4	29	22	3	5	13	15	37	37
20	Oxford	42	7	7	7	23	25	4	4	13	16	34	33
21	York	42	8	3	10	28	34	2	5	14	11	37	28
22	PORTSMOUTH	42	4	6	11	15	23	5	1	15	17	38	25
		924	229	131	102	684	422	102	131	229	422	684	924

Odds & ends

Double wins: (1) Orient.

Double losses: (9) York, Luton, Bristol R, Oxford, Southampton, Bolton, Bristol C, West Brom, Notts Co.

Won from behind: (0).

Lost from in front: (1) York (a).

High spots: Winning 1-0 at first division Birmingham in a FA Cup 3rd Round replay.

Beating Carlisle 1-0 at home in January to secure the first home league win of the season!

Low spots: Club record nine-match losing run between October and December.

Only scored 15 goals at home all season.

Losing to a last-minute goal at home to Southampton.

17 match win-less run from September to December.

Losing 0-3 to Charlton in an FA Cup 4th round replay at Fratton.

Pompey's highest and lowest home attendances of the season came in consecutive matches against Southampton and Orient.

Five players sign on-loan during the season: Ian Collard (Ipswich), John McLaughlin (Liverpool), Tony Macken (Derby, twice), Martyn Busby (QPR) and Jeff King (Derby).

Player of the Year: Norman Piper.

Ever presents: (0).

Hat-tricks: (0).

Leading scorer: Norman Piper (12).

	Appearances						Goals			
	Lge	Sub	LC	Sub	FAC	Sub	Lge	LC	FAC	Tot
Busby, Martin	6						1			1
Cahill, Paul	32	1	1		3					
Collard, Ian	1		1							
Denyer, Peter	5	2								
Eames, Billy	9	2		1	4		1	1	1	3
Ellis, Peter	8	1	3							
Figgins, Phil	9									
Foster, Steve	8	3	1							
Graham, George	39		4		4		2	1		3
Hand, Eoin	17	1	4		1		1			1
Kamara, Chris	21	2					4			4
Kane, Alan	5		2							
King, John	4									
Lawler, Chris	26				4					
Lloyd, Grahame	33		4		4					
Macken, Tony	10						1			1
Marinello, Peter	15	2	3	1			2	1		3
McGuinness, Billy	26	2	3		4		3		1	4
McLaughlin, John	5									
Mellows, Mick	39		3		4		2			2
Piper, Norman	39		4		4		11	1		12
Pullar, David		1								
Reynolds, Richard	19	3	3		4		1			1
Roberts, Phil	33		3		4		1			1
Viney, Keith	6	1								
Went, Paul	29		4		4		1			1
Wilson, Billy	18	3	1				1			1
(own-goal)							1			1
28 players used	462	24	44	2	44	1	33	4	3	40

LEAGUE DIVISION 3

Manager: St John ⇨ Dickinson **SEASON 1976-77**

Line-ups

No	Date	Team	1	2	3	4	5	6	7	8	9	10	11	12 sub used
1	A 21/8	Pompey	Lloyd	Roberts	Wilson	Denyer	Ellis	Lawler	Green*	Piper	Went	Graham	Pollock	Viney
1		Wrexham	Lloyd	Evans	Dwyer	Davis	Roberts	Thomas	Shinton	Sutton	Lee	Ashcroft	Griffiths	
2	H 24/8	Pompey	Lloyd	Wilson	Wilson	Denyer	Ellis	Lawler	Pollock	Green	Piper	Went	Graham	Harris
2		Swindon	Allan	McLaughlin	Taylor	Stroud	Aldenwood*	Prophett	Moss	Goddard	Syrett	Dixon	Anderson	
3	H 28/8	Pompey	Lloyd	Wilson	Wilson	Denyer	Ellis	Cahill	Pollock	Green	Piper	Went	Graham	Graham
3		Chesterfield	Hardwick	Badger	O'Neill	McEwan	Hunter	Cottam	Kowalski	Darling	Fern	Charlton	Bentley	
4	A 4/9	Pompey	Lloyd	Lawler	Wilson	Denyer	Ellis	Cahill	Kamara	Pollock	Green*	Went	Mellows	McGuinness
4		Sheffield Wed	Turner	Walden	Collins	Mullen	Dowd	O'Donnell	Wylde	Johnson	Potts	Prendergast	Feely*	Nimmo
5	H 11/9	Pompey	Lloyd	Lawler	Wilson	Denyer	Ellis*	Cahill	Kamara	Pollock	Green	Went	Mellows	McGuinness
5		Lincoln	Grotier	Brantfoot	Neale	Booth	Ellis	Cooper	Fleming	Ward	Green*	Smith	Harding	
6	A 18/9	Pompey	Lloyd	Lawler	Wilson	Denyer	Ellis	Cahill*	Green	Kamara	Went	Mellows	Pollock	Viney
6		Gillingham	Cawston	Brindley	Spearritt	Galvin*	Shipperley	Tydeman	Williams	Overton	Richardson	Weatherley	Durrell	Hilton
7	H 25/9	Pompey	Lloyd	Lawler	Wilson	Denyer	Ellis	Cahill	Green*	Kamara	Went	Mellows	Pollock	Piper
7		Reading	Death	Peters	Henderson	Cumming	Bennett	Youlden	Murray	Hiron*	Friday	Dunphy	Carnaby	Hollis
8	A 2/10	Pompey	Figgins	Ellis	Wilson	Denyer	Went	Cahill	Roberts	Kamara	Mellows	Mellows	Pollock	Hayward
8		Shrewsbury	Mulhearn	King	Leonard	Turner	Griffin	Atkins	Irvine	Hornsby	Kearney*	Bates	Maguire	
9	H 9/10	Pompey	Figgins	Piper	Viney	Roberts	Ellis	Cahill	Denyer	Kamara*	Pollock	Pollock	Mellows	Green
9		Walsall	Kearns	Hynd	Harrison	Robertson	Serella	Atthey	Dennelly	Caswell	Wright	Buckley	Evans*	Andrews
10	A 15/10	Pompey	Figgins	Piper	Viney	Denyer	Ellis	Cahill	Pollock	Denyer	Wilson*	Wilson	Mellows	Green
10		Northampton	Starling	Gregory	Tucker	Best	Robertson	Phillips	Farrington	McGowan	Reilly	Hall	Christie*	Stratford
11	H 23/10	Pompey	Lloyd	Piper	Viney	Denyer	Ellis	Cahill	Pullar	Kamara*	Green	Pollock	Mellows	Foster
11		Port Vale	Connaughton	Thomson	Griffiths	Ridley	Harris	Tartt	McLaren	Beech	Rogers	Beamish	Williams	

Results

No	Date	Venue	Opponent	Att	Pompey Pos	Opp Pos	Pt	F-A	H-T
1	21/8	A	WREXHAM	4,752	—	—	L 0	0-2	0-0
2	24/8	H	SWINDON	7,898	—	—	W 2	2-1	2-0
3	28/8	H	CHESTERFIELD	8,700	17	4	L 2	0-1	0-0
4	4/9	A	SHEFFIELD WED	12,131	19	13	D 3	1-1	0-0
5	11/9	H	LINCOLN	7,865	16	12	D 4	1-1	1-1
6	18/9	A	GILLINGHAM	6,736	18	7	L 4	1-2	0-1
7	25/9	H	READING	11,937	22	4	L 4	0-2	0-1
8	2/10	A	SHREWSBURY	4,782	22	1	L 4	1-4	0-3
9	9/10	H	WALSALL	7,779	23	19	D 5	1-1	0-0
10	15/10	A	NORTHAMPTON	4,805	24	21	L 5	1-3	0-2
11	23/10	H	PORT VALE	7,516	23	21	D 6	1-1	1-1

Scorers, Times, and Referees

1. Shinton 71, 80. Ref: J Wrennall (Eccleston).
St John's gamble of pushing Went up front surprises Wrexham boss John Neal, but Pompey succumb to debut-making Shinton (£20,000 from Cambridge). First he angles in a header, then loops Griffiths' pass over Lloyd. Local-lad Green impresses, but fighting fans mar the game.

2. Denyer 25, Went 45. Anderson 62. Ref: B Homewood (Sunbury).
Pompey's new-look forward line looks good. Green creates havoc for Denyer to score, then Went crashes in Piper's return pass. Lloyd repeats Saturday's heroics with a stunning early stop from Graham's inadvertent header. Despite Anderson's cool finish the result is rarely in doubt.

3. Fern 78. Ref: D Biddle (Bristol).
St John issues a terse 'no comment' to reporters as Pompey never look like breaking down an organised Chesterfield. Went ruffles Les Hunter early on and hits the bar with a header, but after the break it looks like stalemate until Rod Fern gets away, rounds Lloyd and rolls home.

4. Mellows 60. Prendergast 54. Ref: N Glover (Chorley).
Denyer effectively snuffs out Eric Potts, although he collects an early booking from a fussy referee, and Pompey earn a morale-boosting point against Len Ashurst's side. Mellows turns and fires Pollock's pass into the roof of the net, after Prendergast's header failed to break self-belief.

5. Green 21. Ward 23. Ref: L Burden (Broadstone).
Green caps an impressive first half by hammering home his first senior goal, but lively Imps take advantage of Lloyd's weak punch and Ward strikes. The News calls for Deacon to make a statement on the growing financial crisis, as it is revealed the Board haven't met since April.

6. Mellows 47. Richardson 21p, Weatherley 70. Ref: A Gunn (Southwick).
Generous Gills ease cash-flow worries by giving Deacon a £400 cheque towards Pompey's share of the gate receipts, with the balance to follow next week. Alas, the philanthropy doesn't extend to the pitch and Weatherley's diving header nullifies Mellows' spectacular shot.

7. Hollis 34, Peters 55. Ref: S Bates (Bristol).
Hiron limps off after just 180 seconds, as his fitness gamble fails, but Charlie Hurley's new-boys win easily. Hobbling Peters, with a suspected cracked ankle bone, tucks away the third of his career, after sub Hollis was set up by Eamonn Dunphy. 'The worst in two years,' says St John.

8. Mellows 87. Bates 12, 25, Kearney 28, Atkins 46p. Ref: A Hughes (West Kirby).
St John shuffles his pack, as the League confirm bankruptcy means the end of PFC. Went is back at centre-half, but he will join Cardiff next week for a vital £25,000. Cahill's handball lets Atkins bury the penalty, but by then Bates has netted two easy chances and Kearney chipped in.

9. Piper 85p. Buckley 54. Ref: D Reeves (Uxbridge).
An accountant's report shows Pompey owe £400,000, but Deacon is reluctant to accept its findings. Piper sparks jubilation as his spot-kick, after Green is felled, ends a run of three defeats. The Fratton End turns up the volume and Pollock's late shot is goal-bound, but hits Denyer.

10. Mellows 62. Hall 14, Reilly 24, Robertson 66. Ref: T Bosi (Codsall).
A catastrophic opening dumps Pompey at the foot of the table, as St John wields the axe. Pullar makes a full debut and Pollock nods his first from Piper's centre. Mellows skips past future Fratton boss Ken Gregory to pull one back, but Hall's angled drive and Reilly's looping shot are more than enough.

11. Pollock 26. Beamish 42. Ref: C Downey (Isleworth).
The average age of Pompey's team is 21, as St John bemused: 'Why we can't put things together in the first half?' Ex-Brighton striker Ken Beamish floats his first for Vale, who have a 2-11 away-goal record. Viney's late goal-line clearance saves a point.

Match-by-match record (matches 12–23)

No	V	Opponent	Date	Att	Pos	Res			FT	HT
12	A	ROTHERHAM	26/10	4,428	23	D	11	7	2-2	2-0
13	H	PETERBOROUGH	30/10	8,622	22	D	15	8	0-0	0-0
14	H	CHESTER	2/11	8,480	21	W	16	10	2-1	1-0
15	A	OXFORD	6/11	6,228	21	L	18	10	1-2	1-1
16	H	BURY	13/11	10,252	21	D	10	11	1-1	0-0
17	A	GRIMSBY	27/11	3,836	21	L	22	11	0-1	0-1
18	H	PRESTON	4/12	9,243	22	D	5	12	0-0	0-0
19	A	YORK	18/12	2,058	20	W	24	14	4-1	1-0
20	H	BRIGHTON	27/12	32,368	18	W	3	16	1-0	1-0
21	H	OXFORD	1/1	15,954	17	D	14	17	1-1	0-1
22	A	PETERBOROUGH	3/1	5,424	17	L	19	17	2-4	0-2
23	H	MANSFIELD	18/1	10,720	17	D	5	18	2-2	1-2

12 – ROTHERHAM (A)
Scorers: Pullar 22, Green 32 / Spencer 48, 76. Ref: A Porter (Bolton)
Lineups: Lloyd / McAllister, Piper / Pugh, Viney / Breckin, Denyer / Rhodes, Ellis / Stancliffe, Cahill / Spencer, Pullar / Womble*, Kamara / Phillips, Green* / Gwyther, Pollock / Wagstaff, Mellows / Crawford, Foster / Habbin
St John's Pompey 'babes' pay their first dividend as high-flying Millers are made to look ordinary. Pullar's first-time shot is built-on by Green's pounce on McAllister's fumble. Defender Spencer rumbles forward to angle home his second of the game after a quick counter-attack.

13 – PETERBOROUGH (H)
Ref: R Crabb (Exeter)
Lineups: Lloyd / Waugh, Piper / Lee, Viney / Robson, Denyer / Doyle, Ellis / Turner, Cahill / Jeffries, Pullar / Oakes, Kamara / Cozens, Green / Moss*, Pollock / Carmichael, Mellows / Nixon, Foster / Gregory
With Cahill inspirational, Pompey build on Tuesday's promise by holding Noel Cantwell's Peterborough. Had Green's header from Mellows' centre been a fraction lower, it would have further dented Posh's woeful record of one point from 12 on the road, rather than the crossbar.

14 – CHESTER (H)
Scorers: Kamara 17, Piper 80 / Dearden 72. Ref: D Nippard (Christchurch)
Lineups: Lloyd / Millington, Piper / Edwards, Viney / Raynor, Denyer / Nickeas, Ellis / Delgado, Cahill / Oakes, Pullar / Owen, Kamara / Richardson, Green / Dearden*, Pollock / Mason*, Mellows / Crossley, Foster / Howat
Green is outstanding as Pompey win for the first time since August. The 'babes' show maturity beyond their years to bounce back after Dearden forced home Delgado's header. Kamara opened from 20 yards; then Piper tucked home Kamara's pass. Owen hit a post late on.

15 – OXFORD (A)
Scorers: Pollock 13 / Tait 20, 69. Ref: B James (South Croydon)
Lineups: Lloyd / Milkins, Piper / Fogg, Viney / Shuker, Denyer / Bodel, Ellis / Clarke, Cahill / Jeffrey, Pullar / McGrogan*, Kamara / Housman, Green* / Foley, Pollock / Tait, Mellows / Duncan, Foster / Seacole
Pollock puts Pompey in charge, firing in after Kamara's through ball, but once Tait's free-kick takes a huge deflection, Oxford show more appetite. Lloyd saves twice and has his bar to thank, but it is Shuker who initiates the six-pass move which ends with Tait's gleeful header.

16 – BURY (H)
Scorers: Denyer 87 / Foster 46 (og). Ref: C Gardner (Gloucester)
Lineups: Lloyd / Forrest, Piper / Keenan, Viney / Kennedy, Denyer / Rudd, Ellis / Bailey, Cahill / Hatton, Pullar / Woolfall*, Kamara / Phillips, Green / Rowland, Pollock / McIlwraith, Mellows / Hamstead, Foster / Thompson
One defeat or one win in six? That is the conundrum after Denyer thunders in from the edge of the box. Earlier, Foster's diving diversion of a cross meant a cruel baptism at centre-half, but he will play for England in that position. Striker Kemp (swapped for Graham with Palace) starts.

17 – GRIMSBY (A)
Scorers: Lewis 43. Ref: B Martin (Keyworth)
Lineups: Lloyd / Wainman, Piper / Waters, Viney / Cumming, Denyer / Young, Ellis / Gray, Cahill / Moore, Pullar* / Partridge, Kamara / Lewis*, Green / Wigg, Pollock / Boylen, Mellows / Brolly, Foster / Donovan
Pompey fume at two decisions which change the match. First Lewis's tumble is 'bought' and from the free-kick he scores. Then, on the hour, sub Kemp flashes home, but Mellows is penalised for pushing. Boylen (5'3") and Waters (5'4") dominate midfield for managerless Mariners.

18 – PRESTON (H)
Ref: R Challis (Tonbridge)
Lineups: Lloyd* / Tunks, Piper / McMahon, Viney / Williams, Denyer / Burns, Ellis / Sadler, Cahill / Lawrenson, Pullar / Coleman, Kamara / Brown, Green / Smith, Pollock / Elwiss, Mellows / Bruce, Kamara
Viney dons the green jersey for the final four minutes after Lloyd injures his shoulder and prompts a keeper crisis for next week's FA Cup tie, as Figgins has a knee injury. On a frosty two-tone pitch, potent strike-force Bruce and Elwiss are blunted. Kemp's header hits a post (80).

19 – YORK (A)
Scorers: Kemp 7, Denyer 59, Pollock 61, 66 / Pollard 48. Ref: R Chadwick (Darwen)
Lineups: Lloyd / Crawford, Piper / Hunter*, Viney / Joy*, Denyer / Holmes, Foster / Topping, Cahill / James, Pullar / Pollard, Kamara / Young, Green / Hope, Pollock / Cave, Mellows / Downing, Foster / Hosker
Abysmal York let Pompey record their best away win since 1973. Hunter's back-pass beats his keeper and Kemp taps in on the line. Pollard sweeps in the equaliser out of the blue, but Denyer scores from six yards, then Pollock's shot slithers under Crawford and his header seals it.

20 – BRIGHTON (H)
Scorers: Kemp 7. Ref: L Shapter (Paignton)
Lineups: Lloyd / Grummitt, Piper / Cattlin, Viney / Wilson, Denyer / Horton, Foster / Rollings, Cahill / Cross, Pullar / Towner, Kamara / Ward, Green / Mellor, Pollock / Piper, Mellows / O'Sullivan*, Foster / Morgan
Pompey's potential is underlined as a huge Boxing Day crowd turns out for the derby with Alan Mullery's table-topping Seagulls. They see Pollock intercept Horton's backpass and square the ball for Kemp to sidefoot. Horton's misery is complete when his penalty is saved by Lloyd.

21 – OXFORD (H)
Scorers: Cahill 90 / Foley 42p. Ref: D Smith (Hornchurch)
Lineups: Lloyd / Burton, Piper / Fogg, Viney / Shuker, Denyer / Bodel, Foster / Clarke, Cahill / Jeffrey!, Pullar* / Briggs, Kamara / Housman, Green / Foley, Pollock / Tait, Mellows / Duncan, Foster / Green
Keeper Burton, his waterlogged shorts often revealing more 'cheek' than is decent, defied Pompey time and again. Kemp's header hits the post (83) then Cahill saves it after a late corner flurry. Earlier Jeffrey was sent off for retaliation but within seconds Foley was felled for his penalty.

22 – PETERBOROUGH (A)
Scorers: Mellows 68, Piper 89p / Cozens 40, 42, 69, Heeley 73. Ref: D Jackson (Water Orton)
Lineups: Lloyd / Waugh, Piper / Hindley, Viney / Lee, Denyer / Doyle, Foster / Turner, Cahill / Ross, Pullar / Heeley, Kemp / Gregory, Kamara* / Cozens, Pollock / Carmichael, Mellows / Robson, Foster / Ellis
Posh's first league win since October is on a 'skating-rink'. 'It should have been called off'. St John. Lee misses a pen after Viney's handball, but Cozens takes over. His third, seconds after Mellows' goal, is set up by Villa loanee Ross's great run. Robson handles for Piper's penalty.

23 – MANSFIELD (H)
Scorers: Kemp 43, 77 / Moss 3, Miller 18. Ref: A Hughes (West Kirby)
Lineups: Figgins / Arnold, Piper / Bird, Viney / Foster B, Denyer / Matthews*, Ellis / Saxby, Cahill / Foster C, Pullar* / Morris, Kamara* / Moss, Green / Randall, Pollock / Hodgson, Mellows / Miller, Foster / Cooke
In the dying seconds Kemp muffs a hat-trick chance as he scuffs the rebound from Mellows' bar-thumping 25-yarder. Pollock sets up the fight-back as his pass diverts to Kemp off a divot, then Piper's scissor-kick is finished off. Earlier Stags' player-boss Peter Morris pulled the strings.

LEAGUE DIVISION 3

Manager: St John ⇨ Dickinson

SEASON 1976-77

No 24 — H WREXHAM, 22/1 — L, F-A 0-1, H-T 0-1, Pos 19, Pt 18 — Att 13,505

Pos	1	2	3	4	5	6	7	8	9	10	11	12 sub used
Pompey	Figgins	Piper	Viney	Denyer*	Foster	Cahill	Pullar	Kamara	Kemp	Mellows	Pollock	Green
Opp	Lloyd	Davis	Evans	Cagielski	Roberts	Thomas	Shinton	Sutton	Ashcroft	Whittle	Griffiths	

Scorers: Whittle 21. Ref: K Salmon (Barnet)

While the club toy with the idea of ink-impregnated hessian cover as a frost protector for Duggie Reid's immaculate Fratton turf, third-placed Wrexham put Pompey's revival (13 points in 13 games) in cold storage. Lloyd's long goal-kick splits the defence and Whittle coolly lobs in.

No 25 — A TRANMERE, 28/1 — W, F-A 3-1, H-T 2-0, Pos 18, Pt 20 — Att 3,436

Pos	1	2	3	4	5	6	7	8	9	10
Pompey	Lloyd	Viney	Roberts	Foster	Cahill	Pullar	Kemp	Kamara	Mellows	Pollock
Opp	West	Mathias	Flood	Griffiths	Philpotts	Palios	Peplow	Cliff	Tynan	Allen

Scorers: Foster 31, Pullar 33, Viney 63; Allen 54. Ref: N Midgley (Salford)

A sweetly-struck free-kick gives Viney his first goal and ends Rovers' comeback. Pompey lead when a near-post corner routine meets Foster's head. Kemp and Pollock link to set up Pullar, only for Allen to scramble a goal, but in the end Roberts almost made it four, hitting the bar.

No 26 — A CHESTERFIELD, 5/2 — W, F-A 2-1, H-T 1-0, Pos 17, Pt 22 — Att 3,959

Pos	1	2	3	4	5	6	7	8	9	10	11	12 sub used
Pompey	Lloyd	Viney	Roberts	Foster*	Cahill	Pullar	Kamara	Pollock	Mellows	McGuinness	Denyer	
Opp	Tingay	Chamberlain	Burton	Smith	Cottam	O'Neill	Cammack	Darling*	Fern	Kowalski	Charlton	Bentley

Scorers: Kemp 8, Pollock 62; Fern 56. Ref: K Ridden (Shrewsbury)

McGuinness is back for the first time this season, replacing the injured Mellows. Kemp snaps up Pullar's return pass, but Arthur Cox's side, ten games without a win, level when old-stager Fern poaches on Lloyd's slip. Against the run of play, Pollock's turn and shot seals a vital win.

No 27 — H SHEFFIELD WED, 12/2 — L, F-A 0-3, H-T 0-0, Pos 17, Pt 22 — Att 14,279

Pos	1	2	3	4	5	6	7	8	9	10	11	12 sub used
Pompey	Lloyd	Piper	Viney	Denyer	Foster	Cahill	Pullar*	Kamara	Kemp	Mellows	Pollock	Green
Opp	Turner	Walden	Rushbury	Dowd	Cusack	Leman	Wylde	Johnson	Tynan	Hope	Bradshaw	

Scorers: Tynan 69, 83, Wylde 71. Ref: C White (Harrow)

Foster, impressive of late, comes unstuck as his error gifts Tynan the ball, who then lobs Lloyd from 20 yards. However, St John pleads for patience with him. Owls have come for a point and can't believe their luck. Wylde angles home, then Tynan's free-header clears the terraces.

No 28 — A CRYSTAL PALACE, 22/2 — L, F-A 1-2, H-T 1-2, Pos 19, Pt 22 — Att 16,483

Pos	1	2	3	4	5	6	7	8	9	10	11
Pompey	Lloyd	Lawler	Piper	Denyer	Foster	Cahill	Pullar	Kamara	Kamara	Pollock	Mellows
Opp	Burns	Wall	Sansom	Holder	Cannon	Evans	Chatterton	Hinshelwood	Silkman	Swindlehurst	Harkouk

Scorers: Cannon 12, Harkouk 14. Ref: J Bent (Hemel Hempstead)

Denyer's dream start, thrashing home after Kemp and Piper swap passes inside 59 seconds, is soon undone. Lloyd's gaffe lets Cannon tap home form close-range, then Cahill misses Silkman's through ball and Harkouk scores. Terry Venables' Palace are up to a flattering fourth.

No 29 — H GILLINGHAM, 26/2 — W, F-A 3-2, H-T 2-1, Pos 17, Pt 24 — Att 10,102

Pos	1	2	3	4	5	6	7	8	9	10	11	12 sub used
Pompey	Lloyd	Piper	Viney	Denyer	Foster	Cahill	Pullar	Kamara	Kamara	Pollock	Mellows	Williams
Opp	Hillyard	Knight	Armstrong	Galvin*	Shipperley	Hughes	Nicholl	Crabbe	Weatherley	Westwood	Richardson	Williams

Scorers: Kemp 34, 43 Piper 76p; Westwood 33, 55. Ref: T Bune (Billingshurst)

Pompey secure their first home Saturday league win for 11 months, as St John reckons £20,000 or so will let him to sign two players he wants. Keeper Lloyd makes up for Tuesday's error with some fine saves, but it is Piper's spot-kick cool, after Weatherley shoved Pollock, that wins it.

No 30 — A READING, 5/3 — L, F-A 0-2, H-T 0-1, Pos 18, Pt 24 — Att 7,873

Pos	1	2	3	4	5	6	7	8	9	10	11
Pompey	Lloyd	Piper	Viney	Denyer	Foster	Cahill	Pullar	Kemp	Kamara	Mellows	Pollock
Opp	Death	Peters	Drysdale	Bowman	Hetzke	Moreline	Earles	Williams	Hollis	Carnaby	Dunphy

Scorers: Hetzke 39, 82. Ref: C Thomas (Treorchy)

As SOS Pompey is wound up, having raised £35,000, Maurice Evans' Royals claim their first win in 13 games. Hetzke's two free headers do the damage and brawling visiting fans leave a Reading fan seriously hurt. Earlier in the day Spurs dumped Pompey out of the FA Youth Cup.

No 31 — H SHREWSBURY, 12/3 — W, F-A 2-0, H-T 1-0, Pos 17, Pt 26 — Att 9,904

Pos	1	2	3	4	5	6	7	8	9	10	11	12 sub used
Pompey	Lloyd	Piper	Viney	Roberts	Foster	Cahill	Pullar	Kemp	Gilchrist*	Pollock	Mellows	Kamara
Opp	Mulhearn	King	Leonard	Turner	Griffin*	Atkins	Irvine	Hornsby	Lawrence	Bates	Moore	Loughnane

Scorers: Kemp 49, Mellows 78. Ref: R Crabb (Exeter)

St John gets part of his wish and £5,000 signs Saints' striker Gilchrist, who gets an ovation when replaced. Mulhearn's flap at Pollock's corner allows Kemp a simple header, then Mellows converts Pullar's cross from close in. Alan Durban's side have now earned just one point from 12.

No 32 — A LINCOLN, 15/3 — L, F-A 1-2, H-T 1-0, Pos 18, Pt 26 — Att 4,648

Pos	1	2	3	4	5	6	7	8	9	10	11	12 sub used
Pompey	Lloyd	Piper	Viney	Roberts	Foster	Cahill	Pullar	Kemp	Gilchrist	Pollock*	Mellows	Kamara
Opp	Grotier	Branfoot	Neale	Booth	Ellis	Cooper	Fleming	Hubbard	Graham	Smith	Harding	

Scorers: Kemp 18; Booth 61, Hubbard 76. Ref: D Civil (Birmingham)

Backed by a fierce gale, Dennis Booth bends a corner straight in, but Pompey insist Lloyd was fouled. George Kerr's Lincoln – who have come from behind to win in their last three – scent blood and from a disputed free-kick Hubbard scores after Lloyd only half-punches clear.

No 33 — A WALSALL, 19/3 — D, F-A 1-1, H-T 0-0, Pos 18, Pt 27 — Att 4,871

Pos	1	2	3	4	5	6	7	8	9	10	11	12 sub used
Pompey	Lloyd	Piper	Viney	Roberts	Foster	Cahill	Pullar*	Kemp	Kemp	Pollock	Mellows	Kamara
Opp	Kearns	Taylor	Caswell	Hynd	Serella	Atthey	Dennehy	Bates	Andrews	Buckley	Birch	

Scorers: Pollock 68; Andrews 67. Ref: K Hackett (Sheffield)

The battle of the bosses, both former Scotland caps, is shaded by St John. Dave Mackay, newly-installed at Fellows Park, sees his side lead when Andrews nods in after Piper's header conceded a corner. From the restart, Piper swaps passes with Kemp and Pollock buries the cross.

No 34 — H NORTHAMPTON, 26/3 — W, F-A 2-1, H-T 0-0, Pos 17, Pt 29 — Att 9,195

Pos	1	2	3	4	5	6	7	8	9	10	11	12 sub used
Pompey	Lloyd	Piper	Viney	Roberts	Foster	Cahill	Pullar	Gilchrist	Kemp	Pollock*	Mellows	Denyer
Opp	Ward	Tucker	Bryant	Gregory	Robertson	Martin	Farrington	Williams	Haywood	Stratford	Christie	

Scorers: Gilchrist 85, Kemp 88; Stratford 52. Ref: B Daniels (Brentwood)

Early leavers will not believe it as Pompey turn it round at the end. Cobblers look well set when Stratford nets his eighth in eight games, but Gilchrist stoops for his first in 12 months – his previous goal set Saints on their Wembley way – then Kemp stabs in Foster's near-post flick.

Portsmouth 1979 — Match Log (games 35–46)

#	Venue/Date	Opponent	Pos	Att			Result	HT	FT	Scorers	Referee
35	A 2/4	PORT VALE	19	2,984	16	29	L	0-1	0-1	Cullerton 19	D Lloyd (Fernhill Heath)
36	A 6/4	BRIGHTON	20	25,451	1	29	L	0-2	**0-4**	Ward 13, 55, Rollings 44, Piper 67	L Burden (Broadstone)
37	H 9/4	CRYSTAL PALACE	21	14,108	5	30	D	0-0	0-0	—	A Turvey (Basingstoke)
38	A 11/4	CHESTER	19	3,309	11	31	D	1-0	1-1	Kemp 22; Crossley 67	J Sewell (Leicester)
39	H 16/4	ROTHERHAM	18	10,588	4	33	W	2-1	**5-1**	Denyer 7, 57, Kemp 17, 49, 53; Phillips 27	K Salmon (Barnet)
40	H 19/4	TRANMERE	20	12,710	13	33	L	0-3	0-3	Moore 15, Allen 79, Cliff 86	A Lees (Bridgewater)
41	A 23/4	BURY	20	5,211	6	33	L	0-0	0-1	Entwistle 55	P Richardson (Lincoln)
42	H 30/4	GRIMSBY	21	10,155	24	33	L	1-1	1-2	Moore 10(og), Liddell 28; Viney 62(og)	E Read (Bristol)
43	A 2/5	MANSFIELD	21	10,774	1	33	L	0-1	0-2	Foster C 45, Randall 52	R Chadwick (Darwen)
44	A 7/5	PRESTON	21	5,347	7	34	D	0-0	0-0	—	R Capey (Crewe)
45	H 14/5	YORK	20	14,288	24	36	W	1-1	3-1	Green 35, 74, Kemp 60; Hope 30	B Stevens (Stonehouse)
46	A 17/5	SWINDON	20	6,744	11	36	L	0-3	3-4	Kamara 65p, 68p, Kemp 84 (Aiz'wood 79); Stroud 14, McHale 19, French 40	M Sinclair (Guildford)

Home 11,573 — Away 6,794 — Average 6,794

Line-ups and match reports

35 — Port Vale (A)
Portsmouth: Lloyd, Connaughton, Piper, Viney, Roberts, Foster, Cahill, Pullar*, Kemp, Gilchrist, Denyer, Mellows, Pollock
Port Vale: Brodie*, Dobson, Ridley, Harris, Lamb, Beech, McLaren, Beamish, Cullerton, Brownbill, Osborne
The club announce season-ticket price increases of up to £7, only to see the team get sucked back into the drop zone. The Valiants leap-frog Pompey as Cullerton's leg deflects Brownbill's cross in against the run of play. After that Vale take over and Lloyd keeps the score down.

36 — Brighton (A)
Portsmouth: Lloyd, Steele, Piper, Viney*, Denyer, Foster, Cahill, Kamara, Kemp, Gilchrist, Pollock, Mellows, Green
Brighton: Tiler, Cattlin, Horton, Rollings, Cross, Fell, Ward, Mellor, Piper, O'Sullivan
Classy Peter Ward ensures Albion make up for Boxing Day. His first is a 'Greaves-esque' effort from Mellor's pass, then Rollings, who will later join Pompey, thumps in a header. Ward arrowed in a deflected third, then a low drive by Steve Piper (another future Blue) wrapped it up.

37 — Crystal Palace (H)
Portsmouth: Lloyd, Burns, Piper, Green, Roberts, Foster, Cahill, Kemp, Gilchrist, Pollock, Mellows
Crystal Palace: Hinshelwood, Sansom, Holder, Cannon, Evans, Swindlehurst, Graham, Bourne, Chatterton, Harkouk*, Silkman
An accident with a glass door in the week leaves reserve keeper Figgins with a career-threatening 34 stitches in his wrists. A point in this dour clash with Palace, on course for a blind-side promotion run, is welcome. Cahill faces a ban after his hack on Bourne takes him past 20 points.

38 — Chester (A)
Portsmouth: Lloyd, Millington, Piper, Green, Cahill, Kemp, Gilchrist, Denyer, Mellows, Pullar*
Chester: Edwards, Walker, Storton, Delgado, Richardson, Dearden, Draper, Keaney, Owen, Crossley
Pompey soak up ineffective pressure and are leading thanks to Kemp's mis-hit shot from a swift counter, only for Cahill's block to fall kindly for Crossley and his rising drive levels it. Quickly, Lloyd saves point-blank from Richardson, but Mellows should have sealed it one-on-one.

39 — Rotherham (H)
Portsmouth: Lloyd, McAllister, Piper, Viney, Green, Foster, Cahill, Denyer, Kamara, Kemp, Gilchrist, Pullar
Rotherham: Pugh, Breckin, Rhodes, Stancliffe, Spencer, Finney, Phillips, Gwyther, Wagstaffe, Crawford
St John answers his terrace critics, who bayed for his head last week, as high-riding Millers are thrashed. Jimmy McGuigan's men are floored by early strikes, then Kemp runs 35 yards to float a shot past McAllister to end any comeback hopes. A deflected shot gives Kemp his treble.

40 — Tranmere (H)
Portsmouth: Lloyd, Johnson, Piper, Viney*, Kamara, Foster, Cahill, Green, Gilchrist, Denyer, Mellows
Tranmere: Parry, Flood, Bramhall, Philpots, Palios, Mathias, Cliff, Moore, Tynan, Allen
Tenacious marking and covering from John King's team to poach a win bonus. Moore loops in against the run of play and Rovers have to cling on. A push on Denyer in the box is missed, then Pullar smacks the bar. Allen's soft shot seals it, then Cliff pushes Pompey over the edge.

41 — Bury (A)
Portsmouth: Lloyd, Forrest, Piper, Viney, Kamara, Foster, Ellis, Green*, Kemp, Gilchrist, Denyer, Mellows
Bury: Bailey, Kennedy, Williams, Tucker, Hatton, Thomson, McIlwraith, Rowland, Entwistle, Farrell
England youth international Entwistle gets his crew-cut head to Williams' centre to glance home and wreck hopes of a point. Pompey went in level playing into a windy and wet Lancashire afternoon thanks to two Lloyd saves, but rarely look like breaking down the Shakers' rearguard.

42 — Grimsby (H)
Portsmouth: Lloyd, Wainman, Piper, Viney, Denyer, Foster, Ellis, Green*, Kamara*, Kemp, Pollock, Mellows, Pullar
Grimsby: Cumming, Moore, Waters, Tucker, Lewis, Gray, Harvey, Thomson, Partridge, Liddell, Boylen, Brolly
Pompey are in the bottom four after rock-bottom Grimsby's second away win. Moore gifts the lead when he slices in Kemp's cross, but Liddell levelled. Mellows' tumble gives Piper a spot-kick, but he hits the post, then Viney turns in Hanvey's header to complete a miserable afternoon.

43 — Mansfield (A)
Portsmouth: Lloyd, Arnold, Ellis, Piper, Denyer, Foster, Cahill, Pollock*, Kemp, Gilchrist, Kamara*, Mellows, Pullar
Mansfield: Bird, Foster B, McEwan*, Batter, Mackenzie, Foster C, Morris, Moss, Randall, Hodgson, Matthews
Ian St John is sensationally suspended by Deacon after this loss, with Pompey still needing three points for safety. By contrast, the result puts modest Stags in Division Two for the first time, but their joy is marred when Barry Foster breaks his leg in an accidental clash with Ellis.

44 — Preston (A)
Portsmouth: Lloyd, Tunks, Ellis, Piper, Denyer, Foster, Cahill, Green, Kemp, Gilchrist, Pollock*, Mellows, Pullar
Preston: Cameron, Hunter*, Burns*, Baxter, Lawrenson, Colman, Doyle, Randall, Smith, Elwiss, Bruce, Thomson
Dickinson, 37 years at Pompey, answers Deacon's plea and takes the job he always said he didn't want. His first team sees the experienced Roberts and Wilson recalled and Piper in a more-familiar midfield role. Denyer hits a post and Gilchrist the bar, but the point is fair return.

45 — York (H)
Portsmouth: Lloyd, Roberts, Wilson, Piper, Denyer, Foster, Cahill, Green, Kemp, Gilchrist, Piper, Green, Kamara
York: Neenan, Hunter*, Williams, Young, Topping, James, Lawrenson, Colman, Pollard, Hope, Staniforth, Taylor, Hosker
Deacon pays tribute to the fans, who swarm onto the pitch to celebrate salvation and acclaim Dickinson. Green quickly pounces on defensive confusion, after Hope put doomed York ahead. Kemp converts Mellows' corner, then Green lobs into an empty net with Neenan stranded.

46 — Swindon (A)
Portsmouth: Lloyd, Roberts, Wilson, Kamara, Denyer, Foster, Cahill, Green, Kemp, Gilchrist, Piper, Green, Mellows
Swindon: Allan, Dixon*, Trollope, Stroud, Aizlewood, Prophett, Lawrenson, Syrett, French, Hooper, McHale, Anderson, Taylor
Dickinson's 'Go out and enjoy yourselves' instruction is taken too literally in the first half. Hooper's handball sets hope glimmering, then Allan's foul on Kemp lets Kamara net another spot-kick. Kemp nicks his 17th goal to set up a grandstand finish, after Aizlewood's header.

LEAGUE DIVISION 3 (CUP-TIES) — Manager: St John ⇨ Dickinson — SEASON 1976-77

League Cup

1:1 A CRYSTAL PALACE 14/8 12,936 D F-A 2-2 H-T 1-2
Scorers: Piper 28, Denyer 71 / Kemp 29, 30
Ref: A Turvey (Basingstoke)

1	2	3	4	5	6	7	8	9	10	11	12 sub used
Lloyd	Roberts	Wilson	Kamara	Ellis	Cahill	McGuiness	Piper	Foster*	Mellows	Pollock	Denyer
Hammond	*Wall*	*Sansom*	*Holder*	*Cannon*	*Evans*	*Chatterton*	*Hinsh'wood M Kemp*		*Swindleh'st* Taylor*		*Harkouk*

Kemp impresses Pompey with his finishing power so much he will sign for them in November. England winger Taylor plays a part in the first as watching Leeds' boss Jimmy Armfield ponders a £150,000 bid. Piper levels against the run of play, and sub Denyer seizes on Evans' error.

1:2 H CRYSTAL PALACE 17/8 9,778 L F-A 0-1 H-T 0-0
Scorer: Taylor 59
Ref: T Glasson (Salisbury)
(Pompey lose 2-3 on aggregate)

1	2	3	4	5	6	7	8	9	10	11	12 sub used
Lloyd	Roberts	Wilson	Kamara	Ellis	Cahill	McGuiness*	Piper	Foster	Graham	Mellows	Eames
Hammond	*Wall*	*Sansom*	*Holder*	*Cannon*	*Evans*	*Chatterton*	*Hinsh'wood M Kemp*		*Swindlehurst Taylor*		

Taylor underlines his value with a shot that pings into the net through a ruck of players, but generally Wilson has his match. Pompey's lack of punch up front is apparent again, although Graham hits the bar with a header. Wall hits the woodwork for Terry Venables' Eagles late on.

FA Cup

1 A ALDERSHOT 20/11 10,213 4:11 21 D F-A 1-1 H-T 1-0
Scorers: Mellows 26 / McGregor 67
Ref: L Burden (Broadstone)

1	2	3	4	5	6	7	8	9	10	11	12 sub used
Lloyd	Piper	Viney	Denyer	Foster	Cahill	Pullar	Kamara	Green	Pollock	Mellows	
Johnson	*Howitt*	*Wooler*	*Crosby*	*Mancini*	*Jopling*	*McGregor*	*Morrissey*	*Howarth*	*Butler*	*Brodie*	

McGregor earned a replay with a cool chip, but Pompey aren't complaining too much as the gate receipts will come in handy. Earlier Mellows calmly rounded off a move initiated by Piper and Green was inches away from sealing it. 'Those kids go some,' said Shots boss McAnearney.

1R H ALDERSHOT 23/11 15,089 4:11 21 W F-A 2-1 H-T 1-1
Scorers: Green 36, Foster 62 / McGregor 13
Ref: L Burden (Broadstone)

1	2	3	4	5	6	7	8	9	10	11	12 sub used
Lloyd	Piper	Viney	Denyer	Foster	Cahill	Pullar	Kamara	Green	Pollock	Mellows	
Johnson	*Howitt*	*Wooler*	*Crosby*	*Mancini*	*Jopling*	*McGregor*	*Morrissey*	*Howarth*	*Butler**	*Brodie*	*Walton*

Emerging centre-half Foster recalls his striking instincts to head in from close-range and set up a 'David and Goliath' tie. Shots have only a £7,000 gate share to console them, once a blistering shot by Green – watched again by West Ham boss Ron Greenwood – sets Pompey up.

2 H MINEHEAD 11/12 14,089 SL 22 W F-A 2-1 H-T 1-0
Scorers: Kemp 35, Kamara 58 / Leitch 70
Ref: D Nippard (Christchurch)

1	2	3	4	5	6	7	8	9	10	11	12 sub used
Bennett	Piper	Viney	Denyer	Foster	Cahill	Pullar	Kamara	Kemp	Mellows	Mellows	
Macey	*Impey*	*Clausen*	*Burns*	*Boyd*	*Carter*	*Jenkins*	*Durbin*	*Bryant*	*Brown**	*Leitch*	*Risdale*

Injuries mean rookie keeper Bennett's debut and he excels early on, racing off his line when Jenkins beats the offside trap. Kemp nods his first Pompey goal and Kamara's nonchalant 15-yard finish looks to have sealed it. However, 6' 5" Leitch's header leaves the crowd on tenterhooks.

3 A BIRMINGHAM 8/1 31,598 1:8 17 L F-A 0-1 H-T 0-1
Scorer: Kendall 35
Ref: R Challis (Tonbridge)

1	2	3	4	5	6	7	8	9	10	11	12 sub used
Figgins	Piper	Viney	Denyer	Foster	Cahill !	Pullar*	Kamara	Kemp	Mellows	Pollock	Green
Latchford	*Rathbone*	*Styles**	*Kendall*	*Gallagher*	*Page*	*Jones*	*Francis*	*Burns*	*Hibbitt*	*Connolly*	*Want*

Blues' director Sir Alf concedes Pompey have everything but the win, as Kemp heads against the inside of a post and two penalty appeals are turned down. Kendall fires in from 15 yards after Burns' pass. Cahill sees a red card when he clatters the time-wasting Jones by the corner flag.

Final League Table (Division Three, 1976-77)

			Home				Away					
	P	W	D	L	F	A	W	D	L	F	A	Pts
1 Mansfield	46	17	6	0	52	13	11	2	10	12	20	64
2 Brighton	46	19	3	1	63	14	6	8	9	20	25	61
3 Crys Palace	46	17	5	1	46	15	6	8	9	22	25	59
4 Rotherham	46	11	9	3	30	15	11	6	6	39	29	59
5 Wrexham	46	15	6	2	47	22	9	4	10	33	32	58
6 Preston	46	15	4	4	48	21	6	8	9	16	22	54
7 Bury	46	15	2	6	41	21	8	6	9	23	38	54
8 Sheffield Wed	46	15	4	4	39	18	7	5	11	26	37	53
9 Lincoln	46	12	9	2	50	30	7	5	11	27	40	52
10 Shrewsbury	46	13	7	3	40	21	5	4	14	25	38	47
11 Swindon	46	12	6	5	48	33	3	9	11	20	42	45
12 Gillingham	46	11	8	4	31	21	5	4	14	24	43	44
13 Chester	46	14	4	5	28	20	4	4	15	20	38	44
14 Tranmere	46	10	7	6	31	23	3	10	10	20	30	43
15 Walsall	46	8	7	8	39	32	5	8	10	18	33	41
16 Peterborough	46	11	4	8	33	28	2	11	10	22	37	41
17 Oxford	46	9	8	6	34	29	3	7	13	21	36	39
18 Chesterfield	46	10	6	7	30	20	4	4	15	26	44	38
19 Port Vale	46	9	7	7	29	28	2	9	12	18	43	38
20 PORTSMOUTH	46	8	9	6	28	26	3	5	15	25	44	36
21 Reading	46	10	5	8	29	24	3	4	16	20	49	35
22 Northampton	46	9	4	10	33	29	4	4	15	27	46	34
23 Grimsby	46	10	6	7	29	22	2	3	18	16	47	33
24 York	46	7	8	8	25	34	3	4	16	25	55	32
	1104	287	143	122	903	559	122	143	287	559	903	1104

Appearances & Goals

Player		Appearances						Goals		
	Lge	Sub	LC	Sub	FAC	Sub	Lge	LC	FAC	Tot
Bennett, Paul	42				4		1			1
Cahill, Paul			2							
Denyer, Peter	38	2			4	1	6		1	7
Eames, Billy				1						
Ellis, Peter	19	1	2							
Figgins, Phil	5				1					
Foster, Steve	28	3	2		4		1		1	2
Gilchrist, Paul	16		1				1			1
Graham, George	3		1							
Green, Clive	26	5			2		4	1		5
Kamara, Chris	35	4	1		4		3		1	4
Kemp, David	30	1	1		2		16	1		17
Lawler, Chris	9	1	1							
Lloyd, Grahame	41		2		2					
McGuinness, Bobby	1	2	2							
Mellows, Mick	37	3	2		4		6		1	7
Piper, Norman	42	1	2		4		4		1	5
Pollock, Matt	39	1	2		4		6			6
Pullar, David	27	3			4		2			2
Roberts, Phil	14		2		2					
Viney, Keith	33	2			4		1			1
Went, Paul	8						1			1
Wilson, Billy	13	2			2		1			1
(own-goals)										
23 players used	506	29	22	2	44	2	53	2	5	60

Odds & ends

Double wins: (1) York.

Double losses: (3) Reading, Wrexham, Grimsby.

Won from behind: (3) Gillingham (h), Northampton (h), York (h).

Lost from in front: (4) Oxford (a), Lincoln (a), C Palace (a), Grimsby (h).

High spots: David Kemp scores the first hat-trick for the club since October 1970 in a 5-1 thrashing of Rotherham in April.

Beating local rivals Brighton 1-0 at home on Boxing Day in front of 32,000.

Ensuring survival with a 3-1 win over York in the penultimate game.

Winning 4-1 at York on 18 December.

Low spots: 11 match win-less run from August to October.

Slumping to 24th place after losing 1-3 at Northampton in October.

Losing 0-4 at Sussex rival Brighton in April.

Pompey played in front just over 2,000 fans on 'Black Saturday' in December at York, then in front of more than 32,000 in their next game at home to Brighton on Boxing Day, nine days later.

Player of the Year: Not awarded.

Ever presents: (0).

Hat-tricks: David Kemp (1).

Leading scorer: David Kemp (17).

LEAGUE DIVISION 3 — Manager: Jimmy Dickinson — SEASON 1977-78

No	Date	Att	Pos	Pt	F-A	H-T	1	2	3	4	5	6	7	8	9	10	11	12 sub used
1	A PETERBOROUGH 20/8	6,099	—	D 1	0-0	0-0	Middleton	Roberts	Wilson	Ellis	Foster	Cahill	Gilchrist	Kemp	Green	Mellows	Pollock	Carmichael
	(Peterborough)						*Waugh*	*Hindley*	*Lee*	*Doyle*	*Turner*	*Ross*	*Slough*	*Camp*	*Sargent*	*Robson*	*Rogers**	*Stokes*
2	A SWINDON 27/8	9,396	20/2	L 1	1-3	1-1	Middleton	Roberts	Wilson	Ellis	Foster	Cahill	Green	Kemp*	Green	Pollock	Mellows	Stokes
	(Swindon)						*Allan*	*McLaughlin*	*Trollope*	*Stroud*	*Aizlewood*	*Prophett*	*Moss*	*Kamara*	*Guthrie*	*McHale*	*Anderson*	
3	H CHESTERFIELD 3/9	11,132	13/9	W 3	3-0	2-0	Middleton	Roberts	Wilson	Ellis	Foster	Cahill	Green	Kemp	Stokes	Mellows	Pollock	Pollock
	(Chesterfield)						*Ogrzovic*	*Tartt*	*Burton*	*Kowalski*	*Cottam*	*Pollard*	*Jones**	*Hepplewhite*	*Green*	*Parker*	*Cammack*	*Hunter*
4	A WREXHAM 10/9	5,000	17/10	L 3	0-2	0-2	Middleton	Roberts	Wilson	Denver	Ellis	Foster	Ellis	Kemp	Stokes	Green*	Pollock	Gilchrist
	(Wrexham)						*Niedzwiecki*	*Hill*	*Dwyer*	*Davies*	*Roberts J*	*Thomas**	*Shinton*	*Sutton*	*Lee*	*Cartwright*	*Griffiths*	*Cegielski*
5	H COLCHESTER 13/9	11,757	18/1	D 4	0-0	0-0	Middleton	Roberts	Wilson	Ellis	Foster	Cahill	Pollock	Kemp	Green	Green	Mellows	Mellows
	(Colchester)						*Walker*	*Cook**	*Williams*	*Foley*	*Dyer*	*Davman*	*Garwood*	*Gough*	*Froggatt*	*Bunkell*	*Allison*	*Wignall*
6	H LINCOLN 17/9	11,370	20/22	L 4	0-2	0-1	Middleton	Roberts*	Wilson	Ellis	Foster	Cahill	Green	Kemp	Stokes	Mellows	Pollock	Piper N
	(Lincoln)						*Grotier*	*Neale*	*Leigh*	*Booth*	*Wiggington*	*Crombie*	*Hubbard*	*Graham*	*Fleming*	*Eden*	*Cork*	
7	A EXETER 24/9	5,875	18/11	W 6	1-0	1-0	Middleton	Roberts	Wilson	Piper N	Foster	Denver	Gilchrist	Kemp	Stokes	Mellows	Barnard	Roberts
	(Exeter)						*Key*	*Templeman*	*Hoare*	*Bowker*	*Saxton*	*Hatch*	*Hodge*	*Kellow*	*Randall*	*Holman**	*Jennings*	*Roberts*
8	A OXFORD 28/9	7,769	19/3	D 7	0-0	0-0	Middleton	Roberts	Wilson	Piper N	Foster	Denver	Barnard	Kemp	Gilchrist	Stokes	Mellows	
	(Oxford)						*Burton*	*Kingston*	*Fogg*	*Badel*	*Clarke*	*Jeffrey*	*McGrogan**	*Taylor*	*Foley*	*Curran*	*Duncan*	*Seacole*
9	H SHEFFIELD WED 1/10	12,020	19/24	D 8	2-2	2-1	Middleton	Roberts	Wilson	Piper N	Foster	Denver	Gilchrist	Kemp	Stokes	Mellows	Barnard	Roberts
	(Sheffield Wed)						*Turner*	*Walden*	*Rushbury*	*Mullen*	*Cusack*	*Leman*	*Wylde*	*Johnson*	*Prendergast**	*Gregson*	*Bradshaw*	*Tynan*
10	H CHESTER 4/10	10,465	17/14	D 9	0-0	0-0	Middleton	Roberts	Wilson	Piper N	Foster	Denver	Barnard*	Kemp	Gilchrist	Stokes	Mellows	
	(Chester)						*Lloyd*	*Raynor*	*Walker*	*Storton*	*Delgado*	*Oakes*	*Crossley*	*Jeffries*	*Kearney*	*Edwards*	*Phillips*	*Pullar*
11	A WALSALL 8/10	4,764	19/13	D 10	1-1	0-0	Middleton	Roberts	Wilson	Piper N	Foster	Denver	Barnard	Kemp	Gilchrist	Stokes	Mellows	
	(Walsall)						*Moseley*	*Taylor*	*Newton*	*Hynd*	*Serella*	*Evans*	*Robertson*	*Bates*	*Wood*	*Buckley*	*Birch*	

Scorers, Times, and Referees

1. Ref: A Jenkins (Scunthorpe)
2. Pollock 36 / Kamara 7, McHale 69, Moss 85. Ref: L Shapter (Paignton)
3. Kemp 20, 37p, Stokes 52. Ref: C Gardner (Gloucester)
4. Shinton 29, Davies 37. Ref: A McDonald (Birmingham)
5. Ref: M Sinclair (Guildford)
6. Graham 39, Foster 67 (og). Ref: J Homewood (Sunbury)
7. Kemp 32. Ref: D Lloyd (Fernhill Heath)
8. Ref: D Civil (Birmingham)
9. Foster 2, Kemp 39 / Bradshaw 42, Tynan 83. Ref: R Crabb (Exeter)
10. Ref: D Smith (Hornchurch)
11. Kemp 58 / Evans 51. Ref: A Challinor (Rotherham)

Match reports

1. Keeper Steve Middleton, signed on a free from Saints to replace Lloyd who has retired for 'family reasons', has little to do, as new Posh boss John Barnwell sees his side frustrated. Another summer arrival, Bobby Stokes, also from Saints, via Washington Diplomats, is on the bench.

2. Kamara, sold by Pompey three weeks ago for £17,000, is Town's skipper and he scores with a stooping header, sparking a brawl behind the goal. Pollock levels from an impossible angle, but Moss sets up McHale, then heads in from six yards. Trollope plays his 700th league match.

3. Pompey-born Stokes makes a dream league debut, firing in from ten yards. Earlier Wilson – who is learning the licensing trade – was the toast of the crowd, when his smart cross lets Kemp turn and score. Tartt's foul on Mellows let 'King Kemp' put the team in charge from the spot.

4. Wrexham's new player-boss Arfon Griffiths secures his first league win of the season in blustery North Wales. Facing the wind in the first-half, Pompey are lucky to be only two down. First Roberts' presence causes confusion and Shinton hooks in, then Davies' free-kick flies home.

5. Dickinson warns fans not to chant for substitutes, after his team struggle to break down new-boys Colchester. 'I wasn't thinking of bringing Piper on, but the calls would have stopped me anyway,' he said. Bobby Roberts' U's stay top after a fine start, but they will fade by the spring.

6. The club reveal a vastly-improved balance sheet, 12 months after SOS Pompey, but transfer funds are clearly needed. Green's early one-on-one with Grotier goes begging and the Imps take over. Graham heads a corner, then as Alan Cork (19) goes round Middleton, Foster finishes it.

7. Fred Binney thinks over a move from Brighton, as Dickinson hands Leigh Barnard (19) a debut. A damp day ends in delight as Kemp slides in Roberts' knock, shortly after Pompey fans had been hurt when a wall gave way. Exeter, prompted by ex-Blue Jennings, battle with no reward.

8. After the game Dickinson apologises to Oxford boss Mick Brown. 'We tried to stop them playing, but it doesn't make for an ideal game,' he confessed. Middleton stars, making a string of athletic stops. Meanwhile, Hand turns down a Fratton return, electing to join Shamrock Rovers.

9. Len Ashurst's Owls emerge from a Welsh retreat to earn a point, but they are still winless this season. Gilchrist's cross allows Foster to loop in a header, then Kemp turns his man to fire home. Middleton loses the flight of a corner for Bradshaw. Late on, Tynan's left-footer levels things.

10. Pompey will try to sign Wolves striker Bobby Gould (31) this week, but the £10,000 fee and his wages torpedo the deal. Dickinson's anguish is borne of another barren night against Alan Oakes' Seals. Kemp sees his spot-kick blocked, then he and Gilchrist get in each other's way.

11. Foster bottles up veteran Wood, but is walking a suspension tight-rope after his fifth booking of the season for a foul on Robertson. Saddlers lead when Robertson glides round Wilson and centres to give Evans a simple header. Kemp levels with a header across Derby loanee Moseley.

Portsmouth — Match Log (Nos. 12–23)

No	V	Date	Opponent	Att	Score	Pos	Pompey scorers	Opp scorers	Referee
12	H	15/10	BURY	10,861	1-1	19 D (6/11)	Kemp 83	Rowland 71	A Gunn (Burgess Hill)
13	A	22/10	SHREWSBURY	3,726	1-6	20 L (2/11)	Kemp 75	Atkins 2p, 28p, 50, Hornsby 5, Irvine 72 [Nixon 88]	J Wrennall (Eccleston)
14	A	29/10	PLYMOUTH	6,594	1-3	23 L (15/11)	Kemp 88	Austin 10, Taylor 42, Johnson 46	E Read (Bristol)
15	H	5/11	TRANMERE	8,782	2-5	24 L (3/11)	Kemp 13, 28p	Moore 48, Flood 63, Allen 65p [Palios 72, James 80]	R Lewis (Great Bookham)
16	A	12/11	CARLISLE	3,828	1-3	24 L (20/11)	Carr 85 (og)	Tait 14, McVitie 67, Bonnyman 75	J Hough (Macclesfield)
17	H	15/11	PORT VALE	7,072	1-1	24 D (22/12)	Kemp 55	Hemmerman 44	S Bates (Bristol)
18	H	19/11	HEREFORD	8,077	2-0	23 W (19/14)	Kemp 72, Pollock 87	—	W Gow (Swansea)
19	A	3/12	PRESTON	5,936	1-3	23 L (6/14)	Kemp 85	Bruce 23, Elwiss 55, Smith 65	P Partridge (Cockfield)
20	H	10/12	ROTHERHAM	9,466	3-3	23 D (11/15)	Pollock 37, 52, Kemp 80	Gwyther 13, 88, Finney 20	D Hutchinson (Witney)
21	A	26/12	GILLINGHAM	9,811	0-0	23 D (2/16)	—	—	M Taylor (Deal)
22	H	27/12	CAMBRIDGE	13,152	2-2	23 D (1/17)	Kemp 58, Ruggiero 69p	Biley 12, 23	W Bombroff (Bristol)
23	A	30/12	TRANMERE	4,677	0-2	24 L (2/17)	—	Allen 19, Peplow 26	G Owen (Anglesea)

Match reports

12. BURY — Stokes is pushed up front but struggles to hit it off with Kemp. Bury's third away win looks on when Rowland's shot startles Middleton, but Kemp's fierce free-kick, after Gilchrist was fouled in the 'D', saves it. News of Gould's triple for Bristol Rovers goes down like a lead balloon.

13. SHREWSBURY — Two dodgy pens and a 'goal' that hits the side-netting, all inside half an hour, unhinge Pompey. Hornsby theatrically sprawls twice and bends the free-kick 'wide', then as Middleton shapes to take a goal-kick the referee points to the centre! Even 'Gentleman Jim' is touchy afterwards.

14. PLYMOUTH — Not until first-half injury-time is Barron troubled, while Binney, who turned down a move to Fratton, is on Argyle's bench. Debut-making Gary Megson (18) plays a part in moves for Austin's header and Taylor's curler, but Viney furiously insists he hacked Johnson's effort clear.

15. TRANMERE — Around 100 soaking souls on the Milton End have a close-up view as Kemp stabs home. Allen's pen hits the bar, then Kemp shows him how, after Mellows was fouled. Flood's free-kick starts a deluge and Allen is second-time lucky when Foster handles. Pompey slump to rock-bottom.

16. CARLISLE — Transfer talk surrounds 13-goal Kemp, after he nets as a 'guest' in Derby's midweek friendly with Bruges. Fans put out 'Keep Kemp' posters, but ironically he will end up at Carlisle in March. Bob Moncur's team are hardly in goal-need, as Pompey fold once Tait diverts Lathan's shot.

17. PORT VALE — Pompey stay bottom, despite Kemp's volley from Pollock's corner. Earlier, Hemmerman skilfully turned and shot across Figgins, leaving a mental note for Dickinson, who will sign him in July on a free. The game's original August date was scuppered by Vale's League Cup replay.

18. HEREFORD — John Sillett's Hereford are heading for successive relegations and arrive at Fratton without an away win since March. Even pitiful Pompey are able to take advantage, but Mellor's brilliance keeps them at bay until Kemp's near-post header. Pollock's tap-in ensures a first win in twelve.

19. PRESTON — Pompey move to re-sign Hand, after his Irish adventure goes awry. On this showing his stability will be welcome. By the time Kemp nets his 16th goal, Pompey's defence has buckled three times, but Ellis earns praise for his efforts to keep Harry Catterick's promotion-chasers at bay.

20. ROTHERHAM — Monday's annual report will reveal a £650,000 debt, five years after Deacon joined the board. Plucky Pompey fight back, prompted by loan signing Ruggiero from Brighton. He wins the corner that lets Kemp nod in Pullar's centre, but sloppy defending allows Gwyther to save it.

21. GILLINGHAM — Wasteful Gillingham miss a string of chances to consolidate their promotion push, but could cite Weatherley's header against the bar and Price's shot against the post as evidence of bad luck. Pompey rarely threaten, but Foster causes panic when his shot is hacked from the line.

22. CAMBRIDGE — Ruggiero saves a point when he converts a spot-kick after Smith's innocuous foul on Stokes. Kemp set up a comeback by diverting Ruggiero's shot through a crowd of players, but blond-bombshell Biley, rather of Pompey fame, had earlier fed off Foster's error to put United in charge.

23. TRANMERE — Rovers are unchanged for the 26th successive match and their co-ordination proves enough. With Bill Shankly watching, 16-goal Kemp fails to impress, although a £100,000 bid from Aston Villa may come next week. Tynan makes both goals, but Pompey have only one shot on target.

Line-ups (Pompey / Opponent, by position)

(Best-effort reading of the dense match grid.)

12. BURY — Pompey: Middleton, Roberts, Denyer, Piper N, Wilson, Gilchrist, Kemp, Stokes, Barnard, Mellows, Stanton. Bury: Forrest, Keenan, Kennedy, Thomson, Hatton, Curran*, Suddick, Rowland, McIlwraith, Robins; Maguire.

13. SHREWSBURY — Pompey: Middleton, Roberts, Denyer, Piper N, Foster, Barnard, Kemp, Stokes, Gilchrist, Mellows. Shrewsbury: Mulhearn, King, Leonard, Durban, Griffin, Irvine, Hornsby*, Lindsay, Bates, Maguire; Nixon.

14. PLYMOUTH — Pompey: Middleton, Roberts, Viney, Ellis, Foster, Denyer, Kemp, Gilchrist, Barnard, Mellows. Plymouth: Barron, Smart, Uzzell, Taylor, Foster, Craven, Megson, Hall, Johnson, Austin, Harrison.

15. TRANMERE — Pompey: Middleton, Roberts, Wilson, Ellis, Foster*, Cahill, Pollock, Gilchrist, Green, Mellows. Tranmere: Johnson, Mathias, Flood, Parry, Philpotts, Evans, Peplow, Moore*, Palios, Tynan, Allen.

16. CARLISLE — Pompey: Figgins, Roberts, Wilson, Piper N*, Foster, Denyer, Pullar, Green, Stokes, Mellows, Pollock. Carlisle: Ross, Collins, McCartney, Carr, Lathan, Parker, McVitie, Tait, Bonnyman, Rafferty, Hamilton.

17. PORT VALE — Pompey: Figgins, Piper N, Wilson, Ellis, Denyer, Roberts, Pullar, Stokes, Kemp, Pollock, Mellows. Port Vale: Connaughton/McGifford, Bentley, Harris, Pulson, Brownhill, Sutcliffe, Lamb, Ridley, Hemmerman*, Bailey; Cullerton.

18. HEREFORD — Pompey: Figgins, Piper N, Wilson, Ellis, Denyer, Roberts, Kemp, Carter, Pollock, Davey*, Spring. Hereford: Mellor, Emery, Ritchie, Layton, Marshall, Briley, Stephens, Holmes, Proudlove.

19. PRESTON — Pompey: Figgins, Piper N, Wilson, Denyer, Baxter, Roberts, Pullar, Kemp, Pollock, Mellows, Foster. Preston: Tunks, McMahon, Cameron, Doyle, Burns, Coleman, Haslegrave, Smith, Elwiss, Bruce.

20. ROTHERHAM — Pompey: Figgins, Piper N, Wilson, Denyer, Hand, Ellis, Pullar, Ruggiero, Pollock, Mellows, Pollock. Rotherham: McAllister, Forrest, Breckin, Womble, Stancliffe, Green, Finney, Phillips, Gwyther, Goodfellow, Crawford.

21. GILLINGHAM — Pompey: Figgins, Piper N, Wilson, Denyer, Pullar, Pullar, Kemp, Stokes, Gilchrist, Mellows. Gillingham: Hillyard, Knight, Armstrong, Overton, Shipperley, Crabbe, Nicholl, Hunt*, Price, Westwood, Richardson; Weatherley.

22. CAMBRIDGE — Pompey: Figgins, Piper N, Wilson, Ruggiero, Foster, Hand, Kemp, Stokes, Gilchrist, Mellows. Cambridge: Hansbury, Batson, Smith, Stringer, Fallon, Howard, Watson, Sprigs, Biley, Morgan, Cozens.

23. TRANMERE — Pompey: Figgins, Denyer, Wilson, Ruggiero, Foster, Hand, Kemp, Stokes*, Gilchrist, Mellows, Pollock. Tranmere: Johnson, Mathias, Flood, Parry, Philpotts, Evans, Peplow, Palios, Moore, Tynan, Allen.

LEAGUE DIVISION 3 — Manager: Jimmy Dickinson — SEASON 1977-78

Results

No	Date	Venue / Opponent	Att	Pos	Pt	Res	F-A	H-T	Scorers, Times, and Referees
24	2/1	H BRADFORD C	12,004	23 (22)	19	W	3-1	0-0	Kemp 63, Foster 79, Gilchrist 88; Wright 59. Ref: K Salmon (Barnet)
25	7/1	A PORT VALE	3,481	23 (17)	19	L	0-2	0-2	Beamish 20, 32. Ref: A Hughes (West Kirkby)
26	14/1	H PETERBOROUGH	9,569	21 (6)	20	D	2-2	2-0	Stokes 8, Gilchrist 40; Anderson 65, Turner 85. Ref: K Cooper (Pontypridd)
27	20/1	H SWINDON	11,647	22 (9)	20	L	1-2	1-0	Hand 23; Moss 50, Kamara 58. Ref: J Bent (Hemel Hempstead)
28	28/1	A CHESTERFIELD	4,351	23 (11)	20	L	0-3	0-2	Fern 28 76, Hand 38 (og). Ref: T Jenkins (Scunthorpe)
29	4/2	H WREXHAM	9,223	23 (4)	20	L	0-1	0-1	Whittle 20. Ref: R Challis (Tonbridge)
30	11/2	A LINCOLN	4,100	23 (15)	20	L	0-1	0-0	Jones 61. Ref: J Worrall (Warrington)
31	25/2	A SHEFFIELD WED	10,241	24 (18)	21	D	0-0	0-0	Ref: N Glover (Chorley)
32	28/2	H EXETER	10,260	24 (16)	22	D	1-1	0-0	Cahill 73; Cahill 52 (og). Ref: D Reeves (Uxbridge)
33	4/3	H WALSALL	9,536	24 (6)	22	L	1-2	1-1	Piper S 42; Caswell 41, Dennehy 84. Ref: L Shapter (Paignton)
34	7/3	A COLCHESTER	3,570	24 (10)	22	L	0-4	0-2	Foley 17, Rowles 28, Taylor 55 (og), Allinson 67. Ref: B Daniels (Brentwood)

Line-ups (Pompey in roman; opponents in italics)

No	1	2	3	4	5	6	7	8	9	10	11	12 sub used
24	Figgins	Denyer	Wilson	Ruggiero	Foster	Hand	Piper N	Kemp	Gilchrist	Roberts	Mellows	Ellis
24	*Downsboro'*	*Hardcastle*	*Watson*	*Fretwell*	*Middleton*	*Ratcliffe*	*Grimes*	*Dolan*	*Cooke*	*Wright*	*Hutchins*	
25	Figgins	Denyer	Wilson	Ruggiero	Foster*	Hand	Piper N	Kemp	Gilchrist	Roberts	Mellows	Ellis
25	*Connaughton*	*Beech*	*Griffiths*	*Ridley*	*Harris*	*Bentley*	*Sutcliffe*	*Lamb*	*Cullerton*	*Beamish*	*Bailey*	
26	Figgins	Roberts	Wilson	Ellis	Denyer	Hand	Piper N	Kemp	Gilchrist	Stokes	Mellows	
26	*Barron*	*Hughes*	*Lee*	*Doyle*	*Turner*	*Ross*	*Slough*	*McEwan*	*Sargent*	*Carmichael*	*Anderson*	
27	Figgins	Roberts	Wilson	Ellis	Denyer	Hand	Piper N*	Kemp	Gilchrist	Stokes	Mellows	Pollock
27	*Allan*	*Ford*	*Trollope*	*Kamara*	*Carter*	*Prophett*	*Moss*	*Stroud*	*Guthrie**	*McHale*	*Cunningham*	*Lewis*
28	Figgins	Roberts	Wilson	Ellis	Denyer	Hand	Piper N	Gilchrist	Green	Mellows	Pollock	
28	*Letheran*	*Tartt*	*Burton*	*Hunter*	*Cottam*	*O'Neill*	*Cammack*	*Fern*	*Green*	*Chamberlain*	*Dearden*	
29	Figgins	Roberts	Taylor	Denyer	Hand	Ellis	Piper N*	Kemp	Gilchrist	Stokes	Mellows	
29	*Davies*	*Hill*	*Dwyer*	*Davis*	*Thomas*	*Roberts*	*Shinton*	*Sutton*	*McNeil*	*Whittle*	*Green*	
30	Figgins	Roberts	Taylor	Denyer	Hand*	Ellis	Piper S	Kemp	Gilchrist	Stokes	Mellows	Cahill
30	*Grotier*	*Guest*	*Leigh*	*Neale*	*Wiggington*	*Cooper*	*Jones*	*Graham*	*Harford*	*Hubbard*	*Harding*	
31	Figgins	Roberts	Taylor	Cahill	Ellis*	Denyer	Piper S	Kemp	Gilchrist	Mellows	McCaffery	Piper N
31	*Bolder*	*Walden*	*Grant**	*Rushbury*	*Mullen*	*Hedley*	*Bradshaw*	*Porterfield*	*Tynan*	*Johnson*	*Cusack*	*Leman*
32	Figgins	Roberts	Taylor	Cahill	Denyer	Ellis	Piper S	Kemp	Pullar	Mellows	McCaffery	
32	*Key*	*Templeman*	*Hore*	*Weeks*	*Giles*	*Roberts*	*Hodge*	*Kellow*	*Randell*	*Bowker*	*Pullar*	*Holman*
33	Figgins	Roberts	Taylor	Denyer	Hand*	Cahill	Piper S	Kemp	Gilchrist	Mellows	McCaffery	Piper N
33	*Kearns*	*Macken*	*Caswell*	*Harrison*	*Serella*	*Evans*	*Dennehy*	*Bates*	*Wood*	*Buckley*	*King*	
34	Figgins	Roberts	Taylor	Denyer*	Hand*	Cahill	Piper S	Kemp	Pullar	Mellows	McCaffery	Piper N
34	*Walker*	*Cook*	*Wignall*	*Leslie*	*Packer*	*Davman*	*Foley*	*Gough*	*Rowles**	*Allinson*	*Bunkell*	*Barnard, Dyer*

Match notes

24 — Bradford C: Pompey make heavy-weather of beating fellow-strugglers City. Ruggiero's penalty flies over, after Piper is hauled back. Wright pops up at the far post, but Kemp responds when Hardcastle's back-pass falls short. Foster eases tension from Mellows' cross and Gillie's shot makes it safe.

25 — Port Vale: The week Pompey reveal a partnership with bookmakers Ladbrokes to launch a club lottery, the odds against survival lengthen as Vale win at a canter. Figgins is at fault as much-travelled Beamish gets in front of him to claim his second header. Piper plays his 300th first-team match.

26 — Peterborough: Yesterday, coach Crawford was fired after a court conviction. For an hour, the team defy their position, giving Posh, just 18 goals conceded, the run-around, until Anderson nets. Stokes opened and Gilchrist's first-time shot made it look easy. Doyle hit the post, but Turner poked home.

27 — Swindon: Old-boy Kamara ruins Pompey's hopes once more in a game moved to Friday night at police insistence to avoid clashing with Southampton and Brighton home matches. David Moss's free-kick deflects in off Hand, who had earlier given Pompey the lead, then his run sets up Kamara.

28 — Chesterfield: Frank Burrows is in the stand, considering the coach's job. If he likes a challenge he will come. On a mud-heap, veteran striker Fern, who John Mortimore tried to sign in 1974, poaches two typical goals. His presence also forced Hand into tucking the ball past the on-rushing Figgins.

29 — Wrexham: Burrows (34) takes the job and the club sign Tony Taylor – his rival for the post last week – on a free from Bristol Rovers. The players back his no-nonsense approach and they respond by matching Wrexham, who will end up champions. Only Whittle's glancing header separates them.

30 — Lincoln: Steve Piper, £25,000 from Brighton on Thursday, is in for namesake Norman, while Cahill returns as sub, after a loan spell at Aldershot. On a sandy, icy pitch that Dickinson thought unfit, Hand limps off with a gashed knee. Jones' finishes coolly after Figgins and Ray Harford collide.

31 — Sheffield Wed: Figgins is the hero, clutching Rushbury's penalty after he is harshly judged to have fouled Hedley in a goalmouth scramble. He makes another high-class save to deny Tommy Tynan in the first half, but a point is just reward. Winger Jim McCaffery, £15,000 from Huddersfield, starts.

32 — Exeter: Cahill forces home from close-range after Steve Piper hit the bar to atone for his looped header past Figgins. Before this re-arranged game, ten days after snow postponed it, speculation is rife that Stokes and Norman Piper will be victims of a clear-out ahead of the transfer deadline.

33 — Walsall: Pompey are now three points from safety, having played five games more than 20th-placed Rotherham. Walsall's late promotion bid remains on track, despite Piper's first, a header from McCaffery's palmed-down cross. Dennehy makes up for several earlier misses with a low shot.

34 — Colchester: Pompey's suicidal season continues against a United team without a home win in three months. Foley opens after Rowles' mis-kick, then the roles are reversed as Rowles diverts Foley's off-target effort. Taylor rockets a header past Figgins, then Allinson's cross-shot piles on misery.

The top-of-column player names (reading across): Middleton | Roberts | Taylor | Denyer* | Ellis | Cahill | Lathan | Garwood | Mellows | Pullar | McCaffery | Piper S

---

35 — A BURY — 11/3 — 4,700 — 7 — 23 — D — 0-0 — 0-0

Lineup: Forrest, Thomson, Kennedy, Hatton, Robins, Bailey, Stanton, Suddick, Johnson*, Rowland, McIlwraith, Wilson

Ref: T Mills (Barnsley)

Deadline day sees Kemp go to Carlisle for £75,000, which includes Lathan in return. £25,000 signs Garwood from Colchester, although his wife's reluctance to move south nearly wrecks the deal. A grafting performance atones for Tuesday. Garwood's late shot rolls agonisingly wide.

---

36 — H SHREWSBURY — 18/3 — 8,575 — 15 — 25 — W — 2-0 — 1-0

Lineup: Mulhearn, Leonard, Bowers, Turner, Hayes, Kaye, Irvine, Moore, Atkins, Loughnane, Maguire

Garwood 35, Denyer 66

Ref: L Burden (Wimborne)

Dickinson sets a 15-point safety haul from ten games and two are immediately bagged as Garwood starts to erase Kemp's memory with a well-struck goal from McCaffery's pass. Fans invade the pitch at the end to celebrate a first win since January, sealed by Denyer's near-post touch.

---

37 — H PLYMOUTH — 21/3 — 11,010 — 20 — 25 — L — 1-5 — 0-2   [Fear 70]

Lineup: Barron, James, Uzzell, Bason, Horswill, Foster, Fear, Taylor B, Perrin*, Binney, Megson, Trusson

Piper 73, Trusson 28, Binney 36, 90, Taylor 65

Ref: M Taylor (Deal)

Malcolm Allison's brash brand of management works wonders four days into his reign at Argyle. Dickinson is left 'ashamed' as Pompey give up after a farcical second, when Cahill fails to see his advancing keeper and his throw-in trickles towards the goal leaving Binney a simple job.

---

38 — A CAMBRIDGE — 25/3 — 5,896 — 3 — 25 — L — 0-1 — 0-0

Lineup: Webster, Howard, Buckley, Stringer, Watson, Fallon, Sweetzer*, Spriggs, Biley, Streete, Organ, Barnard / Murray

Fallon 79

Ref: R Kirkpatrick (Leicester)

Deacon pledges himself to Pompey, despite some fearful abuse from the terraces on Tuesday night. He sees his club gain some self-respect, stunning Ron Atkinson's Div Two-bound side when Piper's header hits a post. Fallon volleys in Spriggs' free-kick to calm home fans' jitters.

---

39 — H GILLINGHAM — 27/3 — 8,108 — 4 — 26 — D — 1-1 — 1-1

Lineup: Hillyard, Knight, Armstrong, Overton, Crabbe, Young, Nicholl, Weatherley, Price, Westwood, Richardson, Barnard

McCaffery 14, Weatherley 37

Ref: E Hughes (Weston-super-Mare)

Winger McCaffery turns it on at last, after the 'nightmare' he has endured since his move from Huddersfield. First he nods in Pullar's cross, then is denied a late winner by Hillyard's blinding save. Weatherley levels against the run of play after Westwood's shot breaks kindly.

---

40 — A BRADFORD C — 1/4 — 4,462 — 21 — 26 — L — 0-1 — 0-0

Lineup: Downsboro', Podd, Spark, Johnson*, Baines, —, Watson, Dolan, Wright, Middleton, McNiven, Hutchins / Fretwell

Hutchins 71

Ref: G Courtney (Spennymoor)

Dickinson and Burrows are searching for talent, ready for next season's impending Division Four campaign. City's hopes of avoiding the drop rise when Hutchins snaps up Johnson's low cross. At Fratton Park, 140 police are on duty, as Millwall 'borrow' it after The Den is suspended.

---

41 — H OXFORD — 4/4 — 5,825 — 18 — 26 — L — 0-2 — 0-0

Lineup: Burton, Kingston, Fogg, Briggs, —, Bodel, McGrogan, Foley, Seacole, Duncan, —, Mellows

Taylor 67 (og), Seacole 69

Ref: C Downey (Isleworth)

Any arithmetical hopes of avoiding the drop are ended. Garwood should have made a fight of it, but Burton saves his spot-kick after Duncan's handball. Taylor bags his second o.g. in a month, blocking McGrogan's shot, only to jab the ball past Middleton. Seacole (17) settles things.

---

42 — H CARLISLE — 8/4 — 5,937 — 14 — 27 — D — 3-3 — 2-1

Lineup: Swinburne, Collins, McCartney, MacDonald, —, McLean*, McVitie, Bonnyman, Tait, Parker, Kemp, Hamilton / Sawyers

Foster 7, Wilson 10, Pullar 53; McCartney 37p, Tait 78, Kemp 81

Ref: A Gunn (Burgess Hill)

Kemp gets a warm welcome on his return, but it's his goal that seals United's comeback. Earlier, Foster's back diverted Garwood's free-kick, then Wilson's 35-yarder went in off a post. Pullar restored the two-goal lead, but then Tait kept up his impressive goal-record against Pompey.

---

43 — A HEREFORD — 15/4 — 3,893 — 23 — 29 — W — 2-0 — 2-0

Lineup: Hughes, Bouston, Burrows, Jefferson, Layton, —, Marshall, Proudlove, Crompton, Holmes W, Davey, Emery / Viney

Garwood 27, Denyer 31

Ref: B Stevens (Stonehouse)

A taste of the fourth division – acting-boss Tony Ford's team are about to slip straight through division three – ends on an optimistic note, as Garwood and Denyer's goals are the first on the road for four months. Hereford hit the post twice in the second half, but Pompey hold out.

---

44 — H PRESTON — 22/4 — 6,866 — 2 — 29 — L — 0-2 — 0-0

Lineup: Tunks, McMahon, Cameron, Burns, —, Baxter, Coleman, Haslegrave, Robinson, Cross, Elwiss, Bruce

Bruce 80, Elwiss 83

Ref: D Biddle (Bristol)

Preston are on course to go up, but are made to sweat. Ellis is captain, the fifth man to have been so this season. Elwiss retrieves a 'lost cause' for Bruce's point-blank header, then Robinson's run from deep sets up the second. Figgins, Green and Hider are all released by Dickinson.

---

45 — A CHESTER — 26/4 — 2,837 — 5 — 29 — L — 0-2 — 0-2

Lineup: Lloyd, Nickeas, Raynor, Storton, Jeffries, —, Livermore, Howat, Mellor, Jones, Phillips, —

Livermore 22p, Mellor 44

Ref: A Hamil (Wolverhampton)

Mellows thumps the bar after just 60 seconds, but Pompey self-destruct against a side beaten just twice in their last 23. Player-boss Alan Oakes clears and Mellor breaks, only to be tumbled in the box by Ellis. Mellor scores from an oblique angle and when Denyer hits the bar it's all over.

---

46 — A ROTHERHAM — 29/4 — 3,718 — 19 — 31 — W — 1-0 — 0-0

Lineup (col order Knight, Wilson, Taylor, Ellis, —, Foster, Pullar, Denyer, Lathan, Garwood, Piper S, Mellows):
McAllister, Pugh, Breckin, Forrest, —, Stancliffe, Dawson*, Green, Phillips, Gwyther, Goodfellow / Crawford / Young

Denyer 70

Ref: R Chadwick (Darwen)

Alan Knight (16) has an easy debut against Jimmy McGuigan's men, needing a point to be sure of safety. Wilson bales Knight out early on, clearing off the line, but Denyer's drive settles it. Dickinson hopes to sign Hereford's Davey and Holmes, with Roberts going to Edgar Street.

Home Average 9,683   Away 5,423

LEAGUE DIVISION 3 (CUP-TIES)   Manager: Jimmy Dickinson   SEASON 1977-78

League Cup

				F-A	H-T	Scorers, Times, and Referees	1	2	3	4	5	6	7	8	9	10	11	12 sub used
1:1	H	NEWPORT 13/8	W 3-1	3-1	1:1	Kemp 36, 66p, Green 71 / Woods 41 / Ref: T Spencer (Swindon)	Middleton *Plumley*	Roberts *Derrett*	Wilson *Bell*	Ellis *Kemp*	Foster *Walker R*	Cahill *Jones*	Gilchrist *Preece*	Kemp *Woods*	Green *Clark*	Mellows *Relish*	Pollock *Byrne*	Villars *Villars*
1:2	A	NEWPORT 17/8	L 2-3	2-3	1-3	Pollock 43, Ellis 67 / Clark 9, Walker R 20, Wilson 38 (og) / Ref: D Biddle (Bristol) / (Pompey won 5-4 on aggregate)	Middleton *Plumley*	Roberts *Derrett*	Wilson *Bell*	Ellis *Walker S**	Foster *Walker R*	Cahill *Jones*	Pollock *Preece*	Kemp *Woods*	Gilchrist *Clark*	Green *Relish*	Mellows *Byrne*	Villars *Villars*
2	H	LEICESTER 30/8	W 2-0	2-0	0-0	Green 81, Kemp 85 / Ref: R Lewis (Great Bookham)	Middleton *Wallington*	Roberts *Whitworth*	Wilson *Rofe*	Ellis *Kelly*	Foster *Sims**	Cahill *Woollett*	Pollock *Alderson*	Kemp *Kember*	Stokes *Worthington*	Green *Sammels*	Mellows *Weller*	Weller *Blockley*
3	H	SWINDON 25/10	D 1-1	1-1	1-0	Mellows 32 / Moss 84 / Ref: L Burden (Wimborne)	Middleton *Allan*	Roberts *McLaughlin*	Wilson *Trollope*	Piper N *Stroud*	Foster *Aizlewood**	Cahill *Prophett*	Pullar *Moss*	Kemp *Ford*	Denyer *French*	Stokes *McHale*	Mellows *Anderson*	Kamara *Kamara*
3R	A	SWINDON 1/11	L 3-4	3-4	1-2	Wilson 30, Pullar 49, Denyer 55 / Kamara 8, And'n 15, Moss 46, McHale 75p / Ref: C White (Harrow)	Middleton *Roberts*	Roberts *Ford*	Wilson *Trollope*	Piper N *McLaughlin*	Foster *Aizlewood*	Cahill *Lewis*	Pullar *Moss*	Kemp *Stroud*	Stokes *Kamara*	Denyer *McHale*	Mellows *Anderson*	

Foster bets a £1 for every goal Kemp nets over 25, while the striker stumps up for each one under. Kemp is already only £23 down, as he feeds on Pollock's blocked shot and nets a penalty after Ron Walker handles. It's a struggle against County, who just escaped re-election last season.

Ellis' first goal – and his last until Boxing Day 1982 – spares Pompey's blushes after County's whirlwind start. Three crosses undo a creaking defence, with Clark and Ron Walker netting from close-range, then Wilson heads in almost on the line. Pollock's fine solo goal restores order.

City keeper Wallington's flap at a high ball allows Green to drive home and set up a giant-killing act. Kemp seals it, although he looks offside as he races onto Wilson's pass. Leicester boss Frank McClintock is philosophical: 'You can't teach people to put it in the back of the net.'

Middleton is inconsolable after he drops Moss's hopeful punt into the area over the line. Earlier, Mellows had headed Pompey in front from Piper's corner, and Kemp had been a whisker from toeing home a clincher. 'We did enough to win,' claims a disappointed Dickinson.

Dickinson is delighted with the team's character, but in the end Ray McHale's twice-taken penalty earns Town a trip to Wrexham after Foster catches Lewis' shot on the line. Kamara silences the Fratton boo-boys to score, but headers from Pullar and Denyer make for a thrilling climax.

FA Cup

				F-A	H-T	Scorers, Times, and Referees	1	2	3	4	5	6	7	8	9	10	11	12 sub used
1	H	BIDEFORD 26/11	W 3-1	3-1	1-0	Stokes 27, Pullar 52, Mellows 80 / Wingate 50 / Ref: C Downey (Isleworth)	Figgins *Stevens*	Piper N *Edwards*	Wilson *Hillton*	Ellis *Anthony*	Denyer *Menhenick*	Roberts *Davis*	Pullar *Jordan*	Kemp *Etheridge*	Stokes *Wingate*	Pollock *Druce*	Mellows *Hughes**	Barry
2	H	SWANSEA 17/12	D 2-2	2-2	1-1	Kemp 28, 57 / Curtis 19, Moore K 61 / Ref: L Shapter (Paignton)	Figgins *Barber*	Piper N *Evans*	Wilson *Morris*	Ellis *Lally*	Foster *May*	Hand *Bartley*	Pullar *James R*	Denyer *James A*	Kemp *Curtis*	Pollock *Moore G*	Mellows *Moore K*	
2R	A	SWANSEA 20/12	L 1-2	1-2	0-1	Foster 72 / Denyer 33 (og), Moore G 81 / Ref: L Shapter (Paignton)	Figgins *Barber*	Denyer *Evans*	Wilson *Morris*	Ellis *Lally*	Foster *May*	Hand *Bartley*	Pullar *James A*	Denyer *James A*	Green *Curtis*	Stokes *Moore G*	Mellows *Moore K*	

Western League Bideford's hero is office clerk Norman Stevens, who dislocates a finger in saving Wilson's 30-yarder, then immediately after lengthy repairs, he saves Kemp's penalty, when Pullar is felled on half-time. Wingate's header sends visiting fans wild, but Pompey prevail.

Harry Griffiths' Swans are on a meteoric rise from fourth to first. Unfazed by Fratton, Kevin Moore forces home, despite Wilson's attentions, then Piper's hack off the line spares total embarrassment. Earlier, Kemp's poaching instincts had cancelled out Welsh cap Curtis's classy goal.

Gary Moore nips in after Robbie James' shot hits a post and sends Swans to Walsall. Foster levelled from Hand's pass, ruling out Denyer's inadvertent header from Kevin Moore's cross. Ominously, Pompey have just one win and a draw in four against Div Four teams this season.

League Table

		Home						Away					
		P	W	D	L	F	A	W	D	L	F	A	Pts
1	Wrexham	46	14	8	1	48	19	9	7	7	30	26	61
2	Cambridge	46	19	3	1	49	11	4	9	10	23	40	58
3	Preston	46	16	5	2	48	19	4	11	8	15	19	56
4	Peterborough	46	15	7	1	32	11	5	9	9	15	22	56
5	Chester	46	14	8	1	41	24	2	14	7	18	32	54
6	Walsall	46	12	8	3	35	17	6	9	8	26	33	53
7	Gillingham	46	11	10	2	36	21	4	10	9	31	39	50
8	Colchester	46	10	11	2	36	16	5	7	11	19	28	48
9	Chesterfield	46	14	6	3	40	16	3	8	12	18	33	48
10	Swindon	46	12	7	4	40	22	4	9	10	27	38	48
11	Shrewsbury	46	11	7	5	42	23	5	8	10	21	34	47
12	Tranmere	46	13	7	3	39	19	3	8	12	18	33	47
13	Carlisle	46	10	9	4	32	26	4	10	9	27	33	47
14	Sheffield Wed	46	7	13	3	28	14	2	9	12	22	38	46
15	Bury	46	7	13	3	34	22	6	6	11	28	34	45
16	Lincoln	46	10	8	5	35	26	5	7	11	18	35	45
17	Exeter	46	11	8	4	30	18	4	6	13	19	41	44
18	Oxford	46	11	10	2	38	21	2	4	17	26	46	40
19	Plymouth	46	7	8	8	33	28	4	9	10	28	40	39
20	Rotherham	46	11	5	7	26	19	2	8	13	25	49	39
21	Port Vale	46	7	11	5	28	23	1	9	13	18	44	36
22	Bradford C	46	11	6	6	40	29	1	4	18	16	57	34
23	Hereford	46	9	9	5	28	22	0	5	18	6	38	32
24	PORTSMOUTH	46	4	11	8	31	38	3	6	14	10	37	31
		1104	272	192	88	869	504	88	192	272	504	869	1104

Odds & ends

Double wins: (1) Hereford.

Double losses: (6) Lincoln, Tranmere, Swindon, Wrexham, Plymouth, Preston.

Won from behind: (1) Bradford C (h).

Lost from in front: (2) Tranmere (h), Swindon (h).

High spots: Knocking first division Leicester out of the League Cup 2-0. Beating Chesterfield 3-0 in September.

Low spots: 11-match winless run from January to March. Losing 2-5 at home to Tranmere after leading 2-0 at half-time. Losing 1-5 at home to Plymouth Argyle in March. Selling leading scorer David Kemp to Carlisle for £75,000 on transfer deadline day. Being knocked out of the FA Cup by fourth division Swansea. Failing to score away from home in the league from December to April. Just four home wins in the league all season, including a seven match win-less run at Fratton between September and November.

Player of the Year: Not awarded.

Ever presents: (0).

Hat-tricks: (0).

Leading scorer: David Kemp (21).

Appearances and Goals

	Appearances						Goals			
	Lge	Sub	LC	Sub	FAC	Sub	Lge	LC	FAC	Tot
Barnard, Leigh	8	3	1				1			1
Cahill, Paul	14	1	5				1			1
Denver, Peter	41		2		3		3	1		4
Ellis, Peter	29	1	3		3			1		1
Figgins, Phil	19				3					
Foster, Steve	30	1	5		2		3		1	4
Garwood, Colin	12						2			2
Gilchrist, Paul	22	1	2				2			2
Green, Clive	8	1	3		1			2		2
Hand, Eoin	12				2		1			1
Kemp, David	33		5		3		16	3	2	21
Knight, Alan	1									
Lathan, Jim	12									
McCaffery, Jim	11						1			1
Mellows, Mick	42	1	5		3			1	1	2
Middleton, Steve	26		5							
Piper, Norman	23	3	2		2		2			2
Piper, Steve	13	2					4	1		5
Pollock, Matt	11	3	3		2		1	1	1	3
Pullar, David	22	2	1		3					
Roberts, Phil	33		5		1					
Ruggeiro, John	6						1			1
Stokes, Bobby	23	1	3		2		2		1	3
Taylor, Tony	17									
Viney, Keith	2	2								
Wilson, Billy	36		5		3		1	1		2
(own-goals)										1
26 players used	506	22	55		33		41	11	6	58

LEAGUE DIVISION 4 — Manager: Jimmy Dickinson — SEASON 1978-79

No	Date	Team	Att	Pos	Pt	F-A	H-T	Scorers, Times, and Referees	1	2	3	4	5	6	7	8	9	10	11	12 sub used
1	H 19/8	BRADFORD C	8,268		L 0	0-1	0-1	McNiven 34 — Ref: E Hughes (Weston-super-Mare)	Mellor	Ellis	Viney	Denver	Foster	Hand	Hemmerm'n*	Lathan	Davey	McIlwraith	Pullar	Garwood
		Bradford C							*Downsboro'*	*Reaney*	*Wood*	*Bates*	*Baines*	*Middleton*	*Podd*	*Dolan*	*Jackson*	*McNiven*	*Hutchins*	
2	A 22/8	YORK	2,513		L 0	3-5	1-1	Hemmerman 25, 50, Viney 87p / Stan'th 28, 67p, Randal 65, 73 Loggie 75 — Ref: N Glover (Chorley)	Mellor	Ellis!	Viney	Denver	Foster	Hand*	Hemmerman	Lathan	Davey	McIlwraith	Pullar	Wilson
		York							*Neenan*	*Scott*	*Kay*	*Stronach*	*Faulkner*	*Clements*	*Young*	*Randall*	*Loggie*	*McDonald*	*Staniforth*	
3	A 25/8	HARTLEPOOL	3,074	19 / 16	D 1	1-1	0-1	Davey 85 / Crumplin 25 — Ref: A Challinor (Rotherham)	Mellor	Wilson	Viney	Denver	Foster	Piper	Hemmerman	Lathan	Davey	McIlwraith	Pullar	Goldthorpe
		Hartlepool							*Platt*	*Smith T*	*Garry*	*Smith G**	*Brooks*	*Ayre*	*Linacre*	*Houchen*	*Newton*	*Crumplin*	*Guy*	
4	H 2/9	CREWE	7,429	14 / 24	W 3	3-0	1-0	Hemmerman 29, 56, 75 — Ref: A Gunn (Burgess Hill)	Mellor	Ellis	Viney	Denver	Wilson	Piper	Hemmerman	Lathan	Davey	Barnard	Pullar	Coyne
		Crewe							*Caswell*	*Hughes*	*Cheetham*	*Rimmer*	*Bowles*	*Bevan*	*Davies*	*Roberts*	*Nelson**	*Purdie*	*Wilshaw*	
5	A 9/9	ROCHDALE	1,479	10 / 23	W 5	2-0	2-0	Davey 13, Lathan 44 — Ref: D Richardson (Lincoln)	Mellor	Shyne	Viney	Denver	Piper	Wilson*	Hemmerman	Lathan	Davey	Barnard	Garwood	Mullington
		Rochdale							*Hallows*	*Snookes*	*Hart*	*Scott*	*Scaife*	*Owen*	*Hoy*	*Ashworth*	*Esser*	*O'Loughlin**		
6	H 12/9	SCUNTHORPE	10,965	11 / 9	D 6	0-0	0-0	Ref: M Sinclair (Guildford)	Mellor	Ellis	Viney	Denver	Foster	Piper	Hemmerman	Lathan*	Davey	Barnard	Pullar	Garwood
		Scunthorpe							*Crawford*	*O'Donnell*	*Peacock*	*Oates*	*Deere*	*Cruczman*	*Grimes*	*Kilmore**	*Wigg*	*Gibson*	*Kavanagh*	
7	H 16/9	PORT VALE	9,937	9 / 10	W 8	2-0	1-0	Barnard 7, Garwood 75 — Ref: R Challis (Tonbridge)	Mellor	Ellis	Viney	Denver	Foster	Piper	Hemmerman	Lathan	Davey*	Barnard	Pullar	Garwood
		Port Vale							*Dance*	*Wilkinson*	*Griffiths*	*Bloor*	*Sproson*	*Bentley*	*Bromage*	*Todd*	*Wright*	*Beamish*	*Stenson**	*Chamberlain*
8	A 23/9	ALDERSHOT	8,967	5 / 9	W 10	2-0	1-0	Hemmerman 26, Lathan 83 — Ref: T Glasson (Salisbury)	Mellor	Johnson	Viney	Denver	Foster	Piper	Hemmerman	Lathan	Davey	Barnard*	Pullar	Garwood
		Aldershot							*Johnson*	*Edwards*	*Woller*	*Dixon*	*Youdan*	*Joplin*	*Hooper*	*Brodie*	*Needham**	*Dungworth*	*McGregor*	*Tomlin*
9	H 26/9	WIGAN	13,902	4 / 19	W 12	1-0	0-0	Davey 84 — Ref: T Bune (Billingshurst)	Mellor	Ellis	Viney	Denver	Foster	Piper	Hemmerman*	Lathan	Davey	Barnard	Pullar	Garwood
		Wigan							*Brown*	*Smart*	*Hinnegan*	*Gore*	*Ward*	*Davids*	*Corrigan*	*Wright*	*Moore**	*Brownhill*	*Purdie*	*Wilkie*
10	A 29/9	BOURNEMOUTH	10,056	7 / 6	L 12	1-3	1-1	Viney 35 / Butler M 25, Showers 52, Massey 86 — Ref: T Spencer (Swindon)	Mellor	Ellis	Viney	Denver	Foster	Piper	Hemmerman	Lathan	Davey	McIlwraith!	Pullar	Garwood
		Bournemouth							*Allen*	*Cunningham*	*Miller*	*Impey*	*Brown R*	*Barton*	*Borthwick**	*Showers*	*Butler M*	*Massey*	*Brown K*	*Johnson*
11	H 7/10	HEREFORD	11,949	5 / 14	W 14	1-0	0-0	Denyer 87 — Ref: K Salmon (Barnet)	Mellor	Ellis	Viney	Denver	Foster	Piper	Hemmerman*	Lathan	Davey	Garwood	Pullar	McCaffery
		Hereford							*Hughes*	*Price*	*Marshall*	*Layton*	*Burrows*	*Emery*	*Bailey*	*Holmes K*	*Jones**	*Gould*	*Spring*	*Holmes W*

Match notes

1. Pompey are in charge from start to finish, but end up pointless on their fourth division 'debut'. Previously, the club had never lost on its first game in a new league, but that record ended after ex-Leeds full-back Reaney swung in a cross and Jackson hammered in Foster's mis-header.

2. John Wrennall – from last season's infamous Shrews game – is due to officiate, but retires just days beforehand. Pompey only have themselves to blame tonight, as Ellis is sent off for a 'lunatic' foul and York then net three in eight minutes. Hemmerman snaps up an impressive brace.

3. Bottom place in the Football League beckons, but that ignominy is averted when Hemmerman hits the bar and as Pool fail to clear, Davey glances in Pullar's cross. Fratton old-boy George Smith impresses. Dickinson is launching a clear-out; Gilchrist will join Swindon next week.

4. The fans' have a new hero as Hemmerman's hat-trick leaves Harry Gregg's side with just a solitary point and goal. Foster and McIlwraith are dropped for discipline reasons, but Jeff makes light with an 18-yard shot, a far-post poach and a glancing header. The bar denies him a fourth.

5. Division Four is beginning to look manageable as Pompey comfortably see-off Dale. Piper's conversion to centre-back is a masterstroke, while Davey (a summer free from Hereford) is starting to look the part. He coolly slips a tackle and gets home, then Lathan's bullet-header seals it.

6. Basement reality is underlined as Scunthorpe go home with a £2,000 cheque as the share of the gate, while Pompey got just the minimum £500 from Spotland on Saturday. A £40,000 bid for Hartlepool's Bob Newton fails and his muscularity might have broken down a stubborn defence.

7. Dance leads Dennis Butler's side a merry one. His reckless dash from goal bemuses two defenders and his slice lands at Garwood's feet, who volleys into the empty net from 25 yards, with keeper Trevor frantically retreating. Earlier, Barnard fired in after Davey's header hit the bar.

8. Shots' unbeaten home run, stretching back to April 1977, is ended. Hemmerman heads a three-man queue to nod in Pullar's cross and although Len Walker's side press hard, Lathan's 20-yarder deflects to leave Johnson flat-footed. 5,000 travelling fans sing 'Happy Birthday' to Foster.

9. The referee threatens to abandon the game as drink cans rain down in the goalmouth after he rules out Hemmerman's fine run and shot, only to award a free-kick to Pompey. Davey scores after Garwood's effort squirts to him off a defender. New-boys Wigan put up stout resistance.

10. Bournemouth's roads are jammed as 5,000 travel, earning record receipts. Showers is a handful and Dickinson is so impressed he will sign him in February. His is the vital second after Piper's slip, then police dogs are needed after Massey's clincher. Viney's twice-taken free-kick levels.

11. Pompey force 23 corners, but have to be patient. Denyer finally thrashes in Pullar's pass from 25 yards, but Dickinson, worried at the team's lack of punch, reveals the Board has given him a transfer budget. The club could be in FA hot water after a 1p coin hits Bulls' keeper Hughes.

Match results (games 12–23)

No		Opponent	Date	Att	Pos		Res	Score	Pts
12	A	GRIMSBY	14/10	5,141	5		L	0-1	14
13	A	DONCASTER	17/10	2,480	5		W	3-2	16
14	H	HALIFAX	21/10	12,385	5		W	3-1	18
15	A	TORQUAY	28/10	4,769	5		L	1-2	18
16	H	DARLINGTON	4/11	11,394	5		W	3-0	20
17	A	CREWE	11/11	2,294	4		D	0-0	21
18	H	HARTLEPOOL	18/11	10,717	4		W	3-0	23
19	A	NORTHAMPTON	2/12	3,592	2		W	2-0	25
20	H	HUDDERSFIELD	9/12	11,615	3		W	1-0	27
21	H	READING	23/12	12,541	2		W	4-0	29
22	A	WIMBLEDON	26/12	7,862	2		W	4-2	31
23	A	STOCKPORT	29/12	3,795	2		L	2-4	31

---

12 — A GRIMSBY, 14/10 (L 0-1)

Pompey: Mellor, Ellis, Viney, Denyer, Foster, Piper, Hemmerman, Davey, McIlwraith*, Pullar
Opponents: *Batch, Mawer, Moore, Waters, Barker, Crombie, Ford, Drinkell, Partridge*, Brolly, Young*

Moore 85
Ref: P Willis (Meadowfield)

Mellor hasn't a save to make, but Kevin Moore's late glancing header lets John Newman's team leap-frog Pompey. McIlwraith, recently transfer-listed at his request, prompts numerous counter-attacks. Hemmerman misses a couple and snaps a corner flag when he collides with it.

13 — A DONCASTER, 17/10 (W 3-2)

Pompey: Mellor, Ellis, Viney, Denyer, Foster, Piper, Hemmerman, Davey, McIlwraith*, Pullar
Opponents: *Peacock, Reed, Hemsley, Lally, Bradley, Taylor*, Habbin, Laidlaw, Owen, French, Snodin*

Laidlaw 4, Bentley 60
Ref: P Reeves (Leicester)

In a fine advert for the fourth division, Hemmerman gets away to float home, only for Laidlaw to level from 25 yards. Garwood sets up Hemmerman again, then only a post denies him a 15-minute hat-trick. Denyer deservedly claims the points, hooking home Pullar's nod down.

14 — H HALIFAX, 21/10 (W 3-1)

Pompey: Mellor, Ellis, Viney, Denyer, Foster, Piper, Hemmerman*, Davey, Garwood, McIlwraith, Pullar
Opponents: *Leonard, Trainer, Loska, Smith, Burke, Dunleavy, Bell, Carroll, Bullock, Lawson*, Johnson, Firth*

Garwood 12, 79p, Denyer 72 | *Firth 56*
Ref: L Burden (Corfe Mullen)

The Fratton End proclaim the team 'champions', but it is far from title-winning stuff. Jimmy Lawson's side, already six points adrift in the re-election zone, stun the crowd with Firth's neat chip. Denyer's third in four and a spot-kick, after McIlwraith is scythed, calm jangling nerves.

15 — A TORQUAY, 28/10 (L 1-2)

Pompey: Mellor, Ellis, Viney, Denyer, Foster, Piper, Hemmerman, Davey, Garwood*, McIlwraith, Pullar
Opponents: *Turner, Twitchin, Darke, Davies, Green, Dunne, Wilson, Lawrence, Coffill, Murphy, Parsons*

Denyer 68 | *Lawrence 26, Murphy 71*
Ref: S Bates (Bristol)

A taste of Saturday-night football ends with a bitter defeat. The decider comes as Foster's casual clearance lands at Murphy's feet and he turns and shoots home. 'Foster could have kicked it anywhere in Devon,' moans Dickinson. Denyer levelled after Piper sprang the offside trap.

16 — H DARLINGTON, 4/11 (W 3-0)

Pompey: Mellor, Ellis, Viney, Denyer, Foster, Piper*, Hemmerman, Davey, Garwood, Barnard, Pullar
Opponents: *Burleigh, Nattrass, Cochrane, Hague, Craig, Stone !, Maitland*, Ferguson, Seal, Walsh, Wann, Crosson*

Denyer 45, Garwood, 56 | *[Hemmerman 68]*
Ref: W Bombroff (Bristol)

Stone's first-half dismissal, for punching Hemmerman, changes the game. Pompey had been reeling from Piper's knee injury, which will end his career, but Denyer's bullet breaks Quakers' resolve. Overnight, a daring fan had scaled a floodlight pylon to hang a Pompey Sailor banner.

17 — A CREWE, 11/11 (D 0-0)

Pompey: Mellor, Ellis, Viney, Denyer, Foster, Davey, Hemmerman, Garwood, Barnard, Pullar
Opponents: *Rafferty, Wilkinson, Bowles, Purdie, Dulson, Roberts, Bevan, Rimmer, Davies, Coyne*, Robertson, Nelson*

Ref: G Owen (Anglesey)

A proposed link with an American team, which would see their stars play at Fratton until March, has been put on hold. Battling Crewe have improved considerably on September's sorry showing and Dickinson is pleased with the way Davey has adapted to Piper's defensive position.

18 — H HARTLEPOOL, 18/11 (W 3-0)

Pompey: Mellor, Ellis, Viney, Denyer, Foster, Davey, Hemmerman, Garwood, Lathan, Barnard, Pullar*
Opponents: *Richardson, Smith G, Garry, Lawrence, Brooks, Ayre, Linacre*, Goldthorpe, Newton, Houchen, Loadwick, Norton, Hand*

Garwood 66p, Foster 69, Lathan 80
Ref: C Downey (Isleworth)

Pompey withdrew half-prices on the terraces from today's game in a bid to weed out hooligans, who recently wrecked a service station on the way back from Torquay. Pool boss Billy Horner reckons the penalty, when Garwood tumbles under Richardson's challenge, was 'diabolical'.

19 — A NORTHAMPTON, 2/12 (W 2-0)

Pompey: Mellor, Ellis, Viney, Denyer, Foster, Davey, Hemmerman, Garwood, Lathan, Jayes, Pullar
Opponents: *Jayes, Geldmintis, Mead, Reilly, Robertson, Ashenden, Farrington, Williams, Cordice, Froggatt, Wassall*, Walker*

Garwood 23, Hemmerman 49
Ref: B Homewood (Sunbury)

Dickinson will no doubt enjoy a tot or two, after winning Bells' Division Four 'Manager of the Month' award, but he reckons an away win is an even better tonic. Garwood feeds off Hemmerman's pass, then returns the compliment. 'What's it like to see a crowd,' taunt 1,500 visitors.

20 — H HUDDERSFIELD, 9/12 (W 1-0)

Pompey: Mellor, Ellis, Viney, Denyer, Foster, Davey, Hemmerman, Garwood, Lathan, Barnard, Pullar
Opponents: *Starling, Brown, Branaghan, Lillis*, Sutton, Topping, Fletcher, Hart, Cowling, Robins, Bielby, Gray*

Hemmerman 31
Ref: C White (Harrow)

Full-back Taylor has been freed and he now regrets not taking the youth coach job offered in the summer. Against Town, Pompey have Mellor to thank for preserving the point. He saves from Robins and Fletcher, while at the other end, Starling's fumble allows Hemmerman to pounce.

21 — H READING, 23/12 (W 4-0)

Pompey: Mellor, Ellis, Viney, Denyer, Foster, Wilson, Hemmerman, Davey, Garwood, Barnard, Pullar
Opponents: *Death, Peters, White, Bowman, Hicks, Bennett, Alexander*, Hetzke, Kearney, Sanchez, Earles, Kearns*

Denyer 11, Barnard 19, Hemmerman 48, [Davey 68]
Ref: A Cox (South Croydon)

Pompey rip Reading apart and lay last week's Cup ghost. Against the wind, Denyer's volley and Barnard's shot mean Maurice Evans' side never recapture their poise of seven days ago. Mellor hoists a huge kick, which Hemmerman touches in, then Davey nets from an acute angle.

22 — A WIMBLEDON, 26/12 (W 4-2)

Pompey: Mellor, Ellis, Viney, Denyer, Foster, Wilson, Hemmerman, Davey, Garwood, Barnard, Pullar
Opponents: *Goddard, Bryant, Haverson, Galliers, Galvin, Eames, Briley, Leslie, Knowles, Cork, Cowley, Driver*

Barnard 10, Davey 50, Wilson 60, Knowles 5, 41 [Hemmerman 77]
Ref: B Daniels (Brentwood)

Wilson's 25-yarder sends a huge following home happy and ends table-topping Dons' 18-match unbeaten run at Plough Lane. Davey levels from a tricky angle, and Hemmerman latches onto Lathan's pass to ensure a fifth consecutive win, as Pompey storm back in the second half.

23 — A STOCKPORT, 29/12 (L 2-4)

Pompey: Mellor, Ellis*, Viney, Denyer, Foster, Wilson, Hemmerman, Davey, Wilson, Barnard, Pullar
Opponents: *Ragan, Smith, Rutter, Edwards, Park, Thompson, Henson, Armstrong, Bradd, Summerbee, Lee, Garwood*

Pullar 48, Garwood 71 | *Bradd 45, Lee 49, 57, Summerbee 52*
Ref: C Newsome (Broseley)

Torrential rain threatened the game beforehand, and how Pompey must have wished it had been called off. Bradd converts Lee's cross, but Pullar lobs a leveller soon after half-time. Lee's 20 yard-shot is the first of three in eight minutes, but Garwood pulls one back in a scramble.

LEAGUE DIVISION 4

SEASON 1978-79

Manager: Jimmy Dickinson

Results

No	Date	Venue	Att	Pos	#	Res	Pt	F-A	H-T	Scorers, Times, and Referees
24	13/1	H ROCHDALE	11,595	1	23	D	32	1:1	0:0	Barnard 90 / Owen 87. Ref: R Challis (Tonbridge)
25	3/2	A WIGAN	8,289	4	7	L	32	0:2	0:1	Wright 14, Corrigan 46. Ref: M Peck (Doncaster)
26	10/2	H BOURNEMOUTH	12,172	4	10	D	33	1:1	0:0	Foster 48 / Johnson 65. Ref: D Reeves (Uxbridge)
27	20/2	H NEWPORT	8,206	2	8	W	35	2:1	1:1	Barnard 20, Davey 57 / Moore 15. Ref: L Shapter (Paignton)
28	24/2	H GRIMSBY	12,782	4	5	L	35	1:3	0:2	Hemmerman 66 / Ford 35, 89, Brolly 39. Ref: T Bune (Billingshurst)
29	3/3	A HALIFAX	1,741	5	24	L	35	0:2	0:2	Ellis 28 (og), Johnson 33. Ref: G Owen (Anglesey)
30	10/3	H TORQUAY	8,689	5	12	W	37	1:0	0:0	Showers 90. Ref: M Taylor (Deal)
31	20/3	A PORT VALE	2,738	7	15	D	38	0:0	0:0	Ref: A McDonald (Birmingham)
32	24/3	H YORK	9,353	8	15	D	39	1:1	0:0	Showers 50 / Loggie 65. Ref: R Lewis (Great Bookham)
33	28/3	A BRADFORD C	2,410	8	15	L	39	0:2	0:0	Dolan 47, McNiven 88. Ref: G Tyson (Sunderland)
34	30/3	A BARNSLEY	12,928	8	6	D	40	1:1	0:0	Davey 62 / Graham 67. Ref: G Nolan (Stockport)

Line-ups (Pompey top line, opponent in italics)

No	1	2	3	4	5	6	7	8	9	10	11	12 sub used
24	Mellor	Ellis	Viney	McIlwraith	Foster	Wilson	Hemmerman	Lathan*	Davey	Barnard	Pullar	Denyer
	Felgate	*Creamer*	*Taylor*	*Scaife*	*Scott*	*Snookes*	*Hoy*	*O'Loughlin*	*Jones*	*Owen*	*Esser**	*Bannon*
25	Mellor	Ellis	Viney	Denyer	Foster	Davey	Hemmerman*	Lathan	Garwood	McIlwraith	Pullar	**Showers**
	Brown	*Smart*	*Hinnegan*	*Gore*	*Ward*	*Fretwell*	*Corrigan*	*Wright*	*Houghton*	*Moore*	*Purdie*	
26	Mellor	Ellis	Viney	Barnard	Foster	Davey	Hemmerman	Lathan	Showers	McIlwraith*	Pullar	Denyer
	Allen	*Cunningham*	*Miller*	*Impey*	*Brown R*	*Barton*	*Barthwick*	*MacDougall*	*Scott*	*Brown K**	*Johnson*	*Massey*
27	Mellor	Ellis	Viney	Denyer	Foster	Davey	Hemmerman	Lathan	Wilson	Barnard	Pullar	
	Plumley	*Walden*	*Byrne*	*Warriner*	*Bruton*	*Vaughan I*	*Oakes*	*Lowndes*	*Goddard*	*Thompson*	*Moore*	
28	Mellor	Ellis	Viney*	Denyer	Foster	Wilson	Hemmerman	Lathan	Davey	Barnard	Pullar	Garwood
	Batch	*Moore D*	*Moore K*	*Waters*	*Barker*	*Crombie*	*Brolly*	*Ford*	*Lester*	*Mitchell*	*Cumming*	
29	Mellor	Ellis	Wilson	Denyer	Foster	Davey	Hemmerman	Lathan	Showers*	Barnard	Pullar	Garwood
	Kilner	*Bradley*	*Dunleavey*	*Smith*	*Trainer*	*Burke*	*Firth*	*Kennedy*	*Mountford*	*Loska*	*Johnson*	
30	Mellor	Ellis	Viney	Denyer	Foster	Davey	Hemmerman	Garwood	Lathan	Showers	Barnard	
	Turner	*Darke**	*Ritchie*	*Twitchen*	*Payne*	*Dunne*	*Wilson*	*Lawrence*	*Raper*	*Murphy*	*Davis*	*Cofilll*
31	Mellor	Ellis	Milligan	Denyer	Wilson	Davey	Hemmerman	Lathan	Garwood	Showers	Bryant*	Viney
	Dance	*Keenan*	*Griffiths*	*Bbech*	*Delgado*	*Hawkins**	*Sinclair*	*Farrell*	*Wright*	*Todd*	*Bentley*	
32	Mellor	Ellis	Milligan	Denyer	Foster	Davey	Hemmerman	Lathan	Garwood	Showers	Bryant	Wilson
	Neenan	*Kay*	*Walsh*	*Pugh*	*Faulkner*	*Clements*	*Ford*	*Wellings*	*Loggie*	*McDonald*	*Staniforth*	
33	Mellor	Ellis	Milligan	Denyer	Foster	Davey	Hemmerman	Lathan*	Garwood	Showers	Bryant	
	Smith	*Reaney*	*Wood*	*Bates*	*Baines*	*Middleton*	*Robertson*	*Dolan*	*Johnson*	*McNiven*	*Hutchins*	
34	Mellor	Ellis	Milligan	Denyer	Foster	Wilson	Hemmerman	Lathan	Garwood	Showers	Bryant	
	Springett	*Collins*	*Chambers*	*Pugh*	*Saunders*	*McCarthy*	*Little*	*Clarke**	*Graham*	*Millar*	*Bell*	*Riley*

Match reports

24 — Rochdale: The south beats the arctic weather, but there is ice and snow on the pitch. Pompey go top of a table for the first time since 1967 thanks to Barnard's late volley, but it's unconvincing, especially when Jones breaks against an under-manned defence to cross for Owen to pick his spot.

25 — Wigan: A special chartered train ferries 500 fans to Springfield Park, but Pompey's hopes take a dive on a soft, spongy pitch. Hinnegan's swirling cross fell for Wright to score, then Corrigan angled home just after the break. Showers, a £15,000 signing from Bournemouth, makes his debut.

26 — Bournemouth: A point goes astray for edgy Pompey against Alec Stock's Bournemouth. Ex-Cherry Showers is involved in the goal, turned in by Man-of-the-Match Foster. Johnson's dipping shot equalises after Miller's good work. McIlwraith fouls the scorer in reply and is lucky to only see yellow.

27 — Newport: McIlwraith is off the transfer list, but faces a two-match ban. Vaughan (18) is sent off for swearing over a disputed throw, but while County boss Len Ashurst accepts that, he is less happy about Pullar's jump with Plumley for the opener. Davey angled the winner from Wilson's pass.

28 — Grimsby: BBC's Match of the Day cameras capture the action and Wilson features on the closing credits for his two howlers. First, his back-heel was intercepted by Ford, then he missed a high-ball and Ford ended comeback hopes, which had been raised by Hemmerman's 16th of the season.

29 — Halifax: Halifax win at home for the first time since August, as Pompey's promotion pretensions are exposed. Unlucky Ellis nods home Johnson's free-kick, then Johnson's 20-yarder deceives Mellor. Foster would have played for England Under-21s, but for snow in Holland during the week.

30 — Torquay: Dickinson is hoping for some cash ahead of deadline day to freshen up his squad. Showers, the butt of the crowd, eventually brightens a dreary day by heading past Turner from Garwood's cross. Torquay, player-managed by Mike Green, had recently lost 1-6 to rivals Wimbledon.

31 — Port Vale: Mellor brawls with a fan after he is attacked following his 'pro' foul on Todd. Police separate them, then Mellor is felled by a missile walking off at half-time. Farrell misses a penalty after an innocuous foul, while Bryant (£20,000 from Cobblers) and Blackpool loanee Milligan start.

32 — York: Pullar, transfer-listed last week, gets his chance as Garwood falls ill overnight. Pompey are dropping off the promotion pace, and only have Showers' alertness, as Faulkner and Neenan dither, to thank for a point. Loggie's deflected shot levels, but only after ref and linesman consult.

33 — Bradford C: The Labour Government of Portsmouth-born PM Jim Callaghan falls tonight, and Pompey's promotion hopes are also doomed. On a saturated pitch, which the ref deems playable, Garwood's goal is ruled out after 20 seconds. Dolan's shot and McNiven's near-post header earn the win.

34 — Barnsley: A terrific match is overshadowed by Dickinson's post-match heart-attack, which leaves him in Barnsley hospital fighting for his life. Pompey at last re-discover pre-Christmas form following a post-Bradford crisis meeting. Davey's fierce shot is cancelled out by Graham's nudge home.

Portsmouth FC — Season match-by-match record (matches 35–46)

#	V	Date	Opponent	Att	Opp Pos	Pts	Score	Res	Pompey Pos
35	A	3/4	SCUNTHORPE	1,535	17	41	2-2	D	8
36	H	7/4	NORTHAMPTON	8,066	20	43	1-0	W	7
37	A	13/4	READING	15,054	2	43	0-2	L	8
38	H	14/4	WIMBLEDON	11,453	6	44	0-0	D	7
39	A	16/4	NEWPORT	5,421	8	46	2-1	W	7
40	H	21/4	STOCKPORT	8,177	11	47	1-1	D	7
41	H	24/4	DONCASTER	5,869	20	49	4-0	W	7
42	A	28/4	HUDDERSFIELD	2,895	10	49	0-2	L	7
43	H	5/5	BARNSLEY	8,761	3	49	0-1	L	8
44	A	7/5	HEREFORD	3,707	12	51	1-0	W	8
45	A	11/5	DARLINGTON	1,140	22	51	0-2	L	8
46	H	15/5	ALDERSHOT	6,238	5	52	1-1	D	7

Home Average 10,106 Away Average 4,951

---

35 — A, 3/4 SCUNTHORPE (2-2 D)
Garwood 3, 54 — Couch 65, Bloomer 67. Ref: K Baker (Wolverhampton)
Pompey: Mellor, Ellis, Milligan, Denyer, Foster, Davey, Pullar, Wilson, Garwood, Showers, Bryant*, Lathan
Scunthorpe: Crawford, O'Donnell, Peacock*, Oates, Deere, Hall, Grimes, Kilmore, Bloomer, Cavanagh, Couch, Davy
Garwood seems to have made the perfect Get Well present for Dickinson, as he converts Ellis's centre off the bar, then latches onto Showers' flick. A static defence allows Couch a simple goal, then Bloomer loops in a header. Acting-boss Burrows has some harsh words afterwards.

36 — H, 7/4 NORTHAMPTON (1-0 W)
Garwood 62. Ref: D Biddle (Bristol)
Pompey: Mellor, Ellis*, Milligan, Denyer, Foster, Davey, Pullar, Wilson, Garwood, Showers, Bryant, Lathan
Northampton: Jayes, Geidmintis, Mead, Saunders, Robertson, Farrington, Williams, Matthews, McCaffery*, Reilly, Froggatt, Ashenden
Dickinson is set to return to his Alton home next week and Garwood revives hopes with his tenth goal. Ex-Cobbler Bryant is its architect, sweeping a pass to Pullar, who crosses for Garwood to bullet home a header. Milligan's performances seem to have upped his asking price.

37 — A, 13/4 READING (0-2 L)
Lewis 20, Shipley 71. Ref: D Hutchinson (Cambridge)
Pompey: Mellor, Ellis, Milligan, Denyer*, Foster, Davey, Hemmerman, Wilson, Garwood, Showers, Bryant, Lathan
Reading: Death, Peters, White, Sanchez, Hicks, Bennett, Alexander, Hetzke, Kearney, Shipley, Lewis, Pullar
An insipid display lets down 5,000 fans lured to Elm Park by the prospect of Pompey's promotion 'Alamo'. Instead, they witness an abject surrender as Mellor misjudges the flight of Lewis's shot, then loanee Saint, then George Shipley, seals it. 'We've blown it,' is Burrows' frank view.

38 — H, 14/4 WIMBLEDON (0-0 D)
Ref: B Hill (Wellingborough)
Pompey: Mellor, Ellis, Viney, Barnard, Foster*, Davey, Pullar, Lathan, Garwood, Showers, Bryant, Pullar
Wimbledon: Goddard, Perkins, Haverson, Galliers, Bowgett, Cunningham, Leslie, Briley, Knowles, Cork, Parsons
Pompey show some spirit against Dario Gradi's side and nearly snatch it at the death, but Goddard clutches Hemmerman's header. It will take a miracle to go up now, but Dons are on course for third place. Foster limps off with ankle injury, but Davey bottles up 24-goal Alan Cork.

39 — A, 16/4 NEWPORT (2-1 W)
Garwood 72p, Barnard 80 — Goddard 9p. Ref: C Newsome (Broseley)
Pompey: Mellor, Ellis, Viney, Barnard, Denyer, Davey, Pullar, Lathan, Garwood, Showers, Bryant, Lathan
Newport: Plumley, Waldon, Relish, Davies, Oates, Bruton, Bailey*, Lowndes, Goddard, Tynan, Moore, Thompson
Davey earns Burrows' praise by playing with a swollen jaw after a clash on Saturday. Oakes earns a penalty, tumbling under Denyer's tackle, but then he fouls Garwood to let him deservedly level. Lathan crosses for Barnard's far-post header to earn a first away win since Boxing Day.

40 — H, 21/4 STOCKPORT (1-1 D)
Hand 23 — Lee 32. Ref: B Stevens (Stonehouse)
Pompey: Mellor, Ellis, Viney, Barnard, Hand, Davey, Pullar, Lathan, Garwood, Showers, Bryant, Denyer
Stockport: Lawson, Halford, Rutter, Edwards, Thorpe, Armstrong, Henson, Smith, Bradd, Summerbee, Lee, Denyer
Veteran defender Eoin Hand is hero and villain, fresh from his testimonial last week against an Eire XI. He is on his backside but still forces Bryant's cross home for his first goal in 16 months, but then his poor pass concedes a throw and from it Lee hammers his 23rd of the season.

41 — H, 24/4 DONCASTER (4-0 W)
Garwood 2p, 80, 83, Lathan 42. Ref: B Daniels (Brentwood)
Pompey: Mellor, Ellis, Viney, Barnard*, Hand, Davey, Pullar, Lathan, Garwood*, Showers, Bryant, Mcllwraith
Doncaster: Peacock, Lally, Snodin, Bradley, Cannell, Olney, Bentley, French, Cox*, Lewis, Flanaghan, Pugh
Branded 'too affable' by Burrows when subbed on Saturday, Garwood delights his boss with a triple against Billy Bremner's dreadful Rovers. Burrows is also finalising the retained list, but stalwarts Hand and Wilson won't be on it. Season tickets go up by 10%, in line with inflation.

42 — A, 28/4 HUDDERSFIELD (0-2 L)
Robins 10, Fletcher 52. Ref: N Glover (Chorley)
Pompey: Mellor, Ellis, Viney*, Denyer, Ellis, Davey, Hemmerman, Lathan, Garwood, Showers, Bryant, Hand
Huddersfield: Starling, Brown, Sandercock, Holmes, Sutton, Hanvey, Fletcher, Hart, Cowling, Robins, Gray
Pompey's four-match revival, which had kept hopes flickering, is ruthlessly snuffed out by Mick Buxton's impressive Town, who bounce back from consecutive away defeats. Mellor and Viney get in a muddle to let in Robins, who is then shoved by Denyer for Fletcher's penalty.

43 — H, 5/5 BARNSLEY (0-1 L)
Bell 40. Ref: L Burden (Corfe Mullen)
Pompey: Mellor, Ellis, Viney, Barnard, Ellis, Davey, Hemmerman, Mcllwraith, Garwood, Lathan, Showers*, Pullar
Barnsley: Springett, Collins, Chambers, Pugh, Saunders, McCarthy, Little, Riley, Graham, Bell, Miller, James
Beforehand, popular Mellor receives the Player of the Year award, but he is powerless to stop Bell's looping header silencing the Chimes. The win puts Allan Clarke's Tykes back in Division Three and finally kills off promotion hopes, as Barnsley still have Dons and Reading to play.

44 — A, 7/5 HEREFORD (1-0 W)
Barnard 22. Ref: E Read (Bristol)
Pompey: Mellor, James, Viney, Barnard, Ellis, Davey, Barnard, Lathan, Garwood, Showers, Bryant, Stephens
Hereford: Hughes, Emery, Thomas, Cornes, Layton, Holmes, Spring*, Feely, McGrellis, Gould, White, Stephens
It's Pompey's fourth straight win against Mike Bailey's Hereford, having still to let in a goal against them. Barnard's difficult waist-high finish ends a run of 12 home points from 14. Ex-Bull Davey is superb, ensuring an easy ride for Mellor, voted United's player of the season last term.

45 — A, 11/5 DARLINGTON (0-2 L)
Peachey 47, 57. Ref: M Scott (Nottingham)
Pompey: Mellor, James*, Viney, Barnard, Ellis, Davey, Barnard, Lathan, Garwood, Showers, Bryant, Roberts
Darlington: Burleigh, Nattress, Crosson, Hedley, Craig, Seal*, Stone, Wann, Peachey, Probert, Walsh, Ferguson
Pompey fizzle out at Feethams on Cup Final eve, before the lowest-ever Football League gate for a match involving the club. Trevor Roberts makes his debut, replacing Keith James who did likewise at Hereford. Peachey's double is not quite enough for Darlington to avoid re-election.

46 — H, 15/5 ALDERSHOT (1-1 D)
Garwood 31 — Dungworth 45. Ref: T Glasson (Salisbury)
Pompey: Mellor, James, Viney, Barnard, Ellis, Davey, Barnard, Lathan, Garwood, Showers, Bryant, Roberts
Aldershot: Johnson, Scott, Wooler, Dixon, Youden, Jopling, Crosby, Brodie, Shanahan, Dungworth, Tomlin
What promised to be an all-Hampshire promotion clash, only for a combination of Shots' Cup run and the snow to postpone it, ends up a gentle stroll in front of the second-lowest home gate. Garwood pips Hemmerman to be leading league scorer, while Dungworth bags his 34th goal.

LEAGUE DIVISION 4 (CUP-TIES)   Manager: Jimmy Dickinson   SEASON 1978-79

League Cup

			F-A	H-T	Scorers, Times, and Referees	1	2	3	4	5	6	7	8	9	10	11	12 sub used
1:1 H SWINDON 12/8 9,261 3	D	0-0	0-0		Mellor	Ellis	Viney	Denyer	Foster	Hand	Hemmerman	Lathan	Davey	Piper	Pullar	Carter
						Roberts	*McLaughlin*	*Ford*	*McHale*	*Aizlewood*	*Stroud*	*Miller**	*Kamara*	*Guthrie*	*Bates*	*Williams*	

The hope of last week's draw with Chelsea is dented, as Pompey are slip-shod at times. Town nearly sneak it when Kamara's centre is smashed onto the post by Carter. That close-shave matches those of Ellis, Garwood and McCaffery, now smooth-chinned at boss Dickinson's insistence.
Ref: A Cox (South Croydon)

			F-A	H-T	Scorers, Times, and Referees	1	2	3	4	5	6	7	8	9	10	11	12
1:2 A SWINDON 15/8 7,343 3	L	2-4	0-0	Gilchrist 72, Pullar 82 *(Guthrie 83)*	Mellor	Ellis	Viney	Denyer	Foster	Hand	Hemmerman	Lathan	Gilchrist	McIlwraith	Pullar	Carter
					Aizlewood 50, Williams 79, Miller 81,	*Roberts*	*McLaughlin*	*Ford*	*McHale*	*Aizlewood*	*Stroud*	*Miller**	*Kamara/*	*Guthrie*	*Bates*	*Williams*	

Ref: C Thomas (Treorchy)
(Pompey lost 2-4 on aggregate)

Saturday's stalemate is forgotten after a goal-feast. Guthrie misses a pen, then Hemmerman hits the bar. Aizlewood takes advantage of sloppy defending. £15,000 McIlwraith (Bury) debuts. Gillie's goal sparks a rush, then Kamara is sent off for retaliating against his old mate Viney.

FA Cup

			F-A	H-T	Scorers, Times, and Referees	1	2	3	4	5	6	7	8	9	10	11	12
1 H NORTHAMPTON 25/11 13,338 11	W	2-0	0-0	Hemmerman 78, 89	Mellor	Ellis	Viney	Denyer	Foster	Davey	Hemmerman	Lathan	Garwood*	Barnard	Pullar	Hand
						Jayes	*Geldminitis*	*Mead*	*Woollett*	*Robertson*	*Saunders*	*Farrington*	*Williams*	*Froggatt*	*Reilly*	*Wassell**	*Cordice*

Ref: K Salmon (Barnet)

Town boss Mike Keen has clearly come for a replay. He recalls experienced keeper Jayes, but he fails to hold Barnard's shot and Hemmerman breaks their resistance from the rebound. As Cobblers push forward, a quick counter forces a corner and Hemmerman's head does the rest.

			F-A	H-T	Scorers, Times, and Referees	1	2	3	4	5	6	7	8	9	10	11	12
2 H READING 16/12 17,195 3	L	0-1	0-1	*Alexander 34*	Mellor	Ellis	Viney	Denyer	Foster	Davey	Hemmerman	Lathan	Garwood*	Barnard	Pullar	Hand
						Death	*Peters*	*White*	*Bowman*	*Hicks*	*Bennett*	*Alexander**	*Earles*	*Kearney*	*Sanchez*	*Lewis*	*Hetzke*

Ref: R Challis (Tonbridge)

Reading gain a psychological edge ahead of next week's promotion show-down. Their calm football frustrates a huge crowd, but it might have been different had Garwood's shot not rebounded from the post into Death's arms (17). Alexander pounces as Mellor fumbles Earles' cross.

Home / Away League Table

Pos	Team	P	Home W	D	L	F	A	Away W	D	L	F	A	Pts
1	Reading	46	19	3	1	49	8	7	10	6	27	27	65
2	Grimsby	46	15	5	3	51	23	11	4	8	31	26	61
3	Wimbledon	46	18	3	2	50	20	7	8	8	28	26	61
4	Barnsley	46	15	5	3	47	23	9	8	6	26	19	61
5	Aldershot	46	16	5	2	38	14	4	12	7	25	33	57
6	Wigan	46	14	5	4	40	24	7	8	8	23	24	55
7	PORTSMOUTH	46	13	7	3	35	12	7	5	11	27	36	52
8	Newport	46	12	5	6	39	28	9	5	9	27	27	52
9	Huddersfield	46	13	8	2	32	15	5	3	15	25	38	47
10	York	46	11	6	6	33	24	7	5	11	18	31	47
11	Torquay	46	14	4	5	38	24	4	4	14	20	41	46
12	Scunthorpe	46	12	3	8	33	30	5	8	10	21	30	45
13	Hartlepool	46	7	12	4	35	28	6	6	11	22	38	44
14	Hereford	46	12	8	3	35	18	5	5	15	18	35	43
15	Bradford C	46	11	5	7	38	26	6	4	13	24	42	43
16	Port Vale	46	8	10	5	29	28	6	4	13	28	42	42
17	Stockport	46	11	5	7	33	21	3	7	13	25	39	40
18	Bournemouth	46	11	6	6	34	19	3	5	15	13	29	39
19	Northampton	46	12	4	7	40	30	3	5	15	24	46	39
20	Rochdale	46	11	4	8	25	26	4	5	14	22	38	39
21	Darlington	46	8	8	7	25	21	3	7	13	24	45	37
22	Doncaster	46	8	8	7	25	22	5	3	15	25	51	37
23	Halifax	46	7	5	11	24	32	2	3	18	15	40	26
24	Crewe	46	3	7	13	24	41	3	7	13	19	49	26
		1104	281	141	130	852	557	130	141	281	557	852	1104

Odds & ends

Double wins: (4) Doncaster, Hereford, Northampton, Newport.

Double losses: (2) Bradford C, Grimsby.

Won from behind: (3) Wimbledon (a), Newport (h), Newport (a).

Lost from in front: (1) York (a).

High spots: Unbeaten for 13 home league games from September until February.

Going top of a league table in January for the first time since 1967.

Beating promotion rivals Reading 4-0 and Wimbledon 4-2 in successive matches in December.

Avoiding falling to the bottom of Division Four in August, thanks to a late equaliser from Steve Davey at Hartlepool.

Six games without conceding a league goal twice: Sept, Nov-December.

Low spots: Just five wins in the last 19 matches killed promotion.

Losing 0-2 at bottom club Halifax in March, their first home win since August.

Losing 1-3 at home to promotion rivals Grimsby in Pompey's first 'Match of the Day' appearance since 1971.

Player of the Year: Peter Mellor.

Ever presents: (1) Peter Mellor.

Hat-tricks: Jeff Hemmerman (1), Colin Garwood (1).

Leading scorer: Jeff Hemmerman (16).

Appearances & Goals

Player	Apps Lge	Sub	LC	Sub	FAC	Sub	Goals Lge	LC	FAC	Tot
Barnard, Leigh	28						7			7
Bryant, Steve	15				2					
Davey, Steve	42	4	1		2		7			7
Denyer, Peter	39	2	2		2	2	6			6
Ellis, Peter	44		2		2					
Foster, Steve	35	1	2		2		2			2
Garwood, Colin	27	8	2		2		15			15
Gilchrist, Paul			1					1		1
Hand, Eoin	3	2	1				1			1
Hemmerman, Jeff	37	2	2		2		14		2	16
James, Keith	3	1								
Lathan, John	43	2	2		2		4			4
McCaffery, Jim		1								
McIlwraith, Jim	16	3	1							
Mellor, Peter	46				2					
Milligan, Mike	7									
Piper, Steve	14		1							
Pullar, David	35	3	2		2		1	1		2
Roberts, Trevor		1								
Showers, Derek	19	1					2			2
Viney, Keith	38	1	2		2		2			2
Wilson, Billy	15	3					1			1
22 players used	506	33	22		22	2	62	2	2	66

LEAGUE DIVISION 4   Manager: Frank Burrows   SEASON 1979-80

No	Date	Att	Pos	Pt	F-A	H-T	1	2	3	4	5	6	7	8	9	10	11	12 sub used	Scorers, Times, and Referees
1	A HARTLEPOOL 18/8	3,075		W 2	3-0	1-0	Mellor *Watson*	McLaughlin *Norton*	Styles *Gorry*	Brisley *Goldthorpe*	Aizlewood *Brooks*	Davey *Ayre*	Garwood *Linacre*	Lathan *Smith*	Showers* *Houchen*	Bryant *Harding*	**Rogers** *Lawrence*	Hemmerman	Bryant 35, McLaughlin 66, [Garwood 90] — Ref: P Tyldesley (Stockport). Pool celebrate Harding's 'goal' after Houchen hits the bar, but a linesman's flag rules it out. Davey's quick-thinking puts Bryant away to float a shot over Watson. Home boss Billy Horner is warned and police quell fractious fans. Debut-making McLaughlin nets his only Pompey goal.
2	H TORQUAY 21/8	11,430	1	W 4	3-0	2-0	Mellor *Turner*	McLaughlin *Pethard*	Styles *Twitchin*	Brisley *Larmour*	Aizlewood *Bourne*	Davey *Sermanni*	Garwood *Levy**	**Laidlaw** *Lawrence*	Showers *Cooper*	Bryant *Ritchie*	Rogers *Murphy*	Davies	Showers 17, Garwood 26, 75p — Ref: C Downey (Hounslow). New-look Pompey impress the faithful with a stylish win over Mike Green's Torquay United, who have also reshuffled their squad during the summer. Showers' close-range effort sets up the win, then Styles' pass finds Garwood to angle home. Brisley is bundled over for the spot-kick.
3	H SCUNTHORPE 25/8	12,234	1	W 6	6-1	3-0	Mellor *Crawford*	McLaughlin *Davy*	Styles *Peacock*	Brisley *Kavanagh*	Aizlewood *Partridge*	Davey *Oates*	Garwood *O'Berg*	Lathan *Kilmore*	Showers* *Earl*	Bryant *Pilling*	Rogers *Keeley*	Hemmerman	Brisley 7, Garwood 33, 42, / Pilling 52 [Laidlaw 50, Rogers 80 88] — Ref: W Bombroff (Bristol). Pompey seal their best home win since 1962 and their best home win since 1971. Brisley is tormentor-in-chief and rounds it off with a fine shot. Lathan's sale to Mansfield adds £20,000 to Burrows' transfer kitty.
4	A WIGAN 1/9	8,198	1	W 8	2-1	0-1	Mellor *Shyne*	McLaughlin *Smart*	Styles *Himigan*	Brisley *Gore*	Aizlewood *Ward*	Davey *Fretwell*	Garwood *Corrigan*	Laidlaw *Wright*	Showers *Houghton*	Bryant *More*	Rogers *Purdie*		Brisley 52, Garwood 54 / More 10 — Ref: F Phipps (Wrexham). Purdie's good work for More's goal is noted and he will sign for Pompey shortly. Ward breaks his leg in fouling Showers, then Rogers sets up two in three minutes. Bryant and Aizlewood add to a mounting bookings tally, while Burrows is looking to Sweden to combat spiralling fees.
5	H STOCKPORT 8/9	14,942	1	W 10	1-0	1-0	Mellor *Rogan*	McLaughlin *Sherlock*	Styles *Rutter*	Brisley *Edwards*	Aizlewood *Czuczman*	Davey *Chapman*	Garwood *Summerbee*	Laidlaw *Thorpe*	Showers* *Henson*	Bryant *Galvin*	Rogers *Williams*	Hemmerman	Laidlaw 4 — Ref: L Shapter (Newton Abbot). Skipper Laidlaw curls a glorious 20-yarder, but Pompey's joy is tempered by Showers' serious knee injury. Sub Hemmerman curls an equally spectacular 'goal', but a dubious offside rules it out. Mellor's late save denies former-England star and County player-boss Mike Summerbee.
6	A TRANMERE 14/9	3,550	2	L 10	1-4	1-3	Mellor *Johnson*	McLaughlin 1 *Mathias*	Styles *Flood*	Brisley *Bramhall*	Aizlewood* *Edwards*	Davey *Evans*	Garwood *O'Neill*	Laidlaw *Craven*	Hemmerman *Kerr*	Bryant *Lumby*	Rogers *Peplow*	Ellis	Brisley 2 / Kerr 5, O'Neill 8p, Craven 44, Peplow 90 Johnson — Ref: D Shaw (Sandbach). After Brisley's sharply-taken goal, it all goes wrong. Kerr levels, then McLaughlin handles for O'Neill's penalty. Ten minutes later the full-back is sent off for retaliation and then the Aizlewood limps off. Craven ends hopes, and in injury-time Peplow rubs it in for John King's Rovers.
7	H BOURNEMOUTH 18/9	15,524	1	W 12	4-0	2-0	Mellor *Allen K*	Ellis *Cunningham/ Moore*	Styles *Impey*	Brisley *Impey*	Aizlewood *Townsend*	Davey *Chambers*	Garwood *Holder*	Laidlaw *Thomas*	Hemmerman *Butler**	Bryant *Massey*	Rogers *Evanson*	Borthwick	Brisley 12, 40, Hemmerman 58, 68 — Ref: C White (Harrow). Cherries have no answer to Pompey's power and are already losing to a brace of Brisley goals, the first a volley, when Cunningham is sent off before half-time for kicking Rogers. Hemmerman nets his first goals of the season, rounding it off when he pounces on Kenny Allen's fumble.
8	A ROCHDALE 22/9	2,423	1	W 14	2-1	0-0	Mellor *Watson*	McLaughlin *Cliff*	Styles *Snookes*	Brisley *Weir*	Aizlewood *Bannon*	Davey *Taylor*	Garwood *Hoy*	Laidlaw *Wann*	Hemmerman *Hilditch*	Bryant* *Scaife*	Rogers *Jones*	Ellis	Rogers 62, Garwood 72 / Weir 86 — Ref: K McNally (South Wirral). Cheekiest goal of the season goes to Garwood, as keeper Watson claims a cross, but forgets the striker is there and is dispossessed as he rolls the ball out. Rogers volleyed home after Garwood and Brisley had both hit the bar, but Weir's late strike for Doug Collins' men made it tense.
9	H YORK 29/9	14,917	1	W 16	5-2	2-1	Mellor *Neenan*	McLaughlin *Kamara*	Styles *Kay*	Brisley *Pugh*	Aizlewood *Faulkner*	Davey *James*	Garwood *Eccles*	Laidlaw *Lorimer*	Hemmerman *Wellings*	Bryant* *McDonald*	Rogers *Staniforth*	Barnard	Aizlewood 23, Brisley 43, Garwood / Lorimer 42, Kay 67[54p 72p, Laidlaw 70] — Ref: D Hedges (Oxford). Garwood scores a rare penalty hat-trick chance as Joe Neenan saves after Alan Kamara's push on Rogers late on. Earlier he had netted after Faulkner pushed him, then after a handball. Ex-Leeds star Peter Lorimer's scorching free-kick and Kay's soft goal always kept it competitive.
10	A BOURNEMOUTH 2/10	13,963	1	W 18	1-0	1-0	Mellor *Owers*	McLaughlin *Coleman*	Styles *Ferns*	Brisley *Impey*	Aizlewood *Bainbridge*	Ellis *Chambers*	Garwood *Holder*	Laidlaw *Thomas*	Hemmerman *Butler*	Bryant *Massey*	Rogers *Evanson*		Brisley 39 — Ref: S Bates (Bristol). Brisley's seventh in eight matches sees him pop up to convert Garwood's corner and secure the 'double' over Alec Stock's Cherries. More than 9,000 visiting fans make it virtually a home game, but they are relieved when Mellor turns Chambers' shot onto the bar on the interval.
11	H DARLINGTON 6/10	16,692	1	W 20	4-3	2-2	Mellor *Owers*	McLaughlin *Coleman*	Styles *Cochrane*	Brisley* *Mattress*	Aizlewood *Smith*	Ellis *Smith*	Garwood *McLean*	Laidlaw *Charlton*	Ashworth *Fergusson*	Bryant *Ellis*	Rogers *Walsh*	Todd	Ash 12, 50, Laidlaw 25, Garwood 89p / McLean 10, Walsh 42, Walsh 61p — Ref: L Burden (Corfe Mullen). Burrows nearly spent £60,000 on Wigan striker Peter Houghton, but instead picked up Phil Ashworth from Rochdale reserves on a free. His rags-to-riches tale is complete as he nets a tap-in, cracks in a spectacular shot-on-the-turn, then is fouled for Garwood's decisive late penalty.

12 · Torquay (A) · 10/10 · L 1-2 (HT 0-1) · Att 5,525 · Pos 20
Portsmouth: Mellor, McLaughlin, Styles, Brisley, Aizlewood, Ellis, Garwood, Laidlaw, Hemmerman, Bryant, Rogers*
Torquay: Turner, Pethard, Ritchie, Hagan, Bourne, Sermanni, Davies, Lawrence, Cooper, Smith*, Murphy — sub Coffill
Scorers: Hemmerman 67 / Lawrence 35, Coffill 84
Ref: C Thomas (Porthcawl)
Kenny Todd (£20,000) has become Burrows' 19th signing since he arrived as coach in February 1978, but the ex-Vale striker isn't even on the bench as Torquay gain deserved revenge for August's mauling thanks to substitute Peter Coffill's late goal. Hemmerman's volley had levelled.

13 · Huddersfield (A) · 13/10 · W 3-1 (HT 2-0) · Att 16,540 · Pos 22
Portsmouth: Mellor, McLaughlin, Styles, Brisley, Aizlewood, Ellis, Garwood, Laidlaw, Hemmerman, Bryant, Rogers* — sub Davey
Huddersfield: Starling, Brown, Robinson, Stanton, Sutton, Hanvey, Laverick, Hart, Fletcher, Robins, Cowling
Scorers: Laidlaw 38, 42, Hemmerman 67 / Fletcher 74
Ref: K Redfern (Whitley Bay)
The performance of the season sees Terriers' perfect home start (21-2 goals record) destroyed. Laidlaw reckons no one is a match for Pompey, and his two headers and an assist for Hemmerman prove it. Hemmerman's dismissal for swinging a boot after being fouled is the only blemish.

14 · Bradford City (H) · 20/10 · W 4-1 (HT 3-0) · Att 23,871 · Pos 24
Portsmouth: Mellor, McLaughlin, Styles, Brisley, Aizlewood, Ellis, Garwood, Laidlaw, Ashworth, Bryant, Rogers
Bradford City: Smith, Reaney, Wood, Baines, Cooper, Bates, Dolan, Stainforth, McNiven, Martinez* — sub Padd
Scorers: Ashworth 1, 42, Rogers 34, [Garwood 88] / Dolan 56
Ref: M Bidmead (Chessington)
Ashworth, in for the banned Hemmerman, flicks home Bryant's cross, then buries a marvellous swivel-shot. Beaming Burrows says it is 'real Roy of the Rovers stuff.' Pompey's first-half is awesome, backed by a gate bigger than some in Div One. Dolan's 20-yarder makes it a game.

15 · Newport (H) · 23/10 · L 0-2 (HT 0-1) · Att 20,755 · Pos 24
Portsmouth: Mellor, McLaughlin, Styles, Todd, Aizlewood, Ellis, Garwood, Laidlaw, Hemmerman, Bryant, Rogers — sub Davey
Newport: Plumley, Walden, Relish, Davies, Oakes*, Bailey, Vaughan, Lowndes, Goddard*, Aldridge, Moore — sub Bruton D
Scorers: Lowndes 5, Oakes 80
Ref: R Challis (Tonbridge)
Todd makes his debut, but gifts the ball to Lowndes who scores from 15 yards. Len Ashurst's County out-play Pompey before another bumper crowd, but their joy is marred by Goddard's leg-break after a tackle with Davey. Oakes follows up after Moore hits the underside of the bar.

16 · Doncaster (A) · 26/10 · L 0-2 (HT 0-1) · Att 9,801 · Pos 24
Portsmouth: Mellor, McLaughlin, Styles, Brisley, Aizlewood, Ellis, Garwood, Laidlaw, Hemmerman, Bryant, Rogers — sub Ashworth
Doncaster: Peacock, Russell, Snodin G, Lister, Lally, Dowd, Pugh, Nimmo, Warboys, Lewis, Bentley
Scorers: Lister 43, Warboys 49p
Ref: G Courtney (Spennymoor)
Laidlaw's return to Belle Vue, following his £15,000 summer transfer, ends in disappointment. Brisley sees a shot hacked from the line before Lister's goal, then Lally is up-ended by Davey for Warboys' penalty. Sub Ashworth can't conjure up his magic and seven players are booked.

17 · Hartlepool (H) · 3/11 · W 2-1 (HT 1-1) · Att 14,295 · Pos 26
Portsmouth: Mellor, McLaughlin, Styles, Brisley, Aizlewood, Ellis, Garwood, Laidlaw, Hemmerman, Bryant, Rogers — sub Davey
Hartlepool: Burleigh, Sweeney, Normanton, Lawrence, Carr, Ayre, Linacre, Houchen, Newton, Harding, Loadwick
Scorers: Garwood 42, Brisley 85 / Newton 11
Ref: D Vickers (Ilford)
Piper has played for the stiffs and should soon beef up competition for places; no bad thing after another off-colour display. Former-target Newton runs 60 yards to bundle in off a post at the second attempt, but Garwood levels and 'far-post' Brisley lives up to his nickname late on.

18 · Newport (A) · 6/11 · L 3-4 (HT 2-2) · Att 7,115 · Pos 26
Portsmouth: Mellor, McLaughlin, Styles, Brisley, Aizlewood, Ellis, Garwood*, Laidlaw, Hemmerman, Bryant, Rogers — sub Davey
Newport: Plumley, Walden, Relish, Davies, Oakes*, Bailey, Vaughan, Lowndes, Tynan, Aldridge, Moore — sub Burton D
Scorers: Garwood 24p, Hemmerman 32, 55 / Oakes 5, Aldridge 37, Tynan 50, 70
Ref: K Baker (Wolverhampton)
Tynan's diving header settles a topsy-turvy game. Pompey's run is four losses in seven, far from promotion form. Oakes nods in, but he fouls Hemmerman in the box, who then flicks in Rogers' cross. Aldridge and Tynan see goals pegged back. All Newport's goals were headers.

19 · Walsall (A) · 10/11 · D 1-1 (HT 0-1) · Att 7,468 · Pos 27
Portsmouth: Knight, Ellis, Viney, Brisley, Aizlewood, Davey, Garwood, Laidlaw, Hemmerman, Bryant, Rogers
Walsall: Green, Paul, Mower, Stragia, Serella, Broadhurst, Penn, Williams, McDonough, Buckley, Caswell
Scorers: Garwood 83 / McDonough 19
Ref: R Toseland (Market Harboro')
Keeper Green lets Garwood's mis-hit shot slips through his fingers to earn Pompey a merited draw against their promotion rivals. Davey clamps down on Saddlers' player-boss Alan Buckley, but McDonough nets after Knight (18), in for Mellor, can only deflect Caswell's header.

20 · Lincoln (H) · 17/11 · W 4-0 (HT 1-0) · Att 14,620 · Pos 29
Portsmouth: Knight, Ellis, Viney, Brisley, Aizlewood, Davey, Garwood*, Laidlaw, Ashworth, Bryant, Rogers — sub **Purdie**
Lincoln: Grotier, Carr, Neale, Watson, Saunders, Peake, Hobson, Cockerill, Harford, Cunningham, Ball
Scorers: Garwood 44, 51, Laidlaw 86, 89p
Ref: T Glasson (Salisbury)
Laidlaw's late pen just slithers under Grotier's dive and is the team's 50th league goal of the season. The kick is for a shirt-tug on sub Purdie, a Scots Under-23 cap, signed five weeks ago as cover for Rogers. Imps have been training with the army in Dorset, but wilt under Pompey's fire.

21 · Halifax (H) · 1/12 · W 3-1 (HT 1-0) · Att 14,087 · Pos 31
Portsmouth: Mellor, Ellis, Viney, Brisley, Aizlewood, Davey, Garwood, Laidlaw, Hemmerman, Bryant, Rogers
Halifax: Kilner, Dunleavy, Hutt, Evans, Harris, Goodman*, Firth, Kennedy, Burke, Smith, Stafford — sub Dryhurst
Scorers: Brisley 29, Garwood 58, Laidlaw 72 / Firth 75
Ref: C Maskell (Cambridge)
Pompey's leading scorer Garwood is considering a move to Exeter, but his simple finish, after Hemmerman's shot is saved, is not his swansong … yet. Laidlaw nods his 100th league goal from Rogers' corner. George Kirby's Halifax are one of the most-improved sides so far.

22 · Peterborough (A) · 8/12 · D 0-0 (HT 0-0) · Att 5,371 · Pos 32
Portsmouth: Knight, Ellis, Viney, Brisley, Aizlewood, Davey, Garwood, Laidlaw, Hemmerman, Bryant, Rogers
Peterborough: Waugh, Carmichael, Phillips, Sharkey, Slough, Quow, Foster, Kellock, Cliss, Syrett, Gynn* — sub Robson
Ref: B Martin (Keyworth)
Garwood turns down the move to fans' 'relief', but Bury's Dave Gregory is under view, to add to Perrin's recent £15,000 capture from Argyle. Laidlaw's header thumps a Posh post, but that's it. Mellor is out of the team and out of luck; his sponsored car is dented twice in a week.

23 · Port Vale (H) · 21/12 · D 2-2 (HT 1-1) · Att 12,022 · Pos 33
Portsmouth: Knight, Ellis, Viney, Brisley, Aizlewood, Davey, **Gregory**, Laidlaw, Hemmerman, Bryant, Rogers
Port Vale: Dance, Keenan, Griffiths, Bentley*, Delgado, Bowles, Beech, Farrell, Bromage, Wright, Chamberlain — sub Elsby
Scorers: **Gregory** 13, Bryant 74 / Griffiths 31, 55
Ref: A Cox (South Croydon)
Pompey move the game to Friday to avoid the pre-Xmas 'Black Saturday'. A snow shower at 5.30 leaves the pitch with a light snow covering and the club making a desperate radio appeal for an orange ball. Gregory (£60,000) stabs in on his debut and Bryant's delightful chip saves it.

LEAGUE DIVISION 4   Manager: Frank Burrows   SEASON 1979-80

No	Date	Att	Pos	Pt	F-A	H-T	Scorers, Times, and Referees	1	2	3	4	5	6	7	8	9	10	11	12 sub used
24	A HEREFORD 26/12	4,514 *17*	2 D	34	0-0	0-0	Ref: J Lovatt (Crewe)	Mellor / *Hughes*	McLaughlin / *Price*	Styles / *Burrows*	Barnard / *Marshall*	Aizlewood / *Layton*	Ellis / *Feely*	Gregory / *Stephens*	Laidlaw / *Spring*	**Perrin** / *McGrellis*	Bryant / *Hunt*	Purdie / *White*	
25	H NORTHAMPTON 29/12	15,579 *15*	2 W	36	6-1	4-1	Rogers 4, Hemmerman 18, 51 Aiz'd 25 Bowen 21 [Gregory 30 Laidlaw 59]; Ref: B Stevens (Stonehouse)	Knight / *Poole*	McLaughlin / *Farrington*	Viney / *Sandercock*	Brisley / *Byatt*	Aizlewood / *Gage*	Ellis / *Williams**	Gregory / *Denyer*	Laidlaw / *Sandy*	Hemmerman / *McCaffery*	Bryant / *Bowen*	Rogers* / *Farmer*	*Sargant*
26	H ALDERSHOT 1/1	23,462 *7*	3 L	36	1-3	0-2	Rogers 90 / French 9, Needham 25, 87; Ref: E Read (Bristol)	Knight / *Johnson*	McLaughlin / *Edwards*	Styles / *Howitt*	Brisley* / *Dixon*	Ellis / *Youlden*	Viney / *Wooler*	Gregory / *Crosby*	Laidlaw / *Brodie*	Hemmerman / *French*	Bryant / *Needham*	Rogers / *McGregor*	*Perrin*
27	H WIGAN 12/1	15,625 *8*	3 D	37	1-1	1-0	Brisley 14 / Houghton 90; Ref: B Daniels (Brentwood)	Mellor / *Brown*	McLaughlin / *Fretwell*	Viney / *Hinnigan*	Brisley / *Gore*	Aizlewood / *Methven*	Ellis / *Davids*	Gregory / *Corrigan*	Laidlaw / *Wright*	Hemmerman / *Brownhill*	Bryant / *Quinn**	Rogers* / *Urquhart*	*Garwood / Houghton*
28	A SCUNTHORPE 26/1	2,609 *19*	3 L	37	0-1	0-0	Partridge 59; Ref: D Webb (Radcliffe)	Mellor / *Gordon*	Ellis / *Davy*	Viney / *Peacock*	Brisley / *Deere*	Aizlewood / *Dall*	Roberts / *Kavanagh*	Garwood / *Pugh*	Laidlaw / *Green**	Perrin* / *Pilling*	Bryant / *Partridge*	Rogers / *Stewart*	*Gregory / Cowling*
29	H TRANMERE 2/2	12,821 *14*	3 D	38	1-1	0-1	Todd 80 / Peplow 31; Ref: D Reeves (Uxbridge)	Mellor / *Johnson*	James / *Parry*	Viney* / *Mongall*	Brisley / *Bramhall*	Aizlewood / *Edwards*	Ellis / *Evans*	Gregory / *O'Neill*	Laidlaw / *Craven*	Hemmerman / *Kelly*	Bryant / *Beamish*	Rogers / *Peplow*	*Todd*
30	H ROCHDALE 9/2	12,207 *23*	3 W	40	3-0	0-0	Hemmerman 50, Laidlaw 70, 79; Ref: R Lewis (Great Bookham)	Mellor / *Watson*	McLaughlin / *Hart*	Weir / *Weir*	Barnard / *Bannon*	Aizlewood / *Waldron*	Ellis / *Taylor*	Gregory / *Esser*	Laidlaw / *O'Loughlin*	Hemmerman / *Seal*	Bryant / *Jones*	Purdie / *Hilditch*	
31	A CREWE 12/2	3,315 *24*	3 D	41	1-1	1-0	Laidlaw 30 / Guy 70; Ref: M Scott (Nottingham)	Mellor / *Grobbelaar*	McLaughlin / *Wilkinson*	Viney / *Bowers*	Barnard / *Hunter*	Aizlewood / *Scott*	Ellis / *Prophett*	Gregory* / *McMahon*	Laidlaw / *Guy*	Hemmerman / *Conroy*	Bryant / *Palios*	Purdie / *Nelson*	*Perrin*
32	A YORK 16/2	2,589 *18*	3 L	41	0-1	0-1	Hood 34; Ref: D Richardson (Lincoln)	Mellor / *Crawford*	Ellis / *Hood*	Viney* / *Walsh*	Brisley / *Pugh**	Aizlewood / *Faulkner*	Garner* / *Clements*	Gregory / *Serebee*	Laidlaw / *Lorimer*	Hemmerman* / *Eccles*	Bryant / *McDonald*	Rogers* / *McGhie*	*Todd*
33	H HUDDERSFIELD 23/2	19,203 *2*	3 W	43	4-1	2-1	Brisley 17 Gregory 36, 61 / Kindon 39p [Cowling 78(og)]; Ref: K Salmon (Barnet)	Mellor / *Rankin*	Ellis / *Brown*	Styles / *Purdie*	Brisley / *Stanton**	Perrin / *Sutton*	Davey / *Hanvey*	Gregory / *Laverick*	Laidlaw / *Hart*	Hemmerman / *Kindon*	Bryant / *Robins*	Rogers / *Cowling*	*Perrin / Fletcher*
34	A BRADFORD C 1/3	9,363 *4*	3 D	44	0-0	0-0	Ref: P Partridge (Cockfield)	Mellor / *Smith*	Ellis / *Jones*	Styles / *Wood*	Brisley / *Bates*	Perrin / *Baines*	Davey / *Cooper*	Gregory / *Chapman*	Laidlaw / *Dolan*	Hemmerman / *Campbell*	**Brown** / *McNiven*	Rogers / *Hutchins*	

24. Hereford have still to score against Pompey in five meetings, but the agile Hughes preserves their point. His boss Frank Lord says one save was 'world class'. Gregory hits a post, as a patched-up team play their fourth game in eight days. Perrin debuts and Barnard makes a rare start.

25. Poor Town, unbeaten in six before today, are outclassed. Denyer and McCaffery make an unhappy return as Rogers revels in time and space. He nets as Hemmerman slips rounding Poole and makes three others. Gregory lobs his third in four, but Aizlewood's impending ban is a blow.

26. Knight's confidence is shot to pieces as he fails to deal with three carbon-copy near-post corners, which all result in goals. Brisley's knee-injury is down on the frosty pitch. At the club's AGM Deacon issues a 'hands-off' warning to clubs thinking of poaching manager Burrows.

27. Houghton's late chip over Mellor means Ian McNeill's Wigan are unbeaten in 14. The striker could have been at Fratton in the autumn, had his wife not preferred northern life. Burrows has also been thwarted in his audacious bid for first division Brighton's midfielder Paul Clark.

28. Forest boss Brian Clough tips Pompey to be a 'Team of the 1980s' because of their large crowd, but they won't be on this form. Trevor Roberts makes his full debut and hits a post, but Partridge shrugs off three challenges to score. One league win in seven means third place.

29. Sub Todd makes his mark, guiding in Rogers' cross to level a muddy farce of a game. Peplow ploughs past James to nutmeg Mellor, then Rovers – in Pompey's red due to a kit-bag cock-up – soak up non-stop pressure. Burrows' new weight-watching regime means fines for fatties.

30. Rochdale fail to get a shot on-target, but Pompey only look safe after Laidlaw's strike from Bryant's lay-off. Midfielder Jimmy Brown (ex-Villa) is on a month's trial from Greece. Hemmerman spoons over, having rounded the keeper, but his calm side-step of Hart sets up the opener.

31. Laidlaw's goal is a poor first-half return, but tail-enders Alex, reviving under ex-Stoke boss Tony Waddington (13 points from 16 since he arrived), grab a point after Ellis' error. Garwood goes to Shots this week (£50,000) and defender Alan Garner arrives (£60,000 from Watford).

32. Earlier in the season Crawford let in six for Scunthorpe at Fratton, but there was little danger of a repeat. In fact, Pompey had Mellor to thank for keeping the score down once Hood hit the top corner from the edge of the area in only his second game after a £2,000 move from Hull.

33. Burrows has pledged to resign if Pompey don't go up and his team respond. Terriers' haven't lost in eight, but once Brisley's alertness finishes Aizlewood's flick it's over. Gregory ends a lean spell with two smartly-taken goals, then Rankin punches Rogers' corner onto Cowling's head.

34. Pompey list eight players, including Todd, Ashworth and Purdie signed this season, ahead of this promotion clash. Makeshift defenders Perrin and Davey work hard to keep City at bay. Perrin's snap-shot is just over late on and Brown, signed until May, comes in for the banned Bryant.

No.	H/A	Opponent	Date	Score	Result	Pos	Att	Pts	Scorers	Referee
35	H	DONCASTER	8/3	2-0	W	3	14,382	46	Laidlaw 19p, Brisley 43	M Taylor (Deal)
36	A	STOCKPORT	10/3	1-1	D	3	2,938	47	Hemmerman 4 / Czuczman 75	R Bridges (Deeside)
37	A	DARLINGTON	15/3	1-1	D	3	2,287	48	Rogers 19 / Walsh 69p	D Clarke (Accrington)
38	H	WALSALL	22/3	1-2	L	1	21,785	48	Hemmerman 47 / Macken 33, Buckley 88p	T Bune (Billingshurst)
39	A	LINCOLN	29/3	0-1	L	7	4,682	48	Turner 75	A Grey (Great Yarmouth)
40	A	PORT VALE	1/4	3-2	W	20	3,614	50	Perrin 17, Laidlaw 71, Elsby 73 (og) / Harwood 1, Sealy 24	G Flint (Kirkby-in-Ashfield)
41	H	HEREFORD	5/4	0-0	D	19	15,175	51		L Shapter (Newton Abbott)
42	A	ALDERSHOT	7/4	2-1	W	10	11,989	53	Perrin 7, Laidlaw 47 / Edwards 60	D Lloyd (Fernhill Heath)
43	H	CREWE	12/4	1-1	D	23	13,752	54	Rogers 63 / McLaughlin 22 (og)	S Bates (Bristol)
44	A	HALIFAX	19/4	2-1	W	18	2,950	56	Hemmerman 14, Gregory 51 / Hendrie 57	C Seel (Carlisle)
45	H	PETERBOROUGH	26/4	4-0	W	8	15,095	58	Collins 9 (og), Hemmerman 15, Gynn 60 (og), Rogers 88	M Bidmead (Chessington)
46	A	NORTHAMPTON	3/5	2-0	W	14	10,774	60	Davey 41, Purdie 73	C White (Harrow)

35 — DONCASTER (H)
Pompey: Mellor, Ellis, Styles, Brisley, Aizlewood, Davey, Gregory*, Laidlaw, Hemmerman, Brown, Rogers, Perrin
Doncaster: Peacock, Flanaghan, Snodin, Lister, Lally, Dowd, Lewis*, Nimmo, Warboys, Little, Bentley, Pugh
Pompey's first-half display proves enough for Football League supremo Alan Hardaker. Laidlaw scores from the spot after Dowd handled, then Brisley nets Gregory's flick-on from Rogers' corner. Showers' comeback continues in the reserves against the Navy.

36 — STOCKPORT (A)
Pompey: Mellor*, Ellis, Styles, Brisley, Aizlewood, Davey, Gregory, Laidlaw, Hemmerman, Bryant, Rogers, Perrin
Stockport: Lawson, Rutter, Sherlock, Thorpe, Bradd, Edwards, Williams, Sunley, Czuczman, Galvin, Coyle
Laidlaw goes in goal after Mellor's ankle injury and is caught out of position two minutes later for Czuczman's header. Earlier Hemmerman had converted Bryant's cross and the team squandered several chances. Laidlaw defies County's late push and earns the nickname 'Flying Pig'.

37 — DARLINGTON (A)
Pompey: Knight, Ellis, Styles, Brisley, Aizlewood, Davey, Gregory, Laidlaw, Hemmerman, Bryant, Rogers, Perrin
Darlington: Barry, Mattress, Cochrane, Ball, Craig, Smith, Hawker, Charlton, Stalker, Hamilton, Walsh
Deadline day ends with the status quo intact. Viney turns down Dons, Purdie Halifax and Roberts and Ashworth Bath City. Burrows' eleventh hour bid for Gills' midfielder Terry Nicholl stalls. Rogers' nets the rebound as Hemmerman's shot hits the bar, but then Knight up-ends Walsh.

38 — WALSALL (H)
Pompey: Knight, Ellis, Styles, Brisley, Garner*, Davey, Gregory, Laidlaw, Hemmerman, Bryant, Rogers, Perrin
Walsall: Green, James, Mower, Straglia, Williams J, Williams G, Penn*, Waddington, Rees, Buckley, Caswell, Horne
Davey and James collide to put Penn away and Knight brings him down. Alan Buckley coolly converts and Saddlers will now contest the title with Huddersfield. James had earlier crossed for Hemmerman to drive home, cancelling out former Fratton loanee Macken's dipping shot.

39 — LINCOLN (A)
Pompey: Mellor, Ellis, Styles*, Brisley, Perrin, Davey, Gregory, Laidlaw, Hemmerman, Bryant, Rogers, Roberts
Lincoln: McManus, Thompson, Neale, Shipley, Peake, Carr, Hobson, Hughes, Cunningham, Turner, Bell
With Aizlewood and Garner ruled out for the rest of the season, Pompey's promotion bid looks shaky after Phil Turner (18) snaps up his first league goal from Roberts' poor header. At least Bradford lose to lowly York, but Newport gain their sixth of a ten-match winning run.

40 — PORT VALE (A)
Pompey: Mellor, McLaughlin, Viney, Brisley, Perrin, Davey, Hemmerman, Laidlaw, Perrin, Bryant, Rogers, Chamberlain M
Port Vale: Dance, Keenan, Griffiths, Elsby, Harwood, Sproson, Beech, Chamberlain N, Bromage*, Sealy, Bentley
A pre-match 'clear the air' meeting bears fruit as Pompey roar back from Harwood's early opener. Perrin nets his first goal for the club, then Laidlaw levels again just before confused Elsby knocks the ball past his advancing keeper. John McGrath's side haven't lost at home in 1980.

41 — HEREFORD (H)
Pompey: Mellor, McLaughlin, Viney, Brisley, Ellis, Davey, Hemmerman*, Laidlaw, Perrin, Bryant, Rogers, Gregory
Hereford: Hughes, Price, Burrows, Spiring, Cornes, Harvey, Cunningham, Gilchrist, Binney, McGrellis, Bartley
Hughes defies Pompey for the second time this season, with an early point-blank stop from Laidlaw proving vital. The crowd take out their frustration on Hemmerman, who has subbed for Gregory, but he makes no difference. Newport are a point behind with three games in hand.

42 — ALDERSHOT (A)
Pompey: Mellor, McLaughlin, Viney, Brisley, Ellis, Davey, Hemmerman, Laidlaw, Perrin, Bryant*, Rogers, Gregory
Aldershot: Johnson, Edwards, Wooler, Briley, Howitt, Youden, Green, Brodie, Garwood, French*, McGregor, Lucas
Skipper-for-the-day Garwood gets a huge ovation from 8,000 visitors, but it's not enough. Burrows praises Ellis: 'I had no qualms, Peter's the best marker at the club.'

43 — CREWE (H)
Pompey: Mellor, McLaughlin, Styles*, Brisley, Ellis, Davey, Hemmerman, Laidlaw, Perrin, Bryant, Rogers, Gregory
Crewe: Grobbelaar, Wilkinson, Bowers, Hunter, Scott, Prophett, McMahon, Guy, Davies, Palios, Nelson*, Coyne
Crewe's former Rhodesian army officer Grobbelaar defies Laidlaw with a marvellous stop, but is helpless as Rogers sidefoots in. McLaughlin had put the crowd on edge when he hooked past Mellor under pressure from Palios. Newport hang on against Rochdale to leave Pompey fifth.

44 — HALIFAX (A)
Pompey: Mellor, McLaughlin, Bryant, Brisley, Ellis, Davey, Hemmerman, Laidlaw, Perrin, Brown, Rogers, Smith*
Halifax: Kilner, Dunleavy, Hutt, Evans, Harris, Hendrie, Firth, Kennedy, Mountford, Burke, Allatt
Pompey's promotion train is back on track as their rivals all drop points. Hemmerman glances home Rogers' centre, then hits the bar early in the second half. Man-of-the-Match Brown sets up Gregory for a fierce angled shot, but Hendrie's crisp header means an anxious half-hour.

45 — PETERBOROUGH (H)
Pompey: Mellor, McLaughlin, Bryant, Brisley, Ellis, Davey, Hemmerman, Laidlaw, Perrin, Brown, Rogers, Guy
Peterborough: Waugh, McVay, Phillips, Quow, Collins, Foster, Gynn, Kellock, Cliss*, Syrett, Robson
Two own-goals contribute to Posh's downfall, as Collins turns past Waugh, then Gynn intercepts Brown's pass, only to trump his own keeper. Rogers scores the goal of the game with a rising drive, but Pompey must hope Peter Morris' men do them a favour next week against Bradford.

46 — NORTHAMPTON (A)
Pompey: Mellor, McLaughlin, Bryant, Brisley, Ellis, Davey, Hemmerman, Laidlaw, Perrin, Brown, Purdie
Northampton: Poole, Walker, Sandercock, Byatt, Gage, Denyer, Sargent, Sandy, Heeley, Ingram, Farmer
On an afternoon of unbearable tension, Pompey, given a ticker-tape welcome by 8,000 fans, get the result they need thanks to Davey's looping header and Purdie's drive. Toast of the day, however, is Posh's Tony Cliss, whose goal beats Bradford and puts Pompey up on goal-difference.

Home Average 15,847
Away Average 6,288

LEAGUE DIVISION 4 (CUP-TIES) Manager: Frank Burrows SEASON 1979-80

League Cup

				F-A	H-T	Scorers, Times, and Referees	1	2	3	4	5	6	7	8	9	10	11	12 sub used
1:1	H	SWINDON 11/8	D 1-1 9,978 3	1-1	1-1	Rogers 27 / Rowland 30 / Ref: A Gunn (Burgess Hill)	Mellor *Allan*	McLaughlin *Templeman*	Viney *Ford*	Brisley *McHale*	Aizlewood *Tucker*	Davey *Stroud*	Garwood* *Miller*	Laidlaw *Carter*	Showers *Rowland*	Bryant *Gilchrist**	Rogers *Williams*	Hemmerman *Kamara*
1:2	A	SWINDON 14/8	L 0-2 9,097 3	0-2	0-0	Mellor 75 (og), Carter 77 / Ref: K Salmon (Barnet) (Pompey lost 1-3 on aggregate)	Mellor *Allan*	McLaughlin *Templeman*	Viney *Ford*	Brisley *McHale*	Aizlewood *Tucker*	Davey *Stroud*	Garwood *Miller*	Laidlaw *Carter*	Showers *Rowland*	Bryant *Gilchrist**	Rogers *Williams*	Kamara

1:1 — Pompey have enough chances to have won, as five new faces are fielded, but have to settle for Rogers' (£25,000 from Plymouth) follow-up of Bryant's shot. Andy Rowland levels at once, but Hemmerman clips a post late on. Dickinson's Chief Executive's office is ready for his return.

1:2 — Mellor blunders big-time as he drops Miller's cross over the line and undoes a fine performance. Soon, it's all over as Carter's fine volley ends Pompey's hopes. Showers was earlier denied by Allan's reflex stop. Lathan, transfer-listed over a wage dispute, wants away as soon as he can.

FA Cup

				F-A	H-T	Scorers, Times, and Referees	1	2	3	4	5	6	7	8	9	10	11	12 sub used
1	H	NEWPORT 24/11	W 1-0 19,459 5	1-0	1-0	Brisley 4 / Ref: S Bates (Bristol)	Knight *Dowler*	Ellis *Walden*	Viney *Relsh*	Brisley *Bruton*	Aizlewood *Oakes*	Davey *Vaughan*	Garwood *Bailey*	Laidlaw *Lowndes*	Ashworth* *Tynan*	Bryant *Aldridge*	Rogers *Howey**	Hemmerman *Warriner*
2	A	WIMBLEDON 18/12	D 0-0 10,850 3:24	0-0	0-0	Ref: C Thomas (Porthcawl)	Knight *Goddard*	Ellis *Briley*	Viney *Jones*	Brisley *Galliers*	Aizlewood *Bowgett*	Davey *Downes*	Garwood* *Dziadulewicz*	Laidlaw *Parsons*	Hemmerman *Denny*	Bryant *Cork*	Rogers *Lewington*	Perrin
2R	H	WIMBLEDON 24/12	D 3-3 17,265 3:24	3-3	2-2	Gregory 3, Laidlaw 22, Bryant 53 / Lewington 35, Denny 43, 75 / Ref: C Thomas (Porthcawl)	Knight *Goddard*	Ellis *Briley*	Viney *Jones*	Brisley *Galliers**	Aizlewood *Bowgett*	Davey* *Downes*	Gregory *Dziadulewicz*	Laidlaw *Parsons*	Hemmerman *Denny*	Bryant *Cork*	Rogers *Lewington*	Perrin *Cunnigham*
2 RR	A	WIMBLEDON 5/1	W 1-0 7,484 3:24	1-0	1-0	Hemmerman 12 / Ref: B Hill (Wellingborough)	Mellor *Goddard*	McLaughlin *Briley*	Viney *Jones*	Brisley *Galliers*	Perrin *Bowgett*	Ellis *Cunningham*	Gregory *Perkins*	Laidlaw *Parsons*	Hemmerman *Denny*	Bryant *Cork*	Rogers *Lewington*	
3	H	MIDDLESBROUGH 9/1	D 1-1 31,743 1:10	1-1	0-1	Brisley 62 / Cochrane 13 / Ref: T Spencer (Salisbury)	Mellor *Platt*	McLaughlin *Craggs*	Viney *Johnson*	Brisley *Hedley*	Perrin *Ashcroft*	Ellis *McAndrew*	Gregory *Cochrane*	Laidlaw *Procter*	Hemmerman *Hodgson*	Bryant *Jankovic*	Rogers *Armstrong*	
3R	A	MIDDLESBROUGH 14/1	L 0-3 22,551 1:10	0-3	0-1	Cochrane 10, Johnson 62, Armstrong 63 / Ref: T Spencer (Salisbury)	Mellor *Platt*	McLaughlin *Craggs*	Viney *Johnson*	Brisley *Hedley*	Aizlewood *Ashcroft*	Ellis *McAndrew*	Gregory *Cochrane*	Laidlaw *Procter*	Hemmerman *Hodgson*	Bryant *Jankovic*	Rogers *Armstrong*	

1 — A 'disappointing' gate – 25,000 had been expected – witness a pulsating tie. Brisley heads in off a post after Bryant's dummy is sold to Bruton for the cross. Pompey's young Knight comes of age with a string of saves, the best a second-half point-blank stop to deny John Aldridge.

2 — Rain ruled out the original Saturday tie, but several thousand still travel up the A3 to Plough Lane. Pompey hold their 'superiors', but at a price. Garwood limps off with a hamstring strain and Aizlewood's booking takes him past 20 points and a ban. Perrin misses a sitter late on.

2R — An unprecedented Xmas Eve fixture serves up a thriller for the right to meet first division Middlesbrough. A see-saw affair is finally levelled by Denny, after Bryant's chip had swung the game back to Pompey. After extra-time Wimbledon win the toss, so it's Plough Lane once more.

2 RR — Pompey create an FA Cup 'shock' when Hemmerman springs the offside trap and calmly slots home. Despite bossing the game, Mellor has to save late on as McLaughlin's back-pass sells him short. The team must forego a mid-winter break in Malta, now Boro are coming to town.

3 — A linesman's flag denies Pompey a major scalp at the death, as Hemmerman guides home Rogers' cross, but is just offside. Earlier, Brisley turned in Aizlewood's knock-down to level Cochrane's close-range shot. On half-time, Brisley hit the bar and Ellis saw his shot hacked away.

3R — After travelling through heavy snow on the way to Teesside, Pompey find Ayresome Park is a bog. John Neal's Boro need no time to make class tell. Irish cap Cochrane opens, then Armstrong rounds Mellor for a second in sixty seconds, to book Boro's trip to Birmingham City.

	P	W	D	L	F	A	W	D	L	F	A	Pts
			Home					Away				
1 Huddersfield	46	16	5	2	61	18	11	7	5	40	30	66
2 Walsall	46	12	9	2	43	23	11	9	3	32	24	64
3 Newport	46	16	5	2	47	22	11	9	3	36	28	61
4 PORTSMOUTH	46	15	5	3	62	23	9	7	7	29	26	60
5 Bradford C	46	14	6	3	44	14	10	6	7	33	36	60
6 Wigan	46	13	5	5	42	26	8	8	7	34	35	55
7 Lincoln	46	14	8	1	43	12	8	9	10	21	30	53
8 Peterborough	46	14	3	6	39	22	7	7	9	19	25	52
9 Torquay	46	13	7	3	47	25	2	10	11	23	44	47
10 Aldershot	46	10	7	6	35	23	6	6	11	27	30	45
11 Bournemouth	46	8	9	6	32	25	5	9	9	20	26	44
12 Doncaster	46	11	6	6	37	27	4	8	11	25	36	44
13 Northampton	46	14	5	4	33	16	2	7	14	18	50	44
14 Scunthorpe	46	11	9	3	37	23	3	6	14	21	52	43
15 Tranmere	46	10	4	9	32	24	4	9	10	18	32	41
16 Stockport	46	9	6	8	30	31	5	5	13	18	41	40
17 York	46	9	6	8	35	34	2	4	17	30	48	39
18 Halifax	46	11	9	3	29	20	4	3	16	17	52	39
19 Hartlepool	46	10	7	6	36	28	4	10	13	23	36	38
20 Port Vale	46	8	6	9	34	24	6	13	13	22	46	36
21 Hereford	46	8	7	8	22	21	3	7	13	16	31	36
22 Darlington	46	7	11	5	33	26	2	6	15	17	48	35
23 Crewe	46	10	6	7	25	27	1	7	15	10	41	35
24 Rochdale	46	6	7	10	20	28	1	6	16	13	51	27
	1104	269	159	124	898	562	124	159	269	562	898	1104

Odds & ends

Double wins: (6) Hartlepool, Bournemouth, Rochdale, Huddersfield, Halifax, Northampton.
Double losses: (1) Newport.

Won from behind: (4) Wigan (a), Darlington (h), Hartlepool (h), Port Vale (a).
Lost from in front: (2) Tranmere (a), Newport (a).

High spots: Won promotion on the last day after a victory at Northampton, while Bradford lost at Peterborough.
Scored most goals at home in the league (62).
Unbeaten in last seven matches.
Scored six goals at home twice, against Scunthorpe and Northampton.
Beating promotion rivals Huddersfield 3-1 and Bradford 4-1 in successive matches in October.
Holding first division Middlesbrough to a 1-1 draw in the FA Cup in front of 31,000 at Fratton.
Club-record 91 goals for the season.

Low spots: Four-match winless run in March.
Losing to a late goal at home to promotion rivals Walsall in March.
Losing 1-4 at Tranmere in September.

Player of the Year: Joe Laidlaw.
Ever presents: (0).
Hat-tricks: (0).
Leading scorer: Colin Garwood, Joe Laidlaw (both 17).

Appearances and Goals

	Appearances						Goals			
	Lge	Sub	LC	Sub	FAC	Sub	Lge	LC	FAC	Tot
Aizlewood, Steve	34		2		5		2			2
Ashworth, Phil	3	1				1	4			4
Barnard, Leigh	4	1								
Brisley, Terry	41		2		6		12		3	15
Brown, Jimmy	5									
Bryant, Steve	44		2		6		2		1	3
Davey, Steve	29	4	2	2	3		1			1
Ellis, Peter	37	3			6					
Garner, Alan	3									
Garwood, Colin	23	1	2		3		17			17
Gregory, David	17	4			4		5		1	6
Hemmerman, Jeff	36	2	1		4	1	13		1	14
James, Keith	2									
Knight, Alan	8				3					
Laidlaw, Joe	45		2		6		16		1	17
Lathan, John	1									
McLaughlin, John	29		2		3					
Mellor, Peter	38		2		3					
Perrin, Steve	10	7	1		1	3	2			2
Purdie, Ian	4	1			1		1			1
Roberts, Trevor	1	1								
Rogers, Alan	42		2		6		9	1		10
Showers, Derek	5		2				1			1
Styles, Archie	28									
Todd, Kenny	1	2					1			1
Viney, Keith	16		2		6					
(own-goals)							4			4
26 players used	506	27	22	1	66	4	91	1	7	98

LEAGUE DIVISION 3

Manager: Frank Burrows

SEASON 1980-81

No	Venue	Opponent	Date	Res	F-A	H-T	Att	Pos	Pts	Scorers, Times, and Referees
1	A	BARNSLEY	16/8	W	2-1	1-0	10,253	2	2	Aizlewood 29, Rogers 50 / Parker 78 — Ref: J Lovatt (Crewe)
2	H	SWINDON	19/8	W	1-0	0-0	15,810	2 (22)	4	Laidlaw 60p — Ref: K Salmon (Barnet)
3	H	ROTHERHAM	23/8	W	3-1	1-1	14,767	2 (19)	6	Gregory 33, Showers 52, Bryant 63 / Gooding 34 — Ref: D Reeves (Uxbridge)
4	A	BLACKPOOL	30/8	W	2-0	1-0	8,352	1 (12)	8	Gregory 34, Showers 52 — Ref: C Seel (Carlisle)
5	H	BRENTFORD	6/9	L	0-2	0-0	16,971	2 (8)	8	Booker 48, Funnell 75 — Ref: B Stevens (Stonehouse)
6	A	WALSALL	13/9	L	0-2	0-1	5,738	7 (9)	8	Rees 40, Buckley 73 — Ref: M Dimblebee (Stevenage)
7	H	CHARLTON	16/9	W	1-0	0-0	12,796	5 (3)	10	Laidlaw 48 — Ref: D Hedges (Oxford)
8	A	HULL	20/9	L	1-2	1-1	4,613	7 (19)	10	Brisley 1 / Edwards 44, Swann 68 — Ref: K Redfern (Whitley Bay)
9	H	FULHAM	27/9	W	1-0	0-0	16,460	3 (10)	12	Gregory 61 — Ref: H King (Merthyr Tydfil)
10	H	CHESTERFIELD	4/10	W	1-0	1-0	14,953	6 (3)	14	Rogers 2 — Ref: C White (Harrow)
11	A	COLCHESTER	7/10	L	0-1	0-0	2,702	8 (17)	14	Lee 86 — Ref: A Ward (London)

Line-ups (1–11, and 12 sub used)

No	Team	1	2	3	4	5	6	7	8	9	10	11	12 sub used
1	Pompey	Mellor	McLaughlin	Viney	Brisley	Aizlewood	Garner	Gregory	Laidlaw	Tait	Bryant	Rogers	Reilly
1	*Barnsley*	*New*	*Cooper*	*Chambers*	*Glavin*	*Banks*	*McCarthy*	*Evans*	*Parker*	*Aylott**	*Lester*	*Downes*	*Hamilton*
2	Pompey	Mellor	McLaughlin	Viney	Brisley	Aizlewood	Garner	Gregory	Laidlaw	Tait	Bryant	Rogers	
2	*Swindon*	*Allan*	*Barrett*	*Peach*	*Kamara*	*Rollings*	*Walsh*	*Miller*	*Cockerill*	*Rowland*	*Mayes*	*Carter**	
3	Pompey	Mellor	McLaughlin	Viney*	Brisley	Aizlewood	Garner	Gregory	Laidlaw	Tait	Bryant	Rogers	Showers
3	*Rotherham*	*Brown*	*Forrestt*	*Breckin*	*Halom*	*Stancliffe*	*Mullen*	*Towner*	*Gooding*	*Moore*	*Seasman*	*Carr*	
4	Pompey	Mellor	McLaughlin	Viney	Brisley	Aizlewood	Garner	Gregory	Laidlaw	Showers*	Bryant	Rogers	Tait
4	*Blackpool*	*Harford*	*Gardner*	*Williams*	*Doyle*	*McEwan*	*Greenall*	*Morris*	*Hockaday*	*Fletcher**	*Noble*	*Welsh*	*MacDougall*
5	Pompey	Mellor	McLaughlin	Viney	Brisley*	Aizlewood	Garner	Gregory	Laidlaw	Showers	Bryant	Rogers	Ayrton
5	*Brentford*	*McCullough*	*Shrub*	*Hill*	*Salman*	*Kruse*	*Hurlock*	*Funnell*	*Silkman*	*Booker*	*Walker*	*Crown**	
6	Pompey	Mellor	McLaughlin	Viney	Brisley	Aizlewood	Garner	Gregory	Laidlaw	Showers*	Bryant	Rogers	Perrin
6	*Walsall*	*Freeman*	*Macten*	*Power*	*Serella*	*Baines*	*Hart*	*Penn*	*O'Kelly*	*Rees*	*Buckley*	*Caswell*	
7	Pompey	Mellor	McLaughlin	Viney	Brisley	Aizlewood	Garner	Gregory	Laidlaw	Perrin	Bryant	Rogers	Walker
7	*Charlton*	*Wood*	*Gritt*	*Warman*	*Shaw*	*Barry*	*Tydeman*	*Powell*	*Walsh*	*Hales*	*Smith*	*Robinson**	
8	Pompey	Mellor	McLaughlin	Viney	Brisley	Aizlewood	Garner	Gregory	Laidlaw	Perrin	Bryant*	Rogers	
8	*Hull*	*Norman*	*McNeil*	*Horswill*	*Booth*	*Roberts D*	*Roberts J*	*Nisbet*	*Swann*	*Edwards*	*Moss*	*Haigh*	
9	Pompey	Mellor	McLaughlin	Viney	Brisley	Aizlewood	Garner	Gregory	Laidlaw	Perrin	Bryant*	Rogers	Greenaway
9	*Fulham*	*Peyton*	*Peters**	*Strong*	*Beck*	*Brown*	*Gale*	*O'Driscoll*	*Davies*	*Mahoney*	*Wilson*	*Lock*	
10	Pompey	Mellor	McLaughlin	Viney	Brisley	Aizlewood	Garner	Gregory*	Laidlaw	Perrin	Bryant	Rogers	Showers
10	*Chesterfield*	*Turner*	*Tartt*	*O'Neill*	*Wilson*	*Green*	*Ridley*	*Birch*	*Moss*	*Bonnyman*	*Salmons*	*Walker*	
11	Pompey	Mellor	McLaughlin	Viney	Brisley	Aizlewood	Garner	Gregory	Laidlaw	Perrin	Bryant	Rogers	
11	*Colchester*	*Walker*	*Cook*	*Crouch*	*Leslie*	*Wignall*	*Packer*	*Hodge*	*Gough*	*Rowles*	*Lee*	*Allinson*	

Match reports

1 — Barnsley: Allan Clarke's side, short-priced for promotion, fail to build on a powerful opening. Once Aizlewood hooks in, when Rogers' shot is blocked, Pompey take over. Rogers dives full-length to nod in a cross from Tait. (£100,000 from Hull). Glavin hits the bar, but Parker reduces the lead.

2 — Swindon: Gregory is hauled down by Allan as he looks to pounce on a fumbled back-pass from Andy Rollings, who will join Pompey. Laidlaw makes no mistake from the spot, but Burrows' pours cold water on promotion talk: 'Don't be ridiculous!' he says. Piper quits after his knee fails to mend.

3 — Rotherham: Substitute Showers marks his return just seven minutes after replacing the crocked Viney. Eleven months after a knee injury, his sharp header, as Gregory's effort is saved, floors Millers. Gooding almost levels for a second time, but his shot hits the bar, then Showers sets up Bryant.

4 — Blackpool: Pompey's 10-1 promotion odds are looking generous as Alan Ball's Blackpool fail to score at home again. Ball pitches in 16-year-old defender Colin Greenall for his home debut, but his inexperience is punished, first by Gregory, then as Showers chip in from 25 yards.

5 — Brentford: Bees' boss Fred Callaghan was driving a cab and managing Woking this time last year. Now he is plotting the end of Pompey's winning start, as Bob Booker's shot just creeps over the line, and then as Funnell is left unmarked. Winger Crown stars, and will sign for Burrows next year.

6 — Walsall: Despite a better performance, Pompey lose again. Saddlers' player-boss Alan Buckley makes the first as his cross drifts over Viney's head for Rees to nod in. Paul Hart, who will play for Leeds, centres for Buckley to settle the issue. Pompey want to open a family section at Fratton.

7 — Charlton: Burrows brings in striker Perrin, but incessant rain and a gale make the game a farce. Valiants' boss Mike Bailey keeps faith with 17-year-old England Youth cap Paul Walsh up front, but he is kept quiet. Laidlaw heads home Rogers' inswinging corner to knock Charlton off the top.

8 — Hull: Mellor gaffes as he carries the ball outside his area while taking a drop-kick. He compounds the mistake by watching as Edwards bends home the free-kick, thinking it had been an indirect award for 'steps'. Ex-Wales boss Mike Smith sees Swann secure his strugglers their first win.

9 — Fulham: A promotion First Day Cover is to be issued, franked with this result against ex-PFC coach Bobby Campbell's team. The Match of the Day cameras capture the action as Gregory's low shot breaks the deadlock, but the hero is Mellor, who played for Fulham in the FA Cup final.

10 — Chesterfield: Deacon reveals Burrows has cash to spend, but Blackpool striker Paul Fletcher refuses a £20,000 move. Showers is also staying put, turning down Halifax. Rogers rolls home Bryant's pass, then Frank Barlow's 22-goal team are kept at bay, putting Pompey two points off the top.

11 — Colchester: Astonished Liverpool secretary Peter Robinson pledges every fan will get a ticket for the forthcoming Anfield League Cup-tie and reckons the Kop could be outnumbered. On this showing, it is Pompey's defence which will be over-run. Lee leaves it late, but his miscue creeps in.

No	V	Opponent	Date	Att			Res	Pts	FT	HT	Scorers	Ref
12	A	NEWPORT	11/10	7,003	19	11	L	14	1-2	0-2	Garner 64 / Oakes 44, 45	M Baker (Wolverhampton)
13	H	BURNLEY	18/10	13,459	5	7	W	16	4-2	3-1	Tait 2, Gregory 18p, Rogers 25, [Showers 89] / Scott 44, 76	B Daniels (Brentwood)
14	H	PLYMOUTH	21/10	15,655	2	7	L	16	1-3	1-1	Kemp 6 / Kemp 5, 52, Sims 82	R Lewis (Great Bookham)
15	A	OXFORD	25/10	6,217	17	8	W	18	2-1	0-1	Gregory 49, Barnard 78 / Cooke 7	L Robinson (Sutton Coldfield)
16	H	CARLISLE	1/11	13,913	22	10	W	20	2-1	1-0	Gregory 32, Showers 89 / Beardsley 90	J Deakin (Bedford)
17	H	COLCHESTER	4/11	10,895	17	7	W	22	2-1	1-1	Gregory 33, 69 / Lee 38	E Read (Bristol)
18	A	GILLINGHAM	8/11	6,623	17	5	W	24	1-0	0-0	Gregory 89	G Napthine (Loughborough)
19	A	SWINDON	11/11	8,164	23	5	W	26	2-0	0-0	Laidlaw 66, Showers 85	A Seville (Birmingham)
20	H	BARNSLEY	15/11	14,732	3	6	L	26	0-1	0-1	Riley 36	L Shapter (Newton Abbott)
21	H	CHESTER	29/11	10,515	15	7	W	28	2-0	1-0	Rogers 37, Tait 80	M Bidmead (Chessington)
22	A	SHEFFIELD UTD	6/12	12,158	9	7	L	28	0-1	0-0	Trusson 48	J Worrall (Warrington)
23	A	HUDDERSFIELD	20/12	10,869	5	7	D	29	0-0	0-0		P Richardson (Lincoln)

Line-ups (Portsmouth / Opponent)

12 Newport — Mellor, McLaughlin, Viney, Brisley*, Aizlewood, Garner, Gregory, Tait, Showers, Bryant, Rogers, Barnard / Kendall, Walden, Bailey, Davies, Oakes, Tynan*, Vaughan, Lowndes, Gwyther, Elsey, Moore, Aldridge

13 Burnley — Mellor, McLaughlin, Viney, Brisley, Aizlewood, Garner, Gregory, Tait, Showers, Bryant, Rogers / Stevenson, Laws, Wood, Scott, Overson, Dobson, Cassidy, Potts, Hamilton, Taylor, Cavener

14 Plymouth — Mellor, McLaughlin, Viney, Brisley*, Aizlewood, Garner, Gregory, Tait, Showers, Bryant, Rogers, Barnard / Crudgington, Harrison, James, Randell, Foster, Phill-Masters, Cooper, Kemp, Sims, Bason, Murphy

15 Oxford — Mellor, McLaughlin, Viney, Barnard, Aizlewood, Garner, Gregory, Tait, Showers, Bryant, Rogers / Burton, Griggs, Fogg, Jeffrey, Cooke, Shotton, Brock, Taylor, Berry, Jones*, Lythgoe, Foley

16 Carlisle — Mellor, McLaughlin, Viney, Barnard, Davey, Garner, Gregory, Tait, Showers, Bryant, Rogers / Swinburn, Hoolickin, Coady, MacDonald, Hamilton, Parker, Staniforth, Metcalfe, Bannon, Beardsley, McAuley*, Coughlin

17 Colchester — Mellor, McLaughlin, Viney, Laidlaw, Davey, Garner, Gregory, Tait, Showers, Bryant, Rogers / Walker, Cook, Longhorn, Leslie, Wignall, Packer, Evans, Cotton, Bremner, Lee, Allinson

18 Gillingham — Mellor, McLaughlin, Viney, Laidlaw, Aizlewood, Garner, Gregory, Tait, Showers, Bryant, Rogers / Hillyard, Sharpe, Ford, Overton, Weatherly, Crabbe, White, Nicholl, Bremner, Price, Hughes

19 Swindon — Mellor, McLaughlin, Viney, Laidlaw, Aizlewood, Garner, Gregory, Tait, Showers, Bryant, Rogers / Allan, Lewis, Peach, Kamara, Rollings, Stroud, Miller, Carter, Rowland, Mayes, Williams

20 Barnsley — Mellor, McLaughlin, Viney, Laidlaw, Aizlewood, Garner, Gregory, Tait, Showers, Bryant, Rogers / New, Joyce, Chambers, Cooper, Banks, McCarthy, Evans, Riley, Aylott, Lester, Downes

21 Chester — Mellor, McLaughlin, Viney, Barnard, Aizlewood, Garner, Hemmerman*†, Tait, Perrin, Bryant, Rogers, Davey / Millington, Jeffries, Walker, Storton, Cottam, Oakes, Fear, Phillips, Birch, Jones, Burns

22 Sheffield Utd — Mellor, Ellis, Viney, Doyle, Aizlewood, Davey, Hemmerman*†, Tait, Perrin, Bryant, Rogers, Barnard / Richardson, Ryan, Garner, Kenworthy, MacPhail, Trusson, Jones, Neville, Charles, Hatton, Butlin

23 Huddersfield — Mellor, McLaughlin, Viney, Doyle, Aizlewood, Garner, Gregory, Tait, **Rafferty**, Bryant, Rogers / Rankin, Brown, Robinson, Stanton, Sutton, Hanvey, Lillis, Kennedy, Kindon, Robins, Cowling

Match reports

12 — Mellor gets booked as Pompey bitterly dispute County's two-goal blast. First the linesman's flag for a Newport foul is reversed and from the free-kick Oakes powers home. Then, Oakes gets on the end of Vaughan's kick and it's an uphill struggle. Garner's consolation is his first goal.

13 — Pompey almost blow it as Brian Miller's side fight tooth and nail to save a nine-match unbeaten run. Scott sets up a tense finalé with a looping header, only for Showers to feed eagerly as Gregory's shot rebounds from Stevenson. Showers also earned the pen, when Overson shoved him.

14 — A week ago Kemp was at Fratton, in tandem with Garwood, for Piper's testimonial. Tonight, he squeezes home Bason's cross, for Argyle, who have lost just once in 12. Garner follows up Gregory's free-kick against a post immediately, but Kemp feeds off Bason again, then Sims seals it.

15 — Barnard, in for Brisley, arrives at the far post to head in Rogers' cross and completes a dramatic recovery, leaving Bill Asprey's side without a home win. Earlier Cooke's header had seemingly set U's up. Harland is spying at Anfield, while Pompey have sold 12,500 tickets for Tuesday.

16 — The Board back Deacon's plan to follow in Fulham's footsteps and stage Rugby League at Fratton next season, but Sunday soccer is ruled out. Pompey suffer a cup hangover, but Showers settles it. However, the last word goes to Peter Beardsley, who weaves through from the restart.

17 — Pompey's eighth league win at home is secured by Gregory, who is now in double figures for the season. He heads in Rogers' free-kick, then converts Showers' cross. In between, Lee rounds Mellor to level, but Kevin Bremner, United's record £20,000 signing, has a quiet game.

18 — Just as it seems 0-0 draws can be entertaining, Rogers crosses and Gregory rakes a shot into Hillyard's bottom corner. Westwood is unlucky to hit a post and Gills' unbeaten home record ends.

19 — Pompey's first double of the season is a fortunate affair. Caretaker Danny Williams' Swindon bombard Mellor's goal and he makes two crucial saves from old-boy Chris Kamara. The vital goals come from Laidlaw and Showers, who will both move to Hereford within a fortnight.

20 — Shades of the old Leeds from Norman Hunter's Tykes, as they grind out a result. Riley is at the far post to convert Aylott's cross, but the wind spoils the division's game of the day. New excels to turn away a Gregory effort. Swindon's bid to poach former-coach Burrows is rebuffed.

21 — Pompey's fans get to vote on Deacon's rugby league idea today: the answer is a resounding no, and the idea is shelved. Gregory is still out, a fortnight after a training collision saw him foul onto the Fratton terraces. Rogers' corner is helped in by Storton, then the grafting Tait heads in.

22 — Hemmerman should be celebrating his first goal after his return from a knee injury, but instead he holds his head as he skies over an open goal after Perrin robbed Richardson by the corner flag. Doyle (£70,000 from Blackpool) makes a solid debut, but it's Trusson's volley that wins it.

23 — Pools punters will start perming Pompey again, as they draw for the first time. Striker Rafferty (£100,000 from Newcastle) debuts, but Town's Austin (£120,000 from Mansfield) is only a sub. Mellor suffers vile abuse from home fans. Purdie's contract is ended by mutual consent.

LEAGUE DIVISION 3 — Manager: Frank Burrows — SEASON 1980-81

No	Date		Att	Pos	Pt	F-A	H-T	Scorers, Times, and Referees	1	2	3	4	5	6	7	8	9	10	11	12 sub used
24	H 26/12	READING	17,412	12	30	0-0	0-0	Ref: A Glasson (Salisbury)	Mellor / Death	McLaughlin / Henderson	Viney / Lewis	Doyle / Bowman	Aizlewood / Hicks	Davey / Hetzke	Gregory / Earles	Tait / Kearney	Rafferty / Webb	Bryant / Sanchez	Rogers / Beavon	
25	A 27/12	MILLWALL	8,422	19	31	0-0	0-0	Ref: J Hunting (Leicester)	Mellor / Jackson	McLaughlin / Roberts	Viney / Gregory	Doyle / Martin	Aizlewood / Kitchener	Davey / Blyth	Gregory / Kinsella	Tait / Mitchell	Rafferty / McKenna*	Bryant / Bartley	Rogers / Massey	Harrix
26	H 10/1	SHEFFIELD UTD	14,321	11	33	1-0	1-0	Gregory 37p / Ref: T Bune (Billingshurst)	Mellor / Conroy	McLaughlin / Ryan	Viney / Garner	Doyle / Houston	Aizlewood / MacPhail	Davey / Trusson	Gregory / Charles	Tait / Tibbott	Perrin / Butlin	Bryant / Hatton	Rogers / Peters	
27	A 14/1	EXETER	3,722	8	33	0-2	0-1	Pearson 2, Pullar 81 / Ref: V Callow (Solihull)	Mellor / Bond	McLaughlin / Rogers M	Viney / Hatch	Doyle / Forbes	Aizlewood / Roberts L	Davey / Roberts P	Gregory / Pearson	Tait / Rogers P	Rafferty / Kellow	Bryant* / Delve	Rogers / Pullar	Hemmerman
28	H 24/1	BLACKPOOL	13,265	22	34	3-3	2-0	Hemmerman 8, Rafferty 44, Tait 80 / Hackaday 59, Thompson 69, Morris 76 Hesford / Ref: A Gunn (Burgess Hill)	Mellor / Hesford	McLaughlin / Gardner	Viney / Pashley	Doyle / Ball	Aizlewood* / Thompson	Ellis / Ashurst	Hemmerman / Morgan	Tait / Hackaday	Rafferty / Harrison	Bryant / Morris	Rogers / Simmonite*	Gregory / Entwhistle
29	A 27/1	BURNLEY	6,683	6	36	3-1	1-1	Tait 42, Bryant 71, Hemmerman 83 / Hamilton 6 / Ref: A Hamil (Wolverhampton)	Mellor / O'Rourke	McLaughlin / Laws	Viney / Holt	Doyle / Wood	Ellis / Radaway	Davey / Dobson	Hemmerman / Young	Tait / Potts	Rafferty / Hamilton	Bryant / Taylor	Rogers / Cavener	
30	A 31/1	ROTHERHAM	7,588	3	36	0-3	0-1	Seasman 3, 48, Towner 83 / Ref: A Porter (Bolton)	Mellor / Mountford	McLaughlin / Forrest	Viney / Breckin	Doyle / Rhodes	Aizlewood / Stancliffe	Ellis / Mullen	Hemmerman / Towner	Tait* / Seasman	Rafferty / Moore	Bryant* / Fern	Rogers / Henson	Davey
31	H 7/2	WALSALL	11,921	14	38	2-0	1-0	Doyle 29p, Tait 48 / Ref: C Maskell (Cambridge)	Mellor / Green	McLaughlin* / Harrison	Viney / Mower	Doyle / Serella	Aizlewood / Baines	Ellis / Hart	Hemmerman / Waddington S	Tait / Caswell	Rafferty / Smith*	Bryant / Buckley	Rogers / Waddington P	Penn
32	H 10/2	EXETER	12,743	9	40	5-0	1-0	Bryant 11, Tait 62, 64, 65, Rafferty 69 / Ref: M Taylor (Deal)	Knight / Main	Ellis / Rogers M	Viney / Sparrow	Doyle / Forbes	Aizlewood / Giles	Davey / Roberts P	Hemmerman / Pearson	Tait / Rogers P	Rafferty / Kellow*	Bryant / Prince	Rogers / Hatch	Roberts L
33	A 14/2	BRENTFORD	10,160	11	41	2-2	1-2	Rafferty 17, 87 / Tucker 15p, Roberts 36 / Ref: J Bray (Hinckley)	Mellor / McKellar	Ellis / Tucker	Viney / Hill	Doyle / McNichol	Aizlewood / Kruse	Davey / Hurlock	Hemmerman / Shrub	Tait / Frost	Rafferty / Johnson	Bryant* / Harris	Rogers / Wilson	Gregory
34	A 21/2	FULHAM	9,921	17	41	0-3	0-1	Davies 45, Doyle 64 (og), Lock 75p / Ref: J Warner (Wednesbury)	Mellor / Stannard	Ellis / Strong	Viney / Lock	Doyle / Beck	Aizlewood / Brown	Davey* / Gale	Hemmerman / Davies	Tait / Clement*	Rafferty / Mahoney	Bryant / Wilson	Rogers / Lewington	Gregory / Peters

Match reports

24 — READING: Royals' Death – one of the shortest keepers in the league at 5' 8" – walks tall, despite playing with two cracked ribs. His acrobatics deny both Gregory and Tait. Ex-apprentice Graham Roberts, released in 77, is now Spurs' 'best prospect in years,' according to boss Keith Burkinshaw.

25 — MILLWALL: Like proverbial London buses, you don't get one for ages then three (0-0 draws, that is) turn up at once. The league's senior pro, Lions' keeper John Jackson (38), doesn't have to make a save until Viney's feeble late shot. New player-boss Peter Anderson's young team should have won.

26 — SHEFFIELD UTD: A gentle nudge on Gregory by John MacPhail earns a penalty and the first win since 29 Nov. Blades include World Cup hero and coach Martin Peters (37). In the second half, Aizlewood fouls Hatton, but Mellor saves Ryan's spot-kick. United will go from mid-table to the drop by April.

27 — EXETER: Large numbers of visiting fans mean the referee decides to play, but rain has left the pitch a swamp. In a game re-arranged due to City's FA Cup run, ex-Fratton favourite Dave Pullar makes the opener, then scores. Brisley has turned down Cherries, saying it's London-only for him.

28 — BLACKPOOL: New captain McLaughlin sees a 2-0 lead tossed away, but Tait earns a point with a tap-in after good work by Rogers. Lowly Pool are prompted by player-boss Ball and ex-Man U winger Morgan, whose corner sparked the comeback. Ball's penalty hits a post to the Fratton End's delight.

29 — BURNLEY: Superstitious Hemmerman wears the same clothes as Saturday, after netting his first since April. The charm clearly works as his header seals it. Pompey go ahead after O'Rourke's reckless charge; Rogers beats him to the ball and crosses for Bryant's miscue to screw into the top corner.

30 — ROTHERHAM: Millers, fresh from five days in Spain, put Pompey's promotion hopes in the shade, but the margin is flattering. Seasman pounces early in each half, first after McLaughlin's mistake, then he stays onside and nods in Breckin's centre. Rotherham haven't lost in 16 and will be champions.

31 — WALSALL: Doyle breaks the deadlock with his goal as Tait is hauled down by Caswell in the box after a 35-yard run. Former-Oxford star Tait then seals the points with a deliberate header from Rogers' cross. Full-back Styles must rest his Achilles until April. Defender James has been released.

32 — EXETER: Tait's five-minute hat-trick shatters City, who will draw with Division Two Newcastle away in the FA Cup fifth round on Saturday. Two powerful drives from outside the box and a header complete the feat. Bryant's header started the rout, finished by Rafferty's shot-on-the-turn.

33 — BRENTFORD: Rafferty nets the first away goal at Griffin Park since Boxing Day, then stuns Bees by pulling away to angle Davey's pass wide of a hesitant keeper. Ellis had handled for the penalty, then Mellor made a hash of Roberts' header. Tuesday's hero Tait faces suspension after a booking.

34 — FULHAM: Mellor's Craven Cottage return is a nightmare. Davies latches onto a long-ball deep into first-half injury-time, then Doyle's interception only diverts in. Davies' wriggle into the box ends over a Pompey leg and Lock converts. Mellor has a fractured cheek after clashing heads with Tait.

Season results (matches 35–46)

No	Venue	Date	Opponent	Att	Pos	Opp	Pts	Res	Score	Scorers	Referee
35	H	28/2	HULL	13,596	4	24	43	W	2-1	Rafferty 28, Doyle 74p / Mutrie 35	D Hutchinson (Bourn)
36	A	7/3	CHESTERFIELD	6,895	5	6	43	L	0-3	Salmons 8, Simpson 55, Birch 67	R Chadwick (Darwen)
37	H	14/3	NEWPORT	13,208	4	16	44	D	0-0	—	D Vickers (Ilford)
38	A	21/3	PLYMOUTH	6,042	6	8	44	L	0-1	Murphy 7	E Read (Bristol)
39	H	29/3	OXFORD	12,243	6	16	45	D	1-1	Gregory / Cassells 10	L Burden (Corfe Mullen)
40	A	4/4	CARLISLE	4,429	6	15	46	D	0-0	—	A Dobson (Blackburn)
41	H	11/4	GILLINGHAM	9,172	6	17	47	D	0-0	—	M Bidmead (Chessington)
42	A	14/4	CHARLTON	8,863	5	2	49	W	2-1	Croft 58, Rafferty 65 / Warman 74	A Grey (Great Yarmouth)
43	H	18/4	MILLWALL	13,115	5	12	51	W	2-1	Doyle 9p, Gregory 64 / Horrix 6	S Bates (Bristol)
44	A	20/4	READING	7,061	5	11	51	L	1-2	Perrin 82 / Dixon 35, Hetzke 43	A Ward (London)
45	H	25/4	HUDDERSFIELD	10,218	6	4	51	L	1-2	Doyle 27p / Austin 1, 83	R Challis (Tonbridge)
46	A	2/5	CHESTER	2,153	5	19	53	W	1-0	Gregory 80	H King (Merthyr Tydfil)

Home 13,571 Away 7,158 Average 13,571

Line-ups and reports

35 — Hull
Pompey: Mellor, McLaughlin, Viney, Doyle, Aizlewood, Ellis, Hemmerman, Barnard, Rafferty, Bryant*, Rogers, Bartlett
Hull: Davies, Hoolickin, Booth, Richards, Roberts G, Roberts D, Marwood, McLaren, Edwards, Mutrie, Deacy
Tait's ban means he misses the clash with his old club. Hull are bottom, but unbeaten in four. That record looks over when Rafferty races clear to score, but Mutrie trundles an equaliser and Doyle only settles it after Deacy's silly handball. Marwood then sees one ruled out for offside.

36 — Chesterfield
Pompey: Mellor, McLaughlin, Viney*, Doyle, Aizlewood, Garner, Hemmerman, Barnard, Rafferty, Bryant, Rogers, Ellis
Chesterfield: Turner, Stirk, O'Neill, Wilson, Green, Ridley, Birch, Simpson, Bonnyman, Salmons, Walker
Hull defender Croft is discussing a free transfer and could surely do better. First, a poor clearance falls to Salmons; then Doyle's wayward pass sets up the second. Birch heads past a static defence, but the pitch is a bog, despite having had a new chemical treatment to clear water.

37 — Newport
Pompey: Mellor, McLaughlin, Viney, Doyle, Aizlewood, Ellis, Gregory, Tait, Rafferty, Barnard, Rogers, Bishop
Newport: Plumley, Walden, Relish, Davies, Oakes, Tynan*, Vaughan, Lowndes, Gwyther, Elsey, Moore
County's smothering tactics are a dry-run for their CWC clash with East Germans Carl Zeiss Jena, where a 0-0 will see them into the semi-finals. Alas, Jena get one, but Pompey never look like scoring and it is Davies' 50-yard back-pass that goes closest, bouncing just over the bar.

38 — Plymouth
Pompey: Mellor, McLaughlin, Viney, Doyle, Aizlewood, Ellis, Gregory, Tait, Rafferty, Barnard, Rogers*, Perrin
Plymouth: Crudgington, Nisbet, Harrison, Hodges, Foster, Phill-Masters, Cooper*, Kemp, Sims, Peachey, Murphy, Graves
Burrows has to settle for just signing Croft until May, as a deadline-day move for Brighton's Peter O'Sullivan founders on money. Murphy's cheeky back-heel illuminates a drab game, played in foul weather. The wind holds things up when it rips cladding from one of the stands.

39 — Oxford
Pompey: Mellor, McLaughlin, Viney, Doyle, Aizlewood, Ellis, Gregory, Tait, Rafferty, Barnard, Rogers*, Ayrton*
Oxford: Burton, Fogg, Jeffrey, Briggs, Shotton, Jones, Foley, Smithers, Cassells, Berry*, Seacole
Deacon's Sunday soccer trial is foiled by driving rain, which keeps the gate low. Ironically, Saturday had been glorious. A tame Gregory shot beats Burton as he slips, but Oxford always look the better side. Keith Cassells flicks in, then Mellor dives to keep out a second-half penalty.

40 — Carlisle
Pompey: Mellor, McLaughlin, Viney, Doyle, Croft, Garner, Gregory, Tait, Rafferty, Barnard, Rogers
Carlisle: Swinburne, Coady, Watson, Hamilton, Houghton, Parker, Haigh, Coughlin, Robson, Beardsley, Staniforth
Pompey's hopes are fading after this stalemate, but Burrows sees an improvement and praises debut-making Croft's efforts in a re-jigged back line. Rookie keeper Knight reveals his frustration at being kept out by Mellor. Knight's ex-England Youth rival Lukic is in Leeds' first team.

41 — Gillingham
Pompey: Mellor, McLaughlin, Viney, Doyle, Croft, Garner, Gregory*, Tait, Rafferty, Barnard, Rogers, Bartlett
Gillingham: Hillyard, Young, Ford, Bruce, Overton, Crabbe, Nicholl, Duncan, Price, Lee, White
Pompey look short of quality as struggling Gills grind out a point and a draw. The only chance of the game sees Tait's deflected first-half header miraculously turned away by Ron Hillyard. Styles' career is over, but he will become Youth coach.

42 — Charlton
Pompey: Mellor, McLaughlin, Bryant, Doyle, Aizlewood, Croft, Gregory, Tait, Rafferty, Barnard, Rogers
Charlton: Johns, Gritt*, Warman, Madden, Berry, Tydeman, Powell, Walsh, Hales, Naylor, Robinson, Walker
Promotion dreams are revived, after a run of just one goal in six games. Defender Croft shows the way, rising to nod in a corner, then Doyle's pass releases Rafferty. Warman's reply is not enough for Charlton, whose third defeat in a row leaves their Division Two hopes on a knife-edge.

43 — Millwall
Pompey: Mellor, McLaughlin, Bryant, Doyle, Aizlewood, Croft, Gregory, Tait, Rafferty, Barnard, Rogers
Millwall: Gleasure, Martin, Roberts, Chatterton, Tagg, Kitchener, Dibble, Anderson*, Horrix, Mitchell, Bartley, Hayes
Police separate brawling fans as the game is held up three times. Horrix's spectacular shot gives Lions the lead, only for Tagg's trip on Rogers to allow Doyle the chance to level. Gregory's 25-yard stunner wins it. Burrows is talking to Chelsea's Colin Viljoen about a summer transfer.

44 — Reading
Pompey: Mellor, McLaughlin, Bryant, Doyle, Aizlewood, Croft, Gregory, Tait*, Rafferty, Barnard, Rogers, Perrin
Reading: Fearon, Williams, Lewis, Bowman, Wood, Hetzke, Joslyn, Kearney, Heal, Dixon, Sanchez
Hopes of promotion have gone, as Bowman first sets up Dixon, who will play for England, then his corner is headed in by Hetzke. Maurice Evans' Royals conquer their home 'fear' (four without a win). Aizlewood and Croft are Pompey's sixth central defensive pairing of the season.

45 — Huddersfield
Pompey: Mellor, McLaughlin, Bryant, Doyle, Aizlewood, Croft, Gregory, Tait, Rafferty, Hemmerman, Barnard, Rogers
Huddersfield: Freeman, Brown, Purdie, Kennedy, Sutton, Hanvey, Lillis, Austin, Kindon, Robins, Cowling
Town's Terry Austin keeps their promotion bandwagon on track with early and late goals, but the striker missed a host of other chances. Mick Kennedy, later to play for Pompey, makes the winner. Viney is player of the year and the Board announce Lions' fans are banned from Fratton.

46 — Chester
Pompey: Mellor, McLaughlin, Bryant, Doyle, Aizlewood, Ellis, Gregory, Tait, Rafferty, Barnard, Rogers
Chester: Millington, Needham, Raynor, Zelem, Cottam, Oakes, Fear, Jones, Howatt, Cooke, Ludlam
Burrows bids farewell to Croft and Ellis replaces him. Gregory gets his 13th goal, his header ripping into the net from Rafferty's cross, after good work by Doyle, but it is end-of-season stuff. It is revealed that gates are down by 50,000 on last season: an operating loss is anticipated.

LEAGUE DIVISION 3 (CUP-TIES) Manager: Frank Burrows SEASON 1980-81

League Cup

Match	F-A	H-T	Scorers, Times, and Referees	1	2	3	4	5	6	7	8	9	10	11	12 sub used
1:1 A PLYMOUTH 9/8 — 7,036 — W 1-0	1-0	1-0	Laidlaw 42 — Ref: S Bates (Bristol)	Mellor	McLaughlin	Viney	Brisley	Aizlewood	Garner	Gregory	Laidlaw	Tait	Barnard	Rogers	
				Crudgington	*James*	*McNeil*	*Randall*	*Foster*	*Phil-Masters Hodges*	*Kemp*	*Sims*	*Bason*	*Johnson**	*Graves*	

Some fans, held up in the holiday traffic, only arrive in time to see Laidlaw thump home Brisley's free-kick. Aizlewood and Garner provide the stability missing in the run-in last April and Kemp is kept quiet. Laidlaw is captain again, despite being fined and suspended during pre-season.

Match	F-A	H-T	Scorers, Times, and Referees	1	2	3	4	5	6	7	8	9	10	11	12 sub used
1:2 H PLYMOUTH 12/8 — 11,997 — W 2-1	2-1	1-1	Gregory 20, Rogers 82 / *Kemp 6* — Ref: C Downey (Hounslow) (Pompey won 3-1 on aggregate)	Mellor	McLaughlin	Viney	Brisley	Aizlewood	Garner	Gregory	Laidlaw	Tait	Barnard	Rogers	
				Crudgington	*James*	*Harrison*	*Randall*	*Foster*	*Phil-Masters Hodges*	*Kemp*	*Sims*	*Bason**	*Murphy*	*Graves*	

Ex-Fratton idol Kemp escapes his shackles almost at once to level things, but ex-Argyle winger Rogers breaks his old club's hearts by making one for Gregory, then celebrates as his corner squeezes in at the near post. Pompey's red numbers on blue shirts are unreadable and are scrapped.

Match	F-A	H-T	Scorers, Times, and Referees	1	2	3	4	5	6	7	8	9	10	11	12 sub used
2:1 A OLDHAM 26/8 — 5,251 2:6 — L 2-3	2-3	0-2	Garner 57, Laidlaw 87p / *Keagan 13, Kowenicki 44, Stainrod 78* — Ref: M Heath (Stoke)	Mellor	McLaughlin	Bryant	Brisley	Aizlewood	Garner	Gregory	Laidlaw	Showers	Tait	Rogers	
				McDonnell	*Hoolickin*	*Blair*	*Kowenicki*	*Clements*	*Hurst*	*Wylde*	*Futcher*	*Stainrod*	*Keagan*	*Atkinson*	

Hoolickin's needless handball with time running out will ultimately prove costly, but Pompey match their second division hosts for most of the game. Ged Keegan and Pole Kowenicki puts Latics on easy street, but Garner nods in from a corner. Stainrod's goal is against the run of play.

Match	F-A	H-T	Scorers, Times, and Referees	1	2	3	4	5	6	7	8	9	10	11	12 sub used
2:2 H OLDHAM 2/9 — 18,548 2:10 — W 1-0	1-0	1-0	Laidlaw 12 — Ref: D Vickers (Ilford) (Pompey won on away goals)	Mellor	McLaughlin	Viney	Brisley	Aizlewood	Garner	Gregory	Laidlaw	Showers	Bryant	Rogers	
				McDonnell	*Hoolickin*	*Blair*	*Kowenicki**	*Clements*	*Hurst*	*Wylde*	*Futcher*	*Stainrod*	*Keagan*	*Atkinson*	*Heaton*

Oldham boss Jimmy Frizzell sums up the tie: 'We're out of the Cup because of Peter Mellor and 'THAT penalty.' Once Laidlaw's near-post header squeaks in Pompey are under the cosh, but their blond keeper excels. One plunge to scoop out Wylde's header is in the Banks' class.

Match	F-A	H-T	Scorers, Times, and Referees	1	2	3	4	5	6	7	8	9	10	11	12 sub used
3 A BRISTOL ROV 23/9 — 6,882 2:21 — D 0-0 (at Ashton Gate)	0-0	0-0	Ref: D Civil (Birmingham)	Mellor	McLaughlin	Viney	Brisley	Aizlewood	Garner	Gregory	Laidlaw	Perrin	Bryant	Rogers	
				Thomas	*Jones*	*Bater*	*McCaffery*	*Mabbutt*	*Hughes*	*Pulis*	*Williams*	*Barrowclough Penney**	*Lee*	*Bates*	

Eastville has been ravaged by fire, so a large following travels to Ashton Gate. Mellor makes a couple of smart saves, but it ends a stalemate. Pompey are galvanised by Rovers' boss Terry Cooper's remarks at the draw: 'Magic, we look forward to meeting the big-boys in the last 16.'

Match	F-A	H-T	Scorers, Times, and Referees	1	2	3	4	5	6	7	8	9	10	11	12 sub used
3R H BRISTOL ROV 30/9 — 18,965 2:21 — W 2-0	2-0	1-0	Gregory 9, Perrin 90 — Ref: L Burden (Corfe Mullen)	Mellor	McLaughlin	Viney	Brisley	Aizlewood	Garner	Gregory	Laidlaw	Perrin	Bryant	Rogers	
				Thomas	*Jones*	*Bater*	*Barrowclough Mabbutt*	*Hughes*	*Pulis*	*Williams D*	*Bates*	*Penney*	*Lee*		

With a trip to Anfield the prize, Pompey never look in danger of letting it slip, except when Garner is forced to hack Chic Bates' shot from the line. Bryant crosses for Gregory to power home, then McLaughlin's cross is nodded in by Perrin and the ticket-rush of all-time is under way.

Match	F-A	H-T	Scorers, Times, and Referees	1	2	3	4	5	6	7	8	9	10	11	12 sub used
4 A LIVERPOOL 28/10 — 32,021 1:3 — L 1-4	1-4	1-2	Kennedy A 36 (og) / *Dalglish 22, Johnson 37, 80, [Souness 90]* — Ref: G Owen (Anglesey)	Mellor	McLaughlin	Viney	Barnard	Davey	Garner	Gregory*	Tait	Showers	Bryant	Rogers	Laidlaw
				Clemence	*Neal*	*Irwin*	*Hansen*	*Kennedy A*	*Lee*	*McDermott*	*Souness*	*Kennedy R*	*Dalglish*	*Johnson*	

Pompey sell 12,500 tickets, but the following is even higher, as pockets of jubilation break out all over Anfield when Alan Kennedy can only scuff Rogers' cross past Clemence. The champions steady the ship by restoring their lead at once, but Johnson looks offside as he seals it.

FA Cup

Match	F-A	H-T	Scorers, Times, and Referees	1	2	3	4	5	6	7	8	9	10	11	12 sub used
1 A COLCHESTER 22/11 — 5,387 15 — L 0-3	0-3	0-1	*Lee 26, Allinson 81, Bremner 87* — Ref: C Maskell (Cambridge)	Mellor	McLaughlin	Viney	Barnard	Aizlewood	Garner	Perrin	Tait	Showers	Bryant	Rogers	
				Walker	*Cook*	*Rowles*	*Leslie*	*Wignall*	*Packer*	*Hodge*	*Foley*	*Bremner*	*Lee*	*Allinson*	

United earn their second home win over Pompey in six weeks and avenge their Fratton loss earlier this month. Mike Walker has only one shot to save and the result is rarely in doubt once Lee pounces on Mellor's parry. Burrows leaves out Laidlaw and he will join Hereford next week.

			Home					Away					
		P	W	D	L	F	A	W	D	L	F	A	Pts
1	Rotherham	46	17	6	0	43	8	7	7	9	19	24	61
2	Barnsley	46	15	5	3	46	19	6	12	5	26	26	59
3	Charlton	46	14	6	3	36	17	11	3	9	27	27	59
4	Huddersfield	46	14	6	3	40	11	7	8	8	31	29	56
5	Chesterfield	46	17	4	2	42	16	6	6	11	30	32	56
6	PORTSMOUTH	46	14	5	4	35	19	8	4	11	20	28	53
7	Plymouth	46	14	5	4	35	18	6	4	9	21	26	52
8	Burnley	46	13	5	5	37	21	5	9	9	23	27	50
9	Brentford	46	7	9	7	30	25	7	10	6	22	24	47
10	Reading	46	13	5	5	39	22	5	5	13	23	40	46
11	Exeter	46	9	9	5	36	30	7	4	12	26	36	45
12	Newport	46	11	6	6	38	22	4	7	12	26	39	43
13	Fulham	46	8	7	8	28	29	7	6	10	29	35	43
14	Oxford	46	7	8	8	20	24	6	9	8	19	23	43
15	Gillingham	46	8	8	6	23	19	3	10	10	25	39	42
16	Millwall	46	10	9	4	30	21	4	5	14	13	39	42
17	Swindon	46	10	6	7	35	27	3	9	11	16	29	41
18	Chester	46	11	5	7	25	17	4	6	13	13	31	41
19	Carlisle	46	8	9	6	32	29	6	4	13	24	41	41
20	Walsall	46	8	9	6	43	43	5	6	12	16	31	41
21	Sheffield Utd	46	12	6	5	38	20	2	6	15	27	43	40
22	Colchester	46	12	7	4	35	22	2	4	17	10	43	39
23	Blackpool	46	5	9	9	19	28	4	5	14	26	47	32
24	Hull	46	7	8	8	23	22	1	8	14	17	49	32
		1104	265	162	125	808	529	125	162	265	529	808	1104

Odds & ends

Double wins: (4) Swindon, Charlton, Burnley, Chester.
Double losses: (1) Plymouth.

Won from behind: (3) Oxford (a), Burnley (a), Millwall (h).
Lost from in front: (1) Hull (a).

High spots: Taking 12,500 fans to Liverpool in the League Cup.
Five consecutive league wins in October-November.
Mick Tait's five-minute hat-trick against Exeter in February.
Four-match winning start in the league.

Low spots: First round FA Cup exit at Colchester (0-3).
One goal and just four points in six games costs promotion in March and April.
Drawing 3-3 at home to relegated Blackpool after leading 3-1.

Player of the Year: Keith Viney.
Ever Presents: (0).
Hat-tricks: Mick Tait (1).
Top Scorer: Dave Gregory (15).

	Appearances						Goals		
	Lge	Sub	LC	Sub	FAC	Sub	Lge	LCFAC	Tot
Aizlewood, Steve	41		6		1		1		1
Ayrton, Neil	1	1							
Barnard, Leigh	14	3	3		1		1		1
Bartlett, Kevin		2							
Brisley, Terry	14		6				1		1
Bryant, Steve	42		5				3		3
Croft, Stuart	6				1		1		1
Davey, Steve	12	2	1						
Doyle, Bobby	25						4		4
Ellis, Peter	14	1							
Garner, Alan	23		7				2	1	3
Gregory, David	35	4	7				13	2	15
Hemmerman, Jeff	12	2					2		2
Knight, Alan	1								
Laidlaw, Joe	15		6	1			3	3	6
McLaughlin, John	42		7		1				
Mellor, Peter	45		7		1				
Perrin, Steve	8	3	2		1		1	1	2
Rafferty, Billy	22		6				6		6
Rogers, Alan	45		7		1		4	1	5
Showers, Derek	12	2	3		1		5		5
Tait, Mick	36	2	4		1		8		8
Viney, Keith	41		6					1	1
(own-goals)									1
23 players used	506	22	77	1	11		55	9	64

LEAGUE DIVISION 3

Manager: Burrows → Campbell — SEASON 1981-82

No	Date	Att	Pos	Pt	F-A	H-T	Scorers, Times, and Referees	1	2	3	4	5	6	7	8	9	10	11	12 sub used
1	H LINCOLN 29/8	10,698		1	D 1-1	0-0	Rafferty 85 / Cammack 57 / Ref: J Moules (Ongar)	Knight *Felgate*	McLaughlin *Thompson*	Viney *McVay*	Kamara *Gilbert*	Aizlewood *Peake*	**Rollings** *Carr*	Gregory *Shipley*	Doyle* *Cockerill*	Rafferty *Hobson*	**Berry** *Cunningham*	Rogers *Cammack*	Hemmerman
2	A PRESTON 5/9	6,112	20	1	L 0-1	0-1	Bruce 40 / Ref: G Tyson (Sunderland)	Knight *Litchfield*	McLaughlin *Coleman*	Viney *Westwell*	Kamara *Clark*	Aizlewood *O'Riordan*	Rollings* *Blackley*	Gregory *Houston**	Doyle *Doyle*	Rafferty *McGhee*	Berry *Bruce*	Rogers *Naughton*	Tait *Walsh*
3	H BRENTFORD 12/9	10,364	20	2	D 2-2	0-0	Rafferty 60, Hemmerman 90 / Crown 58, Booker 89 / Ref: S Bates (Bristol)	Knight *McKellar*	McLaughlin *Tucker*	Viney *Hill*	Kamara *Salman*	Aizlewood *Whitehead*	Ellis *Hurlock*	Hemmerman *Walker*	Doyle *Roberts*	Rafferty *Booker*	Berry* *Harris*	Tait *Crown*	Rogers
4	A SOUTHEND 19/9	4,355	22	2	L 0-2	0-1	Spence 2, Gray 78 / Ref: M Dimblebee (Stevenage)	Knight *Keeley*	McLaughlin *Stead*	Viney *Yates*	Kamara *Pountney*	Aizlewood *Moody*	Ellis* *Cusack*	Hemmerman *Gray*	Doyle *Otulakowski*	Rafferty *Spence*	Berry *Mercer*	Tait *Nelson*	Barnard
5	A OXFORD 23/9	4,750	18	5	W 2-0	1-0	Doyle 43p, Rafferty 81 / Ref: A Ward (London)	Knight *Burton*	McLaughlin *Doyle*	Viney *Fogg*	Kamara *Jeffery**	Aizlewood *Briggs*	Rollings* *Shotton*	Hemmerman *Jones*	Doyle *Kearns*	Rafferty *Cassells*	Berry *Thomas*	Tait *Smithers*	Lythgoe
6	H BRISTOL CITY 26/9	10,203	11	8	W 2-0	1-0	Tait 5, Berry 85 / Ref: M James (Horsham)	Knight *Moller*	McLaughlin *Stevens*	Viney *Sweeney*	Kamara *Aitken*	Aizlewood *Rodgers*	Ellis *Nicholls*	Hemmerman *Tainton*	Doyle *Mann*	Rafferty *Mabbutt*	Berry *Harford*	Tait *Hay*	Rogers
7	H EXETER 29/9	10,989	8	11	W 2-0	2-0	Rafferty 24, Hemmerman 41 / Ref: D Civil (Birmingham)	Knight *Bond*	McLaughlin *Davey*	Viney *Sparrow*	Kamara *Lester*	Aizlewood *Cooke*	Ellis *Roberts L*	Hemmerman *Rogers*	Doyle* *Prince*	Rafferty *Kellow*	Berry *Delve*	Tait *Pullar*	Rogers
8	A CHESTERFIELD 3/10	6,169	10	12	D 2-2	1-0	Hemmerman 43, Tait 75 / Windridge 57, Ridley 79 / Ref: T Fitzharris (Bolton)	Knight *Turner*	McLaughlin *Bellamy*	Viney *O'Neill*	Kamara* *Wilson*	Aizlewood *Green*	Ellis *Ridley*	Hemmerman *Windridge*	Doyle* *Henderson**	Rafferty *Bonnyman*	Berry *Kowalski*	Tait *Crawford*	Rogers *Walker*
9	H BURNLEY 10/10	9,891	16	12	L 1-2	0-1	Doyle 47p / Young 12, Wharton 62 / Ref: M Bodenham (Brighton)	Knight *Stevenson*	McLaughlin *Laws*	Viney *Wharton*	Kamara *Scott**	Aizlewood *Overson*	Ellis *Dobson*	Hemmerman *Phelan*	Doyle* *Steven*	Rafferty *Hamilton*	Tait *Taylor*	Rogers *Young*	**Cropley** *Potts*
10	A WALSALL 17/10	4,408	17	12	L 1-3	0-1	Berry 85 / Beech 30, Serella 70, Buckley 79 / Ref: J Lovatt (Crewe)	Knight *Green*	Ellis *Macken*	Viney *Caswell*	Kamara *Beech*	Aizlewood *Serella*	Rollings *Hart*	Hemmerman *Rees*	Doyle *Loveridge**	Rafferty *Penn*	Tait *Buckley*	Cropley* *Waddington*	**Berry** *O'Kelly*
11	A GILLINGHAM 20/10	5,546	18	12	L 2-4	2-1	Tait 5, Rafferty 31 / Bowman 30p, White 77, 89, Price 84 / Ref: R Lewis (Great Bookham)	Knight *Hillyard*	Ellis *Sharpe*	Viney *Ford*	Kamara *Bruce*	Aizlewood ! *Weatherly*	Rollings *Bowman*	Barnard *Powell*	Doyle *Duncan*	Rafferty *White*	Tait *Lee*	Berry* *Price*	Hemmerman

Match notes

1. It will be four more games before Pompey's first three point win-bonus. Rafferty's header rescues a point against newly-promoted Imps, who show the defensive resilience that let in just 25 goals last season. Knight has ousted Mellor as No 1 and Gosport-teenager Steve Berry starts.

2. Summer signing Rollings (free from Swindon) limps off with an ankle injury and Tait is forced into the back-line. Bruce then slips his markers to volley home McGhee's flick for Tommy Docherty's team. Rafferty sees a header cleared off the line, and plenty of graft goes unrewarded.

3. An ordinary game has an extraordinary finish. Persistent-threat Walker crosses and Booker has a free header, but within seconds Hemmerman – in for Rogers – makes space to angle in from Raff's nod down. There is a minute's silence for Jimmy Guthrie, the 1939 cup team skipper.

4. Dave Smith's United prove football is a funny old game, exacting instant revenge for their 1-4 cup defeat. Irish cap Spence is unmarked to nod in Moody's flick after 80 seconds, then Gray heads home from a counter attack. New-boy Cropley (from Toronto Blizzard) has yet to start.

5. The game is going nowhere until Shotton, who will join Pompey in 1987, foolishly fouls Rafferty as the keeper looks set to collect and Doyle converts. As Ian Greaves' side push forward, Burton's hesitancy allows Rafferty to nod in Kamara's looping cross. 'It's a start,' says Burrows.

6. Steve Berry conjures a curler from 20 yards over 6' 5" Moller. 'He's so thin I make sure he's out before we pull the bath plug,' beams Frank Burrows. City boss Bob Houghton took Malmo to a European Cup final, but now he's taking Robins from first to fourth in successive seasons.

7. Two blunders hand Pompey the points, but it is far from convincing. First, Rafferty punishes Rogers' slack control, then the offside trap is sprung and Kamara crosses for Hemmerman's near-post finish. 'We were far the better side in the second-half,' said City boss Brian Godfrey.

8. Pompey hold Spireites in a thriller, but Kamara and Doyle are left injured. Two breakaway goals, the first Hemmerman's sharp turn and shot, then Tait's header, look like sealing it, but slack marking lets Ridley level. A rumoured exchange deal for Kemp is shot down by Burrows.

9. Cropley appears as a sub, but Pompey slump against Brian Miller's side who have lost their last four. Overson's handball is flagged and Doyle buries his sixth penalty in a row, but 18-year-old Wharton's volley delights Frank Casper, standing in for Miller, who has had appendicitis.

10. Burrows read the Riot Act to his team in the week, to no avail. Cropley starts, but is left rubbing his knee after Waddington's tackle and limps off after 18. Beech glances home at the far-post and player-boss Buckley seals it with a glorious chip. Hemmerman's dummy lets in Berry.

11. Three decisions turn the game. Lewis orders a re-take after Knight saves Bowman's pen, then, at 2-1 to Pompey, he sends off Aizlewood for a second booking, but full-back Ellis insists that he should have had the first. Finally, he signals a foul on Knight, only to allow Price's header.

No	Fixture	FT	HT	Pos	Att	Line-ups	Scorers / Referee	Match report
12	H NEWPORT 24/10	0-0	0-0	19 D 14 13	8,787	**Roman:** Knight, Ellis, Viney, Barnard, Rollings, Aizlewood, Berry, Doyle, Rafferty*, Tait, Gregory, Leworthy — *Italic:* Kendall, Walden, Relish, Davies, Bailey, Oakes, Vaughan, Johnson, Goodard, Aldridge*, Elsey, Tynan	Ref: K Salmon (Barnet)	County boss Len Ashurst made his intentions clear beforehand and the result was 90 minutes of unrelieved tedium. Occupying the crowd's thoughts most is Burrows' decision to swap Kamara (only re-signed in the summer for £50,000) for Brentford winger David Crown yesterday.
13	A FULHAM 31/10	1-1	1-1	19 D 7 14	7,542	**Roman:** Knight, Ellis, Viney, Crown, Rollings, Aizlewood, Doyle, Berry, Rafferty*, Tait, Gregory — *Italic:* Peyton, Hopkins, Strong, O'Driscoll, Gale, Brown, Davies, Wilson, Coney, O'Sullivan, Lewington	Hemmerman 73; Wilson 82. Ref: M Taylor (Deal)	Hemmerman's goal after good work by Cropley and Rafferty, looks set to end Fulham's seven-match home winning streak, only for Wilson to touch home after a goalmouth scramble. Burrows has listed Rogers, but moves for Bryant (Torquay) and Todd (Hereford) stall over money.
14	H WIMBLEDON 3/11	1-0	1-0	16 W 24 17	9,063	**Roman:** Knight, Ellis, Viney, Doyle, Rollings, Aizlewood, Garner, Gage, Rafferty*, Cropley, Crown, Gregory — *Italic:* Beasant, Clement, Brown, Bell, Morris, Geddes, Sutton, Leslie*, Lazarus, Downes, Joseph, Fishenden	Cropley 72. Ref: D Lloyd (Ferhill Heath)	Dave Bassett's injury-wracked Dons field a triallist, two apprentices and an unfit player, but should be three-up before half-time. Things get better; Cropley fires in from 20 yards and Tait hits the bar. Goal-machine Senior (£20,000) will sign once Dorchester are out of the FA Cup.
15	A PLYMOUTH 7/11	0-0	0-0	18 D 23 18	6,275	**Roman:** Knight, Ellis, Viney, Doyle, Rollings, Aizlewood, Barnard, Hemmerman, Rafferty*, Tait, Gregory — *Italic:* Crudgington, Nisbet, Uzzell, Cooper, Larkin, Phill-Masters, Hodges, Crabbe, Sims, Randell, Rogers	Ref: D Hutchinson (Bourn) / A Stone	Knight produces one of the displays of his career to deny Argyle (four wins in a row before today) single-handedly. The best saw him plunge backwards to keep out Cook's shot, but Rafferty was unlucky when he hit the post. The ref has to retire after being hit by Crown's clearance.
16	H CARLISLE 14/11	1-2	0-1	19 L 6 18	8,858	**Roman:** Knight, Ellis, Viney, Doyle, Rollings, Aizlewood, Berry, Hemmerman, Rafferty*, Tait, Gregory, Cropley — *Italic:* Swinburne, Parker, Rushbury, Coughlin, Ashurst, Larkin, Robson, Crabbe, Lee, Beardsley, Staniforth	Hemmerman 88; Robson 3, Lee 61. Ref: C Downey (Hounslow)	Peter Beardsley is restored after a clash with Carlisle boss Bob Stokoe and makes both goals. First, his pass put Staniforth clear and his cross leaves Robson with a formality, then he skips away to square for Lee. Hemmerman's stab meant for a dramatic finish, but United hold on.
17	H HUDDERSFIELD 28/11	2-1	2:1	16 W 15 21	8,155	**Roman:** Knight, McLaughlin, Bryant, Doyle, Rollings, Aizlewood, Barnard, Hemmerman, Tait, Cropley, Crown, Berry — *Italic:* Brown, Brown, Purdie, Bell, Harvey, Sutton, Lillis, Laverick, Austin*, Roberts, Cowling, Fletcher	Cropley 35, Tait 66; Aizlewood 21 (og). Ref: L Burden (Corfe Mullen)	Pompey's new skipper Cropley adds the players' backing to Deacon's vote of confidence in Burrows and they respond with a gutsy display after Aizlewood slices past Knight. Cropley scores easily after Hemmerman retrieved a lost cause, then Tait turned to thump home a low shot.
18	A DONCASTER 5/12	0-0	0-0	17 D 10 22	5,912	**Roman:** Knight, McLaughlin, Bryant, Doyle, Rollings, Aizlewood, Barnard, Hemmerman, Tait, Cropley, Crown* — *Italic:* Boyd, Russell, Cooper, Snodin I, Dowd, Lally, Pugh, Nimmo*, Warboys, Snodin G, Lister, Rogers, Dawson	Ref: B Martin (Keyworth)	Concussed Knight – kicked on the head in the first-half – preserves a point with a late double-save from Glynn Snodin's free-kick and Lister's follow-up. From the clearance, sub Rogers – on for struggling Crown – crosses, only for Boyd to match Knight and keep out Barnard's header.
19	H BRISTOL ROV 26/11	0-0	0-0	17 D 12 23	11,395	**Roman:** Knight, McLaughlin, Bryant, Doyle, Rollings, Aizlewood*, Barnard, Hemmerman, Tait, Cropley, Crown — *Italic:* Thomas, Jones, Slatter, Mabbutt, Barrett, Parkin, Gillies, McCaffery, Penney*, Williams D, Williams B, Stephens	Ref: D Vickers (Ilford)	Weather ravages the Boxing Day programme, so Barry Davies and a BBC Match of the Day crew turn up at short notice, only to wonder whether it was worth it. 84 minutes of a dire game ends up on the cutting-room floor and Burrows concedes: 'We let people down badly.'
20	A READING 6/1	1-2	1:2	18 L 8 23	4,018	**Roman:** Knight, McLaughlin, Bryant, Doyle, Rollings, Garner, Barnard, Hemmerman, Tait, Cropley, Crown — *Italic:* Fearon, Williams, Cullen, Webb, Hicks, Hetzke, Beavon, Earles, Dixon, Lewis, Donnellan, Rafferty	Tait 27; Dixon 7, Webb 24. Ref: C Maskell (Cambridge)	Reading, down to eleven fit men, ride their luck as Pompey come bearing gifts. Tait's miscued header is flapped onto the bar for Dixon to follow up, then England-starlet Webb is unmarked for a six-yard header. Tait, 'magnificent' according to Burrows, atones with a bending shot.
21	A CHESTER 19/1	2-3	2:3	19 L 22 23	1,444	**Roman:** Knight, McLaughlin, Bryant, Doyle, Rollings, Aizlewood*, Barnard, Hemmerman*, Tait, Cropley, Crown — *Italic:* Millington, Raynor, Burns, Storton, Cottam, Oakes, Sutcliffe, Jones, Simpson, Blackwell, Henderson	Doyle 43, Hemmerman 71; Sutcliffe 20, Jones 72, Simpson 86. Ref: D Scott (Burnley)	Burrows is 'disgusted' as his team present Chester with their first home win of the season. Hemmerman's diving header from Crown's corner put them ahead, but within seconds Jones' shot swirled home. Knight's reckless charge then gave Simpson the chance to leave him stranded.
22	A LINCOLN 23/1	1-1	1:1	19 D 16 24	3,297	**Roman:** Knight, McLaughlin, Bryant, Doyle, Rollings, Aizlewood, Barnard, Hemmerman, Tait, Bason, Crown* — *Italic:* Felgate, Carr, Neale, Cockerill, Peake, Thompson, Turner, Bell, Cunningham, Beavon*, Gilbert	Tait 56; Bell 77. Ref: B Nixon (Stockport)	Tait's fierce strike lifts the gloom, as Deacon draws up a short-list of contenders for a new coach after firing Stan Harland earlier in the month. Bell atones for a first-half miss with a fine turn and shot to level, leaving Pompey a point clear of the drop zone, having played a game more.
23	H SOUTHEND 30/1	0-0	0-0	19 D 4 25	7,731	**Roman:** Knight, Ellis, Bryant, Doyle, Rollings, Aizlewood, Barnard, Hemmerman, Tait, Bason, Crown* — *Italic:* Keeley, Stead, Yates, Pennyfather!, Nelson, Cusack, Moody, Pountney*, Bell, Greaves, Mercer, Otulakowski, Hadley, Rafferty	Ref: R Milford (Bristol)	Clueless Pompey, with just 24 goals in 23 games, never look like unlocking unlikely promotion candidates United, even after Pennyfather's second booking for stopping Doyle taking a free-kick (50). Brian Bason's loan from Crystal Palace has been extended for another month.

LEAGUE DIVISION 3

Manager: Burrows ⇨ Campbell   **SEASON 1981-82**

No 24 · A BRENTFORD · 6/2 — Att 5,950 · Pos 12 · Pt 26 · D 2-2 · H-T 1-1
Scorers: Rollings 37, Tait 56 / Tucker 31p, Bowles 78 — Ref: E Read (Bristol)

	1	2	3	4	5	6	7	8	9	10	11	12 sub used
Pompey	Knight	McLaughlin	Bryant	Doyle	Aizlewood	Rollings	Hemmerman	Rafferty	Tait	Bason	Crown	Booker
Brentford	McKellar	Salman	Tucker	MacNichol	Whitehead	Hurlock	Kamara	Bowen	Sweetzer	Bowles	Roberts*	Booker

Physio Gordon Neave, by the goal after treating Knight, insists Stan Bowles' shot off the underside never crosses the line. 'It was some way from it and two policemen fell about laughing,' he said. New coach Bobby Campbell is in the stand. If Burrows isn't worried, he should be.

No 25 · H OXFORD · 9/2 — Att 7,095 · Pos 9 · Pt 27 · D 1-1 · H-T 1-1
Scorers: Aizlewood 25 / Thomas 26 — Ref: C Thomas (Porthcawl)

	1	2	3	4	5	6	7	8	9	10	11	12 sub used
Pompey	Knight	McLaughlin	Bryant	Doyle*	Aizlewood	Rollings	Hemmerman	Rafferty	Tait	Bason	Crown	Cropley
Oxford	Burton	Doyle	Fogg	Jeffrey	Briggs	Wright	Jones	Foley	Cassells	Thomas	Smithers	

For the fourth time in five Pompey let a lead slip and the team haven't won since November. The lowest gate of the season boos the team off and furious Burrows lays into his team. 'I have had enough of being spat at and cans thrown at me; the players must take their share,' he rages.

No 26 · H CHESTERFIELD · 13/2 — Att 8,046 · Pos 3 · Pt 30 · W 5-1 · H-T 2-1
Scorers: Aizlewood 4, Crown 7, Bonnyman 15 [Rafferty 51, 80, 85] — Ref: B Stevens (Stonehouse)

	1	2	3	4	5	6	7	8	9	10	11	12 sub used
Pompey	Knight	McLaughlin	Bryant	Doyle	Aizlewood	Garner	Cropley*	Rafferty	Tait	Bason	Crown	Gregory
Chesterfield	Turner	Stirk	O'Neill	Wilson	Green	Ridley	Windridge	Henderson*	Bonnyman*	Kowalski	Crawford	Henson

Burrows 'fight or get out' message gets through him and promotion-hopefuls see their mean reputation (only 19 goals against) torn to shreds. Crown puts indifferent form behind him and Rafferty suggests Burrows' £40,000 bid for Watford's Poskett may not be necessary.

No 27 · A BRISTOL CITY · 20/2 — Att 9,397 · Pos 22 · Pt 33 · W 1-0 · H-T 0-0
Scorers: Rafferty 79 — Ref: M Baker (Wolverhampton)

	1	2	3	4	5	6	7	8	9	10	11	12 sub used
Pompey	Knight	McLaughlin	Bryant	Barnard	Aizlewood*	Garner	Hemmerman	Rafferty	Tait	Bason	Crown	Bartlett
Bristol City	Moller	Stevens	Williams	McCaffery	Nicholls	Muskett	Chandler	Carter	Harford	Newman	Hay	

Cash-strapped City are doomed to relegation, but must wonder how they didn't win. Two bruised posts and Aizlewood's miraculous clearance from Chandler's shot, break acting-boss Roy Hodgson's heart, then Nicholls' poor back-pass lets in Rafferty to notch his 101st league goal.

No 28 · A SWINDON · 23/2 — Att 4,860 · Pos 19 · Pt 33 · L 0-2 · H-T 0-1
Scorers: Carter 45p, Williams 64 — Ref: C White (Harrow)

	1	2	3	4	5	6	7	8	9	10	11	12 sub used
Pompey	Knight	McLaughlin	Bryant	Doyle	Ellis	Garner	Barnard	Rafferty	Tait	Bason*	Crown	Hemmerman
Swindon	Allan	Henry	Baddeley	Williams	Lewis	Stroud	Hughes	Carter	Rideout	Greenwood	Pritchard	

Pompey, shorn of Rollings and Aizlewood and Cropley's creativity, see their revival blown off course in an error-littered game. Swindon, with just one win in four months, are given a gift when McLaughlin's hand intercepted an innocuous cross. Bason is subbed and returns to Palace.

No 29 · A BURNLEY · 27/2 — Att 7,024 · Pos 4 · Pt 33 · L 0-3 · H-T 0-1
Scorers: Taylor 10, Phelan 57, Scott 67 — Ref: J Hough (Macclesfield)

	1	2	3	4	5	6	7	8	9	10	11	12 sub used
Pompey	Knight	McLaughlin	Sullivan	Barnard	Ellis	Garner	Doyle	Rafferty	Gregory	Tait	Rogers*	Crown
Burnley	Stevenson	Laws	Wharton	Cassidy	Phelan	Holt	Dobson	Scott	Hamilton	Taylor*	Young	Potts

Deacon, whose three points-for-a-win proposal was adopted at last year's Football League AGM, now wants lower division clubs given full voting rights. Pompey are well-short of achieving that status on the field, but Burnley, unbeaten since visiting Fratton, will end up champs.

No 30 · H WALSALL · 6/3 — Att 7,133 · Pos 9 · Pt 36 · W 1-0 · H-T 1-0
Scorers: Aizlewood 7 — Ref: B Daniels (Brentwood)

	1	2	3	4	5	6	7	8	9	10	11	12 sub used
Pompey	Knight	McLaughlin	Sullivan	Barnard	Aizlewood	Ellis	Doyle	Rafferty	Gregory	Tait	Crown	
Walsall	Green	Macken	Sinnott	Beech	Serella	Hart	Rees	Loveridge	Penn	O'Kelly	Waddington*	Buckley

Aizlewood battles on despite a knee injury to net his third in four appearances, rifling in after Green turned Gregory's header against the bar. O'Kelly misses a sitter from 12 yards, but Pompey should have won easily. Sullivan, signed until May from Hereford, makes his home debut.

No 31 · H GILLINGHAM · 9/3 — Att 6,711 · Pos 15 · Pt 39 · W 1-0 · H-T 1-0
Scorers: Rafferty 19 — Ref: K Baker (Wolverhampton)

	1	2	3	4	5	6	7	8	9	10	11	12 sub used
Pompey	Knight	McLaughlin	Sullivan	Barnard	Aizlewood*	Garner	Doyle	Rafferty	Gregory	Tait	Crown*	Hemmerman
Gillingham	Hillyard	Sharpe	Adams	Bruce	Shaw	Sitton	Ovard	Tydeman	White	Price	Cascarino*	Bottiglieri

Another host of chances go begging, but Pompey prevail thanks to Rafferty's instincts when Hillyard pushes Crown's corner onto the post. Ex-Marine Ovard sliced a shot wide straight after the break and then saw a shot hit his own defender. Crown slams a shot against the bar late on.

No 32 · A NEWPORT · 13/3 — Att 4,209 · Pos 21 · Pt 40 · D 1-1 · H-T 1-0
Scorers: Crown 13 / Elsey 74 — Ref: G Napthine (Loughborough)

	1	2	3	4	5	6	7	8	9	10	11	12 sub used
Pompey	Knight	McLaughlin	Sullivan	Barnard	Rollings	Garner	Doyle	Rafferty	Gregory	Tait	Crown	Bishop
Newport	Kendall	Lees	Moore	Davies	Oakes	Tynan*	Vaughan	Elsey	Aldridge	Gwyther	Lowndes	

Charlie George's decision to spurn Pompey for Derby on the eve of the game is a disappointment, but the loss of two points here is worse. Crown bursts past Lees and angles home, but County get the crowd off their backs when Elsey fires home after Berry's weak clearance.

No 33 · H FULHAM · 20/3 — Att 10,712 · Pos 4 · Pt 41 · D 1-1 · H-T 1-0
Scorers: Rafferty 43 / Lock 85p — Ref: H King (Merthyr Tydfil)

	1	2	3	4	5	6	7	8	9	10	11	12 sub used
Pompey	Knight	McLaughlin	Sullivan	Barnard	Aizlewood	Ellis	Berry*	Rafferty	Senior	Tait	Crown*	Wimbleton
Fulham	Peyton	Hopkins	Strong	O'Driscoll	Brown	Gale	Davies	Wilson	Tempest*	O'Sullivan	Lock	Parker

Senior is pressed into service as Pompey seek to end a barren goal-run against Malcolm MacDonald's leaders, and he could have had four goals. Rafferty's shot squirms under Peyton, but Lock levels after Ellis up-ended Davies. 'We should have been 3-0 up by then,' said Burrows.

No 34 · H PLYMOUTH · 27/3 — Att 9,551 · Pos 11 · Pt 44 · W 1-0 · H-T 0-0
Scorers: Rafferty 85 — Ref: A Gunn (Burgess Hill)

	1	2	3	4	5	6	7	8	9	10	11	12 sub used
Pompey	Knight	McLaughlin	Sullivan	Doyle	Aizlewood	Ellis	Berry	Rafferty	Senior	Tait	Crown*	Wimbleton
Plymouth	Crudgington	Nisbett	Uzzell	Harrison	Phill-Masters	Cooper	Hodges	Cook	Sims	Randall	Rogers	

Bobby Moncur's Argyle galloped from 24th in October to seventh, but are undone late on, as Senior and Tait set up Rafferty for his 14th goal. Ominously, as it turns out, Deacon halted Burrows deadline-day player search, but Bryant joins Cobblers, while Gregory turns down Dons.

Portsmouth ("Pompey") end-of-season match log — fixtures 35–46

No	V	Opponent	Date	Pos	—	Pts	Res	Score	Scorers	Ref	Att
35	A	CARLISLE	3/4	17	2	44	L	0-2	Staniforth 10, Ashurst 35	D Webb (Radcliffe)	3,919
36	H	PRESTON	6/4	17	18	45	D	1-1	Rafferty 29 / O'Riordan 85	D Reeves (Uxbridge)	6,712
37	A	BRISTOL ROV	10/4	17	13	46	D	1-1	Rafferty 19 / Williams D 22	K Barratt (Coventry)	4,833
38	H	READING	12/4	15	8	49	W	3-0	Senior 6, 73, Doyle 8p	M James (Horsham)	8,427
39	H	DONCASTER	17/4	14	20	50	D	0-0	—	J Deakin (Bedford)	8,657
40	A	HUDDERSFIELD	24/4	14	13	53	W	1-0	Rafferty 75	J Hunting (Leicester)	5,658
41	H	CHESTER	1/5	13	24	56	W	2-0	Rafferty 61, Doyle 65p	C Downey (Hounslow)	6,198
42	A	EXETER	5/5	14	17	57	D	3-3	Rafferty 10, Tait 55, 68 / Kellow 37, Pratt 45, 88	A Hamil (Wolverhampton)	2,596
43	A	MILLWALL	8/5	15	8	57	L	0-1	Shinton 15	L Burden (Corfe Mullen)	4,969
44	H	SWINDON	15/5	14	21	60	W	3-0	Hemmerman 6, 36, 51	M Dimblebee (Stevenage)	6,372
45	A	WIMBLEDON	18/5	15	21	60	L	2-3	Hemmerman 34, Doyle 76p / Morris 27, Joseph 71, Leslie 85	L Shapter (Newton Abbott)	2,642
46	H	MILLWALL	21/5	13	9	61	D	2-2	Doyle 28p, 80p / Massey 68, Chatterton 77p	J Bray (Hinckley)	4,902

Home 8,550 Away 5,038 Average 8,550

---

35 — A CARLISLE
Pompey: Knight, McLaughlin, Sullivan, Doyle, Aizlewood*, Ellis, Berry, Rafferty, Senior, Tait, Crown, Wimbledon
Carlisle: Swinburne, Parker, Rushbury, Larkin, Ashurst, Craig, Ritchie, Haigh, Robson, Lee, Staniforth, Walsh

Caretaker Campbell's reign – Burrows has been fired despite five matches unbeaten – starts on a low note. Aizlewood, wearing a protective head-band, cuts his eye again in a clash with Lee and faces a summer op on his extensive scar tissue. Staniforth and Ashurst claim free headers.

36 — H PRESTON
Pompey: Knight, McLaughlin, Sullivan, Doyle, Garner, Ellis, Berry, Rafferty, Senior, Wimbledon, Crown
Preston: Hodge, Anderson*, McAteer, Naughton, Booth, O'Riordan, Kelly, Doyle, Elliott, Buckley, Bruce, Walsh

Pompey are still not secure, as teams below have games in hand. Knight must have thought he had kept three points safe, when he tipped over McAteer's drive, but from the corner O'Riordan kept Gordon Lee's team, 26 points in 16 games now, on course for a miraculous escape.

37 — A BRISTOL ROV
Pompey: Knight, McLaughlin, Sullivan, Doyle, Garner, Ellis, Berry, Rafferty, Gregory, Senior, Hemmerman, Wimbledon
Bristol Rovers: Kite, Gillies, Randall, Bailey, Parkin, Hughes, Barrett*, Williams D, Stephens, Mabbutt, Williams B, Penney

Gregory comes in from the cold to replace Senior, but it's a familiar tale as Pompey fail to hold on and end up with a 16th draw of the season – the most in the Football League. Rafferty bundles home, but then David Williams shoots home after his first effort was blocked by Garner.

38 — H READING
Pompey: Knight, McLaughlin, Sullivan, Doyle, Garner, Crown*, Wimbledon, Rafferty, Senior, Berry, Rogers, Wimbledon
Reading: Fearon, Williams, Cullen*, Hetzke, Hicks, Barnes, Earles, Kearney, Dixon, Wood, Webb, Donnellan

The Board have yet to discuss the vacant manager's job, but Campbell will have done himself no harm today. Twenty-year-old Senior's two booming headers break his duck, while Doyle's spot-kick (that's 8/8 now) comes after Barnes handles. Royals' Div Two dream is over.

39 — H DONCASTER
Pompey: Knight, McLaughlin, Sullivan, Doyle, Aizlewood, Ellis, Wimbledon*, Rafferty, Senior, Berry, Crown, Pugh
Doncaster: Humphries S, Russell, Humphries G, Snodin I, Cawthorne, Wiggington, Lally, Liddell*, Douglas, Snodin G, Little, Pugh

It will cost £2 on the terraces from next season, but there won't be many takers with games like this. Had Pugh's five-yard free header not gone wide towards the end, it could have been worse. Cropley faces a doctor's verdict on his knee, while Sullivan has earned a one-year contract.

40 — A HUDDERSFIELD
Pompey: Knight, McLaughlin, Sullivan, Doyle, Aizlewood, Viney, Wimbledon*, Rafferty, Senior, Berry, Hemmerman, Cowling
Huddersfield: Cox, Brown, Burke, Stanton, Valentine, Harvey, Lillis, Kennedy, Hotte*, Wilson, Robins, Cowling

Pompey are worthy winners says Campbell. Contract-seeking sub Hemmerman, sets up the goal, after replacing Wimbledon, whose knee injury will wreck his Pompey career. Garner and Gregory have already been released, but Viney and Barnard are also awaiting Campbell's verdict.

41 — H CHESTER
Pompey: Knight, McLaughlin, Sullivan, Doyle, Aizlewood, Viney, Rafferty, Senior, Berry, Tait, Rogers, Burns
Chester: Millington, Raynor, Needham, Storton, Zelem, Cottam, Allen*, Jones, Simpson, Ludlam, Henderson, Burns

Deacon's term as Mayor of Southampton ends soon, and he pledges to revamp costly win-bonuses. The players earn an easy £100 each, as the Seals, in tatty (three without sponsor's logo) yellow shirts, lose for the 24th time. Berry's header is fisted in by Ludlam, but a penalty is given.

42 — A EXETER
Pompey: Knight*, McLaughlin, Sullivan, Doyle, Aizlewood, Viney, Rafferty, Hemmerman, Tait, Berry, Rogers P*, Ellis
Exeter: Main, Kirkup, Sparrow, Marker, Foster, Roberts P, Pratt, Rogers P*, Kellow, Delve, Hatch, Roberts L

Versatile Viney goes in goal at half-time for the second time in his career, after Knight's injury. He is denied a clean sheet when Pratt's low shot skids in to level Tait's earlier mis-hit. At the death, Viney leaps to tip over Hatch's header and earn a gutsy point, but not a contract.

43 — A MILLWALL
Pompey: Gosney, McLaughlin, Sullivan, Doyle, Aizlewood, Viney, Hemmerman, Rafferty, Tait, Ellis, Rogers, West
Millwall: Gleasure, Robinson, Needham, Chatterton, Allardyce, Roberts, Shinton, Hayes, Dibble, Massey, West

Shinton exposes the debut-making Gosney, when his 25-yard chip catches the youngster off his line. Campbell is delighted with the team, despite the end of a seven-match unbeaten run. Lions' slim promotion hopes remain, but a pitch invasion leads to police drawing truncheons.

44 — H SWINDON
Pompey: Knight, McLaughlin, Sullivan, Doyle, Aizlewood, Viney, Hemmerman, Ellis, Tait, Berry, Rogers, Ellis
Swindon: Allan, Henry, Baddeley, Emmanuel, Lewis, Stroud, Williams*, Carter, Rideout, Rowland, Graham, Pritchard

Hemmerman snaps up a sharp hat-trick to send a contract message to Campbell, but his boss is away scouting. The striker latches onto three passes over a square defence; the best is the third, clipped in from an oblique angle. Robins have no fight and will be relegated on Tuesday.

45 — A WIMBLEDON
Pompey: Knight, McLaughlin, Sullivan, Doyle, Ellis, Viney, Hemmerman, Crown, Tait, Senior, Rogers, Elliott
Wimbledon: Beasant, Leslie, Thoams, Brown, Morris, Downes, Shinton, Ketteridge, Joseph, Hodges*, Gage, Elliott

Dons must win 11-0 to stay up, but still go out in style when full-back John Leslie – a survivor from the Southern League team – cracks home Evans' knock-down. Doyle had dragged Pompey level after Downes' handball, but Campbell reckons: 'There several teams worse than Dons.'

46 — H MILLWALL
Pompey: Knight, McLaughlin, Sullivan, Doyle, Tait, Viney, Crown, Hemmerman, Senior, Berry, Rogers, West
Millwall: Gleasure, Chatterton, Robinson, Massey, Allardyce, Roberts, Shinton, Joseph, Neal, Harris, Martin, West

Police man-mark 250 Lions' fans who defy a ticket ban, imposed after trouble in the FA Cup game. Doyle's perfect penalty record (12/12) is maintained, as the released Hemmerman is brought down twice. Chatterton's spot-kick had looked like ending a six-month unbeaten home run.

LEAGUE DIVISION 3 (CUP-TIES)　　　Manager: Frank Burrows　　　SEASON 1981-82

League Cup

		F-A	H-T	Scorers, Times, and Referees	1	2	3	4	5	6	7	8	9	10	11	12 sub used
1:1 A SOUTHEND 2/9	D	0-0	0-0	Ref: A Gunn (Burgess Hill) 4,087	Knight *Cawston*	McLaughlin *Stead*	Viney *Dudley*	Kamara *Hadley*	Aizlewood *Moody*	Rollings *Cusack*	Gregory *Gray**	Doyle *Pountney*	Rafferty *Spence*	Berry *Mercer*	Rogers *Otulakowski*	*Nelson*
1:2 H SOUTHEND 16/9	W 20	4-1	2-1	Rafferty 7, Doyle 21, Berry 70 Spence 5　[Kamara 82] Ref: E Read (Bristol) (Pompey won 4-1 on aggregate) 10,019　15	Knight *Keeley*	McLaughlin *Stead*	Viney *Yates*	Kamara *Nelson*	Aizlewood *Moody*	Ellis *Cusack*	Hemmerman *Gray*	Doyle *Pountney*	Rafferty *Spence**	Berry *Mercer*	Tait *Otulakowski*	*Dudley*
2:1 A QP RANGERS 6/10	L 10	0-5	0-1	[Micklewhite 85, 90] Ellis 13 (og), Gregory 59, 64 Ref: H Taylor (Leicester) 13,502　2:9	Knight *Burridge*	McLaughlin *Gregory*	Viney *Fenwick*	Kamara *Waddock*	Rollings *Hazell*	Ellis *Roeder*	Hemmerman *Micklewhite*	Doyle *Stainrod*	Rafferty *Allen*	Rogers *Currie**	Tait *Gillard*	*Burke*
2:2 H QP RANGERS 27/10	D 19	2-2	2-1	Rafferty 23, Doyle 36p Flanagan 2, Micklewhite 75 Ref: L Shapter (Newton Abbott) (Pompey lost 2-7 on aggregate) 7,677　2:4	Knight *Burridge*	Ellis *Gregory*	Viney *Fenwick*	Barnard *Waddock !*	Aizlewood *Hazell**	Rollings *Roeder*	Hemmerman *Micklewhite*	Doyle *Flanagan*	Rafferty* *Burke*	Cropley *Stainrod*	Tait *Gillard*	Gregory *Stuart*

1:1 Southend boss Dave Smith praises Knight, as he single-handedly denies United a healthy first-leg lead. Aizlewood looped a header onto the bar early on, but after that Knight had to be at full-stretch to keep out Moody, then late on his one-handed effort frustrated Dudley's 35-yarder.

1:2 Burrows' pre-match call for more passion is emphatically answered. Pompey bounce back when Rafferty dips in from 20 yards, then Doyle finishes after Man of the Match Hemmerman's shot is blocked. Berry hooks his first goal, then Kamara's tumbling shot takes a big deflection.

2:1 Pompey's credit soon runs out on QPR's newly-laid plastic, but Burrows refuses to blame the pitch for some shocking defending. Aizlewood is ill before the game, then Ellis's deflection wrong-foots Knight. John Gregory - who becomes Pompey boss in 1989 - kills the tie for TV's men.

2:2 Terry Venables claims the penalty was given for something one of his defenders said. 'Surely that's an indirect free-kick?' he mused. Burrows backs him up and Shapter declines to elucidate. Waddock is dismissed for chopping down Barnard, but Micklewhite chips in for the ten men.

FA Cup

		F-A	H-T	Scorers, Times, and Referees	1	2	3	4	5	6	7	8	9	10	11	12 sub used
1 H MILLWALL 21/11	D 19	1-1	1-0	Hemmerman 14 Chatterton 49p Ref: B Stevens (Stonehouse) 10,113　3	Knight *Gleasure*	McLaughlin *Martin*	Bryant *Warman*	Doyle *Chatterton*	Aizlewood *Allardyce*	Rollings *Slough*	Hemmerman *Hayes*	Tait *Massey*	Barnard *McKenna*	Cropley *Harris*	Crown *West*	
1R A MILLWALL 25/11	L 19	2-3 aet	0-2	Tait 59, Hemmerman 67　[Hayes 110] Allardyce 35, Chatterton 38, Ref: B Stevens (Stonehouse) 6,842　3	Knight *Gleasure*	McLaughlin *Martin*	Bryant *Warman*	Doyle *Chatterton*	Aizlewood *Allardyce*	Rollings *Slough*	Hemmerman *Hayes*	Barnard *Massey**	Tait *McKenna*	Cropley* *Harris*	Crown *West*	Rogers *Dibble*

1 Gerry Francis' presence gets the rumour-mill going, but he is a guest of a Lions player. Cropley's sharp thinking sets up Hemmerman's header, but a dodgy penalty levels. Coins have to be cleared from the goal, after McKenna's tumble sparks furious protests, but Chatterton keeps cool.

1R Ex-Saint Hayes emerges from Bryant's pocket, where he had been for the game, to snatch it. The people of Brighton and Hove heave a sigh of relief, as the Goldstone would have hosted a third match. Soon-to-be-sacked assistant-boss Stan Harland said: 'The players did the club proud.'

League Table

		Home						Away						
		P	W	D	L	F	A	W	D	L	F	A	Pts	
1	Burnley	46	13	7	3	37	20	8	10	5	29	25	80	
2	Carlisle	46	17	4	2	44	21	6	7	10	21	29	80	
3	Fulham	46	12	9	2	44	22	9	6	8	33	29	78	
4	Lincoln	46	13	7	3	40	16	8	7	8	26	24	77	
5	Oxford	46	10	8	5	28	18	9	6	8	35	31	71	
6	Gillingham	46	14	5	4	44	26	6	6	11	20	30	71	
7	Southend	46	11	7	5	35	23	7	8	8	20	28	69	
8	Brentford	46	8	6	9	28	22	11	5	7	28	25	68	
9	Millwall	46	12	4	7	36	28	6	9	8	26	34	67	
10	Plymouth	46	12	5	6	37	24	6	6	11	27	32	65	
11	Chesterfield	46	12	4	7	33	27	6	6	11	24	31	64	
12	Reading	46	11	6	6	43	35	6	5	12	24	40	62	
13	PORTSMOUTH	46	11	10	2	33	14	3	9	11	23	37	61	
14	Preston	46	10	7	6	25	22	6	6	11	25	34	61	
15	Bristol Rov	46	12	4	7	35	28	6	5	12	23	37	61	
16	Newport	46	9	10	4	28	21	5	6	12	26	33	58	
17	Huddersfield	46	10	5	8	38	25	5	7	11	26	34	57	
18	Exeter	46	14	4	5	46	33	2	5	16	25	51	57	
19	Doncaster	46	9	9	5	31	24	4	8	11	24	44	56	
20	Walsall	46	10	7	6	32	23	3	7	13	19	32	53	
21	Wimbledon	46	10	6	7	33	27	4	5	14	28	48	53	
22	Swindon	46	9	5	9	37	36	4	8	11	18	35	52	
23	Bristol City	46	7	6	10	24	29	4	7	12	16	36	46	
24	Chester	46	2	10	11	16	30	5	1	17	20	48	32	
		1104	258	155	139	827	594	139	155	258	594	827	1499	

Appearances / Goals

	Appearances						Goals			
	Lge	Sub	LC	Sub	FAC	Sub	Lge	LC	FAC	Tot
Aizlewood, Steve	36		3		2		3			3
Barnard, Leigh	16	1	1		2					
Bartlett, Kevin		1								
Bason, Brian	9									
Berry, Steve	26	1	2	1			2	1		3
Bryant, Steve	11									
Cropley, Alex	7	2	2		2		2			2
Crown, David	25	2	1		2		2			2
Doyle, Bobby	43		4		2		8	2		10
Ellis, Peter	31	1	3							
Garner, Alan	10									
Gosney, Andy	1									
Gregory, David	12	2	1	1						
Hemmerman, Jeff	29	5	3		2		11		2	13
Kamara, Chris	11		3					1		1
Knight, Alan	45		4		2					
McLaughlin, John	36		3		2					
Rafferty, Billy	35	4	4		2		15	2		17
Rogers, Alan	14	5	2			1				
Rollings, Andy	19		3		2		1			1
Senior, Trevor	9									
Sullivan, Colin	18									
Tait, Mick	35	1	3		2		8		1	9
Viney, Keith	24		4							
Wimbleton, Paul	4	4					2			2
25 players used	506	29	44	2	22	1	54	6	3	63

Odds & ends

Double wins: (2) Bristol C, Huddersfield.

Double losses: (2) Burnley, Carlisle.

Won from behind: (1) Huddersfield (h).

Lost from in front: (2) Gillingham (a), Chester (a).

High spots: Defeating Southampton in the Hampshire Professional Cup. 15-match unbeaten run at home from November.

The 5-1 thrashing of promotion-chasing Chesterfield in February.

One defeat in 13 games from March to May.

Low spots: Losing 2-3 at Chester in January to give them their first home win of the season.

Losing 0-5 on QPR's plastic pitch in the League Cup second round.

Attracting an attendance of less than 5,000 for the last home match of the season.

Eight-match winless run from December to February.

Pompey were the treble chance favourites, drawing 22 of their league and cup games during the season.

Player of the Year: Alan Knight.

Ever Presents: (0).

Hat-tricks: (2) Billy Rafferty, Jeff Hemmerman.

Leading Scorer: Billy Rafferty (17).

LEAGUE DIVISION 3 — Manager: Bobby Campbell — SEASON 1982-83

Column headings for players: 1 · 2 · 3 · 4 · 5 · 6 · 7 · 8 · 9 · 10 · 11 · 12 sub used
(Portsmouth players in roman; opponents in italic.)

---

1 · H · 28/8 · SHEFFIELD UTD · Att 13,361 · W 4-1 · H-T 1-1 · Pt 3

Biley 21, Howe 46, Webb 60, Tait 83; *Edwards 19*
Ref: D Vickers (Ilford)

1	2	3	4	5	6	7	8	9	10	11	12 sub used
Knight	McLaughlin	Sullivan	Doyle	Howe	Aizlewood	Webb	Tait	Rafferty*	Biley	Rogers	Ellis
Conroy	*Henderson*	*Garner*	*McHale*	*MacPhail*	*Kenworthy*	*Morris*	*Arnott*	*Edwards*	*King*	*Curran*	

Biley's £100,000 signing from Everton has raised expectations, but Campbell's new-look team deliver, with three new-boys scoring, before Tait rounds it off against newly-promoted Blades. Edwards pinches a goal, but once Biley heads in Rogers' corner, the result isn't in doubt.

---

2 · A · 4/9 · WALSALL · Att 2,922 · Pos 24 · W 3-0 · H-T 1-0 · Pt 6

Rafferty 21, Tait 81, Biley 82
Ref: D Owen (Wirral)

1	2	3	4	5	6	7	8	9	10	11	12 sub used
Knight	McLaughlin	Sullivan	Doyle	Howe	Aizlewood	Webb*	Tait	Rafferty	Biley	Thomas	Ellis
Green	*Arthur*	*Mower*	*Beech*	*Marshall*	*Hart*	*Teasdale*	*Sinnott*	*Kearns**	*Buckley*	*Preece*	*Round*

Pompey dominate, but it takes Tait and Biley's late one-two to reflect the gulf in class. Rafferty's diving header from McLaughlin's cross looks to be enough, then Kearns is stretchered off with a badly bruised leg after clashing with Tait. Webb is clattered by Mower and limps off.

---

3 · A · 8/9 · EXETER · Att 3,146 · Pos 15 · D 1-1 · H-T 0-1 · Pt 7

Rafferty 85; *Howe 10 (og)*
Ref: E Read (Bristol)

1	2	3	4	5	6	7	8	9	10	11	12 sub used
Knight	McLaughlin	Sullivan	Doyle	Howe	Aizlewood	Webb	Tait	Rafferty	Biley*	Thomas	Rogers
Bond	*Kirkup*	*Viney*	*McEwan!*	*Roberts*	*Rogers M*	*Harle*	*Rogers P*	*Kellow*	*Delve*	*Pullar*	

McEwan's dismissal for foul and abusive changes the game. Within five minutes Rafferty coolly feeds off Doyle's cross, but Pompey had been chasing the game since Kellow had harried Howe into lobbing over Knight. City boss Brian Godfrey paid tribute: 'Pompey are a good side.'

---

4 · H · 11/9 · WREXHAM · Att 10,887 · Pos 17 · W 3-0 · H-T 1-0 · Pt 10

Biley 11, 68, Tait 55
Ref: E Scales (Ware)

1	2	3	4	5	6	7	8	9	10	11	12 sub used
Knight	McLaughlin	Sullivan	Doyle	Howe	Aizlewood	Ellis	Tait	Rafferty	Biley	Thomas	Hill
Niedzwiecki	*Jones*	*Bater*	*Arkwright*	*Dowman*	*Keay*	*Hunt*	*Gregory*	*Fox*	*King**	*Burton*	

Only Oxford's 100% record keeps Pompey off the top. Relegated Wrexham are never in it once Biley cuts inside and bends home. Doyle sees his penalty saved after Bater fouled Rafferty. Dave Gregory, now at the Racecourse, said Pompey – and Doyle – were 'in a different class'.

---

5 · A · 18/9 · OXFORD · Att 9,918 · Pos 1 · D 1-1 · H-T 1-1 · Pt 11

Doyle 17p; *Briggs 35*
Ref: L Robinson (Sutton Coldfield)

1	2	3	4	5	6	7	8	9	10	11	12 sub used
Knight	McLaughlin	Sullivan	Doyle	Howe	Aizlewood	Ellis	Tait	Rafferty	Biley	Thomas	Biggins
Burton	*Limney*	*Fogg*	*Train*	*Briggs*	*Shotton*	*Brock*	*Barnett*	*Vinter**	*Thomas*	*Hebberd*	

Doyle – who missed from the spot for the first time last week – is back to his best after Hebberd's clumsy foul on Tait. Briggs hooks home the equaliser, but the game is far from the expected spectacle. Dickinson is recovering after another heart-attack and Crown wants a transfer.

---

6 · H · 25/9 · NEWPORT · Att 10,833 · Pos 6 · L 1-2 · H-T 0-0 · Pt 11

Biley 67; *Vaughan 53, Aldridge 80*
Ref: M Bodenham (Brighton)

1	2	3	4	5	6	7	8	9	10	11	12 sub used
Knight	McLaughlin	Sullivan	Doyle	Howe	Aizlewood	Ellis	Tait	Rafferty	Biley	Thomas*	Rogers
Kendall	*Jones*	*Relish*	*Bailey*	*Davies*	*Stroud*	*Lowndes*	*Aldridge**	*Tynan*	*Vaughan*	*Elsey*	*Gwyther*

Campbell is still keen to add to his squad and on this evidence he may have to. Pompey are out-thought by Colin Addison's Newport, who clinch it as Aldridge is left unmarked to score off the far-post. Biley heads home Rogers' corner, cancelling out Vaughan's close-range strike.

---

7 · H · 28/9 · MILLWALL · Att 7,615 · Pos 4 · W 2-0 · H-T 0-0 · Pt 14

Rafferty 51, Biley 78
Ref: E Crickmore (Plymouth)

1	2	3	4	5	6	7	8	9	10	11	12 sub used
Knight	McLaughlin	Sullivan	Doyle	Howe	Aizlewood	Ellis	Tait	Rafferty	Biley	Rogers	Massey
Sansome	*Stevens*	*Robinson*	*Chatterton*	*Madden*	*Roberts*	*Shinton**	*Carr*	*Aylott*	*Martin*	*Neal*	

Biley has a goal-of-the-season contender after his classy bender, but the star is Webb, looking a snip at £85,000. However, Campbell reveals he nearly didn't play the 19-year-old, who has been out for a month with a knee injury. Rafferty scores after Doyle's penalty is pushed onto a post.

---

8 · A · 1/10 · SOUTHEND · Att 4,589 · Pos 4 · L 0-4 · H-T 0-1 · Pt 14

[Nelson 59, Pountney 90] Cusack 9p, Otulakowski 55
Ref: C Downey (Hounslow)

1	2	3	4	5	6	7	8	9	10	11	12 sub used
Knight	McLaughlin	Sullivan	Doyle	Howe	Aizlewood	Ellis	Tait	Rafferty	Biley	Rogers	Rogers
Keeley	*Stead*	*Yates*	*Clark*	*Otulakowski*	*Cusack*	*Pountney*	*Phillips*	*Mercer*	*Pennyfather*	*Nelson*	

In the local paper beforehand, Paul Clark says United must stop Doyle. Pompey fail to read the script and the ex-Brighton man carries out the task to perfection. Aizlewood's shove on Mercer looks harsh, but there are no complaints about Rafferty's dismissal for battering Keeley.

---

9 · A · 9/10 · HUDDERSFIELD · Att 6,243 · Pos 9 · D 1-1 · H-T 1-1 · Pt 15

Sutton (og) 32; *Brown 29*
Ref: R Nixon (West Kirby)

1	2	3	4	5	6	7	8	9	10	11	12 sub used
Knight	McLaughlin	Sullivan	Doyle	Howe!	Aizlewood	Webb	Tait	Rafferty!	Biley	Rogers	Rogers
Cox	*Brown*	*Burke*	*Pugh*	*Sutton*	*Hanvey*	*Lillis*	*Doyle*	*Russell*	*Wilson*	*Cowling*	

Deacon reckons Pompey should be involved in a proposed Super League, mooted by first division clubs. Sutton, under pressure from Rafferty, steers home, to level Brown's half-volley. Late on Howe is sent off for a foul on Lillis, who recovers to score, but the free-kick has been given.

---

10 · A · 16/10 · BOURNEMOUTH · Att 10,961 · Pos 10 · L 0-2 · H-T 0-0 · Pt 15

Funnell 49, Heffernan 61
Ref: K Salmon (Barnet)

1	2	3	4	5	6	7	8	9	10	11	12 sub used
Knight	McLaughlin	Sullivan	Doyle	Howe	Aizlewood*	Webb	Tait	Senior	Biley	Rogers	Barry
Leigh	*Heffernan*	*Sulley*	*Spackman*	*Brignull*	*Compton*	*Carter*	*Williams*	*Morgan*	*Funnell*	*Graham*	

Cherries' boss Dave Webb accepts Pompey (13 clear-cut chances) deserved it, but watches gleefully as Funnell nets after a kind break, before Heffernan flicks in. Biley is worst culprit, blazing high and wide from the spot, but Senior, despite hitting the bar, should have had a hat-trick.

---

11 · A · 19/10 · WIGAN · Att 4,504 · Pos 14 · W 1-0 · H-T 0-0 · Pt 18

Biley 56
Ref: C Newsome (Broseley)

1	2	3	4	5	6	7	8	9	10	11	12 sub used
Knight	McLaughlin	Sullivan	Howe	Tait	Doyle	Webb	Rogers	Thomas	Rafferty	Biley	Williams
Tunks	*McMahon*	*Weston*	*Lloyd*	*Methven*	*O'Keefe*	*Langley*	*Cribley*	*Bradd*	*Butler*	*Gemmill*	

Rafferty and Biley combine to set up a win at Springfield Park and calm fans' fears. Despite disagreeing on principle with loans, Campbell has signed Everton's Trevor Ross to cover for the suspended McLaughlin. Ex-Leeds boss Jimmy Armfield, now a journalist, rates Webb highly.

No	V	Club	Date	Pos	Opp Pos	Pts	Res	FT	HT	Att	Scorers	Referee
12	H	PRESTON	23/10	7	17	21	W	3-1	1-1	10,331	Rafferty 9, 71, 74 / Bruce 15	Ref: M Dimblebee (Stevenage)
13	A	CARDIFF	30/10	7	4	21	L	0-1	0-0	7,082	Hemmerman 53	Ref: J Lovatt (Crewe)
14	H	LINCOLN	2/11	7	1	24	W	4-1	2-1	12,529	Biley 19, 32, 46, Rafferty 66 / Bell 3p	Ref: B Stevens (Stonehouse)
15	H	GILLINGHAM	6/11	5	8	27	W	1-0	0-0	12,212	Rogers 78	Ref: K Cooper (Pontypridd)
16	A	BRISTOL ROV	13/11	6	3	27	L	1-5	0-3	9,389	Rafferty 88 [McCaffery 56, Holloway 86] Stephens 3, Parkin 31, Williams D 38	Ref: D Civil (Birmingham)
17	H	DONCASTER	20/11	6	24	30	W	2-1	2-1	9,474	Aizlewood 32p, Webb 42 / Humphries 26	Ref: B Daniels (Brentwood)
18	A	BRADFORD C	4/12	6	9	31	D	2-2	0-1	4,961	Biley 66, 77 / Gray 32, 60	Ref: N Glover (Chorley)
19	A	CHESTERFIELD	18/12	5	19	34	W	1-0	0-0	2,440	Tait 46	Ref: R Bridges (Deeside)
20	H	BRENTFORD	27/12	4	8	37	W	2-1	1-1	14,476	Ellis 29, Webb 56 / Joseph 32	Ref: M James (Horsham)
21	A	READING	28/12	2	19	40	W	2-1	0-0	7,646	Biley 56, Aizlewood 70p / Dixon 64	Ref: D Lloyd (Fernhill Heath)
22	H	PLYMOUTH	1/1	2	8	43	W	2-1	2-0	15,856	Webb 30, Smith 34 (og) / McLaughlin 70 (og)	Ref: A Ward (London)
23	A	SHEFFIELD UTD	15/1	6	16	43	L	1-2	0-0	12,907	Aizlewood 84p / Morris 54, 76	Ref: K Redfern (Whitley Bay)

12 — PRESTON (H) 23/10
Portsmouth: Knight, Ross*, Doyle, Sullivan, Aizlewood, Tait, Thomas, Webb, Rafferty, Biley, Rogers
Preston: Arnold, Walsh*, Clark, McAteer, Westwell, Gowling, Kelly, Bell, Elliott, Naughton, Bruce (Buckley)

Pompey's penalty nightmare is developing as Doyle, despite listening to Ross, misses his third in four. Rogers – so often the butt of the crowd, but now lauded – is fouled by Walsh. Quickly, Rogers crosses for Rafferty to restore the lead, then Webb follows suit for a hat-trick header.

13 — CARDIFF (A) 30/10
Portsmouth: Knight, Ross, Doyle, Sullivan, Aizlewood, Tait, Thomas, Webb, Rafferty, Biley, Rogers
Cardiff: Thomas, Jones, Micaleff, Bodin, Dwyer, Bennett G, Bennett D, Ingram, Gibbins, Hemmerman, Lewis

Webb becomes the third Pompey player to miss from the spot in a month, thundering against the bar after Gibbins flattens Rafferty. Ex-Fratton favourite Hemmerman's header (his eighth in 16 games) seals it for Len Ashurst's side, who bounce back from a 0-4 beating at Huddersfield.

14 — LINCOLN (H) 2/11
Portsmouth: Knight, Ross, Doyle, Sullivan, Aizlewood, Tait, Thomas, Webb, Rafferty, Biley, Rogers
Lincoln: Felgate, Carr, Neale, Cockerill, Peake, Thompson, Burke, Turner, Hobson, Bell, Shipley

It's a nail-biting last 30 as fog swirls around Fratton. The ref said he was always happy and through the gloom Rafferty angled home. Hobson had been felled by Ross for Bell to show Pompey how, but once Biley whips home after Neale's error, title-favourites Imps are outclassed.

15 — GILLINGHAM (H) 6/11
Portsmouth: Knight, Ross, Doyle, Sullivan, Aizlewood, Tait, Thomas, Webb, Rafferty, Biley, Rogers
Gillingham: Hillyard, Sharpe, Bruce, Adams, Shaw, Tydeman, Powell, Johnson, Cascarino, Grewcock*, Weatherly (Price)

'I wasn't too amused': Campbell. Rafferty creates the goal with a run and cross for Rogers to volley home his first in two years, at the far post. Ross prolongs Pompey's agony, making it six misses in seven, as Hillyard saves his shot after Tait's dramatic fall under Shaw's tackle.

16 — BRISTOL ROV (A) 13/11
Portsmouth: Knight, Ross*, Doyle, Sullivan, Aizlewood, Tait, Webb, Rafferty, Biley, Rogers (Thomas)
Bristol Rovers: Kite, Slatter, Williams G, Williams B, Parkin, McCaffery, Holloway, Stephens, Randall, Barrett

A sad week – Dickinson died on Monday – ends with a thrashing at Eastville against a team who have now scored four or more seven times so far this season. Ross is roasted by winger Barrett and will return to Goodison. Rovers' bobby Gould singles out Knight for special praise.

17 — DONCASTER (H) 20/11
Portsmouth: Knight, McLaughlin, Doyle, Sullivan, Howe, Aizlewood, Webb, Rafferty, Biley, Rogers
Doncaster: Peacock, Humphries, Lister, Watson, Wigginton, Cawthorne, Douglas*, Owen, Snodin G, Robertson (Mell)

Aizlewood's trusty right boot ends Pompey's penalty horror, converting after Rafferty's shot is handled by Lister. Rock-bottom Rovers had stunned the crowd when Humphries nodded home Owen's cross, but lose out when Webb accepts a simple chance, after Rogers' wing-play.

18 — BRADFORD C (A) 4/12
Portsmouth: Knight, McLaughlin, Doyle, Sullivan, Howe, Rollings, Webb, Rafferty, Biley, Rogers
Bradford City: McManus, Podd, Chapman, Lester, Cooke, Jackson, Ellis, Campbell, McNiven, Mellor (Gray)

It is costing Deacon £5,000 a week to keep Pompey solvent and the wage-bill has ballooned to over £430,000. Whatever they're paying Alan Biley is money well spent, as he shows class to twice clip the ball over the advancing McManus and save a point after Gray's double-strike.

19 — CHESTERFIELD (A) 18/12
Portsmouth: Knight, McLaughlin, Doyle, Sullivan*, Howe, Rollings, Webb, Rafferty, Biley, Rogers
Chesterfield: Gregory, Pollard*, Wilson, Partridge, Green, Henson, Plummer, Walker, Kowalski, Windridge (Stirk)

The ref plays a good advantage, letting Rafferty cross for Tait to soften the blow as Deacon announces an immediate 25% rise in admission costs to cover Pompey's widening balance-sheet. The election of his wife Joan, doubles the number of female directors in the Football League.

20 — BRENTFORD (H) 27/12
Portsmouth: Knight, McLaughlin, Doyle, Sullivan, Howe, Aizlewood, Webb, Ellis, Rafferty*, Biley, Rogers
Brentford: Roche, Strong, Booker, Wilkins, Whitehead, Hurlock, Kamara, Joseph, Johnson, Bowles*, Roberts (Walker)

Knight ends up a hero, as his string of late saves preserve the points, but Ex-Man U keeper Roche is left blushing as Webb's shot squirms from his grasp and settles it. Ellis gets in front of Hurlock to nod in his first league goal in ten seasons, but Joseph forced home a corner of the bar.

21 — READING (A) 28/12
Portsmouth: Knight, McLaughlin, Doyle, Sullivan, Howe, Aizlewood, Webb, Ellis, Rafferty*, Biley, Rogers
Reading: Judge, Williams, Beavon, Richardson, Hicks, Wood, Bason, Sanchez*, Dixon, O'Sullivan L, Earles (Crown, Donnellan)

Pompey close the gap on leaders Lincoln to three points as Aizlewood keeps his nerve once more after Biley is fouled in front of Reading's biggest gate so far. After a sterile first-half, things livened up when Biley slotted in, only for Dixon to make the most of defensive confusion.

22 — PLYMOUTH (H) 1/1
Portsmouth: Knight, McLaughlin, Doyle, Sullivan, Howe, Aizlewood*, Webb, Ellis, Rafferty, Biley, Rogers
Plymouth: Crudgington, Nisbet, Harrison, Uzzell, Smith L, Cooper, Hodges, Carter*, Sims, McCartney, Cook

The holiday period ends with a fourth win on the trot. Pompey take a firm grip after Webb follows up after Tait's shot is parried. Rafferty then worries Lindsay Smith into an own goal, but the largest Fratton crowd so far is left on tenterhooks after McLaughlin turns in Cooper's corner.

23 — SHEFFIELD UTD (A) 15/1
Portsmouth: Knight, Ellis, Doyle, Sullivan, Howe, Aizlewood, Webb, Tait, Rafferty, Biley, Rogers
Sheffield United: Waugh, Henderson, Brazil, Garner, Houston, Trusson, Morris, West, Edwards, Curran, King

Pompey's seven-match unbeaten league run ends as Blades kick with the wind in the second-half. Morris scrambles home after Edwards and Brazil see efforts blocked. King then falls dramatically over Howe's leg, but Aizlewood profits from West's ungainly challenge on Rafferty.

LEAGUE DIVISION 3

Manager: Bobby Campbell — SEASON 1982-83

Column headings: No | Date | 1 | 2 | 3 | 4 | 5 | 6 | 7 | 8 | 9 | 10 | 11 | 12 sub used | Scorers, Times, and Referees | Att | Pos | Pt | F-A | H-T

---

24 — A ORIENT — 18/1 | Att 3,961 | Pos 6 (opp 13) | Pt 43 | F-A L 1-2 | H-T 1-1

Pos	1	2	3	4	5	6	7	8	9	10	11	12 sub used
Pompey	Knight	Ellis*	Sullivan	Doyle	Howe	Aizlewood	Webb	Tait	Rafferty	Biley	Rogers	Thomas
Orient	*Day*	*Roffey*	*Peach*	*Foster*	*Cunningham*	*Cornwell*	*Gray*	*Godfrey*	*Houchen*	*Kitchen**	*Sussex*	*Smith*

Scorers: Rafferty 5 / *Peach 34p, Sussex 79*. Ref: D Hedges (Oxford)

Campbell stomps off without comment as Pompey snatch defeat from the jaws of victory. Sullivan, in his 500th league match, is the villain. Twice he is skinned by Godfrey and each time a goal results. Aizlewood handles a cross for Peach's pen, then Sussex scores after a scramble.

---

25 — H OXFORD — 22/1 | Att 10,882 | Pos 4 (opp 6) | Pt 46 | F-A W 1-0 | H-T 1-0

Pos	1	2	3	4	5	6	7	8	9	10	11	12 sub used
Pompey	Knight	Ellis	Sullivan	Doyle	Howe	Aizlewood	Webb	Tait	Rafferty	Biley*	Rogers	Thomas
Oxford	*Butcher*	*Fagg*	*Grant*	*Train*	*Briggs*	*Shotton*	*Lawrence*	*Foley**	*Vinter*	*Brock*	*Smithers*	*Barnett*

Scorers: Rafferty 35. Ref: A Gunn (Burgess Hill)

Pompey end Oxford's impressive run of six wins and a draw in their last seven, when Rafferty feeds off Webb's pass and cuts in from the left to smash the ball into the top corner. Shotton almost saves a deserved point near the end when his header loops onto the bar, but Blues hang on.

---

26 — A WREXHAM — 29/1 | Att 3,007 | Pos 3 (opp 18) | Pt 49 | F-A W 2-0 | H-T 0-0

Pos	1	2	3	4	5	6	7	8	9	10	11	12 sub used
Pompey	Knight	McLaughlin	Sullivan	Doyle	Howe	Aizlewood	Webb	Tait	Rafferty	Biley	Rogers	Barker
Wrexham	*Niedzwiecki*	*King*	*Hill*	*Savage*	*Dowman*	*Keay*	*Arkwright*	*Buxton*	*Hunt*	*Steele*	*Baker**	*Barker*

Scorers: Biley 60, Rafferty 73. Ref: K Walmsley (Thornton)

Biley's nudge over the line after Niedzwiecki flaps at Webb's cross changes the game as Bobby Roberts' side relinquish an unbeaten home run stretching back to October. Tait's driving run sets up Rafferty to drill home and leave Wrexham facing a futile battle against the drop.

---

27 — A MILLWALL — 6/2 | Att 5,621 | Pos 2 (opp 23) | Pt 52 | F-A W 2-0 | H-T 1-0

Pos	1	2	3	4	5	6	7	8	9	10	11	12 sub used
Pompey	Knight	McLaughlin	Sullivan	Doyle	Howe	Aizlewood	Webb	Tait	Rafferty	Biley	Thomas	Shinton
Millwall	*Gleasure*	*Martin*	*Stride*	*Madden*	*Allardyce*	*Roberts*	*Hayes*	*Horrix**	*Aylott*	*Massey*	*Chatterton*	*Shinton*

Scorers: Tait 37, Webb 89. Ref: R Milford (Bristol)

Police make this high-risk fixture an 11am Sunday kick-off and their bid to avoid trouble pays off. It is George Graham's Millwall who have all the problems; this loss leaves them in deep trouble. On a mud-heap, Howe's nod-back for Tait silences the Lions' roar, then Webb chips in.

---

28 — H EXETER — 12/2 | Att 10,622 | Pos 2 (opp 17) | Pt 55 | F-A W 3-2 | H-T 2-0

Pos	1	2	3	4	5	6	7	8	9	10	11	12 sub used
Pompey	Knight	McLaughlin	Sullivan	Doyle	Howe	Aizlewood	Webb	Tait	Rafferty	Biley	Rogers	Gibson
Exeter	*Bond*	*Sparrow*	*Viney*	*Harle*	*Davies*	*McEwan*	*Neville*	*Rogers*	*Pullar*	*Delve*	*Gibson*	

Scorers: Biley 14, Tait 21, Howe 60 / *Neville 78, 87*. Ref: J Moules (Ongar)

Complacency almost costs dear as Exeter make a fine come-back. Doyle gifts Neville the first, then the ex-Saint powers home Fratton old-boy Viney's centre. Earlier, headers from Biley and Tait, followed by Howe's jubilant volley, made an eighth home win in a row look inevitable.

---

29 — A LINCOLN — 16/2 | Att 6,311 | Pos 1 (opp 3) | Pt 58 | F-A W 3-0 | H-T 1-0

Pos	1	2	3	4	5	6	7	8	9	10	11	12 sub used
Pompey	Knight	McLaughlin	Sullivan	Doyle	Howe*	Aizlewood	Webb	Tait	Rafferty	Biley	Rogers	Ellis
Lincoln	*Felgate*	*Simmonite*	*Neale*	*Cockerill*	*Peake*	*Carr*	*Burke**	*Turner*	*Hobson*	*Bell*	*Shipley*	*White*

Scorers: Aizlewood 5, Rafferty 55, 61. Ref: J Key (Rotherham)

Lincoln's hope of a shoe-string promotion will fade after this drubbing. Pompey blitz to the top of the table, and inflict only the Imps' second home defeat in 18 months, after Cardiff lose at Bradford. Webb orchestrates the destruction and Campbell purrs: 'A boy grew up tonight'.

---

30 — H HUDDERSFIELD — 22/2 | Att 18,615 | Pos 1 (opp 4) | Pt 61 | F-A W 3-2 | H-T 3-0

Pos	1	2	3	4	5	6	7	8	9	10	11	12 sub used
Pompey	Knight	McLaughlin	Sullivan	Doyle	Rollings	Aizlewood	Webb	Tait	Rafferty	Biley	Rogers	
Huddersfield	*Cox*	*Brown*	*Burke*	*Stanton*	*Sutton*	*Hanvey*	*Lillis*	*Doyle*	*Russell*	*Wilson*	*Cowling*	

Scorers: Aizlewood 13p, Webb 19, 37 / *Russell 48, Brown 55p*. Ref: J Deakin

On a frozen pitch, Hanvey fouls Biley for the first, then Webb snaps up two simple goals. When the ref slips, abandonment is a possibility, but Rollings' foul lets Brown make it competitive and ensures a finish. Hanvey hauls back Biley again in the box, but this time Cox saves the kick.

---

31 — A BOURNEMOUTH — 26/2 | Att 13,406 | Pos 1 (opp 18) | Pt 64 | F-A W 2-0 | H-T 1-0

Pos	1	2	3	4	5	6	7	8	9	10	11	12 sub used
Pompey	Knight	McLaughlin	Sullivan	Doyle	Rollings*	Aizlewood	Webb	Tait	Rafferty	Biley	Rogers	
Bournemouth	*Leigh*	*Heffernan*	*Solley*	*Spackman*	*Brignall*	*Impey*	*Dawtry*	*Beck**	*Morgan*	*Graham*	*Nightingale*	*Lee*

Scorers: Aizlewood 26p, Biley 76. Ref: C Downey (Hounslow)

Seven league wins in a row is a new club record and 10,000 travelling fans celebrate. Rogers is tripped by Heffernan to let Aizlewood get back in the spot-kick groove, then Biley touches home from Ellis's nod-down to seal it. Deacon promises to revamp Fratton Park if the team go up.

---

32 — H WIGAN — 1/3 | Att 16,139 | Pos 1 (opp 11) | Pt 65 | F-A D 0-0 | H-T 0-0

Pos	1	2	3	4	5	6	7	8	9	10	11	12 sub used
Pompey	Knight	McLaughlin	Sullivan	Doyle	Rollings	Ellis	Webb	Tait	Senior*	Biley	Rogers	
Wigan	*Tunks*	*McMahon*	*Glenn*	*Butler*	*Walsh*	*Methven*	*Sheldon*	*Barrow*	*Lowe*	*Houghton*	*Weston*	*Thomas*

Ref: D Reeves (Uxbridge) / C Topliss

Aizlewood is out, so Sullivan takes the spot-kick when the stand-in ref spots a shove on Thomas, but Tunks saves (85). 'The last one I took was ten years ago and I missed that too,' he lamented. The ref had an Achilles injury, giving local linesman Chris Dixon 45 minutes of fame.

---

33 — A PRESTON — 5/3 | Att 5,610 | Pos 1 (opp 23) | Pt 66 | F-A D 0-0 | H-T 0-0

Pos	1	2	3	4	5	6	7	8	9	10	11	12 sub used
Pompey	Knight	Ellis	Sullivan	Doyle	Rollings	Aizlewood	Webb	Tait	Rafferty	Biley	Rogers	
Preston	*Hodge*	*Coleman*	*McAteer*	*O'Riordan*	*Westwell*	*Lodge*	*Walsh**	*Bruce*	*Elliott*	*Naughton*	*Bell*	*Gowling*

Ref: J Hough (Macclesfield)

Suddenly goals are hard to come by, but the returning Rafferty works hard to break down Gordon Lee's team, who will recover to avoid a first trip to Division Four. Pompey are grateful to Knight for a superb tip-over from Willie Naughton, to keep a point intact on a pudding of a pitch.

---

34 — H CARDIFF — 12/3 | Att 24,354 | Pos 1 (opp 2) | Pt 67 | F-A D 0-0 | H-T 0-0

Pos	1	2	3	4	5	6	7	8	9	10	11	12 sub used
Pompey	Knight	Ellis	Sullivan	Doyle	Rollings	Webb	Webb	Tait	Rafferty	Biley	Rogers	
Cardiff	*Steele L*	*Jones*	*Mullen*	*Tong*	*Dwyer*	*Bennett G*	*Bennett D*	*Gibbins*	*Hatton*	*Hemmerman*	*Lewis*	

Ref: L Burden (Corfe Mullen)

The largest Fratton league gate since 1976 sees Biley and old-boy Hemmerman's 'shoot-out' dominated by the agility of the keepers. Steele produces an acrobatic save from Raff's header, then Knight reacts well to stop Hemmerman's shot, before denying the veteran Hatton late on.

Portsmouth season results — matches 35–46

Portsmouth line-up (column headers): Knight · McLaughlin · Sullivan · Doyle · Rollings · Aizlewood · Webb · Tait · Rafferty* · Biley · Rogers · Ellis

No	V	Opponent	Date	Att	Opp Pos	Res	HT	FT	Pts
35	A	GILLINGHAM	19/3	6,489	17	L	0-0	0-1	67
36	H	BRISTOL ROV	26/3	17,828	6	W	1-0	1-0	70
37	A	BRENTFORD	1/4	12,592	11	D	0-1	1-1	71
38	H	READING	2/4	15,327	20	D	1-1	2-2	72
39	H	BRADFORD C	9/4	12,198	11	L	0-1	0-1	72
40	A	NEWPORT	16/4	10,419	3	W	0-0	3-0	75
41	H	CHESTERFIELD	23/4	13,003	24	W	2-0	4-0	78
42	A	DONCASTER	30/4	2,974	23	W	1-0	2-0	81
43	H	ORIENT	2/5	16,232	17	D	2-0	2-2	82
44	H	SOUTHEND	7/5	18,356	14	W	1-0	2-0	85
45	H	WALSALL	10/5	22,244	12	W	1-0	1-0	88
46	A	PLYMOUTH	14/5	14,173	8	W	0-0	1-0	91

Home Average 14,101 · Away 6,970

Scorers & referees

- 35 — Duncan 87. Ref: I Borrett (Eye)
- 36 — Tait 42. Ref: L Shapter (Torquay)
- 37 — Morgan 83; Cassells 5. Ref: H Taylor (Oadby)
- 38 — Dillon 35p, 55p; Price 9, Earles 64. Ref: C Thomas (Porthcawl)
- 39 — McCall 24. Ref: E Scales (Ware)
- 40 — Rafferty 54, 61, Biley 72. Ref: A Seville (Birmingham)
- 41 — Dillon 5, 77, Rogers 60, Biley 73. Ref: B Daniels (Brentwood)
- 42 — Rafferty 1, Webb 47. Ref: R Banks (Manchester)
- 43 — Biley 65, Rafferty 68; McNeil 48, Kitchen 77. Ref: T Bune (Yattendon)
- 44 — Dillon 22, Biley 69. Ref: E Read (Bristol)
- 45 — Aizlewood 7. Ref: D Axcell (Southend)
- 46 — Biley 59. Ref: K Cooper (Pontypridd)

Opponent line-ups (by Portsmouth position column)

No	Knight	McLaughlin	Sullivan	Doyle	Rollings	Aizlewood	Webb	Tait	Rafferty*	Biley	Rogers	Ellis
35	Hillyard	Sharpe	Adams	Bruce	Shaw	Tydeman	Johnson	Horrix*	Weatherly	Mehmet	Duncan	Cascarino
36	Kite	Sherwood	Williams B	Williams G	Parkin	McCaffery	Ball	Pulis*	Randall	Withey	Platnauer	Stephens
37	Roche	Rowe	Booker	McNichol	Whitehead	Hurlock	Kamara	Josephs	Cassells	Bowles	Roberts	
38	Judge	Williams	Richardson	Beavon	Hicks	White	Earles	Price	Dixon	Bason	Sanchez	
39	Ramsbottom / Padd	Jones	Watson	Cavener	Jackson	Cherry	Gray	Black	Campbell	McCall	Chapman	
40	Kendall	Jones	Relish*	Boyle	Oakes	Stroud	Lowndes	Aldridge	Tynan	Bailey	Elsey	Reid
41	Turner	Kendal	Pollard	Kowalski	Green	Bellamy	Plummer	Owen	Gooding	Henderson*	Windridge	Partridge
42	Peacock	Allanson	Johnson	Russell	Humphries	Lister	Mell*	Cawthorne	Douglas	Snodin	Robertson	Wood
43	Day	Rofe	Peach	Foster	Gray	Silkman	Godfrey*	Cornwell	Houchen	Kitchen	McNeil	Smith
44	Cawston	Pennyfather	Stead	May	Moody	Clark	Pountney	Phillips	Mercer	Greaves*	Nelson	Owers
45	Kearns	Caswell	Mower	Shakespeare	Hawker	Hart	Rees	Preece	Summerfield	Buckley	O'Kelly	
46	Crudgington / Nisbet	Uzzell	Smith	Harrison	Smith	Cooper	Hodges	Phillips	Sims	Staniforth	Rowe	

Match reports

35 — A promotion wobble is becoming a wild gyration, after Duncan's late shot skips through a forest of legs from the edge of the box. A first loss in eleven is tempered by news of rivals' failings. Season ticket prices are going up, but a big deadline-day signing is promised for next week.

36 — TV proves the winner belongs to Tait, as his header hits the underside, but Biley bravely dives in to make sure and ends up with a black-eye. The Fratton End taunt ex-Saint Ball unmercifully, as Dillon (£200,000 from Birmingham) and Morgan (£50,000 from Hammers) are unveiled.

37 — Poor Paddy Roche gifted the winner on Boxing Day and he was at it again, letting Biley's shot squirm away for Morgan to score. Earlier, he was the hero, diving to block Aizlewood's pen (Pompey's eighth miss in 15) and forcing Biley to calm fans who rained missiles at the keeper.

38 — Dillon was teased by his new team-mates after he confessed he couldn't remember their names last week, but his was on everyone's lips as his double penalty blast laid the jinx once and for all. First, Hicks held Morgan, then Richardson handled, but lowly-Royals were worth a point.

39 — Two points separate the top four, but Pompey have a game in hand and visit new leaders Newport next week. The jitters set in once 18-year-old Stuart McCall's soft shot trickles in. With eight minutes left, Rafferty nods Rogers' corner against the underside, but it stays out.

40 — Colin Addison's County, with 30 points from their last 36, see their promotion hopes crumble in the face of Pompey's positive approach, aided by some intelligent refereeing. Biley demands a penalty when Kendall clatters him but Rafferty gets the advantage and hooks the killer second.

41 — Chesterfield are all but doomed after Dillon's cross-cum-shot starts the deluge, then rounds off an impressive display by flashing the final goal from the edge of the area. Knight, who played for England Under-21s in the week, is virtually unemployed.

42 — Another nail is hammered in a relegation coffin as Billy Bremner's boys are leaving the division by the trap door. Pompey, meanwhile are in the lift to the second floor, once Webb glides past two to set up Rafferty after just 40 seconds. Rogers' unselfish square-ball lets Webb settle it.

43 — Newport do their bit by losing 0-3 at Millwall, but Pompey miss out on a promotion party as Peter Kitchen – ironically signed by Campbell for £100,000 while he was Fulham boss – levels late on. Biley and Rafferty had seemingly put things on-course with a goal each in four minutes.

44 — Campbell claims we have seen the birth of 'the new Liverpool' as Pompey clinch their return to Division Two, seven years after they left it. Dillon fires home from 18 yards, but Cawston has a case for a foul initially. However, he is helpless as Biley's header sparks a pitch invasion.

45 — Alan Buckley's Walsall (just five losses since Christmas) are clear of danger, and go close to spoiling Pompey's title hopes. Aizlewood dives to head home Rafferty's cross, but then Knight excels, ensuring his 14th clean sheet in the last 24 games. A point at Argyle will seal the title.

46 — Fittingly, it is Player of the Season Biley who fires home from eight yards, from ex-Argyle winger Rogers' cross, earning Pompey's first title since 1962. A bad-tempered pitch invasion causes a hold up of several minutes and Deacon confirms that Fratton will have fences next season.

LEAGUE DIVISION 3 (CUP-TIES)

Manager: Bobby Campbell

SEASON 1982-83

Milk Cup

			F-A	H-T	Scorers, Times, and Referees	1	2	3	4	5	6	7	8	9	10	11	12 sub used
1:1	A CRYSTAL PALACE	L	0-2	0-0		Knight	McLaughlin	Sullivan	Doyle	Howe	Aizlewood	Ellis*	Webb	Tait	Biley	Rogers	Senior
	6,631 2				Hinshelwood 63, 67	*Barron*	*Hinshelwood*	*Williams*	*Hughton*	*Cannon*	*Nebbeling*	*Giles*	*Lovell*	*Langley*	*Mabbutt**	*Hilaire*	*Price*
					Ref: K Baker (Rugby)												

A superb Hinshelwood strike, after good work by Hilaire and Hughton sets up the win, but minutes later Knight looks to be fouled going for Giles' corner. 'We were tremendous,' said Palace boss Alan Mullery. 'They didn't look a division above us,' retorts Campbell enigmatically.

			F-A	H-T	Scorers, Times, and Referees	1	2	3	4	5	6	7	8	9	10	11	12 sub used
1:2	H CRYSTAL PALACE	2 D	1-1	1-1	Biley 39	Knight	McLaughlin	Sullivan	Doyle	Howe	Ellis	Rogers	Tait	Rafferty	Biley	Thomas*	Senior
	10,698 2:6				Lovell 36	*Barron*	*Hinshelwood*	*Williams*	*Hughton*	*Cannon*	*Gilbert*	*Lovell*	*Murphy !*	*Edwards*	*Mabbutt*	*Hilaire*	
					Ref: C Thomas (Porthcawl)												
					(Pompey lost 1-3 on aggregate)												

Clive Thomas courts controversy by dismissing Jerry Murphy just after half-time for three times encroaching – the latter two earn cautions – as Rogers and McLaughlin try to work a short corner. At once Gary Williams does the same and he too is booked. 'It was a joke,' said Mullery.

FA Cup

			F-A	H-T	Scorers, Times, and Referees	1	2	3	4	5	6	7	8	9	10	11	12 sub used
1	H HEREFORD	6 W	4-1	2-0	Biley 6, 11, Rafferty 57, 64	Knight	McLaughlin	Sullivan	Doyle	Howe	Aizlewood	Webb	Tait	Rafferty	Biley	Rogers	
	10,005 4:21				Showers 56	*Plumley*	*Price*	*Bray*	*Hicks*	*Pejic*	*Ross*	*Lane*	*Crabbe*	*Showers*	*McNeil*	*White*	
					Ref: D Vickers (Ilford)												

A poignant minute's silence to mark the death of Dickinson is followed by a workmanlike demolition of Hereford. Two sharp, early headers by Biley from pinpoint crosses kill the game. Old-boy Showers briefly raises Bulls' hopes, only for Rafferty to thrash home from the restart.

			F-A	H-T	Scorers, Times, and Referees	1	2	3	4	5	6	7	8	9	10	11	12 sub used
2	H ALDERSHOT	6 L	1-3	1-2	Webb 4	Knight	McLaughlin	Sullivan*	Doyle	Howe	Ellis	Webb	Tait	Rafferty	Biley	Rogers	Thomas
	13,250 4:13				Briley 5, Banton 44, 67p	*Johnson*	*Scott*	*Gillard*	*Briley**	*Wooler*	*Jopling*	*Shrubb*	*Banton*	*Sanford*	*McDonald*	*Brodie*	*Goddard*
					Ref: M Bodenham (Brighton)												

Shots are 1-6 with the bookies, but turn the form-book upside down. Webb thumps home from 20 yards, but within 40 seconds Briley finds the top corner. Banton is unmarked at the far-post to nod in Briley's corner, then Sanford is felled by Knight and Banton burys come-back hopes.

			Home					Away					
		P	W	D	L	F	A	W	D	L	F	A	Pts
1	PORTSMOUTH	46	16	4	3	43	19	11	6	6	31	22	91
2	Cardiff	46	17	5	1	45	14	8	6	9	31	36	86
3	Huddersfield	46	15	8	0	56	18	8	5	10	28	31	82
4	Newport	46	13	7	3	40	20	10	2	11	36	34	78
5	Oxford	46	12	9	2	41	23	10	3	10	30	30	78
6	Lincoln	46	17	1	5	55	22	6	6	11	22	29	76
7	Bristol Rov	46	16	4	3	55	21	6	5	12	29	37	75
8	Plymouth	46	15	2	6	37	23	4	6	13	24	43	65
9	Brentford	46	14	4	5	50	28	4	6	13	38	49	64
10	Walsall	46	14	5	4	38	19	3	8	12	26	44	64
11	Sheffield Utd	46	16	3	4	44	20	3	4	16	18	44	64
12	Bradford C	46	11	7	5	41	27	5	6	12	27	42	61
13	Gillingham	46	12	4	7	37	29	4	9	10	21	30	61
14	Bournemouth	46	11	7	5	35	20	5	6	12	24	48	61
15	Southend	46	10	8	5	41	28	5	6	12	25	37	59
16	Preston	46	11	10	2	35	17	4	3	16	25	52	58
17	Millwall	46	12	7	4	41	24	2	6	15	23	53	55
18	Wigan	46	12	4	9	35	33	5	5	13	25	39	54
19	Exeter	46	12	4	7	49	43	2	8	13	32	61	54
20	Orient	46	10	6	7	44	38	5	3	15	20	50	54
21	Reading	46	10	8	5	37	28	2	9	12	27	51	53
22	Wrexham	46	11	6	6	40	26	1	9	13	16	50	51
23	Doncaster	46	6	8	9	38	44	3	3	17	19	53	38
24	Chesterfield	46	6	6	11	28	28	2	7	14	15	40	37
		1104	297	137	118	1005	612	118	137	297	612	1005	1519

	Appearances						Goals			
	Lge	Sub	LC	Sub	FAC	Sub	Lge	LC	FAC	Tot
Aizlewood, Steve	42		1		1		7			7
Berry, Steve		1								
Biley, Alan	46		2		2		23	1	2	26
Crown, David		1								
Dillon, Kevin	11						5			5
Doyle, Bobby	44		2		2		1			1
Ellis, Peter	16	10	2		1		1			1
Howe, Ernie	27		2		2		2			2
Knight, Alan	46		2		2					
McLaughlin, John	32		2		2					
Morgan, Nicky	3	3					1			1
Rafferty, Billy	41		1		2		17	2		19
Rogers, Alan	40	2	2		2		2			2
Rollings, Andy	10									
Ross, Trevor	5									
Senior, Trevor	2					2				
Sullivan, Colin	46									
Tait, Mick	44		2		2		6			6
Thomas, Dave	9	4	1		1	1				
Webb, Neil	42		1		2		8	1		9
(own-goals)							1			1
20 players used	506	21	22	2	22	1	74	1	5	80

Odds & ends

Double wins: (7) Walsall, Chesterfield, Wrexham, Millwall, Lincoln, Doncaster, Plymouth.

Double losses: (0).

Won from behind (3) Sheffield Utd (h), Lincoln (h), Doncaster (h).

Lost from in front: (1) Orient (a).

High spots: Won championship with a record points total (91).

Only lost two games at home.

Won nine consecutive home league matches from October to February.

Won a club-record seven consecutive league matches in January and February.

Unbeaten in final six games of the season.

Low spots: Losing 1-3 at home to fourth division Aldershot in the FA Cup second round.

1-5 defeat at Bristol Rovers in November.

0-4 defeat at Southend in October.

Missed eight out of a record 17 penalties awarded during the season.

Player of the Year: Alan Biley.

Ever-presents: (3) Alan Knight, Colin Sullivan, Alan Biley.

Hat-tricks: Billy Rafferty (1), Alan Biley (1).

Leading Scorer: Alan Biley (26).

CANON LEAGUE DIVISION 2 — Manager: Bobby Campbell — SEASON 1983-84

In each match the top (roman) line is Portsmouth; the lower (italic) line is the opponent. The "Pos" figures show Portsmouth's league position (bold) with the opponents' position (italic).

No	Date	Venue	Opponent	Res	F–A	H–T	Att	Pos	Pt
1	27/8	H	MIDDLESBROUGH	L	0-1	0-1	17,547		0
2	3/9	A	FULHAM	W	2-0	1-0	10,672	14 *22*	3
3	6/9	H	BARNSLEY	W	2-1	1-0	12,804	8 *17*	6
4	10/9	H	MANCHESTER C	L	1-2	1-2	18,852	11 *2*	6
5	17/9	A	CARDIFF	D	0-0	0-0	9,033	10 *12*	7
6	24/9	H	SHREWSBURY	W	4-1	1-1	11,909	9 *8*	10
7	27/9	A	CRYSTAL PALACE	L	1-2	0-1	8,486	9 *20*	10
8	1/10	A	NEWCASTLE	L	2-4	0-3	25,411	12 *4*	10
9	8/10	A	BRIGHTON	W	1-0	1-0	17,582	8 *12*	13
10	15/10	H	SHEFFIELD WED	L	0-1	0-0	16,335	10 *1*	13

Match details

1. H MIDDLESBROUGH 0-1 (27/8)
- Portsmouth: Knight, Ellis, Sullivan, Doyle, Tait, Money, Webb, Dillon, Hateley, Biley, Rogers; 12: Mowbray
- *Middlesbrough: O'Hanlon, Wood, Ward, Otto, Baxter, Mattrass, Roberts, MacDonald, Currie, Sugrue*, Bell*
- Scorers: Otto 28. Ref: E Crickmore (Plymouth)
- Keeper Knight lay prone in the goalmouth after colliding with Currie following Sugrue's corner, but the referee lets play continue and Otto eventually finds the bottom corner. Campbell is furious at the decision, but is pleased with the way Money (£50,000 from Luton) slots in.

2. A FULHAM 2-0 (3/9)
- Portsmouth: Knight, Ellis, Money, Doyle, Tait, Aizlewood, Webb, Dillon, Hateley, Biley, Rogers
- *Fulham: Stannard, Parker, Lock, Marshall, Brown, Gale, Davies, Wilson, Coney*, Houghton, Scott; 12: Tempest*
- Scorers: Hateley 3, Biley 61. Ref: D Brazier (Northampton)
- Hateley's far-post header from Rogers' pull-back makes for the perfect start. Fulham boss Malcolm MacDonald fumes when Biley is offside as Doyle runs onto his own pass, but the flag stays down. Doyle then crosses for Biley's head, but the Match of the Day 'panel' vindicate the ref.

3. H BARNSLEY 2-1 (6/9)
- Portsmouth: Knight, Ellis, Money, Doyle, Tait, Aizlewood, Webb, Dillon, Hateley, Biley, Rogers
- *Barnsley: Horn, Joyce, Chambers, Glavin, May, McCarthy!, Wilkes, Campbell, Ronson, Cunningham, Gray*
- Scorers: Hateley 24, Webb 51 / Gray 77p. Ref: K Salmon (Cuffley)
- Hateley's screamer, then Webb's header from Dillon's run and cross, put Pompey in control. Tait protests as Cunningham 'dives' over his leg, to no avail. Deacon acts to curb hooliganism, handing a life-ban to a Fratton Ender arrested against Boro; the Milton End is now visitors only.

4. H MANCHESTER C 1-2 (10/9)
- Portsmouth: Knight, Williams, Money, Doyle, Tait, Aizlewood, Webb, Dillon, Morgan, Biley, Rogers
- *Manchester City: Williams, Ranson, Davies, Bond, Power, Caton, May, Reid, Parlane, Baker, Tolmie*
- Scorers: Morgan 17 / Tolmie 38p, Parlane 44. Ref: D Vickers (Ilford)
- Tait is left indignant for the second time in a week, as he concedes another dodgy pen and it seems he chested May's cross. Tolmie converts and City take over. Ex-Rangers star Parlane nips in between Aizlewood and Tait, but Morgan's header is a poor reward for early domination.

5. A CARDIFF 0-0 (17/9)
- Portsmouth: Knight, Ellis, Money, Doyle, Tait, Howe, Webb, Dillon, Morgan, Biley, Rogers
- *Cardiff: Dibble, Jones, Bodin, Dwyer, Bennett, Tong, Owen, Gibbins, Crawford*, Mullen, Matthews*
- Ref: V Callow (Solihull)
- After seven months injured, Howe makes a steady return, nearly breaking the deadlock, but his header goes over. Pompey look punchless without Hateley (thigh). Fratton's till is ringing, now clubs keep all their gate receipts; last week's crowd was the fifth highest in the country.

6. H SHREWSBURY 4-1 (24/9)
- Portsmouth: Knight, Ellis, Money, Doyle, Tait, Aizlewood, Webb, Dillon, Hateley, Biley, Rogers; 12: Morgan 85
- *Shrewsbury: Ognizovic, Williams, Cross, MacLaren, Pearson, Griffin, McNally, Petts, Brown, Robinson, Hackett*
- Scorers: Hateley 18, Biley 57, Dillon 64p [Morgan 85] / Cross 39. Ref: E Scales (Ware)
- Biley has been working hard to get fitter and lighter after a slow start to the season, but appears back to his best. He sweeps home Hateley's centre to puncture Graham Turner's team's run of one loss in six, then falls over Pearson's leg. Dillon makes sure of the points from the spot.

7. A CRYSTAL PALACE 1-2 (27/9)
- Portsmouth: Knight, Wood, Money, Doyle, Tait, Aizlewood, Webb, Dillon, Hateley, Biley, Rogers
- *Crystal Palace: Wood, Gilbert, Strong, Hughton, Lacy, Nebbeling, Giles, Evans, Wilkins, Murphy, Hilaire*
- Scorers: Biley 63 / Wilkins 16, Hateley 85 (og). Ref: I Borrett (Eye)
- The first own-goal of Hateley's career delivers three lucky points to Alan Mullery's Palace. 'I had my eyes on the free-kick, but John's (McLaughlin) forehead brushed it and it hit my shoulder,' he moaned. Biley's pace allowed him to angle home and set up a storming finish.

8. A NEWCASTLE 2-4 (1/10)
- Portsmouth: Knight, McLaughlin, Money, Doyle, Tait, Aizlewood, Webb, Dillon, Hateley, Biley, Rogers*; 12: Morgan
- *Newcastle: Thomas, Anderson, Ryan, McCreery, Saunders, Carney, Keegan, Beardsley, Waddle*, McDermott, Wharton*; 12: Mills*
- Scorers: Tait 79, Biley 85 [Wharton 54] / Waddle 13, 25, Keegan 40p. Ref: M Scott (Nottingham)
- Arthur Cox's expensive outfit expose some sloppy defending, but it is home-grown Chris Waddle, making his 100th appearance, who puts the skids under Pompey with a neat chip and fierce shot. Keegan converts after Tait trips Beardsley, and then Tait's poor pass is a gift for Wharton.

9. A BRIGHTON 1-0 (8/10)
- Portsmouth: Knight, McLaughlin, Money, Doyle, Tait, Aizlewood, Webb, Dillon, Hateley, Biley, Morgan
- *Brighton: Corrigan, O'Regan, Pearce, Grealish, Young, Stille*, Case, Smith, Ryan, Connor, Ring; 12: Howlett*
- Scorers: Morgan 23. Ref: C Downey (Hounslow)
- A bruising derby against Jimmy Melia's men, who slammed seven past Charlton last week, is settled when Biley clips a cross to the far-post and Morgan's head does the rest. Knight saved Case's free-kick late on. Raff's loan to Blades and Thomas's move to Hartlepool are on hold.

10. H SHEFFIELD WED 0-1 (15/10)
- Portsmouth: Knight, McLaughlin, Money, Doyle, Tait, Aizlewood, Webb, Dillon, Hateley, Biley, Morgan
- *Sheffield Wed: Hodge, Sterland, Shirtliff, Smith, Lyons, Madden, Megson, Bannister, Morris, Pearson*, Shelton; 12: Oliver*
- Scorers: Megson 54. Ref: A Ward (London)
- Tait's luck is out again, as Megson's speculative 35-yarder flicks off him and over Knight. Howard Wilkinson's table-toppers are matched all the way, and Hateley goes closest with a header. Rain renders the South Stand as water-proof as a colander and Deacon pledges to repair it.

Portsmouth match-by-match record (matches 11–21)

For each match: No · Venue · Opponents · Date — League Pos · Result · (two figures, the second being points) · Attendance · Score. Team line-ups are given Pompey first, opponents second (* = substituted, ! = sent off).

---

11 · A · LEEDS · 29/10 — Pos 15 · L · 12 · 13 · Att 16,254 · **1-2**
Morgan 73 — Watson 15, Barnes 52
Ref: G Tyson (Sunderland)
Knight, McLaughlin, Sullivan, Doyle, Tait, Howe, Webb, Dillon, Hateley, Biley, Morgan
Harvey, Aspin, Gray, Watson, Burns, Brown, Thomas, McCluskey, Ritchie, Donnelly, Barnes

Three presentable chances are muffed after Watson pounces on a rebound, then ex-Man C winger Barnes nets from close range. Pompey have just Morgan's finish to show for much hard work, but had Leeds' player-boss Eddie Gray not dragged a penalty wide it could have been worse.

---

12 · H · CAMBRIDGE · 1/11 — Pos 11 · W · 20 · 16 · Att 10,852 · **5-0**
Hateley 8, 48, 86p, Howe 17, Tait 71
Ref: D Reeves (Uxbridge)
Knight, McLaughlin, Sullivan, Doyle, Tait, Howe, Webb, Dillon, Hateley, Biley, Rogers
Webster, Donaldson, Murray, Motes, Fallon, Finney, Pyle, Spriggs*, Cooke, Smith, Nichols · Sinton

Hateley's first was a superb volley. Dillon hands a late penalty over to Hateley, to allow him to bag his second league hat-trick, but Campbell is furious at his midfielder's actions. This fixture had been re-arranged from 22 October, as United had just six fit players due to a flu outbreak.

---

13 · H · GRIMSBY · 5/11 — Pos 7 · W · 8 · 19 · Att 12,906 · **4-0**
Hateley 22, 36, 79, Tait 73
Ref: R Lewis (Great Bookham)
Knight, McLaughlin*, Sullivan, Doyle, Tait, Howe, Webb, Dillon, Hateley, Biley, Rogers* · Morgan
Batch, Cumming, Crombie, Waters, Nicholl, Moore, Ford, Shearer, Drinkell, Speight, Emson* · Whymark

Hateley, 22 on Monday, celebrates his second treble in five days, to eclipse Mariners. He starts by turning Town player-boss Chris Nicholl, before bending home, despite Dillon's plea for a pass, and then a towering header from a corner rounds it off. Ex-boss George Smith has died.

---

14 · A · CARLISLE · 12/11 — Pos 7 · D · 13 · 20 · Att 4,814 · **0-0**
Ref: G Courtney (Spennymoor)
Knight, McLaughlin, Sullivan, Doyle, Aizlewood!, Howe, Webb, Dillon, Hateley, Biley, Rogers*
McKellar, Rushbury, Parker, Ashurst, O'Riordan, Haigh, Hill*, Craig, Poskett, Buckley, Shoulder · Coughlin

Leggy striker Hill tempts Aizlewood into rash tackles twice too often and he is dismissed by FIFA official Courtney. Just before, Webb's cross had come back off the bar, but the ten-men hold out easily for the last 12 mins. Hateley and Knight are being touted for the full England squad.

---

15 · A · BLACKBURN · 19/11 — Pos 10 · L · 8 · 20 · Att 5,551 · **1-2**
Webb 9 — Devine 75, Garner 80
Ref: D Shaw (Sandbach)
Knight, McLaughlin, Sullivan, Doyle, Aizlewood*, Howe, Webb, Dillon, Hateley, Biley, Rogers
Gennoe, Branagan, Hamilton, Barker, Keeley*, Fazackerley, Miller, Lowey, Garner, Patterson, Glenn

Pompey look set to be only the second team to win at Ewood in 12 months, when Webb steals onto Biley's flick to nod home. Once Garner's blocked shot is clipped in by Devine, however, they come apart. Ellis's header falls short and Devine chips Knight for Garner to knock it in.

---

16 · H · OLDHAM · 26/11 — Pos 14 · L · 18 · 20 · Att 11,444 · **3-4**
Biley 80, Howe 90, Webb 90 — Ward 4, Cross 26, 34, Palmer 45
Ref: M James (Horsham)
Knight, McLaughlin, Sullivan, Morgan, Ellis, Howe, Webb, Dillon, Hateley, Biley, Rogers
Grew, Sinclair, Heaton, Hoolickin, Clements, McDonough, Ward, Henry, Cross, Parker, Palmer

Last week, Cross was the first Latics striker to score this season, but his brace of headers puts Joe Royle's team in charge. A calf strain disables Grew and Pompey prosper. The final goal is bizarre; the ball is rolled out for a free-kick, but the ref waves on play and Hateley sets up Webb.

---

17 · A · HUDDERSFIELD · 3/12 — Pos 15 · L · 5 · 20 · Att 8,724 · **1-2**
Hateley 73 — Pugh 35, Stonehouse 77
Ref: M Peck (Kendal)
Knight, McLaughlin, Sullivan, Doyle, Tait, Howe, Webb, Dillon, Hateley, Biley, Rogers*
Cox, Laws, Burke, Stanton, Sutton, Jones, Pugh, Stonehouse, Russell, Wilson, Cowling

Hateley nets from close range after great interplay between Dillon and Biley, but a point is snatched away as Stonehouse poaches a winner. Campbell acts next week to shore up his leaky defence by borrowing Sunderland centre-half Rob Hindmarch, with a view to a £30,000 move.

---

18 · H · DERBY · 10/12 — Pos 12 · W · 19 · 23 · Att 11,834 · **3-0**
Biley 19, Dillon 44p, Morgan 79 [Webb 74]
Ref: A Buksh (London)
Knight, McLaughlin, Sullivan, Doyle, Tait, Hindmarch, Webb, Dillon, Hateley, Biley*, Morgan
Cherry, Attley, Buckley, Gemmill, Watson, Powell, McAlle, Davison, Wilson, Plummer, Harbey* · McFarland

Dillon's penalty, earned after his cross his handled by Watson, breaks Rams' resistance. Earlier, Biley's header was an inaccurate reflection, as Davison's pace troubled Hindmarch. Unbeaten in five, but heading for the drop, Derby include veterans McFarland, Gemmill and McAlle.

---

19 · A · SWANSEA · 17/12 — Pos 10 · W · 22 · 26 · Att 6,404 · **2-1**
Dillon 70, Hateley 72 — Maddy 41
Ref: K Barratt (Coventry)
Knight, McLaughlin, Wimbleton*, Doyle, Tait, Hindmarch, Webb, Dillon, Hateley, Biley, Morgan
Sander, Stanley, Holtham, Marustic, Stevenson, Lewis, Lake, Maddy, Walsh, Loveridge*, Saunders

Struggling Swans – on the return from first to fourth – make eleven changes from the programme, but look set after Maddy's 25-yarder dips in. Rookie keeper Chris Sander blunders twice, first fumbling Dillon's shot, then misjudging Biley's cross. Stanley will soon 'escape' to Fratton.

---

20 · H · CHARLTON · 26/12 — Pos 10 · W · 7 · 29 · Att 15,331 · **4-0**
Hateley 14, Biley 45, Morgan 57 [Webb 74]
Ref: D Allison (Lancaster)
Knight, McLaughlin, Ellis, Morgan, Tait, Aizlewood, Webb, Dillon, Hateley, Biley, Thomas
Lange, Curtis, Dickenson, Gritt*, Dowman, Berry, Harris, Jones, Moore, Smith, Aizlewood · Mountford

Pompey hand out their traditional Xmas 'gift'; an admission price rise, but it is Valiants' debut-making keeper Tony Lange who plays Santa to Deacon's Scrooge, by gifting two goals. Pompey haven't lost on Boxing Day since 1974, and are never in any danger in this morning kick-off.

---

21 · A · CHELSEA · 27/12 — Pos 10 · D · 2 · 30 · Att 25,440 · **2-2**
Hateley 3, Dillon 11p — Canoville 5, Dixon 39
Ref: M Taylor (Deal)
Knight, McLaughlin*, Ellis, Morgan, Tait, Aizlewood, Webb, Dillon, Hateley, Biley, Thomas
Niedzwiecki, Hollins, Jones, Pates, McLaughlin, Bumstead*, Nevin, McAndrew, Dixon, Speedie, Canoville · Lee

Chelsea's sandy desert of a pitch fails to prevent an enthralling game. John Neal's promotion-tips twice peg back Pompey, who take a huge following. The duel between ex-QPR team-mates Thomas and Hollins, 70 years of age between them, is a gem and Knight saves Dixon's pen.

CANON LEAGUE DIVISION 2

Manager: Bobby Campbell

SEASON 1983-84

Note on columns: the figure shown as "Pos" is given as two printed numbers (bold Pompey league position / italic figure). Player cells show "Pompey player / opponent player". `!` = sent off, `*` = substituted.

No	Venue / Opponent	Date	Att	Pos	Pt	F-A	H-T	Scorers, Times, and Referees	1	2	3	4	5	6	7	8	9	10	11	12 sub used
22	H FULHAM	31/12	15,649	10 / 20	30	L 1-4	1-2	Biley 7 / Carr 18, Davies 22, 74, Rosenior 76. Ref: L Burden (Poole)	Knight / Peyton	Ellis / Marshall	Sullivan / Carr	Doyle / Davies	Tait / Hopkins	Aizlewood / Dale	Webb! / Sealy	Dillon / Scott	Hateley / Rosenior	Biley / Houghton	Thomas / Lewington	—
23	A SHREWSBURY	2/1	4,907	11 / 10	30	L 0-2	0-1	Hackett 11, Brown 84. Ref: T Fitzharris (Bolton)	Knight / Orgizovic	Ball / Williams	Sullivan / Turner	Doyle / MacLaren	Tait / Pearson	Morgan / Griffin	Webb / McNally*	Dillon / Petts	Hateley / Stevens	Biley / Brown	Thomas* / Hackett	Rogers / Robinson
24	A MIDDLESBROUGH	14/1	7,971	11 / 12	31	D 0-0	0-0	Ref: L Dilkes (Mossley)	Knight / O'Hanlon	McLaughlin / Wood	Sullivan / Mowbray	Doyle / Otto	Ellis / Baxter	Aizlewood / Nattress	Stanley / Hamilton	Dillon / Kennedy	Wood / MacDonald	Morgan / Sugrue	Thomas* / Currie*	Wimbleton / Ward
25	H CARDIFF	21/1	11,938	11 / 17	32	D 1-1	0-1	Dillon 87p / Lee 42. Ref: A Gunn (Burgess Hill)	Knight / Dibble	McLaughlin / Elsey	Sullivan / Bodin	Doyle / Dwyer	Tait / Bennett	Aizlewood / Tong	Stanley* / Owen	Dillon / Gibbins	Hateley / Baird	Biley / Caughan	Morgan / Lee	Wood
26	H NEWCASTLE	4/2	18,686	11 / 4	32	L 1-4	0-2	Webb 51 / Keegan 3, 73, Beardsley 45, 67. Ref: D Axcell (Southend)	Knight / Carr	McLaughlin / Anderson	Sullivan / Wharton	Doyle / McCreery	Tait / Clarke	Aizlewood / Roeder	Webb / Keegan	Dillon / Beardsley	Hateley / Waddle	Morgan / McDermott	Wood / Ryan*	Carney
27	A MANCHESTER C	11/2	23,138	14 / 3	32	L 1-2	1-0	Wood 42 / Tomie 80p, Reid 90. Ref: K Hackett (Sheffield)	Knight / Williams	McLaughlin / Lomax	Sullivan / May	Doyle / Bond	Tait / Power	Aizlewood / McCarthy	Webb / McNab	Dillon / Baker	Hateley / Parlane*	Morgan / Kinsey	Wood / Tomie	Reid
28	H LEEDS	18/2	13,911	14 / 10	32	L 2-3	2-1	Morgan 9, Hateley 23 / Wright 45, Watson 57, Lorimer 82p. Ref: T Bune (Yattendon)	Knight / Harvey	McLaughlin / Hird	Sullivan / Hamson	Stanley / Watson	Tait / Brown	Aizlewood / Dickinson	Webb / Wright	Dillon / Sellars	Hateley / Ritchie*	Morgan / Lorimer	Wood / Barnes	McCluskey
29	A CAMBRIDGE	25/2	4,359	12 / 22	35	W 3-1	2-0	Biley 6, Hateley 15, 87 / Sinton 55. Ref: B Hill (Kettering)	Knight / Greygoose	McLaughlin / Moyes	Sullivan / Davies	Stanley / Sinton	Tait / Fallon	Aizlewood / Beattie	Webb / Christie	Dillon / Spriggs	Hateley / Cooke	Biley / —	Morgan / Mardenboro'	Cartwright
30	A GRIMSBY	3/3	8,729	12 / 5	38	W 4-3	2-2	Hateley 3, Biley 9, Dillon 66, 89 / Drinkell 21, Ford 43, Cumming 82. Ref: J Worrall (Warrington)	Knight / Batch	McLaughlin / Cumming	Sullivan / Crombie	Doyle / Waters	Tait / Nicholl	Aizlewood / Moore	Webb / Ford	Dillon / Wilkinson	Hateley / Drinkell	Biley / Bonnyman	Stanley / Emson	—
31	H CARLISLE	10/3	10,748	13 / 5	38	L 0-1	0-0	Shoulder 64. Ref: J Deakin (Barry)	Knight / McKellar	Waldron / Rushbury	Sullivan / Parker	Doyle / Ashurst	Tait / O'Riordan	Aizlewood / McCartney	Webb / Buckley	Dillon / Craig	Hateley / Poskett	Biley / Coughlin	Stanley* / Shoulder	Morgan

Match notes

22. Campbell's 'going up' claim looks hollow, as Fulham – winless since 1 October – cruise. Biley clips home, but once Tait trips Davies for Carr's penalty, Fulham clean up. Davies grabs his first for six weeks and Webb is sent off for protesting when Biley tumbles over Peyton.

23. Suddenly, Pompey's boss is under pressure after this sorry display at a soggy Gay Meadow. Hackett knocks in MacLaren's pass via a post, then Brown heads past Knight to seal it. Hindmarch is judged 'slow and ponderous' and will return to Roker, but Stanley is due to sign next week.

24. Illness and injury rob Campbell of key men, but teenager Wood makes a solid debut – Malcolm Allison's Boro rejected him as a lad – in place of Hateley. Ex-boss Mortimore is in the crowd, spying for Saints ahead of the Cup-tie. Dillon strikes the underside of the bar in the first half.

25. City boss Len Ashurst and Campbell were at school together, but the Pompey boss has yet to beat him in nine tries. Lee gleefully shoots across Knight, when Tait and Aizlewood get tangled, but Bluebirds' wings are clipped when Dibble fells Biley after sub Wood's shot was blocked.

26. Ex-Saint Keegan has hinted at a Hampshire return in the summer and Deacon will make an approach next week, to Arthur Cox's fury. KK's drilled shot squirms under Knight, then his vision sets up Beardsley. Webb raises hopes, only for the Magpies' magician to turn it on again.

27. Micky Droy is the latest defender to be linked with Pompey. Wood nods his first league goal, seconds after Hateley had one ruled out, but once Tait handles Power's cross, it's backs to the wall. Reid scores his first goal in 130-odd games when Knight fumbles Baker's shot onto the bar.

28. Lorimer is level with John Charles (154 goals each for Leeds) after his pen earns an unlikely fifth win in a row. When Morgan thumps home and Hateley's low shot goes in-off a post, Pompey's first win in eight looks secure. Sullivan's clearance hits Wright and gets Leeds back in it.

29. Pompey's two-month search for a win is over, but United – 20 games without a win – run them close and might have won had on-loan striker Steve Mardenborough been more accurate. Biley and Hateley had earlier set each other up, but once Sinton scored John Ryan's side dominate.

30. Dave Booth's Mariners are unbeaten at home, with just seven against, and have lost twice since November (both against Pompey). Their unlikely promotion bid comes apart as the teams merrily trade goals, then Dillon's rocket, after Biley's knock-down, provides a fitting finale.

31. Frustration reigns as Carlisle defend in depth, but Pompey are clueless and slip to an eighth home defeat. Shoulder nods home after Aizlewood and the debut-making Waldron (£50,000 from Burnley) dally. The attendance makes worrying reading for Deacon; it is the lowest so far.

Portsmouth FC — Season match-by-match record (matches 32–42)

Match 32 — 17/3 — A BARNSLEY — 3-0 (W)
Position 11 → 17, 41 pts. Att: 7,030
Hateley 30, Biley 64, Webb 70
Ref: A Robinson (Manchester)

Portsmouth: Knight, McLaughlin, Sullivan, Doyle*, Tait, Waldron, Webb, Dillon, Hateley, Biley, Stanley [Hardyman]
Barnsley: Rhodes, Joyce, Chambers, Glavin*, Law, May, McGuire, Thomas, Airey, Geddis, Campbell [Gray]

Aizlewood is dropped for the first time in his career and Doyle takes over as skipper on the ground where he started his English career. Bobby Collins' side are never in the hunt once Hateley's header loops in and next week he will be called up for the England Under-21 squad.

Match 33 — 24/3 — H CRYSTAL PALACE — 0-1 (L)
Position 13 → 19, 41 pts. Att: 10,237
Evans 26
Ref: K Baker (Rugby)

Portsmouth: Knight, McLaughlin, Sullivan, Doyle, Waldron, Aizlewood*, Webb, Tait, Hateley, Biley, Morgan
Crystal Palace: Wood, Locke, Murphy, Stebbing, Cannon, Gilbert, Barber, Evans, Hughton, Nicholas, Hilaire

Deadline day only sees Rogers (to Southend) and Berry (Aldershot) moving, but how the squad needs freshening up. Dillon and Stanley are injured, and the only class comes from Hilaire – who will sign in nine months via Luton. He skips past Webb and sets up Evans for a chip.

Match 34 — 31/3 — H BRIGHTON — 5-1 (W)
Position 11 → 9, 44 pts. Att: 12,724
Webb 58, Doyle 61, Hateley 65; Wilson 21 [Biley 70, Dillon 71]
Ref: B Stevens (Stonehouse)

Portsmouth: Knight, Stanley, Sullivan, Doyle, Waldron, Money, Webb, Dillon, Hateley, Biley, Thomas
Brighton: Corrigan, O'Regan, Hutchings, Case, Gatting, Young W, Wilson, Smillie, Muir, Connor, Penney

Campbell shuffles his pack (Money, Dillon and Stanley back after injury) and his team hold the aces once Webb angles in. Doyle and Hateley fire home from long range, then Corrigan blunders twice. Albion fans are kept behind and endure a radio replay of the goals over the tannoy.

Match 35 — 7/4 — A SHEFFIELD WED — 0-2 (L)
Position 12 → 2, 44 pts. Att: 20,239
Shelton 11, Sterland 71
Ref: N Ashley (Nantwich)

Portsmouth: Knight, McLaughlin, Sullivan, Doyle, Waldron, Money, Webb, Stanley, Hateley, Biley, Thomas
Sheffield Wed: Hodge, Sterland, Shirtliff, Madden, Lyons, Worthington, Megson, Bannister*, Varadi, Cunningham, Shelton [Pearson]

Hateley underlined his England credentials with his five goals in two legs against France Under-21s, but he gets no change out of title-chasing Owls. Bannister is carried off after a clash with Waldron, but by then Shelton has netted from 12 yards. Sterland seals it, but Knight excels.

Match 36 — 14/4 — H BLACKBURN — 2-4 (L)
Position 15 → 7, 44 pts. Att: 8,915
Webb 9, 36; Garner 47, 78, 82, Patterson 72
Ref: A Ward (London)

Portsmouth: Knight, McLaughlin, Sullivan, Doyle, Waldron, Money, Webb, Tait, Hateley, Biley, Thomas
Blackburn: O'Keefe, Glenn, Branagan, Barker, Keeley, Fazackerley, Brotherton, Lowey, Thompson, Garner, Patterson [Stanley]

Pompey unveil the £100 season ticket, ten years after they offered a ten-season one for just £200. It looks value for money when Webb's back-header and shot confirm his return to form, but then Irish cap Brotherton runs Pompey ragged and Garner nets his third while on his backside.

Match 37 — 21/4 — A CHARLTON — 1-2 (L)
Position 15 → 8, 44 pts. Att: 6,328
Morgan 38; Lee 47, 51
Ref: K Cooper (Pontypridd)

Portsmouth: Knight, McLaughlin, **Hardyman**, Doyle, Waldron, Money, Webb, Dillon*, Morgan, Tait, Thomas
Charlton: O'Shea, Dickenson, Smith, Dowman*, Berry, Robinson, Lee, Moore, Aizlewood, Flanagan, Jones

Charlton's 18-year-old ex-turnstile operator Rob Lee put Pompey in a spin. Hardyman marks his debut with a booking and a shot against a post which would have earned a point. Lee's neat shot and well-placed header cancel out Morgan's juggle-and-shot from the edge of the box.

Match 38 — 24/4 — H CHELSEA — 2-2 (D)
Position 15 → 2, 45 pts. Att: 18,660
Biley 60, Dillon 71; Thomas 5, Nevin 55p
Ref: M Bodenham (Brighton)

Portsmouth: Knight, McLaughlin, Sullivan, Doyle, Waldron, Money, Webb, Dillon, Hateley, Biley, Tait
Chelsea: Niedzwiecki, Lee, Jones, Pates, McLaughlin, Nevin, Bumstead, Spackman, Dixon, Speedie, Thomas

Chelsea's promotion party is cut short and their fans riot. Thomas nods in and Nevin converts after Waldron's handball on the line, but then it's all Pompey. Biley diverts Doyle's shot, then turns provider for Dillon. Doyle hits the bar from 25 yards, so Chelsea still need a point.

Match 39 — 28/4 — A OLDHAM — 2-3 (L)
Position 15 → 19, 45 pts. Att: 3,558
Webb 1, Hateley 88; Colville 17, McBride 46, Palmer 70
Ref: T Holbrook (Wolverhampton)

Portsmouth: Knight, McLaughlin, Sullivan, Doyle, Waldron, Money, Webb, Stanley*, Hateley, Biley, Tait [Thomas]
Oldham: Wealands, McDonough, Buchan, Henry, Clements, Hoolickin, Ward, Colville, Parker, Palmer, McBride* [Hodkinson]

Tuesday's bill is put at £15,000 and D section seating is closed for the last two home games. The only damage here is to Pompey's reputation as Latics grasp a relegation lifeline. Tait is absolved from blame, but once McBride nips in as Stanley and Knight dither, the points are bagged.

Match 40 — 5/5 — H HUDDERSFIELD — 1-1 (D)
Position 17 → 12, 46 pts. Att: 7,738
Hateley 8; Robinson 57
Ref: M Dimblebee (Stevenage)

Portsmouth: Knight, McLaughlin, Sullivan, Doyle, Waldron, Money, Webb, Dillon, Hateley, Biley, Tait [Wood]
Huddersfield: Mason, Laws, Burke, Pugh*, Stoutt, Jones, Robinson, Cooper, Eastoe, Wilson, Cowling [Greenwood]

Derby's defeat at Newcastle ensures Pompey will stay up, but Deacon must be bitterly disappointed after his huge outlay. England-dreaming Hateley grabs a typically sharp goal, but it is only once Robinson levels that Pompey show any urgency and Webb begins to impose himself.

Match 41 — 9/5 — A DERBY — 0-2 (L)
Position 19 → 20, 46 pts. Att: 10,189
Davison 57, 74
Ref: D Scott (Burnley)

Portsmouth: Knight, McLaughlin, Sullivan, Doyle, Waldron, Webb, Hardyman, Tait, Hateley, Biley, Wood
Derby: Cherry, Burns, Buckley, Gemmill, Watson, Devine*, Powell, Davison, Garner, Hartley, Robertson [Wilson]

Pompey's recent generosity at Oldham is repeated, but it is too late for Derby who are already down. Davison's double against a spiritless team is the final straw for Deacon and Campbell will be sacked on Friday, less than 12 months after leading Pompey to the third division title.

Match 42 — 12/5 — H SWANSEA — 5-0 (W)
Position 16 → 21, 49 pts. Att: 7,359
Biley 7, 17, 85, Hateley 52 [Morgan 90]
Ref: D Hedges (Oxford)

Portsmouth: Knight, McLaughlin, Sullivan, Doyle*, Waldron, Webb, Tait, Stanley, Hateley, Biley, Morgan
Swansea: Hughes, Marustic, Hottham, Hough, McQuillan, Saunders, Lewis, Richards, Walsh, Loveridge*, Pascoe [Williams]

Alan Ball is put in temporary charge and stakes his claim. Swansea have dropped straight through Division Two and attract the lowest gate of the season. Biley grabs a smart hat-trick and sets up Player-of-the-Year Hateley to reach the 25-goal target set by his father Tony in August.

Home Average 13,161 — Away 11,182

CANON DIVISION 2 (CUP-TIES)   Manager: Bobby Campbell   SEASON 1983-84

Milk Cup

1:1 A HEREFORD 4 L 2-3 1-1 — 4,631

Scorers, Times, and Referees: Hateley 35, Dillon 71p / Phillips 4, 76, Pejic 85
Ref: K Cooper (Pontypridd)

1	2	3	4	5	6	7	8	9	10	11	12 sub used
Gosney	Ellis	Sullivan	Doyle	Tait	Money	Webb	Dillon	Hateley	Biley	Rogers	
Rose	*Emery*	*Leonard*	*Hicks*	*Larkin**	*Dleve*	*Harvey*	*Beacock*	*Phillips*	*Black*	*Dalziel*	*Pejic*

Hereford earn their first success against Pompey in eight attempts. John Newman's plucky band of free-transfers outshine their illustrious visitors and Phillips (21) is the pick of the forwards. He levels Dillon's penalty (awarded for a push on Biley), then Mel Pejic fires the winner.

1:2 H HEREFORD 11 W 3-1 2-1 — 8,363 4.9

Scorers, Times, and Referees: Biley 27, Webb 33, Dillon 57p / Beacock 23
Ref: M Bodenham (Brighton)
(Pompey won 5-4 on aggregate)

1	2	3	4	5	6	7	8	9	10	11	12 sub used
Knight	Ellis	Money	Doyle	Tait	Aizlewood	Webb	Dillon	Hateley	Biley	Rogers	
Rose	*Price*	*Leonard*	*Hicks*	*Pejic*	*Delve*	*Harvey*	*Beacock*	*Phillips*	*Black**	*Dalziel*	*Emery*

Pompey make heavy weather of breaking down Bulls. Beacock is in for the injured Phillips and he stuns the crowd to make it 2-4 on aggregate. Had Price – who will sign for Pompey in ten years' time – done better than hit the side netting just after Dillon's pen, it could have been tense.

2:1 H ASTON VILLA 10 D 2-2 1-0 — 18,484 1:11

Scorers, Times, and Referees: Hateley 40, Gibson 52 (og) / Gibson 85, Evans 89
Ref: J Moules (Ongar)

1	2	3	4	5	6	7	8	9	10	11	12 sub used
Knight	McLaughlin	Money	Doyle	Tait	Aizlewood	Webb*	Dillon	Hateley	Biley	Morgan	Rogers
Spink	*Williams*	*Gibson*	*Evans*	*Ormsby*	*Mortimer*	*Curtishley**	*Shaw*	*Withe*	*McMahon*	*Walters*	*Bremner*

Tony Barton makes a sentimental return to Fratton with his classy outfit. Pompey have Campbell in raptures as Villa are outplayed for long periods, but they bounce back. Gibson atones for his earlier slice past Spink, then Evans rumbles forward to leave the tie beautifully poised.

2:2 A ASTON VILLA 12 L 2-3 1-0 aet — 20,898 1:9

Scorers, Times, and Referees: Biley 7, Dillon 71 / Evans 52p, Withe 82, Walters 102
Ref: D Richardson (Blackburn)
(Pompey lost 4-5 on aggregate)

1	2	3	4	5	6	7	8	9	10	11	12 sub used
Knight	McLaughlin	Money	Doyle	Tait	Aizlewood*	Webb	Dillon	Hateley	Biley	Rogers	Morgan
Spink	*Williams*	*Gibson*	*Evans*	*Ormsby*	*Mortimer*	*Curtishley**	*Shaw*	*Withe*	*McMahon*	*Walters*	*Bremner*

Despite losing Aizlewood and Money (with a serious knee injury) Pompey almost snatch it. Biley is booked for only the second time, insisting Dillon's handball was accidental. Down to ten men, Dillon chips in from 25 yards, but Withe levels and Pompey run out of puff in extra-time.

FA Cup

3 H GRIMSBY 11 W 2-1 0-0 — 12,707 5

Scorers, Times, and Referees: Hateley 61, Morgan 79 / Drinkell 73
Ref: J Moules (Ongar)

1	2	3	4	5	6	7	8	9	10	11	12 sub used
Knight	Ellis	Sullivan	Doyle	Tait	Aizlewood	Webb	Dillon	Hateley	Biley*	Thomas	Morgan
Batch	*Cumming*	*Crombie*	*Waters*	*Nicholl*	*Moore*	*Ford*	*Wilkinson*	*Drinkell*	*Bonnyman*	*Emson*	

Morgan is developing his 'super-sub' status. He replaces the jaded Biley and at once earns the free-kick, which Hateley glances home. With time running out, he then gets to the goal-line and, ignoring Hateley, fires deliberately into the top corner, sparing a long trip to Blundell Park.

4 H SOUTHAMPTON 11 L 0-1 0-0 — 36,000 1:6

Scorers, Times, and Referees: / Moran 90
Ref: L Shapter (Torquay)

1	2	3	4	5	6	7	8	9	10	11	12 sub used
Knight	McLaughlin	Sullivan	Doyle	Tait	Aizlewood	Webb	Dillon	Hateley	Biley	Rogers	
Shilton	*Mills*	*Dennis*	*Williams*	*Wright*	*Agboola*	*Holmes*	*Moran*	*Worthington*	*Armstrong*	*Wallace*	

Moran poaches the winner in stoppage time, allowed for Dennis to receive treatment when hit by a coin. Biley fired over just before the goal and Webb also missed when well-placed. The game is a sell-out, but Pompey upset thousands of supporters with their ticketing arrangements.

		Home					Away					
	P	W	D	L	F	A	W	D	L	F	A	Pts
1 Chelsea	42	15	4	2	55	17	10	9	2	35	23	88
2 Sheffield Wed	42	16	4	1	47	16	10	6	5	25	18	88
3 Newcastle	42	16	2	3	51	18	8	6	7	34	35	80
4 Manchester C	42	13	3	5	43	21	7	7	7	23	27	70
5 Grimsby	42	13	6	2	36	15	6	7	8	24	32	70
6 Blackburn	42	9	11	1	35	19	8	5	8	22	27	67
7 Carlisle	42	10	9	2	29	13	6	7	8	19	28	64
8 Shrewsbury	42	13	5	3	34	18	4	5	12	15	35	61
9 Brighton	42	11	6	4	42	17	6	3	12	27	43	60
10 Leeds	42	13	4	4	33	16	3	8	10	22	40	60
11 Fulham	42	9	6	6	35	24	6	3	9	25	29	57
12 Huddersfield	42	8	6	7	27	20	6	9	6	29	29	57
13 Charlton	42	13	4	4	40	26	3	5	13	13	38	57
14 Barnsley	42	9	6	6	33	23	6	4	11	24	30	52
15 Cardiff	42	11	3	7	32	27	4	3	14	21	39	51
16 PORTSMOUTH	42	8	3	10	46	32	6	4	11	27	32	49
17 Middlesbro	42	9	8	4	26	18	3	5	13	15	29	49
18 Crystal Pal	42	8	5	8	18	18	4	6	11	24	34	47
19 Oldham	42	10	6	5	33	27	3	2	16	14	46	47
20 Derby	42	9	5	7	26	26	2	4	15	10	46	42
21 Swansea	42	7	4	10	20	28	4	4	17	16	57	29
22 Cambridge	42	4	7	10	20	33	0	5	16	8	44	24
	924	234	117	111	761	472	111	117	234	472	761	1269

Odds & ends

Double wins: (5) Barnsley, Brighton, Cambridge, Grimsby, Swansea.
Double losses: (7) Manchester C, Newcastle, Crystal Palace.
Sheffield Wed, Oldham, Blackburn, Leeds.

Won from behind: (2) Swansea (a), Brighton (h).
Lost from in front: (8) Blackburn (h & a), Leeds (h), Fulham (h),
Manchester C (h and a), Charlton (a), Oldham (a).

High spots: Mark Hateley's consecutive hat-tricks in early November.
Scoring five goals in 13 second-half minutes against Brighton.
Winning a seven-goal thriller at Grimsby in March.
Mark Hateley scoring for England in the Maracana against Brazil at the
end of May.

Low spots: Ten home defeats.
Losing 0-1 at home to Southampton in the FA Cup.
Conceding four goals at home on four separate occasions.

Regulars at Fratton see 78 league goals this season; the highest in all
four divisions.

Player of the Year: Mark Hateley.
Ever-presents: (1) Alan Knight.
Hat-tricks: Mark Hateley (2), Alan Biley (1).
Leading Scorer: Mark Hateley (25).

	Appearances						Goals			
	Lge	Sub	LC	Sub	FAC	Sub	Lge	LC	FAC	Tot
Aizlewood, Steve	22		3			2				
Ball, Kevin	1									
Biley, Alan	37		4			2	16	2		18
Dillon, Kevin	36		4			2	9	3		12
Doyle, Bobby	37		4		2	1	1			1
Ellis, Peter	10	2	2		1					
Gosney, Andy			1							
Hardyman, Paul	2	1								
Hateley, Mark	38		4			2	22	2	1	25
Hindmarch, Rob	2									
Howe, Ernie	8						2			2
Knight, Alan	42		3			2				
McLaughlin, John	33		2		1					
Money, Richard	16		4							
Morgan, Nicky	16	9	1	1	1	1	9		1	10
Rogers, Alan	13	1	3	1	1					
Stanley, Gary	11	1								
Sullivan, Colin	30		1			2				
Tait, Mick	36		4			2	3			3
Thomas, Dave	12	2				1				
Waldron, Malcolm	12									
Webb, Neil	40		4			2	10		1	11
Wimbleton, Paul	1	1								
Wood, Paul	7	1					1			1
(own-goals)									1	1
24 players used	462	18	44	2	22	1	73	8	2	83

CANON LEAGUE DIVISION 2

Manager: Alan Ball   SEASON 1984-85

No	Date	Opponents	Att	Pos	Pt	F-A	H-T	Scorers, Times, and Referees	1	2	3	4	5	6	7	8	9	10	11	12 sub used
1	H 25/8	MIDDLESBROUGH	13,070		W 3	1-0	0-0	Biley 87 — Ref: K Cooper (Pontypridd). Ball's new-look team is without banned ex-Boro-boy Kennedy and Gilbert, but Blake (£150,000 from Birmingham), cover for Baxter's illness, plays. In 70 degrees, Hardyman is hamstrung after 15 minutes, but it's his substitute Morgan who crosses for Biley to nudge in at the far-post.	Knight	Stanley	Hardyman*	Doyle	Blake	Waldron	Webb	Tait	McGarvey	Biley	Dillon	Morgan
		Middlesbrough							O'Hanlon	Wood	Ward	Buckley	Mowbray	Nattrass	Mills	Hamilton	Otto	Sugrue	Currie	
2	A 1/9	OXFORD	11,086 *8*	11	D 4	1-1	0-1	Wood 87, Stanley 40 (og) — Ref: T Holbrook (Wolverhampton). Div Three champs Oxford are revitalised under Bob Maxwell and Jim Smith's side are favourites to go up. Stanley, pressured by Hamilton, pokes past Knight, but with time ebbing away Wood springs the offside trap and angles home. Campbell is suing for wrongful dismissal.	Knight	Stanley	Tait	Doyle	Blake	Gilbert	Webb	Kennedy	McGarvey*	Biley	Dillon	Wood
		Oxford							Hardwick	Langan	McDonald	Trewick	Briggs	Shotton	Rh's-Brown	Aldridge	Hamilton	Hebberd	Brock	
3	H 8/9	BARNSLEY	11,509 *17*	13	D 5	0-0	0-0	Ref: L Shapter (Torquay). McGarvey is struggling, but his luck is out, as only an offside, and two saves by Baker, keep him off the score-sheet. Pompey want Norwich's Keith Bertschin as a Hateley-style striker, while Money and Wimbleton face more surgery on their injured knees; the latter will have to retire.	Knight	Stanley	Tait	Doyle	Blake	Gilbert	Webb	Kennedy	McGarvey	Biley	Dillon*	Wood
		Barnsley							Baker	Joyce	Law	Ronson	May	Futcher	Geddis	Thomas	Walsh	Plummer*	Campbell	McGuire
4	A 15/9	LEEDS	19,438 *3*	11	W 8	1-0	0-0	Biley 70 — Ref: R Banks (Manchester). 'And now you've got to believe us!' crows Ball after this impressive win over promotion-contenders Leeds. The catalyst is 'super-sub' Morgan, who replaces McGarvey, then crosses for Biley to head home. Blake and Gilbert look the part and Tait is filling in well at left-back.	Knight	Stanley	Tait	Doyle	Blake	Gilbert	Webb	Kennedy	McGarvey*	Biley	Dillon	Morgan
		Leeds							Harvey	Irwin	Gray	Watson	Linighan	Aspin	Wright	Sheridan	McCluskey*	Lorimer	Sellars	Ritchie
5	A 18/9	BIRMINGHAM	18,012 *1*	6	W 11	1-0	0-0	Webb 83 — Ref: P Tydlesley (Stockport). Birmingham are looking to bounce back after relegation, but are emphatically beaten here. Mick Harford misses an early chance, but then is snuffed out as a threat. Fiery Hopkins is sent off, then the goal arrives as Webb shows great composure to bring down the ball and finish.	Knight	Stanley	Tait	Doyle	Blake	Gilbert	Webb	Kennedy	Morgan	Biley	Dillon	
		Birmingham							Coton	Roberts B	V d Hauwe	Wright B	Armstrong	Daly	Kuhl	Gorman	Harford	Clarke	Hopkins !	
6	H 22/9	SHREWSBURY	12,703 *6*	4	W 14	3-0	0-0	Webb 54, 90, Morgan 85 — Ref: M James (Horsham). A score-line which disguises Shrews' doggedness. Pompey labour, but finally break through when Webb chests down Gilbert's long-pass and angles home. Morgan's header and Webb's second give things a flattering gloss. Pompey offer £70,000 for Bertschin, but refuse arbitration.	Knight	Stanley	Tait	Doyle	Blake	Gilbert	Webb	Kennedy	Morgan	Biley	Dillon	Tester
		Shrewsbury							Green	Williams	Johnson	MacLaren	Griffin	Cross	McNally	Bates	Nardiello*	Robinson	Hackett	
7	A 29/9	CHARLTON	9,251 *8*	7	D 15	2-2	2-1	Biley 25, Morgan 26, Hales 44, Towner 75 — Ref: A Seville (Birmingham). Biley nods in Kennedy's far-post cross and Pompey have a first-half league goal for the first time this season. Inside 60 seconds Dillon and Morgan contrive a carbon copy, then Hales seizes on Dill's over-elaboration. Aizlewood hits a post, and Towner ensures justice for Valiants.	Knight	Stanley	Tait	Doyle	Blake	Gilbert	Webb	Kennedy	Morgan	Biley	Dillon	Flanaghan
		Charlton							Johns	Friar	Dickenson	Gritt	Moore	Berry	Towner	Hales	Lee	Aizlewood		
8	H 2/10	SHEFFIELD UTD	13,439 *14*	3	W 18	2-1	0-1	McGarvey 70, Morgan 71, McHale 10 — Ref: J Moules (Ongar). Two more in a minute put Pompey third – their highest placing since 1968 – but it was close run. Sub McGarvey breaks his duck, hooking in Kennedy's corner, to cancel out McHale's 30-yarder for promoted Blades. At once, Dillon robs Heffernan and Morgan's head trumps Waugh.	Knight	Stanley	Tait	Wood*	Blake	Gilbert	Webb	Kennedy	Morgan	Biley	Dillon	McGarvey
		Sheffield Utd							Waugh	Heffernan	Bolton	Arnott	Stancliffe	Kenworthy	Morris	Cockerill	Edwards	McHale	Henderson	
9	A 6/10	CARDIFF	6,201 *22*	2	W 21	2-1	0-1	Webb 48, McGarvey 68, Elsey 25 — Ref: K Barratt (Coventry). Pompey come from behind again, but are lucky. Ex-England Gerry Francis pulls the strings for City and Ball will sign him soon. Webb turns and shoots to level, then McGarvey nods home Kennedy's centre. 'The players have asked me to apologise for their performance,' said Ball.	Knight	Stanley	Tait	McGarvey	Blake	Gilbert	Webb	Kennedy	Morgan	Biley	Dillon	Micallef
		Cardiff							Smelt	Jones	Grant	Dwyer	Smith	Tong	Francis*	Gibbins	Vaughan	Seasman	Elsey	
10	H 13/10	GRIMSBY	13,624 *10*	1	W 24	3-2	1-0	McGarvey 23, Biley 70, Webb 89, Wilkinson 49, 61 — Ref: A Gunn (Burgess Hill). Biley steals the show, coming on for Morgan and scoring inside a minute. He then loses control of the ball, only to see it turn into a perfect pass and Webb steers past Batch. Dave Booth's Mariners go ahead as Knight and Blake get muddled over a bouncing ball and Wilkinson nets.	Knight	Stanley	Tait	Doyle	Blake	Gilbert	Webb	Kennedy	Morgan*	Biley	Dillon	Biley
		Grimsby							Batch	Robinson	Crombie	Foley	Nichall	Moore	Ford	Wilkinson	Matthews	Bonnyman	Emson	

11. A WIMBLEDON — 20/10 — Att: 8,212 — Pos: 12 — Pts: 24 — L 2-3 (0-2)
Doyle 50, Biley 79 · Cork 44, 66, Blake 45 (og)
Ref: D Axcell (Southend)
Pompey: Knight, Stanley*, Tait, Doyle, Blake, Gilbert, Webb, Kennedy, Morgan, McGarvey, Dillon, Biley
Wimbledon: Beasant, Gage, Winterburn, Galliers, Morris, Hatter, Martin, Ketteridge, Cork, Sayer, Hodges
A ten-match unbeaten run ends against Dave Bassett's men. A wind-aided high-ball barrage sees Cork finally score. From the kick-off, Blake knocks the ball past Knight, without a Dons player touching it! Biley gets his 50th goal, then Beasant saves Dillon's pen; his first miss in ten.

12. H WOLVERHAMPTON — 27/10 — Att: 15,291 — Pos: 16 — Pts: 24 — L 0-1 (0-1)
— · Melrose 20
Ref: D Vickers (Ilford)
Pompey: Knight, Stanley*, Tait, Doyle, Blake, Gilbert, Webb, Kennedy, Morgan, McGarvey, Dillon*, Biley
Wolves: Barrett, Humphrey, Barnes, Cartwright, Pender, Dodd, Ryan*, Evans, Melrose, Buckland, Butler, Ainscow
The first match since terrace prices rose 20p to £3, ends in defeat against Tommy Docherty's Wolves. Melrose is credited with the goal, as his header cannons off Blake. Pompey are encamped in the Wolves' half after that, but Barrett, in for Flowers who has toothache, saves well twice.

13. A OLDHAM — 3/11 — Att: 3,946 — Pos: 14 — Pts: 27 — W 2-0 (0-0)
Webb 56, Morgan 75
Ref: L Robinson (Sutton Coldfield)
Pompey: Knight, Stanley*, Thomas, Blake, Gilbert, Webb, Kennedy, Morgan, McGarvey, Dillon, Biley
Oldham: Goram, Hoolickin, Donachie, McDonough, Clements, Henry, Ward, Palmer, Quinn, Parker, Barlow*, McBride
Knight excels, with five top-quality saves, but his Under-21 understudy Goram – it's a good job Knight kept him out; he went on to play for Scotland – also does well to stop recalled Thomas' shot. Webb neatly finishes Dillon's corner, then Morgan sidefoots in from Stanley's cross.

14. H NOTTS CO — 10/11 — Att: 12,267 — Pos: 22 — Pts: 30 — W 3-1 (3-1)
Doyle 32, McGarvey 40, 43 · Goodwin 10
Ref: L Burden (Poole)
Pompey: Knight, Stanley*, Tait, Doyle, Blake, Gilbert, Webb, Kennedy, Morgan, McGarvey, Dillon
Notts Co: Leonard, Hodson, Benjamin, Richards, Hunt, Goodwin, McParland, Fashanu, O'Neill, Harkouk, Burke
McGarvey – two goals in midweek in a friendly with New Zealand – strikes twice more. An unmarked header is followed by a flicked finish, to put Pompey in control. Doyle's chip levelled Goodwin's 12-yarder. Blake is unhappy and wants a move, but he bottles up Justin Fashanu

15. H CRYSTAL PALACE — 17/11 — Att: 12,656 — Pos: 20 — Pts: 31 — D 1-1 (0-1)
Morgan 75 · Barber 28
Ref: R Groves (Weston-super-Mare)
Pompey: Knight, Stanley*, Tait, Doyle, Blake, Gilbert, Webb, Kennedy, Morgan, McGarvey, Dillon, Thomas*, Biley
Palace: Wood, Hughton, Sparrow, Barber, Nebbeling, Cannon, Irvine, Murphy, Aylott, Nicholas, Mahoney
Pompey would have gone top – Oxford can only draw at Oldham – but in the end they are thankful to Morgan for his tap-in after Biley, a substitute yet again, skins Sparrow. He nearly pinches it, but hits a post. That would have been cruel on Palace, who led after Barber clipped in.

16. A MANCHESTER C — 24/11 — Att: 23,700 — Pos: 8 — Pts: 32 — D 2-2 (2-0)
Webb 8, 45 · Smith 72, Kinsey 78
Ref: M Scott (Nottingham)
Pompey: Knight, Stanley*, Waldron, Doyle, Blake, Gilbert, Webb, Kennedy, Morgan, McGarvey, Dillon
Man C: Williams, Sinclair*, Power, Reid, May, Phillips, Melrose, Baker, Cunningham, Wilson, Kinsey, Smith
The significance of City's comeback will become apparent come the final day. Webb, watched by Forest, Spurs and Arsenal lately, twice finishes classily. Sub Gordon Smith nets after a scramble to get the crowd off City's backs, then Kinsey cuts in and thunders in from 22 yards.

17. H BLACKBURN — 1/12 — Att: 16,284 — Pos: 7 — Pts: 33 — D 2-2 (0-2)
Webb 54p, Hilaire 55 · Blake 29 (og), Tait 44 (og)
Ref: E Scales (Ware)
Pompey: Knight, Stanley*, Tait, Dillon, Blake, Gilbert, Webb, Kennedy, Morgan, McGarvey*, Hilaire, Biley
Blackburn: Gennoe, Branagan, Rathbone, Barker, Keeley, Fazackerly, Miller, Randell, Thompson, Garner, Patterson
Blackburn have scored in every game so far, but rely on Pompey to keep that record going. Miller hits the post and Blake runs it in, then Tait slices out of Knight's hands. Star-man Dillon scores from the spot after Keeley's handball, then Hilaire (£90,000 from Luton) dives full-length.

18. A CARLISLE — 8/12 — Att: 4,006 — Pos: 13 — Pts: 33 — L 0-3 (0-1)
— · Shoulder 3, Poskett 80, Cooke 90
Ref: T Simpson (Sowerby Bridge)
Pompey: Knight, Stanley*, Tait, Dillon*, Blake, Gilbert, Webb, Kennedy, Morgan, McGarvey, Hilaire, Doyle
Carlisle: McKellar, Haigh, McAughtrie, Ashurst, O'Riordan, McCartney, Shoulder, Halsall, Poskett, Bishop, Cooke
Bob Stokoe's shoestring side embarrass Pompey. Shoulder gets a break when the ball hits his back and falls kindly. Poskett pounces as Knight parries Cooke's shot, then Cooke – on-loan from Sunderland – nets from close-range. The Cup draw fails to lift spirits; Blackburn at home.

19. H HUDDERSFIELD — 15/12 — Att: 11,797 — Pos: 8 — Pts: 36 — W 3-2 (1-1)
Stanley 35, Biley 77, Blake 79 · Tempest 7, Waldron 63 (og)
Ref: M Cotton (Camberley)
Pompey: Knight, Stanley*, Tait, Dillon, Blake, Gilbert, Webb, Kennedy, Morgan*, McGarvey, Biley, Doyle
Huddersfield: Cox, Laws, Burke, Doyle, Jones, Allardyce, Lillis, Cooper, Tempest, Wilson, Cowling
Deacon pledges war on the racists; Blake is abused when his error lets in Tempest. Waldron goes one better, hoofing the ball past Knight, but Biley comes to the rescue, thumping into the roof of the net. Irony of ironies, Blake then gets his head on the end of Dillon's cross to win it.

20. H OXFORD — 22/12 — Att: 22,446 — Pos: 4 — Pts: 39 — W 2-1 (0-0)
Biley 90, 90 · Brock 68
Ref: M Bodenham (Brighton)
Pompey: Knight, Stanley*, Tait, Dillon, Blake, Gilbert, Webb, Kennedy, Morgan, McGarvey, Biley
Oxford: Hardwick, Langan, McDonald, Trewick, Briggs, Shotton, Lawrence, Aldridge, Hamilton, Hebberd, Brock
The game is into 'Santa' time, allowed when Father Christmas runs on, when Biley nods in at the near post. From the re-start, Hilaire's quick corner sees Biley rise to nod in Kennedy's cross. There's still time for Hamilton to smack the bar, but Oxford looked safe after Brock's strike.

21. A BRIGHTON — 26/12 — Att: 14,854 — Pos: 11 — Pts: 40 — D 1-1 (1-1)
Hilaire 43 · Ryan 37
Ref: M Dimblebee (Stevenage)
Pompey: Knight, Stanley*, Tait, Dillon, Blake, Gilbert, Webb, Kennedy, Morgan*, McGarvey, Biley, Doyle
Brighton: Moseley, Hutchings, Pearce, Case, Young, O'Reilly, Penney, Wilson, Ryan, Worthington, O'Regan
The tide is turning in Blake's favour, but there is another ebb as his back-pass falls short and Ryan profits. He atones by rumbling up and nodding down Stanley's free-kick for Hilaire. McGarvey turned down a loan to Wolves, while Ball denies a Webb-Mariner swap with Arsenal.

CANON LEAGUE DIVISION 2 — Manager: Alan Ball — SEASON 1984-85

No	Date	Venue/Opponent	Att	Pos	Pt	F-A	H-T	Scorers, Times, and Referees	1	2	3	4	5	6	7	8	9	10	11	12 sub used
22	29/12	A SHEFFIELD UTD	14,396	15	40	L 1-4	0-0	Dillon 89p [Morris 58p, Eves 88] Cockerill 51, Edwards 52. Ref: G Naptuline (Loughborough)	Knight	Stanley	Tait	Dillon	Blake	Waldron	Webb	Kennedy	McGarvey	Sugrue	Hilaire	Cooper
		(Sheffield Utd)						A suicidal second half sees Pompey collapse once Cockerill intercepts Stanley's pass and clips in from 25 yards. Within a minute he sets up Edwards, then Morris converts a disputed pen. Burridge trips Hilaire for Pompey's pen. Pre-Xmas signing Sugrue (from Boro) flops up front.	Burridge	Heffernan	Atkins	Mortimer	Stancliffe*	Thompson	Morris	Cockerill	Edwards	Eves	Arnott	
23	1/1	H FULHAM	17,636	11	41	D 4-4	4-0	W'n 16, Bil' 18, 39, W'b 22 [Lock 90p] Coney 47, Rosenior 74, Barnett 77 Ref: B Stevens (Stonehouse) /1 Carter	Knight	Stanley	Tait	Dillon	Blake	Waldron	Doyle	Kennedy	Webb	Biley	Hilaire	Barnett
		(Fulham)						Roll up! Roll up! for the great Pompey Panto. Three points are in the bag (Oh no they're not!) as Webb and Biley star in a wind-assisted first-half romp. Fulham though, scale the beanstalk and in the final act, Blake turns Ugly Sister as he fells Carr and Lock becomes Prince Charming.	Stannard	Parker	Carr	Marshall	Hopkins	Lock	Rosenior	Wilson*	Coney	Hughton	Lewington	
24	19/1	A MIDDLESBROUGH	4,622	17	42	D 0-0	0-0	Ref: J Hough (Macclesfield)	Knight	Golac	Hardyman	Dillon !	Blake	Gilbert	Francis	Kennedy	Morgan	Webb	Hilaire	Roberts
		(Middlesbrough)						Gilbert returns and Pompey's defence looks the part again. Dillon is sent off for stamping on Nattrass, but the ten men comfortably hold out and, but for an agile save, Webb would have pinched it. Ball has signed Saints' Golac on loan and Francis starts. QPR want to sign Webb.	O'Hanlon	Kay	Hamilton*	Buckley	Mowbray	Nattrass	Ward	Mills	Otto	Currie	McAndrew	
25	2/2	H CHARLTON	12,319	16	42	L 0-1	0-0	Flanagan 80 Ref: K Baker (Rugby)	Knight	Golac	Hardyman	Webb	Blake	Gilbert	Hilaire	Kennedy	Morgan*	O'Callaghan	McGarvey	Tait
		(Charlton)						Webb has rejected a £250,000 move to Loftus Road, reckoning he can reach the top with Pompey; not on this showing though. McGarvey hits a post and goes close twice more, but a classic counter sees veteran Mike Flanagan loop in a header and Pompey are seven adrift of third place.	Johns	Curtis	Friar	Gritt	Dowman	Berry	Lee	Curbishley	Moore	Anderson	Flanagan	
26	9/2	A BARNSLEY	7,382	8	43	D 2-2	1-0	Laws 44 (og), Blake 90 Campbell 55, Wylde 83 Ref: K Redfern (Whitley Bay)	Knight	Golac	Hardyman	Francis	Blake	Gilbert	Hilaire*	Kennedy	Bamber	O'Callaghan	McGarvey	Tait
		(Barnsley)						Debut-making Bamber's burly presence (£20,000 from Walsall in Dec) forces Futcher to head against the back of Laws' head. Tykes salvage their unbeaten home run, Wylde scoring off a post, but seconds from the end Blake heads against the bar and scrambles in the follow-up.	Baker	Joyce	Laws	Ronson	Goodison	Futcher P	Owen	Thomas	Futcher R	Wylde	Campbell	
27	23/2	H OLDHAM	11,108	16	46	W 5-1	3-0	Dillon 28p, 38p, Biley 44, 63, Henry 47p [Hilaire 83] Ref: D Reeves (Uxbridge)	Knight	Golac	Hardyman	Doyle	Blake	Gilbert	Webb	Dillon	Bamber	Biley	Hilaire	Clements
		(Oldham)						Biley is on the list and could have gone to Stoke – who are willing to swap Bertschin – but the league are not happy as Potters have still to pay Norwich. Instead, the fans' darling nets twice and is felled for the second of Dillon's pens. Hilaire is fouled for the first and then rounds it off.	Goram	Boden	Donachie	McDonough	Hoolickin	McGuire	Ward	Henry	O'Callaghan	Colville	Barlow*	
28	2/3	A WOLVERHAMPTON	7,985	20	47	D 0-0	0-0	Ref: D Scott (Burnley)	Knight	Golac	Waldron	Doyle	Blake	Gilbert	Webb	Dillon	Bamber	Biley	Hilaire	
		(Wolverhampton)						Dillon rattles the bar late-on and Blake spurns a one-on-one with Flowers, but Pompey fail to convince. Wolves haven't scored at home since November, but Knight has to be alert. O'Callaghan's loan has been extended, as has Golac's. Biley will shortly go to Brighton for £60,000.	Flowers	Humphrey	Barnes	Chapman	Zelem	Herbert	Ainscow	Cartwright	Eastoe	Langley	King	
29	9/3	H WIMBLEDON	11,444	13	50	W 1-0	1-0	Webb 7 Ref: R Milford (Bristol)	Knight	Golac*	Hardyman	Doyle	Blake	Gilbert	O'Callaghan	Kennedy	Bamber	Webb	Hilaire	Downes
		(Wimbledon)						Three points were essential after the controversial sale of Biley to local (not to mention promotion) rivals. Webb's move up front to cover Biley pays dividends as his back-header from Man-of-the-Match Kennedy's long throw loops in. Dons are leg-weary after FA Cup replays.	Beasant	Gage	Winterburn	Galliers	Morris	Martin	Evans	Fishenden	Cork*	Sanchez	Fairweather	
30	12/3	H LEEDS	16,208	7	53	W 3-1	2-1	Dillon 1, Morgan 13, O'Callaghan 80 Sheridan 35 Ref: C Downey (Hounslow)	Knight	Golac*	Hardyman	Doyle	Blake	Gilbert	O'Callaghan	Kennedy	Bamber	Morgan	Hilaire	Tait
		(Leeds)						Second-placed Brum lose and Pompey are just two points away after Cally's clincher. After 38 secs Dillon's cross-shot opens it, but he misses a pen when Webb is fouled. Moments later, Morgan powers in Hardyman's cross. Knight saves two Lorimer pens, but the first is followed up.	Day	Irwin	Hamson*	Sellars	Linighan	Brown	Baird	Sheridan	Ritchie	Lorimer	Gray	Wright
31	19/3	A GRIMSBY	6,197	9	56	W 3-2	1-1	Dillon 34p, Hilaire 50, Morgan 55 Cumming 43, Wilkinson 62 Ref: J McAulay (Leeds)	Knight	Tait	Hardyman	Dillon	Blake	Gilbert	O'Callagh'n*	Kennedy	Morgan	Webb	Hilaire	Doyle
		(Grimsby)						QPR's second try for Webb is only rebuffed after the Leeds win. Mariners are the latest victims of Pompey's growing self-belief as Morgan wins his personal battle with Nicholl, easing home Webb's pass. Wilkinson kept it interesting, but leaders City are just five points away now.	Felgate	Robinson	Crombie	Foley	Nicholl	Moore*	Ford	Wilkinson	Drinkell	Bannyman	Cumming	Emson

Match-by-match results and line-ups

No	Ven	Opponent	Date	Attendance	Pos	Res	Opp Pos	FT	HT	Pts	Scorers	Referee
32	H	CARDIFF	23/3	13,620	3	D	22	0-0	0-0	57		Ref: K Miller (Harlow)
33	A	SHREWSBURY	30/3	4,140	5	D	9	0-0	0-0	58		Ref: G Aplin (Kendal)
34	A	NOTTS CO	2/4	5,631	3	W	20	3-1	3-1	61	Blake 2, Webb 24, 35 / Harkouk 44	Ref: R Guy (Kirkby)
35	H	BRIGHTON	6/4	22,867	3	D	6	1-1	1-1	62	Webb 26 / Blake 42 (og)	Ref: D Hedges (Oxford)
36	A	FULHAM	8/8	12,542	2	W	8	3-1	2-0	65	Dillon 9, Webb 45, 58 / Rosenior 84	Ref: J Ashworth (Luffenham)
37	A	BIRMINGHAM	13/4	23,983	3	L	2	1-3	1-1	65	Dillon 8 / Geddis 6, 63, 74	Ref: N Butler (East Molesey)
38	A	CRYSTAL PALACE	20/4	10,215	5	L	18	1-2	1-1	65	Webb 20 / Droy 8, Gray 75	Ref: R Smith (Banbury)
39	H	MANCHESTER C	27/4	22,459	6	L	3	1-2	0-0	65	Morgan 57 / Phillips 47, Simpson 82	Ref: M Bodenham (Brighton)
40	A	BLACKBURN	4/5	7,747	4	W	5	1-0	0-0	68	Tait 56	Ref: J Lovatt (Crewe)
41	H	CARLISLE	6/5	12,404	4	W	16	3-1	1-1	71	Hilaire 12, 78, Dillon 90p / Halsall 43	Ref: A Ward (London)
42	A	HUDDERSFIELD	11/5	13,290	4	W	13	2-0	1-0	74	O'Callaghan 19, Hilaire 70	Ref: G Tyson (Sunderland)

Home Average 15,197
Away 10,136

Line-ups (Pompey listed first, opponents in italic)

32 CARDIFF — Knight, Golac, Hardyman, Dillon, Blake, Gilbert, O'Callaghan, Kennedy, Morgan, Webb, Hilaire
Plumley, King, Mullen, Gibbins, Ford, Tong, McLoughlin, Meacock, Vaughan, Withey, Bodin
Rock-bottom Bluebirds frustrate Pompey, with the best chances falling early to Blake, who fired horribly high and Morgan, who dragged wide. Cardiff's Bodin curled into the side-netting and old-boy Hemmerman came on briefly, as City's physio. Sullivan joins Swansea on a free.

33 SHREWSBURY — Knight, Tait, Hardyman*, Doyle, Blake, Gilbert, O'Callaghan, Kennedy, Morgan, Webb, Hilaire
Perks, Williams, Johnson, MacLaren, Griffin, Petts, McNally, Hackett, Stevens, Robinson, Tester
Webb and Hardyman are capped by England Under-21s at Fratton and the pair concede penalties – both converted by Eire's Kennedy! Pompey are unbeaten in eight, but only two fine saves by Knight keep a point at Gay Meadow, where Brum, Man C and Blackburn have all lost lately.

34 NOTTS CO — Knight, Stanley, Tait, Dillon, Blake, Gilbert, O'Callaghan, Kennedy, Morgan, Webb, Hilaire
Leonard, Richards, Davis, Goodwin, Watson, Sims, Harkouk, Fashanu, Dows, Benjamin, Robinson, Waitt*
Webb chimes in with another brace, but wonders whether he will ever score a hat-trick. Twice in the second half he is one-on-one, but the chances go begging. Blake gives Pompey the perfect start with a booming header as Larry Lloyd's County are on a fast-track to division three.

35 BRIGHTON — Knight, Moseley, Tait, Dillon, Blake, Gilbert, O'Callaghan, Kennedy, Morgan, Webb, Hilaire
Keown, Hutchings, Pearce, Young, O'Reilly, Wilson, Biley, Ferguson, Connor, Smillie
Biley is back, but he is subdued by Blake and Gilbert. Webb thrashes home a tremendous goal as Morgan lays Stanley's pass into his path, but Chris Cattlin's Seagulls soar again when Danny Wilson's centre flashes across Knight, and Blake can only touch in his third o.g. of the season.

36 FULHAM — Knight, Payton, Stanley, Dillon, Blake, Gilbert, O'Callaghan, Kennedy, Morgan, Webb, Hilaire
Peyton, Cottington, Carr, Elkins, Marshall, Locke, Scott, Wilson, Rosenior, Houghton, Lewington
Fulham now have a state-of-the-art 'cell-system' pitch and have evicted the Rugby League team. The result is an ideal surface for Ball's Boys. Dillon's cross-shot goes in off both posts, then Webb slides home, before catching Fulham on the counter. Man C lose to Leeds; a perfect day.

37 BIRMINGHAM — Knight, Seaman, Stanley, Hardyman, Blake, Gilbert, O'Callaghan, Kennedy, Morgan, Webb, Hilaire
Seaman, Ranson, Roberts, Wright, Armstrong, Kuhl, Daly, Clarke, Bremner, Geddis, Hopkins
Ron Saunders' Brum have lost their last three away, and might have folded Dillon's early shot gone in, but it hit the post. Quickly, the unmarked Geddis flicks in, only for Dillon to cleverly beat Seaman. More defensive chaos gives Geddis two more; promotion is in the balance.

38 CRYSTAL PALACE — Knight, Wood, Waldron, Dillon, Blake, Gilbert, O'Callaghan, Thomas*, Morgan, Webb, Hilaire
Wood, Locke, Sparrow, Taylor, Dray, Cannon, Irvine, Murphy, Aylott, Gray, Stebbing, McGarvey
Pompey are minus suspended Tait, Kennedy and O'Callaghan, so youth coach Thomas is recalled. Pompey founder on the rock of Mick Droy, who nearly came to Fratton last year. He rifles home after his header is blocked, then his presence leaves Andy Gray (18) free to hook home.

39 MANCHESTER C — Knight, Williams, Clements, Hardyman, Blake, Gilbert, O'Callaghan, Kennedy, Morgan, Webb, Hilaire
Williams, Clements, Power, Reid, McCarthy, Phillips, Simpson, May, Tolmie, Smith, Kinsey
City look the more jittery, but poor marking sees Phillips free at the far post to spark a thriller. Morgan forces in Tait's flick and Billy McNeill's men are on the ropes. Williams' agility saves them, then Simpson lobs Knight. Pompey need a miracle to go up. It nearly happens!

40 BLACKBURN — Knight, Gennoe, Hardyman, Dillon, Blake, Gilbert, O'Callaghan, Kennedy, Wood!, Webb, Hilaire
Gennoe, Branaghan, Rathbone, Barker, Keeley!, Fazackerly, Miller, Randell, Quinn, Garner, Brotherston
Everton have reportedly bid £500,000 for Webb. Pompey remove Rovers from the promotion-equation thanks to Tait's soaring header: his first of the season. Wood and Keeley clash and are sent off, but MotD TV cameras vindicate Wood. City draw 0-0 and hope springs eternal.

41 CARLISLE — Knight, McKellar, Tait, Hardyman*, Blake, Gilbert, O'Callaghan, Kennedy, Wood, Webb, Hilaire
McKellar, Haigh, McCartney, Ashurst, O'Riordan, McAughtrie, Gorman, Halsall, Poskett, Bishop, Halpin, Hill*
The door to Division One is still open, but Pompey make heavy weather of seeing off Carlisle. Ball's half-time team-talk must have had shades of Churchill, as they come out fighting. Hilaire eases tension, then Dillon is tripped and converts. City lose 2-3 at Notts Co; it goes to the wire.

42 HUDDERSFIELD — Knight, Cox, Stanley, Dillon, Blake, Gilbert, O'Callagh'n*, Kennedy, Wood, Webb, Hilaire
Cox, Measham, Tait, Robinson, Webster, Carmody, Allardyce, Lillis, Pugh, Tempest, Wilson, Copper, Butler, Doyle*
If City lose at home to Charlton a draw will do. Alas, Valiants rely on rookie keeper Lee Harmsworth and he lets in five. O'Callaghan's run from halfway is one of the goals of the season, but Hilaire's is academic. Even more so, as news of the Bradford fire filters through to fans.

CANON DIVISION 2 (CUP-TIES) Manager: Alan Ball SEASON 1984-85

Milk Cup

				F-A	H-T	Scorers, Times, and Referees
1:1	H	WIMBLEDON	W	3-0	2-0	Webb 33, 45, Dillon 87p
		8,999				Ref: B Stevens (Stonehouse)
1:2	A	WIMBLEDON 11	L	0-1	0-1	Gage 37
		4,670 17				Ref: T Bune (Newbury)
						(Pompey won 3-1 on aggregate)
2:1	H	NOTT'M FOREST 4	W	1-0	0-0	Biley 64
		20,409 3:1				Ref: R Lewis (Great Bookham)
2:2	A	NOTT'M FOREST 2	L	0-3	0-0	Hodge 46, Wigley 95, Gunn 97
		18,128 2:1				Ref: B Nixon (West Kirby)
						(Pompey lost 1-3 on aggregate)

Match	1	2	3	4	5	6	7	8	9	10	11	12 sub used
1:1	Knight *Beasant*	Stanley *Kay*	Waldron* *Winterburn*	Doyle *Galliers*	Blake *Smith !*	Gilbert *Morris*	Webb *Evans*	Tait *Ketteridge*	McGarvey *O'Berg**	Biley *Gage*	Dillon *Hodges*	Wood *Sayer*
1:2	Knight *Beasant*	Stanley *Kay*	Tait *Winterburn*	Doyle *Hanford**	Blake *Hatter*	Gilbert *Morris*	Webb *Evans*	Kennedy *Ketteridge*	McGarvey *Cork*	Biley *Gage*	Dillon *Hodges*	*Kemp*
2:1	Knight *Sutton*	Stanley *Gunn*	Tait *Swain*	Doyle *Fairclough*	Blake *Smalley**	Gilbert *Bowyer*	Webb *Wigley*	Kennedy *Metgod*	Morgan *Hodges*	Biley *Davenport*	Dillon* *Walsh*	McGarvey *Mills*
2:2	Knight *Sutton*	Stanley *Gunn*	Tait *Swain*	Ball* *Fairclough*	Blake *Hart*	Gilbert *Bowyer*	Webb *Wigley*	Kennedy *Metgod*	Morgan *Christie*	Biley *Davenport**	Dillon *Hodge*	McGarvey *Mills*

1:1 — Newly-promoted Dons show their physical side when Michael Smith is dismissed for a wild tackle on McGarvey. By then Pompey are cruising after Webb snapped up two slick goals. Beasant brings down Biley late on and Dillon preserves his perfect spot-kick record. Gilbert debuts.

1:2 — Ex-Fratton favourite Dave Kemp has signed for Dons, but his neat touch doesn't suit their up-and-under style. He comes on as a late substitute and doesn't touch the ball! Gage's shot pings in through a crowded box, and had Knight not parried Morris's shot it might have been closer.

2:1 — Brian Clough uses all his European experience to try to frustrate Pompey, but Ball's boys rise to the challenge. Kennedy is impressive and it is his long cross which is met by Biley, muscling in front of Mills. Forest rarely commit men forward, but Blake and Gilbert are equal to them.

2:2 — Kevin Ball is given the job of deputising for the injured Doyle and shackling Metgod. Hodge scores from close range, but Morgan claims a penalty late on as Gunn hauls him off the ball. It goes into extra-time, where Wigley accepts a simple chance, then Blake deflects Gunn's shot.

FA Cup

				F-A	H-T	Scorers, Times, and Referees
3	H	BLACKBURN 4	D	0-0	0-0	
		14,966 2				Ref: T Bune (Newbury)
3R	A	BLACKBURN 5	L	1-2	0-0	Kennedy 65
		12,017 1				Quinn 55, 58
						Ref: K Barratt (Coventry)

Match	1	2	3	4	5	6	7	8	9	10	11	12 sub used
3	Knight *Gennoe*	Tait *Branaghan*	Hardyman *Rathbone*	Dillon *Barker*	Blake *Keeley*	Waldron *Fazackerley*	Francis *Miller*	Kennedy *Randell*	Webb *Thompson*	Biley *Quinn*	Hilaire *Brotherston*	
3R	Knight *Gennoe*	Tait *Branaghan*	Hardyman *Rathbone**	Dillon *Barker*	Blake *Mail*	Gilbert *Fazackerley*	Francis* *Miller*	Kennedy *Randell*	Morgan *Thompson*	Webb *Quinn*	Hilaire *Brotherston*	McGarvey *Hamilton*

3 — A frosted pitch makes for poor fare, as Francis makes his debut. Deacon is buying the Telford basketball franchise, to bring it to Portsmouth.

3R — Tea-time snow had claimed this game last Wednesday, but today the pitch is perfect. Thompson finally punishes Blake as his slack pass lets the striker square to Quinn. He then volleys home Brotherston's cross, but Kennedy grabs a spectacular first goal from the edge of the box.

League table

	Team	P		Home					Away					Pts
			W	D	L	F	A	W	D	L	F	A		
1	Oxford	42	18	2	1	62	15	7	7	7	22	21		84
2	Birmingham	42	13	6	2	30	15	12	1	8	29	18		82
3	Manchester C	42	13	4	4	42	16	8	7	6	24	24		74
4	PORTSMOUTH	42	12	6	3	39	25	8	8	5	30	25		74
5	Blackburn	42	13	3	5	38	15	8	7	6	28	26		73
6	Brighton	42	13	6	2	31	11	7	6	8	23	23		72
7	Leeds	42	12	7	2	37	11	7	5	9	29	32		69
8	Shrewsbury	42	12	6	3	45	22	6	5	10	21	31		65
9	Fulham	42	13	3	5	35	26	6	5	10	33	38		65
10	Grimsby	42	13	1	7	47	32	6	4	11	25	32		62
11	Barnsley	42	11	7	3	27	12	3	9	9	15	30		58
12	Wimbledon	42	9	8	4	40	29	7	2	12	31	46		58
13	Huddersfield	42	9	5	7	28	29	6	5	10	24	35		55
14	Oldham	42	10	4	7	27	23	5	4	12	22	44		53
15	Crystal Pal	42	8	7	6	25	27	4	5	12	21	38		48
16	Carlisle	42	8	5	8	27	23	5	3	13	23	44		47
17	Charlton	42	8	7	6	34	30	4	2	15	17	33		45
18	Sheffield Utd	42	7	6	8	31	28	5	2	14	23	38		44
19	Middlesbro	42	6	8	7	22	26	4	2	15	19	31		40
20	Notts Co	42	6	5	10	25	32	3	5	13	20	41		37
21	Cardiff	42	5	3	13	24	42	4	5	12	23	37		35
22	Wolves	42	5	4	12	18	32	3	5	13	19	47		33
		924	224	113	125	734	521	125	113	224	521	734		1282

Odds & ends

Double wins: (5) Leeds, Grimsby, Oldham, Notts Co, Huddersfield.

Double losses: (0).

Won from behind: (6) Sheffield Utd (h), Cardiff (a), Grimsby (h). Notts Co (h), Huddersfield (h), Oxford (h).

Lost from in front: (0).

High spots: Ten-match unbeaten start to league season. Scoring twice in injury-time to beat Oxford in December in front of a crowd of more than 22,000. Eleven-match unbeaten run from February to April puts team on brink of promotion.

Low spots: Three consecutive defeats in April foiled promotion hopes. Manchester City winning 5-1 on the last day to clinch third place. Conceding a 4-0 half-time lead to Fulham on New Year's Day. A last-minute penalty grabbed a point for the Londoners.

Player of the Year: Neil Webb.

Ever-presents: (2) Noel Blake, Alan Knight.

Hat-tricks: (0).

Leading scorer: Neil Webb (18).

Appearances and Goals

Player	Appearances Lge	Sub	LC	Sub	FAC	Sub	Goals Lge	LC	FAC	Tot
Ball, Kevin	4		1							
Bamber, Dave										
Biley, Alan	18	4	3		1		12	1		13
Blake, Noel	42		4		2		3			3
Dillon, Kevin	37		4		2		9	1		10
Doyle, Bobby	19	8	3				2			2
Francis, Gerry	3				2					
Gilbert, Billy	35		4		1					
Golac, Ivan	8									
Hardyman, Paul	15				2					
Hilaire, Vince	26				2		7			7
Kennedy, Mick	37		3		2				1	1
Knight, Alan	42		4		2					
McGarvey, Scott	15	3	3				5			5
Morgan, Nicky	28	2	2		1		8			8
O'Callaghan, Kevin	15						2			2
Stanley, Gary	28	1	4				1			1
Sugrue, Paul	1									
Tait, Mick	30	3	4		2		1			1
Thomas, Dave	3									
Waldron, Malcolm	11		1		1					
Webb, Neil	41		4		2		16	2		18
Wood, Paul	4	2					1			1
(own-goals)							2			2
23 players used	462	23	44		22		69	4	1	74

CANON LEAGUE DIVISION 2

Manager: Alan Ball

SEASON 1985-86

No	Date	Att	Pos	Pt	F-A	H-T	1	2	3	4	5	6	7	8	9	10	11	12 sub used	Scorers, Times, and Referees
1	A HULL 17/8	8,221		1	D 2-2	1-1	Knight	Tait	Swain	Doyle	Blake	Gilbert	O'Callaghan	Kennedy	Morgan	**Channon**	Hilaire		Morgan 25, Hilaire 60 / *Bunn 10, Whitehurst 75* / Ref: T Simpson (Rippenden)
							Norman	*Jobson*	*Pearson*	*Swann*	*Skipper*	*McEwan*	*Williams*	*Bunn*	*Whitehurst*	*Askew*	*Roberts*		Veteran frees Swain and Channon will spearhead a promotion run. Dillon is banned, as new-boys Hull get the perfect start when Bunn rams home Askew's knock-down, but then Pompey run the show. Morgan accepts a simple chance, then Hilaire volleys in, but Whitehurst levels.
2	H SUNDERLAND 20/8	14,681		4	W 3-0	0-0	Knight	Swain	Hardyman	Dillon	Blake	Gilbert	O'Callaghan	Kennedy	Morgan	Channon*	Hilaire	Wood	Hilaire 59, Dillon 66, Morgan 80 / Ref: C Downey (Hounslow)
							McDonagh	*Venison*	*Gray*	*Agboola*	*Bennett*	*Elliott*	*Pickering*	*Wallace*	*Swindlehurst*	*Gates*	*Walker*		Lawrie McMenemy gets a lively reception from the Fratton End, but his big-name Sunderland side flop. McDonagh saves Dillon's first-half pen, but once Hilaire turns and whips in a shot, it's over. Dillon atones with a long-range effort, then Morgan dives to convert Swain's cross.
3	H CARLISLE 24/8	12,595	1	7	W 4-0	3-0	Knight	Swain	Hardyman	Dillon	Blake	Gilbert	O'Callaghan	Kennedy	Morgan	Channon	Hilaire	Gorman	Hilaire 4, Morgan 31, 43 [Hardyman 53] / Ref: R Gifford (Hengoed)
							Carr	*Haigh*	*McCartney*	*Ashurst*	*Baker*	*Bishop*	*Gavin*	*Mayes**	*Entwhistle*	*Hill*	*Halpin*		'Pompey had a better player in every position,' laments Carlisle boss Bob Stokoe, whose side's relegation already looks likely. Morgan and Hilaire keep up goal-a-game records – Morgan now has four in three – then Channon's clever pass sets up Hardyman for a first senior goal.
4	A HUDDERSFIELD 26/8	9,298	1	10	W 2-1	1-0	Knight	Swain	Hardyman	Dillon	Blake	Gilbert	O'Callaghan	Kennedy	Morgan	Channon*	Hilaire	Wood	Hilaire 16, Morgan 83 / *Tempest 67* / Ref: R Guy (Kirkby)
							Cox	*Brown*	*Bray*	*Doyle*	*Webster*	*Jones*	*Curran*	*Cork*	*Tempest*	*Wilson*	*Cowling*		If Saturday showed Pompey's class, tonight shows their resilience. Despite taking an early lead, when Hilaire's cross-cum-shot deflects in off Joey Jones, Town swarm all over Blues and are rewarded when Man-of-the-Match Curran crosses for Tempest. Morgan's volley is a stunner.
5	H NORWICH 31/8	15,504	1	13	W 2-0	1-0	Knight	Swain	Hardyman	Dillon	Blake	Ball	O'Callaghan	Kennedy	Morgan	Channon*	Hilaire	Wood	Morgan 24, 82 / Ref: D Reeves (Uxbridge)
							Woods	*Haylock**	*Spearing*	*Bruce*	*Phelan*	*Watson*	*Barham*	*Drinkell*	*Deehan*	*Mendham*	*Williams*	*Donowa*	Hilaire and Morgan could both set a club record of scoring in the first five of a season, but the honour goes to the burly Londoner, when he nips in to rob Woods of Cally's cross. Canaries are on song, but can't score. Morgan shows them how, burying sub Paul Wood's knock-down.
6	A SHREWSBURY 3/9	3,719	1	14	D 1-1	1-1	Knight	Money	Hardyman	Dillon	Blake	Ball	O'Callaghan	Kennedy	Morgan	Channon*	Hilaire	Wood	O'Callaghan 21 / *Robinson 43* / Ref: D Scott (Burnley)
							Perks	*Williams*	*Kerr*	*Cross*	*Griffin*	*Stevens*	*McNally*	*Hackett*	*Nardiello*	*Robinson*	*Tester*		Money is back, after an 18-month battle to save his career, and he ensures Pompey cash in a point when he crosses for O'Callaghan, then clears off the line early in the second half. Chic Bates' Shrewsbury dominate after that; Nardiello hits the bar and in the scramble Ball hacks clear.
7	A FULHAM 7/9	9,331	1	16	W 1-0	0-0	Knight	Swain	Hardyman	Dillon	Blake	Ball	O'Callaghan	Kennedy	Morgan	Channon*	Hilaire	Tait	O'Callaghan 62 / Ref: I Borrett (Eye)
							Grew	*Cottingham**	*Carr*	*Scott*	*Hopkins*	*Parker*	*Marshall*	*Achampong*	*Sealy*	*Coney*	*Houghton*	*Donnellan*	Ball is Bells' Manager of the Month for August and he is well on the way to becoming September's after this win. Fulham are rebuilding, but dominate a lethargic Pompey. O'Callaghan's winner is their only on-target shot, then Coney holds his head when he hits the underside late on.
8	H STOKE 14/9	13,720	1	20	W 3-0	0-0	Knight	Tait	Swain	Dillon	Blake	Gilbert	O'Callaghan	Kennedy	Morgan	Channon*	Hilaire	Wood	Morgan 53, Dillon 61p, Wood 77 / Ref: A Ward (London)
							Fox	*Parkin*	*Mills*	*Beeston*	*Dyson*	*Berry*	*Williams*	*Maskery*	*Bertschin*	*Saunders*	*Heath*		Pompey's perfect home record now reads four wins and a 12-0 goal record. Stoke player-boss Mick Mills – a former Pompey apprentice – names five under 20 and the class-gulf shows. Channon's back-heel sets up Morgan, and he is then fouled by Dyson. Wood's header seals it.
9	A OLDHAM 21/9	5,814	3	20	L 0-2	0-0	Knight	Tait	Swain	Dillon	Blake	Gilbert	O'Callaghan	Ball	Morgan	Channon*	Hilaire	Stanley	*Palmer 48, Futcher 59* / Ref: J Lovatt (Crewe)
							Goram	*Donachie*	*Ryan*	*McDonough*	*Hoolickin*	*McGuire*	*Palmer*	*Henry*	*Quinn*	*Futcher*	*Atkinson*		Defeat is cruel when you dominate a match. Kevin Ball had chances for a hat-trick, hitting the bar with a header, and twice denied by Goram, who shows the form that will take him to Mexico with Scotland. Quinn sets up Palmer, then Futcher heads home for Joe Royle's Latics.
10	H BLACKBURN 28/9	16,870	3	23	W 3-0	1-0	Knight	Swain	Hardyman	Dillon	Blake	Gilbert	O'Callaghan	Kennedy	Morgan	Channon*	Hilaire	Wood	Channon 7, Hilaire 75, [O'Callaghan 86] / Ref: K Cooper (Pontypridd)
							Gennoe	*Hamilton*	*Branaghan*	*Barker*	*Keeley*	*Fazackerley*	*Miller*	*Lowey*	*Quinn*	*Garner*	*Rathbone*		Channon's wait for his 223rd league goal ends, when he curls home after a clearance falls kindly. Patient Pompey always have Bobby Saxton's Rovers' measure, who would have gone top if they had won. Deacon admits he has been involved in talks about a breakaway Super League.

Portsmouth — Match results (matches 11–21)

No.	V	Opponent	Date	Att.		Pos	Res	Pts	FT	HT
11	A	BARNSLEY	5/10	7,064	1	8	W	26	1-0	1-0
12	H	CHARLTON	12/10	15,549	1	6	W	29	1-0	1-0
13	H	CRYSTAL PALACE	19/10	16,538	1	9	W	32	1-0	1-0
14	A	MILLWALL	26/10	6,810	1	15	W	35	4-0	2-0
15	A	LEEDS	2/11	15,672	1	11	L	35	1-2	1-0
16	A	GRIMSBY	16/11	6,436	1	13	L	35	0-1	0-0
17	H	SHEFFIELD UTD	23/11	17,558	1	2	L	35	0-3	0-2
18	A	BRADFORD C	3/12	4,701	1	17	L	35	1-2	1-1
19	A	SUNDERLAND	7/12	17,229	1	15	W	38	3-1	2-0
20	H	HULL	14/12	13,596	2	13	D	39	1-1	0-0
21	A	CARLISLE	22/12	4,225	2	22	W	42	1-0	0-0

11 — A BARNSLEY (5/10)
Scorer: Blake 13
Ref: M Heath (Stoke)
Pompey: Knight, Swain, Hardyman*, Dillon, Blake, Gilbert, O'Callaghan, Kennedy, Morgan, Channon, Hilaire, Tait
Barnsley: Baker, Joyce, Gray, May, Burns, Futcher, Hirst, Thomas, Walsh, Cross, Campbell, Flanaghan

Tykes unbeaten home run comes to an end. England U-21 Hirst is the only player to ruffle Pompey's composure, and it is the outstanding Blake who hooks home from Hilaire's corner. Rumours of Mark Hateley's impending return are scotched. 'I'm loving it in Italy,' he says.

12 — H CHARLTON (12/10)
Scorer: Dillon 45p
Ref: B Stevens (Stonehouse)
Pompey: Knight, Tait, Swain, Dillon, Blake, Gilbert, O'Callaghan, Kennedy!, Morgan, Channon, Hilaire
Charlton: Johns, Humphrey, Reid, Gritt, Thompson, Pender, Shipley, Lee, Pearson, Curbishley, Friar*

Kennedy becomes the second Pompey player to be dismissed in a week, as he intervenes in a dispute between Hilaire and Reid. By then Dillon had already scored from the spot after Pearson handled, and Pompey hold out comfortably. Money has re-joined his first club, Scunthorpe.

13 — H CRYSTAL PALACE (19/10)
Scorer: Morgan 37
Ref: R Groves (Weston-super-Mare)
Pompey: Knight, Tait, Swain, Dillon, Blake, Gilbert, O'Callaghan, Kennedy, Morgan, Channon*, Hilaire
Crystal Palace: Wood, Locke, Brush, Taylor, Droy, Cannon, Irvine, Finnegan, Wright, Aylott, Barber, Wood

Records are tumbling as the 1948 seven-match winning home start is equalled, with the five-match run of not conceding a goal at home already shattered. The score-line flatters Steve Coppell's Palace, who fall to Morgan's 11th in 17 games, after O'Callaghan nods on Gilbert's free-kick.

14 — A MILLWALL (26/10)
Scorers: O'Callaghan 10, 21, Morgan 48, 89
Ref: P Vanes (Warley)
Pompey: Knight, Stanley, Dillon, Blake, Gilbert, O'Callaghan, Tait, Morgan, Channon*, Hilaire, Sandford
Millwall: Sansome, Stevens, Hinshelwood, Briley, Walker, Nutton, Lowndes, Chatterton, Leslie, Lovell, Kinsella

The league has blanked soccer from the screens, and Deacon is trying to do a unilateral deal with TVS. This performance is worthy of a wider view, although Knight's penalty stop from Chatterton is crucial early in the second half. Pompey refuse their ticket allocation and are fan-less.

15 — A LEEDS (2/11)
Scorer: Morgan 7 — Simmonds 64, 71p
Ref: T Jones (Macclesfield)
Pompey: Knight, Tait, Swain, Dillon, Blake, Gilbert, O'Callaghan, Kennedy, Morgan, Channon*, Hilaire, Stanley
Leeds: Day, Irwin, Phelan, McGregor, Linighan, Aspin, Ritchie, Sheridan, Baird, Hamson, Simmonds

18-year-old debutant Lyndon Simmonds keeps his nerve and sends Knight the wrong way, after Tait's fair-looking tackle ends with Ritchie sprawling. Earlier, he had levelled for Billy Bremner's side as Pompey lost their composure after the break. Channon set up Morgan's tap in.

16 — A GRIMSBY (16/11)
Scorer: Bonnyman 62p
Ref: P Tylesdey (Stockport)
Pompey: Knight, Swain, Sandford, Dillon, Blake, Gilbert, O'Callaghan, Kennedy, Morgan, Channon*, Hilaire, Wood
Grimsby: Batch, Barrett, Crombie, Peake, Lyons, Moore K, Ford, Gilligan, Hobson, Bonnyman, Emson

New Mariners' player-boss Mick Lyons inspires his charges, but Batch is the hero with two stunning saves to deny Hilaire. Dillon chops down Bonnyman, who squeezes the pen past Knight. Grimsby give Channon a plaque – not to mention a black eye – to recall his 700th league game.

17 — H SHEFFIELD UTD (23/11)
Scorers: Foley 10, 80, Withe 33
Ref: M James (Horsham)
Pompey: Knight, Swain, Stanley, Dillon, Blake, Gilbert, Wood, Kennedy, Morgan, Channon*, Hilaire, McGarvey
Sheffield Utd: Burridge, Eckhardt, Smith, Thompson, Stancliffe, McNaught, Morris, Edwards, Withe, Lewington, Foley

Midweek exertions at White Hart Lane catch up with Pompey and Blades overwhelm them. Withe's power sets up Foley, then Edwards centres. Withe and Foley then combine again, slashing Pompey's eight-point lead, at the start of the month, to two.

18 — A BRADFORD C (3/12)
Scorer: Kennedy 38 — Campbell 9, Graham 85
Ref: J Worrall (Warrington)
Pompey: Knight, Swain, Hardyman, Dillon, Blake, Gilbert, O'Callaghan, Kennedy, Morgan, Channon*, Hilaire, Tait
Bradford C: Litchfield, Oliver, Withe, McCall, Jackson, Evans, Hendrie, Abbott, Campbell, Singleton, Graham

Snow and fog claimed this game on Saturday, but it is quickly re-arranged to ease homeless City's cash-flow. Danish triallist Christensen fires home in injury-time, only for the ref to blow up a fraction before. Below-par Pompey struggle on the narrow, boggy Odsal rugby league pitch.

19 — A SUNDERLAND (7/12)
Scorers: Christensen 23, Tait 44, Wood 65 — Gates 88
Ref: K Hackett (Sheffield)
Pompey: Knight, Swain, Sandford, Tait, Blake, Gilbert, O'Callaghan, Kennedy, Wood, Christensen, Hilaire*, Graham
Sunderland: Bolder, Burley, Kennedy A, Pickering, Bennett!, Elliott, Gayle*, Venison, Swindlehurst, Hodgson, Gates, Atkinson

Pompey answer their critics in impressive style, silencing the Roker Roar. Christensen dips home a 25-yard volley, then Tait's subtle touch wrong-foots Bolder. The best comes when Kennedy sets Wood free, who ignores Christensen and rifles home, to send the crowd to the exits.

20 — H HULL (14/12)
Scorers: Christensen 55 — McEwan 81
Ref: K Miller (Harlow)
Pompey: Knight, Swain, Sandford, Tait, Blake, Gilbert, O'Callagh'n*, Kennedy, Channon, Christensen, Hilaire, Sugrue
Hull: Norman, Jobson, Swann, Doyle, Skipper, McEwan, Williams*, Bunn, Saville, Askew, Roberts!, Flounders

Pompey's pre-Xmas price-rise comes into effect, but the team are unable to build on Tuesday's cup heroics. Christensen's flick looked like stealing it, but McEwan drills in a free-kick. Roberts is sent off for tangling with Kennedy and Tigers play Doyle, sold for £30,000 in August.

21 — A CARLISLE (22/12)
Scorer: Channon 75
Ref: K Redfern (Whitley Bay)
Pompey: Knight, Swain, Sandford, Tait, Blake, Gilbert, O'Callaghan, Kennedy, Morgan, Channon, Hilaire, Hill
Carlisle: Endersby, Lomax, McCartney, Ashurst, Saunders, Halsall, Mayes*, Cooke, Baker, Bishop, Halpin

Christensen is injured, but is not in Ball's plans. Morgan, the division's leading scorer returns, and he claims he should have had a goal, when United hack clear his header, but the linesman is un-sighted. Channon's header squirts in, but bookings for Cally and Kennedy mean bans.

CANON LEAGUE DIVISION 2   Manager: Alan Ball   SEASON 1985-86

Match details

No	Date		Att	Pos	Pt	F-A	H-T	Scorers, Times, and Referees
22	26/12	H BRIGHTON	15,265	2 *(8)*	42	L 1-2	1-1	O'Callaghan 35 / Saunders 18, Connor 72 / Ref: L. Shapter (Torquay)
23	28/12	H SHREWSBURY	12,302	2 *(12)*	45	W 4-0	1-0	Kennedy 32, Wood 79, 88, [Channon 86] / Ref: J Moules (Ongar)
24	1/1	A WIMBLEDON	9,025	2 *(3)*	48	W 3-1	2-0	Channon 28, 49, Hilaire 34 / Cork 50 / Ref: M Reed (Birmingham)
25	11/1	H FULHAM	13,666	2 *(21)*	49	D 1-1	0-1	Tait 86 / Coney 19 / Ref: R Hamer (Bristol)
26	18/1	A NORWICH	20,129	2 *(1)*	49	L 0-2	0-0	Barham 77, Drinkell 86 / Ref: N Butler (East Molesey)
27	25/1	H MIDDLESBROUGH	10,611	2 *(20)*	52	W 1-0	0-0	Morgan 74 / Ref: R Groves (Weston-super-Mare)
28	1/2	H HUDDERSFIELD	10,936	2 *(19)*	55	W 4-1	1-0	Tait 23, Dillon 62p, Morgan 76, Tempest 82 [O'Callaghan 80] / Ref: D Axcell (Southend)
29	22/2	H OLDHAM	10,891	2 *(12)*	55	L 1-2	0-1	Hilaire 65 / Colville 10, Henry 76 / Ref: K Cooper (Pontypridd)
30	1/3	A BLACKBURN	4,980	2 *(13)*	55	L 0-1	0-0	Garner 59 / Ref: K Barratt (Coventry)
31	8/3	H BARNSLEY	10,426	2 *(9)*	56	D 1-1	1-1	O'Callaghan 35 / Walsh 23 / Ref: C Downey (Hounslow)

Line-ups (Portsmouth and, in italics, opponents)

No	Team	1	2	3	4	5	6	7	8	9	10	11	12 sub used
22	Portsmouth	Knight	Tait	Swain	Dillon	Blake	Gilbert	O'Callaghan	Kennedy	Morgan	Channon*	Hilaire	Sugrue
22	*Brighton*	*Digweed*	*Jacobs*	*Pearce*	*Wilson*	*Young*	*O'Reilly*	*Saunders*	*Penney*	*Fashanu*	*Connor*	*Mortimer*	
23	Portsmouth	Knight	Tait	Swain	Dillon	Blake	Gilbert	O'Callaghan	Kennedy	Channon	Wood	Hilaire	[Channon 86]
23	*Shrewsbury*	*Perks*	*Gunn*	*Hughes*	*Cross*	*Pearson*	*Griffin*	*Leonard*	*Hackett*	*Stevens*	*Robinson*	*Daly*	
24	Portsmouth	Knight	Tait	Swain	Dillon	Blake	Gilbert	O'Callaghan	Kennedy	Channon	Wood	Hilaire	
24	*Wimbledon*	*Beasant*	*Kay*	*Winterburn*	*Downes*	*Martin*	*Thorn*	*Evans*	*Cork*	*Holloway**	*Sanchez*	*Hodges*	*Wise*
25	Portsmouth	Knight	Stanley	Swain	Ball	Blake	Gilbert	Sugrue*	Tait	Channon	Wood	Hilaire	Morgan
25	*Fulham*	*Peyton*	*Cottington*	*Donnellan*	*Scott*	*Parker*	*Hopkins*	*Marshall*	*Achampong*	*Coney*	*Carr*	*Barnett*	
26	Portsmouth	Gosney	Swain	Sandford	Dillon	Blake	Gilbert	O'Callaghan	Kennedy	Channon	Wood	Hilaire	
26	*Norwich*	*Woods*	*Culverhouse*	*Van Wyk*	*Bruce*	*Phelan*	*Watson*	*Barham*	*Drinkell*	*Biggins*	*Mendham*	*Williams*	
27	Portsmouth	Gosney	Tait	Swain	Dillon	Blake	Gilbert	O'Callaghan	Kennedy	Channon	Wood	Hilaire	Morgan
27	*Middlesbrough*	*McManus*	*Laws*	*McAndrew**	*Mowbray*	*O'Riordan*	*Pallister*	*Hamilton*	*Heard*	*Slaven*	*Stephens*	*Rowell*	*Beagrie*
28	Portsmouth	Gosney	Tait	Swain	Dillon	Blake	Gilbert	O'Callaghan	Kennedy	Morgan	Wood	Hilaire	
28	*Huddersfield*	*Cox*	*Brown*	*Gray*	*Doyle*	*Webster*	*Jones*	*Wilson*	*Stanton**	*Tempest*	*Raynor*	*Cork*	*Curran*
29	Portsmouth	Gosney	Tait	Swain	Dillon	Blake	Gilbert	O'Callaghan	Kennedy	Morgan	Wood	Hilaire	Quinn
29	*Oldham*	*Goram*	*Hoolickin*	*Barlow*	*Jones*	*Linighan*	*Smith*	*Williams*	*McGuire*	*Colville**	*Futcher*	*Henry*	
30	Portsmouth	Knight	Stanley	Hardyman	Dillon	Blake	Gilbert	O'Callaghan	Kennedy	Channon*		Hilaire	Wood
30	*Blackburn*	*Gennoe*	*Branaghan*	*Rathbone*	*Barker*	*Keely*	*Fazackerley*	*Miller*	*Hamilton*	*Quinn*	*Garner*	*Patterson*	
31	Portsmouth	Knight	Tait	Hardyman	Dillon	Blake	Gilbert	O'Callaghan	Kennedy	Morgan	Channon*	Hilaire	Wood
31	*Barnsley*	*Baker*	*Joyce*	*Gray*	*Thomas*	*May*	*Futcher*	*Owen*	*Jonsson*	*Walsh*	*Aylott*	*Cross*	

Match reports

22 — Brighton: Future Fratton forward Connor can't miss, as O'Reilly's long-ball finds Justin Fashanu challenging Knight and the ball squirms to him. Earlier, Fashanu had pounced on Gilbert's back-pass, allowing Saunders his eighth goal. O'Callaghan levelled from an indirect free-kick in the box.

23 — Shrewsbury: Ball proclaims: 'A star is born', as Wood defies the icy surface to latch onto a poor back-pass and lob over Perks. Two more goals – including Channon's glance – put a flattering gloss on the result. Kennedy fired home after Dillon's shot was only parried, but Shrews claim he handled.

24 — Wimbledon: Promotion-rivals Dons are put in their place by the evergreen Channon, aware that Ball is off to watch Fulham's Dean Coney later today. Dave Bassett's boys batter the bar, before Channon strikes from 25 yards. Hilaire scrambles home, then a magnificent glancing header seals it.

25 — Fulham: Deacon baulked at the £350,000 Coney, but he soon proves a point. A classic header looks like giving lowly Fulham a first win in more than a month, but Tait finally gets the better of Peyton with a late header. Arsenal's ex-Saint Williams is the next target, but again proves too costly.

26 — Norwich: Knight's broken hand ends a run of 129 consecutive games. Gosney steps in and is within 13 minutes of preserving stalemate, when Barham gets on the end of Phelan's cross. Ken Brown's team now have their tails up and Gosney makes two more saves before Drinkell makes it safe.

27 — Middlesbrough: The FA Cup exit at Villa allows this game – called off in November because of Boro's flu bug – to be re-scheduled. Morgan forces Kennedy's pass through McManus's dive to score his first since 2 November. Ball's striker search is frustrated again as Wigan's Aspinall joins Everton.

28 — Huddersfield: Ref Axcell diverts Woods pass into Morgan's path for the killer third, against a Town side already smarting from his penalty decision when Webster appeared to clip Hilaire's heel. Tait nodded his second of the season after Hilaire hit the bar and Cally's solo run led to the fourth.

29 — Oldham: Gosney's late gaffe – he fails to hold onto Quinn's soft shot and Henry slams in – is put down to his long periods of inactivity in the biting wind. Dillon too is a villain, as Goram guesses right and stops his penalty. Colville's early bobbler, is cancelled out by Hilaire's overhead kick.

30 — Blackburn: Ball is furious as a leak ends his hopes of loaning Spurs' Clive Allen at an early stage, and how Pompey could have done with his predatory instincts. O'Callaghan's slice defeats Tait and lets in Quinn to set up Garner. Hilaire dragged wide and Dillon hit the side-netting to no avail.

31 — Barnsley: Oldham's Quinn (£150,000) signs before the start, after a £50,000 deal for Leeds' Ritchie foundered on a medical. Tykes' counter-attacking policy pays when Walsh scores, but Cally's free-kick re-take saves it. Referee Downey has 25 bookings and a sending-off in four Fratton apps.

32 A CHARLTON 15/3 — 10,132 — 2 W 59 — 2:1
Channon 9, O'Callaghan 26 / Pearson 19
Ref: M Bodenham (Brighton)

Knight	Swain	Hardyman	Tait	Blake	Gilbert	O'Callaghan	Kennedy	Quinn	Channon*	Hilaire	Wood
Johns	*Humphrey*	*Reid*	*Curbishley**	*Thompson*	*Pender*	*Shipley*	*Lee*	*Pearson*	*Aizlewood*	*Flanaghan*	*Stuart*

Lennie Lawrence says the third promotion spot is between his team and Dons after Pompey's demolition. How wrong can you be? Quinn sets up Channon, then Cally's typical strike seals it. Sugrue (Cobblers) and Bamber (Swindon) have left, while Hardyman plays for England U-21s.

33 H MILLWALL 25/3 — 9,570 — 2 W 62 — 2:1
O'Callaghan 38, Quinn 45 / Lovell 25
Ref: G Napthine (Loughborough)

Knight	Swain	Hardyman	Tait	Blake	Gilbert	O'Callaghan	Kennedy	Quinn	Channon	Hilaire	Wood
Sansome	*Stevens*	*Hinshelwood Briley*	*Walker*	*McLeary*	*Smith*	*Chatterton* Smith*	*Fashanu*	*Lovell*	*Otolakowski Sheringham*		

An ugly game witnesses a 20-man brawl after Briley is flattened by Tait – who escapes with a booking – then Quinn clatters into Sansome and somehow him 100th goal stands. A niggly second half ends with John Fashanu lucky not to be sent off after his forearm smash on O'Callaghan.

34 H WIMBLEDON 29/3 — 18,859 — 2 D 63 — 1:1
Blake 53 / Smith 61
Ref: R Groves (Weston-super-Mare)

Knight	Swain	Hardyman	Tait*	Blake	Gilbert	O'Callaghan	Kennedy	Quinn	Channon	Hilaire	Dillon
Beasant	*Gage*	*Winterburn*	*Galliers*	*Morris*	*Smith*	*Evans*	*Cork*	*Fishenden**	*Sanchez*	*Fairweather Fashanu*	

Ball tries to get sub Dillon on to take a penalty, given when Sanchez trips Hilaire. He fails and O'Callaghan sees Beasant stop his kick. Blake nods in, but £125,000 sub Fash (the bash) is back at Fratton, and fractures Dillon's cheek. Dons level when Smith follows up Evans' header.

35 A BRIGHTON 31/3 — 16,640 — 2 W 66 — 3:2
Quinn 13, 45p, Hilaire 42 / Saunders 54, O'Regan 87
Ref: E Scales (Ware)/P Alcock

Knight	Swain	Hardyman	Ball	Blake	Gilbert	O'Callagh'n*	Kennedy	Quinn	Morgan	Hilaire	Wood
Digweed	*Hutchings*	*Gatting*	*Wilson**	*Young*	*O'Reilly*	*Saunders*	*Penney*	*Biley*	*Connor*	*Mortimer*	*O'Regan*

Albion return Pompey's Boxing Day gift. Kennedy sets up Quinn, then Hilaire nips in front of a pair of dozy defenders. Young crudely stops Hilaire and Quinn converts, his celebrations showing the home fans he has scored two goals. I think. Referee Scales limps off with sciatica.

36 H LEEDS 5/4 — 14,430 — 2 L 66 — 2:3
Blake 11, 88 / Ritchie 55, 83, Baird 62
Ref: J Ball (Kirby Muxloe)

Knight	Swain	Hardyman	Ball	Blake	Gilbert	O'Callaghan	Kennedy	Quinn	Channon*	Hilaire	Morgan
Day	*Aspin*	*Robinson*	*Snodin*	*Ormsby*	*Rennie*	*McCluskey*	*Sheridan*	*Baird*	*Swan*	*Ritchie*	

Nine points clear of fourth spot; promotion looks a formality. Leeds shatter any complacency however, as Ritchie punishes Ball for not signing him. His first is an audacious chip, the killer third (his second) a deflected shot. McGarvey is back from Carlisle to cover a paper-thin squad.

37 A CRYSTAL PALACE 8/4 — 11,731 — 2 L 66 — 1:2
Gray 67 (og) / Gray 18, 44
Ref: V Callow (Solihull)

Knight	Swain	Sandford	Ball	Blake	Gilbert	O'Callagh'n*	Kennedy	Quinn	Channon	Hilaire	Wood
Wood	*Finnegan*	*Brush*	*Taylor*	*Nebbeling*	*Cannon*	*Irvine*	*Ketteridge*	*Gray*		*Higginbottom Wright*	

18-year-old Andy Gray claims an unusual hat-trick. First, he stoops to head in from close-range, then his hit-and-hope from the touch-line drifts over Knight's head. Gray then dives to divert Kennedy's shot past Wood, and in a desperate push, twice the ball sticks in goal-line mud.

38 A MIDDLESBROUGH 12/4 — 7,160 — 2 L 66 — 0:1
Mowbray 63
Ref: K Hackett (Sheffield)

Knight	Ball !	Swain	McGarvey	Blake	Gilbert	O'Callaghan	Kennedy	Quinn	Morgan*	Hilaire	Wood
Pears	*Laws*	*McAndrew*	*Mowbray*	*O'Riordan*	*Pallister*	*Ripley*	*Cooper*	*Steven*	*Currie*	*Hamilton*	

Boro's relegation battle is boosted by an insipid Pompey. In the first half, Quinn fires high when Hilaire is fouled in the box, then Mowbray tucks a shot just inside the post. At once, his tangle with Ball sees the Pompey man sent off. 3-0 wins for Dons and Charlton complete the day.

39 H GRIMSBY 19/4 — 12,967 — 2 W 69 — 3:1
Quinn 57, Hilaire 76, McGarvey 83 / Hobson 59
Ref: J Moules (Ongar)

Knight	Swain	Hardyman	Dillon	Blake	Gilbert	O'Callaghan	Kennedy	Quinn	Channon*	Hilaire	McGarvey
Batch	*Moore A*	*Crombie*	*Peake*	*Lyons*	*Moore K*	*Lund**	*Henshaw*	*Hobson*	*Robinson*	*Cumming*	*Agnew*

The Fratton End upper tier is shut for safety reasons, but Pompey shrug off the blow and are back in the promotion driving seat; Dons and Charlton draw. Quinn steers home, but Hobson heads in after Hardyman is robbed. Hilaire strikes, then McGarvey flicks the goal of the game.

40 A STOKE 22/4 — 8,529 — 3 L 69 — 0:2
Berry 17, Heath 45
Ref: J Worrall (Warrington)

Knight	Swain	Hardyman	Dillon	Blake	Gilbert	O'Callaghan	Kennedy	Quinn	Channon*	Hilaire	McGarvey
Fox	*Mills*	*Hemming*	*Bonnyman*	*Bould*	*Berry*	*Saunders*	*Painter*	*Bertschin*	*Shaw*	*Heath*	

'A second division performance,' is Ball's blunt assessment as heads for the team bus. Results elsewhere mean promotion is fast slipping away. George Berry buries a free header from a corner, then Heath deflects in Painter's cross. Former Pompey target Bertschin also hit a post.

41 A SHEFFIELD UTD 26/4 — 12,234 — 3 D 70 — 0:0
Ref: T Jones (Macclesfield)

Knight	Swain	Hardyman	Dillon	Blake	Gilbert	O'Callaghan	Kennedy	Quinn	Channon	Hilaire*	Wood
Burridge	*Smith P*	*Bolton*	*Arnott*	*Stanliffe*	*Eckhardt*	*Morris*	*Edwards*	*Philliskirk*	*Walshaw*	*Frain*	

Pompey gain their first point at Bramall Lane since 1955, but Billy McEwan's depleted Blades were there for the taking. Instead, the team seem to have lost self-belief and it takes three smart stops from Knight to deny Edwards. Hilaire dwells too long and the best chance has gone.

42 H BRADFORD C 3/5 — 9,568 — 4 W 73 — 4:0
Quinn 20, 69, Dillon 78p, Wood 84
Ref: B Stevens (Stonehouse)

Knight	Swain	Hardyman	Dillon	Blake	Gilbert	O'Callaghan	Kennedy	Quinn	Morgan*	Hilaire*	McGarvey	Russell
Litchfield	*Oliver*	*Evans*	*McCall*	*Jackson*	*Clegg*	*Hendrie*	*Ormondroyd Goodman*	*Abbott*	*Thorne**	*Singleton*		

Dons' win in the week eased Pompey out of the promotion spots for the first time, but at least the team stay down fighting. Quinn poaches on Litchfield's slip, raising brief hopes, but by the time sub Russell's pace unhinges City, Dons and Charlton have all but clinched promotion.

Home 13,624   Away 9,480   Average

CANON DIVISION 2 (CUP-TIES)

Manager: Alan Ball — SEASON 1985-86

Milk Cup

Column positions: 1 | 2 | 3 | 4 | 5 | 6 | 7 | 8 | 9 | 10 | 11 | 12 sub used

2:1 A GILLINGHAM 24/9 — 1 W 3-1 (2-0) · Att 4,617 3:7
Scorers: O'Callaghan 25, Tait 30, Wood 52; *Cascarino 48*. Ref: D Vickers (Ilford)

1	2	3	4	5	6	7	8	9	10	11	12 sub
Knight	Swain	Hardyman	Dillon	Blake	Gilbert	O'Callaghan	Tait	Morgan	Wood	Hilaire	Macowat
Hillyard	*Sage*	*Hinnigan*	*Oakes*	*Collins*	*Shaw*	*Cochrane*	*Weatherley*	*Elsey**	*Mehmet*	*Cascarino*	

Gills have not been beaten in nine but the gap between second and third divisions is clearly apparent. O'Callaghan makes space to shoot home, then Tait nudges home Cally's goal-bound effort. Cascarino's shot lifts Keith Peacock's men, but the impressive Wood's angled finish seals it.

2:2 H GILLINGHAM 8/10 — 1 W 2-1 (0-0) · Att 7,629 3:12
Scorers: Sandford 56, Morgan 76; *Dillon 54 (og)*. Ref: E Scales (Ware) — (Pompey won 5-2 on aggregate)

1	2	3	4	5	6	7	8	9	10	11	12 sub
Knight	Tait	Sandford	Dillon	Blake	Gilbert	O'Callaghan	Kennedy	Morgan	Wood!	Channon	Hilaire
Hillyard	*Sage*	*Elsey*	*Oakes*	*Weatherley*	*Shaw*	*Cochrane*	*Byrne*	*Hales*	*Collins*	*Cascarino!*	

An unsightly first half ends with Cascarino sent off for his challenge on Blake, then Wood follows him for a wild hack at Elsey. Dillon slices Elsey's cross and Gills sense an escape, but debutant Sandford settles nerves, smashing in Tait's back-heel. Morgan then nets his tenth goal.

3 H STOKE 29/10 — 1 W 2-0 (0-0) · Att 13,319 18
Scorers: Dillon 46p, 62p. Ref: A Buksh (London)

1	2	3	4	5	6	7	8	9	10	11	12 sub
Knight	Stanley	Sandford	Dillon	Blake	Gilbert	O'Callaghan	Tait	Morgan	Channon	Hilaire*	McGarvey
Fox	*Bould*	*Mills**	*Hemming*	*Dyson*	*Berry*	*Adams*	*Maskery*	*Bertschin*	*Parkin*	*Heath*	*Saunders*

Potters' player-boss Mick Mills claims Hilaire dived for the first spot-kick, as he tumbled dramatically, but he has no complaints about the second as Hilaire outwits him again. Fox gets his fingers to the first, but is stationary for the second. Knight is forced to make some vital saves.

4 A TOTTENHAM 20/11 — 1 D 0-0 (0-0) · Att 28,619 1:13
Ref: D Axcell (Southend)

1	2	3	4	5	6	7	8	9	10	11	12 sub
Knight	Swain	Hardyman	Dillon	Blake	Gilbert	O'Callaghan*	Kennedy	Morgan	Channon	Hilaire	Wood
Clemence	*Stevens*	*Hughton*	*Roberts*	*Mabbutt*	*Perryman*	*Allen*	*Falco*	*Galvin**	*Hoddle*	*Waddle*	*Cooke*

10,000 visiting fans jam north London, and they are nearly rewarded with a famous win. Midway through the second half Channon is denied by the brilliance of Clemence. Pompey bow to league pressure and move the replay 24 hours, as Saints also have a home replay, with Arsenal!

4R H TOTTENHAM 26/11 — 1 D 0-0 (0-0) · Att 28,100 1:12
Ref: A Gunn (Burgess Hill)

1	2	3	4	5	6	7	8	9	10	11	12 sub
Knight	Hardyman	Swain	Dillon	Blake	Gilbert	O'Callaghan	Kennedy	Morgan	Channon*	Tait	Wood
Clemence	*Stevens*	*Hughton*	*Roberts*	*Mabbutt*	*Perryman*	*Allen*	*Falco*	*Galvin*	*Hoddle*	*Waddle*	

Chaos outside, as thousands of ticket-holders are denied entry after the decision to have pay-on-the-night turnstiles. Peter Shreeves' side go closest, but Knight is equal to Falco and Waddle. The drama switches to the Boardroom: Deacon guesses the toss and it's all-ticket at Fratton.

4 RR H TOTTENHAM 10/12 — 2 W 1-0 (1-0) · Att 26,306 1:10
Scorers: Blake 44. Ref: B Stevens (Stonehouse)

1	2	3	4	5	6	7	8	9	10	11	12 sub
Knight	Swain	Sandford	Tait	Blake	Gilbert	O'Callaghan	Kennedy	Wood*	Christensen	Hilaire	Dillon
Clemence	*Stevens*	*Hughton*	*Roberts*	*Mabbutt*	*Thomas*	*Ardiles**	*Falco*	*Allen C*	*Hoddle*	*Waddle*	*Allen P*

Pompey reach the last eight of the League Cup for the first time since 1961, but Spurs are unlucky when Waddle drifts a late shot against the post. Blake's towering header settles it. Hoddle, back after injury, is stifled by Kennedy and the highly-rated Falco and Allen are anonymous.

QF A OXFORD 22/1 — 1 L 1-3 (0-2) · Att 10,334 1:19
Scorers: *Briggs 2, Phillips 43, Slatter 68*; Stanley 90. Ref: N Ashley (Nantwich)

1	2	3	4	5	6	7	8	9	10	11	12 sub
Gosney	Swain	Sandford	Dillon	Blake	Tait	O'Callaghan	Kennedy	Channon	Wood	Hilaire	Stanley
Judge	*Trewick*	*Slatter*	*Phillips*	*Briggs*	*Shotton*	*Houghton*	*Aldridge*	*Charles**	*Hebberd*	*Brock*	*Jones*

Maurice Evans' side are in the middle of a five-match losing run in the league, but they have far too much class for Pompey. Briggs' back gets the vital deflection for the opener, then Houghton robs Sandford to set up Phillips. Stanley's spectacular 30-yarder is mere consolation.

FA Cup

3 H ASTON VILLA 4/1 — 2 D 2-2 (0-1) · Att 17,732 1:18
Scorers: Blake 57, Dillon 69p; *Kerr 40, Birch 90*. Ref: C Downey (Hounslow)

1	2	3	4	5	6	7	8	9	10	11	12 sub
Knight	Tait	Swain	Dillon	Blake	Gilbert!	O'Callaghan*	Kennedy	Channon	Wood	Hilaire	Stanley
Spink	*Norton*	*Dorigo*	*Evans*	*Elliott*	*Birch*	*Kerr*	*Stainrod*	*Gray*	*Hodge*	*Walters*	

Villa have not lost the last time they were at Fratton in 1983 and lightning strikes twice. Pompey are down to ten men, after Gilbert's clash with Stainrod, but go ahead when Kerr fouls Wood in the box. At the death, Walters crosses and Birch trickles home for Graham Turner's team.

3R A ASTON VILLA 13/1 — 2 L 2-3 (0-1) aet · Att 14,598 1:18
Scorers: Stanley 84, 106p; *Evans 42p, Stainrod 93, 100*. Ref: A Ward (London)

1	2	3	4	5	6	7	8	9	10	11	12 sub
Knight	Swain	Sandford	Stanley	Blake	Gilbert	McGarvey	Tait	Channon*	Wood	Hilaire	Morgan
Spink	*Norton*	*Dorigo*	*Evans*	*Elliott*	*Birch*	*Kerr*	*Stainrod*	*Gray*	*Hodge*	*Walters*	

Patched-up Pompey go down fighting. Knight fouls Walters and Evans converts, but Stanley to blasts the game into extra-time. Knight shatters his hand on Stainrod's head, and the ball bobbles in for the clincher. Stanley's spot-kick sparks a frantic finish and Hilaire is denied by Spink.

League Table

		P	Home					Away					Pts
			W	D	L	F	A	W	D	L	F	A	
1	Norwich	42	16	4	1	51	15	9	5	7	33	22	84
2	Charlton	42	14	5	2	44	15	8	6	7	34	30	77
3	Wimbledon	42	13	6	2	38	16	8	7	6	20	21	76
4	PORTSMOUTH	42	13	4	4	43	17	9	3	9	26	24	73
5	Crystal Pal	42	12	3	6	29	22	7	6	8	28	30	66
6	Hull	42	11	7	3	39	19	6	6	9	26	36	64
7	Sheffield Utd	42	10	7	4	36	24	7	4	10	28	39	62
8	Oldham	42	13	4	4	40	28	4	5	12	22	33	60
9	Millwall	42	12	3	6	39	24	5	5	11	25	41	59
10	Stoke	42	8	11	2	29	16	6	4	11	19	34	57
11	Brighton	42	10	5	6	42	30	6	3	12	22	34	56
12	Barnsley	42	9	6	6	29	26	5	8	8	18	24	56
13	Bradford C	42	14	1	6	36	24	2	5	14	15	39	54
14	Leeds	42	9	7	5	30	22	6	1	14	26	50	53
15	Grimsby	42	11	4	6	35	24	3	6	12	23	38	52
16	Huddersfield	42	10	6	5	30	23	4	4	13	21	44	52
17	Shrewsbury	42	11	5	5	29	20	3	4	14	23	44	51
18	Sunderland	42	10	5	6	33	29	3	6	12	14	32	50
19	Blackburn	42	10	4	7	30	20	2	9	10	23	42	49
20	Carlisle	42	10	2	9	30	28	3	5	13	17	43	46
21	Middlesbro	42	8	6	7	26	23	4	3	14	18	30	45
22	Fulham	42	8	3	10	29	32	2	3	16	16	37	36
		924	242	108	112	767	497	112	108	242	497	767	1278

Appearances and Goals

	Appearances						Goals			
	Lge	Sub	LC	Sub	FAC	Sub	Lge	LC	FAC	Tot
Ball, Kevin	9									
Blake, Noel	42		7		2		4	1	1	6
Channon, Mick	34	4	4		2		6			6
Christensen, Tommy	3		1				2			2
Dillon, Kevin	30	1	6	1	1		6	2	1	9
Doyle, Bobby	1									
Gilbert, Billy	36		6		2					
Gosney, Andy	4		1							
Hardyman, Paul	21		2				1			1
Hilaire, Vince	41		7		2		7			7
Kennedy, Mick	39		5		2		2			2
Knight, Alan	38		6		2					
McGarvey, Scott	2	3			1	1	1			1
Money, Richard	1									
Morgan, Nicky	28	2	5			1	14	1		15
O'Callaghan, Kevin	39		7		1		11	1		12
Quinn, Mick	11						6			6
Russell, Kevin	1									
Sandford, Lee	6	1	4		1			1		1
Stanley, Gary	4	2	2	1	1			1	2	3
Sugrue, Paul	1	2								
Swain, Kenny	39		5		2					
Tait, Mick	23	3	5	1	2		2	1		3
Wood, Paul	10	15	4	1	2		5	1		6
(own-goals)							2			2
24 players used	462	30	77	5	22	1	69	9	4	82

Odds & ends

Double wins: (5) Huddersfield, Sunderland, Charlton, Millwall, Carlisle.

Double losses: (2) Leeds, Oldham.

Won from behind: (1) Millwall (h).

Lost from in front: (2) Leeds (h), Leeds (a).

High spots: Eight-match unbeaten start to the season.
Nicky Morgan sets a club record by scoring in first five league matches.
Milk Cup 4th round second replay victory over Spurs in December.
Seven successive home wins to start the season without conceding a goal.
Winning 4-0 at Millwall in October.
Five consecutive wins in September to October without conceding a goal.

Low spots: Finishing 4th and missing promotion for the second season in succession.
Three successive away defeats in April.
Four points from possible 18 in April.
Four consecutive defeats in November to December.

Player of the Year: Noel Blake.

Ever-presents: (1) Noel Blake.

Hat-tricks: (0).

Leading scorer: Nicky Morgan (15).

TODAY LEAGUE DIVISION 2

Manager: Alan Ball — SEASON 1986-87

Match Results

No	Date	Venue / Opponent	Att	Pos	Pt	Res	F-A	H-T	Scorers (times), Referee
1	23/8	A BRIGHTON	13,723		1	D	0-0	0-0	Ref: J Moules (Ongar)
2	30/8	H IPSWICH	11,849	14 *12*	2	D	1-1	0-0	O'Callaghan 73; Brennan 56. Ref: G Ashby (Worcester)
3	2/9	A HULL	7,706	8 *6*	5	W	2-0	1-0	Quinn 42, 46. Ref: M Peck (Kendal)
4	6/9	A BARNSLEY	4,341	4 *22*	8	W	2-0	1-0	Quinn 40, 88. Ref: J Ashworth (Leicester)
5	13/9	H BLACKBURN	8,773	3 *6*	11	W	1-0	1-0	Kennedy 30. Ref: D Hedges (Oxford)
6	20/9	A STOKE	8,440	3 *19*	12	D	1-1	1-0	Kennedy 30; Kelly 57. Ref: K Baker (Rugby)
7	27/9	H HUDDERSFIELD	9,022	2 *20*	15	W	1-0	0-0	Blake 56. Ref: D Axcell (Southend)
8	4/10	A SUNDERLAND	16,938	3 *11*	16	D	0-0	0-0	Ref: G Napthine (Loughborough)
9	11/10	H BIRMINGHAM	11,252	1 *17*	19	W	2-0	0-0	Quinn 73, 77. Ref: M Dimblebee (Stevenage)
10	18/10	A LEEDS	21,361	3 *2*	19	L	1-3	0-0	Quinn 72p; Sheridan 60p, Ritchie 70, Baird 83. Ref: F Roberts (Prestatyn)

Line-ups (top row = Portsmouth, bottom row = opponents; * = sub used)

No	Team	1	2	3	4	5	6	7	8	9	10	11	12 (sub used)
1	Portsmouth	Knight	Swain	Hardyman	Dillon	Blake	Gilbert	Tait	Kennedy	Mariner	Quinn	Hilaire	
1	Brighton	Digweed	Berry	Hutchings	O'Regan	Gatting	O'Reilly	Penney	Saunders	Armstrong	Connor	Jasper	
2	Portsmouth	Knight	Swain	Hardyman	Dillon	Blake	Gilbert	O'Callaghan	Tait	Mariner	Quinn	Hilaire	D'Avray
2	Ipswich	Cooper	Zondervan	McCall	Atkins	Dozzell	Cranson*	Gleghorn	Brennan	Cole	Deehan	Wilson	
3	Portsmouth	Knight	Swain	Hardyman	Dillon	Blake	Gilbert	O'Callaghan	Tait	Mariner	Quinn	Hilaire	
3	Hull	Norman	Jobson	Swann	Heard	Skipper	Williams	Parker	Bunn	Flounders*	Askew	Roberts	Saville
4	Portsmouth	Knight	Swain	Hardyman	Dillon	Blake	Gilbert	Tait	Kennedy	Mariner	Quinn	Hilaire	
4	Barnsley	Baker	Joyce	Cross	Thomas	Ogley	Futcher	Lowndes	Bradshaw*	Agnew	Gray	Beresford	Plummer
5	Portsmouth	Knight	Swain	Hardyman	Dillon	Blake	Gilbert	Tait	Kennedy	Mariner	Quinn	Hilaire	
5	Blackburn	O'Keefe	Price	Brnagan	Barker	Keeley	Mail	Brotherston	Sellars	Quinn J	Garner	Rathbone*	Patterson
6	Portsmouth	Knight	Swain	Hardyman	Dillon	Blake	Gilbert	Tait	Kennedy	Mariner	Quinn	Hilaire	O'Callaghan
6	Stoke	Fox	Dixon	Hemming	Kelly	Bould	Berry	Ford	Parkin	Bertschin	Shaw	Heath	
7	Portsmouth	Knight	Swain	Hardyman	Dillon	Blake	Gilbert	O'Callaghan	Kennedy	Morgan	Tait	Wood	
7	Huddersfield	Cox	Brown	Bray	Banks	Webster	Jones	Raynor	Winter	Shearer	Wilson	Cowling*	Cork
8	Portsmouth	Knight	Tait	Swain	Dillon	Blake	Gilbert	O'Callaghan	Kennedy	Quinn	Wood	Hilaire	
8	Sunderland	Hesford	Burley	Kennedy A*	Armstrong	Corner	Bennett	Lemon	Doyle	Swindlehurst	Gray	Buchanan	Gates
9	Portsmouth	Knight	Swain	Hardyman	Dillon	Blake	Ball	O'Callaghan	Kennedy	Quinn	Wood	Hilaire	
9	Birmingham	Hansbury	Ranson	Williams	Hagan	Overson	Kuhl	Brenner	Clarke	Whitton	Kennedy	Cooke	
10	Portsmouth	Knight	Swain	Hardyman	Dillon*	Blake	Gilbert	O'Callaghan	Kennedy	Quinn	Morgan	Hilaire	
10	Leeds	Day	Aspin	Robinson	Ormsby	Ashurst	Rennie	Stiles	Sheridan	Baird	Edwards	Ritchie	Ball

Match notes

1. Brighton — Ex-England striker Mariner is denied on his debut by Digweed, who also excels to keep out efforts by Tait and Hilaire. Pompey claim a penalty when Dale Jasper handles, but Albion, with Alan Mullery back at the helm, survive. Ball's other summer signing – Eamonn Collins – is sub.

2. Ipswich — Town contest former favourite O'Callaghan's equalising free-kick. The referee had simultaneously blown to penalise the encroaching defensive wall, but their protests are waved aside. Newly-relegated Ipswich took the lead with a classy strike as Jason Dozzell lays off to Mark Brennan.

3. Hull — Hull lose their way after Flounders' header comes back off the bar. Quinn sets about establishing his 'Noah' nickname, grabbing a brace of sharp strikes either side of half-time. Blake wants a transfer, while Argyle offer £60,000 for Morgan, but decide to sign Tommy Tynan instead.

4. Barnsley — Blake and Gilbert bottle up Barnsley's anonymous attack and Kennedy and Tait are masters of midfield as Pompey arrogantly cruise to a win. Quinn buries Tait's pass, then gives the scoreline a more accurate hue at the death. Blake cap the week by coming off the list.

5. Blackburn — Rovers lose the only 100% record in the league, as Kennedy celebrates his decision with a 25-yarder that fizzes past O'Keefe. The wretched weather means a worrying gate of less than 9,000, who are rewarded with a gritty display and a reflex save from Knight to deny Simon Garner.

6. Stoke — Hardyman has the dubious honour of being carried off and sent off at the same time as he clatters into Ford for a second time, earning another booking and a stretcher ride. Kennedy crashes in his second of the season as Stoke hesitate, but Tony Kelly curls a superb free-kick to level.

7. Huddersfield — A dire game has a happy ending as Blake's header from Dillon's centre defeats Cox, but Town's dodgy finishing helps. The unbeaten run earns Ball the Bells' Manager of the Month award, while Pompey, still without a shirt-sponsor, are accused of ignoring Havant-based CPG's offer.

8. Sunderland — Knight has to be at his sharpest to keep out Blake's inadvertent effort, but that's the closest to a goal. Pompey have the best defensive record in the country – just two conceded in eight – but Deacon is worried about poor gates and announces a cut-price trial at the Wrexham cup game.

9. Birmingham — Pompey force eleven fruitless first-half corners, but Hansbury hasn't a shot to save. A stroke of luck turns the match as Overson's clearance hits a defender and falls perfectly for Quinn to volley. A near-post header gives him his 20th goal in 21 games for the club and sends them top.

10. Leeds — Knight lets in his first in more than seven hours when Gilbert is harshly judged to have fouled Edwards. Three minutes later Dillon is tripped in the box, but play waved on. Ritchie's drive is followed by Quinn's pen – Dillon limped off after the earlier tackle – but Baird's header seals it.

#	Fixture	Att.	Pos		Res	Score	Pts	HT
11	H DERBY 21/10	9,131	1	9	W	3-1	22	0-1
12	H WEST BROM 25/10	11,608	1	7	W	2-1	25	0-1
13	A OLDHAM 1/11	8,635	1	2	D	0-0	26	0-0
14	H BRADFORD C 8/11	10,027	1	16	W	2-1	29	2-1
15	A SHREWSBURY 15/11	3,827	2	18	L	0-1	29	0-1
16	H GRIMSBY 22/11	9,517	2	11	W	2-1	32	0-1
17	A MILLWALL 29/11	5,031	2	13	D	1-1	33	0-0
18	H CRYSTAL PALACE 6/12	10,907	2	15	W	2-0	36	2-0
19	A SHEFFIELD UTD 13/12	9,523	2	8	L	0-1	36	0-0
20	H BARNSLEY 20/12	9,568	1	21	W	2-1	39	0-1
21	A PLYMOUTH 26/12	21,249	1	5	W	3-2	42	2-1

---

11 — H DERBY 21/10
Pompey: Knight, Swain, Hardyman, Dillon, Blake, Gilbert, O'Callaghan, Kennedy, Quinn, Morgan*, Hilaire, Wood
Derby: Wallington, Sage, Forsyth, Williams, Hindmarch, MacLaren, Micklewhite, Gee, Davison, Gregory, Harbey
Quinn 57, 83, 85 / Gregory 25
Ref: M Bodenham (Brighton)
Exactly six years ago Argyle were the last team to beat Pompey under Fratton lights, but Rams have that record in their sights after Gregory's shot sneaks in. Backed by a gale, Pompey storm back and Quinn's poke creeps in. He claims the match-ball with a tap-in and far-post header.

12 — H WEST BROM 25/10
Pompey: Knight, Swain, Hardyman, Dillon, Blake, Gilbert, O'Callaghan, Kennedy, Quinn, Morgan*, Hilaire, Wood
West Brom: Naylor, Whitehead, Cowdrill, Palmer, Dyson, Dickenson, Hopkins, Denniston, Burrows*, Williamson, Crooks, Evans
Hilaire 66, 86 / Crooks 30
Ref: B Stevens (Stonehouse)
Garth Crooks shows his class, rounding Knight and clipping home, to give Pompey yet another second-half mountain to climb. Ron Saunders' Baggies hold out until Hilaire heads in O'Callaghan's cross. Swain sets up the winner for Hilaire, who whisks a shot into the bottom corner.

13 — A OLDHAM 1/11
Pompey: Knight, Swain, Hardyman, Dillon, Ball, Gilbert, O'Callaghan, Kennedy, Quinn, Wood, Hilaire
Oldham: Goram, Irwin, Donachie, Hoolickin, Linighan, Williams, Palmer, Henry, Wright, Futcher, Milligan
Ref: J Key (Rotherham)
After the Albion game Quinn and Wood are cautioned by police for swearing at a linesman. Pompey train at Keele University, after the cup game at Bradford, but Blake is out: a groin strain breaks a run of 117 consecutive matches. Oldham's plastic pitch serves up a game to match.

14 — H BRADFORD C 8/11
Pompey: Knight, Swain, Hardyman, Dillon, Blake, Gilbert, O'Callagh'n*, Kennedy, Mariner, Quinn, Hilaire, Wood
Bradford C: Litchfield, Abbott, Withe, McCall, Oliver, Evans, Hendrie, Goodman, Leonard, Singleton, Ellis
Dillon 16, Quinn 33 / McCall 35
Ref: P Don (Harwood Park)
The goalkeeper's lot is illustrated as Litchfield's one error – misjudging Dillon's swirling cross – costs the game. Quinn quickly taps in Hilaire's cross, but McCall drags City back with a 25-yarder. Litchfield spends the second half keeping Pompey at bay, but few remember that.

15 — A SHREWSBURY 15/11
Pompey: Knight, Swain, Hardyman, Dillon, Blake, Gilbert, O'Callaghan, Kennedy, Mariner, Quinn, Hilaire*, Ball
Shrewsbury: Perks, Williams, Johnson, Leonard, Pearson, Franklin, McNally, Hackett, Brown, Robinson, Daly
Hackett 8
Ref: P Harrison (Heywood)
Shrews somehow cling onto Hackett's early bender, as Gilbert is denied a first goal for the club, first by Perks' brilliant stop, then by a post. Quinn is just wide and Pompey are off the top. Ball refuses to comment. Pompey's balance sheet reveals a £400,000 profit thanks to transfers.

16 — H GRIMSBY 22/11
Pompey: Knight, Swain, Hardyman, Dillon, Blake, Gilbert, Collins, Kennedy, Mariner, Quinn*, Hilaire, Ball
Grimsby: Felgate, Burgess, Agnew, Robinson, Lyons, Moore, Hazell, Walsh, Rawcliffe, O'Riordan, Bonnyman* Straw
Mariner 55, Blake 80 / Hazel 42
Ref: L Shapter (Torquay)
Pompey come from behind for the third time in four home games. Mariners' loanee Des Hazell waltzes round four defenders and Knight to squeeze home a sensational goal. Mariner breaks his goal-drought from a yard after Dillon's free-kick, then Blake heads in Collins' cross.

17 — A MILLWALL 29/11
Pompey: Knight, Tait, Swain, Dillon, Blake, Gilbert, Ball, Kennedy, Mariner, Quinn, Hilaire
Millwall: Horne, Stevens, Coleman, Briley, Walker, McLeary, Byrne, Mehmet, Sheringham, Marks, Salman
Dillon 90 / Sheringham 71
Ref: M Reed (Birmingham)
Teddy Sheringham's near-post header finally sparks Pompey into life and they spend the rest of the game camped in Lions' half. Horne denies Blake, then Mehmet clears from the line, but Millwall finally crack when Coleman muffs a clearance and Dillon eases home a point-saver.

18 — H CRYSTAL PALACE 6/12
Pompey: Knight, Tait, Swain, Collins, Blake, Gilbert, O'Callaghan, Kennedy, Mariner, Quinn, Hilaire
Crystal Palace: Wood, Stebbing, Sparrow, Taylor, Nebbeling, Cannon, Gray, Ketteridge, Bright, Barber, Finnegan
Quinn 16, O'Callaghan 25
Ref: R Milford (Bristol)
Pompey stretch their home run to eleven consecutive wins as Mariner shows his increasing influence on the side. First, he lays off for Quinn to blast home, then his pass splits the Palace defence and Cally stabs home. Morgan – on-loan at Stoke – signs permanently in a £40,000 deal.

19 — A SHEFFIELD UTD 13/12
Pompey: Knight, Tait!, Swain, Dillon!, Blake, Gilbert!, Ball, Kennedy, Mariner, Quinn*, Hilaire, O'Callaghan
Sheffield Utd: Burridge, Barnsley*, Pike, Arnott, Stancliffe, Eckhardt, Morris, Wigley, Daws, Foley, Beagrie!, Dempsey
Mariner 69 (og)
Ref: K Morton (Bury St Edmunds)
Makeshift defender Mariner slices in to give ten-man Blades the win. Hardly impressive though, as Pompey are reduced to eight, thanks to the referee's letter-of-the-law approach. Gilbert goes for something he said, Tait and Beagrie for an off-the-ball clash and Dillon for two bookings.

20 — H BARNSLEY 20/12
Pompey: Knight, Tait, Swain, Dillon, Blake, Gilbert, O'Callaghan, Kennedy, Mariner, Quinn, Hilaire
Barnsley: Baker, Ogley, Gray, Thomas, May, Futcher, Foreman, Agnew, Ferry, MacDonald, Beresford
Quinn 72, Dillon 90p / Ferry 40
Ref: J Deakin (Llantwit Major)
Quinn's tumble over Baker at the death earns a penalty which puts Pompey back on top for 24 hours. Cally set up Quinn for the goal, which levelled Ferry's late arrival from MacDonald's header. Quinn's week is soured when he finds he is likely to be jailed for motoring offences.

21 — A PLYMOUTH 26/12
Pompey: Knight, Tait, Swain, Hardyman*, Dillon, Blake, Gilbert, O'Callaghan, Kennedy, Mariner, Quinn, Hilaire, Tait
Plymouth: Cherry, Nisbet, Coper*, Uzell, McElhinney, Matthews, Hodges, Coughlin, Tynan, Clayton, Nelson, Rowbotham
Quinn 11, Dillon 43, Hilaire 52 / Coughlin 30p, Hodges 77
Ref: K Burge (Tonypandy)
The battle of the ports goes to Pompey, but not until Dave Smith's side pushed them all the way. Promoted Argyle are aiming for division one, but Dillon and Hilaire strike either side of half-time to nullify Coughlin's penalty, after Hardyman fouled Tynan. Hodges pulled one back.

TODAY LEAGUE DIVISION 2 — Manager: Alan Ball — SEASON 1986-87

Column headings: No | Date | Att | Pos | Pt | W | F-A | H-T | Scorers, Times, and Referees | 1 | 2 | 3 | 4 | 5 | 6 | 7 | 8 | 9 | 10 | 11 | 12 sub used

---

22. SHREWSBURY (H) — 29/12 · Att 15,006 · 1 · 15 · 45 · W · 3-0 · H-T 0-0
Scorers: Quinn 58, Hilaire 76, Johnson 87 (og). Ref: K Cooper (Pontypridd)

1	2	3	4	5	6	7	8	9	10	11	12 sub used
Knight	Ball	Williams	Collins	Blake	Mariner	O'Callaghan	Kennedy	Russell	Quinn	Hilaire	
Perks	*Williams*	*Johnson*	*Leonard*	*Pearson*	*Linghan*	*McNally*	*Tester**	*Waller*	*Hackett*	*Daly*	*Robinson*

Injury and suspension-ravaged Pompey draft in Collins and Russell, while Mariner fills in at centre-half again. The wind blows Pompey off-course in the first half, but once Quinn despatches Hilaire's cross the crowd relax. Johnson slices in under pressure from the lively Russell.

---

23. READING (H) — 1/1 · Att 18,289 · 1 · 18 · 48 · W · 1-0 · H-T 1-0
Scorers: Mariner 6. Ref: R Groves (Weston-super-Mare)

1	2	3	4	5	6	7	8	9	10	11	12 sub used
Knight	Swain	Thomas	Dillon	Blake	Tait	O'Callaghan	Kennedy	Mariner	Quinn	Hilaire	
Barron	*Baillie*	*Richardson*	*Hurlock*	*Hicks*	*Wood*	*Williams*	*Taylor*	*Senior*	*Brenner*	*Smillie**	*Beavon*

Ball's old mate George Graham loans Arsenal's England youth defender Michael Thomas and he makes a classy league debut. After Mariner's diving header, Royals graft their way back. Senior earns a penalty, but Knight atones for his foul by reading the ex-Pompey man's intentions.

---

24. BLACKBURN (A) — 3/1 · Att 6,582 · 1 · 21 · 48 · L · 0-1 · H-T 0-0
Scorers: Sellars 54. Ref: P Tyldesley (Stockport)

1	2	3	4	5	6	7	8	9	10	11	12 sub used
Knight	Swain	Thomas	Dillon	Blake	Mariner	O'Callaghan	Kennedy	Mariner	Quinn	Tait*	Hilaire
Gennoe	*Price*	*Rathbone*	*Barker*	*Keeley*	*Mail*	*Branagan*	*Sellars*	*McKinnon*	*Garner*	*Patterson*	

Pompey seem to have problems on northern grounds and frosted Ewood Park is no exception. Sellars bulldozes his way through to score. O'Callaghan nearly saves it as his shot hits the post and Quinn is unable to take advantage of the rebound. At least rivals also dropped points.

---

25. BRIGHTON (H) — 24/1 · Att 12,992 · 1 · 16 · 51 · W · 1-0 · H-T 1-0
Scorers: Dillon 5p. Ref: P Vanes (Warley)

1	2	3	4	5	6	7	8	9	10	11	12 sub used
Knight	Swain	Thomas	Dillon	Blake	Gilbert	O'Callaghan	Kennedy*	Mariner	Collins	Hilaire	Ball
Keeley	*O'Regan*	*Hutchings*	*Wilson*	*Gatting*	*Young*	*Penney*	*Saunders**	*Hughes*	*Connor*	*Jasper*	*Tittman*

With Quinn in Winchester Prison, Pompey respond in style. Ball's lone-striker tactic – so successful in the Full Members Cup – flummoxes Albion. Dillon's 28th penalty out of 32 after Hilaire is nudged settles it, but that record becomes out of 33 when he fires high and wide late on.

---

26. IPSWICH (A) — 7/2 · Att 18,670 · 1 · 5 · 54 · W · 1-0 · H-T 1-0
Scorers: Tait 18. Ref: C Downey (Hounslow)

1	2	3	4	5	6	7	8	9	10	11	12 sub used
Knight	Swain	Hardyman	Dillon	Blake	Daish	O'Callaghan	Tait	Mariner	Quinn	Hilaire	
Cooper	*Yallop**	*McCall*	*Atkins*	*Dozzell*	*Cranson*	*Humes*	*Brennan*	*Cole*	*Wilson*	*Zondervan*	*Stockwell*

After a week's intensive work, the paroled Quinn is back, alongside young defender Daish, who replaces flu-victim Gilbert. Tait muscles in front of a defender to nod in Cally's free-kick, and Hilaire's last-ditch tackle on Brennan and Blake's late goal-line clearance prove vital.

---

27. HULL (H) — 14/2 · Att 11,098 · 1 · 19 · 57 · W · 1-0 · H-T 1-0
Scorers: Quinn 25. Ref: V Callow (Solihull)

1	2	3	4	5	6	7	8	9	10	11	12 sub used
Knight	Swain	Hardyman	Dillon	Blake	Gilbert	O'Callagh'n*	Tait	Russell	Quinn	Hilaire	Ball
Norman	*Palmer*	*Pearson*	*Jobson*	*Skipper*	*Parker*	*Williams*	*Bunn*	*Saville*	*Askey**	*Dyer*	*Flounders*

Portsmouth's best-kept secret can be revealed. Half the side were suffering from a chest infection, which explains a less-than-top-notch display. Quinn's razor-sharp reactions are intact as he whisks home Hilaire's cross. Parker thumps the bar for Hull, then Knight saves from Dyer.

---

28. HUDDERSFIELD (A) — 21/2 · Att 6,229 · 1 · 18 · 57 · L · 0-2 · H-T 0-0
Scorers: Shearer 50, Banks 81. Ref: G Tyson (Sunderland)

1	2	3	4	5	6	7	8	9	10	11	12 sub used
Knight	Swain	Hardyman	Dillon	Blake	Gilbert	O'Callagh'n*	Tait	Mariner	Quinn	Hilaire	Ball
Cox	*Brown*	*Burke*	*Banks*	*Webster*	*Mitchell*	*Winter*	*Cork*	*Shearer*	*Wilson*	*Cowling**	*Jones*

The chest-bug forced Pompey to call off their Full Members' Cup-tie at Norwich, but are back to full strength here. Tyson misses four possible penalties according to Ball, which prove costly when Shearer dives full-length to head home, then Banks coolly drives in the final nail.

---

29. STOKE (H) — 28/2 · Att 14,607 · 1 · 6 · 60 · W · 3-0 · H-T 2-0
Scorers: Quinn 11, 66, Dillon 31p. Ref: A Seville (Birmingham)

1	2	3	4	5	6	7	8	9	10	11	12 sub used
Knight	Swain	Hardyman	Dillon	Blake	Gilbert	O'Callaghan*	Tait*	Mariner	Quinn	Hilaire	Collins
Fox	*Dixon*	*Parkin*	*Talbot**	*Bould*	*Berry*	*Ford*	*Maskery*	*Morgan*	*Bertschin*	*Saunders*	*Hemming*

Stoke's season has been transformed. Since November and the arrival of Morgan, they have zoomed from the foot of the table to the fringes of the play-off zone. Once Quinn jabs home, Potters crumble and Berry hauls down Mariner for Dillon to ensure a 14th straight home win.

---

30. DERBY (A) — 4/3 · Att 21,085 · 1 · 2 · 61 · D · 0-0 · H-T 0-0
Ref: B Hill (Kettering)

1	2	3	4	5	6	7	8	9	10	11	12 sub used
Knight	Swain	Hardyman	Dillon	Blake	Gilbert	Tait	Kennedy	Mariner	Quinn	Hilaire	
Wallington	*Blades*	*Forsyth*	*Williams*	*Hindmarch*	*MacLaren*	*Micklewhite*	*Gee*	*Davison*	*Gregory*	*Callaghan*	*Collins*

This game had everything but goals as Arthur Cox's team fail to close Pompey's six-point lead at the top. Kennedy returns from injury, despite hardly training. The kick-off is delayed 15 minutes to accommodate the crowd, but they see Rams neat passing betrayed by poor finishing.

---

31. LEEDS (H) — 10/3 · Att 13,745 · 1 · 6 · 62 · D · 1-1 · H-T 1-0
Scorers: Mariner 9, Adams 80. Ref: D Elleray (Harrow)

1	2	3	4	5	6	7	8	9	10	11	12 sub used
Knight	Swain	Hardyman	Dillon	Blake	Gilbert	Tait	Kennedy	Mariner	Quinn	Hilaire	
Day	*Aspin*	*McDonald*	*Aizlewood*	*Ashurst*	*Ormsby*	*Stiles*	*Sheridan*	*Pearson*	*Baird*	*Adams*	

Billy Bremner's team were the last to win at Fratton, eleven months ago, and now Adams seizes on Blake's poor header to ease home only the seventh goal conceded at home by Knight. FA Cup semi-finalists Leeds fall behind to Mariner's sharp finish after Day saves Tait's shot.

Football season results table (matches 32–42). The page is a rotated statistics grid; each match lists the Portsmouth XI (roman) against the opponents' XI (italic), followed by match data and a report.

No	V	Date	Opponent	Att	Pos	Res	Pts	FT	HT	Scorers	Referee
32	A	21/3	BIRMINGHAM	9,823	13	2 W	65	1-0	1-0	Hilaire 35	Ref: J Ireland (Warrington)
33	H	28/3	SUNDERLAND	13,371	16	1 W	68	3-1	1-0	Hilaire 29, 87, Blake 72 / Blake 54 (og)	Ref: H King (Merthyr Tydfil)
34	A	4/4	BRADFORD C	8,570	21	2 L	68	0-1	0-0	Futcher 51	Ref: G Courtney (Spennymoor)
35	H	11/4	OLDHAM	19,708	3	2 W	71	3-0	0-0	Dillon 52p, 59p, Quinn 76	Ref: B Stevens (Stonehouse)
36	A	18/4	READING	9,549	13	1 D	72	2-2	1-0	Quinn 29, Hilaire 72 / Peters 47, Bremner 62	Ref: D Vickers (Ilford)
37	H	20/4	PLYMOUTH	17,171	5	2 L	72	0-1	0-0	Summerfield 76	Ref: T Holbrook (Wolverhampton)
38	A	27/4	GRIMSBY	5,085	19	2 W	75	2-0	0-0	Mariner 65, Quinn 78	Ref: K Hackett (Sheffield)
39	A	29/4	WEST BROM	10,007	13	2 L	75	0-1	0-1	Hopkins 16	Ref: T Simpson (W Yorkshire)
40	H	2/5	MILLWALL	15,777	14	2 W	78	2-0	0-0	Mariner 54, O'Callaghan 89	Ref: R Lewis (Great Bookham)
41	A	4/5	CRYSTAL PALACE	18,029	7	2 L	78	0-1	0-0	Wright 87	Ref: R Hamer (Bristol)
42	H	9/5	SHEFFIELD UTD	28,001	9	2 L	78	1-2	1-0	Quinn 35 / Withe 49, Dempsey 70	Ref: R Gifford (Hengoed)

Home Average 13,401 — Away 11,162

---

32 BIRMINGHAM
Pompey: Knight, Swain, Hardyman, Dillon, Blake, Gilbert, O'Callaghan, Tait, Mariner, Ball, Hilaire
Birmingham: Tomlinson, Ranson, Dicks, Williams, Overson, Mortimer, Bremner, North, Whitton, Rees*, Wigley, Handysides
On-loan Tomlinson anticipates Hilaire's header, but the ball hits his shoulder instead and deceives the keeper. Birmingham are in trouble and it shows. Gilbert seems destined not to score; his shot is cleared off the line, but Handysides almost steals a point when his late shot goes wide.

33 SUNDERLAND
Pompey: Knight, Swain, Hardyman, Dillon, Blake, Gilbert, O'Callaghan, Kennedy, Mariner, Quinn, Hilaire
Sunderland: Hesford, Burley*, Gray, Atkinson, Corner, Bennett, Lemon, Procter, Doyle, Bertschin, Gates, Buchanan
Sunderland parade new-boy Bertschin, but he is helpless to halt their plunge towards relegation play-off disaster. Hilaire latches onto Knight's clearance to open but Blake inadvertently levels as Kennedy's clearance cannons off him. He responds with a typical header to restore the lead.

34 BRADFORD C
Bradford C: Litchfield, Mitchell, Goddard, McCall, Oliver, Evans, Hendrie, Abbott, Futcher, Palin, Ellis
Pompey's traditional April wobbles are back as Bantams' boss Terry Dolan reckons his side 'wanted it a bit more.' Ron Futcher's free header separates the teams and Goddard's misplaced back-pass is Pompey's best effort. Blake and Quinn are in the PFA's second division all-stars.

35 OLDHAM
Oldham: Goram, Irwin, Barlow, Henry*, Linighan!, Moore, Palmer, Ormondroyd, Milligan, Williams, Cecere, Wright
Latics' boss Joe Royle remonstrates with Stevens as he gives two penalties – the first for Barlow's trip, then for Linighan's handball – letting Dillon put distance between Pompey and their promotion rivals. Linighan is sent off after a clash with Kennedy, after Quinn forced home.

36 READING
Reading: Francis*, Baillie, Richardson, Beavon, Hicks, Woods, Peters, Taylor, Senior, Bremner, Horrix, Smillie
Senior ends up in goal against his old team as Francis is concussed when Hilaire knocks in the equaliser, but he doesn't have a shot to save in his 12-minute stint. Beavon fired high and wide from an early penalty, but Peters and Bremner lead Royals' fight after Quinn's classy goal.

37 PLYMOUTH
Plymouth: Cherry, Brimacombe, Cooper, Law, Uzzell, Matthews, Hodges, Coughlin, Tynan, Clayton*, Summerfield, Nelson
Fortress Fratton is finally taken as Blake miscues a back-pass and Summerfield – only on for two minutes – fires a cross-shot past Knight. Quinn is strangely subdued, missing the injured Mariner's presence. The loss is tempered by news of Oldham's home draw with Grimsby.

38 GRIMSBY
Grimsby: Prudhoe, McDermott, Burgess, Turner, Moore, Crombie, Halsall, Bonnyman*, O'Riordan, Cumming, Henshaw, McGarvey
Mariner's foot injury has cleared and he eases the tension with a far-post header, shortly after new-dad Knight had made a double save. Quinn wraps it up and Oldham's loss means they are nine behind with four to play. Old-boy McGarvey's foul on Knight sparks an ugly melee.

39 WEST BROM
West Brom: Naylor, Whitehead, Palmer, Bennett, Dyson, Bradley, Hopkins, Goodman, MacKenzie, Anderson, O'Callaghan, Lynex
Had Oldham lost at Stoke – they won 2-0 – this could have been a promotion party. Instead, Hopkins sweeps in the only goal of the game as Albion halt their slide and Pompey still need four points to be sure. Mariner is inches from making this one of them, but his header goes wide.

40 MILLWALL
Millwall: Horne, Morgan, Coleman, Briley, Walker, McLeary, Byrne, Carter, Sheringham*, Salman, Booker, Marks
Cally fires into the roof of the net from an indirect free-kick on the six-yard line, as word spreads that Argyle have levelled at Latics. They haven't, but fences come down and the pitch is invaded. Highly-rated Horne keeps Pompey at bay until Mariner slips his marker and angles in.

41 CRYSTAL PALACE
Crystal Palace: Wood, Nebbeling, O'Doherty, Taylor, O'Reilly, Cannon, Irvine, Gray, Bright, Wright, Salako, Finnegan*
The promised land is three miles away when Ian Wright sweeps home Salako's cross, choking the celebrations of 10,000 fans massed behind Wood's goal. Hilaire's petulant push on Gray sees him sent off at the death, while Mariner had earlier seen a goal ruled out for offside.

42 SHEFFIELD UTD
Sheffield Utd: Burridge, Barnsley, Pike, Kuhl, Stancliffe, Eckhardt, Morris, Frain, Withe, Dempsey, Beagrie
Shrews' midweek defeat of Oldham means Pompey are up, but the title is still alive. Fans invade the closed upper Fratton End tier, delaying the kick-off, but once Withe levels hopes fade. After Beagrie's goal, several pitch invasions hold things up: a promotion party is underway.

TODAY DIVISION 2 (CUP-TIES) Manager: Alan Ball SEASON 1986-87

Littlewoods Cup

	1	2	3	4	5	6	7	8	9	10	11	subs used
2:1 A WREXHAM 3 W 2-1 H-T 1-0	Knight	Pearce	Swain	Dillon	Blake	Gilbert	O'Callaghan	Kennedy	Mariner*	Quinn	Hilaire^	Wood/Collins
24/9 4,110 4:20		*Salathiel*	*Cunnington*	*Williams*	*Cooke*	*Comstive*	*Massey**	*Horne*	*Steel*	*Charles^*	*Conroy*	*Buxton/Emson*
2:2 H WREXHAM 3 W 2-0 0-0	Knight	Pearce	Hardyman	Dillon	Blake	Ball	O'Callaghan	Kennedy	Quinn	Tait	Hilaire	
7/10 8,264 4:16		*Salathiel*	*Cunnington*	*Williams*	*Jones**	*Conroy^*	*Massey*	*Horne*	*Steel*	*Charles*	*Emson*	*C'stive/Wright^*
3 A BRADFORD C 1 L 1-3 1-0	Knight	Swain	Hardyman	Dillon	Blake	Gilbert	O'Callaghan	Kennedy	Quinn	Wood	Hilaire	
29/10 4,885 18	*Litchfield*	*Clegg*	*Withe*	*Abbott*	*Oliver*	*Evans*	*Hendrie*	*Goodman*	*Ormondroyd*	*Singleton*	*Ellis*	

Scorers, Times, and Referees

- 2:1 — O'Callaghan 30, Quinn 56 / *Buxton 90p* / Ref: K Walmsley (Blackpool)
- 2:2 — Quinn 68, 89 / Ref: D Reeves (Uxbridge) / (Pompey won 4-1 on aggregate)
- 3 — Quinn 39 *[Abbott 54p]* / *Goodman 46, Ormondroyd 49* / Ref: G Aplin (Kendal)

Buxton's late pen irritates Ball, but he is more concerned about the injury to Mariner which will keep him out for a month. Ball uses both subs, but still sees his team down to ten men when Quinn tweaks an ankle. By then Pompey are 2-0 up – Cally's angled shot and Quinn's header.

Deacon cuts prices for this game and hoped for 10,000. However, he will repeat the experiment for games over Christmas and New Year with better results. Russell's pace changes the game and his shot deflects off Quinn for the opener; then he fires in and Quinn's touch does the rest.

Nine minutes of madness cost Pompey dear. Quinn slots home from the edge of the box, but 20 seconds into the second half Gilbert stumbles and Goodman is clear. Blake then treads on the ball and Ormondroyd pounces, before Hardyman chops down Hendrie and Abbott converts.

FA Cup

	1	2	3	4	5	6	7	8	9	10	11	subs used
3 H BLACKBURN 1 W 2-0 1-0	Knight	Tait	Swain	Dillon	Blake	Gilbert	O'Callaghan	Kennedy	Mariner	Quinn	Hilaire	
10/1 10,679 21	*O'Keefe*	*Price*	*Rathbone*	*Barker*	*Keeley*	*Mail*	*Brotherston*	*Sellars*	*McKinnon*	*Garner**	*Patterson*	*Miller*
4 A WIMBLEDON 1 L 0-4 0-3	Knight	Swain	Hardyman	Dillon	Blake	Gilbert	O'Callaghan	Kennedy	Mariner*	Quinn	Hilaire	Collins/Russell
31/1 11,329 1:11	*Beasant*	*Kay*	*Winterburn*	*Jones**	*Gayle*	*Thorn*	*Hodges*	*Sayer*	*Fashanu^*	*Sanchez*	*F'weather*	*Downes/Cork*

Scorers, Times, and Referees

- 3 — Quinn 30, 77 / Ref: M James (Horsham)
- 4 — *[Sayer 45]* / *Fashanu 12, 60, Blake 20 (og), Sayer* / Ref: I Hemley (Ampthill)

Pompey have been advertising for a shirt sponsor; but still no takers. They are into the next round of the Cup though, thanks to Quinn's 20th and 21st goals. Mariner's astuteness sets up both strikes, but news of Wood's pelvic injury dampens spirits; he will miss the rest of the season.

Ball will ditch Pompey's white third strip after this surrender in front of the MotD cameras. Quinn's incarceration is no excuse, as Fashanu rolls home after Knight's hesitancy. Blake heads his second own-goal at Plough Lane in three games, then Sayer seizes on Hardyman's error.

Football League Division Two — Final Table

Pos	Team	P	W	D	L	F	A	W	D	L	F	A	Pts
			Home					**Away**					
1	Derby	42	14	6	1	42	18	11	3	7	22	20	84
2	PORTSMOUTH	42	17	2	2	37	11	6	7	8	16	17	78
3	Oldham	42	13	6	2	36	16	9	3	9	29	28	75
4	Leeds	42	15	4	2	43	16	4	7	10	15	28	68
5	Ipswich	42	12	6	3	29	10	5	7	9	30	33	64
6	Crystal Pal	42	12	4	5	35	20	7	1	13	16	33	62
7	Plymouth	42	12	6	3	40	23	4	7	10	22	34	61
8	Stoke	42	11	5	5	40	21	5	5	11	23	32	58
9	Sheffield Utd	42	10	8	3	31	19	5	5	11	19	30	58
10	Bradford C	42	10	5	6	36	27	5	5	11	26	35	55
11	Barnsley	42	8	7	6	26	23	6	6	9	23	29	55
12	Blackburn	42	11	4	6	30	22	4	6	11	15	33	55
13	Reading	42	11	4	6	33	23	3	7	11	19	36	53
14	Hull	42	10	6	5	25	22	3	8	10	16	33	53
15	West Brom	42	8	6	7	29	16	5	6	10	22	27	51
16	Millwall	42	10	5	6	27	16	4	4	13	12	29	51
17	Huddersfield	42	9	6	6	38	30	4	6	11	16	31	51
18	Shrewsbury	42	11	3	7	24	21	4	3	14	17	39	51
19	Birmingham	42	8	9	4	27	21	3	8	10	20	38	50
20	Sunderland	42	8	6	7	25	23	4	6	11	24	36	48
21	Grimsby	42	5	8	8	18	21	5	6	10	21	38	44
22	Brighton	42	7	6	8	22	20	2	6	13	15	34	39
		924	232	122	108	693	438	108	122	232	438	693	1264

Odds & ends

Double wins: (4) Hull, Barnsley, Birmingham, Grimsby.

Double losses: (0).

Won from behind: (4) Derby (h), West Brom (h), Grimsby (h), Barnsley (h).

Lost from in front: (1) Sheffield Utd (h).

High spots: Nine-match unbeaten run at the start of the season.

14 consecutive home league victories from September to March.

Kevin Dillon's hat-trick of penalties in the 3-2 Full Members Cup win against Millwall.

19 clean sheets during the season.

Low spots: Surrendering 0-4 at Wimbledon in the FA Cup 4th round.

Conceding the losing goal at Crystal Palace on May Bank Holiday with just three minutes to go – a point would have clinched promotion.

Player of the Year: Noel Blake.

Ever-presents: (2) Kenny Swain, Alan Knight.

Hat-tricks: Mick Quinn (1), Kevin Dillon (1).

Leading scorer: Mick Quinn (28).

Appearances & Goals

Player	Lge	Sub	LC	Sub	FAC	Sub	Goals Lge	LC	FAC	Tot
Ball, Kevin	9	7	2		1					
Blake, Noel	41		3		2		3			3
Collins, Eammon					1	1				
Daish, Liam	1									
Dillon, Kevin	39		3		2		8			8
Gilbert, Billy	36		2		2					
Hardyman, Paul	33		2		1					
Hilaire, Vince	39	2	3		2		8			8
Kennedy, Mick	35		3		1		2			2
Knight, Alan	42		3		2					
Mariner, Paul	33		1		2		5			5
Morgan, Nicky	4									
O'Callaghan, Kevin	30	3	3		2		3	1		4
Quinn, Mick	39	3	3		1		22	4	2	28
Russell, Kevin	3			1						
Swain, Kenny	42		3		2					
Tait, Mick	25	3	1		2		1			1
Thomas, Michael	3	3		1		2				
Wood, Paul	4	3	1							
(own-goals)							1			1
19 players used	462	19	33	2	22	1	53	5	2	60

BARCLAYS LEAGUE DIVISION 1 Manager: Alan Ball SEASON 1987-88

Columns: No | Date | Att | Pos | Pt | F-A | H-T | Scorers, Times, and Referees | 1 | 2 | 3 | 4 | 5 | 6 | 7 | 8 | 9 | 10 | 11 | subs used

---

1 — A OXFORD — 15/8
Att 9,174 · L · Pt 0 · F-A 2-4 · H-T 0-1

Scorers: Mariner 47, Whitehead 63 / Langan 8, Caton 46, Whitehurst 62, 82 Hucker 63
Ref: N Midgley (Bolton)

	1	2	3	4	5	6	7	8	9	10	11	subs used
Pompey	Knight	Swain	Hardyman	Dillon^	Mariner	Gilbert	Whitehead	Kennedy	Kerr	Quinn	Fillery*	Stewart/Horne
Oxford		*Langan**	*Slatter*	*Shelton*	*Briggs*	*Caton*	*Houghton*	*Foyle*	*Whitehurst*	*Hebbard*	*Rh's-Brown*	*Dreyer*

A long season looks in prospect as Pompey, shorn of banned Baird (Leeds) and the crocked Blake, trade goals merrily with eventual companions in distress. Four debut, with a rags-to-riches tale for US citizen Kerr, who starts after playing in non-league last season.

---

2 — H CHELSEA — 18/8
Att 16,917 · L · Pt 0 · F-A 0-3 · H-T 0-1

Scorers: — / Nevin 28, Dixon 74, Wilson 81
Ref: K Barratt (Coventry)

	1	2	3	4	5	6	7	8	9	10	11	subs used
Pompey	Knight	Swain	Hardyman	Whitehead	Mariner	Gilbert	Sandford	Kennedy	Kerr	Quinn	Fillery*	Horne
Chelsea	*Niedzwiecki*	*Clarke*	*Dorigo*	*Wicks*	*McLaughlin*	*Wood*	*Nevin*	*Hazard*	*Dixon*	*Durie*	*Wilson C*	

Chelsea have too much class once Nevin seizes on Gilbert's error. Dixon and Clive Wilson give the win a flattering complexion, but Pompey's unbeaten run under Fratton lights (31 matches) is over. Police dictate that most home games must be all-ticket and its effect is evident.

---

3 — H SOUTHAMPTON — 22/8
Att 20,161 · Pos 20 · D · Pt 1 · F-A 2-2 · H-T 1-1

Scorers: Hilaire 20, Whitehead 74 / Clarke 25, 48
Ref: R Lewis (Great Bookham)

	1	2	3	4	5	6	7	8	9	10	11	subs used
Pompey	Knight	Swain	Hardyman	Whitehead	Mariner	Gilbert	Fillery*	Kennedy	Baird	Quinn^	Hilaire	Dillon/Sandford
Soton	*Flowers*	*Forrest*	*Statham*	*Case*	*Moore*	*Bond*	*Townsend*	*Cockerill*	*Clarke*	*Hobson*	*Baker G*	

Another poor gate heralds the point which lifts them off the foot of the table. Hilaire wins a race with Flowers and his lob bounces in, but then Clarke shows the prowess that will persuade Burrows to spend £400,000 on him in 1990. Whitehead (free from WBA) finishes smartly.

---

4 — A ARSENAL — 29/8
Att 30,865 · Pos 20 · L · Pt 1 · F-A 0-6 · H-T 0-4

Scorers: — / [Adams 35, Davis 60] Smith 15, 42, 65, Rocastle 18
Ref: J Ashworth (Luffenham)

	1	2	3	4	5	6	7	8	9	10	11	subs used
Pompey	Knight	Swain	Sandford	Whitehead*	Shotton	Gilbert	Fillery	Kennedy	Baird	Mariner	Hilaire	Horne
Arsenal	*Lukic*	*Thomas*	*Sansom*	*Williams*	*O'Leary*	*Adams*	*Rocastle*	*Davis*	*Smith*	*Groves**	*Rix^*	*Merson/Richardson*

Humiliation is the only way to describe this disastrous showing. Shotton (£70,000 from Oxford) has signed to replace long-term injury Blake, but it is Knight who is left red-faced by the opener. He rolls the ball out, but is robbed by Rix and Alan Smith nets his first Gunners' goal.

---

5 — H WEST HAM — 31/8
Att 16,104 · Pos 16 · W · Pt 4 · F-A 2-1 · H-T 1-1

Scorers: Dillon 15, 69p / Strodder 11
Ref: J Deakin (Llantwit Major)

	1	2	3	4	5	6	7	8	9	10	11	subs used
Pompey	Knight	Swain	Horne	Dillon	Shotton	Gilbert	Fillery	Kennedy	Baird	Mariner	Hilaire	
West Ham	*McAllister*	*Stewart**	*McEwan*	*Strodder*	*Martin*	*Brady*	*Ward*	*McAvennie*	*Ince*	*Cottee*	*Robson*	*Parris*

Ball turns to graduate Horne (£60,000 from Wrexham) to shackle Hammers' genius Liam Brady. Kennedy fills in at full-back to mark Ward. The ploy works like a charm. Dillon fired low to level, then converts his 32nd penalty out of 37, after Hilaire had been fouled by McAllister.

---

6 — A DERBY — 5/9
Att 15,071 · Pos 17 · D · Pt 5 · F-A 0-0 · H-T 0-0

Ref: K Hackett (Sheffield)

	1	2	3	4	5	6	7	8	9	10	11	subs used
Pompey	Knight	Swain	Horne	Dillon	Shotton	Gilbert	Fillery	Kennedy	Baird	Mariner	Hilaire	
Derby	*Shilton*	*Sage*	*Forsyth*	*Williams*	*Wright*	*MacLaren*	*Micklewhite*	*Gee**	*Davison*	*Gregory*	*Callaghan*	*Garner*

Pompey tactics are spot on and all Derby's aces are trumped. Kennedy reduces John Gregory to anonymity, while Horne this time snuffs out the rated Nigel Callaghan. Shotton's near-post header is well-saved, but Shilton excels himself to turn away Horne's shot. Dillon hits the bar.

---

7 — H CHARLTON — 12/9
Att 13,136 · Pos 17 · D · Pt 6 · F-A 1-1 · H-T 0-1

Scorers: Quinn 76 / Stuart 44
Ref: K Cooper (Pontypridd)

	1	2	3	4	5	6	7	8	9	10	11	subs used
Pompey	Knight	Swain	Sandford	Dillon	Shotton	Gilbert*	Horne	Kennedy	Baird!	Mariner*	Hilaire	Whitehead/Quinn
Charlton	*Johns*	*Humphrey*	*Reid*	*Gritt*	*Shirtliff*	*Miller*	*Milne*	*Stuart*	*Walsh*	*Mackenzie*	*Croaks*	

Out-of-favour Quinn makes his (and ten-man Pompey's) point, firing a spectacular shot past Johns, just 14 minutes after coming on. Stuart follows up Knight's tip of Walsh's shot onto the bar for Lennie Lawrence's men. Just before, Baird was sent off for two typically wild fouls.

---

8 — A WATFORD — 19/9
Att 13,277 · Pos 17 · D · Pt 7 · F-A 0-0 · H-T 0-0

Ref: B Nixon (West Kirby)

	1	2	3	4	5	6	7	8	9	10	11	subs used
Pompey	Knight	Swain	Sandford	Dillon	Shotton	Gilbert	Horne	Whitehead	Baird*	Quinn	Hilaire	Kerr^/Ball
Watford	*Coton*	*Gibbs*	*Rostron*	*Morris**	*Terry*	*McClelland*	*Chivers*	*Roberts*	*Senior*	*Porter*	*Sterling*	*Blissett*

Kerr becomes the first substitute to be subbed in the Football League as he fails to come to terms with the imposing physiques of Terry and McClelland. Knight is outstanding, twice denying former team-mate Trevor Senior, but Quinn might have pinched it with a header just wide.

---

9 — H WIMBLEDON — 26/9
Att 13,088 · Pos 12 · W · Pt 10 · F-A 2-1 · H-T 1-1

Scorers: Quinn 38, Sandford 85 / Sanchez 26
Ref: R Milford (Bristol)

	1	2	3	4	5	6	7	8	9	10	11	subs used
Pompey	Knight	Swain	Sandford	Fillery	Shotton	Gilbert*	Horne	Kennedy	Mariner	Quinn	Hilaire	
Wimbledon	*Beasant*	*Scales*	*Phelan*	*Jones**	*Young*	*Gayle*	*Wise*	*Gibson*	*Fashanu*	*Sanchez*	*Fairweather*	*Ryan*

Pompey's second win back in the big-time is a fortunate affair. Bobby Gould's Dons are not much better, but Sanchez's header gives them the edge after Gibson's clever flick. Sandford's lay-off set up Quinn, then the young full-back settles it, firing home Gilbert's clipped free-kick.

---

10 — A LIVERPOOL — 3/10
Att 44,366 · Pos 13 · L · Pt 10 · F-A 0-4 · H-T 0-1

Scorers: — / [Aldridge 52p, Whelan 71] Beardsley 29, McMahon 51.
Ref: G Courtney (Spennymoor)

	1	2	3	4	5	6	7	8	9	10	11	subs used
Pompey	Knight	Swain	Sandford	Fillery^	Shotton	Gilbert*	Horne	Whitehead	Quinn	Mariner	Hilaire	Ball/Dillon
Liverpool	*Grobbelaar*	*Gillespie*	*Venison*	*Nicol*	*Whelan*	*Hansen*	*Beardsley*	*Aldridge*	*Johnston**	*Barnes*	*McMahon^*	*Walsh/Lawrensen*

Kenny Dalglish's Pool are almost invincible, but it takes a double second-half strike to kill off plucky Pompey. Beardsley unravels a defensive web, but Mariner might have quickly levelled. McMahon chips in, then wins the penalty for Aldridge to keep his goal-in-every-game record.

Portsmouth match log (matches 11–21)

No.	V	Opponent	Date	Att.	Pompey Pos	Opp Pos	Pompey Pts	Res	Score	HT
11	H	LUTON	10/10	12,391	11	16	13	W	3-1	0-0
12	A	QP RANGERS	24/10	13,171	14	2	13	L	1-2	0-1
13	H	SHEFFIELD WED	31/10	13,582	16	18	13	L	1-2	1-1
14	H	TOTTENHAM	4/11	15,302	17	8	14	D	0-0	0-0
15	A	NOTT'M FOREST	14/11	15,851	18	4	14	L	0-5	0-3
16	H	EVERTON	21/11	17,724	18	5	14	L	0-1	0-0
17	A	NORWICH	28/11	13,099	18	20	17	W	1-0	1-0
18	H	COVENTRY	5/12	13,002	18	16	18	D	0-0	0-0
19	A	NEWCASTLE	12/12	20,455	18	14	19	D	1-1	1-0
20	H	MANCHESTER U	19/12	22,207	18	4	19	L	1-2	0-1
21	A	CHARLTON	26/12	6,686	18	21	19	L	1-2	1-1

11 — H LUTON, 10/10 — W 3-1 (0-0)
Scorers: Dillon 54, 72p, Mariner 79 / Harford 90p. Ref: A Buksh (London)
Pompey: Knight, Swain, Hardyman, Dillon, Shotton, Ball, Horne, Kennedy, Baird*, Quinn, Hilaire, Mariner
Luton: Sealey, Breacker, Grimes, Hill, Foster, Donaghy, Wilson, Stein B, Harford, Johnson R*, Weir^, McDonough/Nwajiobi
Pompey have a blank week coming up (league re-organisation means 21 clubs), but this will tide them over. Weir and Wilson hit bar and post in a featureless first half. Dillon's 30-yarder changes things, then he gets Hilaire in for the penalty and crosses for Paul Mariner's header too.

12 — A QP RANGERS, 24/10 — L 1-2 (0-1)
Scorers: Baird 58 / Byrne 15, Fenwick 85. Ref: M James (Horsham)
Pompey: Knight, Swain, Hardyman, Dillon, Shotton, Whitehead, Horne, Kennedy, Baird, Quinn*, Hilaire, Mariner
QPR: Seaman, Neill, Dawes, Parker, McDonald, Fenwick, Allen, Coney, Bannister, Byrne*, Brock^, Fereday/Maguire
Baird's shock return to Leeds falls through, but Deacon now tries to off-load him to Barnsley. He breaks his Pompey duck from two yards, but future Fratton boss Fenwick fires home a free-kick to flatter QPR. Pompey are in salmon pink – a new change-strip with a link to their roots.

13 — H SHEFFIELD WED, 31/10 — L 1-2 (1-1)
Scorers: Dillon 19p / West 1, 55. Ref: D Hedges (Oxford)
Pompey: Knight, Swain, Hardyman, Dillon, Shotton, Ball, Horne, Fillery^, Baird, Quinn, Connor*, Mariner/Whitehead
Sheffield Wed: Hodge, Sterland*, Worthington, Madden, Pearson, Proctor, Chamberlain, Megson, West, Hirst, Galvin, Fee
Long-term injury Connor (£200,000 from Brighton in the summer) finally starts and Blake, too is approaching fitness. How he is needed after this Hallowe'en horror. West is twice left unmarked for Howard Wilkinson's Owls, although Dillon claws one back when Hilaire is tripped.

14 — H TOTTENHAM, 4/11 — D 0-0 (0-0)
Ref: B Hill (Kettering)
Pompey: Knight, Swain, Hardyman, Dillon, Whitehead, Ball, Horne, Kennedy, Baird, Connor, Hilaire
Tottenham: Parks, Stevens, Hughton, Ruddock, Fairclough, Mabbutt, Moran*, Allen P, Ardiles, Samways, Claesen, Allen C
Dillon's late penalty miss is only the second time in 40 he has failed to hit the target. Managerless Spurs leave out Clive Allen, but Ball's dream is going all wrong; Shotton is a long-term injury, Deacon has told him to cut the wage-bill by a third and gates are well-below budget.

15 — A NOTT'M FOREST, 14/11 — L 0-5 (0-3)
Scorers: Wilson 2, Wilkinson 13, Webb 42, [Rice 77, Clough 81p]. Ref: L Shapter (Torquay)
Pompey: Knight, Swain, Hardyman, Whitehead, Mariner, Ball, Horne, Kennedy, Baird, Quinn*, Hilaire, Starbuck/Glover
Forest: Sutton, Chettle, Pearce, Walker, Wilson*, Carr, Clough, Webb, Wilkinson, Rice, Starbuck/Glover
Not for the first time (or the last) Pompey are a 'crisis club' as nine players are reportedly available. Injuries continue to bite and Mariner fills in – unhappily – at centre-half, although he does hit a post. Wilson, Wilkinson, then old-boy Webb make it safe for Clough Snr by half-time.

16 — H EVERTON, 21/11 — L 0-1 (0-0)
Scorers: Sharp 77. Ref: D Elleray (Harrow)
Pompey: Knight, Swain, Hardyman, Dillon !, Ball, Whitehead, Horne, Kennedy !, Baird, Quinn, Hilaire
Everton: Southall, Stevens, V d Hauwe, Ratcliffe, Watson, Reid, Harper, Heath^, Sharp, Snodin, Sheedy*, Clarke/Pointon
Colin Harvey's champions claim a lucky win as Graham Sharp's 25-yarder sears past Knight. Tempers boil over and Dillon (possibly off to Watford for £150,000) is dismissed for mouthing off, soon to be followed by Kennedy for clattering Reid. Deacon says if he goes, Pompey go.

17 — A NORWICH, 28/11 — W 1-0 (1-0)
Scorers: Horne 37. Ref: T Holbrook (Wolverhampton)
Pompey: Knight, Swain, Hardyman, Dillon, Ball, Whitehead, Horne, Kennedy, Baird, Quinn, Hilaire
Norwich: Gunn, Brown*, Elliott, Bruce, Phelan, Butterworth, Crook, Drinkell, Rosario, Putney, Gordon
Pompey shoot down struggling Canaries to record their first win in seven weeks. Baird's shot is pushed out to Horne, who gleefully hammers his first goal for the club. Kevin Drinkell and Crooks both hit the bar, but Ken Brown's men don't deserve to end a run of one win in twelve.

18 — H COVENTRY, 5/12 — D 0-0 (0-0)
Ref: D Reeves (Uxbridge)
Pompey: Knight, Swain, Hardyman, Fillery, Ball, Whitehead, Horne, Connor, Baird, Quinn, Hilaire
Coventry: Ogrizovic, Borrows, Downs, Emerson, Kilcline, Peake, Bennett, Phillips, Houchen, Speedie, Pickering
Dillon's on-off move finally looks doomed, as Elton John says he is selling out to Bob Maxwell (he thinks). A rare meeting with John Sillett's Sky Blues ends in a first draw in ten clashes, but it couldn't have been much drabber. David Speedie hits a bar and Baird's shot spins to safety.

19 — A NEWCASTLE, 12/12 — D 1-1 (1-0)
Scorers: Hardyman 31 / Mirandinha 76. Ref: N Midgley (Bolton)
Pompey: Knight, Swain, Hardyman, Dillon !, Ball, Whitehead, Horne, Connor, Baird, Quinn, Hilaire
Newcastle: Kelly, Anderson, Wharton, McCreery, Jackson !, Roeder, McDonald, Bogie, Goddard, Mirandinha, Cornwell
Dillon returns from a ban, and is sent off for fighting with Jackson. Hardyman's stunning 30-yarder silences St James', then he turns to more conventional duties as Pompey scrap to keep their lead. Mirandinha's magic from nothing makes Magpies the Geordies' darlings once more.

20 — H MANCHESTER U, 19/12 — L 1-2 (0-1)
Scorers: Dillon 75p / Robson 35, McClair 48. Ref: A Ward (London)
Pompey: Knight, Swain, Hardyman, Dillon, Ball, Whitehead, Horne, Connor, Baird, Quinn, Hilaire
Manchester U: Turner, Duxbury, Gibson, Bruce, Moran, Moses, Robson, Strachan, McClair, Whiteside, Olsen*, Davenport
Hardyman's error hands McClair his first goal in two months, after Robson had earlier headed in for Alex Ferguson's men. Bruce's climb over Quinn earns the penalty. Pompey now turn to a shirt-sponsor – South Coast Fiat – but the deal sparks a row with club car suppliers HCS Toyota.

21 — A CHARLTON, 26/12 — L 1-2 (1-1)
Scorers: Quinn 32 / Jones 1, Shirtliff 69. Ref: I Hemley (Ampthill)
Pompey: Knight, Swain, Hardyman, Connor^, Ball, Whitehead, Horne, Kennedy, Baird, Quinn, Hilaire, Gilbert/Fillery
Charlton: Bolder, Humphrey, Reid, Gritt*, Shirtliff, Thompson, Mackenzie, Campbell, Jones, Williams, Stuart, Bennett
Pompey kick-off, but are still 0-1 down after 19 secs! Reid cuts out Swain's pass and sends Jones away. Quinn nets his first in three months, but Shirtliff's nod hits a post and goes in off Knight's back. Horne has one ruled out and Quinn appealed for a pen, but it's clutching at straws.

BARCLAYS LEAGUE DIVISION 1

Manager: Alan Ball

SEASON 1987-88

No	Date	Att	Pos	Pt	F-A	H-T	Scorers, Times, and Referees	1	2	3	4	5	6	7	8	9	10	11	subs used
22	H WATFORD 28/12	15,003	19	20	1-1	0-0	Connor 60 / *Agana 87*; Ref: L. Shapter (Torquay)	Knight	Swain	Gilbert	Connor	Blake	Ball	Horne	Whitehead	Baird*	Quinn	Hilaire	Mariner
			13				Blake is back after injury, but Pompey struggle against 'For Sale' Watford. Connor and Horne combine for the opener, but Hornets finally sting, when Agana scuffs home after a scramble. Ex-Blue Trevor Senior has a goal ruled out, while Baird picks up his fifth booking in seven.	*Rees*	*Chivers*	*Rostron*	*Jackett*	*Morris*	*McClelland*	*Pullen**	*Agana*	*Senior*	*Porter*	*Sterling*	*Allen*
23	H ARSENAL 1/1	17,366	19	21	1-1	1-0	Connor 8 / *Smith 80*; Ref: R Hamer (Bristol)	Knight	Whitehead	Hardyman	Dillon	Blake	Ball	Horne	Kennedy	Quinn*	Connor	Hilaire	Mariner
			3				Lukic plunges right and Dillon has a 'double' of late penalty misses against the north London rivals on his conscience. The two extra points would have taken Pompey to 14th place. Knight also has his part to play, misjudging a free-kick in the wind to let Alan Smith equalise.	*Lukic*	*Thomas*	*Winterburn*	*Williams*	*Caesar*	*Adams*	*Rocastle*	*Hayes*	*Quinn**	*Groves^*	*Richardson*	*Smith/Merson*
24	A SOUTHAMPTON 3/1	17,002	18	24	2-0	2-0	Horne 16, Connor 23; Ref: A Gunn (Burgess Hill)	Knight	Whitehead	Hardyman	Dillon	Blake	Ball	Horne	Kennedy	Quinn	Connor	Hilaire	Mariner
			13				Pompey's fans – those lucky enough to get in – are in heaven as Horne and Connor pounce on slack defending. Then Clarke misses enough chances to have won two games. There's a sting in the tail though; skipper-for-the-day Kennedy is off to Bradford for £250,000 next week.	*Burridge*	*Baker S*	*Statham*	*Case^*	*Moore*	*Bond*	*Townsend*	*Cockerill*	*Clarke*	*Baker G**	*Wallace D*	*Wallace Rod/Le Tiss'*
25	H OXFORD 16/1	13,417	16	25	2-2	0-1	Ball 48, Quinn 60 / *Briggs 9, Saunders 84p*; Ref: M Reed (Birmingham)	Knight	Whitehead	Swain	Dillon	Blake	Ball	Horne	**Darby***	Baird	Quinn	Hilaire	Gilbert
			19				More late penalty anguish, this time Saunders converts after Ball handles, means the search for a first home win since October goes on. Earlier, Ball had got Pompey back on track with his first senior goal, then Quinn's strike rewarded a bout of pressure. Darby starts, but looks lost.	*Hardwick*	*Bardsley*	*Dreyer*	*Shelton*	*Briggs*	*Caton*	*Hebberd*	*Foyle*	*Saunders*	*Phillips*	*Rh's-Brown*	
26	A CHELSEA 23/1	15,856	15	26	0-0	0-0	Ref: P Danson (Leicester)	Knight	Whitehead	Swain	Dillon	Blake	Ball	Horne	Fillery	Baird	Quinn	Hilaire	
			13				Baird is back from his third ban, but this result does neither team any good in the long run. Knight is on form, but Hazard goes round him, only to hit the side net. Deacon has gagged the players from talking to the media, as the financial crisis looks set for a High Court showdown.	*Freestone*	*Clarke*	*Dorigo*	*Pates*	*McLaughlin*	*Bumstead^*	*McAllister*	*Hazard*	*Dixon^*	*Wilson K*	*Wood*	*Nevin/Wilson C*
27	H DERBY 6/2	14,790	15	29	2-1	1-0	Hilaire 18, Quinn 67 / *Wright 51*; Ref: D Vickers (Ilford)	Knight	Whitehead	Sandford	Dillon	Blake	Ball	Horne	Fillery	Quinn	Connor	Hilaire	
			18				Pompey stretch their unbeaten run to eight, while condemning Arthur Cox's Rams to their ninth successive defeat. Fillery crosses for Quinn – surplus to requirements last summer – to squeeze home. Debut-making Ted McMinn (£300,000 from Seville) sets up Mark Wright's header.	*Shilton*	*MacLaren*	*Forsyth*	*Williams*	*Wright*	*Blades*	*McMinn*	*Gee*	*Garner**	*Gregory**	*Callaghan*	*Penney/Lewis*
28	A WEST HAM 13/2	18,639	15	30	1-1	0-0	Connor 78 / *Cottee 68*; Ref: J Worrall (Warrington)	Knight	Whitehead	Hardyman	Dillon	Blake	Ball	Horne	Sandford^	Baird^	Connor	Hilaire	Gilbert/**Kelly**
			13				Shotton's move to Huddersfield has gone through, but could be scuppered by next week's winding up petition for £738,000 of unpaid debts. Deacon shrugs off the threat, and will be pleased with a point at Upton Park. Connor hooks home after McAllister fails to hold Dillon's centre.	*McAllister*	*Stewart*	*Ince*	*Bonds*	*Strodder*	*Gale*	*Ward*	*Brady*	*Dickens*	*Cottee*	*Robson*	
29	H LIVERPOOL 27/2	**28,117**	17	30	0-2	0-0	*Barnes 49, 84*; Ref: R Lewis (Great Bookham)	Knight	Gilbert	Sandford	Dillon*	Blake	Ball	Horne	Fillery	Quinn	Connor	Hilaire	Hardyman
			1				Liverpool's procession to the title is now 27 without defeat, but Pompey make them fight all the way. Barnes' attempted cross flicks off Gilbert and flies in for the first, that after Quinn had scored a glorious early chance. He then has one ruled out, but Barnes' classy shot seals it.	*Grobbelaar*	*Ablett*	*Venison*	*Nicol*	*Spackman*	*Hansen*	*Beardsley*	*Aldridge*	*Houghton*	*Barnes*	*McMahon*	
30	A SHEFFIELD WED 19/3	13,731	19	30	0-1	0-1	*Sterland 42p*; Ref: R Hart (Darlington)	Knight	Gilbert	Hardyman	Dillon	Blake	Ball	Horne	Fillery*	Baird	Connor	Hilaire	Sandford
			8				Baird has gone back to Leeds (for a cut-price £185,000) and Pompey are out of the Cup. Luck deserts the team; Mel Sterland stumbles over Connor's leg and the penalty looks harsh, but in truth Owls were well worth the win. Director Parkhouse is fired for his role in the cash crisis.	*Pressman*	*Sterland*	*Worthington*	*Madden*	*Fee*	*Proctor*	*Chamberlain*	*Megson*	*Chapman*	*Hirst^*	*Jonsson**	*Marwood/Bradshaw*
31	H QP RANGERS 26/3	13,041	19	30	0-1	0-1	*Coney 11*; Ref: P Vanes (Warley)	Knight	Gilbert	Sandford	Dillon	Blake	Ball	Horne	Fillery	Mariner	Connor	Hilaire	
			4				Ball had set a 15-point target from 30 available; make that 27 now. Former Pompey-target Dean Coney converts Kerslake's cross with a close-range header and the lead is not troubled. Trevor Francis is back from Italy, and his first touch in the league for six years nearly sets up a goal.	*Seaman*	*Neill*	*Dawes*	*Parker*	*McDonald*	*Maddix*	*Allen*	*Kerslake**	*Coney*	*Fereday*	*Channing^*	*Francis/Falco*

Portsmouth — Season fixtures 32–40

No	Venue	Date	Pos		Res	Pts	Score	HT	Att
32	A	29/3	19	9	L	30	1-4	0-1	6,740
33	A	2/4	18	10	W	33	1-0	1-0	18,616
34	H	4/4	19	3	L	33	0-1	0-0	17,528
35	A	9/4	19	3	L	33	1-2	1-1	21,292
36	A	19/4	19	7	D	34	2-2	0-1	9,009
37	H	23/4	19	13	D	35	2-2	0-1	12,762
38	A	30/4	19	9	L	35	0-1	0-1	14,296
39	H	2/5	19	8	L	35	1-2	0-1	12,468
40	A	7/5	19	2	L	35	1-4	0-3	35,105

Home 15,905 — Away 17,615 — Average 15,905

---

32 — LUTON (A)

Dillon 52 [Stein B 87]
Wilson 9, Stein M 53, Mariner 63 (og)
Ref: D Axcell (Southend)

1	2	3	4	5	6	7	8	9	10	11	Sub
Knight	Swain	Sandford	Dillon	Blake	Gilbert	Horne	Fillery	Mariner	Perry*	Hilaire	Kerr
Sealey	Breacker	Grimes	McDonough	Foster	Donaghy	Wilson D	Stein B	Johnson R	Stein M	Allinson	

One of Pompey's games in hand disappears with a tame surrender to Ray Harford's Luton, who have just lost at Wembley in the Simod Cup. Perry – signed from Dulwich Hamlet in the autumn – starts, but is out of his depth. A handful of Pompey fans beat Town's home-only policy.

---

33 — TOTTENHAM (A)

Horne 34
Ref: G Courtney (Spennymoor)

1	2	3	4	5	6	7	8	9	10	11	Sub
Knight	Swain	Sandford	Dillon	Blake	Gilbert	Horne	Whitehead	Mariner	Quinn	Hilaire	
Mimms	Statham	Moncur*	Fenwick	Fairclough	Mabbutt	Walsh	Allen	Hodge^	Samways	Claesen	Moran/Howells

Horne scores his third goal away from home and Pompey have a third win on their travels. Ball's team make a mockery of their position and Terry Venables' side are well-beaten. Horne beats Mimms one-on-one at the second attempt, despite Mabbutt's desperate clearance attempt.

---

34 — NOTT'M FOREST (H)

Wilson 66
Ref: H Taylor (Oadby)

1	2	3	4	5	6	7	8	9	10	11	Sub
Knight	Swain	Sandford	Dillon	Blake	Ball	Horne	Whitehead	Quinn	Connor	Hilaire	
Sutton	Chettle	Pearce	Wassell	Foster	Wilson	Crosby	Webb	Clough	Wilkinson	Glover	

It's one step forward and two back over the Easter period as Forest pinch the points thanks to Wilson's poached effort. Forest boss Brian Clough is not happy afterwards and brushes aside autograph hunters, while Ball insists his side can stay up. Sutton saves from Connor late on

---

35 — EVERTON (A)

Dillon 26
Heath 33, Steven 54
Ref: M Peck (Kendal)

1	2	3	4	5	6	7	8	9	10	11	Sub
Knight	Swain	Sandford	Dillon	Blake^	Ball	Horne	Whitehead	Quinn	Connor*	Hilaire	Mariner/Gilbert
Southall	Steven	Pointon	V d Hauwe	Watson	Reid	Steven	Snodin	Heath	Harper	Sheedy	

Ball is adamant Pompey can survive, as a spirited performance on Grand National morning goes unrewarded. Horne's cross is missed by Quinn, but Dillon strokes home. Blake goofs and Heath is clear to clip in, then Steven's left-foot volley at last lets the Toffees show their class.

---

36 — WIMBLEDON (A)

Mariner 62, Dillon 73
Wise 10, 83
Ref: A Gunn (Burgess Hill)

1	2	3	4	5	6	7	8	9	10	11	Sub
Knight*	Swain	Sandford	Gilbert	Blake	Ball	Horne	Whitehead	Mariner	Quinn	Hilaire	Dillon
Beasant	Scales	Phelan	Ryan	Young	Gayle	Gibson	Cork*	Fashanu	Hazel	Wise	Gannon

Stand-in Sandford excels, as Eric Young's challenge leaves Knight with severe face injuries after just six minutes, but no foul is given. Mariner rolls back the years, then Dillon raises hopes of a win. However, Wise is alive to the possibilities when the ball falls to him 18 yards out.

---

37 — NORWICH (H)

Quinn 59, Mariner 68
Linighan 31, Biggins 90p
Ref: P Don (Harwood Park)

1	2	3	4	5	6	7	8	9	10	11	Sub
Gosney	Swain	Sandford	Gilbert	Blake	Ball	Horne	Whitehead	Mariner	Quinn	Hilaire	
Gunn	Culverhouse	Spearing	Linighan	Phelan	Butterworth	Fox^	Rosario	Fleck*	Goss	Putney	Biggins/Gordon

Mariner handles Putney's corner at the death, and, after the protests subside, Biggins fires high into net to leave Pompey's first division tenure hanging by a thread. Earlier, Mariner's header had turned the game on its head after Quinn had jabbed home to level Andy Linighan's header.

---

38 — COVENTRY (A)

Kilcline 18p
Ref: F Roberts (Prestatyn)

1	2	3	4	5	6	7	8	9	10	11	Sub
Gosney	Swain	Sandford	Gilbert	Blake	Ball	Horne	Fillery	Mariner	Quinn	Hilaire	
Ogrizovic	Borrows	Pickering	Sedgeley	Kilcline	Peake	Emerson	Bannister	Regis	Speedie	Smith	

Penalty controversy stalks Pompey again, when Ball throws his hand in front of his face as Regis smashes a shot towards goal and the referee points to the spot. In midweek, promising youth team winger Mark Kelly came on as an Eire substitute, before he has even made a league start!

---

39 — NEWCASTLE (H)

Quinn 52
Scott 11, Lormor 50
Ref: R Gifford (Hengoed)

1	2	3	4	5	6	7	8	9	10	11	Sub
Gosney	Gilbert	Sandford	Dillon	Blake	Ball	Horne	Fillery	Quinn	Connor	Hilaire	Mariner
Kelly	McDonald	Cornwell	McCreery	Anderson	Scott	Jackson D	Gascoigne	Thomas A	O'Neill*	Bailey	Lormor

Fratton is in turmoil, as it is revealed that Deacon and Ball are not even on speaking terms. Gazza-inspired Magpies end any mathematical hope of avoiding the drop. Fans chant 'Deacon Out', laying the blame squarely on his shoulders; within a month they will have their wish.

---

40 — MANCHESTER U (A)

Quinn 65p
McClair 5, 58p, Davenport 24, [Robson 35]
Ref: G Tyson (Sunderland)

1	2	3	4	5	6	7	8	9	10	11	Sub
Gosney	Whitehead	Hardyman	Sandford	Blake	Ball	Horne	Kelly	Quinn	Connor	Hilaire*	Perry
Turner	Anderson^	Gibson	Bruce	McGrath*	Duxbury	Robson	Strachan	McClair	Davenport	Olsen	Hogg/Blackmore

United clinch second place as Pompey fold in the first half after Davenport sets up McClair. Davenport takes advantage of a stationary back-four, then Robson's free header hints at a cricket score. McClair profits from Hardyman's handball, then sub Perry is up-ended by Gibson.

BARCLAYS DIVISION 1 (CUP-TIES)   Manager: Alan Ball   SEASON 1987-88

Littlewoods Cup

				F-A	H-T	Scorers, Times, and Referees	1	2	3	4	5	6	7	8	9	10	11	subs used
2:1	A	SWINDON 17	22/9	L 1-3	0-2	Quinn 87	Knight	Swain	Sandford	Dillon	Shotton	Gilbert	Horne	Whitehead*	Mariner^	Quinn	Hilaire	Ball/Kerr
			9,878 3:7			*Quinn 2, 10, 82p*	*Digby*	*Hockaday*	*King*	*Kamara*	*Parkin*	*Calderwood Bamber*		*White*￪*	*Quinn*	*Foley*	*Barnard*	*O'Regan*
						Ref: C Downey (Hounslow)												

Ball blames a 'lack of character' as Pompey slump at minnows Town. Jimmy Quinn is only one going to take the pen, after Shotton's foul on Foley; his boss Lou Macari bet £200 he wouldn't score a hat-trick. He gave Robins a dream start, but the other Quinn's late header gives hope.

				F-A	H-T	Scorers, Times, and Referees	1	2	3	4	5	6	7	8	9	10	11	subs used
2:2	H	SWINDON 13	7/10	L 1-3	1-1	Perry 16	Knight	Swain	Sandford	Fillery^	Shotton	Ball	Horne	Perry*	Baird	Quinn	Hilaire	Mariner/Whitehead
			8,727 3:5			*Bamber 45, 83, White 90*	*Digby*	*Hockaday*	*King*	*Kamara*	*Parkin*	*Calderwood Bamber*	*O'Regan*	*Quinn*￪*	*Foley^*	*Barnard*		*White/Henry*
						Ref: L Shapter (Torquay)												
						(Pompey lost 2-6 on aggregate)												

Pompey pound away, but only have debut-making Perry's sharply-taken goal to show for their early dominance. 'With better finishing we'd have made up the deficit,' moaned Ball. A defensive tangle lets Bamber in and Town's late surge sees some in the crowd turn on the boss.

FA Cup

					F-A	H-T	Scorers, Times, and Referees	1	2	3	4	5	6	7	8	9	10	11	subs used
3	A	BLACKBURN 18	9/1	W 2-1	1-1		Quinn 7, Dillon 70	Knight	Whitehead	Hardyman	Dillon	Blake	Ball	Horne	Darby	Quinn	Connor	Hilaire	
			10,352 2:5				*Garner 20*	*Gennoe*	*Price*	*Sulley*￪*	*Barker*	*Hill*	*Mail*	*Dawson*	*Reid*	*Archibald*	*Garner^*	*Sellars*	*Patterson/Curry*
							Ref: G Courtney (Spennymoor)												

Dillon's volley from the best part of 40 yards puts the smile back on fans' faces, furious after the shock sale of Kennedy to Bradford. Deacon refuses to comment, but it is clear Ball is unhappy. Kennedy's place is taken by Darby and he responds well. Quinn netted at the near post.

					F-A	H-T	Scorers, Times, and Referees	1	2	3	4	5	6	7	8	9	10	11	subs used
4	H	SHEFFIELD UTD 15	1/2	W 2-1	2-1		Dillon 25, Quinn 32	Knight	Whitehead	Swain	Dillon	Blake	Ball	Horne	Baird	Quinn	Connor	Hilaire	
			13,388 2:15				*Philliskirk 1*	*Leaning*	*Barnsley*￪*	*Pike*	*Todd*	*Stancliffe*	*Smith*	*Duffield^*	*Philliskirk*	*Cadette*	*Dempsey*	*Beagrie*	*Downes/Morris*
							Ref: D Reeves (Uxbridge)												

Heavy Friday rain claimed Saturday's match, when the weather was perfect. Hastily re-scheduled for Monday, further rain turns the pitch into a barely-playable bog. Blades have just become (Dave) Bassett's all-sorts, and take an early lead, but Dillon's inspired chip is a turning point.

					F-A	H-T	Scorers, Times, and Referees	1	2	3	4	5	6	7	8	9	10	11	subs used
5	H	BRADFORD C 15	20/2	W 3-0	1-0		Blake 15, Quinn 53, Connor 83	Knight	Whitehead	Sandford	Dillon	Blake	Ball	Horne	Fillery	Connor	Quinn	Hilaire	
			19,324 2:5					*Tomlinson*	*Mitchell*	*Goddard*￪*	*McCall*	*Oliver*	*Evans*	*Hendrie*	*Abbott^*	*Ormondroyd Kennedy*	*Sinnott*		*Ellis/Leonard*
							Ref: A Ward (London)												

Bankruptcy is averted as Deacon finds £650,000, but Baird's X-ray is still cancelled over a disputed bill. The Cup cheers though, as Kennedy-led City are easy meat. Blake's header starts the rout; then Connor's cool finish seals it. Pompey last reached the quarter-finals in 1952.

					F-A	H-T	Scorers, Times, and Referees	1	2	3	4	5	6	7	8	9	10	11	subs used
QF	A	LUTON 18	12/3	L 1-3	1-2		Quinn 33	Knight	Gilbert	Hardyman*	Dillon	Blake	Ball	Horne	Fillery	Quinn	Connor	Hilaire	Mariner
			12,857 9				*Wilson 3, Stein M 22, Harford 88*	*Sealey*	*Breacker*	*Grimes*	*McDonough Foster*	*Donaghy*	*Wilson*	*Johnson*	*Harford*	*Stein M*	*Allinson*		
							Ref: J Key (Rotherham)												

Ball is furious at Quinn's dismissal for elbowing Foster just after half-time, earning a booking for arguing with a linesman, but TV seems to vindicate the referee. Two soft goals put Hatters in charge, although Quinn's sharp finish raises hopes. Harford's header settles it on the break.

		P	Home					Away					Pts
			W	D	L	F	A	W	D	L	F	A	
1	Liverpool	40	15	5	0	49	9	11	7	2	38	15	90
2	Manchester U	40	14	5	1	41	17	9	7	4	30	21	81
3	Nott'm Forest	40	11	7	2	40	17	9	6	5	27	22	73
4	Everton	40	14	4	2	34	11	9	6	6	19	16	70
5	QP Rangers	40	12	4	4	30	14	7	6	7	18	24	67
6	Arsenal	40	11	4	5	35	16	7	8	5	23	23	66
7	Wimbledon	40	8	9	3	32	20	6	6	8	26	27	57
8	Newcastle	40	9	6	5	32	23	5	8	7	23	30	56
9	Luton	40	11	6	3	40	21	3	5	12	17	37	53
10	Coventry	40	6	8	6	23	25	7	6	7	23	28	53
11	Sheffield Wed	40	10	2	8	27	30	5	6	9	25	36	53
12	Southampton	40	6	8	6	27	26	6	6	8	22	27	50
13	Tottenham	40	9	5	6	26	23	3	6	11	12	25	47
14	Norwich	40	7	5	8	26	26	5	4	11	14	26	45
15	Derby	40	6	7	7	18	17	4	6	10	17	28	43
16	West Ham	40	6	9	5	23	21	3	6	11	17	31	42
17	Charlton	40	7	7	6	23	21	2	8	10	15	31	42
18	Chelsea*	40	7	11	2	24	17	2	4	14	26	51	42
19	PORTSMOUTH	40	4	8	8	21	27	3	6	11	15	39	35
20	Watford	40	4	5	11	15	24	3	6	11	12	27	32
21	Oxford	40	5	7	8	24	34	1	6	13	20	46	31
		840	182	132	106	610	439	106	132	182	439	610	1128

* relegated after play-offs

Odds & ends

Double wins: (0).

Double losses: (6) Sheffield Wed, Everton, Manchester U, Liverpool, Nott'm For, QPR.

Won from behind: (2) West Ham (h), Wimbledon (h).

Lost from in front: (1) Everton (h).

High spots: Reaching the FA Cup quarter-finals for the first time since 1952.

Beating Southampton 2-0 at The Dell.

Ten matches unbeaten in league and cup from December to February.

Beating Luton 3-1 to go eleventh in October.

Low spots: Relegation after just one season in Division 1.

Failing to win any of our last seven matches.

The 0-6 humiliation at Highbury in August.

Losing 2-6 on aggregate to third division Swindon in the League Cup.

Run of just one win in ten matches from October to December.

Player of the Season: Barry Horne.

Ever-presents: (0).

Hat-tricks: (0).

Leading scorer: Kevin Dillon (12).

	Appearances						Goals			
	Lge	Sub	LC	Sub	FAC	Sub	Lge	LC	FAC	Tot
Baird, Ian	20		1		1				1	1
Ball, Kevin	27	2	1	1	4		1			1
Blake, Noel	19		1		4		1			1
Connor, Terry	19				3		6		1	7
Darby, Lee	1		1		1					
Dillon, Kevin	29	3	1		3		9		3	12
Fillery, Mick	17	1	1		1					
Gilbert, Billy	17	4	1							
Gosney, Andy	4									
Hardyman, Paul	19	1			2		1			1
Hilaire, Vince	38		2		4		2			2
Horne, Barry	36	3	2		4		3			3
Kelly, Mark	1	2								
Kennedy, Mick	18									
Kerr, John	2	2		1						
Knight, Alan	36		2		4					
Mariner, Paul	16	7	1	1			4			4
Perry, Andy	1	3			1			1		1
Quinn, Mick	29	3	2		4		6	1	3	10
Sandford, Lee	19	2	2		1		1			1
Shotton, Malcolm	10		2							
Stewart, Ian		1								
Swain, Kenny	32		2		1		2			2
Whitehead, Clive	30	3	1	1	3					
24 players used	440	37	22	4	44		36	2	8	46

No	Date	Att	Pos	Pt	F-A	H-T	Scorers, Times, and Referees	1	2	3	4	5	6	7	8	9	10	11	subs used
1	A SHREWSBURY 27/8	5,333		3	W 2:1	1:1	Connor 30, Kelly 67 / McNally 40p — Ref: P Tyldesley (Stockport)	Knight	Neill	Hardyman	Dillon	Hogg	Gilbert	Whitehead*	Horne	Quinn	Connor	Sandford	Kelly
								Perks	Williams W	Williams B	Priest^	Green	Finlay	Kasule	McNally	Irvine	Thomas*	Brown	Melrose/Griffin
2	H LEICESTER 29/8	10,737		6	W 3-0	1-0	Connor 15, 50, Quinn 86p — Ref: A Buksh (London)	Knight	Neill	Hardyman	Dillon	Hogg	Gilbert	Whitehead	Horne	Quinn	Connor	Sandford	Sandford
								Cooper	Mauchlen	Spearing	Ramsey^	Walsh	Paris	Turner	Cross^	Newell	McAllister	Weir	Reid/Quinn
3	H LEEDS 3/9	15,263 (21)	1	9	W 4-0	2-0	Taylor 31 (og), Quinn 35, Connor 62 [Chamberlain 75] — Ref: I Hemley (Ampthill)	Knight	Neill	Hardyman	Dillon	Hogg	Gilbert^	Chamberlain	Horne*	Quinn	Connor	Sandford	Kelly/Whitehead
								Day	Haddock	Adams	Aizlewood	Blake	Ashurst	Taylor*	Stiles	Baird !	Pearson	Hilaire	Davison
4	A SWINDON 11/9	11,443 (15)	2	10	D 1-1	1-0	Chamberlain 7 / Foley 85 — Ref: J Ashworth (Luffenham)	Knight	Neill	Hardyman	Dillon	Hogg	Gilbert	Chamberlain	Horne	Quinn*	Connor	Sandford	Aspinall
								Digby	Hockaday	King	MacLaren	Calderwood	Gittens	Foley	Bodin*	Shearer	White	Barnes	Henry
5	H HULL 17/9	11,599 (11)	3	10	L 1-3	0-2	Connor 66 / Edwards 43, 45, Dyer 56 — Ref: M James (Horsham)	Knight^	Neill^	Hardyman	Dillon	Hogg	Gilbert	Chamberlain*	Horne	Quinn	Connor	Sandford	Aspinall/Whitehead
								Norman	Palmer	Jacobs^	Warren	Jobson	Terry	Roberts*	Dyer	Payton	Edwards	Daniel	Saville/De Mange
6	A STOKE 20/9	7,025 (23)	4	11	D 2-2	1-1	Horne 17, Aspinall 83 / Stainrod 28, Hackett 89 — Ref: W Flood (Stockport)	Knight	Sandford	Hardyman	Dillon	Hogg	Whitehead	Chamberlain	Horne	Aspinall	Connor	Kelly	
								Fox	Ford	Carr	Kamara	Hemming	Henry	Hackett	Saunders	Morgan	Stainrod	Beagrie	
7	H CRYSTAL PALACE 24/9	11,249 (20)	4	12	D 1-1	1-0	Aspinall 15p / Wright 68 — Ref: P Danson (Leicester)	Knight	Connor	Hardyman*	Dillon	Hogg	Whitehead	Chamberlain	Horne	Quinn	Aspinall	Kelly	Russell
								Parkin	Pemberton	Burke	Pardew	Hopkins	O'Reilly	Redfearn	Thomas	Bright	Wright	Barber	
8	A BRADFORD C 1/10	11,208 (4)	6	12	L 1-2	1-2	Aspinall 5p / Thomas 26p, Sinnott 29 — Ref: R Bridges (Deeside)	Knight	Neill^	Hardyman	Gilbert	Hogg	Whitehead	Chamberlain	Horne	Aspinall	Connor	Kelly*	Quinn/Sandford
								Tomlinson	Mitchell	Jackson	Oliver	Evans	Banks	Sinnott	Kuhl	Ormondroyd	Kennedy	Leonard*	Jewell
9	A MANCHESTER C 5/10	17,202 (4)	7	12	L 1-4	1-3	Aspinall 44 / White 3, Moulden 5, Biggins 35 [Lake 84] — Ref: A Seville (Birmingham)	Knight	Neill	Hardyman	Kuhl	Hogg	Gilbert	Chamberlain	Horne	Aspinall	Connor*	Kelly	Quinn
								Dibble	Seagraves	Hinchcliffe	Gayle	Biggins	Redmond	White	Moulden	Morley	McNab	Lake	
10	H OXFORD 8/10	9,567 (10)	7	15	W 2-1	1-1	Aspinall 2p, Quinn 81 / Bardsley 17 — Ref: D Vickers (Ilford)	Knight	Neill	Hardyman	Kuhl	Hogg !	Whitehead	Chamberlain	Horne	Aspinall	Connor	Kelly*	Dillon, Quinn/Sandford
								Judge	Bardsley	Phillips J	Phillips I	Briggs	Greenall	Purdie	Foyle	Saunders	Mustoe	Rh's-Brown* Hill	
11	H BOURNEMOUTH 15/10	12,801 (18)	5	18	W 2-1	1-0	Chamberlain 38, Quinn 55 / Close 58 — Ref: P Foakes (Clacton-on-Sea)	Knight	Neill	Hardyman	Kuhl	Hogg	Ball	Chamberlain	Horne	Aspinall	Connor*	Kelly	Quinn
								Peyton	Newson	Morrell*	Bond	Williams^	Whitlock	O'Driscoll	Brooks	Aylott	Bishop	Close	Puckett/O'Connor

Match reports

1. New-boys £110,000 Neill (QPR) and £150,000 Hogg (Man U) are on parade, thanks to Jim Gregory's cheque-book, but Pompey struggle to subdue Shrews. Neill crosses for Connor's header, but Dillon brings down Kasule and McNally converts. Kelly conjures a goal-from-nothing.

2. Fratton is a building site, but has its safety certificate; only with a drastically-reduced capacity. Foxes are tipped for promotion, after reviving last season when David Pleat took over. Injury-prone Terry Connor is keen to make up for lost time however, and Quinn's pen doesn't flatter.

3. Leeds are outclassed once Taylor heads into his own net. Quinn nods in Neill's deep cross, then turns old-boy Blake to set up Connor. Chambo (£200,000 from Owls) smacks a debut goal, and there is still time for Quinn to balloon a penalty, before Ian Baird sees red for fouling Hogg.

4. The Fratton End rebuild is postponed; steel supply problems are cited. Lou Macari's men deserve to level Chambo's classy strike. Quinn is straight down the tunnel after record-fee Aspinall (£315,000 from Villa) subs him; it's OK, he only wants to rush back to his expectant wife.

5. Fixed-odds coupons will be ripped up after this result! Eddie Gray's Tigers bare their teeth, as Edwards twice profits from slack defending, then Dyer bends in after being allowed a free run. Substitute Aspinall peps up things and is involved in the build-up to Connor's consolation.

6. Jim Gregory pledges to dig deeper still as another two points are dropped against Mick Mills' Potters. Quinn is left out, and ponders a transfer-request. Morgan clatters Knight, but Stainrod's goal stands to Ball's indignation, then Aspinall seems to have sealed it until Hackett pounces.

7. Injuries mean Connor lines up at right-back, then rookie Lee Russell (19) comes on when Hardyman is crocked. Aspinall is booked for a wild foul, but three minutes later he converts after a handball. Palace huff and puff, but Ian Wright's chest control and swivel-shot earn a point.

8. Ball's rebuilding goes on with the signing of Bradford's Kuhl (£125,000) but his presence fails to prevent Pompey going down to Sinnott's 25-yarder. Aspinall picks himself up to score, after being brought down by the keeper, but Gilbert then fouls Leonard and Thomas too, is spot-on.

9. Pompey pay for some diabolical early defending, but Ball is upbeat about his team's prospects, despite tabloid rumours that Chairman Jim Gregory's patience is already wearing thin. 'We played some of our best football since Leeds,' he insisted, but it's now seven without a win.

10. Despite the boost of an early penalty, when Briggs held Quinn, a win seems remote as Bardsley's free-kick deflects in, then Hogg chops down speedy Dean Saunders on 74 minutes and gets a second yellow. Quinn's winner is out-of-the-blue after good work by Kelly and Aspinall.

11. Quinn pays for Wednesday's humiliation at Scarborough, but is off the bench at half-time for Connor – for whom Bradford have offered £275,000. Within nine minutes he has settled it with a rising shot from the angle of the box. Hogg's poor back-pass lets Cherries back into it.

12. A WALSALL — 22/10
Att 5,626 · Pos 6 · Opp pos 18 · Pts 19 · **D 1-1** (ht 1-0)
Quinn 17; Hawker 84
Ref: T Simpson (Sowerby Bridge)

	Knight	Neill	Hardyman*	Kuhl	Gilbert	Ball	Chamberlain	Horne	Aspinall	Quinn	Kelly^	subs
Pompey	Knight	Neill	Hardyman*	Kuhl	Gilbert	Ball	Chamberlain	Horne	Aspinall	Quinn	Kelly^	Sandford/Whitehead
Walsall	Barber	Taylor M	Mower	Shakespeare	Forbes	Hart	Hawker	Taylor A	Christie	Bertschin*	Naughton^	Jones P/Pritchard

Unsettled Quinn makes another point with a deft near-post header from Kelly's cross. Ball is unhappy, though when Jones's hit-and-hope enables Hawker to nod in at the far post. Tommy Coakley's Walsall have the meanest defence in the division, but have scored just three in six.

13. A IPSWICH — 25/10
Att 14,796 · Pos 4 · Opp pos 5 · Pts 22 · **W 1-0** (ht 0-0)
Horne 54
Ref: B Hill (Kettering)

Pompey: Knight, Neill, Sandford, Kuhl, Hogg, Ball, Chamberlain, Horne, Aspinall, Quinn, Kelly
Ipswich: Forrest, Yallop, Hill, Zondervan, D'Avray, Stockwell, Lowe, Dozzell, Wark, Atkinson, Kiwomya* (sub Milton)

Horne is being shadowed by Man United and Everton, with a view to a £700,000 move, but Ball insists the Wales cap will see out his recently-signed three-year contract. The 25-year-old does his prospects no harm at all, with a sharp finish to earn a first away win since the opening day.

14. H OLDHAM — 29/10
Att 11,301 · Pos 4 · Opp pos 17 · Pts 23 · **D 1-1** (ht 1-1)
Aspinall 34p; Bunn 44
Ref: R Groves (Weston-super-Mare)

Pompey: Knight, Neill, Sandford, Kuhl, Hogg, Ball, Chamberlain, Horne, Aspinall, Quinn, Kelly
Oldham: Rhodes, Irwin, Barrett, Skipper, Marshall, Warhurst*, Palmer, Kelly, Bunn, Cecere^, Wright (subs Flynn/Phillistkirk)

Paul Warhurst (19), £10,000 from Man C, debuts, but Latics' hero is keeper Rhodes, who produces a wonder save from Quinn as Pompey pile on second-half pressure. Earlier, Aspinall picked himself up to score after Rhodes' rash challenge, but Bunn trundled home the equaliser.

15. A BIRMINGHAM — 5/11
Att 5,866 · Pos 5 · Opp pos 24 · Pts 24 · **D 0-0** (ht 0-0)
Ref: S Lodge (Barnsley)

Pompey: Knight, Neill, Sandford, Kuhl, Hogg, Ball, Chamberlain, Horne, Aspinall, Quinn, Kelly* (sub Whitehead)
Birmingham: Thomas, Ranson, Atkins, Roberts, Bird, Langley, Bremner, Childs, Yates, Sturridge*, Wigley^ (sub Tait)

Injury-wracked Brum include five teenagers in their team, as less than 6,000 rattle around St Andrews. Had Kuhl's free-kick gone in, rather than hit the bar, Pompey might have capitalised, but after the break City dominate. Wily Wigley's pace is noted; he will sign soon for Pompey.

16. H PLYMOUTH — 12/11
Att 11,572 · Pos 3 · Opp pos 20 · Pts 27 · **W 2-0** (ht 2-0)
Chamberlain 26, Quinn 44
Ref: P Don (Harwood Park)

Pompey: Knight, Neill, Sandford*, Kuhl, Hogg, Ball, Chamberlain, Horne, Aspinall, Quinn, Kelly (sub Hardyman)
Plymouth: Cherry, Brown, Cooper*, Burrows, Uzzell, Brimacombe, Plummer, Hodges, McCarthy^, Tynan, Stewart (subs Matthews/Campbell)

Cooper breaks his left leg in a challenge with Horne and play is held up for six minutes early in the second half while he is stretchered off. Earlier, Chambo had shown his class to get away from Cooper and go round Cherry, then Quinn reacted quickest as Uzzell's clearance hit him.

17. H BARNSLEY — 19/11
Att 10,001 · Pos 1 · Opp pos 11 · Pts 30 · **W 3-0** (ht 2-0)
Quinn 17, Horne 27, 47
Ref: B Stevens (Stonehouse)

Pompey: Knight, Neill, Sandford, Kuhl, Hogg, Ball, Chamberlain, Horne, Aspinall*, Quinn, Kelly^ (subs Whitehead/Dillon)
Barnsley: Baker, Joyce, McBugan, Thomas, Shotton, Futcher, Rees, Dobbin, Lowndes, Currie, Broddle

Pompey dethrone Watford from the top of the table after a stylish destruction of Allan Clarke's Tykes – but only on alphabetical order, as they have identical records. Quinn's turn-and-shot is majestic, the Baker muffs Horne's scuffed effort. The clincher is a special strike though.

18. A BLACKBURN — 26/11
Att 8,141 · Pos 5 · Opp pos 2 · Pts 30 · **L 1-3** (ht 1-1)
Chamberlain 19; Hendry 3, Gayle 56, 90
Ref: F Roberts (Prestatyn)

Pompey: Knight, Neill, Sandford, Kuhl, Hogg, Ball, Chamberlain, Horne, Aspinall, Quinn, Hardyman* (sub Dillon)
Blackburn: Gennoe, Atkins*, Millar, Hildersley, Hendry, Gayle, Reid, Kennedy^, Garner, Sellars (subs Dawson/Miller)

Table-topping style this is not, but Rovers aren't much better. Hendry hooks home after Kennedy flicks on a free-kick, but Chambo's alertness lets him roll in Aspinall's deflected shot. Knight is unlucky, as he saves from Sellars, but Gayle's follow-up spins from his grasp and goes in.

19. H WEST BROM — 3/12
Att 12,779 · Pos 5 · Opp pos 6 · Pts 31 · **D 0-0** (ht 0-0)
Ref: P Alcock (Redhill)

Pompey: Knight, Neill, Sandford, Kuhl, Hogg, Ball, Chamberlain, Horne, Aspinall, Quinn, Kelly* (sub Dillon)
West Brom: Naylor, Hodson, Talbot, Alibston, Whyte, North, Bradley, Goodman, Robson*, Anderson, Dillon (subs Palmer I/Paskin)

Football League President Jack Dunnett is in the stand, but can't have been impressed by this shambling affair between two first division aspirants. An X-certificate first half culminates with Carlton Palmer's dismissal for flattening Horne. Winger Ian Stewart has been released.

20. A CHELSEA — 10/12
Att 20,221 · Pos 6 · Opp pos 4 · Pts 32 · **D 3-3** (ht 1-2)
Quinn 42, Kuhl 46, Ball 53; Dixon 4, Durie 35, Wilson K 71
Ref: K Hackett (Sheffield)

Pompey: Knight, Neill, Sandford, Kuhl, Hogg, Ball, Chamberlain, Horne, Aspinall, Quinn, Kelly*
Chelsea: Freestone, Hall, Dorigo, Roberts, Lee, Wood, Wilson K, Nicholas, Dixon*, Durie, McAllister (sub Wilson C)

Bobby Campbell's Chelsea are unbeaten in 13 and on course for an instant return. Dixon and Durie snap up sharp chances, but three goals in nine mins, including a first strike for Kuhl, put Pompey in charge. Chelsea are now ragged, and Kevin Wilson's chip is against the run of play.

21. H BRIGHTON — 17/12
Att 12,467 · Pos 5 · Opp pos 22 · Pts 35 · **W 2-0** (ht 1-0)
Aspinall 14, Hardyman 76
Ref: G Pooley (Bishop's Stortford)

Pompey: Knight, Neill, Sandford, Gilbert, Hogg, Ball, Chamberlain, Dillon, Aspinall, Quinn, Hardyman* (sub Horne)
Brighton: Keeley, Chivers, Dublin, Wilkins, Bissett, Gatting, Nelson, Curbishley, Bremner, Codner, Penney

Pompey keep in touch with the promotion pack, but can count their blessings against their coastal rivals. Aspinall stoops to head in his first in six weeks, then Hardyman makes it safe with a shot in-off a post. Kevin Bremner missed Albion's best chance, scooping over from six yards.

22. A WATFORD — 26/12
Att 15,224 · Pos 6 · Opp pos 4 · Pts 35 · **L 0-1** (ht 0-0)
Redfearn 63
Ref: B Hill (Kettering)

Pompey: Knight, Neill, Sandford, Kuhl, Whitehead, Ball, Chamberlain^, Dillon, Aspinall, Quinn, Hardyman* (subs Kelly/Horne)
Watford: Coton, Gibbs, Jackett, Sherwood, Miller, McClelland, Redfearn, Roberts, Thompson, Porter, Holden

Steve Harrison's Watford have gone off the boil lately, and this is only their second win in eight, but Neil Redfearn's strike is more than enough to see off punchless Pompey. The AGM reveals Pompey's debt under Deacon spiralled from £500,000 in 1974 to £2.5 million in 1988.

23. A SUNDERLAND — 31/12
Att 21,566 · Pos 7 · Opp pos 8 · Pts 35 · **L 0-4** (ht 0-2)
Gates 33, Ord 44, Armstrong 61 [Pascoe 75]
Ref: H Taylor (York)

Pompey: Knight, Neill, Sandford^, Kuhl, Hogg, Ball, Chamberlain*, Horne, Aspinall, Quinn, Kelly (sub Hardyman)
Sunderland: Norman, Bennett, Gray*, Ord, MacPhail, Doyle^, Armstrong, Owers, Gates, Gabbiadini, Pascoe (subs Agboola/Cornforth)

A 700-mile round trip on New Year's Eve is bad enough, and gets worse with the heaviest defeat of 1988, against a team unbeaten at home. Sunderland-born Dillon protests too strongly for a penalty at 0-2, and has now been sent off at all three top North East clubs for Pompey.

BARCLAYS LEAGUE DIVISION 2 Manager: Ball ⇨ John Gregory SEASON 1988-89

No	Date	Att	Pos	Pt	F-A	H-T	Scorers, Times, and Referees	1	2	3	4	5	6	7	8	9	10	11	subs used
24	H SWINDON 2/1	11,681	9/14	35	L 0-2	0-1	Geddis 44, Shearer 67 — Ref: R Hamer (Bristol)	Knight	Neill	Sandford*	Kuhl	Hogg	Ball	Dillon	Horne	Aspinall^	Quinn	Hardyman	Kelly/Powell
								Digby	Hockaday	King	Jones T	Parkin*	Calderwood	Foley^	Shearer	Geddis	MacLaren	Cornwell	Henry/White
25	A LEICESTER 14/1	10,567	13/14	35	L 1-2	1-1	Quinn 40, Turner 17, Reid 58 — Ref: K Burge (Tonypandy)	Knight	Neill	Whitehead	Kuhl	Hogg	Symons	Moran	Horne	Aspinall^	Quinn	Fillery*	Kelly
								Cooper	Mauchlen	Spearing	Ramsey	Paris	Morgan	Reid	Cross	Quinn	McAllister	Turner	
26	H SHREWSBURY 21/1	8,446	10/22	38	W 2-0	1-0	Aspinall 39p, Hogg 81 — Ref: K Barrett (Coventry)	Knight	Neill	Williams W	Priest	Hogg	Symons	Moran*	Horne	Aspinall	Quinn	Fillery*	Kelly
								Hughes	Green	Williams W		Moyes	Pratley	Brown*	Kasule	Griffiths	Irvine	Thomas*	Finley/Steel
27	H MANCHESTER C 4/2	13,207	13/2	38	L 0-1	0-1	Gleghorn 43 — Ref: D Reeves (Uxbridge)	Knight	Neill	Hardyman^	Maguire	Hogg	Whitehead	Moran^	Horne	Aspinall	Aspinall	Kuhl	Kelly/Fillery
								Dibble	Lake	Taggart	Gayle	Megson	Redmond	White	Morley	Gleghorn	McNab	Biggins	
28	A OXFORD 11/2	6,156	13/18	38	L 0-1	0-1	Phillips L 44 — Ref: M James (Horsham)	Knight	Neill	Whitehead	Maguire	Hogg	Fillery*	Chamberlain	Dillon^	Quinn	Aspinall	Kuhl	Kelly/Sandford
								Hucker	Slatter	Phillips J	Phillips L	Lewis	Greenall	Bardsley	Foyle	Durnin	Ford	Hill	
29	H WALSALL 18/2	7,310	14/24	39	D 1-1	0-1	Quinn 59, Rimmer 13 — Ref: K Cooper (Swindon)	Knight	Neill	Whitehead	Maguire	Hogg	Fillery	Chamberlain	Horne	Quinn	Aspinall	Kuhl	Taylor M/Goldsmith
								Barber	Dornan	Mower*	Shakespeare	Forbes	Smith	Goodwin	Rimmer	Banton*	Rees		
30	A BOURNEMOUTH 25/2	9,953	14/6	39	L 0-0? 0-1	0-0	Newson 61 — Ref: D Hedges (Oxford)	Knight	Neill	Whitehead	Kuhl*	Hogg	Maguire	Chamberlain	Horne	Powell	Connor^	Sandford	Dillon/**Ross**
								Peyton	Newson	Morrell	Peake	Williams	O'Driscoll	Cooke	O'Connor	Close	Bishop	Blissett	
31	H IPSWICH 28/2	7,145	14/9	39	L 0-1	0-0	Milton 50 — Ref: M Bodenham (Looe)	Gosney	Neill	Whitehead	Kuhl*	Hogg	Maguire	Chamberlain	Horne	Powell*	Connor	Sandford	Kelly — Baltacha/Harbey
								Fearon	Yallop	Johnson*	Hill	Redford	Linighan	Milton	D'Avray	Wark	Atkinson		
32	A PLYMOUTH 4/3	8,131	14/18	42	W 1-0	0-0	Quinn 81 — Ref: D Hutchinson (Abingdon)	Gosney	Neill	Whitehead	Dillon	Hogg	Maguire	Chamberlain	Horne	Quinn	Connor^	Kelly	Aspinall — Plummer/Pickard
								Wilmot	Brown	Rowbotham	Burrows	Marker	Smith	Matthews*	McCarthy	Tynan	Hodges	Stuart	
33	H BIRMINGHAM 11/3	8,078	13/24	45	W 1-0	0-0	Chamberlain 86 — Ref: A Buksh (London)	Gosney	Neill	Whitehead	Dillon	Hogg	Maguire	Chamberlain	Horne	Quinn	Connor*	Kelly	Aspinall — Robinson/Langley
								Thomas	Ashley	Frain	Atkins	Overson	Roberts*	Brenner	Richards	Yates	Wigley	Langley	
34	A OLDHAM 14/3	5,773	13/17	45	L 3-5	0-2	Aspinall 86, Quinn 87, 89 (Ritchie 73) Holden 37, Wright 38, 79, Milligan 65 — Ref: K Lupton (Stockton-on-Tees)	Gosney	Hardyman	Whitehead	Dillon	Kelly	Chamberlain	Palmer	Horne	Quinn	Aspinall	Kelly*	Fillery
								Halworth	Irwin	Barrett	Kelly	Marshall	Holden	Palmer	Ritchie	Bunn	Milligan	Wright	

24 SWINDON: Gavin Maguire (£215,000 from QPR) has signed, but not in time for today. His 'bad-boy' reputation doesn't worry Ball, who had to defend his team's disciplinary record at the AGM. Lowly Robins blow Pompey's promotion pretensions apart, once David Geddis poaches the lead.

25 LEICESTER: Luck, Filbert Street and Pompey rarely go together and today is no exception. Injuries mean Symons (17) debuts and Awford (16) is sub. Paul Moran (on-loan from Spurs) also starts, but Reid's powerful left-footer means four league defeats in a row and Ball's reign will end next week.

26 SHREWSBURY: John Gregory's regime starts unconvincingly against Ian McNeill's Shrews. Aspinall's penalty prowess continues, after Green's handball, but Town had looked the bet until then. Hogg seals it from just inside the box. A minute's silence is observed for Mick Baxter, who died last week.

27 MANCHESTER C: This match has been designated a 'six-pointer' by Gregory, as Pompey look to get their promotion-bid back on track. The performance is dire however, and City are hardly any better. Gleghorn's strike catches Knight out of position and is the only on-target shot produced by either side.

28 OXFORD: Gregory has pledged to improve Pompey's disciplinary record, backed by his new assistant Steve Wicks, but Quinn and Aspinall both talk themselves into the book and will face suspensions. Fillery has a goal ruled out early on, but Les Phillips' 20-yarder gives Knight no chance.

29 WALSALL: New Saddlers' boss John Barnwell paid £150,000 for Rimmer in the hope of avoiding the drop – Walsall have lost 15 on the trot until his hat-trick last week – and he scores again today. Pompey are now five points adrift of the play-offs, but Quinn's predatory head ensured a reward.

30 BOURNEMOUTH: Problems are piling up. Connor is injured as Newson scrambles home, and he limps off in his comeback after five months out. Teenager Ross comes on, only to end up carried off, Knight is doubtful for Tuesday after clashing with Hogg, and Dillon's pen is saved just after the interval.

31 IPSWICH: John Gregory's bid to sign Saints' £800,000-striker Colin Clarke founders as news of it leaks out. The deal would have been money well-spent, if it ended a wretched record of one goal in more than 450 minutes' play. John Duncan's Ipswich hit Pompey on the counter and prosper.

32 PLYMOUTH: Quinn lifts the gloom around Fratton with his 14th of the season as Dillon and Aspinall combine to set him up from eight yards. However, the future is less clear-cut for Quinn; he has turned down the club's contract offer. Connor's injury jinx strikes again, to dampen Gregory's spirits.

33 BIRMINGHAM: Pompey are thinking of the play-offs again, but this is not promotion form. Birmingham are 15 points adrift of safety, but their blanket defence rarely looks troubled. Gosney makes a fine save from Richards, but the goal is a collector's item; a near-post header from winger Chamberlain.

34 OLDHAM: This looks like a thriller; in reality it was a massacre. Latics' 5-0 lead flattered abysmal Pompey, but once Aspinall knocked in Quinn's pass, the floodgates opened. Quinn then impressed watching scouts with his finishing and another five minutes more and they might have drawn!

Match record (fixtures 35–46)

No	Venue/Date	Opponent	Att	Pos	Res	GS	Pts	Score	Scorers	Referee
35	H 18/3	STOKE	7,624	13	D	9	46	0-0	—	H King (Merthyr Tydfil)
36	A 25/3	LEEDS	27,049	14	L	8	46	0-1	Baird 69	E Parker (Preston)
37	H 27/3	WATFORD	9,364	13	D	8	47	2-2	Quinn 8, Aspinall 20 / Hodges 53, Kuhl 82 (og)	R Groves (Weston-super-Mare)
38	A 1/4	HULL	5,325	14	D	21	48	1-1	Quinn 79 / Edwards 81	G Courtney (Spennymoor)
39	A 5/4	BRIGHTON	10,100	15	L	18	48	1-2	Fillery 13 / Bremner 85, Nelson 90	A Ward (London)
40	H 8/4	SUNDERLAND	7,724	13	W	14	51	2-0	Quinn 15, 53	L Shapter (Torquay)
41	A 15/4	CRYSTAL PALACE	12,358	16	L	4	51	0-2	Wright 63, Bright 81	T Holbrook (Walsall)
42	A 22/4	BRADFORD C	6,909	17	L	16	51	1-2	Aspinall 50 / Palin 40, Quinn 83	R Gifford (Llanbradach)
43	H 29/4	BLACKBURN	6,057	17	L	5	51	1-2	Fillery 66 / Gayle 83p, 86p	D Axcell (Southend)
44	A 1/5	WEST BROM	9,586	18	L	7	51	0-3	Anderson 42p, West 49, 80	D Scott (Burnley)
45	A 6/5	BARNSLEY	5,718	19	L	7	51	0-1	Currie 88p	K Breen (Liverpool)
46	H 13/5	CHELSEA	12,051	20	L	7	51	2-3	Roberts 8 (og), Quinn 75p / McAllister 53, 64, Wilson C 74	M Reed (Birmingham)

Average: Home 10,214 / Away 11,059

Line-ups and reports

35 — STOKE (H), 0-0
Portsmouth: Gosney, Neill, Whitehead, Dillon^, Hogg, Maguire, Chamberlain, Horne, Quinn, Aspinall, Fillery*, Kelly/Kuhl
Stoke: Barrett, Butler, Carr, Kamara, Higgins, Berry, Hackett, Beeston, Bamber*, Shaw, Beagrie, Saunders
Just when you thought it couldn't get worse, Pompey serve up the dreariest fare so far. Home plays as if his mind is on other things – next week's £700,000 transfer to Saints probably. Gregory will invest the cash before deadline day in Beresford (Barnsley) and Wigley (Brum).

36 — LEEDS (A), 0-1
Portsmouth: Gosney, Neill, Whitehead*, Kuhl, Hogg!, Maguire, Moncur, Chamberlain*, Quinn, Aspinall, Fillery, Wigley
Leeds: Day, Aspin, Snodin, Aizlewood, Blake, Fairclough, Sheridan*, Strachan, Baird, Davison*, Hilaire, Williams A/Pearson
Spurs loanee John Moncur starts for new-look Pompey. Strachan debuts for Leeds, but their hero is Baird, who rams visiting fans' taunts down their throats with a booming header. He then tangles with Hogg, who is sent off. Earlier, Gosney saved Sheridan's pen, after Maguire's foul.

37 — WATFORD (H), 2-2
Portsmouth: Gosney, Neill, Beresford*, Kuhl, Hogg, Maguire!, Moncur, Fillery, Quinn, Aspinall, Aspinall, Hodges
Watford: Caton, Gibbs, Pullan, Richardson, Morris*, McClelland, Wilkinson, Thomas, Porter, Thompson^, Hodges, H'worth D'lH'th D'n
Wigley is on fire for 45 minutes. Quinn hits a post, before he dives to nod in his 17th of the season, then Fillery sets up Aspinall for a volley. Hodges pulls one back and Kuhl deflects Porter's free-kick, then Maguire is sent off for retaliation. Beresford cracks an ankle on his debut.

38 — HULL (A), 1-1
Portsmouth: Gosney, Neill, Sandford, Hogg, Whitehead, Maguire, Fillery, Moncur, Quinn, Aspinall, Fillery, Edwards
Hull: Hesford, Brown, Jacobs, Swan, Jobson, Terry, McParland, Thompson*, Whitehurst, Edwards, Bell, Jenkinson
The instinct of the goal-poacher is perfectly illustrated in this dull contest. With the crowd drifting away, Quinn (143 in 300-odd games) is on hand after good work by Aspinall. That's the wake-up call for Keith Edwards (235 in 470-odd), who nods McParland's cross past Gosney.

39 — BRIGHTON (A), 1-2
Portsmouth: Gosney, Neill, Whitehead, Kuhl!, Hogg, Maguire, Moncur*, Fillery, Quinn, Aspinall, Wigley, Hardyman
Brighton: Keeley, Chivers, Dublin, Wilkins, Bissett, Chapman, Trussan*, Nelson, Bremner, Curbishley, Wood, Codner
Kuhl's dismissal for mouthing off is Pompey's third in four, but Gregory is on collision course with the PFA over fines for indiscipline. The kick-off is delayed as Pompey's pink shirts clash with stewards' vests according to the ref. Bremner and Nelson stand the game on its head.

40 — SUNDERLAND (H), 2-0
Portsmouth: Gosney, Neill, Whitehead, Kuhl, Sandford, Maguire, Fillery, Moncur, Quinn, Aspinall, Wigley
Sunderland: Norman, Bennett, Kay, Lemon*, MacPhail, Ord, Doyle, Armstrong, Wharton^, Gates, Atkinson, Gray/Hawke
Quinn meets his personal target of 20 goals for the season with a fierce drive and glancing header, but mid-table Sunderland are clearly snoozing in the Spring sunshine. They don't have a shot until the 76th minute! Gregory will be pleased too, with a card-free afternoon.

41 — CRYSTAL PALACE (A), 0-2
Portsmouth: Gosney, Neill, Whitehead, Kuhl, Sandford, Awford, Fillery, Moncur*, Hardyman, Aspinall, Wigley, Kelly
Crystal Palace: Suckling, Pemberton, Burke, Madden, Hopkins, O'Reilly, McGoldrick*/Pardew, Bright, Wright, Barber, Salako
Andy Awford debuts at 16 years 275 days – Pompey's youngest-ever – and impresses. Steve Coppell's team are on a dash for play-off glory. Wright's bravery and Bright's alertness, as Gosney dithers, makes it seven wins in eight. News from Hillsborough puts things in perspective.

42 — BRADFORD C (A), 1-2
Portsmouth: Gosney, Neill, Whitehead, Dillon, Sandford, Awford, Fillery, Moncur, Hardyman*, Aspinall, Wigley
Bradford C: Evans, Mitchell, Tinnion, Palin, Oliver*, Evans, Campbell, Jewell, Leonard, Quinn, Ellis, Jackson, Russell
Arguments will rage on the bus home over the winning goal. Jimmy Quinn's touch is credited, but Paul Jewell's far-post header looked to be going in. On a sombre day, after an immaculate minute's silence, Aspinall's header from Whitehead's cross looked like sharing the points.

43 — BLACKBURN (H), 1-2
Portsmouth: Gosney, Neill, Whitehead, Dillon, Hogg, Awford, Fillery, Sandford, Aspinall, Aspinall, Wigley, Gilbert
Blackburn: Gennoe, Atkins, Sulley, Reid, Hendry, Mail, Gayle, Millar, Kennedy*, Garner, Sellars, Miller
Hogg's tackle on Gayle looked innocuous, but the referee disagreed. Then Sandford handled Miller's cross and Gayle keeps Rovers on course for the play-offs. Fillery's header had looked like marking the 50th anniversary of Pompey's FA Cup win, until those three mad minutes.

44 — WEST BROM (A), 0-3
Portsmouth: Gosney*, Neill, Whitehead, Hogg, Maguire, Fillery, Sandford, Kuhl, Aspinall, Anderson, Gilbert/Awford
West Brom: Naylor, Raven, Albiston, Talbot, Whyte, North, Ford, Paskin*, West*, Robson, Anderson, Goodman/Bartlett
Gosney's knee is shattered by an early clash with Baggies' Paskin, but Albion fans can only taunt while he is clearly in agony. After a six-minute hold-up, Sandford acquits himself and produces a fine stop to deny ex-Pompey apprentice Bartlett. He can do nothing about the goals.

45 — BARNSLEY (A), 0-1
Portsmouth: Knight, Neill, Whitehead, Hogg, Maguire!, Fillery, Sandford, Kuhl!, Aspinall, Anderson, Macdonald
Barnsley: Baker, Joyce, Broddle, Dobbin, Shotton, Futcher, Robinson, Agnew, Cooper*, Currie, Macdonald, Lowndes
Knight produces three fine saves as Pompey frustrate promotion-dreaming Tykes. It all goes wrong when Kuhl is sent off on the say-so of the linesman, then two minutes later Hogg is adjudged to have handled and Currie scores. Maguire carries on the protests and is also sent off.

46 — CHELSEA (H), 2-3
Portsmouth: Knight, Neill, Whitehead, Hogg, Maguire, Fillery, Sandford*, Quinn, Dillon, Wigley^, Aspinall/Gilbert
Chelsea: Beasant, Clarke*, Dorigo, Roberts, McLaughlin, Hall, McAllister, Nicholas, Dixon^, Wilson K, Wilson C, Le Saux/Monkou
Freed Dillon, Whitehead and Gilbert make their farewells. Ex-Fratton apprentice Roberts heads into his own net, but the champions show their class in the second half. Quinn's penalty, too, is a goodbye gift, but the broadest grin today belongs to Chelsea's ex-Pompey boss Campbell.

BARCLAYS DIVISION 2 (CUP-TIES)   Manager: Ball ⇨ John Gregory   SEASON 1988-89

League Cup

					F-A	H-T	Scorers, Times, and Referees	1	2	3	4	5	6	7	8	9	10	11	Subs used
2:1	H	SCARBOROUGH	4	D	2:2	1-0	Quinn 9, Connor 75	Knight	Sandford	Russell	Dillon	Hogg	Whitehead	Aspinall	Fillery*	Quinn	Connor	Kelly	Kelly
		27/9	4,742	4:5			*Thompson 62, Cook 89p*	*Charlton*	*Kamara*	*Thompson*	*Short*	*Richards*	*Bennyworth*	*Morris*	*Cook*	*Norris*	*Brook**	*Graham*	*Darby* *Adams*
							Ref: J Deakin (Llantwit Major)												

New-boys Scarborough – unfamiliarity appends the superfluous 'Town' to their name on the programme – attract the lowest Fratton crowd for a main cup competition. Ball is forced to squirm as Boro are better by far and Sandford's foul on Norris gave Mitch Cook the chance to level.

					F-A	H-T	Scorers, Times, and Referees	1	2	3	4	5	6	7	8	9	10	11	Subs used
2:2	A	SCARBOROUGH	7	L	1:3	0-1	Aspinall 85	Knight	Neill	Hardyman*	Kuhl	Hogg	Whitehead	Connor	Horne	Aspinall	Quinn	Sandford	Sandford
		12/10	3,802	4:2			*Norris 35, Cook 78, Graham 89*	*Blackwell*	*Kamara*	*Thompson*	*Short*	*Richards*	*Bennyworth*	*Olssen*	*Cook*	*Norris*	*Brook*	*Graham*	*Dillon*
							Ref: K Lupton (Stockton/Tees)												
							(Pompey lost 3-5 on aggregate)												

Ball was confident beforehand, but instead the result flatters his side. Norris runs onto Cook's pass, then rounds Knight. Graham's header hits a post, before Cook seals it with an 18-yard chip. Aspinall heads in too late and Graham sets up a home draw for Boro against….Southampton.

FA Cup

					F-A	H-T	Scorers, Times, and Referees	1	2	3	4	5	6	7	8	9	10	11	Subs used
3	H	SWINDON	9	D	1:1	1-0	Quinn 1	Knight	Neill	Sandford*	Maguire	Hogg	Ball	Dillon	Horne	Quinn	Kuhl	Hardyman^	Kelly/Whitehead
		7/1	10,582	14			*Foley 86*	*Digby*	*Hockaday*	*King*	*Jones T*	*Cornwell*	*Calderwood*	*Foley*	*Shearer*	*Geddis*	*MacLaren*	*Henry**	*White*
							Ref: R Lewis (Great Bookham)												

On Monday Pompey lost to Robins, but get the perfect start when Quinn holds off Calderwood and angles home after just 25 seconds. Maguire makes an impressive debut, as Swindon pile on the pressure, which finally pays when Foley squeezes home after a goalmouth scramble.

					F-A	H-T	Scorers, Times, and Referees	1	2	3	4	5	6	7	8	9	10	11	Subs used
3R	A	SWINDON	9	L	0:2	0-0		Knight	Neill	Sandford*	Kuhl	Hogg	Ball^	Dillon	Maguire	Quinn	Horne	Fillery	Kelly/Whitehead
		10/1	11,457	14			*Foley 81, Shearer 87*	*Digby*	*Hockaday**	*King*	*Jones*	*Calderwood*	*White*	*Foley*	*Cornwell*	*Shearer^*	*MacLaren*	*Geddis*	*McLoughlin/Henry*
							Ref: R Lewis (Great Bookham)												

Pompey look to have survived Town's aerial bombardment, then Foley's shot takes a wicked deflection and Lou Macari's Swindon will host West Ham. Sandford joins the growing casualty list, along with Ball, who is out for four months with a blood-supply problem to his calves.

Final League Table

		P	Home					Away					Pts
			W	D	L	F	A	W	D	L	F	A	
1	Chelsea	46	15	6	2	50	25	14	6	3	46	25	99
2	Manchester C	46	12	8	3	48	28	12	5	6	29	25	82
3	Crystal Pal*	46	15	6	2	42	17	8	6	9	29	32	81
4	Watford	46	14	5	4	41	18	8	7	8	33	30	78
5	Blackburn	46	16	4	3	50	22	6	9	10	24	37	77
6	Swindon	46	13	8	2	35	15	7	8	8	33	38	76
7	Barnsley	46	12	8	3	37	21	8	6	9	29	37	74
8	Ipswich	46	13	3	7	42	23	9	4	10	29	38	73
9	West Brom	46	13	7	3	43	18	5	11	7	22	23	72
10	Leeds	46	12	6	5	34	20	5	10	8	25	30	67
11	Sunderland	46	12	8	3	40	23	4	7	12	20	37	63
12	Bournemouth	46	13	3	7	32	20	5	5	13	21	42	62
13	Stoke	46	10	9	4	33	25	5	5	13	24	47	59
14	Bradford C	46	8	11	4	29	22	6	6	12	23	37	56
15	Leicester	46	11	6	6	29	20	2	10	11	25	43	55
16	Oldham	46	9	10	4	49	32	2	11	10	26	40	54
17	Oxford	46	11	6	6	40	34	3	6	14	22	36	54
18	Plymouth	46	11	4	8	35	22	3	8	12	20	44	54
19	Brighton	46	11	5	7	36	24	4	4	16	21	42	51
20	PORTSMOUTH	46	10	6	7	33	21	3	6	14	20	41	51
21	Hull	46	7	9	7	31	25	4	5	14	21	43	47
22	Shrewsbury	46	4	11	8	25	31	4	7	12	15	36	42
23	Birmingham	46	6	4	13	21	33	2	7	14	10	43	35
24	Walsall	46	3	10	10	27	42	2	6	15	14	38	31
		1104	261	163	128	884	581	128	163	261	581	884	1493

* promoted
after play-offs

Odds & ends

Double wins: (2) Shrewsbury, Plymouth.

Double losses: (3) Manchester C, Bradford C, Blackburn.

Won from behind: (0).

Lost from in front: (4) Brad C (a), Brighton (a), Blackburn (h), Chelsea (h).

High spots: Eight-match unbeaten home run from September to December.

Eight-match unbeaten run in the league from September to November.

Beating Leeds 4-0 at Fratton in September.

Guy Whittingham agrees to sign for £450.

Low spots: Lost last six league matches.

Lost to fourth division Scarborough in League Cup second round.

Seven players sent off in first-team games.

Trailing 0-5 at Oldham with five minutes to go.

Former defender Mick Baxter died after a long illness.

£300,000 signing John Beresford breaks an ankle on his home debut.

Player of the Year: Mick Quinn.

Ever-presents: (0).

Hat-tricks: (0).

Leading scorer: Mick Quinn (21) Including 1 Simod Cup goal.

Appearances and Goals

	Appearances						Goals			
	Lge	Sub	LC	Sub	FAC	Sub	Lge	LC	FAC	Tot
Aspinall, Warren	36	4	2				11	1		12
Awford, Andy	3	1								
Ball, Kevin	14						1			1
Beresford, John	1		1							
Chamberlain, Mark	28				2		6			6
Connor, Terry	14				2		5		1	6
Darby, L		1		1		1				
Dillon, Kevin	24	5	1		1	2				
Fillery, Mick	14	3	1		1		2			2
Gilbert, Billy	9	3								
Gosney, Andy	14									
Hardyman, Paul	23	2	1		1		1			1
Hogg, Graeme	41		2		2		1			1
Horne, Barry	30	1	1		2		4			4
Kelly, Mark	15	13	1		2	2	1			1
Knight, Alan	32		2		2					
Kuhl, Martin	31	1	1		2					
Maguire, Gavin	18		1		2		1			1
Moncur, John	7									
Moran, Paul	3									
Neill, Warren	43		1		2					
Powell, Darryl	2	1								
Quinn, Mick	36	3	2		2		18	2		20
Ross, Mike		1	1							
Russell, Lee		2	1							
Sandford, Lee	28	3	2		2					
Symons, Kit	2									
Whitehead, Clive	27	5	2		2					
Wigley, Steve	11									
(own-goals)							2			2
29 players used	506	49	22	2	22	4	53	3	1	57

BARCLAYS LEAGUE DIVISION 2

Manager: Gregory ⇒ Frank Burrows   **SEASON 1989-90**

No	Date	Venue	Opponent	Att	Pos	Res	Pt	F-A	H-T	Scorers, Times, and Referees
1	19/8	A	WATFORD	10,164	20/15	L	0	0-1	0-1	Wilkinson 20 — Ref: G Ashby (Worcester)
2	26/8	H	STOKE	7,433	20/15	D	1	0-0	0-0	Ref: I Hemley (Ampthill)
3	2/9	A	BRADFORD C	8,425	18/15	D	2	1-1	1-0	Fillery 36 / Quinn 46 — Ref: V Callow (Solihull)
4	9/9	H	HULL	6,469	21/20	D	3	2-2	0-0	Whittingham 51, Ball 89 / Swan 55, 77 — Ref: B Stevens (Stonehouse)
5	12/9	H	PLYMOUTH	6,865	22/5	L	3	0-3	0-1	Tynan 23, 75p, Thomas 88 — Ref: M James (Horsham)
6	16/9	A	NEWCASTLE	19,589	23/6	L	3	0-1	0-0	Thorn 59 — Ref: S Lodge (Barnsley)
7	23/9	H	MIDDLESBROUGH	7,305	20/14	W	6	3-1	3-0	Chamberlain 24, Kuhl 27, Whittingham 41 / Slaven 61 — Ref: R Wiseman (Borehamwood)
8	26/9	H	WEST HAM	12,632	21/3	L	6	0-1	0-0	Rosenior 89 — Ref: D Hutchinson (Marcham)
9	30/9	A	WOLVERHAMPTON	13,677	22/12	L	6	0-5	0-0	Dennison 52, 69, Venus 64, Bull 77, 87 — Ref: R Nixon (West Kirkby)
10	7/10	A	OXFORD	5,193	22/16	L	6	1-2	0-2	Whittingham 65 / Phillips 19p, Durnin 45 — Ref: A Ward (London)
11	14/10	H	BLACKBURN	7,004	22/6	D	7	1-1	1-1	Whittingham 43 / Kennedy 44p — Ref: R Milford (Bristol)

Line-ups (Pompey in roman, opponents in italics)

No	Team	1	2	3	4	5	6	7	8	9	10	11	subs used
1	Pompey	Knight	Neill	Beresford	Fillery^	Sandford	Ball	Wigley	Aspinall*	Kelly	Connor	Black	Hogg/Chamberlain
1	Watford	*Coton*	*Gibbs*	*Jackett*	*Richardson*	*Holdsw'th*	*D'd Roeder*	*Thomas*	*Wilkinson*	*Thompson**	*Porter*	*Redfearn*	*Holdsworth Dean*
2	Pompey	Knight	Neill	Beresford	Fillery	Sandford	Ball	Wigley	Chamberlain	Kelly*	Connor	Black	Whittingham
2	Stoke	*Fox*	*Butler*	*Statham*	*Kamara*	*Cranson*	*Beeston*	*Hackett*	*Scott*	*Bamber*	*Biggins**	*Morgan*	*Beagrie*
3	Pompey	Knight	Neill*	Maguire	Fillery	Sandford	Ball	Wigley	Chamberlain	Kelly	Connor	Black*	Hogg/Kuhl
3	Bradford C	*Tomlinson*	*Abbott*	*Timnin*	*Aizlewood**	*Sinnott*	*Evans*	*Campbell*	*Davies*	*Jewell*	*Quinn*	*Wharton*	*Ellis*
4	Pompey	Knight	Hogg	Maguire	Fillery	Sandford	Ball	Wigley	Chamberlain*	Kelly	Connor	Black	Whittingham/Kuhl
4	Hull	*Kelly*	*Jenkinson*	*Jacobs*	*Swan*	*Terry*	*Jobson*	*Askew*	*Roberts*	*McParland*	*Edwards**	*Doyle*	*Brown*
5	Pompey	Knight	Hogg	Maguire	Fillery	Sandford	Ball	Wigley	Kuhl	Chamberlain	Connor	Black*	Whittingham
5	Plymouth	*Wilmot*	*Brown*	*Brimacombe*	*Marker*	*Burrows*	*Smith*	*Hodges*	*McCarthy*	*Tynan*	*Thomas*	*Stuart*	
6	Pompey	Knight	Kelly	Maguire	Fillery	Sandford	Ball	Wigley	Kuhl	Chamberlain*	Connor	Black*	Hogg/Kelly
6	Newcastle	*Kelly*	*Ranson*	*Stimpson*	*Kristensen**	*Scott*	*Thorn*	*Gallacher*	*Brock*	*Quinn*	*McGhee*	*Fereday*	*Anderson*
7	Pompey	Knight	Maguire	Beresford	Fillery	Sandford	Ball	Wigley	Chamberlain*	Kuhl*	Whittingham	Black	Connor
7	Middlesbrough	*Poole*	*Parkinson*	*Mohan*	*Mowbray*	*Kernaghan*	*Putney*	*Slaven*	*Procter*	*Ripley**	*Brennan**	*Comfort*	*Burke/Davenport*
8	Pompey	Knight	Maguire	Beresford	Fillery	Sandford	Ball	Wigley*	Kuhl	Chamberlain	Connor	Black	Neill
8	West Ham	*Parkes*	*Potts*	*Dicks*	*Gale*	*Martin*	*Keen*	*Allen*	*Slater*	*Rosenior*	*Foster*	*Parris*	
9	Pompey	Knight	Maguire	Beresford	Fillery	Sandford	Ball	Wigley	Kuhl*	Chamberlain*	Connor	Black	Neill/Kelly
9	Wolverhampton	*Kendall*	*Bellamy*	*Venus*	*Westley*	*Clarke**	*Vaughan*	*Bennett*	*Gooding**	*Bull*	*Paskin*	*Dennison*	*Downing/Chard*
10	Pompey	Knight	Neill	Black	Russell	Sandford	Ball	Wigley	Kuhl	Whittingham	Gilligan	Black*	
10	Oxford	*Hucker*	*Smart*	*Phillips*	*Lewis*	*Evans*	*Slatter*	*Penney*	*Mustoe*	*Foyle**	*Stein*	*Simpson*	*Durnin*
11	Pompey	Knight	Neill	Beresford	Maguire	Sandford	Ball	Wigley	Kuhl	Whittingham	Gilligan	Fillery	Hildersley
11	Blackburn	*Collier*	*Atkins*	*Sulley*	*Reid*	*Hill*	*May*	*Kennedy**	*Millar I*	*Stapleton*	*Garner*	*Sellars*	

Match reports

1. Aspinall is carried off late on with a broken ankle, Wilkinson is left unmarked to tap in Rod Thomas's cross, and £250,000 Black (Hearts) is booked, along with Sandford and Beresford. Connor then blazed wide of an open goal; news of Mick Quinn's four for Newcastle caps the day.

2. Knight breaks Milkins' goalkeeping appearance record for the club, with his 334th match and he preserves a point with a point-blank save to deny the unmarked Scott in the second half. Burrows is back as Gregory's assistant, after Steve Wicks resigned to become a football agent.

3. Fillery answers his critics, from Chamberlain's lay-off, by breaking Pompey's league duck. Maguire loses possession and Jimmy Quinn is able to fire home, but after that it's one-way traffic. Chambo heads against the bar and Fillery has two shots well saved, but the winner won't come.

4. Ex-soldier Whittingham rifles home six minutes after replacing Kelly, but Hull defender Swan is twice ignored as he rumbles forward and the points seem lost. Connor has a goal disallowed, but Whit's persistence allows Sandford to cross and Ball's head gets Gregory out of jail.

5. Crestfallen Gregory says: 'We didn't deserve to lose by three'. Tynan shows the Pompey forwards how, with a sharp header and a penalty after Maguire handled a cross. Rhys Wilmot is Argyle's hero, with terrific saves from Kuhl and Fillery, who also raps the bar just before the second.

6. Whittingham makes his full debut and is denied an equaliser by Kelly's plunge. Pompey dominate the first half and Chamberlain hits the bar from 20 yards. Andy's a Thorn in Pompey's side, when he turns in Scott's centre at the far post. Jim Smith's team were booed off at the break.

7. Gregory eases mounting pressure on his job, after the worst start since 1973. Boro, unbeaten in four, are blown away. Wigley crosses for Chamberlain's head, Black centres for Kuhl's header in-off the underside – on the linesman's say-so – then Whits taps in Fillery's nod down.

8. Hammers pinch the points when Rosenior fires home after Slater's cross. It's rough justice on Pompey, but Knight had been the busier keeper, twice denying Rosenior, then Dicks. Gregory denies he's signing Steve Archibald, but £215,000 striker Gilligan (Cardiff) arrives on Friday.

9. Gregory reckoned this would be Pompey's first away win. Instead, Graham Turner's new-boys give them a second-half mauling. Two goals in five minutes, from Dennison and Venus, put Wolves on a different planet, then Bull's right boot claims his sixth and seventh of the season.

10. Maguire is involved in a tunnel clash after being sent off for fouling Stein, just after Whittingham latched onto Gilligan's flick to drag Pompey back into the match. Maguire gave away the penalty by clattering Foyle, who was carried off, then he missed the ball for Durnin to lob Knight.

11. Fratton Park is fence-free for the first time since 1983. Rovers bring the meanest defence (eight conceded in nine), but Whittingham glances home, but at once Ball fouls Garner in the box. Millar is sent off for two bookings. Collier to thank for preserving that.

12	H	LEEDS		22	D	3-3	0-0	Kuhl 60p, Whittingham 89, 90	Knight	Neill	Beresford	Maguire	Sandford^	Ball	Wigley	Kuhl	Whittingham	Gilligan	Fillery*	Connor/Black
	17/10		10,260	*2*	8			*Davison 51, Whitlow 55, Sterland 70*	*Day*	*Sterland*	*Whitlow*	*Jones*	*Fairclough*	*Haddock*	*Strachan*	*Batty*	*Baird*	*Davison*	*Williams A*	
								Ref: K Cooper (Swindon)	Howard Wilkinson's impressive Leeds are cruising, then Whittingham takes over. His magnificent turn-and-shot looks only like a consolation, but deep into injury-time Sterland's backpass fall short, Day is a fraction late to the 50:50 ball and is left pole-axed as Whittingham walks it in.											
13	A	BOURNEMOUTH		22	W	1-0	1-0	Whittingham 36	Knight	Neill	Beresford	Sandford	Hogg	Ball	Wigley	Kuhl	Whittingham	Gilligan	Black	
	21/10		*9,353*	*12*	11				*Peyton*	*Bond*	*Morrell**	*Teale*	*Miller*	*Peacock*	*O'Connor^*	*Moulden*	*O'Driscoll*	*Brooks*	*Blissett*	*Coleman/Shearer*
								Ref: R Hamer (Bristol)	Whittingham's seventh of the season nicks the win. He fires home after Neill's shot is deflected. Seconds before, Kuhl's shot had thumped the bar. Knight makes three excellent stops and Hogg is outstanding as Cherries are frustrated, but Whits could have claimed a hat-trick late-on.											
14	H	IPSWICH		22	L	2-3	0-1	Neill 51, Kuhl 77	Knight	Neill	Beresford	Sandford*	Hogg	Ball	Wigley	Kuhl	Whittingham	Gilligan	Black	Chamberlain
	28/10		7,914	*12*	11			*Milton 28, 48, Dozzell 80*	*Forrest*	*Yallop*	*Thompson*	*Zondervan**	*D'Avray*	*Linighan*	*Lowe*	*Dozzell*	*Kiwomya*	*Stockwell*	*Milton*	*Pennyfather*
								Ref: L Shapter (Torquay)	A hailstorm halts things briefly in the second half. Town are then swamped by Pompey pressure, climaxing with Kuhl hooking in the leveller. However, Dozzell's soft header means the mood matches the skies. Gloomy. Neill nabs his first for the club and Gilligan twice hits a post.											
15	A	SHEFFIELD UTD		23	L	1-2	0-0	Gilligan 55	Knight	Neill	Beresford	Maguire	Hogg	Ball !	Wigley*	Kuhl	Whittingham^	Gilligan	Black	Connor/Chamberlain
	31/10		*14,718*	*1*	11			*Duffield 69p, 85p*	*Tracey*	*Hill*	*Rostron*	*Booker^*	*Stancliffe*	*Morris*	*Bradshaw*	*Gannon*	*Francis*	*Deane*	*Whitehouse**	*Duffield/Todd*
								Ref: K Barratt (Coventry)	This Hallowe'en horror leaves Gregory wondering if he's cursed. Gilligan's 20-yarder had given Pompey the lead, but then Ball is sent off for two bookings. Even Blades' fans think Duffield dived over Beresford's tackle. Then Francis is as surprised as anyone when Hogg is penalised.											
16	A	BARNSLEY		21	W	1-0	0-0	Gilligan 60	Knight	Neill	Beresford	Maguire	Hogg	Ball	Wigley	Kuhl	Whittingham	Gilligan	Black	
	4/11		*5,524*	*19*	14				*Wardle*	*Broddie*	*Cross*	*Dobbin*	*Dunphy*	*Shotton^*	*Banks**	*Agnew*	*Forman*	*Currie*	*Archdeacon*	*Robinson/Tiler*
								Ref: M Bailey (Impington)	Tykes – in dreadful red shirts with white stars – have the leakiest defence (30 in 15 games). Once Gilligan nods in Beresford's cross, the win is safe. Agnew goes close, but the highly-rated Currie is more korma than vindaloo. Pompey pledge to cover the disabled area after complaints.											
17	H	PORT VALE		17	W	2-0	1-0	Black 30, Whittingham 87	Knight	Neill	Beresford	Maguire	Hogg	Ball	Wigley	Kuhl	Whittingham	Gilligan	Black	
	11/11		7,708	*16*	17				*Grew*	*West*	*Jeffers*	*Walker*	*Aspin*	*Millar*	*Miller**	*Earle*	*Cross*	*Beckford*	*Mills*	*Porter*
								Ref: A Gunn (South Chailey)	Gregory's post-Barnsley claim that Pompey can still go up gains credibility as John Rudge's Vale are outclassed. Black scrambles home, as talk of a possible move back to Scotland is subsiding. Whit's goal is pure class; cutting in from the right he tucks a shot just inside the far post.											
18	H	WEST BROM		17	D	1-1	1-0	Kuhl 38p	Knight	Neill^	Beresford	Maguire	Hogg	Symons	Wigley*	Kuhl	Whittingham	Gilligan	Black	Chamberlain/Kelly
	18/11		9,069	*14*	18			*McNally 59p*	*Naylor*	*Hodson*	*Harbey*	*Talbot*	*Raven*	*White*	*Ford*	*Goodman*	*Bartlett*	*McNally*	*Parkin*	
								Ref: D Axcell (Southend)	A tale of two pens has Hodson tripping Beresford, before WBA player-boss Brian Talbot exerts more influence after the break. His reward is when Maguire nudges Bartlett. Awford has signed for four years, but the listed Hogg, Sandford and Neill have prompted no interest so far.											
19	A	SWINDON		21	D	2-2	0-1	Kuhl 48p, Whittingham 49	Knight	Chamberlain	Beresford	Maguire	Hogg	Ball	Wigley	Kuhl	Whittingham	Gilligan	Black	
	26/11		*10,413*	*9*	19			*Shearer 29, 87*	*Digby*	*Kerslake*	*Bodin*	*McLoughlin*	*Calderwood*	*Gittens*	*Jones*	*Shearer*	*White*	*MacLaren**	*Simpson*	*Foley*
								Ref: J Deakin (Llantwit Major)	Ossie Ardiles' Robins ride their luck. Knight fails to hold Fitzroy Simpson's drive and Shearer profits. Then he is then on hand to drive in after Black is harshly penalised for a free-kick. In between, Kuhl is shoved by Calderwood for the penalty, then Whittingham flicks past Digby.											
20	H	WATFORD		22	L	1-2	0-1	Whittingham 62	Knight	Chamberlain	Beresford	Maguire	Hogg	Ball	Wigley^	Kuhl	Whittingham	Gilligan	Black*	Aspinall/Kelly
	2/12		7,933	*16*	19			*Wilkinson 28, Penrice 73*	*Coton*	*Gibbs*	*Ashby*	*Richardson*	*Holdsworth*	*Roeder*	*Falconer**	*Wilkinson*	*Penrice*	*Porter*	*Hodges*	*Pullen*
								Ref: D Vickers (Ilford)	Watford have been slipping of late – one win in eleven – but they dispose of two unwanted records today. Hodges sets up Penrice for his fourth in four since a £500,000 move from Bristol Rovers, and Hornets have their first away win of the season and their first-ever win at Fratton Park.											
21	A	PLYMOUTH		21	W	2-0	1-0	Chamberlain 41, Whittingham 52	Knight	Chamberlain	Beresford*	Maguire	Hogg	Ball	Wigley	Kuhl	Whittingham	Gilligan	Black	Russell
	10/12		*9,988*	*12*	22				*Wilmot*	*Brown*	*Beglin*	*Marker*	*Burrows*	*Hodges*	*Byrne*	*Campbell**	*Tynan*	*Thomas*	*Whiston^*	*Pickard/Damerell*
								Ref: D Hedges (Oxford)	Home defeats against Watford and Dons (in the ZDS Cup) mean the knives are again out for Gregory, whose managerial record stands at eight wins in 41 league games. Make that nine in 42, as reluctant full-back Chamberlain curls home a superb goal. Then Whits is set up by Wigley.											
22	H	SUNDERLAND		20	D	3-3	1-2	Kuhl 4p, Wigley 58, Ball 83	Knight	Neill	Russell	Maguire	Hogg	Ball	Wigley	Kuhl	Whittingham	Gilligan*	Black	Kelly
	16/12		7,127	*3*	23			*Bennett 27, Hardyman 37, Gabbiadini 57*	*Norman*	*Agboola*	*Hardyman*	*Bennett*	*Kay*	*Owers*	*MacPhail*	*Armstrong*	*Gates**	*Gabbiadini*	*Pascoe*	*Hauser*
								Ref: I Hemley (Ampthill)	Two more transfer requests (Gosney and Maguire) suggest poor team-spirit, but Pompey show plenty here to peg back Sunderland. MacPhail's handball is converted, but Gabbiadini's delicate shot seems to have turned it around. Wigley fires home, then Ball nods home Kuhl's free-kick.											
23	A	BRIGHTON		20	D	0-0	0-0		Knight	Neill	Beresford	Maguire	Hogg	Ball	Wigley	Kuhl*	Whittingham	Kelly	Black	Fillery
	26/12		*10,800*	*14*	24				*Keeley*	*Chivers*	*Chapman*	*Curbishley*	*Bissett*	*Dublin*	*Nelson*	*Wood**	*Bremner*	*Codner*	*Wilkins*	*Crumplin*
								Ref: P Alcock (S Mertsham)	With Red Star Belgrade striker Dragisa Binic returning home early after an ineffectual trial, Pompey are still searching for that elusive cutting edge. Albion have the best of the derby, as Nelson sees his flying header hit the bar, then Neill hacks Wilkins' effort off the line near the end.											

BARCLAYS LEAGUE DIVISION 2 — Manager: Gregory → Frank Burrows — SEASON 1989-90

---

24 · A OLDHAM · 30/12
Att 8,815 · Pos 22/4 · Pt 25 · **D** 3-3 (H-T 3-2)
Scorers: Whittingham 4, 10, 34 / Milligan 27, 86, Palmer 33
Ref: G Tyson (Sunderland)

	1	2	3	4	5	6	7	8	9	10	11	subs used
Pompey	Knight	Chamberlain	Beresford	Fillery	Hogg	Ball	Wigley	Kuhl	Whittingham	Gilligan	Black	Kelly
Oldham	Rhodes	Irwin	Barlow	Henry	Barrett	Marshall	Adams	Ritchie*	Bunn	Milligan	Holden	Palmer

Whittingham's first senior hat-trick is nearly enough to end Latics' 26-match unbeaten run on plastic, as fortunes fluctuate. Power, pace, not to mention popping up in the right place, sum up his triple, but Mike Milligan saves it by tapping home after Dennis Irwin's free-kick hit a post.

---

25 · H LEICESTER · 1/1
Att 9,387 · Pos 23/13 · Pt 25 · **L** 2-3 (H-T 2-1)
Scorers: Fillery 14, Wigley 36 / Moran 41, Campbell 59, 81
Ref: K Burge (Tonypandy)

	1	2	3	4	5	6	7	8	9	10	11	subs used
Pompey	Knight	Chamberlain	Beresford	Fillery	Hogg	Ball	Wigley	Kuhl	Whittingham	Gilligan	Black*	
Leicester	Hodge	Mauchlen	Paris	Mills	Walsh	James	Reid	Moran^	Campbell	McAllister	Wright	Russell

'We do seem good at shooting ourselves in the foot,' laments Gregory. Arsenal loanee Campbell's 25-yard stunner seals the comeback, after deflected shots from Fillery and Wigley had appeared to change Gregory's luck. On Wednesday, Chairman Jim will pass him the revolver.

---

26 · A STOKE · 13/1
Att 12,051 · Pos 20/24 · Pt 28 · **W** 2-1 (H-T 2-0)
Scorers: Whittingham 15, Hazard 42 / Sandford 72
Ref: J Watson (Whitley Bay)

	1	2	3	4	5	6	7	8	9	10	11	subs used
Pompey	Knight	Stevens	Beresford	Fillery	Hogg*	Ball	Wigley^	Black	Whittingham	Hazard	Chamberlain	Beresford/Gilligan
Stoke	Fox	Butler	Carr	Kamara	Holmes*	Fowler	Bamber	Beeston	Hazard	Ellis	Sandford	Saunders/Hackett

Caretaker Burrows stakes his claim with a win over Ball's struggling Stoke, where he is assisted by Paddon, who left Fratton last month. New faces Stevens (Spurs) and Hazard (Chelsea) star. Black's penalty hits a post and he holds his head as he instinctively knocks the rebound in.

---

27 · H BRADFORD C · 20/1
Att 8,801 · Pos 17/22 · Pt 31 · **W** 3-0 (H-T 2-0)
Scorers: Fillery 10, Chamberlain 31, Stevens 76
Ref: R Groves (Weston-super-Mare)

	1	2	3	4	5	6	7	8	9	10	11	subs used
Pompey	Knight	Chamberlain	Beresford	Fillery	Hogg	Ball	Wigley	Hazard*	Leonard	Stevens	Black	Campbell
Bradford C	Tomlinson	Mitchell	Tinnion !	Aizlewood !	Sinnott	Abbott	Adcock^	Davies^	McCall	Oliver	Campbell	Jewell

Fans chant for Burrows as City are seen off. They will get their wish next week. Stevens fires home, then Tinnion and Aizlewood are sent off later on after an incident involving Hazard.

---

28 · A MIDDLESBROUGH · 3/2
Att 15,295 · Pos 18/16 · Pt 31 · **L** 0-2 (H-T 0-1)
Scorers: Kerr 45, Slaven 51
Ref: P Wright (Northwich)

	1	2	3	4	5	6	7	8	9	10	11	subs used
Pompey	Knight	Beresford	Stevens	Fillery	Hogg	Ball	Wigley	Hazard	Whittingham^	Black*	Chamberlain	Kuhl/Gilligan
Middlesbrough	Pears	Parkinson	McGee	Mohan	Coleman	Ripley*	Slaven	Procter	Baird	Putney	Kerr	Davenport

The only Portsmouth-born player on the pitch – ironically Boro's Paul Kerr – pounces at the second attempt to break the deadlock. Once Slaven swaps passes with Baird and angles home, there's no way back. But for the post, sub Davenport would have made it three at the death.

---

29 · H NEWCASTLE · 10/2
Att 14,204 · Pos 18/7 · Pt 32 · **D** 1-1 (H-T 0-1)
Scorers: Gilligan 82 / Quinn 41
Ref: K Cooper (Pontypridd)

	1	2	3	4	5	6	7	8	9	10	11	subs used
Pompey	Knight	Stevens	Stevens	Fillery	Hogg	Ball	Wigley	Hazard*	Whittingham	Black*	Chamberlain	Kuhl/Gilligan
Newcastle	Wright	Bradshaw	Simpson	Aitken	Scott	Kristensen*	Brock	Dillon	Quinn	McGhee	Sweeney	Anderson

Old-boy Quinn reminds Pompey what they've been missing, burying his 26th goal of the season after Kristensen cut out Hazard's pass. Roy Aitken and former favourite Dillon drive Magpies on, but sub Gilligan swaps passes with Whittingham and fires in to save an unlikely point.

---

30 · A HULL · 17/2
Att 4,883 · Pos 15/21 · Pt 35 · **W** 2-1 (H-T 0-0)
Scorers: Chamberlain 59, Whittingham 76 / Terry 81
Ref: I Cruikshanks (Hartlepool)

	1	2	3	4	5	6	7	8	9	10	11	subs used
Pompey	Knight	Beresford	Stevens	Fillery	Hogg	Ball	Wigley	Hazard*	Whittingham	Black	Chamberlain	Kuhl
Hull	Hesford	Buckley^	Jacobs	Jobson	Terry	De Mange	Roberts	Payton	Bamber	Askew*	Doyle	Jenkinson/Ngata

Pompey lift themselves five points clear of the relegation dog-fight, but it takes an amazing header from Chamberlain, who redirects Fillery's cross, to break the deadlock. Hazard set up Whittingham for his 17th of the season, but Terry's poke makes for an anxious last nine.

---

31 · H SWINDON · 24/2
Att 10,300 · Pos 16/3 · Pt 36 · **D** 1-1 (H-T 1-0)
Scorers: Black 1 / McLoughlin 65
Ref: A Ward (London)

	1	2	3	4	5	6	7	8	9	10	11	subs used
Pompey	Knight	Stevens	Stevens*	Fillery^	Hogg	Ball	Wigley*	Hazard	Whittingham	Black	Chamberlain	Kuhl/Gilligan
Swindon	Digby	Kerslake	Bodin	McLoughlin	Calderwood	Gittens	Jones	Shearer	White*	MacLaren	Foley	Simpson

Much-criticised midfielder Black weaves some magic after 42 secs, firing low into the corner after being set up by Wigley. After that Swindon – with an unchanged line-up in 18 matches – dominate. White misses a sitter before half-time, but Ball's miscue lets McLoughlin score easily.

---

32 · A WEST BROM · 3/3
Att 10,502 · Pos 16/17 · Pt 37 · **D** 0-0 (H-T 0-0)
Scorers: —
Ref: M Bodenham (Looe)

	1	2	3	4	5	6	7	8	9	10	11	subs used
Pompey	Knight	Stevens	Stevens	Fillery	Hogg*	Ball	Wigley	Hazard	Whittingham	Black	Chamberlain	Kuhl
West Brom	Naylor	Hodson	Harbey	Bradley	North	Burgess	Shakespeare	Goodman*	West	McNally	Bartlett	Hackett

Pompey fans preview the all-seater stadia envisaged by the recent Taylor Report into the Hillsborough Disaster, as safety work means the visitors' terrace is shut. The programme pointed out that the teams had never drawn here in 22 meetings. Murphy's Law served up a dull one.

---

33 · H WOLVERHAMPTON · 6/3
Att 12,284 · Pos 16/5 · Pt 37 · **L** 1-3 (H-T 0-1)
Scorers: Whittingham 69 / Bellamy 36, Fillery 75 (og), Bull 89
Ref: D Elleray (Harrow)

	1	2	3	4	5	6	7	8	9	10	11	subs used
Pompey	Knight	Stevens*	Stevens	Fillery^	Hogg	Ball	Wigley	Hazard^	Whittingham	Black	Chamberlain	Kuhl/Gilligan
Wolverhampton	Kendall	Thompson	Venus	Westley	Downing	Bellamy	Steele	Cook	Bull	McLoughlin	Dennison	

Wolves' England striker Bull is dreaming of Italia 90 after single-handedly destroying Pompey. He nods back Cook's corner for Bellamy, then his presence forces Fillery to head into his own net. Kuhl's back-header gifts him the third. Whits slid home a well-worked free-kick routine.

---

34 · A WEST HAM · 10/3
Att 20,961 · Pos 17/10 · Pt 37 · **L** 1-2 (H-T 0-1)
Scorers: Kuhl 63 / Allen 32, Dicks 81p
Ref: D Axcell (Southend)

	1	2	3	4	5	6	7	8	9	10	11	subs used
Pompey	Knight	Stevens	Stevens	Fillery	Hogg*	Ball	Wigley	Kuhl	Whittingham	Black	Chamberlain	Gilligan
West Ham	Miklosko	Slater	Dicks	Parris	Foster	Gale	Brady^	Allen	Rosenior^	Keen	Kelly	Quinn/Bishop

Hazard is oddly left out; it seems Burrows doesn't rate his attitude. Ball rashly handles Keen's corner and Dicks gives new Irons' boss Billy Bonds a first home win. Earlier, Martin Allen had deflected in Dicks' shot, before the returning Kuhl scuffed home Whittingham's nod down.

35 H OXFORD 17/3 — Pos 18 · W · 2-0 · Att 6,749 · 12 · 40

Gilligan 28, Whittingham 44 · Foster 81 · Ref: T Holbrook (Walsall)

Line-ups: Knight/*Kee*; Stevens/*Evans*; Fillery/*Lewis*; Hogg/*Foster*; Ball/*Ford*; Wigley/*Mustoe*; Gilligan/*Penney**; Whittingham Black/*Durnin Stein*; Chamberlain* Kuhl/*Simpson Heath*

Gilligan's first start in ten pays off as his head powers in Neill's cross, but it is Whittingham's goal that is bizarre. Ex-Fratton star Foster slices a clearance into the air and keeper Kee seems to lose in the sun, leaving an open goal. Connor will turn down a £175,000 move to Bristol C.

---

36 A BLACKBURN 20/3 — Pos 18 · L · 0-2 · Att 8,047 · 5 · 40

Atkins 6, Garner 44 · Ref: M Peck (Kendal)

Line-ups: Knight/*Gennoe*; Stevens/*Atkins*; Fillery/*Sulley*; Hogg/*Moran*; Ball/*Mail*; Wigley/*Gayle**; Gilligan/*Millar*; Whittingham/*Stapleton*; Black/*Garner*; Chamberlain* Kuhl/*Sellars Irvine*

Rovers get a dream start when Atkins side-foots home Sellars' corner. Garner then cuts in and crashes in a 20-yarder, the 161st of his career. Kuhl nearly made a game of it, hitting angle of post and bar. Loanee Stevens signs this week (£250,000), but only after a back X-ray scare.

---

37 A LEEDS 24/3 — Pos 18 · L · 0-2 · Att 27,600 · 1 · 40

Jones 14, Chapman 81 · Ref: N Midgley (Bolton)

Line-ups: Knight/*Day*; Stevens/*Sterland*; Fillery*/*Beglin*; Hogg/*Fairclough*; Ball/*Haddock*; Wigley/*Strachan**; Gilligan/*Batty*; Whittingham*/*Chapman Varadi**; Black/*Steed*; Chamberlain Kuhl/Connor / *Hendrie/Whitlow*

Maguire returns for Ball, who failed a fitness test. Knight had already beaten away a Vinny Jones header and stopped Strachan's weak penalty, before Jones' shot loops in off Gilligan. Substitute Connor gets a warm reception from his old fans, then Lee Chapman's back-header settles it.

---

38 H BOURNEMOUTH 31/3 — Pos 17 · W · 2-1 · Att 8,835 · 16 · 43

Whittingham 48, 61 · Brooks 29 · Ref: I Borrett (Harleston)

Line-ups: Knight/*Kite*; Stevens/*Coleman*; Fillery/*Bond**; Hogg/*Miller*; Ball/*O'Driscoll*; Wigley/*Lawrence*; Gilligan/*Brooks*; Whittingham/*Cadette*; Black/*Holmes^*; Chamberlain/*Blissett Shearer/Aylott*

Blissett cost injury-hit Cherries a point, when he rounds Knight late on, but fires wide. He had earlier set up Brooks, but once Whits scored, Pompey were transformed. After collecting a first yellow, his back-heel starts the move which ends with him sliding in his 21st of the season.

---

39 H SHEFFIELD UTD 7/4 — Pos 16 · W · 3-2 · Att 9,004 · 2 · 46

Fillery 58, Chamberlain 65, Whitt'm 68 · Todd 70, Morris 84 · Ref: B Hill (Kettering)

Line-ups: Knight/*Tracey*; Stevens/*Barnes*; Fillery/*Todd*; Hogg/*Stancliffe*; Ball/*Morris*; Wigley/*Wood**; Gilligan/*Gannon*; Whittingham/*Agana*; Black/*Whitehurst*; Chamberlain/*Bryson Webster/Booker*

Pompey turn it on in the second half against Dave Bassett's Div One-dreaming Blades. Fillery is free to loop in a header, then Chamberlain's diving header and Whittingham's drive look to have made it safe. Mark Morris's glancing header at Knight's misjudgement sets off alarms.

---

40 A IPSWICH 10/4 — Pos 16 · W · 1-0 · Att 11,062 · 10 · 49

Whittingham 12 · Ref: M Bailey (Impington)

Line-ups: Knight/*Forrest*; Stevens/*Stockwell**; Fillery/*Zondervan*; Hogg/*Gayle*; Ball/*Linghan*; Wigley/*Lowe^*; Gilligan/*Stuart*; Whittingham/*Wark*; Black/*Dozzell*; Chamberlain/*Milton Humes/Kiwomya*

Ipswich pound Pompey after Beresford is sent off on the linesman's word for a second booking (77). Stevens' head is swathed in blood-stained bandage, after a clash with Wark, but Pompey hang on to Whittingham's tap-in and Town fail to score at home for the first time this season.

---

41 A LEICESTER 14/4 — Pos 16 · D · 1-1 · Att 8,407 · 17 · 50

Connor 69 · James 65 · Ref: G Tyson (Sunderland)

Line-ups: Knight/*Hodge*; Stevens/*Spearing*; Fillery/*Ramsey*; Hogg/*Walsh*; Maguire/*James*; Wigley/*Reid*; Kelly*/*North*; Connor/*Kelly^*; Beresford/*Oldfield^*; Chamberlain/*Wright Linton/Smith*

Two goals in five minutes liven up a turgid affair. Tony James's near-post header is cancelled out when Stevens puts out-of-contract Connor – playing as Gilligan and Whits are both ill – clear to score his first of the season. Spearing almost pinches it at the death, but Hogg hacks clear.

---

42 H BRIGHTON 16/4 — Pos 13 · W · **3-0** · Att 10,924 · 17 · 53

Whittingham 47, Hogg 53, Gilligan 81 · Ref: K Cooper (Swindon)

Line-ups: Knight/*Digweed*; Stevens/*Chapman*; Fillery/*Curbishley**; Hogg/*Gatting*; Maguire/*Dublin*; Wigley/*Crumplin*; Gilligan/*Gatsaanow*; Whittingham/*Bremner^*; Beresford/*Codner*; Chamberlain/*Wilkins Robinson/Gabbiadini*

Pompey's G-Force – Gilligan and Guy – all but ensure second division football next season. The tannoy gives the opener to Gilligan, but it is Whittingham who got the final touch to Hogg's flick. Hogg finishes Albion off, then Gilligan hits the bar, before heading home Neill's cross.

---

43 A SUNDERLAND 21/4 — Pos 13 · D · 2-2 · Att 14,379 · 6 · 54

Connor 81, Wigley 90 · Armstrong 33, 52 · Ref: D Scott (Burnley)

Line-ups: Knight/*Norman*; Stevens/*Kay*; Fillery/*Hardyman*; Hogg/*Heathcote*; Maguire/*Owers*; Wigley/*Bracewell*; Gilligan*/*Armstrong*; Whittingham/*Gates*; Beresford/*Gabbiadini*; Chamberlain^ Connor/Black / *Agboola*

Wigley stands the game on its head, setting up Connor from ten yards, before steering home, despite the attentions of two defenders with 15 seconds left. Roker's Roar – after Armstrong's looping header and top-corner shot – turns to jeers, as their play-off hopes are in the balance.

---

44 H OLDHAM 24/4 — Pos 13 · W · 2-1 · Att 9,601 · 9 · 57

Wigley 39, Chamberlain 41 · Barrett 33 · Ref: A Gunn (South Chailey)

Line-ups: Knight/*Rhodes*; Stevens/*Irwin*; Fillery/*Barlow*; Hogg/*Henry^*; Ball/*Barrett**; Wigley/*Redfearn*; Connor*/*Ritchie*; Whittingham/*Bunn*; Beresford/*Milligan*; Chamberlain/*Holden R Palmer/Warhurst* · Gilligan

Alex Ferguson reckons Joe Royle's side are the best in the division after their Cup runs, but Pompey outplay them. Their fifth away defeat in a row ends play-off hopes. Barrett heads Holden, as well as the ball, in scoring and has to go off, but Wigley's surging run and shot turns it.

---

45 A PORT VALE 28/4 — Pos 13 · D · 1-1 · Att 7,942 · 11 · 58

Kuhl 35p · Beckford 1 · Ref: P Don (Hanworth Park)

Line-ups: Knight/*Grew*; Stevens/*Mills*; Fillery/*Parkin^*; Hogg/*Aspin*; Maguire/*Glover*; Wigley/*Porter*; Connor/*Earle*; Whittingham*/*Cross*; Beresford/*Beckford**; Chamberlain/*Jeffers Finney/Miller* · Gilligan

Beckford runs onto Cross' pass and races away to give Vale the lead after just 38 seconds. His game turns sour when he is stretchered off, then Kuhl converts after Glover fouls Connor. Grew also has to go off and Vale are down to ten, but Pompey fail to trouble stand-in keeper Millar.

---

46 H BARNSLEY 5/5 — Pos 12 · W · 2-1 · Att 8,415 · 19 · 61

Connor 10, Kuhl 18 · Saville 51 · Ref: M James (Horsham)

Line-ups: Knight/*Baker*; Stevens/*Fleming*; Fillery/*Taggart*; Hogg/*Futcher*; Maguire/*Smith*; Wigley*/*O'Connell*; Connor/*McCord^*; Whittingham*/*Saville*; Beresford/*Agnew*; Chamberlain/*Black Archdeacon/Banks/Lowndes^*

An ankle injury rules out 24-goal Whittingham, but he is still acclaimed and given the Player of the Year award. Connor thunders in from 18 yards, then Kuhl's 25-yard free-kick puts Pompey on top. Saville also has made it safe, after Saville's drive, but his late penalty hit the bar.

Home Average 8,966 · Away 11,643

BARCLAYS DIVISION 2 (CUP-TIES)   Manager: Gregory ⇨ Frank Burrows   SEASON 1989-90

Littlewoods Cup

				F-A	H-T	Scorers, Times, and Referees	1	2	3	4	5	6	7	8	9	10	11	subs used
1:1	A	BRISTOL ROV	L	0-1	0-1	Penrice 10 / Ref: P Jones (Loughborough)	Knight / Martyn	Neill / Alexander	Beresford / Twentyman	Fillery / Yates	Sandford / Mehew	Ball / Jones	Wigley / Holloway	Chamberlain / Reece	Kelly / White	Connor / Penrice	Black / Wilmott	
		4,727		3	23/8													
1:2	H	BRISTOL ROV	W	2-0	0-0	Fillery 47, Black 55 / Ref: P Don (Hanworth Park) / (Pompey won 2-1 on aggregate)	Knight / Martyn	Neill / Alexander	Maguire / Twentyman	Fillery / Yates	Sandford / Mehew	Ball / Jones	Wigley / Holloway	Chamberlain / Reece	Kelly / White	Connor / Penrice*	Black / Wilmott	McClean
		5,287		3:4	29/8													
2:1	H	MANCHESTER U	L	2-3	0-3	Black 74, Kuhl 85 / Ince 20, 40, Wallace 43 / Ref: R Groves (Weston-super-Mare)	Knight / Leighton	Neill / Anderson	Beresford / Donaghy	Fillery / Beardsmore	Sandford / Phelan	Ball / Pallister	Wigley / Robson*	Kuhl / Ince	Whittingham / McClair	Chamberlain / Hughes	Black / Wallace	Duxberry/Sharpe
		18,072		1:11	20/9													
2:2	A	MANCHESTER U	D	0-0	0-0	Ref: J Key (Sheffield) / (Pompey lost 2-3 on aggregate)	Knight / Leighton	Neill / Duxberry	Beresford / Donaghy	Maguire / Bruce	Russell / Phelan	Ball / Pallister	Wigley / Robson	Kuhl / Ince	Whittingham / McClair	Fillery / Hughes	Connor / Wallace	
		26,698		1:14	3/10													

Pompey make a first visit to Twerton Park, Bath. Highly-rated Gary Penrice – who will haunt them again later in the season – races onto a long clearance and slides home. Pompey are in a new 'Brazil' away kit and it is a samba-style move that creates the best chance for Chamberlain.

Rovers' resistance is broken when Wigley's left-wing cross is headed home at the far post by Fillery for Pompey's first competitive strike of the season. Chamberlain picks up Alexander's loose pass, goes round Nigel Martyn and tees up Black to settle it from the edge of the box.

Paul Ince's first for United is a special 25-yarder. Wallace's mis-kick seems to have ended the tie, but Pompey come out fighting and Fillery sets up Black. Beardsmore obstructs Beresford's run and Kuhl curls in the free-kick, but it only stands because Leighton's fingers get a touch.

Ball can't believe his last-minute header came back off the bar and denied Pompey a crack at United in extra-time. Knight makes one excellent save from Robson, but the Old Trafford faithful jeer off their expensively assembled team and the pressure is now on boss Alex Ferguson.

FA Cup

				F-A	H-T	Scorers, Times, and Referees	1	2	3	4	5	6	7	8	9	10	11	subs used
3	A	CRYSTAL PALACE	L	1-2	1-0	Whittingham 40 / Thomas 57, Gray 90p / Ref: R Milford (Bristol)	Knight / Martyn	Neill / Pemberton	Beresford / O'Reilly	Maguire / Gray	Hogg / Hopkins*	Ball / Thorn	Wigley / Salako	Kuhl / Barber	Whittingham* / Bright	Fillery / Wright	Chamberlain / Pardew	Chamberlain Gilligan / Thomas
		12,644		1:14	6/1													

Martyn faces Pompey in a cup match for the third time this season, but his new Palace side are lucky. Andy Gray tumbles over Chamberlain's tackle and he picks himself up to score on 90. Geoff Thomas's long-range shot levelled Whittingham's looping header.

League Table

			Home					Away					
		P	W	D	L	F	A	W	D	L	F	A	Pts
1	Leeds	46	16	6	1	46	18	8	7	8	33	34	85
2	Sheffield Utd	46	14	5	4	43	27	10	8	5	35	31	85
3	Newcastle	46	17	4	2	51	26	5	10	8	29	29	80
4	Swindon	46	12	6	5	49	29	8	8	7	30	30	74
5	Blackburn	46	10	9	4	43	30	9	8	6	31	29	74
6	Sunderland*	46	10	8	5	41	32	10	6	7	29	32	74
7	West Ham	46	14	5	4	50	22	6	7	10	30	35	72
8	Oldham	46	15	7	1	50	23	4	7	12	20	34	71
9	Ipswich	46	13	7	3	38	22	6	5	12	29	44	69
10	Wolves	46	12	5	6	37	20	6	8	9	30	40	67
11	Port Vale	46	11	9	3	37	20	4	7	12	25	37	61
12	PORTSMOUTH	46	9	8	6	40	34	6	8	9	22	31	61
13	Leicester	46	10	8	5	34	29	5	6	12	33	50	59
14	Hull	46	7	8	8	27	31	7	8	8	31	34	58
15	Watford	46	11	6	6	41	28	3	9	11	17	32	57
16	Plymouth	46	9	8	6	30	23	5	5	13	28	40	55
17	Oxford	46	8	7	8	35	31	7	2	14	22	35	54
18	Brighton	46	8	6	7	28	27	5	3	15	28	45	54
19	Barnsley	46	7	9	7	22	23	6	6	11	27	48	54
20	West Brom	46	6	8	9	35	37	6	7	10	32	34	51
21	Middlesbro	46	10	3	10	33	29	3	8	12	19	34	50
22	Bournemouth	46	8	6	9	30	31	4	6	13	27	45	48
23	Bradford C	46	9	6	8	26	24	0	8	15	18	44	41
24	Stoke	46	4	11	8	20	24	2	8	13	15	39	47
		1104	252	165	135	886	640	135	165	252	640	886	1501

* promoted after play-offs

Appearances / Goals

	Appearances						Goals			
	Lge	Sub	LC	Sub	FAC	Sub	Lge	LC	FAC	Tot
Aspinall, Warren	10	2					2			2
Ball, Kevin	36	1	4		1					
Beresford, John	27	2	3		1					
Black, Kenny	36	5	3				2	2		4
Chamberlain, Mark	34	4	3		1		6			6
Connor, Terry	9	6	3				3			3
Fillery, Mick	28	2	4		1		4	1		5
Gilligan, Jimmy	24	8				1	5			5
Hazard, Mick	8						1			1
Hogg, Graeme	36	3			1		1			1
Kelly, Mark	6	7	2							
Knight, Alan	46		4		1					
Kuhl, Martin	30	10	2		1		9	1		10
Maguire, Gavin	29	3	3							
Neil, Warren	35	2	3		1		1			1
Russell, Lee	2	1	1							
Sandford, Lee	13		3							
Stevens, Gary	21									
Symons, Kit	1									
Whittingham, Guy	39	3	2		1		23	1		24
Wigley, Steve	45	1	4		1		4			4
21 players used	506	55	44		11	1	62	4	1	67

Odds & ends

Double wins: (2) Bournemouth, Barnsley.

Double losses: (3) Watford, West Ham, Wolves.

Won from behind: (2) Bournemouth (h), Oldham (h).

Lost from in front: (2) Sheffield Utd (a), Leicester (h).

High spots: Whittingham scoring twice in injury-time to force an unlikely draw with Leeds.

A nine-match unbeaten run at the end of the season to avoid relegation.

A 3-2 home victory over promoted Sheffield United.

Frank Burrows being appointed caretaker manager in January.

Low spots: A 0-5 thrashing at newly-promoted Wolves.

A 0-3 home defeat by Plymouth in September.

Losing 1-2 to a last-minute penalty at Crystal Palace in the FA Cup.

Midfielder Martin Kuhl remains credited with the second goal against Manchester United in the 2-3 Littlewoods Cup defeat, but by rights it should be an own-goal. Kuhl bent an indirect free-kick into the corner of the net, but it was only given because keeper Leighton touched it on the way.

Player of the Year: Guy Whittingham.

Ever presents: (1) Alan Knight.

Hat-tricks: Guy Whittingham (1).

Leading scorer: Guy Whittingham (24).

BARCLAYS LEAGUE DIVISION 2 — Manager: Burrows ⇨ Tony Barton — SEASON 1990-91

No	Date		Att	Pos	Pt	F-A	H-T	Scorers, Times, and Referees	1	2	3	4	5	6	7	8	9	10	11	subs used
1	25/8	H WEST BROM	12,008	–	D 1	1-1	0-1	**Whittingham 74** / **Ford 12** · Ref: B Stevens (Stonehouse)	Knight	Neill	Beresford	Fillery	Symons*	Maguire	Wigley^	Stevens	**Clarke**	Whittingham	Chamberlain	**Powell**/Kelly
									Naylor	Hobson	Harbey	Robson*	Burgess	Stradder	**Ford**	Goodman	Bannister	Bradley	Shakespeare	Hackett
2	29/8	A WEST HAM	20,835	–	D 2	1-1	1-1	**Whittingham 19** / **McAvennie 28** · Ref: I Borrett (Harleston)	Knight	Neill	Beresford	Fillery	Kuhl	Maguire	Wigley	Stevens	Clarke	**Whittingham**	Chamberlain	Powell/Kelly
									Miklosko	Potts	Dicks	Foster	Martin	Keen	Bishop	**McAvennie**	Slater	Allen	Morley	
3	1/9	A OLDHAM	11,657	17/1	L 2	1-3	0-2	**Whittingham 54** / **Holden 17, Kuhl 45 (og), Warhurst 82** · Ref: J Watson (Whitley Bay)	Knight	Neill	Beresford*	Fillery	Kuhl	Maguire	Wigley	Stevens	Clarke	**Whittingham**	Chamberlain	Black/Kelly
									Hallworth	**Warhurst**	Barlow	Henry	Barrett	Jobson*	Adams*	Ritchie	Marshall	Redfearn	**Holden**	Currie
4	8/9	H PORT VALE	8,835	21/9	L 2	2-4	1-1	**Aspinall 30p, Kelly 72** / **Cross 18, Earle 53, Beckford 60, 75** · Ref: J Moules (Erith)	Knight	Neill	Beresford	Kuhl	Hogg	Maguire	Wigley	Stevens	Clarke	**Aspinall***	Chamberlain^	Powell/**Kelly**
									Wood	Mills	Parkin	Walker	Aspin	Glover	Porter	**Earle**	**Cross**	**Beckford**	Jeffers	
5	15/9	A NOTTS CO	6,451	21/4	L 2	1-2	0-1	**Chamberlain 61** / **Draper 10, Thomas 90** · Ref: S Bell (Huddersfield)	Knight	Neill	Beresford	Kuhl	Hogg*	Maguire	Wigley	Stevens	Clarke	Aspinall*	**Chamberlain**	Powell
									Cherry	Palmer	Platnauer	Short	Yates	Robinson	**Thomas**	**Draper**	Bartlett	Lund	Johnson*	Chapman
6	19/9	A BRIGHTON	9,117	22/7	L 2	2-3	1-3	**Kuhl 34, 73p** / **Small 40, Codner 42, Wilkins 44** · Ref: R Wiseman (Borehamwood)	Gosney	Neill	Beresford	**Kuhl**	Black	Maguire^	Wigley	Stevens	Clarke	Aspinall*	Kelly*	Murray/Awford
									Digweed	Crumplin	Chapman^	**Wilkins**	McCarthy	Gatting	Nelson*	Barnham	**Small**	**Codner**	Walker	Byrne/Owers
7	22/9	H BLACKBURN	7,801	19/17	W 5	3-2	1-0	**Stevens 17, Clarke 49, Wigley 51** / **Hill 60, Johnrose 77** · Ref: P Don (Hanworth Park)	Gosney	Neill	Beresford	Kuhl	Hogg^	Black	**Wigley**	**Stevens**	**Clarke**	Aspinall	Kelly*	Murray/Gale
									Collier	Atkins	Miller	Reid	**Hill**	Moran	Irvine	Richardson	Stapleton	Starbuck*	Wilcox	**Johnrose**
8	29/9	H PLYMOUTH	8,636	16/17	W 8	3-1	0-1	**Clarke 48, 89, Kuhl 54** / **Thomas 19** · Ref: G Pooley (Bishop's Stortford)	Gosney	Neill	Beresford	**Kuhl**	Butters^	Black	Wigley	Stevens	**Clarke**	Aspinall	Murray*	Powell/Maguire
									Wilmot	Brown	Morgan	Marker	Burrows	Hodges	Byrne	Fiore*	Turner	**Thomas**	Salmon	Robinson
9	3/10	A MILLWALL	10,393	19/7	L 8	0-2	0-0	**Rae 73, Sheringham 85** · Ref: R Pawley (Cambridge)	Gosney	Neill	Beresford	Kuhl	Maguire	Black	Wigley	Stevens	Clarke	Aspinall	Murray*	Powell
									Horne	Stevens	Dawes	Waddock	Wood	McLeary	Carter	Allen*	**Sheringham**	**Rae**	O'Callaghan	Stephenson
10	10/10	A NEWCASTLE	17,682	20/9	L 8	1-2	0-1	**Anderson 71 (og)** / **Quinn 34, 54** · Ref: W Flood (Stockport)	Gosney	Neill	Beresford	Kuhl	Maguire	Black	Wigley	Stevens	Clarke	Aspinall^	Murray^	Powell/Awford
									Burridge	Scott	Sweeney	Aitken	Anderson	Ranson	Dillon*	Brock	**Quinn**	McGhee	O'Brien	Clark
11	17/10	H BARNSLEY	8,701	20/8	D 9	0-0	0-0	Ref: K Barratt (Coventry)	Gosney	Neill	Beresford^	Kuhl	Maguire	Butters	Wigley*	Stevens	Clarke	Aspinall	Black	Whittingham/Awford
									Baker	Banks	Taggart	McCord	Fleming	Tiler	O'Connell	Rammell	Saville	Agnew*	Archdeacon	Connelly

Match reports

1. Pompey unveil £440,000 signing Clarke (QPR) and he nearly scores inside 120 seconds, but Naylor smothers. Ford gets ahead of Beresford to poach the lead for Baggies, but Kelly crosses and Whittingham's diving header levels. Neill is captain, now that Ball has gone to Sunderland.

2. Thunder and lightning rattle around the Boleyn Ground. Whittingham pops the home fans' bubbles, swapping passes with Clarke before firing home, but £1 million McAvennie rams home his first since his return from Scotland. Knight excels to keep out Bishop's deflected free-kick.

3. Whittingham keeps his goal-a-game record, but Oldham show why they will go up. Holden's drive is followed up by Kuhl's misfortune as he hooks in trying to clear Ritchie's shot, then Chambo misses a sitter just after the break. Warhurst thrashes home and sub Currie hits a post.

4. Hogg is back after injury, but this is a disaster. Wood blocks Kuhl's spot-kick just after Cross's header. Aspin handles again and from the spot Aspinall converts. Earle and Beckford hit Pompey on the break then, despite Kelly's firm shot, Beckford strolls round Knight to seal the win.

5. County skipper Dean Thomas powers home a 25-yard injury-time free-kick to give Neil Warnock's side the win. It is cruel on Pompey, who look the better side once Chamberlain levels, after Cherry blocks Aspinall's penalty. Celtic's Anton Rogan turns down a move to Fratton.

6. Five mad minutes turn the game. Small rams in for his first win. Codner flashes home Small's flick, then Wilkins casually bends in a disputed free-kick. Gosney – in for Knight, paying for his bad start – is unsighted. McCarthy up-ends Clarke and Kuhl regains his nerve, but Albion hold on.

7. Injury-wracked Rovers make Pompey sweat for their first win. Stevens drives in the opener, then Clarke is set up by Wigley for his first for the club. Aspinall's pass put Wigley away, but Hill and Johnrose are able to head in as the defence dozes again. Fillery has been transfer-listed.

8. Guy Butters, £325,000 from Spurs, has been drafted in to shore up the back four, but Thomas is still left unmarked to blast Argyle ahead. Clarke is now flavour of the month, as he nods in Kuhl's cross, then feeds of Powell's shot to seal it. Kuhl put Pompey ahead from 20 yards.

9. Pompey fail to score for the first time, as Powell's super-sub knack – four assists from four introductions – finally fails to deliver. Alex Rae glances Bruce Rioch's Lions ahead, then Sheringham finishes Carter's centre. Knight has asked for a transfer and Hazard moves to Swindon.

10. Mick Quinn's right and left feet earn his first goals in five matches and kick Pompey's hopes into touch. Murray glances past his own keeper and Neill almost saves it, but Burridge smothers the ball at the death. Murray makes his full debut on the ground he was taken to as a boy.

11. Whittingham – out since cracking a cheekbone six weeks ago – is on the bench, but even his introduction can't help a bore draw. Burrows is pleased with a first clean sheet of the campaign. Fillery has ended his Fratton frustration by joining promotion-chasing Oldham for £30,000.

12 H LEICESTER 20/10 — Att 9,286 — Pos 14, 17, 12 — W 3-1 (1-0)
Aspinall 6, Clarke 47, Black 57, Mills 66
Ref: A Gunn (South Chailey)

Gosney	Neill	Beresford	Kuhl*	Butters	Maguire	Wigley	Stevens	Clarke	Aspinall	Black	Whittingham
Hooper	*Mauchlen*	*Paris*	*Ramsey**	*North*	*James*	*Wright*	*Reid*	*Oldfield*	*Mills*	*Kelly*	*Hill*

Aspinall accepted North's charitable back-pass to put Pompey ahead, but the next two had equally stamped all over them. Irish cap Clarke turned James and fired home low, then Black spots Hooper off his line and chips in from 20 yards. Kelly has gone to Spurs on a month's loan.

---

13 A WATFORD 23/10 — Att 8,247 — Pos 11, 24, 15 — W 1-0 (1-0)
Aspinall 16
Ref: P Durkin (Portland)

Gosney	Neill	Beresford	Kuhl	Butters	Maguire	Wigley	Stevens	Clarke	Aspinall	Black	Whittingham
James	*Asbty*	*Williams*	*Falconer*	*Dublin*	*McLaughlin^*	*Thomas*	*Wilkinson*	*Kennedy*	*Devonshire**	*Gavin*	*Porter/Roeder*

Sequence freaks will love this result. Aspinall's far-post header from Beresford's cute cross earns Pompey's first away win in eleven, their first win at Vicarage Road since 1924, and Watford's sixth home defeat in a row. Jim Gregory announces a new Fratton End plan tomorrow.

---

14 A BRISTOL ROV 27/10 — Att 6,500 — Pos 10, 18, 18 — W 2-1 (1-1)
Clarke 4, Stevens 63 — White 42
Ref: P Vanes (Warley)

Gosney	Neill	Beresford	Kuhl	Butters	Maguire	Wigley	Stevens	Clarke	Aspinall !	Black	Whittingham
Parkin	*Bloomer**	*Twentyman*	*Yates*	*Nixon^*	*Jones*	*Holloway*	*Reece*	*White*	*Pounder*	*Purnell*	*Alexander/Mehew*

Ten-man Pompey defy the odds. White springs the offside trap to level Clarke's blindside finish off Wigley's cross. At once, Aspinall is sent off for a clash with Jones. Stevens nets when Parkin slips, then force is with them; Butters clears off the line and late on Pounder hits a post.

---

15 H WOLVERHAMPTON 3/11 — Att 14,574 — Pos 13, 6, 19 — D 0-0 (0-0)
Ref: A Ward (London)

Gosney	Neill	Beresford	Kuhl !	Butters	Maguire	Anderton^	Stevens	Clarke	Aspinall	Black*	Whitt'm/Chamberlain
Stowell	*Ashley*	*Steele*	*Bellamy*	*Hindmarch*	*Downing*	*Thompson*	*Cook*	*Bull*	*Paskin*	*Dennison*	

Anderton starts as Wigley has flu. Chances are at a premium, but a marginal offside rules out Paskin, then Bull hits the bar. Sub Whits goes close, but Hindmarch hoofs clear. 6/62 ROAC will be in blue when they play the US Marines Corps in Saudi, thanks to Pompey's kit donation!

---

16 A SWINDON 10/11 — Att 8,621 — Pos 14, 13, 19 — L 0-3 (0-2)
Lorenzo 29, Foley 40, Shearer 77
Ref: P Alcock (S Merstham)

Gosney	Neill	Beresford^	Kuhl !	Butters	Maguire	Chamberlain	Stevens	Clarke*	Aspinall	Black	Whittingham Wigley/Awford
Digby	*Jones*	*Bodin*	*McLoughlin*	*Viveash*	*Lorenzo*	*Simpson^*	*Shearer*	*White*	*MacLaren*	*Foley*	*Close/Hazard**

Burrows brands this a 'test of character' after the Cup disappointment. Pompey fail it. Argentine Lorenzo starts for Ossie Ardiles' side – his first senior match since the World Cup final – and he heads home from close-range. Kuhl flattens Simpson on half-time and the red card is out.

---

17 H MIDDLESBROUGH 17/11 — Att 8,433 — Pos 17, 4, 19 — L 0-3 (0-1)
Slaven 40, Baird 62, Stevens 76 (og)
Ref: M Bodenham (Looe)

Gosney	Neill	Beresford	Kuhl	Butters^	Awford	Wigley	Stevens	Clarke	Black*	Whittingham Murray/Chamberlain	
Pears	*Cooper*	*Phillips*	*Mowbray*	*Kernaghan*	*Wark*	*Slaven*	*Mustoe^*	*Baird*	*Kerr*	*Hendrie^*	*Ripley/Procter*

Baird is back at Fratton and silences the boo-boys again. His header is pushed out by Gosney and Slaven nets. Then he turns Stevens and smashes a shot in-off a post. Stevens can only help Hendrie's cross into the net to cap a nightmare. Leicester are looking at Hogg and Knight.

---

18 A CHARLTON 24/11 — Att 5,513 — Pos 19, 23, 19 — L 1-2 (0-2)
Clarke 86 — Lee 13, Watson 16
Ref: K Cooper (Swindon)

Knight	Neill	Beresford	Black^	Butters	Awford	Wigley*	Stevens	Clarke	Hogg	Whittingham Chamberlain Anderton/Awford	
Bolder	*Pitcher*	*Minto*	*Peake*	*Balmer*	*Caton*	*Lee*	*Curbishley*	*Dyer*	*Watson*	*Mortimer*	

Minto breezes past Gale to cross for Lee's downward header, then the trick is repeated and Watson nods in. Stevens hits the bar and Clarke's run ends with him easing past Bolder, but it's far too late. £80,000 Daniel (Cardiff) and 6' 4" McFarlane (£20,000 from Cradley) have signed.

---

19 H OXFORD 1/12 — Att 6,902 — Pos 21, 22, 20 — D 1-1 (1-1)
Whittingham 8 — Durnin 73
Ref: M James (Horsham)

Knight	Neill	Beresford	Aspinall	Butters	Awford	Anderton	Stevens	Clarke*	Whittingham Chamberlain Powell		
Veysey	*Robinson*	*Smart*	*Lewis**	*Foster*	*Melville*	*Magilton*	*Stein*	*Foyle*	*Simpson Penney/Durnin*		

Chamberlain puts Whittingham clear to go round Veysey, then Pompey then fail to make possession tell. Clarke's header hits the bar and Foster clears Anderton's shot from the line. Substitute Durnin glances home to keep Brian Horton's side's run of form (now seven unbeaten) going.

---

20 H WEST HAM 8/12 — Att 12,045 — Pos 22, 1, 20 — L 0-1 (0-1)
Morley 59
Ref: R Bigger (Croydon)

Knight	Neill	Beresford	Kuhl	Butters	Awford	Anderton*	Stevens	Clarke	Whittingham Chamberlain Wigley		
Mikiosko	*Breacker*	*Parris*	*Foster*	*Martin^*	*Allen*	*Bishop*	*McAvennie* / Slater*	*Morley*	*Hughton Quinn/Gale*		

Leaders West Ham bring the best defence in the division (12 conceded in 19) to Fratton, but only Miklosko's brilliance keeps that record. His best has him turning Whittingham's point-blank header over, after Morley's head had pinched the lead with Hammers' first on-target effort.

---

21 A WEST BROM 15/12 — Att 7,856 — Pos 21, 13, 21 — D 0-0 (0-0)
Ref: T Lunt (Ashton-in-Makerfield)

Knight	Neill	Beresford	Kuhl	Butters	Awford	Anderton	Stevens	Clarke	Whittingham Aspinall Chamberlain		
Naylor	*Robson^*	*Harbey*	*Roberts*	*Bradley*	*Raven*	*Ford*	*Goodman**	*West*	*McNally Bannister/Hodson*		

Baggies' striker Colin West is given oxygen and is carried off unconscious after Kuhl's free-kick hits him in the face. The game is held up for five minutes, but it merely prolongs the agony for the crowd, who give Albion a hard time. Pompey create nothing, but Awford is composed.

---

22 H IPSWICH 21/12 — Att 7,010 — Pos 18, 12, 22 — D 1-1 (0-1)
Clarke 62 — Palmer 5
Ref: J Moules (Erith)

Knight	Neill	Beresford	Kuhl	Butters	Awford	Anderton	Stevens*	Clarke	Whittingham Aspinall* Chamberlain		
Forrest	*Yallop*	*Thompson*	*Stockwell*	*Linighan*	*Palmer*	*Lowe*	*Redford*	*Hill*	*Dozzell Milton**	*Gregory*	

Stressed Burrows moans: 'It's like Coronation Street; the same every week.' Palmer's dipping shot catches Knight out, but Pompey (three points from 21) recover. Friday night's all right for substitute Clarke, whose 20-yard shot-on-the-turn makes a point in more ways than one.

---

23 A BRISTOL CITY 26/12 — Att 11,892 — Pos 22, 8, 22 — L 1-4 (1-1)
Clarke 44 — Morgan 23, 49, Shelton 71, Rennie 76
Ref: G Willard (Worthing)

Knight	Neill	Beresford	Kuhl	Butters	Awford	Anderton^	Stevens*	Clarke	Whittingham Aspinall* Chamberlain		
Leaning	*Llewellyn*	*Scott*	*May*	*Shelton*	*Rennie*	*Bent^*	*Newman*	*Taylor^*	*Morgan Powell/Daniel*	*Smith Allison/Aizlewood*	

Old favourite Nicky Morgan wrecks Pompey's hopes, seizing on a loose ball after it hits the post to restore City's lead. Clarke is inches from levelling again, but from the clearance May centres for Shelton to put the game beyond salvation. Rennie's 30-yard free-kick is a cruel twist.

BARCLAYS LEAGUE DIVISION 2 — Manager: Burrows ⇒ Tony Barton — SEASON 1990-91

No	Date	V	Opponent	Att	Pos	OppPos	Res	Pt	F-A	H-T	Scorers, Times, and Referees
24	29/12	A	SHEFFIELD WED	22,885	23	3	L	22	1-2	0-1	Whittingham 61 / Hirst 5, 79 / Ref: P Wright (Northwich)
25	1/1	H	HULL	8,004	21	24	W	25	5-1	2-0	Chamberlain 1, Beresford 30, Kuhl 50 7p, [Whittingham 81] / Payton 78 / Ref: J Deakin (Llantwit Major)
26	12/1	H	OLDHAM	10,840	22	2	L	25	1-4	1-2	Kuhl 22p / Holden 19, Palmer 39, Marshall 49, 51 / Ref: K Cooper (Pontypridd)
27	19/1	A	PORT VALE	6,314	22	14	L	25	2-3	2-1	Whittingham 24, 42 / Aspin 13, Glover 86, Beckford 90 / Ref: C Wilkes (Gloucester)
28	2/2	H	NOTTS CO	12,680	22	4	W	28	2-1	1-0	Kuhl 24p, Wigley 47 / Johnson 77 / Ref: R Groves (Weston-super-Mare)
29	9/2	A	BLACKBURN	7,348	22	19	D	29	1-1	1-0	Clarke 34 / Sulley 88p / Ref: D Gallagher (Banbury)
30	23/2	H	SWINDON	8,889	20	11	W	32	2-1	2-1	Whittingham 30, Wigley 35 / White 25 / Ref: L Shapter (Torquay)
31	26/2	A	MIDDLESBROUGH	15,922	16	4	W	35	2-1	1-0	Aspinall 29, Kuhl 80p / Parkinson 70p / Ref: T Fitzharris (Bolton)
32	2/3	A	OXFORD	5,226	20	15	L	35	0-1	0-0	Melville 90 / Ref: P Taylor (Waltham Cross)
33	9/3	H	CHARLTON	8,235	20	16	L	35	0-1	0-1	Peake 23 / Ref: R Milford (Bristol)
34	12/3	H	MILLWALL	7,826	19	6	D	36	0-0	0-0	Ref: M Bailey (Impington)

Line-ups (Portsmouth row / opponent row in italics) and subs used

No	1	2	3	4	5	6	7	8	9	10	11	subs used
24	Knight*	Neill	Beresford	Aspinall	Hogg	Awford^	Wigley	Kuhl	Clarke	Whittingham	Chamberlain	Anderton/Russell
	Turner	*Harkes*	*King*	*Palmer*	*Shirtliff*	*Pearson*	*Wilson**	*Sheridan*	*Hirst*	*Francis*	*McCall**	*Williams/Worthington*
25	Gosney	Neill	Beresford	Aspinall	Hogg	Russell	Wigley	Kuhl	Clarke	Whittingham	Chamberlain	—
	Hesford	*Hockaday^*	*Jacobs*	*Thomas*	*Buckley*	*Shotton*	*McParland^*	*Payton*	*Palin*	*Chamberlain*	*Swan*	*Jenkinson, Mail/Hunter*
26	Gosney	Neill^	Beresford	Aspinall	Hogg	Stevens	Wigley	Kuhl	Clarke*	Whittingham	Chamberlain	Murray/Russell
	Hallworth	*Warhurst*	*Barlow*	*Palmer*	*Barrett*	*Jobson*	*Adams*	*Ritchie*	*Marshall*	*Redfearn*	*Holden*	
27	Gosney	Neill	Beresford	Aspinall	Hogg	Stevens	Wigley	Kuhl	Murray	Whittingham	Chamberlain	Murray
	Wood	*Aspin*	*Agboola*	*Walker*	*Parkin*	*Glover*	*Ford*	*Earle*	*Jepson^*	*Beckford*	*Jeffers*	*Mills*
28	Gosney	Neill	Beresford	Aspinall	Hogg	Stevens	Wigley	Kuhl	Clarke	Whittingham	Chamberlain	Murray
	Cherry	*Palmer*	*Harding*	*Short*	*Yates*	*O'Riordan^*	*Thomas*	*Turner*	*Bartlett*	*Regis*	*Draper^*	*Johnson/Paris*
29	Gosney	Neill	Beresford	Aspinall*	Hogg	Russell	Wigley	Kuhl	Clarke	Whittingham	Chamberlain	Murray
	Mimms	*Atkins*	*Sulley*	*Reid*	*May*	*Dobson*	*Gayle^*	*Richardson*	*Livingstone*	*Garner*	*Sellars*	*Irvine*
30	Gosney	Neill*	Beresford	Aspinall	Hogg	Stevens	Wigley	Kuhl	Clarke	Whittingham	Chamberlain	Russell
	Digby	*Kerslake*	*Bodin*	*Hazard*	*Viveash*	*Simpson*	*Jones**	*Shearer*	*White*	*MacLaren*	*Foley*	*Calderwood*
31	Gosney	Russell	Beresford	Aspinall	Hogg	Stevens	Wigley	Kuhl	Murray	Whittingham	Chamberlain	Murray
	Dibble	*Parkinson*	*Phillips*	*Mowbray*	*Walsh*	*Putney*	*Slaven*	*Wark*	*Baird*	*Mustoe*	*Hendrie**	*Ripley*
32	Gosney	Neill	Beresford	Aspinall*	Hogg	Stevens	Wigley	Kuhl	Clarke*	Whittingham	Chamberlain	Murray
	Veysey	*Robinson*	*Ford*	*Foyle*	*Melville*	*Magilton*	*Phillips*	*Lewis^*	*Nogan*	*Simpson*	*Durnin*	
33	Gosney	Neill	Beresford	Murray	Hogg	Stevens	Wigley	Kuhl	Clarke	Whittingham	Chamberlain*	Anderton
	Bolder	*Pitcher*	*Reid*	*Peake*	*Webster*	*Kernaghan*	*Lee*	*Gritt*	*Dyer*	*Mortimer*	*Minto*	
34	Gosney	Russell	Daniel	Aspinall	Hogg	Stevens	Wigley	Kuhl	Whittingham	Murray	Clarke	Anderton*
	Branagan	*Stevens*	*Dawes*	*Waddock*	*Cunningham*	*McLeary*	*Stephenson*	*Goodman*	*Sheringham*	*Rae*	*Briley*	*Clarke*

Match notes

24. Big Ron's Owls get the breaks. Hirst eases home Carlton Palmer's back-heeled pass, but Whittingham levels, seizing on Pearson's missed header. Knight is injured making a save. Four minutes later he is replaced between the sticks by Clarke, after Hirst clips past the groggy goalie.

25. At last! Pompey's enterprise is rewarded, but anything less against Stan Ternant's Tigers (one point in 15 now) would have been catastrophic. Spirits soar after Chamberlain's acute angle finish after 29 seconds, but Gosney's two fine saves just after half-time are the turning point.

26. In the programme it says Latics can only play on plastic. Joe Royle pins it to the dressing room door and his team respond. Aspinall is fouled by Redfearn and Kuhl converts, but that's as close as it gets. Defender-cum-striker Marshall completes the humiliation with two classy goals.

27. Ex-soldier Whits is on Gulf War-alert. Without him Pompey would be firing blanks. His fifth and sixth in four are not enough however, as Vale snatch an unlikely win. Gosney drops a corner and Glover seems to have saved a point, but Beckford's bullet-header triples the bonus.

28. Wigley – so often the crowd's whipping boy – is their darling, as he races from the halfway line and fires past Cherry. Kuhl's penalty, after Palmer fouls Aspinall, sets up the win but Johnson causes an anxious last few minutes. Magpies are improbably soaring towards play-off glory.

29. More late agony on their travels for Pompey, as Hogg blocks Livingstone's last-ditch shot, only for the ref to deem it handball. Earlier, May had lost his footing to let Clarke angle home. Rovers' undersoil heating means this is the only game in Div Two to survive the Arctic weather.

30. Pompey fans feared the worst when White nodded in Jones' cross, but once Whittingham is put clear to level there's only one winner. Another long through-ball unhinges Town once more. This time Wigley is away to round Fraser Digby and earn a first win over Swindon since 1982.

31. Wark flattens Whittingham and Kuhl steps up to earn Pompey first win at Boro since 1949. That award was clear cut, but even Boro were bemused when the ref penalised Murray as Ripley's point-blank shot hit him. Aspinall's deflected shot had earlier spun under Dibble's dive.

32. That late jinx strikes again, as Stevens' late foul on Simpson ends with Welsh cap Melville firing home from close range as the free-kick pings around the six-yard box. The defeat was harsh, although Magilton had hit the underside, and bookings for Hogg and Beresford mean bans.

33. Lennie Lawrence's side suck Pompey back into the danger-zone, when Gosney goofs Peake's fierce free-kick – he was expecting a cross – and the ball trickles in. The major talking point is the state of the once-carpetlike Fratton turf. Compacted soil is blamed for it being a sandy bog.

34. Lions' keeper Branagan keeps their play-off hopes intact with stunning saves in the first and last minutes to deny Aspinall and Whittingham respectively. Regardless, Burrows has decided to resign – by tomorrow afternoon his office has been cleared – and Barton becomes caretaker.

Portsmouth (Pompey) season — matches 35–46

#	Opponent	H/A	Date	Att	Pos	Res	Pts	FT	HT	Pompey scorers	Opposition scorers	Referee
35	PLYMOUTH	A	16/3	6,586	19/18	D	37	1-1	0-1	Kuhl 82	Brown 44p	R Hamer (Bristol)
36	BARNSLEY	A	19/3	4,921	20/8	L	37	0-4	0-2	—	Saville 25, 87, Rimmer 26, Agnew 71	J Watson (Whitley Bay)
37	NEWCASTLE	H	23/3	9,607	21/11	L	37	0-1	0-1	—	Brock 42	V Callow (Solihull)
38	BRISTOL CITY	H	30/3	10,418	20/8	W	40	4-1	1-0	Clarke 45, 60p, 86, Whittingham 49	Morgan 62	D Axcell (Southend)
39	IPSWICH	A	2/4	11,314	20/16	D	41	2-2	1-1	Kuhl 25, 80p	Dozzell 44, Thompson 64p	J Ashworth (Luffenham)
40	SHEFFIELD WED	H	6/4	10,390	18/3	W	44	2-0	1-0	Whittingham 22, Kuhl 86p	—	J Carter (Christchurch)
41	HULL	A	13/4	4,871	17/24	W	47	2-0	0-0	Russell 78, Kuhl 81p	—	D Allison (Lancaster)
42	BRIGHTON	H	16/4	12,271	17/5	W	50	1-0	1-0	Murray 38	—	A Seville (Birmingham)
43	LEICESTER	A	20/4	10,509	18/20	L	50	1-2	0-1	Wigley 75	Walsh 1, Russell 54	K Hackett (Sheffield)
44	WATFORD	H	27/4	10,074	19/21	L	50	0-1	0-0	—	Falconer 83	J Deakin (Llantwit Major)
45	BRISTOL ROV	H	4/5	9,410	16/12	W	53	3-1	2-1	Beresford 1, Wigley 45, Whittingham 48	Saunders 32	M Bodenham (Looe)
46	WOLVERHAMPTON	A	11/5	12,570	17/12	L	53	1-3	0-1	Clarke 77	Birch 37, Mutch 67, Downing 89	J Moules (Erith)

Home 9,690 Away 10,140 Average 9,690

Line-ups (Pompey on top line, opposition on italic line; subs shown after oblique):

35 Plymouth — Gosney, Stevens*, Daniel, Aspinall, Hogg, Russell, Wigley, Kuhl, Whittingham, Murray, Anderton, Awford. *Wilmot, Brown, Morgan, Marker, Burrows, Salman, Barlow, Hodges, Turner, Morrison, Fiore*, Clement.*

36 Barnsley — Gosney, Awford*, Daniel, Aspinall, Hogg!, Russell, Wigley, Kuhl, Whittingham, Murray, Anderton^ / Clarke/Chamberlain. *Baker, Banks, Fleming, Rimmer, Robinson, Tiler, O'Connell*, Rammell, Saville, Agnew^, Archdeacon / Cross/Dobbin.*

37 Newcastle — Knight, Russell, Daniel, Aspinall^, Hogg, Maguire, Wigley, Kuhl, Whittingham, Murray, Anderton* / Clarke/Black. *Burridge, Watson, Stimson, Aitken, Scott, Kristensen, Dillon, Peacock, Quinn, McGhee^, Brock* / O'Brien/Hunt.*

38 Bristol City — Knight, Russell, Daniel, Murray, Butters, Maguire, Wigley, Kuhl^, Whittingham, Clarke, Anderton^ / Beresford/Black. *Leaning, Llewellyn*, Marden, May, Bryant, Aizlewood, Shelton, Newman, Taylor, Morgan^, Donowa / Allison/Rennie.*

39 Ipswich — Knight, Russell, Daniel, Murray^, Butters, Maguire, Wigley, Kuhl, Whittingham, Clarke, Anderton* / Beresford/Black. *Forrest, Yallop, Thompson, Stockwell, Linighan, Gayle, Palmer, Goddard, Zondervan*, Dozzell, Kiwomya / Houghton.*

40 Sheffield Wed — Knight, Russell, Daniel*, Murray^, Butters, Maguire, Wigley, Kuhl, Whittingham, Clarke, Anderton* / Beresford/Black. *Turner, Nilsson, King, Palmer !, Anderson, Pearson, Hartes, Sheridan, Hirst, Williams, McCall* / Francis.*

41 Hull — Knight, Russell, Daniel*, Murray, Butters, Maguire, Wigley, Kuhl, Whittingham, Clarke, Anderton^ / Beresford. *Hesford, Wilcox, Jenkinson, Buckley, Mail, Shotton, Hockaday, Payton, Swan, Atkinson, Warren^ / Ngata.*

42 Brighton — Knight, Russell, Daniel, Murray, Butters, Maguire, Wigley, Black*, Whittingham, Clarke, Beresford* / Anderton/Aspinall. *Digweed, Crumplin, Gatting, Wilkins^, Pates, Chivers, Barham*, Byrne, Small, Codner, Walker / Nelson/Jovan.*

43 Leicester — Knight, Russell, Daniel*, Murray*, Butters, Maguire, Wigley, Kuhl, Whittingham, Clarke, Beresford / Anderton/Black. *Hodge, North, Spearing, Mauchlen, Walsh, James, Wright*, Kelly, Hill, Mills, Russell^ / Oldfield/Johnson.*

44 Watford — Knight, Russell, Daniel, Murray, Butters, Maguire*, Wigley, Kuhl, Whittingham, Clarke, Beresford / Black. *James, Gibbs, Solomon, Ashby, Roeder, Dublin, Falconer, Wilkinson, Butler*, Porter, Nicholas / Callaghan.*

45 Bristol Rov — Knight, Russell, Daniel, Aspinall*, Butters, Hogg, Wigley, Kuhl, Whittingham, Clarke, Beresford / Murray/Anderton. *Kelly, Alexander, Twentyman, Clarke*, Mehew, Jones, Holloway, Reece, White, Saunders, Purnell / Pounder/Yates.*

46 Wolverhampton — Knight, Russell, Daniel, Aspinall, Butters*, Hogg, Wigley, Kuhl, Whittingham, Clarke, Beresford / Murray/Anderton. *Bartram, Bennett, Thompson, Hindmarch*, Clarke, Downing, Birch, Cook, Paskin^, Mutch, Burke / Dennison/Taylor.*

Match reports

35. Barton has the job he always wanted until the end of the season and Pompey's luck seems to have turned. Trailing to Brown's penalty after Awford hacked down Hodges, Kuhl runs onto Hogg's through ball to clip home, despite Whittingham running back from an offside position.

36. Thirty tons of sand make the surface just about playable. By half-time Pompey wished they hadn't bothered. Saville's speculative 30-yarder slips under Gosney, then Rimmer profits as Archdeacon's effort is deflected. Hogg is sent off for dissent and it's damage limitation after that.

37. The drop is a real threat now, as John Hollins in the stand, fuelling manager speculation. Gosney is dropped, but Brock's dipping shot still divides the sides. Incessant second-half pressure deserved reward, but Whits goes close twice and two good penalty shouts are waved away.

38. A run of one goal in six ends with Daniel setting up Clarke on half-time. Boss Jimmy Lumsden's unlikely bid for City's second successive promotion is derailed by Whit's first in eight and Clarke's first hat-trick for the club, sealed from the spot after May pulled down Wigley.

39. Knight denies Goddard a last-gasp sixth goal in nine, after Maguire's poor pass, to keep a precious point intact. Kuhl's penalty, after Beresford is tapped by Stockwell, cancels out Russell's chop on Kiwomya. Kuhl's free-kick had earlier left Forrest standing, but Jason Dozzell levelled.

40. The form-book is turned upside down, as Wembley-bound Owls' promotion hopes are blunted. Whit's soft shot somehow eludes Turner, then Carlton Palmer cuts down Wigley and Kuhl thumps home the spot-kick. Palmer sees red for his protests and will miss the League Cup final.

41. Barton moves into pole position, as Pompey take a giant step towards safety and condemn Hull. A bobbly pitch and tricky breeze suggests a stalemate, until Russell starts and finishes a slick move from the edge of the box. Whits is fouled by Buckley and the linesman flags a penalty.

42. Pompey have £1 million towards the play-offs, but Barry Lloyd's boys are out-played here. Murray nicks the ball off Beresford for a new Milton End. Albion are incredibly in line for the play-offs, but it now hinges on (doomed) plans for a new Milton End. Murray nicks the ball off Beresford just to score.

43. All runs must end and Pompey's record at Leicester makes this no surprise. Their only win here was in 1929. Old-boy Kevin 'Rooster' Russell clinches it after cutting out Kuhl's pass, and, when he is subbed, City boss Gordon Lee is booed. Wigley makes Foxes sweat for the points.

44. Hornets' late sting gives Steve Perryman's team a sixth win in nine; they sense safety. Pompey still need a win. Wilkinson hit the woodwork in the first half, but he crosses for Falconer to soar. The programme confirms what many had suspected; the Fratton End rebuild is being delayed.

45. Spurred by Beresford's strike after Alexander slips, Pompey save themselves. Saunders' volley sends a frisson of anxiety round the terraces, but Wigley eases the tension after an exchange with Clarke. Whits stabs his 20th of the season and Knight makes his 400th league appearance.

46. This sorry display in the sun ends Barton's hopes of getting the Pompey job, but he doesn't suspect it yet, having sipped champagne last week with Jim Gregory. A win would have kept them out of the Rumbelows Cup first round, but it's never on once Whits misses two early sitters.

BARCLAYS DIVISION 2 (CUP-TIES) Manager: Burrows ⇨ Tony Barton SEASON 1990-91

Rumbelows Cup

					F-A			H-T	Scorers, Times, and Referees	1	2	3	4	5	6	7	8	9	10	11	subs used
2:1	A	CARDIFF	25/9	19	D	1-1	4,224 4:11	1-0	Aspinall 12 Griffith 55 Ref: G Ashby (Worcester)	Gosney	Neill	Beresford	Kuhl	Black	Maguire	Wigley	Stevens	Clarke	Aspinall	Kelly*	Murray
										Hansbury	*Rodgerson*	*Daniel*	*Barnard*	*Matthews*	*Perry*	*Jones*	*Griffith*	*Gibbins*	*Pike*	*Heard**	*Black*

Pompey lost 0-1 at Cardiff in pre-season, but there's no chance of a shock once Aspinall dives to nod in Wigley's centre. He sees another ruled out, then Hansbury's reflexes deny Clarke. Daniel – who will join Pompey soon – creates Griffiths' leveller, shortly after Pike hit a post.

					F-A			H-T	Scorers, Times, and Referees	1	2	3	4	5	6	7	8	9	10	11	subs used
2:2	H	CARDIFF	9/10	20	W	3-1 aet	6,174 4:6	1-0	Clarke 39, 99, Neill 119 Griffith 50 Ref: L Shapter (Torquay) (Pompey won 4-2 on aggregate)	Gosney	Neill	Beresford	Kuhl*	Black	Maguire	Wigley	Stevens	Clarke	Aspinall	Powell^	Awford/Anderton
										Hansbury	*Lewis*	*Daniel*	*Barnard*	*Matthews*	*Perry*	*Jones**	*Griffith*	*Gibbins*	*Blake^*	*Heard*	*Chandler/Morgan*

Len Ashurst's side battle gamely, but it is only veteran Hansbury's brilliance that ensures extra-time. Clarke opened via the post, but Griffiths' close-range effort after Blake's pull-back is against the run of play. Clarke is unmarked to slot in, and Neill's 25-yarder seals a deserved win.

					F-A			H-T	Scorers, Times, and Referees	1	2	3	4	5	6	7	8	9	10	11	subs used
3	A	CHELSEA	31/10	10	D	0-0	16,699 1:15	0-0	Ref: T Holbrook (Walsall)	Gosney	Neill	Beresford	Kuhl	Butters	Maguire	Wigley*	Stevens	Clarke	Aspinall	Black	Whittingham
										Beasant	*Hall*	*Dorigo*	*Townsend*	*Monkou*	*Lee*	*McAllister**	*Nicholas^*	*Wilson*	*Durie*	*Wise*	*Le Saux/Bumstead*

Bobby Campbell's Chelsea haven't lost at home since February. That record is never threatened, but Pompey deserve a second crack at the first division side. Late on Durie goes close, seizing on Aspinall's careless back-pass and clipping over Gosney, but Stevens clears off the line.

					F-A			H-T	Scorers, Times, and Referees	1	2	3	4	5	6	7	8	9	10	11	subs used
3R	H	CHELSEA	6/11	13	L	2-3	16,085 1:11	1-0	Chamberlain 25, Whittingham 47 Lee 81, Wise 84p, Wilson 90 Ref: A Seville (Birmingham)	Gosney	Neill	Beresford	Kuhl	Butters	Maguire	Chamberlain^	Stevens	Clarke	Aspinall*	Whittingham	Black/Wigley
										Hitchcock	*Hall*	*Dorigo*	*Townsend*	*Candy*	*Lee*	*Wise*	*Bumstead*	*Wilson*	*Durie*	*Le Saux**	*Dixon*

For 70 minutes Pompey are superb and Whittingham's overhead kick seems to have made a trip to Oxford in round four a formality. Lee stabs in, then Aspinall looks to be fouled before Butters tumbles Townsend and Wise converts. Wilson bundles past Stevens to break Pompey hearts.

FA Cup

					F-A			H-T	Scorers, Times, and Referees	1	2	3	4	5	6	7	8	9	10	11	subs used
3	A	BARNET	5/1	21	W	5-0	6,209 VC	2-0	Aspinall 17, Whittingham 31, 51, 81, [Clarke 89] Ref: P Durkin (Portland)	Gosney	Neill	Beresford	Aspinall	Hogg	Stevens	Wigley	Kuhl	Clarke	Whittingham	Chamberlain*	Russell
										Phillips	*Poole*	*Cooper^*	*Badley*	*Wilson*	*Richardson**	*Turner*	*Clarke*	*Bull*	*Willis*	*Durham*	*Stein/Hayrettin*

BBC TV's Match of the Day decides this is the potential shock of the round, but once Aspinall draws Bees' early sting with a 20-yard clip, Whittingham goes on to swat the pesky non-leaguers. The Hawthorns is where you should have been Motty, where Woking beat Baggies 4-2!

					F-A			H-T	Scorers, Times, and Referees	1	2	3	4	5	6	7	8	9	10	11	subs used
4	H	BOURNEMOUTH	26/1	22	W	5-1	15,800 3:10	1-0	Clarke 45, Whittingham 56, 70, 75, 85 Fereday 73 Ref: D Elleray (Harrow)	Gosney	Neill	Beresford	Aspinall*	Hogg	Stevens	Wigley	Kuhl	Clarke	Whittingham	Chamberlain	Murray
										Peyton	*Bond^*	*Morrell*	*Teale*	*Watson*	*O'Driscoll*	*Holmes*	*Pulis*	*Jones**	*Lawrence*	*Blissett*	*Ekoku/Fereday*

Harry Redknapp reckons his Cherries should have picked up a pen when Beresford seemed to handle at 1-0, but in truth his side an FA Cup matches. Clarke's cross-shot starts the rout, then Whittingham takes over. He now has eleven goals in six games and seven in two FA Cup matches!

					F-A			H-T	Scorers, Times, and Referees	1	2	3	4	5	6	7	8	9	10	11	subs used
5	H	TOTTENHAM	16/2	22	L	1-2	26,049 1:6	1-0	Chamberlain 41 Gascoigne 60, 84 Ref: T Holbrook (Walsall)	Gosney	Neill	Beresford	Aspinall*	Hogg	Russell	Wigley	Kuhl	Clarke	Whittingham	Chamberlain^	Murray/Anderton
										Thorstvedt	*Edinburgh*	*V d Hauwe*	*Sedgley*	*Nayim*	*Mabbutt*	*Samways**	*Gascoigne*	*Thomas*	*Lineker*	*Allen*	*Gray*

Gazza lives up to the hype, single-handedly taking Spurs through. For the winner the shimmies past a tackle before rolling home. Ex-England star Chambo's cross-shot had Terry Venables' side reeling. Future Fratton boss Fenwick hurts an ankle in the warm-up and Edinburgh wears 2.

		P	Home					Away					Pts
			W	D	L	F	A	W	D	L	F	A	
1	Oldham	46	17	5	1	55	21	8	8	7	28	32	88
2	West Ham	46	15	6	2	41	18	9	9	5	19	16	87
3	Sheffield Wed	46	12	10	1	43	23	10	6	7	37	28	82
4	Notts Co*	46	14	4	5	45	28	9	7	7	31	27	80
5	Millwall	46	11	6	6	43	28	9	7	7	27	23	73
6	Brighton	46	12	4	7	37	31	9	3	11	26	38	70
7	Middlesbro	46	12	4	7	36	17	8	5	10	30	30	69
8	Barnsley	46	13	7	3	39	16	7	3	12	24	32	69
9	Bristol City	46	14	5	4	44	28	6	2	15	24	43	67
10	Oxford	46	10	9	4	41	29	4	10	9	28	37	61
11	Newcastle	46	8	10	5	24	22	6	7	10	25	34	59
12	Wolves	46	11	6	6	45	35	4	6	13	18	28	58
13	Bristol Rov	46	11	7	5	29	20	4	6	13	27	39	58
14	Ipswich	46	9	8	6	32	28	4	10	9	28	40	57
15	Port Vale	46	10	4	9	32	24	5	8	10	24	40	57
16	Charlton	46	8	7	8	27	25	5	10	8	30	36	56
17	PORTSMOUTH	46	10	6	7	34	27	4	5	14	24	43	53
18	Plymouth	46	10	10	3	36	20	2	7	14	18	48	53
19	Blackburn	46	10	10	3	26	27	6	4	13	25	39	52
20	Watford	46	5	8	10	24	32	7	7	9	21	27	51
21	Swindon	46	8	6	9	31	30	4	8	11	34	43	50
22	Leicester	46	12	4	7	41	33	2	4	17	19	50	50
23	West Brom	46	7	11	5	26	21	3	7	13	26	40	48
24	Hull	46	6	10	7	35	32	4	5	14	22	53	45
		1104	253	163	136	866	615	136	163	253	615	866	1493

* promoted
after play-offs

Odds & ends

Double wins: (2) Bristol Rov, Hull.

Double losses: (4) Oldham, Port Vale, Newcastle, Charlton.

Won from behind: (2) Plymouth (h), Swindon (h).

Lost from in front: (2) Brighton (a), Port Vale (a).

High spots: Reaching the FA Cup fifth round with five-goal shows against Barnet and Bournemouth in rounds three and four.

A 2-0 home win over eventually-promoted Sheffield Wednesday.

A run of four wins and a draw in March and April to avoid relegation.

Beating Bristol City 4-1 on Easter Saturday.

Low spots: Failing to win any of the opening six league games.

A ten-match winless run from November to January.

Conceding three goals in four minutes just before half-time at Brighton in September to seal a 2-3 defeat.

Losing 1-4 at Bristol City on Boxing Day.

A 0-4 defeat at Barnsley in March.

In January 1991 Pompey scored 18 goals in five league and cup matches — their most prolific month in the 1970-1999 period.

Player of the Year: Martin Kuhl.

Ever presents: (0).

Hat-tricks: (3) Colin Clarke (1), Guy Whittingham (2).

Leading scorer: Guy Whittingham (20).

Appearances / Goals

Player	Appearances						Goals			
	Lge	Sub	LC	Sub	FAC	Sub	Lge	LC	FAC	Tot
Anderton, Darren	13	7	1	1	1	1				
Aspinall, Warren	32	1	3		3			1	1	2
Awford, Andy	8	6								
Beresford, John	39	3	4		3		1			1
Black, Kenny	14	7	3	1	3		2			2
Butters, Guy	23	3	3				1			1
Chamberlain, Mark	22	3	1		3		2	1	1	4
Clarke, Colin	38	4	4		3		13	2	2	17
Dale, Shaun	2	1								
Daniel, Ray	13	1								
Fillery, Mick	3									
Gosney, Andy	24		4		3		4			4
Hogg, Graeme	20		4		3		1			1
Kelly, Mark	2	3	1				1			1
Knight, Alan	22									
Kuhl, Martin	41		4		3		13			13
Maguire, Gavin	22	1	4							
Murray, Shaun	17	8	1	2						
Neill, Warren	30		4		3			1		1
Powell, Darryl		8	1							
Russell, Lee	16	3			1	1	1			1
Stevens, Gary	31		4		2		2			2
Symons, Kit	1									
Whittingham, Guy	34	3	1	1	3		12	1	7	20
Wigley, Steve	39	2	3	1	3		5			5
(own-goals)							1			1
25 players used	506	61	44	5	33	4	59	6	11	76

BARCLAYS LEAGUE DIVISION 1 — Manager: Jim Smith — SEASON 1991-92

Match summary

No	Date	Team	Att	Pos	Res	Pt	F-A	H-T	Scorers, Times, and Referees
1	17/8	A BLACKBURN	11,118	1	D	1	1-1	0-0	Anderton 49 / Moran 90; Ref: M Reed (Birmingham)
2	24/8	H PORT VALE	8,083	10 / 14	W	4	1-0	1-0	Clarke 29; Ref: I Hemley (Ampthill)
3	31/8	A MIDDLESBROUGH	12,320	16 / 3	L	4	0-2	0-0	Falconer 70, Slaven 90; Ref: J Worrall (Warrington)
4	3/9	H SUNDERLAND	9,621	11 / 10	W	7	1-0	0-0	Burns 68; Ref: A Buksh (London)
5	7/9	H BRIGHTON	10,567	13 / 14	D	8	0-0	0-0	Ref: G Ashby (Worcester)
6	14/9	A CHARLTON	5,707	17 / 7	L	8	0-3	0-2	Nelson 29, Lee 43, 86; Ref: A Smith (Rubery)
7	17/9	A GRIMSBY	5,348	16 / 11	D	9	1-1	0-1	Wigley 78 / Woods 39; Ref: J Rushton (Stoke)
8	21/9	H CAMBRIDGE	7,801	12 / 4	W	12	3-0	2-0	Wigley 12, Burns 27, Kimble 53 (og); Ref: R Milford (Bristol)
9	28/9	A BRISTOL CITY	9,830	7 / 14	W	15	2-0	2-0	Beresford 34, 43p; Ref: D Elleray (Harrow)
10	5/10	H NEWCASTLE	10,175	5 / 24	W	18	3-1	2-0	Beresford 20p, Stimson 40 (og), Clarke 55 / Quinn 68; Ref: L Shapter (Torquay)
11	12/10	A BARNSLEY	6,579	9 / 19	L	18	0-2	0-1	Taggart 16, Graham 88; Ref: N Midgley (Bolton)

Line-ups (Portsmouth in bold above each opposition)

No	Team	1	2	3	4	5	6	7	8	9	10	11	subs used
1	Portsmouth	Knight	Awford	Beresford	**Burns**	Symons	Butters	Anderton	Kuhl	Clarke	Whittingham*	Powell^	Chamberlain/Russell
1	Blackburn	Mimms	Atkins	Sulley	Agnew	Moran	Dobson	Irvine	Richardson*	Livingstone^	Speedie	Sellars	Garner/Gayle
2	Portsmouth	Knight	Awford	Beresford	**Burns**	Symons	Butters	Anderton	Kuhl	Clarke	Doling*	Powell	Chamberlain
2	Port Vale	Grew	Mills S	Hughes	Walker	Aspin	Glover	Jalink	Van der Laan	Houchen*	Foyle	Kent^	Mills B/Swan
3	Portsmouth	Knight	Awford	Beresford	Burns	Symons	Butters	Anderton	Kuhl	Clarke	Chamberlain*	Powell	Russell*/Aspinall
3	Middlesbrough	Pears	Parkinson	Phillips	Mowbray	Kernaghan	Falconer	Mustoe*	Proctor	Wilkinson	Ripley	Hendrie	Slaven
4	Portsmouth	Knight	Awford	Beresford	Burns	Symons	Butters	Anderton	Kuhl	Clarke	Whittingham	Powell	Pascoe
4	Sunderland	Norman	Kay	Hardyman	Bennett	Ball	Owers	Bracewell	Atkinson	Armstrong	Gabbiadini	Hauser*	
5	Portsmouth	Knight	Awford	Beresford*	Burns	Symons	Butters^	Anderton	Kuhl	Clarke	Whittingham	Powell	Wigley/Doling
5	Brighton	Beeney	Crumplin	Chapman	Wilkins	Chivers	O'Reilly	Barham	Byrne	Meade	Codner	Robinson	
6	Portsmouth	Knight	Awford	Beresford*	Burns	Symons	Russell	Anderton	Kuhl	Clarke	Whittingham*	Powell	Aspinall/Doling
6	Charlton	Bolder	Pitcher	Minto*	Peake	Webster	Gatting	Lee	Bacon	Leaburn	Nelson	Walsh^	Gritt/Dyer
7	Portsmouth	Knight	Awford	Beresford	Doling*	Symons	Russell	Anderton	Kuhl	Clarke	Whittingham*	Murray	Wigley/Burns
7	Grimsby	Sherwood	McDermott	Jobling	Futcher	Lever	Dobbin	Childs^	Gilbert	Jones	Agnew	Woods	Smith
8	Portsmouth	Knight	Awford	Russell	Burns	Symons	Butters	Neill	Kuhl	Clarke	Whittingham	Wigley	Powell
8	Cambridge	Vaughan	Fensome	Kimble	Bailie	Clayton*	Chapple	Cheetham	Wilkins	Claridge	Taylor	Philpott*	Dennis/Dublin
9	Portsmouth	Knight	Awford	Beresford	Burns	Symons	Butters	Neill	Chamberlain	Clarke*	Whittingham	Anderton	Powell
9	Bristol City	Welch	Llewellyn	Scott	May	Bryant	Caesar*	Shelton^	Rennie	Allison	Morgan	Smith	Connor/Edwards
10	Portsmouth	Knight	Awford	Beresford	Burns	Symons	Butters	Neill	Chamberlain*	Clarke^	Whittingham	Anderton	Powell/Hebberd
10	Newcastle	Srnicek	Neilson	Stimson	O'Brien	Scott	Bradshaw	Clarke	Peacock	Quinn	Hunt*	Roche^	Carr/Appelby
11	Portsmouth	Knight	Awford	Beresford	Burns	Symons	Butters	Neill	Kuhl !	Clarke	Hebberd*	Anderton^	Whittingham/Doling
11	Barnsley	Butler	Robinson	Archdeacon*	Saville	Taggart	Taggart	O'Connell	Refearn	Pearson	Graham	Rammell	Fleming/Bishop

Match reports

1. Blackburn — New boss Jim Smith gambles with youth and it so nearly pays. Anderton's touch-line curler embarrasses Mimms, but with seconds left Moran scores after a scramble, to save Jack Walkers's cheque-book Rovers. Hogg will move to Hearts next week and Maguire and Aspinall want out.

2. Port Vale — Doling (18) is the next of the Bald Eagle's brood to get his chance. He is put clean away and crosses for Clarke to steady himself and take aim inside Grew's near post. Ex-brickie Burns, signed from Cheltenham (£25,000) last spring, impresses in midfield, as Vale pile on the pressure.

3. Middlesbrough — Pompey ride their luck – Wilkinson's shot somehow sticks between Knight's legs – and the keeper spreads himself twice more to deny Hendrie and Mustoe. Bernie Slaven finally undoes them, crossing for Falconer to head home, then he flicks in a delicate header at the death.

4. Sunderland — Burns' life has been transformed – no more 6.30 am starts – and he enhances his reputation with a sweetly-struck shot after Clarke set him up. Denis Smith's side fade badly, and it takes two flying one-handed saves from Norman to deny Whittingham. Wigley and Black also want away.

5. Brighton — 'Veteran' Knight – he is only 30 though – shows his experience as play-off losers Albion dominate. Ex-Gunner Meade has a diving header stopped, then Chivers, O'Reilly and Barham are all frustrated. Seagulls' red shirts have a white splodge design which looks just like seagull...

6. Charlton — Pompey had won 21 of their 36 visits to Charlton, but their new 'home', Upton Park, clearly inspires them. Nelson had already hit the bar before drilling home, then Robert Lee nets his 50th goal. A mooted move to North Harbour has the backing of fans. Black has gone to Airdrie.

7. Grimsby — Want-away Wigley turns the game. Alan Buckley's Mariners are leading after Woods nips between Awford and Anderton to score, but Wigley sets up Aspinall, then volleys home when the shot is blocked. Whits is off form, but Wimbledon bid £1m for him in the summer, it is revealed.

8. Cambridge — Ironically, Us boss John Beck would, no doubt, have approved of Knight's 'Route-one' hoof, Clarke's flick and Wigley's angled finish, but Pompey destroy Cambridge with football. Wigley provides for Burns at the far post, then Kuhl crosses and Kimble's interception rockets in.

9. Bristol City — Beresford opens with a crisp 18-yard shot from Clarke's knock-down, at a damp Ashton Gate, then he converts a disputed penalty – Kuhl is out injured – when Clarke sprawls under Caesar's challenge. Jimmy Lumsden's team includes Nicky Morgan and second-half sub Connor.

10. Newcastle — Symons cleaned Quinn's boots as an apprentice, now he all but blots him out. Quinn does score, but crocks himself at the same time. Chambo is nudged by Neilson for the pen, then Bradshaw dismissed for a pro foul. Stimson diverts Burns' shot, to seal a disaster half for Ardiles' men.

11. Barnsley — Fergie is spying, ahead of the Man U cup-tie, but won't be worried. Archdeacon's corner is glanced in by Gerry Taggart, then Bishop crosses for Graham's head to settle it. Kuhl is sent off for something he said, but he will be available for Old Trafford. On Ioan Hebberd (Derby) starts.

Portsmouth match-by-match log (matches 12–23)

No	V	Opponent	Date	Att	Pos	—	Res	Pts	FT	HT	Scorers (Pompey; Opposition)	Referee
12	A	DERBY	19/10	13,190	12	6	L	18	0-2	0-0	McMinn 62, Williams P 89	T Fitzharris (Bolton)
13	H	IPSWICH	26/10	8,007	12	5	D	19	1-1	1-1	Burns 43; Milton 18	P Durkin (Portland)
14	A	MILLWALL	2/11	6,060	11	13	D	20	1-1	0-1	Anderton 75; Armstrong 27	M James (Horsham)
15	H	LEICESTER	5/11	7,147	11	6	W	23	1-0	1-0	Whittingham 5	P Foakes (Clacton-on-Sea)
16	H	OXFORD	9/11	7,557	11	23	W	26	2-1	1-0	Butters 30, 63; Magilton 76	G Willard (Worthing)
17	A	SWINDON	16/11	10,738	6	4	W	29	3-2	0-0	Whittingham 57, Anderton 85, Powell 90; White 58, 63	A Gunn (South Chailey)
18	A	WATFORD	23/11	8,135	9	17	L	29	1-2	0-1	Doling 83; Blissett 25, 46	R Gifford (Llanbradach)
19	H	WOLVERHAMPTON	30/11	11,101	10	20	W	32	1-0	1-0	Burns 13	R Wiseman (Borehamwood)
20	H	SOUTHEND	14/12	9,006	10	5	D	33	1-1	1-1	Anderton 25; Scully 17	P Don (Hanworth Park)
21	A	SUNDERLAND	21/12	14,432	10	13	L	33	0-1	0-1	Awford 44 (og)	T Lunt (Ashton-in-Makerfield)
22	H	BRISTOL ROV	26/12	10,710	8	19	W	36	2-0	1-0	Cross 25 (og), Burns 80	A Ward (London)
23	H	MIDDLESBROUGH	28/12	12,324	7	4	W	39	4-0	3-0	Whittingham 9, Powell 34, Beresford 39p, [Kuhl 68]; Pears	R Milford (Bristol)

Match 12 — DERBY (A)
Pompey: Knight, Awford*, Beresford, Burns^, Symons, Butters, Neill, Kuhl, Whittingham, Chamberlain, Anderton. Subs: Aspinall/Hebberd.
Derby: Shilton, Sage, Forsyth, Williams G, Coleman, Comyn, Micklewhite, Ormondroyd, Gee, Williams P, McMinn.
Pompey had five men on international duty in the week, but back in the real world Derby have too much know-how. McMinn nabs a soft goal when Knight flaps under pressure from Ormondroyd, then Paul Williams buries a fierce cross-shot near the end. Shilton denies Whittingham.

Match 13 — IPSWICH (H)
Pompey: Knight, Awford, Beresford, Burns, Symons, Butters, Neill, Chamberlain^, Whittingham, Chamberlain*, Anderton. Subs: Aspinall/Hebberd.
Ipswich: Forrest, Yallop, Thompson*, Stackwell, Wark, Linighan, Lowe^, Zondervan, Whitton, Dozzell, Milton. Subs: Johnson/Moncur.
Whittingham has still to score this season, but how Canadian keeper Forrest kept out his three-yard thunderbolt remains a mystery. Awford's error had let Milton beat Knight's despairing dive, but Burns fires in from ten yards as Butters' shot against the bar falls perfectly for him.

Match 14 — MILLWALL (A)
Pompey: Knight, Awford, Beresford*, Burns, Symons, Butters, Neill, Kuhl, Whittingham, Chamberlain, Anderton. Subs: Chamberlain/Ross.
Millwall: Branagan, Stephenson, Cooper, Armstrong, Thompson, McLeary, Kerr, Colquhoun, Falco*, Rae, Barber. Subs: Goodman.
Lions are run ragged in the second half and Anderton's tap in, after Chamberlain nicks the ball into Branagan, is scant reward. Millwall led when Armstrong steered home a header, but after that it was one-way traffic. Returning Aspinall misses from 12 yards two minutes from time.

Match 15 — LEICESTER (H)
Pompey: Knight, Awford, Russell, Burns, Symons, Butters, Neill, Kuhl, Whittingham, Chamberlain, Anderton. Subs: Ross*/Clarke.
Leicester: Poole, Mills, Gibson*, Smith, Walsh, Fitzpatrick^, Oldfield, Thompson, Wright, Kitson, Gordon. Subs: Coatsworth/Mauchlen.
The corporal is dishing out punishment again. He buries a fierce shot, after Anderton – who must have impressed watching England assistant Lawrie McMenemy – clips the ball into the box. Young Ross is tossed on for the injured Aspinall, but looks to be short of the finished article.

Match 16 — OXFORD (H)
Pompey: Knight, Awford, Russell, Burns, Symons, Butters, Neill, Kuhl, Whittingham, Chamberlain, Anderton*. Subs: Doling/Ross.
Oxford: Keeley, Robinson, Smart, Lewis, Foster, Melville, Magilton, McClaren^, Aylott, Nogan, Simpson. Subs: Durnin.
Guy's in the goals once more, but this time Pompey earn their bread by Butters. His first for the club is a far-post header from Burns' cross, then Kuhl finds him unmarked and he repeats the feat. Brian Horton's side felt they should have had a pen before Magilton's super 20-yarder.

Match 17 — SWINDON (A)
Pompey: Gosney, Awford, Russell*, Burns, Symons, Butters, Neill, Kuhl, Whittingham, Chamberlain, Anderton. Subs: Doling/Powell.
Swindon: Hammond, Kerslake, Summerbee, Jones, Calderwood, Viveash, Hazard, Shearer, Simpson, McClaren, White.
Smith is becoming anxious at the ever-increasing gaggle of scouts at Pompey games, and two of his starlets turn this game around. Whit's shot squirts across goal and Anderton rifles in, then Powell – 20 yesterday – flings himself full-length to nudge his first goal, from Kuhl's corner.

Match 18 — WATFORD (A)
Pompey: Knight, Awford, Beresford, Burns, Symons, Butters, Neill*, Kuhl, Powell, Chamberlain, Anderton. Subs: Doling/Clarke.
Watford: James, Soloman, Drysdale, Dublin, Holdsworth, Ashby, Hessenthaler, Bazeley*, Porter^, Thomas, Nicholas. Subs: Butler/Thomas.
The Board are at a loss to explain low gates, despite being unbeaten at Fratton Park. Shoddy shows like this don't help, but Blissett's second is furiously disputed for offside. £1.5m-rated David James blunders when his throw is intercepted by Whittingham and Doling nets the rebound.

Match 19 — WOLVERHAMPTON (H)
Pompey: Knight, Awford, Beresford, Burns, Symons, Butters, Neill, Kuhl, Whittingham, Chamberlain, Anderton. Subs: Powell.
Wolves: Stowell, Ashley, Venus, Bennett*, Madden, Dennison, Birch, Cook, McLaughlin, Mutch, Mountfield^. Subs: Steele/Thompson.
Wolves were unbeaten in their last ten visits to Fratton, but that all changes when Wigley races away. His shot is blocked by Stowell, but Burns is on hand to steer home. Graham Turner's strugglers are largely toothless. Gosney is back in the reserves after a loan spell at York.

Match 20 — SOUTHEND (H)
Pompey: Knight, Awford, Beresford, Burns, Symons, Butters, Neill, Kuhl, Whittingham, Chamberlain, Anderton. Subs: Clarke/Chamberlain.
Southend: Sansome, Austin, Powell, Jones, Scully, Prior, Ansah, Cornwall, Tilson, Benjamin, Angell. Subs: Benjamin.
Pompey's last game saw them lose 1-2 behind closed doors at Fulham last week, and that lethargy is still there. Dave Webb's side are worth more than their first-ever point at Fratton. Scully's lunging header is his first league goal here too, but Anderton soon levels from close range.

Match 21 — SUNDERLAND (A)
Pompey: Knight, Awford, Beresford, Burns^, Symons, Butters, Neill, Kuhl, Whittingham*, Chamberlain, Anderton. Subs: Wigley/Chamberlain.
Sunderland: Norman, Kay, Rogan, Bennett, Ball, Owers, Bracewell, Goodman, Pascoe, Rush*, Hardyman. Subs: Hauser.
April is the council deadline for Pompey's site search, now the club wonder if Fratton Park is here to hemmed in. Awford also has nowhere to go, so his head gets in the way of Pascoe's hopeful flick to condemn his side. Former Fratton target Anton Rogan clears Anderton's late shot.

Match 22 — BRISTOL ROV (H)
Pompey: Knight, Awford, Beresford, Burns, Symons, Butters, Neill, Kuhl, Whittingham*, Chamberlain^, Anderton. Subs: Wigley/Powell.
Bristol Rov: Parkin, Alexander, Twentyman, Yates, Cross, Skinner, Mehew*, Reece, White, Saunders, Pounder*. Subs: Boothroyd/Stewart.
Kuhl takes 16 corners during this match, to show how much Dennis Rofe's Rovers were under the cosh. From one of them, Whittingham's overhead kick hits Parkin and bounces in off Cross. Burns ensures the points when Chamberlain sends him clear and his shot nutmegs Parkin.

Match 23 — MIDDLESBROUGH (H)
Pompey: Knight, Awford, Beresford, Burns, Symons, Powell, Neill, Kuhl, Whittingham*, Chamberlain^, Anderton. Subs: Aspinall/Daniel.
Middlesbrough: Pears, Fleming*, Phillips, Kernaghan, Mohan, Mustoe, Slaven, Payton, Wilkinson, Pollock^, Peake. Subs: Proctor/Parkinson.
Lennie Lawrence's table-toppers aren't just beaten, they are humiliated. Whittingham poaches the first, swivelling to fire home Anderton's nod down, then Powell converts the second. Pears fouls Anderton for the penalty, then Beresford converts, but Kuhl's is a classic; Chamberlain sets him up 30 yards out.

BARCLAYS LEAGUE DIVISION 1 — Manager: Jim Smith — SEASON 1991-92

No	Date		Att	Pos	Pt	F-A	H-T	Scorers, Times, and Referees	1	2	3	4	5	6	7	8	9	10	11	subs used
24	A 1/1	PLYMOUTH	8,887	9	39	2-3	1-2	Powell 13, Chamberlain 81	Knight	Awford	Beresford	Burns*	Symons	Butters	Neill	Kuhl	Powell	Chamberlain	Anderton*	Aspinall/Wigley
								Turner 7, Morrison 11, Marshall 73 / Ref: G Singh (Wolverhampton)	Wilmot	Spearing	Salmon	Marker	Morrison	Morgan	Barlow	Marshall	Regis	Fiore*	Turner	Edworthy
25	A 11/1	PORT VALE	5,925	17	42	2-0	2-0	Powell 15, Anderton 18	Grew	Awford	Beresford	Powell	Symons	Butters	Neill	Kuhl	Whittingham^	Chamberlain^	Anderton^	Burns/Wigley
								Ref: J Worrall (Warrington)	Mills S	Hughes	Webb*	Aspin	Glover	Swan	Van der Laan	Houchen	Foyle	Mills B*		Porter/Jalink
26	H 18/1	BLACKBURN	20,106	1	43	2-2	0-1	Beresford 79, Whittingham 90	Knight	Mimms	Beresford	Powell	Symons	Butters	Neill	Kuhl	Burns*	Chamberlain^	Anderton	Whittingham/Wigley
								Speedie 27, 56 / Ref: P Durkin (Portland)	Brown	Wright*	Hill	Moran	Cowans	Reid	Sellars	Wilcox	Speedie^	Newell		Hendry/Skinner
27	A 29/1	BRISTOL ROV	5,330	18	43	0-1	0-1	White 20	Knight	Parkin	Beresford	Powell	Symons	Butters*	Neill^	Kuhl	Burns	Whittingham	Anderton	Hendon/Wigley
								Ref: C Wilkes (Gloucester)	Alexander	Moore	Yates	Clark	Skinner*	Mehew	Reece	White^	Saunders	Pounder		Cross/Stewart
28	H 1/2	DERBY	12,008	11	43	0-1	0-0	Gabbiadini 59	Knight	Shilton	Beresford	Powell	Symons	Butters	Neill	Kuhl	Wigley*	Burns^	Anderton	Hendon/Whittingham
								Ref: M Bodenham (Looe)		Kavanagh	Forsyth	Williams G	Coleman	Comyn	Chalk	Ormondroyd	Gabbiadini	Williams P	McMinn	
29	H 4/2	PLYMOUTH	10,467	19	46	4-1	2-0	Powell 24, Whittingham 41, 74, Regis 86 [Marker 67 (og)]	Knight	Wilmot	Beresford	Powell	Symons	Butters	Neill	Kuhl	Whittingham	Burns*	Anderton	Garner
								Ref: K Morton (Bury St Edmunds)	Marker	Spearing	Clement*	Edworthy	Wark	Morgan	Witter	Marshall	Salman	Turner		
30	A 8/2	IPSWICH	13,494	2	46	2-5	1-3	Anderton 10, Powell 53 [Awford 62 (og)]	Knight	Forrest	Beresford	Powell*	Symons	Butters*	Neill^	Kuhl	Whittingham	Burns	Anderton	Clarke/Hendon
								Dozzell 6, 18, Kiwomya 9, 51 / Ref: V Callow (Solihull)	Johnson	Thompson	Stockwell	Wark	Linighan	Milton	Palmer	Dozzell	Kiwomya			
31	A 22/2	WOLVERHAMPTON	15,770	11	47	0-0	0-0		Knight	Stowell	Beresford	Powell^	Symons	Butters	Neill^	Kuhl	Whittingham*	McLoughlin	Anderton	Clarke/Burns
								Ref: G Poll (Berkhamsted)	Ashley*	Venus	Bennett	Mountfield	Rankine	Birch	Cook	Bull	Burke*	Thompson		Dennison/Mutch
32	H 29/2	TRANMERE	16,644	16	50	2-0	2-0	Burns 6, McLoughlin 11	Knight	Nixon	Beresford	Powell*	Symons	Butters	Neill	Kuhl	Clarke	McLoughlin	Anderton	Whittingham/Aspinall
								Ref: R Groves (Weston-super-Mare)	Higgins	Nolan	Irons	Hughes*	Vickers	Mungall	Aldridge	Malkin^	Harvey	Thomas		Branch/Muir
33	A 11/3	LEICESTER	14,207	8	51	2-2	1-0	Burns 29, Clarke 86	Knight	Poole	Beresford	Powell*	Symons	Burns	Butters*	Kuhl	Clarke	McLoughlin	Anderton	Whittingham/Aspinall
								Mills 76, Russell 78 / Ref: M Reed (Birmingham)	Mills	Platnauer	Smith	Walsh	Mauchlen	Thompson	Russell	Wright	Ormondroyd	Gee		Allen/Barber
34	H 14/3	MILLWALL	14,944	15	54	6-1	3-0	Kuhl 3, Whit'm 6, 44, 55, McLoughlin 52, Verveer 85 [Burns 70]	Knight	Davison	Beresford	McLoughlin	Symons	Burns	Neill	Kuhl*	Clarke^	Whittingham	Anderton	Wigley/Aspinall
								Ref: K Burge (Tonypandy)	Stevens	Cooper	Bogie^	Thompson	McLeary	Colquhoun	Verveer	Kerr^	McGinlay	Rae		Allen/Barber

Match reports

24 — Pilgrims' boss Dave Kemp – the ex-Fratton favourite – would have admired Marshall's cool finish to put the game beyond Pompey, who only have themselves to blame. Powell's goal is smartly taken, after Kuhl set him up and Chambo nearly bust the net, but early strikes are decisive.

25 — The Board has pledged not to cash in on their young talent while they can still go up. For John Rudge's side it's D-Day – Darryl and Darren that is – who settle it in a devastating burst. Powell heads into the roof of the net after his shot is blocked, then Anderton wrong-foots Grew.

26 — Rovers are now top the table, under new boss Kenny Dalglish. In an assured first-half display, Newell sets up Speedie, who then tightens their grip with a free header. Beresford curls in a free-kick, then Knight's punt is flashed home by sub Whits and the unbeaten home run stays intact.

27 — White stabs in Yates' cross, but Pompey might have already gone ahead, when Anderton shoots a post after two minutes. Wigley frequently reduces Rovers to panic-stations, but a goal will not come. Gregory repeats his 'no sell' pledge, after Anfield boss Souness watches Anderton.

28 — There are no complaints about this result, but £1 million debutant Gabbiadini's winner will haunt Knight. His soft shot creeps under Knight's dive and Shilton has an easy ride in his 955th match. Rams have their kit raided from their hotel, but a replacement set arrives for the kick-off.

29 — Argyle have already beaten Pompey twice this season, but once Neill springs their offside trap and Powell deftly steers in, it's third time lucky for Smith's men. Whits wallops his 50th goal, and guides in his 51st. Powell tries to claim the third goal, but Marker gets the significant touch.

30 — Four goals in the first 18 are shared unevenly in third-placed Town's favour, who show the form that will win the title. Kiwomya and Powell trade close-range goals, then Awford steers the ball into his own net, off a post, to put John Lyall's team second, seven points clear of Pompey.

31 — Eire's McLoughlin ends his Dell hell, signing on loan, with a view to a £400,000 deal. Defences dominate, but Symons scorns the best chance, heading wide from a first-half corner. Aspinall signs a two-year deal at Cherries, then Gregory pulls the plug. He wants £150,000, not £15,000!

32 — Fratton has its own Supermac, after McLoughlin dazzles. His pass sets up Burns from the edge of the box, but his own goal is even better. After jinking past two defenders, he curls a 20-yard left footer over Nixon. Gary Stevens knee injury means he has been forced to retire.

33 — Cup semi-finalists Pompey almost take their eye off the play-off ball, as Mills surges through to score from 18 yards, then Russell pounces when Gee's shot is blocked. Burns' brave header opened, then he nodded against the bar. Whits flicks on and Clarke chests down to finish.

34 — Bruce Rioch will be out of a job on Monday, as the Lions are mauled in Pompey's den. Whittingham starts for the first time in four games and shows he lost none of his poaching skills. Kuhl opened the account with a 25-yarder and Burns' precise finish puts Pompey well in the black.

No	Date	V	Opponent	Att	Pos	—	Pts	Result	Agg	HT
35	17/3	A	SOUTHEND	6,832	5	9	57	W	3-2	2-2
36	21/3	A	OXFORD	8,432	6	22	57	L	1-2	0-0
37	28/3	H	SWINDON	16,007	7	10	58	D	1-1	0-0
38	31/3	H	CHARLTON	14,539	7	4	58	L	1-2	0-0
39	7/4	A	TRANMERE	6,692	8	12	58	L	0-2	0-1
40	11/4	H	GRIMSBY	10,576	8	18	61	W	2-0	1-0
41	17/4	A	CAMBRIDGE	9,497	8	4	62	D	2-2	0-1
42	20/4	H	BRISTOL CITY	17,151	9	17	65	W	1-0	1-0
43	22/4	H	WATFORD	14,417	9	12	66	D	0-0	0-0
44	25/4	A	NEWCASTLE	25,989	9	20	66	L	0-1	0-0
45	29/4	A	BRIGHTON	11,647	9	23	66	L	1-2	0-1
46	2/5	H	BARNSLEY	11,169	9	16	69	W	2-0	0-0

Home 11,745 Away 10,268 Average 11,745

---

35 — SOUTHEND (A) 17/3
Whittingham 9, Clarke 36, Aspinall 84 / Tilson 21, Jones 27
Ref: J Carter (Christchurch)
Team: Knight, Awford, Beresford, McLoughlin, Symons, Burns, Neill, Kuhl, Clarke, Whittingham, Powell*, Aspinall
Subs: Sansome, Austin, Hyslop, Jones, Scully, Prior, Locke*, Cornwell, Tilson, Benjamin, Angell, Butler

Aspinall is relieved his move collapsed. Since then he has spiked Forest's Keane and now he comes on to seal it after Whittingham sets him up. A pulsating first half saw Whit's volley and Clarke's stab bracket two strikes from outside the box. United's promotion hopes are fading.

36 — OXFORD (A) 21/3
Anderton 49 / Beauchamp 69, Aylott 80
Ref: D Frampton (Poole)
Team: Knight, Awford, Butters^, McLoughlin, Symons, Burns, Neill, Kuhl, Clarke, Whittingham*, Anderton, Aspinall/Powell
Subs: Veysey, Smart, Williams, Lewis, Evans, Melville, Magilton, Beauchamp, Aylott, Durnin, Allen*, Bannister

Referee Frampton is under the spotlight. United are furious he lets Clarke's challenge on Veysey pass and Anderton nets, but Williams handles in the box and gets away with it. In the end, Pompey feel most aggrieved, as the ref ignores an offside and Beauchamp scores in the aftermath.

37 — SWINDON (H) 28/3
Beresford 72p / Jones 49
Ref: D Axcell (Southend)
Team: Knight, Awford, Beresford, McLoughlin, Symons, Burns^, Neill, Kuhl*, Clarke, Whittingham, Anderton, Aspinall/Powell
Subs: Digby, Kerslake, Bodin, Jones, Calderwood, Taylor, Hazard, Gibson, Waddock, Hoddle*, Mitchell, Summerbee

Macca's move has gone through and the only other deal sees wound-up Shots' Kevan Brown arrive on trial. Fratton misfit Micky Hazard lights up the game with a neat pass to set up Jones' cross-shot, but Kerslake's nudge on Beresford lets him maintain his 100% spot-kick record.

38 — CHARLTON (H) 31/3
Minto 64 (og) / Leaburn 67, Whyte 74
Ref: P Vanes (Warley)
Team: Knight, Awford^, Beresford, McLoughlin, Symons, Burns, Neill, Aspinall*, Powell, Whittingham, Anderton, Wigley/Chamberlain
Subs: Bolder, Pitcher, Minto, Pardew, Webster, Balmer, Lee, Bumstead, Leaburn, Nelson*, Walsh, Whyte

Charlton will soon be back at The Valley, but they've got used to playing away. They come from behind for this club-record tenth away win, after Bolder and Minto muff Aspinall's centre. Leaburn nods the equaliser, then Whyte squeezes in. Beresford's saved first-half pen is crucial.

39 — TRANMERE (A) 7/4
Irons 44, Thomas 84
Ref: A Dawson (Jarrow)
Team: Knight, Awford, Beresford^, McLoughlin*, Symons, Burns, Neill, Kuhl, Clarke, Whittingham, Anderton, Aspinall/Powell
Subs: Nixon, Higgins, Nolan, Irons, Harvey, Vickers, Morrissey, Aldridge, Steel, Malkin, Thomas

It will be trial by 'What Happened Next?' for Knight, as his miscued drop kick is volleyed back over his head from 45 yards by Tony Thomas. Jaded Pompey were playing Liverpool just over 48 hours ago, but ex-Red Aldridge lifts spirits when his usual penalty 'shuffle' is scuffed wide.

40 — GRIMSBY (H) 11/4
Doling 28, Aspinall 76
Ref: D Shadwell (Bromsgrove)
Team: Knight, Awford, Daniel, Doling, Symons*, Burns, Neill, Kuhl, Aspinall, Whittingham^, Anderton, Powell/Wigley
Subs: Reece, Jobling, Smith, Rodger, Lever, Cunnington, Ford, Gilbert, Jones*, Mendonca^, Woods, Watson/Hargreaves

Grimsby are in a relegation scrap, but they are happy to saunter in the sun and Pompey make hay. Burns crosses for Doling to ease a shot beyond Reece, then a defender's boot sets up Wigley's cross perfectly for Aspinall. Crucially, there are no injuries ahead of Monday's replay.

41 — CAMBRIDGE (A) 17/4
Kuhl 67, Aspinall 77 / Claridge 4, Wilkins 57
Ref: J Kirby (Sheffield)
Team: Knight, Awford, Daniel*, McLoughlin, Symons, Burns^, Neill, Kuhl, Butters^, Aspinall, Anderton, Powell/Wigley
Subs: Vaughan, Heathcote, Kimble, Dennis, Chapple, O'Shea, Raynor, Wilkins, Dublin, Claridge, Cheetham*, Philpott^/Leadbitter

Gritty Pompey put Monday's cruel defeat behind them and match physical Cambridge. For the second time this season, Beck's boys get a taste of their own medicine, as Daniel's long throw is flicked on by Symons and Aspinall nudges the equaliser. Kuhl's free-kick got them back in it.

42 — BRISTOL CITY (H) 20/4
Wigley 15
Ref: G Ashby (Worcester)
Team: Knight, Awford*, Daniel, McLoughlin, Symons, Doling, Neill, Kuhl, Powell, Aspinall, Wigley^, Burns/McFarlane
Subs: Welch, Atteveld, Scott, Aizlewood, Bryant, Osman, Mellon*, Dziekanowski/Cole, Rosenior, May, Allison

Pompey's play-off dream is still alive, but they get a huge slice of luck when Osman nods the ball out of his keeper's hands and Wigley has an open goal. Resources are stretched, so sub McFarlane can make a lively debut, while Powell slots in a centre-back when Awford is concussed.

43 — WATFORD (H) 22/4
Ref: R Lewis (Great Bookham)
Team: Knight, Awford^, Daniel, McLoughlin, Symons, Burns, Neill, Kuhl^, Powell*, Doling, Anderton, Wigley/Aspinall
Subs: James, Gibbs, Drysdale, Dublin, Holdsworth, Putney, Hessenthaler, Nogan, Bazeley, Soloman*, Porter

Seven games in just over three weeks finally catches up with Pompey, but they still deserve to defeat dour Watford, who have now lost just one in ten matches. Doling goes agonisingly close with six minutes left, but his shot grazes a post after Aspinall's 40-yard pass sent him away.

44 — NEWCASTLE (A) 25/4
Kelly 85
Ref: S Bell (Huddersfield)
Team: Knight, Awford, Daniel, McLoughlin, Symons, Burns, Neill, Doling, Powell, Aspinall^, Anderton^, Wigley/McFarlane
Subs: Wright, Ransom, Nielsen, O'Brien, Kilcline, Scott, Carr, Peacock, Kelly, Sheedy, Brock*, Quinn

Newcastle have one foot in division three as the game drifts into the last five. 'Messiah' manager Keegan seeks divine intervention and Kelly obliges with a vicious cross-shot. Pompey have missed the play-offs and Magpies will stay up…just. Next season's story has already begun.

45 — BRIGHTON (A) 29/4
Aspinall 90 / Robinson 42, Meade 46
Ref: P Alcock (S Merstham)
Team: Knight, Awford, Daniel*, Doling, Symons, Burns, Neill, Kuhl!, Powell^, Whittingham, Wigley, Anderton/Aspinall
Subs: Digweed, Munday, Gallacher, Chapman, McCarthy, Chivers, Barham, Meade!, Gall, Codner, Robinson

Today started badly – Pompey's appeal over plans to build a new Milton End stand have failed – and things get worse as the Seagulls snuff out any mathematical miracle theories about the play-offs and keep their own survival hopes alive. Meade and Kuhl are sent off for fighting.

46 — BARNSLEY (H) 2/5
Symons 48, Whittingham 67
Ref: P Foakes (Clacton-on-Sea)
Team: Knight, Awford^, Daniel, McLoughlin, Symons, Burns, Neill, Kuhl, Powell^, Aspinall, Whittingham, Wigley/Butters
Subs: Butler, Robinson, Taggart, Fleming, Smith, Williams*, Currie^, Bullimore, Redfearn, Archdeacon, Graham/Liddell

Symons celebrates his Player of the Year award with his first senior goal. Butler, under pressure from his own defenders, flaps a corner at his feet. Daniel clips a pass over a square back-line and Whits is off to claim his 13th of the season. The question now is will Gregory cash in?

BARCLAYS DIVISION 2 (CUP-TIES) — Manager: Jim Smith — SEASON 1991-92

Rumbelows Cup

	H/A	Match	W/D/L	F-A	H-T	Scorers, Times, and Referees	1	2	3	4	5	6	7	8	9	10	11	subs used
1:1	H	GILLINGHAM 20/8, 4,801 4:	W	2-1	1-0	Clarke 23, Kuhl 86 / Beadle 75 / Ref: J Carter (Christchurch)	Knight	Awford	Beresford	Burns	Symons	Butters	Anderton	Kuhl	Clarke	Whittingham*	Powell	Chamberlain
							Lim	*O'Shea*	*Martin*	*Elsey*	*Walker*	*Butler*	*Clark*	*Lovell*	*Crown**	*O'Connor*	*Eeles^*	*Beadle/Trusson*
1:2	A	GILLINGHAM 27/8, 5,114 4:4	W	4-3	2-1	And'n 17, Ber'd 30p, Butters 53, Asp'll 89 / Lovell 38, Walker 46, Beadle 86 / Ref: G Pooley (B Stortford) / (Pompey won 6-4 on aggregate)	Knight	Awford	Beresford	Burns	Symons	Butters	Anderton	Doling*	Clarke	Chamberlain	Powell	Aspinall
							Lim	*O'Shea*	*Palmer*	*Elsey**	*Walker*	*Butler*	*Clark*	*Lovell*	*Crown*	*O'Connor^*	*Eeles*	*Trusson/Beadle*
2:1	H	OXFORD 24/9, 4,682 24	D	0-0	0-0	Ref: J Moules (Erith)	Knight	Awford	Beresford	Burns	Symons	Butters	Neill	Kuhl	Clarke*	Wigley	Murray	Anderton
							Kee	*Robinson*	*Smart*	*Phillips*	*Foster*	*Melville*	*Magilton*	*Penney*	*Lewis*	*Nogan*	*Simpson*	
2:2	A	OXFORD 9/10, 4,114 23	W	1-0	1-0	Burns 30 / Ref: P Wright (Northwich) / (Pompey won 1-0 on aggregate)	Knight	Awford	Beresford	Burns	Symons	Butters	Neill	Kuhl	Clarke	Wigley	Chamberlain*	Powell
							Veysey	*Robinson*	*Smart*	*Lewis**	*Foster*	*Melville*	*Magilton*	*Evans**	*Durnin*	*Nogan*	*Simpson*	*Wanless/Beauchamp*
3	A	MANCHESTER U 30/10, 29,543 1:2	L	1-3	0-0	Beresford 60 / Robins 59, 90, Robson 74 / Ref: R Groves (Weston-super-Mare)	Knight	Awford	Beresford	Burns	Symons	Butters	Neill	Kuhl	Clarke*	Chamberlain^	Anderton	Whittingham/Aspinall
							Schmeichel	*Parker*	*Irwin**	*Bruce*	*Webb*	*Pallister^*	*Donaghy*	*Kanchelskis*	*McClair*	*Blackmore*	*Giggs*	*Robins/Robson*

Ex-Fratton winger Crown impresses for Damien Richardson's Gills, but Kuhl has the last word with a controlled volley from Chamberlain's cross. It is no more than Pompey deserve, after Clarke fed on Whittingham's blocked shot, but Peter Beadle outpaces Symons to equalise.

Gills never say die, but Pompey always have a riposte to ensure their passage. Anderton eases home, then Beresford converts after Chambo is felled. Lovell pulls one back, as the ref ignores a flag. Butters hits back after Walker's strike, then Aspinall kills the tie after Beadle's about.

Smith apologises to a new-low gate for a major cup-tie. 'You got rubbish for your money and I'm sorry for you,' he said and calls for the two-leg format to be scrapped. Ex-Pompey star Foster is outstanding. Black stunned Celtic Park on his Airdrie debut as he puts his new team ahead.

Burns slams home Kuhl's pass to ensure Pompey's first win at the Manor in ten years and sets up a mouth-watering clash with Manchester United. Red-faced Chamberlain has to bandage his cycle shorts – FIFA insist they match the white kit – and he is still on a weekly contract.

Beresford – 'brilliant' according to Ferguson – is hero and villain. He hits a post, then curls in a superb free-kick to cancel out Robins' near-post header. However, his back-pass gifts Robson who slides in, then Bruce's slice is touched home by Robins to give United a flattering win.

FA Cup

	H/A	Match	W/D/L	F-A	H-T	Scorers, Times, and Referees	1	2	3	4	5	6	7	8	9	10	11	subs used
3	A	EXETER 4/1, 6,765 3:13	W	2-1	1-0	Whittingham 45, Aspinall 87 / Moran 54 / Ref: I Hemley (Ampthill)	Knight	Awford	Beresford	Powell	Symons	Butters	Neill	Kuhl	Whittingham*	Chamberlain*	Anderton	Aspinall/Wigley
							Miller	*Hiley*	*Cook*	*Williams*	*Daniels*	*Whiston*	*Marshall*	*Wimbleton*	*Moran*	*Brown*	*Cooper*	*Cooper*
4	H	LEYTON ORIENT 25/1, 16,183 3:10	W	2-0	0-0	Anderton 53, 79 / Ref: M Bodenham (Looe)	Knight	Awford	Beresford	Powell*	Butters	Symons	Neill	Kuhl	Whittingham	Burns	Anderton	Wigley
							Turner	*Howard*	*Hackett*	*Burnett*	*Day*	*Whitbread*	*Roeder*	*Castle*	*Jones**	*Nugent*	*Otto^*	*Cooper/Achampong*
5	H	MIDDLESBROUGH 15/2, 18,138 7	D	1-1	0-0	Whittingham 59 / Kernaghan 88 / Ref: B Hill (Kettering)	Knight	Awford	Beresford	Powell	Symons	Murray*	Neill	Kuhl	Whittingham	Burns	Anderton	Chamberlain
							Pears	*Parkinson*	*Phillips*	*Kernaghan*	*Mohan*	*Mustoe*	*Pollock^*	*Peake*	*Wilkinson*	*Hendrie^*	*Ripley*	*Proctor/Payton*
5R	A	MIDDLESBROUGH 26/2, 19,479 7	W	4-2	2-2	Clarke 26, 38, Anderton 58, 72 / Wilkinson 18, 27 / Ref: B Hill (Kettering)	Knight	Awford	Beresford	Powell	Symons	Butters	Neill	Kuhl	Clarke	Burns*	Anderton	Aspinall
							Pears	*Parkinson*	*Phillips*	*Pollock*	*Mohan*	*Mustoe*	*Peake*	*Payton**	*Wilkinson*	*Hendrie*	*Ripley*	*Slaven*
QF	H	NOTT'M FOREST 7/3, 25,402 1:16	W	1-0	1-0	McLoughlin 2 / Ref: S Lodge (Barnsley)	Knight	Awford	Beresford	Powell*	Symons	Burns	Neill	Kuhl	Clarke*	McLoughlin	Anderton	Aspinall/Whittingham
							Crossley	*Laws !*	*Pearce*	*Walker*	*Wassall*	*Keane*	*Crosby*	*Gemmill*	*Clough*	*Sheringham^*	*Glover*	*Chettle*

Exeter boss Ball paid a club-record fee for Aspinall, and he shows his value as he comes off the bench to nod in at the far post and deny City a replay. Former Pompey youngster Wimbleton's class shone for the Grecians, but ex-Saints Moran and Steve Williams would have relished Fratton.

Bad weather across Britain means Pompey are the Match of the Day. Anderton announces his arrival on a national stage, as well as in front of a host of top club scouts. His measured volley goes in off a post, then he powers past Hackett, before exploding a cross-shot past Turner.

Beforehand, Smith tells his team; forget December's result, but Lawrence, no doubt, harped on about little else. The result is a thrilling draw. Whittingham makes sure Burns' shot is going in, but the lead is precarious and Boro are favourites once Kernaghan rifles in from 12 yards.

Clarke hasn't started since November, but his brace keeps Pompey in contention. Anderton now wows a 'Sportsnight' audience, although his first is a total fluke; his corner misses everyone. 'Portsmouth were outstanding, Jim Smith has done a great job,' said presenter Bob Wilson.

McLoughlin puts Pompey in the semis for the first time since 1949. Crossley drops Beresford's free-kick and Macca stabs in. Knight saves from Pearce, then Laws sees red for clattering Beresford from behind. Awford's similar foul on Clough gets only a caution; Forest fans fume.

SF	N	LIVERPOOL	7	D	1-1	0-0	Anderton 108
5/4		41,869 1:4	aet				Whelan 116
		(at Highbury)					Ref: M Bodenham (Looe)

Knight Awford Beresford McLoughlin* Symons Burns Neill Kuhl Clarke Chamberlain^ Anderton Whittingham/Aspinall
Grobelaar Jones* Burrows* Whelan Wright Thomas Houghton^ Rush Barnes McManaman Venison/Marsh

SF	N	LIVERPOOL	9	D	0-0	0-0	
R 13/4		40,077 1:5	aet				
		(at Villa Park)					Ref: M Bodenham (Looe)
							(Pompey lost 1-3 on penalties)

Knight Awford Beresford McLoughlin* Symons Burns Neill Kuhl Clarke Daniel Anderton Aspinall/Whittingham
Grobelaar Jones* Burrows Nichol Whelan^ Wright Saunders Molby Rush Barnes Thomas Walters/Venison

League table

		Home						Away						
		P	W	D	L	F	A	W	D	L	F	A	Pts
1	Ipswich	46	16	3	4	42	22	8	9	6	28	28	84
2	Middlesbro	46	15	6	2	37	13	8	5	10	21	28	80
3	Derby	46	11	4	8	35	24	12	6	6	34	27	78
4	Leicester	46	14	4	5	41	24	9	4	10	31	31	77
5	Cambridge	46	11	9	4	34	19	9	8	6	31	28	74
6	Blackburn*	46	14	5	4	41	21	7	6	10	29	32	74
7	Charlton	46	9	7	7	25	23	11	4	8	29	25	71
8	Swindon	46	15	3	5	38	22	3	12	8	31	33	69
9	PORTSMOUTH	46	15	6	2	41	12	4	6	13	24	39	69
10	Watford	46	9	5	9	25	23	9	6	8	26	25	65
11	Wolves	46	11	6	6	36	24	7	4	12	25	30	64
12	Southend	46	11	5	7	37	26	6	6	11	26	37	62
13	Bristol Rov	46	11	9	3	43	29	5	5	13	17	34	62
14	Tranmere	46	9	9	5	37	32	5	10	8	19	24	61
15	Millwall	46	10	4	9	32	32	7	6	10	32	39	61
16	Barnsley	46	11	4	8	27	25	5	7	11	19	32	59
17	Bristol City	46	10	8	5	30	24	3	7	13	25	47	54
18	Sunderland	46	10	8	5	36	23	4	3	16	25	42	53
19	Grimsby	46	7	5	11	25	28	7	6	10	22	34	53
20	Newcastle	46	9	8	6	38	30	4	5	14	28	54	52
21	Oxford	46	10	6	7	39	30	3	5	15	27	43	50
22	Plymouth	46	11	5	7	26	26	2	4	17	16	38	48
23	Brighton	46	7	7	9	36	37	5	4	14	20	40	47
24	Port Vale	46	7	8	8	23	25	3	7	13	19	34	45
		1104	262	144	146	824	594	146	144	262	594	824	1512

* promoted
after play-offs

Appearances / Goals

	Appearances						Goals			
	Lge	Sub	LC	Sub	FAC	Sub	Lge	LC	FAC	Tot
Anderton, Darren	40	2	3	1	7		7	1	5	13
Aspinall, Warren	9	15	2			5	4	1	1	6
Awford, Andy	45				7					
Beresford, John	35		5		7		6		2	8
Burns, Chris	42	4	5		6		8		1	9
Butters, Guy	32	1	5		3		2		1	3
Chamberlain, Mark	10	6	3		2	1	1			1
Clarke, Colin	19	5	5		3		4	1	2	7
Daniel, Ray	7	1	1							
Doling, Stuart	7	6		1			2			2
Gosney, Andy	1									
Hebberd, Trevor	1	3								
Hendon, Ian	1	3								
Knight, Alan	45		5		7					
Kuhl, Martin	41		4		7		3		1	4
McFarlane, Andy	2									
McLoughlin, Alan	14				3		2		1	3
Murray, Shaun	2	1								
Neill, Warren	38		3		7					
Powell, Darryl	26	10	2		5		6			6
Ross, Mick	3									
Russell, Lee	7	2								
Symons, Kit	46		5		7		1			1
Whittingham, Guy	30	5	1		4	3	11		2	13
Wigley, Steve	8	15	2		2		3			3
(own-goals)							5			5
25 players used	506	83	55	4	77	11	65	8	11	84

Odds & ends

Double wins: (2) Bristol C, Port Vale.
Double losses: (2) Derby, Charlton.

Won from behind: (2) Swindon (a), Southend (a).
Lost from in front: (2) Oxford (a), Charlton (h).

High spots: Beating first division Nottingham Forest to reach the semi-finals of the FA Cup for the first time since 1949.
A 4-0 league victory over eventually-promoted Middlesbrough.
A 4-2 FA Cup 5th round replay win at Middlesbrough.
A 6-1 home win over Millwall.

Low spots: Losing on penalties to Liverpool in the FA Cup semi-final replay at Villa Park.
A fixture pile-up forcing the team to play four games in eight days during April, which meant the play-offs were missed.
A 2-5 thrashing at eventual champions Ipswich.

The 6-1 win over Millwall in March 1992 was the club's biggest since Northampton were beaten by the same score in December 1979.

Player of the Year: Darren Anderton.
Ever presents: (1) Kit Symons.
Hat tricks: Guy Whittingham (1).
Leading scorer: Guy Whittingham & Darren Anderton (both 13).

BARCLAYS DIVISION 1 (New Style)   Manager: Jim Smith   SEASON 1992-93

No	V	Date	Opponent	Att	Pos	Pt	Res	F-A	H-T	1	2	3	4	5	6	7	8	9	10	11	subs used
1	A	15/8	BRISTOL CITY	15,301	—	1	D	3-3	2-2	Knight	Awford	Powell	McLoughlin	Symons	Russell	Neill	Chamberlain^Walsh*	Whittingham	Burns	Clarke/Doling
			italic							Leaning	Mitchell	Scott	Thompson	Bryant	Osman	Mellon	Dziekanowski/Morgan*	Cole	Shelton	Harrison
2	H	22/8	BARNSLEY	11,473	8 / 23	4	W	1-0	0-0	Knight	Awford	Daniel	McLoughlin	Symons	Russell	Neill	Clarke	Walsh*	Whittingham	Burns	Chamberlain
										Butler	Robinson	Taggart	Bishop	Fleming	Bullimore*	Liddell	Rammell*	Pearson	Redfearn	Archdeacon	Smith/Currie
3	A	29/8	LEICESTER	14,780	13 / 3	4	L	0-1	0-1	Knight	Awford	Daniel^	McLoughlin	Symons	Russell	Neill	Powell	Walsh*	Whittingham	Burns	Clarke/Chamberlain
										Muggleton	Mills	Whitlow	Smith*	Walsh	Hill	Oldfield	Thompson	Davison	Ormondroyd	Gee^	Grayson/Fitzpatrick
4	A	1/9	BRENTFORD	8,471	13 / 8	4	L	1-4	1-1	Knight	Awford	Daniel^	McLoughlin	Symons	Russell	Neill	Chamberlain	Walsh	Whittingham	Burns*	Clarke/Powell
										Bayes	Statham	Hughton	Millen	Bates	Ratcliffe	Bennett	Manuel	Gayle	Blissett	Smillie	
5	H	5/9	BIRMINGHAM	12,152	7 / 4	7	W	4-0	1-0	Knight	Awford	Daniel	McLoughlin	Symons	Chamberlain*Neill	Kuhl^	Walsh	Whittingham	Burns	Clarke/Powell
										Gosney	Clarkson*	Frain	Cooper^	Rogers	Matthewson	Donowa	Tait	Sale	Gleghorn	Beckford	Mardon/Rowbotham
6	A	12/9	NEWCASTLE	29,885	11 / 1	7	L	1-3	0-2	Knight	Awford	Daniel^	McLoughlin	Symons	Doling^	Neill	Kuhl	Powell*	Whittingham	Burns	Clarke/Murray
										Wright	Venison	Beresford	O'Brien	Scott	Howey	Carr	Quinn	Kelly*	Clark	Sheedy	Thompson
7	A	18/9	SOUTHEND	5,627	14 / 18	8	D	0-0	0-0	Knight	Awford	Daniel	McLoughlin*	Symons	Aspinall	Neill	Doling^	Clarke	Whittingham^Murray	Burns*	Doling/Powell
										Sansome	Edwards	Powell	Cornwell	Scully	Prior	Ansah	Martin	Locke	Benjamin	O'Callaghan	
8	H	27/9	WEST HAM	12,158	15 / 4	8	L	0-1	0-1	Knight	Awford	Daniel	McLoughlin	Symons	Aspinall	Neill	Doling	Clarke	Whittingham	Murray^	Walsh/Powell
										Miklosko	Breacker	Dicks	Potts	Martin	Allen M	Robson*	Butler	Morley	Allen C	Keen	Holmes
9	A	3/10	LUTON	7,954	11 / 21	11	W	4-1	3-1	Knight	Awford	Daniel	McLoughlin*	Symons	Aspinall	Neill*	Walsh^	Chamberlain	Whittingham	Murray^	Burns/Chamberlain
										Petterson	Linton	James	Salton	Dreyer	Oakes	Kamara	Preece*	Rees^	Claridge	Gray	Campbell/Matthew
10	H	10/10	SWINDON	12,442	10 / 5	14	W	3-1	2-0	Knight	Awford	Daniel*	McLoughlin*Symons	Aspinall	Neill	Chamberlain	Clarke	Whittingham	Maguire	Walsh/Burns
										Hammond	Kerslake	Bodin*	Haddle	Calderwood	Taylor	Hazard^	Summerbee	Maskell	Ling	Mitchell	Horlock/White
11	A	17/10	WOLVERHAMPTON	14,750	9 / 3	15	D	1-1	1-0	Knight	Awford	Daniel	McLoughlin	Symons	Aspinall	Neill	Chamberlain	Clarke^	Whittingham	Maguire	Walsh
										Stowell	Ashley	Edwards	Downing*	Manfield	Blades	Birch	Cook	Bull	Match	Rankine	Dennison

1. BRISTOL CITY — Whittingham 8, 15, 56; *Dziekanowski 2, 49, Cole 27*; Ref: R Gifford (Llanbradach).
Master manager (Smiths) – Jim and Denis – craft a classy contest in the sun. The Pole's early sweep is the pick, but offside-ish Corporal gets the benefit of the doubt for his hat-trick. Cole and 'Jacky' get Robins rockin'. £450,000 Walsh (Spurs) looks the perfect foil for Whits, while Chambo's early cross finds Whits at the near post.

2. BARNSLEY — Whittingham 62; Ref: G Willard (Worthing).
A damp squib (like the weather) after last week's cracker, but no one is complaining. Mel Machin's Tykes take their punishment when sub Chambo's early cross finds Whits at the near post. Did Taggart touch it? 'Not likely' says Guy. Butler excels to deny Guy a second hat-trick.

3. LEICESTER — *Davison 36*; Ref: T Holbrook (Walsall).
Big-money buy Walsh has now been subbed three times and looks far from amused. Bargain basement Davison (£25,000) explodes a shot into the top corner. Smith moans the ref was biased, as Powell's 'goal' is pulled back for a Pompey kick. 'He was most of the afternoon,' he added.

4. BRENTFORD — Symons 25; *Bennett 37, Smillie 64, Gayle 81, [Blissett 83]*; Ref: P Alcock (S Mertsham).
Neil Smillie's 'leg-break' turns this match and puts Pompey on a sticky wicket. His header looks bound for Knight's safe hands, when it rears up off the turf and bobbles into the corner. Earlier Symons had netted from eight yards, but busy Bees don't look like relegation fodder here.

5. BIRMINGHAM — Daniel 21, Walsh 47, Kuhl 62, [Whittingham 65]; Ref: D Frampton (Poole).
Birmingham are blown away after 33-1-to-score Daniel's header; his first for the club. The real Walsh stands up and his delicate clip over old-boy Gosney is class. Inspirational Kuhl is back from suspension. His 22-yard free-kick is top-drawer, but Smith will sell him to Rams soon.

6. NEWCASTLE — Whittingham 85; *Quinn 13, 76, Kelly 41*; Ref: P Wright (Northwich).
Quinn is back in Keegan's plans. He blasts two goals and sets up Kelly, in his first game this season. Magpies' sixth win in succession has the Geordie public responding. The game is a lock-out. Ex-Blue Beresford starts, having signed for Toon when his move to Liverpool fell through.

7. SOUTHEND — Ref: R Wiseman (Borehamwood).
Murray is the man of the match, as patient hours of body-building over the summer seem to have paid off. Macca holds his head as Sansome turns his five-yard bullet over the bar. Ex-Pompey star Cally sees Awford hack his shot from the line, for Colin Murphy's side's best chance.

8. WEST HAM — *Allen 45*; Ref: K Cooper (Swindon).
Knight cites the new back-pass law in mitigation, but accepts he misjudges a long through-ball. He tells Awford to leave it, but Clive Allen pounces and angles home in front of a live ITV audience. Kuhl's Derby move stuns fans. Every player has his price. £650,000 in this case.

9. LUTON — Whittingham 27, 38, 75, Clarke 37; *Dreyer 17*; Ref: B Hill (Kettering).
Torrential rain turns the match into a muddy lottery, but Guy has the winning ticket. Dreyer's 25-yarder would have been great whatever, but Whits levels. His quick-fire 1-2 with Clarke gives Town that sinking feeling, then his second triple is sealed after he swaps passes with Macca.

10. SWINDON — McLoughlin 23, Whittingham 38, White 80, [Chamberlain 87]; Ref: A Buksh (London).
A 'Guy for Forest' story is chopped down, but Premier League clubs are prowling and Whits wants to play there. He makes Macca's goal, then dives full-length for his 14th of the season. White nets the 201st of his career for Glenn Hoddle's team, but Chambo's blistering shot seals it.

11. WOLVERHAMPTON — Whittingham 34; *Birch 66*; Ref: R Nixon (West Kirkby).
Guy stamps on another own-goal theory and Wolves full-back Kevin Ashley is happy to concur as they stretch for a loose ball. Whits also hits a post with a header, but Smith reckons he should have had another hat-trick. Birch chips over Knight and Pompey face a tricky last quarter.

Match 12

12 | H SUNDERLAND | 24/10 — Att 10,689 — Pos 9, W, Opp pos 20, **2-0**, Pts 18

- Pompey: Knight, Burns, Daniel, McLoughlin*, Symons, Aspinall^, Neill, Chamberlain, Clarke, Whittingham, Maguire, Walsh/Powell
- Sunderland: Carter, Kay, Rogan, Owers, Ord, Ball, Cunningham*, Goodman, Davenport^, Atkinson, Armstrong, Colquhoun/Rush
- Scorers: Whittingham 42, Burns 44
- Ref: D Axcell (Southend)

Roker boss Malcolm Crosby, who guided them to Wembley in May, is under pressure as his side slump to their fifth away defeat. Goodman misses a one-on-one with Knight, then Whits strikes in a seething goalmouth. 'Brickie' Burns builds on the lead with a towering header.

Match 13

13 | A GRIMSBY | 31/10 — Att 5,708 — Pos 11, L, Opp pos 12, **0-3**, Pts 18

- Pompey: Knight, Awford*, Daniel, McLoughlin, Symons, Aspinall, Neill, Chamberlain^, Clarke, Whittingham, Maguire, Walsh/Burns
- Grimsby: Beasant, McDermott, Croft, Futcher, Lever, Dobbin, Watson, Gilbert, Groves, Mendonca, Woods*, Rees
- Scorers: Gilbert 32, McDermott 75, Rees 80
- Ref: K Redfern (Whitley Bay)

A thrown fruit pastille fells Knight in the second half and lands Mariners in trouble with the Football Association. Full-back John McDermott nets his first in more than a year, then Rees' tumbling volley rubs it in. Virus-hit Walsh continues his recuperation as a second-half substitute.

Match 14

14 | A OXFORD | 3/11 — Att 5,490 — Pos 11, D, Opp pos 16, **5-5**, Pts 19

- Pompey: Knight, Awford, Daniel, McLoughlin, Symons, Burns, Neill*, Chamberlain, Walsh^, Whittingham, Maguire, Doling/Powell
- Oxford: Reece, Smart, Ford, Lewis*, Evans, Melville, Magilton, Beauchamp, Penney^, Durnin, Allen, Narbett/Cusack
- Scorers: Mcl 18, Wh'm 21, 42, Ev 31 (og), Ch'n 61; P'y 40, M'ton 42, 90p, D'n 77, Allen 90
- Ref: J Rushton (Stoke)

5-2 up with 13 minutes to go and 5-3 in injury-time, then Doling's rash challenge on Allen lets Magilton convert. With a headless chicken apparently marshalling the defence, Reece hoofs, Beauchamp shoots, Knight blocks and Allen's header pays Pompey back for December 1984.

Match 15

15 | H CAMBRIDGE | 7/11 — Att 8,956 — Pos 10, W, Opp pos 18, **3-0**, Pts 22

- Pompey: Knight, Awford, Daniel, McLoughlin*, Symons, Burns, Neill, Chamberlain^, Walsh, Whittingham, Maguire, Clarke/Powell
- Cambridge: Sheffield, Fensome, Kimble, Raynor, Heathcote, O'Shea, Francis, Norbury, White, Clayton*, Philpott^, Leadbitter/Ainsworth
- Scorers: McLoughlin 43, Whittingham 78, 89
- Ref: K Burge (Tonypandy)

Cambridge are safe to rejoin the community now John Beck has gone, but they don't win anymore and will go down. Macca and Walsh are at loggerheads over the opener. 'Ladbrokes have paid me on it and that's final,' trumps the Irishman. Guy now sees 20:20. Goals in games that is.

Match 16

16 | A WATFORD | 14/11 — Att 8,714 — Pos 12, D, Opp pos 14, **0-0**, Pts 23

- Pompey: Knight, Awford, Daniel, McLoughlin*, Symons, Burns, Neill, Chamberlain^, Walsh, Whittingham, Maguire, Charlery/Willis
- Watford: Suckling, Putney, Drysdale, Dublin, Holdsworth, Ashby, Hessenthaler, Nogan*, Furlong, Porter^, Lavin
- Ref: J Brandwood (Lichfield)

Premier scouts jostle for position, but Guy's powder has been dampened by the drizzle. He scorns three chances to win it and Knight's late block has to deny Furlong. Guernsey-based businessman Roy Brehaut has held talks over a £6m buy-out of Gregory's stake, but nothing doing.

Match 17

17 | H TRANMERE | 21/11 — Att 9,982 — Pos 8, W, Opp pos 3, **4-0**, Pts 26

- Pompey: Knight, Awford, Daniel, McLoughlin, Symons, Burns, Neill, Chamberlain, Walsh*, Whittingham, Maguire, Clarke/Agnew
- Tranmere: Nixon, Higgins, Brannan, Irons, Mungall, Vickers, Morrissey, Aldridge, Malkin, Nevin, McNab
- Scorers: McLoughlin 29, Whittingham 41, Walsh 44, [Daniel 77]
- Ref: R Groves (Weston-super-Mare)

John King's team come to Fratton in third place, but are left looking strictly third-class. Macca flicks home Neill's cross and Pompey are on Tranny's wave-length. Whittingham. Who else? Walsh. No arguments this time. Then Daniel runs 50 yards to convert McLoughlin's cross.

Match 18

18 | H MILLWALL | 28/11 — Att 12,445 — Pos 7, W, Opp pos 6, **1-0**, Pts 29

- Pompey: Knight, Awford, Daniel^, McLoughlin*, Agnew, Burns, Neill, Chamberlain, Clarke, Whittingham, Maguire, Aspinall/Powell
- Millwall: Keller, Cunningham, Dawes, May, Cooper, Stevens, Rae^, Morales^, Allen, Byrne, Barber, Roberts/Goodman
- Scorers: McLoughlin 30
- Ref: P Durkin (Portland)

On-loan Agnew – Smith says he's agreed a fee with Blackburn – puts Macca clear to beat Keller. Mick McCarthy's Millwall rarely threaten. Pompey are back from Bari (0-3 in the Anglo-Italian) where Smith had to haul tough-tackling Maguire off to avoid a diplomatic incident!

Match 19

19 | A CHARLTON | 5/12 — Att 8,337 — Pos 8, L, Opp pos 9, **0-1**, Pts 29

- Pompey: Knight, Awford, Daniel^, McLoughlin, Symons, Agnew*, Neill, Chamberlain, Clarke, Whittingham, Maguire, Walsh/Burns
- Charlton: Bolder, Pitcher, Minto, Gritt, Webster, Balmer, Robinson, Powers*, Leaburn, Nelson, Walsh, Grant
- Scorers: Walsh 7
- Ref: A Gunn (South Chailey)

Colin Walsh scores Charlton's first back at The Valley since they left in 1985, hitting the bottom corner. Pompey win the corner count 14-2, but Bolder hasn't a save to make. Ex-Valiant Paul Walsh makes a nostalgic return, as a sub for crocked Agnew, whose transfer is collapsing.

Match 20

20 | A PETERBOROUGH | 12/12 — Att 6,516 — Pos 9, D, Opp pos 13, **1-1**, Pts 30

- Pompey: Knight, Awford, Stimson, McLoughlin, Symons, Burns, Neill, Chamberlain, Walsh, Whittingham, Maguire!, Agnew
- Peterborough: Bennett, Luke, Robinson, Halsall, Bradshaw, Welsh, Sterling, Cooper, Adcock, Philliskirk, Eldon
- Scorers: Whittingham 63; Philliskirk 9
- Ref: R Dilkes (Mossley)

Bennett preserves Posh's point with a string of saves. The best comes just after Whits thrashed in Walsh's lay-off to level, when he reads Walsh's penalty. 'He's not our taker any more': Smith. Maguire is sent off for two innocuous bookings. Stimson (Newcastle) is the latest loan.

Match 21

21 | H NOTTS CO | 19/12 — Att 8,943 — Pos 9, D, Opp pos 22, **0-0**, Pts 31

- Pompey: Knight, Awford, Stimson*, McLoughlin, Symons, Burns, Neill, Chamberlain, Walsh, Whittingham, Clarke, Powell
- Notts Co: Cherry, Palmer, Dijkstra, Thomas*, Turner, William, Draper, Wilson, Agana, Bartlett, Smith D, Smith M
- Ref: M Bodenham (Looe)

Warnock's time at County is running out (one win in ten), but this point helps. Knight blocks Bartlett's point-blank shot. Walsh and Clarke both wear No 9 for five second-half minutes, until the crowd tell the linesman. Walsh reveals his senior penalty record is 3 out of 3. Misses.

Match 22

22 | H BRISTOL ROV | 26/12 — Att 14,288 — Pos 6, W, Opp pos 19, **4-1**, Pts 34

- Pompey: Knight, Awford, Stimson, McLoughlin, Symons, Burns, Neill, Chamberlain, Walsh, Whittingham, Clarke, Clarke/Stimson
- Bristol Rov: Parkin, Alexander, Tillson, Yates, Hardyman, Jones*, Browning, Stewart, Taylor, Saunders, Waddock, Evans
- Scorers: Whittingham 12, 20, 64, 76; Taylor 34
- Ref: G Poll (Berkhamsted)

Big Mal(colm) Allison is back as Rovers boss, but he would have taken his famed fedora off to Whittingham today. Ex-Pompey full-back Hardyman gifts him the second, but his hat-trick is surely the goal of the season. Three swapped passes with Walsh, then a right-foot curler.

Match 23

23 | A DERBY | 28/12 — Att 21,478 — Pos 5, W, Opp pos 8, **4-2**, Pts 37

- Pompey: Knight, Awford, Stimson, McLoughlin, Symons, Burns, Neill, Chamberlain, Walsh*, Whittingham, Aspinall^, Powell
- Derby: Sutton, Forsyth, Short, Wassall, Pembridge, Johnson, Kuhl*, Kitson, Williams, Gabbiadini, McMinn, Coleman/McMinn
- Scorers: Whittingham 7, 50, McLoughlin 64, 88; Johnson 45, Kitson 55
- Ref: J Lloyd (Wrexham)

Crowd congestion delays the kick-off, but the wait is well-worth it. Arthur Cox's £10m team slump to their seventh home defeat as Pompey dig deep. Rams cling to Whit's coat-tails, then McLoughlin dives in. Knight is injured and can't move, but Macca's curler makes it irrelevant.

BARCLAYS DIVISION 1 (New Style) Manager: Jim Smith SEASON 1992-93

No	Date	H/A	Team	Att	Pos		Pt	Res	F-A	H-T	Scorers, Times, and Referees	1	2	3	4	5	6	7	8	9	10	11	subs used
24	9/1	H	SOUTHEND	9,717	4	23	40	W	2-0	1-0	Whittingham, 19, Walsh 54. Ref: P Don (Hanworth Park)	Knight	Awford	Daniel	McLoughlin	Symons	Burns	Neill	Chamberlain	Walsh	Whittingham	Aspinall	Powell/Maguire
												Sansome	Edwards	Powell	Cornwell	Scully	Prior	Locke*	Sussex	Brown	Collymore	Jones	Ashenden
25	16/1	A	WEST HAM	18,127	6	3	40	L	0-2	0-1	Morley 27, Foster 56. Ref: R Gifford (Llanbradach)	Knight	Awford	Daniel	McLoughlin	Symons	Burns*	Neil^	Chamberlain	Walsh	Whittingham	Aspinall	
												Miklosko	Breacker	Dicks	Potts	Foster	Allen M	Robson*	Butler	Morley	Allen C^	Keen	Parris/Holmes
26	23/1	H	BRENTFORD	10,267	5	13	43	W	1-0	0-0	Aspinall 63p. Ref: G Pooley (Bishop's Stortford)	Knight	Awford	Daniel	McLoughlin	Symons	Burns	Russell^	Chamberlain*	Walsh	Whittingham	Aspinall	Powell/Maguire
												Benstead	Buckle	Gayle*	Millen	Bates	Chalmers	Allon	Godfrey^	Bennett	Blissett	Mortimer	Luscombe/Jones
27	30/1	A	BARNSLEY	6,551	5	12	44	D	1-1	0-0	Whittingham 61, Archdeacon 49p. Ref: J Winter (Middlesbrough)	Knight	Awford*	Daniel	McLoughlin	Symons	Burns	Price	Maguire*	Walsh	Whittingham	Aspinall	Powell/Butters
												Butler	Robinson	Fleming	Bishop	Taggart	O'Connell	Currie	Rammell	Pearson	Redfearn	Archdeacon	
28	6/2	H	BRISTOL CITY	10,675	5	17	44	L	2-3	1-1	Walsh 9, Whittingham 48, Shelton 16, Bryant 74, Gavin 83. Ref: P Foakes (Clacton-on-Sea)	Knight	Awford	Daniel	McLoughlin*	Symons	Burns	Price!	Chamberlain	Walsh	Whittingham	Aspinall*	Powell/Russell
												Welch	Llewellyn	Munro	Aizlewood	Bryant	Pennyfather	Shelton	Dziekanowski	Allison*	Cole	Harrison^	Rosenior/Gavin
29	9/2	A	NEWCASTLE	21,028	5	1	47	W	2-0	2-0	Whittingham 13, Symons 40. Ref: D Gallagher (Banbury)	Knight	Awford	Daniel	McLoughlin	Symons	Burns	Price	Chamberlain*	Walsh	Whittingham	Aspinall*	Powell/Maguire
												Srnicek	Venison	Beresford	O'Brien	Kilcline	Scott	Lee	Peacock	Kelly	Clark	Bracewell**	Sheedy
30	13/2	A	BIRMINGHAM	10,935	4	22	50	W	3-2	1-0	McLoughlin 26, Whittingham 51, 84, Sturridge 50, Peschisolido 81. Ref: R Nixon (West Kirkby)	Knight	Awford	Daniel	McLoughlin	Symons	Burns	Price	Chamberlain*	Walsh	Whittingham	Maguire	Powell
												Gosney	Holmes	Potter	Rennie*	Marden	Matthewson	Sturridge	Quinn^	Peschisolido	Foy	Frain	Sale/Fenwick
31	20/2	H	LEICESTER	14,160	4	9	51	D	1-1	0-0	Walsh 77, Philpott 90. Ref: R Milford (Bristol)	Knight	Awford	Daniel	McLoughlin	Symons	Burns	Maguire	Chamberlain*	Walsh	Whittingham	Russell^	Powell/Doling
												Muggleton	Mills	Philpott	James	Walsh	Hill	Oldfield	Thompson	Davison	Lowe	Agnew	
32	27/2	A	SWINDON	14,077	5	4	51	L	0-1	0-0	Bodin 88. Ref: M James (Horsham)	Knight	Awford	Daniel*	McLoughlin^	Symons	Burns	Price	Chamberlain	Walsh	Whittingham	Aspinall	Powell/Murray
												Digby	Kerslake	Bodin	Hoddle	Calderwood	Taylor	Summerbee	McLaren	Mitchell	Ling	White	
33	6/3	H	LUTON	10,457	4	20	54	D	1-1	1-1	Whittingham 17, Aspinall 51p, Gray 16. Ref: S Dunn (Bristol)	Knight	Awford	Daniel*	McLoughlin^	Symons	Burns*	Price	Chamberlain	Walsh	Whittingham	Aspinall	Chamberlain/Russell
												Chamberlain	Dreyer	James	Johnson	Rees*	Peake	Telfer	Dixon	Oakes	Gray	Preece	Hughes^/Williams
34	9/3	H	WATFORD	10,716	3	14	57	W	1-0	0-0	Chamberlain 51. Ref: I Hemley (Ampthill)	Knight	Awford	Russell*	McLoughlin	Maguire	Burns	Price	Chamberlain	Walsh	Whittingham	Aspinall	Butters
												Suckling	Soloman*	Ashby	Dublin	Holdsworth	Willis^	Hessenthaler	Nogan	Furlong	Charlery	Porter	Bazeley/Putney

Match commentaries

24 — Pompey are trying to tie down Whittingham to a long-term contract, but he is having none of it. However, he'll make the top with Pompey the way things are going. Aspinall's shot is turned against the bar and Whits is there. Constant menace Walsh seizes on a loose ball to seal the win.

25 — Hammers gain a vital win, and 0-2 flatters Pompey. Leading scorer Clive Allen has limped off and Morley's diving header leaves him needing treatment. Holmes hits the bar, before Foster's header kills off comeback hopes. Norwegian cap Jan Halvorson trains with Pompey next week.

26 — Aspinall picks himself up after Chalmers' challenge and converts, but that is the prettiest sight on display. The game is brought forward three days as Bees, too, are out of the Cup. Gregory spikes a move for Saints' Speedie. He will join West Ham. Halvorson is tied up by red tape.

27 — Maguire chops Currie and Archdeacon doesn't give Knight a prayer. Whits levels with his 31st goal, then hits the bar. At £50,000, the Price (Blackburn) is right, but surely a striker is needed. Clarke's reserve-team injury will be more serious than thought. Symons signs until 1995.

28 — Managerless City haven't won in nine, but Pompey never get to grips with pacy Andy Cole, who will soon spice up the attack of promotion-rivals Newcastle. Price professionally fouls him and is sent off on his home debut, then sub Gavin curls home the winner from the free-kick.

29 — Magpies have been in Marbella – the Young Tory conference in Southend moved Saturday's match – but they end up well tanned by Pompey. Whits angles in, then Symons converts a corner. Keegan's team fight back, but Knight is equal. New reserve keeper Home faces a long wait.

30 — Whittingham side-foots his second of the game, after McLoughlin leaves Potter standing and Pompey's third away win is in the bag. Macca's cross-shot opened, but Terry Cooper's Blues' response was impressive. Peschisolido looked to have earned only their second point in 15.

31 — This won't be the last time a combination of Roger Milford and Leicester stymie Pompey this season. Smith confronts the referee at the end, convinced there should have been a free-kick just before Maguire nudges Walsh for Philpott to curl home. Walsh deflects Lee Russell's shot.

32 — Automatic promotion is looking a long-shot as second-placed West Ham are nine points ahead after another late defeat. Welsh cap Bodin fires home from the edge of the box, after Mitchell and White see efforts blocked. Clarke sees a specialist on Monday; the prognosis isn't good.

33 — Chelsea supremo Ken Bates is in the crowd, pondering another bid for Luton's Gray, or perhaps a move for Whits. Take your pick. Gray heads in from the edge of the area, only to be trumped at once by Guy's burst of pace and cool finish. Walsh is held by Peake and Aspinall converts.

34 — Watford are never in it, but only Chambo's coolness, clipping home Macca's clever back-heel, kills them off. Whits hits a post soon after, but Pompey are incensed by Soloman's uncarded foul on Russell which sees him carried off. Maguire is desperate for a move. He will join Lions.

Portsmouth (Pompey) — match-by-match record

No		Date	Opponents	Att	Pos / · / Pts	Res		Score	HT	Scorers	Referee
35	A	13/3	CAMBRIDGE	5,975	4 / 21 / 60	W		1-0	1-0	Clayton 37 (og)	Ref: K Barratt (Coventry)
36	H	20/3	CHARLTON	12,854	3 / 9 / 63	W		1-0	1-0	Whittingham 11	Ref: D Frampton (Poole)
37	A	23/3	TRANMERE	7,472	3 / 7 / 66	W		2-0	0-0	Whittingham 54, 82p	Ref: W Flood (Stockport)
38	H	27/3	OXFORD	14,648	2 / 16 / 69	W		3-0	0-0	Robinson 49 (og), McLoughlin 59, Whittingham 68	Ref: A Gunn (South Chailey)
39	A	3/4	MILLWALL	12,921	3 / 5 / 70	D		1-1	1-0	Chamberlain 41 / Kerr 65	Ref: P Vanes (Warley)
40	H	6/4	PETERBOROUGH	15,093	3 / 13 / 73	W		4-0	3-0	Whittingham 13, 21, 61, Butters 27	Ref: D Elleray (Harrow)
41	A	10/4	BRISTOL ROV	5,377	2 / 24 / 76	W		2-1	1-0	Kristensen 33, Whittingham 52 / Stewart 69	Ref: B Hill (Kettering)
42	H	12/4	DERBY	23,805	2 / 11 / 79	W		3-0	2-0	Whittingham 2, 73, Walsh 30	Ref: R Groves (Weston-super-Mare)
43	A	17/4	NOTTS CO	11,014	2 / 17 / 82	W		1-0	0-0	Walsh 70	Ref: W Burns (Scarborough)
44	H	24/4	WOLVERHAMPTON	23,073	1 / 11 / 85	W		2-0	0-0	Daniel 62, Walsh 86	Ref: P Alcock (S Mertsham)
45	A	1/5	SUNDERLAND	21,309	2 / 18 / 85	L		1-4	0-1	Whittingham 86 / Goodman 36p, 51p, Gray Martin 57, [Armstrong 76]	Ref: P Wright (Northwich)
46	H	8/5	GRIMSBY	24,955	3 / 9 / 88	W		2-1	0-1	Daniel 58, Whittingham 83 / Daws 32	Ref: R Hamer (Bristol)

Home — · Away 11,599 · Average 13,695

Line-ups and commentary

35 — Cambridge (A)
Pompey: Knight, Awford, Butters, McLoughlin, Maguire, Burns, Price, Chamberlain*, Whittingham, Aspinall, Powell/Lawrence
Cambridge: Vaughan, Fensome, Kimble, Heathcote, Dennis*, Francis^, O'Shea, Claridge, Clayton, Butler, Rush/Lyne
"Clayton sticks out a leg and makes McLoughlin's cross lethal, but Us pound Pompey in the second half. Ex-Fratton apprentice Claridge hits the bar. Veteran Lawrence debuts – his time-wasting efforts will become a ritual – but signing the Weymouth man suggests a lack of ambition."

36 — Charlton (H)
Pompey: Knight, Awford, Butters, McLoughlin, Symons*, Burns, Price, Chamberlain, Whittingham, Kristensen!, Aspinall/Lawrence
Charlton: Salmon, Pitcher, Gatting, Bacon*, Webster, Houghton, Minto, Balmer, Leaburn, Nelson, Walsh/Dyer
"Whittingham dives to head in Daniel's cross for number 37 and he is closing in on Haines' club goalscoring record. £100,000 Dane Bjorn Kristensen (Newcastle) arrived yesterday. He settles in well, but is then sent off for two fouls. Chambo fumbles late on."

37 — Tranmere (A)
Pompey: Knight, Awford, Butters, McLoughlin, Maguire, Daniel, Price, Chamberlain*, Whittingham, Kristensen, Murray/Lawrence
Tranmere: Nixon, Higgins, Brannan, Nolan*, Proctor, Morrissey, Vickers, Cooper^, Nevin, Thomas, Martindale/Branch
"Guy makes it five wins in-a-row and Hammers are only three points away after they lose at Oxford. He cuts in from the left and fires home, then Higgins halts Chambo's turn of speed. A £300,000 move for Bristol Rovers' striker Taylor stalls, but £100,000 Hall (Torquay) signs."

38 — Oxford (H)
Pompey: Knight, Awford, Butters, McLoughlin, Aspinall*, Daniel, Price, Chamberlain*, Whittingham, Kristensen, Murray/Lawrence
Oxford: Reece, Robinson, Ford, Phillips, Evans, Magilton, Melville, Beauchamp, Durnin, Lewis
"Pompey go second for 24 hours; Hammers are wobbling. Walsh's cross is aimed at Whittingham, but Robinson's head proves just as effective. McLoughlin's calm chip lets the football flow, then Whits shows why he's now got 40. Aspinall's shot is surely going in, but you never know!"

39 — Millwall (A)
Pompey: Knight, Awford, Butters, McLoughlin, Symons*, Daniel, Price^, Chamberlain, Whittingham, Wallace*?, Murray/Lawrence
Millwall: Keller, Cunningham, Dawes, Roberts, Cooper, McCarthy, Maguire, Wallace*, Allen^, Barber, Bogie/Kerr
"Chamberlain's dipping shot from the edge of the area is spectacular, the one that crashed against the inside of the post just after the break would have been even better. Lions make the most of their escape and ex-Pompey Yank Kerr guides in to end Knight's 589 minute clean sheet."

40 — Peterborough (H)
Pompey: Knight, Awford, Butters, McLoughlin, Symons*, Daniel, Price, Chamberlain*, Whittingham, Kristensen, Aspinall/Lawrence
Peterborough: Bennett, Bradshaw, Greenman, Cooper, Howarth, Welsh, Sterling, McGlashen^, Adcock, Barnes, Iorfa
"Sub Aspinall hands a late spot-kick to Whits – he needs one to break Haines' 43-in-a-season – but Bennett guesses right. Smith is not happy. Goals scored may be crucial in the end. His record-equalling goal is a typically sharp finish and his 100th in league and cup for the club."

41 — Bristol Rov (A)
Pompey: Knight, Awford, Butters, McLoughlin, Symons*, Daniel, Price, Chamberlain*, Whittingham, Kristensen, Aspinall/Lawrence
Bristol Rov: Beasley, Alexander*, Tillson, Yates, Clark, Pounder^, Channing, Rees, Taylor, Waddock, Hardyman/Saunders (Stewart)
"Kristensen sets Pompey on their way, trundling through to thump home from the edge of the box, then Guy takes two attempts to scuff home the record-breaker after Beasley blocked Walsh's shot. Stewart's delightful chip spurs Rovers on and Channing is denied by an offside flag."

42 — Derby (H)
Pompey: Knight, Awford, Butters, McLoughlin, Symons, Daniel, Neill, Chamberlain*, Whittingham, Kristensen, Aspinall/Lawrence
Derby: Taylor, Round, Nicholson*, Coleman, Short, Pembridge^, Sturridge, Kuhl, Kitson, Simpson, Stallard/Patterson
"Leaders Newcastle – 19 points away in January – are now within range after this demolition of Derby. It takes just 85 seconds for Whits to nod in Kristensen's deep free-kick, then Walsh twists to volley in. Hammers lose at Luton tomorrow and Pompey are masters of their own destiny."

43 — Notts Co (A)
Pompey: Knight, Awford, Butters, McLoughlin, Symons, Daniel, Neill, Chamberlain, Whittingham, Walsh, Aspinall/Lawrence
Notts Co: Cherry, Short*, Johnson, Thomas, Cox, Walker, Agana, Draper, Reeves, Smith^, Wilson/Lund
"Walsh emerges from Guy's shadow again to glance home the Great Dane's cross, but County run them close. Under new boss Mick Walker they haven't lost at home since January and they give Pompey a torrid time. Lawrence comes on for the ninth time in a row. A lucky mascot?"

44 — Wolverhampton (H)
Pompey: Knight, Awford, Butters, McLoughlin, Symons, Daniel, Neill*, Chamberlain, Whittingham, Walsh, Lawrence
Wolverhampton: Stowell, Simkin, Venus, Burke, Mountfield*, Madden*, Edwards*, Cook, Thomson, Dennison, Steele/Roberts
"Lawrence shuns the corner for once and his cross is nodded in by Walsh – Pompey are on top for 24 hours. Daniel's strike muzzled Wolves. The Parkway Stadium dream is unveiled and Sky will check Fratton camera angles for next season at Tuesday's U-21 international v Holland."

45 — Sunderland (A)
Pompey: Knight, Awford^, Butters!, McLoughlin, Symons, Daniel, Neill^, Chamberlain!, Whittingham, Walsh!, Aspinall/Lawrence
Sunderland: Norman, Gray Martin, Gray Michael/Owers, Butcher, Owers, Bennett*, Cunnington^, Goodman, Davenport, Atkinson, Colquhoun/Howey (Armstrong)
"Where do you start? Butters handles on the line and he's sent off. Symons' 'foul' is seen from 40 yards away, then Martin Gray ends Roker relegation worries. Walsh is sent off on the linesman's say-so and is out of the play-offs. Still, Swindon won't roll over against West Ham."

46 — Grimsby (H)
Pompey: Knight, Awford^, Butters, McLoughlin, Symons*, Daniel, Neill, Chamberlain, Whittingham, Kristensen, Aspinall/Lawrence
Grimsby: Wilmot, McDermott, Croft, Futcher, Rodger, Dobbin, Ford, Gilbert*, Daws, Mendonca^, Groves, Smith/Woods
"Pompey must equal Hammers' result, but score two more in doing so. Inspired Wilmot ensures heartbreak. Daws' long loop is a stunner, but Daniel levels. Hammers are one up. Whits scores then Wilmot somehow stops Kristensen. Some think Cambridge have levelled. They haven't."

BARCLAYS DIVISION 1 (CUP-TIES)

Manager: Jim Smith

SEASON 1992-93

Coca-Cola Cup

		F-A	H-T	Scorers, Times, and Referees	1	2	3	4	5	6	7	8	9	10	11	subs used
2:1 A BLACKPOOL 14	W	4-0	0-0	Clarke 47, McLoughlin 55, 77, Murray 70	Knight	Awford	Daniel*	McLoughlin	Symons	Maguire	Neill	Doling	Clarke	Whittingham	Murray	Powell
4,422 2:19				Ref: K Breen (Liverpool)	Martin	Davies	Murphy	Horner	Briggs	Thornber	Rodwell	Sinclair	Stringfellow* Leitch^	Murray	Eyres	Robinson/Mitchell

Billy Ayre's Blackpool are rocked by a Pompey second-half super show. Before tonight they had lost once at Bloomfield Road in 42 games. Clarke slid home the first then McLoughlin heads in a corner. Murray's is a mint of a goal as he finishes off a sweet move with his left foot.

		F-A	H-T	Scorers, Times, and Referees	1	2	3	4	5	6	7	8	9	10	11	subs used
2:2 H BLACKPOOL 11	W	2-0	1-0	Whittingham 3, 65	Knight	Awford	Daniel	Chamberlain	Symons	Aspinall*	Neill^	Walsh	Burns	Whittingham	Maguire	Doling/Butters
3,096 2:19				Ref: P Durkin (Portland)	McIlhargey	Murphy*	Stoneman	Horner	Briggs	Gore	Rodwell	Sinclair	Robinson^	Gauck	Eyres	Bonner/Stringfellow
(Pompey won 6-0 on aggregate)																

An academic match sees that lowest gate for a major cup-tie shattered again. It is Pompey's 100th League Cup game and Whits effectively ends it as a contest after Walsh and Burns have shots blocked. He then hits the bar, before heading home Chambo's cross from six yards.

		F-A	H-T	Scorers, Times, and Referees	1	2	3	4	5	6	7	8	9	10	11	subs used
3 H IPSWICH 9	L	0-1	0-1	Thompson 6	Knight	Awford	Daniel	McLoughlin	Symons	Aspinall*	Neill	Chamberlain	Clarke	Whittingham	Maguire	Walsh
10,773 P:11				Ref: R Milford (Bristol)	Baker	Johnson	Thompson	Stockwell	Wark	Linighan	Williams	Goddard*	Whitton	Dozzell	Kiwomya	Gregory

Life is uncertain. Ipswich getting a result at Fratton is not. Town haven't lost here since 1966 and Thompson's blistering free-kick sets them up. Baker saves their skins on several occasions and Pompey force 15 second-half corners. Surely we'll beat them before the Millennium?

FA Cup

		F-A	H-T	Scorers, Times, and Referees	1	2	3	4	5	6	7	8	9	10	11	subs used
3 A BRIGHTON 5	L	0-1	0-1	Edwards 28	Knight	Awford	Daniel	McLoughlin	Symons	Burns	Russell^	Chamberlain	Walsh*	Powell	Aspinall	Murray/Ross
17,851 2:9				Ref: A Buksh (London)	Beeney	Chivers	Gallacher	Wilkins	Foster	Bissett	Crumplin	Kennedy	Nogan	Codner	Edwards*	Funnell

Pompey's cup hopes founder on veteran defender Foster, who marshals Albion to a prestigious win over last season's semi-finalists. Edwards heads in after the bounce deceives Symons. Powell's late goal is ruled out for offside and Pompey can concentrate on the league. No bad thing.

Division 1 Play-offs

		F-A	H-T	Scorers, Times, and Referees	1	2	3	4	5	6	7	8	9	10	11	subs used
1:2 A LEICESTER 3	L	0-1	0-0	Joachim 86	Knight	Awford	Price	McLoughlin	Symons	Daniel	Neill	Chamberlain* Powell^	Walsh^	Powell	Whittingham	Burns/Lawrence
24,538 6				Ref: K Hackett (Sheffield)	Poole	Mills	Whitlow	Smith	Walsh	Hill	Oldfield	Thompson	Gee	Gibosa*	Philpott^	Grayson/Joachim
(at Nott'm Forest)																

Joachim's arrival on the hour sparks the City fans into song at last, as Leicester are becoming increasingly desperate. His stunning strike, after his pace took him past three, gives the Foxes the edge. Pompey miss Walsh's guile and Whittingham has only one chance, saved by Poole.

		F-A	H-T	Scorers, Times, and Referees	1	2	3	4	5	6	7	8	9	10	11	subs used
2:2 H LEICESTER 3	D	2-2	0-0	McLoughlin 52, Kristensen 77	Knight	Awford	Butters	McLoughlin	Symons	Daniel	Neill*	Price^	Walsh^	Whittingham	Kristensen	Powell/Hall
25,438 6				Ormondroyd 54, Thompson 68	Poole	Mills	Whitlow	Smith	Walsh	Hill	Oldfield	Thompson	Joachim	Ormondroyd Agnew^	Gibson	
				Ref: R Milford (Bristol)												
				(Pompey lost 2-3 on aggregate)												

The tuning point comes when Ormondroyd, six yards out, steers past Symons on the line, but he should be flagged as keeper Knight is stranded on the penalty spot. Macca had just thumped Pompey deservedly in front. Kristensen's spectacular shot is too late, despite a frantic finish.

Home / Away League Table

	Team	P	W	D	L	F	A	W	D	L	F	A	Pts
				Home						Away			
1	Newcastle	46	16	6	1	58	15	13	3	7	34	23	96
2	West Ham	46	16	5	2	50	17	10	5	8	31	24	88
3	PORTSMOUTH	46	19	2	2	48	9	7	8	8	32	37	88
4	Tranmere	46	15	4	4	48	24	8	6	9	24	32	79
5	Swindon*	46	15	5	3	41	23	6	8	9	33	36	76
6	Leicester	46	14	5	4	43	24	8	5	10	28	40	76
7	Millwall	46	14	6	3	46	21	4	10	9	19	32	70
8	Derby	46	11	2	10	40	33	8	7	8	28	24	66
9	Grimsby	46	12	6	5	33	25	7	1	15	25	32	64
10	Peterborough	46	7	11	5	30	26	9	3	11	25	37	62
11	Wolves	46	11	6	6	37	26	5	7	11	20	30	61
12	Charlton	46	11	6	6	28	19	5	5	11	21	27	61
13	Barnsley	46	12	4	7	29	19	5	5	13	27	41	60
14	Oxford	46	8	7	8	29	21	6	7	10	24	35	56
15	Bristol City	46	10	7	6	29	25	4	7	12	20	42	56
16	Watford	46	8	7	8	27	30	6	6	11	30	41	55
17	Notts Co	46	10	7	6	33	21	2	9	12	22	49	52
18	Southend	46	9	4	10	33	22	4	5	14	21	42	52
19	Birmingham	46	10	4	9	30	32	3	8	12	20	40	51
20	Luton	46	6	13	4	26	26	4	8	11	22	36	51
21	Sunderland	46	9	6	8	34	28	4	5	14	16	36	50
22	Brentford	46	7	6	10	28	30	6	4	13	24	41	49
23	Cambridge	46	8	9	2	29	32	3	10	10	19	37	49
24	Bristol Rov	46	6	6	11	30	42	4	5	14	25	45	41
		1104	263	147	142	859	590	142	147	263	590	859	1509

* promoted after play-offs

Odds & ends

Double wins: (6) Derby, Birmingham, Cambridge, Tranmere, Bristol Rov, Luton.

Double losses: (1) West Ham.

Won from behind: (3) Luton (h&a), Grimsby (h).

Lost from in front: (2) Brentford (a), Bristol C (h).

High spots: Guy Whittingham sets a new club league scoring record by scoring 42 goals, beating Billy Haines' record set in 1927. Run of 11 wins and a draw in 12 matches from March to May. Whittingham scoring four goals in a 4-1 win over Bristol Rovers on Boxing Day.

Low spots: Missing automatic promotion on 'goals scored'. Losing 1-4 at relegation threatened Sunderland in the penultimate game of the season. Conceding two goals in injury-time to allow Oxford to claim a 5-5 draw in November. Getting knocked out of the FA Cup by second division Brighton.

The 5-5 draw at Oxford was the first time the club had been involved in that scoreline in a first team match.

Player of the Year: Paul Walsh.

Ever presents: (3) Alan Knight, Alan McLoughlin, Guy Whittingham.

Hat-tricks: Guy Whittingham (4).

Leading scorer: Guy Whittingham (47). Including 3 in Anglo-Italian Cup.

Appearances and Goals

Player	Lge	Sub	LC	Sub	FAC	Sub	Lge	LC	FAC	Tot
		Appearances						Goals		
Agnew, Steve	3									
Aspinall, Warren	19	8	2		1		2			2
Awford, Andy	44		3		1					
Burns, Chris	28	4	1		1		1			1
Butters, Guy	13	1		1			1			1
Chamberlain, Mark	37	4	2		1		4			4
Clarke, Colin	11	8	2				1		1	2
Daniel, Ray	40		3		1		4			4
Doling, Stuart	2	4	1	1						
Knight, Alan	46		3		3					
Kristensen, Bjorn	10						1			1
Kuhl, Martin	3						1			1
Lawrence, George		12								
Maguire, Gavin	18	3	3							
McLoughlin, Alan	46	2	2		1		9	2		11
Murray, Shaun	2	5	1	1					1	1
Neil, Warren	28	3	1		3					
Powell, Darryl	4	19	1			1				
Price, Chris	13	2								
Ross, Micky						1				
Russell, Lee	12	2	1		1					
Stimson, Mark	3	2								
Symons, Kit	41		3		1		2			2
Walsh, Paul	37	6	1	1	1		9			9
Whittingham, Guy	46		3		3		42		2	44
(own-goals)							3			3
25 players used	506	80	33	4	11	2	80	6		86

ENDSLEIGH LEAGUE DIVISION 1 Manager: Jim Smith SEASON 1993-94

No	V	Opponent	Date	Att	Pos	Pt	F-A	H-T	Scorers, Times, and Referees	1	2	3	4	5	6	7	8	9	10	11	subs used
1	A	OXFORD	14/8	8,550	—	L / 0	2-3	2-2	Chapman 24, 42 / Symons 19 (og), Allen 40, Magilton 64p — Ref: S Dunn (Bristol)	Knight	Awford	Butters*	McLoughlin	Symons	Stimson	Neill	Chamberlain	Chapman	Blake^	Kristensen	Burns/Powell
										Kee	*Smart*	*Ford*	*Lewis*	*Collins*	*Rogan*	*Magilton*	*Beauchamp*	*Dyer*	*Robinson*	*Allen*	*Curbishley*
2	H	CHARLTON	17/8	15,701	—	L / 0	1-2	0-2	Symons 65p / Nelson 20, Walsh 39 — Ref: D Frampton (Poole)	Knight	Awford	Butters*	McLoughlin	Symons	Stimson	Neill	Chamberlain^	Chapman!	Walsh	Blake	Burns/Hall
										Salmon	*Pitcher*	*McLeary*	*Chapple*	*Minto*	*Newton*	*Garland*	*Robinson**	*Walsh*	*Leaburn*	*Nelson*	*Curbishley*
3	H	LUTON	21/8	12,248	10 / 16	W / 3	1-0	1-0	Hall 41 — Ref: G Poll (Berkhamsted)	Knight	Awford	Burns	McLoughlin^	Symons	Stimson	Neill	Hall	Chapman	Walsh^	Blake	Price/Aspinall
										Sommer	*James*	*Johnson*	*Peake*	*Drayer*	*Telfer*	*Hughes*	*Preece*	*Oakes**	*Williams^*	*Dixon*	*Benjamin/Houghton*
4	A	GRIMSBY	24/8	5,259	10 / 18	D / 4	1-1	1-0	McLoughlin 11 / Mendonca 51p — Ref: I Cruickshanks (Hartlepool)	Horne	Awford	Burns	McLoughlin	Symons	Stimson*	Neill	Hall^	Chapman	Walsh^	Blake	Price/Russell
										Crichton	*McDermott*	*Croft*	*Futcher**	*Rodger*	*Dobbin*	*Crosby*	*Gilbert*	*Groves*	*Mendonca*	*Woods*	*Lever*
5	A	CRYSTAL PALACE	28/8	14,428	12 / 6	L / 4	1-5	1-2	Neill 6 [Southgate 64] / Armstrong 18, 68, 83, Gordon 32 — Ref: P Danson (Leicester)	Horne	Awford^	Russell	McLoughlin	Symons	Stimson	Neill	Blake	Chapman	Walsh	Kristensen	Durnin/Price
										Martyn	*Humphrey*	*Gordon*	*Southgate*	*Young*	*Coleman*	*Shaw*	*Bowry*	*Armstrong*	*Williams*	*Rodger*	
6	H	STOKE	4/9	12,552	14 / 16	D / 5	3-3	3-1	Durnin 3, Walsh 10, Gittens 35 / Stein 16, 65, Regis 83 — Ref: R Groves (Weston-super-Mare)	Horne	Awford*	Burns	McLoughlin	Gittens	Daniel	Neill	Blake	Durnin	Walsh^	Butters	Price/Powell
										Prudhoe	*Butler*	*Sandiford*	*Cranson*	*Williams**	*Orlygsson^*	*Gynn*	*Foley*	*Stein*	*Regis*	*Cleghorn*	*Lowe/Carruthers*
7	A	WOLVERHAMPTON	11/9	19,019	18 / 7	D / 6	1-1	0-0	Durnin 64 / Kelly 48 — Ref: J Parker (Preston)	Knight	Gittens	Burns	McLoughlin	Symons	Stimson	Neill	Blake	Durnin*	Walsh	Kristensen	Hall
										Stowell	*Rankine*	*Shirtliff*	*Cook**	*Blades*	*Venus*	*Burke*	*Thomas*	*Regis^*	*Kelly*	*Keen*	*Dennison/Birch*
8	H	SOUTHEND	18/9	11,093	12 / 7	W / 9	2-1	1-1	Durnin 10, Powell 87 / Jones 35 — Ref: D Gallagher (Banbury)	Knight	Gittens	Burns	McLoughlin	Symons	Awford	Neill	Hall	Durnin!	Walsh*	Kristensen	Powell/Allon
										Sansome	*Poole*	*Powell*	*Jones*	*Howell*	*Bressington*	*Ansah*	*Payne*	*Lee*	*Otto*	*Harding**	
9	H	BRISTOL CITY	25/9	10,702	13 / 20	D / 10	0-0	0-0	— Ref: G Willard (Worthing)	Knight	Gittens	Blake*	McLoughlin	Symons	Awford	Neill	Stimson	Durnin	Walsh	Kristensen	Powell/Osman
										Welch	*Burrows*	*Munro*	*Shail*	*Bryant*	*Edwards*	*Martin**	*Allison*	*Baird*	*Robinson*	*Gavin*	
10	A	NOTT'M FOREST	2/10	20,727	13 / 19	D / 11	1-1	0-0	Powell 72 / Stone 89 — Ref: J Rushton (Stoke)	Knight	Gittens	Dobson	McLoughlin	Symons	Awford	Price	Hall^	Powell	Walsh	Kristensen	Aspinall
										Wright	*Laws*	*Lyttle*	*Crosby*	*Chettle*	*Stone*	*Phillips*	*Gemmill*	*Howe*	*Collymore*	*Black*	
11	A	PETERBOROUGH	9/10	6,538	13 / 22	D / 12	2-2	2-1	McLoughlin 22, Walsh 43 / McGlashen 18, Adcock 66 — Ref: P Jones (Loughborough)	Knight	Gittens	Pethick	McLoughlin	Stimson	Awford	Burns	Powell^	Durnin	Walsh	Kristensen*	Aspinall/Dobson
										Bennett	*McDonald*	*Howarth*	*Bradshaw*	*Peters*	*Welsh*	*Adcock*	*Phillskirk*	*McGlashen*	*Brissett**	*Hackett*	*Iorfa*

Match 1 (A, Oxford): Smith has turned to £250,000 Chapman (Leeds) to replace Whits. Two classy strikes seem to do just that, but Smith is furious about United's winner and he will face the FA's wrath (£750 fine). The linesman flags for hands but no one can work out whose. Magilton keeps his cool.

Match 2 (H, Charlton): Chapman makes another mark; with his elbow on McLeary's face and he is sent off. Addicks are already two-up by then, each goal set up by Robinson's back-heel. Symons is now penalty taker and he converts after a handball. Ex-Villain Blake (part of the Whits deal) is labouring.

Match 3 (H, Luton): Bright prospect Hall (20) pays an early dividend, firing home from close range after Stimson (£100,000) crosses. Chapman sees a goal ruled out and also protests his elbow was innocent. There is a minute's silence for ex-player, scout and caretaker boss Barton, who died last week.

Match 4 (A, Grimsby): Walsh is Pompey's fourth skipper so far – the previous three (Kristensen, Chambo and Knight) have all ended up crocked! Happily he remains intact, and sees Macca convert Chapman's flick. Mendonca's penalty is after Awford fouls Woods, then Gilbert hits the inside of the post.

Match 5 (A, Crystal Palace): Whits reveals he has almost stayed in the summer, but even his goals wouldn't have stopped Alan Smith's Eagles preying on Pompey. Neill fires in from 20 yards, but Horne then spills and Armstrong nets. Southgate's 30-yard missile, after running from halfway, is the best of a nap hand.

Match 6 (H, Stoke): Bad-boy Durnin is a £200,000 gamble (Oxford) but he looks a dead-cert in finishing a move from 12 yards. Walsh's goal is glorious. Then Gittens (Middlesbro) nods in to restore the cushion. Horne handles a back-pass and Stein profits, then Regis steers past the advancing keeper.

Match 7 (A, Wolverhampton): Knight has recovered, but Awford makes way for Symons, back from Welsh duty. Big-spending Wolves are awful, but £750,000 Kelly's strike is so bad, it completely deceives Knight and goes in! Durnin sees justice is done, after Walsh's trickery. Parkway faces a crucial council vote.

Match 8 (H, Southend): £250,000 Chapman is back – but he's playing for West Ham! Seems he can't stomach Div One. Sub Powell lashes in and Southend ponder points lost, especially after Durnin's two yellows. Otto misses three sitters and Pompey wear white socks as Southend have only red with them.

Match 9 (H, Bristol City): David Deacon vows to fight on after the Parkway vote is lost, while Smith is shooting down 'Walsh for Saints' stories. Whatever next? Blake sets the tone for this dreary draw by fouling Robinson after just 15 seconds and the referee ends up taking five names in a physical contest.

Match 10 (A, Nott'm Forest): Frank Clark's Forest are short-priced to go up, but have won just two in eight. With £2.2 million Collymore well-shackled, Powell's strike, after Macca nutmegged Lyttle, looks decisive, but Stone has other ideas 25 yards out in injury-time. Loanee Dobson (Blackburn) is impressive.

Match 11 (A, Peterborough): Pompey are unbeaten in nine, but with only one win in the league. That should be two now, after Macca strikes from 25 yards, then Walsh's chip leaves Bennett stranded. £35,000 Pethick (Weymouth) looks to be fouled, but a corner is given and Hackett crosses for Adcock's head.

12. DERBY (H) — 16/10 — W 3-2 · Att 12,404 · (9 / 7) · 15
Scorers: Walsh 37, Durnin 46, Symons 61p / Johnson 16, Kitson 66
Ref: M Bailey (Impington)
Pompey: Knight, Gittens, Pethick, McLoughlin, Symons, Awford, Dobson, Stimson, Durnin*, Walsh, Kristensen; Power
Derby: Taylor, Charles*, Forsyth, Pembridge, Short, Wassell, Harkes, Johnson, Kitson, Gabbiadini^, Simpson; Kavanagh/Hayward
Smith is the loan arranger – Norwich striker Power the latest. New Rams' boss Roy McFarland looks set for a first away win when Johnson strikes, but Dobson robs Charles to set up Walsh, then Durnin snaps up a Walsh's rebound. Short grabs Dobson's shirt and Symons scores.

13. NOTTS CO (A) — 23/10 — D 1-1 · Att 6,681 · (13 / 18) · 16
Scorers: Dobson 8 / Walker 88
Ref: P Wright (Northwich)
Pompey: Knight, Gittens!, Pethick, McLoughlin, Symons, Awford, Dobson, Stimson, Durnin, Walsh, Power*; Hall/Doling
Notts Co: Cherry, Gallagher, King, Turner, Walker, Cos, Devlin, Thomas, McSwegan, Lund, Legg*; Agana
For Forest, read County. Dobson nets from the edge of the area, but at the death Knight fluffs and Walker nods in off Symons. Gittens hoofs into the stand and is sent off in injury-time. Power is short-circuited and will return east. Parkway passes full council muster by one vote.

14. TRANMERE (H) — 30/10 — W 2-0 · Att 12,462 · (8 / 4) · 19
Scorers: Dobson 66, Walsh 80
Ref: I Hemley (Ampthill)
Pompey: Knight, Gittens, Dobson, McLoughlin, Symons, Awford, Neill, Stimson^, Durnin, Walsh, Chamberlain*; Doling/Pethick
Tranmere: Nixon, Higgins, Nolan, Proctor, Mungall, Vickers, Kenworthy*, Muir, Malkin, Nevin, Thomas; Branch
Rovers have lost their three at Fratton now without scoring. Two weeks ago they were top, but have slipped lately and they can have no moans here. Dobbo's loan is extended and he heads in Macca's cross from a narrow angle, then Walsh nips in front of Nixon and angles home.

15. MIDDLESBROUGH (H) — 2/11 — W 2-0 · Att 12,503 · (8 / 7) · 22
Scorers: Hall 75, Durnin 88
Ref: P Alcock (S Mertsham)
Pompey: Knight, Gittens, Doling, Dobson, Symons, Awford, Neill, Stimson, Durnin, Walsh^, Chamberlain*; Hall/Pethick
Middlesbrough: Pears, Barrow, Liburd, Mustoe, Mohan, Whyte, Fleming, Kavanagh, Wilkinson, Johnson, Hignett
Pompey leave it late, but deserve to beat Lennie Lawrence's side, who had lost just one in eight. Doling impresses and it is his 40-yard pass which Hall reaches just ahead of Steve Pears and he clips in. Boro bounce back and hit a post, but Durnin's 20-yard curler clinches it.

16. SUNDERLAND (A) — 9/11 — W 2-1 · Att 17,146 · (6 / 18) · 25
Scorers: Walsh 16, Doling 45 / Smith 48
Ref: J Kirkby (Sheffield)
Pompey: Knight, Butters, Doling*, McLoughlin, Symons, Awford, Neill, Stimson, Durnin, Walsh*, Dobson; Pethick/Powell
Sunderland: Chamberlain, Owers, Gray Mike*, Melville, Ball, Rodgerson, Ferguson, Armstrong, Goodman, Gray Phil, Smith; Bennett
Pompey's search for their first away win ends at Terry Butcher's Sunderland. If only it had come six months ago! Walsh turns Ball and fires home, then Neill gets him to the line and he crosses for Doling to sweep home. Smith's shot deflects in off Symons to subdue restless Roker.

17. BIRMINGHAM (A) — 23/11 — W 1-0 · Att 11,896 · (7 / 16) · 28
Scorers: Stimson 76
Ref: A Flood (Stockport)
Pompey: Knight, Gittens, Blake*, McLoughlin^, Symons^, Awford, Neill, Stimson, Durnin, Walsh, Dobson; Daniel/Kristensen
Birmingham: Miller, Hiley, Parris, Dryden, Potter, Shutt, Moulden*, Saville, Tait, McMinn, Smith; Peschisolido
Stimson gets the terrace critics off his back with a clinical finish when Neill's shot comes back off the bar. Parris then handles, but Durnin puts the penalty wide. In the week Macca's goal takes Eire to USA 94, Ball (Symons (Wales) and Kristensen (Denmark) will have to stay at home.

18. WEST BROM (A) — 30/11 — L 1-4 · Att 13,867 · (9 / 19) · 28
Scorers: McLoughlin 60 / Taylor 18, O'Regan 42, Hunt 85, 88
Ref: P Harrison (Oldham)
Pompey: Knight, Gittens, Dobson, McLoughlin, Symons*, Awford, Neill, Stimson, Durnin, Walsh, Kristensen^; Daniel/Aspinall
West Brom: Lange, Burgess, Williams, Mardon, Raven, Ashcroft*, Hunt, O'Regan, Taylor, Mellon, Hamilton; Heggs
Keith Burkinshaw's side have lost their last six, while Pompey haven't lost since August, but the first half is no contest. Taylor thumps his 14th and O'Regan eases in. Smith's blunt talk improves things, but Hunt profits as Pompey push on. Murray has gone to Scarboro (£25,000).

19. SUNDERLAND (H) — 4/12 — L 0-1 · Att 11,891 · (11 / 19) · 28
Scorers: Smith 45
Ref: P Foakes (Clacton-on-Sea)
Pompey: Knight, Gittens^, Daniel, McLoughlin*, Butters, Awford, Neill, Doling, Durnin, Walsh, Kristensen; Hall/Aspinall
Sunderland: Chamberlain, Owers, Ord, Bennett, Melville, Ball, Ferguson, Cunnington, Goodman, Gray, Smith*; Atkinson
Butcher has paid for six straight losses, and old adversary Mick Buxton is Roker's caretaker. Smith warns in the programme a team with a new boss is rarely a pushover. He is right. Gray's flicked header is scooped away, but Smith is on hand. Durnin wants to catch Jack Charlton's eye.

20. WATFORD (H) — 7/12 — W 2-0 · Att 8,242 · (6 / 23) · 31
Scorers: Durnin 45, Butters 70
Ref: R Milford (Bristol)
Pompey: Knight, Doling*, McLoughlin, Symons, Awford, Neill, Daniel^, Stimson, Durnin, Walsh, Kristensen; Hall/Butters
Watford: Sheppard, Lavin, McCarthy, Hessenthaler, Holdsworth, Watson, Dyer, Soloman, Furlong, Johnson, Nogan*; Alsford
Frost claimed this game a fortnight ago, now Glenn Roeder's team are frozen out. Butters' far-post header makes it safe, after Durnin nodded in Walsh's centre. Is Saints boss Branfoot here to watch Walsh? Environment Minister John Gummer has ordered a public inquiry into Parkway.

21. CHARLTON (A) — 12/12 — W 1-0 · Att 6,975 · (7 / 2) · 34
Scorers: Neill 9
Ref: R Gifford (Llanbradach)
Pompey: Knight, Gittens, Butters, McLoughlin, Symons, Awford, Neill, Doling*, Durnin, Walsh, Kristensen; Russell
Charlton: Salmon, Balmer, Minto, Garland*, Chapple, McLeary, Robinson, Pitcher, Leaburn, Nelson^, Walsh; Robson/Newton
Walsh's cross eludes everyone but Warren Neill coming in at the far post and he tucks home the fourth goal of his Pompey career to settle this televised match. Second-placed Valiants have plenty of possession, but in truth Durnin looks the most likely to score again on the break.

22. OXFORD (H) — 18/12 — D 1-1 · Att 8,980 · (6 / 21) · 35
Scorers: McLoughlin 22 / Beauchamp 83
Ref: E Lomas (Manchester)
Pompey: Knight, Dobson*, Chamberlain^, McLoughlin, Symons, Awford, Neill, Durnin, Daniel^, Walsh, Kristensen; Russell/Hall
Oxford: Whitehead, Elliott, Lewis, Collins, Rogan, Magilton, Beauchamp, Cusack, Penney*, Allen^; Jackson/Druce
Oxford, now managed by Denis Smith, have lost their last three, and Pompey look like extending that when Macca brings down Chambo's cross and slots in. Beauchamp beats the unsighted Knight after Butters' slip. Burns is looking to get his career going again on loan at Swansea.

23. MILLWALL (A) — 27/12 — D 0-0 · Att 12,104 · (8 / 3) · 36
Ref: I Borrett (Harleston)
Pompey: Knight, Gittens, Butters, McLoughlin, Symons, Awford, Neill, Russell*, Durnin, Walsh, Kristensen; Chamberlain
Millwall: Keller, Dolby*, Barber, Roberts, Emblem, Stevens, Rae, Kennedy^, Mitchell, Goodman, Huxford; Beard/Verveer
Pompey have to soak up plenty of pressure on their first visit to Millwall's state-of-the-art Senegal Fields ground, but there is little in the way of goalmouth action to speak of. Mick McCarthy has turned Lions around after a poor start and this result means they are unbeaten in nine.

ENDSLEIGH LEAGUE DIVISION 1

Manager: Jim Smith

SEASON 1993-94

Players are shown as **Portsmouth** / *opponent*. The Pos column shows Portsmouth position / *opponent position*.

No	Date	Venue / Opponent	Att	Pos	Pt	F-A	H-T	Scorers, Times, and Referees	1	2	3	4	5	6	7	8	9	10	11	Subs used
24	28/12	H BOLTON	14,276	7 / *13*	D 37	0-0	0-0	Ref: K Burge (Tonypandy)	Knight / *Davison*	Dobson / *Parkinson*	Daniel / *Burke*	McLoughlin / *Kelly*	Symons / *Seagroves*	Awford / *Winstanley*	Neill / *McAteer*	Blake^ / *Stubbs*	Durnin / *Green*	Walsh / *Fleck*	Kristensen* / *Patterson*	Hall/Powell
25	1/1	A BARNSLEY	6,328	9 / *22*	L 37	0-2	0-1	O'Connell 41, *Redfearn 56* — Ref: I Cruickshanks (Hartlepool)	Knight / *Butler*	Dobson / *Eaden*	Daniel* / *Fleming*	McLoughlin / *Wilson*	Symons / *Taggart*	Awford / *Bishop*	Pethick / *O'Connell*	Chamberlain* / *Redfearn*	Durnin / *Payton*	Walsh / *Rammell*	Russell / *Archdeacon*	Stimson/Kristensen
26	15/1	A DERBY	15,645	12 / *6*	L 37	0-1	0-0	Johnson 90 — Ref: G Cain (Bootle)	Knight / *Taylor*	Neill / *Charles*	Daniel / *Forsyth*	McLoughlin^ / *Kuhl*	Butters / *Short*	Awford* / *Wassall*	Stimson / *Johnson*	Durnin / *Pembridge*	Powell / *Kitson*	Walsh / *Gabbiadini*	Kristensen / *Williams*	Chamberlain/Doling
27	22/1	H PETERBOROUGH	19,534	12 / *24*	L 37	0-2	0-1	Adcock 22, 61 — Ref: D Frampton (Poole)	Knight / *Barber*	Doling^ / *McDonald*	Russell / *Spearing*	McLoughlin / *Greenman*	Dobson* / *Howarth*	Awford / *Walsh*	Neill / *Adcock*	Blake / *Ebdon*	Powell / *Anthrobus**	Walsh* / *Charlery*	Kristensen / *Blissett*	Durnin/Burns, Furnell
28	5/2	H NOTTS CO	9,359	13 / *14*	D 38	0-0	0-0	Ref: P Alcock (S Merstham)	Knight / *Cherry*	Durnin^ / *Palmer*	Daniel / *Sherlock*	McLoughlin / *Turner*	Symons / *Foster*	Awford / *Dijkstra*	Neill / *Devlin*	Chamberlain^ / *Draper*	Creaney* / *Lund*	Walsh / *Reid*	Kristensen / *Agana*	Powell/Burns
29	11/2	A TRANMERE	6,914	14 / *5*	L 38	1-3	0-2	McLoughlin 87; *Aldridge 5, Malkin 35, Branman 63* — Ref: J Key (Sheffield)	Knight / *Nixon*	Gittens / *McGreal*	Daniel / *Nolan*	McLoughlin / *Branman*	Symons / *Hughes*	Awford^ / *O'Brien*	Neill / *Irons*	Blake / *Aldridge*	Creaney / *Malkin*	Walsh* / *Nevin*	Kristensen / *Thomas*	Powell/Pethick
30	19/2	H GRIMSBY	7,794	14 / *17*	W 41	3-1	2-0	Creaney 21, 26p, 46; *Groves 83* — Ref: M Reed (Birmingham)	Knight / *Crichton*	Gittens / *McDermott*	Daniel / *Croft*	Hall / *Futcher*	Symons / *Rodger*	Dobson / *Shakespeare*	Neill / *Childs**	Blake / *Ford*	Creaney / *Rees^*	Powell / *Mendonca*	Kristensen* / *Groves*	Wood, Agnew/Okoreie
31	22/2	A LUTON	6,533	14 / *15*	L 41	1-4	0-2	Symons 55; *Telfer 5, Preece 27, Hughes 50, Oakes 52* — Ref: G Singh (Wolverhampton)	Knight / *Sommer*	Gittens / *Linton*	Daniel* / *James*	Hall / *Harper**	Symons / *Peake*	Dobson / *Dreyer*	Neill^ / *Telfer*	Blake / *Oakes*	Creaney / *Dixon^*	Powell / *Hughes*	Kristensen / *Preece*	Durnin/Wood, Thorpe/Hartson
32	26/2	A STOKE	14,506	15 / *5*	L 41	0-2	0-1	Orlygsson 44p, Carruthers 85 — Ref: J Parker (Preston)	Knight / *Prudhoe*	Stimson^ / *Butler*	Butters / *Sandford*	Burns / *Cranson*	Symons* / *Overson*	Awford / *Orlygsson*	Neill / *Foley*	Durnin / *Carruthers*	Creaney / *Regis*	Walsh / *Clark*	Kristensen / *Gleghorn*	Powell/Wood
33	5/3	H CRYSTAL PALACE	13,508	17 / *1*	L 41	0-1	0-0	Young 63 — Ref: M Bodenham (Looe)	Knight / *Martyn*	Gittens / *Humphrey*	Stimson* / *Gordon*	McLoughlin / *Southgate*	Butters / *Young*	Awford / *Coleman*	Pethick / *Rodger*	Burns^ / *Matthew*	Powell / *Armstrong*	Walsh / *Stewart*	Hall / *Salako*	Durnin/Kristensen
34	12/3	A SOUTHEND	4,437	18 / *10*	L 41	1-2	1-1	Creaney 6; *Beadle 14, Sussex 55* — Ref: G Willard (Worthing)	Knight / *Sansome*	Gittens / *Poole*	Stimson^ / *Powell*	McLoughlin / *Ansah*	Daniel / *Scully*	Awford / *Edwards*	Pethick / *Hunt*	Blake / *Payne*	Creaney* / *Beadle*	Wood / *Otto*	Kristensen / *Sussex*	Hall/Butters

24 BOLTON — Roly-poly Fleck has been borrowed by Bruce Rioch as his team look to consolidate. His rapport with the crowd is better than his forward play. Pompey are firing blanks, but David Deacon hopes to get a result. A decision on delaying Fratton's summer 1994 all-seater deadline is close.

25 BARNSLEY — No doubt Man U and Blackburn were represented here. It's doubtful the Premiership's top two will be quaking, as ex-Pompey apprentice O'Connell sets Tykes on their way. Monday's game with Leicester will be rained off. Smith reveals he is for Southend striker Brett Angell.

26 DERBY — Johnson's shot creeps in through a crowded box, but Stimmo, Butters and Powell face an FA hearing for berating ref Cain; the corner that led to it should have been a goal-kick. Awford and Symons are doubtful for Blackburn. Angell's £500,000 move founders on a dodgy knee X-ray.

27 PETERBOROUGH — Posh won their first game since October last week. Fans flock to Fratton for Man U vouchers; they'll be back again tomorrow to buy the tickets! Chairman-cum-caretaker boss Chris Turner sees Adcock – whom Smith has inquired about – take two sharp chances. Macca hit a post.

28 NOTTS CO — Despite paying a club-record fee for Creaney, Pompey's league drought stretches to 607 minutes. Symons had the perfect chance to end that, when Dijkstra handled Chambo's cross, but Creaney saves the pen. Price has become Hereford coach and Aspinall's off to Cherries (£20,000).

29 TRANMERE — At least Macca scored. Play-off hopes are looking forlorn as Pompey's win-less run is now 13. Blake is back after his hamstring problems, but once Aldridge nods in after McGreal's header hit the bar and Walsh hobbles off, the result is inevitable. Makin and Branman use their heads.

30 GRIMSBY — Gerry finally shows what a great Scot he can be. Powell sets him up for a neat flick, he sends Crichton the wrong way after Hall is clattered, then his bending free-kick 51 seconds into the second half is a gem. Cherry (Paul) Wood has a second coming. He's back at Fratton on loan!

31 LUTON — An inch of snow and first-half blizzard make the pitch a farce for the second season running. This time David Pleat's cup quarter-finalists (one defeat in 12) win 4-1! Telfer heads home, Preece volleys in, Hughes angles home, then Oakes chips from 30 yards. Symons' hardly matters.

32 STOKE — The play-offs seem a dim dream. Pompey are nine points (having played three more) behind Millwall (sixth). Stoke are unbeaten at home since Sept. Symons is hamstrung early on. Orlygsson's pen is for Kristensen felling Carruthers, who then bundles in after Knight spills his shot.

33 CRYSTAL PALACE — Laboured Pompey take 85 minutes to make Martyn save. Walsh's shot makes the keeper stretch, but it will be his last Fratton act (for the time being). Smith will sell him to Man C (£750,000) next week to fans' fury. Palace are well worth Young's close header from Matthew's corner.

34 SOUTHEND — The 1000th competitive match at Roots Hall is settled by Sussex's blinding thirty yarder. Banners urging Gregory to go are unfurled, but the visiting fans cheer up when Walsh's understudy Wood hits the bar and Creaney reacts. Beadle responds with a close-range header on his debut.

Portsmouth match-by-match results (games 35–46)

Game 35 — H 15/3 WOLVERHAMPTON — W 3-0 (17 / 12 / 44) — Att 7,840
Scorers: Chamberlain 35, Creaney 64, 84. Ref: M Bailey (Impington)

Pompey	Opponent
Knight	Stowell
Pethick	Thompson
Daniel	Venus
McLoughlin	Rankine
Gittens	Blades
Dobson	Mountfield*
Kristensen	Marsden^
Chamberlain^	Ferguson
Creaney	Whittingham
Wood*	Kelly
Stimson	Keen
Powell/Hall	Birch/Cook

Wolves play on-loan Whits (this Villa move looks rocky): however he is but a shadow. Chambo's first of the season is a 30-yard special, then Creaney takes his tally to six in eight, muting the moans. Gregory braves fans' fury, but this will be his last visit to Fratton as age takes its toll.

Game 36 — A 19/3 BRISTOL CITY — L 0-1 (17 / 11 / 44) — Att 6,352
Allison 55. Ref: T Holbrook (Walsall)

Pompey	Opponent
Knight	Welch
Dobson	Hoyland
Stimson	Munro
McLoughlin	Shail
Daniel	Bryant
Awford	Tinnion
Pethick^	Harriott
Chamberlain	Hewlett
Creaney	Robinson^
Wood*	Allison
Russell	Scott
Powell/Hall	Baird

Play-offs? Pompey are looking at the relegation zone now! 21st-placed Posh have a game in hand. Scott hits the bar after just two minutes and Knight makes two sharp saves to preserve parity, but he has no chance when Allison turns and tucks away his 18th goal.

Game 37 — H 26/3 NOTT'M FOREST — W 2-1 (17 / 2 / 47) — Att 12,578
Creaney 35, Hall 52 / Collymore 65. Ref: R Groves (Weston-super-Mare)

Pompey	Opponent
Knight	Crossley
Awford	Pearce
Powell^	Cooper
Hall	Chettle
Gittens	Stone
Dobson	Phillips
Neill	Webb
Chamberlain*	Bohinen^
Creaney	Collymore
Wood*	Black
Stimson	Rosario/Lee
McLoughlin/Russell	

Dutch loan striker Boere (West Ham) nods down for Creaney, then high-speed Hall races clear to fire past Crossley. Forest will go up, but they're cut down to size here, but Collymore's class shows. Macca confirms he's happy to see out his contract, but Celtic are still sniffing.

Game 38 — A 30/3 LEICESTER — W 3-0 (16 / 3 / 50) — Att 15,146
Creaney 1, Hall 29, Neill 43. Ref: G Ashby (Worcester)

Pompey	Opponent
Knight	Ward
Awford	Grayson
Powell	Lewis
McLoughlin	Carey
Gittens	Agnew
Butters	Whitlow
Neill	Joachim
Hall^	Blake
Creaney	Roberts
Boere*	Speedie*
Stimson	Roberts
Kristensen/Chamb'n	Ormondroyd^ Walsh/Kerr

Blake - more disciplinary points than games at Pompey - has joined City (£360,000). Creaney motors after 38secs, then he puts Hall away and Foxes looked hunted. Agnew blazes a pen wide, before Neill nearly busts the net. The lights go out at half-time and home fans have their fun.

Game 39 — H 2/4 MILLWALL — D 2-2 (15 / 4 / 51) — Att 11,591
Powell 42, Creaney 85p / Cunningham 46, Mitchell 89. Ref: J Rushton (Stoke)

Pompey	Opponent
Knight	Keller
Awford^	Cunningham
Powell	Dawes
McLoughlin	Roberts
Gittens	Seagraves
Dobson	V d Hauwe
Neill	Hurlock
Chamberlain*	Allen
Creaney	Moralee
Boere^	Mitchell
Hall	Berry^
Kristensen/Wood	Rae

The P-word is bandied about when Creaney converts after Neill is nudged by Stevens, only to choke as Lions save it at the death. Mitchell's toe does the trick in a goalmouth melee. Powell is hit by a clearance and the stiff breezes carries it in, but Kenny Cunningham's header levels.

Game 40 — A 4/4 BOLTON — D 1-1 (15 / 17 / 52) — Att 9,560
Creaney 74 / McGinlay 56. Ref: P Jones (Loughborough)

Pompey	Opponent
Knight	Davison
Awford^	Brown
Powell	Phillips
McLoughlin	Stubbs
Gittens	Seagraves
Dobson	Lydiate
Neill	Fulton
Pethick	McAteer
Creaney	Walker*
Boere^	McGinlay
Kristensen	Roscoe
Hall/Wood	Green

Pompey make their first visit to Burnden Park in 18 years and earn a point thanks to Creaney's 10th goal in 14 games. He reacts quickest when as the ball squirts free on the edge of the area. Wanderers took the lead against the run of play with John McGinlay's low right-foot shot.

Game 41 — H 9/4 BARNSLEY — W 2-1 (13 / 19 / 55) — Att 7,005
Wood 53, Powell 58 / Redfearn 90p. Ref: S Dunn (Bristol)

Pompey	Opponent
Knight	Butler
Gittens	Eaden*
Powell	Fleming
McLoughlin	Sheridan*
Symons	Taggart
Dobson*	Anderson
Neill	O'Connell
Hall	Redfearn
Creaney	Rammell
Wood	Payton
Kristensen	Snodin
Chamberlain	Liddell/Williams

Viv Anderson's team lose their third in a row, but they had won seven out of nine. The game suits the weather. Fans hail Wood's diving lunge into flying boots. Powell's booming header is a ray of sunshine, but the officials are a shower as the find fault with Symons' last-minute tackle.

Game 42 — A 16/4 MIDDLESBROUGH — W 2-0 (10 / 11 / 58) — Att 10,041
Creaney 20, Powell 35. Ref: J Lloyd (Wrexham)

Pompey	Opponent
Knight	Pears
Gittens	Fleming
Powell	Liburd
McLoughlin	Pollock
Pethick	Vickers
Stimson	Whyte
Neill	Hendrie
Hall	Wright*
Creaney	Wilkinson
Wood*	Peake
Kristensen	Moore
Chamberlain	Hignett

Pompey hadn't won at Ayresome for more than 40 years: now they've won three of their last four there! Creaney's sidefoot sets them on their way, then Powell's 30-yard volley is: 'The best I've scored.' That's six unbeaten now. Awford and Powell are holding out for better contracts.

Game 43 — H 23/4 BIRMINGHAM — L 0-2 (14 / 22 / 58) — Att 11,101
Willis 6, Claridge 81p. Ref: K Cooper (Swindon)

Pompey	Opponent
Knight	Bennett
Gittens	Hiley
Powell	Frain
Durnin^	Donowa
Pethick	Whyte
Stimson	Daish
Neill	Ward
Hall	Claridge
Creaney !	Saville*
Wood^	Willis
Kristensen	Doherty
Doling/Boere	De Souza

Creaney is sent off for disputing an innocuous free-kick just after half-time, then Gittens's tackle looks fair, but Claridge tumbles and converts the penalty. It seals Barry Fry's Brum's fourth win in six. They will remain unbeaten, but are doomed. Boere leaves, while Horne wants away.

Game 44 — H 26/4 LEICESTER — L 0-1 (14 / 4 / 58) — Att 7,869
Kerr 17. Ref: P Vanes (Warley)

Pompey	Opponent
Knight	Poole
Gittens*	Grayson
Powell	Lewis
Symons^	Willis
Pethick	Carey
Stimson	Gibson
Neill	Joachim
Hall	Blake
Creaney	Coatsworth
Burton	Kerr
Kristensen	Ormondroyd
Chamberlain/Durnin	

City keep their play-off wagon rolling. This game has been postponed twice and three different programmes have been printed for it! Pompey-born John Kerr is set up by Joachim. Creaney pledges to keep nicking the ball as the keeper clears, despite being penalised four times so far.

Game 45 — A 30/4 WATFORD — L 0-1 (14 / 19 / 58) — Att 10,141
Hessenthaler 18. Ref: R Gifford (Llanbradach)

Pompey	Opponent
Knight	Digweed
Dobson	Lavin
Powell	Drysdale
Durnin^	Foster
Gittens	Dublin
Dobson	Millen
Neill	Hessenthaler*
Hall	Johnson
Creaney	Furlong
Doling^	Porter
Kristensen	Mooney^
Chamberlain/Russell	Ramage/Bailey

Hornets are safe as Pompey saunter once Hessenthaler gets away down the left and cuts in to score. But for Knight, the margin would have been wider. The Parkway public inquiry opens next week. Injured Symons says he wants to play in the Premiership, but won't rock the boat.

Game 46 — H 8/5 WEST BROM — L 0-1 (17 / 21 / 58) — Att 17,629
Ashcroft 45. Ref: D Elleray (Harrow)

Pompey	Opponent
Knight	Lange
Dobson	Strodder
Powell	Darton
Gittens	Ashcroft*
Pethick	Parsley
Dobson	Raven
Neill	Hunt
Chamberlain	Hamilton
Hall	Taylor
Wood	Donovan
Kristensen	McNally
Butters/Burton	Mellon

Ashcroft delights 10,000 visitors with his far-post finish. Albion are in deep trouble with only one win in seven and if Lange hadn't blocked Powell's late point-blank shot it would have been curtains. Brum won at Tranmere. Smith frees seven, but says: 'Don't expect big signings.'

Home 17,629
Away 10,817
Average 11,690

ENDSLEIGH DIVISION 1 (CUP-TIES)   Manager: Jim Smith   SEASON 1993-94

Coca-Cola Cup

				F-A	H-T	Scorers, Times, and Referees	1	2	3	4	5	6	7	8	9	10	11	subs used
2:1	A	ROTHERHAM	12 D	0-0	0-0		Knight	Gittens	Burns	McLoughlin	Symons	Awford	Butters	Powell	Durrin	Young*	Kristensen	Doling
21/9		3,866 2:10				*Mercer*	*Pickering*	*Jacobs*	*Banks*	*Richardson*	*Law*	*Goater**	*Goodwin*	*Helliwell*	*Varadi*	*Marginson*	*Howard*

Ref: A Wilkie (Chester-le-Street) Pompey are down to the bare bones and Romsey-born striker Young makes his only first-team start. The defence is comprised solely of centre-backs, but they cope well. An Achilles niggle denies Price the chance to join the '92-club'. Millmoor is the only ground he hasn't played on.

				F-A	H-T	Scorers, Times, and Referees	1	2	3	4	5	6	7	8	9	10	11	subs used
2:2	H	ROTHERHAM	13 W	5-0	3-0	Stimson 16, McLoughlin 19, Durrin 35, [Walsh 61, Burns 87]	Knight	Gittens	Pethick	McLoughlin*	Symons^	Awford	Powell !	Stimson	Durrin	Walsh	Kristensen	Aspinall/Burns
5/10		4,589 2:15					*Mercer*	*Hutchings*	*Jacobs*	*Banks**	*Richardson*	*Law*	*Page*	*Goodwin*	*Goater^*	*Varadi*	*Wilder !*	*Helliwell/Kiwomya*

Ref: M Bodenham (Looe) Windy Millers are never in it, but only a wicked deflection sets Pompey off. It's Stimmo's goal though. Pethick settles in well, but Smith is not happy when Powell raises his arms after a Wilder's foul and the pair are dismissed. He was also booked on Saturday for inciting Forest fans.
(Pompey won 5-0 on aggregate)

				F-A	H-T	Scorers, Times, and Referees	1	2	3	4	5	6	7	8	9	10	11	subs used
3	H	SWINDON	13 W	2-0	0-0	Durrin 59, Walsh 76	Knight	Gittens	Doling^	McLoughlin	Symons	Awford	Neill	Stimson	Durrin	Walsh	Chamberlain*	Pethick/Burns
26/10		12,554 P:22					*Digby*	*Summerbee*	*Bodin*	*Nijholt*	*Taylor*	*MacLaren**	*Moncur*	*Fjortoft*	*Ling^*	*Mutch*	*Fenwick*	*Horlock/Maskell*

Ref: G Poll (Berkhamsted) Premiership Swindon (12 points behind Pompey) won the play-offs last season. That score is settled. Chambo destroys Town, despite not being match-fit, after a two-month lay-off. Walsh sets up Durrin from 12 yards, then scores at the second attempt after his header is saved.

				F-A	H-T	Scorers, Times, and Referees	1	2	3	4	5	6	7	8	9	10	11	subs used
4	A	PETERBOROUGH	9 D	0-0	0-0		Knight	Gittens	Kristensen	McLoughlin	Butters	Awford	Neill	Stimson	Durrin	Walsh	Dobson*	Daniel
30/11		6,141 22					*Bennett*	*Greenman*	*Spearing*	*Bradshaw*	*Howarth*	*Walsh*	*Adcock*	*Hackett**	*McGalshen*	*Eddon*	*Cooper*	*Barnes*

Ref: J Rushden (Stoke) For the third meeting running at London Road Bennett earns Posh a draw against Pompey. He saves Dobson's fierce free-kick, and also denies Walsh and Durrin. Howarth body-checks Walsh in the box in the 64th minute, but it's only an indirect free-kick and Durrin fires just wide.

				F-A	H-T	Scorers, Times, and Referees	1	2	3	4	5	6	7	8	9	10	11	subs used
4R	H	PETERBOROUGH	8 W	1-0	0-0	Kristensen 119	Knight	Gittens^	Butters	McLoughlin	Symons	Awford	Neill !	Doling*	Durrin	Walsh	Kristensen	Hall/Russell
15/12		9,634 22					*Bennett*	*Greenman*	*Spearing*	*Bradshaw*	*Howarth*	*Walsh*	*Adcock*	*McGalshen*	*Furnell**	*Eddon*	*Halsall^*	*Barnes I/Brissett*

Ref: V Callow (Solihull) Neill has a curious end to this game. He is dismissed for scuffling with Barnes seconds after Kristensen's late-late 25-yarder has taken Pompey through to meet Man U. Two minutes later he's back on again to receive the Man of the Match award! Posh boss Lil Fuccillo will resign soon.

				F-A	H-T	Scorers, Times, and Referees	1	2	3	4	5	6	7	8	9	10	11	subs used
QF	A	MANCHESTER U	9 D	2-2	1-1	Walsh 32, 75	Knight	Durrin	Daniel	McLoughlin	Symons*	Awford	Dobson	Stimson*	Powell	Walsh	Kristensen	Doling/Chamberlain
12/1		43,794 P:1				Giggs 29, Cantona 60	*Schmeichel*	*Parker*	*Irwin*	*Bruce*	*Kanchelskis*	*Pallister*	*Cantona*	*Robson*	*McClair**	*Hughes^*	*Giggs*	*Dublin/Keane*

Ref: K Barrett (Coventry) United are top of the league. Pompey haven't scored in the league for four. Buoyed by their draw at Rovers though, Pompey refuse to be over-awed. Walsh nods in from a corner, then, oh-la-la, he dives to head home Powell's centre to thwart Cantona. 'Pompey are a credit' says Fergie.

				F-A	H-T	Scorers, Times, and Referees	1	2	3	4	5	6	7	8	9	10	11	subs used
QF R	H	MANCHESTER U	12 L	0-1	0-1	McClair 28	Knight	Durrin !	Daniel	McLoughlin	Symons	Awford	Neill	Chamberlain*	Creaney	Walsh	Kristensen	Powell
26/1		24,950 P:1					*Schmeichel*	*Parker*	*Irwin*	*Bruce*	*Kanchelskis*	*Pallister*	*Cantona*	*Ince*	*McClair*	*Keane*	*Giggs*	

Ref: K Cooper (Pontypridd) Creaney signed yesterday from Celtic for a club-record £650,000 and is pitched straight in against United in front of a live ITV audience. United dominate and McClair heads home Giggs' seventh corner of the first half. Durrin's two-footed challenge leads to a second yellow.

FA Cup

				F-A	H-T	Scorers, Times, and Referees	1	2	3	4	5	6	7	8	9	10	11	subs used
3	A	BLACKBURN	9 D	3-3	0-1	McLoughlin 48, 82, 89 / Shearer 21, Gallacher 71, Sherwood 85	Knight	Doling^	Daniel	McLoughlin	Symons	Awford	Stimson*	Dobson	Powell	Walsh	Kristensen	Russell/Durrin
8/1		17,219 P:2					*Flowers*	*Berg*	*Hendry*	*May*	*Le Saux*	*Ripley*	*Sherwood*	*Batty*	*Wilcox*	*Shearer*	*Gallacher*	

Ref: J Kirby (Sheffield) With twenty seconds left Symons flicks Daniel's free-kick into Macca's path and he slots home the first hat-trick of his career. Pompey have stunned big-spending Rovers. Ex-Saint Shearer celebrates his 21st goal, lobbed from the visiting section, mutes them!

				F-A	H-T	Scorers, Times, and Referees	1	2	3	4	5	6	7	8	9	10	11	subs used
3R	H	BLACKBURN	12 L	1-3	0-1	McLoughlin 77 / Shearer 44, May 68, Wilcox 78	Knight	Durrin	Daniel	McLoughlin	Butters*	Awford	Neill	Stimson^	Durrin	Walsh	Kristensen	Dobson/Hall
19/1		23,035 P:2					*Flowers*	*May*	*Berg*	*Sherwood*	*Hendry**	*Le Saux*	*Riley*	*Gallacher*	*Shearer*	*Batty*	*Wilcox*	*Moran*

Ref: J Kirkby (Sheffield) The officials are the only ones who miss Wilcox 'bowl' the ball in, just after Macca's turn-and-shot had Rovers on the rack. TV shows it was an off-break! Shearer deflects in off Awford, then May stoops to conquer. The club have put 'POMPEY' on their shirt backs. Not a good idea.

348

League Table

	P	W	D	L	F	A	W	D	L	F	A	Pts
		Home					Away					
1 Crystal Pal	46	16	4	3	39	18	11	5	7	34	28	90
2 Nott'm Forest	46	12	9	2	38	22	11	5	7	36	27	83
3 Millwall	46	14	8	1	36	17	9	9	5	22	32	74
4 Leicester*	46	11	9	3	45	30	8	8	7	27	29	73
5 Tranmere	46	15	3	5	48	23	6	6	11	21	30	72
6 Derby	46	15	3	5	44	25	8	5	10	29	43	71
7 Notts Co	46	16	3	4	43	26	4	5	14	22	43	68
8 Wolves	46	10	10	3	34	19	7	7	9	26	28	68
9 Middlesbro	46	12	6	5	40	19	6	7	10	26	35	67
10 Stoke	46	14	4	5	35	19	4	9	10	22	40	67
11 Charlton	46	14	4	3	39	22	3	6	13	22	36	65
12 Sunderland	46	14	2	7	35	22	5	5	13	19	35	65
13 Bristol City	46	11	7	5	27	18	5	6	12	20	32	64
14 Bolton	46	10	5	8	40	31	8	6	12	23	33	59
15 Southend	46	10	5	8	34	28	7	3	13	23	39	59
16 Grimsby	46	7	14	2	26	16	6	6	11	26	31	59
17 PORTSMOUTH	46	10	6	7	29	22	5	7	11	23	36	58
18 Barnsley	46	9	3	11	25	26	7	4	12	30	41	55
19 Watford	46	10	5	8	39	35	5	4	14	27	45	54
20 Luton	46	12	4	7	38	25	2	7	14	18	35	53
21 West Brom	46	9	7	7	38	31	4	5	14	22	38	51
22 Birmingham	46	9	7	7	28	29	4	5	14	24	40	51
23 Oxford	46	10	5	8	33	33	3	5	15	21	42	49
24 Peterborough	46	6	9	8	31	30	2	4	17	17	46	37
	1104	276	144	132	864	586	132	144	276	586	864	1512

* promoted after play-offs

Appearances and Goals

Player	App Lge	Sub	LC	Sub	FAC	Sub	Goals Lge	LC	FAC	Tot
Aspinall, Warren	35	5		1						
Awford, Andy	15		7		2					
Blake, Mark	4	1								
Boere, Jeroen	8	4	1		2		1			1
Burns, Chris	1	1								
Burton, Deon	1	1					1			1
Butters, Guy	12	3	3		1		1			1
Chamberlain, Mark	12	7	2	1	1		1			1
Chapman, Lee	5		1				2			2
Creaney, Gerry	18		1				11			11
Daniel, Ray	14	2	2	1	2					
Dobson, Tony	23	1	2	2	1	1	2			2
Doling, Stuart	9	4	2	2		1	1			1
Durnin, John	23	5	7	1	1	1	6	2		8
Gittens, Jon	30		5				1			1
Hall, Paul	16	12	1	1	1	1	4			4
Horne, Brian	3									
Knight, Alan	43		7		2					
Kristensen, Bjorn	31	5	6	1	2		1			1
McLoughlin, Alan	37	1	7	1	2		6	1	4	11
Neill, Warren	35		4	1	1		2			2
Pethick, Robbie	14	4	1	1	1					
Powell, Darryl	17	11	3	1	2		5			5
Power, Lee	1	1								
Price, Chris	1	4								
Russell, Lee	5	5		1		1				
Stimson, Mark	28	1	4	2	2		1	1		2
Symons, Kit	29		6	1	2		1	2		3
Walsh, Paul	30		6		2		5	4		9
Wood, Paul	7	5	1				1			1
Young, Roy										
31 players used	506	82	77	11	22	4	52	10	4	66

Odds & ends

Double wins: (1) Middlesbrough.
Double losses: (2) Crystal Palace, West Brom.

Wins from behind: (1) Derby (h).
Lost from in front: (2) Crystal Palace (a), Southend (a).

High spots: Drawing with Blackburn and Manchester United away in the space of four days.
12 league games undefeated between September and November.
Reaching the quarter-finals of the League Cup for only the third time in the club's history.

Low spots: Four consecutive defeats to the end of the season.
Losing 1-5 at Crystal Palace after taking the lead.
587 minute goalless run in the league from December to February.
Losing to Blackburn and Manchester United in Cup replays in the space of a week.
Selling Paul Walsh to Manchester City in March for £750,000.

Manager Jim Smith used 31 players in league and cup matches during this season; the highest number ever used by the club

Including Anglo-Italian Cup matches the club played 61 competitive first team matches during this season. Another club record.

Player of the Year: Kit Symons.
Ever-presents: (0).
Hat-tricks: (2) Gerry Creaney (1), Alan McLoughlin (1).
Leading scorer: Gerry Creaney & Alan McLoughlin (both 11).

ENDSLEIGH LEAGUE DIVISION 1 Manager: Smith ⇒ Terry Fenwick SEASON 1994-95

No	Date	Opp (H/A)	Att	Pos	Pt	F-A	H-T	Res	Scorers, Times, and Referees
1	13/8	H NOTTS CO	10,487	3	3	2-1	1-0	W	Powell 5, Symons 89 / Sherlock 70 / Ref: P Foakes (Clacton-on-Sea)
2	20/8	A READING	9,106	21	4	0-0	0-0	D	Ref: S Dunn (Bristol)
3	27/8	H CHARLTON	10,566	18	5	1-1	1-1	D	Symons 11 / Nelson 8 / Ref: C Wilkes (Gloucester)
4	30/8	A SOUTHEND	4,333	22	8	2-1	1-1	W	Creaney 26, Powell 54 / Thomson 32 / Ref: I Hemley (Ampthill)
5	10/9	H PORT VALE	8,989	4	8	0-2	0-1	L	Glover L 44, Naylor 72 / Ref: P Alcock (S Merstham)
6	14/9	H TRANMERE	6,383	6	9	1-1	0-0	D	Hall 90 / O'Brien 51 / Ref: G Pooley (Bishop's Stortford)
7	17/9	A BOLTON	11,284	10	10	1-1	0-1	D	Creaney 69 / McGinlay 21 / Ref: P Wright (Northwich)
8	24/9	H WOLVERHAMPTON	13,466	1	10	1-2	1-1	L	Creaney 11p / Walters 34, Kelly 88 / Ref: M Bailey (Impington)
9	28/9	A WEST BROM	13,545	23	13	2-0	1-0	W	Pethick 7, Hall 49 / Ref: J Rushton (Stoke)
10	1/10	A GRIMSBY	4,172	10	13	0-2	0-1	L	Mendonca 17p, Woods 90 / Ref: I Cruikshanks (Hartlepool)
11	8/10	A OLDHAM	7,683	8	13	2-3	0-1	L	Creaney 50, Hall 86 / Holden 27p, 57p, Graham 73 / Ref: J Winter (Middlesbrough)

Line-ups (Portsmouth player, with opposition player in *italics*), positions 1–11 and subs used:

No	1	2	3	4	5	6	7	8	9	10	11	subs used
1	Knight *Cherry*	Gittens *Hoyle*	Stimson *Johnson**	McLoughlin* *Turner*	Symons *Murphy*	Dobson *Yates*	Neill *Garner*	Pethick *Legg*	Powell *Lund*	Creaney^ *McSwegan*	Hall *Simpson*	Daniel/Lee *Sherlock*
2	Knight *Hislop*	Gittens *Bernal*	Stimson *Kerr*	McLoughlin *Widowzyck*	Symons *Williams*	Dobson *Parkinson*	Neill *Taylor**	Lee^ *Gooding*	Powell *Quinn*	Creaney^ *Lovell*	Hall *Osborn*	Daniel/Pethick *Gilkes*
3	Knight *Amman*	Gittens *Brown*	Stimson *Sturgess*	McLoughlin^ *Mortimer*	Symons *Chapple*	Dobson *McLeary*	Neill *Robinson*^	Lee* *Nelson*	Powell *Garland*	Creaney *Whyte*	Hall *Robson**	Daniel/Pethick *Newton/Grant*
4	Knight *Sansome*	Gittens *Poole*	Stimson *Powell*	McLoughlin *Jones*	Symons *Edwards*	Dobson *Bressington*	Neill *Hunt**	Lee^ *Hone*	Powell *Thomson*	Creaney *Otto*	Hall *Sussex*	Daniel *Martin*
5	Knight *Musselwhite*	Gittens *Sandiman*	Stimson *Tankard*	McLoughlin* *Porter*	Symons *Griffiths*	Dobson *Glover D*	Neill^ *Kent**	Lee *Van der Laan Foyle*	Powell *Glover L*	Creaney^ *Naylor*	Hall *Walker*	Daniel/Pethick *Walker*
6	Knight *Nixon*	Gittens *McGreal*	Stimson *Brannan*	McLoughlin *Irons*	Symons *Garnett*	Awford *O'Brien*	Neill *Edwards**	Kristensen *Aldridge*	Powell* *Malkin*	Creaney *Nevin*	Hall *Thomas*	Daniel *Mungall*
7	Knight *Brannagan*	Gittens *Lydiate*	Stimson *Phillips*	McLoughlin *McAteer*	Symons *Kernaghan*	Dobson* *Stubbs*	Awford *Fisher*	Kristensen *Sneekes*	Daniel *Paatelainen*	Creaney *McGinlay*	Hall^ *Kelly**	Pethick/Radosavljevic *Lee*
8	Knight *Stowell*	Gittens *Smith*	Stimson *Thompson*	McLoughlin *Venus*	Symons *Blades*	Awford^ *Shirtliff*	Daniel *Walters*	Kristensen^ *Ferguson*	Powell *Bull*	Creaney *Kelly*	Hall *Froggatt*	Pethick/R savljevic *Kelly*
9	Knight *Naylor*	Gittens *Parsley*	Stimson *Darton**	McLoughlin *Phelan*	Symons *Strodder*	Dobson! *Herbert*	Daniel^ *Hunt*	Kristensen* *Ashcroft*^	Daniel *Taylor*	Creaney *Boere*	Pethick *Donovan*	Radosavljevic/Hall/Awford *Lilwall/McNally*
10	Knight *Crichton*	Gittens *Croft*	Stimson *Agnew*	McLoughlin *Handyside*	Symons* *Lever*	Dobson* *Shakespeare*	Daniel *Dobbin**	Radosavljevic *Gilbert*	Pethick *Woods*	Creaney *Mendonca*	Hall *Groves*	Burton/Rees *Jobling*
11	Knight *Gerrard*	Gittens^ *Halle*	Stimson *Makin*	McLoughlin^ *Henry**	Symons *Jobson*	Pethick *Redmond*	Daniel *Richardson*	Kristensen *Banger*	Daniel *Graham*	Creaney *McCarthy**	Hall *Holden*	Radosavljevic/Rees *Sharp/Brennan*

Match notes

1. Capt Symons rescues his drifting ship with a diving header. Powell powered past Yates to net, then Gittens tackles cleanly from behind, but FIFA's directive means that's a penalty now. McSwegan does the decent thing and misses. Sherlock homed in on Gittens' clearing header.

2. New-boys Reading will be more pleased as Pompey dominate. Joint bosses Quinn and Gooding will steer them to play-off heartbreak, though. Loanee Lee (Chelsea) hits a post, but only signed because ex-Toffee Preki (£100,000) has broken his arm. Symons is NOT going to Anfield.

3. Symons has extended his contract, then hooks in after US keeper Amman flaps Macca's corner. Gittens has signed a new deal too, but is AWOL, as unmarked Nelson nods in Garland's flag-kick. Macca should have scored when through, but hits a post in his 100th Pompey match.

4. Creaney's piledriver hits the stanchion and bounces out; it takes a couple of seconds to register a goal. £100,000 Thomson (QoS) angles home for Peter Taylor's Shrimpers, but when Powell bundles through to fire home, Pompey are up to third. Celtic are linked with a move for him.

5. John Rudge's side confound the pundits, as two of his summer signings pay dividends. Glover (Forest) heads home, then Naylor (Crewe) starts a move on his own penalty area, before waltzing through an undermanned defence to finish. Off-balance Macca muffs Pompey's best chance.

6. In injury-time Hall fires the most speculative of 30-yarders, but Nixon lets it squirm from his grasp. 'Things like that happen,' says phlegmatic Tranmere boss John King. Creaney will stop his ball-pinching party piece after he is booked for robbing Nixon. Lee goes back to Chelsea.

7. Bolton have won three in four and will win the play-offs, but Pompey battle back to deny them here. Macca responds to his critics by cleverly setting up Creaney, whose low shot gives no chance. McGinlay converts Paatelainen's nod down, ensuring a carbon copy of April's meeting.

8. Fratton is apparently one of the worst grounds for racism says a TV report; nonsense retort Gittens and Powell. It's a grim day for Pompey, as Kelly's counter settles a thrilling contest for Graham Taylor's team. Walters' curler is a corker, after Creaney is tugged by Shirtliff for the pen.

9. Pompey rise ten places – this game was postponed earlier due to international call ups – but the night is soured when Awford breaks his leg in four places. Pethick steers home his first for the club and Dobson's injury-time verbal volley at a linesman earns him red and Smith's fury.

10. Pompey's unbeaten away record is in tatters. Pethick chops down Gilbert and Mendonca converts, but Radosavl...Preki, making his first start, and Creaney rattle to woodwork before the interval. Macca is still goal-less, but Crichton denies him, then Woods rolls in to flatter Mariners.

11. A spot of bother unhinges Pompey again. McCarthy and Symons seem to run into one another, but it's Latics' second award and Holden profits again. Kit had no complaints after he tripped Halle though. Hall's diving header suggests an explosive finish, but it quickly fizzles out.

12 · H SWINDON · 15/10 · 12 5 16 · W 4-3 (2-1) · Att 10,610
McLough' 17, 19, Powell 51, Creaney 64p / Bodin 32p, Fjortoft 84, 86
Ref: P Vanes (Warley)

Knight	Gittens	Stimson	McLoughlin	Symons	McGrath	Pethick	Radosavljevic	Powell	Creaney	Hall*	Kristensen
Digby	Robinson	Bodin	Kilcline	Nijholt	Taylor	Webb*	Beauchamp	Fjortoft	Ling*	Scott	Horlock/Mutch

It all comes right for ex-Robin Macca, who twice uses his head to good effect and scores his first goals of the season. Creaney shoves Kilcline, but Powell swaps passes with Creaney to fire home, then Bodin brings down Hall and Gerry atones. Fjortoft's double has nerve-ends jangling.

---

13 · H MIDDLESBROUGH · 23/10 · 14 3 17 · D 0-0 (0-0) · Att 7,281
Ref: P Foakes (Clacton-on-Sea)

Knight	Gittens	Stimson	McLoughlin	Symons	McGrath	Pethick	Radosavljevic	Powell	Creaney	Hall	Hignett
Miller	Cox	Fleming	Vickers	Whyte	Blakmore	Todd	Pollock	Wilkinson	Hendrie	Moreno*	Hignett

This match is beamed to the nation on ITV. Is anyone still watching? Bryan Robson is Boro's boss, and he will take them up, but Smith blames light modern balls for Preki's 35-yarder hitting the bar, rather than dipping in. Martin is running Pompey day-to-day as Gregory snr is ailing.

---

14 · A BRISTOL CITY · 29/10 · 16 21 18 · D 1-1 (0-1) · Att 7,238
Powell 81 / Scott 15p
Ref: A Flood (Stockport)

Knight	Gittens	Stimson	Kristensen	Symons	McGrath	Pethick	Rad'savljevic^	Creaney*	Hall*	Rees	Rees
Welch	Harriott	Scott*	Shail	Bryant	Tinnion	Bent*	Partridge	Baird	Allison	Edwards	Munro/Seal

Pompey unveil their white and navy third strip – 'for when they play teams in red' – and Powell christens it with a fierce right-foot shot to save a point, after Knight had earlier flattened Allison. Recent signing McGrath (ex-Coventry) is booked and City are sliding towards Division Two.

---

15 · A MILLWALL · 2/11 · 14 21 19 · D 2-2 (1-2) · Att 7,108
Rees 30, McLoughlin 90p / Goodman 3, Rae 38
Ref: K Leach (Wolverhampton)

Knight	Gittens	Kristensen	McLoughlin	Symons	McGrath^	Pethick	Rad'savljevic^	Rees	Creaney	Dobson	Hall/Russell
Keller	Cunningham	Rae	Roberts	Witter	Stevens	Savage	Dawes	Cadette	Goodman*	Kennedy^	Mitchell/Beard

Summer free Rees (Luton) has an eventful debut. He levels with a 20-yarder, gives away a free-kick leading to Lions' second, then passes to Kristensen, who feeds Powell to be tumbled by Keller in injury-time. Dive?' 'He impeded me slightly…' Butters has gone to Oxford on loan.

---

16 · H DERBY · 6/11 · 20 17 19 · L 0-1 (0-0) · Att 5,507
Gabbiadini 66
Ref: I Hemley (Ampthill)

Knight	Totten	Stimson	McLoughlin	Symons	Russell	Pethick	Kristensen^	Powell	Creaney	Rees*	Radosavljevic/Durnin
Sutton	Charles	Forsyth	Kuhl	Short*	Williams	Cowans	Carsley	Johnson	Gabbiadini	Simpson	Kavanagh

It's Derby's day for the second time in a fortnight, as they follow up their Coke Cup win by refreshing their league form with a first win in six. TV coverage means the gate is the lowest for 12 years. Creaney has his second call up for Scotland; his diving header is Pompey's best effort.

---

17 · A LUTON · 19/11 · 21 8 19 · L 0-2 (0-2) · Att 8,214
Dixon 2, Preece 55
Ref: J Kirkby (Sheffield)

Knight	Gittens	Dobson	McLoughlin	Symons	Russell	Pethick	Kristensen	Powell	Creaney	Burton^	Rees/Totten
Sommer	James	Johnson	Waddock	Thomas	Peake	Telfer	Oakes	Dixon	Preece	Marshall*	Thorp

Despite their lofty position, David Pleat's Luton have the worst home record in the division (five defeats). Injury-hit Pompey help their cause, but at 0-2 Pethick sees his shot hit both posts, then Powell's rebound is hacked off the line. Burton also saw a header pushed onto the bar.

---

18 · H SUNDERLAND · 26/11 · 21 12 19 · L 1-4 (0-3) · Att 7,527
Powell 53 / Russell 19, Melville 21, Gray P 42p, [Smith 88]
Ref: S Dunn (Bristol)

Knight	Gittens	Dobson	McLoughlin*	Totten	Neill	Pethick	Hall	Powell	Creaney	Burton	Radosavljevic
Chamberlain	Kubicki	Ball	Melville	Ord	Owers	Atkinson	Gray M	Smith	Gray P	Russell	

Fellow strugglers Sunderland put the pressure on Smith. Poor marking leads to the first, and non-existent marking the second. Powell's trip on Gray looks harsh, but 'Cyrille' blasts Pompey back into contention. Smith's tap-in is academic; fans unfurl a banner: 'Div Two here we come.'

---

19 · H STOKE · 30/11 · 21 12 19 · L 0-1 (0-0) · Att 5,272
Beeston 75
Ref: I Hemley (Ampthill)

Knight	Gittens	Daniel	McLoughlin	Symons	Dobson	Pethick	Kristensen	Powell	Creaney	Hall*	Radosavljevic
Muggleton	Butler	Sandford	Cranson	Overson	Orlygsson	Sigurdsson	Beeston	Carruthers	Peschisolido	Gleghorn	

Beeston nets his first for nearly two years, as Lou Macari's side continue their revival (only one loss since he returned to Stoke in October). Creaney hits the bar from ten yards; then Pethick grazes it from 25. Powell lays into fans who booed Dobson: 'His response was brilliant.'

---

20 · A MIDDLESBROUGH · 3/12 · 22 1 19 · L 0-4 (0-2) · Att 17,185
Wilkinson 27, 75, Hignett 29, 59
Ref: J Parker (Preston)

Knight	Gittens	Totten	Russell*	Symons	Dobson	Pethick	Kristensen*	Powell	Creaney !	Newhouse	Radosavljevic/Hall
Miller	Cox	Morris	Vickers	Whyte	Mustoe	Hignett	Pollock	Wilkinson	Hendrie*	Moreno	Moreno

Rampant Boro make it five defeats in a row and just when you thought it couldn't get worse, Creaney chops down Hendrie and gets sent off. Hignett converts the free-kick, then Wilkinson wraps it up. Newhouse (Wimbledon) has signed on loan and shows up well, but is also booked.

---

21 · H READING · 10/12 · 22 6 20 · D 1-1 (1-0) · Att 8,578
Creaney 3 / Quinn 51p
Ref: G Pooley (Bishop's Stortford)

Knight	Gittens	Totten	McGrath	Butters	Wood	Pethick	Rad'savljevic^	Powell	Daniel	Newhouse^	McLoughlin/Hall
Hislop	Bernal	Kerr	Taylor*	McPherson	Parkinson	Gilkes	Gooding	Quinn	Lovell	Osborn	Barnard

Pompey finally stop the slide, but they are still deep in trouble. Powell and Newhouse combine for Creaney to fire in, but Royals' ascent to the play-offs restarts when Gilkes tricks Totten into a foul and player-boss Quinn converts. Woods' two goals for the reserves earned a call up.

---

22 · A NOTTS COUNTY · 17/12 · 21 24 23 · W 1-0 (0-0) · Att 6,382
Wood 60
Ref: T West (Hull)

Knight	Gittens	Butters	McGrath	Symons	Wood !	Pethick	Rad'savljevic^	Daniel	Creaney	Newhouse	McLoughlin/Hall*
Cherry	Mills	Legg	Turner	Yates	Johnson	Devlin	Butter	Lund	Marsden*	Agana^	Jemson/Murphy

Parkway is doomed after a Government inspector turns the plans down. Rock-bottom Magpies – unbeaten at home in three months – don't get the better of Pompey, thanks to Wood's solid finish. Then he turns villain, clattering Yates, and red follows yellow. Devlin hit the bar.

---

23 · A WATFORD · 26/12 · 22 10 23 · L 0-2 (0-0) · Att 9,953
Ramage 63, Shipperley 85
Ref: K Cooper (Swindon)

Knight	Gittens	Butters	McGrath	Symons	Wood^	Pethick^	Daniel	Powell	Creaney	Newhouse	Radosavljevic/Hall
Miller	Lavin	Johnson	Foster	Holdsworth	Ramage	Hessenthaler	Morales*	Shipperley	Porter	Mooney	Beadle

Chelsea's Neil Shipperley – on loan at Hornets – gives Pompey Boxing Day blues, but it's Rammage who ends Watford's six-week home goal drought. 'If Creaney's header had gone in rather than hit the post we'd have been alright,' said Smith. Kristensen and Burns have got frees.

ENDSLEIGH LEAGUE DIVISION 1 — Manager: Smith ⇨ Terry Fenwick — SEASON 1994-95

Key: Each match lists Portsmouth's XI first, then the opponents' XI (in italics). *Pos* = Portsmouth league position; *opp pos* = opponents' league position.

---

24. H 27/12 BARNSLEY — W 3-0 (HT 3-0)
Att 6,751 · Pos 19 · Pt 26 · opp pos 4
Scorers: Newhouse 12, Creaney 20, 35. Ref: G Singh (Wolverhampton)

	1	2	3	4	5	6	7	8	9	10	11	Subs used
POR	Knight	Gittens	Daniel	McGrath	Symons	Butters	Pethick	Radosavljevic	Powell	Creaney	Newhouse	Hall
BAR	*Butler*	*Eaden*	*Fleming*	*Bullock*	*Taggart**	*Davis*	*O'Connell*	*Redfearn*	*Payton**	*Liddell*	*Sheridan*	*Rammell/Bishop*

Preki finally sparkles in the wind and rain. Newhouse slides in for the first – Smith will decide £300,000 is too much for him though – then Creaney's brace moves Pompey out of the bottom four. Danny Wilson's Tykes were the form side of the division with nine wins in 14 games.

---

25. A 31/12 SHEFFIELD UTD — L 1-3 (HT 1-0)
Att 13,467 · Pos 21 · Pt 26 · opp pos 5
Scorers: Creaney 33 / Blake 46, 47, Scott 81. Ref: P Rejer (Tipton)

	1	2	3	4	5	6	7	8	9	10	11	Subs used
POR	Knight	Gittens*	Daniel	McGrath	Symons	Butters	Pethick	Radosavljevic	Powell	Creaney	Newhouse	Hall
SHU	*Kelly*	*Gage*	*Nilsen*	*Hartfield*	*Gayle*	*Scott*	*Rogers*	*Veart*	*Starbuck**	*Hodges*	*Blake*	*Whitehouse*

That elusive Bramall Lane win – nearly 40 years since the last one – looks on when Creaney's sharpness nets after a scramble. Nathan Blake turns first-half jeers to cheers with two quick-fire headers. Creaney hits a post as Pompey maintain self-belief, but soon after Scott seals it.

---

26. H 2/1 BURNLEY — W 2-0 (HT 1-0)
Att 9,097 · Pos 19 · Pt 29 · opp pos 20
Scorers: Radosavljevic 26, Creaney 87. Ref: J Holbrook (Ludlow)

	1	2	3	4	5	6	7	8	9	10	11	Subs used
POR	Knight	Gittens	Daniel	McGrath	Symons	Butters	Pethick	Radosavljevic	Powell	Creaney	Wood*	Hall
BUR	*Beresford*	*Parkinson*	*Armstrong**	*Davis*	*Winstanley^*	*Harrison*	*Saville*	*Heath*	*Robinson*	*Eyres*	*Deary*	*Philliskirk/Brass*

Jimmy Mullen's Burnley are heading straight back to Div Two. Despite being fresh from a 5-1 mauling of Southend, they never adjust to the icy pitch and Preki is in his element. He fires home a dazzler, but concern surrounds Wood, who is knocked out cold and rushed to hospital.

---

27. H 14/1 BRISTOL CITY — D 0-0 (HT 0-0)
Att 8,803 · Pos 19 · Pt 30 · opp pos 23
Ref: M Bailey (Impington)

	1	2	3	4	5	6	7	8	9	10	11	Subs used
POR	Knight	Russell	Daniel	McGrath	Symons	Butters	Pethick	Radosavljevic	Powell	Creaney	Wood*	Hall
BRC	*Welch*	*Hansen*	*Munro*	*Shail**	*Bryant*	*Tinnion*	*Bent*	*Kuhl*	*Fleck^*	*Allison*	*Owers*	*Baird/Dryden*

It's two steps back for Pompey, who undo all their recent good work in this dour draw. Struggling City look marginally the more dangerous side. Runaway midfielder Doing – AWOL since Xmas – is back, but on his last chance. A High Court challenge to Parkway looks unlikely.

---

28. A 22/1 DERBY — L 0-3 (HT 0-0)
Att 11,143 · Pos 19 · Pt 30 · opp pos 8
Scorers: Simpson 47, 75, 88. Ref: I Cruickshanks (Hartlepool)

	1	2	3	4	5	6	7	8	9	10	11	Subs used
POR	Knight	Russell	Daniel	McLoughlin*	Symons	Butters	Pethick	Radosavljevic	Powell	Creaney	Kristensen	Hall
DER	*Sutton S*	*Short**	*Forsyth*	*Nicholson*	*Wassall*	*Kavanagh*	*Simpson*	*Trollope*	*Sutton W*	*Stallard*	*Gabbiadini*	*Wrack*

Pompey are officially 'For Sale' at £7 million. This is a poor advert for the product though, as an ITV audience sees old foe Simpson – Man C, April 1985 – collect a hat-trick. The team are clearly at sixes and sevens, boxing's Frank Maloney.

---

29. A 4/2 STOKE — W 2-0 (HT 0-0)
Att 9,704 · Pos 18 · Pt 33 · opp pos 15
Scorers: Radosavljevic 53, Creaney 90. Ref: W Burns (Scarborough)

	1	2	3	4	5	6	7	8	9	10	11	Subs used
POR	Knight	Gittens	Daniel	McLoughlin	Symons	Butters	Pethick	Radosavljevic*	Powell	Creaney	Rees	Hall
STK	*Sinclair*	*Clarkson^*	*Dreyer**	*Cranson*	*Sigurdsson*	*Allen*	*Orlygsson*	*Peschisolido*	*Scott*	*Downing*	*Gleghorn*	*Butler/Lesley*

Smith has fallen in love with the Leicester curse (Ball and Gregory were fired after losing to Foxes) and Fenwick installed. Preki lifts spirits with a jinking run and finish, then Creaney bustles through. Some are unhappy at Smith's sacking: 'I don't know where my future lies,' says Symons.

---

30. A 18/2 SUNDERLAND — D 2-2 (HT 1-2)
Att 12,372 · Pos 19 · Pt 34 · opp pos 21
Scorers: McLoughlin 43, Doling 79 / Smith 11, 21. Ref: P Harrison (Oldham)

	1	2	3	4	5	6	7	8	9	10	11	Subs used
POR	Knight	Pethick	Daniel	McLoughlin	Symons	Butters	Kristensen*	Radosavljevic	Powell	Creaney	Rees*	Durnin/Doling
SUN	*Norman*	*Ord*	*Ferguson*	*Ball*	*Agnew*	*Gray P**	*Gray M*	*Howey*	*Scott*	*Kubicki*	*Russell*	

Sub Doling levels – his shot bobbles under Norman's dive. Macca sidefoots Pethick's cross as Sunderland lose their way. They were on Easy Street and Smith knew the way past loanee Glass (Palace). Paddon (coach) and Bailey (youth) are out, Keith Waldon and Larry May in.

---

31. A 21/2 LUTON — W 3-2 (HT 0-1)
Att 7,363 · Pos 16 · Pt 37 · opp pos 10
Scorers: McLoughlin 49, Radosavljevic 76, Telfer 11, James 72 [Creaney 79p]. Ref: K Leach (Wolverhampton)

	1	2	3	4	5	6	7	8	9	10	11	Subs used
POR	Knight	Pethick	Daniel	McLoughlin	Symons	Butters	McGrath	Radosavljevic	Powell	Creaney	Rees*	Doling
LUT	*Sommer*	*James*	*Johnson*	*Waddock**	*Thomas*	*Peake*	*Telfer*	*Oakes^*	*Dixon*	*Preece*	*Marshall*	*Woodsford/Harvey*

Coventry's Big Ron strolls down Frogmore Road beforehand. Symons? Creaney? The rumour mill is in overdrive, but Fenwick's wary. Pleat says Creaney 'fouled' Preki for the vital pen, as Pompey twice bounce back. In fact, Sunderland offer £1m for Gerry. 'No way,' says Terry.

---

32. H 25/2 GRIMSBY — W 2-1 (HT 1-1)
Att 8,274 · Pos 14 · Pt 40 · opp pos 7
Scorers: Creaney 43, Symons 89 / Rodger 44. Ref: P Foakes (Clacton-on-Sea)

	1	2	3	4	5	6	7	8	9	10	11	Subs used
POR	Knight	Gittens	Daniel*	McLoughlin	Symons	Butters	Pethick	Radosavljevic	Powell	Creaney	Rees*	Durnin/McGrath
GRI	*Crichton*	*McDermott*	*Jobling*	*Handyside*	*Rodger*	*Groves*	*Watson*	*Dobbin*	*Woods*	*Mendonca*	*Croft*	*Laws/Livingstone*

Call it luck. Call it judgement. Whatever, Fenwick has it by the barrow-load! In injury-time Symons forces his way past two defenders to rifle in. Creaney's looper was swapped with Rodger's free header in to disturb the slumber. 'Linesman' Wendy Toms makes her full Fratton debut.

---

33. A 5/3 WOLVERHAMPTON — L 0-1 (HT 0-0)
Att 23,284 · Pos 15 · Pt 40 · opp pos 4
Scorers: Bull 73. Ref: G Cain (Bootle)

	1	2	3	4	5	6	7	8	9	10	11	Subs used
POR	Knight	Gittens	Russell	McLoughlin	Symons	Butters	Pethick	Raf'savljevic*	Hall*	Creaney	McGrath*	Kristensen/Durnin
WOL	*Stowell*	*Blades*	*Thompson*	*Rankine*	*De Wolf*	*Shirtliff*	*Goodman*	*Kelly*	*Bull*	*Cowans*	*Dennison*	

Paul Wilkinson is poised for a £750,000 move, with Mark Bright an alternative target. Knight accepts the blame for the winning goal. The last place you want a poor punch to land is Steve Bull's feet! Pompey have unveiled plans for a 5,000 seat Fratton End, to be open by Christmas.

---

34. H 8/3 WEST BROM — L 1-2 (HT 1-1)
Att 7,160 · Pos 17 · Pt 40 · opp pos 16
Scorers: Creaney 37 / Taylor 43, 88. Ref: G Pooley (Bishop's Stortford)

	1	2	3	4	5	6	7	8	9	10	11	Subs used
POR	Knight	Gittens	Russell	McLoughlin	Symons	Butters	Pethick	Raf'savljevic*	Hall*	Creaney	Powell	McGrath
WBA	*Naylor*	*Burgess*	*Agnew*	*Phelan*	*Mardon*	*Raven*	*O'Regan*	*Donovan**	*Taylor*	*Hunt*	*Hamilton*	*McNally*

Baggies' boss Alan Buckley had transformed his team, but now they have won once in seven. Knight howls again: Taylor's long shot goes through him, then Fenwick accuses his team of lacking 'mental strength' as Taylor pinches it. Creaney's 18th of the season put Pompey ahead.

Match-by-match record (matches 35–46)

35 · A CHARLTON · 11/3 — 9,443 · 20 · L · 40 · 0-1 · 0-1 · Leaburn 4 · Ref: D Orr (Iver)
Pompey: Knight, Russell^, Gittens, McLoughlin, Symons, Butters, Pethick, Radosavljevic, Powell, Creaney, McGrath*; subs Hall, Durnin.
Charlton: Salmon, Mortimer, Brown, Jones, Rufus, Balmer, Robson*, Leaburn, Pardew, Whyte, Robinson; Newton.
"Fenwick is on a fast learning curve – he now has the pressure of three defeats in a week to deal with. Leaburn's header gives Valiants the edge, but Gittens has a header ruled out for a free-kick retake and offside Creaney would have done better to leave Symons' looping header alone."

36 · H MILLWALL · 15/3 — 6,032 · 17 · W · 43 · 3-2 · 1-1 · Creaney 15, 48, Hall 81 / Oldfield 36, Witter 89 · Ref: R Harris (Oxford)
Pompey: Knight, Russell, Gittens, McLoughlin, Symons, Butters*, Pethick, Radosavljevic, Powell, Creaney, Hall; subs McGrath^/Durnin.
Millwall: Keller, May, Brown, Roberts, Witter, Webber, Savage, Rae*, Oldfield, Mitchell, Kennedy; Thatcher.
"The Wilko deal is dragging on and will founder on his 'Maradona' wages. Hall hits his first goal since October to seal an important win, but sub McGrath seriously injures his knee in an accidental clash with Witter. Fenwick is turning his attentions to Dutch striker Ron Willems."

37 · H SOUTHEND · 18/3 — 6,667 · 15 · D · 44 · 1-1 · 1-1 · McLoughlin 31 / Jones 18 · Ref: S Dunn (Bristol)
Pompey: Knight, Russell, Gittens, McLoughlin, Symons, Rees*, Pethick, Radosavljevic, Powell*, Creaney, Hall; subs Kristensen/Durnin.
Southend: Royce, Powell, Hane, Whelan, Badley, Edwards, Jones, Sussex, Thomson*, Tilson, Dublin; Hails.
"Southend could have been three-up before Pompey get going. Thomson speeds pass Pethick and Jones sweeps in, then Tilson raps one post and Thomson grazes the other. Powell's header is pushed out by Royce and Macca nudges it over the line. Knight saves from Hails at the death."

38 · A PORT VALE · 21/3 — 7,388 · 19 · L · 44 · 0-1 · 0-1 · Allon 39 · Ref: J Parker (Preston)
Pompey: Glass, Rees^, Gittens, McLoughlin, Symons, Butters, Pethick, Rad'savljevic^, Powell, Creaney, Hall; subs Kristensen/Durnin.
Port Vale: Musselwhite, Sandiman, Stokes, Porter, Aspin, Scott, Guppy, Van der Laan, Allon*, Naylor^, Walker; Jeffers/Foyle.
"Fenwick axes Knight and Glass is recalled. Estonian keeper Mart Poom has been injury-plagued all year and is loaned to Leeds to learn. Glass shatters Pompey when he dives over Joe Allon's effort, despite two other good saves. 'I will only be remembered for the mistake,' he rues."

39 · H BOLTON · 25/3 — 7,765 · 18 · L · 45 · 1-1 · 0-1 · Creaney 51 / Paatelainen 12 · Ref: C Wilkes (Gloucester)
Pompey: Glass, Rees, Gittens, McLoughlin, Symons, Butters, Pethick, Rad'savljevic*, Powell^, Creaney, Hall; subs Durnin/Doling.
Bolton: Branaghan, Green, Phillips, McAteer, Seagraves, Stubbs, Sneekes, McDonald*, Paatelainen, Coyle, Thompson; Lee.
"Coca Cola finalists Bolton are held, as Glass picks up the pieces with two smart saves. McAteer surges 70 yards to set up Paatelainen. Pompey improve after the break; Creaney touches in after a furious scramble. The new Fratton End depends on a Safeway store. 'I see trouble ahead…'"

40 · A TRANMERE · 1/4 — 8,722 · 19 · L · 45 · 1-3 · 2-4 · Radosavljevic 19, Mungall 65 (og) / Malkin 2, Aldridge 12, 34, Irons 71 · Ref: R Furmandiz (Doncaster)
Pompey: (Nixon), Durnin, Gittens, McLoughlin, Symons, Russell, Pethick, Rad'savljevic, Powell, Creaney, Hall; subs Jones/Kenworthy.
Tranmere: Nixon, Mungall, Stevens, McGreal, Higgins, O'Brien, Morrissey^, Aldridge, Malkin*, Irons, Nevin.
"Fenwick trots out that old boss's favourite 'We wuz robbed.' Irons did look well offside as Pompey chased an equaliser, but he reserves his ire for his dozy defence, which gives Malkin and Aldridge the freedom of Prenton. Danny Baker would have loved Mungall's slice of bad luck."

41 · H SHEFFIELD UTD · 8/4 — 8,216 · 19 · W · 48 · 1-0 · 0-0 · Creaney 59 · Ref: P Alcock (S Merstham)
Pompey: Knight, Butters, Gittens, McLoughlin, Symons, Russell, Pethick, Rad'savljevic*, Powell^, Creaney, Hall; subs Kristensen/Rees.
Sheffield Utd: Kelly, Gage, Nilson, Hartfield^, Tuttle, Beesley, Starbuck*, Veart, Littlejohn, Flo, Black; Scott/Hodges.
"Creaney's surge from the halfway line ends with him planting the ball past Kelly, but recalled Knight gave him first feel in six months, but is taking it easy. fingertips from Black and his boot from Veart. Black also hit a post. Andy Awford has kicked his first ball in six months, but is taking it easy."

42 · A BARNSLEY · 15/4 — 6,825 · 20 · L · 48 · 0-1 · 0-0 · Payton 65 · Ref: J Lloyd (Wrexham)
Pompey: Knight, Butters, Gittens, McLoughlin, Symons, Russell, Pethick, Rad'savljevic, Rees^, Durnin*, Hall*; subs Gittens/Kristensen.
Barnsley: Watson, Eaden, Fleming, Wilson*, Taggart, Davis, O'Connell, Bullock, Payton, Liddell, Snodin; Redfearn.
"Creaney's face was rearranged outside a Southsea night-club early yesterday. Pompey are punchless without him, but their attrition deserved a point. Bullock beats Russell and Payton nets the cross. Five away defeats running, with trips to rivals coming up, means the outlook is bleak."

43 · H WATFORD · 17/4 — 8,396 · 18 · W · 51 · 2-1 · 1-0 · Durnin 27p, Burton 82 / Phillips 89 · Ref: M Bailey (Impington)
Pompey: Knight, Butters, Gittens, McLoughlin, Symons, Russell, Pethick, Rad'savljevic, Rees, Durnin, Hall; subs Kristensen/Burton.
Watford: Miller, Lavin, Page, Holdsworth, Millen, Pitcher^, Hessenthaler, Payne, Beadle*, Phillips, Porter; Bazeley/Johnson.
"Pompey hang on for four minutes of overtime, after Phillips pulled one back. Durnin's pen is vital and Burton shows maturity to come on and fire in. Fenwick reckons he is still too angry to see Creaney. By Thursday it is revealed he has been 'severely' punished for his indiscretions."

44 · A BURNLEY · 22/4 — 10,666 · 18 · W · 54 · 2-1 · 1-0 · Durnin 36p, Symons 61 / Eyres 81 · Ref: J Winter (Middlesbrough)
Pompey: Knight, Butters, Gittens, McLoughlin, Symons, Russell, Pethick, Burton, Shaw^, Durnin*, Hall*; subs Radosav'/Kristensen.
Burnley: Beresford, Parkinson, Winstanley, Davis, Vinicombe, Randall, McMinn, Phillskirk^, Hoyland, Eyres; Nogan/Robinson.
"Pompey are safe. Durnin nets another crucial pen after Macca is tripped by Davis, then Burton puts Symons clear to go past a defender and roll home. Burnley are down, but Eyres is not out as he slams home Parkinson's pass. Nogan hits the bar and Robinson the post in a frantic finale."

45 · A SWINDON · 29/4 — 9,220 · 18 · W · 57 · 2-0 · 1-0 · Radosavljevic 40, Burton 55 · Ref: J Brandwood (Lichfield)
Pompey: Knight, Butters, Gittens, McLoughlin, Symons, Russell, Pethick, Rad'savljevic*, Burton, Durnin*, Hall^; subs Kristensen/Radosav'.
Swindon: Digby, Todd, Thomson, Viveash, Nijholt, Taylor, O'Sullivan, Beauchamp, Gooden^, Thorne, Ling*; Worrall/Pitman.
"Town are condemned to a second successive drop as Pompey show no mercy to the delight of their 3,000 followers. Serbian sub Preki takes advantage of Taylor and Thomson's confusion to fire in. Burton turns in Pethick's cross and Fenwick's talking of the championship next year."

46 · H OLDHAM · 7/5 — 11,002 · 18 · D · 58 · 1-1 · 0-1 · Hall 62 / McCarthy 43p · Ref: P Vanes (Warley)
Pompey: Knight, Pethick, Butters, McLoughlin, Symons, Russell, Rad'savljevic*, Burton, Rees*, Durnin, Hall; subs Kristensen/Igoe.
Oldham: Gerrard, Makin, Pointon, Richardson, Snodin, Redmond, Bernard, Rickers, McCarthy, Eyre*, Brennan; Beresford.
"Gregory jnr is optimistic new owners will found soon, while Creaney is in training again. Some suggest he might play. A ploy to boost the crowd? Kids for a quid is the more likely explanation. Graeme Sharp's Latics have six kids playing for their futures. Hall saves a point in the sun."

Home Average 8,269 · Away 9,432

ENDSLEIGH DIVISION 1 (CUP-TIES) Manager: Smith ⇒ Terry Fenwick SEASON 1994-95

Coca-Cola Cup

	F-A	H-T	Scorers, Times, and Referees	1	2	3	4	5	6	7	8	9	10	11	subs used
1:1 H CAMBRIDGE W **2-0** 2-0 3,854 2	2-0	2-0	Stimson 35, Powell 44 Ref: D Orr (Iver)	Poom *Filan*	Gittens *Hunter*	Stimson *Barrick*	McLoughlin *Craddock*	Symons *Heathcote*	Dobson *O'Shea*	Neill *Hyde*	Pethick *Rattle*	Powell *Morah**	Daniel *Corazzin*	Hall* *Joseph*	Rees *Butler*
			Estonia's keeper Poom, reportedly bought for £200,000 in the strength of a video, makes a solid start, but Knight will remain between the sticks on Saturday. Stimmo and Powell sees off feeble United, but Smith is unhappy. 'We're playing far too much as individuals,' he reckons.												
1:2 A CAMBRIDGE W **3-2** 1-1 2,571 2:18	3-2	1-1	Creaney 6, Powell 51, 53 Craddock 3, Barrick 72 Ref: K Cooper (Swindon) (Pompey won 5-2 on aggregate)	Poom *Filan*	Gittens *Hunter*	Stimson *Barrick*	McLoughlin *Craddock*	Symons *Heathcote*	Dobson *O'Shea*	Neill* *Hyde*	Pethick *Granville**	Powell *Butler*	Hall* *Corazzin^*	Hall* *Joseph*	Burton/Daniel *Morah/Elad*
			A 'Whits for Pompey' story has surfaced, not for the last time – Villa will offload him, plus £1m, for Symons – 'We want to keep Kit', says Smith. Powell now has four in four, and is praised. Pompey are in charge, but never totally subdue Gary Johnson's men. It's Everton next.												
2:1 A EVERTON W **3-2** 2-0 14,043 P:22	3-2	2-0	Creaney 2, 15, Kristensen 56 Samways 57, Stuart 72p Ref: M Reed (Birmingham)	Knight *Southall*	Gittens *Jackson**	Stimson^ *Burrows*	McLoughlin *Parkinson*	Symons *Watson*	Awford *Unsworth*	Daniel *Samways*	Kristensen *Stuart*	Powell *Amokachi*	Creaney *Rideout^*	Hall* *Hinchcliffe*	Pethick/Radosavljevic *Snodin/Angell*
			The tabloids have a field-day as Mike Walker's Everton are undone by a man they rejected in January. 'Creamy Creams Toffees' is the pick. Walker chose, ironically, £600,000 Brett Angell, but he is out of sorts and has been in the reserves. Stuart's pen placates a seething Goodison.												
2:2 H EVERTON D **1-1** 0-1 13,605 P:22	1-1	0-1	Hall 88 Watson 17 Ref: K Cooper (Pontypridd) (Pompey won 4-3 on aggregate)	Knight *Southall*	Gittens *Snodin*	Stimson *Burrows*	McLoughlin *Parkinson*	Symons *Watson*	Dobson *Unsworth*	Rad'savljevic* *Samways*	Kristensen *Stuart*	Powell *Amokachi*	Creaney *Ferguson*	Pethick *Hinchcliffe**	Hall *Rideout*
			Everton are a different proposition, as they give on-loan Ranger Ferguson a debut and £3m Nigerian Amokachi looks the part. Knight is outstanding, but Watson looks to have forced extra-time. Then Powell flicks on, Hall is clear and his shot nutmegs Southall. Fratton goes wild.												
3 H DERBY L **0-1** 0-0 8,568 19	0-1	0-0	Simpson 46 Ref: S Dunn	Knight *Sutton**	Gittens *Charles*	Stimson *Forsyth*	McLoughlin *Wassall*	Symons *Short*	McGrath *Williams*	Pethick *Cowans*	Radosavljevic *Carsley*	Powell *Johnson^*	Creaney *Gabbiadini*	Hall *Simpson"*	Kristensen/Durnin *Guy/Stallard/Kav'agh*
			Simpson shows he can even score spectacular goals against Pompey with his 'standing' (right) foot to settle this tie. Johnson misses a hat-ful of first-half chances and a late rally can't save it. The Coca-Cola Cup has lost its fizz for fans in a transfer request. Daniel has handed in a transfer request.												

FA Cup

	F-A	H-T	Scorers, Times, and Referees	1	2	3	4	5	6	7	8	9	10	11	subs used
3 H BOLTON W **3-1** 1-1 9,721 4	3-1	1-1	Creaney 31, Radosavljevic 60, 84 Sneekes 42 Ref: P Alcock (S Merstham)	Knight *Branaghan*	Gittens *Green*	Daniel *Phillips*	McGrath *McAteer*	Symons *Coleman*	Butters *Stubbs*	Pethick *Paatelainen**	Radosavljevic *Sneekes*	Powell *Coyle*	Creaney *McGinlay*	Wood *Patterson^*	 *Thompson/Lee*
			Wanderers are cup kings – seeing off a number of top sides lately – but Pompey produce their best of the season to win. With the tie poised, Preki cuts into space, created by Pethick, and his left-footer is the goal of the season. Earlier, Butters had set him up to give Blues the edge.												
4 H LEICESTER L **0-1** 0-1 14,928 P:22	0-1	0-1	Roberts 44 Ref: D Gallagher (Banbury)	Knight! *Poole*	Gittens! *Smith*	Daniel *Whitlow*	McGrath* *Mohan*	Russell *Hill*	Butters *Draper*	Pethick *Grayson*	Radosavljevic *Thompson*	Powell *Robins*	Creaney* *Roberts*	Kristensen^ *Philpott*	McLough/Rees/Flah'n
			Knight slithers out of the box in the wet and handles, but the ref is unbending and it's the first red card of his career, so Flavs debuts. Earlier, Gittens had gone for a last-line tug on Thompson, then Roberts netted at the far post soon afterwards. It's Smith's farewell, but no one suspects.												

League Table

	Team	P	Home W	D	L	F	A	Away W	D	L	F	A	Pts
1	Middlesbro	46	15	4	4	41	19	8	9	6	26	21	82
2	Reading	46	12	7	4	34	21	11	3	9	24	23	79
3	Bolton*	46	15	6	1	43	13	5	8	10	24	32	77
4	Wolves	46	16	5	3	39	18	6	8	9	38	43	76
5	Tranmere	46	17	4	2	51	23	5	6	12	16	35	76
6	Barnsley	46	15	6	3	42	19	5	7	11	21	33	72
7	Watford	46	14	6	3	33	17	5	5	11	19	29	70
8	Sheffield Utd	46	12	9	2	41	21	5	8	10	33	34	68
9	Derby	46	12	6	5	44	23	6	6	11	22	28	66
10	Grimsby	46	12	7	4	36	19	5	7	11	26	37	65
11	Stoke	46	10	7	6	31	21	6	8	9	19	32	63
12	Millwall	46	11	8	4	36	22	5	6	12	24	38	62
13	Southend	46	13	2	8	33	25	5	6	12	21	48	62
14	Oldham	46	12	7	4	34	21	4	6	13	26	39	61
15	Charlton	46	11	6	6	33	25	5	5	13	25	41	59
16	Luton	46	8	6	9	35	30	7	5	9	26	34	58
17	Port Vale	46	11	5	7	30	24	4	8	11	28	40	58
18	PORTSMOUTH	46	9	8	6	31	28	6	5	12	22	35	58
19	West Brom	46	13	3	7	33	24	3	7	13	18	33	58
20	Sunderland	46	5	12	6	22	22	7	6	10	19	23	54
21	Swindon	46	9	6	8	28	27	3	6	14	26	46	48
22	Burnley	46	8	7	8	36	33	3	6	14	13	41	46
23	Bristol City	46	8	8	7	26	28	3	4	16	16	35	45
24	Notts Co	46	7	8	8	26	28	2	5	16	19	38	40
		1104	275	153	124	838	551	124	153	275	551	838	1503

* promoted after play-offs

Odds & ends

Double wins: (3) Swindon, Burnley, Swindon.

Double losses: (3) Port Vale, Wolves, Derby.

Won from behind: (1) Luton (h).

Lost from in front: (3) Wolves (h), Sheffield Utd (a), West Brom (h).

High spots: Four-match unbeaten run at end of the season keeps the team up.

Winning 3-2 at Premiership Everton in the Coca-Cola Cup.

Defeating promotion-chasing Bolton 3-1 in the FA Cup.

Four successive wins in February after Terry Fenwick takes over from Jim Smith as manager.

Low spots: Five consecutive defeats in November.

A 1-4 home defeat by Sunderland.

Gerry Creaney being ruled out for the rest of the season after being attacked outside a nightclub.

Manager Jim Smith who was sacked in February was the sixth most successful manager in the club's history, according to an analysis of their records published shortly after his dismissal. His teams gained 53.6% of league points on offer, just behind Frank Burrows (55.2%), Bobby Campbell (55.6%) and Alan Ball in third place (56.3%). First place went to Bob Jackson (59.8%), then John McCartney (58.3%). Smith also guided the team to the play-offs and the FA Cup semi-finals, as well as making a £3.56 million profit on transfers.

Player of the Year: Alan Knight.

Ever presents: (0).

Hat tricks: (0).

Leading scorer: Gerry Creaney (18).

Appearances & Goals

Player	Lge	Sub	LC	Sub	FAC	Sub	Lge	LC	FAC	Tot
Awford, Andy	3	1	1		1					
Burton, Deon	5	2		1		2	2			2
Butters, Guy	24	8			2	2				
Creaney, Gerry	39		4	2	2		18	3	1	22
Daniel, Ray	17	5	2	1	2					
Dobson, Tony	14		3							
Doling, Stuart	2	3					1			1
Durnin, John	8	1		1			2			2
Flahaven, Aaron					1					
Gittens, Jon	37	1	5		2					
Glass, Jimmy	3									
Hall, Paul	30	13	4	1			5	1		6
Igoe, Sammy	1									
Knight, Alan	43		3	2						
Kristensen, Bjorn	15	10	2	1				1		1
Lee, David	4	1								
McGrath, Lloyd	15	3	1		2					
McLoughlin, Alan	36	2	5		1		6			6
Neill, Warren	7		2							
Newhouse, Adrian	6						1			1
Pethick, Robbie	39	5	4		2		1			1
Poom, Mart			2							
Powell, Darryl	34		5	1	2		5	3		8
Radosavljevic, Pred'g	30	10	2	1	2		5		2	7
Rees, Jason	14	5		1	1		1			1
Russell, Lee	18	1			1					
Stimson, Mark	15		5							
Symons, Kit	40		5		1		4			4
Totten, Alex	3	1								
Wood, Paul	5						1			1
(own-goals)							1			1
30 players used	506	73	55	9	22	3	53	9	2	64

ENDSLEIGH LEAGUE DIVISION 1 — Manager: Terry Fenwick — SEASON 1995-96

No	Date	Opponent / Scorers, Times, and Referees	Att	Pos	Pt	F-A	H-T	1	2	3	4	5	6	7	8	9	10	11	Subs used
1	H 12/8	**SOUTHEND** — Creaney 40, 76, Tilson 42 (og), Rees 73 / *Thomson 4, 78* / Ref: R Gifford (Llanbradach)	10,630		3	W 4-2	2-1	Poom	Pethick	Russell	McLoughlin*	Symons	Butters	Carter"	Durnin	Hall^	Creaney	Rees	Awford/Burton/Igoe
								Royce	*Dublin*	*Powell*	*Bodley*	*Lapper*	*Hails*	*Iorfa**	*Whelan*	*Jones*	*Thomson*	*Tilson*	*Regis*
2	A 19/8	**GRIMSBY** — McLoughlin 81p / *Laws 72, Croft 78* / Ref: K Breen (Liverpool)	4,515	6/12	3	L 1-2	0-0	Poom	Pethick	Russell*	McLoughlin	Awford	Butters	Simpson!	Durnin !	Hall	Creaney^	Rees	Dobson/Burton/Igoe
								Crichton !	*Laws*	*Jobling*	*Handyside*	*Rodger*	*Groves*	*Croft*	*Shakespeare*	*Woods*	*Livingstone*	*Southall*	
3	H 26/8	**READING** — / Ref: G Pooley (Bishops Stortford)	9,917	8/6	4	D 0-0	0-0	Poom	Pethick	Russell	McLoughlin	Gittens	Butters	Carter*	Durnin	Hall^	Burton^	Rees*	Igoe/Griffiths
								Sheppard	*Bernal*	*Gooding*	*Wdowczyk*	*Williams*	*McPherson*	*Gilkes^*	*Parkinson*	*Nogan*	*Lovell*	*Morley.**	*Meaker/Swailes*
4	A 30/8	**LEICESTER** — Creaney 35p, Hall 60 / *Roberts 15, 38, 43, Parker 45* / Ref: G Cain (Bootle)	15,170	19/3	4	L 2-4	1-4	Poom	Pethick	Russell	Simpson	Gittens	Dobson	Carter*	Durnin	Hall	Creaney	Rees*	Igoe/**Bradbury**
								Poole	*Hill*	*Whitlow*	*Willis*	*Walsh*	*Parker*	*Joachim*	*Taylor*	*Roberts*	*Lowe*	*Corica*	
5	H 2/9	**MILLWALL** — / *Dixon 17* / Ref: C Wilkes (Gloucester)	8,023	21/1	4	L 0-1	0-1	Knight	Pethick	Russell	McLoughlin	Gittens	Dobson*	Carter*	Simpson	Hall	Burton^	Rees	Igoe/**Griffiths/Brad'ly**
								Keller	*Newman*	*Thatcher*	*Bowry*	*Witter*	*Stevens*	*Savage"*	*Rae**	*Fuchs^*	*Dixon*	*Van Blerk*	*Rogan/Makin/Doyle*
6	A 9/9	**PORT VALE** — Burton 13, Griffiths 83p / Ref: R Poulain (Huddersfield)	7,374	16/22	7	W 2-0	1-0	Knight	Pethick	Russell	McLoughlin	Gittens	Butters	Carter	Simpson	Hall*	Burton^	Rees	Griffiths/Bradbury
								Musselwhite	*Sandiman*	*Tankard*	*Bogie^*	*Griffiths*	*Glover D*	*McCarthy*	*Porter*	*Mills**	*Glover L*	*Guppy*	*Talbot/Naylor*
7	A 12/9	**SUNDERLAND** — McLoughlin 85p / *Melville 6* / Ref: T Lunt (Ashton-in-Makerfield)	12,282	17/15	8	D 1-1	0-1	Knight	Pethick	Russell	Allen"	Gittens	Butters	Carter*	Simpson	Hall	Burton	Rees*	Mc'n/Durnin/Griffiths
								Chamberlain	*Kubicki*	*Scott*	*Bracewell*	*Ball*	*Melville*	*Gray M*	*Ord*	*Mullin*	*Gray P*	*Russell**	*Aiston*
8	H 16/9	**DERBY** — Gittens 19, McLoughlin 90 / *Van der Laan 32, Flynn 58* / Ref: R Gifford (Llanbradach)	14,434	16/17	9	D 2-2	1-1	Knight	Pethick*	Russell*	Allen	Gittens	Butters	Carter*	Simpson	Hall	Burton*	Rees^	Durnin/Mc'n/Griffiths
								Hoult	*Kavanagh*	*Nicholson*	*Preece*	*Yates*	*Wassall*	*Van der Laan*	*Sturridge^*	*Flynn*	*Gabbiadini^*	*Harkes^*	*Simps'n/Wrack/Tral'p'*
9	H 23/9	**TRANMERE** — Nevin 58, Bennett 62 / Ref: D Orr (Iver)	11,127	17/10	9	L 0-2	0-0	Knight	Pethick	Russell*	McLoughlin	Gittens	Butters	Walsh	Simpson	Hall	Burton^	Nevin	Durnin/Bradbury/Wood
								Coyne	*Stevens*	*Thomas*	*McGreal*	*Garnett**	*Jones*	*Brannan*	*Aldridge^*	*Bennett*	*Irons*	*Moore^*	*Moore/Kenworthy*
10	A 30/9	**LUTON** — Walsh 43 / *Marshall 7, Davis 23, Guentchev 60* / Ref: P Rejer (Tipton)	7,795	22/23	9	L 1-3	1-2	Knight	Pethick*	Russell	McLoughlin^	Gittens !	Butters	Walsh	Simpson	Hall	Bradbury	Rees	Durnin/Igoe/Wood
								Feuer	*Peake*	*Johnson*	*Davis*	*Hughes*	*Vlstrup**	*Alexander^*	*Marshall*	*Taylor*	*Guentchev*	*Harvey*	*Waddock/James*
11	A 7/10	**OLDHAM** — Simpson 49 / *McCarthy 79* / Ref: J Lloyd (Wrexham)	5,937	22/8	10	D 1-1	0-0	Knight	Durnin	Dobson	McLoughlin	Gittens	Butters	Walsh^	Simpson	Wood	Bradbury^	Rees	Pethick/Hall/Igoe
								Gerrard	*McNiven*	*Makin*	*Henry*	*Jobson*	*Redmond*	*Halle*	*Olney^*	*McCarthy*	*Berestord**	*Brennan*	*Snodin/Beckford*

Match notes

1. Creaney has pledged his future to Pompey and Hall sets him up twice to get back in the groove. Hall also crosses for Creaney to nod down for Rees, then Tilson's wild swing denies free Carter (Arsenal) a debut goal. Thomson had earlier shot past Poom, who has the nod over Knight.

2. Mariners' boss Brian Laws' volley trumps Poom, then Durnin is sent off as he moans that Croft was offside. Crichton sees red for pole-axing Burton and Macca converts, but is injured in the process! Symons has gone (Man C £1.2m) but Simpson and Griffiths arrive from Maine Road.

3. Burton, whose parents live in Reading, smacks the best chance over the bar, but Royals' Morley scorns a better one, then is forced off with a head injury. The finger is pointed at Gittens (watch this space) but the ref saw no wrong. Derby and Hammers are linked with bids for Creaney.

4. Poom has a night to forget. His poor judgement hands Roberts a hat-trick as City threaten to score a dozen. Creaney converts a pen to level the game for a while. Ex-soldier Bradbury (20) makes his debut as a sub. Loanee Galloway (Celtic) is set to join, but then suffers a bad car crash.

5. Dixon's strike docks a point from Pompey after Knight saves Fuchs' shot and Rae reacts to cross. Keller's bravery twice denies sub Bradbury, on for ex-Lion Carter, who flops again.

6. Man City's £750,000 Walsh is in the crowd – he signs on Monday in part-exchange for £1.2m Creaney. The kept (Carl) Griffiths out of the City team, but he cheers himself up by converting after namesake Gareth fouls Carter. Burton's volley, too, is down to Gareth's lack of control.

7. £500,000 Martin Allen (West Ham) is on a three-month loan, but a permanent deal is agreed. He limps off at a precaution with a hamstring pull. Sub Macca salvages a point from the spot after Simpson is fouled, but Knight's save from Phil Gray's spot-kick at 0-1 was more crucial.

8. Walshy's second coming puts 6,000 on the gate, but it's Macca's second of the season, a flying header into stoppage time, that gets Pompey out of jail. Jim Smith's Derby were deservedly leading through Van der Laan's long-range effort and Gittens' soft header.

9. Tranmere's veterans Nevin and Bennett have too much know-how for Pompey. Nevin drifts a delicate header across Knight, then Bennett's bullet-header from the edge of the area settles it. Walsh might have had a penalty early on. Target Steve Nichol (ex-Liverpool) is in the stand.

10. Luton are rock-bottom and without a home win since April. Boss Terry Westley has used 24 players so far this season, but today's eleven are more than enough for pathetic Pompey. Gittens is unlucky for the penalty, but is booked and at once he body-checks Taylor and is sent off.

11. Gittens heads past Knight as he is about to gather and McCarthy says thanks very much. Fenwick's side had frustrated Latics up until then, although Halle hit a post, but Makin should have won it when through at the death. Rees's shot is deflected by Walsh and Simpson rolls in.

12	H	BIRMINGHAM	22	L	0-1	0-1		Knight	Durnin	Dobson	McLoughlin	Gittens	Butters	Walsh	Simpson^	Wood	Bradbury"	Rees*	Pethick/Hall/Griffiths
14/10		10,006	*5*	10			*Claridge 24*	*Bennett*	*Poole*	*Cooper*	*Castle*	*Edwards*	*Johnson*	*Hunt*	*Claridge"*	*Finnan^*	*Bowen**	*Tait*	*Otto/Rich'son/Charlery*
							Ref: I Hemley (Ampthill)	Claridge latches onto Durnin's headed back-pass and Pompey haven't won for six. Butters' header hits the bar, then he holds his head after Bennett's one-handed save. It's good news and bad for Gittens. The FA overturn his red at Luton, but Morley (Reading) is saying he'll sue.											
13	A	WEST BROM	24	L	1-2	0-0	McLoughlin 59p	Knight	Durnin	Dobson	McLoughlin	Gittens	Butters !	Walsh^	Simpson	Wood	Hall*	Allen	Pethick/Burton
21/10		*16,257*	*2*	10			*Ashcroft 64, Hunt 89*	*Naylor*	*Burgess*	*Edwards*	*Caldicott*	*Marden*	*Raven*	*Donovan**	*Ashcroft*	*Taylor*	*Hunt*	*Cunnington^*	*Gilbert/Hamilton*
							Ref: U Rennie (Sheffield)	Baggies are second now as Hunt's last-minute header gives them a flattering win. Hall is fouled and Macca converts, but Hunt gets behind the defence to set up Ashcroft soon after. Butters' faintest of touches on Hunt earns a second yellow. Another Wilkinson bid failed last week.											
14	H	WATFORD	21	W	4-2	2-0	Stimson 11, Simpson 15, Allen 66,	Knight	Durnin*	Dobson	McLoughlin	Gittens	Butters	Walsh	Simpson	Stimson^	Hall	Allen	Pethick/Carter
28/10		7,025	*20*	13			*Phillips 50, Ramage 87* [Carter 89]	*Cherry*	*Lavin*	*Bazeley**	*Foster*	*Millen*	*Ramage*	*Holdsworth*	*Palmer*	*Caskey*	*Moralee^*	*Phillips*	*Mooney/Pitcher*
							Ref: K Leach (Brewood)	A cheeky loan bid for Whits (now at Owls) fails, but Pompey find their firepower at last. Stimmo has been out for a year with a back problem, but he fires home, then Simpson thumps in jubilantly. Martin Allen's twice-taken 25-yard free-kick is top drawer, then sub Carter gets his first.											
15	A	SHEFFIELD UTD	22	L	**1-4**	1-2	Simpson 20	Knight	Durnin	Dobson	McLoughlin	**Perrett**	Russell	Walsh	Simpson	Stimson^	Hall*	Allen	Pethick/Carter
4/11		*11,281*	*21*	13			*Veart 32, 74, Flo 34, Battersby 79*	*Kelly*	*Gage**	*Nilson*	*Holland*	*Whitehouse*	*Tuttle*	*Veart*	*Flo*	*Blake"*	*Hodges^*	*Ward*	*Beard/Starb'k/Batt'sby*
							Ref: T Heilbron (Newton Aycliffe)	Dave Bassett's team have Pompey in all sorts of trouble. Sixty mad seconds make Simpson's long-range effort in vain. Veart rolls home, then Flo converts Hodges' cross. Battersby seals it as Knight and debut-making Perrett (Lymington) collide. Warren Smith wants to buy the club.											
16	H	HUDDERSFIELD	22	D	1-1	1-1	Simpson 30p	Knight	Durnin*	Rees"	**Whitbread**	Gittens^	Russell	Walsh	Simpson	Igoe	Hall	Allen	Pethick/Carter/Griffiths
11/11		6,876	*11*	14			*Scully 35*	*Francis*	*Dyson*	*Cowan !*	*Bullock*	*Scully*	*Gray*	*Dalton*	*Makel*	*Booth*	*Jepson*	*Jenkins*	
							Ref: R Harris (Oxford)	Ten-man Town are denied by a shining Knight. Twice he stops Booth, then he turns away Dalton's drive. Cowan goes for two bookings, but the Terriers snap when a push is spotted and Simpson scores. Fans' 'red-card' the watching Gregory, while on-loan Hammer Whitbread starts.											
17	H	STOKE	22	D	3-3	2-1	McLoughlin 16p, 56, Walsh 44	Knight	Pethick	Russell	McLoughlin	Whitbread	Butters	Walsh	Allen	Durnin	Hall	Carter*	Burton
18/11		8,030	*14*	15			*Gayle 33, 61, Sturridge 63*	*Prudhoe*	*Cranson^*	*Sandford*	*Sigurdsson*	*Overson*	*Potter**	*Keen*	*Wallace*	*Gayle*	*Sturridge*	*Gleghorn*	*Devlin/Sheron*
							Ref: C Wilkes (Gloucester)	Pompey snatch a draw from the jaws of victory as they switch off and let Lou Macari's Stoke (one defeat in nine) off the hook. Overson fells Walsh, who restores the lead after Prudhoe's slip. Macca's plunge looks to have sealed it, but Potters hit back, then Durnin raps the bar late on.											
18	A	BARNSLEY	22	D	0-0	0-0		Knight	Pethick	Russell	McLoughlin	Whitbread	Butters	Griffiths*	Allen	Durnin^	Hall	Carter"	Burton/Rees/Igoe
21/10		*6,187*	*14*	16				*Watson*	*Eaden*	*Shirtliff*	*Sheridan*	*Davis*	*De Zeeuw*	*Bullock*	*Redfearn*	*Payton^*	*Liddell**	*Archdeacon*	*Rammell/Hurst*
							Ref: I Cruikshanks (Hartlepool)	Gregory unveils plans to make Fratton all-seater by next December, but it seems to be a take-over bargaining ploy. Unsettled Griffiths is in for Walsh, who's about to be a father again. Fenwick is delighted with a clean sheet. 'For the first time I can say I'm pleased with my defence.'											
19	A	IPSWICH	22	L	2-3	1-2	Walsh 24, Allen 75	Knight	Pethick	Stimson	McLoughlin"	Whitbread	Butters	Walsh	Allen	Durnin	Hall^	Carter*	Rees/Igoe/Griffiths
25/11		*10,286*	*14*	16			*Milton 2, Marshall 25, Thompson 90*	*Forrest*	*Tarricco*	*Thompson*	*Thomson*	*Mowbray*	*Williams*	*Uhlenbeek**	*Tanner*	*Mathie*	*Marshall*	*Milton*	*Stockwell*
							Ref: B Knight	Walsh is hero and villain. He intercepts Uhlenbeek's pass and his chip is sublime, but he concedes the free-kick deep into injury-time and from 25 yards Thompson short-changes Pompey, who slip into the bottom three. Allen fires home unchallenged, not unlike Ian Marshall's effort.											
20	H	OLDHAM	20	W	2-1	1-1	Allen 19, McLoughlin 77p	Knight	Pethick	Stimson*	McLoughlin	Whitbread	Butters	Walsh	Simpson	Durnin	Hall	Allen	Carter
2/12		**6,002**	*14*	19			*Beckford 20*	*Gerrard*	*Snodin*	*Makin*	*Redmond*	*Vonk*	*Fleming*	*Halle**	*Rickers*	*Beckford*	*Brennan*	*Beresford*	*Pemberton*
							Ref: G Barber (Warwick)	Macca undoes Latics from the spot, as Hall is felled by Fleming. A defensive foul-up let Beckford chip in, but Allen's drive was no more than Pompey deserved after a bright opening. Fenwick's former target Vonk is a rock. Gregory says he now thinks Smith's consortium is genuine.											
21	A	TRANMERE	19	W	2-1	2-0	Durnin 9, Hall 36	Knight	Pethick	Stimson	Allen	Whitbread	Butters	Walsh^	Simpson	Durnin	Hall	Carter*	Rees/Griffiths
9/12		*6,678*	*11*	22			*Moore 80*	*Coyne*	*Rogers*	*Thomas*	*Teale*	*Higgins*	*Jones**	*Brannan*	*Branch^*	*Bennett*	*Moore*	*Nevin*	*O'Brien/Morrissey*
							Ref: M Fletcher (Warley)	On Thursday afternoon Smith and Gregory shook on a deal (but how much?) and a new football 'overlord' will be installed (but who?). Tranny are trounced, as the gap in class is as wide as the Mersey. Anfield old-boys Carter and Durnin combine for the first, then Hall floats home.											
22	H	LUTON	17	W	**4-0**	3-0	Hall 30, 43, Walsh 45, Carter 47	Knight	Pethick	Stimson	McLoughlin	Whitbread	Butters	Walsh	Simpson	Durnin	Hall	Carter	
16/12		7,012	*24*	25				*Feuer*	*Patterson*	*Johnson*	*Davis*	*Waddock*	*McLaren*	*Alexander^*	*Oakes*	*Taylor*	*Marshall*	*Harvey**	*Thorpe/Thomas*
							Ref: E Lomas (Manchester)	Hall has had trouble with one-on-ones lately, but not today. He then robs Patterson to set up Walsh and sets up Carter to thump home. Hatters (one win in nine) are going down and Westley will resign soon. In midweek the take-over was off, then on again as Gregory seeks securities.											
23	H	NORWICH	17	W	1-0	0-0	Durnin 56	Knight	Gittens	Stimson	McLoughlin	Whitbread	Butters	Walsh	Allen	Durnin	Hall	Carter*	Igoe
23/12		9,966	*9*	28				*Gunn*	*Polston*	*Bowen*	*Carey*	*Newsome*	*Prior*	*Adams*	*Fleck**	*Ward*	*Johnson^*	*Ullathorne*	*Scott/Sutch*
							Ref: G Pooley (Bishops Stortford)	Gregory jets off on hols, as the take-over turns nasty. Each side blames the other after talks breakdown. Saints have spies in the stand ahead of the cup-tie and they'll have been impressed. Durnin drives in when Carter's shot breaks perfectly and new City boss Gary Megson is a loser.											

ENDSLEIGH LEAGUE DIVISION 1 Manager: Terry Fenwick SEASON 1995-96

No	Date	Att	Pos	Pt	F-A	H-T	Scorers, Times, and Referees	1	2	3	4	5	6	7	8	9	10	11	subs used
24	A 26/12	11,686	17	28	L 1-2	1-0	Hall 8 — Newton 65, Nelson 89 — Ref: M Bailey (Impington)	Knight	Ammann	Stimson	McLoughlin	Whitbread	Butters	Walsh	Allen	Durnin	Hall^	Carter*	Simpson/Burton
								Humphrey	*Stuart*	*Jones*	*Rufus*	*Balmer*	*Newton*	*Leaburn^*	*Robinson*	*White^*	*Bowyer*	*Nelson/Linger*	

Pompey pay the price for missed chances when Nelson angles home in injury-time. Hall fires Pompey ahead from the edge of the box, then Durnin prods against a post. A bid to sign Whitbread and Allen permanently looks doomed; no one is around to sort out the £900,000 needed.

| 25 | A 30/12 | 25,294 | 16 | 29 | D 2-2 | 0-2 | Carter 58, Burton 65 — Bull 5, Goodman 35 — Ref: A Butler (Sutton-in-Ashfield) | Knight | Pethick | Stimson | McLoughlin | Whitbread | Butters | Burton* | Allen | Durnin* | Hall | Carter | Igoe/Simpson |
| | | | | | | | | *Stowell* | *Venus* | *Thompson* | *Atkins* | *Emblem* | *Richards* | *Daley^* | *Goodman* | *Bull* | *Osborn* | *Samways** | *Rankine/Ferguson* |

Carter slapped in a transfer request yesterday and shows his value with a 25-yarder. Burton fires in from close range and Mark McGhee hasn't changed Wolves wretched Molineux form (three wins in 13). Bull and Goodman plough through the blizzard and Pompey looked frozen out.

| 26 | H 1/1 | 12,926 | 17 | 29 | L 2-3 | 0-2 | Butters 57, Simpson 65 — Hopkin 13, 49, Freedman 45 — Ref: J Brandwood (Lichfield) | Knight | Pethick | Stimson* | McLoughlin | Whitbread | Butters | Walsh | Allen | Simpson* | Hall | Carter^ | Durnin/Burton/Igoe |
| | | | | | | | | *Martyn* | *Edworthy* | *Gordon* | *Roberts* | *Cundy* | *Hopkin** | *Pitcher* | *Houghton* | *Freedman* | *Taylor* | *Vincent^* | *McKenzie/Davies* |

Martyn tips Durnin's late effort over the bar, then Knight – 600 league games up today – goes up for a last-second corner as Pompey almost salvage it. 'One or two of the lads didn't get out of bed for the first half,' laments Fenwick. Lloyd McGrath is in line to man-mark Le Tissier.

| 27 | H 13/1 | 6,958 | 16 | 32 | W 3-1 | 2-0 | Walsh 10, Wood 12, Carter 77 — Groves 78 — Ref: I Hemley (Ampthill) | Knight | Pethick | Stimson | McLoughlin | Whitbread | Butters | Walsh | Wood* | Durnin | Hall | Carter | Igoe |
| | | | | | | | | *Crichton* | *Laws* | *Croft* | *Handyside* | *Rodger^* | *Groves* | *Childs* | *Dobbin^* | *Forrester** | *Livingstone* | *Bonetti* | *Woods/Shakesp/Lever* |

Knight passes Peter Bonetti's keeper appearance record today, but he is upstaged by unsettled Carter. Two pin-point crosses find Walsh and Wood's heads. Carter seals it with a shot from the edge of the box. Boss Laws has Mariners on the pitch at half-time to shake off their lethargy.

| 28 | A 20/1 | 5,560 | 16 | 32 | L 1-2 | 1-0 | Hall 41 — McNally 71, Tilson 84 — Ref: G Singh (Wolverhampton) | Knight | Pethick | Stimson | McLoughlin | Whitbread | Butters | Walsh | Wood | Durnin* | Hall | Carter | Gittens |
| | | | | | | | | *Royce* | *Hone* | *Powell* | *McNally* | *Bodley* | *Gridelet** | *Marsh* | *Tilson* | *Regis* | *Charlery* | *Hails* | *Thomson* |

Gregory's 'Pay up or shut up' ultimatum seems to have killed the take-over once and for all. Allen, though, is now in limbo, as cash from Man City isn't due until March. McNally gives the ball away to Hall, but he redeems himself by scrambling the leveller, then Tilson uses his head.

| 29 | A 27/1 | 7,710 | 16 | 33 | D 1-1 | 0-1 | Burton 75 — Van Blerk 24 — Ref: J Kirkby (Sheffield) | Knight | Pethick | Stimson | McLoughlin | Whitbread | Butters | Walsh | Wood* | Durnin* | Hall | Carter^ | Burton/Rees/Thomson |
| | | | | | | | | *Carter* | *Newman* | *Thatcher* | *Culkov* | *Witter* | *Stevens* | *Savage^* | *Connor* | *Malkin* | *Yuran* | *Van Blerk* | *Taylor* |

Pompey could have been playing SV Hamburg in a friendly, but Lions move forward this clash on FA Cup 4th round day. It looks like a bad move after Van Blerk's scrappy finish, then Perrett's rash challenge on Connor sees red. Burton's 20-yard bender caps a spirited comeback.

| 30 | A 4/2 | 7,924 | 14 | 36 | W 1-0 | 0-0 | McLoughlin 69 — Ref: D Orr (Iver) | Knight | Pethick | Stimson | McLoughlin | Perrett ! | Butters | Griffiths* | Wood* | Burton | Hall | Carter | Durnin/Igoe |
| | | | | | | | | *Hammond* | *Booty* | *Gooding* | *Bernal* | *Williams* | *Gilkes* | *Lambert** | *Parkinson* | *Quinn^* | *Nogan^* | *Holsgrove* | *Jones/Lovell/Morley* |

McLoughlin's deflected strike settles this dreary TV game. Griffiths gets his chance due to Walsh's knee. The take-over is finally dead, after last-ditch talks fail. 'We'll be back' says Smith. Poom's work permit extension looks doomed, while Bradbury is impressing on loan at Exeter.

| 31 | H 10/2 | 9,003 | 11 | 39 | W 2-1 | 1-1 | Burton 30, Hall 90 — Roberts 28 — Ref: A D'Urso (Billericay) | Knight | Pethick^ | Awford | McLoughlin | Whitbread | Butters | Walsh | Wood | Burton | Hall | Carter | Durnin/Igoe |
| | | | | | | | | *Poole* | *Grayson* | *Lewis* | *Hill^* | *Walsh* | *Parker* | *Lowe* | *Corica* | *Joachim** | *Roberts* | *Rolling* | *Robins/Carey* |

In injury-time Igoe crosses, Hall volleys in and talk is of a late play-off run, but Martin O'Neill's side will go up. The loss of Walsh – he twists his knee – will prove costly. Corica crosses for Roberts' head, then Burton combines with Wood to level. In limbo Allen's got a calf strain.

| 32 | A 17/2 | 12,241 | 11 | 40 | D 2-2 | 1-1 | Hall 33, Griffiths 89 — Agnew 8, Howey 90 — Ref: C Wilkes (Gloucester) | Knight | Pethick^ | Awford | McLoughlin | Thomson | Butters | Durnin | Walsh* | Burton | Hall | Carter^ | Simpson/Griffiths |
| | | | | | | | | *Given* | *Kubicki* | *Hall* | *Bracewell* | *Ball* | *Melville* | *Gray M** | *Howey* | *Russell^* | *Agnew* | *Cooke^* | *Gray P/Mullin/Bridges* |

Griffiths' gets a faintest touch and another late-show looks on, but Howey silences the cheers with a header. Former Pompey loan Agnew clips in, but Hall denies Given a fifth shut-out in six since being borrowed from Blackburn. Walsh is out for the season and McGrath has to retire.

| 33 | A 24/2 | 16,120 | 12 | 40 | L 2-3 | 0-0 | Hall 61, McLoughlin 86p — Yates 70, Sturridge 75, Gabbiadini 84 — Ref: W Burns (Scarborough) | Knight | Pethick | Awford | McLoughlin | Thomson | Butters | Allen^ | Wood | Burton | Hall | Carter* | Durnin/Griffiths |
| | | | | | | | | *Hoult* | *Rowett* | *Powell C** | *Powell D* | *Yates* | *Wassall* | *V der Laan^* | *Sturridge* | *Willems* | *Simpson* | *Flynn* | *Gabbiadini/Hodges* |

Burton and Hall combine and Pompey might commit highway robbery, but Yates' header responds quickly, then Sturridge makes up for first-half profligacy. Gabbiadini is free to head in, but Macca converts after Yates fouls Griffiths. New director Brady's cash means Allen signs.

| 34 | H 2/3 | 9,323 | 12 | 43 | W 2-1 | 1-1 | Burton 44, 57 — Butters 24 (og) — Ref: N Barry (Scunthorpe) | Knight | Pethick | Awford | McLoughlin | Thomson | Butters | Durnin | Wood | Burton | Hall | Carter | Newton/Nelson/Wns |
| | | | | | | | | *Salmon* | *Brown** | *Stuart* | *Jones** | *Rufus* | *Balmer* | *Robson^* | *Leaburn* | *Robinson* | *Grant* | *Mortimer* | *Newton/Nelson/Wns* |

Charlton have won seven away, but Burton's double ends hopes of another. In first-half injury-time Rufus and Salmon dither and Deon profits, then his 15-yard bicycle kick is a stunner. Butters couldn't get out of the way of Balmer's cross-shot. Fenwick is after Liverpool's Ian Rush.

35 A NORWICH 9/3 — 13,004 · 14 · 44 · 11 · D · 1-1 · 1-1 — Hall 38; Milligan 14 — Ref: P Taylor (Cheshunt)

Knight · Pethick · Awford · McLoughlin · Thomson · Butters · Allen · Wood* · Burton^ · Hall · Carter · Durnin/Griffiths
Gunn · Bradshaw · Newman · Crook · Newsome · Prior · Adams · Goss* · Ward · Milligan · Eadie · Fleck

Canaries have won just once since mid-Nov, but seem on-song when Milligan's sweetly-struck shot leaves Knight helpless. Hall's finish is less spectacular, but just as effective, and Allen bosses the midfield from then on. Thomson (£35,000 from Swindon in December) is impressive.

36 H WOLVERHAMPTON 16/3 — 11,732 · 14 · 44 · 15 · L · 0-2 · 0-2 — Emblem 39, Goodman 41 — Ref: G Barber (Warwick)

Knight · Pethick* · Awford · McLoughlin · Thomson · Butters^ · Allen · Wood · Burton · Hall · Carter · Durnin/Perrett
Stowell · Smith · Thompson · Young · Emblem · Richards · Corica · Goodman · Bull · Froggatt · Osborn

Fenwick's clearing the decks and Stimson's off to Southend (£25,000), but Ipswich's Sedgely (£900,000) is too pricey for him. Emblem strolls through for the first, then Bull's power sets up Goodman. Pompey fight back, but Hall and Perrett both have efforts scrambled clear late on.

37 A CRYSTAL PALACE 23/3 — 17,039 · 3 · 16 · D · 0-0 · 0-0 — Ref: A Wiley (Walsall)

Knight · Hinshelw'd · Awford · McLoughlin* · Thomson · Perrett · Allen · Simpson^ · Burton* · Hall · Carter · Durnin/Bradbury
Martyn · Edworthy · Vincent · Roberts · Tuttle · Hopkin · Pitcher · Houghton · Freedman* · Ndah* · Andersen^ · Dyer/Davies/Veart

Pompey are saved by the whistle as Andy Roberts' searing drive is on its way, when the referee thinks it's all over. Palace boss Bassett is not a happy man afterwards. The only other incident has Simpson hitting Martyn's bar. QPR's Hateley is the next on Fenwick's shopping list.

38 H PORT VALE 27/3 — 6,335 · 13 · 45 · 17 · L · 1-2 · 1-2 — Allen 18; Naylor 6, Griffiths 43 — Ref: S Bennett (Dartford)

Knight · Hinshelwood^ · Awford · Durnin · Thomson · Perrett · Allen · Simpson* · Burton · Hall · Carter^ · Rees/Igoe/Bradbury
Musselwhite · Hill · Stokes · Bogie^ · Griffiths · Aspin · Walker · Porter · Foyle · Naylor* · Guppy · Mills/McCarthy

Allen fires home with only one boot to level after Knight blunders, then Vale sucker Pompey when Griffiths powers in a header. Second-half pressure is fruitless, but Rush, Hateley and Wilkinson (whose flight was booked) all say no, to leave Pompey's striking resources threadbare.

39 H WEST BROM 30/3 — 8,126 · 13 · 45 · 18 · L · 0-2 · 0-1 — Sneekes 20, 79 — Ref: R Gifford (Llanbradach)

Knight · Russell* · Awford · Durnin'' · Thomson · Perrett · Allen · Simpson^ · Hall · Carter^ · Pethick/Rees/Bradbury
Naylor · Holmes^ · Nicholson · Sneekes · Burgess · Raven · Butler · Marden* · Taylor · Hunt · Hamilton · Gilbert/Darby

Baggies have only one defeat in ten, and only one loss in 13 at Fratton. On Grand National Day this game goes by the form-book. Sneekes springs the offside trap for the first, then he seizes on Taylor's flick to seal a comfortable win. Pompey are slipping into the danger zone.

40 A BIRMINGHAM 2/4 — 14,788 · 13 · 45 · 19 · L · 0-2 · 0-1 — Barnes P 17, Devlin 80p — Ref: E Wolstenholme (Blackburn)

Knight · Hinshelwood · Awford* · McLoughlin · Thomson · Perrett · Allen · Simpson^ · Hall · Durnin · Russell/Igoe
Griemink · Edwards · Grainger · Samways · Breen · Johnson · Hunt · Tait · Barnes P · Peschisolido* · Devlin · Francis

Relegation to Div Two will cost £500,000 in Sky TV cash, but it's a real threat now. Allen hits a post, but Pompey are never in it after Barnes' stormer. Devlin's late penalty doesn't flatter Barry Fry's Brum, and Pompey are three above the drop zone, having played two games more.

41 A WATFORD 6/4 — 8,226 · 24 · 48 · 18 · W · 2-1 · 1-1 — Awford 28, McLoughlin 61; Mooney 41p — Ref: R Poulain (Huddersfield)

Knight · Hinshelwood · Awford · McLoughlin · Thomson · Perrett · Allen · Simpson · Burton · Hall · Durnin ! · Pethick
Miller · Bazeley · Ludden · Hessenthaler · Page · Johnson · Porter^ · Palmer · Rammage · Mooney T · Dixon* · White/Simpson

Hornets are doomed, so this is a big win. Awford angles home his first senior goal in his 150th appearance, but Bazeley's flick hits Thommo's hand and Mooney's smiling. Macca's right-foot volley out of the blue is enough, but Durnin's late dismissal for a head butt makes things tense.

42 A SHEFFIELD UTD 8/4 — 8,978 · 12 · 48 · 18 · L · 1-2 · 0-2 — Durnin 56; Whitehouse 33p, White 40 — Ref: I Hemley (Ampthill)

Knight · Hinshelwood* · Awford · McLoughlin · Thomson · Butters · Allen · Simpson · Burton · Hall · Durnin · Pethick
Tracey · Ward* · Nilson · Patterson · Hodgson · Ablett · White · Hutchinson · Taylor · Walker^ · Whitehouse · Beard/Cowans

In 20 games since Howard Kendall took over, Blades have lost just three. They are too sharp for Pompey in the first half. There's no scandal about Whitehouse's penalty, but after the break Durnin's spectacular sets up an escape route, until they lose the plot after Pethick hits a post.

43 A STOKE 13/4 — 11,471 · 5 · 48 · 21 · L · 1-2 · 0-1 — Butters 61; Wallace 8, Sheron 90 — Ref: M Bailey (Impington)

Knight · Pethick ! · Awford · McLoughlin · Thomson · Butters · Allen · Durnin · Burton · Hall · Carter* · Igoe
Prudhoe · Clarkson · Sandford · Sigurdsson · Whittle · Potter · Beeston* · Wallace · Sheron · Sturridge · Gleghorn · Devlin

Pethick's back-chat to a linesman after 20 minutes cost Pompey dear in the end. Wallace has an open goal after the ball breaks from Sturridge, but Butters fires home after Hall gets away. In stoppage-time Sturridge loops a cross and Sheron is there to fire home. The trapdoor is opening.

44 H BARNSLEY 20/4 — 8,744 · 14 · 49 · 21 · D · 0-0 · 0-0 — Ref: D Orr (Iver)

Knight · Pethick* · Awford · McLoughlin · Russell · Butters · Allen · Igoe · Burton^ · Hall · Carter · Rees/Bradbury
Watson · Eaden · Jones · Sheridan · Moses · De Zeeuw · Bullock · O'Connell · Regis · Liddle * · Archdeacon · Hurst

Oldham's win at Lions means they are now level on points. Danny Wilson's mid-table side contest every ball, but chances are few. At least a fifth home defeat on the trot is avoided. Plans to revamp Fratton have gone quiet, but Brady's directorship has been approved by the league.

45 H IPSWICH 27/4 — 12,954 · 7 · 49 · 22 · L · 0-1 · 0-0 — Mathie 80 — Ref: M Riley (Leeds)

Knight · Igoe^ · Awford · McLoughlin · Thomson · Butters · Rees · Simpson · Burton · Hall · Carter* · Russell/Bradbury
Wright · Stockwell · Taricco · Thomson · Wark · Scowcroft · Mason · Sedgeley · Mathie · Marshall · Milton

"We have to win to stand any chance," said Fenwick in the programme, so Alex Mathie's fierce shot across Knight looks fatal. Town look sharper, as they soak up pressure. If they go down, expensive all-seater work can be avoided claim the cynics. No contracts have been signed.

46 A HUDDERSFIELD 5/5 — 14,091 · 8 · 52 · 21 · W · 1-0 · 1-0 — Burton 9 — Ref: J Rushton (Stoke)

Knight · Rees · Awford · McLoughlin · Thomson · Butters · Allen · Simpson · Burton · Hall · Carter · Collins/Baldry
Francis · Jenkins · Cowan · Bullock · Scully · Gray · Edwards · Makel* · Booth* · Jepson · Thornley · Collins/Baldry

Old-boy Creaney kept Latics up in the week and Reading saved themselves too. Millwall, top in December, will drop if they draw and Pompey win. That's what happens. Ipswich 0 Lions 0, while Burton's volley settles it. Relief all round. Gittens is freed and Brady wants to sign eight.

Home 9,407 · Average · Away 11,160

ENDSLEIGH DIVISION 1 (CUP-TIES) Manager: Terry Fenwick SEASON 1995-96

Coca-Cola Cup

			F-A	H-T	Scorers, Times, and Referees	1	2	3	4	5	6	7	8	9	10	11	subs used
1:1	H	CARDIFF	L 0-2	0-1	Dale 17, Bird 65	Knight	Pethick	Russell	McLoughlin	Awford	Butters !	Carter*	Durnin	Hall	Creaney^	Rees	Igoe/Burton
	16/8	4,203 3:			Ref: A D'Urso (Billericay)	*Williams D*	*Brazil*	*Searle*	*Harding*	*Baddeley*	*Perry*	*Wigg*	*Rodgerson*	*Haworth**	*Dale*	*Bird*	*Evans*

Symons is left out; he's off to Man C on Friday in a £2.2 million deal. This is a catastrophe as Kenny Hibbitt's Cardiff stroll. Butters' foul is his second yellow and Blue's Bird's shot flies in. Red tape is slowing Cowes-born Bradbury's army release. 'We were complacent': Fenwick.

			F-A	H-T	Scorers, Times, and Referees	1	2	3	4	5	6	7	8	9	10	11	subs used
1:2	A	CARDIFF	L 0-1	0-0	Dale 56	Poom	Pethick	Russell	Simpson	Awford*	Butters	Burton	Durnin	Hall	Creaney^	Rees"	Igoe/Griffiths/Carter
	22/8	6 3:19			Ref: M Brandwood (Lichfield)	*Williams D*	*Brazil*	*Searle*	*Harding**	*Baddeley*	*Perry*	*Wigg*	*Rodgerson*	*Haworth*^	*Dale*	*Bird*	*Downing/Young*
					(Pompey lost 0-3 on aggregate)												

Fenwick will step up his striker search as his side create nothing, save for Burton's first-half header. 'I'll get onto it in the morning,' he says. Cardiff will play...Southampton. Awford – back after ten months out – has a hairline crack in his knitted shin. The 2nd round draw is made.

FA Cup

			F-A	H-T	Scorers, Times, and Referees	1	2	3	4	5	6	7	8	9	10	11	subs used
3	A	SOUTHAMPTON	L 0-3	0-1	Magilton 12, 46, Shipperley 80	Knight	Pethick	Stimson	McLoughlin	Gittens	Butters	Walsh	Simpson	Durnin	Hall*	Wood^	Burton/Carter
	7/1	15,236 P:16			Ref: M Bodenham (Looe)	*Beasant*	*Dodd*	*Charlton*	*Magilton*	*Neilson*	*Monkou*	*Le Tissier*	*Watson**	*Shipperley*	*Venison*	*Heaney*^	*Maddison/McDonald*

The Hampshire rivals' first FA Cup meeting since 1906 ends in a Saints walk-over once Magilton tucks home. Walsh has a good case for a first half pen, but once Le Tissier's shot is diverted in just after the break it's over as a contest. The post denies sub Carter a late consolation.

League table

	Team	P	Home					Away					Pts
			W	D	L	F	A	W	D	L	F	A	
1	Sunderland	46	13	8	2	32	10	9	9	5	27	23	83
2	Derby	46	14	8	1	48	22	7	8	8	23	29	79
3	Crystal Pal	46	9	9	5	34	22	9	6	6	33	26	75
4	Stoke	46	13	6	4	32	15	7	9	7	28	34	73
5	Leicester*	46	9	7	7	32	29	10	7	6	34	31	71
6	Charlton	46	8	11	4	28	23	9	9	5	29	22	71
7	Ipswich	46	13	5	5	45	30	6	7	10	34	39	69
8	Huddersfield	46	14	4	5	42	23	3	8	12	19	35	63
9	Sheffield Utd	46	9	7	7	29	25	7	7	9	28	29	62
10	Barnsley	46	9	10	4	34	28	5	8	10	26	38	60
11	West Brom	46	11	5	7	34	29	5	7	11	26	39	60
12	Port Vale	46	10	5	8	30	29	5	10	8	29	37	60
13	Tranmere	46	9	9	5	42	29	5	8	10	22	31	59
14	Southend	46	11	8	4	30	22	4	6	13	22	39	59
15	Birmingham	46	11	7	5	37	23	4	6	13	24	41	58
16	Norwich	46	7	9	7	26	24	6	7	10	33	31	57
17	Grimsby	46	8	10	5	27	25	6	4	13	28	44	56
18	Oldham	46	10	7	6	33	20	4	7	12	21	30	56
19	Reading	46	8	7	8	28	30	5	10	8	26	33	56
20	Wolves	46	8	9	6	34	28	5	7	11	22	34	55
21	PORTSMOUTH	46	8	6	9	34	32	5	5	11	27	37	52
22	Millwall	46	7	6	10	23	28	6	7	10	20	35	52
23	Watford	46	7	8	8	40	33	3	10	10	22	37	48
24	Luton	46	7	6	10	30	34	4	6	13	10	30	45
		1104	233	177	142	804	613	142	177	233	613	804	1479

* promoted after play-offs

Odds & ends

Double wins: (1) Watford.

Double losses: (4) Birmingham, West Brom, Sheffield Utd, Ipswich.

Won from behind: (3) Southend (h), Leicester (h), Charlton (h).

Lost from in front: (5) West Brom (a), Sheffield Utd (a), Charlton (a). Southend (a), Derby (a).

High spots: Avoiding relegation on goals scored after a tense 1-0 win at Huddersfield on the last day.

Four-match winning run in December.

Re-signing Paul Walsh in September.

Low spots: Seven-match winless run between September and October.

One win in eleven matches in March and April put the team on brink of relegation.

Losing 0-3 at Southampton in the third round of the FA Cup.

Losing 0-3 on aggregate to third division Cardiff in the Coca-Cola Cup.

Lost in the first round of the League Cup and the third round of the FA Cup, without winning or drawing a game or even scoring a goal. The only comparable performance since the advent of the League Cup in 1961 is the 1969/70 season where the team lost to Brighton and Tranmere in the opening rounds.

Player of the Year: Alan Knight.

Ever presents: (0).

Hat-tricks: (0).

Leading scorer: Alan McLoughlin (10).

Appearances and Goals

Name	Appearances						Goals			
	Lge	Sub	LC	Sub	FAC	Sub	Lge	LC	FAC	Tot
Allen, Martin	27	1	2				4			4
Awford, Andy	17	9					1			1
Bradbury, Lee	3	8								
Burton, Deon	24	8	1	1		1	7			7
Butters, Guy	37		2	1			2			2
Carter, Jimmy	31	4	1		1		4			4
Creaney, Gerry	3		2				3			3
Dobson, Tony	7	2								
Durnin, John	30	11	2				3			3
Gittens, Jon	14	1			1		1			1
Griffiths, Carl	2	12				1	2			2
Hall, Paul	44	2	2		1		9			9
Hinshelwood, Danny	5									
Igoe, Sammy	4	18				2				
Knight, Alan	42		1		1					
McLoughlin, Alan	38	2	2		1		10			10
Perrett, Russell	8	1								
Pethick, Robbie	30	8	2		1					
Poom, Mart	4		1							
Rees, Jason	15	6	2				2			2
Russell, Lee	17	2	2							
Simpson, Fitzroy	27	3	1		1		5			5
Stimson, Mark	14		1				1			1
Symons, Kit	1									
Thomson, Andy	15	1								
Walsh, Paul	21				1		5			5
Whitbread, Adrian	13									
Wood, Paul	13	2			1		1			1
(own-goals)							1			1
28 players used	506	93	22	4	11	2	61			61

NATIONWIDE LEAGUE DIVISION 1 Manager: Terry Fenwick SEASON 1996-97

No	Date	Venue	Opponent	Att	Pos	Pt	Result	F-A	H-T	Scorers, Times, and Referees
1	17/8	A	BRADFORD C	10,007	—	0	L	1-3	1-0	Hall 26 / *Regtop 62p, Duxbury 76, Stallard 88* / Ref: P Richards ((Preston))
2	23/8	H	QP RANGERS	7,501	24	0	L	1-2	0-1	Igoe 76 / *Gallen 7, 77* / Ref: A Butler (Sutton-in-Ashfield)
3	27/8	H	SOUTHEND	5,579	15 *(22)*	3	W	1-0	0-0	Russell 67 / Ref: C Wilkes (Gloucester)
4	31/8	A	GRIMSBY	4,747	10 *(22)*	6	W	1-0	1-0	Rees 45 / Ref: U Rennie (Sheffield)
5	7/9	H	PORT VALE	6,448	11 *(13)*	7	D	1-1	1-0	Russell 23 / *Porter 58* / Ref: P Taylor (Cheshunt)
6	11/9	A	SWINDON	8,685	7 *(15)*	10	W	1-0	0-0	McLoughlin 73 / Ref: K Leach (Wolverhampton)
7	14/9	A	BOLTON	14,248	11 *(1)*	10	L	0-2	0-0	*Blake 49, Fairclough 86* / Ref: K Lynch (Knaresborough)
8	21/9	H	NORWICH	7,511	16 *(3)*	10	L	0-1	0-1	*Crook 36* / Ref: D Orr (Iver)
9	28/9	A	OXFORD	7,626	17 *(10)*	10	L	0-2	0-2	*Beauchamp 18, Ford M 38* / Ref: G Cain (Bootle)
10	1/10	H	CRYSTAL PALACE	7,212	16 *(5)*	11	D	2-2	1-1	Hall 43, Bradbury 86 / *Veart 28, Freedman 63* / Ref: R Harris (Oxford)
11	5/10	A	TRANMERE	5,001	18 *(4)*	11	L	3-4	1-2	Bradbury 43, McLoughlin 78p, Perrett 86 / *Branch 1, 31, Jones G 62, Bonetti 90* / Ref: J Kirkby (Sheffield)

Line-ups (Pompey / opponents)

No	Team	1	2	3	4	5	6	7	8	9	10	11	subs used
1	Pompey	Flahavan!	Pethick	Russell	McLoughlin	Butters	Awford!	Carter*	Simpson	Burton^	Hall	Igoe^	Rees/Bradbury/Thomson
1	Opp	*Gould*	*Liburd^*	*Mitchell*	*Cowans*	*Mohan*	*Sas*	*Hamilton**	*Duxbury*	*Regtop*	*Stallard*	*Kiwomya*	*Shutt/Wright*
2	Pompey	Flahavan	Pethick	Russell	McLoughlin	Butters	Awford	Carter*	Simpson	Burton	Hall	Allen	Igoe
2	Opp	*Sommer*	*Jackson*	*Brevett*	*Barker*	*McDonald*	*Yates*	*Impey^*	*Wilkins*	*Dichio*	*Gallen**	*Sinclair*	*Maddix/Murray*
3	Pompey	Flahavan	Pethick	Russell	McLoughlin	Butters	Awford	Carter*	Simpson	Burton	Hall	Rees	
3	Opp	*Royce*	*Dublin*	*Harris*	*Lapper*	*McNally*	*Gridelet*	*Marsh*	*Roget*	*Rammell*	*Hails**	*Byrne*	
4	Pompey	Knight	Pethick	Russell	Durnin	Butters	Rees	Carter^	Simpson	Burton^	Hall	Igoe	Bradbury/**Waterman**
4	Opp	*Pearcey*	*McDermott*	*Gallimore*	*Handyside*	*Smith*	*Widdington*	*Southall*	*Trollope*	*Livingstone*	*Mendonca*	*Black**	*Childs*
5	Pompey	Flahavan	Pethick	Russell	Dobson	McLoughlin	Awford	Carter*	Simpson	Burton	Hall	**Turner**	Igoe
5	Opp	*Van Heusden*	*Aspin*	*Stokes*	*Bogie*	*Griffiths**	*Glover*	*McCarthy*	*Porter*	*Foyle*	*Mills**	*Guppy*	*Hill/Talbot*
6	Pompey	Flahavan	Pethick	Russell	McLoughlin	Dobson	Awford	Carter	Simpson	Burton^	Hall	Turner	Igoe/Bradbury
6	Opp	*Talia*	*Darras*	*Robinson**	*Leitch*	*Seagraves*	*Culverhouse*	*Walters*	*Watson^*	*Cowe*	*Thorne*	*Horlock*	*Finney/Allison*
7	Pompey	Flahavan	Pethick	Russell	Dobson	McLoughlin	Awford	Carter	Simpson	Burton^	Hall	Turner	Bradbury
7	Opp	*Branaghan*	*McIlhespie**	*Phillips*	*Frandsen**	*Taggart*	*Fairclough*	*Johansen*	*Lee^*	*Blake*	*McGinlay*	*Thompson*	*Todd/Bergsson/Taylor*
8	Pompey	Flahavan	Pethick	Russell	Igoe	McLoughlin	Awford	Carter*	Simpson	Bradbury	Hall*	Turner	Durnin/Perrett
8	Opp	*Gunn*	*Newman*	*Mills*	*Eadie*	*Polston*	*Crook**	*Adams*	*Sutch*	*Akinbiyi*	*Milligan*	*O'Neill*	*Carey*
9	Pompey	Flahavan	Pethick*	Russell	McLoughlin	Butters!	Awford^	Carter	Simpson	Bradbury	Perrett	Turner*	Hall/Igoe/Durnin
9	Opp	*Whitehead*	*Robinson**	*Ford M*	*Smith*	*Elliott*	*Gilchrist*	*Ford B**	*Gray*	*Moody**	*Jemson*	*Beauchamp*	*Murphy/Aldridge/Purse*
10	Pompey	Flahavan	Perrett	Russell	Butters	McLoughlin	Awford	Carter	Simpson	Bradbury	Hall	Igoe	Igoe
10	Opp	*Nash*	*Edworthy*	*Muscat*	*Tuttle*	*Roberts*	*Hopkin*	*Anderson*	*Quinn*	*Freedman*	*Dyer**	*Veart*	*Ndah/Rodger*
11	Pompey	Flahavan	Perrett	Russell	Butters*	McLoughlin	Awford	Carter	Simpson"	Bradbury	Hall	Turner^	Pethick/Igoe/Durnin
11	Opp	*Coyne*	*Stevens*	*Hodges*	*Thorn**	*Teale*	*O'Brien*	*Irons*	*Aldridge*	*Branan*	*Branch*	*Bonetti*	*Jones G*

Match notes

1 — BRADFORD C: New supremo Terry Venables sees Hall fire home Carter's cross. Regtop converts, then Duxbury squeezes past stand-in Pethick. The TV had left before Stallard's clincher. injured – is sent off for fouling Shutt. Awford picks up a second booking and five minutes later, Flavs – Knight is

2 — QP RANGERS: Pompey are suckered by Ray Wilkins' QPR, when Gallen crocks himself, but still converts Sinclair's cross just after sub Igoe's cool finish. Sky TV means this a Friday night game. A female streaker does a 'Klinsmann' dive in the box, but despite wearing a Sky hat, she is edited out!

3 — SOUTHEND: Lee Russell scuffs home the second goal of his Pompey career to secure the first win of the season. Ronnie Whelan's Southend had lost 0-5 at Oxford on Saturday, and haven't scored since the first minute of the season, but Gridelet hits the bar early on. Ex-Fratton loanee Boere plays.

4 — GRIMSBY: Recalled Rees, in for the suspended Awford, rolls home Burton's square pass to give Pompey a flattering half-time lead, then Knight, replacing the banned Flahavan, preserves the points with an instinctive block from Livingstone in injury-time. Subbed Carter is booked for dawdling off.

5 — PORT VALE: Russell can't stop scoring, marking his 100th Pompey game with a well-judged header from Simpson's disputed corner. Vale deserve to level when influential Guppy's corner finds the lurking Porter, who finds the top corner. TV is crowing after his libel suit with Alan Sugar is settled.

6 — SWINDON: Turner (£250,000 from Spurs) crosses for Macca to score, but the referee's assistant concedes after the whistle he got it wrong and should have flagged for offside. FourFourTwo magazine produces figures that a Pompey visit puts 8% on an away club's gate – one of the best in Div One.

7 — BOLTON: Venables is linked with the Man C post after Ball's dismissal, but insists he is staying. Fenwick reckons Pompey were Bolton's equals. He's the only one. Ex-Saint Lee crosses for Blake's emphatic header, then Fairclough nets when Thomson's free-kick catches Pompey off-guard.

8 — NORWICH: Mike Walker's Canaries sneak it with Ian Crook's precise 20-yarder beating Flavs off a post, against the run of play. Bradbury is working hard, but Russell is again the main threat! TV is again the main threat! TV ... and will hint in a TV documentary tomorrow his future may lie abroad.

9 — OXFORD: Pompey fail their Oxford examination and Butters is dismissed for tugging Paul Moody's shirt. He had earlier been booked for protesting that Macca's header had been handled on the line. Beauchamp beat the offside trap and Ford fired home after Gilchrist's effort hit the post.

10 — CRYSTAL PALACE: Palace boss Dave Bassett has also turned down Man C and his team are off the back of consecutive 6-1 wins. A third is never likely, but Veart and Freedman put Pompey two up, until Bradbury rises to head his first senior goal. Forgotten Wood is rehabilitating his knee at Lilleshall.

11 — TRANMERE: Pompey are always chasing after early gifts, but Macca's conversion after Jones handles, then Perrett's shot on the turn, look to have salvaged it. At the death Flavs blunders and Bonetti enjoys an open goal. Bradbury stars and nips between Thorn and Coyne to net. Butters limps off.

Match records 12–23

---

12 · H · CHARLTON · 12/10
6,641 · 14 · W · 2-0 · 0-0 · (23 / 14)
Durnin 78, Bradbury 85
Ref: A D'Urso (Billericay)

Pompey: Flahavan · Pethick* · Russell · McLoughlin · Perrett · Carter · Awford · Simpson · Bradbury · Hall^ · Turner · Igoe/Durnin
Charlton: Salmon · Barness · Otto^ · O'Connell · Chapple · Newton · Balmer · Leaburn · Robinson · Allen* · Kinsella · Whyte/Sturgess

Fenwick says 'Knight's one of the best shot-stoppers; I don't want him to go,' as fans criticise his dropping the legend. Flavs confidence is rebuilt with a clean sheet. Leaburn (bar twice) and Kinsella (post) suggest his luck's changing too. Durnin's 20-yard stunner turns the game.

---

13 · H · WOLVERHAMPTON · 15/10
7,411 · 17 · L · 0-2 · 0-1 · (5 / 14)
Bull 12, 68
Ref: S Bennett (Dartford)

Pompey: Flahavan · Igoe · Russell · McLoughlin · Perrett · Carter · Awford* · Simpson · Bradbury · Durnin · Turner · Hall
Wolves: Stowell · Smith · Froggatt* · Atkins · Venus · V d Laan · Richards · Corica · Bull · Dowe · Crowe^ · Romano/Foley

Pompey have denied a move for Ipswich's Jason Cundy as Butters is off to Gillingham in a shock move. Fenwick is also weighing up a move for Saints' Shipperley, but he will prefer Palace. Old adversary Bull has too much power, as Perrett's poor back-pass leads to the clincher.

---

14 · A · IPSWICH · 19/10
10,514 · 19 · D · 1-1 · 1-1 · (16 / 15)
McLoughlin 40p
Mason 34
Ref: G Pooley (Bishop's Stortford)

Pompey: Flahavan · Pethick · Russell · McLoughlin · Perrett* · Carter* · Awford · Simpson · Bradbury · Durnin · Turner* · Hall/Igoe/Thomson
Ipswich: Wright · Taricco · Vaughan* · Mowbray · Sedgeley · Williams · Uhlenbeek · Sonner · Mathie · Scowcroft · Mason* · Petta

Master craftsman Mason's first-time shot from Mathie's cross zips in. Vaughan bundles Bradbury over almost at once; Macca converts. Flavs makes two sharp saves late on. Venables is talking to Hillier (Arsenal). Ground-works means Brighton won't be sharing Fratton next season.

---

15 · A · STOKE · 26/10
10,259 · 20 · L · 1-3 · 1-0 · (7 / 15)
Bradbury 37
McMahon 59, 75, Sheron 71
Ref: W Burns (Scarborough)

Pompey: Flahavan · Whitbread* · Russell* · McLoughlin · Perrett · Carter* · Awford · Simpson! · Bradbury · Durnin · Turner* · Hall/Igoe/Thomson
Stoke: Muggleton · Devlin · Worthington · Sigurdsson · Whittle · Forsyth · McMahon · Wallace* · Keen" · Sheron" · Kavanagh · Macari/Griffin/Mackenzie

The game goes on for more than 60 seconds after Simpson caught Keen. The ref catches up eventually and a second yellow means an uphill struggle. Two minutes later McMahon gets a break off Russell, then Sheron's shot deflects in. Whitbread (£250,000) signs from West Ham.

---

16 · H · BIRMINGHAM · 29/10
6,334 · 19 · D · 1-1 · 0-1 · (16 / 16)
Bradbury 70
Furlong 22
Ref: A Butler (Sutton-in-Ashfield)

Pompey: Flahavan · Whitbread · Russell" · McLoughlin · Perrett · Carter* · Awford · Simpson · Bradbury · Durnin · Turner" · Burton/Igoe
Birmingham: Bennett · Poole · Ablett · Bruce · Breen · Holland · Devlin · Castle · Furlong · Sheron" · Bowen" · Tait

Fratton's 6,000 extra seats are taking shape – at Venables' behest – as Trevor Francis's Blues look to kick-start a mixed season so far. Furlong capitalises on bad defending, but Bradbury makes it five in a month. After the game Director Brady sensationally resigns at a Board meeting.

---

17 · H · WEST BROM · 2/11
7,354 · 13 · W · 4-0 · 4-0 · (14 / 19)
Bradbury 9, Simpson 20, Durnin 36, Turner 44
Ref: M Bailey (Impington)

Pompey: Flahavan · Whitbread* · Thomson · McLoughlin · Perrett · Carter* · Awford · Simpson · Bradbury · Durnin · Turner" · Pethick/Igoe
West Brom: Crichton · Holmes^ · Nicholson · Sneekes" · Burgess · Raven · Darby · Agnew · Peschisolido Hunt* · Groves · Taylor/Donovan/Ashcroft

West Brom's good Fratton form deserts them. Pompey kick into the wind, but Baggies are blown away; Bradbury's header, Simpson's curler; Durnin's neat finish and Turner's tap-in, turn fans' half-time thoughts to THAT Fulham match (January 1985). Hillier is house-hunting.

---

18 · A · OLDHAM · 9/11
7,639 · 14 · D · 0-0 · 0-0 · (22 / 20)
Ref: G Frankland (Middlesbrough)

Pompey: Flahavan · Whitbread · Thomson · Hillier! · Perrett · Carter" · Awford · Simpson* · Bradbury" · Durnin · Turner · Pethick/Burton
Oldham: Kelly · Fleming · Serrant · Henry · Graham · Redmond · Orlygsson* · Rickers · Ormondroyd Barlow · Beresford · Banger

Hillier starts but sees red when he stamps on Henry – Pompey's fifth red of the season – and the FA's £10,000 suspended fine could well apply. Despite consecutive 3-0 wins, doomed Latics never look like profiting, while Igoe is unlucky to see one ruled out for Bradbury's foul.

---

19 · H · MANCHESTER C · 16/11
12,841 · 13 · W · 2-1 · 2-1 · (21 / 23)
Bradbury 24, Simpson 40
Rodger 16
Ref: B Knight (Orpington)

Pompey: Flahavan · Whitbread · Thomson · McLoughlin* · Perrett · Carter" · Awford! · Simpson* · Bradbury · Durnin · Turner" · Pethick/Burton/Igoe
Man City: Margetson · McGoldrick^ · Brightwell · Lomas · Symons · Wassall · Summerbee Clough* · Rodger · Kinkladze · Rosler" · Kavelashvili/Dickov/Whitley

Rosler's in hot water for gesturing at fans, while Kinkladze's shadow, Awford, sees red for a hack at the Georgian (70). Pompey then have some anxious minutes, but Simpson's special against his old mates is decisive. Turner's dummy set up Bradbury after Rosler could have made it 0-2.

---

20 · A · BARNSLEY · 23/11
7,449 · 15 · L · 2-3 · 0-2 · (3 / 23)
Durnin 65p, Bradbury 72
Wilkinson 17, Hendrie 41, Davis 84
Ref: T West (Hull)

Pompey: Flahavan · Whitbread · Thomson · McLoughlin* · Perrett · Awford · Carter^ · Igoe · Bradbury · Durnin · Turner" · Pethick/Burton/Hall
Barnsley: Watson · Eaden · Appelby · Sheridan · Davis · De Zeeuw · Hendrie · Redfearn · Wilkinson · Liddell" · Thompson* · Marcelle/Bosancic

TV will manage Australia, but also becomes chairman. Danny Wilson's side pass Pompey off the park and a boxing ref would have stopped it until Flav's penalty save from Redfearn. Durnin converts after Bradbury is felled, who then nicks a leveller. Davis's strike now flatters Tykes.

---

21 · H · STOKE · 30/11
7,749 · 11 · W · 1-0 · 1-0 · (7 / 26)
Turner 4
Ref: C Wilkes (Gloucester)

Pompey: Flahavan · Whitbread · Thomson · McLoughlin · Perrett · Igoe · Awford · Carter* · Simpson · Bradbury · Hall · Turner · Kavanagh
Stoke: Pruthoe · Pickering · Devlin" · Sigurdsson · Whittle · Forsyth · Griffin · Wallace · Stein^ · McMahon* · Gayle/Macari/Stokoe

Stoke's top scorer Mike Sheron is ruled out. Turner nods in Bradbury's flick early on, then Thomson could have eased second-half nerves, but blazed over. Stoke boss Lou Macari brings on son Mike to no avail. Swede Svensson's move is tied up in red tape, but it will be cut next week.

---

22 · A · SHEFFIELD UTD · 7/12
16,333 · 18 · L · 0-1 · 0-1 · (2 / 26)
Katchuro 14
Ref: J Brandwood (Lichfield)

Pompey: Flahavan · Whitbread · Thomson · Pethick* · Perrett · Hall^ · Awford · Igoe · Bradbury · Durnin · Turner" · McLoughlin/Carter/Svensson
Sheff Utd: Kelly · Parker · Sandford · Hutchinson* · Holdsworth · Nilson · Spackman · Patterson · Taylor · Katchuro" · Simpson · Walker/Beard

One moment of magic from Petr Katchuro, as he eases past Flav's desperate bid to intercept Taylor's flick, settles this predictably in Blades' favour (two points in 13 visits for Pompey now). £75,000 Svensson (Elfsborg) looks physical, but Thomson's first-half header goes closest.

---

23 · H · HUDDERSFIELD · 14/12
6,954 · 15 · W · 3-0 · 3-1 · (17 / 29)
Simpson 21p, Svensson 41, 44
Makel 51
Ref: P Rejer (Tipton)

Pompey: Flahavan · Whitbread · Thomson · Hillier · Perrett · Hall · Awford · Simpson · Bradbury · Svensson^ · Turner · Pethick/Durnin
Huddersfield: Norman · Tisdale* · Cowan · Bullock · Sinnott · Gray · Makel · Burnett* · Dyson · Payton · Crosby · Edwards/Dunn

Pompey's super Swede mashes the Terriers as he scores two and creates the penalty. He puts Bradbury away to be felled by Norman, then the compliment is returned and Svensson's off the mark. His header from Hillier's cross is thrilling and he earns a standing ovation when subbed.

NATIONWIDE LEAGUE DIVISION 1

Manager: Terry Fenwick

In each match the top row is the Portsmouth XI and the italic/lower row is the opponents' XI. In the "Pos" column the first figure is Pompey's league position and the second figure is the opponents' position.

No	Date	Att	Pos	Pt	F-A	H-T	Scorers, Times, and Referees	1	2	3	4	5	6	7	8	9	10	11	subs used
24	A 21/12 READING	8,520	15 / 19	30	D 0-0	0-0	Ref: D Orr (Iver)	Flahavan	Whitbread	Thomson	Hillier	Perrett	Pethick	Hall	Simpson	Bradbury	Svensson !	Turner*	Cook
	Reading							*Wright*	*Williams*	*Bodin*	*Bernal*	*Hunter !*	*McPherson*	*Gilkes*	*Lambert^*	*Morley*	*Lovell^*	*Gooding*	*Nogan/Bass*
25	H 26/12 SWINDON	10,605	17 / 10	30	L 0-1	0-0	Cowe 57 — Ref: E Lomas (Manchester)	Flahavan	Whitbread	Thomson	McLoughlin^	Perrett	Hillier*	Hall	Simpson	Bradbury	Svensson*	Turner*	Pethick/Durnin/Cook
	Swindon							*Digby*	*Kerslake*	*Horlock*	*Leitch*	*Robinson*	*Elkins*	*Culverhouse*	*Watson*	*Cowe*	*Allison*	*Collins*	
26	A 28/12 PORT VALE	7,382	15 / 9	33	W 2-0	1-0	Hall 11, Svensson 47 — Ref: B Coddington (Sheffield)	Knight	Whitbread	Pethick	Durnin	Perrett	Awford	Hall	Simpson	Bradbury	Svensson*	Cook	Carter
	Port Vale							*Musselwhite*	*Aspin*	*Tankard*	*Smith*	*Griffiths**	*Glover*	*McCarthy*	*Porter*	*Foyle*	*Naylar*	*Guppy*	*Walker*
27	A 1/1 NORWICH	11,946	17 / 6	33	L 0-1	0-0	Jackson 77 — Ref: A Wiley (Burntwood)	Knight	Whitbread	Pethick	McLoughlin^	Perrett^	Awford	Hall	Simpson	Durnin	Svensson*	Cook*	Carter/Thomson/Dobson
	Norwich							*Gunn*	*Newman*	*Jackson*	*Eadie*	*Polston**	*Sutch*	*Adams*	*Fleck*	*Milligan*	*Johnston*	*O'Neill*	*Akinbiyi*
28	H 11/1 BOLTON	10,467	17 / 1	33	L 0-3	0-0	Blake 55, 90, Johansen 74 — Ref: G Singh (Wolverhampton)	Knight	Whitbread^	Pethick	Hillier	Durnin	Awford	Hall^	Simpson	Bradbury	Svensson	Turner*	Carter/Igoe/Thomson
	Bolton							*Ward*	*Todd**	*Small*	*Pollock*	*Taggart*	*Fairclough*	*Lee*	*Sellars*	*Blake*	*Johansen*	*Sheridan*	*Phillips*
29	A 18/1 CRYSTAL PALACE	15,498	14 / 8	36	W 2-1	0-1	Bradbury 55, Thomson 62 / Quinn 30 — Ref: A D'Urso (Billericay)	Knight	Pethick	Thomson	McLoughlin	Hillier	Awford	Hall	Simpson	Bradbury*	Durnin	Cook	Turner
	Crystal Palace							*Day*	*Edworthy*	*Gordon*	*Roberts*	*Tuttle*	*Quinn*	*Muscat*	*Ndah**	*Shipperley*	*Dyer**	*Veart*	*Freedman/Mcenzie*
30	H 28/1 OXFORD	7,301	14 / 11	39	W 2-1	1-1	Hall 37, Svensson 67 / Angel 28 — Ref: M Bailey (Impington)	Knight	Pethick	Thomson	McLoughlin	Perrett	Awford	Hall	Simpson	Bradbury	Svensson^	Hillier*	Igoe/Durnin
	Oxford							*Whitehead*	*Murphy*	*Ford M**	*Smith*	*Purse*	*Gilchrist*	*Angel*	*Gray*	*Ford B^*	*Jemson*	*Beauchamp*	*Moody/Massey*
31	H 1/2 OLDHAM	9,135	11 / 23	42	W 1-0	1-0	Hall 7 — Ref: S Bennett (Dartford)	Knight	Pethick	Thomson	McLoughlin	Perrett	Awford	Hall^	Simpson	Bradbury	Svensson	Hillier	Igoe
	Oldham							*Kelly*	*Fleming !*	*Serrant*	*Henry*	*Snodin*	*Graham*	*Orhlgsson*	*Rickers^*	*McCarthy**	*Ormondroyd*	*Richardson*	*Banger/Beresford*
32	A 8/2 BIRMINGHAM	15,897	8 / 18	45	W 3-0	1-0	Svensson 3, Bradbury 78, McLoughlin 83p — Ref: M Halsey (Welwyn G City)	Knight	Pethick	Thomson	McLoughlin^	Perrett	Awford	Hall	Simpson	Bradbury	Svensson^	Hillier	Igoe/Durnin
	Birmingham							*Bennett*	*Brown**	*Grainger*	*Bruce*	*Johnson*	*Legg*	*Devlin*	*O'Connor*	*Furlong*	*Horne*	*Hunt**	*Bowen/Forster*
33	A 22/2 WEST BROM	15,800	8 / 15	48	W 2-0	2-0	Hillier 27, Burton 45 — Ref: C Foy (St Helens)	Knight	Pethick	Thomson	Igoe	Perrett	Awford	Hall	Simpson*	Bradbury	Burton	Hillier	Dobson
	West Brom							*Crichton*	*Holmes*	*Agnew^*	*Sneekes*	*Murphy^*	*Raven**	*Donovan*	*Smith*	*Hunt*	*Peschisolido*	*Hamilton*	*Caldicott/Darby/Potter*
34	H 1/3 SHEFFIELD UTD	12,715	9 / 4	49	D 1-1	1-0	Hall 19 / Fjortoft 54 — Ref: M Fletcher (Warley)	Knight	Igoe	Thomson	McLoughlin^	Perrett	Awford	Hall	Simpson	Bradbury	Svensson*	Hillier	Burton/Durnin
	Sheffield Utd							*Kelly*	*Short*	*Nilson*	*Hutchison*	*Spackman*	*Holdsworth*	*White*	*Patterson*	*Fjortoft*	*Katchuro**	*Ward*	*Walker*

Match notes

24 — Reading (A): Svensson eventful start in England continues as he clashes angrily for a second time with Hunter and the pair see red, Sven on a stretcher. He also missed a one on one with Wright, as did Bradbury, but McPherson hit the bar for Royals. Loanee Andy Cook (Swansea) comes on as sub.

25 — Swindon (H): Flahavan's luck finally runs out and his howler presents Cowe with a belated Xmas present. He dwells too long on a back-pass, then gives the ball straight to Cowe, who silences the second-biggest crowd of the season. Knight will be back, but Fenwick says he's being cruel to be kind.

26 — Port Vale (A): John Rudge's side are rolling – four wins from four and eleven goals – but they are no match for re-vamped Pompey on a bone-hard pitch. Knight has little to do, but McCarthy's late header hits a post. By then Durnin has set up Hall and Svensson has tucked in Bradbury's cross.

27 — Norwich (A): It's no fun for fans or team as they battle through blizzards to the under-soiled oasis of Carrow Road. A gritty rearguard action looks set for a point when Jackson seizes on Simpson's mistake to score his first of the season. Fenwick reckons all top teams should have under-soil heating.

28 — Bolton (H): Colin Todd's Bolton are impressive as they show their championship class. Blake is especially potent, but he gets a marginal offside decision for the first. He shrugs off Durnin in injury-time to seal it. Fenwick locks his team in the dressing room afterwards, but how will they react?

29 — Crystal Palace (A): Pompey's Selhurst record is dire – no win against Eagles since 1966. When offside-looking Quinn knocks in, it looks like normal service, but Bradbury glances home his first in nine, then Thomson heads in and Roberts and Gordon need the ref's arbitration over who was to blame.

30 — Oxford (H): Svensson enhances his reputation by putting Pompey within four points of sixth-placed Stoke. Bradbury's nod down allows the Swede the chance to hold off Gilchrist and slot in. Angel delighted Oxford, but Hall levelled with only the team's fourth league goal at the Milton End.

31 — Oldham (H): Latics won only one in their first 15 – they're unbeaten in eight away now – but Hall seizes on a mix-up between Snodin and Kelly to roll home and boss Graeme Sharp's days are numbered. Nine players are booked in the first half and one of them – Fleming – sees red in the second.

32 — Birmingham (A): Ex-Pompey midfielder George Graham – now boss at FA Cup fifth round rivals Leeds – is given food for thought as Trevor Francis' Blues are overwhelmed. Live Swedish TV sees Super Sven nod in Hall's cross, but he soon is stretchered off after a sickening clash with Steve Bruce.

33 — West Brom (A): Whisper it quietly, but Pompey are now in play-off prospects, as they claim their seventh win in a row and their fourth in the Midlands since December. Hillier's deflected first goal for his club sets them on their way, then Burton – in for the hamstrung Sven – heads in Pethick's cross.

34 — Sheffield Utd (H): World Cup-dreaming Jamaican Hall runs from halfway to fire spectacularly past Kelly, then Bradbury bobbles a shot against the post on half-time. Fjortoft is given space to turn and fire home, then hits the bar within a minute. Knight is in top form, but a draw is a fair reflection.

Match-by-match record (games 35–46)

---

35. MANCHESTER C (A) — 5/3
Opp pos 11 · D 1-1 · League pos 16 · Pts 50 · Att **26,051**
Simpson 86 / Rösler 58
Ref: R Pearson (Peterlee)
Pompey: Knight, Igoe, Thomson, Cook^, Perrett, Awford, Hall, Simpson, Bradbury, Svensson*, Hillier — subs McLoughlin/Durrin
Man City: Wright, Brightwell, Horlock, Lomas, Symons, Beagrie, Summerbee, McGoldrick, Dickov*, Ingram^, Rösler — subs Brown/Greenacre

City only scored early on, then he tormented Cook, crossing for Horlock to nod home from six yards. 'I was delighted with the attitude,' Fenwick. City had dominated: Summerbee nearly scored early on.

---

36. HUDDERSFIELD (A) — 15/3
Opp pos 9 · W 3-1 · League pos 20 · Pts 53 · Att 10,512
Igoe 58, Hall 61, 62 / Stewart 34
Ref: T Leake (Darwen)
Pompey: Knight, Pethick, Thomson, McLoughlin, Perrett, Awford, Hall, Simpson, Bradbury, Svensson*, Hillier ! — sub Igoe
Huddersfield: Francis, Jenkins, Ryan*, Browning, Edmondson, Gray, Burnett*, Baldry, Stewart, Glover, Reid — subs Dalton/Crosby/Facey

Ten-man Pompey stun the Terriers with three in four second-half minutes, after Hillier received his second, and the team's eighth, red so far. Shortly after, Stewart converts Baldry's cross, but Igoe's glorious floater and Hall's brace of close-range strikes turns the game on its head.

---

37. QP RANGERS (A) — 22/3
Opp pos 12 · L 1-2 · League pos 11 · Pts 53 · Att 15,746
Bradbury 18 / Murray 45, Spencer 77
Ref: K Lynch (Knaresborough)
Pompey: Knight, Pethick !, Thomson*, Igoe, Allen^, Whitbread, Hall, Simpson, Bradbury, Burton*, Hillier — subs McLoughlin/Simpson/Allen
QPR: Sommer, Maddix, Barker, McDonald, Ready, Spencer, Peacock, Dichio, Impey, Sinclair*, Murray — sub Murray

It all goes wrong at Loftus Road, as Pethick is sent off for chopping down Spencer, who profits by angling home the winner from an acute angle seven minutes later. Bradbury fired home, then Murray's shot from 20 yards levels. Fighting fans hold up the game for seven minutes.

---

38. READING (H) — 25/3
Opp pos 8 · W 1-0 · League pos 16 · Pts 56 · Att 9,248
Hall 84
Ref: M Brandwood (Lichfield)
Pompey: Knight, Pethick*, Whitbread, McLoughlin, Perrett, Awford, Hall, Simpson, Bradbury, Svensson*, Hillier — subs Igoe/Durrin
Reading: Mautone, Bernal, Parkinson, Gooding, McPherson, Hopkins, Gilkes, Williams*, Morley, Lovell, Caskey^ — subs Nogan/Holsgrove

Reading make life just as difficult as they did in the Cup, but they would – they have won six out of their last nine. Joint-boss Mick Gooding hits a post in the first half, but Pompey pressure finally pays when Perrett knocks down Macca's free-kick and Hall scores from close range.

---

39. BRADFORD C (H) — 29/3
Opp pos 6 · W 3-1 · League pos 21 · Pts 59 · Att 12,340
Bradbury 30, Hall 39, Svensson 43 / Murray 17
Ref: B Knight (Orpington)
Pompey: Knight, Pethick, Whitbread, Allen*, Perrett, Awford, Hall, Simpson*, Bradbury, Svensson*, Hillier — subs Russell/Burton/Durrin
Bradford C: Davison, Liburd*, Jacobs, Dreyer, Oliveira*, O'Brien, Murray, Kulscar, Newell, Edinho*, Pepper ! — subs Sundgot/Wilder/Blake

Another Murray scores against Pompey, this time it's old-boy Shaun. Pepper had already spiced things up by getting sent off; he fouled Allen, then encroached! Kulscar inadvertently set up Bradbury, who then forces his way to cross for Hall. Sven's 25-yard strike is special.

---

40. SOUTHEND (A) — 31/3
Opp pos 8 · L 1-2 · League pos 24 · Pts 59 · Att 6,107
Hall 54 / Gridelet 27, Rammell 45
Ref: N Barry (Scunthorpe)
Pompey: Knight, Pethick, Whitbread, Allen*, Perrett, Awford, Hall, Cook*, Bradbury, Svensson*, Hillier — subs Russell/Burton/Durrin
Southend: Royce, Harris, Dublin, Lapper, Roget, Gridelet, Marsh, Codner, Rammell, Boere*, Clarke^ — sub Thomson

United keeper Royce denies Pompey a chance of fifth place with a string of saves. Shrimpers hadn't won in eight and are doomed, but poor defending lets Gridelet round Knight, then Boere's flick finds Rammell. Hall's chip drags his side back and Burton has a late goal ruled out.

---

41. GRIMSBY (H) — 5/4
Opp pos 6 · W 1-0 · League pos 22 · Pts 62 · Att 9,854
Carter 55
Ref: D Orr (Iver)
Pompey: Knight, Igoe, Whitbread, McLoughlin, Russell, Awford, Hall, Carter*, Bradbury*, Svensson*, Hillier — subs Burton/Durrin/Waterman
Grimsby: Pearcey, Jobling, Gallimore, Rodger, Lever, Widrington*, Southall, Lee^, Shakespeare, Mendonca, Childs^ — subs Livingstone/Fickling/Lester

Carter peels off his shirt after netting from the edge of the box and his vest proclaims: 'I'm back!' He is too, as this is his first start since November, but Pompey labour against old-boy Kenny Swain's Mariners. Pompey are worth the win though, as they harness the breeze better.

---

42. TRANMERE (H) — 12/4
Opp pos 9 · L 1-3 · League pos 8 · Pts 62 · Att 12,004
Hillier 89 / Cook 16, Jones G 23, Jones L 83
Ref: G Singh (Wolverhampton)
Pompey: Knight, Igoe, Whitbread, McLoughlin, Perrett, Awford, Hall, Carter, Bradbury, Svensson*, Hillier — sub Pethick
Tranmere: Nixon, Thomas^, Rogers, McGreal, Thorn*, Morrissey*, Cook, Jones G, Jones L, Irons — subs Aldridge/Mahon/Branch

David Deacon is here, a minute's silence marks the death of ex-Chairman John. Pompey pick up the sombre mood and John Aldridge's Tranmere look the better play-off bet now. Cook's free header, then Gary Jones' chip, set up the win. A 20-man punch-up sees no one booked!

---

43. CHARLTON (A) — 19/4
Opp pos 11 · L 1-2 · League pos 14 · Pts 62 · Att 12,342
Hall 11 / Bright 10, 65
Ref: M Fletcher (Warley)
Pompey: Knight, Pethick*, Thomson", McLoughlin, Perrett, Whitbread, Hall, Simpson^, Bradbury, Burton*, Hillier — subs Awford/Burton/Durrin
Charlton: Petterson, Stuart*, Barness, Nicholls, Rufus, Balmer, Newton, Bright, Robinson, Lisbie, Kinsella — sub Leaburn

Play-off hopes look forlorn now, but Fenwick protests one-time target Mark Bright – who joined Valiants on deadline day – was offside for both goals. He nudges home Balmer's cross, then loops home Newton's free-kick. Hall had touched home Igoe's cross, straight after the first.

---

44. BARNSLEY (H) — 22/4
Opp pos 7 · W 4-2 · League pos 2 · Pts 65 · Att 8,328
McLoughlin 28p, Bradbury 37, 49, 89 / Redfearn 62, 73
Ref: P Taylor (Cheshunt)
Pompey: Knight, Igoe, Thomson, McLoughlin, Perrett^, Whitbread, Hall, Simpson, Bradbury, Burton*, Hillier* — subs Awford/Durrin/Turner
Barnsley: Watson, Eaden, Shirtliff*, Sheridan, Moses, De Zeeuw, Hendrie, Redfearn, Wilkinson, Marcelle*, Thompson — subs Liddell/Bullock

Bradbury earns the accolades after his England U-21 call-up. Macca converts after De Zeeuw handles, then two Bradbury headers leave Tykes' hopes of clinching promotion ruined. Redfearn rallies, his second from 25 yards, but late on Turner sets up Bradbury for his first hat-trick.

---

45. IPSWICH (H) — 25/4
Opp pos 9 · L 0-1 · League pos 4 · Pts 65 · Att 12,101
Scowcroft 36
Ref: A Wiley (Burntwood)
Pompey: Knight, Igoe, Thomson^, McLoughlin, Awford, Whitbread, Hall*, Simpson, Bradbury, Burton*, Hillier — subs Durrin/Waterman
Ipswich: Wright, Stockwell*, Tanico, Sedgeley, Swailes, Williams, Uhlenbeek, Vaughan, Gregory*, Scowcroft, Mason* — subs Milton/Dyer/Gudmundsson

Pompey's players complete a lap of honour afterwards, but it's George Burley's Ipswich who are celebrating play-off glory, with their fifth win in a row. Knight misses a corner and Scowcroft nods in, but he makes three fine saves. Gregory hits a post as Town are worth their win.

---

46. WOLVERHAMPTON (A) — 4/5
Opp pos 7 · W 1-0 · League pos 3 · Pts 68 · Att **26,031**
Hall 80
Ref: P Richards (Preston)
Pompey: Knight, Igoe, Thomson, McLoughlin, Atkins^, Whitbread, Hall", Simpson*, Bradbury, Burton*, Hillier — subs Durrin/Waterman/Svensson
Wolverhampton: Stowell, Smith, Thompson, Venus, Law, Robinson, Bull*, Ferguson*, Crowe, Thomas, Wright — subs Wright/Dennison/Foley

Hall's first-ever headed goal secures seventh place, as he nods in Macca's free-kick at the far post. Blues are better, but Law hits the top of the bar late on. Wanderers started brightly, but Hall should have made it safe, missing from close in. Pompey just lose the reserve league to Dons.

Average — Home 8,854 · Away 11,928

NATIONWIDE DIVISION 1 (CUP-TIES) Manager: Terry Fenwick SEASON 1996-97

Coca-Cola Cup

	Att	W/L/D	F-A	H-T	Scorers, Times, and Referees	1	2	3	4	5	6	7	8	9	10	11	subs used
1:1 H LEYTON ORIENT 20/8	3,201 (3)	W	2-0	1-0	Burton 9, 56. Ref: S Bennett (Dartford)	Flahavan	Pethick	Russell	McLoughlin	Butters	Awford	Carter*	Simpson	Burton	Hall	Igoe	Bradbury
						Sealey	*Hendon*	*Naylor*	*Garland*	*Martin A*	*Arnott*	*Martin D*	*Ling**	*Ayonide^*	*West*	*McCarthy*	*Hanson/Chapman*
1:2 A LEYTON ORIENT 4/9	3,177 (3:18)	L	0-1	0-0	West 59. Ref: M Fletcher (Warley) (Pompey won 2-1 on aggregate)	Flahavan	Pethick	Russell	McLoughlin	Butters	Awford	Carter	Simpson	Burton	Hall	Igoe*	Turner
						Sealey	*Hendon*	*Naylor*	*Channing*	*Martin A*	*Arnott*	*Martin D**	*Ling*	*Hanson*	*West*	*Kelly*	*Ayonide*
2:1 A WIMBLEDON 18/9	3,811 (P:8)	L	0-1	0-0	Holdsworth 58. Ref: G Barber (Warwick)	Flahavan	Pethick	Russell	McLoughlin	Dobson*	Awford	Carter	Simpson	Perrett	Hall^	Turner	Hall/Bradbury
						Heald	*Jupp*	*Kimble*	*Jones*	*Reeves*	*Blackwell*	*Fear*	*Euell**	*Clarke*	*Holdsworth*	*Leonhardsen^*	*Ardley/Harford*
2:2 H WIMBLEDON 25/9	4,006 (P:6)	D	1-1	1-0	Carter 41; Gayle 47. Ref: M Bodenham (Looe) (Pompey lost 2-1 on aggregate)	Flahavan	Pethick	Russell	McLoughlin	Butters	Awford	Carter	Simpson	Bradbury	Perrett	Turner*	Hall
						Sullivan	*Cunningham*	*Kimble*	*Jones*	*Blackwell*	*Perry*	*Clarke*	*Earle*	*Gayle*	*Holdsworth**	*Fear*	*Leonhardsen*

1:1 — The all-seater Fratton distresses fans. Just 6,000 new seats have been installed and swathes of unusable terracing are left exposed – including the Fratton End. Two Burton strikes seal it, but the second has O's boss Pat Holland fuming. Hendon's careless back-pass is snapped up.

1:2 — Pompey have keeper Flahavan to thank for securing their place in the next round with a last-minute save from Kelly, after West had nodded down Hanson's cross. West pulled O's back into the game with a free far-post header from Naylor's corner. Pompey rarely threatened a goal.

2:1 — Wimbledon boss Joe Kinnear drops ten of the team who started against West Ham on Saturday, but they still win when Jones' long-throw is flicked on by Blackwell for Holdsworth. Turner goes closest for Pompey, but Heald saves, then Hall has a goal ruled out for offside late on.

2:2 — Kinnear beefs up his team a little, as Perry endears himself by claiming Dons will have far too much class for the likes of Pompey. He is lucky not to be sent off for a foul, then Carter's wickedly deflected shot raises hopes. Earle hits a post and Gayle blows Pompey out from the rebound.

FA Cup

	Att	W/L/D	F-A	H-T	Scorers, Times, and Referees	1	2	3	4	5	6	7	8	9	10	11	subs used
3 A WOLVERHAMPTON 7/1	23,626 (4)	W	2-1	0-0	McLoughlin 68, Hall 80; Ferguson 69. Ref: A Wilkie (Chester-le-Street)	Knight	Whitbread	Pethick	McLoughlin	Perrett*	Awford	Hall	Simpson	Bradbury	Durnin	Hillier	Thomson
						Stowell	*Smith*	*Dennison*	*Atkins*	*Venus*	*Emblem*	*Corica**	*Thomas*	*Bull*	*Goodman^*	*Osborn*	*Ferguson/Roberts*
4 H READING 25/1	15,003 (19)	W	3-0	0-0	Hall 68, Bradbury 76, Hillier 86. Ref: D Elleray (Harrow)	Knight	Pethick	Thomson	McLoughlin	Perrett	Awford	Hall	Simpson	Bradbury	Durnin*	Hillier	Svensson
						Bibbo	*Booty*	*Gilkes*	*Caskey**	*Hunter*	*Holsgrove*	*Bernal*	*Williams*	*Morley*	*Lambert*	*Gooding*	*Lovell*
5 A LEEDS 15/2	35,604 (P:11)	W	3-2	1-0	McLoughlin 7, Svensson 67, Bradbury 86; Bowyer 52, 90. Ref: P Alcock (Redhill)	Knight	Thomson	Thomson	McLoughlin*	Perrett*	Awford	Hall	Simpson*	Bradbury	Svensson	Hillier	Igoe/Dobson/Allen
						Martyn	*Kelly*	*Dorigo*	*Palmer*	*Molenaar*	*Halle*	*Jackson**	*Wallace*	*Deane*	*Radebe*	*Bowyer*	*Rush*
QF H CHELSEA 9/3	15,701 (P:7)	L	1-4	0-2	Burton 84; Hughes M 25, Wise 43, 86, Zola 56. Ref: J Winter (Stockton-on-Tees)	Knight	Pethick	Thomson	McLoughlin	Perrett	Awford	Hall	Simpson*	Bradbury	Svensson*	Hillier	Igoe/Burton
						Grodas	*Petrescu*	*Minto*	*Sinclair*	*Lebeouf**	*Calfke*	*Zola*	*Di Matteo^*	*Hughes P*	*Hughes M*	*Wise*	*Johnsen/Barley*

3 — Pompey are Up for the Cup at Molineux and stun Mark McGhee's Wolves with their first win here since 1951. Wanderers have lost six at home, but Macca's joy, after nodding in, is short-lived: Ferguson guides in Dennison's cross. Bradbury nods down for Hall to spare the replay.

4 — Royals are far from flushed – no win in the league since 3 December – but they sent Southampton's Cup hopes down the pan (3-1). Pompey are clearly sterner stuff, but they leave it late. Sub Sven is the catalyst, setting up Hall and Bradbury, before Hillier rolls home his first goal.

5 — 3-2 flatters Leeds, who could have been buried by half-time. Macca is clattered in opening, then reserve spot-kicker Simpson sees Martyn save after Kelly handles. Bowyer levels, but Sven's classy cut inside and Bradbury's two-yard open goal, means Pompey conga their way through.

QF — Chelsea stroll into the semis, as a sea-mist rolls around Fratton. Pompey's Live TV jinx – no win on Sky, no win at Fratton – continues. Old-stager Mark Hughes puts Ruud Gullit's superstars on their way with a typically venomous strike, but Burton's consolation was nearly as good.

League table

	Team	P		Home					Away					Pts
			W	D	L	F	A	W	D	L	F	A		
1	Bolton	46	18	4	1	60	20	10	10	3	40	33		98
2	Barnsley	46	14	4	5	43	19	8	10	5	33	36		80
3	Wolves	46	10	5	8	31	24	12	5	6	37	27		76
4	Ipswich	46	13	7	3	44	23	7	9	7	24	27		74
5	Sheffield Utd	46	13	5	5	46	23	7	8	8	29	29		73
6	Crystal Pal*	46	10	7	6	39	22	9	7	7	39	26		71
7	PORTSMOUTH	46	12	4	7	32	24	8	4	11	27	29		68
8	Port Vale	46	9	9	5	36	28	8	7	8	22	27		67
9	QP Rangers	46	10	5	8	33	25	8	7	8	31	35		66
10	Birmingham	46	11	7	5	30	18	8	8	9	22	30		66
11	Tranmere	46	10	9	4	42	27	7	5	11	21	29		65
12	Stoke	46	15	3	5	34	22	3	7	13	17	35		64
13	Norwich	46	9	10	4	28	18	8	2	13	35	50		63
14	Manchester C	46	12	4	7	34	25	7	6	12	25	35		61
15	Charlton	46	11	8	4	36	28	5	3	15	16	38		59
16	West Brom	46	7	7	9	37	33	8	7	8	31	39		57
17	Oxford	46	14	3	6	44	26	2	6	15	20	42		57
18	Reading	46	13	7	3	37	24	2	5	16	21	43		57
19	Swindon	46	11	6	6	36	27	4	3	16	16	44		54
20	Huddersfield	46	10	7	6	28	20	3	8	12	20	41		54
21	Bradford C	46	10	5	8	29	32	2	7	14	18	40		48
22	Grimsby	46	7	7	9	31	34	4	6	13	29	47		46
23	Oldham	46	6	8	9	30	30	4	5	14	21	36		43
24	Southend	46	9	7	7	32	32	1	6	16	10	54		39
		1104	262	150	140	872	604	140	150	262	604	872		1506

* promoted after play-offs

Odds & ends

Double wins: (3) Grimsby, West Brom, Huddersfield.

Double losses: (4) QPR, Norwich, Bolton, Tranmere.

Won from behind: (5) Man City (h), Crystal Palace (a), Oxford (h). Huddersfield (a), Bradford C (h).

Lost from in front: (3) Bradford C (a), Stoke (a), QPR (a).

High spots: Five consecutive league wins in January and February. Eight-match unbeaten run in the league from January to March. Reaching FA Cup quarter-finals. Winning 3-2 at Premiership Leeds in the FA Cup fifth round. Beating eventually-promoted Barnsley 4-2 at Fratton in April. Scoring four goals in the first half to beat West Brom at Fratton. Striker Lee Bradbury called up for England U-21 squad.

Low spots: Losing 1-4 at home to Chelsea in the quarter-finals of the FA Cup in front of the Sky TV cameras. Nine players sent off during the course of the season.

Player of the Year: Lee Bradbury.

Ever presents: (0).

Hat-tricks: Lee Bradbury (1).

Leading scorer: Lee Bradbury (17).

Appearances and Goals

Player	Appearances Lge	Sub	LC	Sub	FAC	Sub	Goals Lge	LC	FAC	Tot
Allen, Martin	3	1				1				
Awford, Andy	37	2	4		4					
Bradbury, Lee	38	4	1		4	1	15		2	17
Burton, Deon	12	9	2				1	3		4
Butters, Guy	7		3							
Carter, Jimmy	23	4	4				1		1	2
Cook, Andy	6	2								
Dobson, Tony	4	2	1							
Durnin, John	16	18			2		3			3
Flahavan, Aaron	24		4							
Hall, Paul	36	6	3	1	4		13		2	15
Hillier, David	21		2		4		2		1	3
Igoe, Sammy	22	18	2	1	2	2	2			2
Knight, Alan	22				4					
McLoughlin, Alan	33	3	4		4		5		2	7
Perrett, Russell	31	1	2		4		1			1
Pethick, Robbie	27	8	4		4					
Rees, Jason	1	2					1			1
Russell, Lee	18	2	4	2			2			2
Simpson, Fitzroy	40	1	4		4		4			4
Svensson, Mathias	17	2	2	1	2	3	6		1	7
Thomson, Andy	22	6			3	1	1			1
Turner, Andy	22	2	2	1	1		2			2
Waterman, Dave		4								
Whitbread, Adrian	24				1					
25 players used	506	97	44	5	44	6	59	3	9	71

NATIONWIDE LEAGUE DIVISION 1 Manager: Fenwick ⇨ Alan Ball SEASON 1997-98

No	Date	V	Opponent	Att	Pos	Pt	F-A	H-T	1	2	3	4	5	6	7	8	9	10	11	subs used
1	9/8	A	MANCHESTER C	30,474		1	D 2-2	1-1	Knight	Waterman	Thomson	McLoughlin	Whitbread	Hillier	Hall	Simpson F*	Aloisi^	Svensson^	Igoe	Awford/Pethick/Thorp
					1				Margetson	Brightwell	Vaughan	Wiekens	Symons	Beesley*	Braman	Horlock	Bradbury	Kinkladze	Rosler^	Summerbee/Dickov
2	16/8	H	PORT VALE	10,605		4	W 3-1	2-1	Flahaven	Waterman	Thomson	McLoughlin	Whitbread	Hillier	Hall	Simpson F	Aloisi^	Svensson*	Igoe	Thorp
					22				Musselwhite	Hill	Tankard	Aspin	Jansson*	Glover^	Corden	Mills	Talbot	Cordice		Naylor/Stokes
3	23/8	A	SHEFFIELD UTD	15,895		4	L 1-2	0-2	Flahaven	Perrett	Thomson	Pethick	Whitbread	Hillier	Hall	Russell	Aloisi	Svensson^	Igoe^	Thorp/Durnin
					3				Tracey	Borbokis	Quinn*	McGrath	Tiler	Holdsworth	Patterson	Marker	Fjortoft^	Deane	Whitehouse	Hutchison/White
4	30/8	H	OXFORD	10,209		7	W 2-1	1-1	Flahaven	Pethick	Russell	McLoughlin	Whitbread	Perrett	Allen	Turner	Aloisi*	Svensson*	Igoe	Thorp/Durnin
					14				Whitehead	Remy	Angel^	Robinson	Purse!	Wilsterman	Ford B	Smith	Murphy*	Jemson	Beauchamp	Whelan/Aldridge/Powell
5	2/9	H	NORWICH	10,577		8	D 1-1	0-0	Flahaven	Pethick	Russell	McLoughlin	Whitbread	Perrett	Allen!	Turner	Aloisi*	Svensson*	Igoe	Thorp/Durnin
					19				Marshall	Segura"	Newman	Grant	Sutch	Polston	Adams	Fleck*	Roberts	Milligan	Eadie	O'Neill*/Scott/Jackson
6	13/9	A	CREWE	9,505		8	L 2-3	0-1	Flahaven	Pethick	Russell	McLoughlin	Whitbread	Perrett	Hillier	Turner	Aloisi	Svensson*	Igoe	Waterman/Allen/Durnin
					19				Kearton	Bignot	Smith	Unsworth	Watts	Charnock	Lunt*	Rivers	Adebola	Johnson		Anthrobus^/Little*/Lightfoot/Smith
7	20/9	A	NOTT'M FOREST	17,292		8	L 0-1	0-1	Flahaven	Pethick	Russell	McLoughlin	Whitbread*	Perrett*	Hall	Turner	Aloisi	Durnin	Igoe	Waterman/Foster
					1				Beasant	Lyttle	Rogers	Cooper	Chettle	Hjelde	Saunders	Gemmill	V Hooijdonk	Campbell	B Williams	B*Williams/Johnson
8	24/9	A	QP RANGERS	12,620		8	L 0-1	0-1	Flahaven	Pethick	Russell	McLoughlin	Awford^	Perrett	Hall	Waterman	Aloisi	Durnin*	Igoe	Simpson/Turner
					3				Harper	Ready	Brevett	Quashie	Maddix	Morrow*	Spencer	Peacock	Murray	Sheron	Sinclair	Sinclair/Rose
9	29/9	H	READING	9,593		8	L 0-2	0-1	Flahaven	Pethick*	Russell	McLoughlin	Whitbread	Perrett	Hall	Simpson F	Aloisi	Durnin*	Igoe	McLoughlin/Awford/Turner
					22				Mautone	Bernal	Sandford	Williams	McPherson	Primus	Parkinson	Hodges*	Asaba	Houghton	Meaker	Meaker/Swales
10	4/10	A	STOCKPORT	7,824		8	L 1-3	0-2	Flahaven	Pethick	Cook Andy	McLoughlin	Awford*	Perrett	Thomson	Hillier	Aloisi	Durnin	Turner	Carter/Harries
					15				Nixon	Connelly	Woodthorpe	Bennett*	McIntosh	Dinning	Gannon	Marsden	Angell	Armstrong	Cooper	Armstrong/Cooper/Nash
11	18/11	H	WEST BROM	9,158		8	L 2-3	0-1	Flahaven	Pethick	Thomson	Enes*	Whitbread	Awford	Hall	Simpson F^	Aloisi	Foster	Igoe	McLoughlin/Thorp
					3				Miller	Holmes	Smith	Sneekes	Burgess	Mardon	Flynn*	Hamilton	Peschisolido^	Hunt	Kilbane	Butler/Hughes

Scorers, Times, and Referees — with match reports

1. **9/8 — A Manchester C 2-2** — Aloisi 5, Hall 80 / Rosler 16, Wiekens 55. Ref: D Laws (Whitley Bay). Oasis singer Liam Gallagher infuriates Pompey fans with an offensive gesture. £3m Bradbury starts for City, but is upstaged by Pompey's £300,000 Aussie Aloisi (Cremonese). His goal boomerangs as Rosler and Wiekens reward City pressure, but Hall volleys a priceless leveller.

2. **16/8 — H Port Vale 3-1** — Aloisi 24, Svensson 38, 47 / Talbot 43. Ref: R Harris (Oxford). It's a Vale of tears for John Rudge's side as they are never in it once Aloisi latches onto Glover's suicidal headed back-pass. Star of the show, though, is Svensson, who slots home after Pethick and Igoe combine, then restores the two-goal cushion from Hillier's astute pass.

3. **23/8 — A Sheffield Utd 1-2** — Perrett 57 / Fjortoft 4, 15. Ref: R Pearson (Peterlee). Bramall Lane means one thing only these days as Blades blunt Pompey's start. Nigel Spackman's team look set for a promotion bid, when Fjortoft feeds off Thomson's back-pass after Perrett's error had let him chip in. Perrett blindside header atoned, when Tracey missed a corner.

4. **30/8 — H Oxford 2-1** — Aloisi 4, Svensson 66 / Ford B 36. Ref: S Mathieson (Stockport). Purse's sending off for a second foul, costs Oxford, as Sven touches home Pethick's cross. Prompted by Beauchamp, Denis Smith's side had looked a good bet, even after Aloisi nodded in Turner's cross. Ford's neat finish levels. Hall and Simpson are with Jamaica for three weeks.

5. **2/9 — H Norwich 1-1** — Turner 65 / Adams 90p. Ref: B Knight (Orpington). Deep into injury-time Eadie tumbles under Flav's challenge and Adams maintains his perfect pen record. Allen had turned the game City's way after getting sent off for two wild fouls, but Turner races from halfway to out-smart Marshall. Pompey's dogged defending looked set to pay.

6. **13/9 — A Crewe 2-3** — Aloisi 70, 73 / Rivers 1, Anthrobus 57, Adebola 85. Ref: P Taylor (Cheshunt). £300,000 Aussie midfielder Foster is introduced to the crowd. After 28 secs Alex lead as Rivers sweeps in, then Whit's pro foul sees red and 2-0 doesn't flatter Crewe. Aloisi nods in and levels after Pethick's shot rebounds off the bar, but the defence dozes again and Adebola chips in.

7. **20/9 — A Nott'm Forest 0-1** — Van Hooijdonk 34. Ref: A Wiley (Burntwood). Pompey rally, but they've left themselves too much to do against Dave Bassett's Forest, who have wobbled (two defeats in three) after a fine start. Flahaven keeps Pompey in the hunt, but is powerless as Van Hooijdonk fires in from eight yards. Beasant is the busier keeper after that.

8. **24/9 — A QP Rangers 0-1** — Spencer 44. Ref: M Halsey (Welwyn G City). Simpson and Hall are back after World Cup duty, but it's QPR's SAS squad – Sheron and Spencer – who look the class acts. 'Their presence was the difference between the sides,' Fenwick. They combine for Spencer to slide home, but Hall has an early effort clawed away by Harper.

9. **29/9 — H Reading 0-2** — Hodges 16, Williams 85. Ref: M Bailey (Impington). Terry Bullivant's boys have won one in eight and lost 0-6 at Tranny last week, but Royals record their second win at Fratton, almost 21 years to the day since the last. Hodges curls home, then Williams reacts when McPherson's header hits a post. Allen has gone to Southend on loan.

10. **4/10 — A Stockport 1-3** — Aloisi 73 / Cook 7 (og), Angell 45, 90. Ref: P Richards (Preston). Stockport count on Jim Smith's ex-target Brett Angell. Cook nods into his own net, pressured by Cooper, then Gannon sets up Angell. Aloisi jabs in to end a 360-minute goal drought, but at the death Cooper crosses and Angell can't miss. Pompey's squad have had tummy trouble.

11. **18/11 — H West Brom 2-3** — McLoughlin 78, Foster 85 / Mardon 7, Hunt 48, 51. Ref: S Baines (Chesterfield). Pompey's worst league run (six straight defeats) since 1989. Another Aussie, Robbie Enes, debuts and Foster starts, but Mardon's overhead gives Baggies the break. Hunt profits from defensive chaos, but Macca and Foster strike impressively, then Aloisi scores a great late chance.

12 — H BRADFORD C — 21/10 — 6,827 — (23 / 5) — D 1-1 (9)

McLoughlin 17p — Ethino 41
Ref: S Bennett (Redhill)

Knight	Pethick	Thomson!	McLoughlin	Whitbread	Perrett	Hall	Simpson F	Aloisi*	Igoe^	Foster	Thorp/Awford
Walsh	Wilder	Jacobs	Beagrie	Youds	Moore	Kulscar	Pepper!	Steiner*	Murray	Edhino	Lawrence

Pepper is sent off at Fratton for the second time in seven months. His foul on Simpson sparks a brawl, which includes physio Sillett. Macca nets after Aloisi was fouled – the first time Pompey had taken the lead in nine – but Edhino's far-post finish levelled. Thomo sees red for a foul.

13 — A HUDDERSFIELD — 25/10 — 8,985 — (23 / 24 / 10) — D 1-1

Igoe 37 — Dalton 80
Ref: J Robinson (Hull)

Knight	Pethick	Thomson	Awford	Whitbread	Perrett	Hall	Simpson F	Aloisi	Foster	Igoe	
Bartram	Jenkins	Ryan*	Dyson	Morrison	Gray	Dalton	Horne	Stewart	Richardson	Baldry^	Edwards/Lawson

Despite appointing Peter Jackson earlier this month, the Terriers still haven't won. They go close here, buoyed by the midweek capture of ex-Fratton star Horne. Bartram totally misjudges Igoe's cross and the ball drops in at the far post, but Dalton curls in an equaliser from 25 yards.

14 — H SWINDON — 31/10 — 8,707 — (23 / 2 / 10) — L 0-1

Hay 24
Ref: P Danson (Leicester)

Knight	Pethick	Thomson	Awford	Whitbread	Perrett	Hall	Simpson F	Aloisi	Foster*	Igoe^	McLoughlin/Durnin
Mildenhall	Borrows	Culverhouse	Bullock	Taylor	Casper	Watson	Walters	Hay	Allison	Gooden	

The new £2.5m, 4,500-seat Fratton End – now called the KJC – is open, but only after the necessary permission arrived at 5.15! Sky TV are here, so a miserable result is assured. Swindon oblige when Hay nods home Walters' cross. Third-choice keeper Mildenhall denies Pompey.

15 — A MIDDLESBROUGH — 5/11 — 29,724 — (23 / 6 / 11) — D 1-1

Igoe 85 — Townsend 65
Ref: T Leake (Darwen)

Knight	Pethick	Awford	McLoughlin	Whitbread	Perrett*	Durnin	Hillier	Aloisi^	Foster*	Turner	Igoe/Carter/Enes
Schwarzer	Fleming	Kinder*	Festa	Pearson	Emerson	Hignett	Maddison	Beck*	Merson	Townsend	Campbell/Whyte

Bryan Robson's Boro are odds-on tonight, but Igoe's cool finish late on secures a precious point for under-pressure Fenwick. Beck hits a post, then Townsend prods in Merson's cross. A bid to sign Aussie keeper Kalac to Fratton is dragging on, as the work permit rules goes to court.

16 — A BURY — 8/11 — 5,065 — (23 / 15 / 14) — W 2-0

Aloisi 53, Durnin 90
Ref: D Laws (Whitley Bay)

Knight	Pethick	Thomson	McLoughlin	Whitbread	Perrett	Durnin	Hillier	Aloisi	Awford	Turner	Foster
Kiely	Peake^	Woodward*	Daws	Lucketti	Butler	Armstrong	Johnson	Swan	Johnrose	Battersby*	Jepson/Randell/Rigby

Pompey's winless run finally ends, but Shakers' boss Stan Ternant reckons his side were robbed. New-boys Bury had lost just once in 33 games at Gigg Lane and they battered away after Aloisi was set up by Durns' and Macca's good work. Durnin's goal on time soothed nerves.

17 — H SUNDERLAND — 15/11 — 10,702 — (23 / 8 / 14) — L 1-4

Aloisi 7   [Summerbee 64]
Quinn 10, Clark 14, Johnston 32
Ref: A D'Urso (Billericay)

Knight	Thomson	Holloway	Igoe*	Whitbread	Perrett*	Durnin	Hillier	Aloisi^	Awford	Turner	Foster/Enes
Perez	Gray	Clark	Ablett	Williams	Johnston	Rae	Quinn	Phillips	Smith*	Summerbee	

Aloisi's sharp goal was probably the worst thing he could have done, as Sunderland are jolted into action. Within 25 minutes the game is over, as Quinn is left free at a corner, Clark fires in from the edge of the box, and Johnston curls home a free-kick. New signing Summerbee seals it.

18 — A BIRMINGHAM — 29/11 — 17,738 — (24 / 14 / 14) — L 1-2

Hall 35 — Furlong 36, 73
Ref: S Mathieson (Stockport)

Knight	Pethick	Thomson	McLoughlin	Whitbread	Awford	Hall	Simpson F*	Aloisi^	Durnin	Turner	Svensson/Igoe/Perrett
Bennett	Bass	Johnson	Bruce	Ablett	Marsden	McCarthy	Robinson	Furlong	Hughes^	Allen*	Devlin/Ndlovu

It's a double disaster as Chairman TV's Australia fail to reach France 98 after drawing 2-2 with Iran, then Pompey go bottom after this latest defeat. Hall snaps up McCarthy's dreadful back-pass, but he immediately makes amends by crossing for Furlong to score at the third attempt.

19 — H STOKE — 6/12 — 7,072 — (24 / 14 / 17) — W 2-0

Aloisi 31, Svensson 43
Ref: P Rejer (Tipton)

Knight	Pethick	Thomson	McLoughlin	Whitbread	Awford	Hall	Simpson F*	Aloisi^	Foster*	Durnin	Igoe/Durnin
Muggleton	Pickering	Griffin	Sigurdsson	Tweed	Keen	Forsyth	Mackenzie*	Thorne	Kavanagh	McMahon	

November's salaries have gone unpaid, as Fratton's cash-flow crisis – one home game in five weeks – catches up with them. Gregory Jnr has stepped in to cover the loss. TV's position looks insecure, but Fenwick will be happier after Aloisi's volley and returning Svensson's sidefoot.

20 — H WOLVERHAMPTON — 9/12 — 8,042 — (21 / 9 / 20) — W 3-2

Durnin 14, 47, Hillier 74
Westwood 77, Froggatt 87
Ref: D Orr (Iver)

Knight	Pethick	Thomson	McLoughlin	Whitbread	Awford	Hall*	Turner^	Foster*	Durnin	Svensson	Hillier
Stowell	Kubicki*	Froggatt	Sedgeley!	Westwood	Curle	Goodman	Atkins	Keane^	Freedman	Osborn*	Ferguson/Paatelainen/Simpson

Knight's pen save from Curle, after Whitbread brings down Keane proves crucial. Pompey were ahead thanks to Durns' finish and Sedgeley is sent off for 'assaulting' Sven. Durnin runs from halfway to curl home the second, then Hillier has an open goal, but late jitters set in again.

21 — A IPSWICH — 13/12 — 11,641 — (24 / 16 / 20) — L 0-2

Cundy 29, Johnson 68
Ref: K Leach (Wolverhampton)

Knight	Pethick	Thomson	McLoughlin	Whitbread	Awford*	Hall	Simpson F*	Durnin	Svensson	Hillier^	Waterman/Igoe/Turner
Wright	Stockwell	Taricco	Williams	Tanner	Cundy	Dyer	Holland	Johnson	Scowcroft^	Petta*	Sonner/Milton/Mathie

Looking at the table, Ipswich are drop rivals, but the class gulf is huge. George Burley's Town will make the play-offs. US-based Wolanin and Howe want to take over the club and will not be put off by Cundy's free header from Petta's free-kick and David Johnson's fifth in six games.

22 — H CHARLTON — 20/12 — 8,581 — (24 / 4 / 20) — L 0-2

Robinson 44, Leaburn 52
Ref: A Bates (Stoke)

Knight	Pethick	Thomson	McLoughlin	Whitbread	Awford	Hall	Simpson F*	Aloisi^	Svensson	Hillier^	Igoe/Allen
Salmon	Brown	Bowen	Jones	Rufus	Chapple	Newton	Kinsella	Robinson*	Mendonca	Leaburn	Lisbie

Alan Curbishley's promotion-chasing side coast through the game, but it could have been different if Hall had not rolled wide from six yards having gone round Salmon. At once John Robinson sweeps home Newton's cross, then he repays the compliment by setting up Carl Leaburn.

23 — H QP RANGERS — 26/12 — 12,314 — (21 / 12 / 23) — W 3-1

Pethick 35, McLoughlin 62p, Hall 80
Sheron 30
Ref: J Brandwood (Lichfield)

Knight	Pethick	Thomson	McLoughlin	Whitbread	Awford	Hall*	Foster	Aloisi^	Svensson	Turner	Igoe/Durnin
Roberts	Yates	Brazier	Quashie	Ready	Maddix	Spencer*	Peacock	Murray	Sheron	Sinclair	Gallen

Pompey's woe looks set to continue when QPR's £2m striker Sheron poaches, but Pethick's 25-yarder levels almost at once. Led by Foster, the second half is one-sided. Macca converts after Hall is felled just inside the box, then he nods home to seal the first win over R's since 1972.

NATIONWIDE LEAGUE DIVISION 1 — Manager: Fenwick ⇨ Alan Ball — SEASON 1997-98

No	Date	Scorers, Times, and Referees	Att	Pos	Pt	Result	F-A	H-T	1	2	3	4	5	6	7	8	9	10	11	Subs used
24	A 30/12 NORWICH	Jackson 14, Bellamy 70. Ref: K Lynch (Knaresborough)	16,441	12	23	L	0-2	0-1	Knight	Pethick	Thomson	McLoughlin	Waterman*	Awford	Hall	Foster	Aloisi^	Svensson	Turner*	Igoe/Durnin/Enes
		(opp.)							Marshall	Segura	Mills	Grant	Scott	Jackson	Forbes*	Fugelstad	Milligan	Bellamy	O'Neill	Fleck
25	H 10/1 MANCHESTER C	Russell 44, Kinkladze 53, Rosler 89. Ref: P Taylor (Cheshunt)	13,512	18	23	L	0-3	0-1	Knight	Pethick	Thomson	McLoughlin	Waterman	Awford	Hall	Foster	Aloisi^	Svensson	Hillier*	Enes^/Durnin
		(opp.)							Wright	Brightwell	Sheila	Brown	Symons	Edghill	Whitley Jim Russell	Dickov	Kinkladze	Igoe	Rosler	
26	A 17/1 PORT VALE	Durnin 36. Talbot 29, Mills 56. Ref: M Bailey (Impington)	6,028	18	23	L	1-2	1-1	Knight	Waterman^	Thomson!	McLoughlin	Whitbread	Awford	Hall	Simpson F	Durnin*	Foster*	Russell	Aloisi/Carter
		(opp.)							Musselwhite Hill	Tankard	Talbot	Aspin	Beesley	Ainsworth	Porter	Mills	Naylor*	Corden	Foyle	
27	A 24/1 OXFORD	Beauchamp 90. Ref: F Stretton (Nottingham)	7,402	18	23	L	0-1	0-0	Knight	Waterman^	Thomson	McLoughlin	Whitbread	Perrett	Hall	Simpson F	Durnin	Claridge	Carter	Aloisi
		(opp.)							Whitehead	Robinson	Marsh^	Gray	Purse	Gilchrist	Massey*	Smith	Murphy"	Jemson	Beauchamp	Angel/Wretam'n/Weath'stone
28	H 31/1 SHEFFIELD UTD	Foster 18. Knight (og) 32. Ref: M Halsey (Welwyn G City)	12,003	5	24	D	1-1	1-1	Knight	Pethick	Vlachos	McLoughlin	Whitbread	Awford	Igoe*	Foster	Durnin	Claridge	Carter	Svensson
		(opp.)							Tracey!	Short	Sandford	Derry	Barrett	Holdsworth Saunders	Marker	Marcelo	Stuart	Hutchison		
29	H 7/2 NOTT'M FOREST	Chettle 52. Ref: C Wilkes (Gloucester)	15,033	1	24	L	0-1	0-0	Knight	Pethick	Vlachos	McLoughlin	Whitbread	Awford	Hillier*	Foster	Durnin*	Claridge	Carter	Igoe/Aloisi
		(opp.)							Beasant	Lyttle	Rogers	Cooper	Chettle	Johnson A	Johnson D	Thomas	v Hooijdonk Campbell	Bonalair		
30	A 14/2 CREWE	Aloisi 81. Garvey 58, Lunt 72, Little 80. Ref: R Pearson (Peterlee)	5,114	14	24	L	1-3	0-0	Knight	Pethick	Vlachos	McLoughlin	Whitbread	Awford	Foster	Claridge	Durnin*	Svensson^	Carter	Aloisi/Igoe
		(opp.)							Kearton	Bignot*	Smith	Unsworth	Walton	Lunt	Garvey	Whalley	Anthrobus Johnson	Johnson	Little	Street
31	H 17/2 STOCKPORT	Claridge 15. Ref: B Knight (Orpington)	8,622	8	27	W	1-0	1-0	Flahaven	Pethick	Cook Aar'n^	McLoughlin	Whitbread	Awford	Igoe	Cook	Aloisi^	Claridge	Carter^	Svensson/Allen
		(opp.)							Nixon	Connelly	Woodthorpe Byrne	Flynn	Dinning	Gannon*	Cook	Angell	Grant	Cooper^	Nash/Phillips	
32	A 21/2 READING	Whitbread 83. Ref: A Wiley (Burntwood)	9,928	19	30	W	1-0	0-0	Flahaven	Pethick	Robinson	McLoughlin*	Whitbread	Awford	Vlachos	Igoe	Aloisi	Igoe*	Carter*	Thomson/Svensson/Allen Lovell
		(opp.)							Hammond	Booty	Legg	Davies	Primus	Parkinson	Bowen	Houghton	Morley	Asaba	Williams*	
33	A 24/2 WEST BROM	Hillier 12, Claridge 33, McLoughlin 86. Ref: E Wolstenholme (Blackburn)	12,757	10	33	W	3-0	2-0	Flahaven	Pethick	Robinson	McLoughlin	Whitbread	Awford	Vlachos	Claridge	Aloisi*	Hillier^	Thomson	Svensson/Allen Coldicott/Carr
		(opp.)							Miller	Holmes	Potter	Quinn	Murphy	Burgess	Butler	Taylor	Hughes*	Hamilton^	Kilbane	
34	H 28/2 TRANMERE	Aloisi 37. Ref: R Harris (Oxford)	12,250	19	36	W	1-0	1-0	Flahaven	Pethick	Robinson	McLoughlin*	Whitbread	Awford	Vlachos	Claridge	Aloisi*	Hillier*	Thomson	Simpson F/Hall/Allen Kelly/Frail^/Mahon
		(opp.)							Simonsen	Morgan^	Thompson	McCreal Challinor	Irons*	Morrissey	Mellon	Jones	O'Brien	Branch		

Match notes:

24 — Sloppy defending cost Pompey this fixture last year and they were at it again, gifting Jackson a free header from Forbes' corner, then letting Bellamy turn and fire in from 25 yards. Pompey manage one shot on target, a weak effort from Turner, and this result pins them to the bottom.

25 — Fans call for the heads of TV and Fenwick after this surrender against fellow-strugglers City, and they will be gone by Tuesday. Russell scores from close range, then Kinkladze's 25-yarder is unstoppable. Rosler rubs it in, but Wright is reported for making a V-sign to the Fratton End.

26 — Waldon is caretaker – 'I used to do most of the jobs, now I do all of them!' – as take-over talks go on in Paris. On the field nothing changes. Corden crosses for Talbot to head in, but Durns levels at the near post. Mills uses his head, then Thomson doesn't and is sent off for a wild foul.

27 — Ex-apprentice Claridge (Leicester) signs on-loan and hits the bar in the first half. Malcolm Shotton is struggling Oxford's new boss; he is ecstatic when Beauchamp heads in at the death. Rock-star Howe announces on radio tonight that Alan Ball will be the new Pompey boss.

28 — Ball's second coming is an eventful one. Foster fires Pompey ahead as Blades look for a flag, then old-boy Sandford's cross is dropped by Knight. Keeper Tracey is sent off for handling Igoe's shot outside his box and a visiting fan runs on and knocks out linesman Edward Martin.

29 — Wolanin and Howe are here, but the take-over seems to be faltering. Greek free agent Vlachos has steadied the ship, but he can't stop Chettle heading home as Forest – who lost to Oxford last week – move up a gear. Durnin curled one just wide and Aloisi shot across the face of goal.

30 — Ball accepts avoiding relegation is a tall order after this defeat, which leaves them six adrift of safety. Crewe (six wins in their last nine) give them the run-around. Cook Aar'n^ at fault for the second and Foster looks dispirited. One ray of hope. At 0-3 the fans start a barrage of noise.

31 — Claridge's first goal for his home-town club - a header at the Fratton End – wins it, but it's the fans who take the credit with a non-stop barrage of second-half noise, as Gary Megson's County battle to end a run of six away defeats in seven. Flavs replaces Knight and looks assured.

32 — Robinson (£35,000) signs from Saints and proves a good-luck charm as a run of seven consecutive away defeats is ended. Captain Whitbread side-foots home when Claridge sets him up. Royals' early pressure had been weathered and 3,000 travelling fans believe Pompey can stay up.

33 — Claridge has a contender for goal of the season with a 20-yard effort that bends away from Miller. Hillier had put Pompey in charge, with his second at the Hawthorns in two visits. Denis Smith's team haven't won at home in the league since Dec and never look like doing so here.

34 — Pompey are the form team of the league and this win takes them out of the bottom three. Aloisi is put clear by Vlachos to coolly score, then he sees Simonsen make a stunning save. It is now 378 minutes since Pompey conceded a goal, but Tranmere turn up the heat in the second half.

No.	Venue	Team	Date	Attendance	Pos	Result	Score			Scorers	Referee
35	H	BURY	3/3	12,462	20	D	1-1	18	37	Aloisi 68 / Johnrose 19	Ref: S Bennett (Redhill)
36	A	SWINDON	7/3	9,100	18	W	1-0	13	40	Durrin 90	Ref: K Leach (Wolverhampton)
37	H	MIDDLESBROUGH	14/3	17,003	20	D	0-0	2	41		Ref: K Lynch (Knaresborough)
38	A	SUNDERLAND	21/3	38,134	21	L	1-2	3	41	Hall 73 / Phillips 15, Johnston 85	Ref: D Pugh (Wirral)
39	A	WOLVERHAMPTON	29/3	20,718	21	L	0-2	8	41	Goodman 45, Osborn 90	Ref: T Jones (Barrow-in-Furness)
40	H	BIRMINGHAM	4/4	14,591	22	D	1-1	7	42	Thomson 90 / Adebola 83	Ref: A D'Urso (Billericay)
41	A	TRANMERE	7/4	8,020	22	D	2-2	16	43	Durrin 21, Hall 81 / Jones 14, Challinor 53	Ref: W Burns (Scarborough)
42	A	STOKE	11/4	15,569	22	L	1-2	23	43	Durrin 70 / Pickering 78, Lightbourne 90	Ref: R Furnandiz (Doncaster)
43	H	IPSWICH	13/4	15,040	23	L	0-1	5	43	Johnson 8	Ref: J Brandwood (Lichfield)
44	A	CHARLTON	18/4	14,082	23	L	0-1	3	43	Jones 57	Ref: J Kirkby (Sheffield)
45	H	HUDDERSFIELD	25/4	14,013	21	W	3-0	14	46	Pethick 27, Thomson 60, Durrin 70	Ref: M Fletcher (Warley)
46	A	BRADFORD C	3/5	15,890	20	W	3-1	13	49	Durrin 36, 74, Igoe 65 / Ramage 87	Ref: G Cain (Bootle)

35 — BURY (H)
Team: Flahaven, Pethick, Robinson*, McLoughlin, Whitbread, Awford, Vlachos, Claridge, Aloisi, Hillier, Thomson, Hall
Opp/subs: Kiely, Rigby, Small, Daws, Lucketti, Butler, Jemson, Patterson, Armstrong, Johnrose, Matthews*, Battersby
Ternant's side are reviving too (three wins and two draws in five) so a draw is a fair result. Johnrose poaches the lead, but urged on by another large crowd and prompted by Hillier, Aloisi stabs in the equaliser. Ball is reshaping the squad as Aussies Thorp and Enes are being released.

36 — SWINDON (A)
Team: Flahaven, Pethick, Robinson, McLoughlin, Whitbread, Awford, Vlachos, Claridge, Aloisi*, Hillier, Thomson, Durrin
Opp/subs: Talia, Robinson, Burrows, Leitch, Taylor, Collins, Walters, Cuervo, Finney, Cowe, Gooden
Chances are at a premium, but in the dying seconds Pethick crosses and Durrin's left footer takes an age to bobble in off the post. Whitbread's clearing header is clawed out by Flavs, then Cowe rolls Town's best chance wide just before the break. Pethick's 25-yarder stretched Talia.

37 — MIDDLESBROUGH (H)
Team: Flahaven, Pethick, Robinson, McLoughlin*, Whitbread, Awford, Vlachos, Svensson*, Aloisi*, Hillier, Thomson, Hall
Opp/subs: Beresford, Kinder, Harrison, Vickers, Festa, Maddison, Armstrong, Townsend, Branca, Merson, Thomas
Boro are in Pompey's blue socks – they only brought red – and are left hanging on for their point. Aloisi is brought down by Beresford, but he atones by saving the spot-kick after taking advice from Macca's Eire's team-mate Townsend. This is Pompey's first 0-0 since November 1996.

38 — SUNDERLAND (A)
Team: Flahaven, Pethick, Robinson, McLoughlin, Whitbread, Awford, Vlachos*, Waterman^, Hall, Hillier, Thomson, Hall
Opp/subs: Perez, Makin, Gray, Clark, Holloway, Williams, Ball, Rae*, Quinn^, Phillips, Johnston, Summerbee/Dichio
Johnston's late curler keeps Peter Reid's men on course, but Pompey deserved a point after Hall profited when Perez and Williams collided. Phillips nodded in Gray's cross and Aloisi only comes on when Vlachos is hurt. Claridge has returned to Foxes as Pompey can't find the fee.

39 — WOLVERHAMPTON (A)
Team: Flahaven, Pethick, Robinson, McLoughlin*, Whitbread, Awford, Hall^, Simpson F*, Aloisi, Hillier, Thomson, Keane/Bull/Simpson
Opp/subs: Segers, Wright, Froggatt, Sedgeley^, Williams, Curle, Slater*, Emblem, Claridge, Goodman^, Osborn
Claridge plays but it's for Wolves, who have signed him to reinforce a play-off and FA Cup push. He gets a warm reception. McGhee's team had won just two in nine, but Goodman seizes on Flav's slip on half-time, then Osborn chips in at the death to put Ball's back into trouble.

40 — BIRMINGHAM (H)
Team: Flahaven, Pethick, Robinson, McLoughlin, Whitbread, Awford, Allen, Simpson F*, Aloisi*, Durrin, Thomson, Svensson/Simpson R
Opp/subs: Bennett, Bass, Charlton, Purse, Ablett, Marsden, McCarthy*, O'Connor, Adebola, Hughes^, Ndlovu, Grainger^/Forster/Robinson
Pompey are 100-years-old today, but Adebola looks to have pooped the party, nodding in Marston's cross. Flavs then denies Forster another and it proves vital as Thomo stabs in Simpson's last-gasp corner. Then, seconds later, Bennett is forced to save from him again from six yards.

41 — TRANMERE (A)
Team: Flahaven, Pethick, Robinson, McLoughlin*, Whitbread, Awford, Hillier, Simpson F, Aloisi, Durrin, Thomson, Hall
Opp/subs: Simonsen, Kubicki, Thompson, McGreal, Challinor, Irons, Morrissey*, Mellon, Jones, O'Brien, Jones^, Hill/Parkinson
Sub Hall sinks Tranmere's win hopes when his 20-yarder hits the post and bounces in off Simonsen. Gary Jones had earlier put Rovers ahead, having already hit the bar, but Durrin levelled after Aloisi's effort was blocked. Challinor thumped home, but fate was on Pompey's side.

42 — STOKE (A)
Team: Flahaven, Pethick, Robinson, McLoughlin*, Whitbread, Awford, Hillier, Simpson F, Aloisi*, Durrin, Thomson, Hall/Simpson R
Opp/subs: Southall, Pickering, Nyamah, Sigurdsson, Tweed, Keen, Forsyth*, Wallace, Thorne*, Crowe*, Kavanagh, Whittle/Lightbourne/Heath
Pompey had looked on course for a vital win against struggling Stoke, who have won just twice in 25 and whose boss Chris Kamara resigned on Wednesday. Caretaker Alan Durban sees Lightbourne lob Flavs in injury-time to seal a comeback after Durrin squeezed in at the far post.

43 — IPSWICH (H)
Team: Flahaven, Pethick, Robinson, McLoughlin*, Whitbread, Awford, Hillier, Simpson F, Aloisi*, Durrin, Thomson*, Hall/Simpson R
Opp/subs: Wright, Stockwell, Taricco, Dyer, Mowbray*, Cundy, Clapham, Holland, Johnson, Mathie^, Petra, Venus/Scowcroft
Vlachos is back after injury, but Pompey are in trouble from the moment Johnson scores after his first shot hit Whitbread. He then earns a dodgy penalty, falling under Thomo's tackle, but fires well wide. George Burley's side remain in chase, but at least Man C and Stoke lose.

44 — CHARLTON (A)
Team: Flahaven, Pethick, Robinson, McLoughlin, Whitbread, Awford, Vlachos, Igoe*, Aloisi*, Durrin, Thomson, Hall/Svensson
Opp/subs: Ilic, Mills, Bowen, Jones, Rufus, Youds, Newton, Kinsella, Jones*, Mendonca, Heaney, Brown
Relegation looks odds-on now, after Valiants claim a club-record seventh successive win. Ex-Saint Heaney crosses for Steve Jones's simple header at the far post, but Hall is put clear in injury-time, but with just Ilic to beat he scuffs his shot wide. It's six points from six, or bust.

45 — HUDDERSFIELD (H)
Team: Flahaven, Pethick, Robinson, McLoughlin, Whitbread, Awford, Vlachos*, Igoe, Aloisi*, Durrin, Thomson*, Allen
Opp/subs: Harper, Phillips, Edmondson, Dyson, Collins, Richardson*, Baldry^, Home, Stewart, Barnes, Johnson^, Heary/Lawson/Nielsen
Ball has signed a four-year contract and his side's fate is back in their own hands after docile Terriers roll over. Pethick's deflected shot ends it as a contest, then Sven's presence lets Thomo stab in Igoe's cross. He also sets up Durrin. Man C and QPR draw; a win at Bradford C will do.

46 — BRADFORD C (A)
Team: Flahaven, Pethick, Robinson, Waterman, Whitbread, Awford, Vlachos, Igoe, Aloisi*, Hillier, Thomson, Grant^
Opp/subs: Walsh, McAnespie*, Jacobs, Ramage, Sinnott, Moore*, Bolland, O'Brien, Edhino, Pepper, Blake/Steiner/Bower
Igoe is the inspiration as Pompey put early jitters behind them, when he sets up Durrin with an open goal after some dreadful defending. Igoe snaps up the crucial second, then Durrin's start to party as Durns settles it. The Bantams have taken just one point from a possible 15.

Home 11,149
Away 14,628
Average 11,149

NATIONWIDE DIVISION 1 (CUP-TIES) Manager: Fenwick ⇒ Alan Ball SEASON 1997-98

Coca-Cola Cup	Att	F-A	H-T	Scorers, Times, and Referees	1	2	3	4	5	6	7	8	9	10	11	subs used
1:1 A PETERBOROUGH 12/8	3,613 3	D 2-2	2-1	Thorp 8, Hillier 24 / Awford 9 (og), Carruthers 81 / Ref: F Stretton (Nottingham)	Flahaven	Waterman !	Thomson	McLoughlin	Whitbread	Hillier	Durrin	Awford*	Aloisi*	Thorp	Igoe	Pethick
					Tiler	*Linton*	*Lewis*	*Payne**	*Bodley^*	*Edwards*	*Farrell*	*Castle*	*De Souza"*	*Quinn*	*Houghton !*	*Ballmore/Cleaver/Carruthers*
1:2 H PETERBOROUGH 25/8	6,395 P:3	L 1-2	1-1	Svensson 36 / Farrell 44, Quinn 56 / Ref: C Wilkes (Gloucester) (Pompey lost 3-4 on aggregate)	Flahaven	Pethick	Thomson*	McLoughlin	Whitbread	Perrett	Hall	Simpson F	Aloisi^	Svensson"	Hillier	Russell/Turner/Thorp
					Tiler	*Linton*	*Lewis*	*Drury*	*Bodley*	*Edwards*	*Payne*	*Castle*	*Carruthers*	*Quinn*	*Farrell*	

Aussie Thorp gives Pompey the perfect start, nodding in Thomo's knock-back, but within seconds Awford has re-diverted Lewis's cross. Hillier's low shot puts Pompey in charge, but they take their foot off the gas and Carruthers curls home a crucial goal for Barry Fry's side.

Pompey should have steamrollered Posh in an opening burst, but only have Svensson's near-post finish after Hall's run to show for it. On the interval Flavs saves, but Hillier's clearance is weak and Farrell can't miss. Then Jimmy Quinn rolls back the years with a text-book header.

FA Cup	Att	F-A	H-T	Scorers, Times, and Referees	1	2	3	4	5	6	7	8	9	10	11	subs used
3 H ASTON VILLA 4/1	16,013 P:10	D 2-2	2-1	Foster 6, 40 / Staunton 41, Grayson 88 / Ref: U Rennie (Sheffield)	Knight	Pethick	Thomson	McLoughlin	Waterman	Awford	Hall	Foster	Aloisi*	Svensson"	Turner^	Durrin/Igoe
					Bosnich	*Nelson*	*Wright*	*Southgate**	*Ehiogu*	*Staunton*	*Taylor^*	*Draper*	*Milosevic*	*Collymore"*	*Grayson*	*Scimeca/Hendrie/Joachim*
3R A ASTON VILLA 14/1	23,355 P:10	L 0-1	0-1	Milosevic 21 / Ref: U Rennie (Sheffield)	Knight	Pethick	Thomson	McLoughlin	Whitbread	Awford	Hall	Simpson F*	Durrin	Foster^	Russell	Carter/Svensson
					Bosnich	*Grayson*	*Wright*	*Scimeca*	*Ehiogu*	*Staunton*	*Taylor*	*Draper**	*Milosevic*	*Collymore*	*Yorke*	*Hendrie*

Foster impresses as BBC Match of the Day cameras capture his rising 25-yarder, which clips off Staunton, then another which goes in off Ehiogu. Staunton looks offside, but Knight should have stopped his shot anyway, then Thomo dithers late on and Grayson gets Villa out of jail.

Fenwick and Venables departed earlier this week and Waldon picks the team. Pompey pester Villa, who could have wrapped it up before half-time. Milosevic rolled home Collymore's nod down. Wright hit the bar and Colly the post, but plucky Blues always worry Villa on the break.

League Table

Pos	Team	P	W	D	L	F	A	W	D	L	F	A	Pts
			Home					Away					
1	Nott'm Forest	46	18	2	3	52	20	10	8	5	30	22	94
2	Middlesbro	46	17	4	2	51	12	10	6	7	26	29	91
3	Sunderland	46	14	7	2	49	22	12	5	6	37	28	90
4	Charlton*	46	17	5	1	48	17	9	5	9	32	32	88
5	Ipswich	46	14	5	4	47	20	9	9	5	30	23	83
6	Sheffield Utd	46	16	5	2	44	20	3	12	8	25	34	74
7	Birmingham	46	10	8	5	27	15	9	9	5	33	20	74
8	Stockport	46	14	6	3	46	21	5	5	13	25	48	65
9	Wolves	46	13	6	4	42	25	6	5	13	15	28	65
10	West Brom	46	9	7	6	27	26	7	5	11	23	30	61
11	Crewe	46	10	2	11	30	34	8	3	12	28	31	59
12	Oxford	46	10	6	5	36	20	4	15	4	24	44	58
13	Bradford C	46	10	9	4	26	23	4	6	13	20	36	57
14	Tranmere	46	9	8	6	34	26	5	6	12	20	31	56
15	Norwich	46	9	8	6	32	27	5	5	13	20	42	55
16	Huddersfield	46	9	5	9	28	28	5	6	12	20	44	53
17	Bury	46	7	10	6	22	22	4	9	10	20	36	52
18	Swindon	46	9	6	8	28	25	5	4	14	14	48	52
19	Port Vale	46	7	6	10	25	24	6	4	13	31	42	49
20	PORTSMOUTH	46	8	9	6	28	30	5	4	14	23	33	49
21	QP Rangers	46	8	8	9	28	21	2	10	11	23	42	49
22	Manchester C	46	6	6	11	28	26	6	6	11	28	31	48
23	Stoke	46	8	5	10	30	40	3	8	12	14	34	46
24	Reading	46	8	4	11	27	31	3	5	15	12	47	42
		1104	262	145	144	835	575	144	146	262	575	835	1510

* promoted after play-offs

Appearances / Goals

Player	Lge	Sub	LC	Sub	FAC	Sub	Lge	LC	FAC	Tot
	Appearances						Goals			
Allen, Martin	4	10								
Aloisi, John	33	5	1				12			12
Awford, Andy	36	3	1		2					
Carter, Jimmy	6	4								
Claridge, Steve	10						2			2
Cook, Aaron	1									
Cook, Andy	1									
Durnin, John	23	11	1		1	1	10			10
Enes, Robbie	1	4								
Flahaven, Aaron	26		2							
Foster, Craig	13	3			2		2		2	4
Hall, Paul	22	1	1		2		5			5
Harries, Paul		1								
Hiller, David	30	2	2				2	1		3
Igoe, Sammy	21	10	1			1	3			3
Knight, Alan	20		2		2					
McLoughlin, Alan	34	3	2		2		4			4
Perrett, Russell	15	1	1		1		1			1
Pethick, Robbie	43	1	1		1	2	2			2
Robinson, Matt	15									
Russell, Lee	8				1	1				
Simpson, Fitzroy	17	2	1		1					
Simpson, Robbie		2								
Svensson, Mathias	17	9	2		1	1	4	1		5
Thomson, Andy	34	1	2		2		2			2
Thorp, Hamilton		7	1		1				1	1
Turner, Andy	12	4	1				1			1
Vlachos, Michalis	15									
Waterman, Dave	11	4	1							
Whitbread, Adrian	38	2	2		1					
30 players used	506	92	22	4	22	3	50	3	2	55

Odds & ends

Double wins: (0).
Double losses: (5) Crewe, Sunderland, Charlton, Nott'm For, Ipswich.

Won from behind: (1) QPR (h).
Lost from in front: (3) Sunderland (h), Birmingham (a), Stoke (a).

High spots: Avoiding relegation on the last day thanks to a 3-1 win at Bradford City.
Seven-match unbeaten league run in February and March, including five wins.
The return of Alan Ball as manager in January.
Opening of new Fratton End in October.

Low spots: Eleven match winless run from September to November, including six consecutive defeats.
Seven-match winless run from December to February, including six defeats.
Losing 1-3 at Crewe on 14 February to go six points adrift of safety.
Eight-match winless run in March and April puts team on the brink of relegation.

The new £2.5m Fratton End almost caused the postponement of the clash with Bradford C in October and it hadn't even opened! The line of the roof cast a shadow for the floodlights and the extra light installed above the stand weren't enough to compensate. It was only with City boss Chris Kamara's agreement that the game went ahead.

Player of the Year: Andy Awford.
Ever presents: (0).
Hat-tricks: (0).
Leading scorer: John Aloisi (12).

No	Date	Opponent	Att	Pos	F-A	Pt	H-T	Scorers, Times, and Referees
1	H 8/8	WATFORD	15,275		1-2	L 0	1-0	Aloisi 30, Thomson 80 (og), Lee 84. Ref: F Stretton (Nottingham)
2	A 15/8	TRAMMERE	6,714	17 / 21	1-1	D 1	1-1	Aloisi 2, Mellon 12. Ref: J Kirkby (Sheffield)
3	H 22/8	IPSWICH	12,002	18 / 15	0-0	D 2	0-0	Ref: C Wilkes (Gloucester)
4	A 29/8	HUDDERSFIELD	10,085	15 / 13	3-3	D 3	1-1	Aloisi 5, 48, McLoughlin 90p, Stewart 45, 84, Allison 89. Ref: A Bates (Stoke)
5	H 31/8	QP RANGERS	12,106	13 / 21	3-0	W 6	1-0	Aloisi 35, McLoughlin 87, Phillips 90. Ref: K Leach (Codsall)
6	A 6/9	OXFORD	6,626	13 / 18	0-3	L 6	0-2	Marsh 28, Windass 34p, 75. Ref: P Taylor (Cheshunt)
7	A 8/9	BURY	4,310	15 / 5	1-2	L 6	1-2	McLoughlin 39p, Preece 22, D'Jaffo 43. Ref: M Pike (Barrow-in-Furness)
8	H 12/9	SWINDON	10,105	13 / 15	5-2	W 9	2-0	Aloisi 14, 88, Igoe 28, 62, Claridge 64, Onora 65, Ndah 75. Ref: M Fletcher (Warley)
9	A 19/9	PORT VALE	5,992	12 / 23	2-0	W 12	0-0	Aloisi 52, Durnin 89. Ref: M Messias (York)
10	H 26/9	SUNDERLAND	17,022	11 / 1	1-1	D 13	1-0	Igoe 21, Johnston 83. Ref: J Brandwood (Lichfield)
11	H 29/9	BIRMINGHAM	11,843	13 / 5	0-1	L 13	0-0	O'Connor 59p. Ref: S Bennett (Orpington)

Line-ups (Pompey players in roman, opponents in italic)

No	1	2	3	4	5	6	7	8	9	10	11	subs used
1	Flahavan	Hillier	Simpson F*	McLoughlin	Thogersen*	Awford	Vlachos	Kyzeridis*	Aloisi	Durnin	Thomson	Pethick/Soley/Robinson
	Chamberlain Hazan		*Kennedy*	*Page*	*Palmer^*	*Mooney*	*Smart**	*Hyde*	*Lee*	*Easton*	*Rosenthal*	*Bazeley/Millen*
2	Knight	Thomson	Simpson F	McLoughlin	Whitbread	Awford	Vlachos*	Claridge	Aloisi	Durnin	Kyzeridis^	Hillier/Soley
	Simonsen	*Frail*	*Thompson*	*McGreal*	*Hill*	*Irons*	*Morrissey*	*Santos**	*Russell**	*Parkinson*	*Mellon*	*Jones G/Jones L*
3	Flahavan	Thomson	Simpson F	McLoughlin	Whitbread	Awford*	Vlachos	Claridge^	Aloisi	Mathie*	Igoe	Robinson/Kyzeridis
	Wright	*Stockwell*	*Taricco*	*Clapham*	*Mowbray*	*Venus*	*Dyer*	*Holand*	*Johnson*		*Petta*	*Naylor*
4	Flahavan	Thomson	Simpson F	McLoughlin	Whitbread	Thogersen*	Vlachos	Hillier	Aloisi	Claridge	Igoe*	Durnin
	Vaesen	*Hessey**	*Edwards*	*Johnson^*	*Morrison*	*Collins*	*Dalton*	*Horne*	*Stewart*	*Allison*	*Thornley*	*Gray/Browning*
5	Flahavan	Pethick	Simpson F	McLoughlin	Whitbread	Thogersen	Vlachos	Hillier	Aloisi	Claridge	Igoe*	Phillips
	Harper	*Rose*	*Baraclough*	*Murray^*	*Ready*	*Maddix*	*Slade*	*Peacock*	*Sheron**	*Gallen*	*Scully*	*Kiwomya/Rowland*
6	Flahavan	Pethick!	Simpson F	McLoughlin	Whitbread	Awford	Vlachos	Hillier*	Aloisi	Durnin^	Igoe*	Peron/Phillips/Kyzeridis
	Whitehead	*Woodward*	*Marsh*	*Gray^*	*Whelan*	*Gilchrist**	*Powell*	*Windass*	*Cook*	*Murphy*	*Beauchamp*	*Thomson/Hill*
7	Flahavan	Thogersen	Simpson F*	McLoughlin	Whitbread	Awford	Vlachos	Matthews*	Peron	Claridge	Igoe*	Soley/Pethick/Durnin
	Kiely	*Woodward*	*Barrick*	*Daws*	*Lucketti*	*Redmond*	*Swailes*	*D'Jaffo*		*Johnrose*	*Preece*	*Baldry/Ellis*
8	Flahavan	Thogersen	Simpson F*	McLoughlin	Whitbread	Awford	Vlachos*	Peron	Aloisi	Claridge	Igoe*	Pethick/Phillips
	Talia	*Kerslake*	*Hall*	*Leitch*	*Reeves*	*Borrows*	*Walters*	*Ndah*	*Onora*	*Bullock**	*Gooden*	*Robinson*
9	Flahavan	Thogersen	Simpson F*	McLoughlin	Whitbread	Awford	Perrett	Aloisi*	Peron*	Claridge*	Igoe	Soley/Durnin
	Musselwhite Walsh		*Tankard**	*Bogie*	*Barnett*	*Bessley*	*Ainsworth*	*Talbot*	*Beadle*	*Naylor*	*Barker^*	*Corden/Clarke*
10	Flahavan	Thogersen	Simpson F	McLoughlin	Whitbread	Awford	Perrett	Aloisi	Peron*	Claridge*	Igoe	Hillier
	Sorensen	*Williams*	*Gray*	*Ball*	*Melville*	*Butler*	*Summerbee Mullin^*	*Dichio*	*Adebola*	*Bridges**	*Johnston*	*Quinn/Rae*
11	Flahavan	Thogersen	Simpson F	McLoughlin	Whitbread	Awford*	Perrett*	Aloisi	Peron*	Claridge	Soley^	Hillier/Phillips/Durnin
	Poole	*Rowett*	*Charlton*	*Marsden*	*Ablett*	*Johnson*	*McCarthy*	*O'Connor*	*Adebola*	*Grainger*	*Ndlovu**	*Forster*

Match reports

1. Pompey are cruising when Hyde's innocuous cross comes off Thomo's head. Lee then pops up at the far post to nod in, leaving ex-England boss Graham Taylor chuffed for his new-boys. Earlier, Aloisi's finish delighted the sun-basking crowd after Simpson hit the bar from 25 yards.

2. Aloisi is on the mark again with a clinical finish after being set up by Claridge after just 106 seconds. The lead doesn't last long, as Micky Mellon is allowed to run 40 yards before beating Knight from the edge of the area. Dane Thogersen is injured and Greek Kyzeridis anonymous.

3. Pompey live dangerously as impressive Ipswich keep up an unbeaten run at Fratton stretching back to 1966. A lacklustre display is rescued by Flahavan's display. His best save came in the 56th minute to deny Mowbray, then Thomson clears two follow-up efforts off the goal-line.

4. Frustrated Ball claims 'We should have won by a mile.' A first-class attacking display is marred by some sloppy defending, and Town ease ahead in the last ten. Happily, Claridge earns a penalty in injury-time. Macca scores; earlier he missed one, but Aloisi was alive to the rebound.

5. Aloisi nets his seventh goal of the season with a neat lob, but a dreadful miss by Kevin Gallen early in the second half is the turning point. Goals by McLoughlin and the debut-making Phillips wrap up a deserved win over Stewart Houston's Rangers, winless away in nearly a year.

6. Pompey dominate the opening period as Whitehead produces excellent saves from Hillier and Aloisi, only for Marsh to score with the United's first attack. Six minutes later it was all over as Pethick is harshly sent off in conceding a penalty. 'Our football was a delight,' maintained Ball.

7. Neil Warnock's Bury maintain their fine start as they out-muscle Pompey. Frenchman Peron (£125,000 from Walsall) stars in midfield, but all three points are lost as half-time approaches. Goalkeeper Flahavan fails to claim a corner and Laurent D'Jaffo heads home at the near post.

8. A five-star showing by Pompey is overshadowed by the mysterious blackout of goalkeeper Flahavan, which allowed Ndah to pull back a second goal without challenge. Peron again stars, while Claridge scores his first goal of the season with a simple tap in after Aloisi's pass.

9. Vale boss John Rudge is less than complimentary, as Pompey graft to victory thanks to Aloisi's header and a fierce injury-time strike from substitute Durnin. Ball's side control the game for long periods, but Rudge said 'I don't think Pompey are as good as Wolves, who we beat.'

10. After a minute's silence for former chairman Jim Gregory, Pompey turn on the style to match Sunderland. Man of the Match Igoe's precise volley looks set to clinch the points, only for defensive confusion after Hillier replaces Claridge, which allows Johnston to curl an equaliser.

11. Pompey look jaded as impressive Birmingham claim all three points when Flahavan brings down Ndlovu in the box as they go for Charlton's long ball. Birmingham stand-in keeper Poole denies Aloisi with a stunning save after 12 minutes, but City always look the more likely to score.

12 A SHEFFIELD UTD 3/10 — 0-1 (17 L 13) — 15,386 · 7 · 13

Aloisi 48
Saunders 5, Dellas 85
Ref: D Laws (Whitley Bay)

Pompey: Flahavan, Thogersen, Simpson F, McLoughlin, Whitbread, Awford!, Perrett, Peron, Aloisi*, Claridge, Igoe, Hillier
Sheffield Utd: Tracey, Ford^, Quinn, Bruce, Sandford, Twiss^, Saunders, Marker, Marcelo^, Hamilton, Stuart, Devlin/Dellas/Taylor

Luck deserts the side as the referee sends off Awford for an innocuous comment, while Blades' player-boss Bruce is only booked for clattering Claridge. The ten-man are on for a point when Aloisi levels, only for Greek sub Dellas to bury a 'wonder' 30-yarder as time ticks away.

---

13 A BRISTOL CITY 10/10 — 2-2 (15 D 14) — 13,056 · 19 · 14

Igoe 18, Claridge 70
Murray 10, Andersen 85
Ref: A D'Urso (Billericay)

Pompey: Flahavan, Thogersen, Simpson F, Hillier, Whitbread, Awford, Perrett, Peron, Aloisi*, Claridge, Igoe, Durnin
Bristol City: Welch, Murray, Bell, Doherty^, Watts, Carey, Goodridge, Hutchings, Akinbiyi, Cramb*, Tinnion, Andersen/Edwards

Pompey's late jitters see another two points disappear as sub Andersen takes advantage of Flahavan's rash rush from the line to score. Earlier, Pompey had taken control after the livewire Igoe and Claridge delighted 1,500 travelling fans. 'The second goal was a joke,' complained Ball.

---

14 H WOLVERHAMPTON 17/10 — 1-0 (12 W 17) — 13,681 · 10 · 17

McLoughlin 66p
Ref: P Danson (Leicester)

Pompey: Knight, Thogersen, Simpson F, McLoughlin, Whitbread, Thomson, Phillips, Peron^, Aloisi, Claridge, Igoe, Durnin
Wolverhampton: Stowell, Atkins, Gilkes*, Emblem, Sedgeley, Curle, Corica, Robinson, Connolly, Gomez, Ferguson, Naylor

Canny Steve Claridge earns the match-winning penalty and infuriates Wolves boss Mark McGhee. His tumble over Keith Curle's leg gives the defender a second booking and Pompey are lucky to survive a late onslaught, especially when Simpson's handball on the line goes unseen.

---

15 H BRADFORD C 21/10 — 2-4 (16 L 17) — 10,062 · 8 · 17

Aloisi 60, 68
Whalley 23, Rankin 32, Mills 33 [Beagrie 80]
Ref: S Mathieson (Stockport)

Pompey: Knight, Thogersen, Simpson F, McLoughlin, Whitbread, Thomson, Phillips, Pethick^, Aloisi*, Claridge, Igoe, Durnin/Vlachos
Bradford C: Walsh, Todd, Jacobs, McCall, Moore, Dreyer", Rankin*, Blake^, Mills, Whalley, Beagrie, O'Brien/Watson

Ball takes the blame as an early injury to McLoughlin disrupts his game-plan. In the shambles that follows, City help themselves to three goals before the break, the third after a dreadful back-pass by Thomson. Aloisi restores some pride, but Beagrie's 20-yarder seals Bradford's points.

---

16 A BARNSLEY 24/10 — 1-2 (18 L 17) — 15,152 · 16 · 17

Durnin 75
Ward 25, Barnard 59
Ref: D Pugh (Wirral)

Pompey: Knight, Thogersen, Simpson F, McLoughlin, Whitbread, Thomson^, Awford, Durnin, Waterman*, Aloisi*, Claridge, Soley/Phillips
Barnsley: Bullock T, Moses, De Zeeuw, Jones, Tinkler, Appleby, Bullock M, McClare, Ward, Barnard, Dyer*, Fjortoft

Pompey are forced to chase the game again as Ward nets from a tight angle. Then Pompey look doomed after Knight's indecisiveness from Barnard's inswinging corner. Durnin's cool tap-in ignites a grandstand finish, but with Aloisi and Claridge out of sorts, a leveller never comes.

---

17 A CRYSTAL PALACE 7/11 — 1-4 (20 L 17) — 20,188 · 13 · 17

Aloisi 42
Moore 6, Thomson 57 (og), Mullins 64, [Foster 81]
Ref: P Rejer (Leamington Spa)

Pompey: Knight, Thorgersen, Simpson F!, McLoughlin, Thomson, Awford, Vlachos, Waterman*, Aloisi*, Claridge, Peron, Soley/Phillips
Crystal Palace: Digby, Austin, Sun Jihai, Fan Zhiyi, Moore, Foster", Lombardo, Rizzo, Bradbury^, Jansen*, Mullins, Bent/Morrison/Burton

£5-million-rated Jansen orchestrates a Palace command performance after Simpson is foolishly sent off for elbowing Austin. Claridge levels almost at once, but once Thomson deflects Jansen's shot it's all over. Craig Foster rubs it in with a 20-yarder but 1,000 fans stay to praise Ball.

---

18 H NORWICH 10/11 — 1-2 (20 L 17) — 9,335 · 6 · 17

Aloisi 21
Roberts 52, Eadie 73
Ref: E Wolstenholme (Blackburn)

Pompey: Knight, Thogersen, Simpson F, McLoughlin, Waterman*, Awford, Perrett, Peron, Aloisi, Claridge, Igoe, Phillips
Norwich: Marshall, Sutch^, Mackay, Adams, Fleming, Jackson, Marshall, Bellamy^, Roberts, Eadie, O'Neill, Llewellyn/Grant

Aloisi misses a gilt-edged chance in injury-time to save a point, having earlier given Simpson the lead by converting Simpson's cross. After half-time Norwich take control as first Eadie sets up Roberts for a clinical finish before skipping past three feeble challenges to score himself.

---

19 A GRIMSBY 14/11 — 1-1 (20 D 18) — 6,236 · 12 · 18

Aloisi 23
Groves 26
Ref: K Lynch (Kirk Hammerton)

Pompey: Petterson, Thogersen, Simpson F, McLoughlin, Waterman, Awford, Perrett!, Peron, Aloisi, Claridge, Igoe, Phillips
Grimsby: Love, McDermott, Gallimore, Handyside, Livingstone, Widdrington, Coldicott, Smith*, Nogan^, Lester, Groves, Ashcroft/Black

Ball manages to his team's defensive frailty by giving on-loan keeper Petterson his debut. He responds with crucial saves from Black and Ashcroft near the end. Aloisi gives Pompey the lead shortly after Perrett had been dismissed for violent conduct, only for Groves to level.

---

20 H WEST BROM 21/11 — 2-1 (18 W 21) — 11,144 · 11 · 21

Nightingale 38, 55
Hughes 1
Ref: M Halsey (Welwyn G City)

Pompey: Petterson, Thogersen, Robinson, McLoughlin, Waterman, Awford, Perrett, Peron, Aloisi*, Claridge, Igoe, Nightingale
West Brom: Miller, Holmes, Van Blerk, Flynn, Murphy, Carbon, Quinn", Bortolazzi^, De Freitas, Hughes, Kilbane*, Sneekes/Angell/Burgess

'Roy of the Rovers' writes the script as 17-year-old local lad Luke Nightingale comes off the bench, equalises within moments and then goes on to grab the winner. 'He looks like a goalscorer in the making,' said Ball. Earlier, Hughes had given Albion the lead after just 48 seconds.

---

21 A STOCKPORT 28/11 — 0-2 (21 L 21) — 7,504 · 15 · 21

Cooper 47, Dinning 48p
Ref: P Richards (Preston)

Pompey: Petterson, Thogersen, Robinson, McLoughlin, Waterman, Awford, Thomson, Peron, Aloisi, Nightingale*, Igoe, Pethick
Stockport: Nash, Connelly, Dinning!, Cook, Flynn, McIntosh, Matthews, McInnes, Angell^, Cooper^, Moore, Wilbraham/Gannon

Pompey are plunged back into trouble after 60 seconds of madness just after the break. First Cooper thrashes home after Petterson saved from Matthews, then Moore's tumble earns a suspect penalty. Nightingale, in for the injured Aloisi, misses a good chance in the first half.

---

22 H CREWE 5/12 — 2-0 (18 W 24) — 9,800 · 24 · 24

McLoughlin 72, Claridge 90
Ref: K Leach (Codsall)

Pompey: Petterson, Thogersen, Robinson, McLoughlin, Waterman, Awford, Thomson, Peron, Aloisi, Claridge, Igoe, Phillips
Crewe: Kearton, Bignot, Smith, Unsworth, Macauley, Charnock, Wright, Johnson, Anthrobus*, Jack, Streete, Lunt

Patient Pompey make heavy weather of beating rock-bottom Crewe. Sub Phillips does the trick and two minutes later McLoughlin heads home Thogersen's cross. Claridge makes the points safe, but had Streete not blazed over from eight yards early on it might have been another story.

---

23 H GRIMSBY 13/12 — 0-1 (18 L 24) — 8,180 · 9 · 24

Groves 67
Ref: B Knight (Orpington)

Pompey: Petterson, Thogersen, Robinson, McLoughlin, Hillier, Awford, Thomson, Peron^, Aloisi, Claridge^, Igoe, Simpson F/Nightingale
Grimsby: Davison, McDermott, Gallimore, Handyside, Livingstone*, Coldicott, Donovan, Smith, Nogan^, Ashcroft, Groves, Smith/Black

Fans invade the pitch at half-time to protest at chairman Martin Gregory in front of the Sky TV cameras. On the field, the pressure of the club's financial worries seems to tell, and it is no surprise when Grimsby nick the points thanks to Groves' unchallenged header from a corner-kick.

No	Date		Att	Pos	Pt	F-A	H-T	Scorers, Times, and Referees	1	2	3	4	5	6	7	8	9	10	11	subs used
24	A	BOLTON		21	L	1-3	1-0	Igoe 1	Petterson	Thogersen	Robinson	McLoughlin*	Hillier	Awford	Thomson	Peron	Vlachos^	Claridge"	Igoe	Simpson F/Phillips/Night'gale
	19/12		*15,961*	*6*	24			*Taylor 70, Frandsen 78, Holdsworth 84*	*Jaaskelainen*	*Phillips*	*Whitlow*	*Frandsen*	*Warhurst*	*Newsome*	*Johansen*	*Jensen*	*Gunnlaugs'n**	*Taylor*	*Sellars^*	*Gardner/Holdsworth*
								Ref: M Pike (Barrow-in-Furness)	Ball – stripped of his powers to buy and sell – changes tactics. His sole-striker formation looks set to pay off after Igoe poaches a goal inside a minute. Thogersen's mistake gifts Taylor the leveller, then Per Frandsen takes advantage after the referee failed to see a foul on Thomson.											
25	A	IPSWICH		21	L	0-3	0-3		Petterson	Thogersen*	Robinson	Simpson F	Hillier	Perrett	Thomson	Peron	Claridge^	Vlachos"	Igoe	Pethick/Night'gale/**Andreas'n**
	26/12		*21,805*	*2*	24			*Naylor 23, 25, Dyer 31*	*Wright*	*Kennedy*	*Thetis*	*Mowbray*	*Venus*	*Clapham*	*Dyer**	*Holland*	*Petta^*	*Abou"*	*Naylor*	*Bramble/Holster/Johnson*
								Ref: J Robinson (Hull)	Ipswich tear Pompey apart and a furious Ball hauls off three experienced players at half-time. On-loan Norwegian Andreasson comes on, but it's all over after Naylor's one-two with Abou sets up the first and his cool chip the second. Abou sets up Dyer to slip the ball under Petterson.											
26	H	OXFORD		20	D	2-2	0-1	Claridge 48, 70p	Petterson	Thogersen*	Robinson	Simpson F	Hillier^	Perrett	Thomson	Peron	Vlachos	Claridge	Igoe	Andreasson/Pethick
	28/12		12,604	*21*	25			*Banger 44, 73*	*Gerrard*	*Robinson*	*Powell*	*Wright**	*Watson*	*Warren*	*Remy^*	*Murphy*	*Banger"*	*Windass*	*Beauchamp !*	*Smith/Wilsterman/Thomson*
								Ref: E Lomas (Manchester)	Claridge responds to Ball's criticism by heading home Igoe's cross, then notching a penalty when Les Robinson elbows Andreasson. Banger's gestures upset the Fratton End after his acute-angled opener, and he then rubs it in, netting after a save. Beauchamp's foul on Perrett earns a red.											
27	A	WATFORD		20	D	0-0	0-0		Petterson	Robinson	Simpson F	McLoughlin*	Whitbread	Nightingale	Thomson	Peron	Vlachos	Claridge	Igoe	Hillier
	9/1		*12,057*	*5*	26				*Chamberlain*	*Bazeley*	*Kennedy*	*Page*	*Palmer*	*Iroha**	*Smart^*	*Hyde*	*Gift'-Williams*	*Johnson*	*Wright"*	*Bonnot/Mooney/Daley*
								Ref: R Oliver (Sutton Coldfield)	Skipper Whitbread makes a welcome return after injury and his presence inspires the team to a solid defensive performance. Andy Thomson ensured the point with a stunning block on the line from Johnson's shot, but McLoughlin's calf injury is a potential blow to Pompey's hopes.											
28	H	HUDDERSFIELD		20	W	1-0	1-0	Claridge 4	Petterson	Robinson	Simpson F	Hillier	Whitbread	Perrett	Nightingale*	Peron	Vlachos	Claridge	Igoe	Phillips
	16/1		10,334	*10*	29				*Vaesen*	*Jenkings*	*Edwards*	*Johnson*	*Hessey*	*Gray*	*Collins**	*Phillips^*	*Stewart*	*Allison*	*Cowan*	*Branes/Facey*
								Ref: M Brandwood (Lichfield)	Claridge shows his class with a fine curling shot, which earns three vital points against Peter Jackson's Terriers, to pull away from the drop zone. The win is well-deserved, but Pompey have Petterson to thank for three fine saves. 'The players were fantastic,' said a delighted Ball.											
29	A	QP RANGERS		19	D	1-1	0-0	Nightingale 63	Petterson	Robinson	Simpson F	McLoughlin	Whitbread	Perrett	Nightingale	Peron	Vlachos	Whittingham	Igoe	
	30/1		*12,270*	*17*	30			*Peacock 50*	*Miklosko*	*Plummer*	*Baraclough*	*Morrow*	*Ready*	*Maddix^*	*Murray*	*Peacock*	*Dowie*	*Gallen*	*Rose**	*Scully/Rowland*
								Ref: R Furnandiz (Doncaster)	On-loan striker Whittingham, signed from the Owls in the week, can't mark his return with a goal, but Nightingale puts away a classy volley from Simpson's cross to earn a draw after Gavin Peacock swivelled to score despite looking offside. In the first half Murray missed a sitter.											
30	H	TRANMERE		19	D	1-1	1-1	Whittingham 17	Petterson	Robinson	Simpson F	McLoughlin	Whitbread	Awford	Nightingale	Peron	Valchos	Whittingham	Hillier*	Soley^/Phillips
	7/2		10,597	*16*	31			*Taylor 44*	*Coyne*	*Allen*	*Thompson*	*McGreal*	*Challinor*	*Irons"*	*Mahon^*	*Santos*	*Hill*	*Taylor*	*Jones L**	*Parkinson/Jones G/O'Brien*
								Ref: P Taylor (Cheshunt)	Whittingham nets his first Pompey goal for six years, pinching the ball off Peron's toe after he had beaten four defenders and rounded Coyne. Scott Taylor equalises from two yards after Petterson drops a cross. After the break, Nightingale's shot comes closest to breaking the deadlock.											
31	H	BURY		18	W	2-1	1-0	Robinson 37, Whittingham 64	Petterson	Thogersen	Robinson	McLoughlin	Whitbread	Awford	Whittingham	Peron*	Vlachos	Claridge	Durnin^	Phillips/Simpson F
	14/2		9,062	*21*	34			*Kemsel Avdiu 90*	*Kiely*	*Woodward^*	*Williams*	*Daws*	*Swailes*	*Redmond*	*West*	*Patterson*	*James*	*Jemson"*	*Billy**	*Preece/Souter/Kemsel Avdiu*
								Ref: A Bates (Stoke)	A vital win against Neil Warnock's Bury team without an away win all season. Claridge crosses for Robinson to score his first Pompey goal with a diving header, then Whittingham buries McLoughlin's flick with a firm header. Kemsel Avdiu's injury-time tap-in is mere consolation.											
32	A	SWINDON		18	D	3-3	1-3	Claridge 44, 72, Peron 78	Flahavan*	Robinson	Simpson F"	McLoughlin	Whitbread	Awford	Whittingham	Peron	Vlachos	Claridge	Igoe^	Perrett/Thogersen/Nightingale
	21/2		*10,230*	*17*	35			*Hay 31, 40, Onoura 45*	*Talia*	*Robinson*	*Hall*	*Leitch*	*Taylor*	*Borrows*	*Howe**	*Ndah*	*Onuora*	*Hay*	*Davis^*	*Hulbert/Gooden*
								Ref: C Foy (St Helens)	Onuora's challenge puts Flahavan in hospital. Defender Perrett puts on the gloves only to pick the ball out of the net twice more before the break. Pompey then dominate and Claridge nods his second after Whittingham hits the bar. Peron's 25-yarder sends 4,000 visiting fans wild.											
33	H	PORT VALE		18	W	4-0	3-0	McLoughlin 29p, Whittingham 36,39 89	Knight	Thogersen	Robinson	McLoughlin	Whitbread	Awford	Whittingham	Peron	Vlachos	Claridge*	Igoe^	Nightingale/Durnin
	28/2		12,838	*21*	38				*Musselwhite*	*Beesley*	*Talbot*	*Bogie*	*Aspin !*	*Gardner*	*Rougier^*	*Barker*	*Bent*	*Foyle**	*Russell*	*Corden/Walsh*
								Ref: A Hall (Birmingham)	Whittingham rolls back the years, with the best goal seeing Peron run the length of the pitch before crossing for a bullet header to make it 3-0. McLoughlin's penalty sets up the win after Corden's trip on star Peron. Vale crumble after Foyle limps off and Aspin walks for a second foul.											
34	A	SUNDERLAND		18	L	0-2	0-1		Knight	Robinson	Simpson F	Thogersen	Whitbread	Awford	Whittingham	Peron	Vlachos*	Claridge	Igoe^	Perrett/Nightingale
	2/3		***37,656***	*1*	38			*Dichio 9, Phillips 60*	*Sorensen*	*Makin*	*Gray*	*Ball*	*Melville*	*Butler*	*Summerbee*	*Clark**	*Dichio^*	*Phillips*	*Johnston*	*Williams/Bridges*
								Ref: K Lynch (Kirk Hammerton)	Peron's sidefoot over from 12 yards proves crucial, as a minute later Phillips has the freedom of the area to head in Summerbee's cross. Dichio gave Peter Reid's Mackems the lead with a brave header, which forced him out of the game. Knight is on-form and keeps the score down.											

Match-by-match record (matches 35–46)

No	Date	Venue	Opponent	Att	HT	FT	Pos	Res		Pts
35	6/3	A	BIRMINGHAM	20,617	1-1	1-4	18	L	4	38
36	9/3	H	SHEFFIELD UTD	10,287	0-0	1-0	16	W	10	41
37	13/3	H	CRYSTAL PALACE	15,520	0-1	1-1	16	D	13	42
38	20/3	A	NORWICH	16,662	0-0	0-0	16	D	13	43
39	28/3	H	BARNSLEY	13,397	1-0	1-3	16	L	13	43
40	3/4	A	WOLVERHAMPTON	23,262	0-0	0-2	17	L	6	43
41	5/4	H	BRISTOL CITY	13,026	0-0	0-1	18	L	23	43
42	10/4	A	BRADFORD C	13,552	0-2	1-2	18	L	3	43
43	17/4	A	WEST BROM	12,750	2-0	2-2	18	D	12	44
44	24/4	H	STOCKPORT	11,212	2-0	3-1	18	W	16	47
45	1/5	A	CREWE	5,759	0-3	1-3	18	L	19	47
46	9/5	H	BOLTON	16,015	0-1	0-2	19	L	6	47

Home Average 11,976   Away 13,645

---

35. 6/3 A BIRMINGHAM 1-4
Pompey: Knight, Robinson, Simpson F, McLoughlin, Whitbread, Awford, Whittingham, Peron, Vlachos", Durnin*, Igoe^. Subs: Nightingale/Thorgersen/Perrett.
Birmingham: Poole, Bass, Charlton, Hyde", Rowett, Johnson, Adebola, O'Connor, Furlong", Hughes, Ndlovu^. Subs: Forster/Grainger/McCarthy, Cullen/Twiss.
Goals: Whittingham 4; Adebola 25, 59, Forster 50, Hughes 84.
Ref: G Laws (Whitley Bay)
A stiff neck keeps Claridge out, but Whittingham nods in Durnin's cross for a deserved lead. Once Adebola scores his first goal at home since September, Pompey fall apart. Sub Forster heads home, then Adebola again and Hughes' run and mis-hit shot underline Blues' dominance.

36. 9/3 H SHEFFIELD UTD 1-0
Pompey: Knight, Robinson, Simpson F, McLoughlin, Whitbread, Awford, Whittingham, Peron, Vlachos, Durnin, Igoe^. Subs: Nightingale/Thorgersen.
Sheffield Utd: Tracey, Derry, Quinn, Woodhouse*, Jacobsen, Holdsworth, Morris, Hamilton, Marcelo, Devlin, Ford^. Subs: Cullen/Twiss.
Goals: Awford 63.
Ref: P Danson (Leicester)
Andy Awford's first ever goal at Fratton Park, and only the second of his career, settles a hard-fought contest. The defender rose at the far post to head home Whitbread's knock-back in a game of few chances. Knight kept Pompey ahead when he smothered Morris's shot near the end.

37. 13/3 H CRYSTAL PALACE 1-1
Pompey: Knight, Robinson, Simpson F^, McLoughlin, Whitbread, Awford, Whittingham, Peron, Vlachos !, Durnin*, Igoe. Subs: Migliorazi/Nightingale.
Crystal Palace: Miller, Smith, Petric*, Tuttle, Moore, Linighan, Thomson, Fan Zhiye, Morrisson, Bradbury, Mullins. Subs: Evans.
Goals: Whittingham 90; Bradbury 3.
Ref: P Richards (Preston)
Ten-man Pompey earn a point in the last minute thanks to Whittingham's poaching instincts in his last match on loan. Palace led from the third minute after a howler from Knight let in Bradbury, but Palace keeper Miller was in inspired form. Vlachos was sent off for two bookings.

38. 20/3 A NORWICH 0-0
Pompey: Knight, Robinson, Simpson F, McLoughlin, Whitbread, Awford, Claridge, Peron, Migliorazi, Durnin*, Igoe. Subs: Marshall A/Thogerseen.
Norwich: Marshall A, Sutch, Wilson, Russell, Fleming, Jackson, Forbes, Bellamy, Roberts*, Marshall L, Coote. Subs: Llewellyn.
Ref: K Hill (Royston)
Bruce Rioch's side, with just one win in 14, are jeered off as Pompey comfortably hold out. Knight's reflex-stop from Darel Russell's six-yard drive saves the day with five minutes to go. Igoe forces Marshall into a good save and Durnin is just wide with a fierce volley in the first half.

39. 28/3 H BARNSLEY 1-3
Pompey: Knight, Robinson, Simpson F, McLoughlin, Whitbread, Awford, Claridge, Peron, Migliorazi, Durnin, Igoe. Subs: Bullock.
Barnsley: Eaden, De Zeeuw, Richardson* Moses, Appelby, V d Laan*, Hignett, Sheron, Dyer, Jones, Blackmore/Bullock M.
Goals: Durnin 12; Hignett 66, Whitbread (og) 70, Dyer 76.
Ref: M Halsey (Welwyn G City)
Pompey seem to be cruising after keeper Bullock blunders and Durnin is presented with an open goal. A linesman's late flag denies Igoe a second, then it all goes wrong. Hignett is left free, then Whitbread slams a cross past Knight unnecessarily. Dyer's curler, though, is a gem.

40. 3/4 A WOLVERHAMPTON 0-2
Pompey: Knight, Robinson, Simpson F^, McLoughlin, Whitbread, Awford, Migliorazi*, Peron !, Vlachos, Claridge*, Igoe*. Subs: Thorgersen/Durnin.
Wolverhampton: Stowell, Muscat, Gilkes, Sedgley*, Richards, Curle, Robinson, Emblem, Flo, Connolly, Osborn. Subs: Corica.
Goals: Muscat 71, Flo 76.
Ref: C Wilkes (Gloucester)
Peron's sending off for a lunge at Sedgley, moments after he spooned over from close-range, is crucial. Caretaker Colin Lee's Wolves enjoyed possession, but now exploit space. Muscat's 20-yarder pings through a crowd, then Knight inexplicably picks up a back-pass and Flo fires in.

41. 5/4 H BRISTOL CITY 0-1
Pompey: Knight, Robinson, Simpson F, McLoughlin, Whitbread, Awford, Nightingale*, Peron, Vlachos, Durnin, Igoe*. Subs: Durnin/Phillips.
Bristol City: Andersen B, Brennan, Sebok, Locke, Taylor, Carey, Howells, Brown, Akinbiyi, Torpey*, Tinnion. Subs: Andersen S.
Goals: Locke 87.
Ref: F Stretton (Nottingham)
Robins stun Pompey with their first away win in six months, which means an uphill relegation battle. Adam Locke nods home a corner late on, as City suddenly believe they can win. Robinson hits the underside at the death and Ball blames 'media hype' for the team's predicament.

42. 10/4 A BRADFORD C 1-2
Pompey: Knight, Robinson, Simpson F, McLoughlin, Whitbread, Awford, Durnin, Peron*, Vlachos, Claridge, Igoe*. Subs: Thogersen.
Bradford C: Walsh, Sharpe, Jacobs, McCall, Moore, Westwood, Lawrence, Windass*, Mills, Whalley, Beagrie^. Subs: Blake/O'Brien.
Goals: Durnin 67; Mills 26, Sharpe 35.
Ref: S Baines (Chesterfield)
Pompey haven't won away for six months and never look like doing so once Paul Jewell's side go ahead with Mills' curler, then Sharpe, on-loan from Sampdoria, heads in. Ball hauls off Peron, then Durnin causes flutters among home fans with a side-foot from Simpson's cross.

43. 17/4 A WEST BROM 2-2
Pompey: Knight, Whitehead, Simpson F, McLoughlin, Whitbread, Awford, Durnin, Peron*, Vlachos*, Clarge*, Igoe*. Subs: Nightingale/Migliorazi.
West Brom: McDermott, Potter, Murphy, Burgess, Van Blerk, Flynn*, Sneekes, Evans*, Hughes, Kilbane, Maresca/Quinn.
Goals: Durnin 31, 34; Maresca 67, Quinn 78.
Ref: S Mathieson (Stockport)
Durnin strikes twice – the second a volleyed contender for goal-of-the-season – but it is his one-on-one miss at 2-1 which proves to be crucial. Quinn is unmarked to head in almost at once and Denis Smith's Baggies avoid six defeats in a row. A WBA fan runs on and clouts a linesman.

44. 24/4 H STOCKPORT 3-1
Pompey: Knight, Robinson, Simpson F, McLoughlin, Whitbread, Awford, Durnin*, Peron*, Vlachos, Claridge, Igoe^. Subs: Nightingale.
Stockport: Gray, Connelly, Dining, Smith, Flynn, Gannon, Cooper, Moore, Angell*, Ellis, Woodthorpe Matthews.
Goals: Claridge 10, Simpson 17, Durnin 46; Ellis 89.
Ref: S Bennett (Orpington)
Fears of the drop are ended – results on Tuesday will mean only a statistical freak can relegate Pompey – as County clearly are on vacation already. Claridge springs the offside trap and rounds Gray, then a free-kick routine sees Simpson fire home and whip his shirt off to celebrate.

45. 1/5 A CREWE 1-3
Pompey: Knight, Robinson, Simpson F, McLoughlin, Whitbread, Awford, Durnin*, Peron*, Vlachos, Claridge, Igoe. Subs: Migliorazi/Night'gale/Phillips.
Crewe: Kearton, Wright, Smith, Macauley, Watton, Charnock, Wright, Johnson, Little*, Murphy, Rivers. Subs: Street.
Goals: McLoughlin 49; Little 21, 30, Smith 45.
Ref: E Lomas (Manchester)
Obliging Blues let Dario Gradi's Alex complete a Great Escape (three wins in a week), but furious Ball sends the team out five minutes early after the break. By then, Little has pounced, the first after Knight slips, and Smith has curled in a free-kick. Macca's volley pulls one back.

46. 9/5 H BOLTON 0-2
Pompey: Knight, Thogersen, Robinson, McLoughlin, Whitbread, Waterman, Durnin*, Peron*, Vlachos^, Claridge, Migliorazi. Subs: Phillips/Igoe/Nightingale.
Bolton: Banks, Cox, Elliott, Frandsen^, Todd, Fish, Johansen, Jensen, Gudjohnsen Taylor*, Gardner, Warhurst/Hansen.
Goals: Johansen 21, Gudjohnsen 66.
Ref: M Fletcher (Warley)
If Bury win 24-13 against Port Vale and QPR 11-0 against Palace, Pompey could go down. Happily, they won't. Instead, Trotters stroll to the play-offs once Jensen sets up Johansen. Migliorazi produces a wonder-save from Banks, but all the talk is of Serb Milan Mandaric's takeover.

Worthington Cup

	Att		F-A	H-T	Scorers, Times, and Referees	1	2	3	4	5	6	7	8	9	10	11	subs used
1:1 A PLYMOUTH 11/8	4,380 3	W	3-1	2:1	McLoughlin 37p, Vlachos 40, Aloisi 46 / McCarthy 19. Ref: R Furmandiz (Doncaster)	Flahavan*	Pethick	Simpson	McLoughlin*	Whitbread	Awford	Vlachos^	Kyzeridis^	Aloisi	Durnin"	Thomson	Knight/Soley/Claridge
						Sheffield	*Collins*	*Gibbs*	*Mauge*	*Heathcote*	*Wotton*	*Barlow*	*McCarthy*	*Jean*	*Power**	*Hargreaves*	*McCall*
1:2 H PLYMOUTH 18/8	17 5,479 3:17	W	3-2	2:1	Hillier 11, McLoughlin 25p, Aloisi 53 / Jean 3, McCarthy 66. Ref: P Rejer (Leamington Spa) (Pompey won 6-3 on aggregate)	Knight	Thomson	Simpson	McLoughlin*	Whitbread	Awford	Vlachos^	Claridge	Aloisi	Durnin^	Kyzeridis^	Soley/Robinson/Igoe
						Sheffield	*Flash*	*Gibbs*	*McCall**	*Heathcote*	*Wotton*	*Barlow*	*McCarthy*	*Jean^*	*Mauge*	*Hargreaves*	*Ashton/Power*
2:1 H WIMBLEDON 15/9	13 7,010 P:6	W	2-1	2:1	Aloisi 9, McLoughlin 25 / Ekoku 36. Ref: K Burge (Tonypandy)	Knight	Thogersen	Simpson	McLoughlin	Whitbread	Awford	Perrett	Peron"	Aloisi	Durnin"	Igoe^	Phillips/Soley
						Heald	*Jupp*	*Thatcher*	*Perry**	*McAlister*	*Francis*	*Ardley^*	*Fear^*	*Ekoku*	*Cort*	*Kennedy*	*Cunningham/Euell/Leaburn*
2:2 A WIMBLEDON 22/9	12 3,756 P:4	L	1-4 aet	1:1	Whitbread 19 / Ardley 27, Ekoku 54, 112, Leaburn 103. Ref: M Riley (Leeds) (Pompey lost 3-5 on aggregate)	Knight	Thogersen	Simpson*	McLoughlin	Whitbread	Awford	Perrett	Peron^	Aloisi	Claridge^	Igoe	Phillips/Durnin/Soley
						Heald	*Cunningham*	*Perry*	*Thatcher*	*Ekoku*	*Ardley*	*Leaburn*	*Kennedy*	*Jupp^*	*Cort^*	*Francis"*	*Kimble/Roberts/Euell*

1:1 — The sight of Claridge earns a cheer after his protracted move. He is only a sub and sees McCarthy side-foot home before Flahavan is carried off. Kyzeridis and Aloisi combine to earn 'Macca's' penalty. Then Pethick and Durnin set up Vlachos at the far post before Aloisi slides home.

1:2 — Ball is furious with some sloppy defending. Just two in midfield means Pompey are over-run and Jean nets the first then misses a sitter before Hillier's volley. Heathcote trips Claridge for the penalty, then Aloisi rounds Sheffield, only for McCarthy's goal to keep it tense.

2:1 — Aloisi's classy curler from 20 yards is the highlight of a thrilling first half. The players celebrate by mimicking Flahavan's collapse on Saturday. Simpson's cross-shot is deflected in by McLoughlin, then Ekoku taps home for the under-strength Dons after good work by Cort.

2:2 — Dons' boss Joe Kinnear gambles again by leaving out key men. Sub Phillips almost clinches it on full-time, but his shot hits the bar. In extra-time Leaburn's header breaks hearts. Earlier, Aloisi had also been denied by the bar, after Whitbread's near-post opener. Ardley's screamer levelled.

FA Cup

	Att		F-A	H-T	Scorers, Times, and Referees	1	2	3	4	5	6	7	8	9	10	11	subs used
3 A NOTT'M FOREST 2/1	20 10,092 P:22	W	1-0	1-0	Claridge 18. Ref: A Wilkie (Chester-le-Street)	Knight	Robinson	Simpson	McLoughlin	Waterman	Andreasson*	Thomson	Peron	Vlachos	Claridge	Igoe	Nightingale
						Beasant	*Louis/Jean*	*Lyttle**	*Freedman^*	*Chettle*	*Olav Hjelde*	*Stone*	*Gemmill*	*Shipperley*	*Johnson^*		*B't·Williams/Gray/Harewood/Quashie*
4 H LEEDS 23/1	20 18,864 P:6	L	1-5	1:2	Nightingale 9 (Ribeiro 73, Wijnhard 82) / Wetherall 14, Harte 16, Kewell 51. Ref: G Willard (Worthing)	Knight	Simpson	McLoughlin	Whitbread	Woodgate	Waterman	Nightingale*	Peron	Vlachos	Claridge	Igoe	Phillips/Thogersen
						Martyn	*Harte*	*Granville**	*Wetherall*	*Woodgate*	*Halle*	*Hopkin*	*Ribeiro*	*Korsten*	*Hasselbaink*	*Kewell*	*Jones/Wijnhard*

3 — Pompey pull off the shock of the afternoon as Claridge's 18-yard shot beats Beasant after Peron sets him up. Premiership tail-enders Forest are woeful as the crowd bay for boss Bassett's head. Knight, back in the side for the cup-tied Petterson, has only one save to make – from Chettle.

4 — Leeds make class tell, but Pompey thrill a capacity gate when Nightingale scores from close range. Leeds' response is impressive, as Wetherall converts Ribeiro's cross, then Harte's 25-yard free-kick stumps Knight. Kewell's cross-shot seals it, but the score ultimately flatters United.

Home / Away Table

	P	Home					Away					Pts
		W	D	L	F	A	W	D	L	F	A	
1 Sunderland	46	19	3	1	50	10	12	9	2	41	18	105
2 Bradford C	46	15	4	4	48	20	11	5	7	34	27	87
3 Ipswich	46	16	1	6	37	15	10	7	6	32	17	86
4 Birmingham	46	12	7	4	32	15	11	5	7	34	22	81
5 Watford*	46	12	8	3	30	19	9	6	8	35	37	77
6 Bolton	46	13	6	4	44	25	7	10	6	34	34	76
7 Wolves	46	11	10	2	37	19	8	6	9	27	24	73
8 Sheffield Utd	46	12	6	5	42	29	6	7	10	29	37	67
9 Norwich	46	7	12	4	34	28	8	5	10	28	33	62
10 Huddersfield	46	11	9	3	38	23	4	7	12	24	48	61
11 Grimsby	46	11	6	6	25	18	6	4	13	15	34	61
12 West Brom	46	12	4	7	43	33	4	7	12	26	43	59
13 Barnsley	46	7	9	7	35	30	7	8	8	24	26	59
14 Crys Palace	46	11	10	2	43	26	3	6	14	15	45	58
15 Tranmere	46	8	7	8	37	30	4	13	6	26	31	56
16 Stockport	46	7	9	7	24	21	5	8	10	25	39	53
17 Swindon	46	7	8	8	40	44	6	3	14	19	37	50
18 Crewe	46	7	6	10	27	35	5	6	12	27	43	48
19 PORTSMOUTH	46	10	5	8	34	26	1	9	13	23	47	47
20 QP Rangers	46	9	7	7	34	22	3	4	16	18	39	47
21 Port Vale	46	10	3	10	22	28	3	5	15	23	47	47
22 Bury	46	9	7	7	24	27	1	10	12	11	33	47
23 Oxford	46	7	8	8	31	30	3	6	14	17	41	44
24 Bristol City	46	7	8	8	35	36	2	7	14	22	44	42
	1104	250	163	139	846	609	139	163	250	609	846	1493

* promoted
after play-offs

Appearances / Goals

	Appearances						Goals			
	Lge	Sub	LC	Sub	FAC	Sub	Lge	LC	FAC	Tot
Aloisi, John	22		4				14	3		17
Andreasson, Svein		2								
Awford, Andy	35		4							
Claridge, Steve	39		2	1	2		9	1		10
Durnin, John	17	9	3	1			7			7
Flahavan, Aaron	13		2							
Hillier, David	11	5	1							1
Igoe, Sammy	39	1	2	1	2		5			5
Knight, Alan	20		2	1	2					
Kyzeridis, Nikos	2	2								
McLoughlin, Alan	41		4		2		7	3		10
Miglioranzi, Stefani	4	3								
Nightingale, Luke	6	11			1	1	3		1	4
Peron, 'Jeff'	37	1	2		2		1			1
Perrett, Russell	12	3	2							
Pethick, Robbie	4	6	1							
Petterson, Andy	13									
Phillips, Martin	2	14			2	1	1			1
Robinson, Matt	27	3	1		1		1			1
Simpson, Fitzroy	38	3	4		2		1			1
Soley, Steve	1	7		4						
Thogersen, Thomas	29	6	2		4	1				
Thomson, Andy	14		2		1					
Vlachos, Michalis	28	1	1							1
Waterman, David	10				2					
Whitbread, Adrian	33		4		2					
Whittingham, Guy	9						7	1		7
27 players used	506	76	44	11	22	3	57	9	2	68

Odds & ends

Double wins: (1) Port Vale.
Double losses: (4) Bradford, Birmingham, Bolton, Barnsley.

Won from behind: (1) West Brom (h).
Lost from in front: (5) Watford (h), Norwich (h), Bolton (a), Barnsley (h), Birmingham (a).

High spots: Beating Swindon 5-2 in September.
Guy Whittingham's hat-trick in the 4-0 win over Port Vale.
Winning 1-0 at Premiership Nottingham Forest in the FA Cup.
Whittingham's last-minute equaliser against Crystal Palace in March.
Drawing 3-3 at Swindon after losing keeper Flahavan in the first half, then trailing 1-3 at half-time.

Low spots: Aaron Flahavan mysteriously collapsing in the goalmouth at home to Swindon.
Losing 2-4 at home to Bradford C.
Going into administration in January with debts of £7.3 million.
Selling striker John Aloisi for a knock-down £690,000 in December.
The home match with Crystal Palace in March is believed to be the first time two professional clubs in administration have played each other.

Player of the Season: Steve Claridge.
Ever presents: (0).
Hat-tricks: (1) Guy Whittingham.
Leading Scorer: John Aloisi (17).

NATIONWIDE LEAGUE DIVISION 1   Manager: Alan Ball ⇨ Tony Pulis   SEASON 1999-2000

No	Date	Att	Pos	Pt	F-A	H-T	Scorers, Times, and Referees	1	2	3	4	5	6	7	8	9	10	11	subs used
1	H 7/8	17,677	—	W 3	2-0	1-0	SHEFFIELD UTD — Miglioranzi 26, Whittingham 88 / Ref: A Bates (Stoke)	Flahavan / Tracey	Robinson / Ford	Cundy / Quinn	Awford / Woodhouse*	Simpson / Murphy	Newton* / Sandford	Miglioranzi / Smeets	McLoughlin / Derry	Allen / Devlin	Whittingham / Katchuro^	Péron* / Hamilton	Igoe/Thogersen, Hunt/Smith
2	A 14/8	21,024	2 / 6	D 4	1-1	1-0	WOLVERHAMPTON — Allen 28 / Keane 48 / Ref: R Furnandiz (Doncaster)	Petterson / Stowell	Robinson / Muscat	Simpson / Bazeley	Awford / Robinson	Cundy / Curle	McLoughlin / Emblem	Miglioranzi / Naylor	Thogersen / Sedgeley	Allen / Flo	Whittingham / Keane	Péron* / Sinton	Igoe
3	H 21/8	15,002	2 / 5	W 7	2-0	0-0	STOCKPORT — Miglioranzi 65, Allen 74 / Ref: M Halsey (Welwyn G' City)	Petterson / Nash	Robinson / Connelly*	Simpson / Nicholson	McLoughlin / Flynn	Cundy / McIntosh	Whitbread / Cooper	Miglioranzi / Moore	Thogersen / Angell	Whittingham / Smith*	Allen / Dinning	Péron / D'Jaffo	Ellis/Byrne
4	A 28/8	13,792	6 / 7	L 7	0-6	0-1	BARNSLEY — [Barnard 54, Hignett 79] / Van Der Laan 45, 61, Appelby 59, 75, / Ref: S Mattieson (Stockport)	Petterson / Miller	Robinson / Eaden	Simpson ! / Appelby	McLoughlin / Richardson^	Whitbread / Moses	Awford ! / Jones	Thogersen / Barnard	Miglioranzi / Barnard	Whitting'm / Sheron*	Allen / V der Laan" Tuttle	Péron* / Dyer/Bullock/Hristov	Vlachos/Newton
5	H 30/8	13,105	6 / 7	D 8	0-0	0-0	HUDDERSFIELD — / Ref: F Stretton (Nottingham)	Petterson / Vaesen	Robinson / Dyson	Simpson / Armstrong	McLoughlin / Lucketti	Whitbread / Monkou	Cundy / Irons	Thogersen / Horne^	Miglioranzi^ / Beech"	Whitting'm / Sellars	Allen / Stewart^	Péron / Wijnhard	Nightingale/Newton, Allison/Thornley/Edwards
6	H 11/9	16,034	11 / 1	D 9	1-1	0-0	IPSWICH — Whittingham 48 / Scowcroft 88 / Ref: P Alcock (Halstead)	Petterson / Wright	Crowe* / Wilnis*	Whitbread / Clapham	Miglioranzi / Venus	Vlachos / Brown	Péron / McGreal!	Cundy / Holland	Thogersen / Naylor*	Whitting'm* / Wright	Allen* / Scowcroft	Panopoulos / Johnson"	Nightingale/McLoughlin/Igoe, Stockw'll/Magilton/Axeldah
7	A 18/9	5,870	9 / 24	W 12	4-2	3-0	TRANMERE — Péron 2, 18, Whit'm 40, Panopoulos 48 / Kelly 83, Challinor 90 / Ref: D Laws (Whitley Bay)	Petterson / Achterberg	Robinson / Allen^	Vlachos / Thompson"	McLoughlin / Mahon	Panopoulos / Taylor	Awford / Kelly	Thogersen / Yates	Miglioranzi / Challinor	Whittingham / Parkinson^	Durnin / Roberts	Péron / Morgan	Grant/Black/Jones
8	H 25/9	12,073	10 / 13	L 12	1-2	1-1	GRIMSBY — McLoughlin 30p / Ashcroft 10, Caldicott 62 / Ref: R Oliver (Sutton Coldfield)	Petterson / Coyne !	Robinson / Butterfield	Vlachos / Gallimore	McLoughlin / Burnett*	Panopoulos / Groves	Awford / Smith	Thogersen / Donovan	Miglioranzi* / Coldicott	Whittingham / Lester	Durnin* / Ashcroft*	Péron / Smith*	Lovell/Igoe, Croudson/Pouton/Black
9	A 2/10	15,221	15 / 14	L 12	0-4	0-1	CRYSTAL PALACE — [Mullins 90] / Svensson 20, Carlisle 59, Zhiyi 63, / Ref: K Leach (Codsall, Staffs)	Petterson / Digby	Robinson / Smith^	Simpson / Austin	McLoughlin / Mullins	Whitbread / Zhiyi	Awford / Linighan	Thogersen / Fullarton^	Miglioranzi^ / Thomson	Whitting'm* / Svensson^	Péron^ / Bradbury	Péron / Carlisle	Claridge/Miglioranzi, Frampton/de Ornelas/W'zley
10	H 16/10	14,812	19 / 1	L 12	0-2	0-1	CHARLTON — Robinson 42, Salako 90 / Ref: P Rejer (West Midlands)	Petterson / Kiely	Whitbread / Powell	Awford / Rufus	Vlachos^ / Newton"	McLoughlin / Shields	Igoe / Kinsella	Miglioranzi / Youds	Simpson / Robinson	Igoe / Jones	Panopoulos* / Hunt*	Péron* / Mendonca	Rob'son/Tho'sen/Night'gale, Pringle/Salako
11	H 19/10	9,042	13 / 22	W 15	5-1	1-1	WALSALL — Thog'rsen 44, 84, McLoughlin 76p, 80p / Wrack 11 [Bradbury 69] / Ref: B Jordan (Hertfordshire)	Petterson / Walter*	Whitbread / Marsh	Awford / Pointon	Vlachos^ / Viveash	Simpson* / Crowe	Péron* / Wrack	Miglioranzi^ / Keates^	McLoughlin / Larusson	Igoe / Matias"	Thogersen / Claridge	Bradbury / Abou	Robinson/Phillips, Emberson/Bukaran/Robins

Match reports

1. 'You couldn't have written a better script,' says Director David Deacon. 'Saviour' Milan rallied the fans beforehand, Miglioranzi curled a shot beyond Tracey after a flowing move, Devlin skied a penalty just after the break, then Whittingham finished off Allen's headed pass at the end.

2. Coveted Keane showed top class footwork to fire past Petterson – booed after choosing Pompey over Wolves – just after the break. Earlier, Allen had nipped in between Stowell and Curle to score. Keane missed a headed sitter from three feet, then Muscat cleared off the line late on.

3. Allen's class ensures Pompey polish off dogged Stockport. First he burst past a defender to cross for Miglioranzi to scuff home, then he headed in Simpson's cross. 'We had the quality to finish them off,' said Ball afterwards. '2-0 flattered them,' countered County's boss Andy Kilner.

4. At least the fans sang throughout. Awford is sent off for two yellows and Simpson for a two-footed foul before the break. Van Der Laan deflected home a volley on half-time, then Petterson misjudged a 30-yarder from Barnard soon after, and Brazil-kitted Pompey wilt in the heat.

5. Pompey picked up their first-ever point in front of the Sky cameras, but this was a TV turn-off. Ball's showing of Saturday's video nasty tightened up Pompey's rearguard. Petterson is the hero, turning over Sellars' 30-yarder late on, then Wijnhard scoops a shot over the bar.

6. Whittingham's well-timed looping header seemed to have sealed a first home win against Ipswich since 1967. Ten-man Town, after McGreal scythed down Whittingham (40), look dead, but late on Scowcroft sweeps home Stockwell's cross. Allen crocks an ankle and is out for weeks.

7. Péron is pushed further forward and scores twice early on in his 50th match for the club. Rovers are woeful and Whittingham pounces on defensive chaos to lob a third, then Panopoulos hits a post, but the ball rebounds off him into the net. Two late sloppy goals take off the shine.

8. Pompey are deservedly jeered off. Ashcroft rounded Petterson early on to score as Pompey are slow out of the blocks. Keeper Coyne is unlucky to be sent off and McLoughlin converts the penalty, but rookie Croudson is never troubled and then Coldicott scores from close range.

9. 'Some of these players will never play for me again,' rages boss Ball after this capitulation, but he calmed down a bit after 'crisis talks' with Milan. Ex-Blue Svensson curled home the opener after being set up by another former favourite Bradbury. Panopoulos is the pick for Pompey.

10. An improvement against in-form Addicks, but it's not enough. Panopoulos missed a one-on-one, but then Robinson gobbled up a rebound on the stroke of half-time. Petterson kept Pompey in it with four fine saves, but boobed in injury-time failing to claim the ball and Salako pounced.

11. Thogersen's header on half-time is ruled to have gone in and Pompey cruised after that. Lee Bradbury is back at Fratton and he started the rout, then won two converted penalties. Thogersen scored late on after a slick move. Wrack's early goal off the bar shredded nerves for a while.

12 A QP RANGERS — 13,303 — 14 D 0-0 — 9 / 16

Petterson · Whitbread · Crowe · Vlachos · Awford · McLoughlin · Thogersen · Igoe · Simpson · Claridge* · Bradbury · Whittingham
Harper · Breacker · Ready · Darlington · Baraclough · Maddix · Rose · Langley · Wardley · Steiner · Kiwomya

Ref: M Fletcher (Warley)

Luck is on Pompey's side as Steiner hit the post and crossbar for Rangers in a second-half bombardment. In the final minute Awford clears a Baraclough free-kick off the line after he learns from the goal conceded in the week. Thogersen's late flying header almost stole a flukey win.

---

13 A GRIMSBY — 5,912 — 16 L 0-1 — 12 / 16

Petterson · Crowe · McLoughlin · Awford · Robinson · Whitbread · Igoe · Simpson · Claridge* · Bradbury · Phillips/Whittingham
Coyne · Butterfield · Gallimore" · Lever · Smith · Peaton · Groves · Smith · Lester · Allen^ · Caldicott/Ashcroft/Black

Awford 23 (og)
Ref: K Hill (Royston)

Ball throws his cap to the ground in frustration as Pompey's late rally somehow fails to earn a deserved point. McLoughlin is chief villain, heading Igoe's cross wide from close range (82). Simpson also missed a good chance after Awford diverted Gallimore's cross into his own net.

---

14 H CRYSTAL PALACE — 13,018 — 13 W 3-1 — 20 / 19

Petterson · Crowe · McLoughlin · Robinson* · Whitbread · Igoe^ · Thogersen · Simpson · Claridge* · Bradbury · Phillips/Panopoulos/Wh'ham
Digby · Austin · Phelan · Mullins · Woozley · Launders · Rodger · Svensson · De Ornelas · Fullarton · Martin*

Claridge 43, 72, Bradbury 61, Linighan 23
Ref: S Dunn (Bristol)

Once Claridge scrambled home from close in, there was only one winner. Linighan had headed Palace in front, but the soaked travelling fans just knew old-boy Bradbury would score: he did after Linighan's slip, then McLoughlin's quick thinking set up Claridge from a narrow angle.

---

15 A MANCHESTER C — 31,660 — 13 L 2-4 — 1 / 19

Petterson · Crowe · McLoughlin · Awford^ · Whitbread · McLoughlin · Panopoulos · Simpson · Claridge" · Bradbury · Igoe/Whittingham/Berntsen
Weaver · Edgehill · Wiekens · Horlock · Bishop^ · W't-Phillips" · Whitley · Kennedy · Granville · Jobson · Cooke/Pollock/Tiatto*

Bradbury 7, Thogersen 57, Whitley 47, Taylor 66, 69, Pollock 90.
Ref: A Hall (Birmingham)

Jeering City fans – ex-boss Ball their target – are silent for long periods as Pompey match City. Another Maine Road 'flop' Bradbury seizes on Panopoulos's great pass, then Thogersen restores the lead after City's defence flounders. Taylor's brace in four minutes turns the tide of match.

---

16 H BIRMINGHAM — 12,756 — 13 D 2-2 — 6 / 20

Petterson · Crowe · McLoughlin · Berntsen · Whitbread · Panopoulos · Thogersen^ · Simpson^ · Claridge" · Bradbury · Whitting'm* · Lovell/Igoe/Waterman
Bennett · Rowett · Johnson · O'Connor · Purse! · Holdsworth · McCarthy · Holland · Wreh · Marcelo · Adebola/Lazaridis/Hughes*

McLoughlin 35p, 86p, Lazaridis 58, Johnson 62
Ref: S Bennett (Kent)

Sub Lovell's innocuous tumble in the box lets McLoughlin level with his second pen, then Purse is sent off for two yellows, but Pompey can't profit. Macca's first was after Whittingham was fouled, but Lazaridis curled one after a quick break, then his corner was headed in by Johnson.

---

17 A FULHAM — 13,229 — 13 L 0-1 — 4 / 20

Petterson · Crowe · Vlachos · Robinson · Waterman · Whitbread · Awford · Simpson · Claridge* · Bradbury · Lovell
Taylor · Uhlenbeek · Brevett · Melville · Coleman · Symons · Clark · Trollope · Heinz-Riedle · Cadamarteri · Hayward · Collins*

Collins 90
Ref: P Dowd (Stoke)

Another late-late goal – this one an injury-time header from sub Collins – gave big-spending Fulham a barely-deserved win. Simpson scorned a great chance after the break, then Taylor's finger-tips deny Bradbury. Late on Fulham forced seven corners, but Petterson was in inspired form.

---

18 A WEST BROM — 11,463 — 15 L 2-3 — 13 / 20

Flahavan · Crowe · Robinson · Pamarot · Waterman* · Vlachos · Awford · Simpson ! · Whitting'm* · Bradbury · Phillips/Péron
Miller · McDermott/Van Blerk · Flynn · Burgess · Sigurdsson · Raven · Maresca · Quinn · Sneekes · Evans*

Whittingham 20, Awford 29, Maresca 14, Van Blerk 59, Evans 90
Ref: P Danson (Leicester)

Sub Evans fired home with the last kick, so Pompey's late-goal woe – nine in the last ten minutes so far – goes on. It was so different after Whittingham and Awford's headers had put them on top. Van Blerk's shot levelled, then Simpson gets two quick yellows and the die was cast.

---

19 H CREWE — 11,550 — 15 L 0-2 — 22 / 20

Flahavan · Crowe · Robinson · Moore · Whitbread · Panopoulos* · McLoughlin · Simpson · Whitting'm* · Bradbury · Claridge/Igoe
Kearton · Bignot · Wright · Lightfoot · Smith · Collins · Charnock · Sorvel · Jack · Tait^ · Little · Lunt/Cramb*

Jack 34, Tait 63
Ref: P Taylor (Hertfordshire)

£650,000 defender Moore and Man C loanee Brown can't shore up poor Pompey. Jack's shot from outside the box deceives Flavs, then Tait profits from Moore's scuffed clearance. Claridge and Bradbury are denied in one-on-ones. McLoughlin is unhappy and could be off to Wigan.

---

20 A NOTT'M FOREST — 13,841 — 20 L 0-2 — 16 / 20

Flahavan · Crowe · Robinson · Moore^ · Whitbread · Panopoulos* · McLoughlin · Brown · Claridge · Bradbury · Igoe/Pamarot
Crossley · Mannini" · Scimeca · Hjelde · Brennan · Prutton · Johnson · B't-Williams · Rogers^ · John · Beck · Freedman/Quashie/Doig*

John 6, Beck 11
Ref: E Wolstenholme (Blackburn)

Early defensive calamities see John nip in at the near post to volley home, then he found Beck in space to shoot past Flavs. Pompey improved slightly in the second half, but Bradbury wastefully blazed over then saw a shot cleared off the line. The gate is Forest's smallest for a decade.

---

21 H BOLTON — 10,431 — 20 D 0-0 — 8 / 21

Flahavan · Awford · Cundy · Whitbread · Igoe · McLoughlin* · Brown · Simpson · Claridge · Bradbury · Panopoulos
Jaaskel'nen · O'Kane · Whitlow · Jensen · Bergsson · Fish · Johansen · Farrelly · Gudjohns'n^ · Hansen · Gardner · Taylor/Holden*

Ref: D Crick (Worc'r Pk, Surrey)

Cundy is back after injury and Pompey look more solid. Moore is ruled out with 'stiff muscles'. Bradbury sees a shot tipped onto a post early on, then Claridge's curler hits the bar just after the break. Flavs makes a couple of great saves to deny Hansen, then Farelly, so a draw is fair.

---

22 A SHEFFIELD UTD — 10,834 — 20 L 0-1 — 21 / 21

Flahavan · Awford · Cundy · Whitbread^ · Moore · McLoughlin · Panopoulos · Brown · Claridge · Bradbury · Claridge"/Crowe/Igoe
Tracey · Gysbrechts · Murphy · Sandford · Devlin · Derry · Riberio^ · Ford · Quinn · Smith · Bent^ · Kozluk/Hunt/Katchouro*

Devlin 20
Ref: T Leake (Darwen)

Ball fiddles with formations while his reign burns. Allen crocks the other ankle on his return and sub striker Claridge is subbed himself late on. Cundy misses a sitter at the death, Brown hits a post, but Devlin's low 30-yarder seals the win and Ball is fired next week to the players' relief.

---

23 H PORT VALE — 11,869 — 22 D 0-0 — 21 / 22

Flahavan · Hiley · Robinson · Whitbread · Awford · Cundy · Igoe · Mig'lioranzi* · Vlachos · Claridge · Bradbury · Panopoulos
Musselwhite · Tankard · Gardner · Minton · Widdrington · Naylor · Eyre · Rougier · Carragher · Burns · Brisco

Ref: K Lynch (Kirk Hammerton)

Pompey are in the drop zone for Xmas and haven't scored for more than ten hours. Luck isn't on their side as Bradbury twice hits the post – the first inside a minute – with first-half shots, as does Claridge. Vale never threaten. Gary Megson is the favourite to be named new boss shortly.

NATIONWIDE LEAGUE DIVISION 1 — Manager: Alan Ball ⇨ Tony Pulis — SEASON 1999-2000

No	Date	Att	Pos	Pt	F-A	H-T	Scorers, Times, and Referees	1	2	3	4	5	6	7	8	9	10	11	subs used
24	A SWINDON 26/12	10,279	22 / 24	23	1-1	0-1	Claridge 82 / Hay 16 Ref: M Warren (Walsall)	Flahavan	Crowe	Cundy	Awford	Whitbread	Vlachos*	Igoe	Hiley	Whittingham	Claridge	Bradbury	Phillips
								Talia	Hall	Davies*	Reeves		Williams	Collins^	Leitch^	Williams	Hay	Onoura	Willis/Hulbert/Cuervo
							Claridge clips Pompey's first goal in 11 hours, after his initial shot was saved, to claim a point, then all agree he should have had a late pen – except the ref. Hay pounced on a rebound off Flavs as Town dominated the first half. Reeves hit a post on the hour, but then it was all Pompey.												
25	H BLACKBURN 28/12	15,208	22 / 7	23	1-2	1-2	Claridge 15 / Dailly 32, Ostenstadt 45 Ref: P Robinson (Hull)	Flahavan	Crowe	Robinson	Whitbread	Moore	Awford	Igoe	Phillips	Whiting'm*	Claridge	Bradbury	Hiley
								Kelly*	Kenna^	Davidson	McAteer	Daily	Taylor	Carsley	Johnston	Ostenstadt	Duff		Fettis/Grayson
							First Pompey's defence dallies and Dailly smacks home a loose ball, then Dunn has a free cross and ex-Saint Ostenstadt heads home on half-time. Early on Pompey were well worth Claridge's close-range goal from Moore's nod down. Keeper Kelly is carried off with an ankle knock.												
26	A NORWICH 3/1	16,637	22 / 10	23	1-2	0-2	Bradbury 52 / Fleming 9, Roberts 25p Ref: P Rejer (Tipton)	Knight	Crowe	Robinson	Awford	Whitbread	Moore	Migliorani	Igoe	Claridge	Bradbury	Phillips*	Whittingham
								Marshall	Fleming	Jackson	Kenton	Sutch	Fuglestad	Anselin^	De Blasiis*	Russell^	Roberts	Llewellyn	Marshall/Forbes/Wilson
							Old-stager Knight solves a keeper injury crisis, but he can't prevent a nightmare start. First Fleming has a free header from six yards, then Llewellyn tumbles easily in the box and Roberts converts. Bradbury's opportunism sparked a revival and Marshall denied Igoe athletically.												
27	H WOLVERHAMPTON 15/1	13,255	23 / 9	23	2-3	2-0	Igoe 19, Claridge 23 / Sedgeley 76, Branch 85, Akinbiyi 88 Ref: A Butler (Sutton-in-Ashf'ld)	Petterson	Crowe	Robinson	Vernazza	Whitbread	Moore	Awford	Igoe*	Claridge	Bradbury	Phillips*	Panopoulos*/Thogersen/Hiley
								Oakes	Naylor	Muscat	Robinson*	Curle	Pollet	Bazeley	Emblem	Akinbiyi	Branch	Sinton	Sedgley
							New boss Pulis is unveiled and seems to have done the trick as Igoe scores at the far post, then Claridge spins and volleys in. Sedgley's entry turns the game. He heads in off the bar. Then as Pompey wilt Branch meets a cross to level, before Akinbiyi deflects home Muscat's wild shot.												
28	A STOCKPORT 22/1	8,008	23 / 7	24	1-1	1-1	Hughes 44 / Dinning 14p Ref: A Kaye (Wakefield)	Hoult	Crowe	Robinson	Awford	Whitbread	Moore	Vernazza	Thogersen	Claridge	Bradbury	Hughes	
								Gray	Briggs	Nicholson	Fradin	Flynn	Gannon	Cooper	Dinning	D'Jaffo*	Moore^	Allen	Wilbrahin/Bailey
							Dinning's cocky chipped penalty rubbed salt into a debatable decision, then Bradbury smacked the bar from the spot after another soft award. New-boy Hughes (ex-Dons) headed home Bradbury's cross, then Pompey scorned a host of chances to win it as Blues showed character.												
29	H BARNSLEY 29/1	12,201	23 / 3	27	3-0	2-0	Claridge 9, 20, 64 Ref: C Wilkes (Gloucester)	Hoult	Waterman	Awford	Vernazza*	Whitbread	Moore	Panopoulos*	Thogersen	Claridge*	Bradbury	Hughes	Igoe/Whittingham/O'Neil
								Miller	Curtis	Barker*	Appleby	Morgan	Chettle	Eaden	V der Laan*	Hignett^	Shipperley	Barnard	Dyer/Thomas/Sheron
							Claridge claims the match-ball, then faces an FA probe for backing his side to win with four teammates. Two identikit goals from corners, one headed, the second volleyed in at the far post, sandwiched a trademark cross-shot. Late sub O'Neil becomes Pompey's youngest debutant.												
30	A HUDDERSFIELD 5/2	12,753	20 / 5	30	1-0	0-0	Claridge 73 Ref: M Messias (York)	Hoult	Waterman	Awford	Vernazza	Whitbread	Moore	Panopoulos*	Thogersen	Claridge	Bradbury*	Hughes	Whittingham/Hiley
								Vaesen	Jenkins*	Vincent	Irons*	Dyson	Armstrong	Donis	Home*	Smith	Gorre	Thornley	Holland/Facey/Sellars
							A slick set-piece practised on the training ground, as Claridge headed home Hughes' free-kick, gave Pompey another win over a promotion hopeful. Town lacked punch, although Smith hit a post and Donis and Thornley went close. Pompey are unbeaten at the McAlpine in six visits.												
31	H FULHAM 12/2	17,337	20 / 8	30	0-1	0-0	Goldbaek 73 Ref: K Leach (Codsall)	Hoult	Waterman	Awford*	Vernazza	Whitbread	Moore	Panopoulos*	Thogersen	Claridge	Bradbury	Hughes^	Hiley/Igoe/Whittingham
								Taylor	Melville	Coleman	Morgan*	Goldbaek	Phelan	Ball	Clark	Finnan	Hayles	Horsfield	Symons
							Fulham had the linesman and the woodwork to thank for this win. Claridge thought he'd headed in, but it seemed Panopoulos's corner swerved out. He then hit a post and Thogersen the bar. Pulis felt Goldbaek's free-kick, which deflected past Hoult, should have gone the other way.												
32	A BOLTON 22/2	12,672	20 / 9	30	0-3	0-1	Taylor 13, Jensen 68, Elliott 78 Ref: M Reed (Birmingham)	Hoult	Waterman	Waterman	Vernazza	Whitbread	Moore	Panopoulos*	Thogersen	Claridge	Bradbury*	Hughes*	Birming'm/Night'le/W'ham
								Jaasthel'nen	Holden	Whitlow	Bergsson	Fish*	Johansen	Johnston	Elliott	Jensen	Taylor"	Gudjohnson	Gardner/Ritchie/Holdsworth
							Injury-hit Pompey were always second-best once Taylor rose at the far post to head in Johansen's cross. Bolton finally sealed the points when Jensen fired in low from 30 yards, then Elliott scored from a narrow angle. "We need more strength in depth," moaned Whitbread afterwards.												
33	H TRANMERE 1/3	10,759	22 / 16	30	1-2	0-1	Claridge 84p / Hazell 34, Yates 90 Ref: M Fletcher (Warley)	Hoult	Crowe	Waterman	Vernazza	Whitbread	Moore	Panopoulos*	Thogersen	Claridge	Bradbury*	Hughes^	Igoe/Whiting'm/Nightingale
								Murphy	Roberts	Hazell	Yates	Challinor	Hill	Jones	Henry	Mahon	Allison	Taylor^	Koumas
							Hoult misjudges Challinor's long throw in the 94th minute and Yates scores at the far post to break Pompey hearts. Tranmere were supposedly tired after Sunday's League Cup final, but it didn't show. Hazell gave them a deserved lead but Claridge won, then converted, a dodgy late pen.												
34	A IPSWICH 4/3	20,305	21 / 3	33	1-0	1-0	Claridge 27 Ref: P Taylor (Waltham Cross)	Hoult	Crowe	Birmingh'm*	Hiley	Whitbread	Moore	Thogersen	Waterman	Igoe	Claridge	Bradbury*	Fenton
								Wright	Clegg	Clapham	Wilnis	Mowbray	Brown	Holland	Magilton	Scowcroft^	Johnson	Stewart	Wright
							Betting slips up and down the land are torn up as Pompey's sweeper plan dreamt up the day before – with Hiley in the role – works perfectly. Claridge headed home Igoe's cross, then Pompey dug in. Stewart and Johnson missed sitters and Ipswich lose for the first time in 18 games.												

#	Date	H/A	Opponent	Att	Pos	Res	Opp Pos	Pts	Score	HT
35	7/3	A	BIRMINGHAM	19,573	22	L	5	33	0-1	0-0
36	11/3	H	NOTT'M FOREST	14,336	21	W	19	36	2-1	0-0
37	18/3	A	CREWE	6,188	20	W	19	39	3-1	1-0
38	21/3	H	WEST BROM	14,760	18	W	21	42	2-0	1-0
39	25/3	H	SWINDON	15,305	18	W	24	45	4-1	3-0
40	1/4	A	PORT VALE	5,426	18	L	23	45	0-2	0-2
41	8/4	H	NORWICH	14,003	15	W	13	48	2-1	0-1
42	15/4	A	BLACKBURN	17,263	15	D	10	49	1-1	1-1
43	21/4	A	CHARLTON	20,043	15	D	1	50	1-1	1-0
44	24/4	H	MANCHESTER C	19,015	15	D	2	51	2-2	1-2
45	29/4	A	WALSALL	8,151	17	L	22	51	0-1	0-1
46	7/5	H	QP RANGERS	16,301	18	L	10	51	1-3	0-1

Home Average 13,984 Away 13,622

35. A BIRMINGHAM
Portsmouth: Hoult, Whitbread, Waterman, Moore, Crowe, Edinburgh, Thogersen, Igoe, Harper, Claridge, Bradbury
Birmingham: Bennett, Rowett, Charlton, Holdsworth, Purse, Hughes, O'Connor, Grainger, Adebola, Johnson^, Lazaridis* — Marcelo/Ndlovu
Scorer: Marcelo 49
Ref: S Mathieson (Stockport)
"Despite reinforcements in Edinburgh (Spurs) and Harper (Derby), Pompey fail to get a shot on target. Marcelo then gets off the bench to finish O'Connor's charging run from deep. Not much else to report, although Whitbread had to be restrained from tangling with Marcelo at the end."

36. H NOTT'M FOREST
Portsmouth: Hoult, Whitbread, Moore, Crowe, Edinburgh, Igoe*, Thogersen, Waterman, Harper, Claridge^, Bradbury — Allen/Panopoulos
Forest: Beasant, Louis-Jean, Scimeca^, Vaughan^, Brennan, Gray*, Quashie, B't-Williams, Johnson, Rogers, Lester — Harewood/Dawson/Woan
Scorers: Thogersen 84, Claridge 90; Johnson 80
Ref: K Hill (Royston)
"Five minutes into injury-time Claridge sent a cross-shot past Beasant and completed a great escape. Johnson looked to have won it when he fired home from ten yards, but Thogersen's header set up a grandstand finish. Allen scooped over from close in, but his blushes were spared."

37. A CREWE
Portsmouth: Hoult, Whitbread, Waterman, Moore, Crowe, Edinburgh, Derry, Thogersen, Harper, Claridge, Bradbury — Awford/Allen
Crewe: Kearton, Wright D, Lunt, Walton, Macauley, Jack, Sorvel, Rivers, Cramb^, Newby, Tait
Scorers: Claridge 3, Thogersen 63, Harper 86; Cramb 57
Ref: G Laws (Whitley Bay)
"Crewe's passing game was smothered, with new signing Derry (Sheff U) shoring up midfield. Claridge converted Harper's cross early on and even Cramb's leveller didn't break Pompey's stride. Thogersen got lucky as his shot deflected in, then Harper's thumping header sealed it."

38. H WEST BROM
Portsmouth: Hoult, Whitbread, Waterman, Moore, Crowe, Edinburgh, Derry, Thogersen, Harper, Claridge, Bradbury — Bradbury/Sneekes
West Brom: Flahavan, Jensen, Gabbiadon*, Van Blerk, Burgess, Carbon!, Flynn", Quinn, Evans, Hughes, Lyttle/Raven/Oliver
Scorers: Claridge 28p, Derry 86
Ref: G Poll (Tring)
"Ref Poll's generous penalty, as Jensen challenged Claridge, who then converted, turned the game. After that Pompey bossed it and Baggies ended up with four booked and Carbon sent off for hauling back Bradbury. Derry impresses, hitting the bar then racing clear to angle home."

39. H SWINDON
Portsmouth: Hoult, Whitbread, Waterman, Moore, Crowe, Edinburgh, Derry, Thogersen", Harper, Claridge^, Bradbury — Awford/Allen/Myers
Swindon: Talia, Robinson, Reeves, Hall, Willis, Leitch, Collins^, Williams", Cowe", Meaker, Gray — Grazioli/Cuervo/Williams
Scorers: Whitbread 30, Bradbury 40, 42, 50; Gray 70
Ref: T Leake (Darwen)
"Pulis: 'The job isn't done yet', but just two more wins should keep Pompey up. Doomed Swindon collapse after Whitbread forces the ball in from close range. Lee Bradbury collects a quick-fire hat-trick, the first with his left foot, the second with his right, before a far-post header."

40. A PORT VALE
Portsmouth: Hoult, Whitbread I, Edinburgh", Derry", Whitbread!, Moore, Harper, Thogersen", Claridge, Bradbury, Hughes* — Awford/Crowe/Myers
Port Vale: Pilkington, Carragher, Tankard, Cummins, Burton, Snijders, O'Callaghan, Widdrington, Viljanen, Healy, Rougie*. — Eyre
Scorers: Viljanen 16, Widdrington 42p
Ref: P Rejer (Tipton)
"Waterman is unlucky to see red for a handball and, worse, ex-Saint Widdrington converts the penalty. Viljanen, rejected by Pulis in February, had already turned in a cross. Derry spoons a great chance, then Whitbread also walks for a second yellow. 'The ref was not fit,' raged Pulis."

41. H NORWICH
Portsmouth: Hoult, Whitbread, Edinburgh", Derry*, Whitbread, Moore, Harper^, Thogersen^, Claridge", Bradbury, Hughes — Myers/Awford/Allen
Norwich: Marshall A, Sutch, Kenton!, Fleming, Jackson, Mulryne*, Hamilton, Brady", Marshall L, De Waard^, Roberts — Russell/Llewellyn/Mackay
Scorers: Harper 52, Moore 72; Marshall L 45
Ref: P Richards (Preston)
"Suddenly Pompey are targeting a top-half finish. Moore cements his growing popularity with the fans, producing a deft finish with the outside of his boot, after Harper had headed an equaliser. Kenton walked after two fouls on Harper. Lee Marshall's first-half header had flattered City."

42. A BLACKBURN
Portsmouth: Hoult, Crowe, Awford, Derry, Moore, Myers, Harper, Thogersen, Claridge", Bradbury, Hughes — Ostenstadt/Frandsen
Blackburn: Kelly, McAteer, Davidson, Carsley, Short, Dailly, Duff, Filtcroft", Ward, Burgess*, Dunn
Scorers: Hughes 41, Carsley 23p
Ref: M Pike (Barrow-in-Furness)
"Hughes atones for giving away a soft penalty for a foul on Carsley, which the same man converted, by firing a 25-yarder which took a timely bobble on its way past Kelly. That's the keeper's story anyway. Big-spending Blackburn are a strong side, despite a strong start."

43. A CHARLTON
Portsmouth: Hoult, Whitbread, Edinburgh, Derry, Whitbread*, Moore, Harper, Thogersen, Claridge", Bradbury, Hughes — Allen*/Myers/Awford
Charlton: Kiely, Barness, Powell, Stuart, Rufus, Brown, Newton, Kinsella, Svensson, Hunt, Robinson
Scorers: Bradbury 41; Stuart 64
Ref: T Heilbron (Newton Ayc'fe)
"The Addicks need a win to clinch the title, and Sky TV are here, but Pompey should have pooped the party by half-time. Alas, they had only Bradbury's header to show. After a rollicking, Charlton came back strongly and Stuart loops home a leveller, then Hoult makes two fine stops."

44. H MANCHESTER C
Portsmouth: Hoult, Weaver, Edinburgh^, Derry*, Myers, Moore, Harper, Thogersen, Allen", Bradbury, Hughes — Awford/Crowe
Man City: Weaver, Edgehill, Tiatto, Pollack, Prior, Jobson, Whitley, Wiekens", Taylor", Goater, Kennedy" — Dickov/Horlock/Granville
Scorers: Bradbury 45p, 84; Prior 26, Taylor 40
Ref: P Alcock (Halstead)
"City's promotion hopes are stalled by their former boo-boy B(r)adbu(r)y. First he converts a dodgy pen, then nets Hughes' pin-point cross. 'The problem was the ref, not Pompey,' said City boss Joe Royle. Earlier, City were strutting after Prior's header and Taylor's near-post flick."

45. A WALSALL
Portsmouth: Hoult, Walker, Waterman^, Awford, Myers, Moore, Harper, Thogersen, Allen^, Bradbury, Hughes — Crowe/Whitbread/Night'gale
Walsall: Walker, Marsh, Bennett, Viveash, Roper, Keates, Hall, Rammell, Fenton^, Matias, Wrack
Scorer: Matias 12
Ref: M Halsey (Welwyn G City)
"Moore's mistake leads to Matias firing home as his side re-organise after Awford's early knee injury. Pompey clearly have their minds on their holidays, but Walsall are fighting for their lives and dominate throughout. Harper saw a shot pushed onto the bar in a late, but futile, push."

46. H QP RANGERS
Portsmouth: Hoult, Whitbread, Edinburgh, Derry, Myers, Moore, Harper, Thogersen, Allen, Bradbury, Hughes — Murray/Gallen/Kulscar
QP Rangers: Harper, Ready, Plummer, Baraclough, Perry*, Bruce", Wardley, Peacock, Langley, Kiwomya", Koeje
Scorers: Allen 53; Langley 31, Gallen 88, Myers 90 (og)
Ref: C Foy (St Helens)
"Two careless late goals punctured optimism for next season. First Gallen cut in and fired past Hoult, then Myers turned Koeje's cross into his own net. It was harsh on Pompey, who deservedly levelled when Allen clipped home Thogersen's cross. Langley's 25-yarder was top notch."

NATIONWIDE DIVISION 1 (CUP-TIES)   Manager: Alan Ball ⇨ Tony Pulis   SEASON 1999-2000

Worthington Cup

		Att		F-A	H-T	Scorers, Times, and Referees	1	2	3	4	5	6	7	8	9	10	11	subs used
1:1	A TORQUAY 17/8	3,209	D 3	0-0	0-0	Ref: D Crick (Worcester Park)	Flahavan *Southall*	Crowe *Tully*	Robinson ! *Herrara^*	Thogersen *Russell*	Whitbread *Watson*	Vlachos *Aggrey*	Newton* *Platts* *	Igoe *Bedeau*	Nightingale *Williams*	Lovell" *Brandon*	Phillips^ *O'Brien*	Migioranzi/Simpson/Allen *Hill/Simb*

Ball rotates his squad, but gets away with it. £250,000 Lovell, signed from Bournemouth, hits a post and, with strike partner Nightingale, their combined age is less than 41-year-old veteran Gulls' keeper Southall. Even when Robinson walks after two yellows, Pompey are in control.

| 1:2 | H TORQUAY 24/8 | 8,241 | W 3:5 | 3-0 | 2-0 | Nightingale 2, 55, Lovell 27 | Flahavan" *Southall* | Crowe *Tully * * | Simpson *Herrara* | Thogersen *Russell* | Awford *Watson* | Vlachos *Aggrey* | Newton* *Healy* | Igoe *Bedeau* | Nightingale *Williams* | Lovell^ *Brandon* | Phillips *O'Brien* | Robinson/Durnin/Knight *Simb/Platts* |

| | | | | | | Ref: L Cable (Woking) | | | | | | | | | | | | |
| | | | | | | (Pompey win 3-0 on aggregate) | | | | | | | | | | | | |

Despite playing seven players under 23, Pompey cruised. Igoe played in Nightingale after 67 seconds and he fired across Southall, then ref Cable inadvertently set up Lovell to crash home the second. Nightingale's volley settled it, then 'Legend' Knight made appearance 799 late on.

| 2:1 | H BLACKBURN 14/9 | 8,542 | L 15 | 0-3 | 0-0 | Cundy 59 (og), Jansen 73, 78 | Flahavan^ *Kelly* | Crowe *Kenna* | Robinson *Davidson* | McLoughlin *Peacock* | Whitbread* *Dailly* | Cundy *Gill* | Migioranzi *Dunn* | Thogersen *Johnson * * | Panopoulos *Gillespie^* | Whittingham *Blake* | Péron" *Ward* | Pamarot/Petterson/Claridge *Jansen/Harkness* |

| | | | | | | Ref: B Knight (Orpington) | | | | | | | | | | | | |

The result is overshadowed by Flahavan's second fainting fit in a year. Blake earns praise for helping the stricken keeper rather than scoring. After that it all fell apart. Cundy inadvertently headed past sub Petterson, then £4.1 million Matt Jansen scored a classy second and brave third.

| 2:2 | A BLACKBURN 23/9 | 7,512 | L 12 | 1-3 | 1-0 | McLoughlin 7 | Petterson" *Kelly* | Robinson *Kenna* | Simpson *Peacock* | McLoughlin *Harkness * * | Awford *Taylor* | Vlachos *Duff"* | Panopoulos *Dunn* | Migioranzi *Gill* | Durnin* *Gillespie^* | Whitting'm* *Blake* | Péron *Ostenstad* | Igoe/Lovell/Knight *Gallagher/Johnson/Grayson* |

						Duff 59, Dunn 64, Gallagher 90												
						Ref: G Frankland (Middlesbro')												
						(Pompey lose 1-6 on aggregate)												

For an hour there was hope. After McLoughlin side-footed in. Provider Panopoulos hit the bar, but once Panopoulos bundled the ball in, the question was: 'When will Ball bring him on?' After 83 minutes Knight replaced Petterson for his 800th appearance to a standing ovation on all sides.

FA Cup

| 3 | A SUNDERLAND 11/12 | 26,535 | L P:4 | 0-1 | 0-1 | McCann 24 | Flahavan *Sorensen* | Hiley *Makin* | Robinson *Gray* | Moore^ *Bould* | Cundy *Butler* | Panopoul's ! *Summerbee* | Migioranzi* *Roy* * | Awford *McCann* | Vlachos *Schwarz* | Whittingham *Phillips* | Bradbury *Quinn* | Claridge/Crowe *Thirwell* |

| | | | | | | Ref: N Barry (Scunthorpe) | | | | | | | | | | | | |

Caretaker Bob McNab is in charge, in the wake of Ball's sacking, and at least Pompey put up a fight, even if they don't have a shot. The only goal is poked home by McCann after Schwarz's strong run. Panopoulos's dismissal for a bad foul on half-time ends any hopes of a comeback.

League table

	Team	P	Home W	D	L	F	A	Away W	D	L	F	A	Pts
1	Charlton	46	15	3	5	37	18	12	7	4	42	27	91
2	Manchester C	46	17	2	4	48	17	9	5	9	30	23	89
3	Ipswich*	46	16	3	4	39	17	9	9	5	32	25	87
4	Barnsley	46	15	4	4	48	24	9	6	8	40	43	82
5	Birmingham	46	15	3	5	37	16	7	8	8	28	28	77
6	Bolton	46	14	5	4	43	26	6	8	10	26	24	76
7	Wolves	46	15	5	3	45	20	6	6	11	19	28	74
8	Huddersfield	46	14	5	4	43	21	7	6	10	19	28	74
9	Fulham	46	13	7	3	33	13	6	9	10	16	28	67
10	QP Rangers	46	10	9	4	30	20	9	6	10	32	33	66
11	Blackburn	46	9	9	4	33	20	6	10	11	22	31	62
12	Norwich	46	11	6	6	26	22	5	9	11	19	28	57
13	Tranmere	46	10	4	5	35	27	5	4	14	22	41	57
14	Nott'm For	46	10	10	4	29	18	5	4	14	24	37	56
15	Crystal Pal	46	7	11	5	29	26	6	4	13	24	41	54
16	Sheffield Utd	46	10	8	7	38	24	3	7	13	21	47	54
17	Stockport	46	8	8	7	33	31	5	7	11	22	36	54
18	**PORTSMOUTH**	46	8	6	8	36	27	4	6	13	19	39	51
19	Crewe	46	9	5	8	27	31	5	6	14	19	36	51
20	Grimsby	46	10	8	9	27	25	5	4	16	14	36	51
21	West Brom	46	6	11	6	25	26	5	8	11	18	34	49
22	Walsall	46	7	6	10	26	34	4	7	12	26	43	46
23	Port Vale	46	6	6	11	27	30	1	9	13	21	39	36
24	Swindon	46	5	6	12	23	37	3	6	14	15	40	36
		1104	260	159	133	821	570	133	159	260	570	821	1497

* promoted after play-offs

Odds & ends

Double wins: (0).

Double losses: (2) Grimsby, Fulham.

Won from behind: (4) Walsall (h), C Palace (h), Nott'm For (h), Norwich (h).

Lost from in front: (4) Man C (a), West Brom (a), Blackburn (h), Wolves (h).

High spots: Beating Walsall 5-1 in October.

Steve Claridge's hat-trick against high-flying Barnsley at home in January.

Four consecutive wins in March to avoid relegation.

Low spots: Aaron Flahavan collapsing in the goalmouth, for the second time in 12 months, against Blackburn in September.

More than eleven hours without a goal November-December.

14 matches without a league win November-January.

Losing 1-2 at home to ten-man Grimsby in September.

Player of the Season: Steve Claridge.

Ever presents: (0).

Hat-tricks: (2) Steve Claridge, Lee Bradbury.

Leading Scorer: Steve Claridge (14).

Appearances and Goals

Player	Lge	Sub	LC	Sub	FAC	Sub	Goals Lge	LCFAC	Tot
Allen, Rory	10	5		1			3		3
Awford, Andy	28	6	2	1		1	1		1
Bernsten, Tommy	1	1							
Birmingham, Dave	1	1				1			
Bradbury, Lee	35			1		1	10		10
Brown, Michael	4								
Claridge, Steve	31	3	3	1		1	14		14
Crowe, Jason	21	4	3	1		1			
Cundy, Jason	9								
Derry, Shaun	9		1				1		1
Durnin, John	2		1	1					
Edinburgh, Justin	11								
Fenton, Anthony		1							
Flahavan, Aaron	10		3						
Harper, Kevin	12	4			1		2		2
Hiley, Scott	4	4				1			
Hoult, Russell	18								
Hughes, Ceri	15								
Igoe, Sammy	14	12	2	1		1	2		2
Knight, Alan	1		2	2		1	1		1
Lovell, Steve		3	2	1				1	1
McLoughlin, Alan	18	1	2	2		1	5	1	6
Migliorazzi, Stefani	12	1	2	1		1	2		2
Moore, Darren	25		2			1	1		1
Myers, Andy	4	4							
Newton, Adam	1	2	2						
Nightingale, Luke	1	6	2					2	2
O'Neil, Gary		1							
Pamarot, Noë	1	1		1					
Panopoulos, Mike	18	4	2			1	1		1
Péron, 'Jeff'	9	1	2	1			2		2
Petterson, Andy	17		1	1					
Phillips, Martin	2	5	2	2		1			
Robinson, Matt	23	2	3	2	1	1			
Simpson, Fitzroy	17		2	1			5		5
Thogersen, Thomas	32	3	3	3					
Vernazza, Paolo	7								
Vlachos, Michalis	11	1	3		1				
Waterman, David	19	1	1						
Whittingham, Adrian	38		2		1				
Whittingham, Guy	15	10	2	1		2	4		4
41 players used	506	84	44	11	11	2	55	4	59

NATIONWIDE LEAGUE DIVISION 1

Manager: Pulis ⇒ Claridge ⇒ Graham Rix   **SEASON 2000-01**

Match details

No	Venue	Date	Opponent	Att	Pos (Pompey/Opp)	Pt	Res	F-A	H-T	Scorers (Pompey / Opponent)	Referee
1	A	12/8	SHEFFIELD UNITED	15,816	–	0	L	0-2	0-1	— / Devlin 13p, Primus 81 (og)	D Pugh (Bebington)
2	H	19/8	GRIMSBY	12,511	20 / 16	1	D	1-1	0-0	Bradbury 72 / Smith D 84	R Beeby (Northampton)
3	A	25/8	GILLINGHAM	8,741	19 / 22	2	D	1-1	0-1	Moore 68 / Thomson 6	P Danson (Leicester)
4	H	28/8	WOLVERHAMPTON	14,124	10 / 15	5	W	3-1	3-1	Claridge 3, 30, 33p / Ketsbaia 45	A Butler (Sutton-in-Ashf'ld)
5	A	2/9	PRESTON	13,343	15 / 4	5	L	0-1	0-0	— / Basham 46	W Burns (Scarborough)
6	H	9/9	WATFORD	14,012	18 / 2	5	L	1-3	0-2	Quashie 75 / Nielsen 26, Mooney 44, Helguson 59	M Brandwood (Lichfield)
7	H	12/9	TRANMERE	9,235	10 / 7	8	W	2-0	0-0	Mills 81, Bradbury 86 / —	P Alcock (Halstead)
8	A	16/9	BOLTON	14,113	15 / 3	8	L	0-2	0-1	— / Holdsworth 43, Ricketts 85	M Jones (Chester)
9	H	23/9	WEST BROM	11,937	16 / 6	8	L	0-1	0-0	— / Roberts 57	D Crick (Worcester Park)
10	A	30/9	BURNLEY	15,494	18 / 10	9	D	1-1	0-0	Claridge 72 / Weller 88	R Pearson (Peterlee)
11	A	8/10	STOCKPORT	6,212	17 / 20	10	D	1-1	1-0	Mills 15 / Cooper 88	P Joslin (Newark)

Line-ups (positions 1–11) and substitutes used

Match	Team	1	2	3	4	5	6	7	8	9	10	11	subs used
1	Pompey	Hoult	Derry	Awford*	Primus	Edinburgh	Harper	Thogersen	Curtis	Hughes	Bradbury	Mills	Wat'man/Quashie/Rudonja
1	Sheff Utd	Tracey	Uhlenbeek	Weber	Brown^	Murphy	Santos	Devlin	Ford	Bent	Kelly^	Quinn	Woodhouse/Newby
2	Pompey	Hoult	Waterman	Moore	Primus	Edinburgh	Quashie	Derry	Thogersen	Hughes^	Bradbury	Mills*	O'Neil/Claridge
2	Grimsby	Coyne	McDermott	Gallimore	Donovan	Livingstone	Raven	Smith D	Groves	Jeffrey^	Coldicott*	Pouton	Allen/Clare
3	Pompey	Hoult	Derry	Moore	Primus	Edinburgh	O'Neil*	Curtis	Thogersen	Quashie	Bradbury*	Mills	Claridge/Rudonja
3	Gillingham	Bartram	Patterson*	Edge	Ashby	Butters	Hessenthal'r^	Asaba	Gooden*	Hope	Browning	Thomson"	Southall/Lewis/James
4	Pompey	Hoult	Derry	Moore	Primus	Edinburgh	Harper^	Curtis	Thogersen	Quashie	Claridge	Mills^	O'Neil/Bradbury/Waterman
4	Wolves	Oakes	Muscat	Naylor	Thetis	Lescott	Bazeley^	Emblem	Sedgley^	Camara	Ndah"	Ketsbaia	Robinson/Osborn/Taylor
5	Pompey	Hoult	Derry	Moore	Primus	Edinburgh	O'Neil*	Curtis	Thogersen^	Quashie	Claridge	Mills	Bradbury/Waterman
5	Preston	Moilanen	Alexander	Edwards	Gregan	Jackson	Anderson*	Appleton	Rankine	McKenna^	Macken	Basham"	Cartwright/Robinson/Eyres
6	Pompey	Hoult	Lambourde	Moore	Primus^	Edinburgh	Quashie	Derry	Rudonja^	Thogersen	Claridge	Mills	Bradbury/Hughes
6	Watford	Baardsen	Cox	Page	Palmer	Ward	Gibbs	Mooney	Nielsen	Smith	Helguson^	N'l-Williams^	Foley
7	Pompey	Hoult	Lambourde	Moore	Primus	Edinburgh	Quashie	Derry	Thogersen^	Bradbury	Claridge	Mills^	Rudonja
7	Tranmere	Achterberg	Challinor	Hill	Henry^	Allison	Rideout	Flynn^	Yates	Hinds	Hazell!	Taylor^	Parkinson/Barlow/Morgan
8	Pompey	Hoult	Lambourde	Moore	Primus	Edinburgh	Quashie	Derry	Thogersen	Hughes^	Bradbury	Mills	Claridge
8	Bolton	Jaaskelain'n	O'Kane	Bergsson	Fish^	Frandsen	Hansen	Holdsworth*	Barness	Farrelly	Passi	Rankin^	Ricketts/Marshall/Nolan
9	Pompey	Hoult	Lambourde	Moore	Waterman*	Edinburgh	Van Blerk	Derry	Fox*	Keller!	Bradbury	Mills	Claridge/Rudonja
9	West Brom	Jensen	Clement	Butler	Chambers	Lyttle	Van Blerk	Jaardao	Fox	McInnes	Hughes	Roberts^	Sneekes/Taylor
10	Pompey	Hoult	Lambourde	Waterman	Moore	Edinburgh	Keller*	Derry	Thogersen	Quashie	Mills	Claridge^	Harper
10	Burnley	Michapoulos	Thomas"	Davis	Cox	Little	Briscoe	Mellon	Ball	Cook^	Payton	Cooke^	Branch/Weller/Jepson
11	Pompey	Hoult	Lambourde	Moore	Primus	Edinburgh	Quashie	Derry	Thogersen	Quashie^	Mills*	Claridge	Bradbury/Harper/Waterman
11	Stockport	Nash	Connolly	Nicholson	Flynn	Tod	Gibb^	Smith	Clark	Cooper	Moore	Lawson^	Matthews/Wilbraham

Match reports

1. Edinburgh protests he got the ball for Blades early pen, then new-boy Mills misses Pompey's best chance, one-on-one with Tracey. The second is comical. From Derry's bad back-pass, Devlin miscues and Primus slices into his own net. Awford's neck injury looked worse than it was.

2. Pompey look like a team of strangers as they labour to break down Town. The arrival of O'Neil finally sparks things and Bradbury poaches a close-range header from Derry's long throw. Smith's late volleyed equaliser is a quality strike, but means the natives are restless at the end.

3. Tony Pulis's reunion with Gills' Chairman Paul Scally passes off peacefully. After Thomson's close-range header, Pompey are in control. It finally pays when Edinburgh crosses for Moore to lash home at the far post. Mills then sees a header well saved, but Hoult's late stop is vital.

4. A half-hour hat-trick enhances the Claridge cult. First he nods home a near-post corner, then he sidefoots home at the far post from another flag kick. The third is a penalty after Muscat trips O'Neil. Super Steve will sign a new three-year deal this week. Ketsbaia's shot kept Wolves in it.

5. It's back to square one for Pulis as passionless Pompey subside tamely. The only real excitement comes either side of half-time. Mills seems to be fouled by Gregan in the box, but the ref waves play on — 'a disgrace' says Pulis. Then ex-Saint Basham's shot loops over Hoult off Moore.

6. Pompey look well-beaten, but they could have easily drawn. Rudonja hit the bar with a swerving shot before Thogersen's slip let Nielsen in to score. Then Primus did likewise, only for Mooney to volley in just after. Helguson's header sealed it, but a Quashie 20-yarder restored pride.

7. Loanee Lambourde's claim that Pompey are good is given credibility, but they left it late. Hazell's dismissal on half-time for a lunge is harsh, but it takes the arrival of Rudonja to stretch Rovers. Quashie sets up Mills to coolly finish, then Bradbury sweeps home Derry's deflected shot.

8. A fuel crisis means just 300 Blues' fans head north, including the News reporter. 'What a waste of petrol,' sang Bolton's fans as Lambourde's slip let in Holdsworth to angle home, then sub Ricketts profited from an overstretched back line. Until the first goal, Pompey were in control.

9. £2 million Roberts turns in a cross with his knee for his first goal, leaving Pompey in crisis. The ex-Bristol Rover turned down a Fratton move in August. 'He was in talks here for 12 hours. That's a lot of talking,' says Pulis enigmatically. Latest loanee Keller goes close with a curler.

10. Moore boots the ball away in frustration at the end as two points are thrown away. Quashie, Mills and Thogersen all missed good chances. In a frantic finale Burnley almost snatched it. Weller's deflected shot left Blues in a jam, after Claridge's footwork let him fire under the keeper.

11. For the third straight game Pompey concede late on. Things looked great as Mills thumped home a cross shot, but then it all went wrong, after he was stretchered off with a serious knee injury. Chances went begging and Pompey paid when Cooper fired home from the edge of the area.

Portsmouth — Match-by-Match (Nationwide League)

No.		Opponent	Date	Att.	Pos	Res	Score	HT	Opp Pos	Pts
12	H	SHEFFIELD WED	14/10	13,376	13	W	2-1	1-0	24	13
13	H	CREWE	17/10	14,621	10	W	2-1	0-0	20	16
14	A	CRYSTAL PALACE	21/10	15,693	10	W	3-2	1-2	22	19
15	A	NORWICH	24/10	18,772	9	D	0-0	0-0	17	20
16	H	BIRMINGHAM	28/10	15,218	11	D	1-1	1-0	3	21
17	A	QP RANGERS	4/11	12,036	11	D	1-1	0-1	20	22
18	H	BLACKBURN	11/11	14,141	11	D	2-2	1-1	6	23
19	A	FULHAM	18/11	19,005	12	L	1-3	1-1	1	23
20	A	BARNSLEY	25/11	12,853	13	L	0-1	0-0	12	23
21	H	NORWICH	2/12	13,409	12	W	2-0	1-0	20	26
22	A	NOTT'M FOREST	9/12	19,284	13	L	0-2	0-1	6	26
23	H	HUDDERSFIELD	16/12	12,041	13	D	1-1	0-1	24	27

---

12 — H SHEFFIELD WED, 14/10 (W 2-1)
Thogersen 25, Claridge 48, Morrison 66
Ref: D Gallagher (Banbury)

Portsmouth: Hoult, Hiley, Edinburgh, Primus, Moore, Harper*, Derry, Thogersen, Quashie, Bradbury, Claridge^, Panopoulos/Nightingale
Sheffield Wed: Stringer^, Haslam, Harkness, Walker, Hendon, Quinn, O'Donnell, Lescott, Stockdale", Humphreys, Morrison, Di Piedi/Pressman/Cooke

A tumultuous week, as Claridge succeeds the 'on sabbatical' Pulis as caretaker player-boss, ends on a high. In a fairy-tale twist he heads the decisive goal. Thogersen's side-foot from close range left the keeper stranded, but young Morrison's fine finish caused some late jitters again.

13 — H CREWE, 17/10 (W 2-1)
Thogersen 66, Claridge 80p; Smith 59p
Ref: S Tomlin (Lewes)

Portsmouth: Hoult, Hiley, Edinburgh, Primus, Moore*, Harper*, Derry, Thogersen, Quashie, Bradbury*, Claridge, Waterman/Nightingale
Crewe: Kearton, Maybury, Smith, Walton, Wright, Lumsdon, Lunt*, Rivers, Sorvel, Jack, Tait, Sodje

A rogue rat stopped play in the closing minutes, only to be brutally kicked to death by a fan, but Pompey are far from a sinking ship. Claridge converted a pen after Edinburgh was fouled. Thogersen's cross-shot had levelled after Hiley tripped Jack.

14 — A CRYSTAL PALACE, 21/10 (W 3-2)
Claridge 45, Thogersen 59; Black 36, 41
Ref: P Durkin (Portland)

Portsmouth: Hoult, Hiley, Edinburgh, Primus, Moore*, Harper*, Derry, Thogersen, Quashie, Bradbury", Claridge, Panopoulos 80|/Nightingale
Crystal Palace: Kolinko, Smith, Harrison^, Morrison A, Stanton, Black, Pollock, Mullins, Rubens, Forsell", Morrison C, Carlisle/Rodger

Pompey seem dead and buried when Black curls home from 30 yards, then pokes home a second. In first-half injury-time Claridge pounced on Kolinko's error, then Thogersen headed home Hughes' cross. Panopoulos volleyed in Quashie's centre to send 2,500 travelling fans wild.

15 — A NORWICH, 24/10 (D 0-0)
Ref: P Taylor (Cheshunt)

Portsmouth: Hoult, Hiley, Edinburgh, Primus, Moore, Harper*, Derry, Thogersen, Quashie, Bradbury*, Claridge, Hughes*/Miglioranzi/Nightingale
Norwich: Marshall A, Kenton", Derveld^, Mackay, Fleming, Sutch, Mulryne, Marshall L, Llewellyn, Cottee*, Roberts, Dalglish/Russell/McGovern

Veteran striker Cottee spawns a host of chances and 'pays back' Claridge for all the lifts he gave him when the pair trained together while at Leicester. The worst is nine minutes before half-time, when he fires wide with just Hoult to beat. Pompey rarely threaten, but are worth a point.

16 — H BIRMINGHAM, 28/10 (D 1-1)
Bradbury 41; Adebola 48
Ref: M Halsey (Welwyn G City)

Portsmouth: Hoult, Hiley, Edinburgh^, Primus*, Moore, Harper*, Derry, Thogersen, Quashie, Bradbury, Claridge, Miglioranzi/Waterman
Birmingham: Bennett, Eaden, Grainger, Purse, Holdsworth, Marcelo^, O'Connor^, Gill, Johnson M, Johnson A", Sonner, Adebola/Burchill/Hughes

Pompey more than matched high-flying Brum at a rain-soaked Fratton. Bradbury headed home Hughes'' corner then Grainger's pen was tipped onto the bar by Hoult. At once, sub Adebola glanced home a near-post free-kick, then Thogersen was denied at the death by an offside flag.

17 — A QP RANGERS, 4/11 (D 1-1)
Bradbury 50; Peschisolido 9
Ref: E Wolstenholme (Blackb'n)

Portsmouth: Hoult, Hiley, Edinburgh, Primus", Moore, Harper, Derry, Thogersen, Quashie, Bradbury, Claridge, Awford/Waterman
QP Rangers: Harper, Carlisle, Rose, Broomes, Breacker, Warren, Langley, Peacock, Connolly", Crouch, Wardley, Peschisolido

Peschisolido fired home after Pompey fail to clear Peacock's cross, but the team comes out fighting. Miglioranzi slots in well, despite losing a contact lens, then Bradbury forced home Hughes'' cross. Claridge's late header might have won it, but Hoult is lucky to stay on for a rash foul.

18 — H BLACKBURN, 11/11 (D 2-2)
Quashie 44, Panopoulos 61; Bjornebye 45, Jansen 82
Ref: P Walton (Long Buckby)

Portsmouth: Hoult, Hiley, Edinburgh, Primus, Moore, Harper, Derry, Thogersen, Quashie, Panopoulos*, Claridge, Bradbury
Blackburn: Filan, Curtis, Short, Bery, Bjonebye, Johnson^, Hignett, Flitcroft, Dunn, Ostenstad*, Hughes, Jansen/Dailly

Blackburn may have cost £17 million, but Pompey deserve a win. Quashie's vicious 25-yarder is cancelled out at once by Bjonebye's disputed free-kick. Pano turned in Thogersen's cross, but sub Jansen found a gap to level late on. Bradbury's last-gasp shot just went agonisingly over.

19 — A FULHAM, 18/11 (L 1-3)
Claridge 12; Hayles 11, 69, Clark 80
Ref: K Hill (Royston)

Portsmouth: Hoult, Hiley, Edinburgh^, Primus !, Moore, Harper*, Derry*, Thogersen, Quashie, Hughes !, Claridge, Waterman
Fulham: Taylor, Finnan, Brevett, Melville, Coleman, Goldbaek^, Davis^, Clark, Fernandes, Saha, Hayles, Boa Morte/Salhoun

'The ref got a lot of things mixed up,' says Primus diplomatically, after he seemed to win the ball. Then Hughes sees more justifiably. A Pompey fan throws a snooker ball at the linesman. After that Hayles, then Clark, give Fulham a flattering win.

20 — A BARNSLEY, 25/11 (L 0-1)
Dyer 58
Ref: T Parkes (Birmingham)

Portsmouth: Hoult, Hiley, Edinburgh", Primus*, Moore, Harper*, Derry, Thogersen, Quashie, Hughes*, Claridge, Nightingale
Barnsley: Miller, O'Callaghan, Barker, Chettle, Morgan, Ripley, Neil^, Ward, Corbo*, Sheron, Dyer, Barnard/Thomas

Hoult makes a hash of trying to shepherd the ball out for a goal-kick as Dyer robs him and finishes spectacularly. Quashie claims he should have had a pen and saw a free-kick well saved, but Pompey are below par. 'It was the worst performance since I've been boss,' said Claridge.

21 — H NORWICH, 2/12 (W 2-0)
Panopoulos 13, Quashie 57
Ref: U Rennie (Sheffield)

Portsmouth: Hoult, Hiley, Edinburgh*, Primus, Moore, Harper*, Derry, Thogersen, Quashie, Panopoulos*, Claridge, Bradbury/Nightingale
Norwich: Marshall A, Sutch, Derveld*, Fleming, Mackay, Forbes^, Mulryne*, Russell, Llewellyn, Notman, Roberts, Marshall L/de Blasiis/Coote

'If you don't buy a ticket you can't win the raffle,' says Quashie of his 30-yard wonder strike. It sealed the game after Pano's fine volley. Then Bradbury saw a shot turned onto a post, then was subbed with a urinary infection. 'At half-time I just needed to get to the toilet,' he confessed.

22 — A NOTT'M FOREST, 9/12 (L 0-2)
Scimeca 12, Bart-Williams 63
Ref: M Jones (Chester)

Portsmouth: Hoult, Hiley, Crowe, Edinburgh^, Moore, Harper*, Derry !, Thogersen, Quashie, Panopoulos*, Claridge, Nightingale
Nott'm Forest: Beasant, Edwards, B'rt-Williams, Vaughan, Olsen, Foy, Scimeca !, Upson^, Prutton, Lester*, Reid, Harewood/John

Pompey dominate, but miss their chances. Claridge is denied a clear pen and Nightingale fires over from 10 yards, then hits the bar with a chip late on, but Forest are cruising as Scimeca side-footed home, then Bart-Williams curled home a free-kick. Derry walks for two yellows.

23 — H HUDDERSFIELD, 16/12 (D 1-1)
Claridge 77; Dyson 40
Ref: P Rejer (Droitwich Spa)

Portsmouth: Flahavan, Hiley, Crowe, Moore, Hughes, Harper, Derry, Thogersen, Quashie, Panopoulos*Quashie, Claridge, Bradbury/Harper
Huddersfield: Vaesen, Heary, Gray, Vincent, Dyson, Baldry, Armstrong, Holland, Nдlovu, Thornley, Gallen/Nдlovu, Gorre/Sellars

Flavs got a 25th birthday gift when Claridge picked him. He produced a vital one-on-one save as Thornley bore down on goal after Dyson had earlier headed in a corner. Claridge's clever header saved a barely merited point, then Bradbury saw Vaesen clutch his late header on the line.

No	Date		Att	Pos	Pt	F-A	H-T	Scorers, Times, and Referees
24	23/12	H SHEFFIELD UTD	13,606	12 / 10	D 28	0-0	0-0	Ref: A D'Urso (Billericay)
25	26/12	A WIMBLEDON	9,245	14 / 11	D 29	1-1	1-0	Claridge 45; Francis 49; Ref: L Cable (Woking)
26	1/1	H GILLINGHAM	14,526	14 / 13	D 30	0-0	0-0	Ref: M Brandwood (Lichfield)
27	13/1	A WOLVERHAMPTON	20,869	15 / 12	D 31	1-1	1-1	Lescott 27 (og); Sinton 20; Ref: B Curson (Hinckley)
28	20/1	H WIMBLEDON	12,488	12 / 11	W 34	2-1	2-1	Bradbury 16p, Quashie 28; Euell 20; Ref: S Baines (Chesterfield)
29	27/1	A GRIMSBY	4,128	13 / 18	L 34	1-2	0-2	Bradbury 72; Donovan 17, Livingstone 20; Ref: M Pike (Barrow-in-Furness)
30	3/2	H PRESTON	13,331	14 / 9	L 34	0-1	0-1	Healy 26; Ref: F Stretton (Nottingham)
31	10/2	A WATFORD	16,051	16 / 5	D 35	2-2	2-2	Quashie 39, Claridge 45; Smith 13, 17; Ref: B Knight (Orpington)
32	13/2	H BOLTON	11,337	16 / 2	L 35	1-2	0-0	Panopoulos 89; Ricketts 50, Hansen 70; Ref: M Fletcher (Wolverley)
33	24/2	A WEST BROM	17,645	17 / 5	L 35	0-2	0-1	Roberts 10, Chambers 69; Ref: H Webb (Rotherham)
34	3/3	H BURNLEY	12,941	16 / 10	W 38	2-0	0-0	Nightingale 56, Panopoulos 69p; Ref: N Barry (Scunthorpe)

Line-ups (Portsmouth top line; opponents in italics below; subs used at right)

24 — SHEFFIELD UTD:
Flahavan, Crowe, Moore, Hiley*, Hughes, Panopoulos, Quashie, Thogersen, Miglioranzi, Claridge, Bradbury
Tracey, Kozluk, Quinn, Sandford, Murphy, Brown, Woodhouse^Devlin, Ford, Suffo^, Montgom'y^'Kelly/Santos/Curle, Vine
subs used: Vine
"Unsettled keeper Hoult could be off to West Brom as he is left out again. Miglioranzi went closest, but Tracey tipped over, then Flavs was alert late on to block Quinn's fierce shot. Pompey passed the ball well enough, but even the introduction of teen striker Vine couldn't harvest a goal."

25 — WIMBLEDON:
Flahavan, Crowe, Moore, Hiley, Hughes^, Panopoulos, Quashie, Thogersen, Derry, Claridge, Bradbury*
Davis, Holloway, Hawkins, Williams, Gier, Francis, Roberts, Ardley, Agyemang^ Euell, Gayle
subs used: Harper/Whittingham; Gayle
"Claridge's speculative lob from an outrageous angle on the stroke of half-time was no fluke, he insists. 'It is up there with the best I've scored.' Ardley then pulled back a cross for Francis to deservedly level. The crater-strewn mess of a Selhurst Park pitch didn't help the game at all."

26 — GILLINGHAM:
Flahavan, Crowe, Moore, Hiley, Harper, Panopoulos^Miglioranzi^, Quashie, Thogersen, Derry, Claridge, Bradbury^
Bartram, Ashby, Pennock, Hope, Southall, Smith, Edge, Saunder, Lewis, Asaba", Shaw^*
subs used: Nightingale/Harper/Rudonja; Hessenthaler/Onoura/King
"A combination of the icy weather calling the game off at Grimsby and the fact the training ground is shut for the hols means Pompey haven't kicked a ball for a week. It shows with a dismal display against Gills. Bartram is only called into real action once, turning Derry's header aside."

27 — WOLVERHAMPTON:
Flahavan, Crowe*, Moore, Hiley, Harper, Miglioranzi, Quashie, Thogersen, Hughes, Bradbury, Nightingale
Oakes, Muscat, Naylor, Lescott, Dinning, Robinson, Osborn, Andrews^, Proudlock, Sinton^, Branch
subs used: Waterman/Rudonja; Ketsbaia/Emblen
"It's now just one win in 14, but this was close to another one. Moore is harshly penalised as he heads in soon after Lescott had made a hash of Migliorani's cross. Sinton had earlier swept Wolves ahead. Muscat missed a late pen, answering Migsy's prayers after his foul on Emblen."

28 — WIMBLEDON:
Flahavan, Crowe^, Moore, Hiley, Harper, Miglioranzi, Quashie, Thogersen, Hughes*, Bradbury, Nightingale^
Davis, Hawkins, Kimble, Blackwell, Williams, Ainsworth, Francis, Andersen, Karlsson, Hartson, Euell*
subs used: Nightingale^Claridge/Waterman/Rudonja; Gayle
"Quashie pulled out another top-draw long-range finish and earned the penalty converted by Bradbury after being chopped down by Williams. In between, Euell profited from Moore's poor pass. Hughes' inside info on his old club's set-piece routines proved vital in defending the lead."

29 — GRIMSBY:
Flahavan, Crowe, Moore, Hiley, Harper*, Miglioranzi, Quashie, Thogersen, Hughes^, Bradbury, Nightingale
*Coyne, McDermott, Smith, Groves, Enhua, Donovan, Willems, Burnett, Campbell, Livingstone, Jeffrey**
subs used: Panopoulos/Derry/Claridge; Pouton
"Pompey pay for a pitiful opening. Donovan lashed home a rebound off a defender, then Livingstone's presumably easy finish from two yards followed Flav's handling error. Bradbury's neat finish was too little, too late. 'I think we're better than we are,' lamented Hughes."

30 — PRESTON:
Flahavan, Crowe, Moore, Hiley, Panopoulos, Miglioranzi*, Quashie, Derry, Sharpe^, Bradbury!, Claridge^
*Moilanen, Cartwright, Murdock, Jackson, Edwards, McKenna, Rankine, Parkinson, McBride, Macken^, Healy^*
subs used: Thogersen/Rudonja; Barry-Murphy/Gumhaugbs on
"Sharpe debuted, but failed to inspire as his lack of fitness told. After the classy Healy drove home, Preston controlled it and Flavs made several saves to keep the score down. Blues wanted a pen when Jackson handled, but the ref refused. Late on Bradbury kicked Murdock and saw red."

31 — WATFORD:
Flahavan, Crowe*, Moore, Hiley, Panopoulos, Miglioranzi*, Quashie, Derry, Sharpe, Bradbury, Claridge
Chamberlain, Panayi, Robinson, Page, Ward, Nielsen, Vernazza, Palmer, Kennedy, Smith, Helguson*
subs used: Bradbury; Hyde
"Helguson's late header bounced over an open goal to preserve a point for Pompey. Earlier Vernazza's one-two with the ref set up Smith for the first, who then nodded the second from a throw. Quashie glanced home Sharpe's corner, before Claridge pounced on Panayi's poor clearance."

32 — BOLTON:
Flahavan, Crowe, Waterman, Hiley, Panopoulos, Quashie, Thogersen, Derry, Miglioranzi, Sharpe, Claridge
Banks, O'Kane, Bergsson, Hendry, Elliott, Nolan, Farrelly, Frandsen, Hansen, Gardner, Ricketts**
subs used: Mills; Marshall^/Barnes/Passi
"Furious Pompey claimed a late-late pen as Bergsson seemed to punch Hiley's cross, but ref Fletcher was unmoved. Pano had given Blues hope with a 30-yarder. Ricketts got lucky as Crowe's clearance fell kindly to him off Quashie, then Hansen swept in. Mills' arrival livened things."

33 — WEST BROM:
Flahavan, Crowe, Waterman, Derry*, Vincent, Moore, Panopoulos^, Thogersen^, Mills, Nightingale^Sharpe, Claridge
Hoult, Clement, Butler, Carbon, Fox, Sneekes, Taylor, Roberts", Sigurdsson, Chambers, Appleton
subs used: Miglior'zi/Claridge/Thog'sen; Quinn
"48 hours after being fired, Claridge still has to take charge one last time, despite new boss Rix being in the stand. £750,000 Vincent – 'I've had three managers in a week!' – makes an impressive debut, but otherwise it is a sad end for Steve, whose name is chanted by the Pompey fans."

34 — BURNLEY:
Flahavan, Crowe, Vincent, Hiley, Moore, Brady, Panopoulos, Mills, Nightingale*Lovell, Bradbury, Sharpe
*Michopoulos, Thomas, Armstrong, Davis, Weller, Little, Ball", Cook^, Taylor, Moore, Branch^*
subs used: Harper/Rudonja; Briscoe/Mullin/Cox
"Impressive new-boy Brady, signed until the season's end, drives Pompey to a deserved win. Nightingale scores his first since Jan 99, ghosting in from the left to thump home Crowe's cross. Then the league debut-making Lovell – in from the cold – earns the pen which Pano converts."

35 — A 7/3 SHEFFIELD WED — 20,503 — 16 D 19 39 — 0-0 (0-0)
Portsmouth: Flahavan, Crowe, Vincent, Hiley, Moore^, Brady, Thogersen*, Panopoulos*, Harper*, Mills, Sharpe
Sheffield Wed: Pressman, Bromby, Hendon, Walker, Westwood, Sibon, Palmer, Softvedt, Quinn^, Booth^, Ekoku
Subs: Lovell/Waterman//Rudonja | Morrison/Di Piedi
Ref: C Foy (St Helens)

When Moore limps off with 30 minutes to go, Pompey field possibly their shortest ever back four, but they still hold firm against wasteful Wednesday. Soldvedt fired over from six yards, then Di Piedi shot wide late on. Mills forced a fine save and Crowe saw a shot tipped over.

36 — H 10/3 STOCKPORT — 12,202 — 15 W 21 42 — 2-1 (0-0)
Bradbury 76, Lovell 85 / Kuqi 77
Portsmouth: Flahavan, Waterman, Vincent, Hiley, Mills, Brady, Panopoulos, Sharpe, Rudonja^, Wolle'st'n*, Bradbury
Stockport: Dibble, Connolly, Nicholson, Flynn, Roget, Cooper*, Wiss, Fradin^, Grayson, Wilbraham, Kuqi
Subs: Harper/Lovell | Gibb/Carrigan
Ref: A Bates (Stoke)

Super-sub Lovell told manager Rix 'I'll win the game' as he came on. And he delivered as he cut inside and fired home from 20 yards. Another sub, Harper, had perked up Pompey, and Bradbury poked home from close range, only for Kuqi to seize at once on Waterman's misjudgement.

37 — A 14/3 TRANMERE — 9,872 — 14 D 24 43 — 1-1 (0-1)
Harper 57 / Allison 28
Portsmouth: Flahavan, Crowe, Vincent, Hiley, Mills, Brady, Panopoulos, Sharpe, Harper, Wolleaston*, Bradbury
Tranmere: Achterberg, Yates, Roberts, Jobson^, Allen, Parkinson, Hinds, Mellon, Allison, Koumas, Barlow*
Subs: Lovell | Taylor/Challinor
Ref: C Wilkes (Gloucester)

Harper responds to Rix's half-time roasting to round the stranded Acterberg and lob home from a wide angle. He might have won it, but couldn't profit as Lovell's shot came off the bar. Earlier Rovers' direct style caused chaos and Allison converted a Yates' free-kick smartly.

38 — A 17/3 CREWE — 6,182 — 15 L 14 43 — 0-1 (0-1)
/ Ashton 11
Portsmouth: Flahavan, Crowe, Vincent, Hiley, Tiler, Brady*, Panopoulos, Sharpe, Harper, Lovell, Bradbury
Crewe: Bankole, Wright, Smith, Walton, Macauley, Lunt, Sorvel, Street*, Jack, Rivers, Ashton^
Subs: Wolleaston/Nightingale | Charnock/Tait
Ref: A Hall (Birmingham)

17-year-old Ashton's shot on the turn, as new-boy Tiler (from Charlton) is still getting to know Hiley, proves decisive. In the second half Lovell misses from eight yards, then Pano scorns a chance with just the keeper to beat. Pompey look safe, eight points clear of the drop zone.

39 — A 25/3 HUDDERSFIELD — 13,199 — 18 L 22 43 — 1-4 (1-0)
Mills 33 / Booth 55, Facey 71, Gorre 90p, [Baldry 90]
Portsmouth: Flahavan^, Crowe, Vincent, Hiley, Tiler, Brady*, Panopoulos, Sharpe*, Harper, Wolleaston, Mills
Huddersfield: Vaesen, Jenkins, Heary, Dyson, Lucketti, Baldry^, Gorre, Armstrong, Thornley^, Booth, Morris
Subs: Lovell/Tardif/Nightingale | Brennan/Facey
Ref: P Alcock (Halstead)

A second-half capitulation sees angry travelling fans leaving early. Mills' 30-yarder gave them hope, but once Booth prodded in, the white flag was raised. Flavs – later subbed with a finger injury – and Tiler cocked up for Facey's goal. Gorre's been sealed it, then Baldry rubbed in salt.

40 — H 7/4 NOTT'M FOREST — 13,018 — 19 L 7 43 — 0-2 (0-2)
/ Bart-Williams 11p, 37
Portsmouth: Tardif, Crowe, Vincent, Hiley, Tiler, Brady*, Sharpe, Harper, Lovell, Wolleaston^, Mills"
Forest: Beasant, Gray, Doig, Hjelde, Benali, Scimeca, Prutton, Johnson, B'rt-Williams^, Johnson, John
Subs: Panop'los/N'gale/Pettefer
Ref: R Furmandiz (Doncaster)

Skipper Hiley fears Pompey are 'too soft' for the relegation battle as Forest coast. He had conceded an early converted pen as he slithered into an unnecessary handball, then Bart-Williams reacted first as John's 30-yarder hit the post. Disgruntled fans sing for Claridge, now at Millwall.

41 — H 14/4 QP RANGERS — 13,426 — 20 D 23 44 — 1-1 (1-0)
Bradbury 2 / Thomson 55
Portsmouth: Flahavan, Crowe, Vincent, Hiley, Tiler, Brady*, Panopoulos^, Sharpe, Harper, Lovell*, Mills
QPR: Harper, Bignot, Plummer, Ready, Baraclough^, Knight, Rose*, Peacock, Bruce, Crouch, Thomson
Subs: O'Neil/Nightingale | Wardley/Darlington
Ref: S Tomlin (Lewes)

Failure to beat doomed QPR has Pompey in deep trouble. Bradbury's cross-shot is the perfect start, but Harper misses when through and the jitters set in. Flavs can only push out Knight's shot and Thomson reacts first. After that Rangers dominate, but Mills nearly pinches it late on.

42 — A 16/4 BIRMINGHAM — 23,304 — 19 D 4 45 — 0-0 (0-0)
Portsmouth: Flahavan^, Crowe, Vincent, Hiley, Tiler, Brady*, Panopoulos*, Sharpe, Nightingale*, Bradbury, Mills
Birmingham: Bennett, Eaden, Gill, Purse, Johnson M, McCarthy*, Woodhouse, O'Connor, Marcelo, Johnson A^, Lazaridis
Subs: Harper/Tardif | Sonner/Holdsworth
Ref: M Pike (Barrow-in-Furness)

Stressed Rix gets through 20 cigarillos during the game, but Pompey show true grit and promotion-chasing Brum never really dominate, but Lazaridis fires just wide. In fact, only a smart save by Bennett denied Bradbury, and Harper and Mills could have done better with late chances.

43 — H 21/4 FULHAM — 17,651 — 21 D 1 46 — 1-1 (1-0)
Bradbury 10 / Saha 79p
Portsmouth: Petterson, Crowe, Vincent, Hiley, Tiler, Brady, Panopoulos^, Sharpe, Wolleaston*, Lovell*, Mills
Fulham: Taylor, Finnan, Goma*, Melville, Brevett, Goldbaek^, Davis, Clark, Collins, Boa Morte", Saha
Subs: Quashie/Vine | Symons/Riedle/Betsy
Ref: P Dowd (Stoke)

Referee Dowd's bizarre spot-kick award, when Vincent's challenge gets nowhere near ball or man, allows Saha to rescue a point for the title-winners. In truth, Pompey should have wrapped it up by then. Mills' parried shot was gobbled up by Bradbury but then chances went begging.

44 — A 29/4 BLACKBURN — 24,257 — 21 L 2 46 — 1-3 (1-0)
Panopoulos 11 / Hiley 61 (og), Dunn 78, Bent 86
Portsmouth: Petterson, Crowe, Vincent, Hiley, Primus, Brady, Panopoulos^, Sharpe, Wolleaston*, Lovell*, Mills
Blackburn: Friedel, Curtis, Short, Berg, Filtcroft, Bertovic^, Dunn, Hignett*, Johnson, Jansen, Hughes*
Subs: Crowe/Mills | Bent/Gillespie/McAteer
Ref: W Burns (Scarborough)

For an hour Pompey's hopes of an unlikely win are raised after Panopoulos finished Vincent's deep cross. Once Hiley unluckily chested into his own net, Rovers were rampant though. Dunn's pace put him clear for the second, and the defensive confusion allowed Bent an easy third.

45 — H 2/5 CRYSTAL PALACE — 19,013 — 22 L 21 46 — 2-4 (1-3)
Mills 44, Tiler 87 [Freedman 45, 51] / Forssell 18, Riihilahti 25
Portsmouth: Flahavan, Crowe, Vincent, Hiley, Tiler, Brady*, Panopoulos^, Sharpe^, Harper, Mills*, Bradbury
Crystal Palace: Kolinko, Smith, Austin, Mullins, Berhalter, Riihilahti, Thomson, Carlisle*, Freedman, Morrison, Forssell
Subs: Nightingale/Panopoulos | Evans
Ref: P Richards (Darwen)

Pathetic Pompey look doomed. 'You're not fit to wear the shirt!' sang the fans and one even confronted Bradbury late on. The nadir was just after Mills had raised hopes, scuffing home from close range. Tiler's horror pass gifted Freedman a run on goal and he didn't miss. Game over.

46 — H 6/5 BARNSLEY — 17,064 — 20 W 16 49 — 3-0 (1-0)
Bradbury 17, O'Neil 63, Harper 75
Portsmouth: Flahavan, Hiley, Vincent, Tiler, Primus, Brady !, Panopoulos, Sharpe, Harper, Lovell*, Bradbury
Barnsley: Miller, Appleby, Morgan, Parkin, Barker, Bullock, Barnard, Neil, Shipperley*, Dyer^, Crowe
Subs: Crowe | Kay/Sheron/Bertos
Ref: P Walton (Long Buckby)

Results elsewhere ensure safety, despite a comfortable win. Rix can't listen as he waits for Huddersfield's demise to be confirmed. Bradbury wriggled through to score, then O'Neil finished off a slick move. Harper's shot sealed it. Brady's off-the-ball assault late on hardly mattered.

Home Average 13,553 — Away 14,717

NATIONWIDE DIVISION 1 (CUP-TIES)

Manager: Pulis ⇨ Claridge ⇨ Graham Rix   **SEASON 2000-01**

Worthington Cup

	Att	F-A	H-T	1	2	3	4	5	6	7	8	9	10	11	subs used	Scorers, Times, and Referees
1:1 A CAMBRIDGE 22/8	20 D 2,904 2:19	0-0	0-0	Hoult	Edinburgh	Moore	Primus	Waterman	Quashie	O'Neil*	Derry*	Thogersen	Bradbury	Claridge"	Curtis/Rudonja	
(opp)				*Perez*	*Ashbee*	*Mustoe*	*Duncan*	*McAnespie*	*Dreyer*	*Wanless*	*Russell**	*Abbey*	*Hansen^*	*Alexdahl"*	*MacKenzie/Youngs/Slade*	Ref: A Leake (Darwen)
1:2 H CAMBRIDGE 5/9	2 W 5,570 2:7	1-0	0-0	Hoult	Derry	Edinburgh	Moore	Primus	Hughes*	Curtis^	Quashie	Claridge		Mills"	Waterman/O'Neil/Bradbury	Mills 57
(opp)				*Perez*	*Ashbee*	*Duncan*	*Dreyer*	*McAnespie*	*Cowan*	*Mustoe*	*Wanless*	*MacKenzie"*	*Axeldahl**	*Youngs^*	*Russell/Abbey/Taylor*	Ref: W Jordan (Tring) — (Pompey win 1-0 on aggregate)
2:1 A BLACKBURN 19/9	15 L 10,360 7	0-4	0-2	Hoult	Edinburgh"	Bjornebye*	Moore	Derry	Hughes	Quashie"	Thogersen	Rudonja^	Mills	Bradbury	Birmingham/O'Neil/Mig'zi	[Ostenstad 53] Carsley 21, Thomas 23,60
(opp)				*Filan*	*Curtis*	*Taylor*		*Berg^*	*McAteer*	*Johnson*	*Carsley*	*Duff"*	*Ostenstad*	*Thomas*	*Kenna/Dailly/Dunn*	Ref: P Rejer (Droitwich Spa)
2:2 H BLACKBURN 26/9	10 D 2,731 17	1-1	0-0	Hoult	Waterman	Hiley	Primus	Moore	Hughes*	Derry	Thogersen	Quashie	Mills	Bradbury"	Rudonja^/Mig'zi/N'gale	Nightingale 77 / Dunn 88
(opp)				*Miller*	*Kenna*	*Grayson*	*Dailly*	*Taylor*	*McAteer*	*Carsley**	*Johnson*	*Dunn*	*Burgess*	*Ostenstad^*	*O'Brien/Hamilton*	Ref: M Fletcher (Wolverley) — (Pompey lose 1-5 on aggregate)

FA Cup

	Att	F-A	H-T	1	2	3	4	5	6	7	8	9	10	11	subs used	Scorers, Times, and Referees
3 H TRANMERE 6/1	13 L 11,058 19	1-2	1-1	Tardif	Crowe	Hiley	Moore	Harper	Thogersen	Derry	Rudonja*	Quashie	Bradbury	Nightingale^	Hughes^/Hughes/Claridge	Bradbury 8 / Yates 44, Parkinson 68
(opp)				*Achterberg*	*Allen*	*Hill*	*Hinds*	*Jobson*	*Roberts l*	*Yates*	*Flynn*	*Barlow^*	*Parkinson*	*Rideout**	*Gill/Taylor*	Ref: D Gallagher (Banbury)

1:1 — Claridge misses three second-half chances against his old club to put this tie beyond U's reach. First he heads Bradbury's cross against a post, then he scuffed wide with only Perez to beat, before curling a shot just wide late on. O'Neil and Primus also scorned good opportunities.

1:2 — Record striker signing Lee Mills finally gets a goal, swivelling to sweep home Claridge's set up in the second half. The strike gives Pompey a deserved win and will get Mandaric off his back – they are staying at the same hotel and he keeps reminding him of his lack of goals so far.

2:1 — Wearing a new orange away kit for the first time, it becomes synonymous with failure as Rovers rip Pompey apart. At 0-3 Rudonja hit the post, but it was men against boys. Super fan John PFC Westwood parades in his pants at the end and Milan will refund the loyal few's travel costs.

2:2 — With the game over as a contest a record low crowd turns up for a major competitive first team fixture at Fratton. The faithful were even denied a deserved morale-boosting win as Hoult let Dunn's shot squirm through his hands. Nightingale had got the fans singing with a fine finish.

3 — Illness and injury-wracked Pompey are left feeling sick by cynical Rovers. Bradbury coolly finished after Nightingale charged a clearance, but Blues fail to kill the game. Yates heads home on half-time, then Parkinson nets from an acute angle after a surge. Roberts walks for two fouls.

Appearances / Goals

Player	Lge	Sub	LC	Sub	FAC	Sub	Goals Lge	LCFAC	Tot
Awford, Andy	2								
Birmingham, Michael						1			
Bradbury, Lee	35	4	3	1	1		10	1	11
Brady, Garry	8								
Claridge, Steve	24	7	2		1	1	11		11
Crowe, Jason	21	2	2		1				
Curtis, Tom	4					1			
Derry, Shaun	27	1	4	1					
Edinburgh, Justin	16	1	3						
Flahavan, Aaron	20								
Harper, Kevin	15	9			1		2		2
Hiley, Scott	34		1		1				
Hoult, Russell	22		4						
Hughes, Ceri	16	3	3			1			
Keller, Marc	3								
Lambourde, Bernard	6								
Lovell, Steve	5	4					1		1
Miglioranzi, Stefani	8	4				2			
Mills, Lee	22	2	3		1		4	1	5
Moore, Darren	31	1	4				1		1
Nightingale, Luke	7	12		1		1	1	1	2
O'Neil, Gary	7	3				2	1		1
Panopoulos, Michael	26	4	1				6		6
Pettefer, Carl		1							
Petterson, Andy	2								
Primus, Linvoy	23		3						
Quashie, Nigel	29	2	4		1		5		5
Rudonja, Mladen	2	9	1	2	1				
Sharpe, Lee	17								
Tardif, Chris	2	2			1				
Thogersen, Thomas	32	2	4		1		3		3
Tiler, Carl	9								
Vincent, Jamie	14								
Vine, Rowan		2							
Waterman, Dave	12	10	3	1			1		1
Whittingham, Guy		1							
Wolleaston, Robert	5	1							
(own-goals)							1		1
37 players used	**506**	**87**	**44**	**11**	**11**	**2**	**47**	**2**	**50**

League Table

	Team	P	W	D	L	F	A	W	D	L	F	A	Pts
			Home					Away					
1	Fulham	46	16	5	2	49	14	14	6	3	41	18	101
2	Blackburn	46	15	5	3	43	20	11	8	4	33	19	91
3	Bolton*	46	10	10	3	40	28	14	5	4	36	17	87
4	Preston	46	12	6	5	32	18	11	3	9	32	34	78
5	Birmingham	46	14	4	3	34	22	9	6	8	25	26	78
6	West Brom	46	13	5	5	37	23	8	6	9	23	29	74
7	Burnley	46	14	5	4	30	17	7	4	12	20	37	72
8	Wimbledon	46	7	11	5	33	26	10	7	6	38	24	69
9	Watford	46	11	6	6	46	29	9	3	11	30	38	69
10	Sheffield Utd	46	14	4	5	34	18	5	7	11	18	31	68
11	Nott'm For	46	11	3	9	28	24	9	5	9	27	29	68
12	Wolverhampton	46	7	9	7	25	20	7	4	12	20	28	55
13	Gillingham	46	9	6	8	32	28	4	10	9	29	38	55
14	Crewe	46	12	5	6	30	24	3	5	15	17	38	55
15	Norwich	46	10	7	6	25	18	4	5	14	21	40	54
16	Barnsley	46	11	3	9	32	26	4	6	13	17	36	54
17	Sheffield Wed	46	9	4	10	34	38	6	4	13	18	33	53
18	Grimsby	46	10	4	9	26	27	4	6	13	17	35	52
19	Stockport	46	6	11	6	29	26	5	7	11	29	39	51
20	PORTSMOUTH	46	9	8	6	31	25	1	11	11	16	34	49
21	Crystal Palace	46	6	6	11	28	34	6	7	10	29	36	49
22	Huddersfield	46	7	6	10	29	26	4	9	10	19	31	48
23	QP Rangers	46	6	9	8	24	28	1	10	12	21	47	40
24	Tranmere	46	8	7	8	30	33	1	4	18	16	44	38
		1104	247	148	157	781	592	157	148	247	592	781	1508

* promoted
after play-offs

Odds & ends

Double wins: (0).
Double losses: (4) Nottingham Forest, West Brom, Bolton, Preston.

Won from behind: (2) Crewe (h), C Palace (a).
Lost from in front: (2) Huddersfield (a), Blackburn (a).

High spots: Beating Barnsley 3-0 on the final day to avoid the drop.
Three straight wins in October following the appointment of Steve Claridge as caretaker player-manager.

Low spots: Losing 2-4 at home to Crystal Palace in the penultimate match of the season to leave Pompey in the bottom three.
A run of one win in 13 league and cup games from December-February.
A record low gate at Fratton (2,731) for a first class fixture in the second leg of the Worthington Cup against Blackburn.

Player of the Season: Scott Hiley.
Ever presents: (0).
Hat-tricks: (1) Steve Claridge.
Leading Scorer: Steve Claridge and Lee Bradbury (11).

NATIONWIDE LEAGUE DIVISION 1   Manager: Rix ⇨ Harry Redknapp   SEASON 2001-02

No	Date	Opponent	Att	Pos	Res	Pt	F-A	H-T
1	11/8	A WOLVERHAMPTON	23,012	19	D	1	2-2	2-1
2	18/8	H BRADFORD	17,239		L	1	0-1	0-0
3	25/8	A STOCKPORT	5,090	12	W	4	1-0	0-0
4	27/8	H GRIMSBY	13,614	8	W	7	4-2	1-0
5	8/9	H GILLINGHAM	17,224	7	W	10	2-1	0-1
6	12/9	A WIMBLEDON	7,138	5	D	11	3-3	0-1
7	15/9	H CRYSTAL PALACE	18,149	2	W	14	4-2	2-1
8	18/9	A WALSALL	6,153	3	D	15	0-0	0-0
9	22/9	A COVENTRY	18,303	5	L	15	0-2	0-1
10	25/9	H WEST BROM	17,287	7	L	15	1-2	1-1
11	28/9	A BARNSLEY	11,660	5	W	18	4-1	2-1

Line-ups (Pompey starter / opponent in italics), subs used, scorers, times and referees

1. A WOLVERHAMPTON — 1 Beasant/*Oakes*, 2 Hiley/*Muscat*, 3 Vincent/*Naylor**, 4 Zamperini, 5 Moore/*Lescott*, 6 Crowe^/*Butler*, 7 O'Neil/*Dinning*, 8 Miglioranzi*/*Newton*, 9 Quashie/*Kennedy*, 10 Crouch/*Proudlock*, 11 Bradbury"/*Roussel*. Subs used: Panopoulos/Harper/Pitt, *Connelly*.
Crouch 8, Crowe 20; *Newton 45, Roussel 57*. Ref: M Pike (Barrow-in-Furness)
Ex-Saint Beasant comes in for tragic Flavs and emotions still raw Pompey surge into the lead. £1 million Crouch heads home Quashie's cross, then Crowe chips in from 20 yards. Newton taps in after Kennedy hit a post, then Roussel's header levels to temper optimism somewhat.

2. H BRADFORD — 1 Beasant/*Walsh*, 2 Hiley/*Myers*, 3 Vincent/*McCall*, 4 Zamperini/*Whalley*, 5 Moore/*Ward*, 6 Panopoulos"/O'Neil / *Carbone"*, 7 O'Neil/*Jess^*, 8 Derry^/*Molenaar*, 9 Quashie/*Locke^*, 10 Crouch/*Halle*, 11 Bradbury/*Jacobs*. Subs used: Prosinecki/Pitt, *Lawrence/Sharpe/Blake*.
Jess 71. Ref: M Dean (Wirral)
Chain-smoking Croat Prosinecki's work permit red-tape untangled for a sub's cameo, but he can't inspire. His deflected drive almost levelled Jess's header though, after City broke against the run of play. Burchill will finally sign next week from Celtic to provide badly needed punch.

3. A STOCKPORT — 1 Beasant/*Jones*, 2 Hiley/*Briggs*, 3 Vincent/*Van Blerk^*, 4 Zamperini/*Flynn*, 5 Buxton/*Roget*, 6 Harper"/*Gibb*, 7 O'Neil*/*Wiss*, 8 Prosinecki/*Smith*, 9 Barrett/*Taylor*, 10 Crouch/*Wilbraham**, 11 Bradbury^/*Kuqi*. Subs used: Quashie/Burchill/Crowe, *Hardy/Clark*.
Prosinecki 61p. Ref: A Bates (Stoke)
Rix gambles with youth and is rewarded as his side survives a battering. Roget hit the bar, Wilbraham the post and Kuqi missed a sitter, then Pompey pinched it when Bradbury was hauled back in the box. ('On a different planet' says Tommy Docherty) converts with aplomb.

4. H GRIMSBY — 1 Tardif/*Coyne*, 2 Hiley/*McDermott*, 3 Buxton/*Gallimore*, 4 Zamperini*/*Groves*, 5 Harper/*Beharall*, 6 Quashie/*Pouton*, 7 Pitt/*Butterfield*, 8 Prosinecki/*Willems !*, 9 Barrett^/*Campbell*, 10 Crouch/*Rowan**, 11 Burchill"/*Jevons*. Subs used: Crowe/O'Neil/Bradbury, *Jeffrey*.
Burchill 28, 78, Crouch 63, 79; *Butterfield 48, Jeffrey 72*. Ref: P Walton (Northants)
Prosinecki produces a passing master-class that baffles game Grimsby. First Prosi picked out Harper, who crossed for Burchill to nod home, then crosses himself finding Crouch's head. Twice Town pegged Pompey back, but late goals, as Burchill's pace makes and scores one, seal it.

5. H GILLINGHAM — 1 Ilic/*Bartram*, 2 Hiley/*Ashby*, 3 Buxton/*Pennock*, 4 Zamperini/*Hope*, 5 Harper/*Patterson*, 6 Quashie/*Edge*, 7 Pitt/*Smith*, 8 Prosinecki/*Gooden*, 9 Barrett/*Browning^*, 10 Crouch/*King^*, 11 Burchill/*Onuora*. Subs used: *Hessenthaler/Shaw*.
Barrett 58, Zamperini 90; *Onuora 34*. Ref: M Messias (York)
It's the Prosi show again. First his early pen is easily saved, then he conjures up a sublime free-kick for Barrett to head an equaliser. In the final minute Crouch nods down his corner for Zamperini to poke in. Onuora hit the bar before his tap-in and new keeper Ilic made two late saves.

6. A WIMBLEDON — 1 Ilic/*Heald*, 2 Hiley/*Darlington*, 3 Buxton*/*Holloway !*, 4 Zamperini/*Willmott*, 5 Harper/*McAnuff^*, 6 Quashie/*Ardley**, 7 Pitt*/*Roberts*, 8 Prosinecki^/*Andersen*, 9 Barrett/*Cooper*, 10 Crouch/*Shipperley*, 11 Burchill/*Connolly*. Subs used: Bradbury/Vincent/O'Neil, *Hughes/Kimble*.
Burchill 67, Crouch 76, Bradbury 90p; *Cooper 36, Hughes 48, Connolly 53*. Ref: D Gallagher (Oxfordshire)
A triple substitution on the hour, including the jaded Prosi, pays rich dividends. Dons are cruising, although 3-0 flatters them, but then Burchill nods in at the near post, Crouch at the far post and, as Dons panic, Holloway hacks down Bradbury, who converts after the defender is sent off.

7. H CRYSTAL PALACE — 1 Ilic/*Clarke*, 2 Hiley/*Austin*, 3 Crowe/*Mullins*, 4 Zamperini*/*Popovic*, 5 Harper/*Smith^*, 6 Quashie^/*Harrison^*, 7 Pitt/*Rodger"*, 8 Prosinecki*/*Kirovski*, 9 Barrett/*Rihilahti*, 10 Crouch/*Freedman*, 11 Burchill/*Morrison*. Subs used: Buxton/O'Neil/Bradbury, *Black/Rubens/Kabba*.
Zamperini 5, Prosin'ki 38, Burchill 63p, [Crouch 76]; *Rodger 10, Freedman 69*. Ref: D Elleray (Harrow)
Rumours Rix has lost boardroom support are quashed. Zamperini touched home Harper's knock-back, then Rodger was left unmarked to level. Prosi's 25-yard free-kick turned the game. Burchill converted after Pitt was tripped, Freedman tapped in, but Crouch's header made it safe.

8. A WALSALL — 1 Ilic/*Harper*, 2 Hiley/*Brightwell*, 3 Crowe/*Tilson*, 4 Zamperini/*Barras*, 5 Harper/*Gadsby**, 6 Quashie/*Aranalde*, 7 Pitt*/*Bennett*, 8 O'Neil*/*Wrack*, 9 Barrett/*Simpson*, 10 Crouch^/*Goodman*, 11 Burchill/*Leitao^*. Subs used: Vincent/Bradbury/Prosinecki, *Herivelto/Byfield*.
Ref: M Ryan (Preston)
Prosinecki comes on for an 11-minute cameo and produces the defining moment: an uncharacteristic last-ditch tackle to deny Wrack a shooting chance after he had dispossessed debut-making Buxton. The teenage centre-half almost snatched a late winner but his header was blocked.

9. A COVENTRY — 1 Ilic/*Hedman*, 2 Hiley/*Shaw*, 3 Crowe/*Breen*, 4 Zamperini/*Konjic*, 5 Harper/*Edworthy*, 6 Quashie^/*Thompson**, 7 Prosinecki/*Carsley*, 8 O'Neil*/*Safri^*, 9 Vincent/*Chippo*, 10 Crouch/*Hughes*, 11 Bradbury*/*Bothroyd"*. Subs used: Pitt/Vine/Brady, *Martinez/O'Neill/Deloroge*.
Bothroyd 17, Carsley 72. Ref: H Webb (Rotherham)
Pompey's hooligan fringe disgrace themselves at half-time, which lasts 22 mins. The day before, striker Burchill was ruled out for the season with a training-ground knee injury. Zamperini's lazy back-pass gifts the first, then Pompey rally, but Carsley's close-range shot seals the win.

10. H WEST BROM — 1 Ilic/*Hoult*, 2 Hiley/*Sigurdsson*, 3 Buxton/*Butler*, 4 Zamperini/*Clement*, 5 Crowe/*Cummings*, 6 Quashie/*Lyttle*, 7 Pitt/*Appleton*, 8 Barrett/*Johnson*, 9 Prosinecki/*McInnes*, 10 Crouch/*Dobie*, 11 Pitt/*Taylor^*. Subs used: Bradbury/O'Neil, *Chambers*.
Prosinecki 6p; *Clement 28, Dobie 70*. Ref: M Halsey (Welwyn G City)
Blues miss recently left Moore (to Baggies) as their back line has an average age of 19. Prosi's early pen after Pitt was upended promised, but Albion dominated overall: 15 shots to four. Clement curled in the leveller, then saw a pen saved by Ilic. Dobie nodded home Clement's cross.

11. A BARNSLEY — 1 Ilic/*Crowe*, 2 Hiley/*Marriott*, 3 Buxton/*Braker*, 4 Zamperini/*Regan*, 5 Harper/*Tinkler"*, 6 Quashie/*Morgan*, 7 O'Neil/*Donovan*, 8 Prosinecki*/*Barnard*, 9 Barrett/*Gorre"*, 10 Crouch/*Neil*, 11 Burchill/*Dyer*. Subs used: Pitt/Vincent, *Jones/Kay*.
Vinc't 23, Crouch 45, Bradbury 51p, 59!lic; *Barnard 8p*. Ref: P Richards (Lancashire)
Pompey record their first live TV win. Barnard scored a dodgy early pen, but once Vincent's cross-cum-shot flew in, Blues cruised. Crouch nodded in Prosi's cross, then a soft shove let Bradbury convert. His cross shot made it four, then Tykes' faithful applaud lynch-pin Prosi off.

Match 12 — ROTHERHAM (A) 12/10
Att: 6,427 · Pos 7 · Opp 20 · Pts 18 · L · 1-2 (0-1)
Scorers: Crouch 58 / Monkhouse 4, Beech 85
Ref: F Stretton (Nottingham)

- **Pompey:** Beasant, Hiley, Primus, Edinburgh, Harper, Barrett, Prosinecki, Quashie*, Pitt, Crouch, Bradbury, Vine
- **Opp:** Pollitt, Scott, McIntosh, Swailes, Hurst, Sedgwick, Talbot, Daws*, Monkhouse*, Robins, Lee^, Mullin/Barker/Beech

Two turned down spot-kick appeals late on left Pompey fuming, as Beech then curled in his first-ever goal to give Millers' their first home win of the season. Monkhouse's close-range goal ensured a deserved lead, but once Crouch angled home a header there looked only one winner.

Match 13 — SHEFFIELD UTD (H) 20/10
Att: 15,538 · Pos 6 · Opp 21 · Pts 21 · W · 1-0 (1-0)
Scorers: Edinburgh 40
Ref: P Rejer (Worcestershire)

- **Pompey:** Beasant, Hiley, Primus, Edinburgh, Harper, Barrett, Prosinecki, Quashie, Vincent, Crouch, Bradbury*, Lovell
- **Opp:** Tracey, Uhlenbeek, Murphy, Page, Curtis^, Montgomery-Brown, Tonge, Ndlovu, Suffo^, D'Jaffo, Nicholson/Devlin

33-1 shot Edinburgh's goal from six yards secures a barely-merited win. He even defied feeling ill to defend solidly as Blades poured forward. Beasant is on top form, but the bar denies Crouch's hook shot late on. 'Harper should have been booked for diving,' moaned Neil Warnock.

Match 14 — NORWICH (A) 23/10
Att: 19,962 · Pos 9 · Opp 4 · Pts 22 · D · 0-0 (0-0)
Ref: B Curson (Leicestershire)

- **Pompey:** Beasant, Hiley, Primus, Edinburgh, Harper*, Crowe, O'Neil, Quashie, Barrett, Lovell*, Bradbury, Pitt/Vine
- **Opp:** Green, Nedergaard, Mackay, Fleming, Kenton, Rivers*, Holt, Mulryne, McVeigh, Roberts, Libbra, Notman

Patched-up Pompey, missing Crouch and Prosi, battled to a point to celebrate Rix's birthday. City had six home wins behind them, but failed to sparkle. Rivers missed from close range in the first half, but Pompey had their chances too. Roberts headed a good chance wide at the death.

Match 15 — PRESTON (H) 27/10
Att: 15,402 · Pos 12 · Opp 6 · Pts 22 · L · 0-1 (0-1)
Scorers: Cartwright 45
Ref: G Barber (Hertfordshire)

- **Pompey:** Beasant, Hiley, Primus, Edinburgh, Harper, Crowe*, O'Neil, Quashie, Barrett^, Lovell, Bradbury, Pitt/Brady
- **Opp:** Moilanen, Alexander, Lucketti, Jackson*, Murdock, Cartwright, Gregan, Rankine, McKenna, Macken, Healy^, Eaton/Cresswell

Record £1.9m Kawaguchi's arrival causes chaos as Japanese media take over the press box for the national keeper's debut, but he is only a sub. Cartwright heads home Alexander's right-wing cross on half-time to settle it. Lovell glanced Pompey's best chance wide and saw a shot saved.

Match 16 — BIRMINGHAM (H) 30/10
Att: 15,612 · Pos 11 · Opp 6 · Pts 23 · D · 1-1 (1-1)
Scorers: Bradbury 40 / Marcelo 25
Ref: W Jordan (Hertfordshire)

- **Pompey:** Beasant, Hiley, Primus, Edinburgh, Harper, Crowe, O'Neil, Prosinecki, Barrett^, Mills, Bradbury, Bradbury
- **Opp:** Vaesen, Eaden, Purse, Johnson, Grainger, Sonner, Woodhouse, Luntala, Horsfield, Marcelo, Lazaridis

A collector's item in the modern game sees neither side make a substitution. Marcelo profited against the run of play after a comedy of errors, then Beasant saved from Horsfield at once. Bradbury nodded a deserved equaliser. Mills is impressive in Crouch's place and goes close twice.

Match 17 — SHEFFIELD WED (A) 3/11
Att: 18,212 · Pos 11 · Opp 21 · Pts 26 · W · 3-2 (2-1)
Scorers: Crouch 6, 39, Barrett 59 / Donnelly 1, Sibon 67p
Ref: T Parkes (Birmingham)

- **Pompey:** Beasant, Hiley, Primus, Edinburgh, Harper, Barrett, O'Neil, Prosinecki, Pitt, Crouch, Bradbury*, Lovell
- **Opp:** Pressman, Bromby, Soltvedt, Quinn, Sibon, Morrison, Lescott*, Donnelly, Westwood, Geary, Maddix^, Bonvin/Crane

Urban myth has it that Donnelly was 'allowed' to net after 26 secs in a player protest at Beasant's dropping for Yoshi. After that Blues are on top. Crouch lashed home Harper's cross, then hit Bradders' pull-back on the run. Barrett angled home, but Sibon's pen made for a tense finish.

Match 18 — BURNLEY (A) 10/11
Att: 14,123 · Pos 10 · Opp 5 · Pts 27 · D · 1-1 (0-0)
Scorers: Crouch 72 / Taylor 69
Ref: G Frankland (Middlesbro')

- **Pompey:** Beasant, Hiley, Primus, Edinburgh, Harper, Barrett, Waterman, Prosinecki*, Pitt, Crouch, Mills, Lovell/Crowe
- **Opp:** Michopoulos, West, Cox, Gnohere, Briscoe, Little, Weller, Grant, Cook*, Taylor, Moore*, Payton/Johnrose

Classy Crouch, called up by England Under-21s, takes some fearful stick from home fans after he chose Pompey over Clarets in the summer. His revenge is sweet as he spins to fire home after Waterman's deflected shot fell to him just after Taylor's diving header from Cook's cross.

Match 19 — MANCHESTER C (H) 17/11
Att: 19,103 · Pos 10 · Opp 9 · Pts 30 · W · 2-1 (0-1)
Scorers: Bradbury 54, Crouch 77 / Huckerby 28
Ref: P Alcock (Kent)

- **Pompey:** Beasant, Hiley, Primus, Edinburgh, Harper, Barrett, O'Neil, Prosinecki, Pitt, Crouch, Bradbury, Bradbury
- **Opp:** Weaver, Dunne, Howey, Mettomo, Pearce, Wt-Phillips, Negouai, Benarbia, Horlock, Huckerby, Goater*, Mike

Bradbury continues to have the Indian sign over his former club, stooping to head home impressive O'Neil's cross. That levelled Huckerby's glancing header and Yoshi's one-on-one save from sub Mike was crucial. Crouch headed home Prosi's perfect cross then hit the bar late on.

Match 20 — WATFORD (A) 25/11
Att: 15,631 · Pos 10 · Opp 13 · Pts 30 · L · 0-3 (0-2)
Scorers: Robinson 23, Cox 44, Issa 85
Ref: B Knight (Kent)

- **Pompey:** Beasant, Hiley, Primus, Edinburgh, Harper, Barrett*, O'Neil*, Vincent, Pitt, Crouch, Bradbury, Quashie/Lovell/Tiler
- **Opp:** Chamberlain, Cox, Vega, Robinson, Blondeau*, Vernazza, Issa, Hyde", Glass, Gayle^, Smith, Doyley/Noel-Williams/Noble

A Sunday night TV horror show. Big-spending Watford put their indifferent form behind them. Robinson volleys home the 14th time Pompey have gone behind this season) and Cox is unmarked for a header, as is Issa near the end. Crouch missed a one-on-one just after the break.

Match 21 — NOTT'M FOREST (H) 28/11
Att: 14,837 · Pos 9 · Opp 14 · Pts 33 · W · 3-2 (1-2)
Scorers: Hjelde 10 (og), Bradbury 50, 83p / Summerbee 11, Jenas 33p
Ref: P Armstrong (Berkshire)

- **Pompey:** Kawaguchi, Hiley, Crowe, Zamperini*, Harper, Barrett, O'Neil*, Quashie, Pitt^, Crouch, Bradbury*, Thogersen/Lovell/Vincent
- **Opp:** Ward, Louis-Jean, Scimeca, Hjelde, Brennan, Prutton, Williams, Jenas, Reid, Johnson*, John

Two dodgy pens are the talk of this game. Summerbee's tumble looked dramatic, but Jenas converted, then a better shout as Johnson is tripped is waved aside. Late on Crouch misses an overhead kick, but the ref blows up for Bradbury to score. Rix praises the crowd for their passion.

Match 22 — NORWICH (H) 2/12
Att: 13,286 · Pos 10 · Opp 3 · Pts 33 · L · 1-2 (1-1)
Scorers: Harper 10 / Roberts 17, Tiler 85 (og)
Ref: D Pugh (Merseyside)

- **Pompey:** Kawaguchi, Hiley, Crowe^, Tiler, Harper, Barrett, O'Neil, Quashie, Vincent*, Crouch, Bradbury, Pitt/Lovell
- **Opp:** Green, Drury, Mackay, Fleming, Nedergaard, Holt, Mulryne, Russell, McVeigh, Rivers*, Roberts, Notman

'Give him a chance,' pleads Rix as boo-boy Tiler returns, but his fine display is undone as he glances in a decisive OG. Inspired Green saved from Crouch at the death and earlier from Quashie's boomer. Earlier, Harper's curling shot had been matched by unmarked Roberts' header.

Match 23 — CREWE (H) 8/12
Att: 14,430 · Pos 11 · Opp 18 · Pts 33 · L · 2-4 (1-2)
Scorers: Hulse 44, Crouch 81 / Hulse 9, Sodje 28, Charn'k 63, Lunt 68
Ref: S Tomlin (East Sussex)

- **Pompey:** Kawaguchi, Hiley, Crowe, Tiler, Harper, Quashie, O'Neil*, Vincent*, Lovell*, Crouch, Bradbury, Pitt/Thogersen
- **Opp:** Ince, Wright, Foster, Sodje, Smith, Lunt, Thomas, Brammer, Charnock, Ashton*, Hulse, Jack

Crewe railroad Pompey's defence as Hulse and Sodje ram home free headers. Lovell's instinctive overhead kick gives hope, until overlapping Charnock fires in from 20 yards. Lunt followed up after another set-piece caused chaos. Fans are streaming out before Crouch's consolation.

NATIONWIDE LEAGUE DIVISION 1 — Manager: Rix ⇨ Harry Redknapp — SEASON 2001-02

24. A · MILLWALL · 13/12 — L 0-1 (H-T 0-0)
Att 11,527 · Pos 11 · Pt 33 · (6)

Scorers, Times: Sadlier 78
Ref: E Wolstenholme (Blackb'n)

	1	2	3	4	5	6	7	8	9	10	11	subs used
Pompey	Kawaguchi	Buxton	Primus	Tiler	Harper*	Pitt*	O'Neil	Prosinecki	Barrett	Crouch	Bradbury^	Vincent/Lovell
Millwall	*Warner*	*Ryan*	*Nethercott*	*Dyche*	*Green*	*Ifill**	*Livermore*	*Cahill*	*Reid*	*Claridge*	*Sadlier*	*Harris*

A mix-up between Yoshi and Tiler, going for the same ball, lets Sadlier shoot into the roof of the net from six yards, undoing Pompey's hard work. Old-boy Claridge, cheered by both sets of fans, hit the bar in the first half, while Harper hit a post. Bradbury's knee injury looks serious.

25. H · STOCKPORT · 22/12 — W 2-0 (H-T 0-0)
Att 13,887 · Pos 12 · Pt 36 · (24)

Scorers, Times: Crouch 71, Lovell 82
Ref: S Baines (Chesterfield)

	1	2	3	4	5	6	7	8	9	10	11	subs used
Pompey	Kawaguchi	Buxton	Primus	Tiler	Harper	Pitt*	Quashie	Prosinecki	Barrett*	Crouch	Lovell	Vincent
Stockport	*Jones*	*Clark*	*Flynn*	*Raget*	*Gibb*	*Delaney*	*Lescott*	*Briggs**	*Ellison*	*Kuqi*	*Beckett**	*McSheffrey/Taylor*

Cast-adrift County put up plucky resistance, but once Harper's cross is tucked home by Crouch, Pompey relax. Lovell settled it with an angled strike after he burst past a defender. 'We needed that win for the boss,' he said. A defeat would have seen Rix sacked, claimed the rumour mill.

26. A · GILLINGHAM · 26/12 — L 0-2 (H-T 0-2)
Att 10,477 · Pos 13 · Pt 36 · (12)

Scorers, Times: King 21, Shaw 29
Ref: D Crick (Surrey)

	1	2	3	4	5	6	7	8	9	10	11	subs used
Pompey	Kawaguchi	Buxton	Primus	Tiler	Crowe*	Vincent*	Quashie	Prosinecki	Barrett*	Crouch	Lovell	O'Neil/Pitt/Vine
Gillingham	*Bartram*	*Nosworthy*	*Ashby*	*Hope*	*Perpetuini*	*Browning*	*Smith*	*Osborn*	*Taylor*	*King**	*Shaw^*	*Ipoua/Gooden*

White-shirted Pompey surrendered in the winter sun. King's deflected shot left Yoshi flat-footed, then Shaw side-footed home Taylor's cross. Bartram saved at once from Lovell, and Crouch's follow-up was headed off the line. 'I'm at the end of my tether,' lamented Chairman Milan.

27. A · GRIMSBY · 29/12 — L 1-3 (H-T 1-2)
Att 5,217 · Pos 14 · Pt 36 · (22)

Scorers, Times: Crouch 32 / Jevons 40, 79p, Ford 43
Ref: R Pearson (Durham)

	1	2	3	4	5	6	7	8	9	10	11	subs used
Pompey	Kawaguchi	Vincent*	Primus	Tiler	Harper	Pitt	Quashie	Prosinecki	Thogersen*	Crouch	Lovell*	Hiley/Vine/Curtis
Grimsby	*Coyne*	*Groves*	*Neilson"*	*Ford*	*Gallimore*	*Butterfield*	*Coldicott*	*Burnett*	*Chapman*	*Thompson**	*Jevons^*	*Boulding/Jeffrey/Willems*

Yoshi's clangers cost Pompey. First he dropped a corner at Jevons' feet, then he was beaten by Ford to another flag-kick. 'In Japan I would have had two free-kicks, but I'm not making excuses,' he said afterwards. Until then Pompey had been cruising against managerless Mariners.

28. A · BRADFORD · 12/1 — L 1-3 (H-T 1-1)
Att 14,306 · Pos 16 · Pt 36 · (17)

Scorers, Times: Primus 2 / Grant 19, Sharpe 59p, Halle 89
Ref: P Taylor (Hertfordshire)

	1	2	3	4	5	6	7	8	9	10	11	subs used
Pompey	Beasant	Derry	Primus	Tiler !	Barrett^	Pitt*	Quashie	Prosinecki	O'Neil	Crouch	Harper	Crowe !/Buxton
Bradford	*Muggleton*	*Halle*	*Caldwell*	*Myers*	*Emanuel*	*Jorgensen*	*Locke*	*Sharpe*	*Jess*	*Grant*	*Tod*	

Beasant is back, but despite the perfect start – as Primus touched in Crouch's shot – Pompey capitulate again. Grant levelled from close in, then old-boy Sharpe's cocky pen turned the game. Crowe was unlucky to see red, but Tiler's head-butt was stupid. Halle's header settled it at once.

29. H · WOLVERHAMPTON · 17/1 — L 2-3 (H-T 1-1)
Att 13,105 · Pos 16 · Pt 36 · (2)

Scorers, Times: Quashie 11, Prosinecki 79 / Rae 14, Blake 60, Sturridge 84
Ref: M Dean (Wirral)

	1	2	3	4	5	6	7	8	9	10	11	subs used
Pompey	Beasant	Hiley^	Primus	Buxton	Crowe	Vincent	Quashie	Derry	Prosinecki	Crouch	Harper*	Lovell/O'Neil
Wolves	*Oakes*	*Muscat*	*Butler*	*Lescott*	*Camara*	*Newton*	*Rae*	*Cameron*	*Kennedy**	*Blake*	*Sturridge*	*Ndah*

Prosi's stunning left-foot strike looked to have saved a point until the defence dallied and Rae set up Sturridge to clip home. Earlier, Quashie's tackle with Butler saw the ball balloon into the net, then Blake reacted first to a loose ball.

30. A · NOTT'M FOREST · 30/1 — W 1-0 (H-T 0-0)
Att 26,476 · Pos 16 · Pt 39 · (13)

Scorers, Times: Prosinecki 83
Ref: S Mathieson (Stockport)

	1	2	3	4	5	6	7	8	9	10	11	subs used
Pompey	Beasant	Harper*	Primus	Buxton	Crowe	Rudonja*	O'Neil	Prosinecki	Derry	Pitt	Lovell^	Hiley/Thogersen/Curtis
Forest	*Ward*	*Thompson*	*Hjelde*	*Scimeca*	*Vaughan*	*Summerbee*	*Williams*	*Prutton*	*Jenas*	*Lester**	*Harewood^*	*Johnson/Reid*

Pompey skipper and Notts Co fan Shaun Derry is pleased with Pompey's first league win at the City Ground since 1975. 'It's one of my career highlights,' he said after Prosinecki's late deflected free-kick flummoxed Ward. Forest hadn't scored since 1st January and you could see why.

31. H · BARNSLEY · 2/2 — D 4-4 (H-T 2-1)
Att 12,756 · Pos 16 · Pt 40 · (18)

Scorers, Times: Prosinecki 5p, 61, 69, Primus 41 / Lumsd'n 16, 83p, Barker 48, Sheron 90
Ref: P Prosser (Tewkesbury)

	1	2	3	4	5	6	7	8	9	10	11	subs used
Pompey	Beasant	Crowe	Primus !	Buxton	Zamperini	Harper	Quashie	Prosinecki	Derry	Crouch	Pitt*	Hiley
Barnsley	*Miller*	*Mulligan*	*Barker*	*Chettle*	*Morgan*	*Donovan**	*Jones*	*Lumsdon*	*Barnard*	*Dyer^*	*Sheron*	*Bartosi/Bedeau*

Gutted Prosi's sublime hat-trick – a pen, a shot from 20 yards, and a classy free kick – is undone by comical defending. 'I cannot believe it,' he moaned. At 4-2 Primus is harshly red-carded for an alleged elbow and Lumsdon converts before Sheron glances home in stoppage time.

32. A · SHEFFIELD UTD · 9/2 — L 3-4 (H-T 2-3)
Att 17,553 · Pos 16 · Pt 40 · (15)

Scorers, Times: Crouch 6, Prosinecki 45, Quashie 60 / Mont'y 18, Furlong 25, 90p, Asaba 40
Ref: M Clattenburg (Chest'-le-St)

	1	2	3	4	5	6	7	8	9	10	11	subs used
Pompey	Beasant	Crowe	Primus*	Buxton	Vincent	Harper	Quashie	Prosinecki	Derry !	Crouch	Pitt*	Lovell
Sheff Utd	*Tracey*	*Doane*	*Page*	*Curle*	*Ullathorne**	*Montgom'y^*	*Brown*	*Ford*	*Ndlovu*	*Asaba"*	*Furlong*	*Sandford/Peschis'o/Jagielka*

Furlong converts at the death after Derry's foul and there is still time for the Pompey skipper to see red for a hack. It is tough on Blues, who totally dominate the second half. Quashie is booked – one of ten cautions – for celebrating his leveller. Then chance after chance goes begging.

33. H · ROTHERHAM · 16/2 — D 0-0 (H-T 0-0)
Att 13,313 · Pos 16 · Pt 41 · (18)

Scorers, Times: —
Ref: G Hegley (Bishops Stortf'd)

	1	2	3	4	5	6	7	8	9	10	11	subs used
Pompey	Beasant	Harper*	Zamperini	Buxton	Vincent	Pitt*	Quashie	O'Neil*	Derry	Crouch	Biagini	Hiley/Lovell
Rotherham	*Pollitt*	*Hurst*	*Bryan*	*Swailes*	*McIntosh*	*Sedgwick*	*Talbot^*	*Mullins*	*Daws*	*Lee*	*Robins**	*Monkhouse/Barker*

Zamp's return tightened the defence, but despite loanee striker Biagini's bright form, Pompey fire blanks. Pitt missed a one-on-one, then late on already-booked Harper was sent sprawling in the box, but the ref said 'dive' and he walked. 'It looked like a pen to me,' said Millers' Hurst.

34. A · WEST BROM · 23/2 — L 0-5 (H-T 0-4)
Att 21,028 · Pos 17 · Pt 41 · (3)

Scorers, Times: [Balis 45] Roberts 8, 80, Sigurds'n 24, Dobie 38
Ref: M Cowburn (Blackpool)

	1	2	3	4	5	6	7	8	9	10	11	subs used
Pompey	Beasant	Hiley	Zamperini	Buxton	Vincent	Pettefer	Quashie	O'Neil	Thogersen*	Crouch	Biagini	Waterman
West Brom	*Hoult*	*Butler*	*Sigurdsson*	*Gilchrist*	*Balis*	*Clement^*	*McInnes*	*Johnson"*	*Chambers*	*Dobie**	*Roberts*	*Taylor/Cummings/Jordao*

It would take three more weeks to be confirmed, but this loss sealed boss Rix's fate. Ex-Blues' target Roberts started the rout with a tap in and ended it by angling home after rounding Beasant. Wing-back Balis was outstanding. His goal on half-time saw many Blues fans head for home.

#	H/A	Opponent	Date	Att.	Pos		Pts	Res		HT
35	H	COVENTRY	26/2	12,336	17	6	44	W	1-0	0-0

Crouch 54 — Ref: G Barber (Hertfordshire)

Beasant · Hiley* · Waterman · Buxton · Vincent^ · O'Neil · Quashie · Prosinecki · Harper* · Crouch · Pitt
Flowers · Quinn · Konjic · Breen · Hall · Chippo · Safri · Healy · Guerrero* · Thompson · Mills
Subs: Rudonja/Curtis · Joachim

Crouch's far-post header from Prosi's cross helps out under-pressure Rix. In a nervy last ten, City press and Beasant makes a low save from Thompson's shot. Those sure that Mills won't ever again wear a Pompey top were wrong: City cock up change kit, and wear Pompey's orange.

#	H/A	Opponent	Date	Att.	Pos		Pts	Res		HT
36	H	WALSALL	2/3	13,203	17	23	45	D	1-1	0-0

Crouch 66, O'Connor 59 — Ref: L Cable (Woking)

Beasant · Hiley* · Waterman · Buxton · Vincent · O'Neil · Quashie · Prosinecki · Harper* · Crouch · Pitt*
Walker · Shields · Holdsworth · Roper · Aranalde · Wrack · Simpson · O'Connor · Corica^ · Leitao^ · Marcelo
Subs: Curtis/Primus/Biagini · Angell/Biancalani

Milan withholds the players' wages in response to poor performances, but his gesture backfires. 'You don't know what you're doing,' chants the KJC as Rix takes off his wingers after O'Connor rifled in through a ruck. Crouch's looping header from a cross was a rare touch of class.

#	H/A	Opponent	Date	Att.	Pos		Pts	Res		HT
37	A	CRYSTAL PALACE	5/3	15,915	16	7	46	D	0-0	0-0

Ref: P Joslin (Nottinghamshire)

Beasant · Primus · Waterman · Buxton · Vincent · Cooper* · Quashie · Curtis · Derry · Crouch · Pitt*
Clarke · Fleming* · Austin · Murphy · Mullins · Granville · Black · Rihilahti · Gray^ · Morrison · Freedman
Subs: Brady/Barrett · Smith/Akinbiyi

Five matches in the middle frustrates ex-Palace, who have lost their last three at home. Clarke's slice almost gifted an early lead, but Beasant was the busier keeper, saving well from Morrison then brilliantly from a deflected Gray shot. Crouch lifted Pompey's best chance over late on.

#	H/A	Opponent	Date	Att.	Pos		Pts	Res		HT
38	H	MILLWALL	9/3	15,221	16	5	49	W	3-0	2-0

Biagini 5, O'Neil 10, Pitt 52 — Ref: P Danson (Leicester)

Beasant · Primus* · Waterman · Buxton · Vincent · Pitt^ · Quashie · O'Neil* · Derry · Crouch · Biagini
Warner · Lawrence · Ryan · Nethercott · Dyche · Ifill · Bircham · Cahill · Kinet^ · Harris* · Claridge
Subs: Curtis/Lovell/Hiley · Braniff/Bull

Prosi-less Pompey look the better for it. Biagini cuts inside and fires in low, then O'Neil's 25-yarder is bitter-sweet for the ex-Lions season-ticket holder. Pitt's angled shot was helped in by Ryan and Crouch hit a post. At the death Beasant stopped old-boy Claridge's penalty.

#	H/A	Opponent	Date	Att.	Pos		Pts	Res		HT
39	H	WIMBLEDON	12/3	13,118	16	11	49	L	1-2	1-2

Biagini 4, Cooper 77, Connolly 84 — Ref: K Hill (Hertfordshire)

Beasant · Hiley* · Waterman · Buxton · Vincent* · Curtis · Quashie^ · Lovell^ · Derry · Crouch · Biagini*
Davis · Holloway · Willmott · Cunningham Hawkins* · Morgan · Anderson^ · Francis · McAnuff · Connolly · Tait^ · Hulse
Subs: Cooper/Barrett/Vine · Agyemang^ Ardley/Cooper/Nowland

Dons boss Terry Burton is delighted with this McAnuff-inspired comeback. Sub Cooper fired home from the edge of the box, then saw his shot blocked, only for Connolly to score smartly. Earlier Biagini scored a carbon copy of Sat's goal. Lovell's open goal miss at 1-0 proved crucial.

#	H/A	Opponent	Date	Att.	Pos		Pts	Res		HT
40	A	CREWE	16/3	7,170	16	20	50	D	1-1	1-1

Crouch 24, Hulse 38 — Ref: T Leake (Lancashire)

Beasant · Wright* · Waterman · Buxton · Vincent* · Curtis · Quashie · Barrett^ · Derry^ · Crouch · Biagini^
Ince · Wright* · Charnock · Walton · Sodje · Little^ · Lunt · Sorvel · Vaughan · Tait^ · Hulse
Subs: Harper/Lovell/Pettefer · Foster/Jack/Street

Pompey's average age (excluding Beasant) was just 21 and they showed maturity beyond their years to secure a deserved point. Debut-making Vine was the pick of the crop: his reverse pass set up Crouch to slide home. Hulse swept in the equaliser after a misunderstanding at the back.

#	H/A	Opponent	Date	Att.	Pos		Pts	Res		HT
41	H	SHEFFIELD WED	23/3	14,819	15	20	51	D	0-0	0-0

Ref: A Butler (Nottinghamshire)

Beasant · Cooper · Waterman · Buxton · Vincent · Harper^ · Quashie · Pitt^ · Derry^ · Crouch · Todorov
Pressman · Haslam · Burrows · Maddix · Broomes · Hamshaw^ · McLaren · Quinn · Donnelly* · Sibon · Kuqi
Subs: Barrett/Prosinecki/Curtis · Etoku/Crane

A point against struggling Owls is enough to all-but secure safety, but it isn't enough to save Rix who is axed on Monday. Sub Prosi almost wins it with a curling free-kick against a post, but Wednesday dominate, Maddix hitting the bar. New-boy Todorov makes a low-key debut.

#	H/A	Opponent	Date	Att.	Pos		Pts	Res		HT
42	A	PRESTON	30/3	16,832	16	8	51	L	0-2	0-2

Wijnhard 64, Alexander 70 — Ref: M Cooper (Walsall)

Beasant · Buxton · Waterman · Howe* · Vincent* · Harper · Quashie · Sum'erbell · O'Neil · Brady^ · Todorov !
Moilanen · Alexander · Lucketti · Gregan · Edwards* · Cartwright^ Etuhu · McKenna · Anderson · Wijnhard^ · Cresswell
Subs: Cooper/Vine · Eaton/Ainsworth/Healy

Three debuts while Crouch has gone to Villa for £5m. Welcome to management Harry. It all goes wrong after ex-Cherry Howe limps off. Wijnhard profits, scoring and hitting a post, then loan Ranger Wilson gives away a pen. By then Toddy had seen red for an off-the-ball spat.

#	H/A	Opponent	Date	Att.	Pos		Pts	Res		HT
43	H	BURNLEY	1/4	18,020	15	9	52	D	1-1	0-1

Todorov 75, Johnson 21 — Ref: S Tomlin (Walsall)

Beasant · Hiley* · Waterman · Buxton · Vincent* · Harper · Quashie · Summerbell · O'Neil* · Prosinecki · Pitt*
Michopoulos West · Thomas · Gnohere · Briscoe · Weller^ · Ball · Grant* · Moore A · Johnson · Moore I^
Subs: Pitt/Biagini/Miglioranzi · Armstrong/Gascoigne/Little

Toddy lifts the pressure with a cute finish from a tight angle to earn a point. Pacy Johnson had earlier swept past dreaming Wilson to fire home. Gazza's cameo is his Fratton farewell and he gets generous applause. He almost engineers a win for Clarets, but Alan Moore's shot is saved.

#	H/A	Opponent	Date	Att.	Pos		Pts	Res		HT
44	A	BIRMINGHAM	7/4	25,030	17	6	53	D	1-1	0-1

Pitt 84, John 2 — Ref: H Webb (Rotherham)

Beasant · Buxton · Primus · Vincent · Wilson · O'Neil · Quashie · Pitt^ · Derry^ · Prosinecki · Biagini*
Vaesen · Kenna · Johnson M^ Tebily · Grainger · Johnson D · Hughes B · Hughes M · Lazaridis · Mooney^ · John*
Subs: Vine/Miglioranzi · Purse/Horsfield/Devlin

'If we'd been in a relegation battle we'd have gone down,' said Harry of Pompey's run-in, but high-flying Blues should have been beaten. Primus missed a ball for John to score early on, but Pompey settled. Vine swept a sitter after O'Neil hit a post, but Pitt's angled drive saved it.

#	H/A	Opponent	Date	Att.	Pos		Pts	Res		HT
45	H	WATFORD	13/4	16,302	17	14	53	L	0-1	0-0

Webber 50 — Ref: P Walton (Northants)

Beasant · Buxton · Primus · Wilson · Vincent · O'Neil* · Quashie · Summerbell · Harper ! · Summerbell · Pitt*
Chamberlain Doyley · Cox · Robinson · Glass* · Hand · Okon · Hyde · Gayle · McNamee^ · Webber^
Subs: Cooper/Brady · Panayi/Helguson/Smith

Even with 18-year-old O'Neil Pompey's longest-serving player, Harry is promising more upheavals after this inspid surrender. 'You will see a different side here for sure, next season,' he says. Derry will be one to go, after gifting Webber the winner. Harper sees red for kicking Hand.

#	H/A	Opponent	Date	Att.	Pos		Pts	Res		HT
46	A	MANCHESTER C	21/4	34,657	17	1	53	L	1-3	0-2

Pitt 59 — Howey 8, Goater 26, Macken 85 — Ref: R Furmandiz (Doncaster)

Beasant · Buxton · Primus · Wilson · Vincent · O'Neil · Quashie · Summerbell · Harper* · Prosinecki · Pitt*
Nash · Howey* · Dunne · Pearce · Primus · W't-Phillips Benarbia · Horlock · Tiatto^ · Jensen · Goater^ · Huckerby
Subs: Cooper/Brady · Wiekens/Macken/Berkovic · Vine

A soft late pen gives Pearce the chance for his 100th goal in his last-ever match. 'Put it where you like,' says Beasant. Up steps Stu and blasts the ball over the bar. It takes the edge of City's title party, but not much. 'I wonder if that will ever be us,' mused a Pompey fan at the end …

Home 15,233
Away 15,465
Average 15,233

NATIONWIDE DIVISION 1 (CUP-TIES)   Rix ⇨ Harry Redknapp

Worthington Cup

Worthington Cup	Att	F-A	H-T	Scorers, Times, and Referees	1	2	3	4	5	6	7	8	9	10	11	subs used
1 H COLCHESTER 18 L	7,078 2:1	1-2	0-0	Crouch 77 / Stockwell 53, Izzet 81 / Ref: P Taylor (Hertfordshire)	Beasant / Woodman	Hiley / Dunne*	Moore" / Keith	Zamperini / Clark	Panopoulos* / Gregory	Vincent^ / Fitzgerald	O'Neil / Pinault	Prosinecki / Izzet	Quashie / Stockwell^	Crouch / Rapley	Pitt / McGleish	Bradbury/Harper/Miglioranzi / White/Bowry

Prosi's full debut turns into a nightmare as Izzet strolls round Beasant late on to roll home the winner. U's are better than Blues all over the pitch. Stockwell's bullet header gave them the lead, but a classy pass by Prosi gave Pitt the space to cross and Crouch headed in at the far post.

FA Cup

FA Cup	Att	F-A	H-T	Scorers, Times, and Referees	1	2	3	4	5	6	7	8	9	10	11	subs used
3 H LEYTON ORIENT 14 L	12,963 3:15	1-4	1-0	Smith 12 (og) [Christie 90] / Smith 47, Watts 66, Gray 77 / Ref: P Prosser (Tewkesbury)	Kawaguchi / Barrett	Hiley^ / McGhee	Primus / Smith	Tiler / Leigertwood	Harper / Dorrian*	Pitt / Minton	Quashie / Martin	Prosinecki / Harris	O'Neil* / Hones	Crouch / Gray"	Lovell / Watts^	Derry/Crowe / Bernard/Christie/Ibehre

All seemed well when Smith inadvertently chested Pitt's cross in, but then Yoshi fails to line up a wall and Smith levels. Male model Watts nips in, before Gray fires a spectacular third. Substitute Christie has the freedom of the box late on. 'Orient, Orient!' chant the KJC at the end.

	P	Home					Away					Pts
		W	D	L	F	A	W	D	L	F	A	
1 Manchester C	46	19	3	1	63	19	12	3	8	45	33	99
2 West Brom	46	15	4	4	36	11	12	4	7	25	18	89
3 Wolverhampton	46	13	4	6	33	18	12	7	4	43	25	86
4 Millwall	46	15	3	5	43	22	7	9	7	26	26	77
5 Birmingham*	46	14	4	5	44	20	7	9	7	26	29	76
6 Norwich	46	15	6	2	36	16	7	3	13	24	35	75
7 Burnley	46	11	7	5	39	29	10	5	8	31	33	75
8 Preston	46	13	7	3	45	21	7	5	11	26	38	72
9 Wimbledon	46	9	8	6	30	22	9	5	9	33	35	67
10 Crystal Palace	46	13	3	7	42	22	7	3	13	28	40	66
11 Coventry	46	12	4	7	33	19	8	2	13	26	34	66
12 Gillingham	46	12	5	6	38	26	6	5	12	26	41	64
13 Sheffield Utd	46	8	8	7	34	30	6	6	11	19	24	60
14 Watford	46	10	5	8	38	30	6	6	11	24	26	59
15 Bradford C	46	10	1	12	41	39	5	9	9	28	37	55
16 Nott'm For	46	7	11	5	26	21	5	7	11	24	30	54
17 PORTSMOUTH	46	9	6	8	36	31	4	8	11	24	41	53
18 Walsall	46	10	6	7	29	27	3	6	14	22	44	51
19 Grimsby	46	9	7	7	34	28	3	7	13	16	44	50
20 Sheffield Wed	46	6	7	10	28	37	6	7	10	21	34	50
21 Rotherham	46	7	13	3	32	29	3	6	14	20	37	49
22 Crewe	46	8	8	7	23	32	4	5	14	24	44	49
23 Barnsley	46	9	9	5	37	33	2	6	15	22	53	48
24 Stockport	46	5	1	17	19	44	1	7	15	23	58	26
	1104	259	140	153	859	626	153	140	259	626	859	1516

* promoted after play-offs

Appearances / Goals

	Appearances						Goals			
	Lge	Sub	LC	Sub	FAC	Sub	Lge	LC	FAC	Tot
Barrett, Neil	23	3					2			2
Beasant, Dave	27									
Biagini, Leo	6	2					2			2
Bradbury, Lee	17	5			1		7			7
Brady, Garry	1	5								
Burchill, Mark	5	1					4			4
Buxton, Lewis	27	2								
Cooper, Shaun	3	4								
Crouch, Peter	37		1		1		18		1	19
Crowe, Jason	18	4			1		1			1
Curtis, Tom	3	6				1				
Derry, Shaun	12									
Edinburgh, Justin	7						1			1
Harper, Kevin	37	2		1	1		1			1
Hiley, Scott	28	5	1		1					
Howe, Eddie	1									
Ilic, Sasa	7									
Kawaguchi, Yoshi	11				1					
Lovell, Steve	8	12	1		1		2			2
Migljoranzi, Stefani	1	2		1	1					
Mills, Lee	2									
Moore, Darren	2		1							
O'Neil, Gary	27	6	1		1		1			1
Panopoulos, Mike	1	1								
Pettefer, Carl	1	1								
Pitt, Courtney	29	10	1		1		3			3
Primus, Linvoy	21	1	1		1		2			2
Prosinecki, Robert	30	3	1		1		9			9
Quashie, Nigel	33	2	1		1		2			2
Rudonja, Mladen	2	1								
Summerbell, Mark	5									
Tardif, Chris	1									
Thogersen, Thomas	2	3								
Tiler, Carl	7	1			1					
Todorov, Svet	3						1			1
Vincent, Jamie	29	5					1			1
Vine, Rowan	3	8								
Waterman, Dave	8	1								
Wilson, Scott	5									
Zamperini, Aless'ndro	16	1					2			2
(own-goals)							1		1	2
40 players used	506	96	11	3	11	2	60	1	1	62

Odds & ends

Double wins: (1) Stockport.

Double losses: (4) Preston, West Brom, Bradford C, Watford.

Won from behind: (5) Gillingham (h), Barnsley (a), Sheffield W (a), Manchester C (h), Nott'm Forest (h).

Lost from in front: (7) West Brom (h), Norwich (h), Grimsby (a), Bradford C (a), Wolves (h), Sheffield U (a), Wimbledon (h).

High spots: Topping the table in September after beating Palace. Prosinecki's hat-trick against Barnsley at Fratton. Coming back from 0-3 down at Wimbledon to draw in September.

Low spots: Losing 1-2 at home to Colchester in the Worthington Cup. Losing 1-4 at home to Leyton Orient in the FA Cup. Drawing 4-4 with Barnsley at Fratton after leading 4-2 with seven minutes to go. Losing 0-5 at West Bromwich Albion in February.

Player of the Season: Lewis Buxton.
Ever presents: (0).
Hat-tricks: (1) Robert Prosinecki.
Leading Scorer: Peter Crouch (19).

NATIONWIDE LEAGUE DIVISION 1 — Manager: Harry Redknapp — SEASON 2002-03

Column key for line-ups: position 1–11, Portsmouth player (top) / opponent player (italic, bottom); subs used.

---

1. H NOTT'M FOREST — 10/8 · Att 18,910 · Pos — · Pt 3 · W 2-0 (H-T 2-0)
Scorers: Burton 8, Péricard 45. Ref: D Gallagher (Oxfordshire)

1	2	3	4	5	6	7	8	9	10	11	subs used
Hislop	Howe*	Foxe	De Zeeuw	O'Neil	Robinson	Quashie	Taylor	Merson	Burton	Péricard	Primus
Ward	Thompson*	Hall	Hjelde	Walker	Louis-Jean	Williams	Scimeca	Prutton	Brennan^	Johnson	Harewood/Lester

Deon Burton – re-signed on the eve of the season as Rory Allen went lame again – sweeps home an early goal, then Péricard's diving header delights a packed Fratton. Just three pre-Harry players survive. One of them, Linvoy Primus, comes on early as Eddie Howe dislocates a knee.

---

2. H SHEFFIELD UTD — 13/8 · Att 16,093 · Pos 15 · Pt 4 · D 1-1 (H-T 1-1)
Scorers: Burton 25; Ndlovu 12. Ref: A Bates (Staffordshire)

1	2	3	4	5	6	7	8	9	10	11	subs used
Hislop	Howe*	Foxe	De Zeeuw	O'Neil	Robinson^	Quashie	Taylor	Merson	Burton*	Péricard*	Hughes/Burchill
Kenny	Koziuk	Ullathorne*	Yates	Murphy	Brown	Ndlovu*	Jagielka	Tonge*	Asaba	Onuora	Doane/McGovern/McCall

Pompey unveil a new gold away strip and Burton scores a 24-carat equaliser as Merson's clever flick sends him clear to round Kenny. Earlier, Ndlovu had fired home after Taylor's error. After the break, Taylor, Burton and Merson could have given Pompey a first win here since 1955.

---

3. A CRYSTAL PALACE — 17/8 · Att 18,315 · Pos 11 · Pt 7 · W 3-2 (H-T 0-2)
Scorers: Foxe 68, Crowe 69, 72; Freedman 40, Popovic 42. Ref: S Dunn (Bristol)

1	2	3	4	5	6	7	8	9	10	11	subs used
Hislop	Primus	Foxe	De Zeeuw	O'Neil^	Robinson*	Quashie	Taylor	Merson	Burton	Péricard^	Todorov/Hughes/Crowe
Clarke	Powell*	Popovic	Mullins	Butterfield	Thomson^	Derry^	Riihilahti	Granville	Adebola	Freedman	Austin/Fleming/Kabba

At half-time the bubble looks to have burst. Freedman curls in, then Popovic heads home. A double subbing turns the tide, inspired by Merson. Foxe nods in a corner, then sub Crowe is twice on hand to turn the match on its head. 4,000 travelling fans believe something special's afoot.

---

4. H WATFORD — 24/8 · Att 17,901 · Pos 18 · Pt 10 · W 3-0 (H-T 2-0)
Scorers: Merson 42p, Todorov 45, Burton 47. Ref: M Cooper (West Midlands)

1	2	3	4	5	6	7	8	9	10	11	subs used
Hislop	Festa	Foxe	De Zeeuw	Crowe	Hughes^	Quashie	Taylor	Merson^	Burton*	Todorov	Burchill/O'Neil/Robinson
Chamberlain	Cox	Dyche	Gayle	Ardley^	Robinson	Nielsen !	Hyde*	Hand	Smith*	Webber	Vernazza/Doyley/Glass

Italian defender Gianluca Festa is Harry's latest bargain – Boro are paying most of his wages – but he is hardly needed. Crowe is fouled for the pen, then Todorov's sharp turn and shot makes it two. Toddy then crosses for Burton to score with his left foot. Nielsen's mouth leads to a red.

---

5. H GRIMSBY — 26/8 · Att 5,770 · Pos 21 · Pt 13 · W 1-0 (H-T 0-0)
Scorers: Burchill 85. Ref: M Messias (North Yorks)

1	2	3	4	5	6	7	8	9	10	11	subs used
Hislop	Festa	Foxe	De Zeeuw	Crowe^	Hughes	Quashie	Taylor	Merson	Burton*	Todorov^	Burchill/Harper/Robinson
Coyne	McDermott	Gallimore	Ford	Chettle	Campbell	Cooke	Caldicott*	Groves	Barnard*	Kabba	Robinson/Rowan

Pompey are top of the league! Burchill's late left-foot shot from 20 yards, after Todorov flicked on Hislop's punt, found the corner of the net. Mariners dominated for long periods, but Pompey counter-attacked well and Coyne did well to deny Burton, then Taylor in the second half.

---

6. H BRIGHTON — 31/8 · Att 19,031 · Pos 21 · Pt 16 · W 4-2 (H-T 3-2)
Scorers: Taylor 3, Merson 26p, Todorov 45, Cullip 9, Brooker 19 [Crowe 52]. Ref: S Bennett (Kent)

1	2	3	4	5	6	7	8	9	10	11	subs used
Hislop	Festa	Foxe	De Zeeuw	Crowe*	Hughes	Quashie	Taylor	Merson	Burton^	Todorov*	Harper/Burchill/Robinson
Petterson	Pethick	Cullip	Butters	Watson	Marney	Carpenter	Oatway	Melton*	Brooker	Barrett !	Wilkinson

Seagulls have three ex-Blues on show and they stun a full house by leading after Taylor's early 25-yarder. A dodgy pen as Butters fouls Toddy lets Merson level, then Todorov nets from close range on half-time. Crowe's spectacular strike seals it. Barrett tangles with Taylor and walks.

---

7. A GILLINGHAM — 7/9 · Att 8,717 · Pos 10 · Pt 19 · W 3-1 (H-T 2-0)
Scorers: Merson 29, Burchill 45, O'Neil 79; James 68. Ref: S Baines (Derbyshire)

1	2	3	4	5	6	7	8	9	10	11	subs used
Hislop	Primus	Festa	De Zeeuw	Crowe*	Hughes	Quashie	Taylor	Merson	Burchill^	Todorov	Harper/O'Neil
Bartram	Patterson	Ashby	Hope	Edge^	Hessenthaler	Saunders	Shaw	Ipoua	Johnson*		James/Perpetuini

Burchill takes advantage of loanee Burton's misfortune (broken foot in training) and is star-of-the-show. His pass lets Taylor cross for Merse's opener, then he guided home Toddy's pass. James gave Gills hope, but O'Neil chipped a classy third to celebrate an England under-21 call up.

---

8. H MILLWALL — 14/9 · Att 17,201 · Pos 18 · Pt 22 · W 1-0 (H-T 0-0)
Scorers: Todorov 50. Ref: S Tomlin (East Sussex)

1	2	3	4	5	6	7	8	9	10	11	subs used
Hislop	Primus	Festa	De Zeeuw	Harper	Robinson^	Quashie	Taylor	Merson	Péricard^	Todorov^	Burchill/O'Neil/Tiler
Warner	Lawrence	Nethercott	Ward	Bull	Ifill	Roberts	Livermore	Kinet	Claridge	Davies	Harris/Braniff

Despite having 12 players out, Pompey ensure their best-ever start in a lunchtime kick-off. Early on Hislop was in fine form to deny Claridge twice and Kinet. Taylor hit the bar as Pompey improved, then Quashie sent Toddy racing away to coolly lift the ball over the advancing keeper.

---

9. H WIMBLEDON — 17/9 · Att 18,837 · Pos 14 · Pt 25 · W 4-1 (H-T 3-1)
Scorers: Péricard 3, Todorov 31, Williams 39(og), [Taylor 72]; Shipperley 11. Ref: P Danson (Leicestershire)

1	2	3	4	5	6	7	8	9	10	11	subs used
Hislop	Primus	Festa	De Zeeuw	Harper^	Robinson	Quashie	Taylor	Merson	Péricard	Todorov^	Burchill/O'Neil/Tiler
Davis	Darlington	Williams	Gier^	Hawkins	McAnuff	Francis	Andersen	Tapp	Shipperley^	Nowland*	Leigertw'd/Gray/Ainsworth

Péricard hooks in Merson's cross, but pacy McAnuff ('How much?' asks Harry, but £2m is too steep) sets up ex-Saint Shipperley soon after. Toddy restored the lead cutting home from the left, then Davis swings his boot and misses Williams' back-pass. Taylor's blinder goes in off a post.

---

10. A NORWICH — 21/9 · Att 21,335 · Pos 3 · Pt 25 · L 0-1 (H-T 0-0)
Scorers: Roberts 81. Ref: B Curson (Leicestershire)

1	2	3	4	5	6	7	8	9	10	11	subs used
Hislop	Primus	Festa^	De Zeeuw	Harper	Robinson^	Quashie	O'Neil*	Taylor	Merson	Todorov^	Péricard/Burchill/Ritchie
Green	Kenton	Mackay	Drury	Nedergaard	Emblem*	Mulryne	Holt	Heckingb'th*	Roberts	McVeigh	Easton/Nielsen

Harry plays a lone striker, and his tactic almost pays off in this top-of-the-table clash. Quashie and O'Neil both went close to nicking it, but long-time Pompey scourge Roberts got between Festa and De Zeeuw to head home late on. City defender Paul Ritchie is Harry's latest loanee.

---

11. H BRADFORD C — 28/9 · Att 18,459 · Pos 13 · Pt 28 · W 3-0 (H-T 2-0)
Scorers: Quashie 17, 58, Péricard 21. Ref: J Ross (London)

1	2	3	4	5	6	7	8	9	10	11	subs used
Hislop	Primus	Festa^	De Zeeuw	Harper	Robinson*	Quashie	Taylor	Merson	Péricard*	Todorov	O'Neil/Ritchie/Burchill
Banks	Uhlenbeek	Molenaar	Bower	Jacobs	Gray	Evans*	Jorgensen	Warnock	Cadamart'r*	Proctor	Reid/Juanjo

Pompey brush aside Bradford, who include former Blue Dave Beasant on the bench. Once Quashie fires home from the edge of the box it is a question of how many. They settle for two more as Merson first sets up Péricard, then plays a delightful pass to play in Quashie for the third.

Portsmouth — match-by-match (Division One), games 12–23

#	Venue	Opponent	Date	Div	Result	Score	Opp. pos.	Pts	Att.
12	A	ROTHERHAM	5/10	1	W	3–2	8	31	8,604
13	H	COVENTRY	19/10	1	D	1–1	7	32	18,837
14	A	BURNLEY	26/10	1	W	3–0	10	35	15,788
15	H	PRESTON	29/10	1	W	3–2	16	38	18,637
16	H	LEICESTER	2/11	1	L	0–2	2	38	19,107
17	A	WOLVERHAMPTON	6/11	1	D	1–1	9	39	27,022
18	A	DERBY	9/11	1	W	2–1	12	42	26,587
19	H	STOKE	16/11	1	W	3–0	19	45	18,701
20	A	SHEFFIELD WED	23/11	1	W	3–1	23	48	16,602
21	H	WALSALL	30/11	1	W	3–2	19	51	17,701
22	A	READING	7/12	1	D	0–0	5	52	23,462
23	A	STOKE	14/12	1	D	1–1	22	53	13,300

---

12 — A ROTHERHAM
Péricard 15, Todorov 23, Merson 45p, Byfield 34, Lee 73p. Ref: G Laws (Tyne & Wear)
Pompey: Hislop, Festa, Primus, De Zeeuw, Ritchie, Péricard, Diabaté, Quashie, Taylor, Merson, Todorov*, Harper
Rotherham: Pollitt, Swailes!, Scott, McIntosh, Hurst, Sedgwick*, Garner, Daws", Warne, Byfield*, Barker, Lee/Mullin/Monkhouse
When Swailes fouled Toddy in the box and saw red it looked all over as Merson scored from the spot. Sub Lee's pen, after Festa tugged him back, set up a grandstand finish and Hislop tipped Hurst's last-gasp strike onto the bar. Taylor had set up the first two before Byfield's header.

13 — H COVENTRY
Péricard 51, Davenport 60. Ref: D Crick (Surrey)
Pompey: Hislop, Festa, Primus, De Zeeuw, Ritchie, Péricard, Diabaté, Quashie, Taylor, Merson, Todorov*, Harper — Ritchie/Burchill
Coventry: Debec, Caldwell, West, Konjic, Quinn, Pipe*, McAllister, Chippo, Safri, Patridge, Mills*, McSheffrey/Bothroyd
Ex-Pompey villain Lee Mills hits the bar from 25 yards and also a post before Péricard runs onto Merson's pass to lob the opener. Davenport got lucky after pin-ball in the Pompey area, then it's backs-to-the-wall for City. De Zeeuw hits the bar and sub Burchill misses from close in.

14 — A BURNLEY
Quashie 21, Todorov 55, Harper 86. Ref: M Clattenburg (Co Durham)
Pompey: Hislop, Festa, Primus, De Zeeuw, Ritchie, Péricard, Diabaté, Quashie, Taylor, Merson, Todorov*, Robinson/Harper
Burnley: Beresford, Cox", West, Gnohere, Branch^, Little, Davis S, Briscoe, Moore I*, Blake, Taylor, Weller/Maylett/Papadop'los
Another week, another new boy and ex-Villain Stone is at the heart of a great performance. Burnley are unbeaten in 12, but end up outclassed. Todorov's clever pull-back set up Quashie, then Toddy's mis-hit made it two. Harper rounded things off after West hit the bar from the spot.

15 — H PRESTON
Stone 23, Merson 28p, Taylor 34, Cresswell 12, Alexander 47p. Ref: P Armstrong (Berkshire)
Pompey: Hislop, Festa, Primus, De Zeeuw, Ritchie, Diabaté, Quashie, Taylor, Merson, Péricard*, Todorov*, O'Neil/Harper
Preston: Lucas, Broomes, Lucketti, Taggart, Murdock, Edwards", McKenna, Rankine^, Skora, Lewis*, Cresswell, Abbott/Etuhu/Jackson
Stone and Merson look a cut above Div One. Cresswell snaps up an early rebound, but then Stone taps in. Péricard is tripped for Merson to score from the spot, then Taylor lifts a long-shot over the keeper. Cresswell hits the woodwork before Alexander converts after Ritchie's foul.

16 — H LEICESTER
Scowcroft 13, Elliott 39. Ref: A Hall (West Midlands)
Pompey: Hislop, Festa, Primus, De Zeeuw, Ritchie, Diabaté^, Quashie, Taylor, Merson, Péricard, Todorov*, Ritchie/O'Neil/Burchill
Leicester: Walker, Sinclair, Taggart, Elliott, Davidson, McKinlay, Izzet*, Rogers, Dickov, Deane, Scowcroft, Stewart/Benjamin
The game of the season so far turns into a farce as incessant rain turns the pitch into a lake. City's 'route one' approach pays off and Scowcroft is set up from Walker's punt, then Elliott heads home Izzett's corner. 'The ref said he'd call it off if we equalised,' moaned Merson afterwards.

17 — A WOLVERHAMPTON
Merson 56, Sturridge 62. Ref: G Salisbury (Lancashire)
Pompey: Hislop, Primus, Stone, De Zeeuw, Ritchie, Diabaté, Quashie, Taylor, Merson, Robinson*, Todorov*, Harper/Burchill/O'Neil
Wolverhampton: Murray, Edworthy, Lescott, Irwin, Clyde, Ince, Rae, Cooper, Blake, Ndah, Miller, Sturridge/Kennedy/Newton
Pompey turn up in a convoy of cars as their coach breaks down. A scratch side, as De Zeeuw and Festa are ruled out, earns a point with a gutsy display. Merson's sweetly struck free-kick put Pompey ahead, before Sturridge turned home. Diabaté's crude foul on Ndah goes unpunished.

18 — A DERBY
Todorov 27, Burchill 51, Higginbotham 16p. Ref: H Webb (South Yorkshire)
Pompey: Hislop, Primus, Stone, De Zeeuw, Ritchie*, Diabaté, Quashie, Taylor, Merson, Todorov*, Burchill*, Foxe/Péricard/Harper
Derby: Grant, Higginbotham, Evatt, Barton, Boertien, Bolder, Lee, Hunt, Kinkladze, McLeod, Morris, Riggott/Ravanelli/Burton
Diabaté's foul on Morris allows Higginbotham to score from the spot, but Pompey roar back to lead as Todorov converts Taylor's cross, then Merson and Taylor combine to set up Burchill. Rams throw on Pompey target Ravanelli and Burton – earlier on loan at Fratton – to no avail.

19 — H STOKE
Burchill 49, Péricard 87, Todorov 90. Ref: P Taylor (Hertfordshire)
Pompey: Hislop, Primus, Foxe, De Zeeuw, Ritchie, Diabaté, Quashie, Taylor, Merson, Todorov*, Burchill*, Crowe/O'Neil
Stoke: Cutler, Henry, Thomas, Handyside, Clarke, Gudjonsson*, Gunnarsson, Marteins'n^, O'Connor, Hoekstra, Mooney, Iweluma/Gr'nacre/Vand'zen
Hard-working Stoke are the epitome of former Pompey boss Pulis, now at the Potteries, but class tells in the end. Burchill slots home Harper's cross at the near post, then sub Péricard and Todorov put a gloss finish to the scoreline. Loaned Stone is back at Villa with a hamstring injury.

20 — A SHEFFIELD WED
Todorov 11, 50, O'Neil 64, Knight 27. Ref: P Danson (Leicester)
Pompey: Hislop, Primus^, Foxe, De Zeeuw, Ritchie, Diabaté, Robinson, Taylor, Merson*, Péricard, Todorov*, O'Neil/Crowe/Burchill
Sheffield Wed: Pressman, Crane, Haslam, Geary, Bromby, Quinn, Armstrong, Beswetth'k*, Sibon, Knight, Owusu^, Hanshaw/Donnelly
Pompey had never won for Sky TV. Despite losing talisman Merson with an ankle injury, the jinx was buried. His deputy O'Neil ran the show and scored a classy third. Toddy's brace, sandwiched Knight's strike. Diabaté picked up a fifth booking in nine games and will be banned.

21 — H WALSALL
Quashie 45, Todorov 58, Taylor 76, Sonner 31p, 68p. Ref: G Hegley (Hertfordshire)
Pompey: Hislop, Primus, Crowe, De Zeeuw, Ritchie, Diabaté, Quashie, Taylor, Merson, Périard, Todorov, O'Neil/Burchill/Buxton
Walsall: Walker, Pollet, Hay, Roper, Ritchie, Sonner, O'Connor, Wrack, Corica, Junior*, Leitao, Birch
A second half 16-man brawl goes unpunished by the ref. He upsets everyone, awarding two pens for Sonner to convert, sandwiching Quashie's leveller and Toddy's header from a corner. Unhappy Harry is sent to the stands, then Taylor scores after a scramble. Pompey are staying up …

22 — A READING
Ref: T Leake (Darwen)
Pompey: Hislop, Primus, De Zeeuw, Foxe, Ritchie, Robinson, Quashie, Taylor, Merson, Burchill*, Harper
Reading: Hahnemann, Murty, Williams, Upson, Shorey, Rougier, Harper, Newman, Salako, Forster, Hughes, Watson/Cureton/Butler
Patched up Pompey – 'I only had 12 fit players training this week,' whinged Harry – dug deep. Ex-Royal Hislop made a fine double save from Forster, then Salako to preserve a point. The visitors fire blanks and misfit Burchill is subbed at half-time – his Fratton career is winding down.

23 — A STOKE
Crowe 74, Gunnarsson 34. Ref: P Walton (Northants)
Pompey: Hislop, Primus, De Zeeuw, Foxe, Ritchie*, Robinson^, Quashie, Taylor, Merson, Diabaté, Burton, Todorov
Stoke: Banks, Thomas, Shtaniuk, Handyside, Hall, Gudjonsson, Gunnarsson, Henry^, Neal*, Cooke, Greenacre^, Crowe, Mart'ns'n/G'ffe'w/Mooney
Burton is back permanently for a song from cash-strapped Rams. He can't fire Pompey. Stoke are in total control as Gunnarsson prods in Shtaniuk's nod down. After the break a change of tactics is rewarded when sub Crowe, just on, makes sure Primus's goal-bound shot goes in.

NATIONWIDE LEAGUE DIVISION 1 — Manager: Harry Redknapp — SEASON 2002-03

No	Date	Att	Pos	Pt	F-A	H-T	Scorers, Times, and Referees	1	2	3	4	5	6	7	8	9	10	11	subs used
24	H IPSWICH 21/12	19,130	18	54	1-1	1-0	Todorov 19 / Gaardsoe 54, Ref: G Barber (Hertfordshire)	Hislop	Primus	Foxe	De Zeeuw	Makin!	Diabaté	Quashie	Taylor	Merson*	Todorov	Burton^	O'Neil/Burchill/Harper
								Marshall	*Holland*	*Gaardsoe*	*Makin!*	*Miller T*	*Clapham*	*Magilton"*	*Hreidarsson*	*Counago"*	*Naylor"*		*Bent M/Bent D/Wright*
25	H CRYSTAL PALACE 26/12	19,217	12	55	1-1	1-1	Merson 27 / Gray 30, Ref: L Cable (Surrey)	Hislop	Primus	Foxe	De Zeeuw	Crowe^	Diabaté^	Quashie	Taylor	Merson	Todorov	Burton^	O'Neil/Péricard/Harper
								Kolinko	*Symons*	*Powell*	*Popovic*	*Butterfield*	*Mullins*	*Derry*	*Riihilahti*	*Gray*	*Adebola*	*Black^*	*Akinbiyi*
26	A NOTT'M FOREST 28/12	28,165	5	58	2-1	0-0	Taylor 56, Péricard 87 / Dawson 90, Ref: C Foy (Merseyside)	Hislop	Primus	Foxe	De Zeeuw	Walker*	O'Neil	Diabaté	Quashie	Taylor	Todorov	Burton^	Péricard/Crowe
								Ward	*Louis-Jean^*	*Dawson*	*Harper**	*Brennan*	*Prutton*	*Williams*	*Reid*	*Johnson*	*Jess"*		*Doig/Thompson/Westcarr*
27	A WATFORD 1/1	15,048	9	59	2-2	0-0	Burton 54, Harper 58 / Hyde 51, Cox 81, Ref: P Rejer (Worcestershire)	Hislop	Primus	Foxe	De Zeeuw^	Gayle	O'Neil	Diabaté	Quashie	Taylor	Todorov*	Burton^	Crowe/Péricard/Merson
								Chamberlain	*Ardley*	*Cox*	*Pennant*	*Hyde*	*Vernazza*	*Robinson*	*N'l Williams*	*Helguson*			*McNamee/Nielsen/Smith*
28	H SHEFFIELD UTD 13/1	18,872	3	59	1-2	0-1	O'Neil 78 / Ndlovu 24, Brown 87, Ref: C Wilkes (Gloucestershire)	Hislop	Primus	Foxe	Festa^	Page	O'Neil	Quashie	Taylor	Merson	Todorov^	Burton^	Harper/Tavlaridis/Burton
								Kenny	*Jagielka*	*Murphy*	*Quinn*	*Montgomery*	*Brown*	*McCall*	*Tonge*	*Ndlovu*	*Allison*		*Péricard*
29	A BRIGHTON 18/1	6,848	24	60	1-1	0-0	Todorov 64 / Zamora 54, Ref: M Messias (North Yorks)	Hislop	Primus	Foxe	Stone*	Watson	Diabaté	Quashie	Taylor	Merson	Todorov	Péricard^	Harper/Yakubu/Crowe
								Roberts	*Pethick*	*Cullip*	*Mayo*	*Watson*	*Brooker*	*Carpenter*	*Oatway^*	*Jones*	*Barrett^*	*Zamora*	*Blackwell/Kitson*
30	H GRIMSBY 1/2	19,428	22	63	3-0	1-0	Todorov 64 Zamora 54 — Yakubu 4, Ford 75 (og), Quashie 90, Ref: A Bates (Staffordshire)	Hislop	Primus	Foxe^	Tavlaridis*	Harper*	Diabaté	Quashie	Taylor	Merson	Todorov	Yakubu	Crowe/Diabaté/Péricard
								Coyne	*McDermott*	*Chettle*	*Ford*	*Gallimore*	*Campbell*	*Groves*	*Santos**	*Bolder**	*Mansaram*	*Livingstone*	*Soames/Ward*
31	H DERBY 8/2	19,503	14	66	6-2	3-0	Merson 3, Yakubu 17, 80, Taylor 22, Morris 58, Kink!' 67p [Todorov 73, 85], Ref: C Penton (Sussex)	Hislop	Primus	Foxe	Tavlaridis^	Harper*	Diabaté	Quashie	Taylor	Merson	Yakubu	Todorov^	Diabaté/Heikinnen
								Grant	*Barton*	*Evatt*	*Elliott*	*Zavango*	*Bolder*	*Lee*	*Kinkladze*	*Boertien*	*Morris*	*McLeod*	
32	A LEICESTER 17/2	31,775	2	67	1-1	0-1	Taylor 65 / Benjamin 9, Ref: M Pike (Cumbria)	Hislop	Primus	Foxe	De Zeeuw	Taggart	Sherwood	Quashie	Taylor	Merson	Yakubu	Todorov	Péricard/Diabaté
								Walker	*Sinclair*	*Elliott*	*Taggart*	*Rogers*	*McKinlay*	*Izzet*	*Davidson*	*Scowcroft*	*Dickov^*	*Benjamin**	*Summerbee/Wright*
33	H GILLINGHAM 22/2	19,521	15	70	1-0	0-0	De Zeeuw 58, Ref: S Dunn (Bristol)	Hislop	Primus	Foxe	De Zeeuw	Ashby	Sherwood	Quashie	Taylor	Merson^	Yakubu^	Todorov	Péricard/O'Neil
								Brown	*Nosworthy*	*Ashby*	*Hope*	*Edge*	*Hes'enthaler Smith*	*Southall*	*Shaw*	*Wallace*	*Ipoua^*		*Sidibe*
34	A MILLWALL 1/3	9,697	16	73	5-0	4-0	Yakubu 15, 25, Sherwood 31, [Todorov 45, Merson 72p], Ref: H Webb (South Yorkshire)	Hislop	Primus	Foxe	De Zeeuw	Reid	Sherwood	Quashie	Taylor	Merson*	Yakubu	Todorov^	Crowe/Péricard/Diabaté
								Warner	*Reid*	*Robinson*	*Ward*	*Ifill*	*Wise*	*Livermore*	*Kinet*	*Harris*	*Claridge^*		*Sadlier*

24 — Pompey should have lost as Town striker Counago missed three sitters. Toddy had snapped up Marshall's mishandled cross, but Gaardsoe levelled with a thumping header. In a late push, Makin sees red for a bad foul and Marshall atones with a fine save from sub Burchill's header.

25 — Harry lambasts a tabloid hack who suggests Pompey are sliding: 'It's terrible. We've lost twice all season. What a stupid question!' Merse is not fully fit but still runs 70 yards to get on the end of Taylor's cross. Toddy hits the bar, but Gray's sweet volley earns Palace their tenth draw.

26 — Crisis? What crisis? Even without Merson, resting his tender ankle, Pompey outclass a youthful play-off-chasing Forest. Taylor's sublime 25-yarder, with his right foot, is followed up by sub Péricard's poke home as Ward spilled Crowe's shot. Dawson's late header was a consolation.

27 — A heavy pitch meant Harry didn't risk fit-again Merson or Stone. It still looked good as Burton finished a good move, then Harper cut in and curled home to cancel out Hyde's goal. With De Zeeuw limping off early, the defence looked vulnerable and Cox's free header underlined that.

28 — Re-arranged for Monday night Sky after Saturday's frost, Blades won to keep Pompey in reach. Tonge set up Ndlovu, but then O'Neil, but then O'Neil's cool finish on the crocked-again Festa – which let in Brown. and Péricard all knocked on wood. O'Neil's cool finish was erased by Tavlaridis's error – on for the crocked-again Festa – which let in Brown.

29 — Lowly Brighton's high-tempo style shakes Pompey and the Seagulls are flying after Zamora twisted to fire home. The introduction of Yakubu (or is it Ayegbeni?) – signed from Haifa in the week – peps things up and soon after Todorov swivels and buries a shot in the bottom corner.

30 — Yak's pace sets Fratton alight as he burns through early on. Sherwood looks a class above, his protracted move from Spurs complete, and Town are all at sea for an hour. Somehow it stays 1-0 and Groves should have levelled, but once Ford turned a cross into his own net that's it.

31 — Rams were in this game for ten minutes – as a Kinky-inspired second-half comeback looked on – but that apart they were utterly slaughtered. 'Gregory Out!' (as in unpopular ex-Blues boss John) sang the Rams fans and the home crowd joined in – the axe wouldn't be long in falling.

32 — The returning De Zeeuw is at fault for Benjamin's sharp finish. Promotion rivals City are the better side, but after half-time Pompey improve. They have still created little though until Taylor cracks another 30-yarder past Walker. Harper's form has been noted by Scotland boss Vogts.

33 — Merson's pin-point cross to the far post, for De Zeeuw to head home the only goal of the game, was a rare shaft of light in a dour game. Gills came for a point and rarely threatened, while Pompey were off-key. It was a crucial win, with most of their rivals also picking up three points.

34 — Barred Pompey fans made do with a big screen at Fratton, so it was left to give Merson a standing ovation. Sherwood headed the first, Yakubu turned in Harper's cross and then angled home Todorov's pass. Toddy sealed it, before Yak was tripped for the pen.

Portsmouth FC — match results (continued)

#	V	Opponent	Date	Att	Pos	Opp	Pts	HT	FT	Res
35	A	WIMBLEDON	4/3	10,356	1	14	73	1-0	1-2	L
36	H	NORWICH	12/3	19,221	1	8	76	0-0	3-2	W
37	H	WOLVERHAMPTON	15/3	19,558	1	6	79	1-0	1-0	W
38	A	COVENTRY	19/3	13,922	1	15	82	3-0	4-0	W
39	A	PRESTON	22/3	16,665	1	12	83	1-0	1-1	D
40	A	WALSALL	5/4	7,899	1	20	86	2-1	2-1	W
41	H	SHEFFIELD WED	12/4	19,524	2	23	86	1-0	1-2	L
42	A	BURNLEY	15/4	19,221	1	16	89	0-0	0-0	D
43	A	IPSWICH	18/4	29,396	1	7	89	0-3	0-3	L
44	H	READING	21/4	19,535	1	5	92	2-0	3-0	W
45	H	ROTHERHAM	27/4	19,420	1	14	95	3-2	3-2	W
46	A	BRADFORD C	4/5	19,088	1	20	98	1-0	5-0	W

Home 18,955 · Away 16,880 · Average 18,955

---

35 — WIMBLEDON (A)
Portsmouth: Hislop, Primus, De Zeeuw, Festa, Crowe*, Sherwood, Quashie, Taylor, Merson, Yakubu, Todorov^ · subs O'Neil^/Péricard
Wimbledon: Davis, Volz, Williams, Andersen, Hawkins, Ainsworth, Morgan^, Reo-Coker, Tapp, Shipperley, Gray* · subs Agyemang/McAnuff
Merson 26 — Agyemang 66, Ainsworth 87
Ref: P Walton (Northants)
Appeals for a Wimbledon boycott – controversially off to Milton Keynes soon – fall on deaf ears as 9,000 travel to Selhurst Park. Merson's well-placed shot was cancelled out by Agyemang, as Dons exploit Pompey's lack of right-side cover. Reo-Coker's run sets up the winner.

36 — NORWICH (H)
Portsmouth: Hislop, Primus, De Zeeuw, Harper*, Stone^, Sherwood, Quashie^, Taylor, Merson*, Yakubu, Todorov · subs O'Neil/Diabaté/Foxe
Norwich: Green, Nederg 'and' Mackay, Bromby, Drury, Rivers, Holt, Russell*, Abbey, Easton, McVeigh* · subs Nielsen/Roberts/Emblen
Yakubu 57, Todorov 59, 72 — Easton 58, Rivers 62
Ref: D Gallagher (Banbury)
Pompey and City trade four goals in five minutes to delight Sky TV once more. However, it's Toddy's winner, as he spins on a sixpence to fire high into the net, which is the pick. Play-off chasing Norwich pile forward and Hislop saves from Abbey at the death to ensure the win.

37 — WOLVERHAMPTON (H)
Portsmouth: Hislop, Primus*, De Zeeuw, Festa, Stone*, Sherwood, O'Neil, Merson, Yakubu^, Todorov^ · subs Harper/Burton/Diabaté
Wolverhampton: Murray, Edworthy, Clyde, Pollet, Irwin, Rae, Ince, Cameron^, Kennedy, Sturridge, Miller* · subs Newton/Proudlock
Stone 4
Ref: P Dowd (Staffordshire)
Stone's early goal, his shot arcing into the net off Murray, settled a scrappy game. Wolves lose three defenders to illness, while Taylor was out after a heel op. Clyde missed the best chance from 12 yards. On the final whistle the crowd were on the pitch. It wasn't all over: just a fire drill.

38 — COVENTRY (A)
Portsmouth: Hislop, Foxe, De Zeeuw, Festa, Stone, Sherwood, O'Neil, Harper, Merson, Yakubu, Todorov^ · subs Burton/Péricard/Diabaté
Coventry: Hyldgaard, Pead, Shaw, Caldwell, Eustace, McAllister, Chippo^, Safri*, Holdsworth, Joachim, Heikinnen · subs McSheffrey/Whing
Caldwell 14 (og), Stone 17, Harper 23, Merson 68
Ref: M Ryan (Lancashire)
'Goodbye to the Nationwide!' sang Pompey's fans as free-falling (one win in 13) City were thrashed. Toddy hit a post and the ball went in off Caldwell, O'Neil set up Stone and Harper finished Yak's cross with the game only a quarter gone. Merson's rare left-footer wrapped things up.

39 — PRESTON (A)
Portsmouth: Hislop, Primus, De Zeeuw, Festa, Stone, Sherwood, Quashie, Harper, Merson, Yakubu, Todorov^ · sub Burton
Preston: Lucas, Alexander, Broomes", Edwards, Cartwright*, Etuhu, McKenna, Lewis, Koumantis*, Cresswell · subs Lynch/Mears/O'Neil
Yakubu 5 — McKenna 89
Ref: M Messias (North Yorks)
12 months ago Harry took his first Pompey game, near the foot of Div One, to Deepdale. 'I didn't fancy the job,' he said at the time. What a difference now! Yak scored after Stone and Harper combined, but Preston pinched a point through McKenna's 25-yard free-kick at the death.

40 — WALSALL (A)
Portsmouth: Hislop, Primus, De Zeeuw, Festa, Stone, Sherwood, Quashie, Harper, Merson*, Yakubu^, Todorov · subs Burton/O'Neil
Walsall: Ward, Bazeley, Carbon, Aranalde, Samways, Corica*, Wrack^, Junior, Leitao · subs Hay/Zdrilic/Matias
Harper 15, Todorov 33 — Junior 45
Ref: S Mathieson (Cheshire)
Earlier Leicester had knocked Pompey off the top, but Harper's sprint and shot, then Toddy's header put them in arrogant control here. Then Foxe was caught out and Junior took full advantage. Hislop nearly handled outside the box as Saddlers pressed, but Merse missed a sitter to seal it.

41 — SHEFFIELD WED (H)
Portsmouth: Hislop, Primus, De Zeeuw, Festa, Stone, Sherwood, Quashie, Harper*, Merson, Yakubu, Todorov^ · subs Bradbury/Holt
Sheffield Wed: Pressman, Bromby, Smith, Maddix, Westwood, McLaren, Haslam, Quinn, B'ry-Murphy Owusu*, Kuqi^ · subs Reddy/Holt
Bradbury 20 — Westwood 76, Reddy 90
Ref: D Crick (Surrey)
Bradbury, recalled from struggling Owls ten days ago, swivelled to score, but a second wouldn't come. Then Primus sliced a clearance and Westwood netted. In stoppage time the ref let Reddy run through, while Festa thought he had yet to take a free-kick, and he pooped the party.

42 — BURNLEY (A)
Portsmouth: Hislop, Primus, De Zeeuw, Festa, Stone, Sherwood, Quashie, Harper*, Merson, Yakubu, Todorov · sub Péricard
Burnley: Michopoulos, West, Davis S, McGregor, Gnohere", Weller, Pap'dop'los*, Blake, Branch, Moore I, Taylor · subs Maylett/O'Neil^/Chapelow
Ref: B Curson (Leicestershire)
When Merson whacked an early pen against the bar it seemed the Gods were against Pompey again. Chances went begging as Clarets' keeper played a blinder, but with 17 minutes left Quashie's cross-cum-shot was swept in by Todorov and the party could get going. Pompey were up!

43 — IPSWICH (A)
Portsmouth: Hislop, Primus, De Zeeuw, Festa, Stone, Sherwood, Quashie, Harper*, Merson*, Yakubu, Todorov · subs Péricard/O'Neil/Harper
Ipswich: Marshall, Wilnis, Gaardsøe, Makin, Richards, Miller, Magilton^, Holland, Reuser*, Counago, Bent M^ · subs Wright/Westlake/Armstrong
Reuser 11, Miller 27, Counago 30
Ref: E Wolstenholme (Lancs)
Pompey are still mentally partying and play-off-chasing Town profit from some sloppy defending in the first half. Not that the travelling fans mind too much, led in a sing-song by off-key bugler JPFC Westwood. The downside is Pompey's title hopes are now out of their own hands.

44 — READING (H)
Portsmouth: Hislop, Primus, De Zeeuw, Festa, Stone, Sherwood, Quashie, Harper*, Merson*, Yakubu, Todorov · subs De Zeeuw/Diabaté/O'Neil
Reading: Hahnemann, Murty, Williams, Brown^, Shorey, Chadwick^, Hughes*, Newman, Harper, Little, Forster · subs Mackie/Henderson/Salako
Péricard 19, 45, Todorov 71
Ref: G Cain (Merseyside)
Leicester's lunchtime defeat at Blades lifted spirits and rampant Pompey ripped Reading apart. Péricard's future – he is on loan from Juve – is still uncertain, but two well-taken goals will have lifted his value. Toddy ran from deep to score the third as the Royals ran up the white flag.

45 — ROTHERHAM (H)
Portsmouth: Hislop, Gray, De Zeeuw, Festa, Stone, Sherwood, Quashie, Harper*, Merson, Yakubu, Todorov · sub Péricard^
Rotherham: Gray, Barker S, Swailes, McIntosh, Branston, Sedgwick^, Daws, Talbot*, Hurst, Barker R, Lee · subs Warne/Monkhouse
Merson 11p, Todorov 22, 45 — Branston 16, Swailes 29
Ref: R Beeby (Northants)
Foxes drop more lunchtime points, so a win tonight will seal the title. Todorov's fall looks innocuous, but the ref gives it and Merson finally scores at the Fratton End. Four more goals are traded before the break, then it's a countdown to the old trophy being presented to Merson.

46 — BRADFORD C (A)
Portsmouth: Hislop* (75), Primus, De Zeeuw, Festa^, Stone, Sherwood, Quashie, Harper, Merson, Yakubu, Todorov · subs Kawaguchi/Diabaté/O'Neil (Davison)
Bradford C: Uhlenbeek, Wetherall, Molenaar", Bower, Muirhead, Jorgensen, Francis, Myers, Gray, Forrest^, Penfold · subs Ten Heuvel
Festa 20, Todorov 48, 50p, 58, Stone 75
Ref: S Baines (Derbyshire)
All the players wear white boots: 'You'd better win then,' warns Harry. He needn't have fretted. Festa's deflected goal pleases 7,000 visitors, as does Yoshi's cameo. Toddy's quick-fire triple ensures the Golden Boot. 'I wish I'd backed us last summer at 33/1,' rues Harry at the end.

NATIONWIDE DIVISION 1 (CUP-TIES) Manager: Harry Redknapp SEASON 2002-03

Worthington Cup

	Att	F-A	H-T	Scorers, Times, and Referees	1	2	3	4	5	6	7	8	9	10	11	subs used
1 H PETERBOROUGH 1 W	8,581 2:22	2-0	1-0	Quashie 27, Primus 74	Hislop	Primus	Festa	De Zeeuw	Crowe*	Hughes^	Quashie	Taylor	Merson	Todorov	Burchill*	Harper/Robinson/Péricard
				Ref: L Cable (Surrey)	*Tyler*	*Pearce*	*Joseph*	*Rea*	*Burton !*	*Newton*	*Bullard*	*Danielsson*	*Shield**	*Green^*	*Fenn"*	*Gill/Clarke A/MacDonald*

Shot-shy Posh (no goals in 473 minutes) face an uphill task by half-time. Quashie poked home the rebound after Tyler's great save from Burchill, then a linesman sees Sagi Burton's elbow on Todorov and he sees red. Primus slid in to convert Toddy's cross for a popular goal.

	Att	F-A	H-T	Scorers, Times, and Referees	1	2	3	4	5	6	7	8	9	10	11	subs used
2 H WIMBLEDON 1 L	11,754 1:20	1-3	1-2	Péricard 6 [Shipperley 59]	Hislop	Primus	Festa	Ritchie	Harper	O'Neil	Robinson	Taylor	Merson	Péricard	Todorov*	Burchill
				McAnuff 7, Leigertwood 16,	*Davis*	*Holloway*	*Leigertwood*	*Gier*	*Hawkins*	*McAnuff*	*Francis*	*Andersen*	*Tapp*	*Shipperley*	*Nowland**	*Gray*
				Ref: T Parkes (West Midlands)												

Péricard finishes off a Merson free-kick and a repeat of the league game looks on … for 60 seconds. McAnuff's shot deflects off Taylor, then Leigertwood nods in a corner. Pompey press and Taylor has a goal ruled out, but ex-Saint Shipperley silences the boo-boys with a fine header.

FA Cup

	Att	F-A	H-T	Scorers, Times, and Referees	1	2	3	4	5	6	7	8	9	10	11	subs used
3 A MANCHESTER U 1 L	67,222 P:1	1-4	1-2	Stone 38 [Scholes 90]	Hislop	Primus	Foxe	Tavlaridis	Harper	Stone"	Diabaté*	Quashie	Taylor	Merson^	Todorov	Péricard/O'Neil/Burton
				V Nistelrooy 4p, 81p, Beckham 17,	*Carroll*	*Neville G*	*Ferdinand*	*Blanc*	*Silvestre"*	*Beckham*	*Keane"*	*Neville P*	*Richardson^*	*V Nistelrooy*	*Giggs*	*Stewart/Scholes/Brown*
				Ref: P Riley (West Yorkshire)												

9,000 Blues fans get a Premiership pre-taste, but for 35 mins it's embarrassing. Primus's lunge concedes an early pen, then Beckham's bender floors Shaka. Stone's goal changes things, as does a tactical shake-up. Quashie fires over when through. United's two late goals flatter them.

League Table

Pos	Team	P	Home					Away					Pts
			W	D	L	F	A	W	D	L	F	A	
1	PORTSMOUTH	46	17	3	3	52	22	12	8	3	45	23	98
2	Leicester	46	16	5	2	40	12	10	9	4	33	28	92
3	Sheffield Utd	46	13	7	3	38	23	10	4	9	34	29	80
4	Reading	46	13	3	7	33	21	12	1	10	28	25	79
5	Wolves*	46	9	10	4	40	19	11	6	6	41	25	76
6	Nott'm For	46	14	7	2	57	23	6	7	10	25	27	74
7	Ipswich	46	10	5	8	49	39	9	8	6	31	25	70
8	Norwich	46	14	4	5	36	17	5	8	10	24	32	69
9	Millwall	46	11	6	6	34	32	8	3	12	25	37	66
10	Wimbledon	46	12	5	6	39	28	8	6	11	25	45	65
11	Gillingham	46	10	6	7	33	31	8	8	9	23	34	62
12	Preston	46	11	7	5	44	29	6	5	12	24	41	61
13	Watford	46	11	5	7	33	26	6	4	13	21	44	60
14	Crystal Pal	46	8	10	5	29	17	6	7	10	30	35	59
15	Rotherham	46	8	9	6	27	25	7	5	11	35	37	59
16	Burnley	46	10	4	9	35	44	5	6	12	30	45	55
17	Walsall	46	10	3	10	34	34	5	6	12	22	35	54
18	Derby	46	9	5	9	33	32	6	2	15	22	42	52
19	Bradford C	46	7	8	8	27	35	7	2	14	24	38	52
20	Coventry	46	6	6	11	23	31	6	8	9	23	31	50
21	Stoke	46	6	6	8	25	25	3	8	12	23	44	50
22	Sheffield Wed	46	7	7	9	29	32	3	9	11	27	41	46
23	Brighton	46	7	6	10	29	31	4	6	13	20	36	45
24	Grimsby	46	5	6	12	26	39	4	6	13	22	46	39
		1104	247	143	162	845	667	162	143	247	667	845	1513

* promoted after play-offs

Appearances and Goals

Name	Appearances						Goals			
	Lge	Sub	LC	Sub	FAC	Sub	Lge	LC	FAC	Tot
Bradbury, Lee	3						1			1
Burchill, Mark	4	14	1		1		4			4
Burton, Deon	11	4				1	4			4
Buxton, Lewis		1								
Crowe, Jason	7	9	1		1		4			4
De Zeeuw, Arjan	35	3	1		1		1			1
Diabaté, Lassina	16	9								
Festa, Gianluca	27	2	2				1			1
Foxe, Hayden	3	2					1			1
Harper, Kevin	21	16	1	1	1		4			4
Heikkinen, Markus		2			1					
Hislop, Shaka	46		2							
Howe, Eddie	1									
Hughes, Richard	4	2	1							
Kawaguchi, Yoshi		1								
Merson, Paul	44	1	1	2	1		12			12
O'Neil, Gary	11	2					3			3
Péricard, Vincent	18	14	1	1	1	1	9		1	10
Primus, Linvoy	39	1	2					1		1
Quashie, Nigel	42		1		1		5	1		6
Ritchie, Paul	8	4								
Robinson, Carl	11	3	1		1					
Sherwood, Tim	17						1			1
Stone, Steve	18		1		1		4	1		5
Tavlaridis, Efstathios	3		1		1					
Taylor, Matthew	35		2		1		7			7
Tiler, Carl		2								
Todorov, Svetoslav	43	2	2	2	1		26			26
Yakubu, Ayegbeni	12	2	2				7			7
(own-goals)							3			3
29 players used	506	115	22	4	11	3	97	3	1	101

Odds & ends

Double wins: (9) Bradford, Burnley, Derby, Gillingham, Grimsby, Millwall, Nott'm For, Rotherham and Walsall.

Double losses: (0).

Won from behind: (5) C Palace (a), Brighton (h), Preston (h), Derby (a), Walsall (h).

Lost from in front: (1) Sheffield Wed (h).

High spots: Club record number of goals in a season (97) & points (98).
Club record number of wins (29) in a season.
Equalled club record of away wins (11) in a season.
Scoring in 20 consecutive league games (December-April).
Winning 5-0 at Millwall and Bradford C.
Clinching promotion with a 1-0 home win against Burnley on 15 April.
Clinching the title with a 3-2 home win over Rotherham on 27 April.
The performances throughout the season of Paul Merson.

Low spots: Losing 0-2 at home to Leicester in October on a pitch more resembling a lake.
Losing at home to bottom of the table Sheffield Wednesday in April, when a win would have clinched promotion.

Player of the Season: Svetoslav Todorov.
Ever presents: (1) Shaka Hislop.
Hat-tricks: (1) Svetoslav Todorov.
Leading Scorer: Svetoslav Todorov (26).

BARCLAYCARD PREMIERSHIP   Manager: Harry Redknapp   SEASON 2003-04

Match summary

No	Date	H/A	Opponent	Att	Pt	F-A	H-T	Pos	Scorers, Times, and Referees
1	16/8	H	ASTON VILLA	20,101	W 3	2:1	1-0		Sheringham 42, Berger 63 / Barry 84p / Ref: G Barber (Hertfordshire)
2	23/8	A	MANCHESTER C	46,287	D 5	1:1	1-0	6	Yakubu 24 / Sommeil 90 / Ref: M Messias (North Yorks)
3	26/8	H	BOLTON	20,113	W 7	4:0	0-0	1	Stone 48, Sheringham 57, 88, 90p / Ref: D Gallagher (Oxfordshire)
4	30/8	A	WOLVERHAMPTON	28,860	D 8	0:0	0-0	3	Ref: A D'Urso (Essex)
5	13/9	A	ARSENAL	38,052	D 9	1:1	1-1	5	Sheringham 26 / Henry 40p / Ref: A Wiley (Staffordshire)
6	20/9	H	BLACKBURN	20,024	L 9	1:2	0-2	8	De Zeeuw 57 / Neill 35, Cole 43 / Ref: P Durkin (Dorset)
7	27/9	A	BIRMINGHAM	29,057	L 9	0:2	0-1	9	Clemence 21, Lazaridis 50 / Ref: S Bennett (Kent)
8	4/10	H	CHARLTON	20,106	L 9	1:2	1-0	10	Sheringham 34 / Fortune 77, Bartlett 90 / Ref: G Poll (Hertfordshire)
9	18/10	H	LIVERPOOL	20,123	W 12	1:0	1-0	8	Berger 4 / Ref: S Dunn (Gloucestershire)
10	25/10	A	NEWCASTLE	52,161	L 12	0:3	0-2	11	Speed 17, Shearer 28p, Ameobi 61 / Ref: P Durkin (Dorset)

Line-ups (Pompey player / *opponent in italics*)

No	1	2	3	4	5	6	7	8	9	10	11	subs used
1	Hislop *Sorensen*	Zivkovic *Delaney*	Foxe *Johnson*	Stefanovic *Alpay*	De Zeeuw *Samuel*	Stone *Hendrie*	Faye^ *McCann*	Quashie *Barry !*	Berger *Whitting'**	Shering'm Yakubu'* *Allback Angel*	Yakubu'	Péricard/Schemmel, Hitzlsperger/Crouch
2	Hislop *Seaman*	Schemmel *Jihai*	De Zeeuw *Sommeil*	Stefanovic *Distin*	Zivkovic *Tarnat*	Stone *W't-Phillips Barton*	Faye	Quashie *Sibierski^*	Berger^ *Sinclair*	Sheringham Yakubu'* *Anelka Fowler^*	Yakubu'	Péricard/Harper, Wanchope/Berkovic
3	Hislop *Jaaskelain' Barness'**	Schemmel* *N'Gotty*	De Zeeuw *Laville*	Stefanovic *Gardner*	Zivkovic *Okocha*	Stone *Pedersen*	Faye *Campo*	Quashie *Frandsen^*	Berger *Djorkaeff Davies''*	Sheringham Yakubu'	Yakubu'	Primus/Péricard, Charlton/Jardel/Giannok'
4	Hislop *Oakes*	Schemmel *Irwin*	De Zeeuw *Butler*	Stefanovic *Craddock*	Zivkovic *Naylor*	Stone* *Newton*	Faye *Rae**	Quashie *Ince*	Berger *Cameron*	Sheringham Yakubu' *Camara*	Yakubu' *Blake*	**Smertin**/Péricard, Gudjonsson
5	Hislop *Lehmann*	Schemmel *Lauren*	De Zeeuw *Campbell*	Stefanovic *Touré*	Zivkovic *Cole*	Stone *Parlour*	Faye *Vieira*	Quashie *Edu**	Berger* *Pires*	Shering'm* Yakubu' *Bergkamp^ Henry*	Yakubu'	Smertin/**Roberts**/Sherw'd, Ljungberg/Wiltord
6	Hislop *Friedel*	Schemmel *Neill^*	De Zeeuw *Babbel*	Stefanovic *Amoruso*	Zivkovic *Gresko*	Stone *Emerton*	Sherwood* Faye *Ferguson Tugay**	Quashie^	Faye *Thompson*	Sheringham Yakubu *Jansen^*	Yakubu *Cole*	Roberts/Péricard, Baggio/Yorke/Johansson
7	Hislop *Taylor*	Schemmel *Johnson*	De Zeeuw *Cunningh'm Upson*	Stefanovic	Zivkovic *Clapham*	Stone *Dunn*	Smertin *Savage*	Faye* *Clemence*	Taylor^ *Lazaridis^*	Shering'm Yakubu *Dugarry* Forssell^*	Yakubu	Roberts/Sherwood, Cisse/Tebily/Figueroa
8	Hislop *Kiely*	Schemmel *Young*	De Zeeuw *Perry*	Stefanovic *Fish**	Zivkovic *Powell*	Stone *Stuart*	Faye *Holland*	Smertin* *Parker*	Berger* *Jensen^*	Shering'm^ Yakubu *Lisbie*	Yakubu *Bartlett*	Sherwood/Roberts/Taylor, Fortune/Di Canio
9	Hislop *Dudek*	Schemmel *Finnan*	De Zeeuw *Henchoz*	Stefan'vic* *Hyypia*	Zivkovic *Riise*	Stone *Diouf^*	Faye *Gerrard*	Quashie^ *Biscan*	Berger *Smicer**	Sheringham Yakubu *Heskey*	Yakubu *Kewell*	Foxe/Sherwood, Le Tallec/Sinama-Pongolle
10	Hislop *Given*	Schemmel* *Hughes*	De Zeeuw *O'Brien*	Stefanovic *Bramble*	Zivkovic^ *Bernard*	Stone *Bowyer^*	Faye^ *Jenas*	Quashie *Speed*	Berger *Robert^*	Sheringham Yakubu *Shearer*	Yakubu *Ameobi''*	Taylor/Foxe/Sherwood, Ambrose/Viana/LuaLua

Match reports

1. On a sultry lunchtime Pompey kicked the season off. Just before the break, Yakubu's blocked shot was followed up by Sheringham to send Fratton wild. Angel missed a sitter, before Berger jinked through to make it two. Barry converted after being tripped, then saw red for dissent.

2. Pompey are seconds from pooping City's new ground party, then Sommeil rose to head in a free-kick. Earlier Yak had skipped through a static defence to roll home and Harry's League of Nations (ten on display) looked the better side in a venue used for the Commonwealth Games.

3. In injury-time sub Péricard tumbles in the box, Sheringham converts, and Pompey are top of the Premiership. Just before Teddy fired in from ten yards and his bullet header on the hour was top notch. Hislop's save from Davies, and Laville's miss, were crucial after Stone's poke home.

4. Sloppy finishing by Wolves cost them the chance of a first win, but in truth it was dismal fare. Russian skipper Smertin came on for his debut and saw a shot cleared off the line. Harry is sent to the stand for moaning about Ince's scything of Yak. 'I thought the ref was inept,' he said.

5. Arsenal's season-long unbeaten run should have ended almost before it began. Pompey were cruising after Stone crossed for ex-Spur Teddy to upset Gooners. Then Pires fell theatrically as Stefanovic pulled out of a tackle. TV later shows no contact, but Henry converted after two goes.

6. Premiership reality kicks in as Rovers give Pompey a first-half chasing. Neill strolled through to open the scoring, then Cole turned De Zeeuw too easily for the second. DeZ atones with a towering header, then fires over from eight yards. Fans are ejected for standing as rules are rules.

7. Faye lets Clemence escape to head home a free-kick and spoil a promising start. Yak thought he'd levelled, but a flag deprived him, and later the TV replay deemed him onside. Lazaridis slipped home the second, but then Sheringham hit a post and Taylor did well to deny Smertin.

8. Pompey are mugged. With 15 minutes left they deservedly led through Sheringham's near-post header. Di Canio's entrance changed the game. Another sub Fortune got lucky after Young's long throw caused chaos, then Di Canio's corner was met by unmarked Bartlett at the death.

9. Fate decreed Anfield reject Berger should score and he didn't take long, tip-toeing through a static Reds back line to angle home the winner. It could have been different had Heskey's first-minute shot bounced the other way off the inside of a post, but Pompey well deserved their win.

10. For the first time Pompey are given a hiding. Shaka saved from Ameobi after 28 seconds, then he crossed for Speed to open the scoring. Stef handled ('Harsh,' said Harry) and Shearer converted, Given then saved from Yakubu and Sheringham, but Ameobi's looping header sealed it.

Football season match-by-match record.

11 — 1/11 — A MANCHESTER U — 11 — L — 0-3 — 12
Attendance 67,639 — Pos. 3
Forlan 37, Ronaldo 80, Keane 82
Ref: N Barry (North Lincs)
Pompey: Hislop; Zivkovic^, Foxe, Stefanovic, De Zeeuw; Stone; Sherwood*, Quashie; Berger; Sheringham, Yakubu. Subs: Taylor/Roberts
Man U: Howard; Neville G, O'Shea, Ferdinand, Fortune; Fletcher; Butt, Djemba-D*; Forlan^; V Nistel'ry, Giggs". Subs: Keane/Ronaldo/Bellion
United need their big guns (subs Keane and Ronaldo) to end Pompey's resistance. Early on Berger and Yak go close until Van the Man hit the bar. Then Forlan fired home Giggs' knock-down. Berger passed when he should have shot, but Ronaldo's 'freak'-kick broke Pompey hearts.

12 — 8/11 — H LEEDS — 11 — W — 6-1 — 15
Attendance 20,112 — Pos. 20
Stefan'vic 17, O'Neil 45, 71, Foxe 63, Smith 19 [Berger 75, Yakubu 86]
Ref: C Foy (Merseyside)
Pompey: Hislop; Schemmel, Foxe, Stefanovic, De Zeeuw; Stone*; Sherwood, O'Neil^; Berger; Sheringham, Yakubu. Subs: Taylor
Leeds: Robinson; Kelly, Duberry, Matteo, Olembe; Pennant*, Morris, Milner, Roque Jnr^; Johnson S, Smith. Subs: Sakho/Bridges
Leeds collapse and Peter Reid will pay with his job. Stef heads home a corner, then Smith quickly levels. O'Neil's 30-yard volley is a stunner. Pennant goes close, but once Foxe fires home from the edge of the box, Pompey showboat. O'Neil, then Yak are given acres of space.

13 — 24/11 — A FULHAM — 11 — L — 0-2 — 15
Attendance 15,624 — Pos. 5
Saha 30, 33
Ref: A Wiley (Staffordshire)
Pompey: Wapenaar; Schemmel, Foxe*, Stefanovic, De Zeeuw; Stone"; Sherwood, O'Neil^; Berger!; Sheringham, Yakubu. Subs: Taylor/Smertin/Burton
Fulham: Van der Sar; Volz, Melville, Knight, Bonnissel; Legwinski, Clark, Davis S, Malbranque; Saha^, Hayes*. Subs: Inamoto/Sava
O'Neil delays his England Under-20 call up, but he might as well have gone. Subbed after making no impact, Pompey are already down thanks to Saha's sharpness with his head, then his boot. They were against the run of play, but Blues lack punch. Berger sees red for a volley of abuse.

14 — 29/11 — H LEICESTER — 15 — L — 0-2 — 15
Attendance 20,061 — Pos. 13
Ferdinand 31, Bent 59
Ref: M Dean (Wirral)
Pompey: Wapenaar; Zivkovic, Foxe*, Stefanovic, De Zeeuw; Stone; Sherwood, Smertin; Berger; Sheringham, Yakubu. Subs: Taylor
Leicester: Walker; Curtis, Howey, Scimeca, Thatcher; Stewart, McKinlay, Izzet; Scowcroft, Ferdinand*, Bent*. Subs: Davidson/Hignett
Dour Foxes maintain their jinx. An old Harry target, veteran Ferdinand's 30-yard free-kick deflects into the top corner. Then Bent rises to head a second. In between Yakubu might have had a penalty. In a final push, Walker saved well from the Nigerian, and sub Taylor hit the crossbar.

15 — 6/12 — A MIDDLESBROUGH — 16 — D — 0-0 — 16
Attendance 28,031 — Pos. 11
Ref: S Bennett (Kent)
Pompey: Srnicek; Zivkovic, Foxe, De Zeeuw, Taylor; Stone !; Smertin, Faye*; Berger*; Shering'm^, Yakubu. Subs: Quashie/Primus/Sherwood
Middlesbrough: Schwarzer; Mills, Cooper, Southgate, Queudrue; Mendieta, Greening, Boateng, Zenden; Juninho^, Ricketts*. Subs: Maccarone/Nemeth
Third-choice keeper Srnicek is as dodgy as Wapenaar, but he rides his luck when Mills hits the underside of the bar. In fact, patched-up Blues are the better side and might have won when sub Quashie was put through in the second half. Stone is harshly sent off for two innocuous fouls.

16 — 13/12 — H EVERTON — 18 — L — 1-2 — 16
Attendance 20,101 — Pos. 15
Roberts 15
Carsley 27, Rooney 42
Ref: U Rennie (South Yorkshire)
Pompey: Srnicek; Zivkovic, Foxe, Stefanovic, Taylor; Stone; Smertin, Faye; Berger!; Shering'm^, Roberts*, Yakubu. Subs: Péricard
Everton: Martyn; Pistone, Unsworth, Naysmith, Watson*; Gravesen, Carsley, Kilbane; Campbell, Radzinski*, Rooney^. Subs: Rooney/McFadden
Sub Rooney scored the winner as Srnicek flapped, was booked and then walked after punching Stone, only for the ref to just warn him! 'Premier refs, you're having a laugh,' sang the crowd. Indifferent Zivkovic let Naysmith set up Carsley. Earlier Roberts had been set up by Sheringham.

17 — 21/12 — A SOUTHAMPTON — 18 — L — 0-3 — 16
Attendance 31,679 — Pos. 4
[Beattie 90] Schemmel 34 (og), Pahars 67.
Ref: J Winter (Cleveland)
Pompey: Wapenaar; Schemmel*, Primus, Stefanovic, Taylor; Foxe; Hughes^, Sherwood*, Smertin"; Berger, O'Neil^. Subs: Zivkovic/Yakubu
Southampton: Niemi; Dodd, Lundekvam, Svensson, M'Higginboth'; Pahars*, Telfer, Prutton, Marsden"; Beattie, Ormerod^. Subs: McCann/Phillips/Baird
Schemmel wants to go home for family reasons and Harry isn't happy. Even less so when Dodd^'s corner hits a post and goes in off Seb's head. He is later subbed. Wracked by injury and bans, Pompey battle, but a classy Pahars curler settles it. Beattie's late diving header is flattering.

18 — 26/12 — H TOTTENHAM — 15 — W — 2-0 — 19
Attendance 20,078 — Pos. 17
Berger 52, 68
Ref: S Dunn (Gloucestershire)
Pompey: Wapenaar; Primus, Foxe, De Zeeuw, Stefanovic; Stone; Hughes^, Sherwood*, Smertin"; Berger, Sheringham. Subs: Hughes/Roberts/Taylor
Tottenham: Keller; Carr, Gardner, Richards, Taricco; Jackson, Poyet^, King, Dalmat^; Kanouté^, Keane. Subs: Postiga/Ricketts/Zamora
Inconsistent Spurs are perfect fodder for a Boxing Day tonic. Keller saved well from Smertin, but has no chance when Berger drills a 35-yard free-kick into the bottom corner. Another foul on Yak leads to the second, via a deflection. Sherwood breaks a leg and is out for the duration.

19 — 28/12 — A CHELSEA — 16 — L — 0-3 — 19
Attendance 41,552 — Pos. 3
Bridge 65, Lampard 73, Geremi 82
Ref: G Barber (Hertfordshire)
Pompey: Wapenaar; Primus, Foxe, De Zeeuw, Stone*; Stefanovic; Hughes, Smertin^; Berger, O'Neil^, Yakubu". Subs: Schem'el/Robinson/Taylor
Chelsea: Sullivan; Melchiot, Terry, Gallas, Bridge; Geremi, Makelele, Lampard, Gronkjaer; Mutu, Gudjohnsen. Subs: —
Pompey match big-spending Chelsea for an hour, until Stone goes off with a hamstring. His absence lets ex-Saint Bridge push forward to fire in from the edge of the box, then run to bait the travelling fans. Zivkovic gifts Lampard the second, then Geremi's vicious volley ices the cake.

20 — 6/1 — A ASTON VILLA — 17 — L — 1-2 — 19
Attendance 28,625 — Pos. 8
Yakubu 49
Angel 22, Vassell 85
Ref: J Winter (Cleveland)
Pompey: Srnicek; Primus, Foxe, De Zeeuw, Pasanen; Stefanovic; Hughes, Smertin^; Berger, Taylor, Yakubu. Subs: Harper/Sheringham
Aston Villa: Sorensen; Delaney, Mellberg, Dublin, Samuel; Hendrie, McCann, Whitting'*, Barry; Angel^, Vassell^. Subs: Hitzlsperg'r/Moore/Crouch
Villa have led by more than Angel's header as Hendrie also hit the bar, but once Yak heads in Berger's free-kick Pompey are the better side. The home team get lucky as Primus's clearance bounces off Vassell and in. A keeper crisis means Alan Knight MBE (42) is on the bench.

21 — 10/1 — H MANCHESTER C — 17 — W — 4-2 — 22
Attendance 20,120 — Pos. 15
Stefanovic 19, Yakubu 52, 77, Berkovic^
Anelka 21, Sibierski 45 [Shering' 58] Seaman*
Ref: M Messias (North Yorks)
Pompey: Hislop; Primus, Pasanen, De Zeeuw, Stefanovic; Hughes; Smertin, Berger; Berkovic^; Yakubu. Subs: Harper
Manchester C: Seaman*; Sommeil, Dunne, Distin, Tarnat; Sinclair, Bosvelt, Barton, Sibierski; Fowler, Anelka. Subs: Stuhr-Ellegaard
Berkovic signs from City this week and he unlocks Keegan's men. Seaman goes off early on – his final game it turns out – then Stef nods past his understudy. Classy City roar back to lead and knock three times on wood, but once Yak levels, then Barton's goal is ruled out, they fold.

BARCLAYCARD PREMIERSHIP

Manager: Harry Redknapp

SEASON 2003-04

No	Date	V	Opponent	Att	Pos	Pt	F-A	H-T	1	2	3	4	5	6	7	8	9	10	11	subs used
22	17/1	A	BOLTON	26,558	10	22	0-1	0-0	Hislop	Primus*	Pasanen	De Zeeuw	Stefan'vic!	Hughes^	Smertin	Berger	Berkovic	Sheringham	Yakubu	Harper/Taylor
									Jaaskelain'	Hunt	Thome	N'Gotty	Barness	Okocha^	Nolan	Campo	Djorkaeff'	Javi Mor'o	Davies	Ba/Pedersen/Giannakop's
23	31/1	H	WOLVERHAMPTON	20,112	19	23	0-0	0-0	Hislop	Primus	Pasanen	De Zeeuw	Taylor	Smertin"	Faye	Berger	Berkovic^	Sheringham	Mornar*	Yakubu/Stone/Quashie
									Jones	Irwin	Craddock	Butler	Naylor	Cameron	Ince	Rae	Kennedy	Cort*	Miller^	Iversen/Ganea
24	7/2	A	TOTTENHAM	36,107	12	23	3-4	1-2	Hislop	Curtis	Primus	De Zeeuw	Taylor	Smertin	Faye^	Quashie	Berkovic^	Shering'm*	Yakubu	Mornar/LuaLua/Stone
									Keller	Carr	Gardner	Richards	Jackson	Brown	King	Davies	Defoe^	Keane		Ricketts/Poyet
25	11/2	H	CHELSEA	20,140	3	23	0-2	0-1	Hislop	Primus	Pasanen	De Zeeuw	Taylor	Quashie	Faye	Berger*	Berkovic^	Mornar	Yakubu	LuaLua/Taylor
									Sullivan	Melchiot	Terry	Gallas	Bridge	Parker*	Makelele	Lampard	Gronkjaer	Mutu^	Gudjo'ns'n^	Crespo/Cole/Hasselbaink
26	29/2	H	NEWCASTLE	20,140	4	24	1-1	0-1	Hislop	Pasanen	Primus	De Zeeuw	Taylor	Stefanovic	Faye*	Quashie	Berkovic^	LuaLua	Yakubu	Mornar/Harper
									Given	Hughes	Bramble	O'Brien	Bernard	Bowyer^	Speed	Dyer*	Robert^	Shearer	Bellamy	Jenas/Viana/Bridges
27	13/3	A	EVERTON	40,105	14	24	0-1	0-0	Hislop	Pasanen	Primus	De Zeeuw	Curtis	Stone"	Faye	Hughes	LuaLua*	Berkovic^	Yakubu	Taylor/Mornar/Shering'm
									Martyn	Hibbert	Stubbs	Yobo	Naysmith	Watson	Linderoth	Nyarko	Kilbane	Ferguson^	Rooney	Radzinski
28	17/3	A	LIVERPOOL	34,663	6	24	0-3	0-2	Hislop	Primus	De Zeeuw	Stefanovic	Curtis	Smertin"	Faye	Hughes	LuaLua	Todorov^	Mornar	Stone/Taylor
									Dudek	Carragher	Biscan	Hyypia	Riise	Murphy	Hamann	Gerrard*	Kewell^	Owen	Heskey	Cheyrou/Diouf
29	21/3	H	SOUTHAMPTON	20,140	12	27	1-0	0-0	Hislop	Pasanen	De Zeeuw	Higginboth'	Stefanovic	Stone	Faye	Smertin	Taylor	Sheringham*	Yakubu	
									Niemi	Dodd	Lundekvam	Crainey'		Telfer	Delap	Svens'n A*	McCann^	Beattie	Phillips	Prutton/Pahars/Fernandes
30	27/3	A	BLACKBURN	22,855	16	30	2-1	1-1	Hislop	Primus	De Zeeuw	Stefanovic	Stone	Faye	Smertin	Taylor^	Shering'm*	Yakubu		LuaLua/Hughes
									Friedel	Neill	Short	Todd	Gray"	Andresen*	Flitcroft	Tugay	Emerton	Stead^	Cole	Yorke/Reid/Gallagher
31	10/4	A	CHARLTON	26,385	9	31	1-1	0-1	Hislop	Pasanen^	Primus	De Zeeuw	Stefanovic	Stone	Faye			Shering'm^*	Yakubu	Berkovic/LuaLua
									Kiely	Young	Fortune	Heidarsson	Powell	Holland	Euell	Jensen	Konchesky	Johans'on^	Bartlett*	Cole/Di Canio

Scorers, Times, and Referees

22 — BOLTON: Davies 53. Ref: P Dowd (Staffordshire)
Moody Croat Zivkovic has gone to Dortmund, but Yak delays flying to the African Nations Cup to play. Pompey have only 11 fit outfield players, but they deserve little today. Davies's bobbling shot on the turn defeats Hislop, then Stefanovic walks late on for swearing at the ref.

23 — WOLVERHAMPTON: Ref: H Webb (South Yorkshire)
Yakubu is sent home in disgrace and wins a race against time not to sit on the bench. A police escort to do so doesn't go down too well with some. Ex-Saints keeper Jones kept Wolves in it, his best save from Yak, who replaced new-boy Mornar, while Pompey hit the woodwork four times.

24 — TOTTENHAM: Berkovic 39, LuaLua 73, Mornar 84 / Defoe 13, Keane 42, 79, Poyet 89. Ref: P Walton (Northant)
£7m Defoe scored on his debut, Berko nodded in from close range, Keane's 25-yarder on the spin was good, LuaLua's spectacular shot better, Keane's mazy run ended with a goal, then Mornar scored from close range. At the death Poyet kneed home from Richards' knockdown. Phew!

25 — CHELSEA: Parker 17, Crespo 79. Ref: G Poll (Hertfordshire)
Stone dropped out with a stress fracture, then Parker swapped passes with Mutu well-placed then Berger hit a post with a free-kick. Later, an awkward challenge crocked him for the rest of the season, and Crespo chested home JFH's lob off the bar.

26 — NEWCASTLE: LuaLua 89 / Bellamy 78. Ref: A D'Urso (Essex)
LuaLua is a Toon player, but a clause in his loan means he can play. Sir Bobby is apoplectic when his employee volleys home late on. Pompey deserve a point after Dyer had skipped past DeZ and set up Bellamy. Shearer should have wrapped it up, but missed his kick from six yards.

27 — EVERTON: Rooney 78. Ref: N Barry (Lincolnshire)
Rooney remains the scourge of Pompey, settling this dreadful contest with a classy curling effort from the edge of the area. He then races 50 yards to taunt the visiting fans. 'We've got to grind out points,' laments Redknapp, who at least has a contract extension to 2006 to celebrate.

28 — LIVERPOOL: Hamann 6, Owen 28, 58. Ref: B Knight (Kent)
Todorov's return lasts just 45 minutes, by which time Pompey are buried. Hamann's volley from the edge of the box gave Hislop no chance, but the keeper stood between Reds and a cricket score. Owen scored from close range, then headed in Gerrard's cross, before Stef hit the bar.

29 — SOUTHAMPTON: Yakubu 68. Ref: M Halsey (Lancashire)
Before kick-off Saints fans are soaked by a hail-storm and defender Svensson injures a knee. They're good omens as Pompey record their first win over Saints at home since 1963 as Yakubu spears home Stone's cross. Saints rally and Phillips hits the inside of the post in stoppage time.

30 — BLACKBURN: Sheringham 17, Yakubu 82, Taylor 37 (og). Ref: P Durkin (Dorset)
Rovers can't win at home nor Pompey away. Something must give and thanks to Sheri's bender and Yak's coolness (thanks to new striker coach Blissett) Pompey pull away from the drop zone. In between Taylor deflected in Tugay's wayward shot. Cole missed a sitter at the death.

31 — CHARLTON: Yakubu 65 / Bartlett 8. Ref: A D'Urso (Essex)
Harry changes tack at half-time and sub Berko changes the game. He set up Taylor to cross for Yak's classy (or lucky ...) side-foot past Kiely. Bartlett got between two defenders to put Addicks ahead. Di Canio comes on as a sub and thinks he's won it – until an offside flag intervenes.

32	H	BIRMINGHAM		17	W	3-1
12/4		20,104		8		34

Stefan'c 45, LuaLua 62, Yakubu 73p; John 67
Ref: B Knight (Kent)

Hislop	Primus*	De Zeeuw	Stefanovic	Stone	Smertin	Faye"	Taylor	Berkovic^	LuaLua	Yakubu	Pasanen/Quashie/Harper
Taylor Mail Tebily*	Cunningh'm Taylor Mar Upson				Johnson	Hughes	Savage^	Clapham	Forssell"	John	Ben'et/Clemence/Mor'is'n

A tame game erupts on half-time. Taylor handles outside the box but Yak still scores. The ref had blown up so the keeper walks. Pompey fury is abated when Stef curls the free-kick in. LuaLua's pace makes it two and he flip-flops to celebrate. A handball lets Yak seal it from the spot.

33	H	MANCHESTER U		16	W	1-0
17/4		20,140		3		37

Stone 36
Ref: N Barry (North Lincs)

Hislop	Primus	De Zeeuw	Stefanovic	Stone	Smertin	Faye	Stone	Berkovic^	LuaLua^	Yakubu	Quashie/Sheringham
Carroll	Neville G	Brown	Silvestre	O'Shea^	Scholes	Djemba-D^*Butt"	Solskjaer	Giggs	Saha		Ronaldo/Fletcher/Bellion

United rest a couple of big names and pay the price. Stone slots home after the ball falls kindly to him off G Neville, following LuaLua's cross. After that Pompey have their backs to the wall. Stef shows true grit to dive in front of a shot, while Taylor's handball is missed by the referee.

34	A	LEEDS		14	W	2-1
25/4		39,273		18		40

Yakubu 9, LuaLua 51; Harte 83p
Ref: U Rennie (South Yorkshire)

Hislop	Primus	De Zeeuw	Stefanovic	Taylor	Smertin	Faye	Quashie	LuaLua*	Yakubu	Harper/Sheringham
Robinson	Kelly	Caldwell	Duberry	Harte	Pennant	Matteo"	Radebe"	Milner	Smith	J'hnson S^ McPhail/Barmby/Lennon

Pompey outclass Leeds and all but assure their safety. A flowing move sees Yakubu head home at the far post, then early in the second Yak's header loops onto the bar and drops for LuaLua. Harte converts after a dodgy penalty award, then Hislop saves brilliantly from sub Barmby.

35	H	FULHAM		14	D	1-1
1/5		20,065		8		41

Yakubu 80; McBride 85
Ref: S Dunn (Gloucestershire)

Hislop	Primus*	De Zeeuw	Stefanovic	Taylor	Smertin	Faye	Quashie	LuaLua	Yakubu^	Duffy/Sheringham
Van der Sar Volz	Goma	Pearce	Bocanegra	Davis Se	Inamoto	Djetou*	Malbranque Legwinski	Boa Morte^	McBride/John

Pompey technically still need three points to be safe and when Yakubu prods home from close range to wake everyone up, it seems they have them. The defence goes back to sleep again and McBride turns and fires in from 20 yards to level. Youngster Duffy looks assured in his debut.

36	H	ARSENAL		14	D	1-1
4/5		20,140		1		42

Yakubu 30; Reyes 50
Ref: M Riley (West Yorkshire)

Hislop	Curtis	De Zeeuw	Stefanovic	Taylor	Quashie	Faye	Hughes	LuaLua	Yakubu*	Mornar
Lehmann	Lauren	Campbell	Touré	Cole	Bentley*	Parlour	Ljungberg^ Reyes"	Henry	Kanu/Aliadiere/Keown

Leeds' loss on Sunday has done the trick for Pompey and, with Gunners already champions, it is party time at Fratton. Yak nets after Lehmann fails to stop his shot fully. Reyes hits the bar, then profits from some sloppy defending after the break, but in the end a draw suits both sides.

37	A	LEICESTER		14	L	1-3
8/5		31,536		18		42

Quashie 66; Taylor 6 (og), Dickov 27, Scowcr't 71
Ref: G Poll (Hertfordshire)

Hislop	Curtis	De Zeeuw	Stefanovic	Taylor	Smertin	Faye*	Quashie	LuaLua	Yakubu	Mornar/Sheringham
Walker	Sinclair	Dabizas	Heath	Stewart	Scowcroft McKinlay	Izzet"	Guppy^	Dickov	Bent"	Nalis/Ferdinand/Benjamin

Rumours are rife Harry is far from happy – 'They want to sack Jim!' he says - and his bad vibes must have rubbed off. Taylor deflected Bent's shot past Shaka, then Dickov doubled relegated Foxes' lead. Yak set up Quashie to fire in from 20 yards, only for Scowcroft to settle matters.

38	H	MIDDLESBROUGH		13	W	5-1
15/5		20,134		11		45

Yakubu 4, 14p, 31, 83, Shering'm 80; Zenden 27
Ref: M Halsey (Lancashire)

Hislop	Pasanen*	De Zeeuw	Stefanovic	Taylor	Smertin	Quashie"	Berkovic:	LuaLua^	Yakubu	Curtis/Shering'm/Hughes
Schwarzer Mills	Ehiogu	Queudrue	Zenden	Mendieta	Boateng	Greening	Downing* Nemeth^	Job	Morrison/Ricketts

After a week of civil war, Pompey sign off in style. Manager of the month Harry and Milan have called an uneasy truce. Boro's defence must wish they could have done likewise. Yak's pace has a hand in three of his goals, but veteran Sheringham's tap-in really brings the house down.

Home 20,106
Away 34,883
Average

BARCLAYCARD PREMIERSHIP (CUP-TIES)   Manager: Harry Redknapp   SEASON 2003-04

Carling Cup

#	V	Opponent / Date	Att	Pos/Res	F-A	H-T	Scorers, Times, and Referees	1	2	3	4	5	6	7	8	9	10	11	subs used
2	H	NORTHAMPTON 23/9	11,130 3:10	8 W	5-2	3-0	Sherwood 13,83, Roberts 17,60, Hargr'ves 77p, Dud'ld 90 [Taylor 41] Ref: D Crick (Surrey)	Wapenaar	Schemmel*	Primus	Foxe	Taylor	O'Neil	Smertin	Sherwood	Péricard	Sheringham	Roberts	Stone
							Harper	*Chambers*	*Willmott*	*Reid !*	*Caruthers*	*Youngs*	*Trollope*	*Harsley"*	*Hargreaves*	*Richards^*	*Dudfield*	*Sampson/Burgess/Rickers*
3	A	NOTT'M FOREST 29/10	20,078 1:8	11 W	4-2 aet	0-1	Walker 57 (og), Yakubu 64, 108, Bopp 42, 67 [Roberts 101] Ref: H Webb (South Yorkshire)	Wapenaar	Foxe	De Zeeuw	Stefan'vic^	Schemmel	Stone	Sherwood	Quashie^	Taylor	Shering'm"	Roberts	Yakubu/Berger/O'Neil
							Ward	*Louis-Jean*	*Thompson*	*Walker^*	*Morgan*	*Sonner**	*Bopp*	*McPhail"*	*Reid*	*Taylor*	*Harewood*	*Williams/Robertson/Jess*
4	A	SOUTHAMPTON 2/12	29,201 12	15 L	0-2	0-1	Beattie 33, 90p Ref: G Poll (Hertfordshire)	Smicek	Zivkovic^	De Zeeuw!	Stefanovic	Taylor	Stone	Smertin	Faye*	Berger	Sheringham	Yakubu	Sherwood/Foxe
							Niemi	*Dodd*	*Lundekvam*	*Svens'on*	*M'Higginboth'*	*Fernandes*	*Delap*	*Telfer*	*Marsden**	*Beattie*	*Ormerod^*	*Prutton/Delgado*

FA Cup

#	V	Opponent / Date	Att	Pos/Res	F-A	H-T	Scorers, Times, and Referees	1	2	3	4	5	6	7	8	9	10	11	subs used
3	H	BLACKPOOL 4/1	13,479 2:13	17 W	2-1	1-1	Schemmel 36, Yakubu 90, Taylor 43 Ref: S Dunn (Gloucestershire)	Wapenaar	Zivkovic	Pasanen	Stefanovic	Schemmel	Hughes	Smertin	Taylor	Sheringham	Burton	Yakubu*	Robinson
							Jones	*Grayson*	*Flynn*	*Davis*	*Evans!*	*Bullock*	*Wellans**	*Coid*	*Hilton*	*Murphy*	*Taylor^*	*Clarke/Johnson*
4	H	SCUNTHORPE 24/1	17,508 3:16	17 W	2-1	1-0	Taylor 35, 66, Parton 89 Ref: G Barber (Hertfordshire)	Hislop	Primus	Pasanen	Stefanovic	Harper"	Schemmel	Smertin*	Taylor	Hughes	Berger^	Sheringham	Schemmel/Faye/Robinson
							Evans	*Graves**	*Byrne*	*Stanton*	*Sharp*	*Sparrow*	*Barwick*	*Kilford*	*Beagrie*	*Hayes"*	*Torpey*	*Ridley/Parton*
5	A	LIVERPOOL 15/2	34,669 6	17 D	1-1	0-1	Taylor 77, Owen 2 Ref: M Halsey (Lancashire)	Hislop	Primus	Pasanen	De Zeeuw	Stefanovic	Smertin	Faye	Quashie	Berkovic^	Mornar^	Yakubu	Olzar/Taylor
							Dudek	*Finnan*	*Henchoz*	*Hyypia*	*Carragher*	*Kewell^*	*Hamann*	*Gerrard*	*Cheyrou"*	*Owen*	*Heskey*	*Le Tallec/Sinama-Pongolle*
5R	H	LIVERPOOL 22/2	19,529 6	17 W	1-0	0-0	Hughes 72 Ref: M Messias (North Yorks)	Hislop	Primus	Pasanen	De Zeeuw	Stefan'vic"	Hughes	Smertin	Quashie	Taylor	Berkovic	Yakubu	Hughes
							Dudek	*Finnan*	*Henchoz*	*Hyypia*	*Harper*	*Carragher*	*Gerrard*	*Le Tallec^*	*Cheyrou"*	*Owen*	*Heskey^*	*Baros/Murphy/S^-Pongolle*
6	H	ARSENAL 6/3	20,137 1	17 L	1-5	0-3	Sheringham 90 [Touré 45] Henry 25, 50, Ljungberg 43, 57, Ref: J Winter (Cleveland)	Hislop	Primus	Pasanen	De Zeeuw	Taylor	Smertin	Faye	Quashie*	Berkovic^	Mornar"	Yakubu	Stone/Hughes/Sheringh'm
							Lehmann	*Lauren*	*Campbell*	*Touré*	*Cole*	*Ljungberg**	*Vieira^*	*Edu*	*Silva*	*Reyes*	*Henry"*	*Bentley/Clichy/Kanu*

Match reports

Northampton: Cobblers lose Reid for an early cynical foul. Sherwood thumps home a shot and finishes a slick one-two. Roberts chips in his first for the club, then hits a volley, while Taylor returns with a left-foot drive. Pompey could have had ten, but a twice-taken pen and a tap-in flatter the visitors.

Nott'm Forest: Harry's half-time shake-up ensured safe passage. One sub Berger set up the move which saw Walker divert past his own keeper, then another, Yakubu, scored two crackers. Earlier Bopp opened from close range and levelled in similar vein. Roberts' swivel and shot finally broke Forest.

Southampton: Pompey's team bus narrowly avoids an accident on the way and a min's silence for Ted Bates is marred by both sets of fans. The action on the pitch in the first Hants derby in eight years is tame, but Beattie's header gives Saints the edge, and his late pen. for which DeZ sees red, seals it.

Blackpool: Yak spares injury-hit Pompey's blushes, forcing the ball in after Sheri's late header was cleared off the line. 'Perhaps we could have got some rock,' quipped Harry afterwards, discussing the prospect of a replay. Schemmel had earlier headed in, cancelled out by Taylor's sharp strike.

Scunthorpe: Iron travel in numbers and give a good account of themselves on and off the pitch. Taylor snaffled up a rebound off the keeper, then scored with a right-foot drive to end any potential jitters. In the last minute Stefanovic fails to clear a long throw and sub Parton scores from close in.

Liverpool (A): Pompey ride their luck after Owen profits when Berko loses the ball and he clips home the cross. Heskey, Gerrard and Carragher all go close, but Reds can't find the KO punch. They pay when Yak sets up sub Taylor to silence the Kop from 10 yards. He races the field to celebrate.

Liverpool (H, 5R): A tame game goes crazy after half time when the referee awards a penalty to Pool for handball, then changes his mind after protests. Later Taylor's perfect tackle is penalised, but Owen's poor spot kick is saved. Sub Hughes' turn and shot gives patched-up Pompey a famous win.

Arsenal: Arsenal give a masterclass for the TV nation's delectation, but home fans win praise for their sportsmanship. Henry lashed in the first and side footed the fourth. Ljungberg curled in the killer second and Touré and second-half sub Sheringham ended the contest. Late on Yak and Taylor hit wood, before Sheri's header.

League Table

Pos	Team	P	Home W	D	L	F	A	Away W	D	L	F	A	Pts
1	Arsenal	38	15	4	0	40	14	11	8	0	33	12	90
2	Chelsea	38	12	4	3	34	13	12	3	4	33	17	79
3	Manchester U	38	12	3	4	37	15	11	2	6	27	20	75
4	Liverpool	38	10	4	5	29	15	6	5	8	26	22	60
5	Newcastle	38	11	5	3	33	14	2	8	9	19	26	56
6	Aston Villa	38	9	6	4	24	19	6	5	8	24	25	56
7	Charlton	38	7	6	6	29	29	7	5	7	22	22	53
8	Bolton	38	8	8	5	24	21	6	5	8	24	35	53
9	Fulham	38	9	4	6	29	21	5	6	8	23	25	52
10	Birmingham	38	8	5	6	26	24	4	9	6	17	24	50
11	Middlesbro'	38	8	4	7	25	23	5	5	9	19	29	48
12	Southampton	38	8	5	6	24	17	4	5	10	20	28	47
13	**PORTSMOUTH**	38	10	4	5	35	19	2	5	12	12	35	45
14	Tottenham	38	9	4	6	33	27	4	2	13	14	30	45
15	Blackburn	38	5	4	10	25	31	7	4	8	26	28	44
16	Manchester C	38	9	5	5	31	24	4	5	10	24	30	41
17	Everton	38	8	5	6	27	20	1	7	11	18	37	39
18	Leicester	38	3	10	6	19	28	3	5	11	29	37	33
19	Leeds	38	5	7	7	25	31	3	2	14	15	48	33
20	Wolves	38	7	5	7	23	35	0	7	12	15	42	33
		760	167	108	105	572	440	105	108	167	440	572	1032

Odds & ends

Double wins: (1) Leeds.

Double losses: (3) Chelsea, Everton, Leicester.

Won from behind: (1) Manchester C (h).

Lost from in front: (2) Charlton (h), Everton (h).

High spots: Beating Aston Villa 2-1 in our first-ever Premiership match. Going top of the league for 24 hours after beating Bolton 4-0. Not losing in the league to unbeaten Champions Arsenal. Beating Liverpool 1-0 in October at Fratton. Beating Leeds 6-1 at Fratton in November. Yakubu's winning goal against Saints in March. Run of one defeat in the last ten games to avoid the drop.

Low spots: Losing twice at St Mary's to Saints in the league and the Carling Cup. Robert Pires' theatrical dive to win a penalty for Arsenal at Highbury. Losing 1-5 to Arsenal at Fratton in front of national TV in the FA Cup Quarter-finals.

Player of the Season: Linvoy Primus.

Ever presents: (0).

Hat-tricks: (2) Teddy Sheringham, Yakubu.

Leading Scorer: Yakubu (19).

Appearances and Goals

Player	Lge	Sub	LC	Sub	FAC	Sub	Goals Lge	LC	FAC	Tot
Berger, Patrick	20		1	1	4		5			5
Berkovic, Eyal	10	1	1		1		1			1
Burton, Deon										
Curtis, John	5	1								
De Zeeuw, Arjan	36		2		4		1			1
Duffy, Richard		1				1				
Faye, Andy	27		1		2	1	1			1
Foxe, Hayden	8	2	2	1			1			1
Harper, Kevin		7			2	2				
Hislop, Shaka	30				4					
Hughes, Richard	8	3	2	2					1	1
LuaLua, Lomano	10	5			2	2	4			4
Mornar, Ivica	3	5			2		1			1
O'Neil, Gary	3		1	1			2			2
Olzsar, Sebastien						1				
Pasanen, Petri	11	1			4					
Péricard, Vincent		6	1							
Primus, Linvoy	19	2	1		4					
Quashie, Nigel	17	4	1		3		1			1
Roberts, Jason	4	6	2			2	1		3	4
Robinson, Carl		1				2				
Schemmel, Sebastien	12	2	2	1	1					
Sheringham, Teddy	25	7	3	1	2	1	9	1		10
Sherwood, Tim	7	6	2	1						
Smertin, Alexei	23	3	2		5		2			2
Srnicek, Pavel	3		1							
Stefanovic, Dejan	32		2		4		3			3
Stone, Steve	29	3	2	1	1		2			2
Taylor, Matt	18	12	3		4	1		1	3	4
Todorov, Svetoslav	1									
Wapenaar, Harald	5		2		1					
Yakubu, Ayegbeni	35	2	1	1	4		16	2	1	19
Zivkovic, Boris	17	1	1		1					
33 players used	418	82	33	6	55	10	47	8	7	62

BARCLAYCARD PREMIERSHIP   Manager: Redknapp ⇨ Zajec ⇨ Perrin   SEASON 2004-05

No		Opponents	Date	Att	Pos	Pt	F-A	H-T	Scorers, Times, and Referees	1	2	3	4	5	6	7	8	9	10	11	subs used
1	H	BIRMINGHAM	14/8		14	D	1-1	1-1	Unsworth 16p / Savage 10 / Ref: H Webb (South Yorkshire). Brum cost three times as much as Pompey, but it doesn't show. Savage curls in a free-kick but Unsworth converts after Stone was pushed. Yak misses a good chance, then Taylor denies LuaLua. Primus gets away with a handball late on. 'Blatant,' says Bruce, 'Didn't see it,' says Harry.	Hislop	Primus	Stefanovic	De Zeeuw	Unsworth	Stone^	Hughes	Berger*	Quashie	Yakubu	LuaLua	Taylor/Griffin
				20,021	7	1				Taylor Mai	Melchiot	Upson	Taylor Mar	Lazaridis	Grankjaer^	Savage	Izzet	Johnson	Heskey	Forssell^	Gray/Morrison
2	A	CHARLTON	21/8		17	L	1-2	0-1	Berger 53 / Euell 23, Unsworth 87 (og) / Ref: A Wiley (Staffordshire). Shaka's late clanger snatches away a deserved point. Berger's spectacular swivel and 25-yard shot will be a Goal of the Season contender, after Euell peeled off Stefanovic to fire home from 12 yards. A hopeful punt skids off Unsworth's head and Shaka lets the ball squirm over the line.	Hislop	Primus*	Stefanovic	De Zeeuw	Unsworth	Griffin^	Berkovic"	Berger	Quashie	Yakubu	LuaLua	Taylor/Curtis/O'Neil
				25,204	11	1				Kiely	Young	Fish	Fortune	Hreidarsson	Rom'edahl"	Euell	Kishishev	Murphy^	Lisbie	Bartlett*	Jeffers/Konch'/El Kark'ri
3	H	FULHAM	30/8		11	W	4-3	3-2	Berkovic 19, Yakubu 22p, 28, 72 / Cole 39, Boa Morte 41, Bocanegra 72 / Ref: B Knight (Herts). £2.5m Kamara is unveiled, while ex-target Diop is booed. Berko volleyed home, Yak defied Harry to convert after a trip, then fired across the keeper for a third. Pompey fell apart as Cole headed home, then Boa Morte tapped in. Yak side footed a fourth, before Bocanegra's header.	Hislop	Primus	Stefanovic	De Zeeuw	Unsworth	Stone	Berkovic*	Berger	Quashie	Yakubu^	Fuller	LuaLua/Taylor
				19,728	13	4				Van der Sar	Volz	Knight	Goma	Bocanegra	Legwinski^	Diop	Jensen	Boa Morte	Radzinski*	Cole	John/McBride
4	H	CRYSTAL PALACE	11/9		9	W	3-1	1-1	Fuller 3, Berger 47, Popovic 85 (og) / Granville 43 / Ref: P Dowd (Stoke). Fuller sweeps home from 10 yards for the perfect start, but Palace are no pushover and deserve Granville's glancing leveller. Berger fires home another special, but Hislop is the hero, saving Johnson's pen and Popovic's follow up. His bizarre OG, as a cross spins in off his heel, settles it.	Hislop	Primus	Stefanovic	De Zeeuw	Unsworth	Stone	Berkovic*	Berger	Quashie	Yakubu	Fuller^	Taylor/Kamara/Faye
				20,109	20	7				Speroni	Boyce	Hudson	Popovic	Granville	Routledge^	Riihilahti"	Hall	Kolkka'	Johnson	Torghelle	Ventola/Hughes/Derry
5	A	BLACKBURN	18/9		11	L	0-1	0-0	Jansen 76 / Ref: M Clattenburg (Co Durham). Fuller is denied a late penalty as Friedel wrestles him to the ground. To rub in salt, he is booked for diving. At least it's an incident in a feature-free game, settled by sub Jansen's 20-yard strike to give new boss Mark Hughes a good start. Yak missed Pompey's best chance, firing over.	Hislop	Griffin	Stefanovic	Primus	Unsworth	Faye	Berkovic^	Berger^	Quashie	Yakubu	Fuller	Stone/Kamara
				20,647	16	7				Friedel	Neill	Gray	Short*	Matteo	Ferguson	Flitcroft	Pedersen^	Emerton	Stead"	Dickov	Amoruso/Jansen/Bothroyd
6	H	EVERTON	26/9		14	L	0-1	0-0	Cahill 80 / Ref: D Gallagher (Oxford). Everton are the surprise package so far and the Toffees could have won by more. However, Pompey were clinging to a point until Carsley's free-kick to the far post sees Cahill ghost in to head home. A couple of saved long-range efforts from Quashie were the closest Pompey came.	Hislop	Griffin	Stefanovic	Primus	Unsworth	Faye	Berkovic*	Berger	Quashie	Yakubu	Fuller^	LuaLua/Kamara
				20,125	3	7				Martyn	Hibbert	Stubbs*	Weir	Pistone	Watson^	Gravesen	Cahill	Carsley	Kilbane	Bent	Yobo/Ferguson
7	A	NORWICH	2/10		13	D	2-2	1-0	Yakubu 37, Berger 65 / Huckerby 63p, Charlton 67 / Ref: M Messias (York). It's more penalty woe as Taylor's tangle with Huckerby looked innocuous, but he steps up to convert. Berger's blistering free-kick restores the lead, but then tiny Charlton jumps highest to head in. Earlier Yak angled home from 15 yards, but in a late push Holt hit the bar for Canaries.	Hislop	Griffin	Taylor	Charlton	Unsworth*	Faye	Cissé^	Berger	Quashie	Yakubu	Kamara*	Fuller/LuaLua/Hughes
				23,853	19	8				Green	Edworthy	Charlton	Fleming	Drury	Jonson"	Holt	Francis	Bentley	Huckerby	McKenzie*	McVeigh/Svensson
8	H	TOTTENHAM	18/10		12	W	1-0	0-0	Yakubu 63 / Ref: U Rennie (Sheffield). Pompey create five great chances in the first half, Berkovic missing the best of them firing high over an open net, but the Spurs hit back and Gardner nods against a post. Finally Yak heads LuaLua's cross in from close range: the first goal Spurs have let in from open play in 690 mins.	Hislop	Griffin	Stefanovic	Primus	Unsworth*	Faye"	Berkovic"	Berger	Quashie	Yakubu^	LuaLua	Fuller/Kamara/Cissé
				20,121	9	11				Robinson	Pamarot	Naybet	King	Gardner*	Davies	Mendes	Brown"	Atouba"	Keane	Defoe	Kanoute/Carrick/Jackson
9	A	MIDDLESBROUGH	24/10		11	D	1-1	1-0	Kamara 5 / Downing 74 / Ref: M Atkinson (West Yorks). Kamara shows a clean pair of heels to fire home a left-foot cross shot into the corner of the net. Pompey then withstand a Boro barrage in the second half. Hislop saves from Downing and Riggott, then JFH fires over. Downing's well-placed shot levels, then both sides go close late on.	Hislop	Griffin	Stefanovic	Primus	Unsworth*	Faye	LuaLua	Berger	Quashie	Yakubu	Kamara"	Taylor/Fuller/Cooper
				30,964	8	12				Schwarzer	McMahon	Riggott	Southgate	Zenden	Mendieta"	Parlour	Boateng"	Downing	Hasselbaink	Viduka	Nemeth/Cooper
10	H	MANCHESTER U	30/10		9	W	2-0	0-0	Unsworth 53p, Yakubu 72 / Ref: N Barry (Scunthorpe). United are fresh from beating Arsenal, but Harry's bold formation de-railed them. Reds shade the first half, but then Unsworth converts after Ferdinand's tug, before Yak bustles through to dink the ball over Carroll. In between, Smith fires over from two yards after Rooney hit the bar.	Hislop	De Zeeuw	Stefanovic	Primus	Unsworth	Faye	LuaLua	Berger	Quashie	Yakubu	Kamara"	Fuller/Mezague
				20,190	7	15				Carroll	Neville G'	Ferdinand	Silvestre	Heinze	Ronaldo	Neville P"	Scholes	Giggs	Smith"	Rooney	Keane/Saha/Brown

11 — A ASTON VILLA (6/11) — L 0-3 (half-time 0-3) — Pos 10, Pts 15 — Att 32,633

Whitting'm 18, Angel 25, Solano 40
Ref: M Halsey (Lancashire)

Position	Portsmouth	Aston Villa
GK	Hislop	Sorensen
2	De Zeeuw	De la Cruz
3	Stefanovic	Delaney
4	Primus*	Mellberg
5	Unsworth	Samuel
6	Faye"	Solano
7	LuaLua	McCann
8	Mezague^	Hendrie^
9	Quashie	Whitting'm Cole*
10	Yakubu	
11	Fuller	Angel
Subs	Griffin/Hughes/Cissé	Moore/Davis/Hitzlsperger

Pompey are woeful. Cole crosses for unmarked Whittingham to score at the far post. Angel turned and thumped the ball across Hislop from 15 yards then the Solano punishes more slack defending with a lob in Pompey's first on-target shot 15 minutes from the end.

12 — A SOUTHAMPTON (13/11) — L 1-2 — Pos 11, Pts 15 — Att 30,921 (17 15)

Jakobsson 12 (og); Blackstock 18, Phillips 71
Ref: G Poll (Herts)

Position	Portsmouth	Southampton
GK	Hislop	Keller
2	De Zeeuw	Kenton
3	Stefanovic	Le Saux
4	Primus	Lundekvam
5	Unsworth^	Jakobs'on*
6	Faye	Svensson A Delap
7	O'Neil	Telfer
8	LuaLua	Fernandes"
9	Quashie	Blackstock Beattie^
10	Yakubu*	
11	Fuller	
Subs	Fuller/Griffin/Taylor	Dodd/Phillips/Griffit

Saints pull a fast one, signing keeper Keller on loan. His error leads to a headed own-goal, but he saves well from Taylor at the death. Blackstock turns and fires home, then Phillips is unmarked to head the winner.

13 — H MANCHESTER C (20/11) — L 1-3 [Bosvelt 87] — Pos 12, Pts 15 — Att 20,101 (11 15)

O'Neil 8; Wright-Phillips 6, Sibierski 79, [Bosvelt 87]
Ref: M Messias (N Yorks)

Position	Portsmouth	Manchester C
GK	Ashdown	James
2	De Zeeuw	Onuoha
3	Stefanovic	Dunne
4	Primus"	Distin
5	Unsworth	Jordan
6	Faye	W'-Phillips SBosvelt
7	O'Neil	Barton
8	Berger^	Sibierski
9	Quashie	Anelka*
10	Fuller	Macken
11	LuaLua*	
Subs	Berkovic/Taylor/Griffin	Fowler

A grim-faced Harry looks on, in what will be his Pompey swan-song. Wright-Phillips slots home, before O'Neil guides in Unsworth's cross early on, but then City take over. Debutant Ashdown has no chance when Sibierski is set free to angle home, then Bosvelt follows up to score.

14 — A BOLTON (27/11) — W 1-0 — Pos 11, Pts 18 — Att 25,008 (8 18)

De Zeeuw 45
Ref: S Dunn (Gloucestershire)

Position	Portsmouth	Bolton
GK	Ashdown	Jaaskelain' Hunt
2	De Zeeuw	N'Gotty^
3	Stefanovic	Jaidi
4	Primus	Gardner
5	Griffin	Okocha*
6	Stone	Campo"
7	O'Neil	Speed
8	Berger	Giannakop' Davies
9	Quashie	Diouf
10	Fuller	
11	Taylor^	
Subs	Faye	Hierro/Pedersen/Nolan

Caretaker boss Zajec's 4-5-1 formation comes up trumps when O'Neil glances home O'Neil's free-kick. Later Pompey's skipper shows restraint after Diouf spits in his face after trying to dive and win a spot-kick. The ref missed it. Ashdown's first-half stop from Diouf was vital.

15 — H WEST BROM (4/12) — W 3-2 — Pos 9, Pts 21 — Att 20,110 (20 21)

Purse 35 (og), De Zeeuw 85, LuaLua 89; Stefanovic 14 (og), Earnshaw 45
Ref: P Walton (Northants)

Position	Portsmouth	West Brom
GK	Ashdown	Hoult
2	De Zeeuw	Scimeca
3	Stefanovic	Purse
4	Griffin	Moore
5	Unsworth"	Clement
6	Stone	Haas*
7	Faye	Johnson
8	Berger	Greening
9	Quashie"	Gera^
10	Fuller	Kanu
11	Taylor^	
Subs	Primus/LuaLua/Berkovic	Gaardsoe/Sakiri/Hulse

Sub Berkovic sets up LuaLua to fire high into the net to seal a lucky win. Earlier, De Zeeuw had headed home home after Taylor's gaffe. Earlier Stefanovic and Purse both diverted crosses past their keepers. Baggies looked on course when Earnshaw tapped in after Taylor's free-kick.

16 — A NEWCASTLE (11/12) — D 1-1 — Pos 10, Pts 22 — Att 51,480 (12 22)

Stone 30; Bowyer 3
Ref: M Riley (West Yorkshire)

Position	Portsmouth	Newcastle
GK	Ashdown	Given
2	De Zeeuw	Taylor
3	Stefanovic	Bramble
4	Griffin	Hughes
5	Primus	Bernard
6	Stone	Bowyer^
7	Faye	Jenas
8	Berger	Dyer
9	Quashie	Milner^
10	Fuller*	Ameobi
11	LuaLua^	Bellamy
Subs	Taylor/Cissé	Robert/Ambrose

Ex-Saint Strachan is now the top new boss target. Perhaps they don't need him as Zajec's team picks up an impressive point. After Bowyer's splendid strike and Jenas's bad miss, Pompey are the better side. Stone's deflected shot levels, then late on O'Neil's header goes inches wide.

17 — A LIVERPOOL (14/12) — D 0-0 — Pos 10, Pts 23 — Att 35,064 (6 23)

LuaLua 90; Gerrard 70
Ref: M Clattenburg (Co Durham)

Position	Portsmouth	Liverpool
GK	Ashdown	Dudek
2	De Zeeuw	Finnan
3	Stefanovic	Hyppia
4	Griffin	Carragher
5	Primus	Traore
6	Stone	Alonso
7	Faye^	Gerrard
8	Berger	Hamann
9	Quashie	Nunez*
10	Fuller*	Baros^
11	LuaLua	Kewell
Subs	Taylor/Berkovic	Sinama-Pongolle/Josemi

In injury-time Dudek juggles Taylor's cross-cum-shot and the ball sits up for LuaLua to head home a dramatic leveller. Earlier, Pompey had defended stoutly, until Gerrard's unstoppable 30-yard free-kick. Ashdown kept Pompey in it with one superb point-blank stop from Hamann.

18 — A ARSENAL (19/12) — L 0-1 — Pos 10, Pts 23 — Att 20,170 (2 23)

Campbell 75
Ref: H Webb (South Yorkshire)

Position	Portsmouth	Arsenal
GK	Ashdown	Almunia
2	De Zeeuw	Lauren
3	Taylor	Touré
4	Griffin	Campbell
5	Primus	Cole
6	Stone	Pires
7	Faye^	Flamini
8	Berger	Vieira
9	Quashie	Clichy
10	Fuller*	Van Persie*Henry
11	LuaLua	
Subs	Yakubu/Berkovic	Bergkamp

Champions Arsenal ride their luck as Pompey take the game to them, but quality tells. Campbell is the Gunners unlikely hero as he is allowed to stride forward from halfway and bury a low 20-yard shot into the corner of the net. Just before, Berger had forced Almunia into a good save.

19 — A CRYSTAL PALACE (26/12) — W 1-0 — Pos 9, Pts 26 — Att 25,238 (19 26)

Primus 69
Ref: N Barry (Lincolnshire)

Position	Portsmouth	Crystal Palace
GK	Hislop	Kiraly
2	De Zeeuw	Butterfield Hall
3	Taylor	Soronda
4	Griffin	Granville
5	Primus	Watson^
6	Stone	Routledge^
7	Faye*	
8	Berger	Rihilahti"
9	Quashie	Hughes
10	Mezague*	Kolkta
11	Yakubu	Johnson
Subs	Kamara/Fuller	Soares/Fre'dm 'n/Andrews

The kick-off is delayed as ground-staff struggle to clear ice from the cover protecting the pitch. Blues' heroes are Hislop, who produces a stunning late save from Sorondo and Primus, who rumbles forward to head in a corner. Mezague misses a glorious chance from eight yards.

20 — H CHELSEA (28/1) — L 0-2 — Pos 10, Pts 26 — Att 20,210 (1 26)

Robben 79, Cole 90
Ref: A Wiley (Essex)

Position	Portsmouth	Chelsea
GK	Hislop	Cech
2	De Zeeuw	Johnson
3	Taylor	Gallas
4	Griffin	Terry
5	Primus	Ferreira
6	Stone^	Makelele
7	Faye	Lampard
8	Berger	Smertin"
9	Quashie"	Duff
10	Mezague^	Drogba*
11	Yakubu	Robben*
Subs	Fuller/Cissé/Berkovic	Gudjohnson/Cole/Geremi

Robben's extravagant celebration, running 50 yards in only his vest, after his deflected cross-shot found the corner of the net, shows how tough this game was for the champions-elect. Cole's precise finish at the death was cruel. In the first half Quashie had hit the bar with a swirling shot.

21 — H NORWICH (1/1) — D 1-1 — Pos 10, Pts 27 — Att 20,015 (17 27)

Yakubu 61p; Francis 9
Ref: P Dowd (Staffordshire)

Position	Portsmouth	Norwich
GK	Hislop	Green
2	De Zeeuw	Edworthy ! Fleming
3	Taylor"	Doherty
4	Griffin	Charlton
5	Primus	Johnson
6	Stone	Mulryne"
7	O'Neil	
8	Berger*	Francis
9	Quashie	Bentley
10	Kamara*	Huckerby"
11	Yakubu	McKenzie
Subs	Faye/Fuller/Mezague	Brennan/Jarvis/Drury

Edworthy sees red early on for scything Kamara, but City impress. Francis volleys in from the edge of the box and Huckerby sees a goal ruled out for a push. Yak scores three times from the spot, but only one counts: Kamara twice encroached. The award for handball looked generous.

BARCLAYCARD PREMIERSHIP

Manager: Redknapp ⇨ Zajec ⇨ Perrin

SEASON 2004-05

No	Date	Att	Pos	Pt	F-A	H-T	Scorers, Times, and Referees	1	2	3	4	5	6	7	8	9	10	11	subs used
22	A EVERTON 4/1	35,480	13 L	27	1-2	1-1	Yakubu 31 / Stubbs 28, Osman 90; Ref: P Walton (Northants)	Hislop	De Zeeuw	Stefanovic	Primus	O'Neil	Stone	Faye*	Berger	Quashie	Kamara	Yakubu^	Cissé/Taylor
								Wright	Stubbs	Campbell*	McFadden*	Naysmith	Gravesen	Cahill	Yobo	Osman	Hibbert	Carsley	Bent/Kilbane

With two minutes of injury-time indicated, Pompey are well-and-truly aggrieved when Osman swivels to score from the edge of the box deep into the third, as Taylor missed a clearance. Stubbs had headed in a corner at the far post, only to see it cancelled out by Yak's rising cross shot.

No	Date	Att	Pos	Pt	F-A	H-T	Scorers, Times, and Referees	1	2	3	4	5	6	7	8	9	10	11	subs used
23	H BLACKBURN 15/1	19,904	13 L	27	0-1	0-0	/ Pedersen 55; Ref: A D'Urso (Essex)	Hislop	De Zeeuw	Stefanovic	Primus	O'Neil	Stone*	Faye!	Berger	LuaLua!	Kamara^	Yakubu	Taylor/Fuller
								Friedel	Nielsen	Todd	Mokoena	Johansson	Emerton	Thompson	Tugay^	Pedersen	Dickov	Gallacher*	Jansen/Reid

Quashie has gone to Saints for £2m: Pompey could still do with him on this display. Cynical Rovers pick up six yellows, but the game turns as Todd provokes LuaLua into a head-butt. He sees red and Rovers score with a well-worked goal soon after. Faye also walks for two bookings.

No	Date	Att	Pos	Pt	F-A	H-T	Scorers, Times, and Referees	1	2	3	4	5	6	7	8	9	10	11	subs used
24	A CHELSEA 22/1	42,267	14 L	27	0-3	0-3	/ Drogba 15, 39, Robben 21; Ref: M Riley (West Yorkshire)	Ashdown	Taylor	Stefanovic	Primus	Unsworth*	Cissé	O'Neil	Berger	Hughes	Kamara^	Yakubu	Mezague/Fuller
								Cech	Ferreira	Gallas	Terry	Bridge	Duff^	Cole	Makelele	Robben"	Lampard	Drogba*	Gudjohnsn/Tiago/Kezman

It's men against boys as Chelsea go on cruise control after Drogba sidefoots home with Primus and Ashdown in no-man's land. A neat one-two sets Robben up to score at the second attempt, then Drogba nonchalantly lifted a free-kick into the top corner. The second half is a non-event.

No	Date	Att	Pos	Pt	F-A	H-T	Scorers, Times, and Referees	1	2	3	4	5	6	7	8	9	10	11	subs used
25	H MIDDLESBROUGH 1/2	19,620	13 W	30	2-1	1-1	Taylor 40, Queudrue 58 (og), Christie 35; Ref: P Crossley (Kent)	Chalkias	De Zeeuw	Stefanovic	Primus	Taylor	Cissé	O'Neil	Berger*	Hughes	Fuller^	Yakubu	Skopelitis/Rodic
								Schwarzer	Reiziger	Southgate	Cooper*	Queudrue	Morrison	Parlour	Zenden	Downing	Christie^	Hasselbaink	McMahon^/Job/Graham

New keeper Chalkias is a Greek bearing gifts as he spills a shot for Christie to score, but his one-on-one stop from the same player just before Queudrue slid the ball into his own net under pressure from Yakubu was crucial. Taylor levelled with a rising right-foot shot from 10 yards.

No	Date	Att	Pos	Pt	F-A	H-T	Scorers, Times, and Referees	1	2	3	4	5	6	7	8	9	10	11	subs used
26	A TOTTENHAM 5/2	36,105	13 L	30	1-3	1-1	Kamara 28 / Mido 34, 57, Keane 83; Ref: S Dunn (Gloucestershire)	Chalkias	De Zeeuw	Stefanovic	Primus"	Taylor	Cissé	O'Neil^	Berger*	Hughes	Kamara	Yakubu	Fuller/Mezague/Skopelitis
								Robinson	Kelly	Naybet*	King	Atouba	Brown	Carrick	Davies	Reid	Mido^	Defoe	Keane/Bunjevcevic

Kamara clicks in front of England boss Sven with a headed goal from a corner. His pace terrorises Spurs and only a handball denies him again, but by then debutant Mido has made his mark. On the hour he pounces on hesitancy once more, then sub Keane produces a class flicked finish.

No	Date	Att	Pos	Pt	F-A	H-T	Scorers, Times, and Referees	1	2	3	4	5	6	7	8	9	10	11	subs used
27	H ASTON VILLA 12/2	20,160	14 L	30	1-2	1-1	Yakubu 24p / De Zeeuw 17 (og), Hitzlsperger 73; Ref: D Gallagher (Oxfordshire)	Chalkias	De Zeeuw	Stefanovic	Cissé	Mellberg	Stone	Skopelitis^	Berger*	Hughes	Kamara	Yakubu*	LuaLua/Fuller
								Sorensen	De la Cruz	Mellberg	Ridgwell	Samuel	Solano^	Djemba-Dj'	Hendrie*	Barry	Moore^	Angel	Hitzlsperger/Davis/Berson

The 'R' word can be heard around Fratton after sub Hitzlsperger's first-time drive from Salano's cross settles it. Shortly before, Angel's header had hit the bar. Returning Stone won the pen, after De Zeeuw had stuck out a leg and diverted a cross past his own keeper.

No	Date	Att	Pos	Pt	F-A	H-T	Scorers, Times, and Referees	1	2	3	4	5	6	7	8	9	10	11	subs used
28	A MANCHESTER U 26/2	67,989	14 L	30	1-2	0-1	O'Neil 47 / Rooney 8, 81; Ref: M Halsey (Lancashire)	Chalkias	De Zeeuw	Stefanovic	Griffin	Taylor	Cissé	Skopelitis"	Berger*	Hughes^	Kamara	Yakubu	Mezague/Kamara
								Howard	Neville G*	Brown	Silvestre	Heinze	Ronaldo	O'Shea	Neville P	Scholes^	V/Nistel'oy^	Rooney	Smith/Giggs/Fortune

Gary O'Neil's stunning 25 yard half-volley counts for nothing as a slick one-two sees the returning Van Nistelroy set up Rooney to round Chalkias to score late on. In the first half it was all United, but they couldn't build on Rooney's early hooked finish from Gary Neville's cross.

No	Date	Att	Pos	Pt	F-A	H-T	Scorers, Times, and Referees	1	2	3	4	5	6	7	8	9	10	11	subs used
29	A ARSENAL 5/3	38,079	16 L	30	0-3	0-1	Henry 39, 53, 85; Ref: C Foy (Merseyside)	Chalkias	De Zeeuw	Griffin"	Taylor	Cissé	Stone	Skopelitis	Berger	O'Neil*	LuaLua	Yakubu	Primus/Kamara
								Lehmann	Toure	Cygan*	Senderos	Clichy	Fabregas^	Vieira	Flamini	Cole	Henry	Owusu-Ab^	Lauren/van Persie/Ljung'g

Arsenal were never troubled once Henry's shot deflected off DeZ. Earlier Yak had hit the bar with a header. A careless pass set Henry up for a second, then his well-placed free-kick crept in, despite Chalkias getting across to the ball. Saints' win cuts the safety margin to just six points.

No	Date	Att	Pos	Pt	F-A	H-T	Scorers, Times, and Referees	1	2	3	4	5	6	7	8	9	10	11	subs used
30	H NEWCASTLE 19/3	20,165	15 D	31	1-1	1-1	Stone 45 / Dyer 43; Ref: M Messias (West Yorks)	Ashdown	De Zeeuw	Stefanovic	Primus	Taylor	Stone*	Skopelitis	Berger*	Cissé	LuaLua	Yakubu^	Hughes/Fuller/O'Neil
								Given	Carr	O'Brien	Boumsong	Hughes	Bowyer	Faye*	Butt*	Robert*	Shearer	Dyer	Jenas/Milner/Kluivert

Primus misjudges a header and Dyer nipped into score, but Pompey's nerves are calmed at once, as Yak sets LuaLua away and Stone steers his cross in. Ashdown made a fine save from Robert, pushing his shot onto the bar. Toon defensive rock O'Brien will join Pompey in the summer.

No	Date	Att	Pos	Pt	F-A	H-T	Scorers, Times, and Referees	1	2	3	4	5	6	7	8	9	10	11	subs used
31	A FULHAM 3/4	20,502	16 L	31	1-3	1-0	LuaLua 32 / Cole 63, McBride 81, Boa Morte 90; Ref: M Clattenburg (Co Durham)	Ashdown	De Zeeuw	Stefanovic	Primus	Taylor	Stone*	Skopelitis	Berger^	Cissé	LuaLua	Yakubu"	O'Neil/Kamara/Fuller
								Van der Sar	Volz	Knight	Goma	Rosenior	Legwinski^	Jensen*	Clark^	Malbranque	Boa Morte	Cole	McBride/Radz'ski/Bac'gra

For an hour Pompey are in control. LuaLua cut in to fire home, then Ashdown saved Legwinski's pen and the follow up. After Cole side-foots the equaliser, Fulham go for broke. De Zeeuw's weak back-header lets in sub McBride to lob the decider. Then Primus is robbed for the third.

32 · H · CHARLTON · 9/4 — 20,108 · 15 · W · 4-2 · 2-2 · 34 · 9

Yakubu 3, Stone 20, Kamara 83, Fortune 22, Murphy 45 [LuaLua 90]
Ref: G Poll (Hertfordshire)

| Ashdown | De Zeeuw | Stefanovic | Cissé | Taylor" | Stone | Skopelitis* | Berger^ | Hughes | LuaLua | Yakubu | Kamara/Rodic/Primus |
| Kiely | Young | Fortune | Perry" | Hreidarsson | Kishishev* | Holland | Murphy | Konchesky | Jeffers | Bartlett^ | Thomas/Lisbie/Johansson |

New man Perrin's effect is immediate. Yak's bullet and Stone's guided headers get things going, but slackness lets in Fortune at once. Murphy levels with a free-kick, but AP puts on two extra forwards and is rewarded by Kamara's near-post glancing header, before LuaLua rolls home.

---

33 · A · BIRMINGHAM · 16/4 — 28,883 · 15 · D · 0-0 · 0-0 · 35 · 12

Ref: P Walton (Northants)

| Ashdown | De Zeeuw | Primus | Cissé | Griffin | Stone* | Skopelitis" | Hughes | O'Neil | LuaLua | Kamara^ | Berger/Fuller/Mezague |
| Taylor | Mai | Melchiot | Upson | Cunningh'm | Clapham | Pennant | Nafti" | Johnson | Lazaridis* | Heskey | Morrison/Gray/Carter |

Perrin proves he doesn't just do flamboyant, he does disciplined too. A turgid game of few chances will have pay-per-view customers asking for a refund. Primus's spectacular hook off the line denies Heskey's header, then Taylor's sharp reactions deny Kamara a goal from a rebound.

---

34 · H · LIVERPOOL · 20/4 — 20,205 · 16 · L · 1-2 · 1-2 · 35 · 6

Kamara 33, Morientes 4, Garcia 45
Ref: H Webb (South Yorkshire)

| Ashdown | De Zeeuw* | Stefanovic | Cissé | Taylor | Stone^ | Skopelitis | Hughes | O'Neil | LuaLua" | Kamara | Primus/Berger/Fuller |
| Dudek | Finnan | Hyypia | Carragher | Traore | Arne Riise | Alonso | Biscan^ | Garcia" | Baros" | Morientes | Smicer/Gerrard/Cissé |

Pompey are still in danger as classy Reds keep them at arm's length. A flag denied Blues a flying start, but Morientes then scored at the second attempt. Kamara bundled in a corner, but a slick move ends with Garcia's flying header. Stone almost levelled, but just missed Taylor's cross.

---

35 · H · SOUTHAMPTON · 24/4 — 20,210 · 15 · W · 4-1 · 4-1 · 38 · 20

Yakubu 3p, De Zeeuw 17, Camara 20 [LuaLua 22, 26]
Ref: S Dunn (Gloucestershire)

| Ashdown | De Zeeuw | Stefanovic | Griffin | Taylor | Stone | Hughes | Berger^ | O'Neil | LuaLua* | Yakubu" | Kamara/Cissé/Skopelitis |
| Niemi | Delap | Lundekvam | Jakobsson | Higginboth' | Oakley* | Quashie | Redknapp | Telfer | Camara | Phillips | Bernard |

Pumped up Pompey blow away Harry's Saints. Yak converts after Niemi clatters LuaLua, then DeZ thumps home a header. Camara's cross-shot can't stem the tide. Lua lobs home after a defensive error, then fires home from the edge of the box before limping off. All after 26 mins.

---

36 · A · MANCHESTER C · 30/4 — 46,454 · 16 · L · 0-2 · 0-2 · 38 · 8

Distin 4, Fowler 16
Ref: A Mariner (West Midlands)

| Ashdown | De Zeeuw | Stefanovic | Griffin | Taylor | Cissé^ | Kamara | Hughes | O'Neil | Rodic" | Yakubu | Fuller/Mezague |
| James | Onuoha | Distin | Dunne | Jordan" | W't.Phillips | Barton | Reyna | Musampa^ | Sibierski | Fowler* | Croft/Mills/Thatcher |

Pompey need a point for safety, but blow it. Results elsewhere go their way though. Ashdown drops the ball under pressure and Distin heads in the rebound, then Fowler curls in a 20-yard free kick. Rodic wastes Pompey's best chance from six yards as Thatcher hacks his shot away.

---

37 · H · BOLTON · 7/5 — 20,188 · 16 · D · 1-1 · 0-1 · 39 · 8

Yakubu 72, Diouf 11
Ref: M Messias (West Yorks)

| Ashdown | De Zeeuw | Stefanovic | Primus | Taylor | O'Neil | Hughes | Skopelitis* | Mezague^ | Kamara" | Yakubu | Fuller/Cissé/Keene |
| Jaaskelain' | Candela" | Ben Haim | N'Gotty | Gardner | Okocha | Hierro | Speed | Stelios* | Diouf^ | Davis | Nolan/Jaidi/Pedersen |

DeZ refuses to shake Diouf's hand before the start, but the striker gets his revenge with a fierce low shot early on. Europe-chasing Bolton look in control, but once sub Nolan hits a post Pompey get going at last. Yak doesn't know much about his swansong goal from O'Neil's free kick.

---

38 · A · WEST BROM · 15/5 — 27,751 · 16 · L · 0-2 · 0-2 · 39 · 17

Horsfield 58, Richardson 75
Ref: M Riley (West Yorkshire)

| Ashdown | De Zeeuw | Stefanovic | Primus | Taylor | Cissé | Keene" | O'Neil | Hughes* | Kamara^ | Fuller | Skopelitis/Rodic/Mezague |
| Kuszczak | Albrechtsen | Gaardsoe | Clement | Robinson | Gera | Richardson | Wallwork | Greening* | Earnshaw^ | Campbell | Horsfield/Kanu |

With Saints safe at that point, even Pompey fans erupt when sub Horsfield's volley crept in. Richardson's low shot sealed it for Baggies, but the party only gets going once Palace concede late on at Charlton. Saints are down, Baggies stay up, and both sets of fans celebrate together.

Home Average 20,072
Away 33,691

BARCLAYCARD PREMIERSHIP (CUP-TIES)

Manager: Redknapp ⇨ Zajec ⇨ Perrin SEASON 2004-05

Carling Cup

Rd		Opponent	Date	Pos	W/L	Att	F-A	H-T	Scorers, Times, and Referees
2	A	TRANMERE	21/9	11	W	6,966 2:4	1-0	0-0	Kamara 65 — Ref: C Webster (Tyne and Wear)
3	H	LEEDS	26/10	17	W	15,215 C:17	2-1	2-1	Kamara 14, Berkovic 34p / Deane 40 — Ref: S Bennett (Kent)
4	A	CARDIFF	9/11	10	W	13,555 C:18	2-0	0-0	Yakubu 47, 55p — Ref: G Laws (Tyne and Wear)
5	A	WATFORD	30/11	11	L	18,877 C:10	0-3	0-1	Helguson 24, 57, Dyer 61 — Ref: D Gallagher (Oxfordshire)

Line-ups (1–11, subs used):

Match	1	2	3	4	5	6	7	8	9	10	11	subs used
TRANMERE (Pompey)	Ashdown	Griffin	Primus	Unsworth	Taylor	O'Neil	Mezague	Cissé	Berger^	Kamara	Fuller*	Yakubu/Stefanovic
TRANMERE (opp.)	Achterberg	Taylor	Sharps	Goodison	Roberts	Hall	McAteer	Rankine	Whitmore*	Dadi^	Hume	Beresford/Zola
LEEDS (Pompey)	Ashdown	Griffin	Primus	De Zeeuw	Taylor	Berkovic*	Cissé	Hughes	Mezague	Fuller	Kamara^	Yakubu/Berger
LEEDS (opp.)	Sullivan	Kelly	Carlisle	Walton	Pugh	Richardson	Gregan^	Spring	Johnson"	Joachim*	Deane	Lennon/Keogh/Ricketts
CARDIFF (Pompey)	Ashdown	Griffin	De Zeeuw	Stefanovic	Unsworth	Mezague	Faye^	Cissé"	Taylor	Yakubu^	LuaLua	Fuller/Hughes/Pulis
CARDIFF (opp.)	Warner	Vidmar	Gabbidon	Collins	Barker	McAnuff*	Boland	Kavanagh^	Ledley	Parry"	Lee	Bullock/Jerome/Fleetw'od
WATFORD (Pompey)	Ashdown	Primus	De Zeeuw	Unsworth*	Taylor	O'Neil^	Stone	Quashie	Berger	Berkovic^	Fuller	Harper/Griffin/Cissé
WATFORD (opp.)	Lee	Doyley	Cox	Dyche	Darlington	Chambers	Gunnars'n'*	Mahon	Ardley	Helguson"	Dyer^	Blizzard/Fitzgerald/Devlin

TRANMERE: Harry rings the changes, but Pompey have far too much class for Rovers. Kamara side-foots the winner from 12 yards after Berger's cut-back. Dadi misses a good headed chance, but Ashdown doesn't have a save to make until late on. Berger brings a fine save from a 30-yard free-kick.

LEEDS: Kamara is booked for the second time in three days, as he whips off his shirt again after scoring. Mezague is then fouled by Kelly in the box and Berko puts Pompey on cruise control until Deane glances home. Leeds improve significantly after that, and see a goal ruled out for offside.

CARDIFF: Yakubu wrenches the ball of Unsworth and buries a penalty after Taylor was scythed down, suggesting he is serious about taking up Harry's offer of £10,000 if he scores 15 goals this season. City rarely trouble Pompey once Yak had scuffed home the opener just after the break.

WATFORD: Harry and Milan staging a 'clear the air' press conference didn't help preparation, but there were no excuses. Helguson bullied the defence and twice he profited from Ashdown's hesitancy. Dyer rolled home the third to show Hornets' 5-2 win over Saints in the last round was no fluke.

FA Cup

Rd		Opponent	Date	Pos	W/L	Att	F-A	H-T	Scorers, Times, and Referees
3	H	GILLINGHAM	4/1	13	W	14,252 C:22	1-0	0-0	Yakubu 49 — Ref: C Foy (Merseyside)
4	A	SOUTHAMPTON	29/1	14	L	29,453 18	1-2	0-0	Yakubu 57p / Oakley 54, Crouch 90p — Ref: S Bennett (Kent)

Line-ups (1–11, subs used):

Match	1	2	3	4	5	6	7	8	9	10	11	subs used
GILLINGHAM (Pompey)	Ashdown	Griffin^	De Zeeuw	Stefanovic	Unsworth	O'Neil*	Hughes	Berger	Kamara	Fuller"	Yakubu	Stone/Quashie/Primus
GILLINGHAM (opp.)	Banks	Southall	Ashby*	Cox	Rose"	Bodkin^	Hes'nthaler	Smith	Crofts	Byfield	Henderson	Hope/Roberts/Beckwith
SOUTHAMPTON (Pompey)	Chalkias	Primus	De Zeeuw	Stefanovic	Taylor	O'Neil	Hughes	Berger	Kamara	Yakubu*	Kamara !	Fuller
SOUTHAMPTON (opp.)	Niemi	Telfer	Lundekvam	Davenport	Higginboth'	Nilsson*	Delap	Prattan	Oakley^	Svensson A	Crouch	Jones/Jakobsson

GILLINGHAM: Pompey have slapped a £12m price-tag on coveted Yakubu, and he showed his importance to the club by firing in after his first shot was saved. Plucky Gills never threatened, but the home side made heavy weather of breaking them down. A stiff half-time word from Zajec did the trick.

SOUTHAMPTON: Taylor's last-gasp handball is hotly contested, but ex-Blue Oakley stays cool to convert. Earlier Oakley's sweet shot was out of context in a poor game, but at once Kamara – who later saw red for two bookings – was fouled in the box and Yak scored. Sub Fuller missed a late sitter.

League Table

		P	Home					Away					Pts
			W	D	L	F	A	W	D	L	F	A	
1	Chelsea	38	14	5	0	35	6	15	3	1	37	9	95
2	Arsenal	38	13	5	1	54	19	12	3	4	33	17	83
3	Manchester U	38	12	6	1	31	12	10	5	4	27	14	77
4	Everton	38	12	2	5	24	15	6	5	8	21	31	61
5	Liverpool	38	12	4	3	31	15	5	3	11	21	26	58
6	Bolton	38	9	5	5	25	18	7	5	7	24	26	58
7	Middlesbro'	38	9	6	4	25	19	5	7	7	24	27	55
8	Manchester C	38	8	6	5	24	14	5	7	7	23	25	52
9	Tottenham	38	9	5	5	36	22	5	5	9	11	19	52
10	Aston Villa	38	8	6	5	26	17	4	10	5	19	35	47
11	Charton	38	8	4	7	29	29	6	9	4	13	29	46
12	Birmingham	38	8	6	5	24	15	3	6	10	16	31	45
13	Fulham	38	8	4	7	29	26	4	4	11	23	34	44
14	Newcastle	38	7	7	5	25	25	3	7	9	22	32	44
15	Blackburn	38	5	8	6	22	22	5	8	8	11	21	42
16	PORTSMOUTH	38	8	4	7	30	26	2	5	12	13	33	39
17	West Brom	38	5	8	6	17	24	1	8	10	19	37	34
18	Crys Palace	38	6	5	8	21	19	1	7	11	20	43	33
19	Norwich	38	7	5	7	29	32	0	7	12	13	45	33
20	Southampton	38	5	9	5	30	30	1	5	13	15	36	32
		760	173	110	97	570	405	97	110	173	405	570	1030

Odds & ends

Double wins: (1) Crystal Palace.

Double losses: (6) Blackburn, Everton, Aston Villa, Manchester C, Arsenal, Chelsea.

Won from behind: (2) West Brom (h), Middlesbrough (h).

Lost from in front: (3) Southampton (a), Tottenham (a), Fulham (a).

High spots: Thrashing Saints 4-1 in April.

Patrik Berger's wonder volleyed goal at Charlton in August.

Ex-boss Harry Redknapp taking Saints down.

Arjan De Zeeuw's restraint and dignified response after he was spat in the face by El Hadji Diouf in November.

Low spots: Losing twice to Saints at St Mary's in the league and the FA Cup fourth round.

Harry Redknapp resigning in November.

Harry Redknapp joining Saints in December.

Surrendering 0-3 at Championship side Watford in the quarter finals of the Worthington Cup.

Player of the Season: Dejan Stefanovic.

Ever presents: (0).

Hat-tricks: (1) Yakubu.

Leading Scorer: Yakubu (16).

Appearances and Goals

	Appearances						Goals			
	Lge	Sub	LC	Sub	FAC	Sub	Lge	LC	FAC	Tot
Ashdown, Jamie	16		4		1					
Ayegbeni, Yakubu	29	1	1	2	2		12	2	2	16
Berger, Patrick	30	2	2	1	2		3			3
Berkovic, Eyal	6	5	2				1	1		2
Chalkias, Kostas	5									
Cissé, Aliou	12	8	3		1	1				
Curtis John		1								
De Zeeuw, Arjan	32		3		2		3			3
Faye, Amdy	17	3	1							
Fuller, Ricardo	13	18	3	1	1	1	1			1
Griffin, Andy	18	4	3	1	1	1				
Harper, Kevin		1				1				
Hislop, Shaka	17									
Hughes, Richard	13	3	1	1	1	2				
Kamara, Diomansy	15	10	2		2	2	4	2		6
Keene, James	1	1								
LuaLua, Lomano	20	5	1				6			6
Mezague, Valery	3	8	3			1				
O'Neil, Gary	21	3	2		2		2			2
Primus, Linvoy	31	4	3		1	1	1			1
Pulis, Anthony					1					
Quashie, Nigel	19		1							
Rodic, Aleksander	1	3								
Skopelitis, Giannis	9	4								
Stefanovic, Dejan	32		1	1	1	2				
Stone, Steve	22	1	1		1		3			3
Taylor, Matt	21	11	4		1		1			1
Unsworth, David	15		3		1		2			2
(own-goals)							4			4
28 players used	418	95	44	10	22	4	43	5	2	50

With thanks to the following, and their choice of favourite Pompey player

Roland Bedford	Alan Knight
Roger Bryant	Alan Knight
Steve Burghard	
Ashley Cox	Robert Prosinecki
Tim Edwards	
Rodney Elkington	Steve Stone
Steven Lewis	Svetoslav Todorov
Steve Mundy	Alan Biley
Simon Nicholls	Paul Walsh
Chris Owens	Alan Knight
Gordon R Prior	Paul Walsh
Graham Shaw	Robert Prosinecki
Sue Stafford	Warren Neill
Tom Temple	Guy Whittingham
C Vowles	Mick Tait
I M White	Paul Walsh
Paul Wiggett	Mark Hateley